MW00414480

FEDERAL ESTATE AND GIFT TAXATION

Tenth Edition

■ ■ ■

By

Boris I. Bittker

Late Sterling Professor of Law, Emeritus
Yale University

Elias Clark

Lafayette S. Foster Professor of Law, Emeritus
Yale University

Grayson M.P. McCouch

Professor of Law
University of San Diego

AMERICAN CASEBOOK SERIES®

WEST®

A Thomson Reuters business

Mat #40777128

610 Opperman Drive
St. Paul, MN 55123
1–800–313–9378

Printed in the United States of America

ISBN: 978–0–314–19970–6

PREFACE

This book is the tenth edition of a work designed to introduce students to the federal estate, gift, and generation-skipping transfer taxes. Over the years these taxes have undergone numerous changes at the hands of Congress, the courts, and the Internal Revenue Service, rendering many traditional estate planning devices either obsolete or in need of substantial restructuring. Such changes have routinely furnished the occasion for revising casebooks in the field (not to mention countless wills and trusts). Undoubtedly the most striking development in recent years is the enactment in 2001 of legislation calling for repeal of the estate tax—but not until 2010, and then only for a temporary one-year period. In the event, the scheduled repeal was averted at the eleventh hour by fresh legislation which reinstated the estate tax, albeit with an opt-out provision for estates of decedents dying in 2010. While the prospect of permanent estate tax repeal has receded, the skirmishing over rates and exemptions is far from over, and the taxation of inherited wealth is likely to remain the subject of heated controversy for years to come. In the meantime, students, instructors, and practicing attorneys will continue to pay close attention to the existing tax system while remaining alert to the possibility of further statutory changes.

Although the current edition of this book includes revised text and notes in a number of key sections, the basic philosophy of the book is unchanged. Our objective is to provide a book that is complete and up-to-date in coverage, giving equal time to the claims of both the taxpayer and the Internal Revenue Service, while avoiding the temptation of becoming so encyclopedic as to render the book unmanageable in a two-or three-hour course.

Chapter 1 provides an overview of the federal wealth transfer taxes, including their origins, the policy objectives they seek to serve, the method by which they are computed, and the interplay between the marital deduction and the unified credit. Students are also invited to consider the interaction of the transfer taxes with each other, with the income tax, and with state law. Chapters 2 through 4 explore the concept of a taxable transfer for gift and estate tax purposes. Although the gift and estate taxes share a single rate schedule and a unified credit, the two taxes are not fully integrated in that the gift tax receives preferential treatment in several regards and continues to serve mainly as a backstop to the estate tax. Chapter 2 focuses on the application of the gift tax to lifetime transfers (including trusts with retained interests and powers), while Chapters 3 and 4 examine the impact of the estate tax on various property arrangements. The competing claims of the estate and gift taxes are considered in connection with specific situations, including trusts, joint-and-survivor tenancies, employee benefit plans, life insurance, and property subject to powers of appointment. Chapter 5 examines the estate tax deductions and credits, and Chapter 6 presents a bird's-eye view of the tax on generation-skipping transfers. Chapter 7 provides a survey of issues arising with respect to the valuation of property, including special rules concerning transfers of interests in family-owned businesses. Finally, Chapter 8 deals with federal estate and gift tax procedure as well as apportionment of the federal estate tax among those interested in the gross estate.

As noted in Chapter 1, the reach of the federal wealth transfer taxes is limited to a very small group of well-to-do taxpayers; only one out of a hundred decedents will incur any estate tax liability. This does not mean, however, that the study of these taxes is without vocational importance. As attorneys throughout the country will attest, the volume of legal practice in the field remains substantial. Critics may wring their hands in dismay, but the truth remains that this body of law, dealing as it does with an infinite variety of property arrangements, has become a forbidding thicket of complex statutes, regulations, and rulings. As long as this state of affairs continues, the services of informed lawyers will be needed by people planning the disposition of their property.

The subject may lay further claim for attention in its power to stimulate and challenge the student even if he or she never makes vocational use of it. The interplay of legislative, administrative, and judicial action; the attempt to steer a course true to the statute's purpose through the ever-changing and involuted channels cut by reluctant taxpayers; the search for a better tax program—these offer limitless opportunities to the student and instructor alike.

Although the materials in the book can readily be adapted for use in a course on estate planning, that is not our primary orientation. With a few notable exceptions, the writing on estate planning betrays a willingness to sacrifice everything else to a dramatic showing of tax savings, though to be sure there is usually a warning that an estate plan cannot be valued solely by the number of dollars that is diverted from the Treasury to the heirs.

A different approach to the study of these taxes may be simply stated. The federal wealth transfer taxes serve an important social policy. Practicing attorneys, unless they happen to be on a public payroll, can hardly help but regard these levies as burdens to be avoided, if it is legally possible to do so. But students have the time and the independence to reflect on the appropriate status of these taxes in our public policy and on the extent to which they succeed in fulfilling their mission. If such reflection is possible later on, when the problems of clients press on them, so much the better. In any event, they will be better citizens, and probably better lawyers as well, if they have looked at these taxes at least once from the perspective of legislators charged with formulating a tax program.

In editing the cases, rulings, and other materials that follow, we have freely omitted footnotes and renumbered those that were left. Editorial footnotes are marked as such, and parallel citations have been omitted. In general, citations to the Internal Revenue Code refer to current section numbers. In the preparation of this casebook, liberal use has been made of the text and notes in volume 5 of Bittker & Lokken, Federal Taxation of Income,

Estates, and Gifts (2d ed. 1993), where most issues can be pursued in more detail.

We owe an immense debt of gratitude to our senior co-author, Boris Bittker, late Sterling Professor of Law, Emeritus, of Yale University, who passed away on September 8, 2005. Although he did not participate in the preparation of the current edition, this book bears the indelible imprint of his formidable intellect and felicitous writing style. As a colleague and collaborator, he set an exemplary standard of professional integrity and personal generosity. We are also indebted to the many students who served as research and editorial assistants in the preparation of the several editions of this book and to countless other students who have knowingly or unknowingly aided and abetted our education. Finally, we express our appreciation to Pam Siege Chandler, Roxanne Birkel, and West Group for their invaluable assistance in bringing this book to publication.

ELIAS CLARK

GRAYSON M.P. MCCOUCH

April 2011

SUMMARY OF CONTENTS

TABLE OF CONTENTS

TABLE OF CASES

The principal cases are in bold type. Cases cited or discussed in the text are in roman type. References are to pages. Cases cited in principal cases and within other quoted materials are not included.

TABLE OF RULINGS

REVENUE PROCEDURES

REVENUE RULINGS

REVENUE RULINGS

REVENUE RULINGS

REVENUE RULINGS

PRIVATE LETTER RULINGS

TECHNICAL ADVICE MEMORANDA

IRS NOTICES

FEDERAL ESTATE AND GIFT TAXATION

Tenth Edition

Chapter 1

Overview of the Estate and Gift Taxes

■ ■ ■

A. HISTORICAL PERSPECTIVE

The taxes that are the subject of this book are not important sources of government revenue. The federal government has collected $40 billion to $2 trillion in taxes annually since World War II; of this amount, estate and gift taxes have yielded only $500 million to $30 billion a year. With huge federal budgetary deficits projected as far as the eye can see, a dramatic reduction in total tax levies appears unlikely. But estate and gift taxes will continue to produce only a modest part of the total, and any future increases in total collections are not likely to be accompanied by an increase in the relative contribution of the estate and gift taxes. The revenue from these taxes is dwarfed not only by the enormous yields from the taxation of personal and corporate income, but even by the federal taxes on alcohol and tobacco. Before World War II, estate and gift taxes contributed a larger share of total federal tax revenue than they have since then; their proportion during the fiscal period 1935–1941 was approximately 7 percent of the total. But during that period, total federal tax collections averaged only $5 billion per year—a level that will never be approached again. Of the total federal tax revenues of more than $2 trillion for the fiscal year 2009, federal estate and gift taxes contributed around $25 billion or just over 1 percent.

Raising the tax rates, lowering the exemptions, and expanding the coverage of the taxes would increase slightly the yield of the federal estate and gift taxes, but no foreseeable changes in the law could convert them into serious competitors of the federal income tax. In fact, even if a draconian Congress were to transmute the existing estate tax into an escheat measure, its yield would remain only a small part of total revenues. In 2009, for example, of the 33,515 estate tax returns filed, only 8,238 reported gross estates (totals before deductions and credits have been claimed) of $5 million or more, and the other 25,275 reported gross estates of less than $5 million. Outright confiscation of these estates would have produced—along, in all probability, with a flock of new members of Congress—less than 10 percent of total federal revenues. In the same year, federal income taxes produced more than $1.4 trillion, and the federal excise taxes totaled almost $47 billion.

It is not surprising, then, that when confronted with the need to balance the budget, Congress, to the extent it looks to taxes for relief, must focus on the income and excise taxes rather than the estate and gift taxes. Indeed, since 1976 Congress has repeatedly lowered the top marginal estate and gift tax rates and increased the exemptions, thereby limiting the revenue from these taxes. Other steps taken by Congress to protect the tax base may produce modest revenue gains, but any such additional revenue will be only a drop in the bucket, and the relative contribution of these taxes to total revenues can be expected to hover around 1 percent.

State governments, too, have ordinarily looked elsewhere than to death and gift taxes to satisfy the need for funds. In 2009, for example, death and gift taxes produced for the states less than $5 billion out of $715 billion in tax collections, or considerably less than 1 percent of the total. Their yield was relatively more important 60 years ago, but even then they ranked far behind collections from state taxes on retail sales, gasoline, tobacco, alcoholic beverages, and motor vehicles.

The raising of revenue, of course, is not the only function of taxation. Indeed, some taxes are not expected to produce any revenue; if the Treasury reported a sharp increase in the yield from the excise tax on political expenditures by private foundations, Congress would not applaud but rather would start an investigation.

Unconstrained by a conception of taxation for revenue only, many economists have stressed the contribution that taxes may make toward stabilizing the national economy. In this view, tax policy may be a counter-cyclical weapon, deliberately employed to combat manic-depressive fluctuations of the business cycle. Thus, when inflation threatens, taxation can be used to sop up excess consumer purchasing power, to discourage investment, or to encourage savings. By reducing the demand for goods and services, such tax collections would serve to moderate or prevent inflation of the price level. When unemployment develops, on the other hand, taxes can be reduced to encourage spending, thus increasing the demand for goods and services and putting persons and machines back into production. The federal personal income tax is suited to these tasks, it is asserted, because the progressive rate schedule acts rapidly to increase the financial pressure on the taxpayer during a "boom," while it works equally rapidly to diminish that pressure during a recession. This characteristic has been termed "cycle-sensitivity" or, because the tax responds automatically to changes in income (without even a change in the prescribed rates), "built-in flexibility."

Just as estate and gift taxes lag far behind the income tax in the power to raise revenue, so too are they far less promising as counter-cyclical instruments. To be sure, decedents' estates vary in value with changes in the price level, and, therefore, the progressive federal estate tax possesses a degree of "built-in flexibility." If gifts are larger during "booms," as seems likely, the gift tax yields should rise and fall with the business cycle. But the impact of gifts and inheritances on the nation's total pattern of consumption, saving, and investment cannot be great; the force that carries the threat of price inflation during full employment is the generally increased national income, not the fact that the wealth of a few persons may have been augmented to some extent by gift or inheritance. The personal income tax, with stepped-up rates if necessary, can accomplish infinitely more in the way of checking inflation than even a confiscatory estate tax.[1]

What then is the function of these taxes, which neither raise substantial amounts of revenue nor serve to stabilize the nation's economy? The answer may be found in the history of estate and gift taxation, for the proponents of these taxes have not sought to conceal their aims.

In a 1906 message to Congress, advocating a progressive inheritance tax, President Theodore Roosevelt said, "[T]he prime object should be to put a constantly increasing burden on the inheritance of those swollen fortunes which it is certainly of no benefit to this country to perpetuate."[2] A little earlier, in a speech on the occasion of laying the cornerstone of the House of Representatives office building, he had been a bit more detailed:

> I feel that we shall ultimately have to consider the adoption of some such scheme as that of a progressive tax on all fortunes, beyond a certain amount, either given in life or devised or bequeathed upon death to any individual—a tax so framed as to put it out of the power of the owner of one of these enormous fortunes to hand on more than a certain amount to any one individual; the tax, of course, to be imposed by the National and not the State government. Such taxation should, of course, be aimed merely at the inheritance or transmission in their entirety of those fortunes swollen beyond all healthy limits.[3]

The suggestion was greeted with enthusiasm by the liberal and radical press, and with dismay and predictions of doom by more conservative commentators. Somewhat earlier, Andrew Carnegie had announced his support of increased inheritance taxation in a magazine article that attracted widespread attention, including a cordial compliment from John D. Rockefeller. Carnegie said:

> The growing disposition to tax more and more heavily large estates left at death is a cheering indication of the growth of a salutary change in public opinion. The State of Pennsylvania now takes—subject to some exceptions—one tenth of the property left by its citizens. The budget presented in the British Parliament the other

1. For discussions of the economic role of estate taxation, see Gale & Slemrod, Overview, in Rethinking Estate and Gift Taxation (Gale et al. eds., 2001); Aaron & Munnell, Reassessing the Role for Wealth Transfer Taxes, 45 Natl. Tax J. 119 (1992); Jantscher, The Aims of Death Taxation, in Death, Taxes and Family Property 40 (Halbach ed., 1977); Boskin, An Economist's Perspective on Estate Taxation, id. at 56; and Shoup, Federal Estate and Gift Taxes (1966).

2. 17 Works of Theodore Roosevelt 434 (Scribner's, 1925).

3. 18 id. at 571, 578.

day proposes to increase the death duties; and, most significant of all, the new tax is to be a graduated one. Of all forms of taxation this seems the wisest. Men who continue hoarding great sums all their lives, the proper use of which for public ends would work good to the community from which it chiefly came, should be made to feel that the community, in the form of the State, cannot thus be deprived of its proper share. By taxing estates heavily at death the State marks its condemnation of the selfish millionaire's unworthy life.

It is desirable that nations should go much further in this direction. Indeed, it is difficult to set bounds to the share of a rich man's estate which should go at his death to the public through the agency of the State, and by all means such taxes should be graduated, beginning at nothing upon moderate sums to dependents, and increasing rapidly as the amounts swell, until of the millionaire's hoard, as of Shylock's, at least "The other half/Comes to the privy coffer of the State." This policy would work powerfully to induce the rich man to attend to the administration of wealth during his life, which is the end that society should always have in view, as being by far the most fruitful for the people. Nor need it be feared that this policy would sap the root of enterprise and render men less anxious to accumulate, for, to the class whose ambition it is to leave great fortunes and to be talked about after their death, it will attract even more attention, and, indeed, be a somewhat nobler ambition, to have enormous sums paid over to the State from their fortunes.[4]

Although these statements of Roosevelt and Carnegie, like subsequent defenses of our existing estate and gift taxes, were undoubtedly a response to the "robber baron" era of American history, they did not sound a wholly new note. Throughout the nineteenth century, death taxation had been advocated primarily as an instrument for the equalization of wealth. Indeed, Jeremy Bentham had used the very phrase "equalization of fortunes"[5] and John Stuart Mill had suggested "as a possible mode of restraining the accumulation of large fortunes in the hands of those who have not earned them by exertion, a limitation of the amount which any one person should be permitted to acquire by gift, bequest, or inheritance."[6] This drive toward equalization has drawn its strength from several sources: a moralistic abhorrence of idleness or profligacy, thought to be a result of unearned wealth; a belief that the economic well-being of the community requires that all of its members earn their own livings; and an ethical insistence on equality of opportunity. No doubt these sources, and others, have contributed in different degrees to the views of individual supporters of gift and estate taxation.

The history of the relationship of democratic thinking to the institution of inheritance is still to be written, but one may surmise that much of

4. Carnegie, The Gospel of Wealth 14, 21–22 (Harvard Press, 1962).

5. Bentham, Principles of the Civil Code, Part II, ch. III.

6. Mill, Principles of Political Economy, Book V, ch. II, § 3.

the popular support for death taxes in our country has stemmed from the "democratic dogma," no doubt with a strong tinge of puritanical disapproval of idleness. The burgeoning of state inheritance taxes in the 1880s and 1890s must have been an offshoot of agrarian and labor unrest, and, though the present federal estate tax was adopted in 1916 under the pressure of war, its roots and later history are both bound up with the democratic dream of equal opportunity for all. Even before the freedom to *amass* a fortune was challenged by the income tax, there were doubts whether such a fortune should be *passed along* intact to those who had not earned it. American fiction has often glorified the poor boy who became the head of an enterprise by marrying the boss's daughter, but there is no record of similar enthusiasm for the boss's son who acquired his father's place by inheritance.

Theorists have developed a number of other defenses of inheritance taxation. It has been suggested, for example, that the death tax is an appropriate toll charged by the state for use of the probate machinery and for other services in facilitating the transfer of private property at death. Others have argued that the state is collecting a belated fee for protecting the property during the decedent's lifetime or, more cynically, that it is levying a kind of penalty for any tax evasion that the decedent may have indulged in during life. Still others assert that inheritance comes as a windfall; therefore the tax imposes no sacrifice on the heirs, and they have an ability to pay that justifies the levy. One of the most influential of American authorities on public finance, E.R.A. Seligman, based his own support of the inheritance tax on arguments like these, rejecting the equalization of wealth theory as "very distinctly socialistic."[7]

It is hard, however, to resist the conclusion that the case for today's gift and estate taxes rests squarely on equalitarian foundations, to which those other theories are little more than decorative buttresses. Modern writers point out that the federal estate and gift taxes play a significant role in the distribution of the total tax burden and, in particular, are an important mechanism in maintaining progressivity in the federal tax system.[8] It is, of course, the fact that the estate and gift taxes are paid only by the super-rich that makes them effective in this regard. Those who cite this feature as a principal justification for the continuation of a healthy system of transfer taxes stress fairness and the desirability of taxing in accordance with ability to pay. This case for the estate and gift taxes thus appears to rest on equalitarian principles as well. Consequently one's attitude toward the tax is probably governed by the degree to which one wishes to see inequality of inheritance reduced. It is worth noting that for social and economic reasons some may favor equalization of *inherited* wealth without objecting to the same extent, if at all, to fortunes achieved by the personal effort of their owners.

---

7. Seligman, Essays in Taxation 131 (Reprints of Economic Classics, 1969).

8. See Graetz, To Praise the Estate Tax, Not to Bury It, 93 Yale L.J. 259, 272 (1983); Gutman, Federal Wealth Transfer Taxes After ERTA: An Assessment, 69 Va. L. Rev. 1183, 1195–97 (1983).

Without an examination of the Treasury's files and of the financial records of particular families, judgments about the extent to which gift and death taxes have succeeded in breaking up great family fortunes must rest on fragmentary and anecdotal reports. The top federal estate tax rate was 77 percent (imposed on amounts above $10 million) from 1941 to 1976; it is now 35 percent on amounts above $5 million. There have been examples since 1941 of enormous estates that were hard hit by death taxes. The $19.5 million estate of Robert W. Goelet was reduced to a net of less than $3 million by federal taxes of $11.5 million, state taxes of $4 million, and administration expenses of $1 million.[9] The estate of Mrs. Andrew Carnegie fared somewhat better, the federal and state tax bill being a little more than $11.5 million on an estate of $20.5 million, of which $2.5 million was left to charity.[10] After the charitable legacies and taxes were paid, $6.5 million was left for the private beneficiaries. In the case of the largest estates, the tax burden is often greatly reduced by substantial bequests to nonprofit family foundations or other institutions. The Edsel Ford estate paid nearly $25 million in federal estate taxes, but the figure would have been vastly larger if the Ford Foundation had not received all the decedent's nonvoting stock in the Ford Motor Company.[11] Henry Ford's estate, variously estimated at $70 million to $500 million,[12] would also have gone primarily to the federal government had it not been for his huge bequest to the Ford Foundation.

Turning from individual cases to the larger picture, however, a commentator concluded that "the estate tax has done very little to dilute the greatest concentrations of wealth" and that any decline that may have occurred in recent years cannot be persuasively credited to the estate tax.[13] Moreover, for reasons explained in later chapters of this book, the decedent's "taxable estate"—the base on which the federal estate tax is imposed—may be only a small fraction of the wealth that passes from one generation to another.[14] An analysis of returns filed in 2009 reports that only 33,515 of more than 2,400,000 persons who died during the previous twelve-month period (1.4 percent) owned sufficient wealth to require the filing of an estate tax return. Of this number, the vast majority reported ownership of less than $5 million in assets; only 8,238 acknowledged total assets in excess of $5 million. These reports are of gross estates. After subtracting allowable deductions and credits, less than half of these estates actually paid a tax. During the same period, 234,714 gift tax returns were filed, producing $2.7 billion in taxes. In view of the small number of taxpayers and the large amounts sheltered from tax by exclusions, deductions and credits, there can be little doubt that the vast

9. New York Times, Aug. 18, 1950, at 7, col. 6.

10. Id., Sept. 22, 1948, at 36, col. 6.

11. Id., Sept. 28, 1947, at 24, col. 1.

12. Id., April 19, 1947, at 1, col. 4; Oct. 29, 1948, at 22, col. 6.

13. Graetz, supra footnote 8, at 271.

14. See generally Cooper, A Voluntary Tax? New Perspectives on Sophisticated Estate Tax Avoidance (1978); for an earlier version of this work, see 77 Colum. L. Rev. 161 (1977).

majority of gifts and bequests occurring each year escape taxation altogether.

If estate and gift taxes have not fulfilled the hopes of their supporters, they have also fallen short of confirming the fears of their opponents. Enthusiasm for making money may be dampened by knowledge that the government will ultimately be an uninvited heir; on the other hand, there is the tantalizing possibility that an individual may work harder to ensure that his or her chosen beneficiaries will receive a competence after taxes. Similarly, the possibility that business risks will be avoided and investment channeled into placid backwaters because of the tax may be countered by the possibility that greater risks will be undertaken because only thus can substantial sums be accumulated for the beneficiaries. No conclusion as to the effects of estate and gift taxation on individual behavior can be more than a guess.

If we assume for the moment that the individual's pursuit of wealth is neither slackened because the prize is no longer attractive, nor spurred on by a desire to win a greater prize, what is the consequence of a death tax? Adam Smith formulated a classic view of the incidence of death taxes: "Taxes upon the transference of property from the dead to the living fall finally as well as immediately upon the person to whom the property is transferred."[15] Notwithstanding a certain looseness of language, which at times leads us to speak of a tax "on" the deceased, it is obvious that it is the living beneficiaries, not the decedent, who bear the brunt of an inheritance or estate tax. And they can do little or nothing to shift the burden of tax along to others in order to recoup the portion of the legacy to which the government has helped itself. The beneficiaries cannot ask higher prices for their own goods or services, because they are in competition with others who, not having suffered the same burden, are not impelled to raise their prices. They may work more diligently, but though this would increase the amount of work done in the world, thus fulfilling one of the announced aims of death taxation, it would not shift the "incidence" of the tax to others.

The traditional objection to death taxes has been that they destroy productive capital by transferring wealth from private hands to the government. As expounded by Adam Smith, the theory rested on the assumption that taxes on the transfer of property "increase the revenue of the sovereign, which seldom maintains any but unproductive labours, at the expense of the capital of the people, which maintains none but productive."[16] In 1924 Secretary of the Treasury Andrew Mellon urged that the federal estate tax rates be reduced:

> Death taxes are taxes upon capital. It is obvious that, if the government, to maintain itself, were to take 50 percent of every estate, small or large, and if on the average in the course of a generation a man

15. Smith, An Inquiry into the Nature and Causes of the Wealth of Nations, Book V, ch. 2, Part II, Appendix to Articles I and II.

16. Id.

could not double his inheritance, there would be an actual depletion of capital within the country and ultimately nothing would be left to tax. This is clear enough.[17]

Others have echoed the same theme.

The theory, however, cannot be accepted without important qualifications. First, we do not know what adjustments decedents made in the light of their expectations about the tax. Did they save more than they otherwise would have done? If so, the transfer of part of those savings to the government does not reduce what would have been the aggregate of private savings in the absence of a tax. Second, one must compare the use to which the government puts the tax revenue with the use to which the beneficiaries would have put the same funds. If they would have dined on guinea hen and champagne, the government's use of the tax revenue to build dams and bridges would serve to increase total national investment. If, on the other hand, they would have invested in new enterprises while the government increases the salaries of its employees, total national investment is less for the tax.[18] Finally, if the estate finds it necessary to sell part of its assets (for example, shares of a family corporation) to pay the tax, the transfer will have an impact on total investment. This effect will depend on the source from which the new owners of the securities draw the funds that make up the purchase price. If they curtail consumption to finance the purchase, the transfer of the securities will increase the investment of the new owners by as much as it decreases the investment of the estate, leaving total investment unchanged. If, on the other hand, the purchasers of the securities employ funds that otherwise would have gone into another investment, the tax has compelled the estate to reduce its investment without a corresponding increase in the investment of others. Then total private investment would tend to decline.

These three effects of the tax on total national investment (change in the original owner's savings, change in the government's expenditures, and change in the expenditures of those to whom the estate sells) need not be exerted in the same direction, and any conclusion about their net result would be precarious indeed. Consequently, Secretary Mellon's simple prediction, which has enjoyed surprisingly wide acceptance, must be rejected.

Even if the estate tax could be shown, on balance, to discourage investment, it could not be condemned out of hand. For most contemporary economists recognize that the economy may be served better at one

17. Mellon, Economic Aspects of Estate and Inheritance Taxation, 39 Trust Companies 708, 709 (1924).

18. Of course, no government expenditure can be allocated to a specific tax collection, and even the total volume of expenditure is sometimes (for example, during a war) only slightly affected by the volume of revenue. Consequently, it might be argued that the extent of investment by the government is independent of the estate tax yield. Then the effect of the tax on investment would depend on (1) whether the decedent accumulated more during his or her lifetime in anticipation of the tax, and (2) whether, when investments are sold by the estate to pay the tax, the buyers curtail consumption in order to raise the purchase price.

time by increasing total consumption and at another by increasing the volume of investment.

It is sometimes asserted that a great fortune can no longer be accumulated, either because of high income tax rates or for other reasons, and that estate and gift taxation represents an anachronistic relic of happier days. Unrealized appreciation in property, however, is not reached by the income tax, and proposals to alter this aspect of existing law have so far been rejected by Congress. Thus, stock or real estate may generate no income tax liability at all if held until death. A wise, or even a fortuitous, investment may be the seed that grows into a great fortune without any diminution by the income tax. The 2009 edition of the annual journalistic endeavor to identify the 400 richest people in America, whose estimated net worth is $1 billion or more per person, lists only a handful of the 400 as having acquired their wealth through inheritance and implicitly credits the rest as having made their own fortunes.[19] Although the data base for this survey leaves much to be desired, it seems likely that, as long as the income tax laws continue to leave the door open to substantial accumulations, the estate and gift taxes will have a task to perform.

The federal government imposes an *estate* tax, while historically the form of death taxation used by the states was the *inheritance* tax.[20] The traditional distinction between them is that an estate tax is levied on the privilege of transmitting property at death, while an inheritance tax is on the privilege of receiving property from the dead. Terminology aside, the difference is between a tax graduated according to the size of the decedent's entire estate and one that is graduated for each beneficiary according to the size of his or her share and relationship to the decedent.

Theoretically an estate tax is simpler to administer than an inheritance tax, because it is not necessary to place a value on each beneficiary's portion, a task of some complexity when future interests are involved. Yet the federal estate tax does not escape this problem altogether. A deduction for charitable bequests has been allowed since 1918, and in 1948 a "marital deduction" was inaugurated for property passing to a surviving spouse.[21] Both deductions introduce inheritance tax characteristics into the estate tax structure. Moreover, it is becoming ever more common to provide (either by will or by statute) that the federal tax shall be apportioned among the various property interests that constitute the estate, instead of falling, as do other debts and charges, on the residuary

19. The Forbes Four Hundred, 186 Forbes 17 (Oct. 11, 2010).

20. The inheritance tax is no longer the predominant form of state death taxation. By 2001 most states had abandoned their inheritance taxes in favor of a "pick-up" or "sponge" tax geared to the amount allowed as a credit against the federal estate tax under § 2011. Beginning in 2005, however, the § 2011 credit was replaced by a deduction for state death taxes under § 2058. The effect of this change was to abolish state death taxes in states that relied exclusively on a pick-up tax. Several states have responded by converting their pick-up tax to a free-standing estate tax. See infra page 546.

21. See infra Chapter 5, Section C (charitable deduction) and Section D (marital deduction).

alone.[22] Although such an apportionment is not binding on the Treasury, which can collect the tax from any part of the estate, the executor must value each beneficiary's share in order to apportion the tax in accordance with the testamentary or statutory scheme.

Because the inheritance tax is graduated according to each beneficiary's relationship to the decedent, it could be employed to penalize close family control of the decedent's fortune. This is a function that the estate tax, ordinarily taking no account of the beneficiary's identity, could not perform. In point of fact, however, the inheritance tax rate schedules afford preferential treatment to close relatives, the purpose of breaking up family accumulations being overbalanced in this instance by a social view that direct descendants have a birthright claim to the wealth while legacies to collateral relatives and "strangers" are in the nature of windfalls. (The federal "marital deduction" mentioned above makes a similar concession in the case of property passing to the decedent's surviving spouse.)

Neither an estate tax nor an inheritance tax could be very effective if it reached only property owned by the decedent at the time of death. Indeed, the larger the fortune, the easier it would ordinarily be to avoid a death tax by inter vivos gifts. The problem was recognized and met in the first state inheritance tax statute, enacted by Pennsylvania in 1826, which reached out to bring into the tax base any transfer that was "intended to take effect, in possession or enjoyment after the death" of the transferor. It has since become standard operating procedure to include such a provision in death tax statutes; its exegesis is the subject of extended study in this book. In 1891, the New York inheritance tax law introduced another now famous clause, which subjected to the death tax any property that the decedent had transferred during his or her lifetime "in contemplation of death." These clauses, as qualified and amended in later years, have extended the web of both estate and inheritance taxes to catch much peripheral property and add it to property actually owned by the decedent at the time of death in computing the tax.

Property may still be transferred during one's life, and thereby escape death taxation, if the transferor relinquishes all dominion and control. Estate and inheritance taxes are to that extent ineffectual as revenue measures and, more importantly, as instruments for reducing inequality of wealth. Indeed, one commentator observed:

> Until recently, the whole system of levies in the United States could be regarded mainly as a penalty on those whose benefactors failed to pass down their property before death. That any revenues were forthcoming is presumably attributable to untimely deaths, to utter distrust of beneficiaries, or to mere disregard of their interests.[23]

To block this route by which assets may be transmitted from one generation to another without payment of estate or inheritance tax, the

---

22. See infra page 641 (estate tax apportionment).

23. Simons, Personal Income Taxation 131 (1938).

federal government and several states have enacted a gift tax. As will be seen more fully later, an inter vivos transfer may still be cheaper than a transfer at death, especially if the property appreciates in value between the date of the gift and the donor's death. The Code bestows other benefits on lifetime transfers. The exclusions for present-interest gifts and for qualified educational and medical transfers, which are found only in the gift tax, permit large amounts of wealth to be transferred each year free of tax. Furthermore, the gift tax is imposed on the net value of the gift exclusive of the gift tax, while the estate tax applies identical rates to a base that includes the estate tax. If the transferor is not prepared to make an outright gift, however, but instead retains control over the transferred property (e.g., a right to shift enjoyment among a class of beneficiaries), it may be difficult to determine whether the property is subject to gift tax when made, becomes taxable only at the donor's death when the reserved rights terminate, or is subject to both gift and estate taxes. If both taxes apply, the practical effect is not that the tax burden is doubled; instead, the value of the property when transferred is subject to gift tax, and any appreciation between the date of the gift and the donor's death is subject to the estate tax.[24]

In addition to problems in determining whether a transfer is subject to the gift tax, the estate tax, or both, there are problems in the relationship between the gift and estate taxes, on the one hand, and the income tax, on the other. As the law now stands, a transfer of property may be complete enough so that a gift tax must be paid by the donor, yet the yield from the transferred property may still be taxed to the donor for income tax purposes. Conversely, a transfer may be insufficiently final to require payment of gift tax, yet it may be complete enough to terminate the donor's income tax liability. Similarly, a transfer may shift the income tax liability to the donee, even though the property will be subject to the estate tax as part of the transferor's estate, and vice versa. The different concepts of a completed transfer under the various taxing statutes once prompted Judge Jerome Frank to suggest using different words to designate the taxable conduct, calling it "a 'gift' in the gift tax law, a 'gaft' in the income tax law, and a 'geft' in the estate tax law."[25] The statutory anomalies spring from minor differences in phraseology rather than from rational policy, and one proposal for integrating the estate and gift taxes provides for "correlating" an integrated transfer tax with the income tax.[26] The aim is to tax the income from the property to its original owners until they relinquish enough control to warrant payment of the transfer tax, but to relieve them of income tax liability thereafter.

24. See infra pages 19–22, and especially footnote 44.

25. Commissioner v. Beck's Estate, 129 F.2d 243, 246 (2d Cir. 1942).

26. Federal Estate and Gift Taxes: A Proposal for Integration and for Correlation with the Income Tax (1947), prepared jointly by an Advisory Committee to the Treasury Department and by the Office of Tax Legislative Counsel. The proposal is discussed in Platt, Integration and Correlation—The Treasury Proposal, 3 Tax L. Rev. 59 (1947), and Wales, Consistency in Taxes—The Rationale of Integration and Correlation, id. at 173.

Another anomaly in the relation between the gift and estate taxes and the income tax is the transferee's income tax "basis" for property received by gift or inheritance. Suppose the value of stock purchased by the original owner for $100 per share has appreciated to $200 at the time the shares are transferred by gift or bequest. If the recipient later sells the stock for $250 per share, will the gain be $50 or $150? If the transfer was by gift, § 1015(a) of the Internal Revenue Code requires the donee to use the donor's cost "basis" of $100, so that the gain on the sale is $150 per share. But if the stock was received by inheritance, the beneficiary's "basis," prescribed by § 1014(a) of the Internal Revenue Code, is the fair market value at the time of the transferor's death, or $200, so that the gain on the sale is only $50 per share. Thus appreciation in donated property will be charged against the donee, but appreciation in property held until death goes entirely untaxed.[27] The discrimination works against the tax advantages, mentioned above, that inter vivos gifts ordinarily enjoy over transfers at death. Moreover, the prospect of a "stepped-up" basis for appreciated property transmitted at death undoubtedly deters some persons of advanced age from selling such assets or giving them away during life.

More basic in the relationship between the transfer taxes and the income tax is the fact that property received by gift or inheritance is not treated as income to the transferee on receipt. The income tax exemption of gratuitous receipts (assuming it is not compelled by the Constitution[28]) has been defended on various grounds, principally because the transfer itself is subject to gift or inheritance tax, but also because the progressive nature of the income tax would levy a heavy toll on any property that was transferred in a single year rather than over a period of time. Neither objection inheres in the nature of things. The gift and estate taxes could be modified or abolished if it were better tax policy to treat gratuitous receipts as taxable income; and an "averaging" device could be employed to remedy the unfair "bunching" of income in a single year. But Congress has never seriously considered abolishing the existing exemption, despite vigorous advocacy of such action by at least one distinguished tax economist, the late Henry Simons.[29]

---

27. For proposals to tax the gain by treating it as realized when the appreciated property is transferred by gift or at death ("constructive realization"), or by the less drastic device of requiring the beneficiaries to use their decedent's income tax basis in computing gain on disposing of the property ("carryover basis"), see Graetz, Taxation of Unrealized Gains at Death—An Evaluation of the Current Proposals, 59 Va. L. Rev. 830 (1973); Kurtz & Surrey, Reform of Death and Gift Taxes: The 1969 Treasury Proposals, the Criticisms, and a Rebuttal, 70 Colum. L. Rev. 1365, (1970); Zelenak, Taxing Gains at Death, 46 Vand. L. Rev. 361 (1993). Congress enacted carryover basis rules in 1976, but then retroactively repealed them in 1980. In 2001 Congress enacted a modified carryover basis system (in conjunction with estate tax repeal) which took effect in 2010 and expired one year later. See infra page 42.

28. Because these receipts have enjoyed a statutory exemption since the prototype of today's federal individual income tax was enacted in 1913, there has been no occasion for a court to determine whether they constitute income within the meaning of the Sixteenth Amendment. But they were treated as income by the Revenue Act of 1894, the invalidation of which by Pollock v. Farmers' Loan & Trust Co., 158 U.S. 601 (1895), led to the adoption of the Sixteenth Amendment.

29. Simons, supra footnote 23, at 125–47; see also Simons, Federal Tax Reform 136–39 (1950); Schmalbeck, Gifts and the Income Tax—An Enduring Puzzle, 73 L. & Contemp. Probs. 63 (2010);

Somewhat more interest has been displayed in supplementing or replacing the federal income tax with a "consumption tax" on amounts that are consumed rather than saved.[30] In theory, under a consumption tax it would be possible either to treat a gratuitous transfer as consumption by the transferor or to ignore the transfer and tax the recipient on his or her subsequent consumption of the transferred property. Under the latter approach, the exemption of gifts and bequests from the consumption tax base could be counteracted by imposing a separate tax on such transfers.[31]

Another proposal that has attracted much attention is the "accessions" tax, a scheme to replace the existing estate and gift taxes with a single tax imposed on the recipient of property by gift or inheritance.[32] The tax would be cumulative throughout the recipient's life, taxing each accession to his or her unearned wealth more heavily than the previous increment. No distinction would be made between gifts and inheritances or between property received from one benefactor and property received from several. The novel feature of the proposed tax is that it would focus attention on the recipient of wealth rather than on the transferor, treating all gratuitously acquired wealth as a unit. Thus, a taxpayer who received a total of $1 million partly by gift and partly by inheritance from various benefactors over a period of time would incur the same tax liability as one who received the same amount at one time from a single transferor. Because the tax is not imposed until the recipient actually comes into possession of the property, it bypasses many problems inherent in the present system concerning the timing of transfers, the valuation of future interests, and the identification of ultimate beneficiaries.

The accessions tax might be likened to an income tax levied only on gratuitous receipts, but with the lowest tax bracket each year starting where the highest bracket of the previous year ended. It is an effort to achieve more completely the social aim of the gift and estate taxes, not only by taxing more heavily a fortune that is transmitted intact than one

---

cf. Vickrey, Agenda for Progressive Taxation 198–202 (1947). Dissatisfaction with the estate and gift taxes as presently constituted has sparked renewed interest in the proposal to make gifts and bequests subject to the income tax. See McNulty, Fundamental Alternatives to Present Transfer Tax Systems, in Death, Taxes and Family Property 85 (Halbach ed., 1977); Dodge, Beyond Estate and Gift Tax Reform: Including Gifts and Bequests in Income, 91 Harv. L. Rev. 1177 (1978), and the articles and reports cited therein at 1179 n.11.

30. Andrews, A Consumption–Type or Cash–Flow Personal Income Tax, 87 Harv. L. Rev. 1113 (1974); Bradford, Untangling the Income Tax (1986); Graetz, Implementing a Progressive Consumption Tax, 92 Harv. L. Rev. 1575 (1979).

31. Bradford et al., Blueprints for Basic Tax Reform (2d ed. 1984); Dodge, Taxing Gratuitous Transfers Under a Consumption Tax, 51 Tax L. Rev. 529 (1996); Burke & McCouch, A Consumption Tax on Gifts and Bequests?, 17 Va. Tax Rev. 657 (1998). One commentator advocates a "consumption-without-estate tax" to replace the existing income and transfer taxes. McCaffery, The Uneasy Case for Wealth Transfer Taxation, 104 Yale L.J. 283 (1994). For critical responses to this proposal, see Alstott, The Uneasy Liberal Case Against Income and Wealth Transfer Taxation: A Response to Professor McCaffery, 51 Tax L. Rev. 363 (1996); Holtz–Eakin, The Uneasy Empirical Case for Abolishing the Estate Tax, id. at 495; Rakowski, Transferring Wealth Liberally, id. at 419.

32. Andrews, The Accessions Tax Proposal, 22 Tax L. Rev. 589 (1967), and earlier articles cited therein at 589 n.1; Halbach, An Accessions Tax, 23 Real Prop., Prob. & Tr. J. 211 (1988).

that is split up, but also by taxing more heavily a transferee who has already received property from other transferors.[33] The estate tax does neither, while the gift and inheritance taxes do only the first.

A system that imposes the tax on the receipt of property rather than on its transfer might also serve as a solution to the problem that existed in the law as originally written whereby the amount of tax on the transmission of a family fortune depended on the number of transfers that occurred, rather than on the number of generations separating the transferor from the transferee. By way of an example that remains true under current law, if *A* gives property to her brother *B*, and *B* subsequently gives the same property to his sister *C*, two gift taxes must be paid. Similarly, if there are two transfers by will, both *A*'s and *B*'s estates are subjected to estate tax.[34] But only one gift or estate tax is due if *A* transfers the property to *B* for life with remainder to *C*.

Prior to 1976, a transferor could minimize estate and gift taxes by putting property in trust with successive life estates in the transferor's children, grandchildren, etc. The duration of such a trust for multiple generations of beneficiaries was limited only by the local rule against perpetuities. The initial transfer in trust would be subject to tax, but no further gift or estate taxes would be imposed on the property held in trust as benefits shifted from one generation to the next. Had the property been transferred outright to the beneficiaries, a tax would have been imposed at each generational level. Thus, the total burden on a given family fortune was governed by the number of hands, rather than the number of generations, through which the property passed. In some cases the number of transfers was determined by accidents of birth and longevity, resulting in unequal burdens on taxpayers whose economic circumstances were comparable. In others, the number of transfers, and therefore the total tax burden, was determined by ingenuity in the use of life estates and other devices that might unduly constrain family settlements and that in any event were more feasible for the very rich than for others.

The congressional answer to the challenge posed by multi-generational trusts did not take the form of an accessions tax on the receipt of assets by the younger generations. Rather, a new generation-skipping transfer tax was enacted in 1976, and substantially revised in 1986, to tax distributions of wealth from trusts and similar arrangements having beneficiaries more than one generation below the transferor.[35] Thus, in the example in the previous paragraph, the tax is imposed at the death of the transferor's children when beneficial enjoyment shifts to the grandchildren and again

33. Steuerle, Estate or Accessions Tax—An Equity Question, 11 Tax Notes 459 (1980), arguing that if ability to pay and equalization of wealth are the equity principles to be served, an accessions tax is preferable to the current estate and gift taxes. For a proposal to replace the existing wealth transfer taxes with a "comprehensive inheritance tax" combining elements of an accessions tax and an income tax approach, see Batchelder, What Should Society Expect From Heirs? The Case for a Comprehensive Inheritance Tax, 63 Tax L. Rev. 1 (2009).

34. If the two deaths occur within a short time of each other, relief may be available in the form of the credit for previously taxed property under § 2013. See infra page 551.

35. See Chapter 6.

at the death of the grandchildren when beneficial enjoyment shifts to the great-grandchildren. The tax also applies to direct transfers that skip a generation (e.g., a gift from grandparent to grandchild).

Another scheme to ensure that the same burden will be imposed on the transfer of a given sum from one generation to another, regardless of the number of steps in which this is accomplished, is the "bequeathing power succession tax" proposed by Professor William Vickrey.[36] His mechanism for making the tax independent of the number of transfers is to graduate it according to the difference in age between the transferor and transferee, so that the greater the gap the greater will be the tax.

This catalogue of possible reforms should not be closed without mention of the wealth tax, a tax that is now in use in many European countries and that at least one distinguished American authority, Professor George Cooper, has proposed be considered for enactment in this country.[37] Although a wealth tax is a periodic tax on the net value of a person's assets, as distinguished from a tax on the income from those assets, it may be made payable out of either income or capital. Cooper's plan, put forward as he states to generate discussion, though not yet developed in full detail, envisions a low-rate wealth tax payable out of income, plus a supplemental tax at higher rates, payable out of capital, on gratuitously received wealth. He targets two areas of accrued wealth that he believes are not sufficiently covered by the existing tax system, proposing that the income-directed tax be applied to wealth that has been sheltered from the income tax, and that the capital-directed tax be designed, either in lieu of or as a supplement to the estate and gift taxes, to make periodic assessments on concentrations of inherited wealth. Responding to an objection that is usually raised to the enactment of a wealth tax, he suggests procedures for administratively feasible periodic valuations of assets.

Not all contemporary analysts believe that replacement of the existing estate and gift taxes by a new form of wealth tax is called for. Noteworthy in this regard is the Report on Transfer Tax Restructuring, prepared by the Task Force on Transfer Tax Restructuring of the American Bar Association's Section of Taxation, which proceeds on the premise that "a modified version of the present system [is] preferable to untested alternatives."[38] Several of the specific recommendations made in this Report are discussed in later sections of this book.

No doubt the reader has found this kaleidoscope of proposed reforms bewildering. Encountering them without a familiarity with the existing

36. Vickrey, supra footnote 29, at 224–48.

37. Cooper, Taking Wealth Taxation Seriously, 34 Rec. A.B. City N.Y. 24 (1979); the European experience is described in Verbit, Taking Wealth Taxation Seriously, 60 B.U. L. Rev. 1 (1980).

38. The Report is reprinted in 41 Tax Law. 393 (1988), and reviewed in Gutman, A Comment on the ABA Tax Section Task Force Report on Transfer Tax Restructuring, id. at 653. Further reform proposals appear in 2 Treasury Department Report to the President, Tax Reform for Fairness, Simplicity, and Economic Growth 373–405 (1984), and in Report on Reform of Federal Wealth Transfer Taxes, 58 Tax Law. 93 (2004).

law, the reader may also have found the significance of some proposals obscure. But even a casual acquaintance with possible improvements may help to illuminate the study of today's statutes. Further, one or more of the proposals may at some point in the future take the legislative center stage.

No one can chart with certainty the future of the estate and gift taxes. The country at large seems to be either indifferent or hostile to these taxes, and Congress is under no pressure from the voters back home to make them more robust.[39] As a result of legislation enacted in 2001 and 2010, the top marginal tax rate has fallen to its lowest level since the Great Depression and the exemption has increased five-fold. (Indeed, during the year 2010 a decedent's executor was allowed to opt out of the estate tax altogether, albeit at the cost of forgoing the unlimited income tax basis step-up for appreciated property passing from the decedent.) These changes, however, are not cast in stone. Unless Congress acts to extend them, the statutory amendments enacted in 2001 and 2010 will automatically expire at the end of 2012, leaving prior law in effect for 2013 and subsequent years. Admittedly, in today's political climate it seems unlikely that Congress will allow rates and exemptions to revert to pre–2001 levels. Still, in a time of mounting budgetary deficits and increasing economic inequality, the goal of scaling back the estate tax may be overshadowed by more pressing concerns such as meeting the retirement and health care needs of an aging population and forestalling threats to national security. Indeed, there is always the possibility that a swing of the pendulum may prompt future legislatures to consider more vigorous measures to curb the transmission of massive accumulations of hereditary wealth from generation to generation. It may then appear that the estate and gift taxes, with all their problems, still have an important role to play in curbing concentrations of inherited wealth, promoting equality of opportunity, and enhancing fairness in the tax system as a whole.

B. INTRODUCTION TO THE OPERATION OF THE TAXES

1. BASIC STRUCTURE OF THE ESTATE AND GIFT TAXES

We are concerned throughout our study with whether a gratuitous transfer of property has occurred and, if so, when. As the names tell us, a

39. In an illuminating book-length study, Professors Michael Graetz and Ian Shapiro seek to explain how the estate tax, which reaches only the wealthiest 1 or 2 percent of decedents' estates and imposes no burden on the vast majority of taxpayers, became so widely unpopular. In the years before 2001, opponents of the estate tax worked relentlessly to shape public opinion and mobilize political support for repeal. Armed with a store of anecdotes and think-tank studies, they portrayed the estate tax (invariably referred to as the "death tax") as a looming threat to ordinary families and small business owners. Undoubtedly, persistent popular biases and misconceptions also played a role. Most Americans routinely overestimate their own relative wealth and upward mobility; according to some polls, 20 percent of the population believe themselves to be in the wealthiest 1 percent and another 20 percent expect that they will soon join that select group. Many people also believe, erroneously, that the estate tax applies across the board to families at all levels of wealth. In a deft rhetorical move, opponents of the estate tax invoked the populist rhetoric of the "American dream" to attack the tax on grounds of morality and fairness. See Graetz & Shapiro, Death by a Thousand Cuts (2005).

gift tax applies to lifetime gifts and an estate tax to transfers at death (and to quasi-testamentary substitutes therefor), although liability for the former does not always provide immunity from the latter. Before the Tax Reform Act of 1976, the difference in the impact of the two taxes was obvious for all to see. Each had its own exemption, and the gift tax rates were about 25 percent lower than those of the estate tax. Quite simply, it cost substantially more to leave property at death than to give it away during life. The 1976 Act took several important steps toward unifying the estate and gift taxes. After 1976, all taxable transfers made during life and at death are included in a cumulative tax base and are taxed under a single rate schedule, with a unified credit to replace the separate exemptions. Key sections of the Code and many of the cases continue to explore the boundaries between lifetime and deathtime transfers. Why, if the transfer is taxed in the same manner at either time, does it make a difference if the tax is imposed early or late? A first step in the search for an answer requires an understanding of how the taxes are computed.

The estate tax is imposed by § 2001(a) of the Internal Revenue Code on the taxable estate (the gross estate less deductions) of every individual who at death is a citizen or resident of the United States. Section 2033 accounts for the bulk of the gross estate. It subjects to the tax all property owned at death—the so-called probate estate, including such assets as cash, land, securities, mortgages and other claims, unincorporated business interests, works of art, and the like. The gross estate, however, is not limited to such obvious assets. In order to forestall the use of testamentary substitutes to avoid the tax, further provisions are made to recapture transfers that the decedent made while alive over which he or she kept some measure of enjoyment or control.

Section 2038 requires the inclusion of property transferred during life if the transferor possesses at death the power to alter, amend, revoke, or terminate the beneficiaries' interests. This provision is not restricted to the situation where the transferor can reclaim the property by making a call to the trustee. It also applies to powers that cannot be exercised for the transferor's own benefit, such as a power to invade the corpus of a trust for the income beneficiaries or a power to direct how the corpus is to be distributed among the remainder beneficiaries when the trust terminates.

Section 2036 treats as testamentary a lifetime transfer under which the transferor has retained until death the right to the income or the right to designate who shall enjoy the income. Thus, a settlor's instruction in a trust "to pay the income to the settlor for life" will cause the remainder interests that follow the life estate to be included in the settlor's gross estate at death. This provision applies in like manner to powers that enable the settlor to apportion the income of a trust among the beneficiaries or to accumulate it for distribution at a later date.

Section 2037 includes transferred property if the beneficiaries can obtain possession or enjoyment only by surviving the transferor and if the transferor possesses a reversionary interest that is worth more than 5 percent of the value of the property immediately before death.

Section 2039 applies similar tests to determine the includibility of benefits passing at the decedent's death to beneficiaries under a pension plan or other contractual arrangement, to the extent of contributions made by or on behalf of the decedent.

Section 2040 deals with real or personal property owned jointly by the decedent and one or more persons with rights of survivorship. If the tenants are not husband and wife, the property is included in the gross estate to the extent the decedent contributed to the purchase of the property. In the case of a joint tenancy between husband and wife, however, the spouses are deemed equal owners so that one-half of the property's value is included in the gross estate of the first to die.

Section 2041 makes the decedent's estate accountable for any general power of appointment that the decedent held over property transferred by another person, such as the right to invade trust corpus or to designate the beneficiaries who will receive the assets of a trust on its termination.

Section 2042 includes in the gross estate any insurance on the decedent's life if the decedent had at the time of death any "incidents of ownership" in the policy or if the proceeds were payable to the estate.

At one time, § 2035 swept into the gross estate property transferred by the decedent "in contemplation of death" (even if the transferor retained no strings that would subject the property to tax under one of the provisions summarized above), and created a rebuttable presumption that any transfer made within three years of death was such a transfer. In 1976, this test was replaced by a rule that automatically included transfers made within three years of death as well as the gift taxes paid on them. This amendment did not end congressional tinkering with the statute. As the result of a 1981 amendment, the inclusion of transfers made within three years of death has been virtually eliminated except under specified circumstances where § 2035 operates in conjunction with other sections of the Code, most notably § 2042 governing the inclusion of life insurance proceeds. The statute continues to require the inclusion of the gift taxes paid on transfers made within three years of death.

The deductions that are subtracted from the gross estate to arrive at the taxable estate include funeral and administration expenses and claims against the estate (§ 2053), uncompensated casualty losses occurring during the administration of the estate (§ 2054), transfers for public, charitable and religious uses (§ 2055), transfers to the decedent's surviving spouse (§ 2056), and state death taxes (§ 2058). The tax is computed on the taxable estate using the unified rate schedule set out in § 2001(c). The statute authorizes four credits against the estate tax, including the unified credit (§ 2010), as well as credits for gift taxes paid on pre–1977 transfers that are included in the gross estate (§ 2012), estate taxes paid on certain prior transfers (§ 2013), and foreign death taxes (§ 2014).

Section 2501(a) imposes the gift tax on transfers of "property," and § 2511(a) adds that it does not matter whether "the property is real or personal, tangible or intangible." The working sections of the gift tax are deceptively brief. For instance, they do not list special types of transfers (except § 2514 relating to powers of appointment) that are subject to the tax as does the estate tax, although, as we shall see, a number of parallel estate tax concepts have been incorporated into the gift tax by judicial decision. It is clear, however, that the gift tax applies only to beneficial interests in property. Thus, a transfer by a trustee of property in which he or she has only legal title does not constitute a gift subject to the tax. In general, the tax applies to any transfer for which the donor did not receive in return consideration, which is defined in § 2512 as an equivalent "in money or money's worth."

Not all gratuitous transfers of beneficial interests result in gift tax liability. A donor has always been allowed each year to give a specified amount, known as the "annual exclusion," to each donee free of the tax, provided that the donee receives a present as opposed to a future interest in the property. The per-donee exclusion was raised from $3,000 to $10,000 for gifts made after 1981, and that amount is indexed for inflation since 1998. The amount of the exclusion in 2011 was $13,000 ($26,000 in the case of split gifts by married couples).

2. ILLUSTRATIVE COMPUTATIONS

Before the Tax Reform Act of 1976, the estate and gift taxes were separate and distinct. Each had its own exemption ($30,000 for the gift tax and $60,000 for the estate tax), and each was computed on its own rate schedule with the gift tax rates averaging 25 percent less than those of the estate tax.

The 1976 Act "unified" the gift and estate taxes by implementing a unified rate schedule applicable to a single, cumulative base including all taxable transfers made during life and at death. The top unified rate was cut from 77 percent to 70 percent. In addition, a unified credit was enacted in place of the separate specific exemptions. The unified credit automatically offsets the gift and estate taxes on an individual's cumulative taxable transfers up to a specified amount, often referred to as the "exemption" or the "exclusion." §§ 2010 and 2505.

The exemption (i.e., the amount sheltered from tax by the unified credit) has grown by leaps and bounds from its original level of less than $200,000 under the 1976 Act. Gradual increases enacted in 1981 and 1997 raised the taxable threshold first to $600,000 and eventually to $1 million.[40] Under legislation enacted in 2001 and 2010, the exemption soared

40. The Senate Finance Committee presented these increases as necessary "to offset the effects of inflation and to provide estate and gift tax relief to smaller estates, especially those

to new heights, reaching $3,500,000 in 2009 and $5 million in 2010 (indexed for inflation beginning in 2012).[41] As a result, a married couple can leave combined assets of $10 million to their children or other beneficiaries without incurring any gift or estate tax liability.[42]

Legislation enacted since 1976 contained further treats for taxpayers at the uppermost end of the wealth scale, including reductions of the top marginal estate and gift tax rate from 70 percent to less than 50 percent. Beginning in 2010, the top marginal rate plunged to 35 percent. § 2001(c). The 35 percent rate nominally applies to cumulative taxable transfers in excess of $500,000, but because the first $5 million of taxable transfers are sheltered by the unified credit, the estate and gift taxes in effect are imposed at a flat 35 percent rate on taxable transfers in excess of the $5 million exemption (indexed for inflation beginning in 2012).

The gift tax is levied each year. The tax rate schedule is graduated and cumulative in that the tax rate for the current year's taxable gifts is governed by the aggregate sum of all taxable gifts made since 1932. A tentative tax is first computed at current rates on the sum of taxable gifts from 1932 through the current year. Then a tentative tax is computed on the same amount exclusive of the current year's taxable gifts. The difference, less the unified credit (to the extent not previously used), is the tax on the current year's taxable gifts.

For example, suppose a taxpayer makes taxable gifts of $1 million in 2011 and $5 million in 2012, having previously made no taxable gifts. No gift tax is payable on the 2011 gift, because the tentative tax of $330,800 is fully covered by the unified credit. The gift tax liability with respect to the 2012 gift is determined as follows:

Prior years' taxable gifts	$	1,000,000
Plus current year's taxable gifts	+	5,000,000
Cumulative taxable gifts (through 2012)	$	6,000,000
Tentative tax on cumulative taxable gifts	$	2,080,800
Less tentative tax on prior years' taxable gifts	−	330,800
Tentative tax on current year's taxable gifts	$	1,750,000
Less available unified credit ($1,730,800 − $330,800)	−	1,400,000
Gift tax payable on current year's taxable gifts	$	350,000

The estate tax liability at the taxpayer's death is determined by a similar computation, with only a few adjustments. The amounts of taxable

which consist of family businesses." S. Rep. No. 144, 97th Cong., 1st Sess. 124 (1981), reprinted in 1981–2 C.B. 412, 460; see also S. Rep. No. 33, 105th Cong., 1st Sess. 38 (1997), reprinted in 1997–4 C.B. (Vol. 2) 1067, 1119.

41. From 2002 to 2010 the gift tax exemption remained frozen at $1 million despite the steady rise in the estate tax exemption. This anomaly arose not from an explicit policy judgment but rather from concerns about lost revenue. Beginning in 2011, the gift tax exemption once again marches in lockstep with the estate tax exemption.

42. Beginning in 2011, if one spouse dies without using all of his or her exemption, the unused amount may be used by the surviving spouse, in addition to his or her own exemption, if the decedent's executor so elects on a timely filed estate tax return. § 2010(c). The "portability" of the exemption offers married couples considerable flexibility in tax planning and reduces the need for "credit shelter" bequests and lifetime gifts to avoid wasting the exemption. See infra pages 539 and 549.

transfers made during life and at death are added together, and a tentative tax is computed on the total under the unified rate schedule. The gift taxes payable on the lifetime transfers (after the unified credit) and the full unified credit are then subtracted to arrive at the amount of estate tax payable. Assume that the taxpayer in the above example dies in 2016 with a taxable estate of $10 million, having made taxable gifts totaling $6 million during life. Assuming no change in rates or exemptions, the estate tax liability is determined as follows:

Taxable estate	$ 10,000,000
Plus adjusted taxable gifts	+ 6,000,000
Amount subject to tentative estate tax	$ 16,000,000
Tentative estate tax (§ 2001(b)(1))	$ 5,580,800
Less gift tax payable on post–1976 taxable gifts, after unified credit (§ 2001(b)(2))	– 350,000
Less unified credit[43]	– 1,730,800
Estate tax payable	$ 3,500,000

Despite the unified credit and rate schedule, the estate and gift taxes still fall short of a fully integrated system in at least one important respect. A decedent's taxable estate includes amounts used to pay estate taxes, but a donor's taxable gifts do not include amounts used to pay gift taxes. In tax parlance, the estate tax base is said to be "tax inclusive" while the gift tax base is "tax exclusive." This means that for a transfer of a given amount, the effective burden of the estate tax is substantially heavier than that of the gift tax, even though both taxes are imposed at the same nominal rates. The difference may be illustrated by contrasting the tax consequences of a single taxable gift made during life with those of a comparable testamentary transfer.[44]

First, suppose that in 2011 a taxpayer makes a taxable gift of $16 million and pays the resulting gift tax of $3,850,000, thereby increasing the beneficiary's net worth by $16 million:

Taxable gift	$ 16,000,000
Tentative tax	$ 5,580,800
Less unified credit	– 1,730,800
Gift tax payable	$ 3,850,000

Alternatively, suppose that the taxpayer makes no lifetime gifts (and pays no gift tax) but dies in 2011 with a taxable estate of $19,850,000

43. Note that the unified credit previously allowed with respect to lifetime gifts does not directly reduce the estate tax credit under § 2010; instead, the same effect is achieved by reducing the gift tax offset under § 2001(b)(2). The net result is that the unified credit reduces the estate tax liability only to the extent that the credit was not already used against the gift tax during life.

44. It is possible for a single transfer of property to be subject to both a gift tax during life and an estate tax at death. See §§ 2035–2042, discussed in Chapter 4. In such cases, § 2001(b) preserves the benefit of the tax-exclusive gift tax base for the amount of the lifetime gift, leaving only subsequent appreciation to enter the tax-inclusive estate tax base at death. If the gift was made within three years of death, however, the benefit of the tax-exclusive gift tax base is lost due to the operation of § 2035(b), discussed infra at page 225.

(including $3,850,000 of gift tax saved). After payment of the resulting estate tax of $5,197,500 from estate assets, the beneficiary receives a net benefit of $14,652,500:

Taxable estate	$ 19,850,000
Tentative estate tax	$ 6,928,300
Less unified credit	− 1,730,800
Estate tax payable	$ 5,197,500
Net benefit to beneficiary ($19,850,000 − $5,197,500)	$ 14,652,500

In each case, the taxpayer begins with $19,850,000 (before taxes). The estate tax on the deathtime transfer, however, exceeds the gift tax on the lifetime transfer by $1,347,500. This amount represents the cost of including an additional $3,850,000 (the gift tax on the lifetime transfer) in the taxable estate.[45] Of course, if the amount of the gift tax were treated as an additional taxable gift, the total tax liability (and the amount left in the beneficiary's hands after tax) would be the same in both cases.

3. VALUATION OF PROPERTY

Section 2031(a) provides that the value of the decedent's gross estate shall be determined at the time of death, but § 2032 gives the executor a right to elect to value the gross estate as of six months after the decedent's death, provided that the election brings about a decrease in both the value of the gross estate and the amount of the estate tax. The gift tax is applied to the value of the donated property as of the date of the gift. The Code does not, however, prescribe a method for arriving at the "value" of property, which means that the courts must look elsewhere to find the criteria to resolve controversies over the worth of assets that are not publicly traded, such as a family business or farm. The regulations define "fair market value" as "the price at which the property would change hands between a willing buyer and a willing seller, neither being under any compulsion to buy or to sell and both having reasonable knowledge of the relevant facts." Reg. §§ 20.2031–1(b) and 25.2512–1. Most disputes are resolved on the basis of testimony by expert witnesses who submit opinions as to the worth of an asset by reference to various factors such as the historical cost of the asset, prices paid for comparable property, and estimates of its anticipated income and salvage value. These factors and others that may affect fair market value are described in Chapter 7.

Sometimes the estate or gift tax applies to the transfer of only a partial interest in property such as a life estate, term of years, remainder, or reversion. In general, the value of such a partial interest is determined under actuarial tables based on specified assumptions concerning mortality rates and investment returns. For example, suppose a 60–year–old

45. Under the unified rate schedule, the additional $3,850,000 is taxed at a marginal rate of 35 percent, producing an additional tax of $1,347,500.

donor transfers $100,000 in trust to pay income to herself for life with remainder at her death to a named beneficiary. There is no transfer of the retained life estate because the donor cannot make a taxable gift to herself; only the value of the remainder is subject to gift tax. If it is assumed that the trust property produces income of 6 percent per year, the valuation tables set forth in the regulations indicate that the value of a 6 percent annual income stream payable on $1.00 for the life of a 60–year–old is $0.66375, and the value of $1.00 payable at the death of a 60–year–old is $0.33625. Reg. § 20.2031–7T(d)(7) (Table S). Thus, as a general matter, the tables apportion the $100,000 value of the underlying trust property between the income interest ($66,375) and the remainder ($33,625).

The actuarial assumptions on which the tables are based require periodic updating. Under § 7520, added to the Code in 1988, the assumed rate of return on investments is determined on a monthly basis by reference to the average market yield of U.S. Treasury obligations having maturities of three to nine years (see infra page 584).[46] Section 7520 also requires that the tables be revised at least every ten years to reflect the most recent available national mortality experience.

The use of actuarial tables to value partial interests in property has the great advantage of administrative convenience, but in particular cases the tables often yield wildly unrealistic results. During the 1980s, estate planners developed various "estate freezing" techniques which systematically exploited the tables to produce artificially low values for lifetime transfers. Congress responded in 1990 by enacting special rules to govern the gift tax valuation of intrafamily transfers of interests in corporations and partnerships and transfers in trust (§§ 2701 and 2702). The special rules, where they apply, impose unfavorable valuation assumptions that reduce the value of the donor's retained interests and correspondingly increase the value of the interests transferred to family members for gift tax purposes. In the example described above involving a transfer in trust subject to a retained life income interest, if the special rules of § 2702 apply, the donor's retained income interest will be deemed to have a value of zero and the entire value of the trust property will be allocated to the remainder. Accordingly, the creation of the trust will give rise to a taxable gift of $100,000. The special valuation rules are discussed infra at pages 78 and 591.

4. UNLIMITED MARITAL DEDUCTION FOR INTERSPOUSAL TRANSFERS

In determining the amount of the decedent's taxable estate, a marital deduction is allowed in § 2056 for the value of property passing from the decedent to his or her surviving spouse. The deduction is unlimited in amount, but it is subject to several restrictions which generally ensure

46. Prior to May 1989, when the floating discount rate under § 7520 took effect, the tables were based on a fixed discount rate set forth in the regulations.

that the property qualifying for the deduction, if not consumed by the surviving spouse, will eventually be subject to either gift or estate tax when it passes to the couple's children or other beneficiaries.[47]

Because the marital deduction has a gift tax counterpart (§ 2523), a married couple can transfer their assets from one spouse to the other without incurring either gift or estate tax, regardless of which spouse earned, inherited, or otherwise acquired the property. With this freedom, they can protect the property owned by the first spouse from estate tax until the survivor's death, or they can divide their property so that part is taxed in the estate of the first spouse to die and the balance is taxed in the survivor's estate. On the other hand, if both are independently wealthy so that an increase in the estate of either spouse would be disadvantageous, they can arrange to have each spouse's property taxed solely to its owner.

A married couple can also use their unified credits to achieve a tax saving. For example, in 2011 each spouse is entitled to transfer $5 million of property, for a total of $10 million, to their children or other beneficiaries at death without incurring any estate tax. If the family wealth is concentrated in the hands of one spouse, the couple may find it advantageous to rearrange assets, by means of tax-free gifts, to ensure that each spouse will have sufficient assets to make full use of his or her $5 million exemption. Even if one spouse dies without exhausting the available exemption, the surviving spouse can augment his or her own $5 million exemption by the amount of the deceased spouse's unused exemption, with the consent of the decedent's executor.

Section 2056(b) of the estate tax and § 2523(b) of the gift tax ordinarily deny the marital deduction if the interest transferred to the spouse is "terminable," i.e., if the spouse's interest may terminate at some future time and cause beneficial ownership of the property to shift to some other person. For example, if a donor transfers property in trust with income payable to the donor's spouse for life and remainder to their children, the spouse's income interest is "terminable" and ineligible for the marital deduction because it will terminate at the spouse's death, and the children will then succeed to the property as remainder takers. Thus, the "terminable interest rule" strikes a bargain: The initial transfer is exempted from tax on the condition that the donee spouse must receive the property with rights comparable to those of an outright owner, so that the property will eventually be subject to gift or estate tax when it passes to beneficiaries outside the husband-wife unit.

Even if the donee spouse receives a terminable interest, however, a marital deduction may be available under any one of several statutory safe harbors. For example, a deduction is authorized if the donee spouse is entitled to all the income for life and has a general power of appointment, exercisable during life or at death, over the underlying property. The

47. Section 2056(d), enacted in 1988, disallows the marital deduction if the surviving spouse is not a U.S. citizen, but this restriction does not apply to property passing through a "qualified domestic trust." See infra page 487.

existence of the power of appointment ensures that the property will be subject to tax. Since 1981 the statute has also authorized a deduction for "qualified terminable interest property" (QTIP) in which the donee spouse is entitled to all the income for life and the property passes to other beneficiaries at the spouse's death. The QTIP deduction is allowed only if an election is filed agreeing that a tax will be paid on the value of the underlying property when the spouse's interest terminates. The terminable interest rule and the statutory exceptions to it are full of constructional problems and traps for the unwary. They are examined in detail in Chapter 5, Section D.

5. SPLIT GIFTS

The gift tax contains a consent procedure for married couples (§ 2513), under which a gift made by either spouse to a third person can be reported as though each spouse made a gift of one-half of the donated amount. This split-gift procedure makes available two unified credits rather than one and gives a married couple the opportunity to double the number of available per-donee exclusions in computing the amount of the gift.

For example, if a husband and wife join in making taxable gifts of $10 million to third parties, each spouse has a tentative gift tax of $1,730,800, which is fully offset by his or her unified credit. On future gifts, each will have used up his or her unified credit.

6. GENERATION-SKIPPING TRANSFER TAX

In 1976 Congress added a generation-skipping transfer (GST) tax to the Code to ensure that the transmission of hereditary wealth is taxed as it passes from one generation to the next. To illustrate the problem at which the GST tax is aimed, consider a family trust created by a parent, directing that the income be paid to a child for life with remainder at the child's death going to the child's own descendants. As far as the estate tax is concerned, the income interest will terminate at the child's death and nothing will be included in the child's gross estate. The resulting immunity from the estate tax continues even if the child is given limited rights to receive corpus and a nongeneral power to appoint the remainder, a package that functionally approaches the benefits of outright ownership.

In 1986 Congress repealed the original GST tax and replaced it with a completely revised GST tax which appears in §§ 2601–2662. The new provisions continue to impose the tax on terminations of and distributions from trusts that shift wealth into the hands of beneficiaries two or more generations younger than the transferor. Thus, in the example given in the preceding paragraph, the tax is imposed when the trust terminates at the death of the transferor's child. The revised GST tax (unlike the 1976 statute) also applies when property is transferred in a "direct skip" to a beneficiary two or more generations younger than the transferor, as in the case of a gift or bequest from a grandparent to a grandchild.

Each individual transferor is entitled to a special exemption which shelters property up to a specified amount from GST tax. The amount of the exemption was originally fixed at $1,000,000 in 1986 and has been set equal to the estate tax exemption since 2004; beginning in 2010, the exempt amount is $5 million and is indexed for inflation beginning in 2012. The GST exemption operates separately from the unified credit and can be freely allocated to property transferred during life or at death. Once the exemption is exhausted, the GST tax is imposed at a flat rate equal to the highest marginal estate tax rate of 35 percent.

C. EFFECT OF STATE LAW

COMMISSIONER v. BOSCH'S ESTATE

387 U.S. 456 (1967).

MR. JUSTICE CLARK delivered the opinion of the Court.

These two federal estate tax cases present a common issue for our determination: Whether a federal court or agency in a federal estate tax controversy is conclusively bound by a state trial court adjudication of property rights or characterization of property interests when the United States is not made a party to such proceeding.

In No. 673, Commissioner of Internal Revenue v. Estate of Bosch, 363 F.2d 1009, the Court of Appeals for the Second Circuit held that since the state trial court had "authoritatively determined" the rights of the parties, it was not required to delve into the correctness of that state court decree. In No. 240, Second National Bank of New Haven, Executor v. United States, 351 F.2d 489, another panel of the same Circuit held that the "decrees of the Connecticut Probate Court . . . under no circumstances can be construed as binding" on a federal court in subsequent litigation involving federal revenue laws. Whether these cases conflict in principle or not, which is disputed here, there does exist a widespread conflict among the circuits over the question and we granted certiorari to resolve it. 385 U.S. 966, 968. We hold that where the federal estate tax liability turns upon the character of a property interest held and transferred by the decedent under state law, federal authorities are not bound by the determination made of such property interest by a state trial court. . . .

[In *Bosch's Estate*, the decedent had created an inter vivos trust for his wife's benefit and had given her a general power of appointment over the trust property. Before the decedent's death, the wife executed an instrument purporting to convert her general power to a special power. After the decedent's death, his executor obtained a determination from the state trial court that this instrument was a nullity. The Court of Appeals affirmed a Tax Court decision accepting this determination, thereby qualifying the trust for the marital deduction. (See infra page

501.) In *Second National Bank*, the decedent's executor obtained an order from the state probate court permitting the entire federal estate tax to be charged against a testamentary trust established by the decedent for his grandchildren. This increased the amount of the testamentary trust left for his widow, which qualified for the marital deduction. The Court of Appeals agreed with the federal district court that the state probate court's order was not binding for federal tax purposes, and held that a portion of the estate tax was chargeable against the widow's trust, thereby reducing the marital deduction.]

The problem of what effect must be given a state trial court decree where the matter decided there is determinative of federal estate tax consequences has long burdened the Bar and the courts. This Court has not addressed itself to the problem for nearly a third of a century. In Freuler v. Helvering, 291 U.S. 35 (1934), this Court, declining to find collusion between the parties on the record as presented there, held that a prior in personam judgment in the state court to which the United States was not made a party, "[o]bviously ... had not the effect of res judicata, and could not furnish the basis for invocation of the full faith and credit clause...." At 43. In *Freuler*'s wake, at least three positions have emerged among the circuits. The first of these holds that

> ... if the question at issue is fairly presented to the state court for its independent decision and is so decided by the court the resulting judgment if binding upon the parties under the state law is conclusive as to their property rights in the federal tax case.... Gallagher v. Smith, 223 F.2d 218, 225.

The opposite view is expressed in Faulkerson's Estate v. United States, 301 F.2d 231. This view seems to approach that of Erie R. Co. v. Tompkins, 304 U.S. 64 (1938), in that the federal court will consider itself bound by the state court decree only after independent examination of the state law as determined by the highest court of the State. The Government urges that an intermediate position be adopted; it suggests that a state trial court adjudication is binding in such cases only when the judgment is the result of an adversary proceeding in the state court....

We look at the problem differently. First, the Commissioner was not made a party to either of the state proceedings here and neither had the effect of res judicata, Freuler v. Helvering, supra; nor did the principle of collateral estoppel apply. It can hardly be denied that both state proceedings were brought for the purpose of directly affecting federal estate tax liability. Next, it must be remembered that it was a federal taxing statute that the Congress enacted and upon which we are here passing. Therefore, in construing it, we must look to the legislative history surrounding it. We find that the report of the Senate Finance Committee recommending enactment of the marital deduction used very guarded language in referring to the very question involved here. It said that "proper regard," not finality, "should be given to interpretations of the will" by state courts and then only when entered by a court "in a bona fide adversary proceeding." S. Rep. No. 1013, Pt. 2, 80th Cong., 2d Sess., 4. We cannot say that the authors of this directive intended that the decrees of state trial courts were to be conclusive and binding on the computation of the federal estate tax as levied by the Congress. If the Congress had intended state trial court determinations to have that effect on the federal actions, it certainly would have said so—which it did not do. On the contrary, we believe it intended the marital deduction to be strictly construed and applied. Not only did it indicate that only "proper regard" was to be accorded state decrees but it placed specific limitations on the allowance of the deduction as set out in §§ 2056(b), (c), and (d). These restrictive limitations clearly indicate the great care that Congress exercised in the drawing of the Act and indicate also a definite concern with the elimination of loopholes and escape hatches that might jeopardize the federal revenue. This also is in keeping with the long-established policy of the Congress, as expressed in the Rules of Decision Act, 28 U.S.C. § 1652. There it is provided that in the absence of federal requirements such as the Constitution or Acts of Congress, the "laws of the several states ... shall be regarded as rules of decision in civil actions in the courts of the United States, in cases where they apply." This Court has held that judicial decisions are "laws of the ... state" within the section. Erie R. Co. v. Tompkins, supra.... Moreover, even in diversity cases this Court has further held that while the decrees of "lower state courts" should be "attributed some weight ... the decision [is] not controlling ..." where the highest court of the State has not spoken on the point ... [and] that "an intermediate appellate state court ... is a datum for ascertaining state law which is not to be disregarded by a federal court *unless it is convinced by other persuasive data that the highest court of the state would decide otherwise.*" ... Thus, under some conditions, federal authority may not be bound even by an intermediate state appellate court ruling. It follows here then, that when the application of a federal statute is involved, the decision of a state trial court as to an underlying issue of state law should a fortiori not be controlling. This is but an application of the rule of Erie R. Co. v. Tompkins, supra, where state law as announced by the highest court of the State is to be followed. This is not a diversity case but the same principle may be applied for the same reasons, viz., the underlying substantive rule involved is based on state law and the State's highest court is the best authority on its own law. If there be no decision by that court then federal authorities must apply what they find to be the state law after giving "proper regard" to relevant rulings of other courts of the State. In this respect, it may be said to be, in effect, sitting as a state court....

We believe that this would avoid much of the uncertainty that would result from the "non-adversary" approach and at the same time would be fair to the taxpayer and protect the federal revenue as well.

The judgment in No. 240 is therefore affirmed while that in No. 673 is reversed and remanded for further proceedings not inconsistent with this opinion.

It is so ordered.

MR. JUSTICE DOUGLAS, dissenting.

As the Court says, the issue in these cases is not whether the Commissioner is "bound" by the state court decrees. He was not a party to the state court proceedings and therefore cannot be bound in the sense of res judicata. The question simply is whether, absent fraud or collusion, a federal court can ignore a state court judgment when federal taxation depends upon property rights and when property rights rest on state law, as they do here....

I would adhere to Freuler v. Helvering, supra, and Blair v. Commissioner, [300 U.S. 5 (1937)]. There was no indication in those cases that the state court decision would not be followed if it was not from the highest state court.

The idea that these state proceedings are not to be respected reflects the premise that such proceedings are brought solely to avoid federal taxes. But there are some instances in which an adversary proceeding is impossible (see, e.g., Estate of Darlington v. Commissioner, 302 F.2d 693; Braverman & Gerson, The Conclusiveness of State Court Decrees in Federal Tax Litigation, 17 Tax L. Rev. 545, 570–572 (1962)), and many instances in which the parties desire a determination of their rights for other than tax reasons.

Not giving effect to a state court determination may be unfair to the taxpayer and is contrary to the congressional purpose of making federal tax consequences depend upon rights under state law. The result will be to tax the taxpayer or his estate for benefits which he does not have under state law. This aspect is emphasized in Blair v. Commissioner, supra, where the Government attempted to tax the taxpayer for income to which he had no right under state law. In Second National Bank v. United States, the grandchildren's trusts will be assessed for the estate taxes, since the state court held that the proration statute applied; but the estate tax will be computed as if the proration statute did not apply—the marital deduction will be decreased and the tax increased. Or take the case where a state court determines that *X* does not own a house. After *X* dies, a federal court determines that the state court was wrong and that *X* owned the house, and it must be included in his gross estate even though it does not pass to his heirs. I cannot believe that Congress intended such unjust results.

This is not to say that a federal court is bound by all state court decrees. A federal court might not be bound by a consent decree, for it does not purport to be a declaration of state law; it may be merely a judicial stamp placed upon the parties' contractual settlement. Nor need the federal court defer to a state court decree which has been obtained by fraud or collusion. But where, absent those considerations, a state court has reached a deliberate conclusion, where it has construed state law, the federal court should consider the decision to be an exposition of the controlling state law and give it effect as such.

MR. JUSTICE HARLAN, whom MR. JUSTICE FORTAS joins, dissenting. . . .

The issue here, despite its importance in general, is essentially quite a narrow one. The questions of law upon which taxation turns in these cases are not among those for which federal definitions or standards have been provided . . .; it is, on the contrary, accepted that federal tax consequences have here been imposed by Congress on property rights as those rights have been defined and delimited by the pertinent state laws. The federal revenue interest thus consists entirely of the expectation that the absence or presence of the rights will be determined accurately in accordance with the prevailing state rules. The question here is, however, not how state law must in the context of federal taxation ordinarily be determined; it is instead the more narrow one of whether and under what conditions a lower state court adjudication of a taxpayer's property rights is conclusive when subsequently the federal tax consequences of those rights are at issue in a federal court.

The problem may not, as the Court properly observes, be resolved by reference to the principles of res judicata or collateral estoppel . . .; the Revenue Service has not, and properly need not have, entered an appearance in either of the state court proceedings in question here. Nor do the pertinent provisions of the revenue laws, or their legislative history, provide an adequate guide to the solution of the problem; the only direct reference in that lengthy history relevant to these questions is imprecise and equivocal.[48] The cases in this Court are scarcely more revealing; they are, as Judge Friendly remarked below, "cryptic" and "rather dated." 363 F.2d 1009, 1015.

It is, of course, plain that the Rules of Decision Act, 28 U.S.C. § 1652, is applicable here, as it is, by its terms, to any situation in which a federal court must ascertain and apply the law of any of the several States. Nor may it be doubted that the judgments of state courts must be accepted as a part of the state law to which the Act gives force in federal courts, Erie R. Co. v. Tompkins, 304 U.S. 64; it is not, for that purpose, material whether the jurisdiction of the federal court in a particular case is founded upon diversity of citizenship or involves a question arising under the laws of the United States. This need not mean, however, that every state judgment must be accepted by federal courts as conclusive of state law. The Court has, for example, never held, even in diversity cases, where the federal interest consists at most in affording a "neutral" forum, that the judgments of state trial courts must in all cases be taken as conclusive statements of state law; apart from a series of cases decided at the 1940 Term, the Court has consistently acknowledged that the character both of the state proceeding and of the state court itself may be relevant in

48. A supplementary report of the Senate Finance Committee, concerned with the legislation which eventually became the Revenue Act of 1948, said simply that "proper regard should be given to interpretations of the will rendered by a court in a bona fide adversary proceeding." S. Rep. No. 1013, Pt. 2, 80th Cong., 2d Sess., 4. This language is doubtless broadly consistent with virtually any resolution of these issues, but it is difficult to see the pertinence of the sentence's last four words if, as the Court suggests, conclusiveness was intended to be given to the State's highest court, but to none other.

determining a judgment's conclusiveness as a statement of state law. The same result must surely follow a fortiori in cases in which the application of a federal statute is at issue.

Similarly, it is difficult to see why the formula now ordinarily employed to determine state law in diversity cases—essentially that, absent a recent judgment of the State's highest court, state cases are only data from which the law must be derived—is necessarily applicable without modification in all situations in which federal courts must ascertain state law. The relationship between the state and federal judicial systems is simply too delicate and important to be reduced to any single standard.... The inadequacy of this formula is particularly patent here, where, unlike the cases in which it was derived, the federal court is confronted by precisely the legal and factual circumstances upon which the state court has already passed.

Accordingly, although the Rules of Decision Act and the *Erie* doctrine plainly offer relevant guidance to the appropriate result here, they can scarcely be said to demand any single conclusion....

Given the inconclusiveness of these sources, it is essential to approach these questions in terms of the various state and federal interests fundamentally at stake. It suffices for present purposes simply to indicate the pertinent factors. On one side are certain of the principles which ultimately are the wellsprings both of the Rules of Decision Act and of the *Erie* doctrine. First among those is the expectation that scrupulous adherence by federal courts to the provisions of state law, as reflected both in local statutes and in state court decisions, will promote an appropriate uniformity in the administration of law within each of the States. Uniformity will, in turn, assure proper regard in the federal courts for the areas of law left by the Constitution to state discretion and administration, and, in addition, will prevent the incongruity that stems from dissimilar treatment by state and federal courts of the same or similar factual situations. Finally, it must be acknowledged that state courts are unquestionably better positioned to measure the requirements of their own laws; even the lowest state court possesses the tangible advantage of a close familiarity with the meaning and purposes of its local rules of law.

On the other side are important obligations which spring from the practical exigencies of the administration of federal revenue statutes. It can scarcely be doubted that if conclusiveness for federal tax purposes were attributed to any lower state court decree, whether the product of genuinely adversary litigation or not, there would be many occasions on which taxpayers might readily obtain favorable, but entirely inaccurate, determinations of state law from unsuspecting state courts. One need not, to envision this hazard, assume either fraud by the parties or any lack of competence or disinterestedness among state judges; no more would be needed than a complex issue of law, a crowded calendar, and the presentation to a busy judge of but essentially a single viewpoint. The consequence of any such occurrence would be an explication of state law that would not necessarily be either a reasoned adjudication of the issues or a consistent application of the rules adopted by the State's appellate courts.

It is difficult to suppose that adherence by federal courts to such judgments would contribute materially to the uniformity of the administration of state law, or that the taxpayer would be unfairly treated if he were obliged to act, for purposes of federal taxation, as if he were governed by a more accurate statement of the requirements of state law. Certainly it would contribute nothing to the uniformity or accuracy of the administration of the federal revenue statutes if the federal courts were compelled to adhere in all cases to such judgments. . . .

The foregoing factors might, of course, be thought consistent with a variety of disparate resolutions of the questions these two cases present. If emphasis is placed principally upon the importance of uniformity in the application of law within each of the several States, and thereby upon the apparent unfairness to an individual taxpayer if an issue of state law were differently decided by state and federal courts, it might seem appropriate to accept, in all but the most exceptional of circumstances, the judgment of any state court that has addressed the question at issue. This is the viewpoint identified with the opinion of the Court of Appeals for the Third Circuit in Gallagher v. Smith, 223 F.2d 218; it is, in addition, apparently the rule adopted today by my Brother Douglas. Conversely, if emphasis is placed principally upon the hazards to the federal fisc from dubious decisions of lower state courts, it might be thought necessary to require federal courts to examine for themselves, absent a judgment by the State's highest court, the content in each case of the pertinent state law. This, as I understand it, is the rule adopted by a majority of the Court today.

In my opinion, neither of these positions satisfactorily reconciles the relevant factors involved. The former would create excessive risks that federal taxation will be evaded through the acquisition of inadequately considered judgments from lower state courts, resulting from proceedings brought, in reality, not to resolve truly conflicting interests among the parties but rather as a predicate for gaining foreseeable tax advantages, and in which the point of view of the United States had never been presented or considered. The judgment resulting from such a proceeding might well differ only in form from a consent decree. The United States would be compelled either to accept as binding upon its interests such a judgment, or to participate in every state court proceeding, brought at the taxpayer's pleasure, which might establish state property rights with federal tax consequences.

The second position, on the other hand, would require federal intervention into the administration of state law far more frequently than the federal interests here demand; absent a judgment of the State's highest court, federal courts must under this rule re-examine and, if they deem it appropriate, disregard the previous judgment of a state court on precisely the identical question of state law. The result might be widely destructive both of the proper relationship between state and federal law and of the uniformity of the administration of law within a State.

The interests of the federal treasury are essentially narrow here; they are entirely satisfied if a considered judgment is obtained from either a state or a federal court, after consideration of the pertinent materials, of the requirements of state law. For this purpose, the Commissioner need not have, and does not now ask, an opportunity to relitigate in federal courts every issue of state law that may involve federal tax consequences; the federal interest requires only that the Commissioner be permitted to obtain from the federal courts a considered adjudication of the relevant state law issues in cases in which, for whatever reason, the state courts have not already provided such an adjudication. In turn, it may properly be assumed that the state court has had an opportunity to make, and has made, such an adjudication if, in a proceeding untainted by fraud, it has had the benefit of reasoned argument from parties holding genuinely inconsistent interests.

I would therefore hold that in cases in which state-adjudicated property rights are contended to have federal tax consequences, federal courts must attribute conclusiveness to the judgment of a state court, of whatever level in the state procedural system, unless the litigation from which the judgment resulted does not bear the indicia of a genuinely adversary proceeding. I need not undertake to define with any particularity the weight I should give to the various possible factors involved in such an assessment; it suffices to illustrate the more important of the questions which I believe to be pertinent. The principal distinguishing characteristic of a state proceeding to which, in my view, conclusiveness should be attributed is less the number of parties represented before the state court than it is the actual adversity of their financial and other interests. It would certainly be pertinent if it appeared that all the parties had instituted the state proceeding solely for the purpose of defeating the federal revenue. The taking of an appeal would be significant, although scarcely determinative. The burden would be upon the taxpayer, in any case brought either for a redetermination of a deficiency or for a refund, to overturn the presumption . . . that the Commissioner had correctly assessed the necessary tax by establishing that the state court had an opportunity to make, and had made, a reasoned resolution of the state law issues, after a proceeding in which the pertinent viewpoints had been presented. Proceedings in which one or more of the parties had been guilty of fraud in the presentation of the issues to the state court would, of course, ordinarily be entitled to little or no weight in the federal court's determination of state law.

I recognize, of course, that this approach lacks the precision of both the contrasting yardsticks suggested by the Court and by my Brother Douglas. Yet I believe that it reflects more faithfully than either of those resolutions the demands of our federal system and of the competing interests involved.[49] ...

MR. JUSTICE FORTAS, dissenting.

While I join the dissenting opinion of my Brother Harlan, I believe it appropriate to add these few comments. As my Brother Harlan states, in a case in which federal tax consequences depend upon state property interests, a federal court should accept the final conclusion of a competent state court, assuming that such a conclusion is an adjudication of substance arrived at after adversary litigation and on the basis of the same careful consideration that state courts normally accord cases involving the determination of state property interests. The touchstone of whether the state proceeding was "adversary" is not alone entirely satisfactory. I think that this concept has been helpfully embellished by Judge Raum of the United States Tax Court in the *Bosch* case, 43 T.C. 120, 123–124. Judge Raum suggests that among the factors to be considered in determining whether the decision of the state court is to be accepted as final for federal tax purposes are the following: whether the state court had jurisdiction, and whether its determination is fully binding on the parties; whether, in practice, the decisions of the state court have precedential value throughout the State; whether the Commissioner was aware of the state proceedings and had an opportunity to participate; whether the state court "rendered a reasoned opinion and reached a 'deliberate conclusion,' Blair v. Commissioner, 300 U.S. [5], at p. 10"; whether the state decision has potentially offsetting tax consequences in respect of the state court litigant's federal taxes; and, in general, whether the state court decision "authoritatively determined" future property rights, and thus, as Judge Raum stated, "provided more than a label for past events. . . ."

NOTES

1. *Effect of state court adjudications.* Federal tax disputes often turn on a determination (or redetermination) of property rights under state law where precisely the same factual or legal issues have already been adjudicated by a lower state court. The significance of the *Bosch* decision is not limited to the narrow context of the estate tax marital deduction. For example, to determine whether property is includible in a decedent's gross estate under § 2033, it is necessary to ascertain the nature and extent of the decedent's interest in the property at death (see Chapter 3, Section A). Similarly, whether a purported lifetime transfer constitutes a completed gift under § 2511 may turn on whether the donor retains a power under state law to revoke or alter the enjoyment of the property (see Chapter 2, Section C). And, as illustrated by the *Bosch* case, the characterization of a power of appointment as general or

49. It may be doubted, however, whether this approach would actually produce serious practical disadvantages. It is essentially the standard that has been embodied in the Treasury Regulations since 1919, see now Treas. Reg. §§ 20.2053–1(b)(2), 20.2056(e)–2(d)(2), and which was urged before this Court in these cases by counsel for the United States. It is, moreover, similar to the standards employed in various opinions by a number of the courts of appeals. . . . If any practical difficulties actually attend this standard, they have apparently not, despite its wide use, yet appeared.

special under §§ 2041 or 2514 requires an analysis of the terms of the power under state law (see Chapter 4, Section G).

If a state court adjudication is necessary to determine which of two or more competing claimants will ultimately own the property, the parties may be primarily concerned with resolving a bona fide dispute over their respective property rights, with little or no regard for the tax consequences. This might occur, for example, where a decedent attempted while living to give property to *A*, and after the decedent's death the gift is challenged by *B*, who stands to receive the property by will or intestacy. Sometimes, however, there is no dispute over the ultimate disposition of property; all parties agree that one beneficiary is entitled to receive the property, and a state court proceeding is brought for the sole purpose of determining whether the property passed by way of gift, bequest, or purchase. In such cases, the state court decision may have little significance apart from its potential impact on the federal tax consequences of the transfer. See, e.g., Warda v. Commissioner, 15 F.3d 533 (6th Cir.), cert. denied, 513 U.S. 808 (1994) (disregarding constructive trust imposed by probate court for benefit of taxpayer's son, where taxpayer had already been declared the owner of the property in an earlier proceeding and had transferred it to her son).

2. *"Proper regard."* In light of the Supreme Court's holding in *Bosch*, are federal tax authorities free to disregard a lower state court decision concerning the nature and extent of property interests passing to or from a particular taxpayer? Courts often look at whether the state court decision reflects the outcome of a bona fide, adversarial dispute with significant nontax consequences. See, e.g., Warren's Estate v. Commissioner, 981 F.2d 776 (5th Cir. 1993) (allowing charitable deduction based on probate court order approving arm's-length settlement of "truly adversarial, nontax" dispute); Bennett's Estate v. Commissioner, 100 T.C. 42 (1993) (disregarding court-approved trust modification where proceeding was "nonadversarial" and "instituted for the sole purpose of obtaining a marital deduction that was not otherwise available"); Hubert's Estate v. Commissioner, 101 T.C. 314 (1993), affd. on other grounds, 63 F.3d 1083 (11th Cir. 1995), affd., 520 U.S. 93 (1997) (allowing marital and charitable deductions based on court-approved settlement agreement resulting from "bona fide adversary proceeding"). In some cases, courts focus on whether the state court decision represents a correct application of state law, i.e., whether the decision would likely have been affirmed had it been reviewed by the highest state court. See, e.g., Salter's Estate v. Commissioner, 545 F.2d 494 (5th Cir. 1977) (bequest qualified for marital deduction based on probate court's construction of will); Greene v. United States, 476 F.2d 116 (7th Cir. 1973) (marital share bore ratable portion of death tax burden, notwithstanding probate court's contrary conclusion). Does the existence of a bona fide, adversarial dispute between private parties ensure that the state court's decision reflects a correct application of state law? What makes a proceeding "adversarial"?

3. *Standard of review.* In Goree's Estate v. Commissioner, 68 T.C.M. (CCH) 123 (1994) (nonacq.), decedent died intestate, survived by his widow and three minor children. The widow obtained a probate court order directing her, as conservator for the children, to execute partial disclaimers of the children's intestate shares. As a result of the disclaimers, a portion of

decedent's estate passed directly to the widow instead of the children, thereby increasing the marital deduction in decedent's estate. In the federal tax proceeding, the government argued that the disclaimers should be disregarded for federal tax purposes because they were not in the children's "best interests" as required by state law. The Tax Court, however, accepted the probate court's findings, noting that the probate court issued its order after a hearing at which the children's interests were represented by a guardian ad litem:

> The only question we are asked to decide in the instant case is whether the interests in decedent's estate were properly disclaimed under Alabama law. Respondent argues that the interests were not properly disclaimed because the disclaimers were not in the best interests of decedent's children and that we must undertake a de novo review of the Probate Court disclaimer proceedings. We do not agree with respondent's contention that we are required to make such a review. Under Alabama law, the proper standard guiding our review of the Probate Court judge's decision is whether his decision was "plainly and palpably erroneous." Based on the record in the instant case, we hold that the Probate Court judge's decision as to the question of what was in the best interests of decedent's children was not "plainly and palpably erroneous" and that the partial disclaimers were therefore properly made under Alabama law. [68 T.C.M. (CCH) at 128.]

Should the court in a federal tax proceeding assume the posture of a state appellate court in reviewing a lower court's adjudication of property rights? Note that questions of law are subject to de novo review on appeal, but a trial court's findings of fact are ordinarily upheld unless they are clearly erroneous or unsupported by substantial evidence. What if the trial court based its decision on facts stipulated by the parties?

4. *Role of highest state court.* Does *Bosch* prevent federal tax authorities from looking behind a decision of the highest state court concerning the nature and extent of a taxpayer's interest in property? Suppose that *A* gave her son *B* a durable general power of attorney under which *B* made gifts of *A*'s property to himself and *A*'s other descendants during *A*'s lifetime. After *A*'s death, *B* (in his capacity as *A*'s executor) obtains a declaratory judgment from a lower state court confirming the validity of the gifts; with *Bosch* in mind, *B* appeals to the highest state court, which summarily affirms the lower court's judgment. See LeCraw v. LeCraw, 401 S.E.2d 697 (Ga. 1991); cf. Berman v. Sandler, 399 N.E.2d 17 (Mass. 1980) (affirming decree retroactively reforming trust to qualify for marital deduction; "It is appropriate for us to render a decision in this case ... because only an interpretive decision by the highest State court will dispose of contrary interpretations by the Internal Revenue Service."). What if review by the highest state court is not available? See In re Bartholow's Estate, 725 N.W.2d 259 (S.D. 2006) (dismissing taxpayer's appeal from favorable trial court judgment; "Nothing in [*Bosch*] can be construed to suggest this Court should ignore general rules of appellate procedure to provide a rubber stamp affirmance for the benefit of a victorious party.")

5. *References.* For further discussion of the issues raised by *Bosch*, see Caron, The Role of State Court Decisions in Federal Tax Litigation: *Bosch*, *Erie*, and Beyond, 71 Or. L. Rev. 781 (1992); Sobeloff, Tax Effect of State Court Decisions—The Impact of *Bosch*, 21 Tax Law. 507 (1968); Verbit, State Court Decisions in Federal Transfer Tax Litigation: *Bosch* Revisited, 23 Real Prop., Prob. & Tr. J. 407 (1988); Wolfman, *Bosch*, Its Implications and Aftermath: The Effect of State Court Adjudications on Federal Tax Litigation, 3 U. Miami Inst. on Est. Planning ch. 2 (1969), and articles cited therein at footnote 2.

D. CONSTITUTIONALITY

In New York Trust Co. v. Eisner, 256 U.S. 345 (1921), the federal estate tax was attacked "as an unconstitutional interference with the rights of the States to regulate descent and distribution, as unequal and as a direct tax not apportioned as the Constitution requires." The Court, through Justice Holmes, responded:

> It is admitted, as since Knowlton v. Moore, 178 U.S. 41, it has to be, that the United States has power to tax legacies, but it is said that [the estate] tax is cast upon a transfer while it is being effectuated by the State itself and therefore is an intrusion upon its processes, whereas a legacy [i.e., inheritance] tax is not imposed until the process is complete. . . .
>
> Knowlton v. Moore, 178 U.S. 41, dealt, it is true, with a legacy tax. But the tax was met with the same objection; that it usurped or interfered with the exercise of state powers, and the answer to the objection was based upon general considerations and treated the "power to transmit or the transmission or receipt of property by death" as all standing on the same footing. 178 U.S. 57, 59. After the elaborate discussion that the subject received in that case we think it unnecessary to dwell upon matters that in principle were disposed of there. The same may be said of the argument that the tax is direct and therefore is void for want of apportionment. It is argued that when the tax is on the privilege of receiving, the tax is indirect because it may be avoided, whereas here the tax is inevitable and therefore direct. But that matter also is disposed of by Knowlton v. Moore, not by an attempt to make some scientific distinction, which would be at least difficult, but on an interpretation of language by its traditional use—on the practical and historical ground that this kind of tax always has been regarded as the antithesis of a direct tax; "has ever been treated as a duty or excise, because of the particular occasion which gives rise to its levy." 178 U.S. 81–83. Upon this point a page of history is worth a volume of logic. [256 U.S. at 348–49.]

NOTES

1. *Later cases.* In 1929, the Supreme Court rejected a claim that the federal gift tax of 1924 violated the direct tax clause of the Constitution.

Bromley v. McCaughn, 280 U.S. 124 (1929). The estate tax was again upheld as constitutional, against a farrago of additional contentions, in Heitsch v. Kavanagh, 200 F.2d 178 (6th Cir. 1952), cert. denied, 345 U.S. 939 (1953). See generally Eisenstein, Estate Taxes and the Higher Learning of the Supreme Court, 3 Tax L. Rev. 395, 397–408 (1948); see also Ackerman, Taxation and the Constitution, 99 Colum. L. Rev. 1 (1999).

2. *Tax-exempt bonds.* The language of § 2033, applying the estate tax to property owned at death, and § 2511(a), setting out the scope of the gift tax, is sufficiently comprehensive to include tax-exempt state and municipal bonds. Reg. §§ 20.2033–1 and 25.2511–1(a); see also infra page 44, footnote 2 and page 180, footnote 1. The tax, being an excise on the transfer of the bonds, is not unconstitutional. Willcuts v. Bunn, 282 U.S. 216, 230 (1931).

The Housing Act of 1937 authorized the issuance of housing agency bonds (so-called "project notes") to finance the construction of public housing and stated that such notes, including interest thereon, "shall be exempt from all taxation now or hereafter imposed by the United States." In United States v. Wells Fargo Bank, 485 U.S. 351 (1988), the Supreme Court held that Congress did not by this language intend to exempt project notes from the estate tax, emphasizing that exemptions from taxation are not to be implied but must be unambiguously proved. The Court reviewed with approval the authority that identifies the estate tax as an excise tax and as such applicable to tax government bonds without violating the clause of the Constitution governing the imposition of direct taxes.

3. *Retroactivity.* The imposition of a tax on the transfer of property that occurs before the enactment of the taxing statute has given rise to claims of invalidity on the ground that a retroactively imposed tax violates the due process clause of the Fifth Amendment. In a few early cases these challenges were successful. See Nichols v. Coolidge, 274 U.S. 531 (1927) (invalidating 1919 estate tax statute that included trust property, transferred in 1907 with retained life income interest, in gross estate of decedent who died in 1921); Untermyer v. Anderson, 276 U.S. 440 (1928) (invalidating 1924 gift tax statute as applied to gifts made in 1924 while conference report on bill was pending); see also Blodgett v. Holden, 275 U.S. 142 (1927) (four justices concluded 1924 gift tax statute was invalid as applied to pre-enactment gifts, while four others interpreted statute narrowly to avoid constitutional issue).

More recently, however, the Court observed that *Nichols*, *Untermyer* and *Blodgett* "were decided during an era characterized by exacting review of economic legislation under an approach that 'has long since been discarded.' " United States v. Carlton, 512 U.S. 26 (1994). The Court articulated a more lenient due process standard for retroactive tax statutes, requiring only "a legitimate legislative purpose furthered by rational means." In *Carlton*, the Court upheld a retroactive amendment that narrowed the scope of the estate tax deduction under former § 2057, noting that the amendment was intended to cure what Congress "reasonably viewed as a mistake" in the original provision enacted the previous year. Similarly, in United States v. Hemme, 476 U.S. 558 (1986), the Court upheld transitional rules that reduced the newly-enacted unified credit (applicable to transfers made after 1976) to reflect the specific exemption allowed with respect to gifts made late in 1976.

The Court had no difficulty in upholding "subsequent amendments that bring about certain changes in operation of the tax laws, rather than the creation of a wholly new tax." See also Quarty v. United States, 170 F.3d 961 (9th Cir. 1999) (upholding change in top marginal estate tax rate, enacted in August and retroactive to January of same year); NationsBank of Texas v. United States, 269 F.3d 1332 (Fed. Cir. 2001), cert. denied, 537 U.S. 813 (2002) (same).

In several estate tax cases, the Court has avoided constitutional problems by treating death as the final step in a chain of events giving rise to a taxable transfer. Even if some of those events occur before the date of enactment, the Court has repeatedly brushed aside due process challenges to statutes that apply only to estates of decedents dying after the date of enactment. See Reinecke v. Northern Trust Co., 278 U.S. 339 (1929) (revocable trust created before date of enactment); Milliken v. United States, 283 U.S. 15 (1931) (transfer in contemplation of death, made before increase in estate tax rates); United States v. Jacobs, 306 U.S. 363 (1939) (joint tenancy with right of survivorship created before date of enactment). The gift tax has bred less litigation because the statute expressly applies only to gifts made after the date of enactment. See § 2502(c)(1) (gift tax applies only to gifts made after June 6, 1932, the date of enactment of the Revenue Act of 1932).

4. *Double taxation.* United States citizens and resident aliens are taxed by § 2031(a) on "all property ... wherever situated" and hence may be subject to double taxation if they own property within the jurisdiction of another country. The burden of double taxation is partially mitigated by treaties with several foreign countries under which primary taxing jurisdiction is allocated to the country of citizenship or domicile. Specified types of property (e.g., immovables, business property of a permanent establishment, or assets pertaining to a fixed base used for performance of professional services) having its "situs" in the other contracting country may also be subject to that country's taxing jurisdiction, in which case the treaties provide for a credit against the tax imposed by the country of citizenship or domicile. See generally Schoenblum, Multistate and Multinational Estate Planning (2009).

Because treaties have not been negotiated with all foreign countries imposing death taxes on U.S. citizens and resident aliens, and because in some instances the treaties do not produce complete relief against double taxation, Congress in 1951 enacted a statutory credit for foreign death taxes. This provision, § 2014, permits the estate to credit against its U.S. estate tax liability, as a kind of down payment, the death taxes paid to any foreign country "in respect of any property situated within such foreign country and included in the gross estate." The situs rules to be applied are those prescribed by §§ 2104 and 2105 for determining the situs of property includible in the gross estate of a nonresident alien. There are several limitations on the credit; the principal one is that if the United States taxes the property at a lower effective rate than the foreign country, only the lower amount can be credited. Where § 2014 overlaps a treaty, the larger credit may be taken.

5. *Nonresident aliens.* In the case of a nonresident alien, § 2103 provides that the estate tax is imposed on the transfer of only "that part of his

gross estate (determined as provided in § 2031) which at the time of his death is situated in the United States." The situs of real property or tangible personal property is determined by its physical location. Under § 2104, shares of stock are included only if the issuer is a domestic corporation, and debt obligations generally are included only if the obligor is a U.S. citizen or resident or a domestic corporation, partnership, or governmental unit. The scope of these inclusionary rules is limited by § 2105, which exempts certain life insurance proceeds, bank deposits, and works of art. In the case of other intangibles "the written evidence of which is not treated as being the property itself," the regulations require inclusion if the issuer or obligor is a U.S. resident or a domestic corporation or governmental unit. Reg. § 20.2104–1(a)(4).

In 1988 Congress repealed the special estate tax rates formerly applicable to estates of nonresident aliens and replaced them with the same rates that apply to estates of U.S. citizens. § 2101(b). The estate of a nonresident alien is entitled to a unified credit of $13,000 (equivalent to an exemption of $60,000), except where a treaty provides for a different amount based on the portion of the gross estate that is situated in the United States. § 2102(c). This unified credit is reduced by the amount of any unified credit allowed with respect to gifts made by the decedent.

6. *Expatriation to avoid tax.* For many years, § 2107 imposed an enhanced estate tax, computed at the normal rates for U.S. citizens, on the estate of a deceased nonresident alien who lost U.S. citizenship within ten years before death, subject to a few limited exceptions set forth in the statute. Similar provisions applied for gift and income tax purposes. §§ 2501(a)(3) and 877.

In 2008 Congress enacted a new set of provisions to curtail the tax advantages of expatriation. Transfers made during life or at death by a "covered expatriate" are no longer subject to gift or estate tax. Instead, § 2801 imposes a tax on receipt by a U.S. citizen or resident of gifts and bequests from a covered expatriate. The tax is computed at the top marginal gift or estate tax rate and applies to gifts and bequests in excess of the gift tax annual exclusion amount, subject to exceptions for transfers that are otherwise subject to gift or estate tax and transfers that would qualify for a marital or charitable deduction if made by a U.S. person. For income tax purposes, the covered expatriate is treated as selling all his or her property and realizing any built-in gain or loss at the time of expatriation. § 877A.

E. INCOME TAX BASIS OF INHERITED PROPERTY

The timing of a taxable transfer not only determines whether it is subject to gift or estate tax, but also establishes the tax "basis" on which the recipient of the property will compute gain or loss for federal income tax purposes on a later sale or exchange of the property. Under § 1014(a)(1), the income tax basis of an asset acquired from a decedent is "stepped up" to its fair market value on the date of death (or on the alternate valuation date, if the executor elects that date as authorized under § 2032). According to Reg. § 1.1014–3(a), this stepped-up basis is the value of the property "as appraised for the purpose of the Federal estate tax" if the estate is subject to estate tax. Although this valuation does not preclude the heir or legatee from proving a higher value, the estate tax value will at least be entitled to a presumption of correctness. See Rev. Rul. 54–97, 1954–1 C.B. 113 (estate tax value may be rebutted by "clear and convincing evidence," unless taxpayer is estopped by previous actions or statements). Property that has declined in value takes a "stepped-down" basis on the decedent's death, but this fact is counterbalanced by the owner's ability to sell the property during life if the income tax deduction for the loss will be useful to him or her.

A different approach is taken for inter vivos gifts, as § 1015 requires the donee to use the donor's basis in accounting for future capital gains.[50] The lesson to be learned from these contrasting principles is clear: Gifts are to be made of nonappreciated assets, whereas appreciated assets are to be retained until death, thereby acquiring for them a stepped-up, date-of-death basis and eliminating income tax on all pre-mortem appreciation.[51] These rules make it possible for an owner of appreciated assets to give them to an elderly person who at death bequeaths them back to the original owner with the taxable appreciation "laundered" out.[52] Between spouses, this exchange, if made in compliance with the requirements for the marital deduction, can be accomplished without payment of either a gift or an estate tax. Section 1014(e) imposes a minimum control by requiring that the donee hold the property for at least a year before it becomes eligible for the stepped-up value.

From the beneficiary's perspective, a high estate tax value may be advantageous because his or her income tax savings on a sale of the property may exceed any additional estate tax; indeed, the higher basis is advantageous regardless of the increase in estate tax if the latter is borne by a different beneficiary of the estate. Would the executor violate its fiduciary duty of loyalty or impartiality if it deliberately placed a high value on such property or accepted without contest a high valuation asserted by the government? Would it be improper for the beneficiary to reimburse other persons interested in the estate for any additional estate

50. The donee is not entitled to use the donor's basis in computing loss if that basis is greater than the fair market value of the property at the time of the gift. Because of this qualification, which appears in § 1015(a), if property with a basis of $100 and a fair market value of $90 at the time of gift is sold for $85, the donee's loss is only $5. A foresighted donor can avoid this result by selling the property, using the loss on his or her own tax return, and then giving the proceeds to the donee.

Section 1015(d) allows the donee a basis adjustment to reflect gift tax paid on the transfer. For gifts made before 1977, the full amount of the gift tax is treated as if it were a cost incurred by the donee in acquiring the property; for gifts made after 1976, the adjustment is limited to the portion of the gift tax that is allocable to net appreciation in value of the gift (i.e., the excess of fair market value over the donor's basis).

51. An unfortunate by-product of this process of selection is that the investment holdings of elderly people may develop problems of liquidity, as owners retain appreciated property when market and personal considerations might indicate that a sale would be appropriate.

52. Consider the assumption being made here. What if the elderly donee bequeaths the assets to someone other than the original owner?

tax burden that would fall on them? See Pascal's Estate v. Commissioner, 22 T.C.M. (CCH) 1766 (1963), involving an option owned by the decedent to produce a musical play and motion picture based on Shaw's *Pygmalion*, which was reported in the estate tax return as having an "undetermined" value. The government asserted a deficiency based on a value of $200,000, whereupon the estate claimed a value of $1,140,000. The explanation of this curious reversal of roles is, presumably, that the posthumous success of *My Fair Lady* made a high basis for income tax purposes worth more than the added estate tax. The court upheld the value used by the government in asserting the deficiency.

If property received by gift is later included in the donor's gross estate for federal estate tax purposes (e.g., because the donor retained some control over beneficial enjoyment), the donee's basis for the property is no longer governed by § 1015 (property received by gift) but becomes subject to § 1014 (property acquired from a decedent). If the donated property has appreciated in value, the donee is not likely to be upset by the Commissioner's claim that the property must be included in the gross estate. Because the burden of the estate tax will probably not fall on the donee (see Apportionment of the Estate Tax, infra page 641), he or she is in a position to get an increased basis at the expense of the decedent's other beneficiaries. Thus, if the inclusion is disputed by the decedent's executor, the donee may be rooting for the Internal Revenue Service.

In 1976 Congress enacted § 1023, which mandated a carryover basis for property acquired from a decedent to replace the traditional date-of-death basis provided by § 1014. The new provision was added late in the legislative process, without the usual opportunities for deliberation and refinement, and it immediately came under heavy fire from critics who complained that it was technically flawed and administratively unworkable. After extensive hearings, Congress postponed the new provision's effective date in 1978 and repealed it retroactively in 1980.

In 2001 Congress enacted a modified form of carryover basis for property acquired from a decedent, this time in conjunction with projected repeal of the estate tax; both changes were scheduled to take effect in 2010 and to expire one year later. Congress eventually reinstated the traditional date-of-death basis provision (along with the estate tax) as default rules for estates of decedents dying in 2010, and allowed the executor to elect to apply the carryover basis rules as the price for avoiding the estate tax altogether. The carryover basis rules, set forth in § 1022, allowed a tax-free basis step-up of up to $1,300,000 for appreciated property "owned by the decedent at the time of death" (including property held in a revocable trust); property passing in qualifying form to the decedent's surviving spouse was eligible for an additional basis step-up of up to $3,000,000. As a result of these exemptions, a married couple was entitled to a tax-free basis step-up of up to $5,600,000 for their combined property. The allowable basis step-up was to be allocated among the decedent's assets in the discretion of the executor; the statute provided no default rule for making such allocations. The statute also required detailed information reporting by the executor but provided no procedure for auditing information returns or conclusively establishing the basis of inherited property in the hands of beneficiaries. For the vast majority of taxpayers, the net result under § 1022 was much the same as under the traditional date-of-death basis provision for inherited property; only a small group of wealthy taxpayers whose assets had appreciated by more than the exempt amount were directly affected. See Burke & McCouch, Estate Tax Repeal: Through the Looking Glass, 22 Va. Tax Rev. 187 (2002). The election to apply the carryover basis rules (and to avoid the estate tax) is no longer available for estates of decedents dying after 2010.

Reference. On the income tax basis of inherited property, see 2 Bittker & Lokken, Federal Taxation of Income, Estates and Gifts ¶¶ 41.3, 41.4 (3d ed. 2000).

CHAPTER 2

THE GIFT TAX

■ ■ ■

A. TRANSFERS OF PROPERTY BY GIFT: §§ 2501(a)(1) and 2511(a)

1. DEFINITION OF "PROPERTY"

Section 2501(a)(1) imposes the gift tax on "the transfer of property by gift" and § 2511(a) provides that the tax shall apply "whether the gift is in trust or otherwise, whether the gift is direct or indirect, and whether the property is real or personal, tangible or intangible." The definition of "property" finds amplification in the legislative history of the original gift tax statute, stating that "property" is used in the "broadest and most comprehensive sense" to reach "every species of right or interest protected by law and having an exchangeable value,"[1] and in the regulations, which provide that "any transaction in which an interest in property is gratuitously passed or conferred upon another, regardless of the means or device employed, constitutes a gift subject to tax." Reg. § 25.2511–1(c)(1).

This broad concept of property encompasses such assets as cash, real estate, securities, automobiles, jewelry, works of art, and the like.[2] Gifts of insurance and annuity policies, promissory notes, beneficial interests in trust property, partnership interests, and other intangibles are also subject to gift tax, although valuation of such assets may present special problems. As illustrated in the cases that follow, even the most comprehensive statutory language requires interpretation, and the references to property in §§ 2501(a)(1) and 2511(a) are no exceptions.

2. INTEREST–FREE LOANS AND RENT–FREE USE OF ASSETS

DICKMAN v. COMMISSIONER

465 U.S. 330 (1984).

CHIEF JUSTICE BURGER delivered the opinion of the Court.

1. S. Rep. No. 665, 72d Cong., 1st Sess. (1932), reprinted in 1939–1 C.B. (Part 2) 496, 524.

2. Because the gift tax is imposed on the transfer of property rather than on ownership, it applies to government bonds that are otherwise exempt from federal taxation. Phipps v. Commissioner, 91 F.2d 627 (10th Cir.), cert. denied, 302 U.S. 742 (1937). See supra page 38, Note 2.

We granted certiorari to resolve a conflict among the Circuits as to whether intrafamily, interest-free demand loans result in taxable gifts of the value of the use of the money lent.

I

[Between 1971 and 1976 Paul and Esther Dickman loaned substantial sums to their son Lyle Dickman and to a corporation owned by the Dickman family. The loans at issue were evidenced by demand notes bearing no interest. After Paul's death in 1976, the Commissioner determined that the loans resulted in taxable gifts to the extent of the value of the use of the loaned funds and issued notices of gift tax deficiency to Paul Dickman's estate and to Esther Dickman.

On a petition for a redetermination of the deficiencies the Tax Court reaffirmed its earlier decision in Crown v. Commissioner, 67 T.C. 1060 (1977), affd., 585 F.2d 234 (7th Cir. 1978), and concluded that intrafamily, interest-free demand loans do not result in taxable gifts. 41 T.C.M. (CCH) 620 (1980). The Eleventh Circuit reversed, holding that such loans give rise to gift tax liability. 690 F.2d 812 (11th Cir. 1982). The court specifically rejected the contrary position adopted by the Seventh Circuit in *Crown*. The Supreme Court granted certiorari to resolve this conflict.]

II

A

The statutory language of the federal gift tax provisions purports to reach any gratuitous transfer of any interest in property. Section 2501(a)(1) of the Code imposes a tax upon "the transfer of property by gift." Section 2511(a) highlights the broad sweep of the tax imposed by § 2501.... [The opinion here reviewed the gift tax statute and its legislative history, see supra page 44, noting the "expansive sweep of the gift tax provisions" acknowledged in such cases as Commissioner v. Wemyss, infra page 109.]

B

In asserting that interest-free demand loans give rise to taxable gifts, the Commissioner does not seek to impose the gift tax upon the principal amount of the loan, but only upon the reasonable value of the use of the money lent. The taxable gift that assertedly results from an interest-free demand loan is the value of receiving and using the money without incurring a corresponding obligation to pay interest along with the loan's repayment.[3] Is such a gratuitous transfer of the right to use money a "transfer of property" within the intendment of § 2501(a)(1)?

3. The Commissioner's tax treatment of interest-free demand loans may perhaps be best understood as a two-step approach to such transactions. Under this theory, such a loan has two basic economic components: an arm's-length loan from the lender to the borrower, on which the

We have little difficulty accepting the theory that the use of valuable property—in this case money—is itself a legally protectible property interest. Of the aggregate rights associated with any property interest, the right of use of property is perhaps of the highest order. One court put it succinctly:

> "Property" is more than just the physical thing—the land, the bricks, the mortar—it is also the sum of all the rights and powers incident to ownership of the physical thing. It is the tangible and the intangible. Property is composed of constituent elements and of these elements the right to *use* the physical thing to the exclusion of others is the most essential and beneficial. Without this right all other elements would be of little value.... Passailaigue v. United States, 224 F. Supp. 682, 686 (M.D. Ga. 1963) (emphasis in original).

What was transferred here was the use of a substantial amount of cash for an indefinite period of time. An analogous interest in real property, the use under a tenancy at will, has long been recognized as a property right. E.g., Restatement (Second) of Property § 1.6 (1977); G. Thompson, Commentaries on the Modern Law of Real Property § 1020 (J. Grimes ed. 1980). For example, a parent who grants to a child the rent-free, indefinite use of commercial property having a reasonable rental value of $8,000 a month has clearly transferred a valuable property right. The transfer of $100,000 in cash, interest-free and repayable on demand, is similarly a grant of the use of valuable property. Its uncertain tenure may reduce its value, but it does not undermine its status as property. In either instance, when the property owner transfers to another the right to use the object, an identifiable property interest has clearly changed hands.

The right to the use of $100,000 without charge is a valuable interest in the money lent, as much so as the rent-free use of property consisting of land and buildings. In either case, there is a measurable economic value associated with the use of the property transferred. The value of the use of money is found in what it can produce; the measure of that value is interest—"rent" for the use of the funds. We can assume that an interest-free loan for a fixed period, especially for a prolonged period, may have greater value than such a loan made payable on demand, but it would defy common human experience to say that an intrafamily loan payable on demand is not subject to accommodation; its value may be reduced by virtue of its demand status, but that value is surely not eliminated.

This Court has noted in another context that the making of an interest-free loan results in the transfer of a valuable economic right:

> It is virtually self-evident that extending interest-free credit for a period of time is equivalent to giving a discount equal to the value of the use of the purchase price for that period of time. Catalano, Inc. v. Target Sales, Inc., 446 U.S. 643, 648 (1980) (per curiam).

---

borrower pays the lender a fair rate of interest, followed by a gift from the lender to the borrower in the amount of that interest. See Crown v. Commissioner, 585 F.2d 234, 240 (C.A.7 1978).

Against this background, the gift tax statutes clearly encompass within their broad sweep the gratuitous transfer of the use of money. Just as a tenancy at will in real property is an estate or interest in land, so also is the right to use money a cognizable interest in personal property. The right to use money is plainly a valuable right, readily measurable by reference to current interest rates; the vast banking industry is positive evidence of this reality. Accordingly, we conclude that the interest-free loan of funds is a "transfer of property by gift" within the contemplation of the federal gift tax statutes.[4]

C

Our holding that an interest-free demand loan results in a taxable gift of the use of the transferred funds is fully consistent with one of the major purposes of the federal gift tax statute: protection of the estate tax and the income tax. The legislative history of the gift tax provisions reflects that Congress enacted a tax on gifts to supplement existing estate and income tax laws.... Failure to impose the gift tax on interest-free loans would seriously undermine this estate and income tax protection goal.

A substantial no-interest loan from parent to child creates significant tax benefits for the lender quite apart from the economic advantages to the borrower. This is especially so when an individual in a high income tax bracket transfers income-producing property to an individual in a lower income tax bracket, thereby reducing the taxable income of the high-bracket taxpayer at the expense, ultimately, of all other taxpayers and the Government. Subjecting interest-free loans to gift taxation minimizes the potential loss to the federal fisc generated by the use of such loans as an income tax avoidance mechanism for the transferor. Gift taxation of interest-free loans also effectuates Congress' desire to supplement the estate tax provisions. A gratuitous transfer of income-producing property may enable the transferor to avoid the future estate tax liability that would result if the earnings generated by the property—rent, interest, or dividends—became a part of the transferor's estate. Imposing the gift tax upon interest-free loans bolsters the estate tax by preventing the diminution of the transferor's estate in this fashion.

4. Petitioners argue that no gift tax consequences should attach to interest-free demand loans because no "transfer" of property occurs at the time the loan is made. Petitioners urge that the term "transfer" "connotes a discrete, affirmative act whereby a person conveys something to another person, not a continuous series of minute failures to require return of something loaned." Brief for Petitioners 22. We decline to adopt that construction of the statute.

In order to make a taxable gift, a transferor must relinquish dominion and control over the transferred property. Treas. Reg. § 25.2511–2(b), 26 C.F.R. § 25.2511–2(b) (1983). At the moment an interest-free demand loan is made, the transferor has not given up all dominion and control; he could terminate the transferee's use of the funds by calling the loan. As time passes without a demand for repayment, however, the transferor allows the use of the principal to pass to the transferee, and the gift becomes complete. See ibid.; Rev. Rul. 69–347, 1969–1 Cum. Bull. 227; Rev. Rul. 69–346, 1969–1 Cum. Bull. 227. As the Court of Appeals realized, 690 F.2d, at 819, the fact that the transferor's dominion and control over the use of the principal are relinquished over time will become especially relevant in connection with the valuation of the gifts that result from such loans; it does not, however, alter the fact that the lender has made a gratuitous transfer of property subject to the federal gift tax.

III

Petitioners contend that administrative and equitable considerations require a holding that no gift tax consequences result from the making of interest-free demand loans. In support of this position, petitioners advance several policy arguments; none withstands studied analysis.

A

Petitioners first advance an argument accepted by the Tax Court in Crown v. Commissioner:

> [O]ur income tax system does not recognize unrealized earnings or accumulations of wealth and no taxpayer is under any obligation to continuously invest his money for a profit. The opportunity cost of either letting one's money remain idle or suffering a loss from an unwise investment is not taxable merely because a profit *could have been made* from a wise investment. 67 T.C., at 1063–1064.

Thus, petitioners argue, an interest-free loan should not be made subject to the gift tax simply because of the possibility that the money lent *might* have enhanced the transferor's taxable income or gross estate had the loan never been made.

This contention misses the mark. It is certainly true that no law requires an individual to invest his property in an income-producing fashion, just as no law demands that a transferor charge interest or rent for the use of money or other property. An individual may, without incurring the gift tax, squander money, conceal it under a mattress, or otherwise waste its use value by failing to invest it. Such acts of consumption have nothing to do with lending money at no interest. The gift tax is an excise tax on *transfers* of property; allowing dollars to lie idle involves no transfer. If the taxpayer chooses not to waste the use value of money, however, but instead transfers the use to someone else, a taxable event has occurred. That the transferor himself could have consumed or wasted the use value of the money without incurring the gift tax does not change this result. Contrary to petitioners' assertion, a holding in favor of the taxability of interest-free loans does not impose upon the transferor a duty profitably to invest; rather, it merely recognizes that certain tax consequences inevitably flow from a decision to make a "transfer of property by gift." 26 U.S.C. § 2501(a)(1).

B

Petitioners next attack the breadth of the Commissioner's view that interest-free demand loans give rise to taxable gifts. Carried to its logical extreme, petitioners argue, the Commissioner's rationale would elevate to the status of taxable gifts such commonplace transactions as a loan of the proverbial cup of sugar to a neighbor or a loan of lunch money to a colleague. Petitioners urge that such a result is an untenable intrusion by the Government into cherished zones of privacy, particularly where intrafamily transactions are involved.

Our laws require parents to provide their minor offspring with the necessities and conveniences of life; questions under the tax law often arise, however, when parents provide more than the necessities, and in quantities significant enough to attract the attention of the taxing authorities. Generally, the legal obligation of support terminates when the offspring reach majority. Nonetheless, it is not uncommon for parents to provide their adult children with such things as the use of cars or vacation cottages, simply on the basis of the family relationship. We assume that the focus of the Internal Revenue Service is not on such traditional familial matters. When the government levies a gift tax on routine neighborly or familial gifts, there will be time enough to deal with such a case.

Moreover, the tax law provides liberally for gifts to both family members and others; within the limits of the prescribed statutory exemptions, even substantial gifts may be entirely tax free. First, under § 2503(e) of the Code, 26 U.S.C. § 2503(e) (1982 ed.), amounts paid on behalf of an individual for tuition at a qualified educational institution or for medical care are not considered "transfer[s] of property by gift" for purposes of the gift tax statutes. More significantly, § 2503(b) of the Code provides an annual exclusion from the computation of taxable gifts of $10,000 per year, per donee; this provision allows a taxpayer to give up to $10,000 annually to each of any number of persons, without incurring any gift tax liability. The "split gift" provision of Code § 2513(a), which effectively enables a husband and wife to give each object of their bounty $20,000 per year without liability for gift tax, further enhances the ability to transfer significant amounts of money and property free of gift tax consequences. Finally, should a taxpayer make gifts during one year that exceed the § 2503(b) annual gift tax exclusion, no gift tax liability will result until the unified credit of Code § 2505 has been exhausted. These generous exclusions, exceptions, and credits clearly absorb the sorts of de minimis gifts that petitioners envision and render illusory the administrative problems that petitioners perceive in their "parade of horribles."

C

Finally, petitioners urge that the Commissioner should not be allowed to assert the gift taxability of interest-free demand loans because such a position represents a departure from prior Internal Revenue Service practice. This contention rests on the fact that, prior to 1966, the Commissioner had not construed the gift tax statutes and regulations to authorize the levying of a gift tax on the value of the use of money or property. See Crown v. Commissioner, 585 F.2d, at 241; Johnson v. United States, 254 F. Supp. 73 (N.D. Tex. 1966). From this they argue that it is manifestly unfair to permit the Commissioner to impose the gift tax on the transactions challenged here.

Even accepting the notion that the Commissioner's present position represents a departure from prior administrative practice, which is by no means certain, it is well established that the Commissioner may change an earlier interpretation of the law, even if such a change is made retroactive in effect. E.g., Dixon v. United States, 381 U.S. 68, 72–75 (1965)....

IV

As we have noted, Congress has provided generous exclusions and credits designed to reduce the gift tax liability of the great majority of taxpayers. Congress clearly has the power to provide a similar exclusion for the gifts that result from interest-free demand loans. Any change in the gift tax consequences of such loans, however, is a legislative responsibility, not a judicial one. Until such a change occurs, we are bound to effectuate Congress' intent to protect the estate and income tax systems with a broad and comprehensive tax upon all "transfer[s] of property by gift." Cf. Diedrich v. Commissioner, 457 U.S. 191, 199 (1982).

We hold, therefore, that the interest-free demand loans shown by this record resulted in taxable gifts of the reasonable value of the use of the money lent. Accordingly, the judgment of the United States Court of Appeals for the Eleventh Circuit is affirmed.

JUSTICE POWELL, with whom JUSTICE REHNQUIST joins, dissenting.

The Court's decision today rejects a longstanding principle of taxation, and creates in its stead a new and anomalous rule of law. Such action is best left to Congress.

I

[The dissenting opinion here points out that the Internal Revenue Service did not attempt to tax interest-free demand loans until 34 years after the enactment of the gift tax in 1932 and, when it started to do so, was unsuccessful in the *Johnson* and *Crown* cases cited by the Court. It was not until 1982, with the Eleventh Circuit's opinion in this case, that the Service's position was accepted by any court.]

As the above chronology illustrates, until 1982, a long-standing principle of gift tax law, supported by IRS inaction and judicial opinion, was that interest-free demand loans had no gift tax significance. Relying on this principle, taxpayers made loans, tax commentators suggested making loans, and tax counselors used loans as integral parts of complex taxation minimization plans. In my view, petitioners' reliance also was justified.

Despite this justified reliance, the Court today subjects potentially all interest-free loans to gift taxation. The adverse effects of the Court's holding could be substantial. Many taxpayers may have used interest-free loans as an important part of a comprehensive plan to sell their business to a son, to send a daughter to medical school, or to provide for the support of an elderly parent. Such plans are not revamped easily. In addition, the recipients of the loans may not be in a position to help the taxpayers/lenders avoid future gift tax liability by making immediate repayment. The borrowed funds may have been invested in fixed assets or the borrowers simply may have spent the money. The result, in any event, is the assessment of gift taxes that might have been avoided lawfully if the taxpayer could have anticipated the Court's holding in this case. In light of the Commissioner's decision over a 34–year span to attach no significance to such loans, and his lack of success over the past 18 years in attempting to tax such loans, the Court of Appeals' decision is so fundamentally unfair that this Court should be unwilling to add its imprimatur.

II

... The most troublesome issue generated by the Court's opinion is the scope of its new reading of the statute. The Court does not limit its holding to interest-free loans of money. The Court states: "We have little difficulty accepting the theory that the use of valuable property ... is itself a legally protectible property interest." ... Under this theory, potential tax liability may arise in a wide range of situations involving the unrecompensed use of property. Examples could include the rent-free use of a home by a child over the age of minority who lives with his parents, or by a parent over the age of self-support who lives with her child. Taken to its logical extreme, this theory would make the loan of a car for a brief period a potentially taxable event.

The possibility that the generous use by friends or family of property such as homes and even spare bedrooms could result in the imposition of gift tax liability highlights the valuation problems that certainly will result from the Court's holding. It is often difficult to place a value on outright ownership of items of real and personal property. Those difficulties multiply when the interest to be valued is the *use* of the property for varying lengths of time. Even in the simplest case—where the property that is borrowed is cash—valuation problems arise. In the three decided cases in which the Commissioner belatedly pursued the theory that the Court adopts today, the Service used three different methods for determining the interest rate that should be used to establish the use-value of the borrowed money.[5] Thus, it is clear that the Court's decision will generate substantial valuation problems.

The Court downplays the significance of its decision by "assum[ing] that the focus of the Internal Revenue Service is not on such traditional familial matters [as the use of cars or homes]." ... The Court also concludes that the Tax Code's "generous exclusions, exceptions, and credits clearly absorb the sorts of de minimis gifts petitioners envision and render illusory the administrative problems that petitioners perceive." ...

5. In Johnson v. United States, 254 F. Supp. 73 (N.D. Tex. 1966), the Service apparently computed the amount of the gift using the interest rate specified in the regulations for valuing annuities, life estates, terms for years, remainders, and reversions. Id., at 76; see Treas. Reg. § 25.2512–5. In Crown v. Commissioner, 67 T.C. 1060 (1977), the Service used a rate that it considered reasonable under the circumstances. Id., at 1061. In this case, the rate was that specified in I.R.C. § 6621 for determining interest due on underpayments or refunds of taxes. 690 F.2d 812, at 814, n.4 (C.A. 11, 1982). The Service has urged yet another method in a recently docketed Tax Court case, LaRosa v. Commissioner, No. 29632–82. In *LaRosa*, the Service has arrived at a separate interest rate for each month the loan was outstanding. The monthly interest rates were provided by an "expert" who relied on estimated fair market interest rates considering the creditworthiness of the borrowers. On an annualized basis, the rates used in *LaRosa* range from 12.5% to 31.1%.

In effect, the Court has chosen to turn its back on the ramifications of its decision.

The Court, aware of the potential for abuse of its new interpretation, "assume[s]" that the Internal Revenue Service will exercise the power conferred on it in a reasonable way.... This assumption is not likely to afford much comfort to taxpayers and the lawyers and accountants who advise them. The Commissioner, acting with utmost goodwill, is confronted with a dilemma. This Court today holds that the plain language of the statute mandates, and that Congress intended, the "gift tax statute to reach *all* gratuitous transfers of *any* valuable interest in property." ... No discretion is given the Commissioner and the IRS to read "all" and "any" as meaning only such transfers and only such valuable interests in property that it seems reasonable to tax. The Court identifies no statutory basis for such discretion, and even if the Court itself undertook to confer it I am not aware that we have ever before "assumed" that *tax laws* would be enforced—not according to their letter—but reasonably.

III

The Court's answer to these concerns is that the exceptions and exemptions in the Tax Code will render most administrative problems "illusory." ... Although the $10,000 annual per donee exclusion will shield many taxpayers from having to pay gift taxes on intrafamily loans, the taxpayer cannot know whether he has exceeded the annual limit until he has assigned a value to every "transfer" that falls within the Court's definition. In particular, a taxpayer who has made outright gifts during the year, approaching in dollar value the amount of the applicable annual exclusion, must be concerned with the value of intrafamily loans. Once he has exceeded the exclusion, he must file a gift tax return, listing and describing each gift. I.R.C. § 6019(1) (1982 ed.); Treas. Reg. § 25.6019–4.

Nor does it suffice to say that most taxpayers will be protected from payment of gift taxes by the Tax Code's "lifetime exemption." Regardless of the availability of an offsetting credit, all taxpayers who exceed the annual per donee exclusion must go through the uncertain process of valuing intrafamily loans and filing a gift tax return. Moreover, a taxpayer's reduction of the unified credit lessens the amount of credit that will be available to offset estate taxes at the time of his death. In short, the net result of the Court's decision will be to create potential tax liability for many taxpayers who have never been subject to it before, and create legal, tax accounting, and return filing nightmares for many others....

None of the problems and anomalies I have outlined is insurmountable. They do involve, however, delicate issues of policy that should be addressed in the legislative forum. Instead of recognizing the longstanding practice of attaching no gift tax consequences to interest-free loans of money and property, and leaving these difficult issues to the body responsible for legislating tax policy, the Court now allows the Commissioner to decide these questions without guidance. That course is ill-advised and inequitable.

I dissent.

NOTES

1. *Use of the annual exclusion.* A parent who lends money to a child at no interest makes a gift each year in which the loan remains outstanding. Consider the amount that can be loaned before "the reasonable value of the use of the money lent" exceeds the $10,000 annual exclusion ($20,000 if a spouse joins in making the loan).

2. *Statutory treatment of below-market loans.* The Supreme Court stated in *Dickman* that a gift tax on interest-free loans was necessary to minimize the revenue loss "generated by the use of such loans as an income tax avoidance mechanism for the transferor." At the time of the Court's decision, the Service had failed to persuade any court that interest-free loans gave rise to imputed interest payments for federal income tax purposes. In 1984, shortly after the Court announced its decision in *Dickman*, Congress enacted § 7872 to regulate the income and gift tax treatment of below-market loans (including interest-free loans). Where the transaction is "in the nature of a gift," the statute generally treats the lender as making a gift of the forgone interest to the borrower, and then treats the borrower as making an interest payment of the same amount back to the lender. § 7872(a)(1). The amount of forgone interest is measured as the difference between the applicable federal rate (determined under § 1274(d)) and the rate of interest actually payable on the loan. § 7872(e)(2). The statute contains an exception for gift loans between individuals as long as the aggregate outstanding amount of loans does not exceed $10,000; the exception does not apply, however, if the gift loan is "attributable to the purchase or carrying of income-producing assets." § 7872(c)(2).

3. *Sharing assets with family and friends.* Parents may understand that by transferring money, securities, or real estate to their children they are making taxable gifts, but they would be outraged at the suggestion that they may also be making taxable gifts when they invite their children to enjoy a vacation at the family summer home or winter apartment. An area of exemption for family consumption expenses has always been assumed, although its boundary lines defy precise description. See infra page 119.

The Court does not limit its examples to instances of intrafamily sharing, citing in addition the situation where a night's lodging is made available to a friend. Does the host make a taxable gift by taking several friends for a two-week Caribbean cruise on the host's yacht? Does it make a difference whether the yacht is a small ketch or an ocean-going craft that requires a crew of four and, when made available for charters, commands a $20,000 per week rental fee? What if the friends are allowed to stay on board for an additional two weeks after the owner returns home?

4. *Deemed gifts.* The Service has made no attempt to apply the *Dickman* rationale to the uncompensated use of cars, vacation cottages, or other "routine neighborly or familial gifts." In revenue rulings, however, the Service has found a taxable gift where a donor's failure to exercise beneficial rights enhances the value of property previously transferred to family mem-

bers. See Rev. Rul. 81–264, 1981–2 C.B. 185 (child's obligation to repay loan to parent barred by statute of limitations); Rev. Rul. 89–3, 1989–1 C.B. 278 (value shifted from parent to trust for descendants in recapitalization of controlled corporation). The Service reached a similar result where a decedent's surviving spouse acquiesced in a transaction that shifted value from a marital trust (over which the spouse had a general power of appointment) to the spouse's descendants. See Rev. Rul. 84–105, 1984–2 C.B. 197 (underfunding of pecuniary marital bequest increased child's residuary share); Rev. Rul. 86–39, 1986–1 C.B. 301 (recapitalization of closely held corporation shifted value from marital trust to family trust in which child was remainderman).

The government has also sought to apply the *Dickman* rationale to "estate freezing" transactions involving family corporations. Suppose a corporation is capitalized with two classes of stock: noncumulative preferred stock owned by a parent (who also has voting control), and common stock owned by her children. If instead of declaring an annual dividend the corporation retains all of its annual earnings, the value of the forgone dividend on the preferred stock is shifted to the common stock. The Tax Court has refused to treat the forgone dividend as a gift, however, because a shareholder has no legally enforceable right to receive dividends as long as the corporate directors have valid business reasons for retaining earnings. See Snyder v. Commissioner, 93 T.C. 529 (1989) (*Dickman* not applicable to nonpayment of noncumulative preferred dividends; nevertheless, taxpayer's failure to exercise conversion right shifted value from her noncumulative preferred stock to common stock held in trust for her descendants, resulting in periodic taxable gifts). See also Caron, Taxing Opportunity, 14 Va. Tax Rev. 347 (1994). Section 2701, enacted in 1990, imposes special gift tax valuation rules which make it unnecessary for the government to rely on a deemed gift analysis in such cases. Section 2701 is discussed infra at page 591.

5. *Baseball fan's dilemma.* A baseball player hits a record-breaking home run. The ball, which has instantaneously become a valuable collector's item, lands in the bleachers among a crowd of excited fans. In the ensuing scuffle, one of the fans retrieves the ball and promptly returns it to the player. A week later, the player autographs the ball and hands it over to the Hall of Fame where it remains permanently on display. Has the fan made a taxable gift? Has the player? See McGwire's 62nd Home Run: IRS Bobbles the Ball, 89 J. Taxn. 253 (1998).

6. *Limitation on gift tax assessment.* In general, a gift tax deficiency must be assessed within three years after the filing of the gift tax return. § 6501(a). Moreover, once the limitation period has expired for a gift shown on the return, the value of the gift as finally determined becomes binding for purposes of subsequent gift and estate tax computations. §§ 2504(c) and 2001(f). The limitation period does not run, however, for gifts that are not adequately disclosed on the gift tax return. § 6501(c)(9); Reg. § 301.6501(c)–1(f). Thus, if a gift is omitted or not adequately disclosed, the government may assess a gift tax deficiency at any time and may also seek to revalue the gift in order to push subsequent transfers into higher gift or estate tax brackets. A taxpayer who filed a gift tax return but failed to make adequate disclosure ordinarily may start the limitation period running by filing an amended return with the required information. See Rev. Proc. 2000–34, 2000–

2 C.B. 186. For a discussion of disclosure requirements, see Mulligan, Adequate Disclosure: Its Impact on Gift Tax Return Strategies, 28 Est. Planning 3 (2001).

3. PROMISES TO BE PERFORMED IN THE FUTURE

BRADFORD v. COMMISSIONER

34 T.C. 1059 (1960).

DRENNEN, JUDGE.

[In 1938 Mr. Bradford, petitioner's husband, owed a Nashville bank approximately $305,000. The debt had grown out of investment banking ventures he had engaged in prior to the Great Depression. He had pledged most of his assets to the bank as collateral, but the greater part of the indebtedness was unsecured. The brokerage firm of which he was a member held a seat on the New York Stock Exchange. In October 1938 the Exchange adopted a rule requiring each general partner of a member firm to submit a detailed report of his indebtedness. Fearing that disclosure of so much indebtedness might impair the position of his firm with the Exchange, Mr. Bradford persuaded the bank to substitute the note of his wife, the petitioner, for a portion of his indebtedness. Accordingly, petitioner, whose net worth was approximately $15,780, executed her note to the bank for $205,000. Petitioner's note was secured by the same collateral that had previously secured Mr. Bradford's original debt. Mr. Bradford remained the obligor on two notes to the bank totaling $100,000, and so reported to the Exchange.]

The issue here is whether petitioner's substitution of her note in the amount of $205,000 for notes of her husband of equal amount held by a bank in 1938 constituted a taxable gift in the amount of $205,000 by petitioner to her husband in 1938.

Petitioner contends that the transaction did not constitute a transfer of property by gift within [§ 2501(a)(1)], because the note executed by petitioner and delivered to the bank was not "property" in her hands, and, further, that even if she did transfer property to her husband by gift in 1938, the value of the property transferred was substantially less than the exemption and exclusion ... so there is no gift tax liability.

Respondent's position is that the subject of the gift was the entire transaction whereby petitioner's husband was relieved of his indebtedness by the execution and delivery of petitioner's note to the bank, thereby resulting in a transfer of economic benefits which would qualify as a "gift" in the broad and comprehensive sense of that word as used in the statute....

We are of the opinion that the transactions ... did not constitute a taxable gift from petitioner to her husband in the year 1938 within the purview of the statute. We have found no gift tax cases involving facts similar to those here present, but most gift tax cases must be decided on their own facts anyway. Various general principles have developed through case law and the regulations, and our conclusion is based on the application of some of these principles which seem founded on common sense to the facts in this case.

The gift tax is an excise tax on the transfer of property without adequate and full consideration. Gift tax liability is dependent on the transfer of property by the donor, not the receipt of property by the donee, and the measure of the tax is the value of the property passing from the donor at the time the transfer is completed. Estate of Koert Bartman, 10 T.C. 1073.... While the presence of donative intent on the part of the donor is said no longer to be a necessary element to make a transfer subject to gift tax, as it had always been considered to be in the common law connotation of gifts, the transfer must be donative in character, and we think donative intent may still be a material factor in determining whether a taxable gift has been made. See Sarah Helen Harrison, 17 T.C. 1350, 1357. It is true that application of the tax is determined more from the objective facts and circumstances of the transfer and what was accomplished, rather than the subjective motives of the donor, Commissioner v. Wemyss, 324 U.S. 303, but the objective standards used in the tax concept of a gift in effect supply the necessary donative intent of which the donor may not have been conscious. But in any event it seems clear that to constitute a gift for tax purposes there must be a transfer of property owned by the donor with a clear and unequivocal intent on the part of the donor to divest himself presently of the property transferred, and dominion and control thereof. 5 Mertens, Law of Federal Gift and Estate Taxation, secs. 34.01 et seq.

The facts and circumstances surrounding the transaction here involved do not convince us that petitioner intended to divest herself of any property or interest therein owned by her in 1938, or that any of the parties involved anticipated that any of her property would ever be used to satisfy the obligation to the bank. In the first place she did not own property in 1938 that would have come anywhere near satisfying the obligation to the bank, and she had no prospects of acquiring any except through her husband. Secondly, the entire transaction was arranged by [Mr. Bradford], his collateral was retained as security for petitioner's note, and he testified that it was understood that the bank would look first to his collateral for liquidation of the obligation, and he hoped and expected that the collateral would increase sufficiently in value to cover the entire obligation. [Mr. Bradford] paid the interest on the loan and it is reasonable to assume that all parties involved looked to [Mr. Bradford's] assets and his earning power to liquidate the loan.

This does not mean that petitioner was not obligated on the indebtedness evidenced by her note. We assume the bank could have taken judgment against her on the note had it not been paid, and levied on her property to help satisfy the judgment, and that it probably would have done so had that course of action become necessary. But unless and until such action was taken we do not believe petitioner parted with, or intended to part with, dominion and control of any property owned by her which would give rise to a gift tax.

Granted that [§ 2501(a)(1)] is comprehensive enough to "include property, however conceptual or contingent," Smith v. Shaughnessy, 318 U.S. 176, and to reach any passage of control over the economic benefits of property, Estate of Sanford v. Commissioner, 308 U.S. 39; nevertheless, no matter how intangible, the donor must own a property right or interest which is capable of being, and is, transferred. Commissioner v. Mills, 183 F.2d 32 (C.A. 9, 1950), affirming 12 T.C. 468. Petitioner transferred no property or interest in property in 1938 but only made a promise to pay in the future if called upon to do so. John D. Archbold, 42 B.T.A. 453. The fact that [Mr. Bradford] may have derived some economic benefit in 1938 as a result of this promise is not controlling. . . .

This case presents a situation different from those present in Estate of Ira C. Copley, 15 T.C. 17, affd. 194 F.2d 364 (C.A. 7, 1952), and Paul Rosenthal, 17 T.C. 1047, reversed on other grounds 205 F.2d 505 (C.A. 2, 1953). In those cases there was a definite obligation to pay a fixed amount, whereas here there was no certainty in 1938 that petitioner would ever have to pay anything.

We hold that petitioner did not make a transfer of property by gift in 1938. Cf., Minnie E. Deal, 29 T.C. 730. We might add, as suggested in D.S. Jackman, 44 B.T.A. 704, that taxation is a practical matter and it seems incredible that a person having a net worth of only $15,780 could make a gift of $205,000.

Decision will be entered for the petitioner.

NOTES

1. *Discharge of donor's promise.* Does the court in *Bradford* decide that what was transferred in 1938 does not constitute property or that the transfer is incomplete because Mrs. Bradford has not parted with dominion and control? Does a gift occur when these deficiencies are removed? It had previously been held in a related income tax case that Mrs. Bradford did not realize income in 1946 when the bank in effect discharged $100,000 of her liability in return for $50,000. Bradford v. Commissioner, 233 F.2d 935 (6th Cir. 1956). If Mrs. Bradford provided the $50,000, did she make a taxable gift in 1946? The opinion specifically states that the issue of her gift tax liability was not before the court. Id. at 939.

Would the result have been different if in 1938 Mrs. Bradford had executed a promissory note in the amount of $205,000 in favor of her husband and he had endorsed it to the bank in substitution for his own notes? The Service has ruled that a gift of the donor's own note generally is not complete for gift tax purposes until the obligation becomes binding under state law or the note is paid or transferred for value. Rev. Rul. 67–396, 1967–2 C.B. 351; Rev. Rul. 84–25, 1984–1 C.B. 191.

2. *Donor's promise to make a series of gifts.* If a promise to make a series of gifts is enforceable when made, is there a single gift at that time, or a series of separate gifts as the installment commitments are honored? It is established that a gift of a *third-party* obligation, such as an annuity contract, is a gift of the entire contract when made, even though it calls for a series of periodic payments. The courts apply the same single-gift rationale to an enforceable commitment by a donor to make a series of future payments, so that "a binding promise to make a gift becomes subject to gift taxation in the year the obligation is undertaken and not when the discharging payments are made." Rosenthal v. Commissioner, 205 F.2d 505, 509 (2d Cir. 1953) (husband's obligation to make periodic payments to his adult children under an irrevocable agreement incident to divorce). See also Commissioner v. Copley's Estate, 194 F.2d 364 (7th Cir. 1952) (husband made no taxable gifts when he transferred property to wife in 1936 and 1944 as required by a 1931 antenuptial agreement; the opinion implies that there would have been a taxable gift in 1931 when the obligation was created, if the 1932 gift tax law had been in force at that time); Rev. Rul. 84–25, 1984–1 C.B. 191 (gift of donor's own note is complete when obligation becomes binding under state law).

The single-gift principle is not always rigorously applied. For example, if the periodic payments are authorized by a court order and that order is subject to modification at any time, there are no gifts until the payments are actually made. City Bank Farmers Trust Co. v. Hoey, 101 F.2d 9 (2d Cir. 1939). By similar reasoning, the Court of Claims held that a gift of property subject to a mortgage on which the donors remained personally liable was limited to the value of the equity. Because the donors' obligation to pay off the mortgage ran to the lender and was not enforceable by the donees, taxable gifts occurred only when the donors actually made mortgage payments. Alexander v. United States, 640 F.2d 1250 (Ct. Cl. 1981).

3. *Loan guarantees.* Parents often provide personal guarantees to enable a child to obtain a loans from a commercial lender to finance an education, buy a home, or undertake a business venture. Indeed, if a child's net worth is insubstantial, a commercial lender will routinely require the personal guarantee of a parent or other third party as a condition of making an otherwise unsecured loan. In a controversial 1990 private letter ruling (Priv. Ltr. Rul. 9113009, subsequently withdrawn by Priv. Ltr. Rul. 9409018), the Service took the position that the parent's personal guarantee represents an indirect gift of "the economic benefit conferred upon the [child]," and that the gift is complete at the time the guarantee becomes "binding and determinable in value" rather than at the time payment is actually made. How should the parent's gift be valued? To what extent is the amount of the gift offset by the parent's right of subrogation under state law? Should the gift tax be deferred until it becomes clear whether the parent will be called on to make any payments under the guarantee?

4. *Options.* An option to acquire property, like other intangible property rights, ordinarily can form the subject of a completed gift. For example, suppose a parent assigns to a child, for no consideration, an enforceable option to purchase real property at any time during the next ten years for a specified price below the property's current fair market value. The parent has made a completed gift of the difference between the value of the property and

the option price. See Rev. Rul. 80–186, 1980–2 C.B. 280. If the option is not presently exercisable, however, the result may be different. Rev. Rul. 98–21, 1998–1 C.B. 975, involved a nonstatutory stock option granted by an employer to *A*, an employee, as compensation for *A*'s services. The option price was equal to the fair market value of the stock on the grant date, but the option could be exercised only after *A* performed additional services. Before performing the required services, *A* assigned the option to *B* for no consideration. The ruling concluded that no completed gift would occur until *A* performed the required services. "[B]efore *A* performs the services, the rights that *A* possesses in the stock option have not acquired the character of enforceable property rights susceptible of transfer for federal gift tax purposes. *A* can make a gift of the stock option to *B* for federal gift purposes only after *A* has completed the additional required services because only upon completion of the services does the right to exercise the option become binding and enforceable."

5. *Self-executing adjustments.* Taxpayers sometimes attempt to fend off potential gift tax liability by making a transfer of property conditional on the desired gift tax result. For example, in Commissioner v. Procter, 142 F.2d 824 (4th Cir.), cert. denied, 323 U.S. 756 (1944), the court had to pass on the effect of a transfer that by its terms purported to nullify any portion of the transfer that was finally determined to constitute a taxable gift:

> We do not think that the gift tax can be avoided by any such device as this. Taxpayer has made a present gift of a future interest in property. He attempts to provide that if a federal court of last resort shall hold the gift subject to gift tax, it shall be void as to such part of the property given as is subject to the tax. This is clearly a condition subsequent and void because contrary to public policy. A contrary holding would mean that upon a decision that the gift was subject to tax, the court making such decision must hold it not a gift and therefore not subject to tax. Such holding, however, being made in a tax suit to which the donees of the property are not parties, would not be binding upon them and they might later enforce the gift notwithstanding the decision of the Tax Court. It is manifest that a condition which involves this sort of trifling with the judicial process cannot be sustained.
>
> The condition is contrary to public policy for three reasons: In the first place, it has a tendency to discourage the collection of the tax by the public officials charged with its collection, since the only effect of an attempt to enforce the tax would be to defeat the gift. In the second place, the effect of the condition would be to obstruct the administration of justice by requiring the courts to pass upon a moot case. If the condition were valid and the gift were held subject to tax, the only effect of the holding would be to defeat the gift so that it would not be subject to tax.... In the third place the condition is to the effect that the final judgment of a court is to be held for naught because of the provision of an indenture necessarily before the court when the judgment is rendered.... To state the matter differently, the condition is not to become operative until there has been a judgment; but after the judgment has been rendered it cannot become operative because the matter involved is concluded by the judgment. [142 F.2d at 827–28.]

See also Ward v. Commissioner, 87 T.C. 78 (1986) (donors made gifts of stock, retaining power to revoke if value finally determined for gift tax purposes exceeded fixed amount; held, completed gifts of stock valued without regard to adjustment clause).

A taxpayer may also seek to guard against potential gift tax liability on a sale of property by means of a clause providing for a purchase price adjustment to offset any increase in the value of the transferred property as determined for tax purposes. The Service has ruled that such a clause is no more efficacious than the clause purporting to nullify the taxable gift in *Procter*. Rev. Rul. 86–41, 1986–1 C.B. 300 ("Gifts subject to conditions subsequent of [this] kind ... tend to discourage the enforcement of federal gift tax provisions, because operation of the provisions would either defeat the gift or otherwise render examination of the return ineffective."). At least one court, however, has upheld a provision requiring that the purchase price of property transferred by a parent in trust for his children be adjusted to reflect its value as determined for tax purposes. See King v. United States, 545 F.2d 700 (10th Cir. 1976), noted infra page 137, Note 4 (noting that the property was difficult to value and "the transaction was intended as a sale and not as a gift").

Alternatively, a taxpayer may use a "defined value" clause to impose a ceiling on the amount of a taxable gift. Under such a clause, a portion of the transferred property, up to a specified dollar amount, passes to members of the donor's family and the rest of the property, if any, passes to a charitable organization. A defined value clause, if respected, effectively discourages the Service from second-guessing the value reported by the donor as a taxable gift, since any portion of the transfer in excess of the specified dollar amount automatically qualifies for a charitable deduction. Moreover, even if the transferred property is undervalued on the gift tax return, the charitable organization may be reluctant to incur the donor's displeasure by challenging the reported value. In Christiansen's Estate v. Commissioner, 130 T.C. 1 (2008), affd., 586 F.3d 1061 (8th Cir. 2009), the Tax Court allowed a charitable deduction for the increased value of property passing to charity pursuant to a defined value clause in a disclaimer. The court distinguished *Procter* on the ground that the defined value clause "would not undo a transfer, but only reallocate the value of the property transferred among [the beneficiaries]," and concluded that "allowing an increase in the charitable deduction to reflect the increase in the value of the estate's property going to [charity] violates no public policy and should be allowed." On appeal, the Eighth Circuit agreed, finding "no evidence of a clear Congressional intent suggesting a policy to maximize incentives for the Commissioner to challenge or audit returns" but rather "a policy more general in nature ... to encourage charitable donations." See also McCord's Succession v. Commissioner, 461 F.3d 614 (5th Cir. 2006) (upholding defined value clause and refusing to consider subsequent allocation of transferred interests by mutual agreement among family members and charities).

How different in purpose or effect is the defined value clause upheld in *Christiansen* or the purchase price adjustment upheld in *King* from the condition subsequent struck down in *Procter*? In a recent decision upholding a defined value clause, the Tax Court drew a distinction between "a donor who gives away a fixed set of rights with uncertain value—that's *Christiansen*—and a donor who tries to take property back—that's *Procter*," and concluded that "savings clauses are void, but formula clauses are fine." Petter's Estate v. Commissioner, 98 T.C.M. (CCH) 534 (2009). See Zeydel & Benford, A Walk Through the Authorities on Formula Clauses, 37 Est. Planning 3 (Dec. 2010).

DIMARCO'S ESTATE v. COMMISSIONER

87 T.C. 653 (1986).

STERRETT, CHIEF JUDGE.

[Anthony DiMarco was an IBM employee from 1950 until his death in 1979. He was automatically covered by IBM's employee benefit plan, which provided a "survivors income benefit" at the death of each regular employee to certain family members. The plan was noncontributory and unfunded, and was subject to modification or termination in IBM's sole discretion. No employee had any power to designate beneficiaries or to vary the amount, form, or timing of the survivors income benefit payments. At DiMarco's death, his wife Joan became entitled to receive a survivors income benefit equal to three times DiMarco's regular annual compensation, payable in installments.]

The only issue for decision in this case is whether the present value of the survivors income benefit that is payable by IBM to Joan M. DiMarco is an adjusted taxable gift within the meaning of section 2001.[6] ...

We begin our analysis by noting that it is unclear precisely what respondent argues in this case. On brief, he proposes that we adopt as an ultimate finding of fact that "Decedent made a completed gift of the Survivor's Benefit to unnamed beneficiaries upon the commencement of his employment on January 9, 1950." Two pages later in the same brief he argues that "the transfer should be treated as a completed gift in 1979." In the statutory notice of deficiency and the stipulation of facts, respondent appears to take the position that decedent actually made a completed gift of the survivors income benefit at the time of his death in 1979. Respondent finally attempts to clarify his position by stating in his reply brief that it is his "position that the gift of the Survivor's Benefit occurred in 1950 and the inability to value said gift requires ... [respondent] to treat the gift as complete on the date of death when the gift finally became subject to valuation."

After reviewing carefully respondent's briefs, the statutory notice of deficiency, and the stipulation of facts, it appears to us that respondent is making two arguments in this case. First, it appears that respondent argues that decedent made a completed transfer of a property interest in the survivors income benefit for gift tax purposes on January 9, 1950, but that because the interest could not be valued at that time, it was

6. Section 2001(b) defines "adjusted taxable gifts" to include all taxable gifts (as defined in § 2503) made by a decedent after 1976, except for gifts that are drawn back into the decedent's gross estate. Thus, the court must determine whether DiMarco made a taxable gift of the survivors income benefit after 1976.—EDS.

necessary to treat the transfer as an open transaction and to value the transferred property and impose the gift tax on the date of decedent's death, when the property interest finally became subject to valuation. In the alternative, respondent appears to argue that decedent made an incomplete transfer of a property interest in the survivors income benefit for gift tax purposes on January 9, 1950, because the property interest could not be valued at that time, but that the transfer became complete on November 16, 1979, when decedent died, because the transferred property could then and for the first time be valued.

Petitioner argues, for a variety of reasons, that decedent never made a taxable gift of the survivors income benefit. Petitioner argues that decedent never owned a property interest in the survivors income benefit that he was capable of transferring. Petitioner further contends that, even if decedent owned such an interest, he never transferred it, and if he did transfer it, he never did so voluntarily. Petitioner also asserts that transfers of property cannot become complete for gift tax purposes upon the death of the donor, and that decedent never made a completed transfer of any property interest he may have owned in the survivors income benefit before his death because he always had the power to revoke the transfer, if any was made, simply by resigning his employment with IBM. Petitioner finally argues that, if the decedent made a taxable gift of the survivors income benefit, he did so before December 31, 1976, and that such a gift does not qualify as an adjusted taxable gift within the meaning of section 2001. For the reasons set forth below, we find for petitioner....

Respondent argues that decedent transferred a property interest in the survivors income benefit for gift tax purposes on January 9, 1950. This transfer was either complete or incomplete for gift tax purposes. If the transfer was complete, we have little difficulty in disposing of this case because a completed transfer would have been a taxable gift that was made by decedent before December 31, 1976, and section 2001 expressly defines an adjusted taxable gift as a taxable gift that was made after December 31, 1976. On the other hand, if the transfer was incomplete for gift tax purposes, we do not believe that it became complete or that we can deem that it became complete at the time of decedent's death. Section 25.2511–2(f), Gift Tax Regs., provides that—

> The relinquishment or termination of a power to change the beneficiaries of transferred property, *occurring otherwise than by the death of the donor (the statute being confined to transfers by living donors)*, is regarded as the event that completes the gift and causes the tax to apply.... [Emphasis added.]

We believe that this regulation precludes our finding in this case that the alleged transfer of property by decedent on January 9, 1950, became complete for gift tax purposes by reason of decedent's death.

We recognize, of course, that respondent does not assert in this case that the alleged transfer on January 9, 1950, became complete and subject to the gift tax because decedent's death terminated a power to change the beneficiaries of the transferred property. Even so, in view of the fact that a transfer of property that becomes complete because the donor's death terminates a power to change the beneficiaries of the transferred property is not subject to the gift tax, we decline to hold that a transfer of property that becomes complete because the donor's death makes it possible for the first time to value the transferred property is subject to the gift tax. We perceive nothing in the gift tax statute or the regulations that would justify such a result.

In addition, we believe that respondent has confused the issues of completion and valuation in this case. Respondent appears to argue that, because the value of the survivors income benefit could not be determined on January 9, 1950, when the alleged transfer occurred, the transfer should be treated as incomplete for gift tax purposes until the survivors income benefit became susceptible of valuation, when decedent died, at which time the transfer became complete and subject to the gift tax. For the reasons stated above, we have already held that transfers of property do not become complete for gift tax purposes by reason of the death of the donor. We also question, however, whether the fact that the value of transferred property cannot be readily determined at the time of transfer is relevant in determining whether the transfer is complete for gift tax purposes. We have noted above that transfers of property are complete and subject to the gift tax at the time the donor relinquishes dominion and control over the transferred property. Nothing in the statute or the regulations suggests that, even if a donor relinquishes dominion and control over transferred property, the transfer is or can be considered to be incomplete for gift tax purposes if the value of the property is uncertain.... Accordingly, we reject any suggestion by respondent either that transfers of property are incomplete for gift tax purposes simply because "no realistic value can be placed" on the property at the time the transfer occurs, or that transfers of property become complete for gift tax purposes only when the value of the transferred property can be easily ascertained.

Respondent also argues that completed transfers of property for gift tax purposes can and should be treated as open transactions in those cases where the transferred property is difficult to value, and that valuation of the transferred property and the imposition of the gift tax should be postponed until the value of the property can be readily determined. We reject this contention. The clear language of the statute and the regulations requires that transferred property be valued for gift tax purposes at the time the transfer becomes complete. Section 2512(a) provides that, in the case of a gift, "the value thereof *at the date of the gift* shall be considered the amount of the gift." (Emphasis added.) In addition, section 25.2511–2(a), Gift Tax Regs., states as follows:

> The gift tax is not imposed upon the receipt of the property by the donee, nor is it necessarily determined by the measure of enrichment resulting to the donee from the transfer.... On the contrary, the tax

> is a primary and personal liability of the donor, is an excise upon his *act of making the transfer*, [and] *is measured by the value of the property passing from the donor*.... [Emphasis added.]

As a result, property must be valued and the gift tax imposed at the time a completed transfer of the property occurs.

We also agree with petitioner that decedent never made a taxable gift of any property interest in the survivors income benefit because we find no act by decedent that qualifies as an act of "transfer" of an interest in property. His participation in the plan was involuntary, he had no power to select or change the beneficiaries of the survivors income benefit, no power to alter the amount or timing of the payment of the benefit, and no power to substitute other benefits for those prescribed by the plan....

Respondent argues, however, that decedent's simple act of going to work for IBM on January 9, 1950, constituted an act of transfer by decedent for gift tax purposes. We disagree. None of the cases cited by respondent hold that, without more, the simple act of going to work for an employer that has an automatic, nonelective, company-wide survivors income benefit plan similar to the one at issue in this case constitutes a "transfer" of an interest in the benefit for either estate or gift tax purposes. Moreover, we doubt that it can be maintained seriously that decedent began his employment with IBM on January 9, 1950 (when he was 24, unmarried, and without dependents), for the purpose or with any intention of transferring property rights in the survivors income benefit. While we agree with respondent that a taxable event may occur without a volitional act by the donor, as in a case where an incomplete transfer of property becomes complete because of the occurrence of an event outside the donor's control, we do not believe that a taxable event can occur for gift tax purposes unless there is first and in fact an act of transfer by the donor; and there can be no act of transfer unless the act is voluntary and the transferor has some awareness that he is in fact making a transfer of property, that is, he must intend to do so....[7] It is apparent to us that decedent never intended and never voluntarily acted to transfer any interest that he may have owned in the survivors income benefit. There being no act of transfer by decedent, there can be no transfer of property by gift.

Moreover, we question whether decedent ever owned a property interest in the survivors income benefit that he was capable of transferring during his lifetime. He had no voice in selecting the beneficiaries of the survivors income benefit and no ability to affect or determine the benefits payable to them. The categories of beneficiaries, the determination whether a claimant is an eligible beneficiary, and the amounts

---

7. The fact that there can be no taxable gift unless there is a voluntary act of transfer does not mean that the donor also must have donative intent when he makes the transfer. Sec. 25.2511–1(g)(1), Gift Tax Regs.; Commissioner v. Wemyss, 324 U.S. 303, 306 (1945). Any completed transfer of a beneficial interest in property for less than an adequate and full consideration in money or money's worth, unless made in the ordinary course of business, will be subject to the gift tax. Sec. 25.2512–8, Gift Tax Regs.

payable to the beneficiaries all were controlled directly by the provisions of the plan and indirectly by IBM, and payments were made directly to the beneficiaries by IBM. Furthermore, the benefits were payable out of the general assets of IBM, not out of any fund in which decedent had a vested interest, and the benefits did not accrue until decedent's death. Most importantly, IBM had the power and the right to modify the plan and the survivors income benefit at any time and in its sole discretion. Under these circumstances, we have little difficulty in concluding that decedent never acquired fixed and enforceable property rights in the survivors income benefit that he was capable of transferring during his lifetime....

In our opinion, decedent never made a taxable gift of any interest in the survivors income benefit to his wife. It follows that the present value of the survivors income benefit is not an adjusted taxable gift within the meaning of section 2001....

NOTES

1. *Employee death benefits and the "open transaction" approach.* The Service had previously ruled in Rev. Rul. 81–31, 1981–1 C.B. 475, on facts essentially identical to those of *DiMarco*, that a death benefit payable to a deceased employee's surviving spouse was a completed gift occurring at the employee's death when the amount of the benefit first became ascertainable. The Tax Court in *DiMarco* expressly rejected the "open transaction" approach of Rev. Rul. 81–31:

> To the extent that this ruling can be read as holding either that a transfer of property can become complete for gift tax purposes by reason of the death of the donor, or that it is permissible to treat a completed transfer of property as an open transaction and to value the transferred property and impose the gift tax at some time other than when the completed transfer occurs, we regard the ruling as being inconsistent with the gift tax statute and the regulations. [87 T.C. at 661 n.8.]

The Service eventually retreated from its earlier position. See Rev. Rul. 92–68, 1992–2 C.B. 257 (revoking Rev. Rul. 81–31). The Service also acquiesced in the *DiMarco* result "where (1) decedent is automatically covered by the benefit plan and has no control over its terms; (2) decedent's employer retains the right to modify the plan; and (3) decedent's death is the event which first causes the value of the benefit to be ascertainable." 1990–2 C.B. 1. Does the Service's acquiescence imply that a death benefit like the one in *DiMarco* escapes gift and estate tax altogether? Has the Service conclusively abandoned the open transaction approach?

2. *Other transfers as open transactions.* A donor's promise to make future payments generally constitutes a completed gift which is subject to gift tax when the promise becomes binding under state law, even if there is some uncertainty about the amount or timing of the future payments. Rev. Rul. 69–347, 1969–1 C.B. 227. If the promised payments depend on the donor's future income or wealth, however, it may be difficult or impossible to value the transfer at the time the promise becomes binding. In such circumstances the Service may seek to hold the transaction open, waiting to impose the gift tax

until the value of the payments can be determined. For example, in Rev. Rul. 69–346, 1969–1 C.B. 227, a wife promised her husband that she would transfer her share of their community property to his testamentary trust if he included provisions in the trust for her comfort. The Service acknowledged that the agreement became enforceable when it was entered into, but held that the wife did not make a taxable gift until her husband's death when "the amount of the gift first became susceptible of valuation." Does the open transaction approach of Rev. Rul. 69–346 remain viable in light of the Tax Court's decision in *DiMarco*?

Rev. Rul. 75–71, 1975–1 C.B. 309, involved an enforceable contract among three sisters, legatees under the will of another living sister, by which each agreed that if she survived the testator and thereby became entitled to receive her legacy and either or both of the other two sisters did not, she would transfer a portion of her share to the children of the predeceased sisters. The Service ruled that the payments that the sole surviving sister was obligated to make to her nieces and nephews under the contract were taxable as gifts at the testator's death. Why was each sister not treated as making a gift to her own children at the time the contract became enforceable under state law? Compare Rev. Rul. 79–238, 1979–2 C.B. 339 (similar agreement among beneficiaries of irrevocable trust; each party made gift to own children when agreement became enforceable), noted infra page 116, Note 2.

The open transaction approach is discussed in Gans, Valuation Difficulties and Gift Completion, 58 Notre Dame L. Rev. 493 (1983); Macris, Open Valuation and the Completed Transfer: A Problem Area in Federal Gift Taxation, 34 Tax L. Rev. 273 (1979).

4. UNCOMPENSATED SERVICES

COMMISSIONER v. HOGLE

165 F.2d 352 (10th Cir. 1947).

PHILLIPS, CIRCUIT JUDGE.

The Commissioner assessed gift taxes against Hogle for the years 1936 to 1941, inclusive. On review, the Tax Court held there were no deficiencies in gift taxes for those years.

The question presented is whether or not annual earnings of two trusts, one known as the Copley Trust, and one known as the Three Trust, during the years in question, from trading in securities and commodities carried on by the trusts under Hogle's direction, amounted to gifts by Hogle to the trusts. These trusts were before this court in Hogle v. Commissioner, 10 Cir., 132 F.2d 66, and the facts with respect to such trusts are there fully set out.

The Copley Trust was created in 1922 by Hogle and his wife for the benefit of their three children. It consisted of a securities trading account to be managed and operated under Hogle's direction, the property accruing to the trust to be divided among the children on April 15, 1945. The trust was irrevocable and Hogle retained no right to alter or amend the trust instrument, or to change the beneficial interests. None of the principal or income could revest in Hogle. It provided that any losses resulting from trading in excess of the "profits and various income returns thereof" should be made good by Hogle, and that any such losses should not become an indebtedness of the trustee or the beneficiaries, but that any such losses made good by Hogle should be returned to him out of the first profits that accrued from further transactions.

On October 7, 1922, a margin account was opened for the trust with J.A. Hogle & Company, a brokerage partnership, consisting of Hogle and his wife, and in which the three children subsequently became partners. The trading resulted in profits in every year, except 1928 and 1929. In those years, certain securities were given to the trust by Hogle and his wife. The profits and benefits in the trust were divided on April 15, 1945, among the three children, and the trust was terminated.

In 1932, Hogle opened a trading account with the partnership in the name of the Three Trust account and a few days thereafter, Hogle and his wife created the Three Trust, consisting of a securities trading account for the benefit of the three children. The trust was irrevocable and was in all respects like the Copley Trust, with the exception it was to terminate on April 15, 1950, and income could be distributed in the meantime in the discretion of Hogle and any two of the three trustees. Although the trading was conducted in the name of the trust, receipts and disbursements were credited and debited to the individual beneficiaries according to the specified share of each during the term of the trust. Gains and profits were realized in every year, including the taxable years.

The net worth of each trust in each of the years for which the gift taxes were assessed was more than sufficient to provide the margins required to cover the trading carried on for it.

In Hogle v. Commissioner, supra, we held, under the doctrine of Helvering v. Clifford, 309 U.S. 331, that the net income resulting from trading on margin was taxable to Hogle. We do not think it follows, however, that the net income in each of the taxable years derived from trading constituted a gift thereof by Hogle to the trusts....

The net income derived from trading carried on in behalf of the trusts accrued immediately and directly to the trusts, and did not consist of income accruing to Hogle which he transferred by anticipatory gift to the trusts. Hogle never owned or held an economic interest in such income. Likewise, since the funds in the trusts were sufficient to provide the margins required to cover the trading carried on in the taxable years, any losses resulting from trading would have been suffered immediately and directly by the trusts. What, in fact and in reality, Hogle gave to the trusts in the taxable years was his expert services in carrying on the trading, personal services in the management of the trusts. Hogle could give or withhold his personal services in carrying on trading on margin for the trusts. He could not withhold from the trusts any of the income accruing from trading on margin. How could he give what he could not withhold?

There was no transfer directly or indirectly from Hogle to the trusts of title to, or other economic interest in, the income from trading on margin, having the quality of a gift. In short, there was no transfer directly or indirectly by Hogle to the trusts of property or property rights.

The Commissioner places strong reliance upon Hogle v. Commissioner, supra, to sustain the contention that the income arising from the trading on margin represented personal earnings of Hogle; and that Hogle in substance gave to the trusts the profits derived from part of his individual efforts. Certain excerpts from the opinion are emphasized in support of the argument that the net income arising from the trading on margin for the benefit of the trusts represented earnings of Hogle, and that, upon the accrual of such income to the trusts, a transfer having the quality of a gift was effectuated within the meaning of [§ 2501(a)(1)]. But, we think a critical reading of the opinion in that case in its entirety will indicate that it does not support the Commissioner's contention. While the court drew a distinction between the income tax liability of Hogle on profits accruing to the trusts from trading on margin and gains accruing to the trusts from other sources, and held that he was liable for the tax on net income derived from such trading but not on gains accruing from other sources, his liability for tax on the net income derived from trading on margin was predicated upon his power to control indirectly the extent of the profit derived from such trading by determining the extent and amount of such trading. Despite certain statements contained in the opinion on which the Commissioner relies, the basis of the holding that Hogle was liable for income tax on the net income resulting from trading on margin was his power to control the extent of such trading and therefore the extent of the income therefrom. It was predicated on his power to dominate the amount of income that would accrue from trading. That was the essence of our holding. We did not hold that such income accrued first to Hogle and was by him transferred by anticipatory gift to the trusts.

Our holding in Hogle v. Commissioner, supra, was an extreme application of the doctrine of the *Clifford* case, supra. To hold that the profits accruing from trading in margins constitute gifts from Hogle to the trusts, we think, would be an unjustified extension of the doctrine of the *Clifford* case.

Affirmed.

HUXMAN, CIRCUIT JUDGE, concurs in the result.

NOTES

1. *Gifts of uncompensated services and of other wealth-producing opportunities.* Hogle's gift of expert services conferred economic benefit on the three Hogle children, but § 2501(a)(1), by referring to gifts of "property," implicitly exempts gifts of services from the tax. The situation is analogous to parents, who, after giving their children stock in the family business, devote

their talent and energy to making the corporation prosper, thereby causing a substantial appreciation in the value of the children's stock. However, the line separating gifts of property from gifts of services is blurred if the donor's services culminate in transferable property, such as an invention, manuscript, or work of art. Consider the following situations:

1. An author makes a gift to her daughter of a completed manuscript.
2. An author assists her daughter in revising a first draft.
3. The author and her daughter collaborate on the understanding that they will be recognized as co-authors but the daughter will receive all the royalties.

In the last example, does it make a difference if the understanding is entered into before or after the completion of the book?

Parents routinely confer advantages and opportunities on their children, which may include status in the community, contacts with influential friends, access to markets and credit, ideas, tips and advice, and training in work habits, appearance, style and manners. Children who are also lucky enough to inherit their forebears' business acumen may profit handsomely from these opportunities. By the *Hogle* reasoning, no gift tax results. See Blass' Estate v. Commissioner, 11 T.C.M. (CCH) 622 (1952) (gift tax not applicable to taxpayer who brought business opportunity to attention of family trusts and provided services enabling trusts to purchase property and sell it at a profit).

2. *Waiver of compensation for services.* An executor generally is entitled to compensation for administering a decedent's estate. If the executor waives the right to receive commissions, he or she might be treated as constructively receiving the amount of the forgone commissions and then making a gift to the decedent's beneficiaries of the same amount. The Service, however, has ruled that the executor incurs no income or gift tax liability if there is an adequate manifestation of intent to serve on a gratuitous basis. The requisite intent may be express (e.g., a formal waiver executed promptly after the executor's appointment) or it may be implied from surrounding facts and circumstances. See Rev. Rul. 66–167, 1966–1 C.B. 20. Consider the case of a lawyer who drafts a simple will for a family member. The lawyer's regular fee is $500, but she agrees to charge a "courtesy rate" of $200 because of the family relationship. Assuming that the exception for ordinary business transactions does not apply, has the lawyer made a gift of $300? Is there a difference, in economic terms, between performing services for a reduced fee and lending money at a below-market rate?

5. GIFTS OF FUTURE, CONTINGENT, OR DEFEASIBLE INTERESTS

SMITH v. SHAUGHNESSY

318 U.S. 176 (1943).

MR. JUSTICE BLACK delivered the opinion of the Court.

The question here is the extent of the petitioner's liability for a tax under [§ 2511(a)], which imposes a tax upon every transfer of property by gift, "whether the transfer is in trust or otherwise, whether the gift is direct or indirect, and whether the property is real or personal, tangible or intangible; . . ."

The petitioner, age 72, made an irrevocable transfer in trust of 3,000 shares of stock worth $571,000. The trust income was payable to his wife, age 44, for life; upon her death, the stock was to be returned to the petitioner, if he was living; if he was not living, it was to go to such persons as his wife might designate by will, or in default of a will by her, to her intestate successors under applicable New York law. The petitioner, under protest, paid a gift tax of $71,674.22, assessed on the total value of the trust principal, and brought suit for refund in the district court. Holding that the petitioner had, within the meaning of the Act, executed a completed gift of a life estate to his wife, the court sustained the Commissioner's assessment on $322,423, the determined value of her life interest; but the remainder was held not to be completely transferred and hence not subject to the gift tax. 40 F. Supp. 19. The government appealed and the Circuit Court of Appeals reversed, ordering dismissal of the petitioner's complaint on the authority of its previous decision in Herzog v. Commissioner, 116 F.2d 591. We granted certiorari because of alleged conflict with our decisions in Helvering v. Hallock, 309 U.S. 106, and Sanford v. Commissioner, 308 U.S. 39. In these decisions, and in Burnet v. Guggenheim, 288 U.S. 280, we have considered the problems raised here in some detail, and it will therefore be unnecessary to make any elaborate re-survey of the law.

Three interests are involved here: the life estate, the remainder, and the reversion. The taxpayer concedes that the life estate is subject to the gift tax. The government concedes that the right of reversion to the donor in case he outlives his wife is an interest having value which can be calculated by an actuarial device, and that it is immune from the gift tax. The controversy, then, reduces itself to the question of the taxability of the remainder.

The taxpayer's principal argument here is that under our decision in the *Hallock* case, the value of the remainder will be included in the grantor's gross estate for estate tax purposes; and that in the *Sanford* case we intimated a general policy against allowing the same property to be taxed both as an estate and as a gift.

This view, we think, misunderstands our position in the *Sanford* case. As we said there, the gift and estate tax laws are closely related and the gift tax serves to supplement the estate tax. We said that the taxes are not "always mutually exclusive," and called attention to [§ 2012] which charts the course for granting credits on estate taxes by reason of previous payment of gift taxes on the same property. The scope of that provision we need not now determine. It is sufficient to note here that Congress plainly pointed out that "some" of the "total gifts subject to gift taxes . . . may be included for estate tax purposes and some not." House Report No. 708, 72nd Cong., 1st Sess., p. 45. Under the statute the gift tax amounts in some instances to a security, a form of down-payment on the estate tax which secures the eventual payment of the latter; it is in no sense double taxation as the taxpayer suggests.

We conclude that under the present statute, Congress has provided as its plan for integrating the estate and gift taxes this system of secured payment on gifts which will later be subject to the estate tax.

Unencumbered by any notion of policy against subjecting this transaction to both estate and gift taxes, we turn to the basic question of whether there was a gift of the remainder. The government argues that for gift tax purposes the taxpayer has abandoned control of the remainder and that it is therefore taxable, while the taxpayer contends that no realistic value can be placed on the contingent remainder and that it therefore should not be classed as a gift.

We cannot accept any suggestion that the complexity of a property interest created by a trust can serve to defeat a tax. For many years Congress has sought vigorously to close tax loopholes against ingenious trust instruments. Even though these concepts of property and value may be slippery and elusive they can not escape taxation so long as they are used in the world of business. The language of the gift tax statute, "property ... real or personal, tangible or intangible," is broad enough to include property, however conceptual or contingent. And lest there be any doubt as to the amplitude of their purpose, the Senate and House Committees, reporting the bill, spelled out their meaning as follows:

> The terms "property," "transfer," "gift," and "indirectly" [in § 2511(a)], are used in the broadest and most comprehensive sense; the term "property" reaching every species of right or interest protected by law and having an exchangeable value....

The essence of a gift by trust is the abandonment of control over the property put in trust. The separate interests transferred are not gifts to the extent that power remains to revoke the trust or recapture the property represented by any of them, Burnet v. Guggenheim, supra, or to modify the terms of the arrangement so as to make other disposition of the property, Sanford v. Commissioner, supra. In the *Sanford* case the grantor could, by modification of the trust, extinguish the donee's interest at any instant he chose. In cases such as this, where the grantor has neither the form nor substance of control and never will have unless he outlives his wife, we must conclude that he has lost all "economic control" and that the gift is complete except for the value of his reversionary interest.

The judgment of the Circuit Court of Appeals is affirmed with leave to the petitioner to apply for modification of its mandate in order that the value of the petitioner's reversionary interest may be determined and excluded.

It is so ordered.

MR. JUSTICE ROBERTS.

I dissent. I am of opinion that, except for the life estate in the wife, the gift qua the donor was incomplete and not within the sweep of [§§ 2501(a)(1) and 2511(a)]. A contrary conclusion might well be reached were it not for Helvering v. Hallock, 309 U.S. 106. But the decisions in Burnet v. Guggenheim, 288 U.S. 280, and Sanford v. Commissioner, 308 U.S. 39, to which the court adheres, require a reversal in view of the ruling in the *Hallock* case.

The first of the two cases ruled that a transfer in trust, whereby the grantor reserved a power of revocation, was not subject to a gift tax, but became so upon the renunciation of the power. The second held that where the grantor reserved a power to change the beneficiaries, but none to revoke or to make himself a beneficiary, the transfer was incomplete and not subject to gift tax. At the same term, in Porter v. Commissioner, 288 U.S. 436, the court held that where a decedent had given property inter vivos in trust, reserving a power to change the beneficiaries but no power to revoke or revest the property in himself, the transfer was incomplete until the termination of the reserved power by the donor's death and hence the corpus was subject to the estate tax.

When these cases were decided, the law, as announced by this court, was that where, in a complete and final transfer inter vivos, a grantor provided that, in a specified contingency, the corpus should pass to him, if living, but, if he should be dead, then to others, the gift was complete when made, he retained nothing which passed from him at his death, prior to the happening of the contingency, and that no part of the property given was includible in his gross estate for estate tax. McCormick v. Burnet, 283 U.S. 784; Helvering v. St. Louis Union Trust Co., 296 U.S. 39; Becker v. St. Louis Union Trust Co., 296 U.S. 48. So long as this was the law the transfer might properly be the subject of a gift tax for the gift was, as respects the donor, complete when made.

In 1940 these decisions were overruled [by *Hallock*] and it was held that such a transfer was so incomplete when made, and the grantor retained such an interest, that the cessation of that interest at death furnished the occasion for imposing an estate tax. Thus the situation here presented was placed in the same category as those where the grantor had reserved a power to revoke or a power to change beneficiaries. By analogy to the *Guggenheim* and *Sanford* cases, I suppose the gift would have become complete if the donor had, in his life, relinquished or conveyed the contingent estate reserved to him.

In the light of this history, the *Sanford* case requires a holding that the gifts in remainder, after the life estate, create no gift tax liability. The reasoning of that decision, the authorities, and the legislative history relied upon, are all at war with the result in this case. There is no need to quote what was there said. A reading of the decision will demonstrate that, if the principles there announced are here observed, the gifts in question are incomplete and cannot be the subject of the gift tax.

It will not square with logic to say that where the donor reserves the right to change beneficiaries, and so delays completion of the gift until his death or prior relinquishment of the right, the gift is incomplete, but where he reserves a contingent interest to himself the reverse is true,—particularly so, if the criterion of estate tax liability is important to the decision of the question, as the *Sanford* case affirms.

The question is not whether a gift which includes vested and contingent future interests in others than the donor is taxable as an entirety when made, but whether a reservation of such an interest in the donor negatives a completion of the gift until such time as that interest is relinquished.

All that is said in the *Sanford* case about the difficulties of administration and probable inequities of a contrary decision there, applies here with greater force. Indeed a system of taxation which requires valuation of the donor's retained interest, in the light of the contingencies involved, and calculation of the value of the subsequent remainders by resort to higher mathematics beyond the ken of the taxpayer, exhibits the artificiality of the Government's application of the Act. This is well illustrated in the companion cases of *Robinette* and *Paumgarten*.... Such results argue strongly against the construction which the court adopts.

NOTES

1. *Correlation with the estate tax.* The Supreme Court in *Smith v. Shaughnessy* upheld the imposition of a gift tax on the transfer of a contingent remainder, even though it was not known whether that interest would ever become possessory or, if it did, who would take the property. Furthermore, under the Court's holding in Helvering v. Hallock, infra page 333, the value of the trust corpus would have been included in the settlor's gross estate at death. Thus, the Court retreated from earlier dicta in Sanford's Estate v. Commissioner, infra page 89, which had seemed to indicate that a transfer of property might remain incomplete for gift tax purposes as long as the donor retained a power that would cause the property to be included in the donor's gross estate at death.

2. *Valuation of partial interests.* In *Smith*, the settlor transferred a life income interest to his wife and a contingent remainder to her appointees or heirs, retaining a reversion in the trust property. In general, for federal tax purposes, the value of an income interest, remainder, reversion or private annuity is determined under actuarial principles. As mandated by § 7520, the Treasury has promulgated valuation tables reflecting prescribed actuarial assumptions concerning life expectancies and interest rates. Reg. §§ 20.2031–7(d), 20.7520–1, 25.2512–5(d), and 25.7520–1. In effect, the tables apportion the value of the underlying property among the successive interests which, taken together, represent complete beneficial ownership. Thus, if property is held in trust to pay income to *X* for a specified term and then remainder to *Y*, the combined value of the income interest and the remainder is equal to the value of the trust property. And if the value of either interest is known, the

value of the other interest can be determined by subtracting the known value from the value of the underlying property.

The tables reflect three crucial simplifying assumptions. First, all property is assumed to remain constant in principal value; the possibility of future capital appreciation or depreciation is ignored. Second, all property is assumed to generate income at a uniform, constant annual rate based on the current market yield of U.S. Treasury obligations (see explanation, infra page 584). The same annual rate is used in discounting future payments to present value. Finally, each individual is assumed to have a life expectancy consistent with national mortality experience. Based on these assumptions, the tables provide a convenient shortcut for valuing many commonly encountered interests. Consider the following examples, which assume a 6–percent annual rate of return:

1. $100,000 is held in trust to pay income to *A* for ten years with remainder to *B* at the end of the ten-year term. Under the tables, *A*'s income interest is worth $44,160 (the present value of a ten-year stream of $6,000 annual payments), and *B*'s remainder is worth $55,840 (the present value of $100,000 payable in ten years). Reg. § 20.2031–7(d)(6) (Table B).
2. $100,000 is held in trust to pay income to *A* for ten years with remainder at the end of the ten-year term to *B* (presently age 60) if then living, otherwise to *C*. Under the tables, the probability that a 60–year–old will survive for ten years is 85.4 percent (74,794/87,595); the probability of nonsurvival is 14.6 percent. Reg. § 20.2031–7T(d)(7) (Table 2000CM). Accordingly, the value of *B*'s remainder is equal to the present value of $100,000 payable in ten years ($55,840) multiplied by the probability of *B*'s survival (85.4 percent), or $47,680, and the value of *C*'s remainder is $8,160 ($55,840 × 14.6 percent).
3. $100,000 is held in trust to pay income to *A* (presently age 60) for life, with remainder to *B* at *A*'s death. Under the tables, *A*'s income interest is worth $66,375 (the present value of a stream of $6,000 annual payments during the life of a 60–year–old), and *B*'s remainder is worth $33,625 (the present value of $100,000 payable at the death of a 60–year–old). Reg. § 20.2031–7T(d)(7) (Table S).
4. $100,000 is held in trust to pay $5,000 annually to *A* (presently age 60) for life, with the remaining trust property payable to *B* at *A*'s death. Under the tables, *A*'s annuity is worth $54,139 (the present value of a stream of $5,000 annual payments during the life of a 60–year–old), and *B*'s residual interest is worth $45,861 ($100,000 − $54,139). Reg. § 20.2031–7T(d)(2)(iv).

Present value calculations under the tables are discussed in more detail infra at page 584.

A realistic estimate of the value of an income interest, annuity, or remainder often differs markedly from the present value determined under the tables. For example, consider a trust that pays income to *A* for life and remainder to *B*. If the trust is funded with property that produces little current income but appreciates substantially in principal value, the tables will almost certainly overstate the value of *A*'s income interest and understate the value of *B*'s remainder. The misvaluation is even more pronounced if *A* has an unusually short life expectancy due to illness or other circumstances. Section 7520 generally requires that income interests, annuities and remainders be valued under the tables, but the regulations authorize departures from the tables in limited circumstances. Reg. §§ 20.7520–1, 20.7520–3(b), 25.7520–1, and 25.7520–3(b). Furthermore, § 2702, enacted in 1990, sharply restricts the use of the tables in valuing partial interests for gift tax purposes. See infra page 78.

3. *Unappraisable interests.* In Robinette v. Helvering, 318 U.S. 184 (1943), decided the same day as *Smith*, the Court was asked to make an allowance for the value of a reversion that would become possessory only if a 30–year–old woman contemplating marriage should die without issue who reached age 21. The Court refused, pointing out that the petitioners did not offer any recognized method by which the value of such a reversion might be determined. The Court stated:

> It may be true, as the petitioners argue, that trust instruments such as these before us frequently create "a complex aggregate of rights, privileges, powers and immunities and that in certain instances all these rights, privileges, powers and immunities are not transferred or released simultaneously." But before one who gives his property away by this method is entitled to deduction from his gift tax on the basis that he had retained some of these complex strands it is necessary that he at least establish the possibility of approximating what value he holds. Factors to be considered in fixing the value of this contingent reservation as of the date of the gift would have included consideration of whether or not the daughter would marry; whether she would have children; whether they would reach the age of 21; etc. Actuarial science may have made great strides in appraising the value of that which seems to be unappraisable, but we have no reason to believe from this record that even the actuarial art could do more than guess at the value here in question. [318 U.S. at 188–89.]

The rationale of Robinette v. Helvering was applied in Rev. Rul. 77–99, 1977–1 C.B. 295, to hold that a trust instrument that allocated capital gains to income and capital losses to principal rendered the donor's reversionary interest in the corpus incapable of valuation, so the gift tax was imposed on the full value of the trust property. See also Rev. Rul. 76–275, 1976–2 C.B. 299 (trustee had discretion to allocate proceeds of mineral sales to income, even though a portion of such proceeds was treated as principal under state law; held, donor's reversionary interest in the corpus was incapable of valuation, so gift tax was imposed on the full value of the trust property).

Harrison v. Commissioner, 17 T.C. 1350 (1952), involved the valuation for gift tax purposes of a trust under which the trustee was required to pay the settlor's federal and state income taxes. The Commissioner contended that in computing the amount subject to gift tax no allowance could be made for the settlor's reservation of the right to have her income taxes paid by the trustee because the value of that right was not ascertainable with the accuracy required by the *Robinette* case. The court, however, reasoned that "Federal income tax liability may be uncertain as to amount, but it is reasonably sure, if not definite, that the income the petitioner will receive from the trust will require payment of such a tax," and therefore permitted the present value of the future income tax liability to reduce the amount of the gift. Id. at 1355.

4. *Gifts of income interests.* In Lockard v. Commissioner, 166 F.2d 409 (1st Cir. 1948), a settlor transferred property in trust to pay income to her husband for six years or until his prior death; the property was to revert to the settlor at the end of the trust term. The settlor argued, by analogy to the income tax holding in Helvering v. Clifford, 309 U.S. 331 (1940), that she should be treated as owning the trust income until it was actually distributed to her husband. The court responded:

> This suggested mode of treatment may be appropriate and reasonable; the only trouble with it is that it is not sanctioned by the statutory scheme. As we have already pointed out, the income tax and gift tax each has its own independent criteria of taxability. In the trust now before us it may be true, under Helvering v. Clifford, that for income tax purposes the result is the same as if Mrs. Lockard had herself received the income each year and had made a series of assignments of it to her husband. But the fact is that she did not receive the income and then give it away by successive assignments. Upon creating the trust she made a single transfer whereby her husband then and there acquired an irrevocable right to the income for a period of years. Under the plain language of the gift tax, and under the authorities above cited, this intangible right to future income must be valued as of the date of the transfer in trust, and taxed to the donor. [166 F.2d at 412.]

A decision in Mrs. Lockard's favor would have been a mixed blessing for taxpayers. On one hand, characterizing the transaction as a series of annual gifts entitles the donor to a $10,000 per-donee exclusion ($20,000 if the gift is split with the donor's spouse under § 2513) for each year, rather than a single exclusion for the year of the original transfer; it also substitutes a series of small gift tax payments over an extended period for an earlier and larger lump sum payment. On the other hand, the value of the gift when the assignment is made is the discounted present value of the future income payments, not the sum of those amounts.

Another issue in the *Lockard* case involved the value of a separate gift made by Mrs. Lockard in 1941, when she directed that the trust continue after the initial six-year term and that Mr. Lockard receive the trust income for life, plus such amounts of corpus, not in excess of $3,000 in any calendar year, as the trustee "in his uncontrolled discretion shall think necessary" for Mr. Lockard's comfortable maintenance and support. On Mr. Lockard's death, the corpus was to revert to Mrs. Lockard. The Commissioner valued the gift on the assumption that the trustee would pay Mr. Lockard $3,000 per year plus the income from the diminishing corpus. The court upheld the Commissioner's valuation, citing *Robinette* and noting that the taxpayer had not established a sufficient basis for estimating the likelihood of an invasion of corpus.

5. *Correlation with the income tax.* In Commissioner v. Beck's Estate, 129 F.2d 243 (2d Cir. 1942), the grantor of a trust was held liable for gift tax on the entire value of the corpus, although the income was to be used to pay the premiums on insurance on his life and would therefore be taxable to him under § 677(a)(3). After citing several other cases that recognized a lack of coordination among the federal income, estate, and gift taxes, Judge Frank said:

> At the bottom of [taxpayers'] contentions is this implied assumption: The same transaction cannot be a completed gift for one purpose and an incomplete gift for another. Of course, that is not true, as the cases above cited made clear. Perhaps to assuage the feelings and aid the understanding of affected taxpayers, Congress might use different symbols to describe the taxable conduct in the several statutes, calling it a "gift" in the gift tax law, a "gaft" in the income tax law, and a "geft" in the estate tax law. [129 F.2d at 246.]

6. *Income tax treatment of "grantor trusts."* In 1954 Congress enacted the "grantor trust" provisions, §§ 671 to 677, to resolve widespread confusion following the Supreme Court's decision in Helvering v. Clifford, 309 U.S. 331 (1940), concerning the income tax treatment of trust grantors. Under these provisions, a grantor who retains specified beneficial interests or powers may be treated as owning all or a portion of the trust, with the result that a corresponding portion of the trust's items of gross income, deduction and credit will be attributed to the grantor for federal income tax purposes. In general, the grantor trust rules apply where the grantor (or the grantor's spouse) holds any of the following interests or powers:

1. a reversionary interest in trust corpus or income which is worth more than 5 percent of the initial value of the corpus or income (§ 673);
2. a power affecting beneficial enjoyment of trust corpus or income, or a power to revoke, which is exercisable by the grantor or any other person without the consent of an "adverse party" (§§ 674 and 676);
3. certain administrative powers involving the disposition, borrowing, or investment of trust property (§ 675); or
4. an actual or potential right to receive distributions of trust income (§ 677).

Throughout this book, frequent references are made to the estate and gift tax aspects of gifts to minors. An important motive for making such gifts is the desire to shift income tax liability from a high-bracket parent to a low-bracket child. In 1986 Congress curtailed the use of trusts as an income-shifting technique and also introduced the "kiddie tax" of § 1(g), which generally makes the "net unearned income" (above a statutory threshold amount) of a child under age 18 (or older, in some cases) taxable at the marginal rate of the child's parent.

6. VALUATION OF TRANSFERS IN TRUST WITH RETAINED INTERESTS: § 2702

In 1990 Congress added § 2702 to the Code in response to perceived valuation abuses involving gifts of partial interests. The primary target of § 2702 is the "grantor retained income trust" (GRIT), which can be illustrated by a simple example. Assume that *A*, age 60, irrevocably transfers property worth $100,000 in trust to pay income to herself for ten years, with remainder at the end of the term to her child *B*. Under general gift tax principles, *A* has made a completed gift of a remainder in $100,000, which is valued by subtracting the value of her retained income interest from the value of the trust property. According to the tables, assuming a 6–percent annual rate of return, *A*'s income interest is worth $44,160 and the remainder given to *B* is worth $55,840. Reg. § 20.2031–7(d)(6) (Table B).[8] If *A* is still living at the end of the ten–year term, there will be no subsequent taxable gift when the trust property is distributed to *B*.[9]

As long as the assumptions built into the tables hold true, there is no inherent valuation abuse in *A*'s GRIT. In the initial transfer, the tables allocate the bulk of the property's value to *A*'s retained interest based on the assumption that *A* will receive annual income of $6,000. Suppose, however, that the trust property consists of "unproductive" real property or closely held stock that is held for capital appreciation rather than for current income. It now becomes clear that *A* will receive little or no income and any appreciation in the property's value will inure solely to *B*'s benefit. Thus, if the trust property produces no current income but appreciates at an annual rate of 6 percent, it will be worth $179,085 at the end of the ten-year term. Prior to the enactment of § 2702, the bulk of this appreciation arguably would have escaped gift tax altogether.[10]

Section 2702 attacks GRITs and similar arrangements by prescribing special gift tax valuation rules for the initial transfer in trust. The special rules apply when a donor makes a completed "transfer of an interest in trust to (or for the benefit of) a member of the [donor's] family" while retaining an interest in the underlying property. § 2702(a)(1). Property is

---

8. The amount of the gift can be reduced even further if *A* retains a reversionary interest such that the trust property will be payable to *A*'s estate in the event of *A*'s death during the ten-year term. Under the tables, the probability that a 60–year–old will die before reaching age 70 is 14.6 percent (1 − [74,794/87,595]). Reg. § 20.2031–7T(d)(7) (Table 2000CM). Thus, the value of *A*'s additional retained interest under the tables would be $8,160 ($55,840 × 14.6 percent), and the amount of *A*'s gift would be only $47,680.

9. If *A* dies during the ten-year term or transfers the income interest within three years of death, the trust property may be includible in her gross estate under §§ 2035 or 2036, discussed in Chapter 4. For the interaction of § 2702 with these provisions, see infra page 290.

10. A trustee who makes investments that disproportionately favor one beneficiary at another's expense may be liable under state law for breaching the fiduciary duty of impartiality. If the GRIT is intended to shift value to *B* free of gift tax, however, *A* presumably will not complain; *A* may even be the trustee. The government might argue that by failing to enforce her rights *A* makes an indirect gift to *B*. Does the Supreme Court's ruling in *Dickman*, supra page 44, support such an argument? If so, when does such a gift occur and how should it be measured?

considered to be held in trust if beneficial ownership is divided between successive interests such as a life estate or term of years and a remainder. § 2702(c)(1) and (3). Members of the donor's family include the donor's spouse, ancestors and descendants of the donor and his or her spouse, siblings of the donor, and spouses of the foregoing. §§ 2702(e) and 2704(c)(2). Thus, for example, if a donor transfers property irrevocably in trust to pay income to herself for life and remainder at her death to her child, the transfer falls squarely within the terms of the statute. At first glance the special rules appear primarily concerned with the *retained* interest: "The value of any retained interest which is not a qualified interest shall be treated as being zero." § 2702(a)(2)(A). This turns out, however, to be a backhanded method of inflating the value of the *transferred* interest, which is determined by subtracting the value of the retained interest from the value of the underlying property. Thus, unless the donor retains a "qualified" interest (described below), the full value of the underlying property will be allocated to the transferred interest and treated as a taxable gift.

The zero-value rule does not apply to "qualified" retained interests, which continue to be valued under the tables. § 2702(a)(2)(B). There are three types of qualified interests: (1) an annuity interest, i.e., a right to receive annual payments in fixed amounts for life or a specified term of years; (2) a unitrust interest, i.e., a right to receive annual payments equal to a fixed percentage of the annually determined value of the underlying property for life or a specified term of years; and (3) a remainder interest that confers an unconditional right to receive the underlying property following an annuity or unitrust interest. § 2702(b); Reg. § 25.2702–3. These requirements tend to ensure that the holder of a qualified interest will actually receive payments that can be realistically valued under the tables.[11]

The special rules serve the limited function of determining the *gift tax value* of the transferred interest; they do not affect the timing or extent of the completed gift, nor do they govern valuation of the transferred interest for estate, GST or income tax purposes. Furthermore, the special rules apply only to the initial transfer. If the donor subsequently transfers a nonqualified retained interest during life or at death, the subsequent transfer is valued under general principles (i.e., the tables). To alleviate the burden of double taxation that can arise when the retained interest is valued under different methods in the initial and subsequent transfers, the regulations provide for a reduction in the transferor's taxable gifts upon the subsequent transfer. Reg. § 25.2702–6. In general, the amount of the reduction is limited to the lesser of (1) the artificial increase in the transferor's taxable gifts that was caused by applying the special rules in the initial transfer, or (2) the increase in taxable gifts or gross estate resulting from the subsequent transfer. Reg. § 25.2702–6(b).

---

11. The definition of a qualified interest reflects the same concerns that led Congress to impose limitations on charitable deductions for split-interest transfers in 1969. See §§ 170(f), 664(d), 2522(c)(2), and 2055(e)(2). Those limitations are discussed infra at page 473.

To illustrate the operation of § 2702, consider the impact of the special rules on the $100,000 GRIT described above. In creating the GRIT, *A* has made a completed "transfer" of "an interest in trust" to a "member of [her] family" within the meaning of § 2702(a)(1). *A*'s retained income interest is not a qualified interest and therefore must be valued at zero under the special rules. As a result, the entire value of the trust property is allocated to the remainder, producing a taxable gift of $100,000. Assuming that *A* survives the ten-year term and continues to hold the income interest until it expires at the end of the term, there will be no further gift tax consequences. On the other hand, if *A* makes a taxable gift of the income interest before the end of the ten-year term, a reduction will be allowed in calculating *A*'s taxable gifts. The amount of the reduction is limited to the lesser of (1) $44,160 (the amount of the earlier increase in taxable gifts resulting from application of the special rules), or (2) the value (determined under the tables) of the outstanding income interest at the time of the subsequent transfer. This limitation on the allowable reduction ensures that any increase in the value of *A*'s retained income interest after the initial transfer will be subject to gift tax in the subsequent transfer, and also prevents *A* from using any decline in the value of the income interest to reduce her total gift tax liability. The longer *A* waits before disposing of the income interest during the ten-year term, the smaller the allowable reduction in taxable gifts.

Section 2702 also reaches two techniques which arguably would have entirely escaped gift tax under prior law: a sale of a remainder, and a joint purchase. Assume that *A* creates her GRIT in exchange for a cash payment from *B* equal to the value of the remainder interest under the tables ($55,840). Under general valuation principles, *B*'s payment would constitute "adequate and full consideration" for the transfer of the remainder. Under § 2702(c)(1), however, the sale of the remainder is treated as a transfer of an interest in trust, and accordingly *A*'s retained income interest is valued at zero and the transferred remainder is valued at $100,000. Since *B* has paid consideration of only $55,840, the difference of $44,160 constitutes a taxable gift by *A*. Alternatively, assume that an unrelated third person who owns the underlying property sells a ten-year income interest to *A* and simultaneously sells the remainder to *B*; *A* and *B* furnish consideration in proportion to the values of their respective interests under the tables. Under § 2702(c)(2), the transaction is treated as if *A* purchased the underlying property and then sold the remainder to *B* for the consideration actually furnished by *B*, again producing a taxable gift of $44,160.

Despite its apparent harshness, § 2702 has not put an end to intra-family transfers in trust as an estate freezing technique. Instead, it has focused the attention of estate planners on several techniques that either escape the zero-value rule or fall entirely outside the reach of the statute.

a. *Qualified interests.* Under § 2702, the tables still control the valuation of a qualified retained interest such as an annuity or a unitrust interest. Assume that *A* transfers $100,000 irrevocably in trust to make fixed annual payments of $6,000 to *A* (or her estate) for a ten-year term; at the end of the term the remaining trust property will be distributed to her child *B*. This is a "grantor retained annuity trust" (GRAT). Under the tables, assuming a 6–percent annual rate of return, *A*'s retained annuity is worth $44,160 and *B*'s remainder is worth $55,840. Reg. §§ 20.2031–7(d)(6) (Table B) and 25.2512–5(d)(2)(iv). Unlike a GRIT, a GRAT must make fixed annual payments regardless of whether the trust's investment return takes the form of current income or capital appreciation. Thus, *A*'s annuity is valued with reasonable accuracy under the tables. So is *B*'s remainder, as long as the actual investment return on the trust property corresponds to the assumed 6–percent rate. The GRAT may produce substantial gift tax savings if it outperforms the assumed rate over the ten-year term; conversely, if the GRAT performs less well than expected, *A* may incur a heavier gift tax burden than if she had simply made an outright gift to *B* at the end of the term.[12]

As an alternative to a GRAT, suppose that *A* creates an irrevocable $100,000 "grantor retained unitrust" (GRUT). In each year during the ten-year term, the GRUT is required to make a year-end payment to *A* (or her estate) equal to 6 percent of the value of the trust property, determined as of the beginning of the current year; at the end of the term, the remaining trust property will be distributed to her child *B*. Under the valuation method set forth in the regulations, *A*'s retained unitrust interest is worth $44,156 and *B*'s remainder is worth $55,844. Reg. §§ 1.664–4(e)(4) and 1.664–4(e)(6) (Tables D and F). Note that *A*'s unitrust interest and *B*'s remainder have fixed proportional shares in the GRUT's cumulative investment return. Neither interest benefits at the other's expense from a rise or drop in the GRUT's actual rate of return. Indeed, the valuation of the respective interests in a GRUT is virtually independent of the § 7520 interest rate. As a practical matter, the year-to-year fluctuations in annual distributions, combined with the inconvenience of annual valuations of the trust property, may make a GRUT seem less attractive than a GRAT.

b. *Qualified personal residence trusts.* By its terms, § 2702 does not apply to a transfer in trust if the underlying property is "to be used as a personal residence by persons holding term interests in such trust." § 2702(a)(3)(A)(ii). This exception permits a donor's retained interest in a personal residence to be valued under the tables even if it is a nonqualified interest (e.g., an income interest). As a result, the GRIT remains a viable technique for transferring a personal residence at a low gift tax cost. The regulations permit a donor to transfer up to two personal residences in this way, but require that each one be held in a separate "personal

12. Note that if the required annuity payments are sufficiently large, the value of *A*'s retained interest under the tables may be equal to the full value of the underlying property, producing a taxable gift of zero. If *A* survives the ten-year trust term, such a "zeroed-out" GRAT allows any appreciation above the assumed rate to pass to *B* free of gift and estate tax; even if the GRAT fails to meet expectations and the annuity payments to *A* exhaust the trust property, *A* will be no worse off than if she had never created the GRAT. Cf. Walton v. Commissioner, 115 T.C. 589 (2000).

residence trust" or "qualified personal residence trust" (QPRT). Of the two types of trusts, the QPRT is more flexible and therefore more widely used. Detailed requirements concerning the type, use, and disposition of property held in a QPRT are set forth in Reg. § 25.2702–5(c). In addition to a single personal residence, the QPRT may hold only limited amounts of cash for specified purposes (e.g., current expenses). A "personal residence" may be a principal residence or one additional residence (e.g., a vacation home), including appurtenant structures and a "reasonably appropriate" amount of adjacent land; however, the QPRT may not hold personal property (e.g., household furnishings). The QPRT property must be used or held for use as a personal residence by the term holder (or a spouse or dependents). If the residence is sold, damaged or destroyed, any sale or insurance proceeds that are not used to repair or replace the residence within two years must either be distributed outright to the term holder or be converted to a qualified annuity interest for the term holder. During the QPRT term, the trust may not sell or transfer the residence back to the term holder (or his or her spouse). For a sample form of QPRT, see Rev. Proc. 2003–42, 2003–1 C.B. 993.

c. *Tangible property.* The statute contains a special provision for valuing a retained term interest in tangible property where "the nonexercise of rights under [the term interest] would not have a substantial effect on the valuation of the remainder interest in such property." § 2702(c)(4). If the donor can establish the amount for which the retained term interest could be sold to an unrelated third party in a hypothetical arm's-length sale, that value is controlling for gift tax purposes; otherwise, the zero-value rule controls. Reg. § 25.2702–2(c). This provision preserves some of the advantages of a GRIT for tangible, nondepreciable property such as antiques, art works, jewelry, or unimproved land that is expected to appreciate substantially over time. For example, suppose *A* gives an oil painting worth $100,000 to her child *B*, subject to *A*'s retained right to display the painting in her study for a ten-year term. If *A* establishes that the fair market rental value of the painting for the ten-year term is $35,000, she will have made a taxable gift of $65,000. Note that this result, while distinctly more favorable than if the retained interest were valued at zero, ordinarily is less favorable than valuation under the tables.

d. *Transfers outside § 2702.* The special valuation rules of § 2702 apply only if the donor transfers a partial interest in property to a family member while retaining another partial interest in the same property.[13] Thus, the statute does not apply if the donee is a niece, nephew, or other person falling outside the statutory definition of the donor's family. The donor can also avoid the reach of § 2702 by retaining a power to revoke or amend that makes the transfer wholly incomplete for gift tax purposes. See infra page 83. Finally, the statute is inapplicable if the donor makes a

13. The special valuation rules also apply if the retained interest is held by an "applicable family member," which includes the donor's spouse, ancestors of the donor or the donor's spouse, and spouses of such ancestors. §§ 2702(a)(1) and 2701(e)(2).

completed gift of all interests in the property and retains no interest in or control over the property.

e. *Effective date.* Section 2702 applies to transfers occurring after October 8, 1990.

References. For discussions of § 2702, see Blattmachr & Painter, When Should Planners Consider Using Split–Interest Transfers?, 21 Est. Planning 20 (1994); Gans, GRIT's, GRAT's and GRUT's: Planning and Policy, 11 Va. Tax Rev. 761 (1992); McCouch, Rethinking Section 2702, 2 Fla. Tax Rev. 99 (1994); Ponda, Using Qualified Personal Residence Trusts, 67 Tax Notes 947 (1995).

B. INCOMPLETE TRANSFERS

1. RETAINED POWER TO REVOKE

BURNET v. GUGGENHEIM

288 U.S. 280 (1933).

MR. JUSTICE CARDOZO delivered the opinion of the Court.

The question to be decided is whether deeds of trust made in 1917, with a reservation to the grantor of a power of revocation, became taxable as gifts under the Revenue Act of 1924 when in 1925 there was a change of the deeds by the cancellation of the power.

On June 28, 1917, the respondent, a resident of New York, executed in New Jersey two deeds of trust, one for the benefit of his son, and one for the benefit of his daughter. The trusts were to continue for ten years, during which period part of the income was to be paid to the beneficiary and part accumulated. At the end of the ten year period the principal and the accumulated income were to go to the beneficiary, if living; if not living, then to his or her children; and if no children survived, then to the settlor in the case of the son's trust, and in the case of the daughter's trust to the trustees of the son's trust as an increment to the fund. The settlor reserved to himself broad powers of control in respect of the trust property and its investment and administration. In particular, there was an unrestricted power to modify, alter or revoke the trusts except as to income, received or accrued. The power of investment and administration was transferred by the settlor from himself to others in May, 1921. The power to modify, alter or revoke was eliminated from the deeds, and thereby canceled and surrendered, in July, 1925.

In the meanwhile Congress had passed the Revenue Act of 1924 which included among its provisions a tax upon gifts. "For the calendar year 1924 and each calendar year thereafter . . . a tax . . . is hereby imposed upon the transfer by a resident by gift during such calendar year of any property wherever situated, whether made directly or indirectly," the tax to be assessed in accordance with a schedule of percentages upon the value of the property. . . .

At the date of the cancellation of the power of revocation, the value of the securities constituting the corpus of the two trusts was nearly $13,000,000. Upon this value the Commissioner assessed against the donor a tax of $2,465,681, which the Board of Tax Appeals confirmed with a slight modification due to a mistake in computation. The taxpayer appealed to the Court of Appeals for the second circuit, which reversed the decision of the Board and held the gift exempt. 58 F.2d 188. The case is here on certiorari.

On November 8, 1924, more than eight months before the cancellation of the power of revocation, the Commissioner of Internal Revenue, with the approval of the Secretary of the Treasury, adopted and promulgated the following regulation:

> The creation of a trust, where the grantor retains the power to revest in himself title to the corpus of the trust, does not constitute a gift subject to tax, but the annual income of the trust which is paid over to the beneficiaries shall be treated as a taxable gift for the year in which so paid. Where the power retained by the grantor to revest in himself title to the corpus is not exercised, a taxable transfer will be treated as taking place in the year in which such power is terminated. . . .

The substance of this regulation has now been carried forward into [§ 501(c) of] the Revenue Act of 1932. . . .

We think the regulation, and the later statute continuing it, are declaratory of the law which Congress meant to establish in 1924.

"Taxation is not so much concerned with the refinements of title as it is with the actual command over the property taxed—the actual benefit for which the tax is paid." Corliss v. Bowers, 281 U.S. 376, 378. . . . While the powers of revocation stood uncanceled in the deeds, the gifts, from the point of view of substance, were inchoate and imperfect. By concession there would have been no gift in any aspect if the donor had attempted to attain the same result by the mere delivery of the securities into the hands of the donees. A power of revocation accompanying delivery would have made the gift a nullity. Basket v. Hassell, 107 U.S. 602. By the execution of deeds and the creation of trusts, the settlor did indeed succeed in divesting himself of title and transferring it to others . . ., but the substance of his dominion was the same as if these forms had been omitted. Corliss v. Bowers, supra. He was free at any moment, with reason or without, to revest title in himself, except as to any income then collected or accrued. As to the principal of the trusts and as to income to accrue thereafter, the gifts were formal and unreal. They acquired substance and reality for the first time in July, 1925, when the deeds became absolute through the cancellation of the power.

The argument for the respondent is that Congress in laying a tax upon transfers by gift made in 1924 or in any year thereafter had in mind the passing of title, not the extinguishment of dominion. In that view the transfer had been made in 1917 when the deeds of trust were executed.

The argument for the Government is that what was done in 1917 was preliminary and tentative, and that not till 1925 was there a transfer in the sense that must have been present in the mind of Congress when laying a burden upon gifts. Petitioner and respondent are at one in the view that from the extinguishment of the power there came about a change of legal rights and a shifting of economic benefits which Congress was at liberty, under the Constitution, to tax as a transfer effected at that time.... The question is not one of legislative power. It is one of legislative intention.

With the controversy thus narrowed, doubt is narrowed too. Congress did not mean that the tax should be paid twice, or partly at one time and partly at another. If a revocable deed of trust is a present transfer by gift, there is not another transfer when the power is extinguished. If there is not a present transfer upon the delivery of the revocable deed, then there is such a transfer upon the extinguishment of the power. There must be a choice, and a consistent choice, between the one date and the other. To arrive at a decision, we have therefore to put to ourselves the question, which choice is it the more likely that Congress would have made? Let us suppose a revocable transfer made on June 3, 1924, the day after the adoption of the Revenue Act of that year. Let us suppose a power of revocation still uncanceled, or extinguished years afterwards, say in 1931. Did Congress have in view the present payment of a tax upon the full value of the subject matter of this imperfect and inchoate gift? The statute provides that upon a transfer by gift the tax upon the value shall be paid by the donor ... and shall constitute a lien upon the property transferred.... By the act now in force, the personal liability for payment extends to the donee.... A statute will be construed in such a way as to avoid unnecessary hardship when its meaning is uncertain.... Hardship there plainly is in exacting the immediate payment of a tax upon the value of the principal when nothing has been done to give assurance that any part of the principal will ever go to the donee. The statute is not aimed at every transfer of the legal title without consideration. Such a transfer there would be if the trustees were to hold for the use of the grantor. It is aimed at transfers of the title that have the quality of a gift, and a gift is not consummate until put beyond recall.

The respondent invokes the rule that in the construction of a taxing act doubt is to be resolved in favor of the taxpayer.... There are many facets to such a maxim. One must view them all, if one would apply it wisely. The construction that is liberal to one taxpayer may be illiberal to others. One must strike a balance of advantage. It happens that the taxpayer before us made his deeds in 1917, before a transfer by gift was subject to a tax. We shall alleviate his burden if we say that the gift was then complete. On the other hand, we shall be heightening the burdens of taxpayers who made deeds of gift after the Act of 1924. In making them, they had the assurance of a treasury regulation that the tax would not be laid, while the power of revocation was uncanceled, except upon the income paid from year to year. They had good reason to suppose that the tax upon the principal would not be due until the power was extinguished or until the principal was paid. If we disappoint their expectations, we shall be illiberal to them.

The tax upon gifts is closely related both in structure and in purpose to the tax upon those transfers that take effect at death. What is paid upon the one is in certain circumstances a credit to be applied in reduction of what will be due upon the other.[14] ... The gift tax is Part II of Title III of the Revenue Act of 1924; the Estate Tax is Part I of the same title. The two statutes are plainly in pari materia. There has been a steady widening of the concept of a transfer for the purpose of taxation under the provisions of Part I.... There is little likelihood that the lawmakers meant to narrow the concept, and to revert to a construction that would exalt the form above the substance, in fixing the scope of a transfer for the purposes of Part II. We do not ignore differences in precision of definition between the one part and the other. They cannot obscure identities more fundamental and important. The tax upon estates, as it stood in 1924, was the outcome of a long process of evolution; it had been refined and perfected by decisions and amendments almost without number. The tax on gifts was something new. Even so, the concept of a transfer, so painfully developed in respect of taxes on estates, was not flung aside and scouted in laying this new burden upon transfers during life. Congress was aware that what was of the essence of a transfer had come to be identified more nearly with a change of economic benefits than with technicalities of title. The word had gained a new color, the result, no doubt in part, of repeated changes of the statutes, but a new color none the less....

The respondent finds comfort in the provisions of § 302(d) of the Act of 1924, governing taxes on estates.[15] He asks why such a provision should have been placed in Part I [estate tax] and nothing equivalent inserted in Part II [gift tax], if powers for purposes of the one tax were to be treated in the same way as powers for the purposes of the other. Section 302(d) of the Act of 1924 is in part a reenactment of a section of the Revenue Acts of 1918 and 1921, though it has been changed in particulars.... It is an outcome of that process of development which has given us a rule for almost every imaginable contingency in the assessment of a tax under the provisions of Part I. No doubt the draftsman of the statute would have done well if he had been equally explicit in the drafting of Part II. This is not to say that meaning has been lost because extraordinary foresight would have served to make it clearer. Here as so often there is a choice between uncertainties. We must be content to choose the lesser. To lay the tax at once, while the deed is subject to the power, is to lay it on a gift that may never become consummate in any real or beneficial sense. To lay it

14. Section 2012 was repealed for post–1976 gifts because the method of computing the estate tax liability enacted by the Tax Reform Act of 1976 eliminates the need for a special credit for gift taxes paid on a transfer that is also reached by the estate tax. See infra page 550.—EDS.

15. Section 302(d), the predecessor of § 2038, required that any trust created by the decedent during life be included in the gross estate if the decedent held at death a power to "alter, amend, or revoke" beneficial enjoyment.—EDS.

later on is to unite benefit with burden. We think the voice of Congress has ordained that this be done....

The argument for the respondent, if pressed to the limit of its logic would carry him even farther than he has claimed the right to go. If his position is sound that a power to revoke does not postpone for the purpose of taxation the consummation of the gift, then the income of these trusts is exempt from the tax as fully as the principal. What passed to the beneficiaries was the same in either case, an interest inchoate and contingent till rendered absolute and consummate through receipt or accrual before the act of revocation. Congress did not mean that recurring installments of the income, payable under a revocable conveyance which had been made by a settlor before the passage of this statute, should be exempt, when collected, from the burden of the tax.

The judgment is reversed.

THE CHIEF JUSTICE took no part in the consideration or decision of this case.

MR. JUSTICE SUTHERLAND and MR. JUSTICE BUTLER are of opinion that the termination of the donor's power of revocation was not a transfer by gift of any property within the meaning of the statute, and that the judgment of the Circuit Court of Appeals should be affirmed.

NOTES

1. *Repeal of § 501(c), 1932 Act.* Because the Supreme Court in *Guggenheim* expressed the opinion that § 501(c) of the 1932 Revenue Act (providing that a revocable transfer is not a taxable gift) was declaratory only, it was repealed in 1934.

2. *Power of revocation arising by operation of law or indirection.* The principles enunciated in *Guggenheim* apply with equal force even if the power of revocation does not appear in the trust instrument. Under the law of some states, a trust is revocable and hence not a taxable gift if the settlor fails to negate revocability in the instrument. See, e.g., Cal. Prob. Code § 15400 (trust presumed revocable unless expressly made irrevocable). Reserved powers may be construed as tantamount to a power to revoke, even though they are not explicitly so labeled. See Mandels' Estate v. Commissioner, 64 T.C. 61 (1975) (transfer in trust of stock of family business held revocable because trustees were required to vote stock as instructed by donor, refrain from questioning his salary as corporate officer, and allow him to be active in management); see also Touche v. Commissioner, 58 T.C. 565 (1972) (deed of real property mistakenly recited transfer of interest that donor intended to retain; held, no completed gift of interest recoverable in reformation proceeding); Pascarelli v. Commissioner, 55 T.C. 1082 (1971), affd. mem., 485 F.2d 681 (3d Cir. 1973) (funds transferred to woman with whom taxpayer lived not subject to gift tax to extent expended by her pursuant to his direction).

A gift may be subject to recall for many reasons: incompetency of the donor, fraud or undue influence, lack of delivery, failure to comply with the statute of frauds, and so on. In Commissioner v. Allen, 108 F.2d 961 (3d Cir.

1939), cert. denied, 309 U.S. 680 (1940), the court had to decide the proper time for imposing the gift tax on a transfer made by the taxpayer while she was a minor. The applicable local law allowed a minor to recover property transferred by gift at any time before reaching the age of 21 and for a "reasonable time" (depending on "the circumstances of the particular case") thereafter. The transfer occurred in 1932, two days before the gift tax was enacted; the government assessed a deficiency for 1933, when the taxpayer reached age 21. The court rejected the taxpayer's argument that the gift was made in 1932 and upheld the assessment for 1933. There was no contention that the gift occurred in a later year. Should the donor's right to disaffirm the gift for a reasonable period after reaching majority have delayed the effective date of the transfer for gift tax purposes?

3. *Gift of donor's own check.* In Rev. Rul. 67–396, 1967–2 C.B. 351, the Service ruled that the mere delivery of a donor's own check does not give rise to a completed gift:

> The gift of a check does not become complete until it is paid, certified, or accepted by the drawee, or is negotiated for value to a third person. Prior to payment, certification, or negotiation, a check is nothing more than an order on the drawee bank which may be revoked at any time by the drawer by stopping payment and is revoked ipso facto by the death of the drawer.

Under this reasoning, if the donee deposits the donor's check on December 31 and the check clears two days later on January 2 of the next calendar year, the gift would not become complete until the later year. In Metzger's Estate v. Commissioner, 38 F.3d 118 (4th Cir. 1994), however, the court held that "where noncharitable gifts are deposited at the end of December and presented for payment shortly after their delivery but are not honored by the drawee bank until after the New Year's holiday, . . . the gifts should relate back to the date of deposit."

In response to the *Metzger* decision, the Service issued Rev. Rul. 96–56, 1996–2 C.B. 161, which treats the delivery of a check to a noncharitable donee as a completed gift:

> on the earlier of (i) the date on which the donor has so parted with dominion and control under local law as to leave in the donor no power to change its disposition, or (ii) the date on which the donee deposits the check (or cashes the check against available funds of the donee) or presents the check for payment, if it is established that: (1) the check was paid by the drawee bank when first presented to the drawee bank for payment; (2) the donor was alive when the check was paid by the drawee bank; (3) the donor intended to make a gift; (4) delivery of the check by the donor was unconditional; and (5) the check was deposited, cashed, or presented in the calendar year for which completed gift treatment is sought and within a reasonable time of issuance.

The "relation back" doctrine does not apply if the donee receives a check and waits until a later calendar year to present it for payment, see Dillingham's Estate v. Commissioner, 903 F.2d 760 (10th Cir. 1990), or if the donor dies before the check is paid, see Rosano v. United States, 245 F.3d 212 (2d Cir.

2001), cert. denied, 534 U.S. 1135 (2002); Gagliardi's Estate v. Commissioner, 89 T.C. 1207 (1987).

4. *Gifts by or on behalf of an incompetent.* A transfer by an incompetent donor does not constitute a gift if it is ineffective under local law. Bettin's Estate v. Commissioner, 543 F.2d 1269 (9th Cir. 1976). Nevertheless, under the "substituted judgment" doctrine, the guardian of an incompetent may be authorized by local law to make gifts of the ward's property to persons whom the ward is legally, morally or equitably obligated to support if it is likely that the ward would make such gifts if legally competent to do so. Transfers made under this doctrine are subject to gift tax if and to the extent they exceed the ward's obligation to support the donee. Rev. Rul. 73–612, 1973–2 C.B. 322. For Delaware law on the subject, see In re duPont, 194 A.2d 309 (Del. Ch. 1963) (court approved $36 million gift by elderly incompetent's guardians, based on projected net tax savings).

5. *Joint bank and brokerage accounts.* Local law typically provides that a joint account belongs to the parties, during their joint lifetime, in proportion to their respective net contributions. Accordingly, if *A* uses her own funds to create a joint account for herself and *B*, there is no completed gift until *B* draws on the account for his own benefit. Reg. § 25.2511–1(h)(4). Rev. Rul. 69–148, 1969–1 C.B. 226, reaches the same result regarding a joint stock brokerage account.

2. RETAINED NONBENEFICIAL POWER TO ALTER OR AMEND

SANFORD'S ESTATE v. COMMISSIONER

308 U.S. 39 (1939).

MR. JUSTICE STONE delivered the opinion of the Court.

This and its companion case, Rasquin v. Humphreys, [308 U.S. 54 (1939)], present the single question of statutory construction whether in the case of an inter vivos transfer of property in trust, by a donor reserving to himself the power to designate new beneficiaries other than himself, the gift becomes complete and subject to the gift tax imposed by the federal revenue laws at the time of the relinquishment of the power. Correlative questions, important only if a negative answer is given to the first one, are whether the gift becomes complete and taxable when the trust is created or, in the case where the donor has reserved a power of revocation for his own benefit and has relinquished it before relinquishing the power to change beneficiaries, whether the gift first becomes complete and taxable at the time of relinquishing the power of revocation.

In 1913, before the enactment of the first gift tax statute of 1924, decedent created a trust of personal property for the benefit of named beneficiaries, reserving to himself the power to terminate the trust in whole or in part, or to modify it. In 1919 he surrendered the power to revoke the trust by an appropriate writing in which he reserved "the right to modify any or all of the trusts" but provided that this right "shall in no way be deemed or construed to include any right or privilege" in the donor "to withdraw principal or income from any trust." In August, 1924, after the effective date of the gift tax statute, decedent renounced his remaining power to modify the trust. After his death in 1928, the Commissioner following the decision in Hesslein v. Hoey, 91 F.2d 954, in 1937, ruled that the gift became complete and taxable only upon decedent's final renunciation of his power to modify the trusts and gave notice of a tax deficiency accordingly.

The order of the Board of Tax Appeals sustaining the tax was affirmed by the Court of Appeals for the Third Circuit, 103 F.2d 81, which followed the decision of the Court of Appeals for the Second Circuit in Hesslein v. Hoey, supra, in which we had denied certiorari, 302 U.S. 756. In the *Hesslein* case, as in the *Humphreys* case now before us, a gift in trust with the reservation of a power in the donor to alter the disposition of the property in any way not beneficial to himself, was held to be incomplete and not subject to the gift tax under the 1932 Act so long as the donor retained that power.

We granted certiorari in this case, 307 U.S. 618, and in the *Humphreys* case, id. 619, upon the representation of the Government that it has taken inconsistent positions with respect to the question involved in the two cases and that because of this fact and of the doubt of the correctness of the decision in the *Hesslein* case decision of the question by this Court is desirable in order to remove the resultant confusion in the administration of the revenue laws.

It has continued to take these inconsistent positions here, stating that it is unable to determine which construction of the statute will be most advantageous to the Government in point of revenue collected. It argues in this case that the gift did not become complete and taxable until surrender by the donor of his reserved power to designate new beneficiaries of the trusts. In the *Humphreys* case it argues that the gift upon trust with power reserved to the donor, not afterward relinquished, to change the beneficiaries was complete and taxable when the trust was created. It concedes by its brief that "a decision favorable to the government in either case will necessarily preclude a favorable decision in the other."

In ascertaining the correct construction of the statutes taxing gifts, it is necessary to read them in the light of the closely related provisions of the revenue laws taxing transfers at death, as they have been interpreted by our decisions.... When the gift tax was enacted Congress was aware that the essence of a transfer is the passage of control over the economic benefits of property rather than any technical changes in its title. See Burnet v. Guggenheim, 288 U.S. 280, 287....

... The rule was thus established, and has ever since been consistently followed by the Court, that a transfer of property upon trust, with power reserved to the donor either to revoke it and recapture the trust property or to modify its terms so as to designate new beneficiaries other than himself is incomplete, and becomes complete so as to subject the transfer to death taxes only on relinquishment of the power at death.

There is nothing in the language of the statute, and our attention has not been directed to anything in its legislative history to suggest that Congress had any purpose to tax gifts before the donor had fully parted with his interest in the property given, or that the test of the completeness of the taxed gift was to be any different from that to be applied in determining whether the donor has retained an interest such that it becomes subject to the estate tax upon its extinguishment at death. The gift tax was supplementary to the estate tax. The two are in pari materia and must be construed together. Burnet v. Guggenheim, supra, 286. An important, if not the main, purpose of the gift tax was to prevent or compensate for avoidance of death taxes by taxing the gifts of property inter vivos which, but for the gifts, would be subject in its original or converted form to the tax laid upon transfers at death.

Section [2012][16] provides that when a tax has been imposed by [§ 2501(a)(1)] upon a gift, the value of which is required by any provision of the statute taxing the estate to be included in the gross estate, the gift tax is to be credited on the estate tax. The two taxes are thus not always mutually exclusive as in the case of gifts made in contemplation of death which are complete and taxable when made, and are also required to be included in the gross estate for purposes of the death tax. But [§ 2012] is without application unless there is a gift inter vivos which is taxable independently of any requirement that it shall be included in the gross estate. Property transferred in trust subject to a power of control over its disposition reserved to the donor is likewise required by [§ 2038] to be included in the gross estate. But it does not follow that the transfer in trust is also taxable as a gift. The point was decided in the *Guggenheim* case where it was held that a gift upon trust, with power in the donor to revoke it is not taxable as a gift because the transfer is incomplete, and that the transfer whether inter vivos or at death becomes complete and taxable only when the power of control is relinquished. We think, as was pointed out in the *Guggenheim* case, . . . that the gift tax statute does not contemplate two taxes upon gifts not made in contemplation of death, one upon the gift when a trust is created or when the power of revocation, if any, is relinquished, and another on the transfer of the same property at death because the gift previously made was incomplete.

It is plain that the contention of the taxpayer in this case that the gift becomes complete and taxable upon the relinquishment of the donor's power to revoke the trust cannot be sustained unless we are to hold, contrary to the policy of the statute and the reasoning in the *Guggenheim* case, that a second tax will be incurred upon the donor's relinquishment at death of his power to select new beneficiaries, or unless as an alterna-

16. Section 2012 was repealed for post–1976 gifts because the method of computing the estate tax liability enacted by the Tax Reform Act of 1976 eliminates the need for a special credit for gift taxes paid on a transfer that is also reached by the estate tax. See infra page 550.—EDS.

tive we are to abandon our ruling in the *Porter* case.[17] The Government does not suggest, even in its argument in the *Humphreys* case, that we should depart from our earlier rulings, and we think it clear that we should not do so both because we are satisfied with the reasoning upon which they rest and because departure from either would produce inconsistencies in the law as serious and confusing as the inconsistencies in administrative practice from which the Government now seeks relief.

There are other persuasive reasons why the taxpayer's contention cannot be sustained. By [§ 6324(b)], the donee of any gift is made personally liable for the tax to the extent of the value of the gift if the tax is not paid by the donor. It can hardly be supposed that Congress intended to impose personal liability upon the donee of a gift of property, so incomplete that he might be deprived of it by the donor the day after he had paid the tax. Further, [§ 2522] exempts from the tax, gifts to religious, charitable, and educational corporations and the like. A gift would seem not to be complete, for purposes of the tax, where the donor has reserved the power to determine whether the donees ultimately entitled to receive and enjoy the property are of such a class as to exempt the gift from taxation. Apart from other considerations we should hesitate to accept as correct a construction under which it could plausibly be maintained that a gift in trust for the benefit of charitable corporations is then complete so that the taxing statute becomes operative and the gift escapes the tax even though the donor should later change the beneficiaries to the non-exempt class through exercise of a power to modify the trust in any way not beneficial to himself.

The argument of petitioner that the construction which the Government supports here, but assails in the *Humphreys* case, affords a ready means of evasion of the gift tax is not impressive. It is true, of course, that under it gift taxes will not be imposed on transactions which fall short of being completed gifts. But if for that reason they are not taxed as gifts they remain subject to death taxes assessed at higher rates, and the Government gets its due, which was precisely the end sought by the enactment of the gift tax.

Nor do we think that the provisions of [§ 676(a), relating to income tax,] have any persuasive influence on the construction of the gift tax provisions with which we are now concerned. One purpose of the gift tax was to prevent or compensate for the loss of surtax upon income where large estates are split up by gifts to numerous donees. Congress was aware that donors in trust might distribute income among several beneficiaries, although the gift remains so incomplete as not to be subject to the tax. It dealt with that contingency in [§ 676(a)] which taxes to the settlor the income of a trust paid to beneficiaries where he reserved to himself an unexercised power to "revest in himself title" to the trust property

17. In Porter v. Commissioner, 288 U.S. 436 (1933), noted infra page 239, the Court held that a settlor's reserved power to modify or alter a trust indenture in any manner except in favor of himself or his estate required inclusion of the trust property under the predecessor of § 2038.—EDS.

producing the income. Whether this section is to be read as relieving the donor of the income tax where the power reserved is to modify the trust, except for his own benefit, we do not now decide. If Congress, in enacting it, undertook to define the extent to which a reserved power of control over the disposition of the income is equivalent to ownership of it so as to mark the line between those cases on the one hand where the income is to be taxed to the donor and those on the other where, by related sections, the income is to be taxed to the trust or its beneficiaries, we do not perceive that the section presents any question so comparable to that now before us as to affect our decision. We are concerned here with a question to which Congress has given no answer in the words of the statute, and it must be decided in conformity to the course of judicial decision applicable to a unified scheme of taxation of gifts whether made inter vivos or at death. If Congress, for purpose of taxing income, has defined precisely the amount of control over the income which it deems equivalent to ownership of it, that definition is controlling on the courts even though without it they might reach a different conclusion, and even though retention of a lesser degree of control be deemed to render a transfer incomplete for the purpose of laying gift and death taxes.

The question remains whether the construction of the statute which we conclude is to be derived from its language and history, should be modified because of the force of treasury regulations or administrative practice. [The Court went on to hold that the regulations were "ambiguous and without persuasive force in determining the true construction of the statute" and that the administrative practice was too inconsistent to be accepted as an expert interpretation of the statute.]

Affirmed.

MR. JUSTICE BUTLER took no part in the consideration or decision of this case.

NOTES

1. *Exceptions to the Sanford rule.* In *Sanford* the Supreme Court established the general rule that a transfer of property is not complete for gift tax purposes to the extent that the donor reserves a power to alter or amend beneficial enjoyment, even if the power cannot be exercised for the donor's own benefit. Nevertheless, there are several well-established exceptions to the general rule. A retained power to vary the beneficial interests of others does not prevent the transfer from being complete for gift tax purposes if the power is: (1) one that affects only the "manner or time" of enjoyment (Reg. § 25.2511–2(d)); (2) a power exercisable only with the consent of a person having a "substantial adverse interest" (Reg. § 25.2511–2(e)); or (3) a fiduciary power limited by a "fixed or ascertainable standard" enforceable by the beneficiaries (Reg. § 25.2511–2(g)). Note also that the gift tax regulations do not attempt to distinguish powers of "disposition" from powers of "administration." In the ordinary course of trust administration, a trustee normally is authorized by the terms of the trust or state law to manage the trust

property, to make investments, to allocate receipts and expenditures between principal and income, and so on. Could such administrative powers, if held by a settlor acting as trustee, be exercised to alter or amend beneficial enjoyment? In the estate tax context, courts generally rely on fiduciary constraints imposed by state law in holding that routine administrative powers do not amount to powers of disposition. See Old Colony Trust Co. v. United States, infra page 307.

2. *Overlap of gift and estate taxes.* The Court in *Sanford* found nothing in the statute or the legislative history to suggest "that the test of the completeness of the taxed gift was to be any different from that to be applied in determining whether the donor has retained an interest such that it becomes subject to the estate tax upon its extinguishment at death." Nevertheless, the Court went on to acknowledge that "[t]he two taxes are . . . not always mutually exclusive," noting that in certain cases a taxable gift might be drawn back into the donor's gross estate at death.

Despite the "unification" of the gift and estate taxes in the 1976 Act, some powers held by a donor over property transferred during life may render the transfer incomplete for estate tax purposes even though they did not prevent completion for gift tax purposes. Consider, for example, a power affecting only the "manner or time" of beneficial enjoyment by others, or a power to revoke or amend that is exercisable only with the consent of a person having a "substantial adverse interest." Such powers, if held at death, may cause the underlying property to be included in the gross estate under § 2038, discussed infra at page 238. As part of the cumulative estate tax computation, § 2001(b)(2) allows an offset against the tentative estate tax equal to the gift tax (determined under the rate schedule in effect at death) payable with respect to all taxable gifts made by the decedent after 1976. For transfers that are subject to both gift and estate taxes, the § 2001(b)(2) offset replaces the analogous § 2012 credit applicable to pre–1977 gifts.

3. *Simplifying the completed transfer rule.* There is widespread dissatisfaction with the current rules defining when a transfer is complete for estate and gift tax purposes, and several proposals for achieving better coordination of the two taxes have been put forward. One proposal, for example, would overrule the *Sanford* result. It would treat a transfer as incomplete as long as "the transferor can recover the transferred property [or receive income from it], through exercise of a power retained by him or conferred by him on another." An inter vivos transfer would be complete and therefore subject to gift tax even though the transferor retained a power to alter and amend beneficial enjoyment in favor of persons other than the transferor. ABA Tax Section Task Force, Report on Transfer Tax Restructuring, 41 Tax Law. 395, 405 (1988). For further discussion of the completed transfer rules and proposals for their reform, see infra page 342.

3. RETAINED POWER EXERCISABLE ONLY WITH CONSENT OF PERSON HAVING SUBSTANTIAL ADVERSE INTEREST

CAMP v. COMMISSIONER

195 F.2d 999 (1st Cir. 1952).

MAGRUDER, CHIEF JUDGE.

Frederic E. Camp petitions for review of a decision of the Tax Court entered November 7, 1950, holding that petitioner was deficient in his gift tax for the year 1937 in the amount of $55,737.08, and for the year 1943 in the amount of $1,839.99. Primarily, the issue relates to the year 1937; the Tax Court's determination as to 1937 resulted in an upward revision of the figure for taxpayer's net gifts for the years prior to 1943, and thus, as a mere matter of mathematical computation, in a determination of a deficiency in taxpayer's gift tax liability for other gifts made by him in 1943.

The dispute centers about the effect of a transfer in trust made by the taxpayer in 1932, prior to the enactment of the Revenue Act of 1932, § 501 of which imposed a tax on gifts.... Petitioner insists that this transfer in trust was a completed gift of the whole corpus, so that the transaction in its entirety was outside the incidence of the gift tax subsequently enacted. The Tax Court has held, however, that there was no completed gift at all in 1932, because the donor reserved in the deed of trust full power to alter, amend or revoke, in conjunction with his half brother, who, the court concluded, had no "substantial adverse interest" in the trust property; and that there was a completed gift of the whole of the corpus of the trust in 1937, when the trust instrument was amended so as to vest the power of further amendment or revocation in the donor in sole conjunction with the donor's wife, who had a life interest in the trust income.

We are unable to accept altogether either the taxpayer's argument or the conclusion of the Tax Court. This segment of tax law, as to when a transfer in trust is to be deemed a completed gift for purposes of the gift tax, has been in a somewhat cloudy state, as perhaps is evident from the fact that in the present case the Commissioner has taken several successive positions, each asserting a larger deficiency for the years in question.

The case was tried in the Tax Court upon a stipulation of facts, supplemented by a deposition by petitioner which was read into evidence.

On October 30, 1931, the taxpayer married Alida Donnell Milliken. No children have issued from this marriage; but at various dates within the period January 19, 1937, to October 3, 1942, taxpayer and his wife have adopted four children.

On February 1, 1932, taxpayer executed a trust indenture naming Bankers Trust Company of New York as trustee, and transferred to said trustee, as corpus of the trust, securities then having a fair market value of $416,131.72.

The trust instrument provided that the income should be payable to taxpayer's wife Alida during her life, and that upon her death the principal of the trust should be paid to the then living issue of the donor per stirpes; and in default of such issue, that the trustee should continue to hold the principal in trust, paying the income therefrom to Johnanna R. Bullock, mother of the donor, during her life, and upon her death, that the trustee should pay the principal of the trust fund unto H. Ridgely Bullock, half brother of the donor, or if he be then dead, unto the then living issue of said H. Ridgely Bullock per stirpes, or if there be none, to the trustees of Princeton University.

The tenth article of the trust indenture provided:

> This indenture shall not be subject to revocation, alteration or modification by the Donor, alone, but nevertheless, he may, in conjunction with either H. Ridgely Bullock or Johnanna R. Bullock, beneficiaries hereunder, during the continuance of this trust, by instrument, in writing, executed and acknowledged by the Donor and either the said H. Ridgely Bullock or the said Johnanna R. Bullock, . . . modify or alter in any manner, or revoke in whole or in part, this indenture and the trusts then existing, and the estates and interests in property hereby created. . . .

When the trust was thus created in February, 1932, taxpayer's wife Alida was 23 years of age, his mother Johnanna R. Bullock was 63, and his half brother H. Ridgely Bullock was 22.

On August 30, 1934, the taxpayer, in conjunction with Ridgely, exercised the power to alter or amend by inserting a provision that Alida, wife of the donor, should receive the income of the trust only so long as she, during the donor's lifetime, should continue to be his wife and to reside with him.

On December 11, 1937, the taxpayer, in conjunction with Ridgely, exercised the amendatory power so as to provide that the term "issue of the Donor," as used in the trust instrument, should be deemed to include any child or children then or thereafter legally adopted by the donor and his said wife, and their issue. At the same time the trust instrument was further modified so as to strike out the above-quoted provision in the tenth article with reference to the power to alter, amend or revoke, and to substitute in lieu thereof a provision containing the same words except that the name of Alida Donnell Milliken Camp was substituted for the names of H. Ridgely Bullock and Johnanna R. Bullock. Thus, on and after December 11, 1937, taxpayer reserved the power to alter, amend or revoke the trust in sole conjunction with his wife Alida, who was entitled to all the income from the trust during her lifetime, with the qualification previously stated.

The fair market value of the corpus of the trust, as of December 11, 1937, was $518,089.76.

On June 6, 1946, the taxpayer, in conjunction with his wife Alida, further modified the trust instrument by striking out in its entirety the provision of the tenth article, as amended, dealing with the power to alter, amend or revoke, and substituting in lieu thereof an unqualified provision that the trust indenture "shall not be subject to revocation, alteration or modification."

Section 501(c) of the Revenue Act of 1932 contained the following specific provision:

> The tax shall not apply to a transfer of property in trust where the power to revest in the donor title to such property is vested in the donor, either alone or in conjunction with any person not having a substantial adverse interest in the disposition of such property or the income therefrom, but the relinquishment or termination of such power (other than by the donor's death) shall be considered to be a transfer by the donor by gift of the property subject to such power, and any payment of the income therefrom to a beneficiary other than the donor shall be considered to be a transfer by the donor of such income by gift.

This subsection was repealed in 1934 . . . for the reason, as explained in the committee reports, that "the principle expressed in that section is now a fundamental part of the law by virtue of the Supreme Court's decision in the *Guggenheim* case [supra page 83]." . . .

It is to be noted that the facts of the *Guggenheim* case were narrower than the situations specifically covered in § 501(c), in that the Supreme Court was not passing upon the case where the donor did not reserve to himself alone the power of revocation, but vested such power in himself in conjunction with some other person who might or might not have had a substantial adverse interest in the disposition of the property or the income therefrom. However, the committee reports in 1934 expressed the view that this latter situation was covered in principle by the Supreme Court's decision in the *Guggenheim* case, and therefore recommended the repeal of § 501(c) because it had become unnecessary and superfluous.

What, then, was this "principle" recognized in the *Guggenheim* case? We think it is to be found in the Court's opinion . . . that the gift tax was not aimed at every transfer of the legal title without consideration, which would include a transfer to trustees to hold for the use of the grantor, but was aimed, rather, "at transfers of the title that have the quality of a gift, and a gift is not consummate until put beyond recall."

Subsequent cases have elaborated upon the concept of a "gift," and have settled that a transfer in trust is incomplete as a gift, not only where the donor reserves the power to revest the trust property in himself, but also where he reserves the power to alter the disposition of the property or the income therefrom in some way not beneficial to himself. Estate of Sanford v. Commissioner, 1939, 308 U.S. 39. . . .

Treasury Regulations [§ 25.2511–2] contain the following provisions, which we take to be declaratory of the intent of the Act and of the gloss which later cases have put upon the concept of a "gift" as expressed in Burnet v. Guggenheim:

> . . . As to any property, or part thereof or interest therein, of which the donor has so parted with dominion and control as to leave in him no power to change the disposition thereof, whether for his own benefit or for the benefit of another, the gift is complete. But if upon a transfer of property (whether in trust or otherwise) the donor reserves any power over the disposition thereof, the gift may be wholly incomplete, or may be partially incomplete, depending upon all the facts in the particular case. Accordingly, in every case of a transfer of property subject to a reserved power, the terms of the power must be examined and its scope determined.
>
> A gift is incomplete in every instance where a donor reserves the power to revest the beneficial title to the property in himself. A gift is also incomplete where and to the extent that a reserved power gives the donor the right to name new beneficiaries or to change the interests of the beneficiaries as between themselves. . . .
>
> A donor shall be considered as himself having the power where it is exercisable by him in conjunction with any person not having a substantial adverse interest in the disposition of the transferred property or the income therefrom. A trustee, as such, is not a person having an adverse interest in the disposition of the trust property or its income.
>
> The relinquishment or termination of a power to change the disposition of the transferred property, occurring otherwise than by the death of the donor (the statute being confined to transfers by living donors), is regarded as the event which completes the gift and causes the tax to apply. . . .

Where a donor makes a transfer in trust for numerous beneficiaries, it is obvious that there may be several distinct gifts or potential gifts. For purposes of the gift tax, some of the interests created may be completed gifts, and others may not be, depending upon the facts of the particular case—as is stated in the first paragraph of the above quotation from [§ 25.2511–2] of the regulations.

From the foregoing, we think the following propositions are reasonably clear:

(1) If the trust instrument gives a designated beneficiary any interest in the corpus of the trust property or of the income therefrom, which is capable of monetary valuation, and the donor reserves no power to withdraw that interest, in whole or in part, except with the consent of such designated beneficiary, then the gift of that particular interest will be

deemed to be complete, for the purposes of the gift tax. See accord, our discussion in Commissioner v. Prouty, 1 Cir., 1940, 115 F.2d 331, 334.... This is true, though at the time of the creation of the trust there might be extraneous considerations, whether of a pecuniary or sentimental nature, which would give the donor every confidence that such designated beneficiary would acquiesce in any future desire of the donor to withdraw the gift, in whole or in part. See Commissioner v. Prouty, supra at page 335–336. In that respect the donor is taken at his word; he has legally given away something which he cannot take back except with the consent of the donee. The transfer fulfills the concept of a completed gift, quite as much as if a husband makes an outright gift of securities to his wife, being confident that his wife would reconvey the securities to him if he ever asked for them. If there were an advance agreement between the donor and the donee, prior to the transfer in trust, to the effect that the donee would acquiesce in any future exercise of the power of modification proposed by the donor, then the situation would be different. The trust instrument would not express the true intention of the parties. A real gift is not intended, where the purported donee has agreed ahead of time to hold the "gift" subject to the call and disposition of the purported donor.

(2) If the only power reserved by the donor is a power to revoke the entire trust instrument (not a power to modify the trust in any particular), and this power may be exercised only in conjunction with a designated beneficiary who is given a substantial adverse interest in the disposition of the trust property or the income therefrom, then the transfer in trust will be deemed to be a present gift of the entire corpus of the trust, for purposes of the gift tax. In such cases, the gift of the entire corpus will be deemed to have been "put beyond recall" by the donor himself.

(3) If the trust instrument reserves to the donor a general power to alter, amend or revoke, in whole or in part, and this power is to be exercised only in conjunction with a designated beneficiary who has received an interest in the corpus or income capable of monetary valuation, then the transfer in trust will be deemed to be a completed gift, for purposes of the gift tax, only as to the interest of such designated beneficiary having a veto over the exercise of the power. As to the interests of the other beneficiaries, the gifts will be deemed to be incomplete, for as to such interests the donor reserves the power to take them away in conjunction with a person who has no interest in the trust adverse to such withdrawal. The gifts to the other beneficiaries have not been "put beyond recall" by the donor; in such cases the regulation recognizes realistically that when the donor has reserved the power to withdraw any of the donated interests with the concurrence of some third person who has no interest in the trust adverse to such withdrawal, it is in substance the same as if the donor had reserved such power in himself alone. In further support of this proposition, see the discussion in Estate of Sanford v. Commissioner, 1939, 308 U.S. 39, 46–47.

Coming back, then, to the terms of the trust which petitioner created in February, 1932: It is clear that there was not at that time a completed gift of the life income to petitioner's wife Alida. Under the original provisions of the trust indenture, this life estate was subject to revocation by the donor in conjunction either with the donor's half brother Ridgely or his mother Johnanna, neither of whose interests in the trust were adverse to the withdrawal of the life estate from Alida.

When the trust instrument was amended on December 11, 1937, so as to transfer to Alida alone the veto power over any further proposals by the donor for amendment of the trust, there was on that date a completed gift to Alida of the interest which she then held in the trust. It is stipulated that the value on December 11, 1937, of the income of a trust having a principal value of $518,089.76, payable during life of a woman of 29 (Alida's age), was $356,492.38. However, it is to be noted that Alida did not at this time hold an absolutely unqualified life interest in the income. By prior amendment, the indenture provided that the income of the trust was to be payable to Alida, wife of the donor, only "as long as she, during his lifetime, shall continue to be his wife and to reside with him." Whether, in the valuation of the gift to Alida on December 11, 1937, some allowance should be made for this qualification upon the life estate, we do not undertake to say. Cf. Robinette v. Helvering, 1943, 318 U.S. 184, 188. The Tax Court was in error, we think, in ruling that upon the execution of the amendment of December 11, 1937, petitioner made a taxable gift of the whole corpus of the trust, valued then at $518,089.76. There were at that time no completed gifts to the succeeding income beneficiaries and beneficiaries in remainder, for Alida's interest in the trust was not adverse to the donor's revocation of those succeeding interests by an exercise of the reserved power.

By the amendment of June 6, 1946, whereby all power to revoke, alter or modify the trust was eliminated, there resulted a taxable gift of the then value of the corpus, minus the sum determined to be the value of the gift to Alida on December 11, 1937, and minus also the values of any completed gifts which may be deemed to have been made at the time of the creation of the trust on February 1, 1932. This latter point we do not have to determine in the present case, because petitioner's liability for the year 1946 is not before us. In passing, we simply allude to a possible difficulty, in that the donor originally reserved a power to revoke or modify the trust in conjunction with either Ridgely or Johnanna. Ridgely's contingent remainder interest might have been revoked by the donor, in conjunction with Johnanna, whose interest in the trust was not adverse to such revocation. Johnanna's contingent life estate could have been revoked by the donor in conjunction with Ridgely, whose interest in the trust was not adverse to such revocation. Where the veto power is thus lodged in the alternative, it may be that, for purposes of the gift tax, there is not a completed gift to either of such beneficiaries. But cf. Estate of Leon N. Gillette, 1946, 7 T.C. 219; Commissioner v. Betts, 7 Cir., 1941, 123 F.2d 534.

The decision of the Tax Court is vacated, and the case is remanded to that court for further proceedings not inconsistent with this opinion.

NOTES

1. *"Substantial adverse interests" and the happy family.* In rejecting the theory that a "substantial adverse interest" cannot exist within a happy family unit, the *Camp* court relied on its earlier decision in Commissioner v. Prouty, 115 F.2d 331 (1st Cir. 1940). In *Prouty*, the court observed:

> Examining these intimate family trusts, one must recognize an element of unreality in the inquiry whether a beneficiary's interest is substantially adverse to the grantor. The supposition is that, given a sufficient stake in the trust, the beneficiary is not likely to yield to a wish of a grantor to revoke the trust. In many cases the grantor may have full confidence in the compliant disposition of the member of the family he selects to share his power of revocation, even though such member is named as beneficiary of a handsome interest in the trust. The very fact that the grantor reserved a power to revoke indicates a mental reservation on his part as to the finality of the gift; and if the grantor wishes to hold on to a power of recapture, it stands to reason he will vest the veto power in someone whose acquiescence he can count on. Cf. Helvering v. City Bank Farmers Trust Co., 296 U.S. 85, 90. However, we cannot read into the gift tax, any more than into [§§ 676 and 677], the proposition that a member of the grantor's immediate family can never be deemed to have "a substantial adverse interest." So far as the gift tax is concerned, it is fair enough to take the grantor at his word. As to the income tax, it might be rational for Congress to tax all family income as a unit. But as the law now stands—both gift tax and income tax—we must give weight to the formal rights conferred in the trust instrument in determining whether a given beneficiary has a substantial adverse interest, bearing in mind the admonition of Helvering v. Clifford, 309 U.S. 331, 335, that "where the grantor is the trustee and the beneficiaries are members of his family group, special scrutiny of the arrangement is necessary...." [115 F.2d at 335–36.]

The *Prouty* court also commented on a cognate problem: whether a trustee or other person whose consent is required to an amendment or other change in a trust has an adverse interest if an exercise of the power will adversely affect a member of that person's family. In *Prouty*, a settlor retained a power, exercisable with her husband's consent, to revoke or amend two trusts that she had created for the benefit of their children. The court held that the creation of the trusts was not a completed gift, despite the requirement of the husband's consent:

> "It is natural to assume," said the Board [of Tax Appeals], "that his desire and concern for the support, maintenance, and welfare of his children after his death would prompt him to resist any effort on the part of the grantor of the trust to alter, amend or revoke that part of the trust so as to revest in her title to such property." No doubt this is an interest of a sort. But we think the phrase "substantial adverse interest," as it was used in Section 501(c) of the Revenue Act of 1932 and as it is used in [§§ 676 and 677], means a direct legal or equitable interest in the trust

property and not merely a sentimental or parental interest in seeing the trust fulfilled for the advantage of other beneficiaries. [115 F.2d at 335.]

What if the beneficiaries whose enjoyment will be adversely affected by the trustee's action are his minor children, whom he is obligated to support? In Latta v. Commissioner, 212 F.2d 164 (3d Cir.), cert. denied, 348 U.S. 825 (1954), the court held that the estranged husband of the settlor of a trust did not have a substantial adverse interest, although their minor children were the remaindermen.

2. *Relation to income tax.* The term "substantial adverse interest" was taken by the gift tax regulations from § 501(c) of the Revenue Act of 1932, as the *Camp* case points out, and this statute took it from the statutory provisions governing the grantor's *income tax* liability on the income of a revocable trust. The common use of the term thus effected a degree of coordination between the gift tax and the income tax. In 1954, the term "substantial adverse interest" was dropped from the income tax provisions and the concept of "adverse" and "nonadverse" parties was substituted. Section 672(a) defines an "adverse party" as a person "having a substantial beneficial interest in the trust which would be adversely affected by the exercise or nonexercise of the power which he possesses respecting the trust." No substantive change in the law was intended. For an analysis of the "substantial adverse interest" test as applied to a family trust in the income tax context, see Joseloff v. Commissioner, 8 T.C. 213 (1947).

3. *Power held by person other than donor.* If the settlor of a trust retains no enforceable rights to receive distributions or to control beneficial enjoyment by others, the creation of the trust is normally a completed gift. A power held by a person other than the settlor to reshuffle the interests of the beneficiaries does not prevent the transfer from being complete for gift tax purposes. See Reg. § 25.2511–2(b); Higgins v. Commissioner, 129 F.2d 237 (1st Cir.), cert. denied, 317 U.S. 658 (1942). Furthermore, the possibility that the settlor might receive distributions of income or corpus through the exercise of a "completely voluntary" power held by a third-party trustee normally does not prevent gift completion. Rev. Rul. 77–378, 1977–2 C.B. 347. If, on the other hand, the trustee's power to make distributions to the settlor is governed by an external standard that can be enforced by the settlor, the gift is incomplete to the extent of the settlor's retained rights. The Service can ordinarily tax the transfer in full if the settlor cannot establish the value of the retained rights with reasonable accuracy. Although this is a normal result of the taxpayer's burden of proof, the courts have been willing in a few cases involving transfers by infirm and elderly settlors to look outside the trust instrument in order to determine that vague support provisions rendered the gift incomplete. In these cases the external circumstances indicated that the trust was created to protect the property against loss during the settlor's lifetime, rather than to make gifts to the remaindermen. See Holtz's Estate v. Commissioner, 38 T.C. 37 (1962); Commissioner v. Vander Weele, 254 F.2d 895 (6th Cir. 1958); Gramm's Estate v. Commissioner, 17 T.C. 1063 (1951).

Since no gift tax is imposed on a transfer if the donor retains a power to revoke or amend with the consent of a "neutral" third party (i.e., a person having no substantial adverse interest), why should a power held solely by a neutral third party be treated differently?

4. INDIRECT RETAINED POWER

OUTWIN v. COMMISSIONER

76 T.C. 153 (1981).

DAWSON, JUDGE.

... We must decide whether the transfers by the petitioners to their respective discretionary trusts in 1969 constituted completed gifts subject to tax under section 2501. The gift tax provisions of the Internal Revenue Code do not define the term "completed gift" but it is well settled that a conveyance in trust will not be subject to gift tax where the donor retains dominion and control over the property transferred. Estate of Sanford v. Commissioner, 308 U.S. 39 (1939); Burnet v. Guggenheim, 288 U.S. 280 (1933); Estate of Mandels v. Commissioner, 64 T.C. 61 (1975); Hambleton v. Commissioner, 60 T.C. 558 (1973); Estate of Holtz v. Commissioner, 38 T.C. 37 (1962); sec. 25.2511–2(b), Gift Tax Regs. In the present cases, the discretionary trusts are irrevocable under the terms of the written trust agreements. In each instance, the grantor may receive lifetime distributions of trust income or corpus only in the "absolute and uncontrolled discretion" of the trustees. The trustees are empowered to distribute the entire corpus to the grantor even though such distribution results in the termination of the trust. Additionally, the trust agreements require the grantor's spouse to give his or her prior written consent in an individual capacity to any such distributions. Upon the death of the grantor, the surviving spouse acquires the right to mandatory distributions of trust income on at least an annual basis, plus distributions of principal in the unfettered discretion of the trustees. The grantor's spouse is also given a special testamentary power of appointment over the trust corpus. Under these circumstances, we must decide whether petitioners have sufficiently parted with dominion and control over their property so as to qualify the transfers as completed gifts.

Petitioners contend that no completed gifts resulted because the trustees of the discretionary trusts had orally agreed prior to the execution of the written agreements to (1) distribute the trust income or corpus whenever the grantors requested such funds, and (2) terminate the trusts upon their request by making liquidating distributions of all the remaining corpus. Consequently, petitioners maintain that they never relinquished dominion and control over the property transferred. In the alternative, they argue that under Massachusetts law the creditors of a grantor-beneficiary of a discretionary trust can reach the assets of the trust for satisfaction of their claims, notwithstanding the veto power over discretionary distributions vested in the grantor's spouse. Accordingly, they contend that the gifts are incomplete under the principle established in Paolozzi v. Commissioner, 23 T.C. 182 (1954).

Respondent contends that the evidence is insufficient to prove the existence of the oral agreements alleged by the petitioners, and that, even if such agreements did exist between the grantors and the trustees, there was no agreement between the grantors (petitioners) which would restrict the right of either grantor to veto distributions from the other's discretionary trust(s). Respondent further argues that the transfers in trust were completed gifts under sections 25.2511–2(b) and 25.2511–1(g)(2), Gift Tax Regs., since there are no fixed or ascertainable standards enforceable by or on behalf of the grantor which limit the trustees' discretion to make distributions. Finally, respondent contends that under Massachusetts law the assets of a discretionary trust cannot be subjected to the claims of the grantor's creditors where (1) distributions are subject to the approval of the grantor's spouse, who is also a secondary beneficiary, and (2) there are no enforceable standards to limit the trustees' discretion in making such distributions. Thus, respondent maintains that the rule of law in *Paolozzi* is inapplicable. We hold for petitioners.

Where the trust agreement specifies, as here, that distributions to the settlor are to be made in the absolute discretion of the trustees, with no enforceable standard provided, the transfer is generally held to be complete for gift tax purposes. Herzog v. Commissioner, 116 F.2d 591 (2d Cir. 1941); Rheinstrom v. Commissioner, 105 F.2d 642 (8th Cir. 1939); Estate of Holtz v. Commissioner, 38 T.C. 37, 42 (1962); sec. 25.2511–2(b), Gift Tax Regs.... A different result obtains, however, where State law permits creditors of the settlor-beneficiary to pierce the trusts for satisfaction of claims.

In Paolozzi v. Commissioner, 23 T.C. 182 (1954), the taxpayer created a trust under the terms of which the trustees were authorized to pay her so much of the trust income as they in their absolute discretion determined to be in her best interest. Upon her death, the trust assets were to be distributed to her issue. She reported a taxable gift when the trust was established in an amount equal to the value of the assets transferred reduced by the value of a life estate for an individual her age. Respondent determined that the amount of the gift should be undiminished by the value of the life estate since her interest in the trust income was at best an expectancy, and not susceptible of valuation by actuarial methods. This Court rejected respondent's determination on the ground that, under Massachusetts law, the creditors of a settlor-beneficiary of a discretionary trust could reach for satisfaction of claims the maximum amount which the trustee could pay to the settlor or apply for her benefit. Thus, we concluded that the taxpayer could at any time obtain the economic benefit of the trust income simply by borrowing and then forcing her creditors to look to her interest in the trust income for a source of repayment. On this basis, we held that the gift was incomplete to the extent of the value of her life estate. Accord, Vander Weele v. Commissioner, 27 T.C. 340, 343–344 (1956), affd. 254 F.2d 895 (6th Cir. 1958) (involving Michigan law)....

Under the rule of *Paolozzi*, then, we must determine whether the assets of the Edson S. Outwin and Mary M. Outwin discretionary trusts could be subjected to the claims of the grantor's creditors under Massachusetts law, which governs the interpretation and administration of the trusts.

The general rule in this country regarding the rights of creditors of a settlor-beneficiary of a discretionary trust is expressed in 1 Restatement, Trusts 2d, sec. 156(2) (1959): "Where a person creates for his own benefit a trust for support or a discretionary trust, his transferee or creditors can reach the maximum amount which the trustee under the terms of the trust could pay to him or apply for his benefit." An example of the application of this rule is set forth in E. Griswold, Spendthrift Trusts, sec. 481 (2d ed. 1947).

> § 481. *Discretionary trusts.* The settlor may attempt to retain a beneficial interest free from the claims of his creditors, by giving his property to a trustee and investing the trustee with complete discretion to decide whether the income shall be paid to him and, if so, how much of it. Thus, *A* may convey property to *T* on trust to pay to *A* during *A*'s life so much of the income as in *T*'s uncontrolled discretion he deems wise, with a provision that on *A*'s death the principal and any accumulated income shall be conveyed to *B*. The remainder, so far as the principal is concerned, being a present vested remainder in *B* and not subject to *A*'s control, is beyond the reach of *A*'s creditors, unless the transfer is a fraudulent conveyance. Does the fact that the trustee is given discretion over the disposition of the income exempt the income, likewise, from the claims of creditors? The courts have very properly held that in such a case creditors of the settlor may reach the entire income from the trust property during his life. A person can not settle his own property so that it will be free from the claims of creditors and yet retain the right to receive the income, if it is paid to any one, during his lifetime....

The Supreme Judicial Court of Massachusetts formally adopted this general rule in Ware v. Gulda, 331 Mass. 68, 117 N.E.2d 137 (1954)....

Respondent does not dispute the correctness of *Gulda* or its continued viability as a part of Massachusetts trust law. Nor does he challenge the propriety of our decision in *Paolozzi*. Rather, he seeks to distinguish those cases on the ground that discretionary distributions from the trusts herein require the prior individual consent of the grantor's spouse, who is also a remainderman beneficiary thereof. The presence of such a veto power in an interested party, respondent contends, imposes a significant limitation on the trustees' discretion and thereby removes these cases from the general rule of *Gulda*. We disagree.

... [I]t is our opinion that the veto power bestowed upon the grantor's spouse in connection with the trusts herein is insufficient to render the *Gulda* rule inapplicable. The *Gulda* opinion and the cases cited therein evidence a strong public policy in Massachusetts against persons placing property in trust for their own benefit while at the same time insulating such property from the claims of creditors. That policy would be easily frustrated if creditors were prevented from reaching the trust assets merely because the settlor's spouse is given an interest in the trust and the right to veto discretionary distributions which might deplete that interest. It is not unreasonable to assume that, because of the marital relationship, the settlor could anticipate the complete acquiescence of his spouse in any discretionary distributions which he might receive, regardless of their effect on her interest as a remainderman. Thus, in the absence of unforeseen circumstances, such as divorce, the possibility of a spousal veto in such a situation may be at best a remote possibility. This is particularly true in the present cases, where the fact that each spouse has the right to veto distributions from the other's discretionary trust(s) could discourage the exercise of that authority through fear of reprisal. For these reasons, we think that the veto powers held by the petitioners do not, by themselves, place the trusts outside the scope of the *Gulda* decision....

We hold, therefore, that creditors of the petitioners could reach the assets of their respective discretionary trusts for reimbursement under Massachusetts law, and under the holding of *Paolozzi* the petitioners have failed to surrender dominion and control over the trust assets.[18]

In reaching our decision in this case, we expressly disavow any reliance on the oral understandings between the petitioners and the trustees to the effect that the trustees would be totally responsive to any requests from the petitioners for discretionary distributions. On occasion, this Court has considered extrinsic evidence, such as the settlor's financial condition, his purpose in establishing the trust, and oral assurances by the trustees that the funds would be made available upon request, to help determine whether a right to discretionary distributions rendered a transfer in trust incomplete for gift tax purposes. See Estate of Holtz v. Commissioner, 38 T.C. 37, 43–44 (1962); Vander Weele v. Commissioner, 27 T.C. 340, 345–346 (1956), affd. 254 F.2d 895 (6th Cir. 1958); Gramm v. Commissioner, 17 T.C. 1063, 1066 (1951). In each of these cases, however, a standard limiting the trustee's discretion was provided in the trust instrument and the extrinsic evidence served primarily to indicate the probability that the trust funds would be used to satisfy that standard. There are no ascertainable standards in the trust agreements before us. In fact, other than the requirement that the trustees act in good faith, there are absolutely no limitations placed on the trustees' discretionary authori-

18. Although the transfers in trust in these cases are not subject to gift tax, the settlor's ability to secure the economic benefit of the trust assets by borrowing and relegating creditors to those assets for repayment may well trigger inclusion of the property in the settlor's gross estate under secs. 2036(a)(1) or 2038(a)(1). See Estate of Uhl v. Commissioner, 25 T.C. 22 (1955), revd. 241 F.2d 867 (7th Cir. 1957) (Seventh Circuit disagreed with this Court's finding that creditors of the settler had the right to reach the trust assets under Indiana law, but did not directly dispute the conclusion that such a right, had one existed, would cause inclusion in the settlor's gross estate under the predecessor to section 2036(a)); Rev. Rul. 76–103, 1976–1 C.B. 293 (inclusion required under sec. 2038(a)); see also C. Lowndes, Some Doubts About the Use of Trusts to Avoid the Estate Tax, 47 Minn. L. Rev. 31, 36–37 (1962).

ty. They are specifically directed to exercise their discretion without regard to the independent financial resources of any beneficiary, and without regard to whether any anticipated distributions would lead to the termination of the trust. Yet, these provisions vesting absolute discretion in the trustees are flatly contradicted by the oral understandings to which the petitioners and the trustees testified. We are inclined to give such testimony little weight for several reasons: (1) The petitioners' testimony is self-serving; (2) the trustees are close personal friends of the petitioners; and (3) the petitioners have yet to receive any distributions from their respective discretionary trusts. Furthermore, we note that, while the testimony indicates that the petitioners received the specified assurances from trustees Henry B. Thielbar and Morris H. Bergreen, there is insufficient evidence to prove that either of the petitioners agreed in advance to consent to any proposed distributions from the other's trust(s). Accordingly, we rest our decision in this case solely on the creditor's rights theory set forth in *Paolozzi*.

Decisions will be entered for the petitioners.

NOTES

1. *Portion of gift subject to tax.* The settlor in *Guggenheim* reserved the right to revoke the entire trust, but if a transfer is revocable only in part, the transfer is incomplete only as to the revocable portion, and there is a gift of the portion beyond the settlor's control. Reg. § 25.2511–2(b). By similar reasoning, a transfer is not taxable to the extent of any beneficial interest retained by the grantor. How did the Internal Revenue Service justify its claim for a tax on the full amount of the 1969 transfers made by Mr. and Mrs. Outwin? Note the Service's acquiescence in *Outwin*, 1981–2 C.B. 2.

2. *Power held by donor subject to consent of adverse party.* Although the settlors in *Outwin* did not expressly retain any beneficial interests or powers, the court found that under state law each settlor could indirectly realize the economic value of his or her respective trust by incurring debts and relegating creditors to the trust property for repayment. Mrs. Outwin had a beneficial interest in her husband's trusts and a right to veto any invasion of corpus for his benefit. Mr. Outwin had similar rights with respect to the trust created by his wife. Normally, a donor's retained power to revoke a transfer does not prevent completion if the power can be exercised only with the consent of a person having a substantial adverse interest. See Reg. § 25.2511–2(e); Camp v. Commissioner, supra page 95. Since distributions could be made to the settlors in *Outwin* only with the consent of a spouse having a substantial adverse interest, why did the court not find that the gifts were complete? Should each spouse have been treated as the settlor of the other spouse's trust under the "reciprocal trust" doctrine of *Grace's Estate*, infra page 262?

3. *"Neutral" trustees.* In spite of their close friendship with the settlors, the *Outwin* trustees were classified as "neutral." They had no beneficial interest in the trusts nor were they under any legal obligation to make trust distributions in accordance with the settlors' wishes. Despite their own admission that they were prepared to return the funds to the settlors on

request, the court was unwilling to treat them as the settlors' agents. As a general proposition, what is the likelihood of any trustee being unresponsive to the settlor's desires during the latter's lifetime? One commentator has observed:

> Even a corporate fiduciary may be susceptible to pressure from the grantor in its exercise of discretionary powers as trustee. The grantor may be a customer of the commercial department as well as the trust department, or the corporate fiduciary may anticipate serving as executor of the grantor's estate and as trustee under his will if no untoward development should mar the relationship. Quite apart from such specific pressures is the more general one that arises from the nature of a fiduciary's business. As the name implies, it is engaged in the administration of trusts. A reputation in the community for being hard to get along with is unlikely to assist the work of the new business department. [Westfall, Trust Grantors and Section 674: Adventures in Income Tax Avoidance, 60 Colum. L. Rev. 326, 340 (1960).]

If a settlor retains an unrestricted power to remove and replace a trustee, any powers held by the trustee are attributed to the settlor. Should the same analysis apply if the trustee can be removed only for cause, or if any successor trustee must be an "independent" third party? See Vak's Estate v. Commissioner, 973 F.2d 1409 (8th Cir. 1992) (no attribution where donor retained power to replace original trustee with independent successor); Rev. Rul. 95–58, 1995–2 C.B. 191 (no attribution where terms of retained power precluded appointment of "related or subordinate" person as successor trustee).

4. *Informal side agreements.* Should a settlor be able to supplement or vary the terms of a formal trust agreement by reference to an informal understanding or side agreement between the settlor and the trustee? Should it matter whether the purported side agreement is raised by the taxpayer or the government? In *Outwin*, the court refused to take account of alleged oral agreements between the settlors and the trustees which would have varied the terms of their written trust agreements. In *Camp*, supra page 95, where there was no attempt to vary the terms of the formal trust agreement, the court remarked that the settlor should be "taken at his word" in determining whether his retained powers were subject to veto by a person having a substantial adverse interest. At the same time, the *Camp* court distinguished the hypothetical situation where a donee agreed in advance to acquiesce in any future modification that the donor might request; in that case, "[t]he trust instrument would not express the true intention of the parties." For an application of this principle, see Publicker v. Miles, 48 A.F.T.R. 1968 (E.D. Pa. 1955), where the terms of a trust which would have been a taxable gift if taken at face value were disregarded on evidence that the trustee had agreed with the donor that the corpus would be returned to her on request and that a provision permitting the donor to revoke only with the consent of her husband was inserted by an attorney without the donor's knowledge and in violation of her intention.

5. *Relation to the estate tax.* If a transfer is held to be incomplete because the trustee has the power to maintain and support the settlor, is it open to the settlor's executor following the settlor's death to exclude the

property from the gross estate on the inconsistent theory that it was put beyond the settlor's control by the lifetime transfer? Compare the *Outwin* court's discussion of the possible estate tax consequences of these arrangements in footnote 18 supra, with the discussion in German's Estate v. United States, 7 Cl. Ct. 641 (1985).

Under the traditional rule regarding self-settled trusts, a spendthrift clause is ineffectual to prevent a settlor's creditors from reaching any beneficial interest retained by the settlor; in the case of a discretionary trust, creditors can reach the maximum amount of income or corpus that the trustee could distribute to the settlor-beneficiary. Beginning in the 1990s, however, several states have enacted statutes repudiating the traditional rule and expressly allowing a settlor-beneficiary to fend off creditors by means of an "asset protection trust." Such a trust typically must be irrevocable and may be administered by an independent corporate trustee who has sole discretion to distribute income and corpus to the settlor and members of her family. In the absence of any other interests or powers retained directly or indirectly by the settlor, the Service has held in a private letter ruling that the creation of the trust is a completed gift and that the trustee's discretionary power will not cause the trust property to be included in the settlor's gross estate under § 2036. Priv. Ltr. Rul. 200944002 (July 15, 2009).

C. TRANSFERS FOR CONSIDERATION OR IN DISCHARGE OF LEGAL OBLIGATIONS: §§ 2512(b), 2043(b), AND 2053(c)(1)(A)

1. DONATIVE INTENT

Many of the cases that first gave purpose and definition to §§ 2501 and 2511 and continue to be recognized as landmarks in the development of the gift tax involved transfers of property made before marriage or at the marriage's dissolution. Were these fact situations to arise today, the gift tax consequences would often be significantly different due to the enactment of the marital deduction in 1948 and its expansion in 1981 to allow an unlimited amount of tax-free gifts between spouses. Nevertheless, the marital deduction has not diminished the importance of the principles developed in the earlier cases. The marital deduction will be unavailable in many cases, either because the donee is not married to the donor at the time of the gift or because the transfer runs afoul of the terminable interest rule which precludes a deduction for interests that may terminate on an event such as divorce or remarriage. A transfer that is not covered by the marital deduction may still escape gift tax if it qualifies as a sale or exchange for consideration in money or money's worth.

COMMISSIONER v. WEMYSS

324 U.S. 303 (1945).

MR. JUSTICE FRANKFURTER delivered the opinion of the Court.

In 1939 taxpayer proposed marriage to Mrs. More, a widow with one child. Her deceased husband had set up two trusts, one half the income of which was for the benefit of Mrs. More and the other half for that of the child with provision that, in the event of Mrs. More's remarriage, her part of the income ceased and went to the child. The corpus of the two trusts consisted of stock which brought to Mrs. More from the death of her first husband to her remarriage, about five years later, an average income of $5,484 a year. On Mrs. More's unwillingness to suffer loss of her trust income through remarriage the parties on May 24, 1939, entered upon an agreement whereby taxpayer transferred to Mrs. More a block of shares of stock. Within a month they married. The Commissioner ruled that the transfer of this stock, the value of which, $149,456.13, taxpayer does not controvert, was subject to the Federal Gift Tax.... Accordingly, he assessed a deficiency which the Tax Court upheld, 2 T.C. 876, but the Circuit Court of Appeals reversed the Tax Court, 144 F.2d 78. We granted certiorari to settle uncertainties in tax administration engendered by seemingly conflicting decisions. 323 U.S. 703.

The answer to our problem turns on the proper application of [§§ 2501(a)(1) and 2512(b)] to the immediate facts....

In view of the major role which the Tax Court plays in Federal tax litigation, it becomes important to consider how that court dealt with this problem. Fusing, as it were, [§§ 2501(a)(1) and 2512(b)], the Tax Court read them as not being limited by any common law technical notions about "consideration." And so, while recognizing that marriage was of course a valuable consideration to support a contract, the Tax Court did not deem marriage to satisfy the requirement of [§ 2512(b)] in that it was not a consideration reducible to money value. Accordingly, the Court found the whole value of the stock transferred to Mrs. More taxable under the statute and the relevant Treas. Reg. [§ 25.2512–8]: "A consideration not reducible to a money value, as love and affection, promise of marriage, etc., is to be wholly disregarded, and the entire value of the property transferred constitutes the amount of the gift." In the alternative, the Tax Court was of the view that if Mrs. More's loss of her trust income rather than the marriage was consideration for the taxpayer's transfer of his stock to her, he is not relieved from the tax because he did not receive any money's worth from Mrs. More's relinquishment of her trust income, and, in any event, the actual value of her interest in the trust, subject to fluctuations of its stock earnings, was not proved. One member of the Tax Court dissented, deeming that the gift tax legislation invoked ordinary contract conceptions of "consideration."

The Circuit Court of Appeals rejected this line of reasoning. It found in the marriage agreement an arm's length bargain and an absence of "donative intent" which it deemed essential: "A donative intent followed by a donative act is essential to constitute a gift; and no strained and artificial construction of a supplementary statute should be indulged to tax as a gift a transfer actually lacking donative intent." 144 F.2d 78, 82.

Sections [2501(a)(1) and 2512(b)] are not disparate provisions. Congress directed them to the same purpose, and they should not be separated in application. Had Congress taxed "gifts" simpliciter, it would be appropriate to assume that the term was used in its colloquial sense, and a search for "donative intent" would be indicated. But Congress intended to use the term "gifts" in its broadest and most comprehensive sense.... Congress chose not to require an ascertainment of what too often is an elusive state of mind. For purposes of the gift tax it not only dispensed with the test of "donative intent." It formulated a much more workable external test, that where "property is transferred for less than an adequate and full consideration in money or money's worth," the excess in such money value "shall, for the purpose of the tax imposed by this title, be deemed a gift...." And Treasury Regulations have emphasized that common law considerations were not embodied in the gift tax.

To reinforce the evident desire of Congress to hit all the protean arrangements which the wit of man can devise that are not business transactions within the meaning of ordinary speech, the Treasury Regulations make clear that no genuine business transaction comes within the purport of the gift tax by excluding "a sale, exchange, or other transfer of property made in the ordinary course of business (a transaction which is bona fide, at arm's length, and free from any donative intent)." Treas. Reg. [§ 25.2512–8]. Thus on finding that a transfer in the circumstances of a particular case is not made in the ordinary course of business, the transfer becomes subject to the gift tax to the extent that it is not made "for an adequate and full consideration in money or money's worth." See 2 Paul, Federal Estate and Gift Taxation (1942) p. 1113.

The Tax Court in effect found the transfer of the stock to Mrs. More was not made at arm's length in the ordinary course of business. It noted that the inducement was marriage, took account of the discrepancy between what she got and what she gave up, and also of the benefit that her marriage settlement brought to her son. These were considerations the Tax Court could justifiably heed, and heeding, decide as it did. Its conclusion on the issue before it was no less to be respected than were the issues which we deemed it was entitled to decide as it did in Dobson v. Commissioner, 320 U.S. 489, Commissioner v. Heininger, 320 U.S. 467, Commissioner v. Scottish American Co., 323 U.S. 119.

If we are to isolate as an independently reviewable question of law the view of the Tax Court that money consideration must benefit the donor to relieve a transfer by him from being a gift, we think the Tax Court was correct. See Commissioner v. Bristol, 121 F.2d 129. To be sure, the Revenue Act of 1932 does not spell out a requirement of benefit to the transferor to afford relief from the gift tax. Its forerunner, [the 1924 Act], was more explicit in that it provided that the excess of the transfer over "the consideration received shall ... be deemed a gift." It will hardly be suggested, however, that in re-imposing the gift tax in 1932 Congress meant to exclude transfers that would have been taxed under the 1924 Act. The section [§ 2512(b)] taxing as gifts transfers that are not made for "adequate and full [money] consideration" aims to reach those transfers which are withdrawn from the donor's estate. To allow detriment to the donee to satisfy the requirement of "adequate and full consideration" would violate the purpose of the statute and open wide the door for evasion of the gift tax. See 2 Paul, supra, at 1114.

Reversed.

MR. JUSTICE ROBERTS dissents, and would affirm the judgment for the reasons given in the opinion of the Circuit Court of Appeals.

MERRILL v. FAHS

324 U.S. 308 (1945).

MR. JUSTICE FRANKFURTER delivered the opinion of the Court.

This is a companion case to Commissioner v. Wemyss. . . .

On March 7, 1939, taxpayer, the petitioner, made an antenuptial agreement with Kinta Desmare. Taxpayer, a resident of Florida, had been twice married and had three children and two grandchildren. He was a man of large resources, with cash and securities worth more than $5,000,000, and Florida real estate valued at $135,000. Miss Desmare's assets were negligible. By the arrangement entered into the day before their marriage, taxpayer agreed to set up within ninety days after marriage an irrevocable trust for $300,000, the provisions of which were to conform to Miss Desmare's wishes. The taxpayer was also to provide in his will for two additional trusts, one, likewise in the amount of $300,000, to contain the same limitations as the inter vivos trust, and the other, also in the amount of $300,000, for the benefit of their surviving children. In return Miss Desmare released all rights that she might acquire as wife or widow in taxpayer's property, both real and personal, excepting the right to maintenance and support. The inducements for this agreement were stated to be the contemplated marriage, desire to make fair requital for the release of marital rights, freedom for the taxpayer to make appropriate provisions for his children and other dependents, the uncertainty surrounding his financial future and marital tranquillity. That such an antenuptial agreement is enforceable in Florida is not disputed, . . . nor that Florida gives a wife an inchoate interest in all the husband's property, contingent during his life but absolute upon death. . . . The parties married, and the agreement was fully carried out.

On their gift tax return for 1939, both reported the creation of the trust but claimed that no tax was due. The Commissioner, however, determined a deficiency of $99,000 in taxpayer's return in relation to the transfer of the $300,000. Upon the Commissioner's rejection of the taxpayer's claim for refund of the assessment paid by him, the present suit against the Collector was filed. The District Court sustained the taxpayer, 51 F. Supp. 120, but was reversed by the Circuit Court of Appeals for the Fifth Circuit, one judge dissenting. 142 F.2d 651. We granted certiorari in connection with Commissioner v. Wemyss . . . and heard the two cases together. . . .

This case, unlike the *Wemyss* case, does not come here by way of the Tax Court. No aid can therefore be drawn from a prior determination by the tribunal specially entrusted with tax adjudications. (See Griswold, The Need for a Court of Tax Appeals (1944) 57 Harv. L. Rev. 1153, 1173.) But like the *Wemyss* case, this case turns on the proper application of [§ 2512(b)].... Taxpayer claims that Miss Desmare's relinquishment of her marital rights constituted "adequate and full consideration in money or money's worth." The Collector, relying on the construction of a like phrase in the estate tax, contends that release of marital rights does not furnish such "adequate and full consideration."

We put to one side the argument that in any event Miss Desmare's contingent interest in her husband's property had too many variables to be reducible to dollars and cents, and that any attempt to translate it into "money's worth" was "mere speculation bearing the delusive appearance of accuracy." Humes v. United States, 276 U.S. 487, 494. We shall go at once to the main issue.

The guiding light is what was said in Estate of Sanford v. Commissioner, 308 U.S. 39, 44: "The gift tax was supplementary to the estate tax. The two are in pari materia and must be construed together." The phrase on the meaning of which decision must largely turn—that is, transfers for other than "an adequate and full consideration in money or money's worth"—came into the gift tax by way of estate tax provisions. It first appeared in the Revenue Act of 1926. Section 303(a)(1) of that Act ... allowed deductions from the value of the gross estate of claims against the estate to the extent that they were bona fide and incurred "for an adequate and full consideration in money or money's worth." [§ 2053(c)(1)(A).] It is important to note that the language of previous Acts which made the test "fair consideration" was thus changed after courts had given "fair consideration" an expansive construction.

The first modern estate tax law had included in the gross estate transfers in contemplation of, or intended to take effect in possession or enjoyment at, death, except "a bona fide sale for a fair consideration in money or money's worth." ... Dower rights and other marital property rights were intended to be included in the gross estate, since they were considered merely an expectation, and in 1918 Congress specifically included them.... This provision was for the purpose of clarifying the existing law.... In 1924 Congress limited deductible claims against an estate to those supported by "a fair consideration in money or money's worth," ... employing the same standard applied to transfers in contemplation of death.... Similar language was used in the gift tax, first imposed by the 1924 Act, providing, "Where property is sold or exchanged for less than a fair consideration in money or money's worth" the excess shall be deemed a gift....

The two types of tax thus followed a similar course, like problems and purposes being expressed in like language. In this situation, courts held that "fair consideration" included relinquishment of dower rights....

Congress was thus led, as we have indicated, to substitute in the 1926 Revenue Act, the words "adequate and full consideration" in order to narrow the scope of tax exemptions. See Taft v. Commissioner, 304 U.S. 351, 356. When the gift tax was re-enacted in the 1932 Revenue Act, the restrictive phrase "adequate and full consideration" as found in the estate tax was taken over by the draftsman.

To be sure, in the 1932 Act Congress specifically provided that relinquishment of marital rights for purposes of the estate tax shall not constitute "consideration in money or money's worth." [§ 2043(b)(1).] The Committees of Congress reported that if the value of relinquished marital interests "may, in whole or in part, constitute a consideration for an otherwise taxable transfer (as has been held to be so), or an otherwise unallowable deduction from the gross estate, the effect produced amounts to a subversion of the legislative intent. . . ." H. Rep. No. 708, 72d Cong., 1st Sess., p. 47; S. Rep. No. 665, 72d Cong., 1st Sess., p. 50. Plainly, the explicitness was one of cautious redundancy to prevent "subversion of the legislative intent." Without this specific provision, Congress undoubtedly intended the requirement of "adequate and full consideration" to exclude relinquishment of dower and other marital rights with respect to the estate tax. Commissioner v. Bristol, 121 F.2d 129; Sheets v. Commissioner, 95 F.2d 727.

We believe that there is every reason for giving the same words in the gift tax the same reading. Correlation of the gift tax and the estate tax still requires legislative intervention. Commissioner v. Prouty, 115 F.2d 331, 337; Warren, Correlation of Gift and Estate Taxes (1941) 55 Harv. L. Rev. 1; Griswold, A Plan for the Coordination of the Income, Estate and Gift Tax Provisions (1942) 56 Harv. L. Rev. 337. But to interpret the same phrases in the two taxes concerning the same subject matter in different ways where obvious reasons do not compel divergent treatment is to introduce another and needless complexity into this already irksome situation. Here strong reasons urge identical construction. To hold otherwise would encourage tax avoidance. Commissioner v. Bristol, supra at 136; 2 Paul, Estate and Gift Taxation (1942) p. 1118. And it would not fulfill the purpose of the gift tax in discouraging family settlements so as to avoid high income surtaxes. . . . There is thus every reason in this case to construe the provisions of both taxes harmoniously. Estate of Sanford v. Commissioner, supra.[19]

Affirmed.

MR. JUSTICE ROBERTS dissents.

MR. JUSTICE REED, dissenting.

This case differs from Commissioner v. Wemyss. . . . Whether the transferor of the sums paid for the release of dower and other marital rights, received adequate and full consideration in money and money's

19. Treasury Regulations [§ 25.2512–8] is inapplicable. To find that the transaction was "made in the ordinary course of business" is to attribute to the Treasury a strange use of English.

worth is a question of fact. The agreement recites that the parties contemplate marriage and provides that the trust shall be set up only in the event of and following the marriage. Petitioner was obligated to create the trust upon consideration of the relinquishment of marital rights and did so, and hence this is not a case involving marriage alone as consideration. Through the tables of mortality, the value of a survivor's right in a fixed sum receivable at the death of a second party may be adequately calculated. By adopting present value as the accepted future value, the uncertainty inherent in fluctuations of an estate's value is theoretically eliminated. The trial court thus found the present value of the release of the taxpayer's estate from the wife's survivorship rights largely exceeded the amount paid by the taxpayer and that the transactions between the parties were made in good faith for business reasons and not an attempt to evade or avoid taxes. Thus the District Court findings bring this transaction within the express language of the applicable Treasury Regulation [§ 25.2512–8, relating to transfers in the ordinary course of business].... Its determination, we think, also makes it clear that the husband's estate received practical advantages of value in excess of the cost paid. See Henderson v. Usher, 125 Fla. 709, 727, 170 So. 846.

The question of the taxability as gifts of transfers to spouses in consideration of the release of marital rights had been a matter of dispute in courts before the passage of the Revenue Act of 1932.... It seems to us clear that with the judicial history of the difficulties in estate and gift taxes as to the transfer of marital rights, when Congress expressly provided [in 1932] that relinquishment of dower, curtesy or other statutory estate was not "consideration" for estate tax purposes and left the gift tax provision without such a limitation, it intended that these rights be accorded a different treatment under these sections....

In our view this judgment should be reversed.

THE CHIEF JUSTICE and MR. JUSTICE DOUGLAS join in this dissent.

NOTES

1. *Common law consideration.* The opinion in *Wemyss* refuses to engraft detriment to the transferee onto § 2512(b) as an acceptable form of consideration, explaining that a contrary view would "open wide the door for evasion of the gift tax." Performance of a promise by the donee to complete college, marry Mabel, or refrain from smoking, drinking and swearing constitutes good consideration at common law, but it fails to satisfy the statutory test because neither the donee's promise nor the anticipated performance offsets the depletion of the donor's estate. Assume that a parent promises to pay $10,000 to a child if the child graduates from college. When the child eventually graduates, the parent is treated as making a gift of $10,000; the child's performance does not constitute "consideration in money or money's worth" under § 2512(b). See Rev. Rul. 79–384, 1979–2 C.B. 344. Suppose instead that the parent dies after the child's graduation, without having made the promised payment. The child files a claim with the parent's executor and

in due course receives $10,000 from the estate. Are the funds that are used to pay the child's claim subject to estate tax? See Rev. Rul. 84–25, 1984–1 C.B. 191 (funds included in parent's gross estate, with no offsetting deduction for child's claim; gift excluded from adjusted taxable gifts under § 2001(b)).

2. *Mutual promises as consideration.* If two family members enter into an enforceable agreement to transfer property of equal value to each other's children, each is treated as making a gift to his or her own children, despite the appearance of an exchange for adequate consideration in money's worth. Thus, in Rev. Rul. 79–238, 1979–2 C.B. 339, an irrevocable trust named the settlor's twin children as equal remainder beneficiaries; if one predeceased the life income beneficiary, the surviving twin would take the entire remainder. The twins agreed that if one of them predeceased the life income beneficiary, the survivor would transfer half of the remainder to the other's children. The Service treated each twin as making a gift to his or her own children. This result can be justified either on the ground that the consideration benefits the children rather than the contracting parties themselves, see *Wemyss* (324 U.S. at 307–08), or by realigning the transferors under the "reciprocal trust" doctrine of *Grace's Estate* (infra page 262). Should the result in Rev. Rul. 79–238 be different if the agreement provides for half of the remainder to be paid to the predeceased twin's estate?

3. *Net gifts.* A donor who makes a taxable gift is primarily liable for payment of the resulting gift tax. § 2502(c). If, as a condition for making the gift, the donor requires that the donee agree to pay the gift tax, the amount of the gift tax is subtracted from the value of the transferred property in determining the amount of the gift. For purposes of § 2512(b), the donee's payment of the tax, whether made directly to the government or as reimbursement to the donor, is treated as consideration received by the donor. See Rev. Rul. 75–72, 1975–1 C.B. 310 (illustrating interrelated gift tax computation). What if the donee agrees merely to pay any additional gift tax resulting from an increase in the value of the transferred property as finally determined for gift tax purposes? See Armstrong's Estate v. United States, 277 F.3d 490 (4th Cir. 2002) (denying net gift treatment due to the "speculative and illusory" nature of donee's obligation).

For income tax purposes as well, the transaction is treated as if the donor sold the property to the donee for the amount of the gift tax paid, thereby making a part-gift, part-sale of the transferred property. Accordingly, if the gift tax exceeds the adjusted basis of the transferred property, the donor recognizes gain on the transfer. See Diedrich v. Commissioner, 457 U.S. 191 (1982).

4. *Arm's-length transactions.* Under Reg. § 25.2512–8, a transfer occurring "in the ordinary course of business (a transaction which is bona fide, at arm's length, and free from any donative intent)" is not subject to gift tax because the transferor is treated as receiving full money's-worth consideration. Is this consistent with the Supreme Court's observation in *Wemyss* that the gift tax has "dispensed with the test of 'donative intent' " in favor of "a much more workable external test [of § 2512(b)]"?

The Tax Court on several occasions has held that a payment in settlement of a family dispute over property was made for "adequate and full consideration in money or money's worth." In Beveridge v. Commissioner, 10 T.C. 915 (1948), for example, the court concluded that a payment by the taxpayer to settle a controversy with her estranged daughter was not a gift:

> The testimony of petitioner's advisors and attorneys convinces us that in making the transfer petitioner was not actuated by love and affection or other motives which normally prompt the making of a gift, and, further, that the settlement to which she agreed on her attorneys' advice was that which they and she regarded as advantageous economically under the circumstances. Perhaps she could have successfully resisted the daughter's threatened suit, but her attorneys were not certain of the outcome of the litigation and so advised her; the value of the property defended was substantial, and by accepting that settlement, she avoided additional legal expenses. She acted, in our opinion, as one would act in the settlement of differences with a stranger. [10 T.C. at 918.]

Compare Friedman's Estate v. Commissioner, 40 T.C. 714 (1963) (settlement of will contest held not subject to gift tax), with Housman v. Commissioner, 105 F.2d 973 (2d Cir. 1939), cert. denied, 309 U.S. 656 (1940) (contestant's claim was groundless; settlement held subject to gift tax).

5. *Income tax aspects of antenuptial agreements.* On the issue of whether an antenuptial property settlement is a gift or a sale for income tax purposes, § 1041 states that no gain or loss is recognized on a transfer of property to a spouse or former spouse (if incident to a divorce). Instead, the transfer is treated as a gift with the transferee taking the transferor's adjusted basis. See infra page 131, Note 3.

2. PAYMENTS TO DISCHARGE SUPPORT OBLIGATIONS

REVENUE RULING 68–379

1968–2 C.B. 414.

... A husband and wife entered into an agreement incident to a legal separation. Pursuant to the agreement, the husband transferred property to the wife in full settlement of her property and support rights. The question arises as to the application of the gift tax to such transfer.

Section 2512(b) ... provides that where property is transferred for less than an adequate and full consideration in money or money's worth, the amount by which the value of the property exceeds the value of the consideration shall be deemed a gift.

Section 25.2512–8 of the Gift Tax Regulations provides that a consideration not reducible to a value in money or money's worth is to be wholly disregarded and the entire value of the property transferred constitutes the amount of the gift. A relinquishment or promised relinquishment of dower or curtesy, or of a statutory estate created in lieu of dower or curtesy, or of other marital rights in the spouse's property or estate, shall not be considered to any extent a consideration in money or money's worth.

Generally, a husband has a duty to support his wife during their joint lives or until she remarries. The satisfaction of this legal obligation does not have the effect of diminishing the husband's estate any more than the satisfaction of any other legal obligation. A transfer to a wife in settlement of inheritance rights is, on the other hand, a present transfer of what would otherwise be a major portion of the husband's estate on death. Section 25.2512–8 of the regulations specifically states that the release of dower or curtesy or a statutory substitute for dower or curtesy (inheritance rights) is not a consideration in money or money's worth which would prevent taxation of the transfer. The regulations make no reference to support rights. Consequently, since support rights are distinguishable from inheritance rights, a surrender of support rights is not a surrender of "other marital rights," as that phrase is used in the regulations. A release of support rights by a wife constitutes a consideration in money or money's worth.

Accordingly, it is held that the transfer of property pursuant to the property settlement agreement of the parties incident to a legal separation results in a taxable gift to the extent that the value of the transferred property may exceed the value of any support rights surrendered....

NOTE

Payments in discharge of support obligations. Revenue Ruling 68–379 superseded E.T. 19, 1946–2 C.B. 166, which conveyed the same message but also contained other statements that became obsolete with changes in the statute and case law. E.T. 19 made this comment on the allocation of payments between support rights and other marital rights:

> The establishment of a reasonable allocation is regarded as a proper matter for administrative determination by the [Internal Revenue Service] in the absence of a reasonable allocation or segregation by the parties. In making this determination the facts and circumstances of each case will be separately considered. Elements to be considered are the amount of the husband's annual income, the extent of his assets, also, the life expectancies of the parties and the probability of the wife's remarriage, alimony almost universally being limited to such periods. An agreement of the parties may provide for payments extending beyond the period of their joint lives. The required allocation in such a case will involve a determination of the question whether the aggregate amounts paid and payable exceed normal support rights, which ordinarily would terminate upon the death of the husband. The contingency of the wife's remarriage may be measured by actuarial standards. [1946–2 C.B. at 169.]

On the basis of the reasoning in Rev. Rul. 68–379, a deduction for the commuted value of support rights that had been relinquished under a valid separation agreement was allowed as a claim against the estate in computing the estate tax. Rev. Rul. 71–67, 1971–1 C.B. 271. These rulings presuppose an *enforceable* release of the donee's support rights. Cf. Ellis v. Commissioner, 51 T.C. 182 (1968), affd., 437 F.2d 442 (9th Cir. 1971) (husband's creation of trust for wife in consideration of her purported release of support rights under antenuptial agreement was not made for money's-worth consideration because release was unenforceable under state law).

3. EXPENDITURES FOR FAMILY CONSUMPTION: § 2503(e)

Rev. Rul. 68–379 is concerned only with transfers under an agreement incident to legal separation. Presumably the proposition that one does not incur a gift tax liability by supporting a spouse and children in an amicable family setting was thought so obvious as not to require an explicit statement. In the case of a united family, are amounts paid for support subject to gift tax if the family is maintained at a level above the parents' legal obligation and, a fortiori, if they live beyond their means? Is the cost of food, clothing, and shelter exempt no matter how luxurious? What about jewelry, fur coats, vacation trips, education, and the use of summer homes and yachts?

The $10,000 annual per-donee exclusion (indexed for inflation since 1998) was enacted to make it unnecessary to report small gifts, as well as wedding and Christmas gifts. S. Rep. No. 665, 72d Cong., 1st Sess., reprinted in 1939–1 C.B. (Part 2) 496, 525–26. Does this imply that wedding, birthday, and Christmas gifts to the donor's spouse and minor children are taxable gifts (to the extent they exceed the exclusion), or can a station-in-life concept of support be invoked to avoid a gift tax if the gift (e.g., a Lamborghini, chinchilla wrap, or diamond brooch) is no more than is expected in the donor's environment?

Does Rev. Rul. 68–379 eliminate gift tax liability if the transfer discharges a support obligation under state law, no matter how far it may enlarge the concept of "support"? In a number of states, either by statute or by the common law, a parent is legally required to support an incompetent or disabled adult child. What if the parent's duty were expanded to include a college and professional education for any adult child? An obligation to support the child (and the child's spouse and offspring, if any) until the child gets established in an occupation and becomes self-supporting?

The American Law Institute's Estate and Gift Taxation Project (1969) proposed an explicit gift tax exemption for "transfers for consumption." Under the proposal, the gift tax would not apply to expenditures for:

> 1. The benefit of any person residing in the transferor's household, or the benefit of a child of the transferor under 21 years of age, whether or not he resides in the transferor's household, which does not result in [such person or child] acquiring property that will retain any significant value after the passage of one year from the date of [such expenditure]; or
>
> 2. Current educational, medical or dental costs of any person; or

3. Current costs of food, clothing and maintenance of living accommodations of any person or persons in fact dependent on the transferor, in whole or in part, for support, provided such expenditures are reasonable in amount.

Section 2503(e), enacted in 1981, adopts the A.L.I.'s concept but changes the coverage in two important respects. The exclusion is limited to transfers made for tuition or medical expenses, while the class of permissible beneficiaries is opened up to include anyone, whether or not a member of the family. The statute exempts any "qualified transfer" from the gift tax and goes on to define such a transfer as any amount paid on behalf of an individual—

(A) as tuition to an educational organization ... for the education or training of such individual, or

(B) to any person who provides medical care ... with respect to such individual as payment for such medical care. [§ 2503(e)(2).]

NOTES

1. *Qualified transfers.* Tuition payments on behalf of an individual qualify for the § 2503(e) exclusion only if the payments are made directly to a "qualifying educational organization" that fits the description set out in § 170(b)(1)(A)(ii) and normally maintains a regular faculty, curriculum, and enrolled student body. The exclusion does not cover payments for books, dormitory fees, board, or other expenses that do not constitute direct tuition costs. Reg. § 25.2503–6(b)(2).

The exclusion covers medical expenses as defined in § 213(d), including expenses incurred for the diagnosis, treatment, and prevention of disease (to the extent not reimbursed by the donee's medical insurance), as well as medical insurance premiums. Reg. § 25.2503–6(b)(3).

Transfers for tuition or medical care qualify for the § 2503(e) exclusion only if payment is made directly to an educational organization or medical care provider. Thus, if a donor reimburses a donee for tuition or medical expenses previously paid by the donee, the exclusion is not available. Similarly, a donor who makes a completed gift of property in trust is not entitled to the § 2503(e) exclusion, even if the trust is established for the exclusive purpose of paying tuition and medical expenses of the beneficiaries. Reg. § 25.2503–6(c) (Examples 2 and 4). Suppose instead that the donor pays a lump sum directly to a college to cover a freshman student's tuition costs for the current year and three succeeding years. Does the entire payment qualify for the § 2503(e) exclusion?

2. *GST and estate tax treatment of tuition and medical expenses.* There is no estate tax counterpart to § 2503(e), and so a bequest for the purpose of defraying an individual's tuition or medical expenses is subject to the estate tax. Section 2611(b)(1), however, does exempt payment of such expenses from the generation-skipping transfer tax. See infra page 564, footnote 20.

3. *Qualified tuition programs.* Several states maintain "qualified tuition programs" pursuant to § 529. Such programs allow a contributor to purchase

tuition credits or certificates on behalf of a designated beneficiary or to make cash contributions to an account for the purpose of paying the beneficiary's qualified higher education expenses. Contributions do not constitute qualified transfers for purposes of § 2503(e), but instead are treated as completed gifts of present interests eligible for the annual exclusion under § 2503(b). A donor who makes contributions in excess of the allowable annual exclusion amount may elect to take the contributions into account ratably over a five-year period for purposes of § 2503(b). A transfer occurring due to a change of beneficiary (or a rollover of credits or account balances) is generally disregarded for gift tax purposes, unless the new beneficiary is not a member of the old beneficiary's family or is assigned to a generation below that of the old beneficiary. Moreover, for estate tax purposes, any unexpended funds remaining in an account at the contributor's death are generally excluded from the contributor's gross estate, notwithstanding the contributor's power to designate new beneficiaries. See § 529(c); Prop. Reg. § 1.529–5.

4. PROPERTY SETTLEMENTS IN CONTEMPLATION OF DIVORCE OR SEPARATION: §§ 2516 AND 2053(c)(1)(A)

HARRIS v. COMMISSIONER

340 U.S. 106 (1950).

MR. JUSTICE DOUGLAS delivered the opinion of the Court.

The federal estate tax and the federal gift tax, as held in a line of cases ending with Commissioner v. Wemyss, 324 U.S. 303, and Merrill v. Fahs, 324 U.S. 308, are construed in pari materia, since the purpose of the gift tax is to complement the estate tax by preventing tax-free depletion of the transferor's estate during his lifetime. Both the gift tax [§ 2512(b)] and the estate tax [§ 2053(c)(1)(A)] exclude transfers made for "an adequate and full consideration in money or money's worth." In the estate tax this requirement is limited to deductions for claims based upon "a promise or agreement"; but the consideration for the "promise or agreement" may not be the release of marital rights in the decedent's property [§ 2043(b)]. In the *Wemyss* and *Merrill* cases the question was whether the gift tax was applicable to premarital property settlements. If the standards of the estate tax were to be applied ex proprio vigore in gift tax cases, those transfers would be taxable because there was a "promise or agreement" touching marital rights in property. We sustained the tax, thus giving "adequate and full consideration in money or money's worth" the same meaning under both statutes insofar as premarital property settlements or agreements are concerned.

The present case raises the question whether *Wemyss* and *Merrill* require the imposition of the gift tax in the type of post-nuptial settlement of property rights involved here.

Petitioner divorced her husband, Reginald Wright, in Nevada in 1943. Both she and her husband had substantial property interests. They reached an understanding as respects the unscrambling of those interests, the settlement of all litigated claims to the separate properties, the assumption of obligations, and the transfer of properties.

Wright received from petitioner the creation of a trust for his lifetime of the income from her remainder interest in a then-existing trust; an assumption by her of an indebtedness of his of $47,650; and her promise to pay him $416.66 a month for ten years.

Petitioner received from Wright 21/90 of certain real property in controversy; a discontinuance of a partition suit then pending; an indemnification from and assumption by him of all liability on a bond and mortgage on certain real property in London, England; and an indemnification against liability in connection with certain real property in the agreement. It was found that the value of the property transferred to Wright exceeded that received by petitioner by $107,150. The Commissioner assessed a gift tax on the theory that any rights which Wright might have given up by entering into the agreement could not be adequate and full consideration.

If the parties had without more gone ahead and voluntarily unravelled their business interests on the basis of this compromise, there would be no question that the gift tax would be payable. For there would have been a "promise or agreement" that effected a relinquishment of marital rights in property. It therefore would fall under the ban of the provision of the estate tax which by judicial construction has been incorporated into the gift tax statute.

But the parties did not simply undertake a voluntary contractual division of their property interests. They were faced with the fact that Nevada law not only authorized but instructed the divorce court to decree a just and equitable disposition of both the community and the separate property of the parties. The agreement recited that it was executed in order to effect a settlement of the respective property rights of the parties "in the event a divorce should be decreed"; and it provided that the agreement should be submitted to the divorce court "for its approval." It went on to say, "It is of the essence of this agreement that the settlement herein provided for shall not become operative in any manner nor shall any of the Recitals or covenants herein become binding upon either party unless a decree of absolute divorce between the parties shall be entered in the pending Nevada action."

If the agreement had stopped there and were in fact submitted to the court, it is clear that the gift tax would not be applicable. That arrangement would not be a "promise or agreement" in the statutory sense. It would be wholly conditional upon the entry of the decree; the divorce court might or might not accept the provisions of the arrangement as the measure of the respective obligations; it might indeed add to or subtract from them. The decree, not the arrangement submitted to the court, would fix the rights and obligations of the parties. That was the theory of Commissioner v. Maresi, 156 F.2d 929, and we think it sound.

Even the Commissioner concedes that that result would be correct in case the property settlement was litigated in the divorce action. That was what happened in Commissioner v. Converse, 163 F.2d 131, where the divorce court decreed a lump-sum award in lieu of monthly payments provided by the separation agreement. Yet without the decree there would be no enforceable, existing agreement whether the settlement was litigated or unlitigated. Both require the approval of the court before an obligation arises. The happenstance that the divorce court might approve the entire settlement, or modify it in unsubstantial details, or work out material changes seems to us unimportant. In each case it is the decree that creates the rights and the duties; and a decree is not a "promise or agreement" in any sense—popular or statutory.

But the present case is distinguished by reason of a further provision in the undertaking and in the decree. The former provided that "the covenants in this agreement shall survive any decree of divorce which may be entered." And the decree stated "It is ordered that said agreement and said trust agreements forming a part thereof shall survive this decree." The Court of Appeals turned the case on those provisions. It concluded that since there were two sanctions for the payments and transfers—contempt under the divorce decree and execution under the contract—they were founded not only on the decree but upon both the decree and a "promise or agreement." It therefore held the excess of the value of the property which petitioner gave her husband over what he gave her to be taxable as a gift. 178 F.2d 861.

We, however, think that the gift tax statute is concerned with the source of rights, not with the manner in which rights at some distant time may be enforced. Remedies for enforcement will vary from state to state. It is "the transfer" of the property with which the gift tax statute is concerned, not the sanctions which the law supplies to enforce transfers. If "the transfer" of marital rights in property is effected by the parties, it is pursuant to a "promise or agreement" in the meaning of the statute. If "the transfer" is effected by court decree, no "promise or agreement" of the parties is the operative fact. In no realistic sense is a court decree a "promise or agreement" between the parties to a litigation. If finer, more legalistic lines are to be drawn, Congress must do it.

If, as we hold, the case is free from any "promise or agreement" concerning marital rights in property, it presents no remaining problems of difficulty. The Treasury Regulations [§ 25.2512–8] recognize as tax free "a sale, exchange, or other transfer of property made in the ordinary course of business (a transaction which is bona fide, at arm's length, and free from any donative intent)." This transaction is not "in the ordinary course of business" in any conventional sense. Few transactions between husband and wife ever would be; and those under the aegis of a divorce court are not. But if two partners on dissolution of the firm entered into a transaction of this character or if chancery did it for them, there would seem to be no doubt that the unscrambling of the business interests would satisfy the spirit of the Regulations. No reason is apparent why husband

and wife should be under a heavier handicap absent a statute which brings all marital property settlements under the gift tax. . . .

Reversed.

MR. JUSTICE FRANKFURTER, whom MR. JUSTICE BLACK, MR. JUSTICE BURTON, and MR. JUSTICE MINTON join, dissenting.

. . . Unless we are now to say that a settlement of property in winding up, as it were, a marriage, smacks more of a business arrangement than an antenuptial agreement and therefore satisfies the requirement of "an adequate and full consideration in money or money's worth" which we found wanting in Merrill v. Fahs, and unless we are further to overrule Merrill v. Fahs insofar as it joined the gift tax and the estate tax of the Revenue Act of 1932, so as to infuse into the gift tax the explicitness of the estate tax in precluding the surrender of marital rights from being deemed to any extent a consideration "in money or money's worth," we must hold that a settlement of property surrendering marital rights in anticipation of divorce is not made for "an adequate and full consideration in money or money's worth."

The same year that it enacted the gift tax Congress amended the estate tax by adding to the provision that "adequate and full consideration" was prerequisite to deduction of "claims against the estate" the phrase, "when founded upon a promise or agreement." [§ 2053(c)(1)(A).] . . .

. . . The statute does not say "founded solely upon a promise or agreement." The statute does not say that the tax should not fall on "property transferred under the terms of a judgment or decree of the court." Nor is the phrase "founded upon agreement" a technical term having a well-known meaning either in law or in literature. The question is whether the transfer made by the taxpayer to her husband was, within the fair meaning of the language, "founded" upon her agreement with her husband. Did the Nevada judge in decreeing the divorce describe what actually took place here when he said that on the "date of February 27, 1943, the plaintiff and defendant entered into an agreement and trust agreements forming a part thereof, under the terms of which the parties settled all obligations arising out of their marriage"?

The fact that the undertakings defined by this agreement would come into force only on the occurrence of a condition, to wit, the entering of a decree of divorce, is apparently regarded as decisive of taxability. But does this make any real difference? The terms of that decree might be different from the terms of the agreement; but "nevertheless the covenants in this agreement shall survive any decree of divorce which may be entered." If the divorce court had disapproved the agreement and had not decreed the transfer of any property of the wife to her husband, it is difficult to see how transfers which she made, solely because of the compulsion of the agreement, would be effected by court decree and for that reason not subject to tax. The condition on which an agreement comes into force does not supplant the agreement any more than a deed in escrow ceases to be a deed when it comes out of escrow. In the *Wemyss* and *Merrill* cases, would the gifts have been any the less founded upon an agreement if, as a condition to the antenuptial arrangements in those cases, the consent of the parents of the fiancée had been made a condition of the marriage? Nor can excluding the transfers here involved from the gift tax be made tenable by resting decision on the narrower ground that to the extent the divorce decree "approved" the agreement or embodied its provisions so as to make them enforceable by contempt the transfers were not "founded upon" the agreement within the meaning of the statute.[20] If the taxpayer had been sued by her husband for the sums she was obligated to transfer to him could he not have brought the suit on the contract? Even though a promise for which inadequate consideration was given has been reduced to a judgment, a claim based upon it has been held not deductible from the gross estate and thus must have been deemed to be "founded upon a promise." Markwell's Estate v. Commissioner, 112 F.2d 253. If a transfer does not cease to be "founded upon a promise" when the promise is merged into a judgment, is not a transfer pursuant to an agreement which survives a ratifying decree a fortiori "founded upon" that agreement?

Judge Learned Hand's treatment of this matter is so hard-headed and convincing that it would be idle to paraphrase his views.

> In some jurisdictions contracts, made in anticipation of a divorce, are held to persist ex proprio vigore after the divorce decree has incorporated their terms, and has added its sanctions to those available in contract. That, for example, is the law of New York, where the contract remains obligatory even after the court has modified the allowances which it originally adopted; and where the promises will be thereafter enforced by execution and the like. Perhaps, that is also the law of Nevada, which the parties provided should govern "all matters affecting the interpretation of this agreement or the rights of the parties." Be that as it may, in the case at bar, the Nevada decree having declared that the agreement was "entitled to be approved," that included the provision that its "covenants" should "survive" as well as any of its other stipulations. Thus the payments made under it were "founded" as much upon the "promise or agreement" as upon the decree; indeed, they were "founded" upon both; the parties chose to submit themselves to two sanctions—contempt under the divorce court and execution under the contract. The payments were therefore subject to the gift tax. [178 F.2d at 865.]

I would affirm the judgment.

20. The ground adopted for reversal of the court below is important to the disposition of the case. On the broader ground apparently employed, no gift tax is due. But if the narrower basis be used, it is probable that some liability should be imposed. One of the transfers required by the agreement—the wife's assumption of a $47,650 indebtedness of her husband—was not incorporated into the divorce decree and therefore is presumably enforceable only under the contract. If enforceability under the decree is the criterion, a gift tax is due to the extent this indebtedness is reflected in the amount determined by the Commissioner to represent the value attributable to release of marital rights.

NOTE

Rationale of Harris and the enactment of § 2516. Does the *Harris* exemption rest on the incorporation of the property settlement into the divorce decree, the stipulation that the settlement was contingent on a decree of absolute divorce, or the involuntary character of the transaction? The usual reading of the decision emphasizes the incorporation feature as essential to the argument that the settlement was not founded on the parties' promise or agreement. See McMurtry v. Commissioner, 203 F.2d 659 (1st Cir. 1953); Commissioner v. Watson's Estate, 216 F.2d 941 (2d Cir. 1954). Immunity from tax, however, is not automatically achieved by incorporating the settlement into the decree, because even under *Harris* the decree would not be efficacious if the divorce court lacked discretion to modify the parties' agreement. See Barrett's Estate v. Commissioner, 56 T.C. 1312 (1971). Property settlements incident to a divorce are typically the product of lengthy negotiations between the parties, both of whom are represented by counsel. Is it realistic to assume that the divorce court judge, when vested with power to modify the settlement, will exercise that power in a manner unacceptable to the parties? Or that the judge will make an *independent* finding that the negotiated settlement is not just and equitable if the parties are each represented by counsel and express their satisfaction with the arrangement? For further discussion of the rationale and implications of the *Harris* decision, see Pedrick, The Gift Tax Jurisdiction of the Divorce Court, 46 Ill. L. Rev. 177 (1951).

Recognizing that many uncertainties concerning the gift tax status of divorce settlements remained even after *Harris*, Congress in 1954 enacted § 2516, which is discussed in the following case.

SPRUANCE v. COMMISSIONER

60 T.C. 141 (1973).

DAWSON, JUDGE.

. . . The facts, as we have found them, can be summarized as follows: Preston Lea Spruance (Lea) and his wife, Margaret, entered into a written separation agreement in July 1955 settling their marital (including support) and property rights and their minor children's support rights. The agreement was conditioned upon the wife being granted a divorce and was to become effective when the divorce was granted. Pursuant to the agreement, when read together with a supplemental agreement, Lea transferred duPont and Christiana Securities stock having a fair market value of $1,058,575.13 in trust for the benefit of Margaret and their four children. On the date of the transfer one child was an adult and the others were age 20, 17, and 10. The income interest in the stock—called "separately held stock" in the separation agreement—was transferred in part to Margaret for her support and maintenance and in part to his children for their support and maintenance while minors. Upon the death of Lea and Margaret the remainder interest in the stock will pass to the children. The Delaware divorce court adopted the separation agreement; it did not have the power to modify the agreement, so the agreement survived the court's decree....

Respondent views the 1955 transaction as a transfer of stock to the trust that was in fact part sale to the wife under a long line of authority including United States v. Davis, 370 U.S. 65 (1962), and part gift to the children. Taxation of the sale is barred by the statute of limitations. Taxation of the gift is still possible because no Federal gift tax return was filed.

After the 6–year statute of limitations had run on his 1955 personal income tax return, Lea obtained a ruling by the Delaware courts that the separation agreement and the supplemental agreement had together provided for the creation of a trust. Up to that time, the character of the 1955 transaction was unclear to strangers to the dealings....

... Respondent determined that there was a gift for gift tax purposes to the extent that the total value of the separately held stock at the time of transfer exceeded the value of the income interest in the stock transferred to Margaret and the value of the income interest in the stock transferred to the minor children. Petitioner contends that the entire transfer was for full and adequate consideration.

We hold that there was a taxable gift in the amount determined by the respondent.

Section 2512(b) provided, on the date of the transfer, as follows:

> Where property is transferred for less than an adequate and full consideration in money or money's worth, then the amount by which the value of the property exceeded the value of the consideration shall be deemed a gift, and shall be included in computing the amount of gifts made during the calendar year.

Section 2516 of the Code provides:

> Where husband and wife enter into a written agreement relative to their marital and property rights and divorce occurs within 2 years thereafter[21] (whether or not such agreement is approved by the divorce decree), any transfers of property or interests in property made pursuant to such agreement—
>
> (1) to either spouse in settlement of his or her marital or property rights, or
>
> (2) to provide a reasonable allowance for the support of issue of the marriage during minority,
>
> shall be deemed to be transfers made for a full and adequate consideration in money or money's worth.

We interpret these sections to mean, in the context of this case, that petitioner must prove that the transfer of stock in trust was either to settle his wife's marital or property rights or to provide a reasonable

21. In 1984 the statute was amended to apply where divorce occurs "within the 3–year period beginning on the date 1 year before such agreement is entered into."—EDS.

allowance for the support of the minor children. Having failed to prove this with respect to a portion of the property transferred, that portion must be taxed as a gift. Incident to the problem of proof, we observe that respondent has not determined that the value of the income interest going to the minor children was excessive, i.e., that the transfer provided for more than a reasonable support allowance. Respondent has simply calculated the value of Margaret's income interest and the children's minority income interests—all according to the tables appearing in section 20.2031–7(f), Estate Tax Regs.—and subtracted the sum of these values from the total value of the stock transferred.[22] The end result is that the value of the taxable gift is $448,158.37. Petitioner does not challenge respondent's calculations or his use of the estate tax tables.

Petitioner argues that no gift was intended and that, in fact, no gift occurred, citing United States v. Davis, supra, and Matthews v. United States, 425 F.2d 738 (Ct. Cl. 1970). But it is well settled that donative intent on the part of the transferor is not an essential element in the application of the gift tax to a given transfer. Sec. 25.2511–1(g)(1), Gift Tax Regs.; Commissioner v. Wemyss, 324 U.S. 303 (1945); Merrill v. Fahs, 324 U.S. 308 (1945); May T. Hrobon, 41 T.C. 476, 499 (1964). And as for the two cases cited by the petitioner, both deal with the gift concept under income tax as opposed to gift tax law. Thus, in *Davis*, where the Supreme

---

22. Respondent explains his approach in the following manner:

The value of the stock transferred, the value of the income interest transferred to Margaret, together with the value of the income interest transferred to the children while minors, and the value of the taxable gift is shown as follows:

Value of stock on 10/28/55	$1,058,075.13
Value of Margaret's income interest together with value of income interest of the children while minors	610,416.76
Value of taxable gift	448,158.37

The value of Margaret's income interest, together with the value of the income interest of the children while minors, was determined under section 20.2031–7(f), Table I, of the Estate Tax Regulations, using the factor used in determining the value of a life estate in property for the life of one whose present age is 45 years or a factor of .57664. The remaining value of the property transferred, the value of the taxable gift, is broken down into two parts, shown as follows:

Children's income interest that will "fall in" upon the death of Margaret	$101,834.94
Children's remainder interest as survivors of Preston and Margaret	346,323.43
Value of taxable gift	448,158.37

The factor used in determining the remainder value of the children's interest as survivors of Preston and Margaret was determined under section 20.2031–7(f), Table III, of the Estate Tax Regulations, using the factor used in determining the value of a remainder interest in property to take effect upon the death of the survivor of two persons whose ages are both 45 years or a factor of .32716. The value of the children's income interest that will "fall in" upon the death of Margaret was determined by subtracting from the factor in Table I used in determining the value of a remainder interest in property to take effect after an estate for the life of one whose present age is 45 years, .42336, the above factor of .32716 taken from Table III, to arrive at a factor of .09620.

A simpler method is available in arriving at the value of the taxable gift. One can simply apply the factor of a remainder interest per Table I of the Estate Tax Regulations to take effect upon the death of a person whose present age is 45 (0.42336) to the value of the stock transferred in trust ($1,058,575.13), as was done by the respondent in his statutory notice. Using either method, one will arrive at the value of the taxable gift made by Preston.

Court states in a footnote that "To intimate that there was a gift to the extent the value of the property exceeded that of the rights released not only invokes the erroneous premise that every exchange not precisely equal involves a gift but merely raises the measurement problem ... [discussed elsewhere in the opinion]," the Court is speaking of "gift" for income tax purposes. The next sentence in the footnote makes this clear: "Cases in which this Court has held transfers of property in exchange for the release of marital rights subject to gift taxes are based not on the premise that such transactions are inherently gifts but on the concept that in the contemplation of the gift tax statute they are to be taxed as gifts." United States v. Davis, supra at 69 fn. 6. And in *Matthews*, the plaintiff argued that there was a gift, hoping to avoid a finding that the transaction was a transfer for consideration to which the income tax rule of *Davis* would apply. However, the Court of Claims found that there was no gift under Federal income tax law. Matthews v. United States, supra at 748–754. Moreover, neither case involved a transfer of appreciated property to persons other than a spouse or minor children. Here we have, among other things, a transfer of present and future interests in part to adult children.

Petitioner next argues that the case of Harris v. Commissioner, 340 U.S. 106 (1950), blocks respondent's path. We disagree. The Supreme Court in *Harris* was presented with the question whether petitioner was liable for a gift tax where she and her husband mutually exchanged certain interests in property and certain rights that they had against each other, including the surrender of marital inheritance rights, pursuant to a separation agreement, and where it was conceded that the value of what she gave exceeded the value of what she received. The agreement was conditioned upon the subsequent divorce; it was to be (and was) submitted for approval to the divorce court; it was not operative unless the divorce followed. The agreement was also written so as to survive the divorce decree. And, it is noted, the Nevada divorce court there involved has the power to accept or discard the settlement agreement provisions, to add or subtract from them as it saw fit. The Court held that the transfer in question was not made pursuant to a "promise or agreement" but was "founded" upon the divorce decree; therefore, the transfer was not a taxable gift under gift tax rules imported from the estate tax area. Respondent makes two arguments to support his circumvention of *Harris*: First, *Harris* is distinguishable. There the divorce court had the power to vary the terms of the parties' separation agreement, a factor that has been considered as significant in subsequent cases. McMurtry v. Commissioner, 203 F.2d 659 (C.A.1, 1953); Commissioner v. Watson's Estate, 216 F.2d 941 (C.A.2, 1954) (an estate tax case). Here the divorce court had no such power. Consequently, "the rationale of the *Harris* case does not apply." Estate of Chester H. Bowers, 23 T.C. 911 (1955), acq. 1955–2 C.B. 4; Rev. Rul. 60–160, 1960–1 C.B. 374. Second, the holding in *Harris* does not immunize from the gift tax all transfers that are enforceable as court decrees. Stated another way:

> Thus, although the crux of the *Harris* case was that the transfer was made pursuant to a court decree rather than a promise or agreement, *Harris* did not incorporate a broad rule that all transfers based on a court decree need not be supported by adequate consideration, and that all involuntary transfers are free from gift tax. It would seem that the *Harris* rationale is to be limited only to those cases involving relinquishment of marital rights.... [Surrey & Warren, Federal Estate and Gift Taxation 222–23 (1966).]

We agree that respondent's second route is a correct one on the authority of In Re Estate of Hartshorne, 402 F.2d 592 (C.A.2, 1968); Rosenthal v. Commissioner, 205 F.2d 505 (C.A.2, 1953); Karl T. Wiedemann, 26 T.C. 565 (1956); Roland M. Hooker, 10 T.C. 388 (1948), affd., 174 F.2d 863 (C.A.5, 1949); Edmund C. Converse, 5 T.C. 1014 (1945), affd., 163 F.2d 131 (C.A.2, 1947). These cases are precedent for the rule that a taxpayer-transferor who transfers property (a) in return for his or her spouse's marital rights or property rights, (b) to provide a reasonable allowance for the support of their minor children, and (c) to put the property in the hands of adult children, has made a taxable gift to the extent of (c). "To construe the statute as suggested by petitioner would open a means for a divorcing parent to transfer property to his adult child free of both gift tax and estate tax." Estate of Hubert Keller, 44 T.C. 851, 860 (1965).

Finally, with regard to this issue, petitioner stresses that the portion of the transfer determined to be taxable by the respondent is not a gift because Margaret bargained her own rights in return for the transfer to the children. Estate of Robert Rodger Glen, 45 T.C. 323 (1966). We cannot assume, however, that this was the case. The lone statement of the petitioner, in response to his attorney's question, that the wife did so insist is not sufficient evidence on this vital point, especially where other sources of the desired information were not explored and where the petitioner's memory admittedly was not very good with respect to what transpired approximately 17 years ago. Karl T. Wiedemann, supra; Estate of Hubert Keller, supra; Estate of Harold Hartshorne, 48 T.C. 882 (1967)....

NOTES

1. *Scope of Harris after the enactment of § 2516.* Section 2516 applies by its terms whether the agreement is approved by the divorce decree or not. The importance of *Harris*, so far as divorce settlements are concerned, is thus much reduced. But does *Harris* control the status of marital settlements that do not meet the requirements of § 2516? Consider the following possibilities:

   1. A property settlement under an agreement that was approved by the divorce court, but the divorce did not occur within the time period specified in the statute.
   2. A property settlement under an agreement that was approved by a decree of legal separation, but the parties do not obtain a divorce.

3. Transfers approved by the divorce court to adult children or to minor children in excess of a "reasonable allowance" for support. Does the *Spruance* decision assume that the divorce court's decree, to the extent it adopted the 1955 agreement, was a nullity that could have been disregarded by the taxpayer with impunity? Or does the decision rest on the narrower premise that the court, on its own motion, could not have required the taxpayer to support the children after their majority? What if local law authorized the court to require such payments, at least to children who are mentally or physically incapable of self-support?

Section 2516, as initially enacted in 1954, had no estate tax counterpart. Consequently, although a divorced individual could make payments during life pursuant to an approved property settlement free of gift tax under § 2516, any installments that remained unpaid at death did not automatically qualify for an estate tax deduction. This disparity was finally remedied in 1984 when Congress amended § 2043(b)(2) of the estate tax to incorporate the § 2516(1) exemption. As a result, payments to a former spouse under an agreement that meets the requirements of § 2516(1) are treated as made for money's-worth consideration and are deductible under § 2053. See infra page 436, Note 1.

2. *Concessions to obtain benefits for persons whom the transferor is not obligated to support.* The taxpayer in *Spruance* asserted unsuccessfully that his wife bargained a part of her own rights away in return for a transfer of property to their adult children. The argument is equally available if a wife bargains on behalf of her children from a first marriage to whom her second husband never owed an obligation of support, or if a father agrees to make payments to the children during their majority because they agreed to accept less than they were entitled to during their minority. Rev. Rul. 79–363, 1979–2 C.B. 345, states that if one spouse "specifically and deliberately" releases support rights to induce the other spouse to make payments to a third person, § 2516 applies to the transfer, but the transaction constitutes a gift by the spouse who relinquishes his or her rights to induce the payments. The reasoning of the ruling is equally applicable to separation and divorce settlements that do not satisfy the conditions of § 2516. See Rev. Rul. 77–314, 1977–2 C.B. 349 (Situation 2); Glen's Estate v. Commissioner, 45 T.C. 323 (1966); see also Leopold v. United States, 510 F.2d 617 (9th Cir. 1975), infra page 433 (for estate tax purposes, decedent's bequest to daughter pursuant to divorce settlement was supported by money's-worth consideration because former wife accepted reduced alimony payments in return); Keller's Estate v. Commissioner, 44 T.C. 851 (1965) (payments to transferor's adult children pursuant to divorce decree not deductible for estate tax purposes; payments were "requested" by decedent's ex-wife, but no showing that she correspondingly reduced her own claims for support).

3. *Income tax aspects of property transfers pursuant to divorce settlements.* In United States v. Davis, 370 U.S. 65 (1962), the Supreme Court held that a husband recognized gain for income tax purposes on a transfer of appreciated assets to his wife in exchange for her release of marital rights under a divorce settlement. In 1984, Congress overturned the *Davis* result by enacting § 1041, which provides nonrecognition treatment for any transfer of property between spouses during marriage or, subject to several qualifica-

tions, between former spouses incident to a divorce. Thus, the transferor recognizes no gain as a result of the transfer, and the transferee, having received the property in effect by gift, takes the transferor's adjusted basis ("carryover basis") for purposes of determining gain or loss on a subsequent disposition.

5. BUSINESS TRANSACTIONS

ANDERSON'S ESTATE v. COMMISSIONER

8 T.C. 706 (1947).

ARUNDELL, JUDGE.

[Gift tax deficiencies of about $870,000 were determined by the Commissioner on transfers, in the circumstances related below, by M.D. Anderson and W.L. Clayton of 18,675 shares of common stock of Anderson–Clayton Securities Corporation to executives of the Corporation. The Corporation was the successor of an unincorporated enterprise, referred to in the opinion as "association."]

At the threshold we are met with the question of whether the sales of stock by Anderson and Clayton to the six individuals actively engaged in the Anderson–Clayton business enterprise are in any event subject to gift tax. Respondent concedes that these sales were bona fide and at arm's length; but he contends that they were not made in the ordinary course of business, that the value of the stock was greater than the value of the consideration received, and that the excess is therefore taxable as a gift under [§ 2512(b)]. He relies primarily upon Commissioner v. Wemyss, 324 U.S. 303, for the proposition that the absence of donative intent is immaterial.

It is quite true that in *Wemyss* the Supreme Court held that Congress in [§ 2512(b)] had dispensed with the subjective test of donative intent and substituted the more workable external or objective test of whether the consideration for the transfer is full and adequate in money or money's worth. It must not be overlooked, however, that at the same time the Court was careful to point out that genuine business transactions—"business transactions within the meaning of ordinary speech"—are not within the scope of the gift tax. Citing Treasury Regulations [§ 25.2512–8] it said that:

> . . . the Treasury Regulations make clear that no genuine business transaction comes within the purport of the gift tax by excluding "a sale, exchange, or other transfer of property made in the ordinary course of business (a transaction which is bona fide, at arm's length, and free from any donative intent)." . . . Thus on finding that a transfer in the circumstances of a particular case is not made in the ordinary course of business, the transfer becomes subject to the gift tax to the extent that it is not made "for an adequate and full consideration in money or money's worth."

The first issue therefore reduces itself to the question of whether the sales of common stock of corporation were "made in the ordinary course of business." Petitioners contend that the sales were so made. They argue that, while donative intent may not be material in determining whether a gift has been made, the presence or absence of donative intent is an important circumstance in determining whether a sale or other disposition of property is made in the ordinary course of business. The regulations, they say, define a transfer made in the ordinary course of business as "a transaction which is bona fide, at arm's length, and free from any donative intent."

For the purposes of deciding the first issue thus raised, we shall assume that the stock had a value in excess of the consideration.

All the sales of stock were made pursuant to what was essentially a profit-sharing plan. Profit participation by the active management was a common practice in the cotton merchandising business generally. The evidence makes clear that cotton merchandising is primarily a management business and one of the most difficult and complex merchandising operations in the world, and that the success of the business is dependent, by and large, upon efficient and well trained management having long experience in all phases of cotton merchandising.

Prior to the organization of corporation, Clayton, Fleming, and Whittington held profit sharing or commission contracts with association which yielded them large annual returns and removed considerable cash from the business. When corporation was organized, its common stock was substituted for the profit sharing contracts; and that had the two-fold effect of keeping cash in the business as invested capital and compelling the executives to acquire a proprietary interest in the business. From the beginning, the common stock of corporation was designed to be held only by persons actively engaged in the Anderson–Clayton business enterprise. Clayton and Anderson were the holders of the largest equities in the business, and the real value of their large investments in preferred stock could be maintained and preserved only by a continued efficient management. In order to build up a responsible management which could continue the business in the event of the retirement or death of Anderson or Clayton, they believed it essential that the junior executives acquire proprietary interests in the business and that such proprietary interests should grow in proportion to the shifting of responsibilities from the seniors to the juniors.

And so the plan was put into operation upon the organization of corporation. All the common stockholders understood that the relative proportions of their holdings would change from time to time as responsibilities were shifted from the older to the younger executives. At the beginning of each cotton season it was customary to reexamine the management situation and the relative contributions to management on the part of the several executives and to determine what readjustments, if any, in the relative ownership of common stock should be made. All the sales of common stock here in issue, as well as other sales not in issue, were made pursuant to the agreement between corporation and all the common stockholders, all of whom were actively engaged in the business. Under that agreement a method was provided for determining annually, in accordance with a consolidated balance sheet adjusted so as to reflect the true net worth of the consolidated business enterprise, a price at which transfers of the common stock should be made. The holders of 75 percent of the common stock could direct any party to sell all or any part of his stock to corporation or to such person as they might designate. No party could sell or otherwise dispose of his common stock without the written consent of 75 percent of the holders. If any party should elect to withdraw from the business, he had to sell his stock to corporation. If any party should die, his stock was to be purchased by corporation. No cash dividend could be paid on common stock so long as corporation was indebted in any sum whatever. Other provisions of the agreement are set out in our findings and need not be repeated here. It was contemplated not only that Clayton and Anderson would sell some of their common stock from time to time to their juniors, but also that as the latter should pass the peak of responsibility, they in turn would sell part of their holdings to their juniors who were taking on more responsibility. In other words, the common stock was designed not to be marketable, but to be held in direct proportion to the active participation of each stockholder in the business enterprise.

It is obvious from all these circumstances that the sales of common stock were motivated by the peculiar importance of expert and continuous management to the cotton merchandising business. They were intended to preserve or augment the value of the estates of Clayton and Anderson, as well as to relieve them of obligations to corporation. All the vendees of the stock were, either at the time of the sales or shortly thereafter, managing executives in association and held qualifying shares to make them fully liable for the debts of association. Association being a modified form of partnership, the vendees were partners with Anderson and Clayton in the operating entity of the business enterprise. There was no intent on the part of Anderson and Clayton in selling the stock to confer, nor intent on the part of their vendees to receive, gratuitous benefits. Clearly, then, these transactions were not gifts in any ordinary sense of the word.

In contending that the sales of stock were not "made in the ordinary course of business," respondent's position appears to be that it was neither ordinary for Anderson and Clayton nor ordinary for business men in general to enter into transactions of the type here involved. We do not agree. On the contrary, it is apparent from the numerous occasions on which Clayton and Anderson sold common stock to their junior executives, both those in issue and others not in issue, that it was a quite customary and ordinary thing for them to do. The record also proves that profit sharing or participation among the active management was quite the ordinary and customary practice in the cotton merchandising business generally. Furthermore, from facts within the range of judicial knowledge, we know that nothing is more ordinary, as business is conducted in this country, than profit-sharing arrangements and plans for the acquisition of proprietary interests by junior executives or junior partners, often for inadequate consideration, if consideration is to be measured solely in terms of money or something reducible to a money value.

The cases of Deputy v. DuPont, 308 U.S. 488, and Welch v. Helvering, 290 U.S. 111, relied on by respondent, have little if any bearing on the problem here presented. Both cases deal with expense deductions for income tax purposes under a statute providing for the allowance of "ordinary and necessary expenses paid or incurred ... *in carrying on any trade or business.*" (Italics supplied.) It does not follow that considerations which are relevant in determining whether an item of expense is an "ordinary and necessary" business expense for purposes of income tax deduction are relevant in determining whether a transfer of property is made "in the ordinary course of business" for purposes of the gift tax.

The pertinent inquiry for gift tax purposes is whether the transaction is a *genuine business* transaction, as distinguished, for example, from the marital or family type of transaction involved in *Wemyss* and its companion case, Merrill v. Fahs, 324 U.S. 308. Surely it will not be said that there may not be a genuine business transaction not directly connected with the taxpayer's trade or business or even though the taxpayer be not engaged in "carrying on any trade or business," within the scope of that term as limited by Higgins v. Commissioner, 312 U.S. 212. Bad bargains, sales for less than market, sales for less than adequate consideration in money or money's worth are made every day in the business world for one reason or another; but no one would think for a moment that any gift is involved, even in the broadest possible sense of the term "gift."

It appears that this is the first attempt on the part of the respondent to apply the gift tax to transactions such as those presented here. To sustain the attempt, in our judgment, would be to work a perversion of the whole purpose and spirit of the gift tax law. However broadly Congress may have used the term "gifts" in the gift tax law, and however much it may have dispensed with common law concepts of gifts, we are certain that the law was neither designed nor intended in its operation to hamper or strait-jacket the ordinary conduct of business.

We have found that the sales of stock in issue were bona fide and made at arm's length, in the ordinary course of business. Therefore, assuming, without deciding, that the value of the stock was greater than the value of the consideration, we hold that the transfers are not subject to gift tax....

Decisions will be entered for the petitioners.

NOTES

1. *Buy-sell agreements.* A typical form of buy-sell agreement among the owners of a closely held corporation or partnership provides that upon the

death or retirement of a shareholder or partner, the survivors will have the right to purchase the deceased or retired owner's interest at book value (i.e., without taking goodwill or appreciation in the value of real estate or other assets into account). Does *Anderson's Estate* provide an effective shield against gift tax liability, both when the agreement is entered into and when a retired owner's interest is sold at book value? Does such an agreement conclusively establish the value of a deceased owner's interest for estate tax purposes? Does it make any difference if the owners are members of the same family? In 1990 Congress enacted § 2703, which limits the use of buy-sell agreements and similar restrictive arrangements in determining the value of transferred property. Section 2703 is discussed infra at page 608.

2. *Family business succession.* When a parent brings a child into the family business as a partner, the transaction may give rise to a gift tax if the child contributes less than full consideration in exchange for his or her partnership interest. For example, if the business is a going concern with valuable assets (including goodwill), a capital shift from the existing partners to the new partner is likely to be treated as a taxable gift. See Gross v. Commissioner, 7 T.C. 837 (1946). On the other hand, if the business has no substantial assets and the value of the partners' interests is attributable solely to their personal services, the transaction may escape gift tax, either on the ground that no transfer occurred or on the alternative ground that any transfer was of negligible value or was offset by full consideration. See Rothrock v. Commissioner, 7 T.C. 848 (1946).

3. *Family limited partnerships.* In recent years family limited partnerships (and limited liability companies) have become widely used as vehicles to hold and manage business and investment assets, to protect assets from creditors' claims, and to shelter family wealth from gift and estate taxes as it passes from one generation to the next. In general, the transfer of wealth involves two formally distinct steps: (1) the initial formation of the partnership with assets contributed by the partners in proportion to their respective interests in the partnership, followed by (2) a gift or bequest by one partner of limited partnership interests to other family members at discounted values. For example, in a typical case *A* contributes 99 percent of the partnership assets in exchange for a 99–percent limited partnership interest, and her child *B* (or an entity owned by *B*) contributes the other 1 percent of the assets in exchange for a 1–percent general partnership interest. Subsequently *A* transfers her limited partnership interest to *B* during life or at death, claiming substantial valuation discounts on the gift or estate tax return due to lack of marketability and lack of control. (These valuation discounts are discussed infra at page 598.) On liquidation of the partnership, *B* will ultimately receive the assets in a tax-free distribution.

Focusing on the formation of the partnership, the Service has argued that *A* makes a taxable gift equal to the difference between the value of the assets she contributes and the discounted value of the limited partnership interest she receives in exchange. The courts, however, have rejected this argument, concluding that the formation of the partnership does not give rise to a taxable gift as long as each partner's contribution is properly reflected in his or her capital account and does not enhance the value of any other partner's interest in the partnership. See Strangi's Estate v. Commissioner, 115 T.C.

478 (2000), affd. on this issue and revd. on another issue, 293 F.3d 279 (5th Cir. 2002); Jones v. Commissioner, 116 T.C. 121 (2001). Does this conclusion rest on the notion that the formation of the partnership is an ordinary business transaction within the meaning of Reg. § 25.2512–8? That the partners receive full consideration in exchange for their respective contributions? That the partners retain sufficient dominion and control to prevent a completed gift? That no taxable transfer can take place in the absence of a capital shift from one partner to another?

Failure to complete the formation and funding of the partnership prior to the transfer of limited partnership interests may prove costly. If, through inadvertence or poor planning, *A* contributes assets to the partnership and simultaneously assigns her limited partnership interest to *B*, the Service may invoke the "step transaction" doctrine to recharacterize the transaction as an indirect gift by *A* of the contributed assets (rather than a gift of a limited partnership interest), resulting in denial of valuation discounts and nullifying the purported tax benefits of the partnership transaction. See Senda v. Commissioner, 433 F.3d 1044 (8th Cir. 2006) ("integrated and simultaneous" transactions treated as gifts of assets, not partnership interests); Shepherd v. Commissioner, 283 F.3d 1258 (11th Cir. 2002); cf. Holman v. Commissioner, 130 T.C. 170 (2008), affd. on another issue, 601 F.3d 763 (8th Cir. 2010) (declining to apply step transaction doctrine where partnership was formed five days before transfer of partnership interests).

4. *Nondonative transfers outside the "ordinary course of business."* The regulations refer to "ordinary business transactions" and to transfers "made in the ordinary course of business." Reg. §§ 25.2511–1(g)(1) and 25.2512–8. These terms have been construed broadly to include any transaction that is bona fide, at arm's length, and free from donative intent, even though there is no showing that a business motive (i.e., hope of future profits) is paramount. See, for example, Galluzzo v. Commissioner, 43 T.C.M. (CCH) 199 (1981) (transfer to reduce transferor's association with business during a criminal investigation not taxable); and cases discussed supra at page 116, Note 4. Recognizing the difficulty of establishing that intrafamily transfers are bona fide business transactions, the taxpayer in King v. United States, 545 F.2d 700 (10th Cir. 1976), took the precaution, when selling stock to trusts for his children, to provide that the purchase price would be readjusted to conform to the Internal Revenue Service's valuation if it differed from the price ($1.25 per share) fixed in the contract. The Service determined that the stock was worth $16 per share and assessed a gift tax based on the original purchase price. The court, however, treated the sale as a bona fide business transaction and went on to note that the price adjustment clause was consistent with the parties' intent that the father receive full money's-worth consideration for the transferred stock.

5. *Installment sales and other transactions among family members.* The Service views with skepticism claims that sales and other transactions within the family should not be taxed because they are bona fide and ostensibly supported by adequate consideration. Taxpayers have been attracted to the installment sale as a device to avoid the gift tax. For example, suppose a parent sells real property to a child, taking in return the child's promissory note for the fair market value of the property, payable in annual installments

equal to the gift tax annual exclusion and secured by a mortgage on the property. The parent then forgives each annual installment as it becomes due. The parent's contention that no gift occurs on the original sale because the child's note constitutes money's-worth consideration, or on the forgiveness of each annual installment because the transfer falls within the annual exclusion, has prevailed in several cases. Haygood v. Commissioner, 42 T.C. 936 (1964); Kelley's Estate v. Commissioner, 63 T.C. 321 (1974) ("the notes and vendor's liens, without evidence showing they were a 'facade,' are prima facie what they purport to be"); contra, Deal v. Commissioner, 29 T.C. 730 (1958). The Service has announced that it will not follow the *Kelley* and *Haygood* decisions but will treat a purported installment sale as a disguised gift where the donor intends to forgive the notes as part of a prearranged plan. Rev. Rul. 77–299, 1977–2 C.B. 343. Can "prearrangement" be inferred after the fact from a practice of forgiving payment of each year's installment?

6. *Business "gifts," prizes, and rewards.* The *Anderson* reasoning will exempt from gift tax most transfers from an employer to an unrelated employee. See Rev. Rul. 80–196, 1980–2 C.B. 32 (transfer of stock by major shareholders to unrelated employees as bonus for past services and inducement to continued employment was a bona fide business transaction). What if a business executive gives a friend an expensive car in gratitude for some business advice, or a corporation pays a $25,000 prize for the best essay on a topic of public interest, or a philanthropist gives a reward for information leading to the capture of a public enemy or the return of lost property, or sponsors a contest in which the participants win large prizes? Are these payments taxable gifts or do they escape the tax as business transactions? Compare DuPont v. United States, 97 F.Supp. 944 (D. Del. 1951) (contribution to the National Economic Council to encourage private enterprise and further the general welfare was a taxable gift), with Rev. Rul. 68–558, 1968–2 C.B. 415 (contribution to a manufacturing company to attract it to the community not taxable, presumably because the contributors obtained the response they hoped to induce).

7. *Political contributions.* In 1975 Congress added a special exemption from the gift tax for transfers made to a political organization, party, committee, or fund, whether incorporated or unincorporated, which is organized to receive and expend funds for an "exempt function." § 2501(a)(4). Section 527(e)(2) defines "exempt function" as "the function of influencing . . . the selection, nomination, election, or appointment of any individual to any Federal, State, or local public office or office in a political organization, or the election of Presidential or Vice–Presidential electors, whether or not such individual or electors are selected, nominated, elected, or appointed." Does this statute, by negative implication, require a gift tax on contributions to a single-issue lobbying organization that does not support a candidate but seeks to secure world peace, promote health, or save the environment? Prior to the enactment of § 2501(a)(4), the Service took the position that political contributions were subject to the gift tax. See Rev. Rul. 59–57, 1959–1 C.B. 626; Rev. Rul. 72–583, 1972–2 C.B. 534. A number of courts have taken the opposite view. See Carson v. Commissioner, 641 F.2d 864 (10th Cir. 1981) (Congress did not intend the gift tax to apply to campaign contributions); Stern v. United States, 436 F.2d 1327 (5th Cir. 1971) (transfer to a political

action group was "permeated with commercial and economic factors" because taxpayer wanted to promote a slate of candidates that would advance her personal and property interests, and therefore was exempted under the "business transaction" exception to the tax).

How might a donor exploit the § 2501(a)(4) exemption to shelter gifts to family members from gift tax? See Reis, Mr. Soros Goes to Washington: The Case for Reform of the Estate and Gift Tax Treatment of Political Contributions, 42 Real Prop., Prob. & Tr. J. 299 (2007).

D. ANNUAL EXCLUSION: § 2503(b) AND (c)

Since the inception of the gift tax in 1932, the statute has provided an annual per-donee exclusion for gifts up to a specified amount. In recommending the exclusion, the Senate Finance Committee described its purpose as follows:

> Such exemption, on the one hand, is to obviate the necessity of keeping an account of and reporting numerous small gifts, and, on the other, to fix the amount sufficiently large to cover in most cases wedding and Christmas gifts and occasional gifts of relatively small amounts. [S. Rep. No. 665, 72d Cong., 1st Sess. (1932), reprinted in 1939–1 C.B. (Part 2) 496, 525–26.]

The committee's description implicitly acknowledges that it would be unrealistic to expect taxpayers to keep track of and report numerous small gifts, and that any attempt by the government to do so would be fraught with administrative difficulties. In view of these practical limitations, Congress allowed taxpayers each year to make tax-free gifts, up to a specified amount for each donee, to an unlimited number of donees.

By its terms, the exclusion does not apply to gifts of "future interests." § 2503(b). Accordingly, only gifts of "present interests"—a term that appears in the regulations but not in the statute—are eligible for the exclusion. The distinction between present and future interests has never been elaborated with great precision for gift tax purposes, and the boundary between the two categories has been the site of intermittent skirmishing between taxpayers and the government from an early date.

1. PRESENT INTEREST REQUIREMENT

UNITED STATES v. PELZER

312 U.S. 399 (1941).

MR. JUSTICE STONE delivered the opinion of the Court.

Decision in this case turns on the question whether certain gifts of property in trust for the benefit of several beneficiaries are gifts of "future interests" which, in the computation of the gift tax, are, by [§ 2503(b)], denied the benefit, otherwise allowed, of exclusion from the computation to the extent of the first $5,000 of each gift "made to any person by the donor" during the calendar year. . . .

In 1932 the taxpayer, respondent here, created a trust for the benefit of his eight grandchildren and any other grandchildren who might afterward be born during the term of the trust. The trustee was directed to accumulate the income for a period of ten years and thereafter to pay an "equal grandchild's distributive share" of the income to each of the named grandchildren who were then living and twenty-one years of age and to pay a like share of income to each other named grandchild for life after that child should reach the age of twenty-one years. Provision was made whereby grandchildren born after the creation of the trust and during its life were to receive like participation in the income of the trust except as to distributions of income made prior to the birth of such after-born grandchildren, and except that the after-born grandchildren should be paid their shares of the income during their respective minorities after the termination of the ten-year accumulation period. The trust instrument also made gifts over of the share of the income of each grandchild at death, the details of which are not now material. It was further provided that the trust should terminate twenty-one years after death of the last survivor of the named grandchildren, when the corpus of the trust, with accumulated income, was to be distributed in equal shares among the surviving grandchildren and the issue per stirpes of all deceased grandchildren.

During the years 1933, 1934, and 1935, the taxpayer added further amounts of property to the 1932 trust. . . .

Upon claims for refunds of overpaid taxes upon the transfers made in the years 1933, 1934, and 1935, the commissioner recomputed the tax and allowed one $5,000 exclusion only from the net amounts subject to gift tax given or added in each year to each trust. In the present suit, brought in the Court of Claims, respondent sought to recover overpaid taxes for the years in question on the grounds that the gifts to the beneficiaries were gifts of present, not future, interests and that the taxpayer in the computation of the tax for each year was entitled to one exclusion of $5,000 for each beneficiary. The court sustained both contentions and gave judgment for respondent accordingly. 31 F. Supp. 770. We granted certiorari, 311 U.S. 634, to resolve the conflict of the decision below with that of the Seventh Circuit in United States v. Ryerson, 114 F.2d 150.

The Government challenges both grounds of decision below. It argues that only a single $5,000 exclusion is allowable under [§ 2503(b)] from the total gifts made to the trust in each calendar year and that if the gifts are deemed to be made to the named beneficiaries of the trust no deduction can be allowed in the case of gifts to the 1932 trust because they were of future interests for which no exclusion is allowed by [§ 2503(b)].

We have this day decided the first question, in Helvering v. Hutchings, [312 U.S. 393], in which we held that in the case of gifts in trust the beneficiaries are the persons to whom the gifts are made and that for purposes of computation of the tax [§ 2503(b)] excludes the first $5,000 in value of the gift to each beneficiary from the taxable amount of the gifts made in the calendar year. For the reasons stated in our opinion in that case we hold that the first beneficiaries of the trusts in this case are the persons to whom the gifts were made and that the taxpayer is entitled to the benefit of the $5,000 exclusion for each gift to such beneficiary if it is not of a future interest.

But the Government argues here, as it did below, that the gifts to the beneficiaries of the 1932 trust are of future interests within the meaning of the statute and treasury regulations. While the eight named grandchildren are the first beneficiaries of the trust, and the persons to whom the gifts were made, none of them takes any benefit from the trust before the end of the ten-year accumulation period or until he is twenty-one, whichever last occurs, and then only if he survives that event. And the question is whether such a gift is a gift of a "future interest" within the meaning of [§ 2503(b)]. Respondent, relying on statutes and judicial decisions of Alabama, where the trust was created and is being administered, insists that the gifts to the named grandchildren are present, not future, interests as defined by Alabama law. He argues that as [§ 2503(b)] does not define the "future interests" gifts of which are excluded from its benefits, they must be taken to be future interests as defined by the local law, and it is the local law definition of future interests which must be adopted in applying the section. But as we have often had occasion to point out, the revenue laws are to be construed in the light of their general purpose to establish a nationwide scheme of taxation uniform in its application. Hence their provisions are not to be taken as subject to state control or limitation unless the language or necessary implication of the section involved makes its application dependent on state law. Burnet v. Harmel, 287 U.S. 103, 110; Morgan v. Commissioner, 309 U.S. 78, 81.

We find no such implication in the exclusion of gifts of "future interests" from the benefits given by [§ 2503(b)]. In the absence of any statutory definition of the phrase we look to the purpose of the statute to ascertain what is intended. It plainly is not concerned with the varying local definitions of property interests or with the local refinements of conveyancing, and there is no reason for supposing that the extent of the granted tax exemption was intended to be given a corresponding variation. Its purpose was rather the protection of the revenue and the appropriate administration of the tax immunity provided by the statute. It is this purpose which marks the boundaries of the statutory command. The committee reports recommending the legislation declared (H. Rept. No. 708, 72d Cong., 1st Sess., p. 29; S. Rept. No. 665, 72d Cong., 1st Sess., p. 41):

> The term "future interests in property" refers to any interest or estate, whether vested or contingent, limited to commence in possession or enjoyment at a future date. The exemption being available only in so far as the donees are ascertainable, the denial of the exemption in the case of gifts of future interests is dictated by the apprehended difficulty, in many instances, of determining the number of eventual donees and the values of their respective gifts.

[The Treasury regulations] declared that "future interests" include any interest or estate "whether vested or contingent, limited to commence in use, possession, or enjoyment at some future date or time." . . .

We think that the regulations, so far as they are applicable to the present gifts, are within the competence of the Treasury in interpreting [§ 2503(b)] and effect its purpose as declared by the reports of the Congressional committees, and that the gifts to the eight beneficiaries of the 1932 trust were gifts of future interests which are excluded from the benefits of that section. Here the beneficiaries had no right to the present enjoyment of the corpus or of the income and unless they survive the ten-year period they will never receive any part of either. The "use, possession, or enjoyment" of each donee is thus postponed to the happening of a future uncertain event. The gift thus involved the difficulties of determining the "number of eventual donees and the value of their respective gifts" which it was the purpose of the statute to avoid.

We have no occasion to consider the definition of future interests in other aspects than those presented by the present case. The judgment of the Court of Claims will be reversed so far only as it excluded the gifts to the 1932 trust from the computation of the tax for each of the years in question.

Reversed.

NOTES

1. *Scope of the annual exclusion.* The amount of the annual exclusion has fluctuated over time. Originally set at $5,000 in 1932, the exclusion was reduced in 1938 to $4,000 and then in 1942 to $3,000, where it remained until 1981 when Congress raised it to $10,000.[23] By a 1997 amendment, the exclusion was made subject to an annual adjustment for inflation, and by 2011 the amount of the exclusion had reached $13,000.

A married couple with three children can transfer $78,000 ($26,000 per child) each year free of gift tax, by pooling their exclusions as permitted by the "split gift" provision in § 2513. In 15 years more than $1 million can be transferred in this manner without encroaching on either parent's unified credit. If there are also grandchildren to whom annual gifts can be made, the amount that can be transferred tax free can, of course, be enlarged still further.

Estate planners frequently use the full amount of the annual exclusion to illustrate the tax advantages of transferring cash, real estate, stocks and securities to the donor's children or other relatives, as if the donor had done nothing for them on their birthdays, at holidays, during vacations, etc., that should be charged against the exclusion. Thus, from its origin as a method of

23. The Senate Finance Committee justified the 1981 increase on the ground that inflation had substantially reduced the real value of the exclusion since 1942, noting that "because of the effect of inflation, the [$3,000] present level of gift tax exclusion is often insufficient to cover amounts paid by parents to provide higher education for their children." S. Rep. No. 144, 97th Cong., 1st Sess. 129 (1981), reprinted in 1981–2 C.B. 412, 462.

protecting such occasions from gift tax, the exclusion has come to be thought of as an estate planning device for transfers *in addition* to birthday and holiday presents. Are the latter transfers protected by the "duty of support" rationale against gift tax, or are the estate planners skating on thin ice? Is the ice made more treacherous by the enactment of § 2503(e) exempting tuition and medical payments from the tax? See supra page 119.

2. *Identifying the donees.* In Helvering v. Hutchings, 312 U.S. 393 (1941), decided the same day as *Pelzer*, the Court held that, for purposes of the annual exclusion, a gift in trust is treated as made to the trust beneficiaries, not to the trust itself. The Court explained its reasoning as follows:

> The gift tax provisions are not concerned with mere transfers of legal title to the trustee without surrender by the donor of the economic benefits of ownership and his control over them. A gift to a trustee reserving to the donor the economic benefit of the trust or the power of its disposition, involves no taxable gift. It is only upon the surrender by the donor of the benefit or power reserved to himself that a taxable gift occurs, ... and it would seem to follow that the beneficiary of the trust to whose benefit the surrender inures, whether made at the time the trust is created or later, is the "person" or "individual" to whom the gift is made.
>
> But for present purposes it is of more importance that in common understanding and in the common use of language a gift is made to him upon whom the donor bestows the benefit of his donation. One does not speak of making a gift to a trust rather than to his children who are its beneficiaries. The reports of the committees of Congress used words in their natural sense and in the sense in which we must take it they were intended to be used in [§ 2503(b)] when, in discussing [§ 2501(a)], they spoke of the beneficiary of a gift upon trust as the person to whom the gift is made. Similarly they spoke of gifts effected by transfer of money or property to another as consideration for the payment of money or other property to a third person as a gift to the third person.... It is of some significance also that the denial by [§ 2503(b)] of the exemption in the case of gifts of "future interests" has little scope for practical operation unless the gifts to which the exemption applies include those gifts made to beneficiaries of a trust, since it is by resort to the conveyance in trust that most future interests are created.
>
> Moreover, the very purpose of allowing a gift tax exemption measured by the number of donees, would be defeated if a distinction were to be taken between gifts made directly to numerous donees and a gift made for their benefit by way of a single trust, and we are unable to discern in the statute or its legislative history any purpose to make such a distinction. While one object of the exemption was to permit small tax free gifts, and at the same time "to fix the amount sufficiently large to cover in most cases wedding and Christmas gifts" without the necessity of keeping accounts and reporting the gifts, ... nevertheless the statute extended the exemption in the specified amount to all gifts, whether large or small, "made to any person."
>
> In the face of an exemption thus made broadly applicable to all gifts to all donees and in the absence of some indication of an intention to

discriminate between gifts made directly to the donees and those made indirectly to the beneficiaries of a trust, we can hardly assume a purpose to favor one class of donees over the other or find such a purpose in the words of the statutory definition of "person" which may indicate either the trust or each individual beneficiary of the trust as the person to whom the gift is made. Further, such an assumption would open the way to avoid the $5,000 limitation upon the allowed exemption, by resort to the simple expedient of the creation by a single donor of any number of trusts of $5,000 each for the benefit of a single beneficiary. A construction so dependent upon an artificial meaning of the words of the statute and so out of harmony with the statutory scheme and purpose is not to be favored. [312 U.S. at 396–98.]

In *Hutchings* the Court recognized the possibility that a legal entity might be the donee for purposes of the exclusion in the case of gifts "for impersonal, public or charitable purposes where there are no designated or ascertainable first beneficiaries." 312 U.S. at 398. The Service will presumably resort to this approach when determining the number of exclusions allowable for a taxable contribution to a political action group not exempted under § 2501(a)(4). See Reg. § 25.2511–1(h)(1); Rev. Rul. 72–355, 1972–2 C.B. 532, amplified in Rev. Rul. 74–199, 1974–1 C.B. 285.

3. *Establishing the number of donees.* The excerpt from the congressional reports set out in *Pelzer* justifies the denial of the exclusion to gifts of future interests because of the "apprehended difficulty, in many instances, of determining the number of eventual donees and the value of their respective gifts." Is the rationale convincing as to vested remainder interests where there is no potential for additional takers (other than the donee's estate)? Is there any difficulty in determining that there will be at least *one* "eventual donee" of the 1932 trust in the *Pelzer* case? In Rev. Rul. 55–679, 1955–2 C.B. 390, the Service addressed itself to the proper number of exclusions for a trust under which the income was to be paid quarterly for a ten-year period to the settlor's grandchildren (or their surviving issue), whether born before or after the creation of the trust, who were living at the time of payment. Although the precise number of eventual donees was not ascertainable at the time of the gift, the Service ruled that exclusions were allowable for the ten grandchildren living when the trust was created, since recognized valuation methods made it possible to determine a minimum value for their respective income interests—e.g., on the assumption that the maximum number of additional grandchildren who could share in the income during the ten-year trust term was 50.

4. *Gift of income for life or a term.* At one time, the government took the position that a life estate was a future interest, except for the income to be paid to the donee in the year of the gift, because the annual installments are to be paid at future times. Several cases holding to the contrary were apparently approved by the Supreme Court in Fondren v. Commissioner, 324 U.S. 18, 21 (1945): "[I]t has been held that if the income of a trust is required to be distributed periodically, as annually, but distribution of the corpus is deferred, the gift of the income is one of a present interest, that of the corpus one in futuro." In Charles v. Hassett, 43 F.Supp. 432 (D. Mass. 1942), the

court pointed out some of the implications of holding that a life estate is a present interest but a remainder is a future interest:

> If a gift of $5,000 to trustees to pay the income to *A* for life is a present interest, what is to be said of these gifts: (1) $200 to *A* each year so long as he lives; (2) $200 to *A* the first year, if he lives, $300 to *A* the second year, if he lives, $400 to *A* the third year, if he lives, etc.; (3) $200 to *A* the first year, if he lives, $200 to *A* the second year, if he lives, etc. and $5,000 to *A* the fifteenth year, if he lives; and finally, (4) the income on $5,000 to *A* each year he lives for the next fifteen years, and then $5,000 to *A* in the fifteenth year?
>
> To the argument implied in that progression, the answer is that historically lawyers have treated gifts of income beginning at once and lasting for life, or for a period of years, as a "present interest" and gifts of principal at a future date as a "future interest"; that Congressional committees and the Treasury appear to have had some such distinction in mind; and that this and other circuits in construing the gift tax statute have used that line of distinction in cases where the gifts of income and of principal were to different persons.... No historical reason justifies abandoning the distinction in cases where the gifts of income and of principal are to the same person and are therefore regarded by donor and donee as one gift. [43 F.Supp. at 434–35.]

The court then pointed out the "anomalous" result that the donor may pay a heavier gift tax if he gives his donee the income of a short-term trust than if the trust is of longer duration, even though the remainder is to go to the same donee on the termination of the trust, because the smaller value of the income interest in the short-term trust may not use up the entire annual exclusion.

The taxpayer has the burden of establishing the value of the present gift, including the obligation of showing that none of that value is attributable to a future interest. See Rev. Rul. 55–678, 1955–2 C.B. 389 (valuation of income interests when the class of beneficiaries is open to let in after-born members); Rev. Rul. 55–679, 1955–2 C.B. 390 (same); see also Rev. Rul. 75–506, 1975–2 C.B. 375 (gift of income from trust in equal shares to two beneficiaries and of entire income to survivor; held, each donee's right to one-half the income is a present interest, but right to receive the additional half on surviving the other donee is a future interest).

5. *Merger of remainder and income interests.* If the donor does not create a future interest, but transfers one that is already in existence (e.g., a remainder interest under a trust created by the donor's parent), does the exclusion apply? In Clark v. Commissioner, 65 T.C. 126 (1975), gifts to the income beneficiaries of part of the retained principal interests in two previously established "*Clifford*" trusts were held to be present interests because the beneficiaries' income and principal interests "merged," resulting in a partial termination of the trusts. Accord, Rev. Rul. 78–168, 1978–1 C.B. 298 (gift of remainder interest to income beneficiary qualifies as present interest in state where merger results from union of both interests in same person). Is there an inconsistency in allowing two exclusions, one for the initial gift of

income and another for the subsequent gift of principal, where there would be only a single exclusion for an outright gift of the same property?

HACKL v. COMMISSIONER

335 F.3d 664 (7th Cir. 2003).

EVANS, CIRCUIT JUDGE.

Most post-retirement hobbies don't involve multi-million dollar companies or land retirees in hot water with the IRS, but those are the circumstances in this case. Albert J. (A.J.) and Christine M. Hackl began a tree-farming business after A.J.'s retirement and gave shares in the company to family members. The Hackls believed the transfers were excludable from the gift tax, but the IRS thought otherwise. The Tax Court agreed with the IRS, Hackl v. Comm'r, 118 T.C. 279 (2002), resulting in a gift tax deficiency of roughly $400,000 for the couple. The Hackls appeal.

Our story begins with A.J. Hackl's retirement and subsequent search for a hobby that would allow him to keep his hand in the business world, diversify his investments, and provide a long-term investment for his family. Tree-farming fit the bill and, in 1995, A.J. purchased two tree farms (worth around $4.5 million) and contributed them, as well as about $8 million in cash and securities, to Treeco, LLC, a limited liability company that he set up in Indiana. . . .

A.J. and his wife, Christine, initially owned all of Treeco's stock (which included voting and nonvoting shares), with A.J. serving as the company's manager. Under Treeco's operating agreement, the manager served for life (or until resignation, removal, or incapacity), had the power to appoint a successor, and could also dissolve the company. In addition, the manager controlled any financial distributions, and members needed his approval to withdraw from the company or sell shares. If a member transferred his or her shares without consent, the transferee would receive the shares' economic rights but not any membership or voting rights. Voting members could run Treeco during any interim period between managers, approve any salaries or bonuses paid by the company, and remove a manager and elect a successor. With an 80-percent majority, voting members could amend the Articles of Organization and operating agreement and dissolve the company after A.J.'s tenure as manager. Both the voting and the nonvoting members had the right to access Treeco's books and records and to decide whether to continue Treeco following an event of dissolution (such as the death, resignation, removal, retirement, bankruptcy, or insanity of the manager). During A.J.'s watch, Treeco has operated at a loss and not made any distributions to its stockholders. While Treeco has yet to turn a profit, A.J. was named "Tree Farmer of the Year" in Putnam County, Florida, in 1999.

Shortly after Treeco's creation, A.J. and Christine began annual transfers of Treeco voting and nonvoting shares to their children, their children's spouses, and a trust set up for the couple's grandchildren. After January 1998, 51 percent of the company's voting shares were in the hands of the couple's children and their spouses. The Hackls attempted to shield the transfers from taxation by treating them as excludable gifts on their gift tax returns. While the Internal Revenue Code imposes a tax on gifts, 26 U.S.C. § 2501(a), a donor does not pay the tax on the first $10,000 of gifts, "other than gifts of future interests in property," made to any person during the calendar year, 26 U.S.C. § 2503(b)(1). Unfortunately for the Hackls, the IRS thought that the transfers were future interests and ineligible for the gift tax exclusion. The Hackls took the dispute to the Tax Court which, as we said, sided with the IRS.

The Hackls contend that the Tax Court was in error. Although we owe no special deference to the Tax Court on a legal question, when we consider the application of the legal principle to the facts we will reject the Tax Court decision only if it is clearly erroneous....

The crux of the Hackls' appeal is that the gift tax doesn't apply to a transfer if the donors give up all of their legal rights. In other words, the future interest exception to the gift tax exclusion only comes into play if the donee has gotten something less than the full bundle of legal property rights. Because the Hackls gave up all of their property rights to the shares, they think that the shares were excludable gifts within the plain meaning of § 2503(b)(1). The government, on the other hand, interprets the gift tax exclusion more narrowly. It argues that any transfer without a substantial present economic benefit is a future interest and ineligible for the gift tax exclusion.

The Hackls' initial argument is that § 2503(b)(1) automatically allows the gift tax exclusion for their transfers. The Hackls argue that their position reflects the plain—and only—meaning of "future interest" as used in the statute, and that the Tax Court's reliance on materials outside the statute (such as the Treasury regulation definition of future interest and case law) was not only unnecessary, it was wrong. We disagree. Calling any tax law "plain" is a hard row to hoe, and a number of cases (including our decision in Stinson Estate v. United States, 214 F.3d 846 (7th Cir. 2000)) have looked beyond the language of § 2503(b)(1) for guidance. See, e.g., United States v. Pelzer, 312 U.S. 399, 403–04 (1941), and Comm'r v. Disston, 325 U.S. 442, 446 (1945) (stating that regulatory definition of future interest has been approved repeatedly). The Hackls do not cite any cases that actually characterize § 2503(b)(1) as plain, and the term "future interest" is not defined in the statute itself. Furthermore, the fact that both the government and the Hackls have proposed different—yet reasonable—interpretations of the statute shows that it is ambiguous. Under these circumstances, it was appropriate for the Tax Court to look to the Treasury regulation and case law for guidance.

Hedging their bet, the Hackls say that the applicable Treasury regulation supports the conclusion that giving up all legal rights to a gift automatically makes it a present interest. The applicable Treasury regulation states that a "future interest" is a legal term that applies to interests "which are limited to commence in use, possession, or enjoyment at some future date or time," Treas. Reg. § 25.2503–3. The regulation also provides that a present interest in property is "[a]n unrestricted right to the immediate use, possession, or enjoyment of property or the income from property (such as a life estate or term certain)." We don't think that this language automatically excludes all outright transfers from the gift tax....

We previously addressed the issue of future interests for purposes of the gift tax exclusion in *Stinson Estate*. In that case, forgiveness of a corporation's indebtedness was a future interest outside the gift tax exclusion because shareholders could not individually realize the gift without liquidating the corporation or declaring a dividend—events that could not occur upon the actions of any one individual under the corporation's bylaws. See 214 F.3d at 848. We said that the "sole statutory distinction between present and future interests lies in the question of whether there is postponement of enjoyment of specific rights, powers or privileges which would be forthwith existent if the interest were present." Id. at 848–49 (quoting Howe v. United States, 142 F.2d 310, 312 (7th Cir. 1944)). In other words, the phrase "present interest" connotes the right to substantial present economic benefit. See Fondren v. Comm'r, 324 U.S. 18, 20 (1945).

In this case, Treeco's operating agreement clearly foreclosed the donees' ability to realize any substantial present economic benefit. Although the voting shares that the Hackls gave away had the same legal rights as those that they retained, Treeco's restrictions on the transferability of the shares meant that they were essentially without immediate value to the donees. Granted, Treeco's operating agreement did address the possibility that a shareholder might violate the agreement and sell his or her shares without the manager's approval. But, as the Tax Court found, the possibility that a shareholder might violate the operating agreement and sell his or her shares to a transferee who would then not have any membership or voting rights can hardly be called a substantial economic benefit. Thus, the Hackls' gifts—while outright—were not gifts of present interests.

The Hackls protest that Treeco is set up like any other limited liability corporation and that its restrictions on the alienability of its shares are common in closely held companies. While that may be true, the fact that other companies operate this way does not mean that shares in such companies should automatically be considered present interests for purposes of the gift tax exclusion. As we have previously said, Internal Revenue Code provisions dealing with exclusions are matters of legislative grace that must be narrowly construed. See *Stinson Estate*, 214 F.3d at 848. The onus is on the taxpayers to show that their transfers qualify for the gift tax exclusion, a burden the Hackls have not met.

The decision of the Tax Court is affirmed.

NOTES

1. *Outright gifts of restricted shares.* The *Hackl* decision came as a surprise to many practitioners who had assumed that outright gifts of corporate stock or partnership interests automatically qualified as present interests for purposes of the annual exclusion. In earlier rulings, however, the Service had taken the position that in some circumstances outright gifts of stock could be treated as gifts of future interests. See Rev. Rul. 76–360, 1976–2 C.B. 298 (denying exclusion for gifts of non-dividend-paying stock subject to a two-year restriction on sale, despite donees' limited power to pledge stock or give it to relatives). Does the *Hackl* court's conclusion that the donees received no "substantial present economic benefit" rest on (1) the donees' inability to transfer their shares freely, (2) their inability to compel distributions, (3) their inability to redeem shares or to liquidate the company on demand, or (4) the company's lack of earnings available for distribution? Would the gifts qualify as present interests if the donees could freely transfer their shares? If the company turned a regular profit, even though its earnings were retained rather than distributed? If the manager expected to make regular distributions from future profits?

If the Hackls had chosen a discretionary trust rather than a limited liability company as the vehicle for making gifts to their children, it seems clear beyond argument that no annual exclusion would have been allowed. See infra Notes 3 and 4 and the authorities there cited. Are there fundamental differences between a gift of an interest in a limited liability company (or a limited partnership) and a gift of a trust interest that should be taken into account in applying the present-interest test? One commentator has observed:

> In many respects a limited partner who has no withdrawal rights is much like a beneficiary of a discretionary trust whose only rights with respect to the trust consist of the right to trust distributions which may be withheld at the discretion of the trustee. Regardless of the general partner's fiduciary duties, there is no certainty that the limited partner will receive current distributions from the partnership. [Kalinka, Should the Gift of a Limited Partnership Interest Constitute a Future Interest?, 76 Taxes 12, 18 (Apr. 1998), quoted in Price v. Commissioner, 99 T.C.M. (CCH) 1005, 1010 n.10 (2010).]

2. *Indirect gifts to shareholders.* A gift made to a corporation generally is treated as a gift to the individual shareholders, in proportion to their respective interests in the corporation. Reg. § 25.2511–1(h)(1). This veil-piercing approach, however, has brought taxpayers little satisfaction, because the shareholders have no immediate right to use, possess or enjoy corporate assets or earnings. The shareholders' enjoyment is dependent on the declaration of dividends or the liquidation of the corporation, which usually require approval by the corporate directors. Thus, the gift to the corporation is a future interest for which no exclusion is allowed. See Stinson Estate v. United States, 214 F.3d 846 (7th Cir. 2000); Georgia Ketteman Trust v. Commissioner, 86 T.C. 91 (1986); Chanin v. United States, 393 F.2d 972 (Ct. Cl. 1968); Heringer v. Commissioner, 235 F.2d 149 (9th Cir.), cert. denied, 352 U.S. 927 (1956); Rev. Rul. 71–443, 1971–2 C.B. 337. In the case of a partnership,

however, the unrestricted right of a donee general partner to demand repayment of his or her capital account has been held sufficient to qualify a gift to the partnership as a present interest. See Wooley v. United States, 736 F.Supp. 1506 (S.D. Ind. 1990).

3. *Trustee powers.* In Commissioner v. Disston, 325 U.S. 442 (1945), the trustees were to distribute currently such income "as may be necessary for the education, comfort and support" of minor beneficiaries and to accumulate the balance of the income for distribution to the beneficiaries at age 21. The Court held that no exclusion was allowable:

> [E]ven though the trustees were under a duty to apply the income for support, irrespective of outside sources of revenue, there is always the question how much, if any, of the income can actually be applied for the permitted purposes. The existence of a duty so to apply the income gives no clue to the amount that will be needed for that purpose, or the requirements for maintenance, education and support that were foreseeable at the time the gifts were made. In the absence of some indication from the face of the trust or surrounding circumstances that a steady flow of some ascertainable portion of income to the minor would be required, there is no basis for a conclusion that there is a gift of anything other than for the future. The taxpayer claiming the exclusion must assume the burden of showing that the value of what he claims is other than a future interest. [325 U.S. at 448–49.]

Accord, Hamilton v. United States, 553 F.2d 1216 (9th Cir. 1977) (no exclusion allowed where trustees had discretion to accumulate or distribute principal and income). An interest is future even though possession or enjoyment is postponed for only a short time. Hessenbruch v. Commissioner, 178 F.2d 785 (3d Cir. 1950) (exclusion not allowed because 20–year–old donee's right to income commenced at age 21); Rev. Rul. 75–415, 1975–2 C.B. 374 (exclusion not allowed for right to income commencing three years after gift or donee's earlier withdrawal from educational institution).

An interest that is future because possession or enjoyment may be withheld by trustees or others is not made present by the fact that the donee can immediately sell or assign it. Blasdel v. Commissioner, 58 T.C. 1014 (1972), affd., 478 F.2d 226 (5th Cir. 1973) (beneficiary's interest in trust); Chanin v. United States, 393 F.2d 972 (Ct. Cl. 1968) (shares in closely held corporation). Conversely, a spendthrift provision does not disqualify an interest for the exclusion. Rev. Rul. 54–344, 1954–2 C.B. 319.

A trustee's normal administrative powers do not impair the exclusion even if they impose minor restrictions on the donee's immediate enjoyment of the transferred property. See Mercantile–Safe Deposit & Trust Co. v. United States, 311 F.Supp. 670 (D. Md. 1970) (various fiduciary powers, including discretionary powers over investments and power to apportion receipts and expenses between principal and income, did not disqualify income interests for the exclusion because exercise of powers was judicially reviewable); Martinez v. Commissioner, 67 T.C. 60 (1976) (powers to make investments and to apportion items between principal and income treated as judicially reviewable, despite inclusion of "commonplace boilerplate trust powers" purporting to confer uncontrolled discretion). There is, however, a risk that discretionary powers will be held to make the value of a donee's interest unascertainable. See Van den Wymelenberg v. United States, 397 F.2d 443 (7th Cir.), cert. denied, 393 U.S. 953 (1968) (trustee's broad administrative powers made the value of income interest uncertain despite evidence that powers had not been used to vary amount of net income).

4. *Gifts in trust of nonproductive property.* Suppose a settlor creates a trust with all the income payable to a named beneficiary for life, and funds the trust with nonproductive property (e.g., shares in a family corporation that pays no dividends) that cannot readily be sold or exchanged for income-producing property. Courts have denied the annual exclusion, on the theory that the actuarial tables "are designed to calculate the value of a present interest, not create it" and can be used only if the taxpayer proves that the income beneficiaries will actually receive some income. Maryland Natl. Bank v. United States, 609 F.2d 1078 (4th Cir. 1979) (no exclusion for gift in trust of interest in real estate partnership with history of losses, despite prospects for development, where trustees could not convert to other assets). See also Berzon v. Commissioner, 534 F.2d 528 (2d Cir. 1976) (same for gift in trust of shares in closely held corporation, where payment of dividends was not intended and shareholders' agreement restricted sale and reinvestment in income-producing assets); Calder v. Commissioner, 85 T.C. 713 (1985) (no exclusion for gift in trust of art works that were not expected to generate a "steady flow of income" by rental or other means). But cf. Rosen v. Commissioner, 397 F.2d 245 (4th Cir. 1968) (exclusion allowed where trustees had power to sell non-dividend-paying stock, but believed prospect of future dividends warranted retention); Rev. Rul. 69–344, 1969–1 C.B. 225 (Service will not follow *Rosen*). Should the exclusion be allowed for an income interest in trust property if the trustee is authorized, but not required, to invest in nonproductive property? See Gilmore v. Commissioner, 213 F.2d 520 (6th Cir. 1954) ("It is the right of a donee to the income, rather than the accident of whether there is income at any given time, that is the criterion of present interest.").

5. *Gifts of contractual rights to future payments.* The regulations provide that an outright gift of a bond or note qualifies for the exclusion even if the obligation bears no interest or bears interest payable only at maturity. The same is true of an outright gift of a policy of life insurance and of premium payments on an existing policy owned by the donee, even though no proceeds will be paid until the insured's death. Reg. § 25.2503–3(a) and (c) (Example 6); see also Commissioner v. Kempner, 126 F.2d 853 (5th Cir. 1942) (non-interest-bearing notes maturing in three or four years); Rev. Rul. 55–408, 1955–1 C.B. 113 (absence of cash surrender value does not nullify exclusion). If, however, such contractual obligations are transferred in trust to pay the income from the property to *A* for life and the remainder to *B*, *A*'s income interest does not qualify for an exclusion because no income will be available for distribution to *A* until the bond, note, or policy matures. Reg. § 25.2503–3(a) and (c) (Example 2); see also Rev. Rul. 79–47, 1979–1 C.B. 312 (no exclusion for premiums paid on life insurance policy after assignment to irrevocable trust). Why this distinction between future payments under a contract, the value of which is a present interest qualifying for the exclusion, and a remainder or similar interest in a trust, which does not qualify? How is

a gift of an annuity contract to be treated, if payments are to commence at a future date? See Roberts v. Commissioner, 143 F.2d 657 (5th Cir. 1944), cert. denied, 324 U.S. 841 (1945) (postponement of use and enjoyment coupled with survival contingency made premium payments gifts of future interests).

2. POWERS TO DEMAND PAYMENT

CRISTOFANI'S ESTATE v. COMMISSIONER

97 T.C. 74 (1991).

RUWE, JUDGE:

... The sole issue for decision is whether transfers of property to a trust, where the beneficiaries possessed the right to withdraw an amount not in excess of the section 2503(b) exclusion within 15 days of such transfers, constitute gifts of a present interest in property within the meaning of section 2503(b).

[In 1984 and 1985, decedent made annual contributions of property worth $70,000 to an irrevocable inter vivos trust (the "children's trust"). Decedent's two children, Frank Cristofani and Lillian Dawson, were named as trustees. Decedent had five minor grandchildren: Frank Cristofani's two children and Lillian Dawson's three children.

By the terms of the children's trust, each child was entitled to receive one-half of the net income and, if living 120 days after decedent's death, one-half of the corpus. In addition, the trustees had discretion to invade corpus for the children's support, health, maintenance, and education, taking into account decedent's desire to consider her children as "primary beneficiaries" and the other beneficiaries "of secondary importance." If either child failed to survive decedent by 120 days, the deceased child's share of corpus would pass to his or her issue. Under Article Twelfth, the trustees were required to notify the beneficiaries of any contributions to the children's trust, and during the 15-day period following a contribution each beneficiary had the right to withdraw an amount not exceeding the amount of the annual exclusion specified in § 2503(b).

Decedent died in 1985. Both of her children survived her by 120 days and received their respective shares of corpus upon termination of the children's trust.

Decedent did not report her 1984 and 1985 contributions to the children's trust as taxable gifts. Rather, for each year she claimed seven $10,000 exclusions—one for each of her two children and five grandchildren.]

There was no agreement or understanding between decedent, the trustees, and the beneficiaries that decedent's grandchildren would not exercise their withdrawal rights following a contribution to the children's trust. None of decedent's five grandchildren exercised their rights to withdraw ... during either 1984 or 1985. None of decedent's five grandchildren received a distribution from the children's trust during either 1984 or 1985.

Respondent allowed petitioner to claim the annual exclusions with respect to decedent's two children. However, respondent disallowed the $10,000 annual exclusions claimed with respect to each of decedent's grandchildren claimed for the years 1984 and 1985. Respondent determined that the annual exclusions that decedent claimed with respect to her five grandchildren for the 1984 and 1985 transfers ... were not transfers of present interests in property. Accordingly, respondent increased petitioner's adjusted taxable gifts in the amount of $100,000....

In the instant case, petitioner argues that the right of decedent's grandchildren to withdraw an amount equal to the annual exclusion within 15 days after decedent's contribution of property to the children's trust constitutes a gift of a present interest in property, thus qualifying for a $10,000 annual exclusion for each grandchild for the years 1984 and 1985. Petitioner relies upon Crummey v. Commissioner, 397 F.2d 82 (9th Cir. 1968), revg. on this issue T.C. Memo 1966–144.

In Crummey v. Commissioner, T.C. Memo. 1966–144, affd. in part and revd. in part 397 F.2d 82 (9th Cir. 1968), the settlors created an irrevocable living trust for the benefit of their four children, some of whom were minors. The trustee was required to hold the property in equal shares for the beneficiaries. Under the terms of the trust, the trustee, in his discretion, could distribute trust income to each beneficiary until that beneficiary obtained the age of 21. When the beneficiary was age 21 and up until age 35, the trustee was required to distribute trust income to each beneficiary. When the beneficiary was age 35 and over, the trustee was authorized, in his discretion, to distribute trust income to the beneficiary or his or her issue. Upon the death of a beneficiary, his or her trust share was to be distributed to that beneficiary's surviving issue subject to certain age requirements. If a beneficiary died without issue, then his or her trust share was to be distributed equally to the trust shares of the surviving children of the grantors. In addition, each child was given an absolute power to withdraw up to $4,000 in cash of any additions to corpus in the calendar year of the addition, by making a written demand upon the trustee prior to the end of the calendar year.

Relying on these powers, the settlors claimed the section 2503(b) exclusion on transfers of property to the trust for each trust beneficiary. Respondent permitted the settlors to claim the exclusions with respect to the gifts in trust to the beneficiaries who were adults during the years of the additions. However, respondent disallowed exclusions with respect to the gifts in trust to the beneficiaries who were minors during such years. Respondent disallowed the exclusions for the minor beneficiaries on the ground that the minors' powers were not gifts of present interests in property.

In deciding whether the minor beneficiaries received a present interest, the Ninth Circuit specifically rejected any test based upon the likelihood that the minor beneficiaries would actually receive present enjoyment of the property.[24] Instead, the court focused on the legal right of the minor beneficiaries to demand payment from the trustee.[25] ... The court found that the minor beneficiaries had a legal right to make a demand upon the trustee, and allowed the settlors to claim annual exclusions, under section 2503(b), with respect to the minor trust beneficiaries.

The Ninth Circuit recognized that there was language in a prior case, Stifel v. Commissioner, 197 F.2d 107 (2d Cir. 1952), affg. 17 T.C. 647 (1951), that seemed to support a different test.

> As we read the *Stifel* case, it says that the court should look at the trust instrument, the law as to minors, and the financial and other circumstances of the parties. From this examination it is up to the court to determine whether it is likely that the minor beneficiary is to receive any present enjoyment of the property. If it is not likely, then the gift is a "future interest." [Crummey v. Commissioner, supra at 85.]

As previously stated, the Ninth Circuit rejected a test based on the likelihood that an actual demand would be made. Respondent does not rely on or cite *Stifel* in his brief. We believe that the test set forth in Crummey v. Commissioner, supra, is the correct test.

Subsequent to the opinion in *Crummey*, respondent's revenue rulings have recognized that when a trust instrument gives a beneficiary the legal power to demand immediate possession of corpus, that power qualifies as a present interest in property. See Rev. Rul. 85–24, 1985–1 C.B. 329 ...; Rev. Rul. 81–7, 1981–1 C.B. 474.... While we recognize that revenue rulings do not constitute authority for deciding a case in this Court, ... we mention them to show respondent's recognition that a trust beneficiary's legal right to demand immediate possession and enjoyment of trust corpus or income constitutes a present interest in property for purposes of the annual exclusion under section 2503(b).... We also note that respon-

---

24. The Ninth Circuit stated:

> Although under our interpretation neither the trust nor the law technically forbid a demand by the minor, the practical difficulties of a child going through the procedures seem substantial. In addition, the surrounding facts indicate the children were well cared for and the obvious intention of the trustors was to create a long term trust.... As a practical matter, it is likely that some, if not all, of the beneficiaries did not even know that they had any right to demand funds from the trust. They probably did not know when contributions were made to the trust or in what amounts. Even had they known, the substantial contributions were made toward the end of the year so that the time to make a demand was severely limited.... We think it unlikely that any demand ever would have been made. [Crummey v. Commissioner, 397 F.2d at 87–88.]

25. The Ninth Circuit stated:

> ... As we visualize the hypothetical situation, the child would inform the trustee that he demanded his share of the additions up to $4,000. The trustee would petition the court for the appointment of a legal guardian and then turn the funds over to the guardian. It would also seem possible for the parent to make the demand as natural guardian....
>
> All this is admittedly speculative since it is highly unlikely that a demand will ever be made or that if one is made, it would be made in this fashion. However, as a technical matter, we think a minor could make the demand. [397 F.2d at 87.]—EDS.

dent allowed the annual exclusions with respect to decedent's two children who possessed the same right of withdrawal as decedent's grandchildren.

In the instant case, respondent has not argued that decedent's grandchildren did not possess a legal right to withdraw corpus from the children's trust within 15 days following any contribution, or that such demand could have been legally resisted by the trustees. In fact, the parties have stipulated that "following a contribution to the children's trust, each of the grandchildren possessed the *same right of withdrawal* as ... the withdrawal rights of Frank Cristofani and Lillian Dawson." (Emphasis added.) The legal right of decedent's grandchildren to withdraw specified amounts from the trust corpus within 15 days following any contribution of property constitutes a gift of a present interest. Crummey v. Commissioner, supra.

On brief, respondent attempts to distinguish *Crummey* from the instant case. Respondent argues that in *Crummey* the trust beneficiaries not only possessed an immediate right of withdrawal, but also possessed "substantial, future economic benefits" in the trust corpus and income. Respondent emphasizes that the children's trust identified decedent's children as "primary beneficiaries," and that decedent's grandchildren were to be considered as "beneficiaries of secondary importance."

Generally, the beneficiaries of the trust in *Crummey* were entitled to distributions of income. Trust corpus was to be distributed to the issue of each beneficiary sometime following the beneficiary's death. See Crummey v. Commissioner, T.C. Memo. 1966–144. Aside from the discretionary actions of the trustee, the only way any beneficiary in *Crummey* could receive trust corpus was through the demand provision which allowed each beneficiary to demand up to $4,000 in the year in which a transfer to the trust was made. The Ninth Circuit observed:

> In our case ... if no demand is made in any particular year, the additions are forever removed from the uncontrolled reach of the beneficiary since, with exception of the yearly demand provision, the only way the corpus can ever be tapped by a beneficiary, is through a distribution at the discretion of the trustee. [Crummey v. Commissioner, 397 F.2d at 88.]

In the instant case, the primary beneficiaries of the children's trust were decedent's children. Decedent's grandchildren held contingent remainder interests in the children's trust. Decedent's grandchildren's interests vested only in the event that their respective parent (decedent's child) predeceased decedent or failed to survive decedent by more than 120 days. We do not believe, however, that *Crummey* requires that the beneficiaries of a trust must have a vested present interest or vested remainder interest in the trust corpus or income, in order to qualify for the section 2503(b) exclusion.

As discussed in *Crummey*, the likelihood that the beneficiary will actually receive present enjoyment of the property is not the test for determining whether a present interest was received. Rather, we must examine the ability of the beneficiaries, in a legal sense, to exercise their right to withdraw trust corpus, and the trustee's right to legally resist a beneficiary's demand for payment. Crummey v. Commissioner, 397 F.2d at 88. Based upon the language of the trust instrument and stipulations of the parties, we believe that each grandchild possessed the legal right to withdraw trust corpus and that the trustees would be unable to legally resist a grandchild's withdrawal demand. We note that there was no agreement or understanding between decedent, the trustees, and the beneficiaries that the grandchildren would not exercise their withdrawal rights following a contribution to the children's trust.

Respondent also argues that since the grandchildren possessed only a contingent remainder interest in the children's trust, decedent never intended to benefit her grandchildren. Respondent contends that the only reason decedent gave her grandchildren the right to withdraw trust corpus was to obtain the benefit of the annual exclusion.

We disagree. Based upon the provisions of the children's trust, we believe that decedent intended to benefit her grandchildren. Their benefits, as remaindermen, were contingent upon a child of decedent's dying before decedent or failing to survive decedent by more than 120 days. We recognize that at the time decedent executed the children's trust, decedent's children were in good health, but this does not remove the possibility that decedent's children could have predeceased decedent.

In addition, decedent's grandchildren possessed the power to withdraw up to an amount equal to the amount allowable for the 2503(b) exclusion. Although decedent's grandchildren never exercised their respective withdrawal rights, this does not vitiate the fact that they had the legal right to do so, within 15 days following a contribution to the children's trust. Events might have occurred to prompt decedent's children and grandchildren (through their guardians) to exercise their withdrawal rights. For example, either or both of decedent's children and their respective families might have suddenly and unexpectedly been faced with economic hardship; or, in the event of the insolvency of one of decedent's children, the rights of the grandchildren might have been exercised to safeguard their interest in the trust assets from their parents' creditors. In light of the provisions in decedent's trust, we fail to see how respondent can argue that decedent did not intend to benefit her grandchildren.

Finally, the fact that the trust provisions were intended to obtain the benefit of the annual gift tax exclusion does not change the result. As we stated in Perkins v. Commissioner, [27 T.C. 601 (1956)],

> regardless of the petitioners' motives, or why they did what they in fact did, the legal rights in question were created by the trust instruments and could at any time thereafter be exercised. Petitioners having done what they purported to do, their tax-saving motive is irrelevant. [27 T.C. at 606.]

Based upon the foregoing, we find that the grandchildren's right to withdraw an amount not to exceed the section 2503(b) exclusion, represents a present interest for purposes of section 2503(b). Accordingly, petitioner is entitled to claim annual exclusions with respect to decedent's grandchildren as a result of decedent's transfers of property to the children's trust in 1984 and 1985.

Decision will be entered for the petitioner. . . .

NOTES

1. *Internal Revenue Service position on demand powers.* Rev. Rul. 73–405, 1973–2 C.B. 321, revoking an earlier contrary ruling, holds that a gift in trust for a minor beneficiary subject to a demand power will not be denied the exclusion merely because a guardian has not been appointed, provided there is no impediment under the terms of the trust or state law to the appointment of a guardian and the minor has the right to demand distribution. Must the minor be aware of the demand power or of the right to apply for the appointment of a guardian? In a ruling involving a demand trust for the benefit of an adult beneficiary, the Service held that "the donor's intent . . . is a relevant consideration in determining when the rights actually conferred are meant to be enjoyed," and that the donor's failure to inform the beneficiary of the demand right before it lapsed at the end of the year of the transfer rendered it "illusory," with the result that the gift was a future interest and not entitled to the exclusion. Rev. Rul. 81–7, 1981–1 C.B. 474. In a subsequent ruling, the Service distinguished Rev. Rul. 81–7 and allowed the exclusion for a gift made on December 29 even though the donee became aware of the demand power only on January 6 of the following calendar year; the demand power remained exercisable for 45 days after notice, which was required to be given within 10 days of the gift. Rev. Rul. 83–108, 1983–2 C.B. 167. What constitutes an adequate time period for the exercise of a *Crummey* withdrawal power will depend on the circumstances of each case. A 15–day period was held sufficient in *Cristofani*, but many practitioners recommend a longer period (60 days, for example) as the more prudent course.

2. *Aftermath of Cristofani.* The Service has announced its acquiescence in the result in *Cristofani*, while disagreeing with the Tax Court's lenient view of demand powers:

> The Service does not contest annual gift tax exclusions for *Crummey* powers where the trust instrument gives the power holders a bona fide unrestricted legal right to demand immediate possession and enjoyment of trust income or corpus. See Rev. Rul. 85–24, 1985–1 C.B. 329; Rev. Rul. 81–7, 1981–1 C.B. 474. Current income beneficiaries and persons with vested remainder interests have a continuing economic interest in the trust and must weigh the benefit of a present withdrawal against their long term interests. Generally, the Service will not contest annual gift tax exclusions for *Crummey* powers held by these beneficiaries.
>
> . . . However, the Service will deny the exclusions for *Crummey* powers, regardless of the power holders' other interests in the trust, where the withdrawal rights are not in substance what they purport to be in form. See Gregory v. Helvering, 293 U.S. 465, 469 (1935). If the facts and circumstances of a particular case show that there was a prearranged

understanding that the withdrawal right would not be exercised or that doing so would result in adverse consequences to its holder (e.g., losing other rights or gifts under the instant trust instrument or other beneficial arrangement), the creation of the withdrawal right is not a bona fide gift of a present interest in property. Cf. Heyen v. United States, 945 F.2d 359 (10th Cir. 1991)....

Although the Service did not appeal [the *Cristofani* decision], the Service disagrees with the Tax Court's sweeping interpretation of *Crummey*. To extend the benefit of the annual exclusion to illusory gifts of present interests would undermine significantly the unified system of estate and gift taxation and invite flagrant abuse of the benefit which Congress intended in enacting section 2503(b). Accordingly, the Service will continue to litigate cases whose facts indicate that the substance of the transfers was merely to obtain annual exclusions and that no bona fide gift of a present interest was intended. [AOD 1996–10 (Jul. 15, 1996).]

Can a tacit "agreement or understanding" be inferred from a donee's subsequent failure to exercise a demand power? Does it matter whether the donor expects that the power will not be exercised? In Heyen v. United States, 945 F.2d 359 (10th Cir. 1991), the donor transferred separate blocks of stock valued at less than $10,000 to 29 recipients; all but two of the recipients promptly endorsed stock certificates in blank so that the stock could be retransferred to members of the donor's family. Invoking "substance over form," the court disregarded the intermediate recipients, noting that the donor "merely used those recipients to create gift tax exclusions to avoid paying gift tax on indirect gifts to the actual family member beneficiaries." 945 F.2d at 363.

3. *Gift tax treatment of lapsing withdrawal powers.* To obtain the benefit of the annual exclusion, a *Crummey* withdrawal power must be exercisable immediately by the donee with no substantial restrictions. The power constitutes a general power of appointment, and its exercise, release or lapse during the holder's life generally is treated as a transfer of the underlying property for gift and estate tax purposes. §§ 2514 (gift tax) and 2041 (estate tax). The *Crummey* power, however, usually is designed to take advantage of a statutory exemption for the lifetime lapse of a general power over up to $5,000 (or 5 percent of the value of the underlying property, if larger). §§ 2514(e) and 2041(b)(2). Thus, if appropriately limited in amount, a *Crummey* power can be structured to avoid gift tax both to the original donor at the time of its creation (§ 2503(b)) and to the donee at the time of lapse (§ 2514(e)). If the power is held at death, the underlying property is includible in the holder's gross estate under § 2041. The treatment of lapsing powers is discussed infra at page 418.

4. *Demand power as a target for reform.* The *Crummey* power is a gimmick, pure and simple. The donor has no intention that it be used; indeed, a teenage donee who toys with the idea of making the demand must consider the possibility that because of this rash act the donor may withhold additional gifts in future years. In recent years demand powers have repeatedly been identified as a target for legislative reform.

One proposal advocates continuation of the $10,000 per-donee exclusion, subject to a limit of $30,000 on the total amount that can be claimed each year ($60,000 if the donor's spouse joins in making gifts). An additional de minimis per-donee exclusion ($100 is put forward for illustrative purposes) would be available for donees not covered by the $30,000. The "present interest" rule would be replaced by a requirement that the gift be "vested." ABA Tax Section Task Force, Report on Transfer Tax Restructuring, 41 Tax Law. 395, 401 (1988). These proposals are subject to critical review in Gutman, A Comment on the ABA Tax Section Task Force Report on Transfer Tax Restructuring, id. at 653, 657–60. Professor Gutman would prefer to return to the original purpose of the exclusion and set an amount representing "a realistic appraisal of the aggregate value of incidental 'hard to keep track of' gifts an individual would be expected to make to a single donee." The exclusion would be coordinated with an expanded exclusion for consumption expenses under a revised version of § 2503(e). The exclusion would be available for gifts in cash or specific property but not for transfers in trust, nor for transfers "which must be recorded by an intermediary," such as stocks, registered debt obligations, real property and life insurance policies, on the theory that donors should have no difficulty keeping track of such gifts.

Other proposals would curtail the tax benefits of demand powers by denying the exclusion for all transfers in trust, or by allowing the exclusion for trust transfers only in limited circumstances. For example, the exclusion might be allowed only if the donee were the sole beneficiary of the trust and held either beneficial interests tantamount to absolute ownership of the trust property or a nonlapsing, unrestricted power of withdrawal. See Sherman, 'Tis a Gift to Be Simple: The Need for a New Definition of "Future Interest" for Gift Tax Purposes, 55 U. Cin. L. Rev. 585 (1987); Smith, Should We Give Away the Annual Exclusion? 1 Fla. Tax Rev. 361 (1993); Steinkamp, Common Sense and the Gift Tax Annual Exclusion, 72 Neb. L. Rev. 106 (1993); Staff of Joint Comm. on Taxation, Options to Improve Tax Compliance and Reform Tax Expenditures 405–08 (2005).

3. TRANSFERS TO MINORS

LEVINE'S ESTATE v. COMMISSIONER

526 F.2d 717 (2d Cir. 1975).

KAUFMAN, CHIEF JUDGE.

One suspects that because the Internal Revenue Code ... piles exceptions upon exclusions, it invites efforts to outwit the tax collector. The case before us is an example of adroit taxpayers seizing upon words in the Code which, if interpreted as they urge, would distort congressional intent and violate well-established rules of statutory construction. We therefore reverse the decision of the Tax Court favoring the taxpayers, 63 T.C. 136 (1974).

I

The facts in this case have been stipulated. On December 30, 1968 David H. Levine, a Connecticut resident, established identical irrevocable trusts for five grandchildren whose ages then ranged from 2 to 15 years. The corpus of each trust consisted of common stock of New Haven Moving Equipment Corporation. The shares were valued at $3,750. Unless a designated "Independent Trustee" saw fit in his discretion to direct otherwise, the trustees were to retain all income generated until the grandchild-beneficiary reached age 21. At that time, the accumulated income would be distributed in toto. Thereafter, the beneficiary would receive payments at least annually of all income earned by the trust. If the grandchild died before his or her twenty-first birthday, all accumulated income would go to the estate of the grandchild.

During the lifetime of the beneficiary, control over the trust corpus was vested exclusively in the "absolute and uncontrolled discretion" of the Independent Trustee. He could permit the principal to stand untouched or he could pay out any portion directly to, or for the benefit of, the beneficiary. In addition, the trustee could terminate the trust at any time by distributing the entire corpus. The trust also provided the beneficiary with a limited power of appointment in the event that any of the principal remained in the trust upon his or her death. The corpus, or any part of it, could be designated to pass to some or all of David H. Levine's lineal descendants. The original beneficiary could not elect to leave corpus to his or her own estate, his or her creditors, or the creditors of the original beneficiary's estate. . . .

II

The dispute focuses on the interpretation and interrelation of §§ 2503(b) and (c) of the Internal Revenue Code. . . .

At first blush, it might seem that the Levine trusts clearly fail to satisfy the requirements of § 2503(c)(2). The "property"—if defined as the corpus—would not pass to the donee when the beneficiary turned 21. Nor would it be payable to the donee's estate if death occurred before the age of 21 years. The power of appointment established by each trust over the corpus also fails the tests set forth in § 2514(c).

The problem, however, is somewhat more complex. The Supreme Court in *Disston* [325 U.S. 442 (1945)] and *Fondren* [324 U.S. 18 (1945)] recognized that a gift may be divided into component parts for tax purposes. One or more of those elements may qualify as present interests even if others do not. The Tax Court applied these principles in a 1961 decision involving a trust similar to Levine's. Herr v. C.I.R., 35 T.C. 732 (1961). Treating the income to be accumulated to age 21 (the "pre–21 income interest") as a separate element of "property," id. at 737, the Tax Court held that this segment satisfied the requirements of § 2503(c) and the taxpayer could therefore benefit from the § 2503(b) exclusion. The Third Circuit affirmed the Tax Court, 303 F.2d 780 (3d Cir. 1962). The Commissioner has acquiesced in the *Herr* decision, 1968–2 Cum. Bull. 2, and accordingly concedes in the present case that the pre–21 income interest is eligible for the gift tax exclusion.

The pre–21 income interests in the Levine trusts do not, however, exhaust the $3,000 per donee annual exclusion. Knowing that the remainder interests cannot qualify as present interests under either § 2503(b) or § 2503(c), the Levines have concentrated their attention on the post–21 income interests. Although the taxpayer in *Herr* did not suggest that the post–21 segment could properly be considered a present interest, the Tax Court explicitly spoke to the issue: "[I]ncome [after] 21 ... [is a] future interest." 35 T.C. at 736. And the Court of Appeals commented similarly: "[T]he right[s] to income and principal after minority are future interests." 303 F.2d at 782. The taxpayers ask us to disregard these views and to extend the holding of *Herr* so that the post–21 income interests will be treated as present interests. We decline to do so.

III

If the post–21 income interests are looked upon as separate gifts, they cannot be considered present interests under § 2503(b). As in the case of the remainder interests, initial enjoyment is delayed until a time in the future. Moreover, the requirements of § 2503(c)(2) are not satisfied.

The taxpayers urge that we are required to treat the post–21 income interests as one with the pre–21 income interests, but that the remainder interests should be considered a separate gift. The taxpayers recognize that the combined pre– and post–21 income interests do not qualify as a present interest when viewed solely in the light of § 2503(b). This is so because the accumulation of income before age 21 works as a postponement of immediate enjoyment. In addition, the combined income interests fail to meet the criteria of § 2503(c)(2).

The Levines seek to overcome these obstacles by means of an ingenious argument. The combination of pre–21 and post–21 income interests resembles a unitary life estate, they argue. The only reason it cannot qualify as a § 2503(b) present interest, they urge, is the accumulation provision that permits enjoyment to be delayed until age 21. But, they say, § 2503(c) as interpreted by *Herr* permits the future interest characteristic of the pre–21 income interests to be disregarded for the purpose of receiving the § 2503(b) exclusion. In other words, they assert that *Herr* and § 2503(c) in effect transform the pre–21 income interests into present interests. Then, by a giant leap, the taxpayers conclude that a single, lifetime present interest is produced by linking the pre–21 *constructive* present interests with the post–21 income interests.

A study of the statutory language, however, convinces us that Congress did not contemplate such an "off-again, on-again" elusive treatment of the pre–21 segment of the transfers in trust. Moreover, we cannot be unmindful of the rule of construction that Congress permits exclusions only as a matter of grace, and the exclusions sections are to be strictly construed against the taxpayer. See Standard Oil Co. v. United States, 338 F.2d 4, 8 (2d Cir. 1964); Bingler v. Johnson, 394 U.S. 741, 752 (1969). Nor does the legislative history prove more helpful to the taxpayers. The

House Report, H.R. Rep. No. 1337, 83d Cong., 2d Sess. A322, 3 U.S. Code Cong. & Admin. News, p. 4465 (1954), explained that § 2503(c)

> *partially* relaxes the "future interest" restriction contained in [§ 2503(b)], in the case of gifts to minors, by providing a *specific type of gift* for which the exclusion will be allowed. If *the gift* may be expended by, or for the benefit of, the minor donee prior to his attaining the age of 21 years, and, to the extent not so expended, will pass to the donee at that time, but if the donee dies prior to that time, will pass to the donee's estate or as he may appoint by will under a general power of appointment, *the gift* will not be treated as a future interest. [emphasis added]

See also 3 U.S.Code Cong. & Admin. News at p. 5123 (Senate Report, refers to a "*certain type* of gift to a minor which will not be treated as a gift of a future interest" [emphasis added]). The special treatment of pre–21 income interests in *Herr* could be justified as not *penalizing* the taxpayer for linking pre–21 income interests with other interests. But, the Levines would have us *reward* such a combination, since the post–21 income interest clearly could not, by itself, qualify for the annual exclusion.

There is one additional factor that we cannot ignore. The *Herr* opinions rejecting the contention that a post–21 income interest can be a § 2503 present interest were rendered more than a decade ago. Extensive attention has been paid by the treatises, commentators, and tax services to the *Herr* decisions, and "no other field of legislation receives as much continuous, sustained and detailed attention" from Congress as does tax law. 3 Sutherland on Statutory Construction § 66.02 at 184 (4th ed. 1974). Congress has had ample opportunity to amend the Code if it disagreed with the interpretation of §§ 2503(b) and (c) set forth in *Herr*. See Georgia v. United States, 411 U.S. 526, 533 (1973).

Accordingly, we reverse the decision of the Tax Court and remand.

NOTES

1. *Internal Revenue Service position on gifts to minors.* Rev. Rul. 54–400, 1954–2 C.B. 319, sets out the following position on gifts to minors:

> An unqualified and unrestricted gift to a minor, with or without the appointment of a legal guardian, is a gift of a present interest; and disabilities placed upon minors by State statutes should not be considered decisive in determining whether such donees have the immediate enjoyment of the property or the income therefrom within the purport of the Federal gift tax law.... In the case of an outright and unrestricted gift to a minor, the mere existence or nonexistence of a legal guardianship does not of itself raise the question whether the gift is of a future interest.... It is only where delivery of the property to the guardian of a minor is accompanied by limitations upon the present use and enjoyment of the property by the donee, by way of a trust or otherwise, that the question of a future interest arises.

If the taxpayer gives an imported sports car to his daughter and warns that it will be taken away if she misbehaves, has the parent made a gift or a revocable transfer? If a gift, is the exclusion allowable?

2. *State custodianship statutes.* Every state has enacted in some form the Uniform Transfers to Minors Act (or its predecessor, the Uniform Gifts to Minors Act), which authorizes gifts to a minor by transferring cash, securities, or other property to a custodian, who may be the donor, another adult individual, or a bank; the statute further authorizes the custodian to apply the property and the income therefrom for the minor's benefit with a minimum of legal supervision. The property, together with any unexpended income, is paid to the minor at age 21; if the minor dies before then, the payment is made to the minor's estate. The Service has ruled that gifts under these statutes are complete and eligible for the exclusion. Rev. Rul. 59–357, 1959–2 C.B. 212. If the age when the property will pass to the donee is reduced from 21 to 18 years, to accord with the age of majority under state law, gifts pursuant to the amended statute continue to qualify for the exclusion. Rev. Rul. 73–287, 1973–2 C.B. 321.

If a parent makes a gift by taking title to property in his or her name as custodian, why is the transfer a completed gift rather than a revocable transfer, in view of the custodian's power to apply the property to the minor's support, maintenance, and education—i.e., to expenses for which the parent is legally responsible?

3. *Trustee's power to expend property for donee's benefit.* Does § 2503(c) apply if the trustee may use trust income only for specified extraordinary needs of the minor? According to Reg. § 25.2503–4(b), the trustee may have discretion over the amounts and the purposes of expenditures "provided there are no substantial restrictions under the terms of the trust instrument on the exercise of such discretion." In Rev. Rul. 67–270, 1967–2 C.B. 349, the Service ruled that if "a trust instrument provides that the trust property may be expended during the donee's minority for purposes which have no objective limitations (i.e., 'welfare,' 'happiness,' and 'convenience') and [such] provisions when read as a whole approximate the scope of the term 'benefit,' as used in § 2503(c)," the "no substantial restriction" requirement of the regulations is satisfied. See also Williams v. United States, 378 F.2d 693 (Ct. Cl. 1967) (trustee authorized to use income and corpus if in his opinion the minor beneficiary needed funds for maintenance, education, medical care, support, or general welfare, and "the cost and expenses incident thereto are not otherwise adequately provided for"; held, quoted phrase does not place a substantial restriction on the trustee's discretion); but see Faber v. United States, 439 F.2d 1189 (6th Cir. 1971) (limitation on use of income to provide "for accident, illness or other emergency" constituted a substantial restriction on trustee's discretion to use income for minor's benefit; exclusion disallowed).

What if a trustee is given the same powers that a guardian would have under state law to expend property for the minor's benefit? In Ross v. United States, 348 F.2d 577 (5th Cir. 1965), the court noted that "[t]he trust instruments, in spirit and in letter, give the trustees, at the very least, all the powers of a guardian under Texas law," and concluded that the requirements of § 2503(c)(1) were met:

> It is true that under Texas law, a guardian may spend the corpus of his ward's estate (1) only for the maintenance and education of the ward, (2) only where the parents of the ward cannot provide adequate support, and (3) except in cases of emergency, only after obtaining a court order. But these restrictions, in themselves, do not require that a gift through a Texas guardian be treated as a future interest for purposes of section 2503. An outright gift by a donor to the guardian of a minor is considered a gift of a present and not a future interest under section 2503(b); and limitations imposed by state law on the guardian's use of the property do not make the gift one of a future interest. Beatrice B. Briggs, 1960, 34 T.C. 1132. A gift in trust for a minor "as if the trustee herein were holding the property as guardian" for the donee has been held to be a gift of a present interest under section 2503(b) of the Code and is, therefore, entitled to the [annual] exclusion for taxable gifts permitted by that section. That state laws pertaining to guardianships might pose barriers to the immediate enjoyment of a gift in trust will not cause the gift to be denied present-interest status. United States v. Baker, 4 Cir. 1956, 236 F.2d 317.... The district court in Arizona has held that a gift to minors in trust qualified for the annual exclusion even though "resort to a court of equity might be necessary" in order for the trustee to invade the trust principal. DeConcini v. Wood, D.C. Ariz. 1960, 60–1 U.S.T.C. par. 11,938. In light of the authorities—such as they are—we read the words "*may be expended*" in section 2503(c) to mean "*may be expended within the limitations imposed on guardians by state law.*" ...
>
> We find that the existence of reasonable, prudent, and ordinary restrictions imposed by state law on the powers of a guardian do not, in themselves, disqualify a gift to a minor represented by a guardian. Here the trustees had all the powers of a guardian, and more. We hold, therefore, that the taxpayers were entitled to the annual exclusion for the gifts in question. [348 F.2d at 579, 581.]

4. *Disposition if donee dies before age 21.* Section 2503(c)(2)(B) requires that the unexpended property and income be payable to the donee's estate or to such persons as the donee may appoint under a general power of appointment as defined in § 2514(c). Is § 2503(c)(2)(B) satisfied if the unexpended property and income are payable as the donee may appoint if he dies before age 21, but in default of appointment are to be paid to specified persons rather than to his estate? Note that in such a case the property would go to persons designated by the donor if the donee dies before he is old enough to exercise a power of appointment. Does § 2503(c)(2)(B) require, in other words, that the property must go either to the donee's estate or to persons whom he (rather than the donor) designates? Even if the property is so payable, it will go to the donee's intestate successors if he dies before he is old enough to make a will or exercise a power of appointment. See Reg. § 25.2503–4. If the terms of the gift require the unexpended property and income to be distributed to the donee's descendants, next of kin, or heirs at law, the gift does not qualify as a disposition to the donee's "estate" because these takers are not necessarily identical with those who would take the

estate. Ross v. Commissioner, 652 F.2d 1365 (9th Cir. 1981) (heirs at law); Clinard v. Commissioner, 40 T.C. 878 (1963) (next of kin).

5. *Extending a § 2503(c) trust.* Reg. § 25.2503–4(b) permits the donor to grant the donee a power to extend the trust on reaching age 21 without disqualifying the gift under § 2503(c). The Service originally took the position that a trust would not qualify for the annual exclusion if the donee had to perform a positive act upon reaching age 21 in order to receive the property. After losing several cases on the issue (notably Heidrich v. Commissioner, 55 T.C. 746 (1971)), the Service modified its position in Rev. Rul. 74–43, 1974–1 C.B. 285:

> [A] gift to a minor in trust, with the provision that the beneficiary has, upon reaching age 21, either (1) a continuing right to compel immediate distribution of the trust corpus by giving written notice to the trustee, or to permit the trust to continue by its own terms, or (2) a right during a limited period to compel immediate distribution of the trust corpus by giving written notice to the trustee which if not exercised will permit the trust to continue by its own terms, will not be considered to be the gift of a future interest. . . .

E. DISCLAIMERS: § 2518

Section 2518, enacted in 1976, provides that if a person makes a "qualified disclaimer" of an interest in property, the federal gift, estate, and generation-skipping transfer taxes apply as if the disclaimed interest "had never been transferred to such person." To illustrate the operation of this provision, assume that in her will a decedent left a bequest of $100,000 to *A* and the rest of her estate to *B*. Assume further that *A*, for whatever reason, is willing to give up the benefit of the decedent's largesse in favor of *B*. Of course, *A* could simply accept the bequest and then immediately transfer $100,000 to *B*; this would result in a taxable gift from *A* to *B*. Alternatively, *A* could disclaim the bequest and thereby cause the $100,000 to fall into the residuary estate passing to *B*. If *A*'s disclaimer qualifies under § 2518, the bequest will be treated as passing directly from the decedent to *B* without ever passing through *A*'s hands, even though *B* is richer by $100,000 as a result of *A*'s act of generosity. Although the decedent's initial transfer is subject to estate tax, no further gift tax is imposed. In effect, *A*'s role in shifting the bequest to *B* is disregarded.

Basically, a disclaimer is a refusal to accept a donative transfer of an interest in property. To qualify under § 2518, a disclaimer must be irrevocable, unconditional, and made in writing. The writing must be received by the original transferor (or the transferor's legal representative or the holder of title to the transferred property) not later than nine months after the date of the transfer creating the interest or, if later, the date on which the disclaimant reaches age 21. The disclaimant must not have accepted the interest or any of its benefits, and the interest must pass, as a result of the disclaimer and without any direction by the disclaimant, to the original transferor's surviving spouse or some person other than the disclaimant. § 2518(b).

MONROE'S ESTATE v. COMMISSIONER

124 F.3d 699 (5th Cir. 1997).

JONES, CIRCUIT JUDGE:

I. Background

This case requires interpretation of § 2518(b) of the Internal Revenue Code and its accompanying regulations, which describe "qualified disclaimer" of benefits, a device commonly used for "post-mortem" estate and other tax planning. The disclaimants here were 29 legatees of the wife's will, all of whom were asked by her husband and did irrevocably disclaim the proffered bequests. Shortly afterward, the husband gave them gifts equaling or exceeding the bequests, and not long after that he died at age 93. The Tax Court concluded that the disclaimers were induced or coerced by "the implied promise that [the disclaimants] would be better off if they did what Monroe wanted them to do . . .," even though he made no explicit promises. Finding that the "coerced/induced" standard is inconsistent with the regulations and a fair reading of the statute, we reverse on nearly all of the disclaimers.

On April 28, 1989, Louise S. Monroe died at the age of 91, leaving a multimillion dollar estate. J. Edgar Monroe (Monroe), her husband, became executor of the estate. Monroe, who was then 92 years old, sought help from Robert Monroe, his nephew, in administering the estate. An estate tax return was timely filed in March 1990. Edgar Monroe died in May 1990.

The Monroes had no children, but Louise Monroe's will made 31 specific cash bequests to extended family members, long-time employees, and friends, as well as 4 bequests to corporate entities. Louise Monroe also made bequests in trust to two grandnieces and a grandnephew, giving each a treasury bond with a $500,000 face value. Monroe was the residual beneficiary of his wife's estate.

. . . Deeply concerned about the high tax burden on the individual bequests, Monroe and Robert Monroe decided to pursue disclaimers as a means of reducing the overall federal tax liability. Before requesting the disclaimers, Monroe received assurance from Touche Ross [an accounting firm retained by the estate] that he could independently make gifts to the legatees and include bequests to them in his own will. The accountants also advised Robert Monroe that a disclaimer was only valid if it was done without the promise of anything in return.

With assistance from the accountants, Monroe and Robert Monroe identified 29 legatees to approach about renouncing. Robert Monroe rehearsed with one of the accountants his presentation to the legatees. In substance, Robert Monroe made the following points: his uncle was upset about the amount of taxes that would have to be paid by the estate and the legatees; each bequest would be significantly reduced by taxes; his uncle would like each legatee to disclaim his or her bequest; each legatee who disclaimed would be giving up a right; and any disclaimer had to be voluntary and without consideration.

Monroe personally asked Kathleen Gooden Hayward, Monroe's grand-niece and one of the legatees of a $500,000 treasury bond, as well as four household employees to give up their bequests. Robert Monroe made some version of his presentation to the remaining 24 legatees on the list. In December 1989, each of the 29 legatees signed a disclaimer, conceded by the Commissioner to be valid and effective under Louisiana law. The total amount disclaimed was $892,781, and this amount was included in the marital deduction on the estate tax return as money which passed to Monroe.

In late December 1989 and January 1990, Monroe wrote each of the disclaimants a personal check in an amount approximately equal to the gross amount of the bequest renounced....

After an audit, the Commissioner disallowed the marital deduction claimed in the estate tax return....

On the estate's petition for redetermination, the Tax Court, although noting that each disclaimer was motivated by different factors, analyzed the disclaimers as a group, citing only a few examples. The Tax Court summarized the motivation for the disclaimants' actions as follows:

> Some of the disclaimants were told by the nephew that Monroe had always taken care of them and had never cheated them or that Monroe was a generous man. Many of the disclaimants anticipated that Monroe would continue to care for them financially or was likely to make a bequest to them in his will. Some disclaimants believed that executing the disclaimer would be in their best long-term interest, because they did not wish to upset Monroe by refusing to renounce.

The Tax Court agreed with the Commissioner on 28 of 29 disclaimers and, although it denied a fraud penalty, on the imposition of a negligence penalty. The Tax Court concluded that the disclaimers were not "qualified disclaimers" under I.R.C. § 2518(b). The resulting deficiency was $625,552.73, plus a negligence penalty of $125,104.55. The taxpayer appealed.

II. The Tax Court Decision

When a legatee, other than a surviving spouse, makes a qualified disclaimer that causes the surviving spouse to be entitled to the property, the disclaimed interest is treated as if it passed directly to the surviving spouse. See Estate Tax Regs. § 20.2056(d)–1(b). An estate may take a marital deduction for property passing directly from the decedent to a surviving spouse. See I.R.C. § 2056(a). Thus, the estate's marital deduction depends on whether the 29 disclaimers at issue are qualified disclaimers....

Section 2518(b) provides that "the term 'qualified disclaimer' means an irrevocable and unqualified refusal by a person to accept an interest in property but only if ... (3) such person has not accepted the interest or any of its benefits...."

In concluding that all but one of the disclaimers were not qualified within the meaning of § 2518, the Tax Court reasoned that the disclaimants

> expected, for one reason or another, that they would receive their renounced bequests in the form of a gift or legacy from Monroe. Furthermore, the testimony of many of the disclaimants suggests that they feared what would happen if they refused to renounce their bequests....
>
> The disclaimants may not have explicitly negotiated with or bargained with Monroe or the nephew for consideration in return for executing their disclaimers. Each of the disclaimants other than Helene Tebo, however, was induced or, in some instances, coerced, into executing a disclaimer. Under these circumstances, the consideration for their disclaimers was the implied promise that they would be better off if they did what Monroe wanted them to do than if they refused to do so. Their disclaimers thus were not "unqualified" as required by section 2518.

The Tax Court analyzed the 29 disclaimers as a group, citing excerpts of trial testimony from three disclaimants as "representative of that of a majority of the disclaimants." First, the Tax Court cited the testimony of Lawrence Lee, who had served as a butler and chauffeur to the Monroes since 1949. Lee renounced a specific bequest of $50,000 as well as a bequest in the amount of his annual salary, or $10,000. Approximately three weeks later, he received a check from Monroe for $60,000 bearing the notation "gift." Lee testified in part:

> Q. What did he [J. Edgar Monroe] ask you?
>
> A. He asked us to renounce, give it—turn it over to him.
>
> Q. Did he say why?
>
> A. No, I don't think. I can't remember exactly for what reason, other than to turn it over to him, and he would take care of it.
>
> Q. He would take care of you if you turned it over to him.
>
> A. Yes.

The Tax Court also relied on the testimony of Betsy Richardson, a niece of the Monroes. Before Louise Monroe's death, Richardson's daughter, Lisa, had been sick with cancer, and Monroe had paid $10,000 toward Lisa's treatment as well as $10,000 upon her high school graduation. At trial, Richardson testified why she renounced a $5,000 bequest from Louise Monroe:

Q. Why did you ultimately decide to sign the act of renunciation?

A. Because, like I said, I didn't know if I would need help for her [Lisa] later, and you just—you don't go against Edgar if you ever want anything from him.

The Tax Court also cited testimony from Kathleen Hayward, Monroe's grand niece. Hayward disclaimed her right to income from the $500,000 bond bequeathed to her in trust.... Testifying that she thought of the Monroes as her parents, Hayward described a long, consistent pattern of the Monroes' generosity toward her....

After Louise Monroe died, Robert Monroe approached Hayward about the renunciation. She also talked with Monroe about renouncing.... Hayward talked over the idea with her husband and with an attorney, who cautioned her that she was giving up a right. After stating that she received nothing in exchange for her disclaimer, was not promised anything by Robert or Edgar Monroe, and had no agreement that Edgar Monroe would do anything for her later, Hayward gave the testimony seized upon by the Tax Court:

Q. Isn't it true that you told the agents that you knew from the conversation with J. Edgar Monroe that you would get the inheritance money, if not shortly after renouncing the bequest, then in his will?

A. He didn't state that. I sort of certainly assumed that.

The Tax Court next highlighted testimony from Robert Monroe. He stated that he had not bargained with the disclaimants and had not made any promises that Edgar Monroe would make payments to the legatees in return for the disclaimers. On cross-examination, he was asked why he mentioned his uncle's generosity as a part of his presentation to the legatees:

Q. What has generosity got to do with disclaiming on the part of a person being disclaimed in favor of it?

A. It puts into perspective the fact that someone is asking you to do something and he's not promising you anything. He's not giving you anything, but at least you're identifying what type of person he is or was, anyway.

Focusing upon this testimony, the Tax Court concluded that Robert Monroe

> intended to buttress the legatees' confidence in Monroe's continued generosity....
>
> The nephew's testimony demonstrates that he intended to inform the disclaimants that the probability that they would receive something from Monroe in the future was good. Conversely, if the legatees refused to disclaim, they were unlikely to receive anything from Monroe subsequently, because their refusal would be against Monroe's wishes.

Thus, the Tax Court concluded that the disclaimers were not "unqualified" within the meaning of § 2518, and that the subsequent payments by Monroe were not "merely part of a pattern of generosity" but were in return for the execution of the disclaimers. . . .

IV. Discussion

. . . If the disclaimers in this case fail to meet the requirements of § 2518, it is either because they were not "irrevocable and unqualified," or because the disclaimants had "accepted the interest or any of its benefits." The Treasury Regulations further explain that acceptance of the interest within the meaning of § 2518(b)(3) includes not only explicit or implied acceptance of the interest or any of its benefits, but also the receipt of consideration in return for executing the disclaimer. See Treas. Reg. § 25.2518–2(d)(1).

Unqualified means "not modified by reservations or restrictions." Id. Under the plain meaning of the statute, an "irrevocable and unqualified" disclaimer is a relinquishment of a legal right that is incapable of being retracted or revoked by the disclaimant and is not modified by reservations or restrictions that limit its enforceability. None of the written disclaimers challenged by the Commissioner can be attacked as being subject to revocation or subject to some condition: the documents executed by the disclaimants are irrevocable and unqualified on their face.

Monroe's gifts, given after the disclaimants renounced their bequests, do not change the irrevocability of the disclaimers: once executed, the disclaimers were effective to give up the legatees' rights to their respective bequests from Louise Monroe's estate. . . .

But irrevocability is a side issue. The real bone of contention is whether the disclaimers were "unqualified," and whether unqualified has some meaning beyond the possibilities carefully delineated in the applicable Treasury Regulations. None of the written disclaimers articulates any kind of disabling qualification, of course. Nevertheless, the Tax Court and the Commissioner assert that because all but one of the disclaimants "expected," because they were "induced" or "coerced" by Monroe, that they would eventually receive their bequests in the form of a gift or legacy, their renunciations were "qualified" to the extent of the expectation. As the Tax Court later put it, a disclaimer is not "unqualified" if it rests on an "implied promise" that the disclaimant will be better off executing the disclaimer than not doing so. Further, according to the Tax Court, the "implied promise" may exist even though the disclaimants did not negotiate or bargain with Monroe for later recompense.

We disagree with this interpretation of "unqualified." It is inconsistent with a holistic reading of section 2518(b), contrary to the governing Treasury Regulations . . ., and intolerably, unnecessarily vague.

Section 2518(b) describes a covered disclaimer as one which is "unqualified . . . but only if [the disclaimant] . . . has not accepted the interest or any of its benefits." A "qualification," therefore, would seem to depend on the tangible receipt of property, i.e., the "interest or any of its benefits." That is also the most sensible understanding of an unqualified disclaimer. One who disclaims an interest in property must do so without getting something in exchange; and since property has been given up, it follows that a "qualified disclaimer" would be one in which the renunciation is not complete because property has been kept or received in return.

The Commissioner and Tax Court would eliminate this statutory symmetry by holding that a disclaimer of property is "qualified" even though something less than property, e.g. an "expectation" or "implied promise," is received in return. While their reading would enhance the government's ability to disqualify disclaimers, it also rests on an incomprehensible subjective standard. How likely is it, in tax terms, that people would disclaim "a bird in the hand" purely altruistically? Yet the clear inference to be drawn from the Tax Court's approach to this case is that a "qualified disclaimer" demands no less than disinterest in the "property or its benefits." The court voided all of the disclaimers here except that of Ms. Tebo, who acted solely for personal reasons in executing a disclaimer. On the contrary, ... a primary purpose of the law authorizing qualified disclaimers is to facilitate post-mortem estate tax planning and to increase family wealth on the "expectation" that there will thus remain more wealth to pass on to disclaimants in the future. Consequently, if the Tax Court's subjective interpretation of "unqualified" disclaimer is accepted, it undermines the very purpose for which the provision was enacted. It also ensures litigation in virtually every disclaimer situation, because it can be assumed that heirs and legatees rarely execute disclaimers for tax purposes without having had some "expectations" or "inducements" based on conversations with advisers on the prospective benefits of such a course of action.

Not only does the statutory language conflict with the Tax Court's interpretation of an "unqualified disclaimer," but the Treasury Regulations are also incompatible with the "expectation" or "implied promise" theory.... The regulations set forth two situations in which a disclaimer expresses a mere qualified refusal to accept an interest in property: when the disclaimant accepts, expressly or impliedly, the interest or any of its benefits; and when the disclaimant receives "consideration" in return for executing the disclaimer. Treas. Reg. § 25.2518–2(d)(1). Consistent with our interpretation, a disclaimant cannot purport to disclaim, while taking actual advantage of the property "or any of its benefits." Further, the disclaimant cannot accept "benefits" from the property by receiving consideration in exchange for the disclaimer. The juxtaposition in the regulation between the "implied" acceptance of the interest or any of its benefits and the "consideration" that must be received in exchange for a disclaimer is not accidental. One may impliedly accept the benefits of property, for instance by pledging it as security for a loan, and therefore act inconsistently when making an alleged disclaimer. On the other hand, only by receiving "consideration" in the classic sense does one receive "property" or any of its benefits in exchange for executing the disclaimer.

We thus agree with the estate that to have accepted the benefits of a disclaimed interest, the disclaimant must have received actual consideration in return for renouncing his legacy.

A disclaimant's mere expectation of a future benefit in return for executing a disclaimer will not render it "unqualified." "Consideration," used deliberately in the regulations, is a term of art. See Philpot v. Gruninger, 81 U.S. 570, 577 (1872); Fire Ins. Assn. v. Wickham, 141 U.S. 564, 579 (1891) (to constitute consideration, promise "must have been offered by one party, and accepted by the other, as one element of the contract").... Thus, the question for each disclaimer is whether the decision to disclaim was part of mutually-bargained-for consideration or a mere unenforceable hope of future benefit, whether that unenforceable hope springs from family ties, long-term friendship or employment, or a generalized fear that benefits will be withheld in the future absent execution of the disclaimer.

Accordingly, we also agree with the estate that the Tax Court was required to evaluate each disclaimer under the requirements of § 2518. The statutory requirements are applicable to each interest disclaimed. The estate submitted documentary evidence supporting all 29 disclaimers and testimony regarding all but two. Although the Tax Court singled out Helene Tebo, finding that she disclaimed her bequest for personal reasons, its opinion lumps the remaining 28 disclaimers together. As the Commissioner argues, the Tax Court may have focused on alleged inducement and/or coercion of the disclaimants by Robert and Edgar Monroe, rather than on each legatee's motivation for disclaiming. But the correct standard requires a finding whether there was actual bargained-for consideration for the disclaimers.

The rehearsed presentation by Robert Monroe does not in itself support a finding that there was consideration. He explained the estate tax problems created by the decedent's will and how executing the disclaimers would affect the distribution of property. He informed the legatees that they were giving up a right and that he could not promise them anything in return for that. The only potentially questionable part of the presentation was the reference to his uncle's generosity. The Tax Court found that the intent of this statement was

> to inform the disclaimants that the probability that they would receive something from Monroe in the future was good. Conversely, if the legatees refused to disclaim, they were unlikely to receive anything from Monroe subsequently, because their refusal would be against Monroe's wishes.

Even assuming that the Tax Court correctly ascertained Robert Monroe's intention, his statements merely reminding the disclaimants of Monroe's history of generosity, without demonstrating that the individual legatee did or could reasonably be expected to interpret such a reminder as a promise, do not invalidate the disclaimers. It is only where the evidence indicates that Robert or Edgar Monroe went further than this rehearsed presentation, or that a particular legatee interpreted this as a promise, that the Tax Court's findings might be supported. Furthermore, even if the record shows that Robert or Edgar Monroe went too far in their representations to a specific legatee, that does not support a generalization applicable to other disclaimants.

Turning to an evaluation of the record relevant to each disclaimer, we conclude that for the majority of the disclaimants, the evidence as a matter of law does not support a finding of any agreement that would amount to consideration for the execution of the disclaimers....

[The court reviewed evidence relating to each of the 29 disclaimers and concluded that 23 of them were "qualified disclaimers" within the meaning of § 2518(b). The other six disclaimers presented fact issues to be resolved on remand to the Tax Court.]

Finally, we disagree with the Commissioner's contention that the Tax Court's decision should be affirmed on substance-over-form or step-transaction grounds. While the disclaimants, to varying degrees, may have thought they would eventually receive something from Monroe, even the actual amount of their legacy, the evidence shows that most really believed they were, in fact, giving up their legacy under Louise Monroe's will. Several legatees sought outside counsel before making their decision. As long as there was no implicit agreement that they would receive something from Monroe in return for their disclaimers, the fact that the legatees understood they were giving up their rights and actually did, in a manner effective under Louisiana law, give up their rights is sufficient. There is no evidence that any of the legatees who executed disclaimers that we have held to be "qualified disclaimers" under § 2518(b) believed they were receiving their inheritance under Louise Monroe's will when they received Edgar Monroe's gifts. Accordingly, Monroe's subsequent gifts do not change the legitimacy or legal effect of the legatees' renunciations....

For the foregoing reasons, we reverse in part and remand for reconsideration of the status of the disclaimers executed by the 6 named individuals.

Reversed and remanded.

KING, CIRCUIT JUDGE, dissenting:

... The majority tells us that consideration consisting of a promise, the existence of which is fairly implied or inferred from what is actually said and done, of a gift or bequest in the full amount of the bequest disclaimed is not enough to disqualify a disclaimer. Instead, the majority requires explicitly negotiated or bargained-for consideration, presumably of the sort required to support a contract....

Section 2518 of the Internal Revenue Code defines an "unqualified disclaimer" as "an irrevocable and unqualified refusal by a person to accept an interest in property but only if ... such person has not accepted the interest or any of its benefits." I.R.C. § 2518(b). The two statutory rationales for the Tax Court's decision represent a fair reading of the statute. First, giving up the bequest "in return for" a gift is akin to accepting the benefits of the bequest.[26] Second, a refusal to accept a bequest from Mrs. Monroe "in return for" a gift from Mr. Monroe is not an unqualified refusal. Contrary to the reading adopted by the majority, the statute makes no mention of bargaining, tangible property, consideration or an enforceable obligation, and there is no warrant in the statute for compelling the Commissioner to litigate over these matters when challenging a disqualification.

The majority supports its reading of the statute by misreading Treas. Reg. § 25.2518–2(d)(1) to require that a disclaimant receive consideration in exchange for the disclaimer. As the Commissioner points out, the regulation describes several circumstances in which a disclaimant is deemed to have accepted the benefits of a legacy, the last among them (or, in the words of the regulation, "in addition" to the other circumstances listed in the regulation) being where the disclaimant accepts consideration in return for the disclaimer. The regulation cannot fairly be read to require consideration before disqualifying a disclaimer.

The majority likens the promise of gift or bequest implied from Mr. Monroe's words and actions to a "mere expectation" or unenforceable hope of future benefit and rejects the implied promise along with the mere expectation.... [I]n the absence of an express or implied agreement, the mere expectation or hope that a disclaimant may one day benefit from the disclaimed property (generally in the form of an inheritance) is too speculative to form the basis for disqualifying a disclaimer. But the crux of the inquiry is whether there is an express or implied agreement. Based on all of the evidence before it, including evidence of the words and deeds of Mr. Monroe and Robert Monroe, as well as the legatees' agreement to disclaim, the Tax Court reasonably deduced that an implied agreement existed between Mr. Monroe and the legatees. The Tax Court cannot fairly be read to have based its decision on a "mere expectation" or hope of future benefit on the part of the legatees.

Finally, the majority opinion contains a great deal of fact-finding, and the majority fails to acknowledge it as such. This case requires, first and foremost, credibility determinations about the testimony of Robert Monroe and the disclaimants, determinations properly relegated to the Tax Court. The Tax Court was not required to accept that testimony at face value, nor was it required to go through each piece of testimony and say that the court did not credit it. The Tax Court's opinion makes very clear that the court simply did not credit much of what it heard. We overstep the bounds of our authority as appellate judges when we go back through an appellate record and make our own credibility assessments about the witnesses' testimony. The majority opinion errs in that respect.

---

26. Treas. Reg. § 25.2518–2(d)(1) tells us that "[a]cceptance is manifested by an affirmative act which is consistent with the ownership of the interest in property." Exchanging a bequest from Mrs. Monroe for a gift from Mr. Monroe can fairly be said to constitute an act that is consistent with ownership of the bequest.

As is apparent from the majority opinion, no law addressing factual scenarios even remotely similar to the facts at issue here exists at the appellate level. The Commissioner accepts the concept of post-mortem tax planning, and until now the rules have been relatively clear. As Robert Monroe testified in the Tax Court, "the person renouncing ... can't receive a benefit for signing a renunciation." As for a subsequent gift or bequest, in Robert's words, "you just couldn't have a promise." The Tax Court found as facts that the disclaimants received a benefit for signing a renunciation, and that just such a promise existed. In order to overturn those fact-findings, the majority has now imported concepts of explicit bargaining, consideration and tangible receipt of property into a statute conspicuously devoid of them. I respectfully dissent.

NOTES

1. *Distinguishing disclaimers from transfers.* In general, the relinquishment of an interest in property, such as the cancellation of a debt or the forgiveness of a loan, is a transfer subject to the gift tax. Reg. § 25.2511–1(a). See, e.g., Lang's Estate v. Commissioner, 613 F.2d 770 (9th Cir. 1980) (parent made completed gift to child by allowing statute of limitations to run on loan); accord, Rev. Rul. 81–264, 1981–2 C.B. 185. In theory, there is no obstacle to treating a disclaimer as a "transfer" for gift tax purposes. "Since the practical effect of [taxpayer's] disclaimers [is] to reduce the expected size of his taxable estate and to confer a gratuitous benefit upon the natural objects of his bounty, the treatment of the disclaimers as taxable gifts is fully consistent with the basic purpose of the statutory scheme." Jewett v. Commissioner, 455 U.S. 305, 310 (1982).

Nevertheless, in an early decision the Sixth Circuit insisted that a disclaimer was not subject to gift tax, relying on a perceived distinction under state law between a "transfer of an interest in property" and an "exercise of a right to refuse a gift of property." Brown v. Routzahn, 63 F.2d 914, 917 (6th Cir.), cert. denied, 290 U.S. 641 (1933). Although today this analysis seems unduly formalistic, the "no transfer" approach enunciated in *Brown* became entrenched in state disclaimer statutes and ultimately in the gift tax regulations and § 2518. Thus, the treatment of qualified disclaimers represents "an exception to the general rule of taxability," and any disclaimer that fails to meet the requirements of § 2518 or the applicable gift tax regulations is treated as a taxable gift. United States v. Irvine, 511 U.S. 224 (1994).

2. *Timely disclaimers of future interests and survivorship rights.* Section 2518 applies only to disclaimers of property interests created after 1976. In the case of interests created before 1977, the gift tax treatment of disclaimers is governed by Reg. § 25.2511–1(c)(2), which generally requires that a disclaimer be "unequivocal and effective under [state] law" and be made "within a reasonable time after knowledge of the existence of the transfer" and before any acceptance of ownership. Assume that a settlor creates a trust to pay income to the settlor's spouse for life, with remainder at the spouse's death to the settlor's issue then living. If a child of the settlor waits until the spouse's death to disclaim a share of the remainder, is the disclaimer timely under Reg.

§ 25.2511–1(c)(2)? In Jewett v. Commissioner, 455 U.S. 305 (1982), the Supreme Court held that the "transfer" referred to in the regulation occurs when the interest is created, not when the interest becomes indefeasibly vested under state law. As a result, if the child waits more than a reasonable time after learning of the existence of the remainder interest, the disclaimer will be treated as a taxable gift. See also United States v. Irvine, 511 U.S. 224 (1994) (same result where interest was created before enactment of federal gift tax). The *Jewett* decision makes clear that Reg. § 25.2511–1(c)(2), like § 2518, imposes an independent federal timeliness requirement in addition to the requirements of state law.

For interests created after 1976, § 2518(b)(2) provides that a qualified disclaimer must be made no later than nine months after the date of the "transfer creating the interest" (or, if later, the disclaimant's 21st birthday). Determining when the disclaimer period begins to run raises special problems in the case of a joint tenancy with right of survivorship (or a tenancy by the entirety). For example, assume that *A* and *B* acquire property as joint tenants with right of survivorship; *A* then dies survived by *B*, whose right of survivorship ripens into absolute ownership. May *B* disclaim the survivorship interest at *A*'s death, or does the disclaimer period run from the creation of the joint tenancy? Should the result depend on whether *A* or *B* furnished the funds used to purchase the property? On whether state law would have permitted either tenant, acting alone, to sever the joint tenancy while both tenants were alive?

The Internal Revenue Service initially took the position, in accordance with then existing regulations, that the disclaimer period ran from the creation of the joint tenancy. Several appellate courts, however, rejected this position and held the regulations invalid. See Kennedy v. Commissioner, 804 F.2d 1332 (7th Cir. 1986); McDonald v. Commissioner, 853 F.2d 1494 (8th Cir. 1988), cert. denied, 490 U.S. 1005 (1989); Dancy's Estate v. Commissioner, 872 F.2d 84 (4th Cir. 1989). In response to these decisions, the regulations have been amended. Under the amended regulations, if the creation of a joint tenancy (or tenancy by the entirety) gives rise to a completed gift, the donee tenant generally has nine months from the creation of the tenancy to make a qualified disclaimer of the interest received from the donor tenant. (No disclaimer is possible with respect to the donor tenant's retained interest.) If the tenancy remains intact until one tenant dies, the survivor generally has nine months from the first tenant's death to make a qualified disclaimer of the one-half interest received by right of survivorship, regardless of whether state law permits unilateral severance and regardless of the portion of the property attributable to consideration furnished by the disclaimant. Reg. § 25.2518–2(c)(4)(i). If the creation of the tenancy does not give rise to a completed gift (i.e., a bank, brokerage or other investment account from which each tenant can unilaterally regain his or her own contributions without the other tenant's consent), the transfer creating the survivor's interest is treated as occurring at the first tenant's death. Accordingly, the survivor generally has nine months from the first tenant's death to make a qualified disclaimer of the funds contributed by the deceased tenant; no disclaimer is possible with respect to the survivor's own contributions. Reg. § 25.2518–2(c)(4)(iii).

Section 2518 prescribes a fixed nine-month disclaimer period, with no mention of knowledge on the disclaimant's part. Thus, the period for disclaiming an interest created after 1976 may expire before the disclaimant ever learns of the existence of the interest (although in no event before the disclaimant reaches age 21).

3. *Requirement of no acceptance.* Section 2518(b)(3) permits a qualified disclaimer of an interest only if the disclaimant "has not accepted the interest or any of its benefits." The regulations define acceptance as "an affirmative act which is consistent with ownership of the interest," such as use or disposition of property in a nonfiduciary capacity or acceptance of income from property. Reg. § 25.2518–2(d). See Engelman's Estate v. Commissioner, 121 T.C. 54 (2003) (decedent's exercise of testamentary general power of appointment constituted acceptance, precluding subsequent disclaimer by executor). Moreover, the receipt of any consideration in exchange for making a disclaimer is treated as acceptance of the benefits of the disclaimed interest. Merely receiving title to property by delivery of a deed or by operation of law, however, does not constitute acceptance. Thus, a surviving spouse who claims an elective share of a decedent's estate is not thereby precluded from disclaiming the elective share in whole or in part. Rev. Rul. 90–45, 1990–1 C.B. 176. See also Rev. Rul. 2005–36, 2005–1 C.B. 1368 (allowing IRA beneficiary to disclaim remaining account balance after receiving required minimum distribution for year of owner's death).

4. *Disposition of disclaimed interest.* Section 2518(b)(4) generally requires that the disclaimed interest pass to a person other than the disclaimant "without any direction on the part of the [disclaimant]." In effect, this provision requires that the disclaimer be effective under the terms of the original transfer or state law to remove the disclaimed interest from the disclaimant's ownership and control. Thus, a disclaimant may not disclaim a specific bequest under a will and then turn around and accept the same property as part of a residuary or intestate share. An exception is made for the original transferor's surviving spouse, who is permitted to disclaim a bequest in one capacity even if he or she receives an interest in the same property by an alternative route. For a detailed exposition of these rules, see Reg. § 25.2518–2(e).

A problem arises where a disclaimant receives property by operation of law and state law fails to authorize an effective disclaimer. At common law, for example, it was technically impossible for an heir to disclaim an intestate share, and an heir who attempted to do so was treated as making a taxable gift to the ultimate takers. See Hardenbergh v. Commissioner, 198 F.2d 63 (8th Cir.), cert. denied, 344 U.S. 836 (1952). Most states have enacted statutes that specifically authorize an heir to disclaim an intestate share, but the same problem may arise in connection with other transfers falling outside the scope of the state disclaimer statutes. See Bishop v. United States, 338 F.Supp. 1336 (N.D. Miss. 1970), affd. mem., 468 F.2d 950 (5th Cir.), cert. denied, 409 U.S. 878 (1972) (surviving joint tenant's attempted disclaimer of survivorship interest "amounted to nothing more than a transfer of property owned absolutely by him," and hence constituted a taxable gift); Maxwell v. Commissioner, 17 T.C. 1589 (1952) (same, as applied to attempted disclaimer of community property). In 1981, Congress responded by enacting § 2518(c)(3).

Under this provision, a "written transfer" that fails to meet the definition of a disclaimer under state law—e.g., because state law does not recognize a disclaimer of the type of interest involved—is nevertheless treated as a qualified disclaimer for tax purposes if the other requirements of § 2518(b) are met.

5. *Partial disclaimers.* A disclaimant generally is prohibited from retaining beneficial ownership or control of the disclaimed interest, and from accepting the interest or any of its benefits. These prohibitions, however, do not prevent the disclaimant from disclaiming only a portion of "severable property." For example, a legatee who is entitled to 500 shares of stock may make a qualified disclaimer of 100 shares while accepting the remaining 400; the result would be the same in the case of a bequest of money or an aggregation of tangible property. Reg. § 25.2518–3(a)(1)(ii). Similarly, § 2518(c)(1) authorizes a qualified disclaimer of an "undivided portion" of an interest. Thus, a devisee of a fee simple interest in Blackacre may disclaim an undivided 30–percent interest in Blackacre while retaining the remaining 70 percent. But the devisee may not disclaim a remainder interest in Blackacre while retaining a life estate in the same property. Reg. § 25.2518–3(b); Walshire v. United States, 288 F.3d 342 (8th Cir. 2002); Christiansen's Estate v. Commissioner, 586 F.3d 1061 (8th Cir. 2009).

In general, a person may disclaim one interest while accepting another interest in the same property where the interests are separately created by the original transferor. For example, if a trust beneficiary has a life income interest and a contingent remainder, the beneficiary may disclaim the remainder interest while retaining the income interest. Reg. § 25.2518–3(a)(1)(i). The regulations impose special restrictions on partial disclaimers of interests in specific property held in trust. Reg. § 25.2518–3(a)(2). For examples of partial disclaimers, see Reg. § 25.2518–3(d).

6. *Powers.* Section 2518(c)(2) provides that a power with respect to property is treated as an interest in the property. As a result, the holder of a power of appointment may disclaim the power while retaining other separately created interests in the underlying property. Special problems may arise under state law concerning the validity and effect of a disclaimer of a power. See Rev. Rul. 90–110, 1990–2 C.B. 209 (trustee's attempted disclaimer of power to invade corpus for remainderman ineffective under state law because remainderman did not consent; no qualified disclaimer); see also Bennett's Estate v. Commissioner, 100 T.C. 42 (1993) (trustee's attempted disclaimer ineffective under state law).

7. *Relation to state law.* Section 2518 was enacted to secure geographically uniform rules for tax-free disclaimers. See H.R. Rep. No. 1380, 94th Cong., 2d Sess. 65–68 (1976), reprinted in 1976–3 C.B. (Vol. 3) 735, 799–802. How well does the statute achieve this objective? What law governs the devolution of disclaimed property? To what extent does tax-free treatment of a disclaimer under § 2518 depend on its validity under state law?

8. *Post-mortem estate planning.* Disclaimers offer a decedent's beneficiaries extraordinary opportunities for after-the-fact estate planning. Disclaimers are often used to preserve a deduction for a marital or charitable bequest or to fine-tune the amount of the deduction. For example, if a bequest in trust for a

surviving spouse or charity fails to qualify for a marital or charitable deduction due to provisions for other beneficiaries, the deduction may be salvaged if those beneficiaries disclaim their interests. Similarly, a child may disclaim a specific bequest in order to increase the value of the residuary share passing to a surviving spouse or charity. In addition to *Monroe's Estate*, see DePaoli v. Commissioner, 62 F.3d 1259 (10th Cir. 1995) (settlement of will contest treated as qualified disclaimer, making property relinquished by decedent's son and received by decedent's widow eligible for marital deduction). Conversely, a surviving spouse may disclaim part of an "over-funded" marital bequest (see infra page 537 for this concept) and let the disclaimed property fall into a residuary trust for other beneficiaries. The executor may also have a role to play. See, for example, Rolin's Estate v. Commissioner, infra page 413 (disclaimer by widow's executors increased her predeceased husband's estate tax by $35,000 but reduced hers by $99,000; held, disclaimer valid—"taxpayers are generally permitted to arrange their affairs to minimize estate tax liability").

9. *References.* On disclaimers, see Frimmer, A Decade Later: Final Disclaimer Regulations Issued Under Section 2518, 1987 Inst. on Est. Planning ch. 6; Hastings, The Discriminate "No," 125 Tr. & Est. 39 (Oct. 1986); Martin, Perspectives on Federal Disclaimer Legislation, 46 U. Chi. L. Rev. 316 (1979); Newman & Kalter, The Need for Disclaimer Legislation—An Analysis of the Background and Current Law, 28 Tax Law. 571 (1975).

CHAPTER 3

THE GROSS ESTATE: PROPERTY OWNED AT DEATH

■ ■ ■

A. PROPERTY OWNED AT DEATH: § 2033

Section 2033 requires that "the value of all property" be included in the gross estate "to the extent of the interest therein of the decedent at the time of his death." This provision reaches "all property, whether real or personal, tangible or intangible, and wherever situated," including cash, real estate, works of art, securities, and unincorporated business interests. Reg. § 20.2033–1(a). Congress has exempted certain bonds and other debt instruments issued by the federal government or its agencies from federal taxation, but such instruments are nevertheless included in the gross estate because the estate tax is "an excise tax on the transfer of property" rather than "a tax on the property transferred." Reg. § 20.2033–1(a).[1] A cemetery lot owned by the decedent is included in the gross estate, but its value is limited to the "salable value" of any portion of the lot which is not to be used for the burial of the decedent or members of the decedent's family. Reg. § 20.2033–1(b).

Section 2033 is concerned primarily with "interests in property passing through the decedent's probate estate," but it is not narrowly confined to property that is subject to administration or to creditors' claims. Reg. § 20.2031–1(a)(1).[2] For example, property owned by the decedent which qualifies for homestead or some other exemption under state law is included in the gross estate even though it may pass by court order without being subject to administration or creditors' claims. Reg.

1. In United States v. Wells Fargo Bank, 485 U.S. 351 (1988), the Supreme Court held that the exemption under the Housing Act of 1937 of certain public housing agency bonds from "all taxation ... imposed by the United States" did not apply to the federal estate tax. The Court noted "the distinction between an excise tax, which is levied upon the use or transfer of property even though it might be measured by the property's value, and a tax levied upon the property itself."

2. The original estate tax statute, enacted in 1916, provided for inclusion of the decedent's interest in property "which after his death is subject to the payment of the charges against his estate and the expenses of its administration and is subject to distribution as part of his estate." Under this provision, the inclusion of real property in the gross estate hinged on the vagaries of state probate law, and in 1926 the limiting language was dropped "[i]n the interest of certainty." H.R. Rep. No. 1, 69th Cong., 1st Sess. (1925), reprinted at 1939–1 (Part 2) C.B. 315, 324.

§ 20.2033–1(b). The regulations emphasize that § 2033 is aimed at interests in property that are "beneficially owned by the decedent" at the time of death. Thus, property held by the decedent in a fiduciary capacity (e.g., as trustee) for the benefit of another person is not included in the gross estate; conversely, the decedent's beneficial interest in property held by another person as trustee is included in the gross estate unless the interest expired at the decedent's death.

Section 2033 has traditionally been viewed as the workhorse of the estate tax; property owned at death accounts for the bulk of value included in the gross estate. Although the concepts of "property" and a decedent's "interest" therein are notoriously slippery, the basic contours of the general inclusionary rule are reasonably well established. To be sure, the outer limits of § 2033 are not always clearly demarcated. However, those limits are seldom tested because, in most cases, transfers that arguably fall outside the comprehensive scope of § 2033 are adequately covered by specific provisions dealing with revocable transfers (§ 2038), survivor annuities (§ 2039), joint-and-survivor tenancies (§ 2040), powers of appointment (§ 2041), or life insurance (§ 2042). These provisions function as a backstop to § 2033 and also allow courts to sidestep difficult interpretive issues arising under the general inclusionary rule.

1. DOMINION AND CONTROL AS OWNERSHIP

HELVERING v. SAFE DEPOSIT & TRUST CO.

316 U.S. 56 (1942).

MR. JUSTICE BLACK delivered the opinion of the Court.

Because of the importance in the administration of the Federal Estate Tax of the questions involved, we granted certiorari to review the judgment of the Circuit Court of Appeals, 121 F.2d 307, affirming a decision of the Board of Tax Appeals, 42 B.T.A. 145.

Zachary Smith Reynolds, age 20, died on July 6, 1932. At the time, he was beneficiary of three trusts: one created by his father's will in 1918, one by deed executed by his mother in 1923, and one created by his mother's will in 1924. From his father's trust, the decedent was to receive only a portion of the income prior to his twenty-eighth birthday, at which time, if living, he was to become the outright owner of the trust property and all accumulated income. His mother's trusts directed that he enjoy the income for life, subject to certain restrictions before he reached the age of 28. Each of the trusts gave the decedent a general testamentary power of appointment over the trust property; in default of exercise of the power the properties were to go to his descendants, or if he had none, to his brother and sisters and their issue per stirpes.

The Commissioner included all the trust property within the decedent's gross estate for the purpose of computing the Federal Estate Tax.

The Board of Tax Appeals and the Circuit Court of Appeals, however, held that no part of the trust property should have been included.

I

The case presents two questions, the first of which is whether the decedent at the time of his death had by virtue of his general powers of appointment, even if never exercised, such an interest in the trust property as to require its inclusion in his gross estate under [§ 2033]. . . .

The Government argues that at the time of his death the decedent had an "interest" in the trust properties that should have been included in his gross estate [under § 2033], because he, to the exclusion of all other persons, could enjoy the income from them; would have received the corpus of one trust upon reaching the age of 28; and could alone decide to whom the benefits of all the trusts would pass at his death. These rights, it is said, were attributes of ownership substantially equivalent to a fee simple title, subject only to specified restrictions on alienation and the use of income. The respondents deny that the rights of the decedent with respect to any of the three trusts were substantially equivalent to ownership in fee, emphasizing the practical importance of the restrictions on alienation and the use of income, and arguing further that the decedent never actually had the capacity to make an effective testamentary disposition of the property because he died before reaching his majority.

We find it unnecessary to decide between these conflicting contentions on the economic equivalence of the decedent's rights and complete ownership.[3] For even if we assume with the Government that the restrictions upon the decedent's use and enjoyment of the trust properties may be dismissed as negligible and that he had the capacity to exercise a testamentary power of appointment, the question still remains: Did the decedent have "at the time of his death" such an "interest" as Congress intended to be included in a decedent's gross estate under [§ 2033]? It is not contended that the benefits during life which the trusts provided for the decedent, terminating as they did at his death, made the trust properties part of his gross estate under the statute. And viewing [§ 2033] in its background of legislative, judicial, and administrative history, we cannot reach the conclusion that the words "interest . . . of the decedent at the time of his death" were intended by Congress to include property subject to a general testamentary power of appointment unexercised by the decedent.

The forerunner of [§ 2033] was § 202(a) of the Revenue Act of 1916, 39 Stat. 777. In United States v. Field, 255 U.S. 257, this Court held that property passing under a general power of appointment *exercised* by a

3. In declining to pass upon this issue, we do not reject the principle we have often recognized that the realities of the taxpayer's economic interest, rather than the niceties of the conveyancer's art, should determine the power to tax. See Curry v. McCanless, 307 U.S. 357, 371, and cases there cited. Nor do we deny the relevance of this principle as a guide to statutory interpretation where, unlike here, the language of a statute and its statutory history do not afford more specific indications of legislative intent. Helvering v. Clifford, 309 U.S. 331.

decedent was not such an "interest" of the decedent as the 1916 Act brought within the decedent's gross estate. While the holding was limited to *exercised* powers of appointment, the approach of the Court, the authorities cited, and certain explicit statements in the opinion left little doubt that the Court regarded property subject to *unexercised* general powers of appointment as similarly beyond the scope of the statutory phrase "interest of the decedent."

After the *Field* case, the provision it passed upon was reenacted without change in the Revenue Act of 1921 ... and in the Revenue Act of 1924.... If the implications of the *Field* opinion with respect to unexercised powers had been considered contrary to the intendment of the words "interest of the decedent," it is reasonable to suppose that Congress would have added some clarifying amendment....

When it was held in the *Field* case that property subject to an *exercised* general testamentary power of appointment was not to be included in the decedent's gross estate under the Revenue Act of 1916, this Court referred to an amendment passed in 1919 which specifically declared property passing under an *exercised* general testamentary power to be part of the decedent's gross estate. The passage of this amendment, said the Court, "indicates that Congress at least was doubtful whether the previous act included property passing by appointment." In the face of such doubts, which cannot reasonably be supposed to have been less [greater?] than doubts with respect to *unexercised* powers, Congress nevertheless specified only that property subject to exercised powers should be included. From this deliberate singling out of *exercised* powers alone, without the corroboration of the other matters we have discussed, a Congressional intent to treat *unexercised* powers otherwise can be deduced....

In no judicial opinion brought to our attention has it been held that the gross estate of a decedent includes, for purposes of the Federal Estate Tax, property subject to an unexercised general power. On the contrary, as the court below points out, "the courts have been at pains to consider whether property passed under a general power or not so as to be taxable under Section 302(f), a consideration which would have been absolutely unnecessary if the estate were taxable under [§ 2033] because of the mere existence of a general power whether exercised or not." 121 F.2d 307, 312. In addition, the uniform administrative practice until this case arose appears to have placed an interpretation upon the Federal Estate Tax contrary to that the Government now urges. No regulations issued under the several revenue acts, including those in effect at the time this suit was initiated, prescribe that property subject to an unexercised general testamentary power of appointment should be included in a decedent's gross estate. Because of the combined effect of all of these circumstances, we believe that a departure from the long-standing, generally accepted construction of [§ 2033], now contested for the first time by the Government, would override the best indications we have of Congressional intent....

NOTES

1. *General power of appointment.* A few months after the Supreme Court's decision, Congress intervened prospectively to put an end to the preferential treatment of unexercised general powers of appointment. Under § 2041(a)(2), discussed infra page 395, property subject to a general power of appointment that was created after October 21, 1942 and held by the decedent at death is includible in the gross estate, without regard to whether the power was exercised. Thus, under current law, if Zachary Reynolds were to die holding an unexercised general power of appointment (created after October 21, 1942), the property subject to the power would be included in his gross estate under § 2041. Section 2033, however, would have no application. In this respect, the doctrine of *Field* and *Safe Deposit & Trust Co.*, holding that a general power of appointment does not constitute an "interest" in property for purposes of § 2033, remains valid.

2. *"Dominion and control" and § 2033.* The significance of the *Safe Deposit & Trust Co.* case is that the Supreme Court refused to read what is now § 2033 as expansively as it had read the predecessor of § 61(a) two years earlier in Helvering v. Clifford, 309 U.S. 331 (1940). In the *Clifford* case, the grantor was subjected to income tax on the income from a short-term trust that he had set up for the benefit of his wife, on the theory that his retained powers of administration preserved his "dominion and control" over the transferred assets despite the "temporary reallocation of income within an intimate family group." The Court observed that "[i]t is hard to imagine [the grantor] felt himself the poorer after this trust had been executed or, if he did, that it had any rational foundation in fact." 309 U.S. at 336. As will be seen, a trust may be includible in the grantor's gross estate if the grantor retained (1) the power to alter, amend, revoke or terminate it, (2) the right to possess or control the income, or (3) a reversionary interest. Since the *Safe Deposit & Trust Co.* decision, § 2033 has not been applied to transfers that escape the technical requirements of these provisions on the ground that the grantor was still "in substance" the owner of the property.[4]

3. *Remainder payable to income beneficiary's estate.* In Keeter v. United States, 461 F.2d 714 (5th Cir. 1972), the decedent was the beneficiary of an

4. On one occasion, the Supreme Court asked counsel in a pending case to argue the relation of the *Clifford* case to estate tax liability. Spiegel's Estate v. Commissioner, 335 U.S. 701 (1949). The government took the following position in its brief on reargument:

> Indeed, it is even arguable that a trust covered by the *Clifford* doctrine should be included in the gross estate under [§ 2033], which in a sense corresponds to the general provisions in [§ 61(a)] defining gross income. Section [2033] is the basic provision requiring the inclusion in the gross estate of all property owned by the decedent at his death. And where the settlor remains in substance the owner of the trust property for purposes of Section [61(a)] under the *Clifford* case, it is highly persuasive that it should be included in his gross estate under Section [2033], unless there is a specific statute providing otherwise. See Helvering v. Safe Deposit & Trust Co., 316 U.S. 56, 58–59 (1942). However, the Government has sought in the present cases merely to include these trusts in Section 811(c) [of the 1939 Code].

The case was decided, as the government intimated it should be, under § 811(c) of the 1939 Code (the predecessor of § 2037, discussed infra page 328), rather than under the general language of § 2033. The *Clifford* problem, opened up on the Court's own motion, was discussed only in a dissenting opinion by Justice Burton, who denied that the doctrine of that case was applicable to the estate tax without citing the *Safe Deposit & Trust Co.* case.

insurance policy on her deceased husband's life. Under a settlement option elected by her husband, the decedent received interest on the proceeds for life and the proceeds were payable at her death to her estate. The court held that the decedent in her will had exercised a general power of appointment over the proceeds, causing them to be included in her gross estate under § 2041. See infra page 409, Note 2.c. Accordingly, there was no need to consider whether the proceeds were beneficially owned by the decedent under § 2033. Compare the result in Second Natl. Bank of Danville v. Dallman, 209 F.2d 321 (7th Cir. 1954), where the court held on similar facts that life insurance proceeds were not includible in the decedent's gross estate under § 2041 because she had "no power to dispose of the insurance proceeds by will"; § 2033 also did not apply because the proceeds were paid to the executor "not by reason of decedent's will but because of the [insurance company's] contractual obligation with [the insured]." See Rev. Rul. 55–277, 1955–1 C.B. 456 (nonacquiescence in *Dallman*).

In Royce's Estate v. Commissioner, 46 B.T.A. 1090 (1942), the government sought to apply § 2033 to property that the decedent had the right to withdraw on demand from a trust created by her husband. Apparently the government thought that the *Safe Deposit & Trust Co.* case was distinguishable because it involved a testamentary power of appointment, whereas the decedent in *Royce* had a power exercisable during life. The court held, however, that the decedent had no "interest" in the trust corpus. See also Rev. Rul. 75–145, 1975–1 C.B. 298 (uncashed Social Security check payable solely to decedent was not includible in his gross estate under § 2033 because decedent's right to payment terminated at death, but was includible under § 2041 because decedent had unlimited power of disposition while alive; § 2041 would not apply, however, if check were jointly payable to decedent and spouse).

TECHNICAL ADVICE MEMORANDUM 9207004[5]

(October 21, 1991).

Issues

(1) Are the drugs that were in the decedent's possession at the time of his death includible in his gross estate under section 2033 of the Internal Revenue Code?

(2) If the drugs are includible in the decedent's gross estate, how is the fair market value determined for purposes of section 2031 of the Code?

---

5. The Internal Revenue Service furnishes guidance concerning the interpretation and application of the tax laws to specific facts in the form of a letter ruling (issued to a particular taxpayer in connection with a prospective transaction or return) or technical advice (issued to a director or appeals area director in connection with a proceeding such as the examination of a particular return). See Rev. Proc. 2011–1, 2011–1 C.B. 1 (letter rulings); Rev. Proc. 2011–2, 2011–1 C.B. 90 (technical advice). Although a taxpayer may not rely on letter rulings or technical advice issued to or for other taxpayers, tax practitioners view these documents as significant statements of the Service's policy. See Rogovin & Korb, The Four R's Revisited: Regulations, Rulings, Reliance and Retroactivity in the 21st Century: A View From Within, 87 Taxes 21 (Aug. 2009).—EDS.

(3) Does the forfeiture of the drugs and cash under the drug enforcement laws result in a deduction under section 2053 or section 2054 of the Code?

Facts

[For several years before his death, federal and local law enforcement authorities suspected decedent of drug smuggling. On January 4, 1987, decedent met his two accomplices in Florida and drove with them to an unopened stretch of highway that was under construction and deserted at night. Decedent told the two accomplices that it was a good place to land an airplane and offload drugs, and told them to meet him at the site the next night between 10:00 and 10:30 p.m. with a truck. Under the plan, as later revealed, the two accomplices were to offload the marijuana that the decedent was bringing in by airplane; one accomplice was to drive the truck, loaded with the marijuana, to City; the other accomplice and the decedent were to fly in the decedent's airplane to City; and both accomplices were then to be paid by the decedent.

On January 5, 1987, the two accomplices drove to the landing site as directed; due to a severe storm, however, they arrived late. While they were still setting up landing lights, the decedent attempted to land; the airplane struck a tree and power lines and crashed, killing decedent. When the police arrived on the scene, they found bales of marijuana. Shortly afterwards, the police apprehended the two accomplices driving the truck loaded with more bales of marijuana. The accomplices stated that they had been hired by decedent to offload the drugs from the plane and that they had obtained the marijuana from the crash site. Tire impressions made at the scene of the airplane crash confirmed that the accomplices' truck had been there.

All the marijuana found at the crash site and in the truck, totaling 662.50 pounds, was ordered forfeited and confiscated under the drug enforcement laws of Florida. The grade of the marijuana was not ascertained. Both of the accomplices were convicted of conspiracy to traffic marijuana and of possession of marijuana.]

Under the laws of Florida (and Tennessee), an individual's possession of personal property is prima facie evidence of the individual's ownership of the property.... This, however, is rebuttable upon proof of ownership in another person....

Law and Analysis

Issue 1: Section 2033

Section 2033 of the Code provides that the value of the gross estate shall include the value of all property to the extent of the interest therein of the decedent at the time of death....

In determining the nature of ownership that is required for inclusion of property in a decedent's gross estate under section 2033, we note that the estate tax inclusionary statutes, including section 2033, include property in a decedent's gross estate based upon the decedent's possession of the economic benefits of the property. For this reason, if a decedent possessed the economic equivalence of outright ownership of property, it is not necessary to establish that the decedent possessed the legal title to the property. Thus, for example, the Supreme Court stated in Burnet v. Wells, 289 U.S. 670 (1933):

> Taxation is ... concerned with ... the *actual command* over the property taxed—the actual benefit for which the tax is paid.... Liability may rest upon the enjoyment by the taxpayer of privileges and benefits so substantial and important as to make it reasonable and just to deal with him as if he were the owner and to tax him on that basis. 289 U.S. at 678 [Emphasis supplied.] ...

In this case, the decedent, rather than an unknown third party, employed the accomplices. The role of the accomplices, in awaiting the decedent's arrival at the makeshift landing strip, was to unload the plane and assist the decedent in transporting the marijuana to City. The evidence indicates that the two accomplices were the decedent's employees, having no apparent interest in the marijuana. See, for example, Erickson v. Commissioner, T.C. Memo. 1989–552, affd., 937 F.2d 1548 (10th Cir. 1991).

In *Erickson*, a case involving the income tax, the Tax Court noted that the taxpayer's ownership of an airplane and his possession of a planeload of drugs (seized from the airplane) were sufficient to put the taxpayer to the burden of proof as to the ownership of the drugs. Likewise, the circuit court, in affirming the Tax Court's finding that the taxpayer was the owner of the planeload of drugs, stated, "Considering the Byzantine ways of drug trafficking, it is ... easy to argue that ... marijuana in one's possession belongs to someone else." ...

In this case, the decedent's ownership of the airplane and his possession of a planeload of drugs that he was flying into Florida sufficiently established (i) the decedent's exclusive possession and control over the drugs, and (ii) that it was the decedent who was to receive the economic benefits of the drugs. See Erickson v. Commissioner, above cited. (We note that, under Florida law, the decedent's possession of the drugs is prima facie evidence of his ownership.)

Thus, (1) at the time of the decedent's death, he had the exclusive possession and control over the drugs, and (2) his possession and control over the drugs were to continue until the drugs were sold for cash which the decedent was to retain for himself (or transfer to his heirs). Consequently, the decedent's possession, control, and power of disposition over the marijuana were tantamount to his ownership of it for purposes of section 2033 of the Code....

Issue 2: Section 2031—Valuation

Section 2031(a) of the Code provides that the value of the gross estate shall be determined by including the value at the time of death of all property wherever situated.

Section 20.2031–1(b) of the regulations provides that the value of every item of property includible in a decedent's gross estate is its fair market value at the time of the decedent's death. The fair market value is the price at which the property would change hands between a willing buyer and a willing seller, neither being under any compulsion to buy or to sell and both having reasonable knowledge of the relevant facts.

For federal tax purposes, in determining the value of illicit drugs held by a taxpayer and subsequently destroyed pursuant to drug enforcement laws, so that the grade or quality of the drugs cannot be determined, the Service is given latitude in establishing (1) the grade of the drugs, and (2) the selling price of the drugs. See, for example, Jones v. Commissioner, T.C. Memo. 1991–28, and Graff v. Commissioner, T.C. Memo. 1986–550, in which the court stated that, in determining the value of narcotics sold by the taxpayer, in order to reconstruct the income that the taxpayer failed to report, the Commissioner is under no obligation to assume the lowest price supported by the evidence. See also Erickson v. Commissioner, above cited, in which the circuit court stated:

> The problem facing the Commissioner where criminal activity of the type involved in drug trafficking is concerned, is that the activity is characterized by cash transactions and a lack of records, or concealed or deceptive records. [937 F.2d at 1554.]

Thus, in applying section 2031 of the Code, to determine the fair market value of drugs that have been confiscated, the Service is entitled to use any reasonable means to establish the grade of the drugs held by the decedent at his death and the market in which the drugs would have been sold....

In this case, because the decedent obtained the marijuana through a smuggling operation in which he expected to sell the drugs, it is reasonable to assume that the marijuana that was held by the decedent, at death, and confiscated by drug enforcement authorities was, at a minimum, of an average grade.... Further, because the willing buyers of the marijuana could have included street dealers (as well as distributors to street dealers), it is reasonable to determine the fair market value of the marijuana based on the retail street value in the City area.... Consequently, for purposes of section 2031 of the Code, the value of the 662.5 pounds of marijuana is determined based on retail street value of average grade marijuana (in the City area at the time of the decedent's death)....

Issue 3: Section 2053(a) and Section 2054—Deduction

Section 2053(a) of the Code provides, in part, that, for purposes of the estate tax, the value of the taxable estate shall be determined by deducting from the value of the gross estate such amounts for administration expenses and claims against the estate as are allowable by the laws of the jurisdiction under which the estate is being administered.

Section 2054 of the Code provides that the value of the taxable estate shall be determined by deducting from the value of the gross estate losses incurred during the settlement of estates arising from fires, storms, shipwrecks, or other casualties, or from theft, when such losses are not compensated by insurance or otherwise.

[Fla. Stat. § 893.12(1)] provides that all controlled substances which may be possessed are declared to be contraband and shall be subject to seizure and confiscation. The court having jurisdiction shall order such controlled substances forfeited and destroyed.

21 U.S.C. § 881(f) provides that all controlled substances that are possessed in violation of the provisions of the subchapter shall be deemed contraband and seized and summarily forfeited to the United States....

Is a federal estate tax deduction allowable for a seizure and forfeiture made pursuant to drug enforcement laws?

The courts, holding that the allowance of an income tax deduction for the confiscation of drugs and the proceeds of drug dealing would frustrate a sharply defined public policy against drug trafficking, have consistently denied any income tax deduction for the loss....

21 U.S.C. § 881 was enacted to sanction forfeiture as a law enforcement tool in combatting drug trafficking, one of the most serious crime problems facing the United States today. The legislative history of the amended 21 U.S.C. § 881 states, in H.R. [Rep.] No. 98–1030, 98th Cong. 2d Sess. 191 (1984):

> Profit is the motivation for this criminal activity, and it is through economic power that it is sustained and grows.... [T]he traditional sanctions of fine and imprisonment are inadequate to deter or punish the enormously profitable trade in drugs which, with its inevitable attendant violence, is plaguing the country. Clearly, if law enforcement efforts to combat ... drug trafficking are to be successful, they must include an attack on the economic aspects of these crimes. Forfeiture is the mechanism through which such an attack may be made.

... Because state drug enforcement laws of forfeiture and 21 U.S.C. § 881 are based on the same principles, any forfeiture made pursuant to a state drug enforcement law is regarded as made in furtherance of the same public policy that underlies 21 U.S.C. § 881. Therefore, in considering whether a tax deduction is allowable for a forfeiture under drug enforcement laws, and in denying a tax deduction for public policy reasons, it does not matter whether the forfeiture was made pursuant to a state law or federal laws.

As with the income tax, the sharply defined public policy against drug trafficking (as particularly expressed in the legislative history of 21 U.S.C. § 881 and by Congress' enactment of forfeiture statutes to attack the economic power of drug trafficking) likewise overrides any deduction that might otherwise be allowable under the federal estate tax statutes for a forfeiture (of a decedent's property) made pursuant to drug enforcement laws.

In this case, the decedent held cash and drugs at his death that were included in his gross estate. The cash and drugs were forfeited under the drug enforcement laws of Florida. Because the allowance of any estate tax deduction for the forfeiture would violate the sharply defined public policy against drug trafficking, no deduction is allowable under section 2053 or section 2054 of the Code for the value of any of the property that was forfeited....

No deduction is allowable under section 2053 or section 2054 of the Code for the confiscated property.

NOTES

1. *Estate tax and ill-gotten gains.* The Service invokes a "sharply defined public policy against drug trafficking" to justify imposing an estate tax on the value of contraband drugs possessed by the decedent at death and subsequently seized by law enforcement officers. The tax, however, is an imperfect device for achieving the policy objective. Assume the decedent dies owning assets, legally obtained, worth $500,000. What becomes of these assets if at the time of death decedent also possesses marijuana worth $8 million? What if the seizure of the marijuana occurred during decedent's lifetime rather than after his death? See Turnier, The Pink Panther Meets the Grim Reaper: Estate Taxation of the Fruits of Crime, 72 N.C. L. Rev. 163, 194–95 (1993).

The Service issued a similar ruling in a case involving stolen property. While stationed in Europe in 1945, decedent, a United States serviceman, stole art objects from a church in Germany and china and silverware from a villa in France, and mailed the stolen articles to his home in Texas. When the decedent's activities came to light, he was court-martialed and discharged with a fine and a reprimand. Upon his death in 1980, decedent bequeathed the china and silverware to two nieces and a nephew and the rest of his property to his brother and sister. A Texas inheritance tax form listed assets of about $120,000 but made no mention of the stolen articles. Because of the small size of the estate, no federal estate tax return was filed. During the next ten years, the brother and sister tried to sell articles from the stolen collection on both legitimate and illicit art markets, leading to the identification of the collection as stolen property. The church recovered its treasures, having an estimated value of $50 to $100 million, upon payment to the heirs of a $2.75 million "finder's fee." In Tech. Adv. Memo. 9152005 (Aug. 30, 1991), the Service ruled that the stolen property was includible in the gross estate under § 2033, that its value at the time of decedent's death was to be determined by reference to prices on both the legitimate and illicit markets, and that no § 2053(a) deduction was allowable for claims made by the rightful owners.

In Hester's Estate v. United States, 99 A.F.T.R.2d 1288 (W.D. Va. 2007), affd. per curiam, 102 A.F.T.R.2d 6714 (4th Cir. 2008), cert. denied, 129 S.Ct. 2168 (2009), the decedent, while acting as trustee of a family trust, improperly withdrew trust assets and commingled them with his own funds. After his death, the executor sought to exclude the misappropriated assets from the gross estate, arguing that the decedent held them as a constructive trustee for the trust beneficiaries. The court disagreed, noting that the decedent "exercised dominion and control over the assets as though they were his own without an express or implied recognition of an obligation to repay and without restriction as to their disposition." Because the decedent "controlled the misappropriated assets and did not reimburse them before his death," the assets were included in his gross estate under § 2033. Furthermore, although in theory the trust beneficiaries could have sued to recover the assets, they never did so and the court refused to allow a deduction for a "hypothetical, unasserted, and unpaid claim."

2. *Effect of local property law.* To determine whether property is includible in the decedent's gross estate, it is necessary first to determine the nature and extent of the decedent's interest under local property law. Is property includible in the gross estate if the decedent held title as trustee for the benefit of others? If he was the beneficial but not the record owner? See Reg. § 20.2033–1(a). What of property transferred to the decedent to hinder, delay, or cheat the transferor's creditors? Of property so transferred by the decedent? See McCann v. Commissioner, 87 F.2d 275 (6th Cir. 1937). An inter vivos transfer by the decedent may be vulnerable for various reasons (lack of delivery, legal incapacity, and so on); conversely, the decedent may have received property in a tainted transaction. Should taxability turn on whether the transfer was "void" rather than "voidable"? On whether the transferor, or only his creditors, may recover the property? On whether an action for its recovery has or has not been brought by the decedent's executor (or by the transferor against the executor)? See Safe Deposit & Trust Co. v. Tait, 54 F.2d 383 (D.Md. 1931).

Suppose that *T* established a testamentary trust to pay income "at such times and in such amounts as the trustee shall deem best" equally to *A*, *B*, and *C*. At *A*'s death, the trustee holds a substantial sum of accumulated, undistributed income. This sum is eventually distributed by order of the probate court to *B* and *C*, who are the residuary beneficiaries of both *T* and *A*, as "the only persons interested in *T*'s estate." Does this order preclude an independent finding by federal tax authorities that one-third of the accumulated trust income was an asset of *A*'s estate? See Earle v. Commissioner, 157 F.2d 501 (6th Cir. 1946), cert. denied, 330 U.S. 822 (1947). On the effect of a prior state court adjudication, see *Bosch*, supra page 26.

2. DECEDENT'S INTEREST IN PROPERTY

BARR'S ESTATE v. COMMISSIONER

40 T.C. 227 (1963).

PIERCE, JUDGE. . . .

[The decedent's widow received a "wage dividend death benefit" of about $4,500 from his employer, Eastman Kodak Company, under the following circumstances: The directors of Kodak were authorized by the shareholders to pay "wage dividends" in any year in which a dividend was paid on the common stock, if in the directors' opinion the corporation's cash position and earnings warranted such action, and wage dividends were paid in every year but one during the period 1912–1961. In November 1957, eight months after the decedent's death, Kodak's directors declared such a "wage dividend" for all employees on the payroll as of the end of 1957, based on the employee's wages for the five preceding years, to be paid in March 1958. If an employee died after the end of 1957 but before the payment date in March 1958, the wage dividend was paid to his estate as a matter of right. If he died before the end of 1957, his estate was not entitled to a wage dividend; but it was the company's practice to pay a "death benefit wage dividend" in such cases to the employee's spouse, children, or parents, and the company had regularly informed its employees that "the immediate survivors of Kodak people may expect" such a death benefit. In each such case, there was an investigation to determine whether "the circumstances of the deceased employee's family" justified payment; usually, but not always, a death benefit was paid equal in amount to the wage dividend that the employee would have received had he survived to the end of the year. From time to time, the company altered the eligibility rules for wage dividends; for example, in 1956 employees whose compensation exceeded $45,000 were made ineligible.

The decedent's widow also received a "salary death benefit" of about $1,750, under a company practice of paying an amount equal to the salary that would have been earned by a deceased employee during the balance of the pay period in which he died. The decedent was paid at four-week intervals; he died at the end of the first week of his pay period and the payment was equal to three weeks' salary. The company's policy in paying "salary death benefits" was the same as its policy in paying "wage dividend death benefits," namely, payment was not guaranteed but depended on an exercise of judgment based on an investigation of the family's circumstances.]

I

The first issue relates to the so-called wage dividend death benefit which Eastman Kodak Co. paid to decedent's widow in March 1958 (approximately 1 year after decedent's death). And the question presented with respect to this, is whether the amount of such payment is includable in the gross estate of the decedent for Federal estate purposes, under either section 2033 or section 2039 of the 1954 Code. . . .

It will be observed that [§ 2033] relates only to *interests in property* which the decedent had at the time of his death. And, as the Supreme Court pointed out in the leading case of Knowlton v. Moore, 178 U.S. 41, the justification for the Government's power to subject such interests to the Federal estate tax rests on the principle that such interests *pass* from the decedent at death, and that the estate tax is an excise tax on the privilege of transmitting property at death to the survivors of the decedent. To the same effect see New York Trust Co. v. Eisner, 256 U.S. 345.

It is our opinion that, in the present case, the decedent did not have at the time of his death any property interest, either in the "wage dividend" which Eastman's board of directors subsequently declared for the benefit of its living eligible employees (after it had declared a cash dividend for the benefit of its stockholders), or in the related death benefit which these directors then authorized to be paid to decedent's widow. Accordingly, there was no such interest which passed, or could have passed, from him to his widow; and hence no such interest upon which the excise tax on the privilege of transmitting property at death may be imposed under section 2033.

Both this Court and others have recognized that there is a distinction between *rights* of an employee to death benefits, and, on the other hand, mere hopes and expectancies on the part of an employee that death benefits may be paid. Thus, in the early case of Dimock v. Corwin, 19 F. Supp. 56 (E.D.N.Y.), affirmed on other issues 99 F.2d 799 (C.A.2), affd. 306 U.S. 363, it was shown that the Standard Oil Company had adopted an annuity and insurance plan, subject to withdrawal or modification by Standard at its discretion, under which death benefits roughly equal to a year's salary of an employee might be paid to the widow of a deceased employee. The District Court concluded that the decedent had "only the right to render it possible for [his surviving spouse] to receive a grant from the Standard Oil Co., and that this did not constitute property of his" under the then applicable statute, section 302 of the Revenue Act of 1926, a statutory provision cognate to section 2033 of the 1954 Code....

Authorities reaching differing results on the basis of the decedents having *enforceable vested* rights to have their employers pay death benefits to survivors, are typified by Estate of Charles B. Wolf, 29 T.C. 441, 447, in which case we stated:

> At the date of decedent's death he had *enforceable vested* rights in the three trusts [one profit-sharing trust, and two pension trusts], procured by the rendition of services and by continuing in the employ of the respective corporations. He could be deprived of those rights only by deliberately terminating his employment or being discharged for cause. He had unlimited power to designate or change beneficiaries, and payments to his named beneficiaries were obligatory. The rights thus created were valuable property rights, capable of valuation, and in fact valued by the parties. The decedent's death was the decisive event that resulted in the passage of those rights to the beneficiary. It seems clear to us that they are includible in his gross estate either under the sweeping provisions of [§ 2033] or under the more specific provisions of [§ 2041, dealing with powers of appointment]....
>
> This case is to be sharply distinguished from cases such as Dimock v. Corwin, ... where the employer retained the unfettered right to withdraw or modify the pension plan and where it was thought that the employee's interest could not rise above that of a mere expectancy....

We are convinced that in the instant case, decedent had no more than a hope or expectancy that his surviving spouse might receive a wage dividend death benefit. There were so many events that had to occur before such hope could be realized that we find it impossible to conclude that, at the date of death, he had any property right which he could pass to her. Eastman had to realize earnings and profits for the year 1957; the directors, in the exercise of their discretion, had to declare a dividend to its stockholders; the directors, in further exercise of their discretion, had to declare a wage dividend payment to those employees who were alive and employed by the company on the last day of the Kodak year; and the directors, in the still further exercise of their discretion, had to approve a wage dividend death benefit to the widow of the instant decedent who had theretofore died. Moreover, the company, in its Rules of Eligibility and Participation and in the pamphlet distributed to its employees, made it clear that whether it might approve a wage dividend death benefit to the estate or beneficiary of a deceased employee was solely within its "option"; and that such situation would be distinguishable from that of an employee who had continued to live until after the close of the Kodak year for which the wage dividend was declared, and who thereby had acquired a "right" to the same.

We hold that section 2033 is not here applicable.

[Discussion of § 2039 omitted; see infra page 357, Note 4.a.]

II

The second issue is whether the salary death benefit which was paid to the decedent's widow is includable in the decedent's gross estate, under [sections] 2033 or 2039.

It is our opinion that what we have stated with respect to each of these sections in our consideration of the wage dividend death benefit is equally applicable to this salary death benefit....

NOTES

1. *Employee death benefits.* If employee benefits are "created" at or by death, the Internal Revenue Service may seek to include the benefits in the gross estate under § 2033, arguing that they represent an interest in property arising from the decedent's employment and passing to the survivors by reason of the decedent's death. This argument has not been notably successful. In addition to the *Barr* case, see Tully's Estate v. United States, 528 F.2d 1401 (Ct. Cl. 1976), reprinted infra page 245 (decedent had only minimal associations with an employment contract requiring the employer to pay decedent's widow an amount equal to twice his salary for the year preceding his death because "he could not reach [the benefits] for his own use"); Bogley's Estate v. United States, 514 F.2d 1027 (Ct. Cl. 1975) (resolutions of two companies expressing intent to pay death benefits created expectancies, not enforceable contract rights).

The Service may also seek to tax employee death benefits under other sections of the Code. For instance, § 2039 was enacted in 1954 to reach survivorship annuities; in addition, property transferred during life subject to a power to alter or amend may be includible under § 2038, and property subject to a general power of appointment may be includible under § 2041. See, e.g., Rev. Rul. 76–304, 1976–2 C.B. 269 (death benefit taxable under § 2038 because of employee's retained right to change beneficiaries; § 2033 not mentioned).

One reform proposal would amend § 2039 to make it the exclusive estate tax provision for survivor benefits and expand its coverage to include all "contractual or statutory survivor benefits economically attributable to the decedent." ABA Tax Section Task Force, Report on Transfer Tax Restructuring, 41 Tax Law. 395, 411 (1988). Under this approach, the benefits in the *Barr* case would be subject to estate tax, as would the statutory death benefits described infra Note 3.

2. *Interests arising at death: Wrongful death recoveries.* In Rev. Rul. 54–19, 1954–1 C.B. 179, the Service ruled that the estate of a decedent who died in an airplane crash did not include the executor's claim against the carrier for damages. The state wrongful death statute provided that the decedent's executor or administrator could sue, but for the benefit of the decedent's intestate successors rather than for the benefit of his estate or legatees:

> The decedent in his lifetime never had an interest in the right of action or in the proceeds. He did not create the right, it was created by statute and vested in the persons designated in the statute. Inasmuch as the decedent had no right of action or interest in the proceeds at the time of his death, nothing "passed" from the decedent to the beneficiaries. Accordingly, the amounts recovered by the beneficiaries would not be includible in the decedent's gross estate for Federal estate tax purposes.

After litigating and losing several cases, most notably Connecticut Bank & Trust Co. v. United States, 465 F.2d 760 (2d Cir. 1972), the Service conceded in Rev. Rul. 75–127, 1975–1 C.B. 297, that § 2033 also does not include amounts recovered under wrongful death statutes of the "survival type" which provide that a decedent's action for damages survives his death (as opposed to a new action being created by his death, as in Rev. Rul. 54–19):

> These cases hold that the wrongful death proceeds are not includible in the decedent's gross estate under either section 2033 or section 2041 because the wrongful death action cannot exist until the decedent has died. Thus, the decedent possessed neither a property interest in such cause of action nor a power of appointment over such cause of action at the time of his death.

See also Rev. Rul. 75–126, 1975–1 C.B. 296 (wrongful death proceeds not includible in gross estate notwithstanding state statute subjecting proceeds to decedent's debts and liabilities). Revenue Ruling 75–127 stated, however, that any proceeds representing damages to which the decedent had become entitled during his lifetime (such as for pain and suffering or medical expenses) would be included in the gross estate.

3. *Other statutory recoveries.* Social Security benefits paid on the death of an employee are not part of the gross estate, the Service has ruled, because "the decedent had no control over the designation of the beneficiary or the amount of the payment since these are fixed by statute. Furthermore, the

decedent had no property interest in the 'Federal Old Age and Survivors Insurance Trust Fund' from which the payment is made." Rev. Rul. 67–277, 1967–2 C.B. 322. Does this suggest the surprising result that if a minor dies before he is capable of making a will, his estate will not be subject to federal estate tax because he did not have an opportunity to choose his beneficiaries? If the power to designate a beneficiary is essential to estate tax liability for employee and Social Security death benefits, why is that element not supplied (even if the benefits are to be paid to persons selected by the employer or by Congress) by the decedent's decision to accept employment with a particular employer knowing that such benefits will be (or are likely to be) paid?

The no-inclusion principle of the wrongful death cases (see supra Note 2) has been applied in rulings to exclude from the gross estate various statutory death benefits, such as military allotments paid to the beneficiaries of members of the armed forces dying in active duty (Rev. Rul. 55–581, 1955–2 C.B. 381); awards paid under a worker's compensation act to the employee's dependents (Rev. Rul. 56–637, 1956–2 C.B. 600); wrongful death recoveries under the Federal Death on the High Seas Act (Rev. Rul. 69–8, 1969–1 C.B. 219); benefits payable to an employee's surviving spouse under the Federal Coal Mine Health and Safety Act of 1969 (Rev. Rul. 76–102, 1976–1 C.B. 272); certain benefits payable to a veteran's surviving spouse (Rev. Rul. 76–501, 1976–2 C.B. 267); survivors' loss benefits under no-fault automobile insurance (Rev. Rul. 82–5, 1982–1 C.B. 131); and death benefits under the Public Safety Officers' Benefits Act (Rev. Rul. 79–397, 1979–2 C.B. 322).

4. *Speculative and contingent claims.* Section 2033 brings into the gross estate a wide range of unliquidated, speculative, contingent and defeasible claims and interests, even though the value of the asset may not be readily ascertainable. See infra page 203, Note 3. For example, the Service has ruled that the right of an attorney's estate to receive payment on a quantum meruit basis for legal services performed by the decedent under a contingent fee contract constitutes an interest in property within the meaning of § 2033. (Under state law, in the event of the death of an attorney who was employed on a contingent fee basis, the estate ordinarily is entitled to recover the reasonable value of the attorney's services if the case is terminated successfully.) Rev. Rul. 55–123, 1955–1 C.B. 443. Since the right to collect on a quantum meruit basis arises only because of the attorney's death (and is contingent on a successful outcome of the litigation), does it come within the terms of § 2033? If it does, how can its value at the time of death be ascertained? The Tax Court addressed both questions in Curry's Estate v. Commissioner, 74 T.C. 540 (1980). At issue was the taxability of an attorney's right to receive a percentage of any contingent fees subsequently awarded in thirteen cases pending before the Indian Claims Commission, which passed to his estate on his death. The court held that the contingent nature of the claims bore solely on their value and did not place them beyond the reach of § 2033:

> The fact that the legal fees we are concerned with were contingent upon future recovery by the Indian tribes is a critical consideration in trying to determine what the contract right was worth as of the date of death. However, the contingent nature of the contract right must bear on the factual question of valuation. It cannot, as a matter of law, preclude the inclusion of the interest in the decedent's gross estate or command that

> the value be fixed at zero. Although uncertainty as to the value of a contract right may postpone the inclusion of the income until it is actually realized for *income* tax purposes, for *estate* tax purposes, the value of an asset must be determined in order to close the estate.... We therefore hold that, under the circumstances before us, the contractual right herein to share in future attorney's fees which are contingent in nature, is property to be included in the decedent's gross estate under section 2033. [74 T.C. at 546–47.]

The same facts that make the process of valuation speculative may give rise to a more fundamental defense that there is no "interest in property" within the meaning of § 2033 to be valued. For example, in Rodiek v. Commissioner, 33 B.T.A. 1020 (1936), affd., 87 F.2d 328 (2d Cir. 1937), the court excluded from the gross estate a claim against the United States for compensation for an erroneous seizure of property under the Trading with the Enemy Act. Pursuant to a Senate resolution passed after the decedent's death, a proceeding was commenced in the Court of Claims, which was to report its findings to the Senate. The Tax Court said: "What that report may turn out to be, no one can now foretell, and even the most favorable recommendation which may be made by that court to the Senate will be of no force to establish an enforceable legal right. The Senate will then act upon its own judgment upon a broad standard of sovereign justice, and may uncontestably refuse what the Court of Claims may recommend." 33 B.T.A. at 1045–46. What if the Senate had acted favorably before the tax proceeding was commenced but after the decedent's death? What if the resolution had been passed *before* the decedent's death? See also Bary's Estate v. Commissioner, 24 T.C.M. (CCH) 1790 (1965), affd. per curiam, 368 F.2d 844 (2d Cir. 1966) (1940 value of a claim to be compensated for property confiscated by the Soviet government in 1918–1919 was zero, despite legislation creating a claims procedure against assets assigned by Soviet government to United States in 1933).

In First Victoria Natl. Bank v. United States, 620 F.2d 1096 (5th Cir. 1980), the executor argued that decedent's "rice history acreage" was not an interest in property subject to tax, claiming, secondarily, that if it was within § 2033, it had no value. The decedent's many years as a large-scale rice farmer was the basis for his "rice history acreage," a record on which his annual allotment of acreage for growing and marketing rice free from payment of statutory penalties was established. Although the farmer concededly had "no enforceable right to a continuation of the allotment program or to any specific number of acres of allotment" until the Department of Agriculture set the production quotas each year, the court held that the "rice history acreage" was a valuable entitlement that passed with the farm to the decedent's heirs and was includible in his gross estate under § 2033. The court brushed aside the argument that uncertainties concerning the continuation of the program and the size of future allotments made the entitlement worthless, noting that the price at which allotments and production histories were traded reflected a discount for such uncertainties.

5. *Partnership interests.* In the absence of an agreement to the contrary, a general partnership is automatically dissolved on the death of a general partner. See Uniform Partnership Act § 31(4). To avoid this result, the

partnership agreement may provide for continuation of the partnership and liquidation of the deceased partner's interest at a price equal to a specified share of the partnership's assets at the time of death as well as a share of profits earned during a specified period after death. The deceased partner's rights under the agreement must be valued as of the date of death and included in the gross estate under § 2033. Riegelman's Estate v. Commissioner, 253 F.2d 315 (2d Cir. 1958). This result would seem too obvious to require explication if it were not for an early Supreme Court decision, Bull v. United States, 295 U.S. 247 (1935), holding a deceased partner's share of post-death profits to be beyond the reach of the estate tax. Although *Bull* has never been expressly overruled, modern authority accepts the *Riegelman* court's judgment: "we think [*Bull*] no longer states the applicable law."

Although it did not rest its decision on the point, the Court in *Bull* expressed concern at the apparent unfairness of subjecting the value of the deceased partner's share to estate tax when it was clear that the future payments would eventually be subject to income tax when received by the decedent's successors. Income received under these circumstances has come to be known as "income in respect of a decedent" (IRD), and is subject to income tax in the hands of the recipient under § 691(a). To alleviate the burden of the combined estate and income taxes, § 691(c) authorizes the person who includes an item of IRD in gross income to take an income tax deduction for the estate tax attributable to the item. In general, the deduction is calculated by determining the amount of the estate tax imposed on the "net value" of IRD in the decedent's estate and allocating that amount among the items of IRD in proportion to their estate tax values. Reg. § 1.691(c)–1. Income in respect of a decedent comes in various forms, including, for example, salary earned but not received during life, interest accrued but unpaid at death, dividends payable after death on stock owned by the decedent on the record date, post-death distributions from qualified retirement plans, commissions on insurance policy renewals, and unpaid installments of lottery winnings. See generally 3 Bittker & Lokken, Federal Taxation of Income, Estates and Gifts ¶ 84.1 (3d ed. 2001).

6. *Lottery winnings. D*, an irrepressible optimist and purchaser of lottery tickets, defied the overwhelming odds and won a $20 million grand prize. Applicable state law requires that the prize money be paid in annual installments of $1 million over 20 years and prohibits the sale or assignment of future installments except by court order, effectively preventing the winner from using such installments as collateral for a loan. (These restrictions may be defended as measures to protect the winner from his or her own improvidence. Unstated, of course, is the fact that the state can finance a 20–year annuity of $1 million per year for a present payment of around $12 million.) *D* claimed the prize on behalf of herself, her husband and their five children pursuant to a partnership agreement which allocated all lottery winnings equally among the seven partners. Before receiving the first installment, *D* died. What interest does *D* own at death and how is it valued? Did she make a completed lifetime gift of an interest in the ticket, the partnership, or the prize money? Does it matter whether the partnership agreement was executed before or after the drawing of the winning number? See Winkler's Estate v. Commissioner, 73 T.C.M. (CCH) 1657 (1997). On the valuation of future

lottery payments, see infra page 587. See also Aghdami, The Morning After: Tax Planning for Lottery Winners, 90 J. Taxn. 228 (1999).

GOODMAN v. GRANGER

243 F.2d 264 (3d Cir.), cert. denied, 355 U.S. 835 (1957).

KALODNER, CIRCUIT JUDGE.

When does the federal estate tax attach?

More specifically stated, when does such tax attach to a decedent-employee's contractual right to annual deferred compensation payments from his employer, payable to his estate after his death?

That problem, of first impression, is presented by this appeal by the government from a judgment in favor of the taxpayer, Eleanor D. Goodman, administratrix of the estate of Jacques Blum, deceased, in a suit brought by her in the District Court for the Western District of Pennsylvania to recover estate taxes and interest alleged to have been erroneously assessed and collected.

The District Court, subscribing to the taxpayer's contention, concluded as a matter of law that the decedent's contractual right was to be "... valued during decedent's lifetime and *at the moment before death* ..." and made the factual finding that at such moment the contractual right was "valueless," for reasons which will subsequently be discussed. In its opinion the District Court stated "It must be admitted that if the value in the contracts is to be fixed *the moment after death*, then the Government is correct in its contention in this case." (Emphasis supplied.)

The undisputed facts may be summarized as follows:

The decedent, Jacques Blum, for several years prior to his sudden death of a heart attack at the age of 52 on May 2, 1947, was executive vice-president of Gimbel Brothers, Inc. ("Gimbels") in charge of its Pittsburgh store.

On October 19, 1944, June 1, 1945 and May 26, 1946, decedent entered into identical contracts of employment with Gimbel Brothers covering the years ending January 31, 1945, January 31, 1946 and January 31, 1947, respectively. Each contract provided for a basic salary of $50,000 per year, and for additional "contingent benefits" of $2,000 per year for fifteen years "after the employee ceases to be employed by the employer" by reason of death or otherwise. The post-employment "contingent payments" were to be made only if the employee duly performed the services agreed upon and did not engage in a competing business within a specified period after termination of his employment; and they were to be reduced if his post-employment earnings from a non-competing business plus the contingent payments exceeded seventy-five percent of his yearly average compensation under the contracts. Any of the fifteen annual contingent payments which fell due after the employee's death were to be paid to his estate, or to a nominee designated in his will.

The third contract for the period of employment ending January 31, 1947 was, by its terms, renewed on a month-to-month basis and was in effect at the time of decedent's death. At the latter time there was every prospect that he would continue to advance in his highly successful career in retailing.[6]

After the decedent's death Gimbels paid the $6,000 annual installments provided by the three separate contracts ($2,000 each) to the taxpayer in her capacity as administratrix as they became due. She filed with the Collector a timely federal estate tax return and included the three contracts at a value of $15,000. Upon audit of the return the Internal Revenue Agent in Charge, Pittsburgh, increased the value of the three contracts from $15,000 to $66,710.34, the present worth of $90,000, payable in equal annual installments of $6,000 a year over a period of fifteen years. The increase in the value of the contracts resulted in a deficiency of $15,958.18, including interest, which was assessed against and paid by the taxpayer, and for the recovery of which she brought the suit here involved.

At the trial the taxpayer offered the testimony of three witnesses to the effect that the three contracts created no property right having any market value in the decedent while he lived.

The government offered the testimony of one witness who testified that the deficiency assessment was based upon his conclusion that the contracts created in the decedent valuable vested interests, subject to being divested, and on that theory the contracts were considered by the government to have the marketable monetary value which it had determined and assessed.

The federal estate tax is imposed upon "the transfer" of a decedent's property, Internal Revenue Code [§ 2001], and the gross estate of the decedent is determined by including "the value at the time of his death of all property" to "the extent of the [decedent's] interest therein." [§ 2033.] Treasury Regulations [§ 20.2031–1(b)] provide that the measure of value for the purpose of determining the gross estate in federal estate taxation is the fair market value of the estate.

The sum of the taxpayer's position is (1) what is taxed is "the value" of the decedent's interest in his contract that "ceased by reason of death," not the value of what is received by the recipient (the administratrix); otherwise stated, "the value" of the decedent's interest in his contract was to be determined as "of the moment before death."

---

6. Each of the contracts provided for payment of amounts falling due after the employee's death, in the following language:

> 6. Any of the fifteen (15) annual contingent payments which fall due after the death of the Employee shall be paid either (1) to such person as shall furnish evidence satisfactory to the Employer showing that under the last will and testament of the Employee or for other reason he is duly authorized in law to receive such payment, or (2) to such person as shall furnish the Employer with evidence of appointment as representative of the estate of the Employee. The receipt of any such person for such payments shall release the Employer of any further obligation in respect thereof. "Person" as used in this Article 6 may include one or more individuals, trusts, firms or corporations.

The government's position may be summarized as follows: (1) the estate tax is measured by the value of property transferred by death and here an absolute right to the fifteen deferred compensation payments passed by decedent's death to the taxpayer inasmuch as the possibility of forfeiture was extinguished by decedent's death; (2) the government properly valued the right to the deferred compensation payments in the same manner as an annuity for a term certain, i.e., at the commuted value in accordance with the applicable Treasury Regulations. . . .

It is clear that the decedent's interest in the employment contracts was "property" includible in his gross estate under [§ 2033]. Determination of the time when that interest is to be valued is the crux of the dispute. . . .

The taxpayer has ignored the very nature of the tax which it is urged is dispositive of this case. True, the tax reaches the ". . . interest which ceased by reason of the death," Knowlton v. Moore, [178 U.S. 41, 49 (1900)], but the reference there was to the distinction between an estate tax and an inheritance tax. The inheritance tax is levied upon the individual shares of the decedent's estate after distribution to the legatees; the estate tax is imposed upon the total estate of the decedent which is transferred to the legatees. [§ 2001.] The estate tax has been characterized as "an excise imposed upon the transfer of or shifting in relationships to property at death." United States Trust Co. of New York v. Helvering, 1939, 307 U.S. 57, 60. The estate and inheritance taxes have the common element of being based upon the transmission of property from the dead to the living. New York Trust Co. v. Eisner, 1921, 256 U.S. 345. In Knowlton v. Moore, supra, the Supreme Court recognized this basic principle when it said 178 U.S. at page 56:

> . . . tax laws of this nature in all countries rest in their essence upon the principle that death is the generating source from which the particular taxing power takes its being, and that it is the power to transmit, or the transmission from the dead to the living, on which such taxes are more immediately rested.

Since death is the propelling force for the imposition of the tax, it is death which determines the interests to be includible in the gross estate. Interests which terminate on or before death are not a proper subject of the tax. Assets may be acquired or disposed of before death, possibilities of the loss of an asset may become actualities or may disappear. Upon the same principle underlying the inclusion of interests in a decedent's gross estate, valuation of an interest is neither logically made nor feasibly administered until death has occurred. The taxpayer's theory of valuing property before death disregards the fact that generally the estate tax is neither concerned with changes in property interests nor values prior to death. The tax is measured by the value of assets transferred by reason of death, the critical value being that which is determined as of the time of death.

As was so succinctly stated by Judge Hartshorne in Christiernin v. Manning, D.C.D.N.J. 1956, 138 F. Supp. 923, 925:

> There can not be a decedent, till death has occurred. A decedent's estate is not transferred either by his will or by intestacy, till death has occurred.... And the decedent's interest in the property taxable is to be such interest "at the time of his death." ...

Here the employment contracts provided for additional "contingent" compensation of $6,000 per year for fifteen years to be paid to Blum or his estate after the termination of his employment by reason of death or otherwise. True, the right to these payments was forfeitable upon the occurrence of any of the specified contingencies. However, forfeiture as a result of the contingencies never occurred during Blum's lifetime, and any possibility of their occurrence was extinguished by his death. Gimbels has been making and the estate has been collecting the payments provided by the contracts. Valuation of the right to these payments must be determined as of the time of Blum's death when the limiting factor of the contingencies would no longer be considered. Death ripened the interest in the deferred payments into an absolute one, and death permitted the imposition of the tax measured by the value of that absolute interest in property.

In Mearkle's Estate v. Commissioner of Internal Revenue, 3 Cir., 1942, 129 F.2d 386, we considered the proper method of valuing an annuity upon the death of the decedent which by its terms was payable to the decedent during his life and to his wife for her life. The criterion adopted was the purchase price of an annuity contract upon the life of the wife measured by her life expectancy on the date of her husband's death. There is no reference in this test to the husband's life expectancy upon the date of his death or to the joint expectancies of the decedent and his wife. See Christiernin v. Manning, supra. The value of decedent's interest in the annuity up to the time of his death is not considered, and, as in the situation here involved, death cuts off prior limiting factors.[7]

For the reasons stated the judgment of the District Court will be reversed with directions to proceed in accordance with this opinion.

NOTES

1. *Post-death events.* The fair market value standard requires consideration of "[a]ll relevant facts and elements of value as of the applicable valuation date." Reg. § 20.2031–1(b). In some cases, a contingency affecting the value of property—for example, the possibility that the annual payments in *Goodman* might have been reduced or forfeited—is resolved at death. In

7. In Estate of Harper, 1948, 11 T.C. 717, cited by taxpayer, there were included in decedent's gross estate notes of insolvent makers who by reason of the receipt of legacies under the decedent's will became solvent. The Commissioner valued the notes at face value. The Tax Court held to the contrary, subscribing to the view that the estate tax was "measured by the value of the interest transferred or which ceases at death," viz., the actual value of the then insolvent maker's assets. The result reached is consistent with our approach in the instant case, although the language used by the Tax Court was perhaps something less than fortunate.

many cases, however, the value of property depends on future events or conditions that cannot be predicted with certainty. In general, post-death events may not be used directly to prove value. Nevertheless, the courts have permitted events that were "reasonably foreseeable" at the valuation date to be taken into account "for the 'limited purpose' of establishing what the willing buyer and seller's expectations were on the valuation date and whether these expectations were 'reasonable and intelligent.' " Gilford's Estate v. Commissioner, 88 T.C. 38, 52 (1987) (quoting Jephson's Estate v. Commissioner, 81 T.C. 999 (1983)). Does this mean that a post-death takeover bid may be taken into account in valuing a decedent's stock? Does it matter whether the bid is successful? Whether the existence of the bid, or its terms, were reasonably foreseeable at the date of death? See Gilford's Estate, supra (disregarding post-death merger); Jung's Estate v. Commissioner, 101 T.C. 412 (1993) (admitting post-death events "as evidence of value rather than as something that affects value"); see also Polack v. Commissioner, 366 F.3d 608 (8th Cir. 2004) (financial statements for subsequent years not relevant in valuing gift of stock). The effect of post-death events on the valuation of claims against the estate under § 2053 is discussed in McMorris' Estate v. Commissioner, infra page 446, and in Note 2, infra page 456.

2. *Interests terminating at death.* The court in *Goodman* stated that "[i]nterests which terminate on or before death are not a proper subject of the tax." Assume that *D* is the life income beneficiary of a trust created by her parents; at *D*'s death the trust property is payable to her issue then living. Since *D*'s income interest terminates at death, no portion of the trust property is includible in her gross estate. Moreover, if one of *D*'s children predeceases her, the child's contingent remainder is defeated and therefore is not includible in the child's gross estate. See Dickinson's Estate, 41 T.C.M. (CCH) 787 (1981) (life estate); Rev. Rul. 55–438, 1955–2 C.B. 601 (contingent remainder). One of the principal targets of the generation-skipping transfer tax, discussed in Chapter 6, is a dynastic trust created to pay income for life to successive generations of beneficiaries.

It does not follow, however, that a debt owed to the decedent may be canceled by will without incurring a tax. Reg. § 20.2033–1(b). Because the will is freely revocable during the testator's lifetime, cancellation of the debt by will is functionally equivalent to a bequest, and the debt must be included in the decedent's gross estate under § 2033. See Buckwalter's Estate v. Commissioner, 46 T.C. 805 (1966) (forgiveness of son's debt at death did not avoid inclusion of the debt in father's gross estate under § 2033); cf. Moss' Estate v. Commissioner, 74 T.C. 1239 (1980) (promissory notes not included when their cancellation occurred at holder's death pursuant to an irrevocable agreement made during life at arm's length for full consideration).

3. *Property of unascertainable value.* In exceptional cases, a transaction may be held "open" for income tax purposes if property has no ascertainable value. See, e.g., Burnet v. Logan, 283 U.S. 404 (1931); see also *DiMarco's Estate*, supra page 61, and Note 2, supra page 65, concerning the "open transaction" approach in the gift tax context. In contrast, for purposes of the estate tax, property must be valued at once or not at all. Estimating the present value of a stream of future payments is especially difficult where the amount or timing of the payments depends on uncertain future events. For

example, in Andrews' Estate v. United States, 850 F.Supp. 1279 (E.D. Va. 1994), the asset to be valued was the "name" of V.C. Andrews, a best-selling paperback novelist. After Andrews' death, her executor authorized the ghostwriting of several novels which eventually were published under Andrews' name. The court determined a value of just over $700,000 for Andrews' name, based on estimated net revenues from the initial posthumous novel (measured by Andrews' customary advance payments, less agent's and ghostwriter's fees and other production costs), discounted by 33 percent to reflect the risk that the ghostwriter might fail to produce a manuscript acceptable to the publisher. See also Pascal's Estate v. Commissioner, 22 T.C.M. (CCH) 1766 (1963) (option to produce a musical play based on Shaw's *Pygmalion*, which resulted after the decedent's death in the production of *My Fair Lady*, valued at $200,000 although claims made by the parties ranged up to $1,140,000); Smith's Estate v. Commissioner, 57 T.C. 650 (1972), affd. on other issues, 510 F.2d 479 (2d Cir.), cert. denied, 423 U.S. 827 (1975) (deceased sculptor's inventory of unsold pieces valued at $2,700,000, roughly splitting the difference between the executor's appraisal of $714,000 and the Service's of approximately $4,300,000).

Another source of difficulty in valuing property is uncertainty concerning the extent of the decedent's enforceable rights under local law. In Newhouse's Estate v. Commissioner, 94 T.C. 193 (1990), the decedent held all of the common stock and family members held all of the preferred stock in Advance Publications, Inc. Due to Advance's unusual and complex capital structure, the respective rights of the common and preferred shareholders under state law were largely "unclear." Several prominent experts took "diametrically opposed" positions, for example, on whether a purchaser of the common stock could obtain more than a ratable share of the value of Advance's assets in a forced merger. The Tax Court noted the effect of this uncertainty on the fair market value of the common stock:

> A prospective buyer of the Advance common stock would want to know the rights of the preferred shareholders to gauge what corporate affairs the common stock could control and to project how to maximize the value of the investment. The prospective buyer would have received contradictory expert legal opinions on the relative rights and privileges of the common and preferred stock. This uncertainty would significantly depress the purchase price of the common stock. The prospective buyer would have been sure of protracted and expensive litigation. [94 T.C. at 214.]

Ultimately, the Tax Court found it unnecessary to resolve the disputed state law issues and valued the common stock at $176 million based on a hypothetical recapitalization and public offering.

4. *Qualified conservation easements.* Under § 2031(c), enacted in 1997, the executor may elect to exclude from the gross estate a portion of the value of land that is subject to a "qualified conservation easement." To qualify for the exclusion, the land must be located in the United States or its possessions and must have been owned by the decedent or a family member throughout the three-year period ending at death. The easement must impose a perpetual restriction on the use of the land and must be granted by the decedent or a family member (or by the decedent's executor or a trustee) to a qualifying

organization "exclusively for conservation purposes." In this context, conservation purposes include the preservation of land for outdoor recreation or education of the general public, protection of a natural habitat, or preservation of open space for scenic enjoyment or pursuant to a governmental conservation policy. §§ 2031(c)(8) and 170(h).

The amount of the exclusion under § 2031(c) is generally based on the value of the land includible in the decedent's gross estate (net of any estate tax charitable deduction with respect to the easement). The excludable amount is generally equal to 40 percent of the net value of the land, up to a maximum amount of $500,000. The full benefit of the 40–percent exclusion is available only if the easement reduces the value of the land by at least 30 percent; for every percentage point below the 30–percent threshold, the exclusion drops by two percentage points. Thus, if the easement reduces the value of the land by less than 10 percent, the exclusion disappears entirely. The estate tax benefit of the exclusion comes at the price of forgoing a stepped-up basis for income tax purposes. § 1014(a)(4).

See generally Lindstrom & Small, New Estate Tax Relief for Land Under Conservation Easement, 78 Tax Notes 1171 (1998); Sawyer, Conservation Easements Help Preserve Real Estate for an Owner's Family, 26 Est. Planning 68 (1999); Levin, You're Not Too Late: Post–Mortem Donations of Conservation Easements, 89 Tax Notes 661 (2000).

B. MARITAL ESTATES (DOWER, ELECTIVE SHARE, AND COMMUNITY PROPERTY) AND THE ORIGINS OF THE MARITAL DEDUCTION

1. ESTATES CREATED BY DOWER AND ELECTIVE SHARE

Section 2034, which provides that the gross estate shall include all property to the extent of the surviving spouse's "dower or curtesy"[8] or statutory substitute therefor (i.e., elective share), buttresses § 2033 by preventing the gross estate from being reduced by the value of these marital estates.[9] Nor is a taxpayer able to circumvent § 2034 by having

8. The estate of curtesy, which granted a surviving husband rights in his wife's property if a child was born to the marriage, is for all practical purposes nonexistent today; it has been merged with the rights of dower or elective share which typically are made equally available to both spouses.

9. An action was brought at an early date attacking the inclusion of dower in the gross estate as unconstitutional. The argument was developed as follows: (a) the wife's dower interest arises as an incident of her marriage, not from the husband's death; (b) therefore, there is no "transfer" at the time of her husband's death; (c) therefore, the tax is imposed not on a transfer but on the surviving wife's "property"; (d) therefore, the tax is not an excise but a "direct" tax; (e) therefore, the tax violates Sections 2 and 9 of Article I of the Constitution, which require that direct taxes be apportioned among the several states according to their population. The obvious weak links in the syllogism are (a) and (b); in upholding the tax, the Eighth Circuit in Allen v. Henggeler, 32 F.2d 69, 72 (8th Cir.), cert. denied, 280 U.S. 594 (1929), asserted that the husband has very substantial rights over his real property during life and that it is only on his death that the wife "comes into" her property. Although the Supreme Court has never ruled directly on the

his or her spouse relinquish marital rights in return for a claim as a creditor against the taxpayer's estate at death or in return for a transfer of assets during life. The claim against the estate will not be deductible in computing the taxable estate because § 2043(b)(1), paralleling § 2034, states that the relinquishment of marital rights is not treated as consideration in money or money's worth. By similar reasoning, the lifetime transfer is not supported by consideration and therefore is subject to the gift tax. See Merrill v. Fahs, supra page 112. Under current law, however, interspousal transfers of property, pursuant to a written agreement settling marital and property rights in connection with a divorce proceeding, are deemed, for both gift and estate tax purposes, to have been made for full and adequate consideration. See § 2516, discussed in Spruance v. Commissioner, supra page 126, and § 2043(b)(2), discussed infra page 436, Note 1.

2. COMMUNITY PROPERTY AND THE MARITAL DEDUCTION

Although the federal estate tax does not grant immunity to the surviving spouse's dower or elective share in computing the decedent's gross estate, the surviving spouse's interest in community property has been treated differently. As early as 1919, the Attorney General ruled that only one-half of the value of community property was includible in the gross estate of the first spouse to die. T.D. 2450, 19 Treas. Dec. Int. Rev. 38 (1919); T.D. 3138, 23 Treas. Dec. Int. Rev. 238 (1921). The ruling was predicated on the nature of community property: Each spouse is regarded as having an equal, vested interest in the property throughout the marriage, and the first spouse to die has testamentary power only over his or her one-half interest. See Poe v. Seaborn, 282 U.S. 101 (1930). Several scholars, however, contended that under the state law as it existed at that time the husband's control over both halves of the community property during the marriage was so substantial that it would be appropriate to include the entire property in his gross estate if he predeceased his wife. See Eisenstein, Estate Taxes and the Higher Learning of the Supreme Court, 3 Tax L. Rev. 395, 538–40 (1948). Subsequent changes in state statutes that grant the spouses equal rights of management over the community property undermine this argument for a more inclusive tax in the husband's estate. See, e.g., Cal. Fam. Code §§ 1100 (personal property) and 1102 (real property).

Congress was less concerned with the theoretical justification for the tax than with the practical necessity of achieving a measure of equality in tax impact on the citizens of community property and common law states. In 1942, it moved to put the estate tax on the same footing for the two systems by requiring that the entire value of the community property be included in the gross estate of the first spouse to die, "except such part

constitutionality of § 2034, its validity is assumed in Merrill v. Fahs, supra page 112, and follows a fortiori from the reasoning of Fernandez v. Wiener, infra footnote 10.

thereof as may be shown to have been received as compensation for personal services actually rendered by the surviving spouse or derived originally from such compensation or from separate property of the surviving spouse." I.R.C. § 811(e)(2), as amended by § 402 of the Revenue Act of 1942, 56 Stat. 798. Even if the community property was entirely attributable to the surviving spouse's personal services or separate property, however, the 1942 amendment required inclusion of one-half of the property in the gross estate of the spouse who died first because of his or her testamentary power over that half.[10] The Revenue Act of 1942 also sought to equalize the community property and common law systems in the gift tax field by requiring that a gift of community property be treated as a gift by the husband unless it was attributable to the wife's personal services or separate property.

Because of widespread dissatisfaction with the 1942 legislation, Congress in 1948 restored the pre–1942 deference to the community property system, under which only one-half of the property was included in the gross estate of the first spouse to die. By itself, this would have revived the discrimination against the common law states, but Congress simultaneously enacted the marital deduction—an equalizing mechanism similar to the income-splitting joint return, which was also adopted in 1948. The Senate Finance Committee explained the new provision as follows:

> With the repeal of the 1942 amendments your committee recommends estate and gift tax splitting which is similar in its effects to the splitting of the income tax provided for in this bill. It is recognized that complete equalization of the estate and gift taxes can not be achieved because of the inherent differences between community property and noncommunity property. However, the new provisions will result in equality in the important situations.
>
> Under the estate-tax provision of your committee's bill a decedent spouse is allowed a marital deduction from his gross estate in the amount of the value of all interests in property passing outright from the decedent to the surviving spouse by way of bequest, devise, transfer, right of survivorship in jointly held property, etc. The deduction is limited to an amount not in excess of 50 percent of the adjusted gross estate.
>
> Under the gift-tax provisions of your committee's bill a donor spouse is allowed a deduction for every outright transfer by gift to his

10. An attack on constitutional grounds, similar to that made against the inclusion of dower in the gross estate in Allen v. Henggeler, supra footnote 9, was leveled against the economic source rule in the 1942 legislation. It was argued that by operation of state law, the surviving spouse already owned one-half of the community property at the death of the other spouse, so that inclusion of this half in the decedent's gross estate violated the direct tax and due process clauses of the Constitution. The Supreme Court in Fernandez v. Wiener, 326 U.S. 340 (1945), rejected this argument and upheld the tax, asserting that the death of either spouse brings about "changes in the legal and economic relationships" of the survivor to the property being taxed sufficient to justify an indirect tax as authorized by the Constitution. The constitutionality of the gift tax provisions of the 1942 Act was upheld on the authority of Fernandez v. Wiener in Francis v. Commissioner, 8 T.C. 822 (1947), and Beavers v. Commissioner, 165 F.2d 208 (5th Cir. 1947), cert. denied, 334 U.S. 811 (1948).

spouse, such deduction to be an amount equal to one-half of the value of the interest transferred. In the case of a transfer by gift by a married person to persons other than his spouse, the interest transferred may be considered as made one-half by each, if the spouses so elect.

Under both the estate and gift taxes the marital deduction does not apply to the decedent's or the donor's interest in community property. This exception was necessary because after the repeal of the 1942 amendments the surviving spouse in a community property State will receive one-half of the community property tax-free. Similarly, a donor spouse will be taxable on only one-half the value of any gifts made out of the community property. Although the marital deduction does not apply to community property, it will apply, in general, to the separate property of a decedent or a donor in a community-property State. [S. Rep. No. 1013, 88th Cong., 2d Sess. (1948), reprinted in 1948–1 C.B. 285, 305.]

Over the years, a number of proposals were forthcoming recommending that interspousal transfers be free from estate and gift taxation altogether.[11] In 1976, Congress took a first step in this direction by increasing the maximum marital deduction to equal the greater of $250,000 or one-half of the decedent's adjusted gross estate. A similar concession, limited to $100,000, was enacted for the gift tax, but if the decedent exercised this privilege for gifts, the $250,000 estate tax deduction was correspondingly reduced. This modest beginning was deemed insufficient, and in 1981 Congress eliminated all quantitative limits on the marital deduction, so that transfers in qualifying form between husband and wife are now fully exempt from estate and gift taxes. By these amendments, the marital deduction has become more than a device to secure the same estate and gift tax results for citizens in common law states as in community property states. The deduction now has the independent function of treating a husband and wife "as one economic unit for purposes of estate and gift taxes, as they generally are for income tax purposes." S. Rep. No. 144, 97th Cong., 1st Sess. 127 (1981), reprinted in 1981–2 C.B. 412, 461.

NOTES

1. *Impact of the unlimited marital deduction on taxation of marital estates under §§ 2034 and 2043(b).* The 1981 conversion of the marital deduction into an unlimited allowance for interspousal transfers makes §§ 2034 and 2043(b) of no practical consequence for marital estates that pass to the surviving spouse outright or in another form that qualifies for the marital deduction under § 2056. However, common law dower consummate and the elective share in some states (see, e.g., Conn. Gen. Stat. § 45a–436)

11. For reports that advocated a 100–percent marital deduction, see U.S. Treasury Department, Tax Reform Studies and Proposals, 91st Cong., 1st Sess. (Part 3) 357–60 (1969); American Law Institute, Federal Estate and Gift Taxation 31–37 (1969).

are awarded to the surviving spouse as interests in the decedent's property for life only, an estate that has traditionally been considered a nondeductible terminable interest. Although § 2056(b)(7), which also came into the Code in 1981, may be invoked to make a life estate eligible for the marital deduction, the executor must file an election to that effect and no other disqualifying conditions may be imposed on the estate by the state statute that creates it. For a discussion of marital estates and the terminable interest rule, see Chapter 5, Section D.

2. *Current status of community property and the marital deduction.* Consistent with the marital deduction's function as a device to give common law states the same tax advantages that existed in community property states, the pre–1981 statutes (viz., § 2056(c)(1)(C) (estate tax) and § 2523(f) (gift tax)) specifically made the deduction unavailable for community property, although a married couple in a community property state was allowed to apply the deduction against their separate property. When the role of the marital deduction was changed in 1981, these restrictions were removed, which enabled interspousal transfers of community property to qualify for the 100–percent marital deduction.

C. JOINT INTERESTS WITH RIGHT OF SURVIVORSHIP: § 2040

1. INTRODUCTION

The estate tax status of real or personal property held in joint tenancy by two or more persons with right of survivorship[12] is governed by § 2040, which establishes two different sets of rules, one for joint interests held by husband and wife and the other for nonmarital joint interests. The divergent principles applicable to these two areas can be summarized as follows:

1. *Joint interests of husband and wife.* If property is held by husband and wife as joint tenants with right of survivorship or as tenants by the entirety, one-half of its value is included in the gross estate of the first spouse to die under § 2040(b), regardless of how the property was acquired or who supplied the consideration for its acquisition.

2. *Nonmarital joint interests.* If the joint tenants are not husband and wife, § 2040(a) requires inclusion of the full value of the

12. Section 2040 is aimed at property held jointly with a right of survivorship, a form of ownership under which the deceased tenant's interest does not pass by will or intestacy, but terminates at his or her death, so that the surviving tenant's interest ripens into absolute ownership. Under a nonsurvivorship tenancy, such as a tenancy in common, each tenant owns a proportionate share of the property and has the power to dispose of that share at death, making it includible in his or her gross estate under § 2033. It is necessary to look at local law to determine whether a particular asset held by the decedent and another person "as joint tenants" meets the survivorship requirement of § 2040. In some states, the term "joint tenants" in a conveyance or will implies a right of survivorship unless this implication is expressly negated; other states, by contrast, treat the document as creating only a tenancy in common unless it expressly provides for a right of survivorship.

property in the gross estate of the first to die, unless (a) the tenants did not themselves acquire the property but received it by gift or inheritance from someone else (e.g., a parent devises a summer home to two children as joint tenants with right of survivorship; each owns half) or (b) the survivor or survivors furnished part or all of the consideration with which the property was acquired.

The economic source rule enunciated in § 2040(a) for nonspousal joint interests is described as the "general rule," to which § 2040(b), relating to joint interests held by married couples, is an exception.[13] In point of fact, husband-wife joint interests are more important both in numbers and values, so that § 2040(b) could more properly bear the label "general rule." For this reason, and also because § 2040(b) is a simpler provision that can be applied without reference to § 2040(a), it is examined first.

2. QUALIFIED JOINT INTERESTS OF HUSBAND AND WIFE: § 2040(b)

Section 2040(b) provides that only one-half of a "qualified joint interest" held by the decedent and the decedent's spouse is includible in the gross estate, regardless of which spouse furnished the consideration with which the property was acquired. The half-and-half approach was first enacted in 1976, but the term "qualified joint interest" was then defined in a more restrictive manner than under current law. The 1976 rules applied only to joint tenancies (including tenancies by the entirety) created after 1976 by the decedent, the decedent's spouse, or both, and only if (1) in the case of personal property, the creation of the interest constituted a gift for gift tax purposes, or (2) in the case of real property, the donor elected under former § 2515 of the gift tax to treat the creation of the joint interest as a gift. In 1981, these restrictions were deleted and § 2515 was repealed. Section 2040(b) now defines a "qualified joint interest" as any interest in property which is held exclusively by a husband and wife as tenants by the entirety or joint tenants with right of

13. Section 2040(a) is the "general rule" in the sense that it was the original rule and governed the application of the estate tax to joint tenancies, including those between husband and wife, from 1916 to 1976. In Tyler v. United States, 281 U.S. 497 (1930), the Supreme Court upheld as constitutional § 202(c) of the Revenue Act of 1916, the forerunner of § 2040(a), as applied to a tenancy by the entirety created after the statute was enacted. The attack focused on the extent to which the death of the first spouse affected the surviving spouse's rights to her half of the tenancy. The Court held that death was the "generating source" of important accessions to the property rights of the survivor and that the tax was therefore an excise tax on that enlargement of rights and not an unapportioned direct tax on the property. In Third Natl. Bank & Trust Co. v. White, 287 U.S. 577 (1932), the Court affirmed, per curiam, a judgment applying the same principle to a pre-1916 tenancy by the entirety.

Where property is held in joint tenancy, rather than in tenancy by the entirety, either co-tenant can terminate the tenancy and get an undivided one-half interest in the property, provided he or she acts while the other co-tenant is living. Despite this possibility of severance, the Supreme Court upheld the application of what is now § 2040(a) to property held in joint tenancy, whether the tenancy was created before or after 1916. United States v. Jacobs, 306 U.S. 363 (1939).

survivorship.[14]

At first reading, the 1981 legislation appears to contain a paradox. On one hand, § 2040(b) requires inclusion in the decedent's gross estate of one-half the value of any qualified joint interest; on the other hand, § 2056 grants a marital deduction that offsets in full the amount included under § 2040(b). The Senate Finance Committee Report offers an explanation:

> [T]he committee believes that the taxation of jointly held property between spouses is complicated unnecessarily. Often such assets are purchased with joint funds making it difficult to trace individual contributions. In light of the unlimited marital deduction adopted by the committee bill, the taxation of jointly held property between spouses is only relevant for determining the basis of property to the survivor [under § 1014].... Accordingly, the committee believes it appropriate to adopt an easily administered rule under which each spouse would be considered to own one-half of jointly held property regardless of which spouse furnished the consideration for the property. [S. Rep. No. 144, 97th Cong., 1st Sess. 127 (1981), reprinted in 1981–2 C.B. 412, 461.][15]

In short, § 2040(b) is designed not to raise revenue under the estate tax but rather to establish one-half as the maximum amount of marital survivorship property that is eligible for the date-of-death basis prescribed by § 1014. Thus, if Blackacre was purchased by a married couple for $200,000, was held in a joint-and-survivorship tenancy, and was worth $500,000 when the decedent died, one-half of its value, or $250,000, is included in the decedent's gross estate under § 2040(b). The surviving spouse is entitled, in the event of a future sale of the property, to an income tax basis of $350,000—$100,000 for the one-half interest acquired by the survivor when the property was initially purchased, plus $250,000 for the one-half interest passing by right of survivorship and included in the decedent's gross estate. Moreover, the stepped-up basis for the one-half interest included in the decedent's estate is acquired without any countervailing tax burden, because the inclusion is matched by a marital deduction of the same amount under § 2056.

---

14. The 50–percent inclusion rule of § 2040(b)(1), as enacted in 1976, originally applied only to "qualified joint interests" created after 1976. The current definition of "qualified joint interests" was enacted in 1981, effective for decedents dying after 1981. Although Congress in 1981 may have intended to make the half-and-half rule prospectively applicable to all marital joint tenancies, whenever created, the courts have held that the 1981 amendment did not alter the original effective date of § 2040(b)(1). As a result, the tracing rule of § 2040(a) continues to apply to marital joint tenancies created before 1977. See Gallenstein v. United States, 975 F.2d 286 (6th Cir. 1992); Patten v. United States, 116 F.3d 1029 (4th Cir. 1997); Hahn v. Commissioner, 110 T.C. 140 (1998).

15. Another explanation for the 50–50 principle of § 2040(b) was offered by the House Ways and Means Committee in its report on the 1976 statutory predecessor of § 2040(b): "[I]ncluding only one-half the value of the property in the [decedent's gross estate] implicitly recognize[s] the services furnished by [the surviving] spouse toward the accumulation of the jointly owned property even though a monetary value of the services cannot be accurately determined." H.R. Rep. No. 1380, 94th Cong., 2d Sess. 20 (1976), reprinted in 1976–3 C.B. (Vol. 3) 735, 754.

By including the decedent's half of the survivorship property in decedent's gross estate, § 2040(b) also has an impact on three statutory allowances, the availability of which depends on the size and composition of the gross estate. These allowances are as follows:

1. Section 303(b), relating to the income taxation of redemptions of stock to pay administration expenses and death taxes;
2. Section 2032A, relating to special use valuation for qualified real property; and
3. Section 6166, granting an extension of time for the payment of estate taxes attributable to closely held business interests.

By the enactment of the half-and-half principle, joint-and-survivorship tenancies between husband and wife are put on a par with tenancies in common, where each tenant has separate ownership of a proportionate share of the property. In contrast, § 2040(a), which is applicable to non-spousal joint tenancies, allocates the estate tax to the estate of the tenant who furnished the consideration. This means that the estate of the decedent who was the source of the consideration is taxed on the value of the tenancy, but because it passes through the decedent's estate under § 2040(a), that amount is accorded a stepped-up (or stepped-down) basis. In like manner but with the estate tax removed by the marital deduction, a husband and wife can obtain a full new basis if the spouse who acquired complete ownership of the property retains it until death and transfers it by will to the surviving spouse.

NOTES

1. *Basis on succession to an entire interest in community property.* On the death of spouse *A*, spouse *B* automatically succeeds to one-half of the community property by operation of local law. If *A* transfers the other half to *B* by will, *B* acquires the full title, in a manner similar to a surviving joint tenant in a common law state. Because the transfer of *A*'s share to *B* qualifies for the marital deduction, *A*'s estate will not be liable for an estate tax on the property. Is *B* entitled to a stepped-up basis for all or only one-half of the property? Section 1014(b)(6) states that the surviving spouse's one-half share of community property receives the stepped-up basis provided that the other half is included in the decedent's gross estate. Is that condition satisfied? There is no comparable provision in § 1014 dealing with joint-and-survivorship property.

2. *Other considerations that arise when creating husband-wife survivorship interests.* Although there is no federal tax incentive for doing so, many married couples hold a substantial amount of their property in joint tenancy with right of survivorship. Their reasons may include a need to express their sense that they own everything collectively, a desire to avoid the costs and delay of putting the property through probate and administration, and a hope of reducing state death taxes.[16] Concentration of all the family wealth in joint-

16. This hope may be realized to some extent in a state that has no gift tax and that treats husband-wife joint tenancies as belonging half to each spouse for inheritance tax purposes.

and-survivorship tenancies, however, may produce unfortunate tax consequences. For example, assume the first spouse dies in 2011 and the survivor succeeds to a $10 million estate by right of survivorship. Because of § 2040(b) and the marital deduction, no estate tax is paid. In 2012 the surviving spouse dies, leaving the $10 million estate to the children by will. The survivor's estate may incur an estate tax liability of $1,750,000 ($3,480,800 tentative tax less $1,730,800 unified credit). With foresight, how might the couple have arranged their affairs to avoid payment of any estate tax? For an example of a credit shelter bequest, see infra page 538, Note 1. In 2010 Congress amended the statute to allow the surviving spouse to make use of the deceased spouse's unused exemption, if the latter's executor so elects on a timely filed estate tax return. § 2010(c). The "portability" of the exemption reduces the need for a credit shelter bequest and mitigates the adverse tax consequences of holding all of the couple's combined assets in joint-and-survivorship form. See infra pages 539 and 549.

3. *Tenancy held by decedent and noncitizen surviving spouse.* As part of a broader amendment in 1988 denying the marital deduction for transfers to a spouse who is not a U.S. citizen, the Code provides that marital survivorship tenancies owned by a decedent and a noncitizen surviving spouse are governed by the general rule in § 2040(a) rather than the husband-and-wife rule in § 2040(b). It will therefore be necessary to determine the amount of consideration furnished by the deceased spouse to determine the amount to be included in his or her estate. Gifts to a noncitizen spouse are no longer eligible for the marital deduction, but the statute provides that the creation of a survivorship tenancy in real property is not a taxable gift. See §§ 2056(d) and 2523(i), discussed infra page 487.

3. NONSPOUSAL JOINT TENANCIES: § 2040(a)

GOLDSBOROUGH'S ESTATE v. COMMISSIONER

70 T.C. 1077 (1978), affd. mem., 673 F.2d 1310 (4th Cir. 1982).

FEATHERSTON, JUDGE. . . .

Section 2040 provides in general that the decedent's gross estate includes the entire value of jointly held property but that section "except[s] such part thereof as may be shown to have originally belonged to . . . [the surviving joint tenant(s)] and never to have been received or acquired by the latter from the decedent for less than an adequate and full consideration in money or money's worth." Section 2040 further provides that if the decedent owned property jointly with another, the amount to be excluded from the decedent's gross estate is "only such part of the value of such property as is proportionate to the consideration furnished by . . . [the surviving joint tenant(s)]." Mathematically this "consideration furnished" exclusion can be expressed as follows:

$$\text{Amount excluded} = \text{Entire value of property (on the date of death or alternate valuation date)} \times \frac{\text{Survivor's consideration}}{\text{Entire consideration paid}}$$

In the instant case, the decedent (Goldsborough) acquired on May 12, 1937, real property (St. Dunstans) in her individual name. On April 4, 1946, decedent transferred St. Dunstans, valued at $25,000 on that date, to her two daughters (Eppler and O'Donoghue) as a gift. On July 17, 1949, the daughters sold St. Dunstans to H.W. Ford and his wife for $32,500. Sometime in that same year, each daughter invested her share of the proceeds from the sale of St. Dunstans in various stocks and securities; each daughter took title to her respective stocks and securities in joint tenancy with decedent. These stocks and securities remained in joint tenancy until December 21, 1972, the date of decedent's death, and during the period of joint tenancy the stocks and securities appreciated in value to $160,383.19, the value on the alternate valuation date.

Thus, the section 2040 exclusion depends on the amount, if any, of the consideration Eppler and O'Donoghue, the surviving joint tenants, furnished toward the $32,500 purchase price of the jointly held stocks and securities.

Respondent contends that all the funds used to purchase the stocks and securities in question were derived from decedent and thus the entire value of the jointly held property ($160,383.19) is includable in her gross estate.

Petitioners Buppert and Eppler argue that only the value of St. Dunstans at the time the gift was made to decedent's two daughters (i.e., $25,000) is includable in decedent's gross estate. In the alternative, petitioner Eppler contends that the gain of $7,500, measured by the appreciation in value from the time St. Dunstans was given to the two daughters in 1946 until that property was sold by them in 1949, constitutes consideration furnished by the daughters toward the $32,500 purchase price of the jointly held stocks and securities. Thus Eppler argues that $37,011.50 ($7,500/$32,500 of $160,383.19), the value of the jointly held property on the alternate valuation date, should be excluded from decedent's gross estate. We agree with this alternative argument.

To be sure, section 2040 is not a paragon of clarity, and the courts and Internal Revenue Service have wrestled with the question of whether a contribution made out of gain representing appreciation in value of property received gratuitously from decedent is attributable to the decedent or, instead, is to be treated as income from the property and thus separate funds of the surviving tenant.[17] The law, as we perceive it, recognizes two distinct situations and treats the two differently. In one situation, the surviving joint tenant receives property gratuitously from the decedent; the property thereafter appreciates, and the property itself is contributed in an exchange for jointly held property. In this circumstance section 20.2040–1(c)(4), Estate Tax Regs., treats all the property as

17. It is clear that income from property acquired gratuitously from the decedent constitutes a contribution from a surviving joint tenant's separate funds. Sec. 20.2040–1(c)(5), Estate Tax Regs.

having been paid for by the decedent, and the entire value of the property is included in the decedent's gross estate. See Estate of Kelley v. Commissioner, 22 B.T.A. 421, 425 (1931).

In the second situation, the surviving joint tenant receives property gratuitously from the decedent; the property thereafter appreciates or produces income and is sold, and the income or the sales proceeds are used as consideration for the acquisition of the jointly held property. In this situation, the income or the gain, measured by the appreciation from the time of receipt of the gift to the time of sale, has been held to be the surviving joint tenant's income and a part of that joint tenant's contribution to the purchase price. Harvey v. United States, 185 F.2d 463, 467 (7th Cir. 1950); First National Bank of Kansas City v. United States, 223 F. Supp. 963, 967 (W.D. Mo. 1963); Swartz v. United States, 182 F. Supp. 540, 542 (D. Mass. 1960). Thus, in the words of the statute, "such part of the value of such property as is proportionate to the consideration furnished by [the surviving joint tenant]" is excluded. See also Estate of Kelley v. Commissioner, supra; cf. Dimock v. Corwin, 99 F.2d 799 (2d Cir. 1938), affd., 306 U.S. 363 (1939); Stuart v. Hassett, 41 F. Supp. 905 (D. Mass. 1941).

The facts of the instant case fall precisely within this second situation. In Harvey v. United States, supra at 465, the court characterized the facts and framed the issue as follows:

> The jointly held property is not the gift property itself, in either its original or transmuted form, but property traceable to (1) the profits made through sales of the original gift property and successive reinvestments of the proceeds of such sales or (2) the rents, interest and dividends produced by such property in its original or converted form, while title thereto was in the wife. The question presented by this appeal, then, is whether such profits and income, realized from property originally received by the wife as a gift from her husband and traceable into property which was held by them as joint tenants at the time of the husband's death, came within the exception to the requirement of Section 811(e) [predecessor to sec. 2040] that the entire value of property held in joint tenancy shall be included in the decedent's gross estate.

The Government in *Harvey* argued that the full value of the jointly held property should be included in the decedent's gross estate, and the court dealt with that argument in the following manner (185 F.2d at 467):

> It seems clear that none of the cases cited contains any support for the novel proposition that income produced by gift property, after the gift has been completed, belongs to the donor and is property received or acquired from him by the donee; nor is there, in these cases, anything to impeach the conclusion of the trial court, or that of the Tax Court in [Estate of Howard v. Commissioner, 9 T.C. 1192, 1202–1203 (1947)], that the income produced by property of any kind belongs to the person who owns the property at the time it produces

> such income and does not originate with a donor who has made a completed gift of that property prior to its production of the income....
>
> Moreover, no reason is suggested for holding that one form of income, i.e., "profit gained through a sale or conversion of capital assets," ... is outside the exception, whereas other forms of income, such as dividends, rentals and interest, fall within its terms. It follows that the government's contention that the full value of the property held in joint tenancy by decedent and his wife at the time of his death should have been included in decedent's gross estate must be rejected. [Citations omitted.]

Thus we conclude that Eppler and O'Donoghue furnished $7,500 toward the $32,500 purchase price paid for the stocks and securities they held in joint tenancy with decedent until her death on December 21, 1972. Under the terms of the statute, such part of the value of the property, i.e., $160,383.19 on the alternate valuation date, as is proportionate to the $7,500 of consideration Eppler and O'Donoghue furnished is excluded from decedent's gross estate. Under the mathematical formula, set out above, the amount of the exclusion is $37,011.50....

NOTES

1. *Gift tax on creation or termination of joint tenancy.* In general, if *A* uses her own property to create a joint tenancy with her child *B*, *A* makes a completed gift of one-half of the value of the property. Reg. § 25.2511–1(h)(5). Does the amount of the gift accurately measure the value of the interest conferred on *B*? If the joint tenancy is subsequently terminated while both tenants are living and in such a way that *B* acquires the full title, *A* makes a completed gift of the other half of the property.

If *A* creates a joint tenancy with *B* while retaining the right to regain the entire property without *B*'s consent (as in the case of a typical joint bank account or a U.S. savings bond payable to *A* or *B* or the survivor), there is no completed gift until *B* actually receives some or all of the property. Reg. § 25.2511–1(h)(4).

On *A*'s death survived by *B*, the entire value of the property is includible in *A*'s gross estate where it will be subject to estate tax (subject to an offset for any gift tax attributable to the creation of the joint tenancy). §§ 2040(a) and 2001(b)(2). What are the tax results if *B* unexpectedly dies before *A*?

In the case of a joint tenancy between husband and wife, the gift resulting from the creation or termination of the tenancy automatically qualifies for the marital deduction, which ensures that no gift tax is payable. Reg. § 25.2523(d)–1. At the death of one spouse, the marital deduction similarly prevents any estate tax from being imposed on the one-half interest included in the decedent's gross estate. §§ 2040(b) and 2056.

2. *Contributions by survivor.* The inclusionary rule of § 2040(a) exempts "such part ... as may be shown to have originally belonged to [the survivor or survivors] and never to have been received or acquired by the latter from

the decedent for less than an adequate and full consideration in money or money's worth." This principle has been tested in various situations.

a. *Income and capital gains from property received by gift from the decedent.* Consider the application of the *Goldsborough* holding to the following hypothetical situations, assuming in each case that *A* gave *B* stock worth $100,000:

1. *B* receives dividends amounting to $25,000 and uses them to acquire property in joint tenancy with *A*.
2. *B* sells the stock for $125,000 and deposits the proceeds in a bank account; thereafter, *B* withdraws $25,000 to purchase property in joint tenancy with *A*.
3. When the stock is worth $125,000, *B* uses one-fifth of the shares to purchase property worth $25,000 in joint tenancy with *A*.

The *Goldsborough* decision recognizes the principle that income (e.g., cash dividends, rent, interest) and capital gains realized by the survivor from donated property belong to the survivor and are within the exception. Despite its initial reluctance, the Service appears to have accepted the ample body of case law equating capital gains with income as a contribution from the survivor (see the cases cited in *Goldsborough*). See Rev. Rul. 79–372, 1979–2 C.B. 330 (realized appreciation on property purchased by the survivor with funds received by gift from the decedent qualifies as a contribution from the survivor). The third hypothetical, however, as the decision notes, is controlled by Reg. § 20.2040–1(c)(4), which explicitly provides that if the donated property itself is used to acquire the joint tenancy, the entire value of the property, including appreciation, is taxed to the decedent. Is there any justification for a difference in result between the second and third hypotheticals? If *B* uses a stock dividend from donated property to purchase a joint tenancy with *A*, does the dividend qualify as a contribution from *B* or from *A*? See English v. United States, 270 F.2d 876 (7th Cir. 1959) (survivor not credited with stock dividends); Tuck v. United States, 282 F.2d 405 (9th Cir. 1960) (same where stock dividends reflected corporate earnings realized before the donated stock was received from the decedent); Rev. Rul. 80–142, 1980–1 C.B. 197 (same with statement that in case of dividend of common on common, period to which capitalized profits are attributable should not be controlling).

Assume that *A* contributes $100,000 to create a joint-and-survivor brokerage account with *B*, directing that all income and capital gains be reinvested. At *A*'s death the account is worth $500,000. How much, if any, can be excluded from *A*'s gross estate as a contribution from *B*? See Endicott Trust Co. v. United States, 305 F.Supp. 943 (N.D.N.Y. 1969) (property was held at all times in joint-and-survivorship form, capital gains never belonged exclusively to the survivor); but see Rev. Rul. 80–142, 1980–1 C.B. 197 (if shareholders had option to take dividends in cash or additional shares and elected the latter, stock dividends are treated by local law as belonging equally to both tenants, with the survivor's share therefore excluded from decedent's gross estate).

b. *Post-acquisition contributions.* Assume that *A* purchases Blackacre for $200,000, taking title in the names of *A* and *B* as joint tenants with right of survivorship. A few years later, when Blackacre is worth $300,000, *B* pays $100,000 for improvements (e.g., driveway, tennis court, etc.). Subsequently *A* dies survived by *B* when Blackacre is worth $600,000. Should the amount excluded from *A*'s gross estate on account of *B*'s contribution be $100,000 (amount contributed), $200,000 (amount based on proportionate share of total contributions), or $150,000 (amount based on hypothetical sale and repurchase at time of improvements)? See Peters' Estate v. Commissioner, 46 T.C. 407 (1966), affd., 386 F.2d 404 (4th Cir. 1967) (exclusion from decedent's gross estate limited to amount of survivor's cash contribution, in absence of evidence of appreciation in value of improvements; the court noted that had there been a showing of appreciation "it might have been necessary for us to devise a formula or ratio of our own").

c. *Services as contributions.* If the survivor worked for or with the decedent in the conduct of a business, pursuant to an understanding that the profits would be invested in jointly held property as compensation for the survivor's services, is the value of the services counted as a contribution by the survivor to the purchase of the tenancy? For the proposition that the survivor's services may constitute qualifying contributions, see Berkowitz v. Commissioner, 108 F.2d 319 (3d Cir. 1939) (remanding case to Board of Tax Appeals to determine whether widow's half interest in jointly held property was compensation for her services under "agreement that half is mine and half his"); Singer v. Shaughnessy, 198 F.2d 178 (2d Cir. 1952) (equal contributions based on showing of 50–50 partnership agreement); United States v. Neel, 235 F.2d 395 (10th Cir. 1956) (same, although partnership agreement was oral and records were not kept in partnership form). If the joint tenants are closely related (virtually all the cases involve husband and wife and the pre–1981 law), the services may have been rendered out of love for the decedent, rather than for compensation, and, conversely, the decedent may have been similarly motivated in giving the survivor an interest in the jointly held property. See Bushman v. United States, 8 F.Supp. 694 (Ct. Cl. 1934), cert. denied, 295 U.S. 756 (1935) (wife's services in husband's law practice and real estate business were of "inestimable value" but were rendered out of love and affection); Loveland's Estate v. Commissioner, 13 T.C. 5 (1949) (wife's nursing services were not shown to be beyond those required by the marriage contract).

d. *Assumption of mortgage as contribution.* Assume that (1) *A* and *B* purchase Blackacre as joint tenants for $100,000, of which *A* pays $20,000; (2) *A* and *B* execute a purchase money mortgage for the $80,000 balance; (3) *A* dies before *B* and before any payments of principal are made; and (4) Blackacre is worth $150,000 at *A*'s death. What contribution, if any, has *B* made to the acquisition of the tenancy? See Bremer v. Luff, 7 F.Supp. 148 (N.D.N.Y. 1933) (*B* credited with $40,000 contribution; 40/100 times $150,000 equals $60,000 attributable to *B* at *A*'s death). Payments to amortize the mortgage do not alter this outcome if rent from Blackacre is used or if *A* and *B* contribute equal amounts of their own funds, but an adjustment is required if one of them contributes a disproportionate amount. See Rev. Rul. 79–302, 1979–2 C.B. 328 (illustrative computations of amounts includible where decedent and survivor were jointly liable on mortgage, on which all payments were made by decedent).

3. *Simultaneous death of joint tenants.* *A* and *B* own Blackacre as joint tenants, *A* having paid the entire consideration for its acquisition. They are killed in an accident under circumstances that make it impossible to determine the order of deaths. The jurisdiction has adopted the Uniform Simultaneous Death Act, which provides that under these circumstances each tenant is deemed to have survived with respect to one-half of the property. What portion of the property is includible in the gross estates of *A* and *B*, respectively? See Rev. Rul. 76–303, 1976–2 C.B. 266 (*A*'s estate taxed on entire value; *B*'s estate on one-half). What are the arguments for and against this result?

CHAPTER 4

THE GROSS ESTATE: TRANSFERS DURING LIFE

■ ■ ■

A. GIFTS WITHIN THREE YEARS OF DEATH: § 2035

Earlier versions of § 2035 had important responsibilities for determining the content of a decedent's gross estate for estate tax purposes. In 1981 these responsibilities were curtailed so that in its current form § 2035 basically performs only two functions. First, it ensures that §§ 2036, 2037, 2038 and 2042 will still apply to certain lifetime transfers made by the decedent even if the decedent attempts during the last three years of life to sever the "taxable string" that would have brought one or more of those sections directly into operation; and second, it requires that the gross estate be increased by the amount of any gift tax paid by the decedent on transfers made by the decedent or the decedent's spouse within a three-year period ending with the decedent's death. These provisions are examined in detail below, but because the current version of § 2035 is only the latest in the complicated history concerned with so-called gifts in contemplation of death, a brief summary is required to explain how it is that this once key section of the Code evolved into its present form.

1. 1916 TO 1976: GIFTS IN CONTEMPLATION OF DEATH

In the estate tax enacted in 1916, Congress sought to prevent depletion of the tax base by requiring that two types of lifetime transfers be included in the gross estate: (1) transfers "intended to take effect in possession or enjoyment" at or after the decedent's death, and (2) transfers made by the decedent "in contemplation of death." The postponed-possession-and-enjoyment clause is the statutory predecessor of §§ 2036 through 2038, which are discussed later in this chapter. The second clause of the 1916 legislation, which gradually evolved into § 2035, required that gifts made "in contemplation of death" be included in the gross estate, even if the decedent had cut all strings to the property so that absolute ownership passed to the donee during the decedent's life.

Throughout the period from 1916 to 1976 there was considerable litigation as to whether particular gifts were made in contemplation of death. In United States v. Wells, 283 U.S. 102 (1931), the Supreme Court explained the requisite determination as follows:

> It is recognized that the reference is not to the general expectation of death which all entertain. It must be a particular concern, giving rise to a definite motive. The provision is not confined to gifts causa mortis, which are made in anticipation of impending death, are revocable, and are defeated if the donor survives the apprehended peril.... Death must be "contemplated," that is, the motive which induces the transfer must be of the sort which leads to testamentary disposition. [283 U.S. at 115–17.]

Formulation of the test as one of motive led to litigation in which decedents' representatives argued that disputed gifts were made for "life" not "death" motives. A flavor of those cases can be found in Johnson's Estate v. Commissioner, 10 T.C. 680 (1948), in which a 90–year–old man who made substantial gifts to his children was found not to be contemplating death. Evidence of his "life" motives included his health (at age 89, "he jumped into the air and clicked his heels together 2 or 3 times before descending to the floor"), his nature ("cheerful, sanguine and optimistic"), and his general attitude toward life ("he bought ready-made clothes, and liked bright-colored neckties"). The court speculated that the "verbal picture" of the decedent created at trial might bear "more resemblance to a synthesis of decedents whose transfers had been held in many reported cases to have been made not in contemplation of death than to the real [decedent]," but nevertheless concluded that there was sufficient evidence of "life" motives to avoid inclusion of the gifts in the decedent's gross estate. 10 T.C. at 691.

The difficulties inherent in reconstructing the subjective state of mind of a person who is necessarily dead at the time the inquiry is made led Congress to enact various statutory presumptions to assist the fact-finding process. From 1916 to 1950, the statute contained a rebuttable presumption that a transfer by the decedent "of a material part of his property in the nature of a final disposition or distribution thereof," which was made within two years of death, was a transfer in contemplation of death. Transfers made outside the presumptive period could be included in the gross estate if, without recourse to the presumption, they were made in contemplation of death. In 1950, the statute was amended to exempt gifts made more than three years before death from inclusion in the gross estate; at the same time, the rebuttable presumption was extended to cover transfers made within the three-year period, and the requirement that the transfer be of a "material part" of the estate was removed. These presumptions did not bring the desired precision to the process, however, and the flow of litigation continued unabated, causing increasing dissatisfaction with the contemplation-of-death concept.

2. 1976 TO 1981: GIFTS WITHIN THREE YEARS OF DEATH

Difficulty with the administration of the test was the first but by no means the only reason for the eventual repeal of the contemplation-of-death section and its successor section that taxed transfers made within three years of death. With the enactment of the gift tax in 1932 and the unification of the gift and estate taxes in 1976, the function of the rule requiring the inclusion of these transfers in the gross estate was correspondingly diminished, which led ultimately to the conclusion that there was no need for the rule's continued existence.

In 1916, when the contemplation-of-death provision was enacted, there was no gift tax; thus, property transferred by gift during life was free of any tax unless brought back into the gross estate. The enactment of the gift tax in 1932 left intact several substantial advantages that attached to lifetime gifts. The two taxes had separate exemptions; the gift tax rates were consistently lower than the estate tax rates; the two rate schedules applied separately rather than cumulatively; and the gift tax was based on the value of the property at the time of the gift rather than at the donor's death. As a result, a wealthy taxpayer could still reduce his or her potential estate tax liability by making lifetime gifts, as long as those gifts were not drawn back into the gross estate under the contemplation-of-death provision. Recognizing in the light of these possibilities that the contemplation-of-death provision still had a function, Congress preserved the provision; but because it would often reach transfers that were subject to the new gift tax, the 1932 legislation authorized a credit for the gift tax paid on lifetime transfers if the same property was included in the decedent's gross estate.

A crucial change in the relationship between the gift tax and the estate tax occurred in 1976, when Congress unified the two taxes by creating a single, cumulative rate schedule and a single credit to replace the separate schedules and exemptions of prior law. Because of these changes, a transfer theoretically generates the same tax liability whether it is subject to the gift tax or to the estate tax, except that gifts continue to enjoy the benefit of the annual gift tax exclusion, whereas deathtime transfers are taxed at full value. The 1976 legislation left intact this advantage enjoyed by lifetime transfers but attacked two other distinctions favoring gifts over deathtime transfers—the gift tax's failure to reach the appreciation in value occurring between the time of the gift and the donor's death,[1] and the removal of the funds used to pay the gift tax

---

1. The House Ways and Means Committee noted that the section now had as its objective the taxing of appreciation in the value of gifts made within three years before death:

> With the adoption of a single unified rate schedule, the tax impact of a rule requiring the inclusion of all transfers made within 3 years of death is not as significant as would be the case

from the transfer tax base. The 1976 statute eliminated the contemplation-of-death provision, and substituted a flat rule that drew back into the gross estate all transfers made during the three-year period before the decedent's death as well as any gift tax paid thereon.

The enactment of an automatic three-year rule came as no surprise given the widespread dissatisfaction with the old rule that had the courts looking back in time to delve into the innermost thoughts of persons who made gifts late in life.[2] Time became the sole criterion for inclusion; the courts no longer needed to search out the facts and circumstances that under prior law had been examined to determine whether a gift was made in contemplation of death.

The so-called gross-up of the gift tax paid on transfers during the three-year period represented a new concept in the estate tax and requires a brief explanation. From the time of its enactment the gift tax has been levied on a net basis; gift taxes paid are not included in the gift tax base. The estate tax, on the other hand, is levied on a gross basis, so that estate taxes paid are included in the amount taxed.

The manner in which this difference between the two taxes could be put to taxpayer advantage was dramatically demonstrated in a 1963 decision by the Delaware Court of Chancery, authorizing the guardians of an 86-year-old man, suffering from total physical and mental disability, to make gifts to his already wealthy children and grandchildren of property worth $36 million, incurring a gift tax of $21 million.[3] If the gifts were not made, the anticipated federal estate tax on an estate of $57 million (at the then maximum rate of 77 percent) would be $44 million, leaving only $13 million for the beneficiaries. Under the proposed plan, the beneficiaries would receive $36 million of the $57 million. (A mitigating disadvantage was the loss of a stepped-up income tax basis for the transferred property.)

Even if the gift was later held to be made in contemplation of death under the pre-1976 law, there would be a tax saving: The estate tax would be $28 million (77 percent of $36 million), less a credit under § 2012 of $21 million for the gift tax paid, or a net estate tax payable of $7 million, leaving $29 million ($36 million less $7 million) in the hands of the beneficiaries. Thus, they would still realize $16 million more than if the property had been retained by the donor until his death because the funds used to pay the gift tax would have been removed from the estate tax base.

---

where either no separate gift tax is imposed or a dual tax system providing rate differentials between lifetime and deathtime transfers is imposed. The most significant adverse consequence would result where the property transferred substantially appreciates in value between the date of the transfer and the date of the decedent's death. [H.R. Rep. No. 1380, 94th Cong., 2d Sess. 14 (1976), reprinted in 1976-3 C.B. (Vol. 3) 735, 748.]

2. The House Ways and Means Committee justified the proposal as a means of eliminating the "substantial problems for executors, beneficiaries, and the Internal Revenue Service" caused by the "considerable litigation concerning the motives of decedents in making gifts." Id. at 12, reprinted in 1976-3 C.B. (Vol. 3), at 746.

3. In re duPont, 194 A.2d 309 (Del. Ch. 1963). The tax computations in that case reflect rates, exemptions, and credits under pre-1976 law.

In 1976, Congress acted to curtail this advantage by requiring in situations of this kind that the gift tax paid by the decedent on transfers made within three years of death be included in the gross estate and be subjected to the estate tax.[4]

3. AFTER 1981: THE REMAINS OF THE THREE-YEAR RULE

The principal feature of the 1976 reform of § 2035—the inclusion in the gross estate of all gifts made within the three-year period before the donor's death—lasted for only five years. In 1981 Congress amended § 2035 to make the three-year rule inapplicable to all but a few special cases for decedents dying after 1981.[5] Accordingly, the vast majority of gifts completed during life are no longer drawn back into the gross estate, even if made within three years before death. Today, § 2035(a) applies only where the decedent, within three years before death, transferred an interest (or relinquished a power) which, had it been retained until death, would have triggered inclusion of the underlying property under §§ 2036, 2037, 2038 or 2042.[6] In such a case, the value of the property is includible in the gross estate just as if the decedent had actually retained the interest (or power) until death.

In its present form, the three-year rule is aimed at a narrow range of deathbed transfers that would otherwise remove substantial value from the gross estate at little or no gift tax cost. For example, suppose that *A* created a trust many years ago to pay income to herself for life with remainder at her death to her children. Having discovered that if she continues to receive income until death the trust property will be includible in her gross estate under § 2036(a), *A* assigns her outstanding income interest to the children for no consideration. If she survives for at least three years after the assignment, *A* will succeed in removing the trust property from her gross estate. If she dies within three years, however, the trust property will be includible under § 2035(a). Section 2035(a), in conjunction with § 2042, also plays a significant role in the taxation of life

---

4. The Treasury, in its 1969 tax reform proposals, recommended that the gift tax be imposed on a tax-inclusive basis. In the *DuPont* example in text, the donor would be treated as having made a transfer of $57 million, comprising the sum of the net value passing to the donees and the amount of gift tax imposed on the transfer. (Tables would be promulgated to simplify the "gross-up" calculation for a donor who wished to transfer a specified net amount to the donee.) Thus, the transfer tax would be paid out of the taxed amount, as has always been the case with the federal estate tax. See U.S. Treasury Department, Tax Reform Studies and Proposals, 91st Cong., 1st Sess. (Part 3) 355 (1969).

5. In recommending this change, the Senate Finance Committee made the following comments: "The committee generally does not believe it appropriate to tax appreciation that accrues after a gift has been made under the unified estate and gift taxes merely because the donor died within 3 years of the gift. The present rule often results in needless administrative burdens in valuing property twice." S. Rep. No. 144, 97th Cong., 1st Sess. 138 (1981), reprinted in 1981–2 C.B. 412, 466.

6. Section 2035(a) reached its present form in 1997, when Congress consolidated and restated the provisions of former § 2035(a) and (d).

insurance policies transferred within three years of death. See infra page 388.

The scope of § 2035(a) is limited by § 2035(d), which makes the three-year rule inapplicable to bona fide sales for adequate and full consideration. In the above example, suppose that *A* sells her outstanding income interest for its present value (determined under the applicable tables) and then dies one year later. In United States v. Allen, 293 F.2d 916 (10th Cir.), cert. denied, 368 U.S. 944 (1961), on similar facts, the court held that for purposes of § 2035 the adequacy of the consideration received by the decedent must be measured by reference to the value of the underlying property that would have been drawn back into her estate, not the value of the transferred income interest. Accordingly, the full deathtime value of the trust property was drawn back into the gross estate, with an offset under § 2043 for the consideration received in the sale. See Lowndes, Cutting the "Strings" on Inter Vivos Transfers in Contemplation of Death, 43 Minn. L. Rev. 57 (1958). More recently, however, several courts have refused to follow the lead of *Allen* in the analogous context of § 2036(a). See D'Ambrosio's Estate v. Commissioner, infra page 298.

Despite the limited reach of § 2035(a), the pre–1981 version of the three-year rule continues to have collateral tax consequences as a result of § 2035(c). Transfers made within three years before death are drawn back into the gross estate in determining the availability of the following three statutory allowances, which depend on the size and composition of the gross estate: § 303(b), relating to redemptions of stock to pay death taxes; § 2032A, establishing special valuation rules for qualified real property; and § 6166, granting an extension of time for the payment of estate taxes attributable to closely held businesses. In addition, property transferred within three years before death remains subject to the tax liens created by §§ 6321 through 6327. Even when applicable for these special purposes, the three-year rule is limited by the exception set out in § 2035(c)(3), which makes the rule inapplicable to any gift of property (other than a life insurance policy) that was not required to be reported on a gift tax return when made (e.g., a gift fully covered by the annual exclusion).

Section 2035(b)[7] increases the decedent's gross estate by the amount of any gift taxes paid by the decedent or the estate on gifts made by the decedent (or by the decedent's spouse) within three years before death. The function of this gross-up of gift taxes, as explained by the Staff of the Joint Committee on Taxation, is to eliminate "any incentive to make deathbed transfers to remove an amount equal to the gift taxes from the transfer tax base." General Explanation of the Tax Reform Act of 1976, 94th Cong., 2d Sess. 529 (1976), reprinted in 1976–3 C.B. (Vol. 2), at 541. Note that § 2035(b) operates independently of § 2035(a); thus, the gross-up requirement applies to gift taxes paid by the decedent on gifts made

7. This provision, originally enacted in 1976 as § 2035(c), was redesignated in 1997 without substantive change.

within three years before death, even if the underlying gift is immune from inclusion.

The simplest gross-up situation is a taxable gift by an unmarried decedent who uses his own resources both to make the gift and to pay the resulting gift tax. The gross-up requirement also applies where the decedent paid gift tax on gifts made by his spouse within three years before death. If the spouse's gift was treated under § 2513 as made half by the spouse and half by the decedent, each of them is jointly and severally liable for the entire gift tax, and it is consistent with underlying policy for the statute to require that the gift tax paid by the decedent from his own funds be drawn back into his gross estate except to the extent reimbursed by the spouse.

BROWN v. UNITED STATES

329 F.3d 664 (9th Cir.), cert. denied, 540 U.S. 878 (2003).

BERZON, CIRCUIT JUDGE:

[Willet Brown created an irrevocable trust to hold life insurance on the life of his wife Betty. Willet gave Betty $3,100,000 to fund the trust, and Betty promptly wrote a check for the same amount in favor of the trust. The funding of the trust constituted a taxable gift, which Willet and Betty elected to treat as made one-half by each spouse pursuant to the "split gift" provisions of § 2513. At the time of the gift, it was clearly a better "actuarial bet" for Betty (age 71) rather than Willet (age 87) to pay the resulting gift tax liability of $1,415,732, because she was more likely than Willet to outlive the three-year period prescribed by § 2035(b). Betty, however, had little property of her own and was unable to pay the gift tax from her separate funds. Accordingly, on the advice of his attorney, Willet gave Betty two checks totaling $1,415,732 with the "understanding" that she would use the funds to satisfy their joint and several gift tax liability. Betty deposited the funds in her own account and the next day wrote two checks for the same amount to the Internal Revenue Service.

Willet died in 1993, less than three years after the funding of the life insurance trust. Willet's estate took the position that the gift tax payment was made not by Willet but by Betty and was therefore not includible in Willet's gross estate under § 2035(b). The Service disagreed and assessed a deficiency. The estate paid the additional tax and sued for a refund. The district court awarded summary judgment in favor of the government, and the estate appealed.]

... [W]e must determine whether the Internal Revenue Service ("IRS") properly increased the estate tax owed by the estate of Willet Brown ("the Estate") under [§ 2035(b)], a provision which increases the estate tax to account for gift taxes paid in the three years immediately prior to death. To answer that question, we must consider whether the IRS was entitled to apply the "step transaction" doctrine, treating gift taxes paid by Betty Brown as if paid by Willet Brown....

The "step-transaction" doctrine collapses "formally distinct steps in an integrated transaction" in order to assess federal tax liability on the basis of a "realistic view of the entire transaction." Commissioner v. Clark, 489 U.S. 726, 738 (1989).... As such, the doctrine is part of the "broader tax concept that substance should prevail over form." Associated Wholesale Grocers, Inc. v. United States, 927 F.2d 1517, 1521 (10th Cir. 1991). Under these principles, the IRS argues, the two transactions which resulted in the payment of gift taxes (gift from Willett to Betty, payment by Betty) should be collapsed into one (payment by Willet).

The substance-over-form doctrines are, however, bound by, and in some tension with, the principle, equally lauded in tax law, that "anyone may so arrange his affairs that his taxes shall be as low as possible; he is not bound to choose the pattern which will best pay the Treasury." Grove v. Commissioner, 490 F.2d 241, 242 (2d Cir. 1973). We look to two principles to reconcile these competing concerns.

First, we attempt to distinguish between legitimate "tax avoidance"—actions which, although motivated in part by tax considerations, also have an independent purpose or effect—and illegitimate "tax evasion"—actions which have no, or minimal, purpose or effect beyond tax liabilities. See Stewart v. Commissioner, 714 F.2d 977, 987–988 (9th Cir. 1983) (citing Bittker, Pervasive Judicial Doctrines in the Construction of the Internal Revenue Code, 21 How. L.J. 693, 695 (1978)).

Second, we scrutinize whether the facts presented "fall within the intended scope of the Internal Revenue provision at issue." Stewart, 714 F.2d at 988. This second step is crucial in areas, such as estate planning, in which it is common for Congress to create, and taxpayers to exploit, various tax planning incentives.... For example, § 2513 allowed Willet and Betty, by exercising certain elections, to treat the underlying $3,100,000 gift from Willet to the life insurance trust as if made by both of them, when in reality Willet supplied the entirety of the funds. The IRS has never argued that the substance-over-form doctrine invalidated that election, for obvious reasons: That approach would deny taxpayers the tax benefits intentionally created by the plain language of the Code.

Applying these two principles with appropriate caution, we conclude that the two-step transaction between Willet, Betty, and the IRS, was properly treated as if Willet had paid the gift taxes directly.

1. Betty as a Mere Conduit of Funds

Navigating the murky distinction between "tax avoidance" and "tax evasion" requires careful stewardship. In the context of the step transaction doctrine, however, we have identified a class of cases in which the form of the transaction is particularly suspect. Where a party acts as a "mere conduit" of funds—a fleeting stop in a predetermined voyage toward a particular result—we have readily ignored the role of the intermediary in order appropriately to characterize the transaction. Robino Inc. Pension Trust v. Commissioner, 894 F.2d 342, 344 (9th Cir. 1990) (where taxpayers sold options on land to two trusts but the trusts acted as mere "conduits" for the ultimate sale to a third party, role of trust disregarded under step transaction doctrine); Stewart, 714 F.2d at 991 (where corporation acted as "merely a conduit" for the sale of appreciated securities by the taxpayer, several steps collapsed into one under the substance-over-form principle). See also Estate of Sachs v. Commissioner, 856 F.2d 1158, 1163 (8th Cir. 1988) (because donor of net gift used donee as a "conduit" to pay taxes, donor deemed to have paid the gift tax).

Viewing the historical facts in the light most favorable to the Estate, it is nonetheless clear that Betty was a "mere conduit" of Willet's funds. The Browns do not advance any argument that the payment to Betty had any purpose or effect other than as a step towards facilitating Willet's payment of the gift tax liability and Betty owned Willet's funds for exactly one day. Betty's fleeting ownership can therefore be disregarded under the principles of *Robino* and *Stewart*.

True, Betty was under no binding commitment to complete the prearranged plan. "Despite intimations to the contrary in the early cases," however, "there is ample authority for linking several prearranged or contemplated steps, even in the absence of a contractual obligation or financial compulsion to follow through." Boris I. Bittker, Fed. Inc. Tax'n of Indiv. § 1.03[5] (2d ed.). See, e.g., Kornfeld v. Commissioner, 137 F.3d 1231, 1235–1236 (10th Cir. 1998).... Where the two parties to the transaction were sufficiently related or commonly controlled, we have twice applied the step transaction analysis without any finding that the intermediary was legally bound to complete the prearranged plan. See Robino, 894 F.2d at 345 (transactions between two taxpayers and trust controlled by taxpayers and spouse of one taxpayer); Stewart, 714 F.2d at 984 (transaction between taxpayer and corporation he controlled).

Particularly apt is the Tenth Circuit's analysis in *Kornfeld*, applying the step transaction doctrine where, as here, family members colluded to accomplish a prearranged plan. In *Kornfeld*, the taxpayer, an experienced tax attorney, gave cash payments to his daughters and secretary. 137 F.3d at 1232–33.

The gift recipients then immediately used those funds to purchase remainder interests in bonds. Id. The Tenth Circuit determined that the series of transactions should be treated as if the taxpayer had purchased the bonds in fee simple and given the remainder interests to his daughters and secretary (a determination which had negative tax consequences for the taxpayer). Id. In so determining, the Tenth Circuit applied a heightened level of skepticism to transactions between related parties. Id. at 1235. In addition, the court was swayed by the facts that the "taxpayer [had] stipulated that his intention in making gifts was to enable the donees to make the purchases," and that the donees would be unlikely to flout the taxpayer's intention. Id. at 1236. As the court noted, "one does not look a gift horse in the mouth." Id.

The same factors which applied in *Kornfeld* apply here: The parties are related, so heightened scrutiny is appropriate. Willet's admitted intention in giving the funds to Betty was to enable her to make the gift tax payments. Finally, Betty was unlikely to flout the desires of her husband because it was she, as the initial beneficiary of the Estate, who stood to gain if the gift tax wager was successful. The two transactions culminating in gift tax payments should therefore be treated as one integrated whole despite the lack of a legally binding commitment.

2. The End Run Around § 2035

Our conclusion is reinforced by a consideration of the statute here at issue, [§ 2035(b)]. We begin, in considering that statute, with the Eighth Circuit's analysis of a quite similar situation in Estate of Sachs v. Commissioner, 856 F.2d 1158 (8th Cir. 1988). In *Sachs*, Samuel Sachs gave stock in trust to his grandchildren within three years of his death. Id. at 1159. The gift was structured as a "net gift," meaning that the donees were legally bound to pay the gift taxes otherwise chargeable to the donor. Id. Relying in part on the plain language of § 2035, and in part on the substance-over-form doctrine, the Eighth Circuit held that "the gift tax paid under this arrangement is a 'tax paid ... by the decedent or his estate' under § 2035." Id. at 1164.

The instant case differs from *Sachs*, however, in that Betty was jointly liable under § 2513(d) to pay the gift tax liability. In comparison, no matter how the beneficiaries in *Sachs* received funds to pay the gift taxes, the gift tax payment was attributable to the donor, if for no other reason than because only the donor was liable for the debt owed to the IRS. Id. at 1163–64.

The question then is whether the Willet–Betty–IRS transaction, though on its face an end-run around [§ 2035(b)], is nonetheless authorized by § 2513. Had Betty truly paid the gift tax from her own funds, § 2035 would not apply to Betty's payments of the gift tax, because of § 2513.[8] Id. at 1165. The Estate argues that because § 2513 authorizes the very "actuarial bet" the couple made, the source of Betty's funds is irrelevant.

The source of the funds *is* pertinent. Sachs, 856 F.2d at 1165 (because the gift tax was paid with funds from decedent's estate, fact that gift was split between decedent and his wife under § 2513 did not alter application of [§ 2035(b)]). The language and the history of [§ 2035(b)] emphasize that this section applies to actual gift tax payments, regardless of the relative gift tax liability among spouses.

First, [§ 2035(b)] requires that the decedent include in his estate gift taxes "*paid* ... on any gift made by the decedent *or his spouse*." (Emphasis added). Second, the legislative history states:

> The amount of the gift tax subject to this rule would include tax paid by the decedent or his estate on any gift made by the donor.... It

8. Section 2513 applies only for purposes of the gift tax, not for the estate tax. Estate of Flandreau v. Commissioner, 994 F.2d 91, 93 n.1 (2d Cir. 1993). As discussed in the text, therefore, the [§ 2035(b)] liability is not altered by the split-gift election when the decedent in fact pays the gift taxes.

would not, however, include any gift tax paid by the spouse on a gift made by the decedent within three years of death which is treated as made one-half by the spouse [e.g., under § 2513], *since the spouse's payment of such tax would not reduce the decedent's estate at the time of death.* [H. Rep. No. 94–1380, 14, 94th Cong., 2d. Sess. (1976) (emphasis added).]

The reason the source of funds matters is that [§ 2035(b)] was designed to reverse the effect of funds transferred out of an estate within three years of death. If Willet pays the gift tax, it is his net worth that is reduced and therefore his estate that will escape estate tax liability on the funds if he outlives the three-year reach of [§ 2035(b)]. Accordingly, it is his estate that must reverse the effect of the transfer if he dies within the three-year period. Only if Betty pays the gift tax by using her own financial resources is her estate reduced, such that her estate should bear the risk that the payment be included in her estate via [§ 2035(b)].

By channeling Willet's funds through Betty's estate, the Browns created a transaction sequence in which the tax risk diverged from the economics of the payment. Where one spouse has significantly fewer assets than the other spouse, shifting the risk of § 2035 inclusion onto the estate of the less wealthy spouse, while actually transferring the assets out of the estate of the more wealthy spouse, could have tax evasion advantages for the couple beyond the effect of divergent mortality probabilities: The smaller estate may be subject to lower tax rates, see § 2001(c), or to no tax at all, see § 2010, so that the inclusion risk does not adequately reverse the effect of the reduction in the larger estate. We do not know whether this was the case in the Brown estate. We note the effect, however, to demonstrate that requiring, as the text and legislative history plainly do, that the § 2035 inclusion risk follow the economics of the gift tax payment is not a pointless formality. Thus, the fact that the "actuarial bet" the Browns attempted may have been proper under § 2035 and § 2513 had Betty actually paid the gift taxes does not imply that the Browns' maneuvering here was similarly appropriate.

In Magneson v. Commissioner, 753 F.2d 1490, 1497 (9th Cir. 1985), we distinguished between a taxpayer's right to choose "[b]etween two equally direct ways of achieving the same result" the method "which entailed the most tax advantages" and the inability to "secure by a series of contrived steps, different tax treatment than if he had carried out the transaction directly." That distinction is illuminating: Had Betty and Willet both had adequate funds with which to pay the gift tax, they would be entitled to choose the most advantageous method from among two equally direct ways of paying the tax (check from Willet to IRS vs. check from Betty to IRS). Here however, Willet actually supplied the funds, and Betty's involvement was merely a "contrived step" to secure tax treatment different from that which would have resulted if Willet had paid the IRS directly. The contrived step did not alter the economic reality that Willet paid the tax, and Betty's transient ownership over the funds for one day had no independent purpose or effect beyond the attempt to alter tax liabilities.

3. Impact of Lack of Certainty of Tax Benefit

In a variant of its assertion that the actuarial bet was entirely proper, the Estate, noting that the end result of the machinations did not create a *certain* tax advantage, contends that the transaction sequence is therefore immune from the step transaction doctrine. That the tax advantages flowing from Willet's plan were uncertain does not, as the Estate contends, distinguish this case from other instances in which the step transaction or substance over form doctrine has been applied.

For example, in *Sachs*, Samuel Sachs' decision to route gift tax payments through his grandchildren's trust created a tax advantage only because he died within three years of the gift, such that § 2035 would apply if the gift tax payment were attributed to him. Just as Willet's actuarial bet had an uncertain payoff, Sachs' attempt to evade § 2035 could have been rendered useless by subsequent events.

Similarly, in *Robino*, we looked through the form of a transaction even though the choice of form did not create a certain tax advantage. In *Robino*, individuals devised a complicated cross-option scheme, using two trusts as conduits to hold, and ultimately sell, real property. This arrangement "let the taxpayers keep the parcel if it did not appreciate in value but shift the gain on the parcel to the trusts if it did increase in value." 894 F.2d at 345. The real estate market was "volatile" during the relevant time period, id. at 343, so a gain on the real property, and therefore the tax advantage of the scheme, was by no means assured. As both *Robino* and *Sachs* therefore demonstrate, a certain tax advantage is not a prerequisite to application of the step transaction doctrine.

Tax consequences aside, the nature of the Browns' transaction sequence (ultimately, a transfer of funds from Willet to the IRS) was fixed the moment Betty wrote out the check to the IRS. Focusing only on Betty's role within that predetermined result, it is clear that her participation had no significance beyond the attempt to alter tax liabilities. Unlike a situation in which Betty paid the gift taxes by reducing her own net worth, a decision with independent economic effect on Betty's estate, Betty's role as a conduit altered the economics of the transaction *only* by shifting the risk of § 2035 inclusion from Willet's estate to Betty's estate. Where, as here, that risk shift did not reflect the reality of the underlying transaction sequence, application of the step transaction is appropriate.

The final component of the Estate's uncertainty argument relates to its complaint that the step transaction doctrine can be, and often is, applied asymmetrically: Had Betty died within three years of the gift tax payments, it is quite unlikely that the IRS would adamantly advocate in favor of treating the funds as if paid by Willet, so as to relieve Betty of the estate tax liability. The IRS's lawyer so indicated at oral argument.

The possibility of a one-way ratchet does give us pause. We are not alone: Both courts and commentators have struggled with whether the substance over form principle is a one- or two-way street, and whether, even if a two-way street, it nonetheless "run[s] downhill for the Commissioner and uphill for the taxpayer." Bittker & McMahon, Fed. Inc. Tax'n of Indiv., § 1.03 (quoting Rogers' Estate v. CIR, 70,192 P–H Memo. TC (1970), affd. 445 F.2d 1020 (2d Cir. 1971)). . . .

Had Betty indeed died first, we would be faced with the difficult question of whether symmetry required application of the step transaction doctrine, or whether the taxpayer, having complete control over the form of the transaction, must bear the consequences of the chosen form without recourse to the step transaction doctrine. Whether the doctrine must be applied symmetrically is not, however, the issue now before us, and we do not reach it.

4. Effect on Estate Planning

The Estate also maintains, somewhat grandiosely, that our holding vitiates the entire estate tax planning profession. For example, notes the Estate, a typical estate planning tool, employed by many parents, involves annual gifts of approximately $10,000 per parent in order to take advantage of the annual gift exclusion of § 2503(b). Because those transactions are also motivated by a desire to avoid estate taxes, the Estate suggests, applying the substance-over-form doctrine to the instant case would require that we apply the substance-over-form doctrine to such annual gift giving and treat the gifts as if they were instead taxable estate transfers.

Rather than supporting the result the Estate favors, the inter vivos gift example usefully illustrates the boundaries of the substance-over-form doctrine. When parents elect to make an inter vivos gift to their children rather than bequeathing those assets, that decision does have effects independent of the tax consequences: The children receive the funds earlier, and the parent loses control over the assets. In comparison, Betty's ownership over the funds from Willet was transitory. She was simply a conduit, and her role in the transaction was a temporary artifice rather than an event with independent economic significance.

The inter vivos gift example differs from the present situation for a second reason as well. The plain language of § 2503(b) reveals that Congress intended to allow, and perhaps to encourage, small annual gifts free of tax, when it enacted § 2503(b). Otherwise, there would not be an annual dollar exclusion from the gift tax. In stark contrast, [§ 2035(b)] discourages manipulation of the tax code by large inter vivos transfers, by reversing the tax benefits of those transfers. It can hardly be argued that the purpose of § 2035 is advanced by Willet's maneuvering to create the appearance that Betty paid the gift tax when in all practical effect, Willet did so. . . .

For the reasons stated, we affirm.

NOTES

1. *Gross-up of gift taxes.* In the *Brown* case there would have been no gift tax gross-up under § 2035(b) if both spouses had survived for three years after the funding of the life insurance trust. If, contrary to all expectations, Betty Brown died one year after the funding of the trust and her husband survived for another five years, should Betty's gift tax payment be drawn back into her gross estate? What if both spouses died within the three-year period?

Suppose that a wife makes a substantial taxable gift. Her husband, although under no legal obligation to do so, voluntarily pays the resulting gift tax and dies within three years after the date of the gift. Is it open to the husband's executor to argue that the husband made a gift to his wife (which would not be subject to gross-up) rather than a gift tax payment? If the gift tax payment must be included in the husband's gross estate under § 2035(b), should the husband's payment of his wife's gift tax liability give rise to a marital deduction? Cf. Rev. Rul. 79–383, 1979–2 C.B. 337 (allowing marital deduction for bequest to satisfy surviving spouse's debt, and noting that transaction is substantially equivalent to an outright bequest to the spouse).

For gifts made within three years before death, the gross-up requirement of § 2035(b) erases one of the most conspicuous tax advantages of lifetime gifts over testamentary transfers. Recall the difference between the "tax-exclusive" gift tax base and the "tax-inclusive" estate tax base, illustrated by the example at page 21 supra. In that example, if the $16 million gift was made within three years before the donor's death, the $3,850,000 gift tax must be included in the gross estate, generating an additional estate tax of $1,347,500 (see supra page 22, footnote 45); the total transfer taxes thus amount to $5,197,500, the same as in the case of a single testamentary transfer.

2. *Net gifts.* Section 2035(b) requires the gross-up of any gift tax paid by the "decedent or his estate." This wording was cited in support of a taxpayer's argument that in the case of a net gift the gift tax is paid by the donee and therefore is not covered by the statute. The Tax Court was not persuaded. Sachs' Estate v. Commissioner, 88 T.C. 769 (1987), affd. on this issue, 856 F.2d 1158 (8th Cir. 1988) ("we may go beyond the literal language of the Code if reliance on that language would defeat the plain purpose of Congress").

Suppose that a donor makes a gift conditioned on the donee's promise to pay the resulting gift tax as well as any additional estate tax liability resulting from the § 2035(b) gift tax gross-up if the donor dies within three years. In determining the amount of the net gift, should the donee's promise to pay a contingent estate tax liability be treated as consideration received by the donor? Compare Armstrong's Estate v. United States, 277 F.3d 490 (4th Cir. 2002) (disregarding "speculative and illusory" obligation), with McCord's Succession v. Commissioner, 461 F.3d 614 (5th Cir. 2006) (taking commuted value of obligation into account). If the donor dies within three years, should the donee's estate tax payment reduce the amount includible under § 2035(b)? See Armstrong's Estate v. Commissioner, 119 T.C. 220 (2002).

3. *Estate tax treatment of reincluded split gifts.* The dispute in the *Brown* case arose over the application of the gift tax gross-up provision of § 2035(b); the underlying $3,100,000 gift was not drawn back into the decedent's gross estate under § 2035(a). Suppose, however, that Betty made a taxable gift by assigning all incidents of ownership in an insurance policy on her own life to an irrevocable trust. Suppose, further, that Willet consented to be treated as making one-half of the gift under § 2513 and that he paid all of the resulting gift tax. If Betty died one year after assigning the life insurance policy, the full amount of the proceeds would be included in her gross estate under § 2035(a). Moreover, in computing her estate tax, Betty's half of the split gift would be excluded from her adjusted taxable gifts (§ 2001(b)(1)(B)), and the gift tax paid by Willet would be credited against her tentative estate tax. § 2001(b)(2) and (d). If Willet survived Betty and then died one year later, how would Willet's half of the split gift and the amount of his gift tax payment be treated in computing his estate tax? See § 2001(b)(1), (b)(2), and (e); Rev. Rul. 82–198, 1982–2 C.B. 206. Would the result be different if Willet died first? See Rev. Rul. 81–85, 1981–1 C.B. 452.

4. *Transfers from revocable trust.* Transfers made from a decedent's revocable trust within three years before death pose a special problem under § 2035. If such a transfer is treated as a pro tanto relinquishment of the decedent's power to revoke, it is includible in the gross estate under § 2035(a). Inclusion may be avoided, however, if the transfer is viewed as a constructive withdrawal of trust property followed by a gift from the decedent to the recipient. See Jalkut's Estate v. Commissioner, 96 T.C. 675 (1991) (distinguishing relinquishment from exercise of power). Although the distinction between a relinquishment and an exercise of a power to revoke may be more a matter of form than of substance, the stakes can be substantial. For example, if the decedent made annual exclusion gifts from a revocable trust, the benefit of the exclusion is lost if the gifts are drawn back into the gross estate; on the other hand, if the gifts are treated as made directly by the decedent, they escape both gift and estate tax.

Section 2035(e), added in 1997, treats transfers from the decedent's revocable trust as if they were made directly by the decedent for purposes of §§ 2035 and 2038. The legislative history offers the following rationale:

> The inclusion of certain property transferred during the three years before death is directed at transfers that would otherwise reduce the amount subject to estate tax by more than the amount subject to gift tax, disregarding appreciation between the times of gift and death. Because all amounts transferred from a revocable trust are subject to the gift tax, the Committee believes that inclusion of such amounts is unnecessary where the transferor has retained no power over the property transferred out of the trust. [H.R. Rep. No. 148, 105th Cong., 1st Sess. 624 (1997), reprinted in 1997–4 C.B. (Vol. 1) 319, 946.].

Note that § 2035(e) applies only if at the time of the lifetime transfer the trust was treated as a grantor trust under § 676 for income tax purposes by reason of the decedent's power to revoke. Not all powers that give rise to estate tax inclusion under § 2038 meet this requirement. Consider, for example, a power exercisable only in favor of beneficiaries other than the decedent (see Porter v. Commissioner, infra page 239) or only with the consent of an adverse party (see Helvering v. City Bank Farmers Trust Co., infra page 258). Should transfers made from a trust subject to such retained powers within three years before death be included in the gross estate?

5. *Relationship of §§ 2035 and 2036 to § 2040.* Section 2035(a) requires that certain transfers made within three years before death be drawn back into the gross estate. The list of tainted transactions, however, makes no reference to joint tenancies. At one time, the Internal Revenue Service attempted to combine §§ 2035 and 2040 in situations such as that presented in Sullivan's Estate v. Commissioner, 175 F.2d 657 (9th Cir. 1949), where in contemplation of husband's death, husband and wife made a gift to their son of property that they owned as joint tenants with right of survivorship. The husband was the economic source of the tenancy, and the Service argued that, had he died with the tenancy intact, the entire value would have been included in his gross estate under § 2040, as then written to apply to husband-wife tenancies. The court, emphasizing that under local law both tenants had the independent right to transfer their respective shares, held that only one-half of the value of the property was treated as a gift made by the husband in contemplation of death. Accord, Borner's Estate v. Commissioner, 25 T.C. 584 (1955) (tenancy by the entirety).

The Service had no greater success in integrating § 2040 with § 2036. In 1946, a decedent transferred property, for which he had furnished the entire consideration, into a joint tenancy with his wife; in 1948, they transferred the property to their children, reserving joint-and-survivor life estates. On decedent's death (after his wife's death), the government asserted that the full value of the property was includible in his estate, on the ground that, but for the 1948 transfer, it would have been so includible. The court held that only one-half of the property was includible under § 2036, on the ground that the decedent owned only one-half in 1948, when the transfer reserving the life estate was made. United States v. Heasty, 370 F.2d 525 (10th Cir. 1966); accord, Rev. Rul. 69–577, 1969–2 C.B. 173. This immunity from inclusion for joint tenancies is further illustrated in Black v. Commissioner, 765 F.2d 862 (9th Cir. 1985) (§ 2040 inapplicable where joint tenancy was severed by transfer into a revocable trust shortly before the death of one of the tenants).

6. *Amount includible.* Property that is transferred during life and then drawn back into the gross estate under § 2035 is valued at the date of the decedent's death (or the alternate valuation date, if applicable). A provision in the pre–1981 regulations generally required that the transferred property be valued without regard to any enhancement attributable to "improvements or additions" made by the transferee as well as any income received after the transfer. Reg. § 20.2035–1(e). What happens if the transferee consumes the property or disposes of it before the decedent's death? In a case arising under pre–1981 law, it was held that "the very property" transferred, not any substitute property, was includible under § 2035. Humphrey's Estate v. Commissioner, 162 F.2d 1 (5th Cir.), cert. denied, 332 U.S. 817 (1947) (decedent made outright gifts of cash in contemplation of death, which the donee invested in property that subsequently declined in value; held, amount of original cash gift included in gross estate); see also Commissioner v. Gidwitz's Estate, 196 F.2d 813 (7th Cir. 1952) (decedent transferred shares of

stock in trust in contemplation of death; held, gross estate included deathtime value of original stock but not subsequent accumulations of income); Rev. Rul. 72–282, 1972–1 C.B. 306. This result reflects the notion that the inclusionary rule is intended to produce the same estate tax result as if the decedent had never transferred the property during life. Nevertheless, where the decedent created a trust in contemplation of death and the original trust property was subsequently sold or exchanged, it has been held that it is the trust property as it exists at death (rather than at inception) that is includible under § 2035. In Kroger's Estate v. Commissioner, 2 T.C.M. (CCH) 644 (1943), affd., 145 F.2d 901 (6th Cir. 1944), cert. denied, 324 U.S. 866 (1945), the Tax Court explained:

> The estate tax is imposed upon the value of the net estate as it exists at the date of the death of the decedent. If the decedent had made an inter vivos gift of property in contemplation of death that property would have to be valued as of the date of death whether that value be more or less than at the date of the gift; and if property has been converted into other property the value of such other property at the date of death is the measure of the tax. The same rule applies where property is transferred to a trust in contemplation of death.

See also DeWitt's Estate v. Commissioner, 68 T.C.M. (CCH) 1136 (1994) (following *Kroger's Estate* and distinguishing *Humphrey's Estate*).

7. *Income tax "basis" of deathbed gifts.* Section 1014(b)(9) sets as the income tax basis of inherited property its value as of the decedent's death (or the alternate valuation date, if applicable). There is, however, a condition that the stepped-up basis is available only if "the property is required to be included in determining the value of the decedent's gross estate." Is this condition satisfied by § 2035(a)?

The availability of a stepped-up basis is limited where a donor transfers appreciated property to a donee who is nearing death, with the knowledge that the property will return to the donor under the soon-to-be-deceased donee's will. Under § 1014(e), the property retains its old basis if the first transfer is made within one year of the donee's death. What result if the donor resorts to extraordinary measures to keep the donee alive for 53 weeks? What if the property does not return directly to the original owner but passes instead to the owner's spouse or a trust that includes the owner as a beneficiary?

4. REFORM PROPOSALS

In 1976, a single rate schedule and unified credit were made applicable to the estate and gift taxes. The purpose of this unification was to render the taxes a neutral factor in an individual's decision whether to make transfers during life or at death. Much attention continues to be given to the need to simplify the complex rules that define when a transfer is complete so that the transfer is subject either to gift tax or to estate tax, but not both. The proposed solution is to treat an inter vivos transfer as incomplete and therefore not subject to gift tax if the transferor retained a beneficial interest in the property or if title to the property could be revested in him or her. The transfer would be complete for gift tax purposes, however, if it was irrevocable and made to beneficiaries other than the transferor, even if the transferor retained the right to determine who would receive the income or principal. If this proposal (and the reform outlined below) were enacted, the need for § 2035 would be greatly reduced.

The Treasury Department's 1984 Report to the President, entitled Tax Reform for Fairness, Simplicity, and Economic Growth, made these proposals but stated that in fairness to taxpayers the issue of existing preferences favoring lifetime gifts must first be addressed. (The differential treatment of the transferee's basis in property acquired by gift or bequest is discussed supra at page 40.) After conceding that the annual exclusion (which is available only for lifetime gifts) may be justified on practical, administrative grounds, the report (at 376–77) argued for the gross-up of all gift taxes as follows:

> . . . [N]either tax policy concerns nor administrative convenience support application of the gift tax on a tax-exclusive basis while the estate tax is computed on a tax-inclusive basis. Such a rule hampers the overall fairness of the transfer tax system because the individuals it benefits are those who can afford to give away a significant portion of their property during life. Those individuals who are unable or unwilling to make lifetime gifts, and who therefore retain their property until death, are subject to tax at a higher effective rate.[9]
>
> In addition, the preferential treatment accorded lifetime gifts encourages individuals to make lifetime transfers solely to reduce their overall transfer tax burden. The transfer tax system should not treat an individual wishing to retain his or her property until death either more or less favorably than it treats an individual wishing to make lifetime gifts.
>
> Finally, the preference given lifetime gifts has resulted in a complex and often arbitrary set of rules that attempt, with uneven results, to prevent taxpayers from taking unintended advantage of the preference. In some cases, these rules do not fully remove the preference given to lifetime gifts; in others, the rules are punitive and cause transfer tax consequences that are more severe than if the individual had not made a lifetime gift.
>
> [*Proposal:*] The gift tax would be computed on a tax-inclusive basis. Under this system, the gift tax payable on a transfer of a fixed net amount to a donee would be determined by calculating the gross amount that, when subject to the transfer tax rate schedule, would be

9. The difference between tax-exclusive and tax-inclusive rates can be illustrated by a simple example. Suppose *A* wishes to use $150 to make a transfer and pay the resulting tax (which is imposed at a flat 50–percent rate). On one hand, *A* can make a lifetime gift of $100 and pay a gift tax (based on the amount received by the donee) of $50. On the other hand, if *A* retains the $150 until death, the estate tax (imposed on the total outlay of $150) amounts to $75, leaving only $75 for the beneficiary. In effect, a 50–percent tax-exclusive rate is equivalent to a 33⅓–percent tax-inclusive rate. See supra page 21.—EDS.

sufficient to pay the gift tax on the transfer and leave the net amount for the donee. Stated differently, the amount of the gift would be "grossed up" by the amount of the gift tax payable with respect to the transfer. The tax imposed on a decedent's estate would be computed by adding the amount of the decedent's taxable estate to the sum of the decedent's adjusted taxable gifts and the gift tax paid by the decedent.

In order to prevent taxpayers from having to make somewhat complicated gross-up calculations, the gross-up factor would be built into the rate table contained in the statute. Under this method, the stated rate applicable to gifts would be higher than the stated rate applicable to estates, but the effective rate imposed on a net transfer would be the same regardless of whether subject to the gift tax or the estate tax....

NOTE

References. See Report on Transfer Tax Restructuring, 41 Tax Law. 395, 402–04 (1988) (arguing in favor of continuing existing differentials because they encourage lifetime giving causing "business and investment capital to be moved into the hands of younger, more vigorous owners" and because gift tax may be "analogized to a discount for early payment" of the transfer tax); Gutman, A Comment on the ABA Tax Section Task Force Report on Transfer Tax Restructuring, id. at 653, 656–57 (no evidence, studies or other data to support Task Force's justification of status quo); Aucutt, Further Observations on Transfer Tax Restructuring: A Practitioner's Perspective, 42 Tax Law. 343, 345–46 (1989); Gutman, A Practitioner's Perspective in Perspective: A Reply to Mr. Aucutt, id. at 351, 353; see also Sims, Timing Under a Unified Wealth Transfer Tax, 51 U. Chi. L. Rev. 34 (1984).

B. REVOCABLE TRANSFERS: § 2038

From 1916 to 1924, the estate tax statute did not refer specifically to revocable transfers, but they were includible in the gross estate by virtue of a clause reaching any transfer by trust or otherwise "intended to take effect in possession or enjoyment at or after death." Moreover, it was held that revocable transfers made before 1916 could be reached if the transferor died after 1916; the claim that to include such property in the gross estate was retroactive legislation in violation of the due process clause of the Fifth Amendment was rejected on the ground that the transfer was not complete until the transferor's death and that the tax was imposed on the shifting of economic benefits at death. Reinecke v. Northern Trust Co., 278 U.S. 339 (1929).

In 1924 the prototype of what is now § 2038 was enacted, reaching transfers where enjoyment was subject at the date of the decedent's death "to any change through the exercise of a power, either by the decedent alone or in conjunction with any person, to alter, amend, or revoke, or where the decedent relinquished any such power in contemplation of his death." This provision has been amended from time to time since 1924; some of those amendments, as will be seen, were declaratory rather than substantive.

1. WHERE TRANSFEROR'S POWER IS UNRESTRICTED

Over the years, the Internal Revenue Service has construed § 2038 in an expansive manner and has met with few setbacks along the way. In Porter v. Commissioner, 288 U.S. 436 (1933), the Supreme Court held that § 2038 brought into the gross estate property transferred in trust by the decedent during his lifetime subject to a nonbeneficial power to amend, i.e., a power to alter or modify the trust indentures in any manner except in favor of himself or his estate. The Court held that the decedent's retained power triggered application of § 2038, even though the decedent had no "interest" in the underlying property within the meaning of § 2033 and even though the decedent had no power to "revoke" the trusts or to "alter" or "amend" them in favor of himself or his estate. The Court said:

> We need not consider whether every change, however slight or trivial, would be within the meaning of the clause. Here the donor retained until his death power enough to enable him to make a complete revision of all that he had done in respect of the creation of the trusts even to the extent of taking the property from the trustees and beneficiaries named and transferring it absolutely or in trust for the benefit of others. So far as concerns the tax here involved, there is no difference in principle between a transfer subject to such changes and one that is revocable. [288 U.S. at 443.]

The Court also rejected the argument that, so construed, § 2038 measured the decedent's tax by property belonging to others, in violation of the due process clause:

> [The taxpayers] treat as without significance the power the donor reserved unto himself alone and ground all their arguments upon the fact that deceased, prior to such enactment, completely divested himself of title without power of revocation. It is true that the power reserved was not absolute as in the transfer considered in Burnet v. Guggenheim [supra page 83], in which this court, in the absence of any provision corresponding to [§ 2038], held that the donor's termination of the power amounted to a transfer by gift within the meaning of [the Revenue Act of 1924]. But the reservation here may not be ignored, for, while subject to the specified limitation, it made the settlor dominant in respect of other dispositions of both corpus and income. His death terminated that control, ended the possibility of any change by him, and was, in respect of title to the property in question, the source of valuable assurance passing from the dead to the living. That is the event on which Congress based the inclusion of

> property so transferred in the gross estate as a step in the calculation to ascertain the amount of . . . the net estate. Thus was reached what it reasonably might deem a substitute for testamentary disposition. United States v. Wells, 283 U.S. 102, 116. There is no doubt as to the power of Congress so to do. [288 U.S. at 444.]

In Commissioner v. Chase Natl. Bank, 82 F.2d 157 (2d Cir.), cert. denied, 299 U.S. 552 (1936), § 2038 was held applicable to an irrevocable inter vivos trust created by the decedent in 1920, under which the corpus was payable on her death to her lawful descendants in such proportions as she should appoint by will, or in equal shares per stirpes in default of such appointment:

> We think [§ 2038] authority for the inclusion of the trust corpus in the decedent's gross estate. Up to the time she died she had the power to alter the proportions in which her descendants should take the property in accordance with the original terms of the trust instrument. She could have limited any, or all but one, of them to a nominal amount and given all of real value to one or to such of them as she pleased. Her death eliminated the possibility of any such change in the provisions of the deed of trust and made it certain that her lawful descendants would take the property in equal shares per stirpes. The power she reserved was not to change the trust provisions in a trivial way, but went right to the heart of them and gave the decedent a substantial though qualified control over the trust property until her death. Such a power to alter or amend the substance of the transfer by trust brought it within the scope of the decision in Porter v. Commissioner [supra page 239], and justified the inclusion of the property in the gross estate of the decedent. . . . The decedent, having the right to change the economic benefit, had the power to alter within [§ 2038] even though she could not benefit herself in a pecuniary way by the change. . . . She lived several years after the act took effect and she was on notice of its provisions, retaining the reserved powers when she might have given them up to rid her estate of this tax liability. So there has been no denial of rights under the Fifth Amendment. [82 F.2d at 158.]

A further step was taken in Commissioner v. Holmes' Estate, 326 U.S. 480 (1946), where the decedent during his lifetime had created three irrevocable trusts, one for each of his sons, retaining with respect to each trust a power to accumulate income and a power of termination. Upon termination of any son's trust, corpus and accumulated income were to be distributed to the son if living, otherwise to the son's surviving issue, if any; if the son left no surviving issue the property was to be distributed to the other sons if living or their surviving issue, if any, with an ultimate gift over. The Court held that the decedent's power of termination constituted a power to "alter, amend, or revoke" within the meaning of § 2038:

> It seems obvious that one who has the power to terminate contingencies upon which the right of enjoyment is staked, so as to make certain that a beneficiary will have it who may never come into it if the power is not exercised, has power which affects not only the time of enjoyment but also the person or persons who may enjoy the donation. More therefore is involved than mere acceleration of the time of enjoyment. The very right of enjoyment is affected, the difference dependent upon the grantor's power being between present substantial benefit and the mere prospect or possibility, even the probability, that one may have it at some uncertain future time or perhaps not at all. A donor who keeps so strong a hold over the actual and immediate enjoyment of what he put beyond his own power to retake has not divested himself of that degree of control which [§ 2038] requires in order to avoid the tax. [326 U.S. at 487.]

Because the trusts were created before 1936, they were included under § 2038(a)(2), which does not expressly refer to a power of termination. The Court held that the express reference in § 2038(a)(1) to a power to "terminate," added by Congress in 1936, was intended as declaratory of existing law rather than as a substantive change.

LOBER v. UNITED STATES

346 U.S. 335 (1953).

MR. JUSTICE BLACK delivered the opinion of the Court.

This is an action for an estate tax refund brought by the executors of the estate of Morris Lober. In 1924 he signed an instrument conveying to himself as trustee money and stocks for the benefit of his young son. In 1929 he executed two other instruments, one for the benefit of a daughter, the other for a second son. The terms of these three instruments were the same. Lober was to handle the funds, invest and reinvest them as he deemed proper. He could accumulate and reinvest the income with the same freedom until his children reached twenty-one years of age. When twenty-one they were to be paid the accumulated income. Lober could hold the principal of each trust until the beneficiary reached twenty-five. In case he died his wife was to be trustee with the same broad powers Lober had conveyed to himself. The trusts were declared to be irrevocable, and as the case reaches us we may assume that the trust instruments gave Lober's children a "vested interest" under state law, so that if they had died after creation of the trusts their interests would have passed to their estates.[10] A crucial term of the trust instruments was that Lober could at any time he saw fit turn all or any part of the principal of the trusts over

10. The lower court noted that the trust instrument did not provide for a gift over to another beneficiary in the event a child died before reaching age 25. Lober v. United States, 108 F. Supp. 731 (Ct. Cl. 1952). If that event occurred, it would be necessary to construe the trust instrument to determine whether the trust property should be distributed to the deceased child's estate or to Lober. The Court assumes the former construction, which makes the imposition of the estate tax harder to justify.—EDS.

to his children. Thus he could at will reduce the principal or pay it all to the beneficiaries, thereby terminating any trusteeship over it.

Lober died in 1942. By that time the trust property was valued at more than $125,000. The Internal Revenue Commissioner treated this as Lober's property and included it in his gross estate. That inclusion brought this lawsuit. The Commissioner relied on [§ 2038]. That section, so far as material here, required inclusion in a decedent's gross estate of the value of all property that the decedent had previously transferred by trust "where the enjoyment thereof was subject at the date of his death to any change through the exercise of a power ... to alter, amend, or revoke...." In Commissioner v. Holmes, 326 U.S. 480, we held that power to terminate was the equivalent of power to "alter, amend, or revoke" it, and we approved taxation of the Holmes estate on that basis. Relying on the *Holmes* case, the Court of Claims upheld inclusion of these trust properties in Lober's estate. 124 Ct. Cl. 44, 108 F. Supp. 731. This was done despite the assumption that the trust conveyances gave the Lober children an indefeasible "vested interest" in the properties conveyed. The Fifth Circuit Court of Appeals had reached a contrary result where the circumstances were substantially the same, in Hays' Estate v. Commissioner, 181 F.2d 169, 172–174. Because of this conflict, we granted certiorari. 345 U.S. 969.

Petitioners stress a factual difference between this and the *Holmes* case. The *Holmes* trust instrument provided that if a beneficiary died before expiration of the trust his children succeeded to his interest, but if he died without children, his interest would pass to his brothers or their children. Thus the trustee had power to eliminate a contingency that might have prevented passage of a beneficiary's interest to his heirs. Here we assume that upon death of the Lober beneficiaries their part in the trust estate would, under New York law, pass to their heirs. But we cannot agree that this difference should change the *Holmes* result.

We pointed out in the *Holmes* case that [§ 2038] was more concerned with "present economic benefit" than with "technical vesting of title or estates." And the Lober beneficiaries, like the Holmes beneficiaries, were granted no "present right to immediate enjoyment of either income or principal." The trust instrument here gave none of Lober's children full "enjoyment" of the trust property, whether it "vested" in them or not. To get this full enjoyment they had to wait until they reached the age of twenty-five unless their father sooner gave them the money and stocks by terminating the trust under the power of change he kept to the very date of his death. This father could have given property to his children without reserving in himself any power to change the terms as to the date his gift would be wholly effective, but he did not. What we said in the *Holmes* case fits this situation too: "A donor who keeps so strong a hold over the actual and immediate enjoyment of what he puts beyond his own power to retake has not divested himself of that degree of control which [§ 2038] requires in order to avoid the tax." Commissioner v. Holmes, supra, at 487.

Affirmed.

MR. JUSTICE DOUGLAS and MR. JUSTICE JACKSON dissent.

NOTES

1. *Scope of the phrase "alter, amend, revoke, or terminate."*

a. *Dispositive powers.* In Porter v. Commissioner, supra page 239, the Supreme Court reserved judgment about the status of powers to make "slight or trivial" changes in the beneficiaries' enjoyment of transferred property, hinting that the statute might be construed to embody an implied de minimis exception. Although the *Lober* decision does not foreclose a de minimis argument, no cases have been decided in the taxpayer's favor on this ground, and the regulations now provide that § 2038 applies "to any power affecting the time or manner of enjoyment of property or its income, even though the identity of the beneficiary is not affected." Reg. § 20.2038–1(a). For a discussion of "speculative" powers, see Tully's Estate v. United States, infra page 245.

b. *Powers not affecting "enjoyment."* Section 2038(a) does not reach powers to alter, amend, revoke or terminate unless an exercise of the power will change "enjoyment" of the transferred interest in property. Under this theory, trust property has escaped inclusion under § 2038 despite the settlor's retention of the following powers: a power to add property to the trust, Central Trust Co. v. United States, 167 F.2d 133 (6th Cir. 1948); a power to substitute property of "equal value," Jordahl's Estate v. Commissioner, 65 T.C. 92 (1975); a power to amend the trust to clarify the original language, if it does not enable the settlor to "shift economic benefits," Theopold v. United States, 164 F.2d 404 (1st Cir. 1947); a power to amend the trust to enlarge the power of a trustee to shift enjoyment of the property among the beneficiaries, on the theory that the power does not enable the settlor to alter enjoyment, United States v. Winchell, 289 F.2d 212 (9th Cir. 1961); but see Fidelity Union Trust Co. v. United States, 126 F.Supp. 527 (Ct. Cl. 1954) (contra). Elaborating on the holding of *Jordahl's Estate*, the Service has ruled that a trust settlor's retained power, exercisable in a non-fiduciary capacity, to acquire trust assets by substituting property of equivalent value will not give rise to inclusion under § 2038, provided that the trustee has a fiduciary obligation to ensure that the substituted property is in fact of equivalent value and further provided that the power of substitution cannot be exercised to shift benefits among the trust beneficiaries. Rev. Rul. 2008–22, 2008–1 C.B. 796. For the effect of a settlor's retained power to remove a trustee and name himself or a third person as successor, see infra page 261, Note 3.

c. *Administrative powers.* The Service had some early success in applying § 2038 to broad powers of trust administration—e.g., powers to select investments, to manage trust property, and to allocate receipts and disbursements to principal and income—whether held by the decedent as trustee or in an individual, nonfiduciary capacity, because § 2038(a) reaches powers held by the decedent "in whatever capacity exercisable." See, e.g., Commissioner v. Hager's Estate, 173 F.2d 613 (3d Cir.), cert. dismissed, 337 U.S. 937 (1949); State Street Trust Co. v. United States, 263 F.2d 635 (1st Cir. 1959). Its campaign met a major setback when the First Circuit overruled its *State Street* decision and held that § 2038 did not reach a settlor's retained discretionary powers to acquire investments not normally held by fiduciaries and to determine which items were to be charged or credited to income or principal. The court refused to treat "purely administrative powers" as powers to alter beneficial enjoyment because in exercising such powers the trustee was subject to fiduciary standards enforceable in a court of equity. Old Colony Trust Co. v. United States, 423 F.2d 601 (1st Cir. 1970), infra page 307. See also United States v. Byrum, 408 U.S. 125 (1972), infra page 312.

2. *Source of powers.* Although most powers are expressly reserved by the decedent when creating a trust, § 2038(a)(1) applies "without regard to when or from what source the decedent acquired such power."

a. *Powers arising by operation of law.* Section 2038 applies to a revocable trust where the settlor's power to revoke arises by implication under local law in the absence of a contrary provision in the trust instrument. Reg. § 20.2038–1(c); Hill's Estate v. Commissioner, 64 T.C. 867 (1975), affd. mem., 568 F.2d 1365 (5th Cir. 1978) (Texas law); Davis' Estate v. Commissioner, 51 T.C. 361 (1968) (California law). Apart from the express or implied terms of the transfer, a power to rescind may arise from circumstances that would prevent the transfer from being complete for gift tax purposes, e.g., the transferor's lack of capacity, fraud on the beneficiary's part, or a formal defect in the transfer. See supra page 87, Note 2. Compare Casey's Estate v. Commissioner, 948 F.2d 895 (4th Cir. 1991) (unauthorized transfers by decedent's son under durable power of attorney were rescindable, hence includible in gross estate), with Ridenour's Estate v. Commissioner, 36 F.3d 332 (4th Cir. 1994) (no inclusion where transfers were authorized under durable power of attorney).

b. *Powers arising under state custodianship statutes.* Under state custodianship statutes, a custodian typically has broad discretion to expend custodial property for the minor donee's "use and benefit." Uniform Transfers to Minors Act § 14(a), infra page 287, Note 2. If the donor of custodial property dies while acting as custodian before the donee reaches majority, the donor-custodian is treated as having a power to alter beneficial enjoyment under § 2038. See Stuit v. Commissioner, 452 F.2d 190 (7th Cir. 1971) (statutory power equivalent to power to terminate); Rev. Rul. 59–357, 1959–2 C.B. 212.

3. *Amount includible under § 2038.* In *Lober*, the full value of the three trusts was included in Mr. Lober's gross estate. Would a lesser amount have been appropriate had he retained only the power to terminate the trusts? Each child would then have had a vested right to receive the income until he or she reached age 25, subject to their father's reserved power to terminate the trusts and pay over the principal to them. See the discussion of § 2038 under similar circumstances in Leopold v. United States, infra page 254, and the authorities there cited.

4. *Gift tax treatment of retained powers.* Is a gift tax payable on the creation of a trust of the type involved in the *Lober* case? Of the type involved in Commissioner v. Chase Natl. Bank, supra page 240? See Higgins v. Commissioner, 129 F.2d 237 (1st Cir.), cert. denied, 317 U.S. 658 (1942). Of

the type involved in Commissioner v. Holmes' Estate, supra page 240? See generally Chapter 2, Section B; Reg. § 25.2511–2.

TULLY'S ESTATE v. UNITED STATES

528 F.2d 1401 (Ct. Cl. 1976).

KUNZIG, JUDGE.

The single issue presented in this estate tax case is the includability in decedent Edward A. Tully, Sr.'s gross estate of death benefits paid directly to Tully's widow by his employer. Plaintiffs (co-executors) move for partial summary judgment claiming that no estate tax provision compels such treatment. Defendant's cross-motion counters that the death benefits must be added to the gross estate as required either by section 2038(a)(1) or section 2033 of the Internal Revenue Code of 1954. We agree with plaintiffs and hold the sum at issue not includable in Tully's gross estate.

The facts in this case are uncontested. Before his death, Tully was employed by Tully and DiNapoli, Inc. (T & D), a company owned 50% by decedent and 50% by Vincent P. DiNapoli. On July 1, 1959, Tully, DiNapoli and T & D entered into a contract whereby T & D promised to pay death benefits to the Tully and DiNapoli widows. Later, in October 1963, the same parties amended the 1959 agreement to limit the maximum amount of death payments to $104,000. On March 7, 1964, Tully died. T & D paid his widow the $104,000 called for in the contract.

Because the death benefits were paid directly by T & D to the widow, plaintiffs did not include this sum in Tully's gross estate when they filed the estate tax return. On audit, the Internal Revenue Service (IRS) concluded that the $104,000 was part of Tully's gross estate and assessed an estate tax deficiency. Plaintiffs paid the deficiency, filed a refund claim and by timely petition filed in this court, brought the present action after the IRS disallowed their claim.

In essence, plaintiffs say section 2038(a)(1) is inapplicable because Tully never transferred an interest in the death benefits, either at the time of their creation or thereafter, and even if he had, he kept no power to "alter, amend, revoke or terminate" the interest. Further, plaintiffs assert, decedent had no "interest" in the death benefits at the time of his death within the meaning of estate tax section 2033. Defendant takes an opposing viewpoint. It contends that Tully made a transfer of his interest in the benefits prior to his death, but kept a power to "alter, amend, revoke or terminate" such transfer until the time of his death. Defendant claims this power requires addition of the benefits to Tully's gross estate under section 2038(a)(1). Alternatively, the Government argues, Tully still had sufficient "interest" in the benefits at the time of his death to force the $104,000 into his gross estate under section 2033.

. . . [O]ur inquiry takes two avenues. First, did Tully transfer the death benefits but keep a power to change or revoke them until the time of his death? If so, section 2038(a)(1) applies. Second, did Tully have an "interest" in the benefits at his death? If he had an "interest," section 2033 applies....

I. Section 2038(a)(1)

Defendant argues that Tully transferred an interest in the death benefits at some point prior to his death and kept a section 2038(a)(1) power to "alter, amend, revoke or terminate" the enjoyment of the benefits after the transfer until his death. Plaintiffs counter that there was no "transfer" in the 1959 contract or thereafter because decedent never had any interest in the benefits which he could transfer. Even if a transfer is found, plaintiffs claim Tully did not keep a section 2038(a)(1) "power" after such transfer.

Contrary to plaintiffs' position, Tully did transfer an interest in the death benefits to his wife by executing the 1959 contract. In one of the three death benefit plans at issue in Estate of Bogley v. United States, 514 F.2d 1027, 206 Ct. Cl. 695 (1975), the decedent (an employee, officer, director and 34% shareholder) entered into an enforceable contract with his employer. In consideration of decedent's past and future services, the employer promised to pay decedent's *widow* or the estate two years' salary after his death. We found that where decedent was married at the time of the execution of the contract he "did make a transfer of his interest to his wife during his lifetime by making the contract with [the employer]." Bogley, supra, 514 F.2d at 1039, 206 Ct. Cl. at 715. In the instant case, the basic facts are nearly identical. The 1959 agreement looked to Tully's past and future services to T & D for consideration. The benefits here were also payable to the "widow" and decedent was married at the time of the 1959 contract. Tully in substance, if not in form, made a gift of a part of his future earnings to his wife.

However, within the meaning of section 2038(a)(1), Tully did not keep a power to "alter, amend, revoke or terminate" the death benefit transfer after the 1959 contract. There was no express reservation of such power in either the 1959 or 1963 contracts and no indication in the record of any other express agreements in which Tully obtained a section 2038(a)(1) power.

The Government implies that Tully's 50% stock ownership of T & D gave him unfettered power to change the death benefit plan to suit his own tastes. The facts do not bear this out. To the contrary, Tully's every movement could have been blocked by the other 50% shareholder. Tully did not have individual control of T & D and could not by himself, alter the terms of the death benefit agreement. As stated by the court in Harris v. United States, 29 Am. Fed. Tax R. 2d 1558 (C.D. Cal. 1972), section 2038(a)(1) powers must be *demonstrable*, *real*, *apparent* and *evident*, not speculative. See also Hinze v. United States, 29 Am. Fed. Tax R. 2d 1553 (C.D. Cal. 1972). We agree with this test and find Tully did not have a section 2038(a)(1) power to "alter, amend, revoke or terminate" through his 50% stock ownership in T & D at the time of his death.

Moreover, the death benefits are not includable in Tully's gross estate despite the fact that Tully *might* have altered, amended, revoked or terminated them in conjunction with T & D and DiNapoli. A power to "alter, amend, revoke or terminate" expressly exercisable in conjunction with others falls within section 2038(a)(1), but "power" as used in this section does not extend to *powers of persuasion*. If section 2038(a)(1) reached the possibility that Tully might convince T & D and DiNapoli to change the death benefit plan, it would apply to *speculative* powers. Section 2038(a)(1) cannot be so construed. Harris, supra; Hinze, supra. In addition, if section 2038(a)(1) applies to situations where an employee *might* convince an employer to change a death benefit program, it would sweep all employee death benefit plans into the gross estates of employees. It would always be at least possible for an employee to convince the employer that it would be to their mutual benefit to modify the death benefit plan. In light of the numerous cases where employee death benefit plans similar to the instant plan were held not includable in the employee's gross estate, we find that Congress did not intend the "in conjunction" language of section 2038(a)(1) to extend to the mere possibility of bilateral contract modification. Therefore, merely because Tully might have changed the benefit plan "in conjunction" with T & D and DiNapoli, the death benefits are not forced into Tully's gross estate.

Tully also did not obtain a section 2038(a)(1) "power" from the remote possibility that he could have altered the amount of death benefits payable to his widow by changing his compensation scheme. The death benefits here were to be paid based on decedent's annual salary. From this, defendant reasons that up until the time of his death, Tully could have accepted lesser compensation or terminated his employment in order to alter or revoke the death benefits.[11] In practical terms, we reject this *possibility*. This is not a factor which rises to the level of a section 2038(a)(1) "power." An employee might accept lesser compensation or terminate his employment for a myriad of reasons, but to conclude that a motive for such action would be the death benefit plan itself is not only speculative but ridiculous. And we have already made clear that a section 2038(a)(1) "power" cannot be speculative, but must be *demonstrable*, *real*, *apparent* and *evident*. Harris, supra; Hinze, supra. In addition, modification of Tully's employment contract would have required the cooperation of T & D or a breach by Tully. Neither of these two events constitutes a section 2038(a)(1) "power." Further, it is a common practice to "peg" employee death benefit plans to the employee's salary. To our knowledge, no court has ever held that such practice subjects death benefits to

11. Defendant does not argue that the failure to set a specific dollar amount on the death benefits gave Tully a section 2038(a)(1) "power." Instead it contends this represents a section 2033 "interest" held by decedent until his death. Such position is misplaced. Section 2033 is not a "catch all," but taxes property over which the owner has kept so much control that he has never really transferred it. In this context, the only control that Tully *might* have had over the death benefits by virtue of the failure to set a specific dollar figure was an ability to change or terminate the payments. This is a section 2038(a)(1) "power." Having once given away the benefits, he could not have obtained any part of the benefits to spend for his own use or anyone else's use and, therefore, did not have a section 2033 "interest."

inclusion in the employee's gross estate. On the contrary, in Estate of Whitworth v. Commissioner, 22 CCH Tax Ct. Mem. 177 (1963), the court concluded that although the decedent could have terminated his widow's benefits by leaving his employ or by breaching his employment contract, the death benefits at issue were *not* includable in his estate as a section 2038(a)(1) revocable transfer. Due to the practicalities of death benefit contracts and using the rationale of the *Whitworth* case, we hold that no section 2038(a)(1) power was created by the remote possibility that Tully might have changed the amount of death benefits prior to his death.

Finally, Tully did not retain a section 2038(a)(1) "power" to revoke or terminate the transfer to his wife by virtue of the *possibility* that he could have divorced her. The contract called for T & D to make the death benefit payments to Tully's *widow*. It might be argued that Tully could have divorced his wife to terminate her interest in the death benefits, but again such an argument ignores practicalities, reduces the term "power" to the speculative realm, and is not in accord with prior cases. In reality, a man might divorce his wife, but to assume that he would fight through an entire divorce process merely to alter employee death benefits approaches the absurd. Further, in various cases, death benefits payable to the "widow," Estate of Porter v. Commissioner, 442 F.2d 915 (1st Cir. 1971), or "wife," Estate of Kramer v. United States, 406 F.2d 1363, 186 Ct. Cl. 684 (1969), were not thereby held includable in the gross estate. The possibility of divorce in the instant situation is so de minimis and so speculative rather than *demonstrative*, *real*, *apparent* and *evident* that it cannot rise to the level of a section 2038(a)(1) "power." Harris, supra; Hinze, supra. Thus the use of "widow" in the death benefit contract did not give Tully a real power to revoke or terminate the death benefit transfer to his wife.

In short, in the 1959 contract Tully transferred certain interests to his wife by obtaining T & D's promise to pay death benefits. While it may be argued that Tully kept a certain de minimis association with the death benefit plan, such association never rose to the dignity of a power to "alter, amend, revoke or terminate" the transfer. In *Kramer*, supra, we held that a substantially similar plan did not create section 2038(a)(1) powers. The facts here are not significantly different. Therefore, section 2038(a)(1) does not operate to compel inclusion of the death benefits in decedent's gross estate.

II. Section 2033

Nor does section 2033 require addition of the benefits to Tully's gross estate. The Government argues that corporate control, "pegging" the benefits to Tully's salary, and naming "widow" as beneficiary constituted section 2033 "interests" kept by Tully until his death. We found above that these facts did not give rise to a section 2038(a)(1) "power." We also determine that they did not create a section 2033 "interest."

Having found that Tully transferred the death benefits to his wife and that he could not reach them for his own use, he could not have kept a section 2033 "interest." The de minimis associations Tully may have still had with the benefits are not strong enough to force a conclusion that decedent never transferred his interests in the benefits to his wife....

Accordingly, plaintiff's motion for partial summary judgment is granted and defendant's cross-motion for partial summary judgment is denied....

NOTES

1. *"Transfer" by the decedent.* An employee's promise to perform services, or the actual performance of them, constitutes a sufficient "transfer" to bring § 2038 into force, with the result that the value of the survivors' benefits under an employment contract or benefit plan is includible in the employee's gross estate if he or she has the right to name or change the beneficiaries. Rev. Rul. 76–304, 1976–2 C.B. 269; Levin's Estate v. Commissioner, 90 T.C. 723 (1988), affd. mem., 891 F.2d 281 (3d Cir. 1989) (decedent, as controlling shareholder and chairman of employer's board of directors, held power to terminate benefits); Siegel's Estate v. Commissioner, 74 T.C. 613 (1980) (same result where employer's consent is required); cf. Kramer v. United States, 406 F.2d 1363 (Ct. Cl. 1969) (cited and discussed in principal case). The same result follows where the decedent became entitled to receive life insurance proceeds and elected a settlement option that allowed her to withdraw the proceeds or change the interests of successor beneficiaries. Morton's Estate v. Commissioner, 12 T.C. 380 (1949). If a father gives property to his daughter and the daughter uses the property to establish a trust, naming the father as a trustee with fiduciary powers to alter or amend, has the father made a "transfer" within the meaning of § 2038? See Reed's Estate v. Commissioner, 36 A.F.T.R.2d 6413 (M.D. Fla. 1975) (no; the two transactions were "totally unrelated"); see also Skifter's Estate v. Commissioner, infra page 379 (same where husband transferred insurance policies on his life to his wife, who subsequently transferred policies in trust naming husband as trustee).

2. *Retained power.* The court in *Tully's Estate* notes that Tully did not expressly reserve a power to alter, amend, revoke, or terminate the death benefits payable to his widow under the contracts with T & D. If the contracts had stated that those benefits could be changed with the consent of Tully, DiNapoli, and T & D, would the court have reached a different result? See Siegel's Estate v. Commissioner, 74 T.C. 613 (1980) (§ 2038 applicable where decedent expressly retained powers exercisable with employer's consent which "appear[ed] to be greater than those arising from local contract law"; *Tully's Estate* distinguished).

3. *Interest owned at death.* At the time of his death Tully did not directly own an "interest" in the death benefit payable to his widow. He did, however, own a 50–percent stock interest in T & D, which paid the death benefit from its corporate assets. Should the amount of the death benefit be included in the appraised value of T & D and thus indirectly reflected in the value of Tully's stock? Or should T & D's value be reduced dollar-for-dollar by the company's contractual obligation to pay the death benefit? On an analogous question

arising when a corporation owns an insurance policy on the life of a controlling shareholder, see infra page 385, Note 3.

2. WHERE TRANSFEROR'S POWER IS RESTRICTED

a. Power Subject to a Standard or Contingency

JENNINGS v. SMITH

161 F.2d 74 (2d Cir. 1947).

SWAN, CIRCUIT JUDGE.

. . . [T]he question presented at the trial and renewed here, is whether the value of [property transferred in trust by the decedent prior to his death in 1936] should have been included in the gross estate. The district court held it includible under [§ 2038]. Accordingly judgment was given for the defendant, and the plaintiffs have appealed.

In December 1934 the decedent set up two trusts: one for the family of his elder son, B. Brewster Jennings, the other for the family of his younger son, Lawrence K. Jennings. The trust instruments were identical, except for the names of the beneficiaries and the property transferred. In discussing the terms of the trusts it will suffice to refer to the one set up for the elder son's family. The trust was irrevocable and in so far as legally permissible its provisions were to be interpreted and enforced according to Connecticut law. It reserved no beneficial interest to the settlor. He and his two sons were named as the trustees; in case a vacancy should occur provision was made for the appointment of a successor trustee having like powers; there were always to be three trustees and they were authorized to act by majority vote. At the end of each year during the life of the son, the trustees were to accumulate the net income by adding it to the capital of the trust but they were given power, "in their absolute discretion" at any time during the year and prior to the amalgamation of that year's net income into capital, to use all or any part of it for the benefit of the son or his issue provided "the trustees shall determine that such disbursement is reasonably necessary to enable the beneficiary in question to maintain himself and his family, if any, in comfort and in accordance with the station in life to which he belongs." Upon the death of the son the capital of the trust was to be divided into separate equal trust funds, one for each of his surviving children and one for each deceased child who left issue surviving at the death of the son. The trustees also had power to invade the capital upon the terms set out in paragraph 3(f) of the trust deed. In the Lawrence K. Jennings trust all current net income for the years 1935 and 1936 was paid to him, the trustees, of whom the decedent was one, having unanimously determined that such payments were necessary to enable Lawrence to maintain himself and his family in comfort and in accordance with his station in life. No payment or application of income of the B. Brewster Jennings trust, and none of capital of either trust, was made or requested during the life of the decedent.

Gift tax returns covering the transfers in trust were duly filed and taxes paid thereon. The trusts were not created in contemplation of death, nor to reduce estate taxes on the settlor's estate.

[The court held that a power exercisable in a fiduciary capacity falls within the scope of § 2038(a)(2), and that the parenthetical clause "in whatever capacity exercisable" in § 2038(a)(1), added in 1936, was declaratory of prior law. See Commissioner v. Newbold's Estate, 158 F.2d 694 (2d Cir. 1946).]

The next question is whether the powers conferred upon the trustees in the case at bar are powers of the character described in [§ 2038(a)(2)], which requires that enjoyment of the trust property must be subject at the date of the decedent's death to change through the exercise of a power. The trustees' power to invade the capital of the trust property was exercisable only if the son or his issue "should suffer prolonged illness or be overtaken by financial misfortune which the trustees deem extraordinary." Neither of these contingencies had occurred before the decedent's death; hence enjoyment of the capital was not "subject at the date of his death to any change through the exercise of a power." In Commissioner v. Flanders, 2 Cir., 111 F.2d 117, although decision was rested on another ground, this court expressed the opinion that a power conditioned upon an event which had not occurred before the settlor's death was not within the section.... The question has recently been explored by the Tax Court in Estate of Budlong v. Commissioner, 7 T.C. 758 [affd. in part, revd. in part sub nom. Industrial Trust Co. v. Commissioner, 165 F.2d 142 (1st Cir. 1947)]. There it was held in a convincing opinion that the power of trustees to invade corpus in case of "sickness or other emergency," which had not occurred before the decedent's death, was not a power to "alter, amend or revoke" within the meaning of the statute. The court reasoned that the trustees had not unlimited discretion to act or withhold action under the power, since the trust instrument provided an external standard which a court of equity would apply to compel compliance by the trustees on the happening of the specified contingency or to restrain threatened action if the condition were not fulfilled. In the case at bar the district judge was of opinion that even if the trustees found that the stated conditions had been fulfilled, "their finding created no enforcible rights in any of the beneficiaries." 63 F. Supp. 834, at page 837. In this view we are unable to concur. The condition upon which the power to invade capital might arise is sufficiently definite to be capable of determination by a court of equity. As Judge L. Hand said in Stix v. Commissioner, 2 Cir., 152 F.2d 562, 563, "no language, however strong, will entirely remove any power held in trust from the reach of a court of equity." ... Since the trustees were not free to exercise untrammeled discretion but were to be governed by determinable standards, their power to invade capital, conditioned on contingencies which had not happened, did not in our opinion bring the trust property within the reach of [§ 2038(a)(2)].

Similar reasoning leads to the same conclusion with respect to the trustees' power over net income. At the end of each calendar year they were to accumulate the net income of that year unless prior to its amalgamation into capital they exercised their power to disburse it to, or for the benefit of, the son or his issue. The power the trustees had with respect to disbursing income was exercisable year by year; and at the date of the decedent's death the only income of which the enjoyment was subject to change through exercise of a power was the income of the B. Brewster Jennings trust for the year 1936. But the exercise of this power was conditioned on the trustees' determination that disbursement of the income was necessary to enable the beneficiary to whom it might be allotted to maintain himself and his family "in comfort and in accordance with the station in life to which he belongs." The contingency which would justify exercise of the power had not happened before the decedent's death; consequently the 1936 net income of the B. Brewster Jennings trust was not subject at the date of the decedent's death "to any change through the exercise of a power." Hence it was not includible in the gross estate of the decedent under [§ 2038]. This conclusion is not inconsistent with Commissioner v. Newbold's Estate, 2 Cir., 158 F.2d 694, for there the trustees had unlimited discretion, the trust instrument expressly providing that no beneficiary should have any vested right to receive any payment from income.

[The court held that the limitations on the decedent's retained powers also prevented inclusion of the trust property under § 2036(a)(2).]

The judgment is reversed and the cause remanded with directions to enter judgment for the plaintiffs.

NOTES

1. *Supervision of discretion by a court of equity.* How restricted was the discretion of the trustees in the *Jennings* case? This question gives rise to several subsidiary questions. What was the likelihood of either son petitioning the court to exercise its supervisory power? The trustees were given "absolute discretion" to disburse income when "reasonably necessary to enable the beneficiary in question to maintain himself and his family, if any, in comfort and in accordance with the station in life to which he belongs." Did this language compel distributions when the necessity arose, or was it designed merely to insulate the trustees from challenges by the remainder beneficiaries in making discretionary distributions to the income beneficiaries? If one son had fallen on hard times, would the court have interfered with any exercise of discretion that ranged, say, from a floor of $20,000 to a ceiling of $200,000? If not, did the trustees not in effect have "untrammeled discretion" within those limits? These issues are explored in the *Leopold* case, which follows.

2. *Contingent powers under § 2038.* In accord with the *Jennings* court's statement that a contingent power is not within the reach of § 2038 if the contingency has not occurred before the decedent's death, is Reg. § 20.2038–1(b), which states that "section 2038 is not applicable to a power the exercise

of which was subject to a contingency beyond the decedent's control which did not occur before his death (e.g., the death of another person during the decedent's life).'' But see Rev. Rul. 68–538, 1968–2 C.B. 406, stating that a trust was includible in the gross estate of a decedent who had originally reserved the power to revoke, but who had relinquished this power for a period of two years and had died during the period. The ruling is reminiscent of a provision in the pre–1954 regulations which stated that a power to alter, amend, or revoke ''will be considered to have existed on the date of the decedent's death, ... though the exercise of the power was restricted to a particular time which had not arrived, or the happening of a particular event which had not occurred, at decedent's death.'' Reg. 105, § 81.20(d).

What is the status of a power contingent on an event that the decedent could, but did not, bring about, if the event's nontax consequences greatly overshadow its significance for tax purposes, such as a power exercisable only if the transferor marries, gets divorced, bears a child, or quits a job? Recall the discussion on the point in *Tully's Estate*, supra page 245 (dismissing as ''speculative'' and ''absurd'' the notion that decedent could have altered enjoyment of employee death benefits payable to widow by quitting his job or divorcing his wife); see also Rev. Rul. 80–255, 1980–2 C.B. 272 (power to bear or adopt children involves acts of ''independent significance,'' whose effect on a trust that included after-born and after-adopted children was ''incidental and collateral'').

3. *Power subject to requirement of notice or lapse of time.* Transferred property is includible under § 2038 only if enjoyment ''was subject *at the date of [the decedent's] death* to any change through the exercise of a power ... by the decedent.'' What if the decedent was required to give twelve months' notice of his intention to exercise the power or if the change was to take effect only twelve months after exercise of the power? In proposing an amendment to the predecessor of § 2038, the House Committee on Ways and Means offered the following explanation:

> [I]f the retained right to alter, amend, or revoke could be exercised only after a precedent notice of, say, a year, or if the alteration, amendment, or revocation would become effective only after a lapse of time after [the decedent] performed the act which gave rise to the alteration, amendment, or revocation, it might be contended that under existing law the property is not includible in the decedent's gross estate. While it is believed that such contention would not be well founded, your committee believes it desirable to clarify the law so that under such circumstances it will be entirely clear that all the property of which the decedent at the date of his death has to all intents and purposes practical, if not technical, ownership, is to be included in his gross estate. [Section 2038(b)] clarifies the existing law on the subject and expressly provides that, although a notice may be required as a condition precedent to exercising the right to alter, amend, or revoke, nevertheless the full value of the property at the date of the decedent's death must be included in the gross estate, less only the outstanding estate (measured by the period required to elapse between the giving of the notice and the taking effect of any alteration, amendment, or revocation) which at the decedent's death is irrevocably

beyond his control. [H.R. Rep. No. 704, 73d Cong., 2d Sess. (1934), reprinted in 1939–1 C.B. (Part 2) 554, 581.]

Does the decedent have a power "at the time of his death" under § 2038 if he could not exercise it immediately before his death because of incompetence, perhaps caused by the last illness itself? In Hurd v. Commissioner, 160 F.2d 610 (1st Cir. 1947), a power held by the settlor as trustee was charged against him despite his incapacity, but the court indicated that the result would have been otherwise had he resigned or been removed before death. It also hinted, however, that if a successor fiduciary had been appointed to act on his behalf, he would be considered as still possessing the power at the time of his death.

LEOPOLD v. UNITED STATES

510 F.2d 617 (9th Cir. 1975).

GOODWIN, CIRCUIT JUDGE.

The district court awarded the executors of the estate of Hans G.M. de Schulthess a refund of federal estate taxes, and the government appeals.

The government asserts: (1) that the entire value of the corpus and the undistributed accumulated income of two identical inter vivos trusts created by the decedent for the benefit of two of his daughters is includible in his gross estate; and (2) that a payment made by the executors to the guardian of a third daughter was a nondeductible testamentary gift and not a deductible claim against the estate. [The portion of the opinion dealing with the second issue is reprinted infra at page 433.]

The decedent died in an automobile accident in 1962 at the age of 44. He was not married at the time of his death. Two former wives, Amelie de Schulthess and Constance Trevor de Schulthess, and three daughters, Catherine, Celeste and Beatrice Tina survived. Catherine and Celeste were the children of his first wife, Amelie, and Beatrice Tina was the child of his second wife, Constance. All three daughters were minors at the time of his death....

The first issue is the includibility in the decedent's gross estate of the entire corpus and accumulated income of two inter vivos trusts, one for the primary benefit of his daughter Catherine, and the other for the primary benefit of his daughter Celeste.

The relevant portions of the trust for Catherine are quoted below. The trust for Celeste was identical except for the difference in names. Decedent designated himself and a friend as trustees of both trusts.

> First: The Trustees shall receive, hold, manage, sell, exchange, invest and reinvest such property and every part thereof in the manner hereinafter specified, and shall collect, recover and receive the rents, issues, interest and income thereof, hereinafter called "income" and, after deducting such expenses in connection with the administration of the trust as, in the opinion of the Trustees, are

> properly payable from income, shall pay the balance of the said income to Catherine J.H. de Schulthess, the daughter of the Donor, during the term of her natural life, at such intervals as the Trustees, in their sole discretion, may determine. During the minority of the said Catherine J.H. de Schulthess the said income may be accumulated or paid to Amelie de Schulthess, the mother of the said Catherine J.H. de Schulthess, or to the guardian of Catherine J.H. de Schulthess, for the support, education, maintenance and general welfare of the said infant, but such decision to accumulate or pay the income during such minority is to be made solely in the uncontrolled discretion of the Trustees. Any income accumulated when the said Catherine J.H. de Schulthess shall attain the age of twenty-one (21) years shall be paid over to her at that time.
>
> Second: Upon the death of the said Catherine J.H. de Schulthess, this trust shall terminate, and the principal thereof shall then be paid and distributed to the issue of the said Catherine J.H. de Schulthess, in equal shares per stirpes and not per capita. If the said Catherine J.H. de Schulthess shall die leaving no issue then the trust principal shall be paid and distributed to her sister....
>
> Third: The Donor hereby authorizes and empowers the Trustees at any time during the continuance of the trust to pay to the said Catherine J.H. de Schulthess, or to apply for her benefit out of the principal of the trust, such amounts, if any, as the Trustees may deem necessary or proper, and their judgment with respect to the time and amount of any such payments of principal shall be final and conclusive beyond any dispute or appeal. Any payment or payments of principal under this Article may only be made in the event both Trustees hereunder concur in such payment or payments, and such payment or payments may in no manner be applied, directly or indirectly, to the benefit of the Donor....

Each trust was created in December 1956 with a corpus of approximately $641,000. Prior to the decedent's death each trust earned approximately $63,000 in net income, $37,000 of which was paid to each beneficiary in five annual installments and $26,000 of which was allowed to accumulate in the trust.

On decedent's federal estate tax return, the trusts were identified, but no portion of either was included in the gross estate. The Commissioner determined that the entire corpus and undistributed accumulated income of each trust were includible under sections 2036 and 2038 of the Internal Revenue Code, 26 U.S.C. §§ 2036, 2038, and asserted a deficiency in estate taxes. The district court, rejecting part of the Commissioner's determination, held that none of the accumulated income and only the actuarial value of the remainder interests (21.187 per cent of the corpus of Catherine's trust and 20.021 per cent of the corpus of Celeste's) was includible in the gross estate.

The appeal asserts the Commissioner's original position. The taxpayers have not cross-appealed from the district court's holding that the actuarial value of the remainder interests is includible, and that issue is not before us.

Section 2038(a)(1) of the Code provides that there shall be included in a decedent's gross estate all property gratuitously transferred by the decedent "where the enjoyment thereof was subject at the date of his death to any change through the exercise of a power . . . by the decedent alone or by the decedent in conjunction with any other person . . . to alter, amend, revoke, or terminate. . . ." Similarly, section 2036(a)(2), which often overlaps section 2038 in its coverage, requires the inclusion of all gratuitously transferred property over which the decedent has retained "the right, either alone or in conjunction with any person, to designate the persons who shall possess or enjoy . . . the income therefrom."

The government contends that the powers of decedent and his co-trustee to distribute principal to decedent's daughters whenever they deemed such payments to be "necessary and proper" and to accumulate trust income or to pay it out in their "uncontrolled discretion" for the girls' "support, education, maintenance and general welfare" constituted a power "to alter, amend, revoke, or terminate" within the meaning of section 2038. The government also contends that these powers gave the decedent the ability to shift income from his daughters to their heirs and, thus, to designate the persons who would receive the enjoyment of the property within the meaning of section 2036(a)(2).

The district court concluded, and the taxpayers do not dispute, that since the decedent had the power to pay out principal as he deemed "necessary and proper," he retained sufficient control over the remainder interest of each trust to justify its inclusion in his gross estate. However, the court also held that the decedent had retained no power to affect the beneficial enjoyment of the income of either trust, except to the extent that such power was limited by an ascertainable, external, objective standard. Although the question is a close one, we agree with the district court that the standard was ascertainable. The Court of Appeals for the First Circuit has said:

> The trust provision which is uniformly held to provide an ascertainable standard is one which, though variously expressed, authorizes such distributions as may be needed to continue the beneficiary's accustomed way of life. . . . Old Colony Trust Co. v. United States, 423 F.2d 601, 604 (1st Cir. 1970).

The provision at issue here, authorizing payments of income for the "support, education, maintenance and general welfare" of decedent's daughters, requires the trustees to maintain the daughters in their accustomed way of life and, hence, provides a sufficiently objective standard. . . .

From this conclusion it follows that the present value of a portion of the income interests was properly excluded from the decedent's gross estate. At the time of decedent's death, the daughters had an enforceable right to enjoy that portion of the trust income necessary to maintain them in their accustomed way of life. The government has elsewhere conceded the propriety of excluding from the gross estate the present value of a fixed, indefeasible income right even though the decedent retained the power to pay corpus prematurely to the income beneficiary. See Walter v. United States, 295 F.2d 720 (6th Cir. 1961). See also Revenue Ruling 70–513, 1970–2 Cum. Bull. 194, which holds that under section 2038 only the value of the remainder interest, and not the entire corpus, of a trust is includible in the decedent's gross estate where the enjoyment of a life estate is vested in the beneficiary and is not subject to reduction through exercise of the decedent's reserved power to terminate the trust and to pay over the corpus to the life beneficiary.

But the daughters here had an enforceable right to enjoy currently only a *portion* of the full income stream prior to reaching twenty-one years of age—i.e., that amount necessary to maintain them in their accustomed way of life. With respect to the remaining income, the decedent had two options: He could either allow that income to accumulate until the girls reached 21, or he could provide for present enjoyment of the income by paying over the corpus with its full income-generating capacity. Thus, the decedent possessed a degree of control over the enjoyment of that segment of the future income he was not required to distribute currently which precludes exclusion of its actuarial value from his gross estate. See United States v. O'Malley, 383 U.S. 627, 631 (1966); Lober v. United States, 346 U.S. 335, 337 (1953). . . .

The amount of previously accumulated income was properly excluded. Once the decision had been made to accumulate part of the income, this accumulation was placed beyond the reach of the trustees. The accumulated income would be paid to the children when they reached 21. Although the trustees could pay out the principal early, they could not prematurely distribute the accumulated income. Unlike the accumulated income held taxable in United States v. O'Malley, the accumulated income here did not become part of the trust principal and was not subject to the powers decedent reserved over the principal.

We hold, then, that under sections 2036(a)(2) and 2038(a)(1) the decedent's reserved power to distribute the principal of the trusts at any time requires the inclusion of the corpus of each trust, reduced by the actuarial value of that segment of the future income stream which the decedent would be obligated to distribute currently to his daughters.[12] We further hold that the exclusion of previously accumulated income was

12. The government also contends that these trusts are includible in decedent's gross estate under section 2036(a)(1), 26 U.S.C. § 2036(a)(1), because the decedent retained the right to apply trust income in satisfaction of his legal obligation to support his daughters. See Treas. Reg. § 20.2036–1(b)(2) (1960). However, this issue was never raised at the time of audit or in the district court, but only for the first time on this appeal. Since this issue presents genuine factual questions, we decline to consider it now. . . . [This concept is discussed infra at page 287, Note 2.—EDS.]

proper. The case must be remanded to the district court for a factual determination of the amount of the includible sum....

NOTE

The "enforceable external standard." Although the assumptions on which it is founded are dubious, the external standard doctrine is routinely applied by the courts, and, although the doctrine is not included in the regulations, it is recognized in revenue rulings. See, e.g., Rev. Rul. 73–143, 1973–1 C.B. 407 (power to invade principal for "special need" limited to support and education is sufficiently definite to avoid § 2038). The courts have approved a host of provisions that reserve to the settlor-trustee a large measure of control over the transferred property. See, e.g., Wilson's Estate v. Commissioner, 13 T.C. 869 (1949), affd. per curiam, 187 F.2d 145 (3d Cir. 1951) ("need for educational purposes or because of illness or for any other good reason"); United States v. Powell, 307 F.2d 821 (10th Cir. 1962) ("maintenance, welfare, comfort or happiness"); Budd's Estate v. Commissioner, 49 T.C. 468 (1968) ("sickness, accident, misfortune or other emergency").

The prediction of a particular court ruling is a risky business, however, because other courts have found similar language to be too open-ended to justify an escape from the application of § 2038. See, e.g., Michigan Trust Co. v. Kavanagh, 284 F.2d 502 (6th Cir. 1960) ("special emergency"); Bell's Estate v. Commissioner, 66 T.C. 729 (1976) ("funds for a home, business, or for any other purpose believed by the Trustees to be for her benefit"); Yawkey's Estate v. Commissioner, 12 T.C. 1164 (1949) ("the best interest of the beneficiary"); Hurd v. Commissioner, 160 F.2d 610 (1st Cir. 1947) ("The word 'circumstances' ... is as wide as the world and to say it imposes a legal limitation, or imports a controlling contingency, is to stretch it far beyond good sense.").

Where the trust instrument permits but does not require the distribution of funds for the "beneficiary's support, education, and comfort," the settlor-trustee has unrestricted discretion to make or withhold the payment. Such discretion has been held to be a taxable power because, even though the prescribed external standard limits the uses for which funds may be distributed, it does so only "in the sense of creating a ceiling on distributions rather than the floor required to avoid inclusion of the assets in the gross estate." Carpenter's Estate v. United States, 45 A.F.T.R.2d 1784 (W.D. Wis. 1980).

b. Power Exercisable in Conjunction With Another Person

By its terms, § 2038 applies if enjoyment is subject to a power to alter, amend or revoke, exercisable by the decedent alone or in conjunction with any other person. In Helvering v. City Bank Farmers Trust Co., 296 U.S. 85 (1935), the Supreme Court held the statute applicable where a decedent who had created an inter vivos trust retained a power to revoke the trust with the consent of the trustee and a beneficiary. The Court rejected a due process challenge, finding nothing "unreasonable or arbitrary" in applying the statute to powers exercisable by a decedent in conjunction with another person:

> The purpose of Congress in adding [§ 2038(a)(2)] to the section as it stood in an earlier act was to prevent avoidance of the tax by the device of joining with the grantor in the exercise of the power of revocation someone who he believed would comply with his wishes. Congress may well have thought that a beneficiary who was of the grantor's immediate family might be amenable to persuasion or be induced to consent to a revocation in consideration of other expected benefits from the grantor's estate. [296 U.S. at 90.]

The specific reference to powers exercisable by the decedent in conjunction with another person was added to the statute in 1924. A predecessor provision, which reached transfers only if they were in contemplation of death or "intended to take effect in possession or enjoyment" at or after the transferor's death, was held inapplicable where inter vivos trusts were revocable by the settlor only with the consent of the beneficiaries. Reinecke v. Northern Trust Co., 278 U.S. 339 (1929); cf. Reg. § 20.2038–1(d) (adverse party exception for pre–1924 transfers).

Because § 2038 speaks of a power exercisable "by the decedent alone or by the decedent in conjunction with any other person," a power held solely by a third person is not attributed to the grantor. By contrast, for income tax purposes, a power held by a "nonadverse party" is ordinarily treated the same as if it were held by the grantor, §§ 674(a) and 676(a); for limited exceptions, see § 674(c) and (d). In *City Bank Farmers Trust Co.*, the Supreme Court rejected the argument that the estate tax provision should be construed in light of the analogous income tax provision:

> The two sections have a cognate purpose but they exhibit marked differences of substance.... It is true, the Report of the Ways and Means Committee on [§ 2038] said "this provision is in accord with the principle of [§ 676(a)] which taxes to the grantor the income of a revocable trust." But to credit the assertion that the difference in phraseology is without significance and in both sections Congress meant to express the same thought, would be to disregard the clear intent of the phrase "any person" employed in § 2038. We are not at liberty to construe language so plain as to need no construction, or to refer to Committee reports where there can be no doubt of the meaning of the words used. [296 U.S. at 89.]

Is there any reason why powers held by a nonadverse party should be imputed to the grantor for purposes of the income tax but not the estate tax?

For gift tax purposes, a donor's retained power affecting beneficial enjoyment of transferred property does not prevent completion of the gift if the power can be exercised only with the consent of a person having a substantial adverse interest. Reg. § 25.2511–2(e), discussed in Camp v. Commissioner, supra page 95. Section 2038, however, contains no "adverse party" exception. Is a transfer of the type involved in *City Bank Farmers Trust Co.* subject to both gift tax and estate tax?

Could a third person be treated as the decedent's alter ego under § 2038? See Delaney v. Gardner, 204 F.2d 855 (1st Cir. 1953) (property transferred to nonstock membership corporation; held, not decedent's instrumentality); Kneeland v. Commissioner, 34 B.T.A. 816 (1936) (power to revoke vested in decedent's wife; held, trust not within § 2038). Recent cases tend to analyze this issue in terms of the grantor's retention of enjoyment of the trust property as defined in § 2036. See discussion infra at page 282, Note 3. Does a trustee concede that he is the grantor's agent if he testifies in a proceeding involving grantor's gift tax liability that he is prepared at all times to comply with the grantor's bidding, including a direction to return the trust property to the grantor? Consider the estate tax consequences of the trusts in Outwin v. Commissioner, supra page 103. Is it possible that transfers of this type will avoid both the gift and estate taxes?

NOTES

1. *Power vested in all beneficiaries jointly.* In Helvering v. Helmholz, 296 U.S. 93 (1935), the Supreme Court denied the application of the statutory predecessor of § 2038 to a trust that could be terminated with the consent of all the beneficiaries, a group that included the settlor. Because a trust can be terminated under local law if all parties agree and if the purposes of the trust have been accomplished, the Court held as one ground for its decision that the provision for termination "added nothing to the rights which the law conferred" and therefore did not create a "power" within the meaning of § 2038. Reg. § 20.2038–1(a)(2), which adopts the *Helmholz* rationale, states that a power does not count under § 2038 if it can "be exercised only with the consent of all parties having an interest (vested or contingent) in the transferred property, and if the power adds nothing to the rights of the parties under local law." An unresolved issue is whether the expression "all parties" means "all living persons beneficially interested" or whether it also includes beneficiaries who are yet to be born. A New York statute, E.P.T.L. § 7–1.9, has been interpreted to authorize the living beneficiaries to give the necessary consent, but the law in most other jurisdictions does not permit living beneficiaries to cut off the rights of unborn or unascertained beneficiaries unless the trust instrument so provides.

2. *Power to initiate or veto action by third person.* In Thorp's Estate v. Commissioner, 164 F.2d 966 (3d Cir. 1947), cert. denied, 333 U.S. 843 (1948), the corpus of a trust was held to be includible under § 2038 because it could be terminated on request by the beneficiaries, provided the decedent consented to such action: "regardless of who could set in motion the termination machinery, the trust could be terminated only by the action of the decedent in conjunction with others." See also Du Charme's Estate v. Commissioner, 164 F.2d 959 (6th Cir. 1947) ("Regardless of who initiates or requests such a change, the consent of both parties is required to make the change effective."); Grossman's Estate v. Commissioner, 27 T.C. 707 (1957) (same); Rev. Rul. 70–513, 1970–2 C.B. 194 (same for settlor's power to veto trustee's decision to terminate trust).

Does such a veto power come within the "contingency" exception of Reg. § 20.2038–1(b) (§ 2038 not applicable "to a power the exercise of which was subject to a contingency beyond the decedent's control which did not occur before his death")? In Kasch's Estate v. Commissioner, 30 T.C. 102 (1958), the trustees were empowered to invade corpus for "the proper care, support and medical attention" of the beneficiaries, provided the decedent consented. The court held that his power was "contingent" within the meaning of Jennings v. Smith (supra page 250). Assuming that the trust instrument permitted the trustees to invade corpus only under an enforceable external standard, but the decedent's power to veto their decision was wholly discretionary, should the corpus have been included in his estate under § 2038?

3. *Decedent's power to remove trustee in whom power is vested.* If a power to revoke or amend was held by a trustee who could be removed at will by the decedent, and the decedent could have appointed himself as successor trustee, the property is includible under § 2038. Reg. § 20.2038–1(a)(3); Van Beuren v. McLoughlin, 262 F.2d 315 (1st Cir. 1958), cert. denied, 359 U.S. 991 (1959). But if the decedent could have named himself only if the trustee had voluntarily resigned, it has been held that § 2038 is inapplicable unless the event occurred. United States v. Winchell, 289 F.2d 212 (9th Cir. 1961). What if the decedent retained the unfettered power to remove trustees, but not the right to take over the office himself? In a controversial 1979 revenue ruling, the Service took the position that a trust was includible in the settlor's gross estate under §§ 2038(a)(1) and 2036(a)(2) because the settlor could remove the corporate trustee without cause and designate a successor, even though the successor had to be another corporate trustee. Rev. Rul. 79–353, 1979–2 C.B. 325 (limited to prospective effect by Rev. Rul. 81–51, 1981–1 C.B. 458). The Tax Court, however, has rejected the ruling's underlying assumption that a settlor's power to remove a trustee amounts to a "de facto power to exercise the powers vested in the trustee," since the trustee is accountable to the beneficiaries, not the settlor, and the settlor has no legally enforceable right to control the trustee's exercise of its discretion. Wall's Estate v. Commissioner, 101 T.C. 300 (1993) (power to remove initial trustee and substitute another independent corporate trustee); see also Vak's Estate v. Commissioner, 973 F.2d 1409 (8th Cir. 1992) (gift tax). In Rev. Rul. 95–58, 1995–2 C.B. 191, the Service revoked its earlier ruling and announced that a retained power to remove a trustee and appoint a successor trustee who is "not related or subordinate to the decedent (within the meaning of section 672(c) of the Code)" will not cause the trustee's powers to be attributed to the decedent. What if the decedent retained the power to appoint his spouse as a successor trustee? What if the decedent's spouse held a power to appoint the decedent as a successor trustee? The tax implications of the settlor's power to remove the trustee are further discussed in Farrel's Estate v. Commissioner, infra page 322.

3. WHERE DECEDENT MAY MODIFY A TRANSFER MADE BY ANOTHER: "RECIPROCAL TRUSTS"

UNITED STATES v. GRACE'S ESTATE

395 U.S. 316 (1969).

MR. JUSTICE MARSHALL delivered the opinion of the Court.

This case involves the application of [§ 2036(a)(1)] to a so-called "reciprocal trust" situation. After Joseph P. Grace's death in 1950, the Commissioner of Internal Revenue determined that the value of a trust created by his wife was includible in his gross estate.[13] A deficiency was assessed and paid, and, after denial of a claim for a refund, this refund suit was brought. The Court of Claims, with two judges dissenting, ruled that the value of the trust was not includible in decedent's estate under [§ 2036(a)(1)] and entered judgment for respondent. Estate of Grace v. United States, 183 Ct. Cl. 745, 393 F.2d 939 (1968). We granted certiorari because of an alleged conflict between the decision below and certain decisions in the courts of appeals and because of the importance of the issue presented to the administration of the federal estate tax laws. 393 U.S. 975 (1968). We reverse.

I

Decedent was a very wealthy man at the time of his marriage to the late Janet Grace in 1908. Janet Grace had no wealth or property of her own, but, between 1908 and 1931, decedent transferred to her a large amount of personal and real property, including the family's Long Island estate. Decedent retained effective control over the family's business affairs, including the property transferred to his wife. She took no interest and no part in business affairs and relied upon her husband's judgment. Whenever some formal action was required regarding property in her name, decedent would have the appropriate instrument prepared and she would execute it.

On December 15, 1931, decedent executed a trust instrument, hereinafter called the Joseph Grace trust. Named as trustees were decedent, his nephew, and a third party. The trustees were directed to pay the income of the trust to Janet Grace during her lifetime, and to pay to her any part of the principal which a majority of the trustees might deem advisable. Janet was given the power to designate, by will or deed, the manner in which the trust estate remaining at her death was to be distributed among

13. Section 2036(a)(1) provides that if a decedent transferred property during his lifetime, retaining the right to receive the income, the property is includible in his gross estate. The ramifications of this provision are considered infra at page 268. It is sufficient for present purposes to note that the Court in *Grace* was concerned with the scope of the "reciprocal trust" doctrine, it being conceded that if the decedent had created, with his own property, a trust identical to the one his wife created for him, its corpus would have been includible in his estate under § 2036.—EDS.

decedent and their children. The trust properties included securities and real estate interests.

On December 30, 1931, Janet Grace executed a trust instrument, hereinafter called the Janet Grace trust, which was virtually identical to the Joseph Grace trust.[14] The trust properties included the family estate and corporate securities, all of which had been transferred to her by decedent in preceding years.

The trust instruments were prepared by one of decedent's employees in accordance with a plan devised by decedent to create additional trusts before the advent of a new gift tax expected to be enacted the next year. Decedent selected the properties to be included in each trust. Janet Grace, acting in accordance with this plan, executed her trust instrument at decedent's request.

Janet Grace died in 1937. The Joseph Grace trust terminated at her death. Her estate's federal estate tax return disclosed the Janet Grace trust and reported it as a nontaxable transfer by Janet Grace. The Commissioner asserted that the Janet and Joseph Grace trusts were "reciprocal" and asserted a deficiency to the extent of mutual value. Compromises on unrelated issues resulted in 55% of the smaller of the two trusts, the Janet Grace trust, being included in her gross estate.

Joseph Grace died in 1950. The federal estate tax return disclosed both trusts. The Joseph Grace trust was reported as a nontaxable transfer and the Janet Grace trust was reported as a trust under which decedent held a limited power of appointment.[15] Neither trust was included in decedent's gross estate.

The Commissioner determined that the Joseph and Janet Grace trusts were "reciprocal" and included the amount of the Janet Grace trust in decedent's gross estate. A deficiency in the amount of $363,500.97, plus interest, was assessed and paid.

II

. . . The doctrine of reciprocal trusts was formulated in response to attempts to draft instruments which seemingly avoid the literal terms of [§ 2036(a)(1)], while still leaving the decedent the lifetime enjoyment of his property. The doctrine dates from Lehman v. Commissioner, 109 F.2d 99 (C.A. 2d Cir.), cert. denied, 310 U.S. 637 (1940). In *Lehman*, decedent and his brother owned equal shares in certain stocks and bonds. Each brother placed his interest in trust for the other's benefit for life, with remainder to the life tenant's issue. Each brother also gave the other the right to withdraw $150,000 of the principal. If the brothers had each reserved the right to withdraw $150,000 from the trust that each had

14. That is, the Janet Grace trust included provisions for Joseph Grace which were similar to those made for Janet Grace in the Joseph Grace trust.—EDS.

15. By itself, this limited power of appointment over the Janet Grace trust (permitting decedent to designate by will or deed the manner in which the trust estate was to be distributed among his wife and their children) would not have required its inclusion in his gross estate. See Section G of this chapter.—EDS.

created, the trusts would have been includible in their gross estates as interests of which each had made a transfer with a power to revoke. When one of the brothers died, his estate argued that neither trust was includible because the decedent did not have a power over a trust which he had created.

The Second Circuit disagreed. That court ruled that the effect of the transfers was the same as if the decedent had transferred his stock in trust for himself, remainder to his issue, and had reserved the right to withdraw $150,000. The court reasoned: "The fact that the trusts were reciprocated or 'crossed' is a trifle, quite lacking in practical or legal significance.... The law searches out the reality and is not concerned with the form." 109 F.2d, at 100. The court ruled that the decisive point was that each brother caused the other to make a transfer by establishing his own trust.

The doctrine of reciprocal trusts has been applied numerous times since the *Lehman* decision. It received congressional approval in § 6 of the Technical Changes Act of 1949, 63 Stat. 893. The present case is, however, this Court's first examination of the doctrine.

The Court of Claims was divided over the requirements for application of the doctrine to the situation of this case. Relying on some language in *Lehman* and certain other courts of appeals' decisions, the majority held that the crucial factor was whether the decedent had established his trust as consideration for the establishment of the trust of which he was a beneficiary. The court ruled that decedent had not established his trust as a quid pro quo for the Janet Grace trust, and that Janet Grace had not established her trust in exchange for the Joseph Grace trust. Rather, the trusts were found to be part of an established pattern of family giving, with neither party desiring to obtain property from the other. Indeed, the court found that Janet Grace had created her trust because decedent requested that she do so. It therefore found the reciprocal trust doctrine inapplicable.

The court recognized that certain cases had established a slightly different test for reciprocity. Those cases inferred consideration from the establishment of two similar trusts at about the same time. The court held that any inference of consideration was rebutted by the evidence in the case, particularly the lack of any evidence of an estate tax avoidance motive on the part of the Graces. In contrast, the dissent felt that the majority's approach placed entirely too much weight on subjective intent. Once it was established that the trusts were interrelated, the dissent felt that the subjective intent of the parties in establishing the trusts should become irrelevant. The relevant factor was whether the trusts created by the settlors placed each other in approximately the same objective economic position as they would have been in if each had created his own trust with himself, rather than the other, as life beneficiary.

We agree with the dissent that the approach of the Court of Claims majority places too much emphasis on the subjective intent of the parties in creating the trusts and for that reason hinders proper application of the federal estate tax laws. It is true that there is language in *Lehman* and other cases that would seem to support the majority's approach. It is also true that the results in some of those cases arguably support the decision below. Nevertheless, we think that these cases are not in accord with this Court's prior decisions interpreting related provisions of the federal estate tax laws.

Emphasis on the subjective intent of the parties in creating the trusts, particularly when those parties are members of the same family unit, creates substantial obstacles to the proper application of the federal estate tax laws. As this Court said in Estate of Spiegel v. Commissioner, 335 U.S. 701, 705–706 (1949): "Any requirement ... [of] a post-death attempt to probe the settlor's thoughts in regard to the transfer, would partially impair the effectiveness of ... [§ 2036(a)] as an instrument to frustrate estate tax evasions." We agree that "the taxability of a trust corpus ... does not hinge on a settlor's motives, but depends on the nature and operative effect of the trust transfer." Id., at 705....

We think these observations have particular weight when applied to the reciprocal trust situation. First, inquiries into subjective intent, especially in intrafamily transfers, are particularly perilous. The present case illustrates that it is, practically speaking, impossible to determine after the death of the parties what they had in mind in creating trusts over 30 years earlier. Second, there is a high probability that such a trust arrangement was indeed created for tax-avoidance purposes. And, even if there was no estate-tax-avoidance motive, the settlor in a very real and objective sense did retain an economic interest while purporting to give away his property.[16] Finally, it is unrealistic to assume that the settlors of the trusts, usually members of one family unit, will have created their trusts as a bargained-for exchange for the other trust. "Consideration," in the traditional legal sense, simply does not normally enter into such intrafamily transfers.[17]

For these reasons, we hold that application of the reciprocal trust doctrine is not dependent upon a finding that each trust was created as a quid pro quo for the other. Such a "consideration" requirement necessarily involves a difficult inquiry into the subjective intent of the settlors. Nor do we think it necessary to prove the existence of a tax-avoidance motive. As we have said above, standards of this sort, which rely on subjective factors, are rarely workable under the federal estate tax laws. Rather, we hold that application of the reciprocal trust doctrine requires only that the trusts be interrelated, and that the arrangement, to the extent of mutual

16. For example, in the present case decedent ostensibly devised the trust plan to avoid an imminent federal gift tax. Instead of establishing trusts for the present benefit of his children, he chose an arrangement under which he and his wife retained present enjoyment of the property and under which the property would pass to their children without imposition of either estate or gift tax.

17. The present case is probably typical in this regard. Janet Grace created her trust because decedent requested that she do so; it was in no real sense a bargained-for quid pro quo for his trust....

value, leaves the settlors in approximately the same economic position as they would have been in had they created trusts naming themselves as life beneficiaries.[18]

Applying this test to the present case, we think it clear that the value of the Janet Grace trust fund must be included in decedent's estate for federal estate tax purposes. It is undisputed that the two trusts are interrelated. They are substantially identical in terms and were created at approximately the same time. Indeed, they were part of a single transaction designed and carried out by decedent. It is also clear that the transfers in trust left each party, to the extent of mutual value, in the same objective economic position as before. Indeed, it appears, as would be expected in transfers between husband and wife, that the effective position of each party vis-à-vis the property did not change at all. It is no answer that the transferred properties were different in character. For purposes of the estate tax, we think that economic value is the only workable criterion. Joseph Grace's estate remained undiminished to the extent of the value of his wife's trust and the value of his estate must accordingly be increased by the value of that trust.

The judgment of the Court of Claims is reversed and the case is remanded for further proceedings consistent with this opinion.

It is so ordered.

MR. JUSTICE STEWART took no part in the consideration or decision of this case.

MR. JUSTICE DOUGLAS, dissenting.

The object of a reciprocal trust, as I understand it, is for each settlor to rid himself of all taxable power over the corpus by exchanging taxable powers with the other settlor. Yet Joseph P. Grace and his wife did not exchange taxable powers. Each retained a sufficient power over the corpus to require the inclusion of the corpus in his or her taxable estate. Each settlor, as one of the three trustees, reserved the right to alter the trust by paying to the chief beneficiary "any amounts of the principal of the said trust, up to and including the whole thereof, which the said Trustees or a majority of them may at any time or from time to time deem advisable." I have quoted from Janet Grace's trust. But an almost identical provision is in the trust of Joseph P. Grace.

I would conclude from the existence of this reserved power that the corpus of the Janet Grace trust was includible in her estate for purposes of the estate tax. Lober v. United States, 346 U.S. 335.

That is to say the use of a reciprocal trust device to aid the avoidance of an estate tax is simply not presented by this case.

---

18. We do not mean to say that the existence of "consideration," in the traditional legal sense of a bargained-for exchange, can never be relevant. In certain cases, inquiries into the settlor's reasons for creating the trusts may be helpful in establishing the requisite link between the two trusts. We only hold that a finding of a bargained-for consideration is not necessary to establish reciprocity.

I would dismiss the petition as improvidently granted.

NOTES

1. *"Crossed" powers.* The Court's holding in *Grace* leaves open the question whether the reciprocal trust doctrine can be applied if the decedent had no economic interest in the property to be included in his estate. In Bischoff's Estate v. Commissioner, 69 T.C. 32 (1977), a husband and wife had made identical transfers in trust for the benefit of their grandchildren; each spouse was named trustee of the other's trust and in that capacity had discretionary power to accumulate income and distribute corpus for the benefit of the grandchildren. The Tax Court applied *Grace* to "uncross" the trusts and included the corpus in the decedent's estate under §§ 2036 and 2038, even though neither spouse could derive any personal benefit from either trust. See also Exchange Bank & Trust Co. v. United States, 694 F.2d 1261 (Fed. Cir. 1982) (reciprocal custodianships); but see Green's Estate v. United States, 68 F.3d 151 (6th Cir. 1995) (divided court refused to apply *Grace* where settlors had discretionary fiduciary powers, but no economic benefits, under trusts for their grandchildren).

See Rev. Rul. 56–397, 1956–2 C.B. 599, ruling that the reciprocal transfer doctrine is not applicable to the common arrangement among partners or other business associates, by which each purchases insurance on the life of the other in order to meet his obligation under an agreement to buy out the interest of the first to die.

2. *Gift tax consequences of reciprocal transfers.* Three brothers each had three children. Each brother and his wife simultaneously made identical gifts of stock to each of their own children and to each of their six nieces and nephews. Is each donor entitled to nine annual exclusions? In Sather v. Commissioner, 251 F.3d 1168 (8th Cir. 2001), the court applied the reciprocal trust doctrine to uncross the gifts, with the result that each donor was allowed only three annual exclusions:

> We do not believe that the Supreme Court [in *Grace*] meant to limit the doctrine to cases involving life estate trusts, or even to cases where the donor retains an economic interest.... In this case, the parents transferred stock to their nieces and nephews in exchange for transfers to their own children by the nieces' and nephews' parents. Though the [donors] received no direct economic value in the exchange, they did receive an economic benefit by indirectly benefitting their own children. The donors were in the same economic position—the position of passing assets to their children—by entering into the cross transactions as if they had made direct gifts of all of their stock to their own children.... Thus, using the reciprocal trust doctrine to identify the actual transferor, each donor made transfers to each of his or her own children but no gifts to any of the nieces and nephews. [251 F.3d at 1174–75.]

Accord, Schuler's Estate v. Commissioner, 282 F.3d 575 (8th Cir. 2002); Schultz v. United States, 493 F.2d 1225 (4th Cir. 1974); Rev. Rul. 85–24, 1985–1 C.B. 329 (reciprocal powers of withdrawal).

3. *Income tax consequences of reciprocal transfers.* Krause v. Commissioner, 57 T.C. 890 (1972), affd., 497 F.2d 1109 (6th Cir. 1974), cert. denied, 419 U.S. 1108 (1975), applied *Grace* under the income tax to uncross reciprocal trusts created by a husband and wife. The realigned "grantors" were then taxed on the income of the trusts under § 677(a)(2), based on the trustees' power to accumulate income for future distribution to the grantors.

4. *Amount included in the gross estate.* Rev. Rul. 74–533, 1974–2 C.B. 293, involved reciprocal trusts created on the same day by a husband and wife. Each spouse's trust named the other spouse as life income beneficiary, with remainder payable to the couple's surviving issue. The trust created by the husband was initially funded with $400,000 and at the wife's death held assets worth $600,000. The trust created by the wife was initially funded with $300,000 and at the husband's death held assets worth $500,000. Citing *Grace*, the Service uncrossed the trusts and ruled that the full value of the smaller trust ($500,000) was includible in the husband's estate; however, based on the relative values of the two trusts at inception, only three-quarters of the value of the larger trust ($450,000) was includible in the wife's estate.

5. *Identifying the transferor.* Aside from the reciprocal trust area, it is sometimes necessary to determine whether the decedent was the transferor of property if he gave it to someone else on condition that the latter place it in trust, or if the decedent placed property in trust after receiving it from another person. See First Natl. Bank of Shreveport v. United States, 224 F.Supp. 747 (W.D. La. 1963), affd. per curiam, 342 F.2d 415 (5th Cir. 1965), and cases there cited.

C. TRANSFERS WITH RETAINED RIGHT TO RECEIVE INCOME OR DESIGNATE INCOME BENEFICIARY: § 2036

Development of "postponed-possession-or-enjoyment" clause. From its enactment in 1916 until the adoption of the 1954 Code, the federal estate tax reached transfers "intended to take effect in possession or enjoyment at or after [the transferor's] death." It has already been noted (supra page 238) that from 1916 to 1924 revocable trusts were included in the gross estate by virtue of this statutory provision, and that in 1924 the predecessor of § 2038 was enacted to deal in a more explicit fashion with transfers under which the transferor retained the right to alter, amend, or revoke. Thereafter, despite an overlapping area, the taxability of transfers of this type was primarily governed by the explicit statutory language of § 2038 as modified from time to time, rather than by the more vague standard of the "postponed-possession-or-enjoyment" clause. The scope of § 2038 is studied in Section B of this chapter.

A second type of transfer that was originally tested by the "postponed-possession-or-enjoyment" clause was a gift of property with a reservation by the donor of the right to receive or to control the income. In 1931, however, this type of disposition also received explicit statutory recognition. The governing statute is now § 2036.

A third type of transfer that was formerly subject to the "postponed-possession-or-enjoyment" clause was a gift of property that might revert to the transferor's estate at or after his death. The statute eventually was amended to deal specifically with this type of transfer too, but this did not occur until 1949. The current version of the 1949 legislation is § 2037.

This development of a progressively more detailed statute culminated, in 1954, in the elimination of the original postponed-possession-or-enjoyment clause.[19] But the current provisions can hardly be understood without a few words of history.

Original understanding of the "postponed-possession-or-enjoyment" clause. In 1916, when the postponed-possession-or-enjoyment clause was enacted, it apparently was generally believed that it brought into the gross estate property that had been transferred by the decedent during his lifetime if he reserved to himself the income from the property. The pre–1916 understanding of the clause has been described by the Supreme Court in Commissioner v. Church's Estate, 335 U.S. 632 (1949), as follows:

> The "possession or enjoyment" provision ... seems to have originated in a Pennsylvania inheritance tax law in 1826. As early as 1884 the Supreme Court of Pennsylvania held that where a legal transfer of property was made which carried with it a right of possession with a reservation by the grantor of income and profits from the property for his life, the transfer was not intended to take effect in enjoyment until the grantor's death: "One certainly cannot be considered, as in the actual enjoyment of an estate, who has no right to the profits or incomes arising or accruing therefrom." Reish, Admr. v. Commonwealth, 106 Pa. 521, 526. That court further held that the "possession or enjoyment" clause did not involve a mere technical question of title, but that the law imposed the death tax unless one had parted during his life with his possession and his title and his enjoyment. It was further held in that case that the test of "intended" was not a subjective one, that the question was not what the parties intended to do, but what the transaction actually effected as to title, possession and enjoyment.

19. In 1942, Randolph Paul complained:

> We have been like Englishmen who never clean their slates; no language could be thrown away if anyone thought in optimistic vein that he understood its meaning. Amendments consisted of addition, duplication and overlapping. No one suggested the heroic remedy of fresh language which would clear away the debris and say simply what was plainly dictated by disillusioning experience with a statute that had repeatedly failed to say what the Treasury, at least, thought it meant. It was easier to repair at damaged points in a makeshift way, always hoping for a dim best. Some day we shall learn that sound revenue laws are not made in such a piecemeal way, and that postponing such important tax problems may be an expensive luxury. [1 Paul, Federal Estate and Gift Taxation § 7.01 (1942).]

In the years that have followed Mr. Paul's complaint, the process of shoring up, rather than rebuilding, the structure has continued; and even the 1954 elimination of the original "postponed-possession-or-enjoyment" clause falls short of the "heroic remedy of fresh language" that he urged, since a truncated version was retained, albeit for a limited purpose, in §§ 2036(a) and 2037.

> Most of the states have included the Pennsylvania-originated "possession or enjoyment" clause in death tax statutes, and with what appears to be complete unanimity, they have ... substantially agreed with this 1884 Pennsylvania Supreme Court interpretation. Congress used the "possession or enjoyment" clause in death tax legislation in 1862, 1864, and 1898.... In referring to the provision in the 1898 Act, this Court said that it made "the liability for taxation depend, not upon the mere vesting in a technical sense of title to the gift, but upon the actual possession or enjoyment thereof." Vanderbilt v. Eidman, 196 U.S. 480, 493. And five years before the 1916 estate tax statute incorporated the "possession or enjoyment" clause to frustrate estate tax evasions, ... this Court had affirmed a judgment of the New York Court of Appeals sustaining the constitutionality of its state inheritance tax in an opinion which said: "It is true that an ingenious mind may devise other means of avoiding an inheritance tax, but the one commonly used is a transfer with reservation of a life estate." Matter of Keeney, 194 N.Y. 281, 287, 87 N.E. 428, 429; Keeney v. New York, 222 U.S. 525. [335 U.S. at 637–38.]

Treasury practice from 1916 to 1930 accorded with the interpretation of the postponed-possession-or-enjoyment clause described above. See Commissioner v. Church's Estate, 335 U.S. at 639.

The "bombshell" of 1930: May v. Heiner. In 1930, however, the Supreme Court rejected this construction of the clause in May v. Heiner, 281 U.S. 238 (1930). The decedent in this case had transferred property in trust in 1917 to pay the income to her husband for his life and to her for her life if she survived him; on the survivor's death, the trust was to terminate and the property was to be distributed to her children. The record did not disclose whether she had survived her husband, so as to come into present enjoyment of the income, or not; but the Court thought this was not relevant. Holding that the trust property was not part of the decedent-settlor's gross estate, the Court said:

> [The transfer in 1917] was not testamentary in character and was beyond recall by the decedent. At the death of Mrs. May no interest in the property held under the trust deed passed from her to the living; title thereto had been definitely fixed by the trust deed. The interest therein which she possessed immediately prior to her death was obliterated by that event. [281 U.S. at 243.]

After May v. Heiner was decided, there remained for the Treasury the hope that it could be confined to its own peculiar facts: The decedent had retained a contingent, or secondary, life estate, rather than a primary one. This hope was dashed the next year when the Supreme Court decided Burnet v. Northern Trust Co., 283 U.S. 782 (1931), involving a trust under which the settlor retained a life income interest, without the intervention of any other beneficiary's interest. In a per curiam decision, the Court stated:

> The question in this case is that of the construction of [the postponed-possession-or-enjoyment clause. A similar provision] has already been construed by this Court, and, in this view, there being no question of the constitutional authority of the Congress to impose prospectively a tax with respect to transfers or trusts of the sort here involved, the judgment of the Circuit Court of Appeals for the Seventh Circuit is affirmed upon the authority of May v. Heiner.... [283 U.S. at 783.]

The Joint Resolution of March 3, 1931. There was a dramatic climax to Burnet v. Northern Trust Co. and to Morsman v. Burnet, 283 U.S. 783 (1931), and McCormick v. Burnet, 283 U.S. 784 (1931), two companion cases decided the same day:

> March 3, 1931, the next day after the three per curiam opinions were rendered, Acting Secretary of the Treasury Ogden Mills wrote a letter to the Speaker of the House explaining the holdings in May v. Heiner and the three cases decided the day before. He pointed out the disastrous effects they would have on the estate tax law and urged that Congress "in order to prevent tax evasion," immediately "correct this situation" brought about by May v. Heiner and the other cases. 74 Cong. Rec. 7198, 7199 (1931). He expressed fear that without such action the Government would suffer "a loss in excess of one-third of the revenue derived from the Federal estate tax, with anticipated refunds in excess of $25,000,000." The Secretary's surprise at the decisions and his apprehensions as to their tax evasion consequences were repeated on the floor of the House and Senate. 74 Cong. Rec. supra. Senator Smoot, Chairman of the Senate Finance Committee, said on the floor of the Senate that this judicial interpretation of the statute "came almost like a bombshell, because nobody ever anticipated such a decision." Both houses of Congress unanimously passed and the President signed the requested resolution that same day. [Commissioner v. Church's Estate, 335 U.S. 632, 639–40 (1949).]

Because Congress was scheduled to adjourn the following day, the resolution was adopted under a suspension of the rules and without having been printed, in reliance upon statements from the floor.

The Joint Resolution of March 3, 1931, enacted in such haste, provided for the inclusion in the gross estate of transferred property if the transferor retained for his life or any period not ending before his death (1) the possession or enjoyment of, or the income from, the property, or (2) the right to designate the persons who should possess or enjoy the property or the income therefrom. In 1932, this provision was amended so as to give it the form now found in § 2036(a).

Although the Supreme Court in Burnet v. Northern Trust Co. had taken the unusual step of advising that there was "no question of the constitutional authority of the Congress to impose prospectively a tax with respect to transfers of trusts of the sort here involved," the constitutionality of the Joint Resolution of March 3, 1931 was challenged by a taxpayer in Helvering v. Bullard, 303 U.S. 297 (1938). The Supreme Court did not retreat, holding that the Joint Resolution was "reasonably calculated" to prevent tax avoidance and consequently did not violate the Fifth Amendment. On the same day that the *Bullard* case was decided, the Court held that the Joint Resolution, and the 1932 amendment thereof, were both intended by Congress to be prospective only. Hassett v. Welch, 303 U.S. 303 (1938).

1. TRANSFERS SUBJECT TO RETAINED LIFE ESTATES

a. Retention of Rights

RAPELJE'S ESTATE v. COMMISSIONER

73 T.C. 82 (1979).

DAWSON, JUDGE.

[In August 1969 the decedent made a gratuitous conveyance of his personal residence in Saratoga Springs, New York, to his two daughters, Mrs. Mulligan and Mrs. Wright. He reported the transfer as a taxable gift. Except for a vacation in Florida from November 1969 to May 1970, he continued to live in the house until his death in November 1973. In July 1970, the decedent suffered a stroke that left him paralyzed on his right side and unable to speak.]

The issue presented here is whether the value of decedent's residence must be included in his gross estate pursuant to section 2036. . . .

This section requires property to be included in the decedent's estate if he retained the actual possession or enjoyment thereof, even though he may have had no enforceable right to do so. Estate of Honigman v. Commissioner, 66 T.C. 1080, 1082 (1976); Estate of Linderme v. Commissioner, 52 T.C. 305, 308 (1969). Possession or enjoyment of gifted property is retained when there is an express or implied understanding to that effect among the parties at the time of transfer. Guynn v. United States, 437 F.2d 1148, 1150 (4th Cir. 1971); Estate of Honigman v. Commissioner, supra at 1082; Estate of Hendry v. Commissioner, 62 T.C. 861, 872 (1974); Estate of Barlow v. Commissioner, 55 T.C. 666, 670 (1971).[20] The burden is on the petitioner to disprove the existence of any implied agreement or understanding, and that burden is particularly onerous when intrafamily arrangements are involved. Skinner's Estate v. United States, 316 F.2d 517, 520 (3rd Cir. 1963); Estate of Hendry v. Commissioner, supra at 872; Estate of Kerdolff v. Commissioner, 57 T.C. 643, 648 (1972).

---

20. We note here that under sec. 2036 it is irrelevant whether the parties *intended* at the time of transfer that the decedent would retain possession and enjoyment *for his life*. The statute requires only that the decedent retain possession or enjoyment "for any period which does not *in fact* end before his death." See Estate of Honigman v. Commissioner, 66 T.C. 1080 (1976). Thus, even if the donees in the present case understood at the time of transfer that decedent would remain in the house only until he found a new home, there would still be inclusion under sec. 2036 because he retained possession or enjoyment of the property up to the time of his death.

In the present case, there was no express agreement allowing decedent to retain possession and enjoyment of the home. Respondent, however, contends that the facts support an inference of an implied understanding between the decedent and his daughters whereby decedent was allowed to live in the house until he was able to locate a new home. Petitioners maintain that although such an understanding may have arisen after decedent suffered his stroke, there was no such agreement in existence at the time of the gift. Based on our review of the record before us, we conclude that petitioners have failed to meet their burden of proving that a tacit agreement did not arise contemporaneously with the transfer.

In determining whether there was an implied understanding between the parties, all facts and circumstances surrounding the transfer and subsequent use of the property must be considered. The continued exclusive possession by the donor and the withholding of possession from the donee are particularly significant factors. Guynn v. United States, supra at 1150; compare Estate of Linderme v. Commissioner, supra at 309, with Estate of Gutchess v. Commissioner, 46 T.C. 554, 557 (1966). In the present case, the donor maintained almost exclusive occupancy of the residence until his death in 1973. The transfer took place in August 1969. Decedent continued to live there alone until September 1969. Sometime in September, Mrs. Mulligan's niece moved in with her husband and they stayed until January 1970. In November 1969, the decedent went to Florida and did not return until May 1970. From May 1970 until September 1971, the decedent lived alone at the residence. In September 1971, Mrs. Mulligan's daughter moved in and stayed for several months. Thereafter, the decedent was the sole occupant of the residence.

A plausible argument could be made that the donees were making indirect use of the property by allowing their relatives to stay there, particularly if they did so over the decedent's objection. There is nothing in the record, however, to support that proposition. Decedent may have been wholly indifferent to their use of the property, or he may even have invited them himself. Even if he had violently opposed the presence of the guests, that would only tend to show an intent by the donees to exercise dominion and control over the property, which is only one factor to be considered in deciding whether decedent retained possession pursuant to an implied agreement.

In spite of the donees' continued residence in their original houses after the gift, petitioners argue that the conduct of the parties subsequent to the transfer negates the existence of any implied agreement. For example, they contend that the primary purpose of decedent's 6–month sojourn in Florida soon after the transfer was to purchase a new house. We disagree. Although decedent did look at one house for sale in Fort Lauderdale, the record does not reveal any extensive house hunting activity. Moreover, the decedent had made identical winter trips to Florida every year for the past 10 years. Thus, we are not convinced that the decedent felt any compelling need to locate a new home on this particular visit.

Petitioners also maintain that Mrs. Mulligan intended to move into the residence in 1971 when her husband was due to retire. In anticipation of this event, the couple visited the home frequently on weekends and vacations and made some repairs. Mrs. Mulligan also notified her employer in Buffalo that she would be leaving in 1971. This planned move was abandoned, of course, when the decedent suffered his stroke. We think that Mrs. Mulligan did intend to move into the residence eventually, but the facts suggest to us that the move was implicitly conditioned on the successful conclusion of the decedent's search for a new home.

There are other facts which support an inference of an implied understanding between the parties. The decedent paid no rent to his daughters for the continued use of the property. Although Mrs. Wright did pay some utility bills relating to the property, the decedent continued to pay the real estate taxes. Neither daughter made any attempt to sell her own house. Nor did they ever attempt to sell or rent the residence prior to the decedent's death. The plain fact of the matter is that with the exception of the change in record title, the gift of the property did not effect any substantial changes in the relationship of the parties to the residence. Thus, we find that there was an implied understanding between the parties arising contemporaneously with the transfer whereby the decedent was allowed to retain possession or enjoyment of the residence for a period which did not in fact end before his death.

Accordingly, we hold that under section 2036 the value of the residence must be included in decedent's gross estate....

NOTES

1. *Transfer of family residence.* In cases where a parent has given the family residence to a child but has continued to live in it as the sole occupant, the courts have regularly inferred that the parent's continued occupancy was intended from the outset and that such retained life use was subject to § 2036(a). The courts have not been so ready to infer an intent to retain possession and enjoyment where one spouse has given the residence to the other and they have continued to occupy it jointly. Gutchess' Estate v. Commissioner, 46 T.C. 554 (1966) (acq.); but see Hendry's Estate v. Commissioner, 62 T.C. 861 (1974) (working farm, with residence, included in husband's gross estate despite gift of it to wife, where husband retained farm income).

Should it make a difference if the donee-child occupies the residence jointly with the donor-parent? Compare Spruill's Estate v. Commissioner, 88 T.C. 1197 (1987) (refusing to apply § 2036 "based solely on the family relationship without a showing of an express or implied agreement that the donor would have the right to continue to live in the residence," where decedent did not have exclusive possession at any time after the gift), with Rev. Rul. 78–409, 1978–2 C.B. 234 (full value of residence included because decedent continued to enjoy unrestricted use and possession); see also Rev. Rul. 70–155, 1970–1 C.B. 189 (distinguishing husband-wife cases from parent-child cases). What if a parent gives a vacation home to a child, retaining the right to use the property for one month each year? See Rev. Rul. 79–109, 1979–1 C.B. 297 (include fractional share of property's value, corresponding to decedent's retained share of annual use value).

In Stewart's Estate v. Commissioner, 617 F.3d 148 (2d Cir. 2010), the decedent owned an apartment building where she lived with her adult son on the lower two floors; the upper floors were leased to an unrelated tenant. Six months before her death, the decedent retitled the property in the names of herself and her son as tenants in common. There was no change in use or possession of the property; the decedent and her son continued to occupy the residential portion, and the decedent paid most of the expenses and collected all the rent from the leased portion until her death. The Tax Court held that the entire property was includible in the decedent's gross estate under § 2036, but on appeal the Second Circuit took a different view. With respect to the residential portion of the property, the court held that "mere co-occupancy between the donor and the donee" could not support a finding of an implied agreement for the decedent's retained possession of the interest that she transferred to her son. In determining the extent of the decedent's retained economic benefit in the transferred interest, the court indicated that the use value of the residential portion must be taken into account in addition to the rental income from the leased portion, net of expenses. A vigorous dissent argued that under § 2036 the analysis should focus on the benefits retained by the decedent rather than the interest formally transferred to the son. The dissent pointed out that the decedent retained possession or enjoyment of the entire transferred interest—"not only the income stream from the rent that was paid, but also the substantial economic benefits of residence"—and that "her relationship to the property changed in not one significant respect from the period preceding transfer to the period after."

2. *Reservation of income for a fixed period.* Suppose the decedent transferred property, retaining the right to receive the income for five years, and then died during that period. Would inclusion depend on whether the decedent's life expectancy at the time of the transfer was more or less than five years? The pre–1954 regulations provided that § 2036(a) was applicable if the decedent reserved the income of property "for such a period as to evidence his intention that it should extend at least for the duration of his life and his death occurs before the expiration of such period." Reg. 105, § 81.18(a)(1). This provision does not appear in § 20.2036–1 of the current regulations. Cf. Fry's Estate v. Commissioner, 9 T.C. 503 (1947) (gift of stock with retained right to first $15,000 of dividends).

3. *Reservation of contingent life estate.* Suppose a settlor creates a trust to pay income to his wife for her life, then income to himself if he survives his wife, with remainder to the couple's issue. If the settlor survives his wife, the property is clearly includible in his gross estate under § 2036(a) because he has reserved the income either for "life" or for a "period which does not in fact end before his death." If he predeceases his wife, however, so that his secondary life estate does not ripen into present enjoyment, is the property includible? Although § 2036(a)'s phrase "for any period not ascertainable

without reference to his death" seems to describe the transfer, it has been argued that by referring explicitly to the taxability of a contingent life estate where the settlor survives the primary life tenant, the House committee report on the 1932 amendment to the 1931 Joint Resolution implies by negative inference that the tax does not apply if he does not survive. Since May v. Heiner itself involved a secondary life estate and a transferor who apparently did not survive the primary life tenant, however, the Court of Appeals for the Second Circuit refused to accept this argument, pointing out that it would produce the "astonishing result" that the 1931 Joint Resolution "failed of its intended purpose" of reversing May v. Heiner. Marks v. Higgins, 213 F.2d 884 (2d Cir. 1954). See also Commissioner v. Arents' Estate, 297 F.2d 894 (2d Cir.), cert. denied, 369 U.S. 848 (1962); Commissioner v. Nathan's Estate, 159 F.2d 546 (7th Cir. 1947), cert. denied, 334 U.S. 843 (1948); Hubbard's Estate v. Commissioner, 250 F.2d 492 (5th Cir. 1957) (contra).

If the settlor dies before his wife, how much of the trust is included in his gross estate? Note that the wife's life estate is already in existence and is in no way affected by his dying. Reg. § 20.2036–1(b)(ii) indicates that the amount drawn back into the gross estate does not include the wife's outstanding life estate, with the result that the includible amount is limited to the present value of the children's right to receive the property at the wife's death.

MAXWELL'S ESTATE v. COMMISSIONER

3 F.3d 591 (2d Cir. 1993).

LASKER, SENIOR DISTRICT JUDGE. . . .

I

On March 14, 1984, Lydia G. Maxwell (the "decedent") conveyed her personal residence, which she had lived in since 1957, to her son Winslow Maxwell, her only heir, and his wife Margaret Jane Maxwell (the "Maxwells"). Following the transfer, the decedent continued to reside in the house until her death on July 30, 1986. At the time of the transfer, she was eighty-two years old and was suffering from cancer.

The transaction was structured as follows:

(1) The residence was sold by the decedent to the Maxwells for $270,000;[21]

(2) Simultaneously with the sale, the decedent forgave $20,000 of the purchase price (which was equal in amount to the annual gift tax exclusion to which she was entitled);

(3) The Maxwells executed a $250,000 mortgage note in favor of decedent;

(4) The Maxwells leased the premises to her for five years at the monthly rental of $1800; and

21. The parties have stipulated that the fair market value of the property on the date of the purported sale was $280,000.

(5) The Maxwells were obligated to pay and did pay certain expenses associated with the property following the transfer, including property taxes, insurance costs, and unspecified "other expenses."

While the decedent paid the Maxwells rent totaling $16,200 in 1984, $22,183 in 1985 and $12,600 in 1986, the Maxwells paid the decedent interest on the mortgage totaling $16,875 in 1984, $21,150 in 1985, and $11,475 in 1986. As can be observed, the rent paid by the decedent to the Maxwells came remarkably close to matching the mortgage interest which they paid to her....

Not only did the rent functionally cancel out the interest payments made by the Maxwells, but the Maxwells were at no time called upon to pay any of the principal on the $250,000 mortgage debt; it was forgiven in its entirety. As petitioner's counsel admitted at oral argument, although the Maxwells had executed the mortgage note, "there was an intention by and large that it not be paid." Pursuant to this intention, in each of the following years preceding her death, the decedent forgave $20,000 of the mortgage principal, and, by a provision of her will executed on March 16, 1984 (that is, just two days after the transfer), she forgave the remaining indebtedness....

She continued to occupy the house by herself until her death. At no time during her occupancy did the Maxwells attempt to sell the house to anyone else, but, on September 22, 1986, shortly after the decedent's death, they did sell the house for $550,000....

On the decedent's estate tax return, the Estate reported only the $210,000 remaining on the mortgage debt (following the decedent's forgiveness of $20,000 in the two preceding years). The Commissioner found that the 1984 transaction constituted a transfer with retained life estate—rejecting the petitioners' arguments that the decedent did not retain "possession or enjoyment" of the property, and that the transaction was exempt from section 2036(a) because it was a bona fide sale for full and adequate consideration—, and assessed a deficiency against the Estate to adjust for the difference between the fair market value of the property at the time of decedent's death ($550,000) and the reported $210,000.

The Estate appealed to the tax court, which, after a trial on stipulated facts, affirmed the Commissioner's ruling, holding:

> On this record, bearing in mind petitioner's burden of proof, we hold that, notwithstanding its form, the substance of the transaction calls for the conclusion that decedent made a transfer to her son and daughter-in-law with the understanding, at least implied, that she would continue to reside in her home until her death, that the transfer was not a bona fide sale for an adequate and full consideration in money or money's worth, and that the lease represented nothing more than an attempt to add color to the characterization of the transaction as a bona fide sale.

There are two questions before us: Did the decedent retain possession or enjoyment of the property following the transfer. And if she did, was the transfer a bona fide sale for an adequate and full consideration in money or money's worth.

II

[Here the court noted that the Tax Court had applied § 2036(a) in numerous cases where an elderly person transferred a residence to a family member but continued to live there until death. Quoting *Rapelje*, supra page 272, the court noted that the statute had been held applicable based on the decedent's actual retained possession and enjoyment pursuant to an "express or implied understanding" even in the absence of an "enforceable right."]

As indicated above, the tax court found as a fact that the decedent had transferred her home to the Maxwells "with the understanding, at least implied, that she would continue to reside in her home until her death." This finding was based upon the decedent's advanced age, her medical condition, and the overall result of the sale and lease. The lease was, in the tax court's words, "merely window dressing"—it had no substance.

[The court upheld this finding as not clearly erroneous.] The decedent did, in fact, live at her residence until she died, and she had sole possession of the residence during the period between the day she sold her home to the Maxwells and the day she died. There is no evidence that the Maxwells ever intended to occupy the house themselves, or to sell or lease it to anyone else during the decedent's lifetime. Moreover, the Maxwells' failure to demand payment by the estate, as they were entitled to do under the lease, of the rent due for the months following decedent's death and preceding their sale of the property, also supports the tax court's finding.

The petitioner argues ... that the decedent's status was no more than that of a tenant, and that such a status was insufficient to cause the property to be includible in her estate or to qualify as "possession or enjoyment" under section 2036(a). However, the petitioner misapprehends the tax court's ruling. That court held, on the basis of all the facts described above, that the decedent's use of the house following the transfer depended not on the lease but rather on an implied agreement between the parties that the decedent could and would continue to reside in the house until her death, as she actually did. It found that the lease "represented nothing more than an attempt to add color to the characterization of the transaction as a bona fide sale." The tax court did not rely on the tenancy alone to establish "possession or enjoyment."

Just as petitioner argues that the decedent's tenancy alone does not justify inclusion of the residence in her estate, so it argues that the decedent's payment of rent sanctifies the transaction and renders it legitimate. Both arguments ignore the realities of the rent being offset by mortgage interest, the forgiveness of the entire mortgage debt either by gift or testamentary disposition, and the fact that the decedent was eighty-two at the time of the transfer and actually continued to live in the residence until her death which, at the time of the transfer, she had reason to believe would occur soon in view of her poor health.

The Estate relies primarily on Barlow v. Commissioner, 55 T.C. 666 (1971). In that case, the father transferred a farm to his children and simultaneously leased the right to continue to farm the property. The tax court held that the father did not retain "possession or enjoyment," stating that "one of the most valuable incidents of income-producing real estate is the rent which it yields. He who receives the rent in fact enjoys the property." Barlow, 55 T.C. at 671 (quoting McNichol's [Estate] v. Commissioner, 265 F.2d 667, 671 (3d Cir.), cert. denied, 361 U.S. 829 (1959)). However, *Barlow* is clearly distinguishable on its facts: In that case, there was evidence that the rent paid was fair and customary and, equally importantly, the rent paid was not offset by the decedent's receipt of interest from the family lessor.

Nor is there any merit to petitioner's contention that the "decedent's status as a tenant" exempts her from § 2036(a) "as a matter of law." *Barlow* itself recognized that where a transferor "by agreement" "reserves the right of occupancy as an incident to the transfer," § 2036(a) applies. Barlow, 55 T.C. at 670. The court there simply reached a different conclusion on its facts: "[The] substance-versus-form argument, *while theoretically plausible*, depends upon the facts, and we do not think the record as a whole contains the facts required to give it life...." Id. at 670 (emphasis added).

For the reasons stated above, we conclude that the decedent did retain possession or enjoyment of the property for life and turn to the question of whether the transfer constituted "a bona fide sale for adequate and full consideration in money or money's worth."

III

Section 2036(a) provides that even if possession or enjoyment of transferred property is retained by the decedent until her death, if the transfer was a bona fide sale for adequate and full consideration in money or money's worth, the property is not includible in the estate. Petitioner contends that the Maxwells paid an "adequate and full consideration" for the decedent's residence, $270,000 total, consisting of the $250,000 mortgage note given by the Maxwells to the decedent, and the $20,000 the decedent forgave simultaneously with the conveyance.[22]

The tax court held that neither the Maxwells' mortgage note nor the decedent's $20,000 forgiveness constituted consideration within the meaning of the statute.

22. As noted above, the parties have stipulated that the fair market value of the property on the date of the purported sale was $280,000. The Estate contends that $270,000 was full and adequate consideration for the sale, with a broker, for a house appraised at $280,000. We assume this fact to be true for purposes of determining whether the transaction was one for "an adequate and full consideration in money or money's worth."

$250,000 Mortgage Note

As to the $250,000 mortgage note, the tax court held that:

> Regardless of whether the $250,000 mortgage note might otherwise qualify as "adequate and full consideration in money or money's worth" for a $270,000 or $280,000 house, the mortgage note here had no value at all if there was no intention that it would ever be paid. The conduct of decedent and the Maxwells strongly suggest[s] that neither party intended the Maxwells to pay any part of the principal of either the original note or any successor note.

There is no question that the mortgage note here is a fully secured, legally enforceable obligation on its face. The question is whether it is actually what it purports to be—a bona fide instrument of indebtedness—or whether it is a facade. . . .

We agree with the tax court that where, as here, there is an implied agreement between the parties that the grantee would never be called upon to make any payment to the grantor, as, in fact, actually occurred, the note given by the grantee had "no value at all." We emphatically disagree with the petitioner's view of the law as it applies to the facts of this case. As the Supreme Court has remarked,

> the family relationship often makes it possible for one to shift tax incidence by surface changes of ownership without disturbing in the least his dominion and control over the subject of the gift or the purposes for which the income from the property is used.

Commissioner v. Culbertson, 337 U.S. 733, 746 (1949). There can be no doubt that intent is a relevant inquiry in determining whether a transaction is "bona fide." As another panel of this Court held recently, construing a parallel provision of the Internal Revenue Code, in a case involving an intrafamily transfer:

> when the bona fides of promissory notes is at issue, the taxpayer must demonstrate affirmatively that "there existed at the time of the transaction a real expectation of repayment and an intent to enforce the collection of the indebtedness." Estate of Van Anda v. Commissioner, 12 T.C. 1158, 1162 (1949), affd. per curiam, 192 F.2d 391 (2d Cir. 1951). See also Estate of Labombarde v. Commissioner, 58 T.C. 745, 754–55 (1972), affd., 73–2 U.S. Tax Cas. (CCH) ¶ 12953 (1st Cir. 1973).

Flandreau v. Commissioner, 994 F.2d 91, 93 (2d Cir. 1993) (case involving I.R.C. § 2053(c)(1)). In language strikingly apposite to the situation here, the court stated: "it is appropriate to look beyond the form of the transactions and to determine, as the tax court did here, that the gifts and loans back to decedent were 'component parts of single transactions.' " Id. (citation omitted).

The tax court concluded that the evidence "viewed as a whole" left the "unmistakable impression" that "regardless of how long decedent lived following the transfer of her house, the entire principal balance of the mortgage note would be forgiven, and the Maxwells would not be required to pay any of such principal." Id.

The petitioner's reliance on Haygood v. Commissioner, 42 T.C. 936 (1964), not followed by Rev. Rul. 77–299, 1977–2 C.B. 343 (1977), Kelley v. Commissioner, 63 T.C. 321 (1974), not followed by Rev. Rul. 77–299, 1977–2 C.B. 343 (1977), and Wilson v. Commissioner, 64 T.C.M. (CCH) 583 (1992), is misplaced. Those cases held only that intent to forgive notes in the future does not per se disqualify such notes from constituting valid consideration....

By contrast, in the case at hand, the tax court found that, at the time the note was executed, there was "an understanding" between the Maxwells and the decedent that the note would be forgiven.

> In our judgment, the conduct of decedent and the Maxwells with respect to the principal balance of the note, when viewed in connection with the initial "forgiveness" of $20,000 of the purported purchase price, strongly suggests the existence of an understanding between decedent and the Maxwells that decedent would forgive $20,000 each year thereafter until her death, when the balance would be forgiven by decedent's will....

$20,000 Initial Forgiveness

We also agree with the tax court that, as to the $20,000 which was forgiven simultaneously with the conveyance, "In the absence of any clear and direct evidence that there existed an obligation or indebtedness capable of being forgiven ..." the $20,000 item had "no economic substance."

To conclude, we hold that the conveyance was not a bona fide sale for an adequate and full consideration in money or money's worth.

Section 2043

The petitioner argues finally that the tax court should be reversed because, under 26 U.S.C. § 2043, if there was any consideration in money or money's worth paid to the decedent, even if the payment was inadequate, the Estate is at least entitled to an exclusion pro tanto. The argument has no merit in the circumstances of this case. The tax court held, and we do also, that the transfer was without *any* consideration. Section 2043 applies only where the court finds that some consideration was given.

The decision of the tax court is affirmed.

[Dissenting opinion omitted.]

NOTES

1. *Retained possession or enjoyment under a lease.* As the *Maxwell* case illustrates, a taxpayer who transfers property to a family member and immediately leases it back is likely to be viewed as having retained possession

and enjoyment for purposes of § 2036(a). This result is almost certain if the lease provides for below-market rental payments. See, e.g., duPont's Estate v. Commissioner, 63 T.C. 746 (1975) (decedent transferred residential property to a controlled corporation, subject to his right to lease back the property at a below-market rent, then transferred his stock in the corporation to an irrevocable family trust). On the other hand, in Barlow's Estate v. Commissioner, 55 T.C. 666 (1971), distinguished in the *Maxwell* opinion, the Tax Court held that § 2036(a) did not apply where a parent gave a farm to his children who then leased the farm back to the parent at a fair market rent; the government argued unsuccessfully that the parent had retained possession and that the rental payments constituted additional gifts to his children. Might the *Maxwell* court have reached a different result if the son and his wife, upon receiving legal title in 1984, had offered the residence for rental on the open market for a few months before leasing it back to Mrs. Maxwell? What if Mrs. Maxwell had arranged a sale-and-leaseback transaction with an unrelated third party?

2. *Consideration in money or money's worth.* Note that Mrs. Maxwell's 1984 transfer of her house was structured as a sale in which Mrs. Maxwell received a legally binding promissory note from her son and his wife. In the *Haygood*, *Kelley*, and *Wilson* cases, distinguished in the *Maxwell* opinion, the Tax Court found that promissory notes given in exchange for transferred property constituted "consideration in money or money's worth" for gift tax purposes, even though the notes were subsequently forgiven. In Deal v. Commissioner, 29 T.C. 730, 746 (1958), however, the Tax Court found that "the notes executed by the [recipients] were not intended to be enforced and were not intended as consideration for the transfer by the petitioner, and that, in substance, the transfer of the property was by gift." In an omitted portion of the *Maxwell* opinion, the court rejected the notion that "the intent to forgive notes has no effect on the question of whether the notes constitute valid consideration" as "inconsistent with controlling tax principles and tax court decisions," citing *Deal*. Might Mrs. Maxwell have achieved a more favorable result if, instead of annually forgiving the $20,000 principal installments on the promissory note, she had collected the scheduled payments from her son and his wife and then made annual cash gifts back to them in similar amounts?

3. *Distributions of income to settlor in trustee's discretion.* Boardman's Estate v. Commissioner, 20 T.C. 871 (1953), involved a transfer of property in trust under which the trustees were to make such distributions to the settlor from income and corpus as they "deem necessary for her comfort, support and/or happiness." The court found that the trust instrument "offered no basis upon which the trustees could have withheld any of the income of the trust which the decedent might have desired during her life" and held that in these circumstances she retained the right to the income for life. The principal purpose of the trust was to support the decedent, the court said that the trustees "could not resist her demand for the income," and she did in fact receive the income therefrom during her life. Compare the Tax Court's statement with its later refusal in a case involving gift tax liability to give credit to the trustees' testimony that they were prepared at all times to do the settlors' bidding. Outwin v. Commissioner, supra page 103.

If the decedent created a trust under which the trustee had unfettered discretion to distribute income and corpus to the decedent, can the trust property be included in the gross estate if under state law the decedent's creditors could have levied on it? See Uhl's Estate v. Commissioner, 241 F.2d 867 (7th Cir. 1957). Note that a transfer that can be reached by the transferor's creditors is deemed to be revocable and not subject to gift tax. See Outwin v. Commissioner, supra page 103; see also Paxton's Estate v. Commissioner, 86 T.C. 785 (1986) (understanding that the trustees would exercise discretion in decedent's favor at his demand inferred from facts that (1) distributions were regularly made to decedent during life, and (2) the trust was funded with almost all of decedent's property, including his house and household furnishings; moreover, decedent had the power to incur debts enforceable against the trust). In contrast, if the transferred property cannot be reached by the decedent's creditors and the decedent retained no other interests or powers, the property may escape inclusion under § 2036. See Priv. Ltr. Rul. 200944002 (July 15, 2009), discussed supra at page 108, Note 5.

4. *"Family estate" trusts.* In Rev. Rul. 75–259, 1975–2 C.B. 361, the decedent created a "family estate trust" to which he assigned his "lifetime services" as well as certain real and personal property in exchange for 100 units of "beneficial interest" in the trust. The trustees, whose powers were "in effect, without limitation," included the settlor, his spouse, and a third party. Each week the settlor would deposit his pay check in the bank account of the trust, which the "trustees" used to pay the living expenses of the settlor's family. The Service held that all the assets of the trust transferred to it by the settlor were includible in his estate under §§ 2036 and 2038. The value of the 100 units of "beneficial interest" was includible under § 2033 to the extent not includible under §§ 2036 and 2038. In Notice 97–24, 1997–1 C.B. 409, the Service offered several examples of "abusive trust arrangements" that purport to offer "tax benefits with no meaningful change in the taxpayer's control over or benefit from the taxpayer's income or assets." The Service warned that such arrangements do not produce the promised tax benefits and may lead to civil or criminal penalties.

5. *Family limited partnerships.* A family limited partnership may be open to challenge under § 2036(a) if the decedent retained unfettered lifetime access to partnership assets. See infra page 318, Note 2.

b. Support Trusts

GOKEY'S ESTATE v. COMMISSIONER

72 T.C. 721 (1979).

WILES, JUDGE.

[In 1961, the decedent established an irrevocable trust agreement, naming his wife as trustee and creating separate trusts for their three children, Bridget, Gretchen, and Patrick. The trust agreement provided:

> *Section 2:* Until each beneficiary becomes twenty-one (21) years of age, the Trustee shall use such part or all of the net income of his or her trust for the support, care, welfare, and education of the

beneficiary thereof, payments from such net income to be made to such beneficiary or in such other manner as the Trustee deems to be in the best interest of the beneficiary, and any unused income shall be accumulated and added to the principal of such beneficiary's trust. After each beneficiary becomes twenty-one (21) years of age, the Trustee shall pay to him or her, in convenient installments, the entire net income of his or her trust. In the Trustee's discretion, said income payments may be supplemented at any time with payments of principal from a beneficiary's share whenever the Trustee deems any such payments necessary for the support, care, welfare, or education of the beneficiary thereof.

At decedent's death in 1969, Gretchen was 15 years old and Patrick was 13; the value of their trusts totaled approximately $800,000. Bridget, who was then 18 years old, had reached the Illinois statutory age of majority, and no issue was raised concerning her trust.]

The first issue is whether decedent retained the possession or enjoyment of, or the right to the income from, property transferred by him to irrevocable trusts for the benefit of Gretchen and Patrick. If so, the value of the property in those trusts is properly includable in decedent's gross estate under section 2036. The resolution of this issue depends upon whether, within the meaning of section 20.2036–1(b)(2), Estate Tax Regs., the income or property of the trusts was to be applied toward the discharge of the decedent's legal obligation to support Gretchen and Patrick during his lifetime.

Respondent contends that under Illinois law, decedent was under a legal duty to support his minor children, Gretchen and Patrick; that the terms of the children's trusts clearly require the trustees to use the trusts' income and property for their support; and that, therefore, the value of the trust property is includable in decedent's gross estate.

Petitioners do not dispute decedent's obligation to support Gretchen and Patrick under Illinois law; however, they contend that the use of the property or income therefrom for the children's support was within the unrestricted discretion of the trustees; that even if trusts did not give the trustees any discretion in this matter, the decedent nevertheless intended to grant them this discretion; that the use of the term "welfare" in the trusts creates an unascertainable standard which, even if ascertainable, is much broader than the standard for support; and that, therefore, the value of the trust property is not includable in decedent's gross estate. We agree with respondent on this issue.

Respondent relies upon section 20.2036–1(b)(2), Estate Tax Regs., which states that the use, possession, right to the income, or other enjoyment of the transferred property is considered as having been retained by or reserved to the decedent within the meaning of section 2036(a)(1) to the extent that the use, possession, right to the income, or other enjoyment *is to be applied* toward the discharge of a legal obligation of decedent which includes an obligation to support a dependent. "Is to be applied" is not to be read as "may be applied," which exists where an independent trustee is vested with discretion over distributions. Estate of Mitchell v. Commissioner, 55 T.C. 576, 580 (1970). This creates a factual question as to whether the income from the trust property must be restricted or confined to fulfilling the settlor's obligation to support his dependents. Estate of Lee v. Commissioner, 33 T.C. 1064, 1067 (1960).

We believe the language of the children's trusts found in section 2 of the 1961 trust agreement which relates "shall use such part or all of the net income ... for the support, care, welfare, and education of the beneficiary" clearly manifests decedent's intent to require the trustees to apply the income for the stated purpose. In our view, it is impossible to construe the instrument as one which gives the trustees discretion as to whether or not income shall be used for "support, care, welfare, and education." That standard completely controls the application of the trusts' funds. If those needs exceed the trusts' income, principal may be utilized. If those needs do not absorb all the trusts' income, the remaining income is accumulated and added to principal. Moreover, the section 2 phrase "payments from such net income to be made to such beneficiary or in such other manner as the Trustee deems to be in the best interest of the beneficiary" does not alter our interpretation. Clearly, this phrase only grants the trustee discretion in the method of payment adopted. Since we find decedent's intent clearly expressed in the trust instrument, we need not look beyond the four corners of the instrument to determine intent.

Petitioners next argue that the use of the word "welfare" within the phrase "the Trustee shall use such part or all of the net income of his or her trust for the support, care, welfare, and education of the beneficiary thereof" in section 2 of the 1961 trust instrument, gives the trustee authority to make nonsupport expenditures which, in turn, violates the "is to be applied" language of section 20.2036–1(b)(2), Estate Tax Regs. They support this theory by arguing that the standard "support, care, welfare, and education" is not ascertainable under, among others, sections 2036(a)(2) and 2041; and even if ascertainable, "welfare" is broader than "support" under Illinois law.

In determining whether "support, care, welfare, and education" is subject to an ascertainable external standard, we must rely upon Illinois law. Estate of Budd v. Commissioner, 49 T.C. 468, 474 (1968); Estate of Pardee v. Commissioner, 49 T.C. 140, 144 (1967). In Estate of Wood v. Commissioner, 39 T.C. 919, 923–924 (1963), we held that the phrase "support, maintenance, welfare, and comfort" was subject to an ascertainable standard:

> We think that these four somewhat overlapping nouns were intended in the aggregate to describe the life beneficiary's standard of living in all its aspects.... Admittedly, the words "support," and "maintenance" are regarded as referable to a standard of living, and the addition of the naked words "comfort" and "welfare" in the context

of the instrument before us merely rounds out the standard of living concept.

In Estate of Bell v. Commissioner, 66 T.C. 729, 734–735 (1976), we found that the phrase "well being and maintenance in health and comfort" was subject to an ascertainable standard in Illinois:

> Although providing a modicum of discretion to the trustees, this language created a standard enforceable in a court of equity. Under Illinois law, a court of equity would look to the beneficiary's accustomed living standard in compelling compliance by the trustees, either to require income distributions for the stated purposes or to restrain distributions for unauthorized purposes. In Re Whitman, 22 Ill. 511 (1859) ("support, education, and maintenance"); French v. Northern Trust Co., 197 Ill. 30, 64 N.E. 105, 106 (1902) ("properly maintained and comfortably provided for out of such property"); Burke v. Burke, 259 Ill. 262, 102 N.E. 293, 294 (1913) ("the comforts and necessities of life").

We similarly believe that under Illinois law, a court of equity would look to Gretchen's and Patrick's accustomed living standard in compelling compliance by the trustee to require income distributions for the stated purposes. As a result, we find that the terms "support, care, welfare, and education," when viewed in the aggregate, were intended to describe the children's standard of living and are, therefore, subject to an external ascertainable standard. See Estate of Wood v. Commissioner, supra; Leopold v. United States, 510 F.2d 617, 620 (9th Cir. 1975). Having found that the phrase in the aggregate created an ascertainable standard requiring the trustee to make expenditures for the children's accustomed living standard, we must reject petitioners' argument that the term "welfare" in the phrase allows the trustee to make nonsupport payments because "welfare" is broader than "support" under Illinois law.

Thus, it only remains for us to decide whether, under Illinois law, support is synonymous, for this purpose, with accustomed standard of living. In Rock Island Bank & Trust Co. v. Rhoads, 353 Ill. 131, 187 N.E. 139, 144 (1933), the Illinois Supreme Court stated: "The word 'comfort' must be construed as relating to her *support* and ease.... Had this clause provided only for her comfort, it cannot be doubted that such would be a limitation ... to maintain her in the *station in life to which she was accustomed*." (Emphasis added.) We view this language as indicative that, under Illinois law, support is equivalent to accustomed standard of living. We are satisfied that the instrument before us provides an ascertainable standard under Illinois law. Accordingly, we find that decedent's gross estate includes the value of Gretchen's and Patrick's trusts since we find them to be support trusts within the meaning of section 2036(a)(1) and section 20.2036–1(b)(2), Estate Tax Regs....

NOTES

1. *Value of remainder subject to power of invasion.* Another issue in the *Gokey* case involved a separate trust created by the decedent in 1961 to pay income to his wife for life, with remainder at her death in equal shares to the children's trusts. A corporate trustee had discretion to invade the principal for the wife's "care, comfort, support or welfare." In an omitted portion of the opinion, the Tax Court held that the remainder shares payable to Gretchen's and Patrick's trusts at their mother's death constituted additional assets of their trusts which were includible in the decedent's gross estate. In an unpublished opinion, the Seventh Circuit affirmed the Tax Court's holding that the remainder interests were includible in the decedent's gross estate, but remanded for a redetermination of value in light of the trustee's power of invasion. 735 F.2d 1367 (7th Cir. 1984). On remand, the Tax Court observed that "where an ascertainable standard exists, the petitioner must establish with reasonable certainty the needs of the owner of the life estate for the rest of her life and the extent to which corpus might be invaded under the standard." In view of the trustee's broad power to invade principal for the benefit of the life income beneficiary, the Tax Court ultimately valued the remainder interests at less than 25 percent of their value under the Treasury tables. 49 T.C.M. (CCH) 367 (1984).

2. *Support of dependents required.* As the court notes in the principal case, citing Mitchell's Estate v. Commissioner, 55 T.C. 576 (1970), Reg. § 20.2036–1(b)(2) contemplates inclusion of property if the income "is to be applied" to defray decedent's legal obligations; it is not enough that the income "may be" so applied. If, however, the settlor is the trustee, § 2036(a)(1) applies to income that could be used to relieve the settlor of a support obligation, whether or not the income was actually or likely to be so used. To the effect that the application of income by a third-party trustee must be mandatory and not permissive or discretionary, see, in addition to the cases cited in *Gokey*, Commissioner v. Dwight's Estate, 205 F.2d 298 (2d Cir.), cert. denied, 346 U.S. 871 (1953). In these cases, the courts recognize that § 2036(a)(1) will reach only part of the transferred property if it generates more income than will be required to defray the decedent's legal obligation. See, e.g., Pardee's Estate v. Commissioner, 49 T.C. 140 (1967) (analysis of the amount required under Michigan law to support a minor child); Sullivan's Estate v. Commissioner, 66 T.C.M. (CCH) 1329 (1993) (settlor-trustee's right to invade corpus for wife's support).

Section 14 of the Uniform Transfers to Minors Act provides:

> (a) A custodian may deliver or pay to the minor or expend for the minor's benefit so much of the custodial property as the custodian considers advisable for the use and benefit of the minor, without court order and without regard to (i) the duty or ability of the custodian personally or of any other person to support the minor, or (ii) any other income or property of the minor which may be applicable or available for that purpose.
>
> (b) On petition of an interested person or the minor if the minor has attained the age of 14 years, the court may order the custodian to deliver

or pay to the minor or expend for the minor's benefit so much of the custodial property as the court considers advisable for the use and benefit of the minor.

(c) A delivery, payment, or expenditure under this section is in addition to, not in substitution for, and does not affect any obligation of a person to support the minor.

If a donor dies while acting as custodian for his or her minor child, courts have held that the custodial property is includible in the donor-custodian's gross estate under § 2036(a). Eichstedt v. United States, 354 F.Supp. 484 (N.D. Cal. 1972) (inclusion under §§ 2036(a)(1) and 2038(a)(1)); Prudowsky's Estate v. Commissioner, 55 T.C. 890 (1971), affd., 465 F.2d 62 (7th Cir. 1972) (same; decedent's intent not to use power immaterial). These cases were decided under an earlier version of the uniform statute which did not include the language of § 14(c). Does the revised statute produce a different result under § 2036(a)?

3. *Contradicting the terms of the trust instrument.* Is it open to the executor to bring in evidence that the decedent never intended to have the trust used to discharge a support obligation? In *Dwight's Estate*, supra Note 2, the court held that the parol evidence rule precluded the admission of such evidence. Note also that the cases cited in Note 2 state that the decedent's intent is immaterial. See, e.g., Pardee's Estate v. Commissioner, 49 T.C. 140 (1967) (§ 2036(a) "does not require that the transferor pull the 'string' or even intend to pull the string on the transferred property; it only requires that the string exist"). What if the shoe is on the other foot: The instrument contains no reservation of the income, but the government offers evidence that the income was in fact received by the decedent and asks the court to infer from this fact that there was a secret arrangement between him and the trustee amounting to a reservation of the income? In Skinner's Estate v. United States, 316 F.2d 517 (3d Cir. 1963), the court upheld a finding that such an understanding existed, but noted that it was "breaking new and perhaps dangerous ground" by placing "a heavy burden upon the estate of a settlor of a discretionary trust to avoid the inference of secret prearrangements with the trustee when the settlor has in fact received all income during his life." Accord, McNichol's Estate v. Commissioner, 265 F.2d 667 (3d Cir.), cert. denied, 361 U.S. 829 (1959); Green's Estate v. Commissioner, 64 T.C. 1049 (1975); Rapelje's Estate v. Commissioner, supra page 272.

4. *Reimbursement of settlor's income tax liability.* The settlor of an irrevocable trust may retain sufficient powers to be treated as the owner of the trust's income under the "grantor trust" rules of §§ 671 to 677 (see supra page 77, Note 6), even though the creation of the trust constitutes a completed gift and removes the trust property from the settlor's gross estate. If the trust instrument requires or permits the trustee to reimburse the settlor for the income tax imposed on the trust's income, will the trust property be drawn into the settlor's gross estate under § 2036? In Rev. Rul. 2004–64, 2004–2 C.B. 7, the Service ruled that (1) a provision requiring that the settlor be reimbursed by the trust for the income tax attributable to the trust's income will cause the trust property to be included in the settlor's gross estate under § 2036(a)(1), but (2) the existence of a discretionary reimbursement

power in the trustee, whether or not exercised, will not by itself give rise to estate tax inclusion. (The Service warned, however, that the latter conclusion might be altered by additional facts, such as an understanding between the settlor and the trustee regarding the exercise of the reimbursement power, a power retained by the settlor to substitute himself as trustee, or a provision of state law subjecting the trust property to claims of the settlor's creditors.) In neither case will the payment of income tax by the settlor or the reimbursement by the trust give rise to a taxable gift on the part of the settlor or the trust beneficiaries. See Gans, Heilborn & Blattmachr, Some Good News About Grantor Trusts: Rev. Rul. 2004–64, 31 Est. Planning 467 (2004).

5. *Income tax aspects of support trusts.* Section 677(b) provides that the income of a "support" trust is not to be taxed as income of the grantor "merely because such income in the discretion of another person, the trustee, or the grantor acting as trustee or co-trustee, may be applied or distributed for the support or maintenance of a beneficiary ... whom the grantor is legally obligated to support or maintain, except to the extent that such income is so applied or distributed." This provision was enacted after it was held in Helvering v. Stuart, 317 U.S. 154 (1942), that if a trustee had the power to use the income of a trust for the support of the grantor's minor children, the income came within the language of what is now § 677(a)(1) and (a)(2). May a support trust be included in the gross estate even though the income was not taxed to the decedent during his lifetime, or be excluded from the estate even though the income was taxed to the decedent? Should different tests be applied? On the income tax consequences of support trusts, see 3 Bittker & Lokken, Federal Taxation of Income, Estates and Gifts ¶ 80.4.4 (3d ed. 2001).

6. *Gift tax consequences of support trusts.* When is a gift tax due on a trust of the type that Mr. Gokey created for his children in the principal case? On the trust's creation? On the date that each child reaches majority? If and when distributions are made?

7. *Divorce settlements.* In Keller's Estate v. Commissioner, 44 T.C. 851 (1965), the husband, pursuant to a divorce decree, created a trust, directing that the income be paid to himself for his life, then to his divorced wife for her life, with corpus to be distributed at the survivor's death to their adult children. On the husband's death survived by his divorced wife, the Tax Court held that § 2036(a) brought the value of the children's remainder into their father's gross estate; the former wife's life estate, which was founded on the divorce decree, was excluded because that interest was transferred for full and adequate consideration in the form of her relinquishment of her right to support and maintenance. In 1984, the provisions of § 2516(1) of the gift tax, pertaining to spousal property settlements incident to divorce, were incorporated into the estate tax by § 2043(b)(2). Under pre–1984 law, courts were required to determine the value of rights relinquished by the decedent's spouse in order to determine the extent to which an includible transfer of property by the decedent was offset by consideration under § 2043(a). See, e.g., Commissioner v. Nelson's Estate, 396 F.2d 519 (2d Cir. 1968); United States v. Past, 347 F.2d 7 (9th Cir. 1965); Glen's Estate v. Commissioner, 45 T.C. 323 (1966). Under § 2043(b)(2), a transfer of property to either spouse in settlement of his or her marital rights that meets the requirements of

§ 2516(1) is deemed to be made for adequate and full consideration. See infra page 436, Note 1.

c. Estate Freezing Techniques Involving Trusts

Over the years, taxpayers seeking to limit or avoid exposure to estate taxation have resorted, with mixed success, to various "estate freezing" techniques. In general, these techniques call for a lifetime transfer of property that is expected to appreciate substantially, subject to a retained interest representing limited income or other rights in the same underlying property. A successful estate freeze (from the taxpayer's point of view) not only removes the appreciated value of the underlying property from the transferor's gross estate at the cost of a modest gift tax, but also leaves the transferor with a retained interest that will have little or no value at death. One technique that became especially popular during the 1980s is the grantor retained income trust (GRIT), introduced supra at page 78. In the initial transfer, the donor retains an income interest for a fixed term of years and makes a completed gift of a remainder in the underlying property. The amount of the taxable gift is determined by subtracting the value of the retained income interest from the value of the underlying property; the higher the value of the retained interest, the lower the taxable gift. If the donor survives the fixed term and continues to hold the income interest until it expires, no further gift or estate tax is imposed on the transfer.

The objectionable feature of GRITs and other estate freezing techniques (from the government's point of view) is that they often shift substantial value from the donor to the donee free of gift and estate tax. For example, assume that *A* creates a trust funded with low-dividend, high-growth stock in a closely held corporation, to pay the income to *A* for a fixed ten-year term with remainder at the end of the term to her child *B*. Prior to the enactment of § 2702, *A*'s retained income interest would be valued on the assumption that she would receive annual income distributions at the current § 7520 rate for ten years, and the remainder given to *B* would be discounted at the same rate. If, as expected, the trust property actually produced little or no current income but grew substantially in capital value, the income interest would disappear without a trace at the end of the ten-year term, and *A* would have transferred the appreciated stock to *B* at a greatly reduced gift tax cost. *A*'s GRIT illustrates a typical use of a trust as an estate freezing vehicle; for analogous techniques involving outright transfers of interests in corporations and partnerships, see infra page 591. The policy concerns raised by estate freezing techniques have been summarized as follows:

> First, because frozen interests are inherently difficult to value, they can be used as a means of undervaluing gifts. Second, such interests entail the creation of rights that, if not exercised in an arms' length manner, may subsequently be used to transfer wealth free of transfer tax. Third, "frozen" interests may be used to retain substantial ownership of the entire property while nominally transferring an

interest in the property to another person. [Staff of Joint Comm. on Taxation, 101st Cong., 2d Sess., Present Law and Proposals Relating to Federal Transfer Tax Consequences of Estate Freezes 17–19 (Comm. Print 1990).]

One possible response to estate freezing techniques would be to impose a gift or estate tax on the underlying property at its appreciated value when the donor's retained strings over the property are finally cut. Congress experimented briefly with such a "back-end" approach in the late 1980s with former § 2036(c), which applied to a broad range of estate freezing transactions including GRITs. Under § 2036(c), the transferred interest (including any post-gift appreciation, but excluding any amount previously taxed in the initial transfer) was drawn back into the donor's transfer tax base upon the ultimate disposition or termination of the retained interest. Widespread complaints about the statute's "complexity, breadth, and vagueness"[23] led in 1990 to the retroactive repeal of § 2036(c) and its replacement with Chapter 14 (§§ 2701 to 2704).

At the heart of Chapter 14 are special gift tax valuation rules for intrafamily transfers of interests in corporations or partnerships (§ 2701) and transfers in trust (§ 2702). In contrast to the back-end approach of former § 2036(c), §§ 2701 and 2702 adopt a "front-end" approach focusing on valuation of the retained and transferred interests in the initial transfer. These provisions do not attempt to draw post-gift appreciation back into the donor's transfer tax base, but merely impose unfavorable valuation assumptions which tend to increase the amount of the taxable gift in the initial transfer. Estate planners have several reasons to prefer a front-end approach, especially as applied to transfers in trust: § 2702 is widely perceived as simpler, clearer, less intrusive, and less burdensome than former § 2036(c). To understand the impact of § 2702, however, it is necessary to consider the estate tax treatment of trusts with retained interests.

In general, § 2702 applies where a donor carves beneficial ownership of property into successive interests (i.e., a term interest and a remainder) and transfers one interest to a family member while retaining another interest in the same underlying property. Under the special rules, nonqualified retained interests are normally valued at zero, with the result that the full value of the underlying property may be subject to gift tax in the initial transfer. See supra page 78. If the donor retains an income interest for life or a related period, the underlying property may also be subject to estate tax at death. For example, assume that *A* transfers property worth $100,000 in trust to pay income to herself for ten years with remainder to her child *B*. Under § 2702, *A* has made a taxable gift of $100,000. If *A* dies six years later, still holding her income interest, when the value of the trust property has risen to $200,000, the full value of the property at the time of *A*'s death will be includible in her gross estate under § 2036. See Cooper's Estate v. Commissioner, 74 T.C. 1373 (1980).

---

23. 136 Cong. Rec. S15629, S15680 (Oct. 18, 1990).

However, the gift tax attributable to the initial gift will reduce the tentative estate tax under § 2001(b)(2), so that only the $100,000 of subsequent appreciation is actually subject to estate tax. Disregarding any intervening changes in *A*'s marginal rate and unified credit, the total amount of gift and estate taxes will be precisely equal to the tax that would have been imposed on a single taxable transfer of $200,000. No further adjustment is necessary to prevent double taxation.

The situation is somewhat more complicated if *A* retained a qualified annuity or unitrust interest that was valued under the tables in the initial transfer. If *A* dies during the ten-year trust term, still holding her qualified interest, when the trust property is worth $200,000, the retained interest will still give rise to inclusion in *A*'s gross estate under § 2036, but the includible amount may be less than the full value of the underlying property. Under the regulations, the includible amount will not exceed the principal amount which, if invested at the § 7520 rate in effect at death, would generate annual income equal to the annuity or unitrust payment. Thus, assuming an annual payment of $6,000 and a § 7520 rate of 6 percent, the amount included under § 2036 would be limited to $100,000 ($6,000 ÷ .06). Reg. § 20.2036–1(c)(2); see also Prop. Reg. § 20.2036–1(c)(2) (similar computation for graduated annual payment). May the government seek to include a larger amount under another provision such as § 2039? See Reg. § 20.2039–1(e).

The enactment of § 2702 was not accompanied by any change in the estate tax provisions concerning lifetime transfers. Thus, § 2036(a) continues to require inclusion in the gross estate of transfers made by the decedent subject to a retained life estate. If the transferor's retained interest is to last for a fixed term of years, inclusion depends on whether the transferor has the misfortune to die before the end of the trust term. If the transferor expires on the last day of the term, § 2036(a) applies with full force; one day later, and the trust property escapes estate tax altogether. The estate tax consequences do not turn on how closely the transaction approximates a testamentary transfer or whether it is undertaken for the purpose of avoiding taxes. For estate tax purposes, it makes very little difference whether the transferor's retained interest was valued under the tables or under the zero-value rule of § 2702 in the initial transfer.

In a sense, § 2702 may be viewed as something of a stopgap solution to the problem of estate freezing techniques involving trusts. Section 2702 focuses exclusively on the initial transfer in trust, imposing special valuation rules which appear at first glance to be both simple and effective. The special rules, however, do not simplify the overall gift and estate tax treatment of trusts with retained interests. Such trusts remain potentially subject to overlapping gift and estate taxes, and the resulting risk of double taxation accentuates the need for corrective adjustments. Furthermore, the effectiveness of § 2702 is open to question: Despite the unfavorable valuation assumptions of the special rules, the statute perpetuates the estate freezing advantages of fixed-term trusts with qualified retained interests (or even nonqualified retained interests, in the case of a personal residence). More generally, the limited front-end approach of § 2702 may ultimately impede more fundamental structural reform. Both before and after the unification of the estate and gift taxes in 1976, reformers have repeatedly called for a uniform completion rule under which a transfer in trust would be subject to a single gift tax or estate tax but not to both. See, for example, the Treasury Department's 1984 Report to the President, infra page 342. In theory, such a rule could adopt either a front-end or a back-end approach: Is one approach preferable to the other?

d. Private Annuities

BERGAN'S ESTATE v. COMMISSIONER

1 T.C. 543 (1943).

... Margaret L. Goggin and the decedent, Sarah A. Bergan, were sisters. The decedent died in 1939. Kate A. Johnson, a third sister, died intestate December 6, 1932, leaving an estate of approximately $500,000, and her only distributees were her two above named sisters. Shortly after Mrs. Johnson's death, Miss Bergan, who was then 74 but in good health, approached Mrs. Goggin, who was five years younger, with the proposition that Mrs. Goggin was to take all of Mrs. Johnson's estate, except $50,000 in bonds which were to be transferred to Miss Bergan, and that there was to be an oral understanding between the two that Miss Bergan would live with Mrs. Goggin for the remainder of Miss Bergan's life and that Mrs. Goggin was to defray all of the living expenses. That proposition was agreed upon by both sisters and was fully executed. The respondent determined that Miss Bergan in 1933 made a transfer of her share of Mrs. Johnson's estate in excess of the $50,000 of bonds, which excess the respondent has determined was subject to both the gift tax and the estate tax. Petitioner by appropriate assignments of error has contested these determinations....

BLACK, JUDGE.

... Is this transfer of Miss Bergan's share of Mrs. Johnson's estate in excess of the $50,000 block of bonds includible in Miss Bergan's gross estate under [§ 2036(a)] of the Internal Revenue Code? ...

The respondent strongly contends that in substance Miss Bergan retained for her life the right to the income from the property transferred, and that for this reason the property must be included in Miss Bergan's gross estate under [§ 2036(a)]. In this connection the respondent points out that the living expenses of Miss Bergan, Mrs. Goggin and her two adult sons, all of which were paid by Mrs. Goggin, were between $25,000 and $30,000 a year, and that, if it took $7,500 a year for Mrs. Goggin to support Miss Bergan, the income from the property transferred (1933 agreed value, $133,662.37) would hardly be sufficient. From this the respondent argues that the result of the agreement between the two sisters was in substance the same as if Miss Bergan had transferred the property in trust with instructions to pay her the income therefrom for life and upon her death to deliver the principal to Mrs. Goggin, citing Tips v. Bass [21 F.2d 460 (W.D. Tex. 1927)] and Updike v. Commissioner [88 F.2d 807 (8th Cir.), cert. denied, 301 U.S. 708 (1937)]. . . .

We think these cases are distinguishable from the instant estate tax proceeding. In both these cases relied upon by the respondent actual trusts were created to secure the annuities, whereas no trust was created in the instant proceeding. Mrs. Goggin was free to use the property transferred to her in any way that she pleased. The title vested in Mrs. Goggin and not in any trustee. Miss Bergan did not reserve to herself the income from the property transferred. She had entered into a contract with her sister for support and transferred the property in question as consideration for the contract. In the *Tips* case the Government conceded that the real property transferred of the value of $86,000, which was not placed in trust, was not includable in the gross estate. Although the entire property in the *Updike* case was not placed in trust, the entire transfer in that case was made in contemplation of death, a fact which clearly distinguishes that case from the instant proceeding. In other words, the property transferred in the *Updike* case was included in the gross estate because the transfer was made in contemplation of death and not because the decedent there had in effect reserved to himself for life the income from the property transferred. . . . The *Updike* case is therefore not controlling. . . . On this issue we sustain petitioner.

We shall now consider the question whether any part of Miss Bergan's share of Mrs. Johnson's estate in excess of the $50,000 block of bonds is taxable as a gift made in 1933. . . .

In deciding the estate tax question we held that Miss Bergan made a "transfer" during the year 1933 of her share of Mrs. Johnson's estate in excess of the $50,000 block of bonds in consideration for Mrs. Goggin's promise to support Miss Bergan for the remainder of Miss Bergan's life. The parties agree that in 1933 the value of the property thus transferred by Miss Bergan was the amount of $133,662.37. Petitioner contends that the transfer was for an adequate and full consideration in money or money's worth, and that there was, therefore, no gift. In the alternative, petitioner contends that if the transfer was for less than an adequate and full consideration, the minimum value of such consideration computed under [the Treasury tables], would be $38,880.15, and that only the difference between $133,662.37 and $38,880.15 should be deemed a gift under [§ 2512(b)]. The respondent contends that the transfer was for less than an adequate and full consideration; that petitioner has failed to prove the value of the consideration, namely, Mrs. Goggin's promise to support Miss Bergan for the remainder of Miss Bergan's life; and that, therefore, the entire value of the property transferred ($133,662.37) should be deemed a gift under [§ 2512(b)].

The Committee on Ways and Means, in its report accompanying the Revenue Bill of 1932, referred to [§ 2512(b)] (Cumulative Bulletin 1939–1, Part 2, p.477) as follows:

> Since the tax is designed to reach all transfers to the extent that they are donative, and to exclude any consideration not reducible to money or money's worth, it is provided in this section that where the transfer is made for less than an adequate and full consideration in money or money's worth, the excess in value of the property transferred over such consideration shall be deemed a gift. For example, if *A* sells property worth $10,000 to *B* for $1,000, there is a gift of $9,000....

In the instant gift tax proceeding there was a valid consideration for the transfer in question, namely, Mrs. Goggin's promise to support Miss Bergan for the remainder of Miss Bergan's life, but it was less than an adequate and full consideration for the property which was transferred. Is that consideration reducible to a money value? We think it is. Mrs. Goggin was to support Miss Bergan according to the standard then being enjoyed by the four adults which was at a cost of between $25,000 and $30,000 a year, or an average of between $6,250 and $7,500 for each adult. We adopt the lower figure in view of the insufficiency of the evidence to adequately establish a higher figure than that. We think such a consideration may be valued in the same way that an annuity of $6,250 for Miss Bergan's life would be valued. At the time of the transfer in 1933 Miss Bergan was 74 years of age. According to [the Treasury tables], the present value of $1 due at the end of each year during the life of a person 74 years of age is $5.18402, or $32,400.13 for an annuity of $6,250.[24] This is the same method of computation as petitioner used in arriving at the figures of $38,880.15 as being the value of Mrs. Goggin's agreement to support and maintain Miss Bergan during the remainder of her life. The difference in our figure and that arrived at by petitioner is that we use a figure of $6,250 as the cost of annual support and maintenance for Miss Bergan, whereas petitioner used $7,500 as such annual figure. We find, therefore, that Miss Bergan transferred property of the value of $133,662.37 for an equivalent in money of $32,400.13, and, under [§ 2512(b)], we hold that the excess of the value of the property transferred over the value of the consideration, or $101,262.24, shall be deemed a gift and shall be included in computing the amount of gifts made by Miss Bergan during the calendar year 1933....

NOTES

1. *"The income from the property."* If *A* owns 1,000 shares of *XYZ* stock, on which the annual dividend for many years has been $9 per share, and transfers these shares in trust, reserving for himself the income for life, the value of the shares at the date of his death will be includible in his gross estate under § 2036(a)(1). If the remainder takers are members of *A*'s family (as defined in § 2704(c)(2)), the transfer in trust will be treated as a gift of the full value of the shares under § 2702(a). Are the gift or estate tax

24. This computation is based on the valuation tables in Reg. 108, § 86.19, which used a 4 percent annual rate of return for gifts made before 1952.—EDS.

consequences different if *A* transfers the shares to his children and they agree (a) to hold the shares and pay him the dividends therefrom for his life; (b) to pay him $9,000 per year for his life whether they hold the shares or not; or (c) to pay him each year, whether they hold the shares or not, an amount equal to the dividends declared by *XYZ* on 1,000 shares?

If any of these three cases are treated differently under § 2036(a) from a transfer of the shares in trust with a reserved life estate, is there any policy reason for the difference? See Greene v. United States, 237 F.2d 848 (7th Cir. 1956) (transfer of property to donee on latter's agreement to pay the income to donor, but not less than $1,500 per year; held, § 2036(a) embraces transfer by trust "or otherwise," including this transaction). Rev. Rul. 55–378, 1955–1 C.B. 447, involved a trust of $100,000 created by the settlor for the benefit of his children, under which he reserved the right to withdraw $2,500 a year or all of his living expenses:

> The decedent did not transfer the property to his children absolutely in consideration of their agreement to pay him $2,500 a year or all of his living expenses but instead he transferred the property into a trust account reserving the right to receive $2,500 a year or all of his living expenses out of the transferred property. Accordingly, it is held that the transfer was not a bona fide sale for an adequate and full consideration in money or money's worth and is includible in decedent's gross estate under [§ 2036(a)].

Is the ruling based on a distinction without a difference? Does it matter whether the underlying property is pledged to secure the transferee's obligation to make the required payments to the transferor? See Loftis, When Can a Trust Be Used to Fund a Private Annuity Without Creating a Retained Interest?, 14 Est. Planning 218 (1987).

2. *Private annuity as an estate planning technique.* The private annuity achieves optimal estate and gift tax savings if the annuitant dies soon after the annuity has been created. The findings of fact in Fabric's Estate v. Commissioner, 83 T.C. 932 (1984), included the following report on the annuitant's health:

> Mollie P. Fabric (hereinafter referred to as decedent) was born on May 1, 1909, and died, testate, on February 21, 1977, a resident of Florida. She was survived by her four sons. . . .
>
> Decedent's family had a history of myocardial infarctions (heart attacks) and hypertension (elevated blood pressure). The decedent had had hypertension since at least 1962. On May 31, 1974, the decedent was hospitalized, suffering from multiple medical problems, including kidney problems, ulcerative colitis, and hypertension. Decedent was treated and released on July 3, 1974.
>
> During the first 9 months of 1975, the decedent had severe chest pains, which were alleviated only with nitroglycerine. On September 5, 1975, the decedent's chest pains had increased in their intensity, resulting in an unexpected hospitalization. Medical tests conducted on the decedent revealed that she had a blockage in a single coronary artery. The obstruction, or occlusion, was determined to be in the range of 95 to

99 percent. To alleviate this blockage, the decedent underwent coronary artery bypass surgery (open-heart surgery) on September 24, 1975. Prior to the surgery, the decedent's physicians predicted that she had a 60– to 75–percent chance of survival. Decedent survived the surgery, but it was not the end of her medical treatment.

On October 8, 1975, decedent had a permanent intravenous pacemaker inserted. The pacemaker was inserted in order to regulate the decedent's heartbeat, which had slowed somewhat after her surgery. Decedent was discharged from the hospital on October 11, 1975.

During October, November, and early December 1975, the decedent had pleural effusion, which is retention of excessive fluid in the chest and lungs. Pleural effusion is very common after open-heart surgery and is not a serious problem. The decedent entered the hospital in December 1975 to have this condition treated.

After the decedent was discharged, her followup care was entrusted to Dr. Morton Diamond, a cardiologist practicing in Hollywood, FL. Dr. Diamond first met and began treating the decedent in January 1976. At that time the decedent had hypertension, arteriosclerotic heart disease, hypertensive heart disease, chronic renal disease, and ulcerative colitis. Even with decedent's medical problems, Dr. Diamond was of the opinion that as of the latter part of 1975 and as of January 1976 he would have expected the decedent to live easily several years, possibly even in excess of 5 years.

Decedent was hospitalized on January 6, 1977, because of congestive heart failure. The decedent was hospitalized for the last time on February 11, 1977, and died on February 21, 1977, from congestive heart failure. Decedent's death occurred approximately 1 year and 5 months after her September 24, 1975, operation. [83 T.C. at 933–35.]

In September 1975, shortly before her open-heart surgery, Mrs. Fabric created a trust, naming a bank as trustee and her four sons as the ultimate beneficiaries of the balance in the trust at her death. She agreed to transfer assets worth $1,150,000 to the trust and, in return, the bank agreed to pay her $2,378.48 per week for the rest of her life. The annuity was a fixed obligation and was not dependent on the trust's income; in the event the trust assets were exhausted, the bank was liable to make the annuity payments from its own assets. The amount of the annuity was determined under the Treasury tables, and an expert actuary testified that the purchase of a private annuity with identical terms and conditions would have cost approximately $1,215,000.

Following Mrs. Fabric's death one year and five months later, her estate contended that the transfer created no gift or estate tax liability because Mrs. Fabric received adequate and full consideration (i.e., the bank's agreement to make the annuity payments). The Commissioner responded that Mrs. Fabric had not purchased an annuity but had retained a life income interest in the transferred assets. Alternatively, even if a valid annuity agreement existed, the Commissioner argued that Mrs. Fabric had not received adequate and full consideration; the use of the Treasury tables was inappropriate because her "death was clearly imminent and her medical condition was incurable."

The Tax Court ruled against the Commissioner on both counts. Existing authority required that the arrangement be treated as a valid annuity agreement. Moreover, the use of the valuation tables was justified by "administrative necessity," and departures from the tables were authorized only in "exceptional circumstances"—for example, where a particular individual's maximum life expectancy was less than one year. See also Costanza's Estate v. Commissioner, 320 F.3d 595 (6th Cir. 2003) (parent died four months after selling property to child for self-canceling installment note secured by mortgage on transferred property; held, transaction was bona fide sale).

3. *Joint purchase.* On its face, § 2036(a) applies when property is transferred subject to a retained income interest for life or a related period. Suppose that *A* and *B* purchase real property from an unrelated third party for its fair market value, taking title in the names of *A* as life tenant and *B* as remainderman. Each party furnishes consideration in proportion to the value of his or her respective interest. If *A* dies five years later, survived by *B*, is any portion of the property includible in *A*'s gross estate?

Although the Service has not directly challenged a pure version of the joint purchase technique, there is always the possibility that a purported purchase of a life estate may be recast as a transfer subject to a retained interest. In the above example, should *A* and *B* be viewed as purchasing a life estate and a remainder, respectively, or should each party be treated as purchasing an undivided interest in the property and then exchanging a life estate in one portion for a remainder in the other portion? Cf. Mahoney v. United States, 831 F.2d 641 (6th Cir. 1987), cert. denied, 486 U.S. 1054 (1988) (father created trust of stock for son's benefit; son's payment to father for stock treated as transfer with retained income interest); cf. Giannini v. Commissioner, 148 F.2d 285 (9th Cir.), cert. denied, 326 U.S. 730 (1945) (parents and children created trust to pay income to children for their lives).

D'AMBROSIO'S ESTATE v. COMMISSIONER

101 F.3d 309 (3d Cir. 1996), cert. denied, 520 U.S. 1230 (1997).

NYGAARD, CIRCUIT JUDGE.

Vita D'Ambrosio, executrix of the estate of Rose D'Ambrosio, appeals from a judgment of the United States Tax Court upholding a statutory notice of deficiency filed against the estate by the Commissioner of Internal Revenue. The tax court held that, even though the decedent had sold her remainder interest in closely held stock for its fair market value, 26 U.S.C. § 2036(a)(1) brought its entire fee simple value back into her gross estate. We will reverse and remand with the direction that the tax court enter judgment in favor of appellant.

I

The facts in this case have been stipulated by the parties. Decedent owned, inter alia, one half of the preferred stock of Vaparo, Inc.; these 470 shares had a fair market value of $2,350,000. In 1987, at the age of 80, decedent transferred her remainder interest in her shares to Vaparo in exchange for an annuity which was to pay her $296,039 per year and retained her income interest in the shares. There is no evidence in the record to indicate that she made this transfer in contemplation of death or with testamentary motivation. According to the actuarial tables set forth in the Treasury Regulations, the annuity had a fair market value of $1,324,014. The parties stipulate that this was also the fair market value of the remainder interest.

Decedent died in 1990, after receiving only $592,078 in annuity payments and $23,500 in dividends. Her executrix did not include any interest in the Vaparo stock when she computed decedent's gross estate. The Commissioner disagreed, issuing a notice of deficiency in which she asserted that the gross estate included the full, fee simple value of the Vaparo shares at the date of death, still worth an estimated $2,350,000, less the amount of annuity payments decedent received during life.[25] The estate then petitioned the tax court for redetermination of the alleged tax deficiency.

The tax court ... ruled in favor of the Commissioner.... The executrix now appeals....

II

... There is no dispute that Rose D'Ambrosio retained a life interest in the Vaparo stock and sold the remainder back to the company. The issue is whether the sale of a remainder interest for its fair market value constitutes "adequate and full consideration" within the meaning of § 2036(a). Appellant argues that it does. The Commissioner takes the position that only consideration equal to the fee simple value of the property is sufficient. Appellant has the better argument.

A

The tax court and the Commissioner rely principally on four cases, Gradow v. United States, 11 Cl. Ct. 808 (1987), affd. for the reasons set forth by the claims court, 897 F.2d 516 (Fed. Cir. 1990); United States v. Past, 347 F.2d 7 (9th Cir. 1965); Estate of Gregory v. Commissioner, 39 T.C. 1012 (1963); United States v. Allen, 293 F.2d 916 (10th Cir. 1961). We find these cases either inapposite or unpersuasive; we will discuss them in chronological order.

In *Allen*, the decedent set up an irrevocable inter vivos trust in which she retained a partial life estate and gave the remainder (as well as the remaining portion of the income) to her children. Apparently realizing the tax liability she had created for her estate under the predecessor of § 2036, she later attempted to sell her retained life interest to her son for an amount slightly in excess of its fair market value. After she died, the estate took the position that, because decedent had divested herself of her retained life interest for fair market value, none of the trust property was includable in her gross estate. The Court of Appeals disagreed, holding

25. The Commissioner now concedes that the estate must be credited for the fair market value of that annuity rather than the lifetime payments received under it.

that consideration is only "adequate" if it equals or exceeds the value of the interest that would otherwise be included in the gross estate absent the transfer. See 293 F.2d at 917. . . .

Allen, however, is inapposite, as the Commissioner now concedes, because it involved the sale of a life estate after the remainder had already been disposed of by gift, a testamentary transaction with a palpable tax evasion motive. This case, in contrast, involves the sale of a remainder for its stipulated fair market value. Nevertheless, we agree with its rationale that consideration should be measured against the value that would have been drawn into the gross estate absent the transfer. As the tax court persuasively reasoned in a later case:

> [W]here the transferred property is replaced by other property of equal value received in exchange, there is no reason to impose an estate tax in respect of the transferred property, for it is reasonable to assume that the property acquired in exchange will find its way into the decedent's gross estate at his death unless consumed or otherwise disposed of in a nontestamentary transaction in much the same manner as would the transferred property itself had the transfer not taken place. . . .
>
> In short, unless replaced by property of equal value that could be *exposed to inclusion* in the decedent's gross estate, the property transferred in a testamentary transaction of the type described in the statute must be included in his gross estate. [Estate of Frothingham v. Commissioner, 60 T.C. 211, 215–16 (1973) (emphasis added).]

Gregory presents a closer factual analogy to D'Ambrosio's situation. *Gregory* was a "widow's election" case involving the testamentary disposition of community property. Typically in such cases, the husband wishes to pass the remainder interest in all of the marital property to his children, while providing for the lifetime needs of his surviving spouse. In a community property state, however, half of the marital property belongs to the wife as a matter of law, so he cannot pass it by his own will. To circumvent this problem, the will is drafted to give the widow a choice: take her one-half share in fee simple, according to law, or trust over her half of the community property in exchange for a life estate in the whole. Put another way, she trades the remainder interest in her half of the community property in exchange for a life estate in her husband's half.

In *Gregory*, the widow exchanged property worth approximately $66,000 for a life estate with an actuarial value of only around $12,000; by the time she died eight years later, the property she gave up had appreciated to approximately $102,000. The tax court compared the $102,000 outflow to the $12,000 consideration and concluded that the widow's election did not constitute a bona fide sale for an adequate and full consideration. 39 T.C. at 1015–16. It also stated that "the statute excepts only those bona fide sales where the consideration received was of a comparable value *which would be includable in the transferor's gross estate*." Id. at 1016 (emphasis added).

We believe that the *Gregory* court erred in its analysis, although it reached the correct result on the particular facts of that case. There is no way to know ex ante what the value of an asset will be at the death of a testator; although the date of death can be estimated through the use of actuarial tables, the actual appreciation of the property is unknowable, as are the prevailing interest, inflation and tax rates. Consequently, there is no way to ever be certain in advance whether the consideration is adequate and thus no way to know what tax treatment a transfer will receive. This level of uncertainty all but destroys any economic incentive to ever sell a remainder interest; yet, Congress never said in § 2036 that *all* transfers of such interests will be taxed at their fee simple value or that those transfers are illegal. Instead, it clearly contemplated situations in which a sale of a remainder would not cause the full value of the property to fall into the gross estate. Without some express indication from Congress, we will not presume it intended to eliminate wholesale the transfers of remainder interests. Therefore, rather than evaluate the adequacy of the consideration at the time the decedent dies, we will compare the value of the remainder transferred to the value of the consideration received, measured as of the date of the transfer. Here, we need not address that valuation issue, because it is stipulated that the fair market value of the stock was the same on the date of transfer as it was on the date of death.

In *Gregory*, however, the $12,000 the decedent received was grossly inadequate against the value of the property she transferred, regardless of the valuation date. The court was therefore correct that the transfer was not for adequate and full consideration. Because of that gross inadequacy, however, the holding of *Gregory* does not extend to the issue now before us: whether, when a remainder is sold for its stipulated fair market value, the consideration received is inadequate because it is less than the fee simple value of the property.

The *Past* case was factually somewhat different, in that it involved a divorce settlement, but the substance of the transaction was the same as in *Gregory*: the sale of a remainder in one-half of the marital property in exchange for a life estate in the whole. . . .

B

The facts in *Gradow* were similar to those in *Gregory*; both are "widow's election" cases. That case is particularly significant, however, because the court focused on the statutory language of § 2036. . . .

We examine first the *Gradow* court's construction of the statute. It opined that

> there is no question that the term "property" in the phrase "The gross estate shall include . . . all property . . . of which the decedent has at any time made a transfer" means that part of the trust corpus attributable to plaintiff. If § 2036(a) applies, all of [decedent's] former community property is brought into her gross estate. Fundamental

> principles of grammar dictate that the parenthetical exception which then follows—"(except in case of a bona fide sale . . .)"—refers to a transfer of that same property, i.e. the one-half of the community property she placed into the trust. [Id. (ellipses in original).]

We disagree; although the *Gradow* court's rationale appears plausible, we note that the court, in quoting the statute, left out significant portions of its language. Below is the text of § 2036, with the omitted words emphasized:

> The *value of the* gross estate shall include *the value of* all property *to the extent of any interest therein* of which the decedent has at any time made a transfer (except in case of a bona fide sale for an adequate and full consideration in money or money's worth), by trust or otherwise, under which he has retained for his life . . . (1) the possession or enjoyment of, or the right to the income from, the property . . .

After parsing this language, we cannot agree with the *Gradow* court's conclusions that "property" refers to the fee simple interest and that adequate consideration must be measured against that value. Rather, we believe that the clear import of the phrase "to the extent of any interest therein" is that the gross estate shall include the value of the remainder *interest*, unless it was sold for adequate and fair consideration. . . .

The *Gradow* court also believed that its construction of § 2036 was "most consistent" with its purposes. 11 Cl. Ct. at 813. The tax court in this case, although recognizing that the issue has spawned considerable legal commentary and that scholars dispute its resolution, 105 T.C. at 254, was persuaded that decedent's sale of her remainder interest was testamentary in character and designed to avoid the payment of estate tax that otherwise would have been due. Id. at 260. It noted particularly that the transfer was made when decedent was eighty years old and that the value of the annuity she received was over $1 million less than the fee simple value of the stock she gave up. Id. Again, we disagree.

We too are cognizant that techniques for attempting to reduce estate taxes are limited only by the imagination of estate planners, and that new devices appear regularly. There is, to be sure, a role for the federal courts to play in properly limiting these techniques in accordance with the expressed intent of Congress. Under long-standing precedent, for example, we measure "consideration" in real economic terms, not as it might be evaluated under the common law of contract or property. E.g., Commissioner v. Wemyss, 324 U.S. 303 (1945) (promise of marriage insufficient consideration, for gift tax purposes, for tax-free transfer of property); Merrill v. Fahs, 324 U.S. 308 (1945) (same). Likewise, when the transfer of the remainder interest is essentially gratuitous and testamentary in character, we focus on substance rather than form and require that the full value of trust property be included in the gross estate, unless "the settlor absolutely, unequivocally, irrevocably, and without possible reservations, parts with all of his title and all of his possession and all of his enjoyment of the transferred property." See Commissioner v. Estate of Church, 335 U.S. 632, 645 (1949). . . .

On the other hand, it is not our role to police the techniques of estate planning by determining, based on our own policy views and perceptions, which transfers are abusive and which are not. That is properly the role of Congress, whose statutory enactments we are bound to interpret.[26] As stated supra, we think the statutory text better supports appellant's argument.

Even looking at this case in policy terms, however, it is difficult to fathom either the tax court's or the Commissioner's concerns about the "abusiveness" of this transaction. A hypothetical example will illustrate the point.

A fee simple interest is comprised of a life estate and a remainder. Returning to the widow's election cases, assume that the surviving spouse's share of the community property is valued at $2,000,000. Assuming that she decides not to accept the settlement and to keep that property, its whole value will be available for inclusion in the gross estate at death, but only as long as the widow lives entirely on the income from the property. If she invades principal and sells some of the property in order to meet living expenses or purchase luxury items, then at least some of that value will not be included in the gross estate. Tax law, of course (with the exception of the gift tax), imposes no burdens on how a person spends her money during life.

Next, assume that same widow decides to sell her remainder and keep a life estate. As long as she sells the remainder for its fair market value, it makes no difference whether she receives cash, other property, or an annuity. All can be discounted to their respective present values and quantified. If she continues to support herself from the income from her life estate, the consideration she received in exchange for the remainder, if properly invested, will still be available for inclusion in the gross estate when she dies, as *Frothingham* and *Gregory* require. On the other hand, if her life estate is insufficient to meet her living expenses, the widow will have to invade the consideration she received in exchange for her remainder, but to no different an extent than she would under the previous hypothetical in which she retained the fee simple interest. In sum, there is simply no change in the date-of-death value of the final estate, regardless of which option she selects, at any given standard of living.

On the other hand, if the full, fee simple value of the property at the time of death is pulled back into the gross estate under § 2036(a), subject only to an offset for the consideration received, then the post-sale appreciation of the transferred asset will be taxed at death. Indeed, it will be double-taxed, because, all things being equal, the consideration she received will also have appreciated and will be subject to tax on its increased value. In addition, it would appear virtually impossible, under the tax

26. Indeed, subsequent to the transfer at issue here, Congress *did* enact legislation dealing with abusive transfers of remainder interests. See 26 U.S.C. §§ 2036(c) (repealed), 2701 [2702?].

court's reasoning, ever to sell a remainder interest; if the adequacy of the consideration must be measured against the fee simple value of the property at the time of the transfer, the transferor will have to find an arms-length buyer willing to pay a fee simple price for a future interest. Unless a buyer is willing to speculate that the future value of the asset will skyrocket, few if any such sales will take place.

Another potential concern, expressed by the *Gradow* court, is that, under appellant's theory, "[a] young person could sell a remainder interest for a fraction of the property's [current, fee simple] worth, enjoy the property for life, and then pass it along without estate or gift tax consequences." 11 Cl. Ct. at 815. This reasoning is problematic, however, because it ignores the time value of money. Assume that a decedent sells his son a remainder interest in that much-debated and often-sold parcel of land called Blackacre, which is worth $1 million in fee simple, for its actuarial fair market value of $100,000 (an amount which implicitly includes the market value of Blackacre's expected appreciation). Decedent then invests the proceeds of the sale. If the rates of return for both assets are equal and decedent lives exactly as long as the actuarial tables predict, the consideration that decedent received for his remainder will equal the value of Blackacre on the date of his death. The equivalent value will, accordingly, still be included in the gross estate.... We therefore have great difficulty understanding how this transaction could be abusive.

On this appeal, the Commissioner likewise argues for the *Gradow* rule on the rationale that "the retained life interest is in closely held stock whose dividend treatment is subject to the control of decedent and her family. In such circumstances, the amount of the dividend income that decedent was to receive from her life income interest in the Vaparo preferred stock was susceptible of manipulation[.]" Commissioner's Brief at 33. There is no evidence, however, that the Vaparo dividends *were* manipulated, and the Commissioner directs us to no authority that we should presume so. In addition, implicit in her argument is the proposition that the life estate was overvalued by the executor and the remainder correspondingly undervalued. Such a position, however, is directly contrary to the Commissioner's own stipulation regarding the values of those interests.

The Commissioner also asserts that the D'Ambrosio estate plan is "calculated to deplete decedent's estate in the event that she should not survive as long as her actuarially projected life expectancy." Commissioner's Brief at 34–35. We note first that the Commissioner does not argue that decedent transferred her remainder in contemplation of imminent death under such circumstances that the tables should not be applied. Leaving aside the untimely death of Rose D'Ambrosio, any given transferor of a remainder is equally likely to *outlive* the tables, in which case she would collect more from her annuity, the gross estate would be correspondingly larger and the Commissioner would collect more tax revenue than if the remainder had never been transferred....

III

Because we conclude that the tax court erred as a matter of law when it determined that the consideration received by Rose D'Ambrosio for her remainder interest was not adequate and full, we will reverse and remand for it to enter judgment in favor of the estate.

COWEN, CIRCUIT JUDGE, dissenting.

Today the majority holds that a tax-avoidance approach previously considered "too good to be true" can, at least in limited circumstances, actually be true. I respectfully dissent. The tax court's opinion is supported by well-established case law and the plain language of the Internal Revenue Code. It should be affirmed. . . .

The value of a gross estate includes the value of all property held by the decedent on the date of death. I.R.C. § 2033. Pursuant to section 2036(a), for federal estate tax purposes the gross estate also includes any property that is the subject of an inter vivos transfer and in which the taxpayer reserves an income interest in that property until death. The sole exception authorized by section 2036(a) is a "bona fide sale" in which the transferor receives "adequate and full consideration" in exchange for the transferred property. I.R.C. § 2036(a). The majority holds that under section 2036(a), "adequate and full consideration" must be provided merely for that portion of the taxpayer's property interest actually transferred, rather than for the full value of the property that is the basis for the ongoing income interest.

The majority excludes from the computation of "full and adequate consideration" the value of decedent's life interest in the transferred stock, on the grounds that D'Ambrosio retained that interest. The intended purpose of section 2036 is to prevent decedents from avoiding estate taxes by selling their property to a third party but retaining the benefits of ownership during their lives. . . . When a taxpayer makes a transfer with a retained life interest, the powerful arm of section 2036(a) pulls into the gross estate the full value of the transferred property, not merely the value of the remainder interest.

The majority accepts the view of the estate that the decedent "sold" only the remainder interest to Vaparo. This view of section 2036 sanctions tax evasion: It enables strategic segmentation of the property into multiple interests, with "adequate and full consideration" now required only for a specific transferred segment, rather than the indivisible whole. Such an interpretation of section 2036(a) thwarts its very purpose, enabling taxpayers to avoid paying estate taxes on property while retaining the income benefits of ownership. I would affirm the tax court's holding that "adequate and full consideration" assesses whether the consideration received is equal to the value of *the property that would have remained in the estate but for the transfer*, not whether it is commensurate with the value of the artfully separated portion of the property technically transferred. . . .

The paramount purpose of section 2036(a) is to prevent the depletion of estate assets when individuals retain the use and enjoyment of those assets until death. In Commissioner v. Estate of Church, 335 U.S. 632 (1949), the Supreme Court emphatically noted that

> an estate tax cannot be avoided by any trust transfer except by a bona fide transfer in which the settlor, absolutely, unequivocally, irrevocably, and without possible reservations, parts with all of his title and all of his possession and all of his enjoyment of the transferred property. [Id. at 645.]

D'Ambrosio clearly fails this requirement that all title, enjoyment, and possession of the transferred property be unequivocally halted. Commenting on the forerunner to section 2036(a) more than a half century ago, the Supreme Court stated that the law

> taxes not merely those interests which are deemed to pass at death according to refined technicalities of the law of property. It also taxes inter vivos transfers that are too much akin to testamentary dispositions not to be subjected to the same excise. [Helvering v. Hallock, 309 U.S. 106, 112 (1940).]

These cases clearly demonstrate that the concept of "adequate and full consideration," as used in sections 2035 through 2038, must be construed with reference to the special problems posed by trying to prevent testamentary-type transfers from evading estate tax. The bona fide sale analysis, which exempts property from inclusion in the gross estate pursuant to section 2036(a), cannot focus merely on the value of the limited property interest that is sold. It must also consider the property that would otherwise be included in the decedent's gross estate....

I would affirm the decision of the tax court. I respectfully dissent.

NOTES

1. *Bona fide sale exception.* Section 2036, like §§ 2035, 2037 and 2038, carves out an exception in the case of a "bona fide sale for an adequate and full consideration in money or money's worth." The *D'Ambrosio* majority accepts the taxpayer's argument that a sale of a remainder for its actuarial value removes the underlying property from the reach of § 2036(a), and other courts have followed suit. See Wheeler v. United States, 116 F.3d 749 (5th Cir. 1997) ("the sale of a remainder interest for its actuarial value ... constitutes an adequate and full consideration under section 2036(a)"); Magnin's Estate v. Commissioner, 184 F.3d 1074 (9th Cir. 1999).

In theory, the sale of a remainder for its actuarial value does not deplete the taxpayer's gross estate because the present value of the retained income interest, combined with the consideration received, equals the value of the underlying property. Thus, it may be expected that the compounded value at death of the income stream and the sale proceeds will fully replace the value of the underlying property in the gross estate, leaving the taxpayer in much the same position as if the entire property were transferred at death.

This theoretical equivalence, however, depends on the presumed accuracy of the valuation tables. If the property turns out to generate substantial capital appreciation but little or no current income, or if the taxpayer dies prematurely, the assets included in the gross estate may prove to be worth much less than their expected value under the tables. In *D'Ambrosio*, for example, the tables indicated an actuarial value of $1,025,986 in 1987 for the decedent's retained income interest in the Vaparo stock, but she received only $23,500 of dividends before her death in 1990; similarly, the tables indicated an actuarial value of $1,324,014 for the transferred remainder, but the decedent received only $592,078 in annuity payments. Is the court on solid ground in assuming that "any given transferor of a remainder is equally likely to *outlive* the tables"?

2. *Consideration offset.* If the decedent transferred property subject to a retained life estate and received less than "adequate and full" consideration, the amount includible in the gross estate under § 2036 is reduced by the amount of consideration received. § 2043(a). Note, however, that while the property included under § 2036 is valued at the decedent's death (or alternate valuation date, if applicable), the consideration offset under § 2043(a) is frozen at the time of the lifetime transfer. As a result, any appreciation in the transferred property between the time of the lifetime transfer and the decedent's death remains exposed to estate taxation. Furthermore, the property received as consideration, unless consumed or disposed of before death, is also includible in the gross estate under § 2033 at its deathtime value.

3. *Impact of § 2702.* The tax advantages of transfers with retained income interests have been narrowed, though not entirely foreclosed, by § 2702. The special valuation rules of § 2702 usually treat a retained income interest as having a value of zero, resulting in a correspondingly higher value for the transferred remainder. Nevertheless, if the donor retains a qualified annuity or unitrust interest (or even a simple income interest, in the case of a qualified personal residence trust), the values of the retained and transferred interests continue to be determined under the tables. See supra pages 78–83. What advantages, if any, might a taxpayer find in selling a remainder for its actuarial value, even if the transfer is subject to the zero-value rule of § 2702? See Jensen, Estate and Gift Tax Effects of Selling a Remainder: Have *D'Ambrosio*, *Wheeler* and *Magnin* Changed the Rules? 4 Fla. Tax Rev. 537 (1999).

2. TRANSFERS SUBJECT TO RETAINED POWER TO DESIGNATE BENEFICIAL ENJOYMENT

OLD COLONY TRUST CO. v. UNITED STATES

423 F.2d 601 (1st Cir. 1970).

ALDRICH, CHIEF JUDGE.

The sole question in this case is whether the estate of a settlor of an inter vivos trust, who was a trustee until the date of his death, is to be charged with the value of the principal he contributed by virtue of reserved powers in the trust. The executor paid the tax and sued for its recovery in the district court. All facts were stipulated. The court ruled for the government, 300 F. Supp. 1032, and the executor appeals.

The initial life beneficiary of the trust was the settlor's adult son. Eighty per cent of the income was normally to be payable to him, and the balance added to principal. Subsequent beneficiaries were the son's widow and his issue. The powers upon which the government relies to cause the corpus to be includible in the settlor-trustee's estate are contained in two articles. . . .

Article 4 permitted the trustees to increase the percentage of income payable to the son beyond the eighty per cent, "in their absolute discretion . . . when in their opinion such increase is needed in case of sickness, or desirable in view of changed circumstances." In addition, under Article 4 the trustees were given the discretion to cease paying income to the son, and add it all to principal, "during such period as the Trustees may decide that the stoppage of such payments is for his best interests."

Article 7 gave broad administrative or management powers to the trustees, with discretion to acquire investments not normally held by trustees, and the right to determine, what was to be charged or credited to income or principal, including stock dividends or deductions for amortization. It further provided that all divisions and decisions made by the trustees in good faith should be conclusive on all parties, and in summary, stated that the trustees were empowered, "generally to do all things in relation to the Trust Fund which the Donor could do if living and this Trust had not been executed."

The government claims that each of these two articles meant that the settlor-trustee had "the right . . . to designate the persons who shall possess or enjoy the [trust] property or the income therefrom" within the meaning of section 2036(a)(2) . . . and that the settlor-trustee at the date of his death possessed a power "to alter, amend, revoke, or terminate" within the meaning of section 2038(a)(1). . . .

If State Street Trust Co. v. United States, 1 Cir., 1959, 263 F.2d 635, was correctly decided in this aspect, the government must prevail because of the Article 7 powers. There this court, Chief Judge Magruder dissenting, held against the taxpayer because broad powers similar to those in Article 7 meant that the trustees "could very substantially shift the economic benefits of the trusts between the life tenants and the remaindermen," so that the settlor "as long as he lived, in substance and effect and in a very real sense . . . 'retained for his life . . . the right . . . to designate the persons who shall possess or enjoy the property or the income therefrom. . . .' " 263 F.2d at 639–640, quoting 26 U.S.C. § 2036(a)(2). We accept the taxpayer's invitation to reconsider this ruling.

It is common ground that a settlor will not find the corpus of the trust included in his estate merely because he named himself a trustee. Jennings v. Smith, 2 Cir., 1947, 161 F.2d 74. He must have reserved a power to himself that is inconsistent with the full termination of ownership. The government's brief defines this as "sufficient dominion and control until his death." Trustee powers given for the administration or management of the trust must be equitably exercised, however, for the benefit of the trust as a whole. Blodget v. Delaney, 1 Cir., 1953, 201 F.2d 589; United States v. Powell, 10th Cir., 1962, 307 F.2d 821; Scott, Trusts §§ 183, 232 (3d ed. 1967); Rest. 2d, Trusts §§ 183, 232. The court in *State Street* conceded that the powers at issue were all such powers, but reached the conclusion that, cumulatively, they gave the settlor dominion sufficiently unfettered to be in the nature of ownership. With all respect to the majority of the then court, we find it difficult to see how a power can be subject to control by the probate court, and exercisable only in what the trustee fairly concludes is in the interests of the trust and its beneficiaries as a whole, and at the same time be an ownership power.

The government's position, to be sound, must be that the trustee's powers are beyond the court's control. Under Massachusetts law, however, no amount of administrative discretion prevents judicial supervision of the trustee. Thus in Appeal of Davis, 1903, 183 Mass. 499, 67 N.E. 604, a trustee was given "full power to make purchases, investments and exchanges . . . in such manner as to them shall seem expedient; it being my intention to give my trustees . . . the same dominion and control over said trust property as I now have." In spite of this language, and in spite of their good faith, the court charged the trustees for failing sufficiently to diversify their investment portfolio.

The Massachusetts court has never varied from this broad rule of accountability, and has twice criticized *State Street* for its seeming departure. Boston Safe Deposit & Trust Co. v. Stone, 1965, 348 Mass. 345, 351, n.8, 203 N.E.2d 547; Old Colony Trust Co. v. Silliman, 1967, 352 Mass. 6, 8–9, 223 N.E.2d 504. . . . We make a further observation, which the court in *State Street* failed to note, that the provision in that trust (as in the case at bar) that the trustees could "do all things in relation to the Trust Fund which I, the Donor, could do if . . . the Trust had not been executed," is almost precisely the provision which did not protect the trustees from accountability in *Appeal of Davis*, supra.

We do not believe that trustee powers are to be more broadly construed for tax purposes than the probate court would construe them for administrative purposes. More basically, we agree with Judge Magruder's observation that nothing is "gained by lumping them together." State Street Trust Co. v. United States, supra, 263 F.2d at 642. We hold that no aggregation of purely administrative powers can meet the government's amorphous test of "sufficient dominion and control" so as to be equated with ownership.

This does not resolve taxpayer's difficulties under Article 4. Quite different considerations apply to distribution powers. Under them the trustee can, expressly, prefer one beneficiary over another. Furthermore, his freedom of choice may vary greatly, depending upon the terms of the individual trust. If there is an ascertainable standard, the trustee can be compelled to follow it. If there is not, even though he is a fiduciary, it is not unreasonable to say that his retention of an unmeasurable freedom of choice is equivalent to retaining some of the incidents of ownership. Hence, under the cases, if there is an ascertainable standard the settlor-trustee's estate is not taxed, United States v. Powell, supra; Jennings v. Smith, supra; Estate of Budd, 1968, 49 T.C. 468; Estate of Pardee, 1967, 49 T.C. 140, but if there is not, it is taxed. Henslee v. Union Planters Natl. Bank & Trust Co., 1949, 335 U.S. 595; Hurd v. Comr., 1st Cir., 1947, 160 F.2d 610; Michigan Trust Co. v. Kavanagh, 6th Cir., 1960, 284 F.2d 502.

The trust provision which is uniformly held to provide an ascertainable standard is one which, though variously expressed, authorizes such distributions as may be needed to continue the beneficiary's accustomed way of life. Ithaca Trust Co. v. United States, 1929, 279 U.S. 151.... On the other hand, if the trustee may go further, and has power to provide for the beneficiary's "happiness," Merchants Natl. Bank v. Comr. of Internal Revenue, 1943, 320 U.S. 256, or "pleasure," Industrial Trust Co. v. Comr. of Internal Revenue, 1st Cir., 1945, 151 F.2d 592, cert. denied, 327 U.S. 788, or "use and benefit," Newton Trust Co. v. Comr. of Internal Revenue, 1st Cir., 1947, 160 F.2d 175, or "reasonable requirement[s]," State Street Bank & Trust Co. v. United States, 1st Cir., 1963, 313 F.2d 29, the standard is so loose that the trustee is in effect uncontrolled.

In the case at bar the trustees could increase the life tenant's income "in case of sickness, or [if] desirable in view of changed circumstances." Alternatively, they could reduce it "for his best interests." "Sickness" presents no problem. Conceivably, providing for "changed circumstances" is roughly equivalent to maintaining the son's present standard of living. But see Hurd v. Comr. of Internal Revenue, supra. The unavoidable stumbling block is the trustees' right to accumulate income and add it to capital (which the son would never receive) when it is to the "best interests" of the son to do so. Additional payments to a beneficiary whenever in his "best interests" might seem to be too broad a standard in any event. In addition to the previous cases see Estate of Yawkey, 1949, 12 T.C. 1164, where the court said, at p. 1170,

> We can not regard the language involved ["best interest"] as limiting the usual scope of a trustee's discretion. It must always be anticipated that trustees will act for the best interests of a trust beneficiary, and an exhortation to act "in the interests and for the welfare" of the beneficiary does not establish an external standard.

Power, however, to decrease or cut off a beneficiary's income when in his "best interests," is even more troublesome. When the beneficiary is the son, and the trustee the father, a particular purpose comes to mind, parental control through holding the purse strings. The father decides what conduct is to the "best interests" of the son, and if the son does not agree, he loses his allowance. Such a power has the plain indicia of ownership control. The alternative, that the son, because of other means, might not need this income, and would prefer to have it accumulate for his widow and children after his death, is no better. If the trustee has power to confer "happiness" on the son by generosity to someone else, this seems clearly an unascertainable standard....

The case of Hays' Estate v. Comr. of Internal Revenue, 5 Cir., 1950, 181 F.2d 169, is contrary to our decision. The opinion is unsupported by either reasoning or authority, and we will not follow it. With the present settlor-trustee free to determine the standard himself, a finding of ownership control was warranted. To put it another way, the cost of holding onto the strings may prove to be a rope burn. State Street Bank & Trust Co. v. United States, supra.

Affirmed.

NOTES

1. *External standard under § 2036(a)(2).* The external standard doctrine is now well entrenched and is applied with like effect whether the claim is made under § 2038 or § 2036. See, e.g., Leopold v. United States, supra page 254. Recall that in Jennings v. Smith, supra page 250, the court suggested that a power exercisable only in accordance with an external standard could be viewed as a contingent power, which can be exercised only if and after the prescribed event occurs. Because in *Jennings* the event had not occurred, this theory buttressed the result that the power was not in existence at decedent's death, as is required under § 2038, and that therefore no tax was due. Does this theory similarly render § 2036(a)(2) inapplicable or does this section reach contingent powers even if the specified event has not occurred during the decedent's lifetime? See supra page 275, Note 3; see also the discussion in Farrel's Estate v. United States, infra page 322.

2. *"Transfer" requirement under § 2036(a).* Section 2036, like §§ 2035, 2037 and 2038, requires as a condition of inclusion in the gross estate that the decedent have made a "transfer" of property during life. In United States v. O'Malley, 383 U.S. 627 (1966), Edward Fabrice created irrevocable trusts for his wife and each of his children. Until his death he served as one of three trustees who were empowered to distribute the trust income annually or to accumulate the income and add it to principal. It was undisputed that the power to accumulate income constituted a power to designate beneficial enjoyment, so that the original trust property as it existed at Fabrice's death was includible in his gross estate under § 2036(a)(2). The issue before the Supreme Court was whether Fabrice made a lifetime "transfer" not only of the property that he originally contributed to the trust but also of the income accumulations that were subsequently added to trust principal. The Court answered in the affirmative and explained its reasoning as follows:

> At the time Fabrice established these trusts, he owned all of the rights to the property transferred, a major aspect of which was his right to the present and future income produced by that property. Commissioner v. Estate of Church, 335 U.S. 632, 644. With the creation of the trusts, he relinquished all of his rights to income except the power to distribute that income to the income beneficiaries or to accumulate it and hold it for the remaindermen of the trusts. He no longer had, for example, the right to income for his own benefit or to have it distributed to any other than the

trust beneficiaries. Moreover, with respect to the very additions to principal now at issue, he exercised his retained power to distribute or accumulate income, choosing to do the latter and thereby adding to the principal of the trusts. All income increments to trust principal are therefore traceable to Fabrice himself, by virtue of the original transfer and the exercise of the power to accumulate. Before the creation of the trusts, Fabrice owned all rights to the property and to its income. By the time of his death he had divested himself of all power and control over accumulated income which had been added to the principal, except the power to deal with the income from such additions. With respect to each addition to trust principal from accumulated income, Fabrice had clearly made a "transfer" as required by [§ 2036(a)(2)]. Under that section, the power over income retained by Fabrice is sufficient to require the inclusion of the original corpus of the trust in his gross estate. The accumulated income added to principal is subject to the same power and is likewise includable. [383 U.S. at 632–33.]

In Miller's Estate v. Commissioner, 58 T.C. 699 (1972), the decedent was the income beneficiary of a residuary trust under the will of her predeceased husband. Although the decedent was entitled to practically all of the net income earned by the estate during administration, she allowed it to be used to pay estate administration expenses which should have been charged to trust corpus. The court held that by not claiming the income to which she was entitled, the decedent in effect transferred it to the trust corpus; since she retained her life income interest in the trust, the transfer was includible in her gross estate under § 2036(a)(1). See also Sexton v. United States, 300 F.2d 490 (7th Cir.), cert. denied, 371 U.S. 820 (1962) (beneficiary who consented to extend trust term transferred her share of trust corpus); Thomson's Estate v. Commissioner, 495 F.2d 246 (2d Cir. 1974) (settlor made periodic transfers of income by failing to exercise retained distribution power and allowing income to be added to corpus); Pyle v. Commissioner, infra page 392 (owner-beneficiary of insurance policy on another's life made transfer by electing interest-only settlement option which became irrevocable at insured's death); Rev. Rul. 81–166, 1981–1 C.B. 477 (owner of insurance policy on another's life made transfer at insured's death when proceeds became payable to insured's revocable trust).

3. *Administrative powers.* For an extensive review of the cases involving the retention of administrative powers, see Greer v. United States, 448 F.2d 937 (4th Cir. 1971).

UNITED STATES v. BYRUM

408 U.S. 125 (1972).

MR. JUSTICE POWELL delivered the opinion of the Court.

[In 1958 the decedent, Milliken Byrum, created an irrevocable inter vivos trust to which he transferred stock in three unlisted corporations controlled by him. The sole trustee was a bank, and the beneficiaries of the trust were Byrum's children (or, if they died during the trust term, their surviving children). Byrum reserved the rights to vote the transferred stock, to veto the disposition of any trust assets (including the transferred stock), to veto trust investments, and to remove the trustee and appoint another corporate trustee as successor. The right to vote the transferred stock, coupled with the right to vote the stock owned by him outside the trust, gave Byrum a majority vote in each of the three corporations during his lifetime. After Byrum's death in 1964, the Service determined that the transferred stock was includible in his gross estate under §§ 2036(a)(1) and 2036(a)(2). The District Court ruled in favor of the taxpayer, 311 F. Supp. 892 (S.D. Ohio 1970), and its decision was affirmed by the Court of Appeals with one judge dissenting, 440 F.2d 949 (6th Cir. 1971).]

I

The Government relies primarily on its claim, made under § 2036(a)(2), that Byrum retained the right to designate the persons who shall enjoy the income from the transferred property. The argument is a complicated one. By retaining voting control over the corporations whose stock was transferred, Byrum was in a position to select the corporate directors. He could retain this position by not selling the shares he owned and by vetoing any sale by the trustee of the transferred shares. These rights, it is said, gave him control over corporate dividend policy. By increasing, decreasing, or stopping dividends completely, it is argued that Byrum could "regulate the flow of income to the trust" and thereby shift or defer the beneficial enjoyment of trust income between the present beneficiaries and the remaindermen. The sum of this retained power is said to be tantamount to a grantor-trustee's power to accumulate income in the trust, which this Court has recognized constitutes the power to designate the persons who shall enjoy the income from transferred property.

At the outset we observe that this Court has never held that trust property must be included in a settlor's gross estate solely because the settlor retained the power to manage trust assets. On the contrary, since our decision in Reinecke v. Northern Trust Co., 278 U.S. 339 (1929), it has been recognized that a settlor's retention of broad powers of management does not necessarily subject an inter vivos trust to the federal estate tax. Although there was no statutory analogue to § 2036(a)(2) when *Northern Trust* was decided, several lower court decisions decided after the enactment of the predecessor of § 2036(a)(2) have upheld the settlor's right to exercise managerial powers without incurring estate-tax liability. In Estate of King v. Commissioner, 37 T.C. 973 (1962), a settlor reserved the power to direct the trustee in the management and investment of trust assets. The Government argued that the settlor was thereby empowered to cause investments to be made in such a manner as to control significantly the flow of income into the trust. The Tax Court rejected this argument, and held for the taxpayer....

Essentially the power retained by Byrum is the same managerial power retained by the settlors in *Northern Trust* and in *King*. Although neither case controls this one—*Northern Trust*, because it was not decided under § 2036(a)(2) or a predecessor; and *King*, because it is a lower court opinion—the existence of such precedents carries weight. The holding of *Northern Trust*, that the settlor of a trust may retain broad powers of management without adverse estate-tax consequences, may have been relied upon in the drafting of hundreds of inter vivos trusts. The modification of this principle now sought by the Government could have a seriously adverse impact, especially upon settlors (and their estates) who happen to have been "controlling" stockholders of a closely held corporation. Courts properly have been reluctant to depart from an interpretation of tax law which has been generally accepted when the departure could have potentially far-reaching consequences. When a principle of taxation requires reexamination, Congress is better equipped than a court to define precisely the type of conduct which results in tax consequences. When courts readily undertake such tasks, taxpayers may not rely with assurance on what appear to be established rules lest they be subsequently overturned. Legislative enactments, on the other hand, although not always free from ambiguity, at least afford the taxpayers advance warning.

The Government argues, however, that our opinion in United States v. O'Malley, 383 U.S. 627 (1966), compels the inclusion in Byrum's estate of the stock owned by the trust....

In our view, and for the purposes of this case, *O'Malley* adds nothing to the statute itself. The facts in that case were clearly within the ambit of what is now § 2036(a). That section requires that the settlor must have "retained for his life ... (2) the *right* ... to designate the persons who shall possess or enjoy the property or the income therefrom." *O'Malley* was covered precisely by the statute for two reasons: (1) there the settlor had reserved a legal right, set forth in the trust instrument; and (2) this right expressly authorized the settlor, "in conjunction" with others, to accumulate income and thereby "to designate" the persons to enjoy it.

It must be conceded that Byrum reserved no such "right" in the trust instrument or otherwise. The term "right," certainly when used in a tax statute, must be given its normal and customary meaning. It connotes an ascertainable and legally enforceable power, such as that involved in *O'Malley*. Here, the right ascribed to Byrum was the power to use his majority position and influence over the corporate directors to "regulate the flow of dividends" to the trust. That "right" was neither ascertainable nor legally enforceable and hence was not a right in any normal sense of that term.

Byrum did retain the legal right to vote shares held by the trust and to veto investments and reinvestments. But the corporate trustee alone, not Byrum, had the right to pay out or withhold income and thereby to designate who among the beneficiaries enjoyed such income. Whatever power Byrum may have possessed with respect to the flow of income into the trust was derived not from an enforceable legal right specified in the trust instrument, but from the fact that he could elect a majority of the directors of the three corporations. The power to elect the directors conferred no legal right to command them to pay or not to pay dividends. A majority shareholder has a fiduciary duty not to misuse his power by promoting his personal interests at the expense of corporate interests. Moreover, the directors also have a fiduciary duty to promote the interests of the corporation. However great Byrum's influence may have been with the corporate directors, their responsibilities were to all stockholders and were enforceable according to legal standards entirely unrelated to the needs of the trust or to Byrum's desires with respect thereto.

The Government seeks to equate the de facto position of a controlling stockholder with the legally enforceable "right" specified by the statute. Retention of corporate control (through the right to vote the shares) is said to be "tantamount to the power to accumulate income" in the trust which resulted in estate-tax consequences in *O'Malley*. The Government goes on to assert that "[t]hrough exercise of that retained power, [Byrum] could increase or decrease corporate dividends . . . and thereby shift or defer the beneficial enjoyment of trust income." This approach seems to us not only to depart from the specific statutory language, but also to misconceive the realities of corporate life.

There is no reason to suppose that the three corporations controlled by Byrum were other than typical small businesses. The customary vicissitudes of such enterprises—bad years; product obsolescence; new competition; disastrous litigation; new, inhibiting Government regulations; even bankruptcy—prevent any certainty or predictability as to earnings or dividends. There is no assurance that a small corporation will have a flow of net earnings or that income earned will in fact be available for dividends. Thus, Byrum's alleged de facto "power to control the flow of dividends" to the trust was subject to business and economic variables over which he had little or no control.

Even where there are corporate earnings, the legal power to declare dividends is vested solely in the corporate board. In making decisions with respect to dividends, the board must consider a number of factors. It must balance the expectation of stockholders to reasonable dividends when earned against corporate needs for retention of earnings. The first responsibility of the board is to safeguard corporate financial viability for the long term. This means, among other things, the retention of sufficient earnings to assure adequate working capital as well as resources for retirement of debt, for replacement and modernization of plant and equipment, and for growth and expansion. The nature of a corporation's business, as well as the policies and long-range plans of management, are also relevant to dividend payment decisions. Directors of a closely held, small corporation must bear in mind the relatively limited access of such an enterprise to capital markets. This may require a more conservative policy with respect to dividends than would be expected of an established corporation with securities listed on national exchanges.

Nor do small corporations have the flexibility or the opportunity available to national concerns in the utilization of retained earnings. When earnings are substantial, a decision not to pay dividends may result only in the accumulation of surplus rather than growth through internal or external expansion. The accumulated earnings may result in the imposition of a penalty tax.

These various economic considerations are ignored at the directors' peril. Although vested with broad discretion in determining whether, when, and what amount of dividends shall be paid, that discretion is subject to legal restraints. If, in obedience to the will of the majority stockholder, corporate directors disregard the interests of shareholders by accumulating earnings to an unreasonable extent, they are vulnerable to a derivative suit. They are similarly vulnerable if they make an unlawful payment of dividends in the absence of net earnings or available surplus, or if they fail to exercise the requisite degree of care in discharging their duty to act only in the best interest of the corporation and its stockholders.

... We conclude that Byrum did not have an unconstrained de facto power to regulate the flow of dividends to the trust, much less the "right" to designate who was to enjoy the income from trust property. His ability to affect, but not control, trust income, was a qualitatively different power from that of the settlor in *O'Malley*, who had a specific and enforceable right to control the income paid to the beneficiaries. Even had Byrum managed to flood the trust with income, he had no way of compelling the trustee to pay it out rather than accumulate it. Nor could he prevent the trustee from making payments from other trust assets, although admittedly there were few of these at the time of Byrum's death. We cannot assume, however, that no other assets would come into the trust from reinvestments or other gifts.

We find no merit to the Government's contention that Byrum's de facto "control," subject as it was to the economic and legal constraints set forth above, was tantamount to the right to designate the persons who shall enjoy trust income, specified by § 2036(a)(2).

II

The Government asserts an alternative ground for including the shares transferred to the trust within Byrum's gross estate. It argues that by retaining control, Byrum guaranteed himself continued employment and remuneration, as well as the right to determine whether and when the corporations would be liquidated or merged. Byrum is thus said to have retained "the ... enjoyment of ... the property" making it includable within his gross estate under § 2036(a)(1). The Government concedes that the retention of the voting rights of an "unimportant minority interest" would not require inclusion of the transferred shares under § 2036(a)(1). It argues, however, "where the cumulative effect of the retained powers and the rights flowing from the shares not placed in trust leaves the grantor in control of a close corporation, and assures that control for his lifetime, he has retained the 'enjoyment' of the transferred stock." Brief for United States 23.

... The Government points to the retention of two "benefits." The first of these, the power to liquidate or merge, is not a *present* benefit; rather, it is a speculative and contingent benefit which may or may not be realized. Nor is the probability of continued employment and compensation the substantial "enjoyment of ... [the transferred] property" within the meaning of the statute. The dominant stockholder in a closely held corporation, if he is active and productive, is likely to hold a senior position and to enjoy the advantage of a significant voice in his own compensation. These are inevitable facts of the free-enterprise system, but the influence and capability of a controlling stockholder to favor himself are not without constraints. Where there are minority stockholders, as in this case, directors may be held accountable if their employment, compensation, and retention of officers violate their duty to act reasonably in the best interest of the corporation and all of its stockholders. Moreover, this duty is policed, albeit indirectly, by the Internal Revenue Service, which disallows the deduction of unreasonable compensation paid to a corporate executive as a business expense. We conclude that Byrum's retention of voting control was not the retention of the enjoyment of the transferred property within the meaning of the statute.

For the reasons set forth above, we hold that this case was correctly decided by the Court of Appeals and accordingly the judgment is affirmed.

MR. JUSTICE WHITE, with whom MR. JUSTICE BRENNAN and MR. JUSTICE BLACKMUN join, dissenting....

Byrum's lifelong enjoyment of the voting power of the trust contravenes § 2036(a)(2) as well as § 2036(a)(1) because it afforded him control over which trust beneficiaries—the life tenants or the remaindermen—would receive the benefit of the income earned by these shares. He secured this power by making the trust to all intents and purposes exclusively dependent on shares it could not sell in corporations he controlled. Thus, by instructing the directors he elected in the controlled corporations that he thought dividends should or should not be declared Byrum was able to open or close the spigot through which income flowed to the trust's life tenants. When Byrum closed the spigot by deferring dividends of the controlled corporations, thereby perpetuating his own "enjoyment" of these funds, he also in effect transferred income from the life tenants to the remaindermen whose share values were swollen by the retained income....

O'Malley makes the majority's position in this case untenable. *O'Malley* establishes that a settlor serving as a trustee is barred from retaining the power to allocate trust income between a life tenant and a remainderman if he is not constrained by more than general fiduciary requirements. See also Commissioner v. Estate of Holmes, 326 U.S. 480 (1946), and Lober v. United States, 346 U.S. 335 (1953). Now the majority would have us accept the incompatible position that a settlor seeking tax exemption may keep the power of income allocation by rendering the trust dependent on an income flow he controls because the general fiduciary obligations of a director are sufficient to eliminate the power to designate within the meaning of § 2036(a)(2)....

The majority would prop up its untenable position by suggesting that a controlling shareholder is constrained in his distribution or retention of dividends by fear of derivative suits, accumulated earnings taxes, and "various economic considerations ... ignored at the director's peril." I do not deny the existence of such constraints, but their restraining effect on an otherwise tempting gross abuse of the corporate dividend power hardly guts the great power of a controlling director to accelerate or retard, enlarge or diminish, most dividends....

NOTES

1. *Retention of right to vote transferred stock.* In 1976 Congress acted to overrule the *Byrum* result. The anti-*Byrum* rule, as amended in 1978, now appears as § 2036(b). This provision states that for purposes of § 2036(a)(1), a decedent's "retention of the right to vote (directly or indirectly) shares of stock of a controlled corporation shall be considered to be a retention of the enjoyment of transferred property." A "controlled corporation" is defined as a corporation in which, at any time after the transfer and within three years before death, the decedent owned, either actually or constructively, or had the right to vote at least 20 percent of "the total combined voting power of all classes of stock." As in the general operation of § 2036, it is no defense that the decedent possessed the voting rights as trustee or could vote the stock only in conjunction with another person. Section 2036(b) is prospective, applying only to transfers made after June 22, 1976.

Section 2036(b) applies where the decedent retained voting rights "directly or indirectly." For example, if the decedent transferred stock in trust with an understanding or agreement that the trustee would vote stock in accordance with directions from the decedent, the trustee's voting rights may be attributed to the decedent. Rev. Rul. 80–346, 1980–2 C.B. 271. However, a decedent is not treated as having retained the right to vote stock transferred in trust "merely because a relative was the trustee who voted the stock." S. Rep. No. 745, 95th Cong., 2d Sess. 90 (1978). Suppose that *D* owns all of the voting and nonvoting stock of a corporation. *D* transfers the nonvoting stock to an irrevocable trust, retaining no interests or powers, and retains control of the corporation through ownership of the voting stock until death. Are the nonvoting shares includible in *D*'s gross estate under § 2036? See Rev. Rul. 81–15, 1981–1 C.B. 457 (no; decedent had no right to vote the transferred stock).

2. *Family limited partnerships.* Although § 2036 now reaches transfers like the one in *Byrum*, where the decedent retained voting rights in stock of a closely held corporation, the rationale of *Byrum* remains relevant in situations not governed by § 2036(b). Note that by its terms § 2036(b) applies to transfers of stock in a controlled corporation; it has no application to transfers of interests in a partnership. Does it follow that wealth can be passed from

parent to child free of estate tax through transfers of interests in a family limited partnership, even if the parent retains control of the partnership until death?

Suppose that a parent and child form a family limited partnership with the parent as a 99–percent limited partner and the child (or an entity owned by the child) as a 1–percent general partner; parent and child each contribute assets in proportion to their respective interests in the partnership. Although the parent has exchanged assets for a limited partnership interest of substantially less value, due to lack of marketability and lack of control, the courts have held that the formation of the partnership does not give rise to a taxable gift, as long as capital accounts are properly maintained and no capital is shifted from one partner to the other. See the cases cited supra at page 136, Note 3. Does this holding rest on the notion that there is no completed gift because the parent has not fully relinquished dominion and control of the contributed assets, or, alternatively, on a finding that the parent received full consideration in money's worth for the contributed assets? The distinction may be significant in determining the estate tax consequences for the parent who still holds a limited partnership interest at death. If the parent retained sufficient dominion or control to prevent a completed gift upon formation of the partnership, the same interests or powers, if held at death, presumably would justify drawing 99 percent of the partnership assets back into the parent's gross estate under § 2036. In contrast, if the parent's limited partnership interest constituted full consideration for the contributed assets, the transfer presumably would come within the bona fide sale exception to § 2036, leaving only the value of the limited partnership interest (discounted for lack of marketability and lack of control) to be included in the gross estate under § 2033.

In several cases the Internal Revenue Service has successfully invoked § 2036 based on the decedent's retained enjoyment of assets contributed to a family limited partnership. For example, in Thompson's Estate v. Commissioner, 382 F.3d 367 (3d Cir. 2004), the decedent at age 95 formed limited partnerships with his two children. The decedent contributed the bulk of his assets, consisting mostly of marketable securities, in exchange for limited partnership interests, and did not retain sufficient assets to support himself for his actuarial life expectancy. Indeed, the partnerships made cash distributions as needed during the decedent's life to meet his personal expenses (including the funding of gifts to family members) and after his death to pay bequests and estate taxes. In light of the "general testamentary character" of the arrangement, the court inferred that the decedent had retained enjoyment of the transferred assets pursuant to an implied agreement. The court also found that "there was no transfer for consideration within the meaning of § 2036(a)," and concluded that the transfers did not come within the bona fide sale exception because neither partnership conducted any "legitimate business operations" or provided any "nontax benefit." See also Harper's Estate v. Commissioner, 83 T.C.M. (CCH) 1641 (2002) ("Without any change whatsoever in the underlying pool of assets or prospect for profit ... there exists nothing but a circuitous 'recycling' of value."); Reichardt's Estate v. Commissioner, 114 T.C. 144 (2000) (decedent retained exclusive control over management of assets as well as timing and amount of distributions; "nothing changed . . . except legal title" after decedent's transfer of residence and other assets to partnership); Korby's Estate v. Commissioner, 471 F.3d 848 (8th Cir. 2006); Abraham's Estate v. Commissioner, 408 F.3d 26 (1st Cir. 2005), cert. denied, 547 U.S. 1178 (2006). Note that these cases were decided on the basis of the decedent's retained enjoyment under § 2036(a)(1). If the decedent was a general partner, could the same result be reached on the basis of a retained power to control beneficial enjoyment under § 2036(a)(2), or does the rationale of *Byrum* suggest that the decedent's powers were sufficiently constrained by fiduciary duties and practical business exigencies to block the application of that provision? See Strangi's Estate v. Commissioner, 85 T.C.M. (CCH) 1331 (2003), affd. on another issue, 417 F.3d 468 (5th Cir. 2005) (decedent's rights were "of a different nature" and "not accompanied by comparable constraints"; *Byrum* distinguished).

In other cases courts have refused to apply § 2036 on the ground that the decedent's contribution of assets to the partnership came within the bona fide sale exception. In Kimbell v. United States, 371 F.3d 257 (5th Cir. 2004), the court found that the family partnership transaction was "not a disguised gift or sham transaction," noting that the decedent retained sufficient assets for her own support and did not commingle partnership assets with her own assets; that the requisite formalities were satisfied in creating the partnership; that the assets contributed to the partnership included working interests in oil and gas properties that required active management; and that the formation of the partnership rested in part on "non-tax business reasons" relating to management and asset protection. The court concluded that the transfer to the partnership was a bona fide sale for adequate and full consideration which removed the partnership assets from the decedent's gross estate. The court dismissed the notion that a contribution of assets in exchange for a discounted pro rata partnership interest precluded a finding of adequate consideration:

> The business decision to exchange cash or other assets for a transfer-restricted, non-managerial interest in a limited partnership involves financial considerations other than the purchaser's ability to turn right around and sell the newly acquired limited partnership interest for 100 cents on the dollar. Investors who acquire such interests do so with the expectation of realizing benefits such as management expertise, security and preservation of assets, capital appreciation and avoidance of personal liability. Thus there is nothing inconsistent in acknowledging, on the one hand, that the investor's dollars have acquired a limited partnership interest at arm's length for adequate and full consideration and, on the other hand, that the asset thus acquired has a present fair market value, i.e., immediate sale potential, of substantially less than the dollars just paid—a classic informed trade-off. [371 F.3d at 266.]

See also Stone's Estate v. Commissioner, 86 T.C.M. (CCH) 551 (2003) (decedent's receipt of discounted pro rata partnership interest constituted full consideration for contributed assets, despite difference in value; contrary argument "reads out of § 2036(a)" the bona fide sale exception). In *Kimbell*, did the decedent receive property of equivalent value in exchange for the assets she contributed to the partnership? Did the "financial considerations" mentioned by the court supply the necessary consideration "in money or money's worth" to make up the difference in value between the transferred assets and the limited partnership interest received in exchange? Or does the court's explanation suggest that the exchange was an ordinary business transaction (Reg. § 25.2512–8), making it unnecessary to account for the difference in value? For further discussion, see Hellwig, On Discounted Partnership Interests and Adequate Consideration, 28 Va. Tax Rev. 531 (2009).

What factors should be considered in determining whether a partnership contribution comes within the bona fide sale exception of § 2036? In Bongard's Estate v. Commissioner, 124 T.C. 95 (2005), the Tax Court articulated the following test:

> In the context of family limited partnerships, the bona fide sale for adequate and full consideration exception is met where the record establishes the existence of a legitimate and significant nontax reason for creating the family limited partnership, and the transferors received partnership interests proportionate to the value of the property transferred. ... The objective evidence must indicate that the nontax reason was a significant factor that motivated the partnership's creation. ... A significant purpose must be an actual motivation, not a theoretical justification. [124 T.C. at 118.]

The requirement of a "legitimate and significant nontax reason" has been variously interpreted by the courts. Is it necessary that the partnership actively carry on business operations or manage a pool of investments? See Bigelow's Estate v. Commissioner, 503 F.3d 955 (9th Cir. 2007) (transfer lacked "business purpose"; court refused to credit purported purposes of asset protection and consolidated ownership and management); Rector's Estate v. Commissioner, 94 T.C.M. (CCH) 567 (2007) (partnership entailed "no change in the underlying pool of assets or the likelihood of profit" and was "more consistent with an estate plan than an investment in a legitimate business"). Is it sufficient that the partnership was formed to promote the partners' financial and estate planning goals? Compare Mirowski's Estate v. Commissioner, 95 T.C.M. (CCH) 1277 (2008) (joint management and pooling of investments and providing for descendants held legitimate and significant nontax purposes), with Erickson's Estate v. Commissioner, 93 T.C.M. (CCH) 1175 (2007) (partnership was "a mere collection of mostly passive assets intended to assist [decedent's] tax planning and benefit the family"; no significant nontax purpose where partnership was "just a vehicle for changing the form of the investment in the assets, a mere asset container"). In a few decisions the perpetuation of a decedent's idiosyncratic "investment philosophy" has been held sufficient. Schutt's Estate v. Commissioner, 89 T.C.M. (CCH) 1353 (2005) ("buy and hold" philosophy); Black's Estate v. Commissioner, 133 T.C. 340 (2009) (same, coupled with protection from improvident grandchildren and potential creditors); Miller's Estate v. Commissioner, 97 T.C.M. (CCH) 1602 (2009) (active trading strategy based on charting stocks).

3. *Private trust companies.* In *Byrum*, the decedent reserved the right to remove the original corporate trustee and replace it with another corporate trustee. Suppose that before his death Mr. Byrum exercised that power and named as successor trustee a private trust company of which he was the

founder and sole shareholder. Suppose further that the trustee held discretionary powers over trust income which, if held directly by Mr. Byrum, would cause the trust property to be included in his gross estate under § 2036(a)(2). Should those powers be attributed to Mr. Byrum by virtue of his position as the trust company's sole shareholder? Should the result depend on whether the trustee's powers were lodged in a special committee that did not include Mr. Byrum as a member? On whether Mr. Byrum, in his capacity as sole shareholder of the trust company, had the right to appoint its directors and officers or to hire and fire its employees? On whether Mr. Byrum was the trust company's sole shareholder or merely a controlling shareholder? See Notice 2008–63, 2008–2 C.B. 261 (proposed guidelines allowing use of private trust company to achieve results "not more restrictive" nor more lenient than those that could be achieved by a taxpayer directly). Cf. Rev. Rul. 95–58, 1995–2 C.B. 191, supra page 261, Note 3, confirming that a decedent's retained power to remove a trustee and appoint a successor trustee who is "not related or subordinate to the decedent" will not cause the trustee's powers to be attributed to the decedent.

4. *References.* For discussions of the estate tax treatment of retained interests and powers in light of the *Byrum* decision, see Pedrick, Grantor Powers and the Estate Tax: End of an Era?, 71 Nw. L. Rev. 704 (1977); Dodge, Retentions, Receipts, Transfers, and Accumulations of Income and Income Rights: Ruminations on the Post–*Byrum* Role of Sections 2036, 2037, 2039, and 2043(a), 58 Tex. L. Rev. 1 (1979); Hellwig, Revisiting *Byrum*, 23 Va. Tax Rev. 275 (2003).

FARREL'S ESTATE v. UNITED STATES

553 F.2d 637 (Ct. Cl. 1977).

DAVIS, JUDGE.

The stipulated facts in this tax refund suit thrust upon us a narrow but knotty issue of estate tax law under Section 2036(a)(2) of the Internal Revenue Code of 1954. In 1961 Marian B. Farrel established an irrevocable trust with a corpus of various securities and her grandchildren as beneficiaries. Two individuals were named as trustees. They were given discretionary power to pay or apply all or part of the net income or principal to or for the benefit of any one or more of the beneficiaries (and their issue). The instrument also provided for a "time of division" when the corpus was to be divided into various portions, each of which (according to specified circumstances) was either to be paid over immediately to a specified beneficiary, or held in a new trust with the trustees having discretionary power to make payments to or for the benefit of specified beneficiaries until a later time when required payments were to be made. No provision was made in the trust for any distribution to Mrs. Farrel in any circumstances.

The trust called for two trustees at all times, and provided for Mrs. Farrel to appoint a successor trustee if a vacancy occurred in that position through death, resignation or removal by a proper court for cause. However, neither the instrument nor Connecticut law (which governed the trust) permitted Mrs. Farrel to remove a trustee and thereby create a vacancy. The trust was silent as to whether Mrs. Farrel could appoint herself as a successor trustee in the event of a vacancy, but neither the trust instrument nor Connecticut law would have prevented her from doing so.

Two vacancies occurred in the office of trustee during Mrs. Farrel's life. In 1964 a named trustee died and Mrs. Farrel appointed a third person as successor trustee. In 1965 that successor trustee resigned and Mrs. Farrel, as settlor, appointed another individual to succeed him.

Mrs. Farrel died in October 1969. Her estate, plaintiff here, filed in 1971 a federal estate tax return which did not include the trust property in the gross estate, and paid the tax shown on the return.[27] In 1973 the Internal Revenue Service assessed a deficiency on the ground that the trust property should have been included in the gross estate under Section 2036(a)(2) of the 1954 Code. Plaintiff paid the deficiency, filed a timely refund claim, and after the appropriate waiting period instituted the present refund suit.

Both parties agree that (a) the trustees had "the right, either alone or in conjunction with any person, to designate the persons who shall possess or enjoy the property or the income therefrom" within the meaning of Section 2036(a)(2); (b) Mrs. Farrel, the decedent-settlor, could lawfully designate herself (under the trust and Connecticut law) as successor trustee if a vacancy occurred during her life; (c) the occurrence of a vacancy in the office of trustee was a condition which Mrs. Farrel could not create and which was beyond her control; and (d) Mrs. Farrel had the opportunity, before her 1969 death, to appoint a successor trustee only during the two periods in 1964 and 1965 mentioned above. The legal conflict is whether the right of the trustees (as to who should enjoy or possess the property or income) should in these circumstances be attributed to the decedent under Section 2036(a) for any of the three periods designated in that statutory provision—her life; any period not ascertainable without reference to her death; any period which does not in fact end before her death. The Government's answer is yes and the plaintiff of course says no.

Only Section 2036(a) is now before us but, since taxpayer's presentation emphasizes a comparison of that provision with Section 2038 (a cognate but separate part of the estate tax), it is important to set out, at the beginning, the relevant aspects of the latter.... Plaintiff's primary point is that (i) it is now and has long been settled that Section 2038 does not cover a power or right subject to a conditional event which has not occurred prior to and does not exist at the decedent's death, such as a discretionary power to distribute income or principal under specified conditions which have not occurred before the death, and (ii) the same rule has been and is applicable to Section 2036(a).

---

27. Mrs. Farrel and her husband reported the transfers to the trust as a gift in 1961 and paid the federal gift taxes.

There is no question that taxpayer is correct as to the construction of Section 2038. That slant was given by the courts to the provision's predecessor under the 1939 Code (see Jennings v. Smith, 161 F.2d 74, 77–78 (2d Cir. 1947); Estate of Want v. Commissioner, 29 T.C. 1223 (1958), revd. on other grounds, 280 F.2d 777 (2d Cir. 1960); Estate of Kasch v. Commissioner, 30 T.C. 102 (1958)), and the Treasury has itself adopted the same interpretation for the 1954 Code as well. Treasury Regulations on Estate Tax (1954 Code), Section 20.2038–1(a) and (b); see also Rev. Rul. 55–393, 1955–1 Cum. Bull. 448.

The initial and fundamental question we have to face is whether this settled understanding of Section 2038 necessarily governs Section 2036(a), as it now stands. We think not for two reasons which we shall consider in turn: first, that the critical points-of-view of the two provisions differ, and, second, that the regulations governing the two sections take diametrically opposed positions on the narrow issue of contingent rights and powers of the kind involved here.

The two separate provisions appear to diverge sharply in their perspective—the point from which the pertinent powers and rights are to be seen. Section 2038(a) looks at the problem from the decedent's death—what he can and cannot do at that specific moment. Excluded are contingent rights and powers (beyond the decedent's control) which are not exercisable at that moment because the designated contingency does not exist at that time. Section 2036(a), on the other hand, looks forward from the time the decedent made the transfer to see whether he has retained any of the specified rights "for his life or for any period not ascertainable without reference to his death or for any period which does not in fact end before his death." This language makes the transferor's death one pole of the specified time-span but the whole of the time-span is also significant. Because of the statute's reference to the time-span, differences of interpretation are quite conceivable. It is possible for instance, to hold the words to mean that the retained right has to exist at all times throughout one of the periods, but it is also possible to see the language as covering contingencies which could realistically occur at some separate point or points during the designated periods—always including the moment of decedent's death. We take it (from the argument's insistence on the parallel to 2038) that the taxpayer would not stand on the former ("at all times") interpretation if a vacancy in the trusteeship existed and had not been filled at Mrs. Farrel's death. But under the language of 2036(a) there is no compelling reason why the moment of death has to be exclusively important. Unlike Section 2038, this provision seems to look forward from the time of transfer to the date of the transferor's death, and can be said to concentrate on the significant rights with respect to the transferred property the transferor retains, not at every moment during that period, but whenever the specified contingency happens to arise during that period (so long as the contingency can still occur at the end of the period).

There is nothing unreasonable about this latter construction, which accords with Congress' over-all purpose to gather into the estate tax all transfers which remain significantly incomplete—on which the transferor still holds a string—during his lifetime. It is hard to believe, for instance that, whatever may be true of 2038, 2036(a) would have to be seen as failing to cover a trust where the trustee, with discretionary powers, could be removed by the settlor, and the settlor substituted as trustee, whenever economic conditions fell below a stated level (e.g., a designated level on a certain stock exchange index or a level of earnings of the trust) even though fortuitously that condition did not happen to exist at the time of death. In a case like that, the lifetime link between the decedent and the trust property (and income) would be so strong as plainly to measure up to both the letter and the spirit of 2036(a) if the Treasury chose to see it that way. This case, though perhaps less clear, falls into the same class of a continuing substantial tie.

The other element which leads us to reject plaintiff's attempt to equate 2036(a) with 2038, for this case, is that the Treasury has affirmatively chosen to separate the two sections—there is a Treasury regulation under the former § 20.2036–1 which, to our mind, clearly covers this decedent's situation (in contrast to the regulation under 2038 which excludes it). Taxpayer urges us to read the regulation otherwise, and if we cannot to hold it invalid.

The regulation says flatly ... that it is immaterial "(iii) whether the exercise of the power was subject to a contingency beyond the decedent's control which did not occur before his death (e.g., the death of another person during the decedent's lifetime)." This would seem on its surface to blanket this decedent's position under her trust, but plaintiff would read it very literally and narrowly to apply only where the contingency relates to the "exercise" of an already existing power, and conversely, to be inapplicable where the power only springs into existence when a trustee vacancy occurs. Similarly, taxpayer sees in the broad sweep of the last sentence of § 20.2036–1(b)(3) ... the implied negative pregnant that a restricted power in the decedent to appoint herself a substitute trustee only in the event of a vacancy lies outside 2036(a). We cannot accept these strained (if not casuistic) analyses of the regulation because they go directly counter to its apparent purpose to cover just such contingencies as we have here. If proof of that objective is needed it is fully supplied by the companion regulation under 2038 (Treasury Regulation on Estate Tax (1954 Code), § 20.2038–l(b)) which declares in coordinate terms that "section 2038 is not applicable to a power the exercise of which was subject to a contingency beyond the decedent's control which did not occur before his death (e.g., the death of another person during the decedent's life). *See, however, Section 2036(a)(2) for the inclusion of property in the decedent's gross estate on account of such a power*" (emphasis added).

We are required, then, to consider whether § 20.2036–1(b)(3) should be overturned as invalid. Recognizing the deference due Treasury Regulations (Commissioner v. South Texas Lumber Co., 333 U.S. 496, 501

(1948); Bingler v. Johnson, 394 U.S. 741, 749–751 (1969)), we cannot take that step. We have pointed out that 2036 is not the same as 2038 in its wording or in the viewpoint from which it appraises the decedent's link to the transferred property. We have also said that it is not unreasonable to regard 2036(a), in the way the Treasury does, as a blanket overall sweeping-in of property over which the decedent still has at death some significant, though contingent, power to choose those who shall have possession or enjoyment.

To this, plaintiff's ultimate response is double-barreled: (i) the regulation was not contemporaneous with the adoption of the predecessor of 2036 but came years later, and (ii) for taxable years before the regulation was adopted courts applied the same rule to the predecessors of 2036 as they have to 2038 and its predecessors. Both points may be technically correct. The relevant regulation was promulgated in 1958 many years after the first predecessor of 2036 was enacted. And in 1947 Jennings v. Smith, supra, seemed to use, as an alternative holding, the same rule for the forerunner of 2036 that it applied to the predecessor of 2038. To the same effect was Estate of Kasch v. Commissioner, supra (1958) (predecessor section). Nevertheless the Treasury was not foreclosed, in our view, from taking the position it did in 1958. As we have stressed, neither the text nor the purpose of 2036 demands that it be treated the same as 2038. The judicial observations lumping the two predecessor provisions responded to Government arguments treating the two sections as fully parallel on this point. Moreover, Jennings v. Smith was the only appellate decision on the point which was outstanding when the 1958 regulations were promulgated, and its statement was, at best, a rather summary alternative holding, not truly necessary to the ultimate decision. Thus, the judicial interpretation of Section 2036's predecessor was neither so strong nor so encrusted that Congress may be thought to have embodied it in Section 2036 when it adopted the 1954 Code. On the contrary, we think the Treasury was free to take a new look under that new Code as it evidently did. In sum, the current regulation under 2036 is a reasonable reading of the text and objective of the statute and the previous contrary judicial interpretation was not such that the Treasury was forced to bow to it despite the prima facie acceptability of the administrative stance.

We end by noting that the contingent right of Mrs. Farrel to make herself a trustee in the event of a vacancy—unlike the de facto "powers" involved in United States v. Byrum, 408 U.S. 125 (1972) and in Estate of Tully v. United States, [528 F.2d 1401 (Ct. Cl. 1976)]—was a legally enforceable right, in effect imbedded in the trust instrument, which bore directly on the designation of the persons to possess or enjoy the trust property or income. That the exercise of this right was foreseeable when the trust was created—that it was a real right, neither insignificant nor illusory—is shown by the fact that Mrs. Farrel had two opportunities to exercise it in eight years and, if she had lived, may well have had more....

For these reasons we hold that plaintiff is not entitled to recover and the petition is dismissed.

[Concurring opinion omitted.]

NOTES

1. *Overlap between §§ 2036 and 2038.* Has § 2036(a)(2) completely swallowed up § 2038, or is it possible for the transferor to retain a power to alter, amend, or modify (taxable under § 2038) that will not also constitute a power under § 2036(a)(2) to designate the persons who will enjoy the property or its income? Assuming transfers after March 3, 1931, could *Porter* (supra page 239), *Holmes* (supra page 240), *City Bank Farmers Trust Co.* (supra page 258), and *Lober* (supra page 241) all have been decided in the government's favor under § 2036(a)(2)? What argument can be made that § 2038 and not § 2036(a)(2) applies to tax a trust on decedent's death that directs the income to be paid to *A* for the settlor's life, remainder to *B* and *C* equally unless the settlor provides otherwise by will? Section 2036(a)(2) covers the right to designate "who shall possess or enjoy the property or the income therefrom," but the regulations emphasize that the section is concerned with control over the income or use of the property. See Reg. § 20.2036–1(b)(3) ("The phrase, however, does not include a power over the transferred property itself which does not affect the enjoyment of the income received or earned during the decedent's life.").

When a transfer is subject to both provisions, the amount includible in the decedent's gross estate is frequently but not necessarily the same. If there is a difference, which section can be expected to produce the larger tax? Recall that § 2036 authorizes inclusion of the entire corpus of a trust if the settlor retained control over its income, whereas § 2038 taxes only those parts of the trust that are subject to the settlor's power to alter, amend, revoke, or terminate.

The *Farrel* opinion makes the point that the two sections diverge in their perspective—§ 2038 looks at the problem from the decedent's death, whereas § 2036 "looks forward from the time the decedent made the transfer to see whether he has retained any of the specified rights" (supra page 324). The court then holds that only § 2036 applies to a trust in which the decedent retained a power to designate beneficial enjoyment contingent on an event that had not occurred at decedent's death; § 2038 does not apply because the power was not exercisable at the time of death. Does the court's reasoning support an assertion that § 2036 will tax any trust which is taxable under § 2038 if the settlor has powers over the trust income (except one created before March 3, 1931)? Consider the case in which the settlor creates a family trust giving the trustee discretionary powers over income and principal. Settlor is not named as trustee and does not have the power to nominate successor trustees. A vacancy develops, and the court appoints the settlor as successor trustee. At settlor's death, are §§ 2036(a) and 2038 equally applicable to this trust? See Rev. Rul. 70–348, 1970–2 C.B. 193 (custodianship property).

2. *Estate tax apportionment.* Where property is included in the gross estate under § 2036 due to a retained interest or power, § 2207B gives the executor a right to recover the resulting federal estate tax from the recipient, unless the decedent's will (or revocable trust) directs otherwise. This provision is intended to prevent the incremental tax burden generated by the included property from being inadvertently shifted to the recipients of the decedent's probate assets. See infra page 638. There is no corresponding provision for property included under § 2038.

D. TRANSFERS TAKING EFFECT AT DEATH: § 2037

Scope of § 2037. Section 2037, dealing with transfers taking effect at death, is a 1954 revision of a provision that came into the statute in 1949. From 1916 to 1949, transfers of the type now reached by § 2037 were included in the gross estate only to the extent that they came within the general provision covering transfers "intended to take effect in possession or enjoyment at or after [the decedent's] death." See supra page 268.

The operation of § 2037 can be illustrated by a simple example. Assume that *H* creates an irrevocable inter vivos trust to pay income to his wife *W* for life, with corpus payable at her death to *H* if he survives her, otherwise to their child *C* (or *C*'s estate). The requirement of § 2037(a)(1) is satisfied because *C* can obtain possession or enjoyment of the property only by surviving *H*, the transferor. Whether § 2037(a)(2) is satisfied depends on whether immediately before *H*'s death the actuarial value of his reversionary interest exceeds 5 percent of the value of the property.

If at the time of *H*'s death *H* and *W* are both age 40, the value of *H*'s reversionary interest, determined immediately before his death under the Treasury tables (and assuming a 6–percent annual rate of return), is about 7.10 percent of the value of the trust property.[28] Put another way, the present value of $1.00, payable at the death of a 40–year–old to another person of the same age in the event the latter survives, is $0.0710. Because *H*'s reversionary interest is worth more than 5 percent of the corpus, § 2037 requires that the trust corpus, reduced by the value of *W*'s outstanding income interest, be included in *H*'s gross estate.

In contrast, if at the time of *H*'s death *H* and *W* are both only age 30, the value of *H*'s reversionary interest (still assuming a 6–percent annual rate of return) is less than 5 percent of the value of the corpus.[29] Because

28. Assuming a 6–percent annual rate of return, a remainder payable at the death of a 40–year–old is worth 14.201 percent of the value of the property. Reg. § 20.2031–7T(d)(7) (Table S). Since a person has an even chance of surviving another person of the same age, the value of *H*'s reversionary interest is one-half of 14.201 percent, or 7.10 percent. If *H* and *W* are of different ages, calculating the probability of *H*'s survival becomes more complicated. In the case of an actual decedent, special actuarial factors can be obtained from the Internal Revenue Service at the executor's request. Reg. § 20.2031–7(d)(4).

29. Assuming a 6–percent annual rate of return, a remainder payable at the death of a 30–year–old is worth 8.820 percent of the value of the property. Reg. § 20.2031–7T(d)(7) (Table S).

H's reversionary interest is worth less than 5 percent of the corpus, the trust corpus is not includible under § 2037. Is *H*'s reversionary interest nevertheless includible under § 2033?

The language of § 2037 is relatively straightforward, presenting no more than its fair share of minor difficulties. But why *are* these the tests for including transfers taking effect at death? A study of the evolution of § 2037 from the primitive postponed-possession-or-enjoyment clause (§ 811(c) of the 1939 Code) will aid in answering these questions; otherwise, § 2037 is like a military order sent from headquarters to a distant unit that must act on it in ignorance of its setting or purpose. At the same time, the taxation of transfers taking effect at death has had so tortuous a history that abbreviation is essential. What follows is only a summary. For a comprehensive history of the period from 1916 to 1945, see Eisenstein, Estate Taxes and the Higher Learning of the Supreme Court, 3 Tax L. Rev. 395, 421–502 (1948); for later developments, see Bittker, The *Church* and *Spiegel* Cases: Section 811(c) Gets a New Lease on Life, 58 Yale L.J. 825 (1949); Bittker, *Church* and *Spiegel*: The Legislative Sequel, 59 Yale L.J. 395 (1950).

The decedent's life as a measuring stick. By accident or otherwise, the first three cases in this area to reach the Supreme Court arrived in an order inversely related to the strength of the government's position.

In Shukert v. Allen, 273 U.S. 545 (1927), a settlor transferred property in trust to accumulate the income for 30 years and then to distribute the corpus and accumulated income to his children or their issue. Upon the settlor's death shortly after creating the trust, the government asserted that the trust property was includible in his estate. Because the term of the trust exceeded the settlor's life expectancy (about 16 years) when the transfer was made, the government argued that the transfer was "intended to take effect in possession or enjoyment at or after his death." The Supreme Court held to the contrary, but the ground of its decision was not altogether clear:

> The transfer was immediate and out and out, leaving no interest remaining in the testator. The trust in its terms has no reference to his death but is the same and unaffected whether he lives or dies.... It seems plain from the little evidence that was put in that the testator was not acting in contemplation of death as a motive for his act, or otherwise, except in the sense that he was creating a fund intended to secure his children from want in their old age, whoever might dissipate the considerable property that he retained and left at his death; and that being fifty-six years old, if he thought about it, he would have contemplated the possibility or probability of his being dead before the emergency might arise. Of course it was not argued that every vested interest that manifestly would take effect in actual enjoyment after the grantor's death was within the statute. There

---

Since a person has an even chance of surviving another person of the same age, the value of *H*'s reversionary interest is one-half of 8.820 percent, or 4.410 percent.

> certainly is no transfer taking effect after his death to be taxed under [the postponed-possession-or-enjoyment clause].
>
> It is not necessary to consider whether the petitioner goes too far in contending that [this clause] should be construed to refer only to transfers of property the possession or enjoyment of which does not pass from the grantor until his death. But it seems to us tolerably plain, that when the grantor parts with all his interest in the property to other persons in trust, with no thought of avoiding taxes, the fact that the income vested in the beneficiaries was to be accumulated for them instead of being handed to them to spend, does not make the trust one intended to take effect in possession or enjoyment at or after the grantor's death. [273 U.S. at 547–48.]

Believing that it might have lost Shukert v. Allen because the term of the trust (30 years) was not expressly linked to the settlor's death, the government soon sought review of a case involving trusts whose duration was dependent on the settlor's death. In Reinecke v. Northern Trust Co., 278 U.S. 339 (1929), the decedent had created five trusts, four of which were to end five years after his death or on the death of the life tenants, whichever occurred earlier. The fifth trust was to terminate five years after his death or on the death of the life tenant, whichever occurred later. The Court held that these five trusts were not reached by the postponed-possession-or-enjoyment clause:

> But the question much pressed upon us remains, whether, the donor having parted both with the possession and his entire beneficial interest in the property when the trust was created, the mere passing of possession or enjoyment of the trust fund from the life tenants to the remaindermen after the testator's death, as directed, and after the enactment of the statute, is included within its taxing provisions. That question, not necessarily involved, was left unanswered in Shukert v. Allen, 273 U.S. 545. There the gift of a remainder interest, having been made without reference to the donor's death, although it did in fact vest in possession and enjoyment after his death, was held not to be a transfer intended to take effect in possession or enjoyment at or after the donor's death, and for that reason not to be subject to the tax. But here the gift was intended to so take effect, although the transfer which effected it preceded the death of the settlor and was itself not subject to the tax unless made so by the circumstances that the possession or enjoyment passed as indicated.
>
> In its plan and scope the tax is one imposed on transfers at death or made in contemplation of death and is measured by the value at death of the interest which is transferred.... It is not a gift tax, and the tax on gifts once imposed by the Revenue Act of 1924 ... has been repealed.... One may freely give his property to another by absolute gift without subjecting himself or his estate to a tax, but we are asked to say that this statute means that he may not make a gift inter vivos, equally absolute and complete, without subjecting it to a

tax if the gift takes the form of a life estate in one with remainder over to another at or after the donor's death. It would require plain and compelling language to justify so incongruous a result and we think it is wanting in the present statute.

It is of significance, although not conclusive, that the [tax is imposed] on the net estate of decedents, and that the miscellaneous items of property required ... to be brought into the gross estate for the purpose of computing the tax, unless the present remainders be an exception, are either property transferred in contemplation of death or property passing out of the control, possession or enjoyment of the decedent at his death. They are property held by the decedent in joint tenancy or by the entirety, property of another subject to the decedent's power of appointment, and insurance policies effected by the decedent on his own life, payable to his estate or to others at his death. The ... sections, read together, indicate no purpose to tax completed gifts made by the donor in his lifetime not in contemplation of death, where he has retained no such control, possession or enjoyment. In the light of the general purpose of the statute and the language ... explicitly imposing the tax on net estates of decedents, we think it at least doubtful whether the trusts or interests in a trust intended to be reached by the phrase ... "to take effect in possession or enjoyment at or after his death," include any others than those passing from the possession, enjoyment or control of the donor at his death and so taxable as transfers at death.... That doubt must be resolved in favor of the taxpayer.... Doubts of the constitutionality of the statute, if construed as contended by the government, would require us to adopt the construction, at least reasonably possible here, which would uphold the act. [278 U.S. at 347–49.]

After Reinecke v. Northern Trust Co. was decided, the government gave up the effort to tax transfers merely because they were contingent on the transferor's death—where his life was only a measuring stick, as it were. Nor did the Treasury ask Congress to change the law, possibly because of the constitutional doubts voiced in the last sentence quoted above. Not until 1949, as will be seen, was this type of transfer again threatened by the estate tax.

In the meantime, the government sought to make the most of the statements in Shukert v. Allen and Reinecke v. Northern Trust Co. that the proper province of the postponed-possession-or-enjoyment clause was a transfer under which possession or enjoyment passes "from" the transferor at his death. One branch of the Treasury's attack was on transfers with reservation of income; this attack was routed in 1931 by May v. Heiner, described supra page 270, and Congress had to come to the aid of the Treasury by enacting what is now § 2036(a). The other type of transfer which the Treasury sought to tax after Reinecke v. Northern Trust Co. was a trust under which the transferor retained a reversionary interest, as described at the beginning of this section. If such a transfer was not reached by the postponed-possession-or-enjoyment clause, the Treasury might have reasoned, what *was* that clause's function?

The early "reversionary interest" cases. In seeking to apply the postponed-possession-or-enjoyment clause to transfers with reversionary interests, the Treasury seemed at long last to be on the right track. In Klein v. United States, 283 U.S. 231 (1931), the Supreme Court unanimously held for the government with respect to such a transfer. The settlor had created a trust to pay the income to his wife for her life. At her death, the property was to revert to the settlor if living; but if he predeceased her, she was to get the property in fee simple. He died before his wife, and the court held that the property was includible in his estate:

> Nothing is to be gained by multiplying words in respect of the various niceties of the art of conveyancing or the law of contingent and vested remainders. It is perfectly plain that the death of the grantor was the indispensable and intended event which brought the larger estate [i.e., fee simple ownership] into being for the grantee and effected its transmission from the dead to the living, thus satisfying the terms of the taxing act and justifying the tax imposed. [283 U.S. at 234.]

But only four years later, the "niceties of the art of conveyancing" turned out to be more durable, and profitable, than was thought. The Supreme Court was asked to review two cases, each involving a trust to pay the income to a child of the settlor for the child's life. In one, Helvering v. St. Louis Union Trust Co., 296 U.S. 39 (1935), there were gifts over on the child's death, but if the child predeceased the settlor, the trust was to terminate and the property was to revert to the settlor. The settlor predeceased the life income beneficiary. The Supreme Court, in a five-to-four decision, held that the property was not includible:

> The grantor here, by the trust instrument, left in himself no power to resume ownership, possession or enjoyment except upon a contingency in the nature of a condition subsequent, the occurrence of which was entirely fortuitous so far as any control, design or volition on his part was concerned. After the execution of the trust he held no right in the trust estate which in any sense was the subject of testamentary disposition. His death passed no interest to any of the beneficiaries of the trust, and enlarged none beyond what was conveyed by the indenture. His death simply put an end to what, at best, was a mere possibility of a reverter by extinguishing it—that is to say, by converting what was merely possible into an utter impossibility. [296 U.S. at 43.][30]

The *Klein* case was distinguished on the ground that:

> only a life estate was vested, the remainder being retained by the grantor; and whether that should ever become vested in the grantee depended upon the condition precedent that the grantor die during the life of the grantee. The grantor having died first, his death clearly

30. The other case, Becker v. St. Louis Union Trust Co., 296 U.S. 48 (1935), involved a similar trust and was decided in the same way.—EDS.

effected a transmission of the larger estate to the grantee. But here the grantor parted with the title and all beneficial interest in the property, retaining no right with respect to it which would pass to any one as a result of his death. Unlike the *Klein* case, where the death was the generating source of the title, here, as the court below said, the trust instrument and not the death was the generating source. The death did not transmit the possibility, but destroyed it. [296 U.S. at 45–46.]

Helvering v. Hallock: the end of verbal niceties? There was, clearly enough, only a verbal distinction between the taxable *Klein* reversionary interests (retained by the settlor subject to divestment if he predeceased the beneficiary) and the nontaxable *St. Louis Union Trust Co.* reversionary interests (contingent on the beneficiary's predeceasing the settlor). The distinction was administratively unworkable, and within five years the problem was back in the Supreme Court when certiorari was granted in three cases involving reversionary interests created by diverse legal formulas. Under the style of Helvering v. Hallock, 309 U.S. 106 (1940), the Supreme Court decided all three cases for the government:

> The terms of these grants [in the cases before the Court] differ in detail from one another, as all three differ from the formulas of conveyance used in the *Klein* and *St. Louis Trust* cases. It therefore becomes important to inquire whether the technical forms in which interests contingent upon death are cast should control our decision. If so, it becomes necessary to determine whether the differing terms of conveyance now in issue approximate more closely those used in the *Klein* case and are therefore governed by it, or have a greater verbal resemblance to those that saved the tax in the *St. Louis Trust* cases.... The law of contingent and vested remainders is full of casuistries. There are great diversities among the several states as to the conveyancing significance of like grants; sometimes in the same state there are conflicting lines of decision, one series ignoring the other.... The importation of these distinctions and controversies from the law of property into the administration of the estate tax precludes a fair and workable tax system. Essentially the same interests, judged from the point of view of wealth, will be taxable or not, depending upon elusive and subtle casuistries which may have their historic justification but possess no relevance for tax purposes. These unwitty diversities of the law of property derive from medieval concepts as to the necessity of a continuous seisin. Distinctions which originated under a feudal economy when land dominated social relations are peculiarly irrelevant in the application of tax measures now so largely directed toward intangible wealth.
>
> Our real problem, therefore, is to determine whether we are to adhere to a harmonizing principle in the construction of [the postponed-possession-or-enjoyment clause] or whether we are to multiply gossamer distinctions between the present cases and the three earlier ones. Freed from the distinctions introduced by the *St. Louis Trust*

cases, the *Klein* case furnishes such a harmonizing principle. Does, then, the doctrine of stare decisis compel us to accept the distinctions made in the *St. Louis Trust* cases as starting points for still finer distinctions spun out of the tenuosities of surviving feudal law? We think not. We think the *Klein* case rejected the presupposition of such distinctions for the fiscal judgments which [the statute] demands. [309 U.S. at 116–19.]

Questions after Hallock. The *Hallock* case at first seemed to be the final step of a long journey; it soon became apparent that it was only the end of the beginning. Two questions that particularly called for decision were as follows:

1. Did the statute reach a reversionary interest that was not expressly reserved by the settlor but instead arose by operation of law? In the cases passed on by the Supreme Court, the reversionary interest had been created by the express language of the trust indenture. But what if *H* transfers property in trust to pay the income to *W* for *H*'s life, remainder to *H*'s children living at the time of his death, with no gift over if the children all predecease *H*? In these circumstances *H* would have a reversionary interest by operation of law. It was argued that such a trust was not reached by the statute, however, at least not without proof that the transfer was "intended" to take effect in possession or enjoyment at or after death. It was of course possible that *H* had no intention of reserving anything, and that his reversionary interest existed only because the drafter failed to provide for a final gift over. But even an *express* reservation of a reversionary interest might result from a drafter's caution rather than the settlor's deliberation, and the *Hallock* case did not make any inquiry into the question of whether the reversionary interests there involved were *deliberately* retained.

2. Was the "remoteness" of the reversionary interest relevant? The principal Supreme Court cases had all concerned settlors who would recapture transferred property if they outlived a wife or a child. The possibility of survivorship was sufficiently substantial that the settlor might have retained the reversionary interest deliberately, and perhaps a conclusive presumption that the transfer was "intended" to take effect in possession or enjoyment at or after his death was warranted. But what if a settlor transfers property in trust for his wife for the settlor's life, remainder to her if she survives him, otherwise to those of his children and their issue who survive him, with a reversionary interest in the settlor's estate if his wife, his children, and the issue of his children all predecease him? See Estate of Goodyear v. Commissioner, 2 T.C. 885 (1943), where a trust fund of about $350,000 would have reverted to the decedent only if she had survived a son, four grandchildren and their issue, eight great-grandchildren being alive at the time of her death; the value of the reversionary interest was $0.0000000000876. If the settlor's reversionary interest was virtually worthless, because conditioned on a remote possibility, was the transfer "intended to take effect in possession

or enjoyment at or after his death," as that clause was interpreted in the *Hallock* case?

The answers to Hallock's questions: Church and Spiegel. In October 1947, Spiegel's Estate v. Commissioner, 335 U.S. 701 (1949), and Commissioner v. Church's Estate, 335 U.S. 632 (1949), which raised both of these questions, were argued in the Supreme Court. In both cases, the government asserted that the settlor of a trust possessed a remote reversionary interest arising by operation of law, because the instrument of transfer did not provide for all contingencies. In the *Spiegel* case, the corpus was worth about $1.1 million when the decedent died, and its inclusion in the estate produced an estate tax of about $450,000; the settlor's reversionary interest (dependent on outliving his children and their issue) was worth $4,500 when the trust was created and about $85 just before he died. On the last day of the 1947 term, the Supreme Court ordered reargument, requesting counsel to discuss nine questions which in effect inquired whether the Court had been mistaken in its view of the postponed-possession-or-enjoyment clause in every important case before Helvering v. Hallock. 68 S.Ct. 1524 (1948). The cases were reargued in accordance with these orders in October 1948 and were decided in January 1949. In deciding the *Church* case, in which the decedent had not only a reversionary interest but also a pre–1931 life income interest, the Court (three justices dissenting) did not confine itself to the reversionary interest issue, but decided the case by overruling May v. Heiner. The Court ruled that Church's life income interest in the transferred property was "a most valuable property right" and that under the reasoning in the *Hallock* case the gift "passed" and became "complete" for the first time at Church's death.

Unlike Church, Spiegel had not retained a life income interest. In deciding the *Spiegel* case, therefore, the Court had to decide the effect of a remote reversionary interest arising by operation of law. It held that reversionary interests arising by operation of law were as fatal as those that were expressly reserved, and that the remoteness of the decedent's interest was irrelevant: "In either event the settlor has not parted with all of his presently existing or future contingent interests in the property transferred." There were forceful dissents in both cases. See Bittker, The *Church* and *Spiegel* Cases: Section 811(c) Gets a New Lease on Life, 58 Yale L.J. 825 (1949).

The legislative sequel to Church and Spiegel: Technical Changes Act of 1949. As soon as the *Church* and *Spiegel* cases were decided, speculation commenced on whether Reinecke v. Northern Trust Co. (supra page 330) had been overruled sub silentio. When the Supreme Court said that to avoid the postponed-possession-or-enjoyment clause, a transfer "must be unaffected by whether the grantor lives or dies," did it mean that a transfer was taxable if (as in the *Northern Trust Co.* case) the transferor's life was used as a yardstick to measure the term of a trust, even though the transferor reserved no interest for himself? Even if the Supreme Court did not intend to take this step, was there any reason to tax the trust in the *Spiegel* case, which was to terminate on the settlor's death, because he would recapture the corpus in the highly unlikely event that he outlived his children and their issue, but exclude a trust that was identical in all respects except that the virtually worthless residual interest was vested in someone else? The impact of the *Spiegel* case on Reinecke v. Northern Trust Co. was not settled by the judiciary, however, because Congress intervened by enacting the Technical Changes Act of 1949. This statute commenced the task of obliterating the *Church* case, a job that was completed in 1953 when Congress restored the rule in May v. Heiner to effectiveness for all pre–1931 transfers. The 1949 statute was more generous to the *Spiegel* case. For transfers after October 7, 1949, it provided that the transferred property would be included if the transferee was required to survive the transferor to obtain possession or enjoyment of the property. Thus Reinecke v. Northern Trust Co. was overruled prospectively.[31] A transfer to trustees to accumulate the income during the settlor's life, with distribution to a child or the child's estate to be made on the settlor's death, was taxable under this part of the 1949 Act even though the settlor retained no interest of any type. In the case of transfers made on or before October 7, 1949, however, the 1949 Act rejected the sweeping position of the *Spiegel* case. Such transfers were not to be included in the gross estate unless the reversionary interest (a) arose by the express terms of the instrument of transfer and not by operation of law and (b) had a value immediately before the decedent's death of more than 5 percent of the value of the transferred property. The 1949 legislation is discussed in detail in Bittker, *Church* and *Spiegel*: The Legislative Sequel, 59 Yale L.J. 395 (1950); Pavenstedt, Congress Deactivates Another Bombshell: The Mitigation of *Church* and *Spiegel*, 5 Tax L. Rev. 309 (1950).

The 1954 legislation: Restoration of Reinecke v. Northern Trust Co. In 1954, Congress intervened once more. Section 2037 of the 1954 Code retained the 1949 rules for transfers on or before October 7, 1949, but revised the treatment of transfers made after October 7, 1949. The rule of Reinecke v. Northern Trust Co. was restored, so that the use of the settlor's life as a measuring stick was not fatal unless a reversionary interest was retained. Moreover, the 5–percent rule was extended to post–1949 transfers, and was made applicable to interests arising by operation of law as well as to those created by the express language of the instrument of transfer. In recommending this change, the Senate Finance Committee said:

> Where the decedent has disposed of all, or substantially all, of his rights to property long before his death, it appears unduly harsh to

31. Reinecke v. Northern Trust Co., supra page 330, warned of a constitutional problem if Congress attempted to impose an estate tax on such transfers. In the *Bullard* case, supra page 271, however, the Supreme Court said: "Since Congress may lay an excise upon gifts it is of no significance that the exaction is denominated an estate tax or is found in a statute purporting to levy an estate tax." Does this rationale dispose of the constitutional doubts expressed in the *Northern Trust Co.* case? See Lowndes, The Constitutionality of the New Federal Estate Tax Definition of a Transfer Taking Effect at Death, 3 Vand. L. Rev. 203 (1950).

subject the property to estate tax merely because the ultimate taker of the property is determined at the time of the decedent's death. [S. Rep. No. 1622, 83d Cong., 2d Sess. 123 (1954).]

After all the sound and fury that attended its birth, § 2037 might have been expected to play a major role in the administration of the estate tax. The contrary has been true. Unlike §§ 2036 and 2038, § 2037 has generated very few judicial or administrative rulings since its enactment. It has probably functioned primarily as a trap for the unwary, because the reversionary interests that bring it into force are usually retained more by mistake than by design.

The "necessary survivorship" requirement. Section 2037(a)(1) reaches only those transfers under which "possession or enjoyment can ... be obtained only by surviving the decedent." This requirement is met, for example, where *H*, the decedent, created an inter vivos trust to pay income to his wife *W* for life, with corpus payable at her death to *H* if then living, otherwise to their surviving issue. Reg. § 20.2037–1(e) (Example 3). The result is different, however, if the trust corpus is payable at *W*'s death to their surviving issue, with a reversion to *H* or his estate if no issue survive *W*. Reg. § 20.2037–1(e) (Example 1). In this case, the issue will take if and only if they survive *W*, regardless of whether *H* is still living. Their rights, in other words, are not affected by *H*'s death: If he dies the day after the trust is created, they are no closer to possession or enjoyment than if he were still alive. Thus, § 2037 does not apply, but if *H* dies before *W* the actuarial value of his reversionary interest is includible in his gross estate under § 2033.

By the same token, the "necessary survivorship" requirement is not met if the beneficiary could have obtained possession or enjoyment "either by surviving the decedent or through the occurrence of some other event such as the expiration of a term of years." The regulations warn, however, that the "other event" may be ignored "if a consideration of the terms and circumstances of the transfer as a whole indicates that the 'other event' is unreal and if the death of the decedent does, in fact, occur before the 'other event.' " Reg. § 20.2037–1(b). Suppose that the decedent created an inter vivos trust to accumulate income for a 20–year term or until the decedent's earlier death, with the corpus and accumulated income to be paid at the end of the term to the decedent's child if then living. If the decedent was 30 years old at the time of the transfer, § 2037 would not apply because the child could obtain the property at the end of the 20–year term even if the decedent were still living. But if the decedent was 80 years old at the time of the transfer and actually died within the 20–year term, the possibility that the child might have taken the property without surviving the decedent would be so remote that it would be ignored. Reg. § 20.2037–1(e) (Example 5).

In Commissioner v. Marshall's Estate, 203 F.2d 534 (3d Cir. 1953), the decedent created inter vivos trusts to pay income to his wife for life, with corpus payable at her death "to such person or persons as would be entitled thereto under the intestate law of the State of Pennsylvania if she had at that time died seized and possessed of the trust estate." Under Pennsylvania law, the decedent would have been entitled to a one-third intestate share of his wife's estate if he had survived her; since he died before his wife, his one-third share passed instead to her other heirs. The court found that the "necessary survivorship" requirement of § 2037 was not met:

> At the moment preceding Marshall's death it was possible for beneficiaries to take the one-third interest without surviving him. This could have resulted (1) by a change in the intestate laws of Pennsylvania, mitigating or eliminating the surviving spouse's share; (2) under the present intestate laws if Marshall had divorced his wife or she had divorced him; (3) if Marshall either wilfully neglected or refused to provide for Mrs. Marshall for one year previous to her death, or if he wilfully and maliciously had deserted her for that period. Had any one of those things occurred, the one-third interest which decedent would otherwise have gotten, would have gone to persons (the children, if they survived their mother) who would not have had to survive the decedent....
>
> The possible contingencies taken together under which beneficiaries could have taken the interest without surviving Marshall cannot be regarded as so remote as to be "unreal."[32] [203 F.2d at 539–40.]

For the sequel to the *Marshall* case, involving the treatment of the trusts at the wife's death, see Marshall's Estate v. Commissioner, 51 T.C. 696 (1969).

Under the last sentence of § 2037(b), the statute does not apply if a beneficiary could have obtained possession or enjoyment of the underlying property "during the decedent's life through the exercise of a general power of appointment ... which in fact was exercisable immediately before the decedent's death." Evidently, if a beneficiary or third party has the power to cut off the decedent's reversionary interest by exercising a *general* power of appointment, the decedent's death cannot be realistically regarded as a necessary condition to possession or enjoyment. By similar reasoning, should the "necessary survivorship" requirement of § 2037(a)(1) be deemed not satisfied if the decedent's reversionary interest could be destroyed by the exercise of a *nongeneral* power of appointment?

The decedent's reversionary interest. Section 2037(a)(2) requires that the decedent have retained a reversionary interest which is worth more than 5 percent of the value of the underlying property immediately before death. The term "reversionary interest" is defined by § 2037(b) to include not only a possibility that the property may return to the decedent or his

---

32. In an omitted footnote, the court illustrated an "unreal" event with the following example taken from Bittker, *Church* and *Spiegel*: The Legislative Sequel, 59 Yale L.J. 395, 404 (1950): "[S]uppose the remainderman were a member of the Communist Party and could take either by becoming President of Yale University or by surviving the settlor. Under the '*Hallock* regulation' no doubt the 'other event' would be unreal."—EDS.

estate, but also a possibility that it may be subject to a "power of disposition by him." What if a trust is created under which the settlor, if he survives the life income beneficiary, will have only a restricted power to affect the remainder takers or other beneficiaries, such as a power to alter the proportions of their shares? In Klauber's Estate v. Commissioner, 34 T.C. 968 (1960), the executor argued that a power to invade principal for the income beneficiary was too narrow to be considered a retained "power of disposition." The Tax Court rejected the argument and refused to distinguish between broad and narrow powers, noting that they are treated the same in an analogous context (the reference in § 2036(a)(2) to a retained power to "designate" the persons to possess or enjoy income). See also Costin v. Cripe, 235 F.2d 162 (7th Cir. 1956) (statute applied to power by which grantor was empowered, if he survived his wife and son, to designate different beneficiaries of the remainder, not including himself or his creditors).

In speaking of a possibility that property "may be subject to a power of disposition by [the decedent]," does § 2037(b)(2) contemplate a power exercisable by the decedent alone? In *Klauber's Estate*, supra, the power of disposition was exercisable by a trustee; the court held that it was in effect exercisable by the decedent because he could have removed the trustee and appointed someone amenable to his wishes.

ROY'S ESTATE v. COMMISSIONER

54 T.C. 1317 (1970).

STERRETT, JUDGE. . . .

The facts involved are not complex and they are largely uncontested. On October 27, 1959, the decedent, who was then approximately 41 years old, and his brother transferred certain property in trust. Decedent's father, Benjamin, who was then approximately 69 years of age, was to have a life interest in the trust's net income. Upon Benjamin's death the trust corpus was to revert to the grantors, if living. If either grantor predeceased Benjamin his share of the trust corpus was to be administered for the benefit of his family.

Although the decedent was in relatively good health at the inception of the trust, in 1952 it was discovered that he was afflicted with glomerulonephritis. He, nonetheless, remained clinically well for approximately 11 years. In November of 1963 his condition began to steadily worsen until he succumbed to uremia on April 28, 1965. Benjamin did not die until approximately 4 years later, on April 6, 1969.

The controversy at issue arises because just prior to the decedent's death the state of his health indicated a severely limited, actual life expectancy, while the respondent's mortality tables indicate an expectancy for a man of 47, in normal health, of considerably longer duration. If we consider the decedent's actual health in valuing his reversionary interest, that interest would have been less than 5 percent. If we are bound to consider only the average life expectancy of those in normal health as reflected in the mortality tables, his interest would have been approximately 70 percent as the respondent contends. The issue is thus narrowed to whether the decedent's personal life expectancy may be considered for purposes of valuing his reversionary interest under section 2037(a)(2).

Section 2037(b) prescribes the methods of evaluating reversionary interest as follows:

> The value of a reversionary interest immediately before the death of the decedent shall be determined (without regard to the fact of the decedent's death) by usual methods of valuation, including the use of tables of mortality and actuarial principles, under regulations prescribed by the Secretary or his delegate.

Since it is the method of evaluation that is at issue here, construction of the language quoted above will be determinative.

The predecessor of section 2037(a)(2) and (b) was enacted ... by section 8 of the Technical Changes Act of 1949. Prior to the enactment of this section, [the statute] simply provided for the inclusion in the decedent's gross estate of interests that the decedent had transferred which were "intended to take effect in possession or enjoyment at or after his death."

Consequently, in Estate of Spiegel v. Commissioner, 335 U.S. 701 (1949), the Supreme Court required inclusion of a trust of approximately $1,140,000 due to the retention of a $70 reverter. See Estate of Spiegel v. Commissioner, supra at 727 (Burton, J., dissenting). It was the congressional reaction to this decision which provided the impetus for the enactment of section 8 of the Technical Changes Act of 1949. S. Rept. No. 831, 81st Cong., 1st Sess., p.8.

The circumstances surrounding this enactment indicate Congress' intention to reverse the holding in Estate of Spiegel v. Commissioner, supra, by the incorporation of a de minimis standard determinable with some mathematical precision. Certainty is of benefit to taxpayer and Internal Revenue Service alike.

As the statute obviously recognizes, no single method of valuation of a reversion can be prescribed in view of the large variety of reversionary interests. There must necessarily be some flexibility in the means used to make the appraisal. Thus, it is that mortality tables would be of little use in valuing an interest the receipt of which is contingent upon someone dying without issue. Yet there are, it is equally obvious, certain reversionary interests where the use of a mortality table is the fairest and most equitable method to be used.

In the case at bar petitioner would have us ignore the life expectancy as reflected in the mortality tables and use, in lieu thereof, the actual life expectancy of the decedent here involved. Admittedly such a position has appeal and ignites a sympathetic reaction under the facts here present. Further, the position is ably argued in the briefs.

Yet we feel its acceptance would emasculate section 2037 thereby vitiating the congressional intent to bring certainty to the law through the enactment of a de minimis provision. It would effectively write the words "including the use of tables of mortality" out of the statute. Surely Congress had certain reversionary interests in mind when it prescribed mortality tables as a means of evaluation. It is difficult to conceive of a "section 2037 reversion" where the use of such tables would be more appropriate than the one before us. Thus, to deny the applicability of the "tables of mortality" language here would be to ignore what appears to be the specific mandate of Congress.

Should we accept the petitioner's arguments herein, section 2037 would not apply to comparable reversionary interests in any instance where the decedent was terminally ill prior [to] death. In cases of that sort a drastically foreshortened actual life expectancy would bring any retained reversion below the 5–percent level. Section 2037 would then be applicable only in cases of sudden death; e.g., when a healthy individual is killed in an accident or when an ostensibly healthy individual dies as the result of a sudden coronary. We do not feel it reasonable to assume that Congress intended section 2037 to be limited to such narrow circumstances. Nor can we believe that Congress intended the mode of death, lingering or sudden, to be determinative of estate tax consequence.

Section 2037(b) states that the value of a retained reversionary interest "shall be determined (without regard to the fact of the decedent's death)...." If we were in the future to consider the manner of cause of a decedent's death we would, it seems to us, be in violation of this requirement....

NOTES

1. *Valuing the reversionary interest under the 5–percent rule.* Section 2037(b) states that in applying the 5–percent test, the value of a reversionary interest shall be determined "by usual methods of valuation, including the use of tables of mortality and actuarial principles." The Conference Committee's report on the Technical Changes Act of 1949, in recommending adoption of the 5–percent rule, stated:

> The value [of a reversionary interest] shall be ascertained as though the decedent were, immediately before his death, making a gift of the property and retaining the reversionary interest. The rule of Robinette v. Helvering (318 U.S. 184), under which a reversionary interest not having an ascertainable value under recognized valuation principles is considered to have a value of zero, is to apply. [H.R. Rep. No. 1412, 81st Cong., 1st Sess. (1949), reprinted in 1949–2 C.B. 295, 297.]

The Senate Report on the 1954 Code states:

> The decedent's reversionary interest is to be valued by recognized valuation principles and without regard to the fact of the decedent's death. Where it is apparent from the facts that property could have reverted to the decedent under contingencies that were not remote, the reversionary

> interest is not to be necessarily regarded as having no value merely because the value thereof cannot be measured precisely. [S. Rep. No. 1622, 83d Cong., 2d Sess. 469.]

If the value of the reversionary interest cannot be determined by recognized principles of valuation, is it to be treated as having no value, as the 1949 Conference Report states—or does the 1954 Senate Report mean that it will be treated as worth more than 5 percent because the taxpayer will be unable to prove that it is worth less? In Thacher's Estate v. Commissioner, 20 T.C. 474 (1953), property would revert to the decedent if his wife was divorced or legally separated from him. In the absence of evidence that the value of the reversionary interest either could not be measured or, if measurable, was not more than 5 percent of the value of the trust property, the court presumed that the value of the interest exceeded the 5 percent threshold. Can this conclusion be reconciled with the 1949 Conference Report? The case was decided in 1953. If it had come up after the 1954 Senate Report, would the reversionary interest be fatal even if there was evidence that its value could not be calculated by recognized valuation methods? See also Cardeza's Estate v. United States, 261 F.2d 423 (3d Cir. 1958) (decedent's reversionary interest conditioned on son's death without issue; held, in view of financial incentive for son to have issue, no value can be reliably ascribed to decedent's reversionary interest and, under 1939 Code, it must be treated as having value of zero).

2. *Reform proposals.* A recurring theme in reform proposals is the desirability of simplifying the rules concerning completed transfers for gift and estate tax purposes. For example, the Treasury Department's 1984 Report to the President, entitled Tax Reform for Fairness, Simplicity, and Economic Growth, at pages 378–80, proposed a uniform completion rule along the following lines:

> *Simplification of Rules Pertaining to Completed Gifts and Testamentary Strings*
>
> . . . The complex retained interest rules would be replaced with a simpler set of rules determining when a transfer of less than an entire interest constitutes a completed gift for Federal transfer tax purposes. These new rules would ensure that a transfer is subject to gift or estate tax, but not to both taxes. . . .
>
> *Retained beneficial enjoyment.* The proposal would simplify present law by providing that a transfer tax would be imposed only once, when the beneficial enjoyment retained by the donor terminates. Thus, if a donor makes a gift of a remainder interest in property, but retains the intervening income interest, no gift would occur until the termination of the donor's income interest. At that time, the property would be subject to gift or estate tax at its full fair market value. Because the transferor would be treated as the owner of the property during the interim, any distributions made to beneficiaries other than the transferor would be treated as transfers when made. . . .
>
> *Revocable transfers.* The rules of present law would continue with respect to any transfer where the transferor retains the right to regain possession or enjoyment of the property. Such a transfer would be treated as incomplete for gift and estate tax purposes, and would be treated as

complete only when the transferor's retained right or power to revoke terminates. Distributions from the property to beneficiaries other than the donor would be treated as gifts when made, thereby providing consistency with the rules governing the income taxation of trusts as well as the rules governing the income and gift tax treatment of demand loans.

Retained powers. In determining whether a gift is complete for transfer tax purposes, the proposal would treat a retained power to control the beneficial enjoyment of the transferred property as irrelevant where the power could not be used to distribute income or principal to the donor. Thus, the fact that the transferor as trustee or custodian can exercise control over the identity of the distributee of the property or over the amount or timing of a distribution would be irrelevant in determining whether a gift is complete (although such factors may be relevant in determining whether the transfer qualifies for the annual gift tax exclusion). Under this rule, a transfer would be complete for gift tax purposes where the grantor creates an irrevocable trust but retains the absolute right to determine who (other than himself) will receive the trust income or principal.

Reversionary interests. Current rules regarding retained reversionary interests would be replaced by a rule that disregards reversionary interests retained by the grantor in valuing transferred property for Federal gift tax purposes. The existence of the reversionary interest would be relevant only for purposes of determining the timing of the transfer for estate and gift tax purposes.

If the donor makes a gift of property for a term of years or for the life of one or more beneficiaries, and if the donor retains a reversionary interest that is more likely than not to return the property to the donor or his or her estate, the transfer would be treated as incomplete. Interim distributions of income or principal (or the value of the use of the property) would be treated as gifts by the donor on an annual basis. On the other hand, if it is more likely than not that the reversionary interest will not return the property to the donor or his or her estate, the transfer will be treated as complete and the full fair market value of the property will be subject to gift tax, without reduction for the actuarial value of the reversionary interest. If the donor dies with the reversion outstanding, the value of the reversionary interest will be excluded from the donor's estate, whether or not the reversion terminates at that time. If the property reverts to the donor prior to his or her death, the donor would have the right to retransfer the property at any time free from additional gift tax liability. If not retransferred during the donor's lifetime, the property would be excluded from the donor's estate. In order to prevent disputes arising from the reversion and subsequent retransfer of fungible assets, however, the proposal would require the donor to place the reverted property in a segregated account in order to benefit from the exclusion.

The determination of whether a reversionary interest is more likely than not to return property to the donor during his lifetime generally would depend on the life expectancy of the donor and the anticipated duration of the intervening interest. For example, a reversion following a term of years less than the donor's life expectancy or following the life of a beneficiary older than the donor would be more likely than not to return the property to the donor. Similar actuarial determinations would be made for multiple intervening income beneficiaries.

A uniform completion rule along the lines proposed in the Treasury report would make the existing estate and gift tax system considerably simpler, and would also eliminate the need for the special gift tax valuation rules of § 2702. How would a uniform completion rule apply to powers that are subject to an external standard or can only be exercised with the consent of others? How would it deal with retained voting rights in transferred stock? Consider also how an accessions tax (discussed supra at page 13) would address the problem of timing. For further discussion of reform proposals, see ABA Tax Section Task Force, Report on Transfer Tax Restructuring, 41 Tax Law. 395, 404–10 (1988); Gutman, A Comment on the ABA Tax Section Task Force Report on Transfer Tax Restructuring, id. at 653, 674–81; Dodge, Redoing the Estate and Gift Taxes Along Easy-to-Value Lines, 43 Tax L. Rev. 241 (1988).

E. SURVIVORSHIP ANNUITIES: § 2039

1. PURCHASED COMMERCIAL ANNUITIES

Section 2039, governing the taxability of survivorship annuities, was added to the Code in 1954. Before 1954, the value of the rights of a beneficiary under a survivorship annuity was included in the gross estate of the purchaser of the annuity contract only if the transaction could be fitted into some other provision of the estate tax law. To see the 1954 statute in perspective, it is necessary to sketch in the background.

Suppose that *H* purchases a commercial annuity contract under which he will receive $10,000 a year for his life, and his wife *W*, if she survives him, will receive the same (or lesser) amount for her life. This is a "self-and-survivor" contract. Disregarding the insurance company's expenses and profit, *H*'s purchase of the contract might be compared to a transfer of property in trust, under which *H* is to receive annual distributions for life consisting of (1) the net trust income, plus (2) sufficient corpus to bring each annual distribution up to $10,000. Since a transfer in trust with reservation of the income for life is taxable under § 2036, *H*'s annuity contract would also seem to be includible under § 2036. The parallel is not perfect, to be sure, since *H* is entitled to receive $10,000 per year under the contract, but no more; if instead of buying the contract he had transferred an equal amount in trust with a reservation of the income, his return in any one year might be greater or less than $10,000. But the cost of the annuity is based on the assumption that *H* for his life, and then *W* for hers, will get not only the income produced by the funds paid for the annuity, but also returns of capital. At one time it was argued that *H* had not "retained" possession or enjoyment of any property or the income therefrom, as required by § 2036, because the consideration he paid for the annuity contract was entirely at the disposal of the commercial issuer. The courts finally adopted the view, however, that the value of *W*'s rights under such a contract, measured at the time of *H*'s death, was includible in *H*'s gross estate under what is now § 2036. Commissioner v. Clise, 122 F.2d 998 (9th Cir. 1941), cert. denied, 315 U.S. 821 (1942); Forster v. Sauber, 249 F.2d 379 (7th Cir. 1957), cert. denied, 356 U.S. 913 (1958). Of course, if *W* predeceased *H*, the issuer's obligation to make payments would terminate at *H*'s death and there would be no value to be included in his gross estate.

Another common annuity contract provides for payments to *H* and *W* while they both live, with payments continuing to the survivor (a "joint-and-survivor" annuity). Suppose *H* and *W* are each entitled to receive $5,000 while they are both alive, and after the death of one spouse the survivor is to receive $10,000 for the rest of his or her life. If *H* predeceases *W*, can the value of her rights at the time of his death be included in his gross estate under § 2036? It is of course possible that *H*'s $5,000 per year during *W*'s life was substantially less than the income that would have been produced if the purchase price of the annuity had been transferred in trust. Does this destroy the analogy suggested earlier? Even if it does, recall that in Marks v. Higgins, supra page 276, a transfer under which the grantor reserved a "contingent" or secondary life estate was held to be within § 2036. Does not *H*, under the joint-and-survivor annuity, have at least the equivalent of a secondary life estate—namely, his right to receive $10,000 per year if he survives *W*? Such annuities were held to be taxable under what is now § 2036. Mearkle's Estate v. Commissioner, 129 F.2d 386 (3d Cir. 1942).

Section 2039, enacted in 1954, takes over from § 2036 the responsibility for annuities such as these. Accepting the analogy of transfers with reserved life estates, § 2039 (like § 2036) applies only to transactions after March 3, 1931, and the last clause of § 2039(a) is adopted verbatim from § 2036(a). The House version of § 2039 required that "an annuity or similar payment" be payable to the decedent; the Senate changed this phrase to "an annuity or other payment" to make it clear that § 2039 applied if the decedent could get a lump-sum payment in lieu of an annuity. S. Rep. No. 1622, 83d Cong., 2d Sess. 470 (1954). Note that § 2039(a) is applicable if "an annuity or other payment *was payable* to the decedent, or the decedent *possessed the right to receive such annuity or payment*." (Emphasis supplied.) Is there a difference between an annuity that was "payable" to the decedent and one that he "possessed the right to receive"? Is § 2039 applicable if the decedent's *spouse* was to receive the annuity for her life and the decedent was to receive payments only if he survived her? Suppose that *H*, instead of buying a "self-and-survivor" annuity, buys two contracts: an annuity for himself, and one for *W* under which payments are to be made only if she survives him. Is § 2039 applicable?

The Senate Report states (at page 472) that the provisions of § 2039 "shall not prevent the application of any other provision of law relating to the estate tax." Consider these possibilities:

1. If § 2039 is inapplicable because the decedent had no right to receive payments himself, would § 2038 be applicable if the decedent reserved a power to alter or amend the beneficiary's rights?
2. If the decedent purchased an annuity for himself alone, with no provision for payments to a survivor, § 2039 is inapplicable and there is no value at the date of death to be included under any other provision. But if such a contract provides for a refund to the purchaser's estate if he dies before receiving a specified number of payments, § 2033 would reach the refund. If the refund is payable to a named beneficiary rather than to the purchaser's estate, apparently § 2039 would be applicable.
3. If the purchaser of an annuity contract had, until his death, the power to surrender the contract for cash, would the amount he could obtain just before his death by a surrender of the contract be taxable under § 2033?
4. *H* buys a contract providing an annuity for *W*, who is younger than he. His only right under the contract is that he or his estate will receive a refund if *W* should die before the aggregate payments to her under the contract equal the price he paid for it. *H* dies before *W* has received back the cost of the contract. Is anything includible in *H*'s estate? Note that if *W* lives out her life expectancy, there will be no refund. Would the answer depend on the state of *W*'s health when *H* dies? See Hofford's Estate v. Commissioner, 4 T.C. 542 (1945).

In the case of a survivorship annuity, the surviving beneficiary may be required to pay income tax on payments which were reflected in the value of the annuity that was subject to estate tax under § 2039 at the primary annuitant's death. For income tax purposes, a portion of the annuity payments may be treated as a tax-free return of capital under § 72(b), but the balance is includible in gross income by virtue of § 72(a). The exclusion determined under § 72(b) is available until the investment in the annuity contract is recovered, i.e., the primary annuitant and then the surviving beneficiary are entitled to exclude a portion of each payment received during their respective lives until the aggregate amount excluded equals the investment in the annuity contract. (If both die before the investment is fully recovered, a deduction is allowed for the unrecovered amount.) It is possible, of course, that the value of the annuity taxed in the primary annuitant's estate under § 2039 may exceed the aggregate amount that the surviving beneficiary is entitled to exclude as a return of capital under § 72(b), thus creating a double tax problem. To ameliorate this result, § 691(d) states that the payments received by the survivor shall, to the extent included in gross income under § 72(a), be treated as income in respect of a decedent under § 691(a). As a result, the survivor is entitled to an income tax deduction for an allocable portion of the estate tax that was imposed on the annuity in the primary annuitant's estate. See Reg. § 1.691(d)–1 (illustrating the deduction and limiting it to the period of the survivor's life expectancy); 1 Bittker & Lokken, Federal Taxation of Income, Estates and Gifts ¶ 12.3.4 (3d ed. 1999).

2. BENEFITS UNDER EMPLOYEE RETIREMENT AND PENSION PLANS AND INDIVIDUAL RETIREMENT ACCOUNTS

As the foregoing material indicates, the taxable status of typical joint-and-survivor annuities was moderately clear even before the enactment of § 2039 in 1954, and the minor unsettled issues are still in doubt. In point of fact, however, the primary function of the new section was to clear up the status of survivorship annuities purchased by employers for their employees.

Under pre–1954 law, if an employee, in an effort to provide financial security for his surviving spouse, bargained with his employer for an increased salary and used the increased wages to purchase a joint-and-survivor annuity contract, the survivor's rights under the contract were treated like similar rights under any other purchased annuity contract. But if, instead of increasing wages, the employer agreed to provide a retirement annuity to the employee, with payments to be made to the spouse after the employee's death, the pre–1954 law was far less clear. Because such retirement annuities were customarily payable only if the employee had not died, quit, or been discharged for cause before the scheduled retirement date, there was some doubt as to whether the employee had any "property" to transfer, and it was almost as doubtful under the cases whether he made a "transfer" by designating his spouse as the beneficiary under the contract or plan. The Internal Revenue Service primarily attacked contracts under which the employee could choose between (a) an annuity for his life alone and (b) an annuity at a reduced rate for his life with payments to continue to his spouse after his death. If the employee elected to take the reduced annuity, the Service asserted that he had made a transfer with a retained income interest within the meaning of what is now § 2036. The courts in general rejected this position and distinguished the cases involving purchased commercial annuities. Commissioner v. Twogood's Estate, 194 F.2d 627 (2d Cir. 1952); Higgs' Estate v. Commissioner, 184 F.2d 427 (3d Cir. 1950).

Section 2039(a) eliminated these obstacles of pre–1954 law by requiring that the value of the survivor's benefits be included in the employee's gross estate if the employee contributed to the cost of the contract. The statute made clear that contributions by the employer are attributed to the employee for this purpose. This change in the law, however, was mitigated by the simultaneous enactment of § 2039(c), which exempted qualified pension and profit-sharing plans from the inclusionary rule of § 2039(a).

The reason for this exemption, which was combined with generous concessions under the income tax, was not apparent. A plan was "qualified" if it met the standards set out in §§ 401(a) and 403(a), income tax provisions that had no relationship to the estate and gift taxes. Qualified pension and profit-sharing plans came to be known as the quintessential tax shelter. In 1982, Congress imposed a $100,000 cap on the aggregate exemption for benefits under qualified plans and, in 1984, finally repealed § 2039(c) for decedents dying after 1984. It was reasoned that the unlimited marital deduction protects death benefits payable to a surviving spouse from taxation and that death benefits payable to others should be subject to tax to the extent they exceed the amount sheltered by the unified credit.

SCHELBERG'S ESTATE v. COMMISSIONER

612 F.2d 25 (2d Cir. 1979).

FRIENDLY, CIRCUIT JUDGE.

This appeal by a taxpayer from a decision of the Tax Court, 70 T.C. 690 (1978), raises a serious question with respect to the interpretation of § 2039, which was added to the Internal Revenue Code in 1954.

I

Decedent William V. Schelberg was born on March 14, 1914 and died on January 6, 1974 from lung cancer after a week's illness. He was survived by his wife, Sarah, and two daughters, one aged 23 and the other 19. He had been employed by International Business Machines Corp. (IBM) since 1952. At his death he was serving as assistant director of international patent operations at a salary of $4,250 per month.

IBM maintained a variety of employee benefit plans, each adopted at a different time and separately administered. Those here relevant are the Group Life Insurance Plan, the Retirement Plan, the Sickness and Accident Income Plan, and the Total and Permanent Disability Plan. Schelberg was entitled to participate in each.

The Group Life Insurance Plan provided two basic benefits—a group term life insurance, which is not here at issue,[33] and an uninsured and unfunded survivors income benefit, which is. This benefit, determined on the basis of the employee's compensation at the time of death and the amount of the aforementioned life insurance, was payable to a decedent's "eligible" survivors in an order of preference stated in the plan. Payment was to be made monthly, at the rate of one-quarter of the decedent's regular monthly compensation, until the total benefit was exhausted.

33. Section 2039(a) is expressly inapplicable to payments receivable "as insurance on the life of the decedent."

Payments continued only so long as at least one eligible survivor remained.

The Retirement Plan was a qualified pension plan under I.R.C. § 401. Under IBM's general employment policy, Schelberg would have been required to retire at age 65 and would have been entitled to the retirement benefits provided in the plan.

Under the Sickness and Accident Plan all regular IBM employees were entitled to receive full salary (reduced by any workmen's compensation payments) while absent from work on account of sickness or accident for up to 52 weeks in any 24–month period. Benefits could be continued for more than 52 weeks at IBM's discretion in individual cases; these were known as "individual consideration" benefits.

The Disability Plan covered all IBM employees with more than five years' service. Eligibility was based on determination of "total and permanent disability" by a corporate panel on the basis of medical evidence. The quoted phrase was defined to mean that the employee was unable to perform any employment for pay or profit and had no reasonable expectation of becoming able to do so. Benefits were calculated on the basis of the employee's regular compensation prior to disability, taking account of eligibility for Social Security payments and workmen's compensation. They began on the expiration of the 52–week period of Sickness and Accident benefits plus any period of individual consideration benefits and continued until normal retirement date, at which time the employee became eligible for benefits under the Retirement Plan.[34] During the period of disability an employee remained covered by a variety of other IBM employee plans[35] and could, under certain conditions, accrue further credits under the Retirement Plan. If, contrary to expectation, the employee became able to work again, he was entitled to return, but few did so. As of January 1, 1974, a total of 393 IBM employees out of 150,000 were receiving benefits under the Disability Plan.

At the time of his death Schelberg was not receiving benefits under any of these plans. By virtue of his decease his widow became entitled under the Group Life Insurance Plan to a death benefit of $23,666.67 under the group life insurance policy, and to a survivors benefit of $1,062.50 per month. The value of the latter amount was not included in decedent's gross estate in his federal estate tax return, although its existence was reported. The Commissioner of Internal Revenue entered a notice of deficiency on the sole ground that the present value of the

---

34. Disability benefits began at 75% of regular compensation and continued at that rate for the first 18 months less any period during which the employee had received "individual consideration" benefits under the Sickness and Accident Plan. Thereafter the benefits were the greater of 40% of regular compensation at the time of disability or accrued retirement income under the Retirement Plan based on actual service and imputed earnings during the receipt of payments under the Sickness and Accident Plan, with an upward adjustment for employees disabled before attaining age 55. . . .

35. These included the Family Hospitalization Plan, the Major Medical Plan, the Dental Plan, the Medical Plans with Medicare, the Special Care for Children Assistance Plan, the Adoption Assistance Plan and various educational benefit plans.

survivors annuity, which is stipulated to have been $94,708.83, was includible in the estate pursuant to I.R.C. § 2039.... The Tax Court upheld the Commissioner in a considered but somewhat *dubitante* opinion by Judge Raum, see 70 T.C. at 705 and infra, and the estate has appealed.

II

The estate does not dispute that the survivors benefit constituted "an annuity or other payment receivable by any beneficiary by reason of surviving the decedent under any form of contract or agreement entered into after March 3, 1931 (other than as insurance under policies on the life of the decedent)" within the opening clause of § 2039(a). It is likewise indisputable that this alone would not suffice to make the survivors benefit includible in the gross estate. The Commissioner must also satisfy the condition that "under such contract or agreement, an annuity or other payment was payable to the decedent, or the decedent possessed the right to receive such annuity or payment, either alone or in conjunction with another for his life or for any period not ascertainable without reference to his death or for any period which does not in fact end before his death."

Not contending that he can satisfy this requirement within the four corners of the Group Life Insurance Plan, the Commissioner asserts that, as provided by the Treasury Regulations, 26 C.F.R. § 20.2039–1(b), he is entitled to consider "any arrangement, understanding or plan, or any combination of arrangements or plans arising by reason of the decedent's employment." Although this is a rather sharp departure from the letter of the statute, see Pincus, Estate Taxation of Annuities and Other Payments, 44 Va. L. Rev. 857, 868–69 (1958), we accept it with the caveat that while the Commissioner is entitled to "consider" such arrangements, this does not mean that the mere possibility of an employee's receiving some benefit under an arrangement other than that giving rise to the survivors benefit necessarily satisfies the condition of § 2039(a). The Commissioner does not rely on either the Retirement Plan or the Sickness and Accident Plan to satisfy the condition that "an annuity or other payment" was payable to Schelberg. Apart from other considerations, any such reliance is precluded by previous revenue rulings. Revenue Ruling 76–380, 1976–2 C.B. 270, concluded that qualified plans, like the Retirement Plan, and non-qualified plans, like the Survivors Income Benefit Plan, were not to be considered together in determining the applicability of § 2039(a) and (b). See also Estate of Brooks v. C.I.R., 50 T.C. 585, 594–95 (1968). Revenue Ruling 77–183, 1977–1 C.B. 274, held that benefits such as those Schelberg might have been entitled to under the Sickness and Accident Plan had he lived longer "were in the nature of compensation" and thus no more meet the test set out in the condition than would compensation payments themselves, Estate of Fusz v. C.I.R., 46 T.C. 214 (1966), acq. 1967–2 C.B. 2; see also Kramer v. United States, 406 F.2d 1363, 186 Ct. Cl. 684 (1969). This left as the Commissioner's sole reed the fact that, at the time of his death, Schelberg possessed the right that after 52 weeks (or more if he qualified for "individual consideration") under the Sickness and Accident Plan, he might become entitled to payments under the Disability Plan. The estate contends that Schelberg's rights under the Disability Plan were too dissimilar in nature from an "annuity or other payment" and too contingent to meet the condition of § 2039(a). We agree.

It is worth repeating that the Commissioner's position here would apply to every IBM employee having more than five years' service who dies before attaining age 64 (or taking early retirement) although he neither received nor had any reasonable expectation of receiving anything under the Disability Plan. On the other hand, if he died after attaining age 64 but before taking retirement, the survivors benefit would not be includible since the first twelve months away from work would be covered by the Sickness and Accident Plan and he could never become eligible for the Disability Plan. And, of course, if he died after actually taking retirement, the most common case, the survivors benefit would not be includible by virtue of Revenue Ruling 76–380, 1976–2 C.B. 270. We find nothing in the language of § 2039, in its legislative history, or in the Treasury Regulations sufficient to justify a conclusion that the action of an employer in creating a plan whereby a handful of employees can receive disability benefits because of a rare health or accident syndrome should bring the survivors of all within § 2039.

As recognized by a learned commentator shortly after § 2039 was enacted, the statute was aimed at "annuity contracts under which the purchaser (alone or with a joint annuitant) was entitled to payments for his life, with payments to continue after his death, at either the same or a reduced rate, to a survivor." Bittker, Estate and Gift Taxation under the 1954 Code: The Principal Changes, 29 Tul. L. Rev. 453, 469 (1955)....

Both text and context show that § 2039 was conceived as dealing only with the problem of what in substance was a joint annuity, although to be sure in all its various ramifications, not with the whole gamut of arrangements under which an employee, his employer or both may create benefits for the employee's survivors. The new section applied only "if, under such contract or agreement, an annuity or other payment was payable to the decedent, or the decedent possessed the right to receive such annuity or payment, either alone or in conjunction with another for his life or for any period not ascertainable without reference to his death or for any period which does not in fact end before his death." If Congress had wished to legislate more broadly, it would have eliminated this clause or chosen more general language for it. The intended sphere of application is made quite clear by the illustrations given in the House and Senate reports "as examples of contracts, but ... not necessarily the only forms of contracts to which this section applies." Under all of these the decedent was receiving or entitled to receive at death what anyone would consider an "annuity or other payment" for the duration of his life or for a stipulated term.[36] Furthermore, in each case the beneficiary succeeded to the inter-

36. The sole exception is example (4) which omits any requirement of annuity or other payment to the decedent. However, it has been recognized that this example simply cannot be correct unless amplified....

est of the decedent, as in the classic instance of a joint and survivor annuity, quite unlike the present case. Although the term "other payment" is literally broad, Congress was clearly thinking of payments in the nature of annuities—the same types of payments which, if made to the survivor, would be includible in the estate. See Estate of Fusz, supra, 46 T.C. at 217. None of the examples is even close to payments receivable only if the deceased employee might have become totally and permanently disabled had he lived.

We do not consider the case to be altered in the Government's favor by the Treasury Regulations. While these contain some broad language, there is nothing to indicate that their framers addressed the problem here presented. The closest of the illustrations is example (6).[37] While we have no quarrel with this, it is inapposite since the payments both to the employee and to the beneficiary were life annuities. Without endeavoring to be too precise, we deem it plain that, in framing the condition on § 2039(a), Congress was not going beyond benefits the employee was sure to get as a result of his prior employment if he lived long enough. Even more plainly Congress was not thinking of disability payments which an employee would have had only a remote chance of ever collecting had he lived. Not only are the disability payments in this case extremely hypothetical, they are also far from the "annuity or other payment" contemplated by Congress. Courts have, consistent with basic principles of statutory construction, recognized that "annuity or other payment" does not mean "annuity or any payment," but that the phrase is qualitatively limited by the context in which it appears. See Estate of Fusz, supra, 46 T.C. at 217–18. The Service itself has acquiesced in and furthered this view. See Rev. Rul. 77–183, supra. Thus, it seems clear to us that Congress did not intend the phrase to embrace wages, Estate of Fusz, supra, 46 T.C. at 217; Kramer v. United States, supra, 406 F.2d 1363, 186 Ct. Cl. 684; Eichstedt v. United States, 354 F. Supp. 484, 491 (N.D. Cal. 1972); possible sickness and accident payments, which were a substitute for wages, Rev. Rul. 77–183, supra; or the disability payments involved in this case, which likewise were a partial continuation of wages when an employee's physical health deteriorated even further. The disability payments theoretically achievable here by the decedent in his lifetime are closer to the sickness benefits which he would have received at an early stage of his illness than they are to post-retirement benefits. The Tax Court's treatment of possible disability benefits as presupposing a post-

37. *Example (6).* The employer made contributions to two different funds set up under two different plans. One plan was to provide the employee, upon his retirement at age 60, with an annuity for life, and the other plan was to provide the employee's designated beneficiary, upon the employee's death, with a similar annuity for life. Each plan was established at a different time and each plan was administered separately in every respect. Neither plan at any time met the requirements of section 401(a) (relating to qualified plans). The value of the designated beneficiary's annuity is includible in the employee's gross estate. All rights and benefits accruing to an employee and to others by reason of the employment (except rights and benefits accruing under certain plans meeting the requirements of section 401(a) (see § 20.2039–2)) are considered together in determining whether or not section 2039(a) and (b) applies. The scope of section 2039(a) and (b) cannot be limited by indirection.

retirement status linked to the widow's ultimate succession thereto seems to us to be unsupported in fact....

III

... The most influential decision on what the decedent must receive or be entitled to receive in order to trigger application of § 2039 is Estate of Bahen v. United States, 305 F.2d 827, 158 Ct. Cl. 141 (1962) (Davis, J.). The opinion is indeed a virtuoso performance which has tended to dominate the field to the extent that, with the significant exception of Judge Aldisert's dissent in Gray v. United States, [410 F.2d 1094, 1112–14 (3d Cir. 1969)], courts seem to look to the *Bahen* opinion rather than to the statute and the committee reports as indicative of the legislative intent. Beyond all this it is of peculiar importance here since it involved a sum payable only in the event of disability, and the Commissioner quite properly relies heavily upon it.

The case involved payments by the Chesapeake & Ohio Ry. to Mr. Bahen's widow under two benefit plans. Under the more significant, a non-qualified Deferred Compensation Plan applicable only to 40 officers and executives, on Mr. Bahen's death the C. & O. would pay $100,000 to his widow or surviving children in 60 equal monthly installments; if, prior to retirement, he became totally incapacitated, the payments would be made to him so long as he survived, any amounts unpaid at the time of his death to go to his widow or minor children. Another plan provided that if an employee with more than 10 years service died while in the company's employ and before becoming eligible for retirement, the company would pay a sum equal to three months salary to his widow or minor children. Mr. Bahen died suddenly while in the railway's employ and before becoming eligible for retirement. The court held that payments to Mrs. Bahen under both plans were includible in the estate since "[e]very requirement [of § 2039] is squarely met, not only in literal terms but in harmony with the legislative aim." 305 F.2d at 829, 158 Ct. Cl. at [146]. Most relevantly for our purposes, the court held that the provision for payments to Mr. Bahen under the Deferred Compensation Plan in the event of his disability prior to retirement satisfied the condition of § 2039(a), for the purposes of both payments to Mrs. Bahen, since at the time of his death he possessed the right to receive such payments.

While, as indicated, the case bears some resemblance to ours, there is a different flavor about it, at least so far as concerns the payments under the Deferred Compensation Plan. There was in fact a unitary right to receive deferred compensation of $100,000 in 60 equal monthly payments, this to be paid to Mrs. Bahen if Bahen died or to him if he became totally disabled prior to retirement. There was no question of grouping separate plans together, since both Mr. and Mrs. Bahen's rights were pursuant to the same Deferred Compensation Plan. Even more to the point, if payments were being made to Mr. Bahen due to his disability and he died prior to exhausting the fund, the remaining payments would be made to Mrs. Bahen. In this respect the Deferred Compensation Plan was much like the joint and survivor annuity at which § 2039 was aimed. Here, of course, Mrs. Schelberg had no rights to any payments under the Disability Plan. The possible payments to Mr. Bahen were not, as under IBM's Disability Plan, true disability payments intended to cover a portion of previous salary; they were deferred compensation, as the plan's title indicates, payable by the railway in any event, to be made available to Mr. Bahen at a date earlier than death if his needs so required. They thus met the test laid down in *Estate of Fusz*, supra, 46 T.C. at 217–18, as IBM's disability benefits do not, of being of the same nature as the payments to the beneficiary. We are not sure that the distinction is sufficient or—what is more or less the same thing—that we would have decided *Bahen* as the Court of Claims did. For the moment we shall leave the matter that way. . . .

We here decide only that to consider a deceased employee's potential ability to have qualified at some future time for payments under a plan protecting against total and permanent disability—a disagreeable feat that had been accomplished as of January 1, 1974, by only a quarter of one percent of IBM's employees—as meeting the condition in § 2039(a) that there must be a contract or agreement under which the decedent received or be entitled to receive "an annuity or other payment," is such a departure from the language used by Congress, read in the light of the problem with which it was intending to deal, as to be at war with common sense. Cf. United States v. American Trucking Associations, Inc., 310 U.S. 534, 543 (1940). The only decision by which we are bound, All v. McCobb, [321 F.2d 633 (2d Cir. 1963)], does not come near to the problem here presented. Of the other decisions cited to us, there are clear grounds of distinguishing all with the possible exception of the leading one, *Estate of Bahen*, supra, 305 F.2d 827, 158 Ct. Cl. 141, and the certain exception of *Gaffney*, [200 Ct. Cl. 744 (1972)]. Although we have been able to distinguish the cases other than *Gaffney* and possibly *Bahen* on grounds that seem to us sufficient, we would not wish to be understood as necessarily agreeing with all of them or with the general approach taken in *Bahen*, see 305 F.2d at 833, 158 Ct. Cl. 141. Some other case may require complete rethinking whether courts, under the influence of the *Bahen* opinion, have not unduly eroded the condition in § 2039(a), as is pointedly suggested by Judge Aldisert's dissent in Gray v. United States, supra, 410 F.2d at 1112–14; on the other hand, Congress might decide to cast its net more widely and eliminate or broaden the condition, as it could have done in 1954. We simply decline to carry the erosion of the condition to the extent here urged by the Commissioner.

The judgment is reversed and the cause remanded with instructions to annul the determination of a deficiency.

NOTES

1. *Aftermath of the Bahen and Schelberg decisions.* In Van Wye's Estate v. United States, 686 F.2d 425 (6th Cir. 1982), the Sixth Circuit agreed with

the reasoning in the *Schelberg* case and ruled that the Commissioner's effort to read the disability benefit plan in tandem with the survivors benefit plan and thereby create an "annuity" covered by § 2039(a) was unreasonable. But see Looney v. United States, 569 F.Supp. 1569 (M.D. Ga. 1983) (contra, adopting the *Bahen* analysis). Subsequently, the Internal Revenue Service decided not to contest the holdings in *Schelberg* and *Van Wye* and settled the *Looney* case in the estate's favor, leading one commentator to conclude: "The Service's concession appears to resolve in favor of the taxpayer the issue of whether contingent, future benefits under a disability plan must be combined with death benefits in applying Section 2039." Holz, Properly Structured Death Benefit Plans Can Avoid Estate and Gift Tax Consequences, 15 Est. Planning 100, 101 (1988).

In *Schelberg*, the government was precluded from relying on Schelberg's pension benefits under the Retirement Plan as an "annuity or other payment" receivable during life. At the time of Schelberg's death in 1974, benefits payable to a surviving beneficiary under a qualified plan were exempt from estate taxation under former § 2039(c), and in Rev. Rul. 76–380, 1976–2 C.B. 270, the Service conceded that qualified plans would not be considered together with other plans in determining the applicability of § 2039(a). This obstacle was removed with the repeal of § 2039(c) in 1984, and the Service is now free to consider a qualified plan together with other plans. See Rev. Rul. 88–85, 1988–2 C.B. 333 (declaring Rev. Rul. 76–380 obsolete). Thus, if *Schelberg* were to arise under current law, Schelberg's pension benefits would clearly qualify as an annuity or payment receivable for his life, and the survivors income benefit payable to his widow would be fully includible in his gross estate under § 2039(a).

At the conclusion of the *Schelberg* opinion, Judge Friendly invited Congress to reexamine the requirement in § 2039 that the decedent either received or was entitled to receive an annuity or other payment. Recall the origins of this requirement. It, along with other sections of the estate tax, was shaped by the statement in Reinecke v. Northern Trust Co., 278 U.S. 339 (1929), supra page 330, that the statutory forerunner of these sections was intended by Congress to require that some interest pass out of the possession, enjoyment or control of the decedent at death and that without this feature the statute would be of doubtful constitutionality. Even in their own time, these propositions were debatable; today, elimination of the "right to receive an annuity or other payment" language would not raise constitutional issues. The ABA Tax Section Task Force recommends just such a move, commenting: "All contractual or statutory survivor benefits economically attributable to the decedent would thus be includible in the gross estate." Report on Transfer Tax Restructuring, 41 Tax Law. 395, 411 (1988).

2. *Survivorship.* To be subject to § 2039(a), the annuity or other payment must be "receivable by [the] beneficiary by reason of surviving the decedent." This requirement is less demanding than the survivorship test of § 2037(a)(1), which is not satisfied unless the beneficiary can obtain possession or enjoyment of the transferred property only by surviving the decedent. Assume an annuity is payable to a 40–year–old primary annuitant for life or ten years, whichever is shorter, and a secondary annuitant is to receive the annuity for life if living when the specified period ends. The primary annui-

tant dies during the ten-year period. Is the survivorship test set out in § 2039(a) satisfied? The test in § 2037(a)(1)? If in the above example the primary annuitant or the annuitant's estate was to receive the payments for ten years, and no mention was made of termination on death, would the value of the annuity payable to the secondary beneficiary be subject to § 2039(a)?

3. *Decedent's right to receive "annuity or other payment."* The question of what constitutes an "other payment" is the central issue in the *Schelberg* case. The court takes the view that Congress meant the payments to be "in the nature of annuities," similar to those to be received by the survivor on the employee's death. The regulations appear to take a more expansive view, and state that the term "other payments" is not limited to annuity payments, but applies to "one or more payments" and that they "may be equal or unequal, conditional or unconditional, periodic or sporadic." Reg. § 20.2039–1(b)(1). The litigated cases in this area have been concerned with four principal problems.

a. *Wages.* As pointed out in the *Schelberg* decision, decedent's regular wages have not been accepted as meeting the "other payment" test of § 2039. Fusz's Estate v. Commissioner, 46 T.C. 214 (1966); see also Siegel's Estate v. Commissioner, 74 T.C. 613 (1980) (disability benefits were in the nature of salary or wage continuation payments because the employee was expected to return to work, so they were not to be integrated with survivor benefits in applying § 2039); Rev. Rul. 77–183, 1977–1 C.B. 274 (same for sickness and accident income benefits). On the basis of this ruling, Schelberg's rights under the Sickness and Accident Plan were viewed as "compensation payments" that did not meet the test of "other payment."

b. *Payments in the event of disability.* Although the facts in the cases are, as the *Schelberg* opinion notes, distinguishable, there is in *Bahen* and *Schelberg* a common issue as to whether payments in event of a disability qualify as an "other payment" within the meaning of § 2039, with the *Schelberg* analysis having emerged as the dominant view. See supra Note 1.

c. *Forfeiture on an event other than retirement.* If conditions other than surviving to retirement age are required, e.g., honesty, loyalty, or compliance with a no-competition agreement, Reg. § 20.2039–1(b)(1) provides that the decedent will be regarded as qualifying "so long as he had complied with his obligations under the contract or agreement up to the time of his death." In Wadewitz's Estate v. Commissioner, 339 F.2d 980 (7th Cir. 1964), the decedent was entitled to a pension on retirement provided he kept himself available for consultation and did not accept employment with a competitor. The court held that the retirement benefits constituted an "annuity or other payment" receivable by decedent since forfeiture would only occur on activity initiated by the decedent. Accord, Silberman v. United States, 333 F.Supp. 1120 (W.D. Pa. 1971) (pension contingent on performance of advisory services after retirement); Rev. Rul. 71–507, 1971–2 C.B. 331 (partnership plan obliged decedent-partner to provide post-retirement consulting services). In Kramer v. United States, 406 F.2d 1363 (Ct. Cl. 1969), however, the court held that § 2039 did not apply to the value of payments receivable by the decedent's widow under a contract providing (a) that the decedent was employed at $12,000 per year for life as the general manager of a family corporation, (b) that if by reason of disability or otherwise it was impossible for him to continue as general manager, he was to become a consultant-adviser to the corporation at the same salary, and (c) that if he died while serving either as general manager or consultant-adviser, his widow would receive $150 weekly for life. The court implied that the result would be different if the services to be rendered were nominal or the prescribed payments were really a retirement annuity. Two dissenting judges expressed fear of "an easy device by which businesses could actually pension off their officers while protecting [their] estates by exacting amorphous undertakings from them to give 'advice' when called upon," but called attention to the fact that the decision, resting on stipulated facts, did not explore the substance of the decedent's consulting arrangement and hence should not be of major precedential importance.

The court in *Kramer* also rejected the government's argument that the value of the widow's weekly payments for life was includible in the decedent's estate under §§ 2036 and 2038, holding that decedent had not retained the requisite powers to bring those sections into operation, nor did § 2033 reach decedent's interest which terminated at his death. One commentator has written that in reliance on authority of this kind agreements between corporations and their top executives have become popular, "whereby, in consideration of the executive continuing to work for the corporation until his death, it will pay a substantial sum to his surviving spouse or other beneficiary." Cooper, A Voluntary Tax? New Perspectives on Sophisticated Estate Tax Avoidance, 77 Colum. L. Rev. 161, 189 (1977).

d. *Combining two or more contracts.* The regulations provide that the term "contract or agreement" includes "any combination of arrangements, understandings or plans arising by reason of decedent's employment." Reg. § 20.2039–1(b)(1). The *Schelberg* opinion describes this regulation as "a rather sharp departure from the letter of the statute" and accepts it with the caveat that the mere possibility that a deceased employee might have received benefits under one plan does not necessarily mean that death benefits payable to a surviving beneficiary under some other plan are automatically includible in the employee's gross estate under § 2039.

4. *Contract or agreement.* This requirement has created two types of problems:

a. *Voluntary payments.* The employer in *Bahen* was contractually obligated to make the payments. In Barr's Estate v. Commissioner, supra page 191, the government cited § 2039 (as well as § 2033) as authority for including benefits paid to the employee's widow in his gross estate, but the court rejected the § 2039 claim for want of a contract or agreement:

> The repeated reference [in § 2039(a) and (b)] to the requirement for some form of contract or agreement, indicates that the rights of both the decedent and the survivor must be enforceable rights; and that voluntary and gratuitous payments by the employer are not taxable under section 2039. This is expressly recognized in Example (4) of [Reg. § 20.2039–1(b)(2)]. However, this same example does state that where the terms of an enforceable retirement plan have been modified by consistent practice of the employer, the annuity received pursuant to such modification will be considered to have been paid under a "contract or agreement." We do

> not think that the latter statement was intended to mean that where there was no enforceable arrangement, contract, or agreement whatever, the mere consistency of an employer in making voluntary or gratuitous payments would be sufficient to supply the essential "contract or agreement." Congress, for reasons satisfactory to it, has made the existence of some form of "contract or agreement" an indispensable prerequisite to the application of section 2039. [40 T.C. at 235–36.]

For an example of an employer's consistent practice of paying death benefits, see Rev. Rul. 75–505, 1975–2 C.B. 364 (state judicial retirement system).

b. *Statutory rights.* Survivorship benefits under plans maintained by the government, such as monthly Social Security payments, are not includible in the employee's gross estate under § 2039(a) because they are payable by virtue of a statute rather than pursuant to a "contract or agreement" and because the amounts withheld from the employee's wages are taxes rather than contributions generating a contractual obligation. Rev. Rul. 81–182, 1981–2 C.B. 179 (Social Security benefits); Rev. Rul. 60–70, 1960–1 C.B. 372 (Railroad Retirement Act benefits).

5. *Life insurance.* Section 2039 does not apply to amounts payable "as insurance under policies on the life of the decedent." In All v. McCobb, 321 F.2d 633 (2d Cir. 1963), a determination by the district court that a payment by Standard Oil Company (New Jersey) under its "death benefit plan" constituted life insurance was reversed:

> The statute thus clearly calls for inclusion in the decedent's gross estate of the death benefits paid to the widow, unless these benefits can be found to have been insurance, as the district court found. It based this finding upon the ground that "the payments in this case were designed to provide partial protection for one year to her as a dependent beneficiary against loss of retirement allowances to her husband through his untimely death." 206 F.Supp. at 903. We hold that this finding is without support and cannot be sustained. The fact that a payment is designed to afford a widow partial protection against the difficulties presented by her husband's death does not, ipso facto, convert that payment into insurance. The function of providing partial protection to widows is characteristic of a great many survivorship annuities and payments which nevertheless are not insurance for purposes of federal estate taxation and which are includable within a decedent's gross estate and taxable as such under § 2039.... [321 F.2d at 636.]

The court then quoted from the definitions of "life insurance" in the *LeGierse* and *Treganowan* cases, infra page 369, Note 1, and concluded:

> Judged by the standards of *LeGierse* and *Treganowan*, the Death Benefit Plan bears no resemblance to a life insurance program. The Plan was unfunded and the company did not make periodic contributions to it in the employee's name. "Premium payments [were] not required, nor [was] there a shifting and spreading of the risk of death in any meaningful sense." Essenfeld v. Commissioner, 311 F.2d 208, 209 (2 Cir., 1962). The decedent in no way shifted to the company the risk that his death would come prematurely and before the company, as insurer, had received

premiums by or on his account in a sum equal to the amount required to be paid to the beneficiary. The company in no way gambled with the decedent that he would live a long life and that it would recover by periodic assessments before his death the amount to be paid to the beneficiary. It made no difference to the company, so far as any fund was concerned, whether the decedent died prematurely or not. . . . Nor did the company in any way undertake to distribute among a larger group of employees, on the basis of actuarial data from which the appropriate size of a terminal reserve could be computed, the risk of the premature death of a single employee. The company did nothing more than promise to pay a sum certain to a named beneficiary upon the death of a retired employee. If payments resulting from such a promise were under the present facts to be regarded as insurance, the effectiveness and significance of § 2039 would be greatly diminished, if not vitiated. [321 F.2d at 637.]

6. *Application of gift tax to employee annuities.* In the absence of specific statutory provisions, the gift tax treatment of employee annuities is governed by general principles, which were summarized in the pre–1986 regulations as follows: "Where an employee has an unqualified right to an annuity but takes a lesser annuity with the provision that upon his death a survivor annuity or other payment will be paid to his designated beneficiary, the employee has made a gift to the beneficiary at the time he gives up his power to deprive the beneficiary of the survivor annuity or other payment." Reg. § 25.2517–1(a)(1). Section 2503(f) expressly exempts the waiver of a spouse's right to a qualified joint and survivor annuity (or qualified preretirement survivor annuity) from the application of the gift tax.

Having conceded that death benefits are not reached by § 2039 in the absence of an annuity or other payment receivable by the decedent during life, the Service has invoked the gift tax in an attempt to prevent such death benefits from escaping transfer tax altogether. This approach received a setback in DiMarco's Estate v. Commissioner, supra page 61, involving death benefits paid to a deceased employee's widow under an unfunded plan maintained by the employer. The court questioned whether the employee ever owned a transferable property interest in the death benefits and found that in any event he made no "transfer" subject to gift tax. Compare the analysis of the "transfer" requirement under § 2038 in Tully's Estate v. United States, supra page 245; see also the cases cited in Note 1, supra page 249. See generally Wolk, The Pure Death Benefit: An Estate and Gift Tax Anomaly, 66 Minn. L. Rev. 229 (1982).

F. LIFE INSURANCE

1. POLICIES ON THE LIFE OF THE DECEDENT: § 2042

Pre–1942 treatment of insurance on the decedent's life. The Revenue Act of 1916 made no mention of life insurance, with the consequence that proceeds of insurance policies on the life of the decedent were included in the gross estate only when the predecessor of § 2033 (property owned by decedent at death) was applicable. This meant that policies payable to the decedent's estate were taxable but policies payable to designated beneficiaries were not. In the Revenue Act of 1918, however, Congress included a provision—the forerunner of § 2042—dealing specifically with insurance on the life of the decedent. Although the principal purpose of the 1918 legislation was to reach policies payable to designated beneficiaries, it also provided that insurance proceeds "receivable by the executor" were includible in the gross estate. The latter provision has been carried forward to the present, and it now appears as § 2042(1). It reaches insurance proceeds that are available for payment of the decedent's debts even though not in form payable to the executor. Reg. § 20.2042–1(b)(1); Matthews' Estate v. Commissioner, 3 T.C. 525 (1944) (portion of proceeds payable to bank in satisfaction of decedent's debts was "receivable by the executor"); Rev. Rul. 77–157, 1977–1 C.B. 279 (life insurance proceeds not receivable by executor where beneficiary has discretion to pay taxes, debts and other charges against insured's estate but is not required to do so). The same tax result was reached where a beneficiary killed the insured and thereby forfeited the right to receive the proceeds, which passed instead to the insured's heirs or devisees under state law as though paid to the insured's executor. Draper's Estate v. Commissioner, 536 F.2d 944 (1st Cir. 1976); First Kentucky Trust Co. v. United States, 737 F.2d 557 (6th Cir. 1984). Conversely, proceeds payable in form to the executor may escape § 2042(1) if state law immunizes them from liability for the decedent's debts so that the executor holds them for the benefit of others. Commissioner v. Jones, 62 F.2d 496 (6th Cir. 1932) (executor held to be mere conduit under local law); United States v. First Natl. Bank & Trust Co., 133 F.2d 886 (8th Cir. 1943) (insurance proceeds payable to decedent's testamentary trustees not receivable by executors, although same bank served in both capacities).

The more troublesome part of the 1918 legislation dealt with policies payable not to the executor but to other beneficiaries. It provided for the inclusion of amounts "receivable by all other beneficiaries as insurance under policies taken out by the decedent upon his own life," except that the first $40,000 of such proceeds was exempt. The innocent phrase "taken out by the decedent" was productive of nothing but trouble. If the 1918 legislation was to be of any consequence, it could not be limited to policies actually applied for by the decedent. Whether the decedent signed the formal application or not, the policy would serve as a device for transmitting wealth from one generation to another if the decedent paid the premiums. Moreover, even if the decedent neither applied for the policy nor paid the premiums, he could affect the transmission of wealth if he held until his death the power to name or change the beneficiary, to assign or pledge the policy, or to surrender it for its cash value. Was a policy "taken out by the decedent" if he paid the premiums or if he possessed "incidents of ownership"? Were both necessary? During the long period that the statute included the phrase "taken out by the decedent," regulation succeeded regulation as the Treasury Department turned from one construction to another like a whirling dervish. Its dizzy antics, which were in part an effort to propitiate the courts, are described in Eisenstein, Estate Taxes and the Higher Learning of the Supreme Court, 3 Tax L. Rev. 395, 513–36 (1948).

1942–1954: The "premiums paid" and "incidents of ownership" tests. Congress finally intervened. The Revenue Act of 1942 wiped out the $40,000 exemption for policies payable to beneficiaries (simultaneously increasing the overall estate tax exemption from $40,000 to $60,000) and eliminated the troublesome phrase "taken out by the decedent." It went on to provide that insurance proceeds payable to designated beneficiaries were includible in the decedent's gross estate if the decedent *either* (1) paid the premiums directly or indirectly, *or* (2) possessed at the time of death any of the "incidents of ownership," exercisable either alone or in conjunction with any other person.

Because the "premiums paid" test required the insurance proceeds to be included in the insured's gross estate even though the decedent retained no control over the policy, its constitutionality was attacked on the ground that it was a "direct tax" on the property, invalid because not apportioned among the states in proportion to population. This theory was rejected by the Supreme Court in United States v. Manufacturers Natl. Bank, 363 U.S. 194 (1960):

> Under the statute, the occasion for the tax is the maturing of the beneficiaries' right to the proceeds upon the death of the insured. Of course, if the insured possessed no policy rights, there is no transfer of any interest *from him* at the moment of death. But that fact is not material, for the taxable "transfer," the maturing of the beneficiaries' right to the proceeds, is the crucial last step in what Congress can reasonably treat as a testamentary disposition by the insured in favor of the beneficiaries. That disposition, which began with the payment of premiums by the insured, is completed by his death. His death created a genuine enlargement of the beneficiaries' rights. It is the "generating source" of the full value of the proceeds.... The maturing of the right to proceeds is therefore an appropriate occasion for taxing the transaction to the estate of the insured. Cf. Tyler v. United States, 281 U.S. 497, 503, 504....
>
> It makes no difference that the payment of premiums occurred during the lifetime of the insured and indirectly effected an inter vivos transfer of property to the owner of the policy rights. Congress can properly impose excise taxes on wholly inter vivos gifts. Bromley v. McCaughn, 280 U.S. 124. It may impose an estate tax on inter vivos transfers looking toward death. Milliken v. United States, 283 U.S. 15. Surely, then, it may impose such a tax on the final step—the maturing of the right to proceeds—in a partly inter vivos transaction completed by death. The question is not whether there has been, in the strict sense of the word, a "transfer" of property owned by the decedent at the time of his death, but whether "the death has brought

> into being or ripened for the survivor, property rights of such character as to make appropriate the imposition of a tax upon that result...." Tyler v. United States, supra, at 503. [363 U.S. at 198–99.]

The alternative basis for including life insurance proceeds in the insured's gross estate under the 1942 law was retention by the decedent of any of the "incidents of ownership." The House and Senate committee reports include the following statement:

> There is no specific enumeration of incidents of ownership, ... as it is impossible to include an exhaustive list. Examples of such incidents are the right of the insured or his estate to the economic benefits of the insurance, the power to change the beneficiary, the power to surrender or cancel the policy, the power to assign it, the power to revoke an assignment, the power to pledge the policy for a loan, or the power to obtain from the insurer a loan against the surrender value of the policy. [H.R. Rep. No. 2333, 77th Cong., 2d Sess. 163 (1942), reprinted in 1942–2 C.B. 372, 491; S. Rep. No. 1631, 77th Cong., 2d Sess. 235 (1942), reprinted in 1942–2 C.B. 504, 677.]

Cf. Reg. § 20.2042–1(c)(2) (listing essentially the same examples).

The 1942 law did provide, however, that a reversionary interest was not an "incident of ownership." But if the decedent possessed a reversionary interest (e.g., if the proceeds would be payable to his estate should the beneficiary predecease him), the proceeds might have been reached by the postponed-possession-or-enjoyment clause.

The 1954 Code: Elimination of "premiums paid" test. The 1954 Code made two changes in this pattern of taxing proceeds payable to designated beneficiaries. It eliminated the premiums paid test, and it provided that a reversionary interest is an "incident of ownership" if its value exceeded 5 percent of the value of the policy immediately before the death of the decedent.

The elimination of the premiums paid test was perhaps the 1954 Code's most important innovation in the estate tax law. The Senate Finance Committee report stated:

> No other property is subject to estate tax where the decedent initially purchased it and then long before his death gave away all rights to the property and to discriminate against life insurance in this regard is not justified. [S. Rep. No. 1622, 83d Cong., 2d Sess. 124 (1954).]

Opposing the change, a minority of the House Ways and Means Committee said:

> Under present law, if a husband transfers ownership of an insurance policy on his life to his wife, but continues to pay the premiums himself, the proceeds are still considered to be a part of the estate he leaves his wife on his death and are, therefore, included in his estate in computing the estate tax.

It is sought to justify the change as merely putting life insurance on a par with other property which may be given away free from estate tax if the gift is not made "in contemplation of death." But life insurance is not like other property. It is inherently testamentary in nature. It is designed, in effect, to serve as a will, regardless of its investment features. Where the insured has paid the premiums on life insurance for the purpose of adding to what he leaves behind at his death for his beneficiaries, the insurance proceeds should certainly be included in his taxable estate.

We predict that if this provision becomes law, it will virtually do away with the estate taxation of life insurance. To avoid the tax, the insured need only assign the policy to his wife or other beneficiary. Since estates of less than $60,000 are nontaxable, only the wealthy will benefit. Nevertheless, we predict that the estate-tax revenue loss will be substantial. Doubtless life insurance will come into great favor among persons of wealth as a means of avoiding estate taxes.

The proposal goes even further than the method of taxing life-insurance proceeds as a part of estates that prevailed prior to 1942, when an exclusion of $40,000 was provided, which Congress eliminated in the Revenue Act of 1942. [H.R. Rep. No. 1337, 83d Cong., 2d Sess. B14–15 (1954).]

From 1942 to 1954, the incidents of ownership test was not of great importance, since in most cases the head of the family could not avoid paying the premiums on the insurance directly or indirectly, and consequently the proceeds would be includible under the premiums paid test. As a result of the 1954 changes, however, the insured can pay the premiums himself and at the same time keep the proceeds out of his estate by ridding himself of all incidents of ownership. The rights to change beneficiaries, to surrender the policy for cash, to pledge it for a loan, and to assign it, can be given up easily enough, if the insured wishes to do so. A reversionary interest can be avoided by providing that the proceeds are to be paid to a designated beneficiary or, if the beneficiary predeceases the insured, to the beneficiary's estate. Moreover, the regulations provide, in § 20.2042–1(c)(3), that the terms "reversionary interest" and "incidents of ownership" do not include the possibility that the insured might receive a policy or its proceeds by inheritance or as a surviving spouse by election.

Gift tax on transfers of insurance policies and payments of premiums. The repeal of the premiums paid test in 1954 brought in its train many transfers of policies that had been in force for some time. The transfer of such a policy is a "gift" under § 2511(a), and a gift tax may be due. How is the policy to be valued? In Guggenheim v. Rasquin, 312 U.S. 254 (1941), a donor made a gift of three single-premium life insurance policies (with an aggregate face amount of $1 million) immediately after purchasing them. Although she had paid about $852,000 in premiums, the cash surrender value of the policies was only about $717,000, and she valued them at the lower amount on her gift tax return. The Supreme Court held that the proper value was her cost:

> Cash-surrender value is the reserve less a surrender charge. And in case of a single-premium policy the reserve is the face amount of the contract discounted at a specified rate of interest on the basis of the insured's expected life. If the policy is surrendered, the company will pay the cash-surrender value. It is asserted that the market for insurance contracts is usually the issuing companies or the banks who will lend money on them; that banks will not loan more than the cash-surrender value; and that if policies had an actual realizable value in excess of their cash-surrender value, there would arise a business of purchasing such policies from those who otherwise would surrender them. From these facts it is urged that cash-surrender value represents the amount which would be actually obtained for the policies in a willing buyer-willing seller market. . . .
>
> That analysis, however, overlooks the nature of the property interest which is being valued. Surrender of a policy represents only one of the rights of the insured or beneficiary. Plainly that right is one of the substantial legal incidents of ownership. . . . But the owner of a fully paid life insurance policy has more than the mere right to surrender it; he has the right to retain it for its investment virtues and to receive the face amount of the policy upon the insured's death. That these latter rights are deemed by purchasers of insurance to have substantial value is clear from the difference between the cost of a single-premium policy and its immediate or early cash-surrender value—in the instant case over $135,000. All of the economic benefits of a policy must be taken into consideration in determining its value for gift-tax purposes. To single out one and to disregard the others is in effect to substitute a different property interest for the one which was the subject of the gift. In this situation as in others . . . an important element in the value of the property is the use to which it may be put. Certainly the petitioner here did not expend $852,438.50 to make an immediate gift limited to $717,344.81. Presumptively the value of these policies at the date of the gift was the amount which the insured had expended to acquire them. Cost is cogent evidence of value. And here it is the only suggested criterion which reflects the value to the owner of the entire bundle of rights in a single-premium policy—the right to retain it as well as the right to surrender it. Cost in this situation is not market price in the normal sense of the term. But the absence of market price is no barrier to valuation. . . . [312 U.S. at 256–58.]

Although the Supreme Court held that the cost of the policy was the proper measure of its value in this case, the cash surrender value of a policy that has been in force for some time might exceed the aggregate premiums paid. Moreover, neither the cash surrender value nor the aggregate cost is a fair index of the value of the policy if the insured has become uninsurable. In United States v. Ryerson, 312 U.S. 260 (1941), the Court said of a gift of such policies:

> The cost of duplicating the policies at the dates of the gifts is, in absence of more cogent evidence, the one criterion which reflects both their insurance and investment value to the owner at that time.... The fact that the then condition of an insured's health might make him uninsurable emphasizes the conclusion that the use of that criterion will result in placing a minimum value upon such a gift. [312 U.S. at 261–62.]

The value of a policy that has been in force for some time and on which further premiums are to be paid is the "interpolated terminal reserve," at the date of the gift, plus the proportionate part of the last premium paid that covers the period beyond the date of the gift. The value is adjusted to take into account an outstanding dividend or indebtedness. See Reg. § 25.2512–6(a) (Example 4) (illustrative computation). Each premium payment made by the donor thereafter constitutes an additional gift. It is of obvious concern in planning an estate whether the irrevocable transfer of a policy of life insurance and the subsequent payment of premiums are gifts of present or future interests. An outright gift of a policy, even if it has no cash surrender value, and of premiums on a previously transferred policy, are considered present interests eligible for the $10,000 annual exclusion. Reg. § 25.2503–3(a); Rev. Rul. 55–408, 1955–1 C.B. 113; see also Rev. Rul. 76–490, 1976–2 C.B. 300 (premiums paid by employer on group-term policy after employee assigned rights in policy treated as gifts by employee). If, however, the policy is transferred in trust so that no income or principal is presently available to the beneficiaries, the gift will not be entitled to the exclusion. See supra page 151, Note 5. In this situation, taxpayers have resorted to the use of *Crummey* powers, conferring on a beneficiary a noncumulative power to withdraw each year the full amount of any premiums paid (up to the amount of the annual exclusion) during that year. Such a device may give rise to tax problems for a beneficiary who does not exercise the power of withdrawal. The lapse of such a power is considered a release of a general power of appointment, which may trigger gift and estate tax consequences under §§ 2514(e) and 2041(b)(2) to the extent that the lapsed amount exceeds the greater of $5,000 or 5 percent of the aggregate value of the assets subject to the power. See discussion infra page 418.

Under these several provisions, an insured can remove the proceeds of life insurance from the reach of the estate tax by making the proceeds payable to a third person and by transferring all incidents of ownership in the policies to the beneficiary or some other person. If full advantage is taken of the $10,000 annual exclusion ($20,000 per donee for a married couple), the initial gift and the subsequent payment of premiums may incur little or no gift tax. With an outright gift, if the donee survives the insured and the proceeds become payable to a third person, the donee will be treated as making a gift of the full amount of the proceeds to the beneficiary. Goodman v. Commissioner, 156 F.2d 218 (2d Cir. 1946).

Furthermore, there is a risk that the donee may die before the insured, leaving his or her estate, including the life insurance, to the insured. This unexpected development would wipe out the anticipated tax advantages and, unless the transfers are covered by the marital deduction, may prove costly in additional taxes. The value of the policy will be included in the donee's gross estate under § 2033, and the insured will have to make arrangements to transfer the policy to a new beneficiary. This risk may be avoided by transferring the policy in trust with provisions for alternative beneficiaries, although such a transfer may fail to qualify for the annual exclusion.

With the repeal of the premiums paid test in 1954, there has been a revival of interest in a form of irrevocable insurance trust by which income-producing property is transferred to a trustee to pay premiums on insurance on the settlor's life. The settlor either transfers existing policies with the other property or the trustee takes out new policies. On the settlor's death, the beneficiaries receive both the insurance proceeds and the property whose income was previously used to keep up the policies.[38] Section 2042(2) does not reach the insurance proceeds because the insured does not possess any incidents of ownership, nor has the Service been successful in applying §§ 2036 or 2038 to them. Crosley's Estate v. Commissioner, 47 T.C. 310 (1966). What argument can be made for applying § 2036(a) to the rest of the trust property? Note that the income of a trust of this kind continues to be taxed to the settlor under § 677(a)(3). The 1954 repeal of the premiums paid test for the estate tax was not accompanied by a revision of the theory that the payment of premiums on life insurance is so important an expenditure for the average taxpayer that the income of a trust which relieves him of that expense is taxed to him even if the policies have been irrevocably assigned.

For the tax consequences of a gift of life insurance within three years of the insured's death, see infra page 388.

COMMISSIONER v. NOEL'S ESTATE

380 U.S. 678 (1965).

MR. JUSTICE BLACK delivered the opinion of the Court.

This is a federal estate tax case, raising questions under § 2042(2) of the Internal Revenue Code of 1954, ... which requires inclusion in the gross estate of a decedent of amounts received by beneficiaries other than the executor from "insurance under policies on the life of the decedent" if the decedent "possessed at his death any of the incidents of ownership, exercisable either alone or in conjunction with any other person...." The questions presented in this case are whether certain flight insurance policies payable upon the accidental death of the insured were policies "on

38. The objective here is to provide either liquidity (i.e., cash to pay the estate tax) or security for dependent family members (i.e., income to replace the insured's earnings in the event of premature death), rather than maximum return. The settlor who lives out a full life expectancy is likely to realize a higher return from alternative investments.

the life of the decedent" and whether at his death he had reserved any of the "incidents of ownership" in the policies.

These issues emerge from the following facts. Respondent Ruth M. Noel drove her husband from their home to New York International Airport where he was to take an airplane to Venezuela. Just before taking off, Mr. Noel signed applications for two round-trip flight insurance policies, aggregating $125,000 and naming his wife as beneficiary. Mrs. Noel testified that she paid the premiums of $2.50 each on the policies and that her husband then instructed the sales clerk to "give them to my wife. They are hers now, I no longer have anything to do with them." The clerk gave her the policies, which she kept. Less than three hours later Mr. Noel's plane crashed into the Atlantic Ocean and he and all others aboard were killed. Thereafter the companies paid Mrs. Noel the $125,000 face value of the policies, which was not included in the estate tax return filed by his executors. The Commissioner of Internal Revenue determined that the proceeds of the policies should have been included and the Tax Court sustained that determination, holding that the flight accident policies were insurance "on the life of the decedent"; that Mr. Noel had possessed exercisable "incidents of ownership" in the policies at his death; and that the $125,000 paid to Mrs. Noel as beneficiary was therefore includable in the gross estate. 39 T.C. 466. Although agreeing that decedent's reserved right to assign the policies and to change the beneficiary amounted to "exercisable incidents of ownership within the meaning of the statute," the Court of Appeals nevertheless reversed, holding that given "its ordinary, plain and generally accepted meaning," the statutory phrase "policies on the life of the decedent" does not apply to insurance paid on account of accidental death under policies like those here. 332 F.2d 950. The court's reason for drawing the distinction was that under a life insurance contract an insurer "agrees to pay a specified sum upon the occurrence of an *inevitable* event," whereas accident insurance covers a risk "which is *evitable* and not likely to occur." (Emphasis supplied.) 332 F.2d, at 952. Because of the importance of an authoritative answer to these questions in the administration of the estate tax laws, we granted certiorari to decide them. 379 U.S. 927.

I

In 1929, 36 years ago, the Board of Tax Appeals, predecessor to the Tax Court, held in Ackerman v. Commissioner, 15 B.T.A. 635, that "amounts received as accident insurance" because of the death of the insured were includable in the estate of the deceased. The Board of Tax Appeals recognized that "there is a distinction between life insurance and accident insurance, the former insuring against death in any event and the latter ... against death under certain contingencies...." The Court of Appeals in the case now before us considered this distinction between an "inevitable" and an "evitable" event to be of crucial significance under the statute. The Board of Tax Appeals in *Ackerman* did not, stating "we fail to see why one is not taken out upon the life of the policy-holder as much as the other. In each case the risk assumed by the insurer is the loss of the insured's life, and the payment of the insurance money is contingent upon the loss of life." This view of the Board of Tax Appeals is wholly consistent with the language of the statute itself which makes no distinction between "policies on the life of the decedent" which are payable in all events and those payable only if death comes in a certain way or within a certain time. Even were the statutory language less clear, since the Board of Tax Appeals' *Ackerman* case it has been the settled and consistent administrative practice to include insurance proceeds for accidental death under policies like these in the estates of decedents. The Treasury Regulations remain unchanged from the time of the *Ackerman* decision and from that day to this Congress has never attempted to limit the scope of that decision or the established administrative construction of § 2042(2), although it has re-enacted that section and amended it in other respects a number of times. We have held in many cases that such a long-standing administrative interpretation, applying to a substantially re-enacted statute, is deemed to have received congressional approval and has the effect of law. See, e.g., National Lead Co. v. United States, 252 U.S. 140, 146; United States v. Dakota–Montana Oil Co., 288 U.S. 459, 466. We hold here that these insurance policies, whether called "flight accident insurance" or "life insurance," were in effect insurance taken out on the "life of the decedent" within the meaning of § 2042(2).

II

The executors' second contention is that even if these were policies "on the life of the decedent," Mrs. Noel owned them completely, and the decedent therefore possessed no exercisable incident of ownership in them at the time of his death so as to make the proceeds includable in his estate. While not clearly spelled out, the contention that the decedent reserved no incident of ownership in the policies rests on three alternative claims: (a) that Mrs. Noel purchased the policies and therefore owned them; (b) that even if her husband owned the policies, he gave them to her, thereby depriving himself of power to assign the policies or to change the beneficiary; and (c) even assuming he had contractual power to assign the policies or make a beneficiary change, this power was illusory as he could not possibly have exercised it in the interval between take-off and the fatal crash in the Atlantic.

(a) The contention that Mrs. Noel bought the policies and therefore owned them rests solely on her testimony that she furnished the money for their purchase, intending thereby to preserve her right to continue as beneficiary. Accepting her claim that she supplied the money to buy the policies for her own benefit (which the Tax Court did not decide), what she bought nonetheless were policy contracts containing agreements between her husband and the companies. The contracts themselves granted to Mr. Noel the right either to assign the policies or to change the beneficiary without her consent. Therefore the contracts she bought by their very terms rebut her claim that she became the complete, unconditional owner of the policies with an irrevocable right to remain the beneficiary.

(b) The contention that Mr. Noel gave or assigned the policies to her and therefore was without power thereafter to assign them or to change the beneficiary stands no better under these facts. The contract terms provided that these policies could not be assigned nor could the beneficiary be changed without a written endorsement on the policies. No such assignment or change of beneficiary was endorsed on these policies, and consequently the power to assign the policies or change the beneficiary remained in the decedent at the time of his death.

(c) Obviously, there was no practical opportunity for the decedent to assign the policies or change the beneficiary between the time he boarded the plane and the time he died. That time was too short and his wife had the policies in her possession at home. These circumstances disabled him for the moment from exercising those "incidents of ownership" over the policies which were undoubtedly his. Death intervened before this temporary disability was removed. But the same could be said about a man owning an ordinary life insurance policy who boarded the plane at the same time or for that matter about any man's exercise of ownership over his property while aboard an airplane in the three hours before a fatal crash. It would stretch the imagination to think that Congress intended to measure estate tax liability by an individual's fluctuating, day-by-day, hour-by-hour capacity to dispose of property which he owns. We hold that estate tax liability for policies "with respect to which the decedent possessed at his death any of the incidents of ownership" depends on a general, legal power to exercise ownership, without regard to the owner's ability to exercise it at a particular moment. Nothing we have said is to be taken as meaning that a policyholder is without power to divest himself of all incidents of ownership over his insurance policies by a proper gift or assignment, so as to bar its inclusion in his gross estate under § 2042(2). What we do hold is that no such transfer was made of the policies here involved. The judgment of the Court of Appeals is reversed and the judgment of the Tax Court is affirmed.

It is so ordered.

MR. JUSTICE DOUGLAS dissents.

NOTES

1. *General definition of "life insurance."* Section 2042 does not define "life insurance." The starting point for most analyses of the subject is the statement from Helvering v. LeGierse, 312 U.S. 531, 539 (1941), that "[h]istorically and commonly insurance involves risk-shifting and risk-distributing." Under this test, an amount does not qualify as "life insurance" merely because it becomes payable by reason of death, if the risk that is insured is not the victim's early death. Rev. Rul. 57-54, 1957-1 C.B. 298, involved a contract of insurance under which the insurer agreed to pay the owner of an

airplane all sums that the latter might become liable to pay by reason of liability for accident to any passenger, provided the passenger or his representatives executed a full release of all claims for damages against the insured. The Service ruled that the amounts received by the personal representatives of a deceased passenger are not life insurance within the meaning of the statute, even though paid without proof of the insured's legal liability for the passenger's death. The ruling goes on to say:

> However, if the contract between the insurance carrier and the owner of the airplane had provided that the insurance company would unconditionally pay an agreed amount to the estate of any passenger who died as a result of an accident while a passenger on the airplane, the acceptance of such amount would have constituted insurance receivable by the executor of the decedent's estate and includible in the decedent's gross estate for Federal estate tax purposes under section 2042 of the Code.

See also Rev. Rul. 68–88, 1968–1 C.B. 397 (amounts recoverable for wrongful death under the uninsured motorist endorsement of an automobile liability insurance policy required by state statute are not proceeds of life insurance within meaning of § 2042).

The statutory reference to "policies" on the decedent's life might be construed as reaching only contracts written by regular insurance companies, but Reg. § 20.2042–1(a) states expansively: "The term 'insurance' refers to life insurance of every description, including death benefits paid by fraternal beneficial societies operating under the lodge system." In Commissioner v. Treganowan, 183 F.2d 288 (2d Cir.), cert. denied, 340 U.S. 853 (1950), the court had to determine whether the gross estate included a "death benefit" of $20,000 paid to the decedent's widow by the Trustees of the Gratuity Fund of the New York Stock Exchange, of which the decedent had been a member:

> ... Since 1873 the Exchange has had a plan providing for the payment by the surviving members of a certain sum to the families of deceased members. The constitution of the Exchange sets up for this purpose a Gratuity Fund and provides that before any one may be elected to membership in the Exchange he must make a contribution to the Gratuity Fund of $15. By the constitution the member also "pledges himself to make, upon the death of a member of the Exchange, a voluntary gift to the family of each deceased member in the sum of fifteen dollars." The constitution also pledges the faith of the Exchange to pay, out of these assessments, $20,000, or so much thereof as may have been collected, to the persons named in the next section of the document. The persons there named were the widow and children of the member or issue of a deceased child or children, or if he died leaving neither widow, child, nor issue of a child, then to his legal heirs or the persons who would, under the laws of New York, take the same by reason of relationship to him had he owned the same at the time of his death. No member has at any time had the right to name, select, or designate any beneficiary or beneficiaries other than those named above, nor may the proceeds be assigned or pledged for the payment of any debt.
>
> Although the constitution provides that the beneficiaries of a deceased member are to receive the full $20,000 only if that amount is

collected, practically it is certain that the full amount will be paid. Under Art. X, § 5, of the constitution of the Exchange, members are subject to loss of their seats for failure to meet any assessment, including the contribution due on decease of a member. When the assessments against all 1374 living members are met, the Exchange has actually received $610 more than is necessary to cover the payment of $20,000; thus default of more than forty members would be required before the benefit would be decreased, and in fact the full amount has invariably been paid. Moreover, the Fund itself has reached such an amount that the Exchange in 1941 took steps for its reduction by the device of foregoing such contributions. [183 F.2d at 289–90.]

2. *Statutory constraints.* The traditional concept of life insurance developed by the courts is broad enough to include some financial products which function primarily as investment vehicles (e.g., "flexible premium" or "universal life" policies). In 1984, however, Congress enacted § 7702, which adopts a narrower definition of a "life insurance contract" for federal tax purposes. Although § 7702 serves mainly to restrict the income tax benefit of deferral under § 101, it also applies for estate and gift tax purposes. If a policy falls within the statutory definition, the full amount paid by reason of the insured's death is treated as life insurance proceeds under § 2042; otherwise, only the amount in excess of the net surrender value is so treated, though in this case the net surrender value presumably will be included under another provision (e.g., § 2033 or § 2038). § 7702(g)(2).

3. *Life insurance-annuity combinations.* In Helvering v. LeGierse, 312 U.S. 531 (1941), the Court had to pass on the status of proceeds under a life insurance policy purchased by an 80–year–old person in conjunction with an annuity contract, the issuer having required that both contracts be purchased in combination so that its loss on the insurance policy in the event of an early death would be counterbalanced by gain on the annuity contract. The issue was whether in these circumstances, the proceeds of the insurance policy qualified for the $40,000 exemption allowed for insurance proceeds under the pre–1942 law. The Court held that the contracts in combination eliminated the mortality risk that is characteristic of insurance, so that the proceeds were not "receivable as insurance" under the statute. In Fidelity–Philadelphia Trust Co. v. Smith, 356 U.S. 274 (1958), the decedent purchased a similar insurance-annuity combination at age 76, but made an irrevocable assignment of the insurance policy during her life. On her death, the Court rejected the government's argument that the proceeds were includible in the estate under § 2036:

> To establish its contention, the Government must aggregate the premiums of the annuity policies with those of the life insurance policies and establish that the annuity payments were derived as income from the entire investment. This proposition cannot be established. Admittedly, when the policies were purchased, each life insurance-annuity combination was the product of a single, integrated transaction. However, the parties neither intended that, nor acted as if, any of the transactions would have a quality of indivisibility. Regardless of the considerations prompting the insurance companies to hedge their life insurance contracts with annuities, each time an annuity-life insurance combination

was written, two items of property, an annuity policy and an insurance policy, were transferred to the purchaser. The annuity policy could have been acquired separately, and the life insurance policy could have been, and was, conveyed separately. The annuities arose from personal obligations of the insurance companies which were in no way conditioned on the continued existence of the life insurance contracts. These periodic payments would have continued unimpaired and without diminution in size throughout the life of the insured even if the life insurance policies had been extinguished. Quite clearly the annuity payments arose solely from the annuity policies. The use and enjoyment of the annuity policies were entirely independent of the life insurance policies. Because of this independence, the Commissioner may not, by aggregating the two types of policies into one investment, conclude that by receiving the annuities, the decedent had retained income from the life insurance contracts. [356 U.S. at 280–81.]

The proceeds payable at decedent's death from a life insurance-annuity combination are now subject to estate tax under § 2039(a), which had not been enacted at the time the *Fidelity–Philadelphia Trust Co.* case arose. See Montgomery's Estate v. Commissioner, 56 T.C. 489 (1971), affd., 458 F.2d 616 (5th Cir.), cert. denied, 409 U.S. 849 (1972).

UNITED STATES v. RHODE ISLAND HOSPITAL TRUST CO.

355 F.2d 7 (1st Cir. 1966).

COFFIN, CIRCUIT JUDGE.

This appeal presents the question whether the proceeds of a life insurance policy on decedent's life are properly includable in the gross estate of the decedent by reason of the alleged possession at his death of "any of the incidents of ownership, exercisable either alone or in conjunction with any other person," under Section 2042 of the Internal Revenue Code. . . .

The Commissioner of Internal Revenue having included the proceeds of an insurance policy on the life of Holton W. Horton (decedent) in his gross estate and the sum of $14,185.85 in federal estate taxes and $1,004.67 in interest having been paid, the plaintiffs, coexecutors under his will, made timely claim for refund and brought this action for recovery under 28 U.S.C. § 1346(a), alleging that such sums were erroneously assessed. The matter was submitted to the district court upon an agreed statement of facts and depositions. The district court found for the plaintiffs, D.R.I., 1965, 241 F. Supp. 586, and the government appeals.

The facts, undisputed, are of two kinds: "intent facts"—those relating to the conduct and understanding of the insured and his father, who was the instigator, premium payer, and primary beneficiary of the policy; and the "policy facts"—those revealed by the insurance contract itself.

Decedent's father, Charles A. Horton, was a textile executive, a prominent businessman in his community, and, according to the testimony, "a man with strong convictions and vigorous action." Charles and his wife, Louise, had two sons, decedent and A. Trowbridge Horton. In 1924, when decedent was 18 and Trowbridge 19, their father purchased an insurance policy on the life of each boy from Massachusetts Mutual Life Insurance Company. The policies were identical, each having the face amount of $50,000, the proceeds being payable to Charles and Louise, equally, or to the survivor.

Charles Horton's purpose was to assure that funds would be available for his wife, should he and either son die. Charles kept the policies in his safe deposit box and paid all premiums throughout his life. Under the policies, however, the right to change beneficiaries had been reserved to the sons. In January, 1952, the boys' mother, Louise, died. In March, 1952, Charles told each of his sons to go to the insurance company's office and sign a change of beneficiary form. The amendment executed by decedent named his father as primary beneficiary, with decedent's wife, brother, and the executors or administrators of the last survivor being the successive beneficiaries. After this amendment, decedent continued to retain the right to make further changes, but none was made. Decedent died on April 1, 1958, survived by his wife and father. His father died on October 2, 1961.

The father, Charles, regarded the policies as belonging to him, saying at one point that it would be "out of the question" for the sons to claim them. Decedent's brother never discussed the policies with his father, never asked for a loan based on the policies, obediently signed the change of beneficiary form at his father's request, and considered the policy on his life as the property of his father. Decedent's widow recalled only that decedent had once told her that his father had a policy on himself and his brother but that "in no way did it mean anything to us or would it ever. It was completely his." She added that her husband, the decedent, had wanted more insurance of his own, but was not able to obtain it.

Coming to what we call "policy facts," a careful reading of the policy, captioned "Ordinary Life Policy—Convertible," reveals the following rights, privileges, or powers accorded to the decedent.

> *Right to change beneficiary.* In the application, an unrestricted change of beneficiary provision was elected by striking out two alternative and more limited provisions. The policy itself indicated reservation of "the right successively to change the beneficiary" by the insertion of typewritten dashes where, otherwise, the word "not" would have been inserted.
>
> *Assignment.* No assignment would be recognized until the original assignment, a duplicate, or a certified copy was filed with the company. The company did not assume responsibility for the validity of an assignment.
>
> *Dividends.* The insured had the option to have dividends paid in cash, used to reduce premiums, used to purchase paid-up additions, or accumulate subject to withdrawal on demand.

Loans. On condition that the unlimited right to change the beneficiary was reserved, as in this case, the company would "loan on the signature of the insured alone."

Survival. Should no beneficiary survive the insured, the proceeds were payable to his executors and administrators.

Alteration. The policy could be altered only on the written request of the insured and of "other parties in interest."

Discharge of company's obligations. The company would not be responsible for the conduct of any trustee or for the determination of the identity or rights of beneficiaries. Payment at the direction of a trustee or in good faith to a beneficiary would discharge the company of its contractual obligations. Beneficiaries were advised by the policy that they need hire no firm or person to collect the amount payable under the policy, but that they would save time and expense by writing to the company directly.

The plaintiffs contend that the district court properly held that decedent possessed no incidents of ownership in the policy; that the term "incidents of ownership" refers to the rights of insured or his estate to the economic benefits of the policy; that the question of possession of such incidents is one of fact; that such possession depends upon all relevant facts and circumstances, including the intention of the parties; and that these facts and circumstances clearly establish that decedent's father was the real owner of the policy, while decedent was merely the nominal owner, having no real economic interest in it.

The government asserts that, as a matter of law, the facts bring this case squarely within the reach of Section 2042, as applied by the cases, notwithstanding the evidence as to the intentions and extra-policy circumstances of the parties, and the lack of economic benefit to decedent.

At the outset we are confronted with the issue of the nature of this review. It is undoubtedly true that the question of possession of incidents of ownership of a life insurance policy is one of fact, the plaintiff having the burden of proving non-possession of all.... But where all of the evidentiary facts appear, we are faced with a question of law not of fact. Were we to proceed otherwise, cases presenting identical or closely similar facts in this technical and complex field could be decided oppositely, to the disadvantage of equitable tax administration.

Taking the subsidiary facts as presented to the district court, we differ with its conclusion that "the decedent's father was actually the real owner of the various incidents of ownership in said policy." But in differing we recognize that early holdings and occasional dicta, early and late, have invited litigation. This is the kind of case where the government enters, appearing to seek its pound of flesh on the basis of petty technicality, while the taxpayer's decedent generally appears as a person who had very little to do with the insurance policy which is causing so much trouble to his estate. If such hard cases have not made bad law, they have at least made bad dicta. Although the Supreme Court has recently (indeed, since the principal hearing of this case before the district court) spoken strongly and succinctly on this issue in Commissioner of Internal Revenue v. Estate of Noel, 1965, 380 U.S. 678, of which more will be said, we think it appropriate to set forth the considerations of fact, law, and policy which have persuaded us.

To begin, the statute which bears on this case has a reason for being, is part of a general rationale and tax law pattern, and is deliberately precise. Before the Revenue Act of 1942, the tax criterion governing cases in this area was "policies taken out" by the decedent on his own life.... This led to difficult problems of interpretation, which the courts resolved by creating two criteria: "payment of premiums" and possession of "incidents of ownership." The Revenue Act of 1942 ... eliminated the "policies taken out" language, and sanctified the judicial gloss, with Congress, in its committee reports, including an illustrative list of the kinds of rights included under "incidents of ownership." These included decedent's right to change beneficiaries, to borrow, to assign, to revoke an assignment, and to surrender or cancel. H. Rep. No. 2333, 77th Cong., 2d Sess., p.164, 1942–2 Cum. Bull. 372, 491.

In acting this way, Congress was, we think, trying to introduce some certitude in a landscape of shifting sands. In the provision which was the predecessor of Section 2042, it was not trying to tax the *extent* of the interest of the decedent. That it knew how to do this is evident, for example, from a reading of Section 2033 ..., which includes in the gross estate of the decedent "the value of all property ... to the extent of the interest therein...." What it was attempting to reach in Section 2042 and some other sections was the *power* to dispose of property, the same power that the Supreme Court recognized as a basis for exercise of the tax instrument in Chase National Bank of City of New York v. United States, 1929, 278 U.S. 327. Power can be and is exercised by one possessed of less than complete legal and equitable title. The very phrase "incidents of ownership" connotes something partial, minor, or even fractional in its scope. It speaks more of possibility than of probability.

Plaintiffs seize on Section 20.2042–1(c)(2) of the Treasury Regulations on Estate Tax, which says "... the term 'incidents of ownership' is not limited in its meaning to ownership of the policy in the technical legal sense. Generally speaking, the term has reference to the right of the insured or his estate to the economic benefits of the policy." Plaintiffs urge that there must be "a real control over the economic benefits." To this there are two answers. First, it is clear that the reference to ownership in the "technical legal sense" is not abandoned and supplanted by reference to "economic benefits." Second, the regulation goes on to list illustrative powers referred to by Congress in its reports. All of these are powers which may or may not enrich decedent's estate, but which can affect the transfer of the policy proceeds.

Viewed against this background, what power did decedent possess? This is the relevant question—not how did he feel or act. Did he have a capacity to do something to affect the disposition of the policy if he had wanted to? Without gaining possession of the policy itself, he could have borrowed on the policy. He could have changed the method of using dividends. He could have assigned the policy. He could have revoked the assignment. Should he have gained possession of the policy by trick (as by filing an affidavit that the policy was lost), force, or chance, he could have changed the beneficiary, and made the change of record irrevocable.... Other such possibilities might be imagined. We cite these only to evidence the existence of some power in decedent to affect the disposition of the policy proceeds. In addition, he always possessed a negative power. His signature was necessary to a change in beneficiary, to a surrender for cash value, to an alteration in the policy, to a change in dividend options. Even with this most limited power, he would be exercising an incident of ownership "in conjunction with" another person....

The existence of such powers in the decedent is to be distinguished from such rights as may have existed in decedent's father or duties owed the father by decedent. It is, therefore, no answer that decedent's father might have proceeded against him at law or in equity. The company made it clear in the contract that it bore no responsibility for the validity of an assignment, that it could pay a beneficiary without recourse, and that it was under no obligation to see to the carrying out of any trust. It even made clear that a beneficiary need only write to the home office to receive payment. Should a third party—for example, an innocent creditor who had given valuable consideration to decedent—receive the proceeds of the policy, the proceeds of a loan on the policy, or the cash value, it could not be said that the transaction between decedent and such third person would in all such cases be nugatory. For decedent had some powers—perhaps not rights, but powers—which could, if exercised alone or in conjunction with another, affect the disposition of some or all of the proceeds of the policy.

Nor is it a compelling argument that decedent lacked physical possession of the policy. Commissioner of Internal Revenue v. Estate of Noel, 1965, 380 U.S. 678.... Moreover, as we have noted, some rights could be exercised without physical possession of the policy.

The cases arising from similar facts over nearly a quarter of a century give little support, in their holdings, to plaintiffs.... Decisions in [these] cases have, on the evidence presented, almost uniformly held the "policy facts" (reservation of rights in the policy) impregnable to attack from the "intent facts." ...

To the principle of heavy predominance of the "policy facts" over the "intent facts" there must be added the caveat that, where the insurance contract itself does not reflect the instructions of the parties, as where an agent, on his own initiative, inserts a reservation of right to change a beneficiary contrary to the intentions which had been expressed to him, no incidents of ownership are thereby created. National Metropolitan Bank of Washington v. United States, 1950, 87 F. Supp. 773, 115 Ct. Cl. 396; Schongalla v. Hickey, 2 Cir. 1945, 149 F.2d 687. The case before us presents no such issue, for the right in decedent to change beneficiaries was recognized on the one occasion when it was exercised and this right continued thereafter.

While decisions against the estate of a passive but power-possessing decedent may often conflict with the honest intentions and understanding of premium-paying beneficiaries and insureds, the alternative of abandoning the insistence on the governing nature of the contract, in most cases, is less desirable. The drawing of a useful line would be impossible; there would be a much wider range of varying decisions on similar facts; and there would be an invitation to unprincipled estate manipulation. As government counsel has pointed out, there could always be a formally executed side agreement under which the insured clearly surrenders to the beneficiary all his rights to the policy, such agreement to be brought to light only in the event of the decedent's dying before the beneficiary.

In any event, the statute has been on the books since the Revenue Act of 1942. This is only one of a number of cases applying it in the face of considerable external evidence of intent. Charles Horton, who caused the policy to be taken out, saw fit to vest decedent with rights in the policy and to allow such rights to continue for thirty-four years. Charles was a successful businessman and with as much incentive, opportunity, and capacity to be aware of the laws of the land as most people. It is difficult to speculate what purpose he thought was being served by his son's retention of rights in the policy. Had he wished to deprive his son of all incidents of ownership in the policy, this result could easily have been accomplished. But the step was not taken. We find that the decedent died, possessing at least an incident of ownership in the policy on his life.

Judgment will be entered vacating the judgment of the district court and ordering judgment for the defendant.

NOTES

1. *Incidents of ownership.* In both *Noel* and *Rhode Island Hospital Trust Co.*, life insurance proceeds were includible in the gross estate despite the decedent's inability, as a practical matter, to exercise incidents of ownership over the policy. See also O'Daniel's Estate v. United States, 6 F.3d 321 (5th Cir. 1993) ("Incidents of ownership connote the legal power to exercise ownership, not the decedent's practical ability to do so.") Conversely, a decedent who misappropriates the economic benefits of a life insurance policy does not necessarily possess incidents of ownership. See Bloch's Estate v. Commissioner, 78 T.C. 850 (1982) (decedent, as trustee, took out policies on his own life and pledged them as collateral for personal debt in breach of fiduciary duty; held, proceeds not includible in gross estate).

2. *Contingent rights.* Nothing in § 2042 excludes contingent rights from the scope of the term "incidents of ownership." Is a retained right to

withdraw the cash surrender value of a policy if the consumer price index exceeds a specified figure an incident of ownership, even though the specified event is not subject to decedent's control and does not occur during his life?

The issue in Smith's Estate v. Commissioner, 73 T.C. 307 (1979), involved an employment agreement under which the decedent's employer was obligated to allow the decedent to purchase for their cash surrender value two policies of insurance on the decedent's life, if and when the employer dropped or surrendered the policies. The court refused to find that decedent's option was an incident of ownership, pointing out that decedent's rights "were contingent ones dependent on an event which never occurred and over which he had no control." 73 T.C. at 309. Smead's Estate v. Commissioner, 78 T.C. 43 (1982), presented similar facts. The employee was entitled, under a group insurance policy maintained by his employer, to convert his coverage into individual insurance, without medical examination or other evidence of insurability, on either voluntary or involuntary termination of his employment. On the *Smith* authority, the court held that the conversion privilege was not an incident of ownership within the meaning of § 2042(2), noting that quitting a job is "too high a price to pay for the right to convert to another policy" and that termination by the employer was a contingency beyond the employee's control. For an additional justification of rulings of this kind, see Rev. Rul. 72–307, 1972–1 C.B. 307 (employee's power to cancel coverage under group-term policy by terminating employment is "a collateral consequence of the power that every employee has to terminate his employment," not an incident of ownership in the policy). See also Rev. Rul. 84–130, 1984–2 C.B. 194 (employee's right under group-term policy to convert to individual policy on termination of employment not an incident of ownership).

Does the decedent possess an incident of ownership if it is subject to divestment by the action of another person? In Margrave's Estate v. Commissioner, infra page 398, the decedent's wife took out insurance on his life, naming as beneficiary a revocable trust created by the decedent. The wife retained the right to change the beneficiary of the policy. The court rejected the Service's claim that the decedent's power to revoke the trust constituted an incident of ownership in the policy, noting that while alive he never possessed more than a power over an expectancy that was subject to elimination at his wife's "absolute whim." See Rev. Rul. 81–166, 1981–1 C.B. 477 (acquiescence in *Margrave*; the gift tax aspect of the ruling is discussed in the Note, infra page 400). Compare Terriberry v. United States, 517 F.2d 286 (5th Cir. 1975), cert. denied, 424 U.S. 977 (1976) (decedent possessed incidents of ownership even though they could have been eliminated had wife chosen to exercise her right to revoke trust).

3. *Joint powers.* The opinion in the *Rhode Island Hospital Trust Co.* case recognizes that decedent's "negative power" to block unilateral action by his father was encompassed in the statutory language requiring inclusion of an incident of ownership exercisable "in conjunction with" another person. See also Commissioner v. Karagheusian's Estate, 233 F.2d 197 (2d Cir. 1956) (policy on decedent's life held in trust that was revocable by his wife with consent of decedent and their daughter; § 2042(2) applicable because "[i]t makes no difference whether under the trust instrument the decedent may initiate changes or whether he must merely consent to them"); Goldstein's

Estate v. United States, 122 F.Supp. 677 (Ct. Cl. 1954), cert. denied, 348 U.S. 942 (1955) (same where owner of policy could act only with decedent's consent); Schwager v. Commissioner, 64 T.C. 781 (1975) (same where decedent's employer could not change beneficiary of split-dollar policy without decedent's consent). The rule applies with like force to an incident of ownership exercisable only in conjunction with a person who is adversely affected by their joint action, such as a right in the decedent to obtain the cash surrender value with the consent of a person who is a designated beneficiary of the proceeds. See Gesner v. United States, 600 F.2d 1349 (Ct. Cl. 1979) ("if the concept of adversity of interest is to be introduced into considerations of shared powers under section 2042(2), it is for the Congress to do, not this court").

SKIFTER'S ESTATE v. COMMISSIONER

468 F.2d 699 (2d Cir. 1972).

LUMBARD, CIRCUIT JUDGE.

The Commissioner of Internal Revenue appeals from a decision of the Tax Court holding that proceeds of nine insurance policies on decedent's life were not includible in decedent's estate. The Tax Court, 56 T.C. 1190, held incorrect the Commissioner's inclusion of these proceeds in decedent's gross estate and his assessment of a deficiency thereon.

In 1961 Hector Skifter, the decedent, assigned all his interest in nine insurance policies on his life to his wife Naomi, effectively making her the owner of those policies. Skifter retained no interest in the policies and retained no power over them. Several months later, Naomi died and left a will directing that her residuary estate, which included the nine insurance policies, be placed in trust. She directed that the income was to be paid to their daughter, Janet, for life and, upon Janet's death, there were provisions for the distribution of corpus and income to other persons.

Naomi appointed Skifter as trustee and authorized him, in his absolute discretion, at any time and from time to time, to pay over the whole or any part of the principal of the trust to the current income beneficiary whether or not this would result in the termination of the trust. It was explicitly provided that, in making these payments, the trustee could disregard any rules of trust law that may require impartiality between income beneficiaries and remaindermen. In addition, Skifter, as trustee, was given broad powers of management and control over the trust, including the powers to sell and mortgage the property and invest and reinvest the proceeds.

In 1964 Skifter died and a successor trustee was named. Contending that, under the terms of the trust established under Naomi's will, Skifter possessed at his death "incidents of ownership" so as to require that the proceeds of the insurance be included in his estate under § 2042(2) of the Internal Revenue Code, the Commissioner assessed a deficiency against the estate. From the Tax Court's holding in favor of the estate, the Commissioner appeals.

... The essential issue before this Court is whether the broad fiduciary powers that were granted to Skifter under Naomi's will constitute "incidents of ownership" within the meaning of § 2042(2). We hold that they do not, and thus affirm the decision of the Tax Court.

In enacting the predecessor of § 2042(2), the Senate and House Committee Reports of the Seventy-seventh Congress acknowledged that, while the new provision introduced the term "incidents of ownership," it failed to suggest a definition of it. The Reports then went on to list the sort of powers and interest that the Congress was concerned with:

> Examples of such incidents are the right of the insured or his estate to the economic benefits of the insurance, the power to change the beneficiary, the power to surrender or cancel the policy, the power to assign it, the power to revoke an assignment, the power to pledge the policy for a loan, or the power to obtain from the insurer a loan against the surrender value of the policy.

See 1942–2 Cum. Bull., pp. 491, 677. The Treasury relied on this legislative history in promulgating its regulations on § 2042(2). Reg. § 20.2042–1(c)(2) states:

> For purposes of this paragraph, the term "incidents of ownership" is not limited in its meaning to ownership of the policy in the technical legal sense. Generally speaking, the term has reference to the right of the insured or his estate to the economic benefits of the policy. Thus, it includes the power to change the beneficiary, to surrender or cancel the policy, to assign the policy, to revoke an assignment, to pledge the policy for a loan, or to obtain from the insurer a loan against the surrender value of the policy, etc....

It seems significant to us that the reference point in the regulation for "incidents of ownership" is "the right ... to the economic benefits of the policy," since there was no way in which Skifter could have exercised his powers to derive for himself any economic benefits from these insurance policies.

The predecessor of § 2042 provided that, if the decedent continued to pay the premiums on the policy, even if he had divested himself of all interest therein, the proceeds therefrom would be included in his estate at death. In reenacting this predecessor provision as § 2042 of the Internal Revenue Code of 1954, Congress eliminated this premium test. In explaining this change, the Senate Finance Committee stated:

> No other property is subject to estate tax where the decedent initially purchased it and then long before his death gave away all rights to the property and to discriminate against life insurance in this regard is not justified.

S. Rep. No. 1622, 83rd Cong. 2d Sess., p.124, U.S. Code Cong. & Admin. News 1954, p. 4757. The inference from this statement is very strong that it was the intent of Congress that § 2042 should operate to give insurance policies estate tax treatment that roughly parallels the treatment that is given to other types of property by § 2036 (transfers with retained life estate), § 2037 (transfers taking effect at death), § 2038 (revocable transfers), and § 2041 (powers of appointment)....

Although this legislative history is hardly conclusive on the matter, we feel that there is sufficient support to justify our conclusion that Congress intended § 2042 to parallel the statutory scheme governing the interests and powers that will cause other types of property to be included in a decedent's estate. This conclusion is reinforced by the types of interests and powers that Congress indicated were exemplary of what it meant to be included within the scope of "incidents of ownership." The interests there listed are interests that would cause other types of property to be included in a decedent's estate under § 2036 or § 2037; and the powers that Congress discussed are also powers that would result in the property being included in the decedent's estate under § 2038 or § 2041. Therefore, in ruling on the Commissioner's contention that the fiduciary power here involved is an "incident of ownership," a question that has not been considered under § 2042, we feel that we should look to the experience under the statutory scheme governing the application of the estate tax to other types of property. Indeed, the Commissioner, in making his contentions before us, relies on numerous analogies to decisions under these other statutory provisions.

The core of the controversy here centers on the decedent's power, as trustee, to prefer the current income beneficiary over the remainderman and all later income beneficiaries through payment of the entire trust corpus. He did not have the power to alter or revoke the trust for his own benefit and he could not name new, additional, or alternative beneficiaries. In this regard, Reg. § 20.2042–1(c)(4) provides:

> A decedent is considered to have an "incident of ownership" in an insurance policy on his life held in trust if, under the terms of the policy, the decedent (either alone or in conjunction with another person or persons) has the power (as trustee or otherwise) to change the beneficial ownership in the policy or its proceeds, or the time or manner of enjoyment thereof, even though the decedent has no beneficial interest in the trust.

The Commissioner contends that this regulation requires that the proceeds of the policies here be included in decedent's estate.

The Tax Court declined to interpret that regulation so as to make it applicable here, but concluded that, since the power could not be exercised to benefit the decedent or his estate, it would not cause the proceeds to be included in his estate. If the power had been exercisable for the benefit of decedent, or for the benefit of whomever the decedent selected, it would have been necessary to include the proceeds in the estate; for there would be a powerful argument that this was an incident of ownership since he would have had the equivalent of a power of appointment, which under § 2041 would cause other types of property to be included in the estate of the holder of such a power. This distinction causes us to concur in the Tax

Court's conclusion that the Commissioner's reliance on our decision in Commissioner v. Karagheusian's Estate, 233 F.2d 197 (2d Cir. 1956), is misplaced.

The power that the decedent possessed was over the entire trust corpus, which included property other than the insurance policies. But there is no serious doubt that this power did not result in this other property being in decedent's estate for tax purposes. This type of power would fall under both § 2036 and § 2038. The former provision is clearly not triggered in this case because it only applies to a power retained by the grantor over the income from property when he transferred it to another. Thus, for purposes of § 2036, it would not matter that the decedent effectively had the power to deprive later income beneficiaries of the income from the corpus in favor of an earlier income beneficiary. However, the latter provision, § 2038, would apply because decedent had the power "to alter, amend ..., or terminate" the trust. The Commissioner has pointed to many cases holding that such a power would result in the property interest over which the power could be exercised being included in the estate of the holder of the power. See e.g. Lober v. United States, 346 U.S. 335 (1953); United States v. O'Malley, 383 U.S. 627 (1966) (decided under § 2036); Commissioner of Internal Revenue v. Newbold's Estate, 158 F.2d 694 (2d Cir. 1946). Therefore, he argues, this power must be an incident of ownership for § 2042 purposes also.

But the Commissioner's reliance on § 2038 cases exposes the fatal flaw in his position. The cases he cites dealt with powers that were retained by the transferor or settlor of a trust. That is not what we have here; the power the decedent had was given to him long after he had divested himself of all interest in the policies—it was not reserved by him at the time of the transfer. This difference between powers retained by a decedent and powers that devolved upon him at a time subsequent to the assignment is not merely formal, but has considerable substance. A taxpayer planning the disposition of his estate can select the powers that he reserves and those that he transfers in order to implement an overall scheme of testamentary disposition; however, a trustee, unless there is agreement by the settlor and/or beneficiaries, can only act within the powers he is granted. When the decedent is the transferee of such a power and holds it in a fiduciary capacity, with no beneficial interest therein, it is difficult to construe this arrangement as a substitute for a testamentary disposition by the decedent....

Accordingly, we conclude that, although such a power might well constitute an incident of ownership if retained by the assignor of the policies, it is not an incident of ownership within the intended scope of § 2042 when it has been conveyed to the decedent long after he had divested himself of all interest in the policies and when he cannot exercise the power for his own benefit. We justify this interpretation of "incidents of ownership" on the apparent intent of Congress that § 2042 was not to operate in such a manner as to discriminate against life insurance, with regard to estate tax treatment, as compared with other types of property.... Therefore, we must reject the contention of the Commissioner that the language of § 2042 requires that it be given a broader scope of operation than the statutes covering other types of property....

[The Court here analyzed the origins of § 2038 and concluded that] § 2038 has not been applied when the power possessed by decedent was created and conferred on him by someone else long after he had divested himself of all interest in the property subject to the power. Therefore, because of our view that Congress did not intend § 2042 to produce divergent estate tax treatment between life insurance and other types of property, we conclude that the fiduciary power that Skifter possessed at his death did not constitute an "incident of ownership" under § 2042; hence, that provision does not require that the life insurance proceeds at issue be included in Skifter's estate.

The Tax Court was thus correct in holding that Reg. § 20.2042–1(c)(4) must be read to apply to "reservations of powers by the transferor as trustee" and not to powers such as that in issue. Accordingly, the decision of the Tax Court is affirmed.

NOTES

1. *Incidents of ownership held by decedent in a fiduciary capacity.* In Rose v. United States, 511 F.2d 259 (5th Cir. 1975), the decedent's brother created trusts for the decedent's children, naming the decedent as trustee. The decedent, as trustee, took out insurance policies on his own life and designated the trusts as beneficiaries. At his death, the decedent held fiduciary powers affecting beneficial enjoyment of the trust property, including the life insurance proceeds. The Fifth Circuit disagreed with the *Skifter* analysis and result:

> The Second Circuit has concluded that Reg. § 20.2042–1(c)(4) "must be read to apply [only] to '*reservations* of powers by the transferor as trustee.' " Estate of Skifter v. Commissioner, 1972, 468 F.2d 699, 705 (emphasis added). In so holding, the *Skifter* court relied primarily upon the observation that *Lober*, *O'Malley*, and their judicial descendants applying the "substantial control" approach all "dealt with powers retained by the transferor or settlor of a trust." 468 F.2d at 703. But we indicated our disagreement with *Skifter*'s reading of § 2042 in [Lumpkin's Estate v. Commissioner, 474 F.2d 1092, 1097 (5th Cir. 1973)], and we adhere to that position now. Under § 2036 Congress specifically levied the estate tax upon interests *retained* by a decedent in connection with an incomplete transfer; and § 2038 is similar in effect. Under § 2042, however, Congress applied the tax to insurance over which a decedent *possessed* any incidents of ownership. The difference in statutory language is significant. *Lober* and *O'Malley* quite naturally involved retained interests because they arose under statutes designed to reach only interests so held. But nothing in those cases suggests that the substantiality of the control possessed by the decedents there depended upon whether the decedents' interests were retained in connection with an incomplete transfer rather than derived in some other fashion. We agree with the

Second Circuit that § 2042 "roughly parallels" its cousin sections of the Estate Tax Code in regard to the substantiality of the decedent's control which is prerequisite to includability in decedent's gross estate. But we cannot ignore Congress' conspicuous variety in statutory idiom, so as to make the tax treatment of insurance identical with the taxation of other interests: § 2042 was not drawn in terms to catch only *retained* incidents of ownership, and we find no basis to infer such a design. Here, where the decedent-trustee's rights to alter the time and manner of enjoyment of the insurance proceeds were procured by the decedent-trustee himself, we have no difficulty in concluding under *Lumpkin* and Reg. § 20.2042–1(c)(4) that the value of the insurance proceeds was properly included in his gross estate under § 2042(2). [511 F.2d at 263–65.]

In Rev. Rul. 76–261, 1976–2 C.B. 276, the Service came down four-square on the side of the Fifth Circuit, specifically rejecting the conclusion in *Skifter* that § 2042(2) applies to fiduciary powers only if they were retained by the trustee-insured as transferor of the trust. By 1982, the Service was having second thoughts about its 1976 ruling. In Bloch's Estate v. Commissioner, 78 T.C. 850, 857 (1982), an excerpt from the government's reply brief was quoted, saying that on reconsideration the Service was "in agreement with the Second Circuit in [*Skifter*]." On the basis of this concession, the court refused to declare the decedent's powers as trustee over a trust created by his father and others to be incidents of ownership. Arguments seeking to justify the tax on other grounds were also rejected. The court held that there was insufficient evidence that the decedent had paid a fraction of the premiums to qualify him as a co-settlor of the trust and that the policies were not available for his personal use because his pledge of them to secure his personal loans was in violation of his fiduciary duty. 78 T.C. at 861–64.

In Rev. Rul. 84–179, 1984–2 C.B. 195, the Service revoked Rev. Rul. 76–261, relying on the reasoning of *Skifter* and repudiating its victory in *Rose*:

> [A] decedent will not be deemed to have incidents of ownership over an insurance policy on decedent's life where decedent's powers are held in a fiduciary capacity, and are not exercisable for decedent's personal benefit, where the decedent did not transfer the policy or any of the consideration for purchasing or maintaining the policy to the trust from personal assets, and the devolution of the powers on decedent was not part of a prearranged plan involving the participation of decedent.

The Service, however, continues to view a fiduciary power as grounds for including life insurance in the gross estate if the decedent (1) could have exercised the power for his own benefit, (2) paid premiums on the policy, directly or indirectly, or (3) transferred the policy to the trust, directly or through an intermediary. Under the reasoning of *Skifter* and Rev. Rul. 84–179, does § 2042(2) still have an independent role to play, or does it merely replicate the coverage of §§ 2036 through 2038?

2. *"Incidents of ownership."* Reg. § 20.2042–1(c)(2) observes that the term "incidents of ownership" is not limited to technical legal ownership of the policy but has a broader meaning:

> [T]he term "incidents of ownership" is not limited in its meaning to ownership of the policy in the technical legal sense. Generally speaking,

> the term has reference to the right of the insured or his estate to the economic benefits of the policy.

Is it to be inferred from this language that a right that is of no economic benefit to the insured does not count? Some of the rights that constitute ownership of an insurance policy, like the right to select a settlement option, have been held to qualify as "incidents of ownership" even though they would not be regarded as "economic benefits" of the policy. Compare Lumpkin's Estate v. Commissioner, 474 F.2d 1092 (5th Cir. 1973) (decedent's right to select settlement option under group term policy constituted incident of ownership, even though it affected only time and manner of beneficiary's enjoyment of proceeds), with Connelly's Estate v. United States, 551 F.2d 545 (3d Cir. 1977) (contrary result on similar facts). The Service announced in Rev. Rul. 81–128, 1981–1 C.B. 469, that it will not follow *Connelly* except in cases appealable to the Third Circuit. In light of its change of position in the *Skifter–Rose* controversy, the Service may no longer be so firm in its resolve. The Third Circuit has had occasion to reaffirm the position it took in the *Connelly* case. In Rockwell's Estate v. Commissioner, 779 F.2d 931 (3d Cir. 1985), decedent transferred eight policies on his life to his wife, who subsequently transferred the policies in trust for their children. Decedent's only retained power was the right to veto any assignment of the policies to a person who did not have an insurable interest in decedent's life. The court concluded that this retained power was not an incident of ownership because it conferred no "economic benefit," citing *Skifter* and Rev. Rul. 84–179 in support of this result.

The value of the economic benefit may be only a fraction of the value of the insurance proceeds that are included in the gross estate under § 2042(2). See Rev. Rul. 79–129, 1979–1 C.B. 306 (decedent's right to borrow against cash surrender value of policy, amounting to $12,000 at death, triggered inclusion of $12,000 under § 2042(1) and $138,000 balance of proceeds under § 2042(2)). A right may be an economic benefit but not an incident of ownership. See, for example, Bowers' Estate v. Commissioner, 23 T.C. 911 (1955) (right to receive dividends not an incident of ownership because dividends merely reduce the cost of keeping the policy in force); Jordahl's Estate v. Commissioner, 65 T.C. 92 (1975) (accord as to dividends; in addition, decedent's power to reacquire policies in trust by substituting other policies of equal value not an incident of ownership).

3. *Incidents of ownership held by corporation controlled by decedent.* If a decedent owned stock of a closely held corporation that was named as beneficiary of an insurance policy on the decedent's life, the proceeds are indirectly taken into account in valuing the decedent's stock under § 2033 (relating to property owned at death). See Reg. § 20.2031–2(f); Huntsman's Estate v. Commissioner, 66 T.C. 861 (1976) (insurance proceeds included in same manner as other nonoperating assets in valuing stock); Rev. Rul. 82–85, 1982–1 C.B. 137 (accord); but cf. Blount's Estate v. Commissioner, 428 F.3d 1338 (11th Cir. 2005) (contra). If the decedent possessed the incidents of ownership or was chargeable with them because of his control of the corporation, the proceeds may also be subject to tax under § 2042(2). Although the statute makes no mention of the possibility of double counting, Reg. § 20.2042–1(c)(6) does take the problem into account in establishing guide-

lines to govern the attribution of incidents of ownership from a controlled corporation to the decedent:

> In the case of economic benefits of a life insurance policy on the decedent's life that are reserved to a corporation of which the decedent is the sole or controlling stockholder, the corporation's incidents of ownership will not be attributed to the decedent through his stock ownership to the extent the proceeds of the policy are payable to the corporation. Any proceeds payable to a third party for a valid business purpose, such as in satisfaction of a business debt of the corporation, so that the net worth of the corporation is increased by the amount of such proceeds, shall be deemed to be payable to the corporation for purposes of the preceding sentence.... [I]f any part of the proceeds of the policy are not payable to or for the benefit of the corporation, and thus are not taken into account in valuing the decedent's stock holdings in the corporation for purposes of section 2031, any incidents of ownership held by the corporation as to that part of the proceeds will be attributed to the decedent through his stock ownership where the decedent is the sole or controlling stockholder. Thus, for example, if the decedent is the controlling stockholder in a corporation, and the corporation owns a life insurance policy on his life, the proceeds of which are payable to the decedent's spouse, the incidents of ownership held by the corporation will be attributed to the decedent through his stock ownership and the proceeds will be included in his gross estate under section 2042. If in this example the policy proceeds had been payable 40 percent to decedent's spouse and 60 percent to the corporation, only 40 percent of the proceeds would be included in decedent's gross estate under section 2042. For purposes of this subparagraph, the decedent will not be deemed to be the controlling stockholder of a corporation unless, at the time of his death, he owned stock possessing more than 50 percent of the total combined voting power of the corporation.

Test the application of these rules in a situation where the decedent owned at death 60 percent of the stock of a corporation that had the right to borrow against a $100,000 policy on decedent's life, the proceeds of which were payable 50 percent to the corporation and 50 percent to a former employee. How much of the proceeds would be includible under § 2042(2)? under § 2033? What difference would it make if the policy was payable 100 percent to the former employee, but the corporation possessed (but never exercised) a right to change the beneficiary and designate itself? The evolution of Reg. § 20.2042–1(c)(6) is traced in Levy's Estate v. Commissioner, 70 T.C. 873 (1978), which upholds as valid the rule requiring attribution to a controlling as well as a sole shareholder.

The regulations are silent about the treatment of a partnership that holds incidents of ownership in a policy on a partner's life, but the Service has ruled that the partnership's incidents are attributable to the insured partner if the proceeds are payable "other than to or for the benefit of the partnership." Rev. Rul. 83–147, 1983–2 C.B. 158. Cf. Knipp's Estate v. Commissioner, 25 T.C. 153 (1955), affd. on other grounds, 244 F.2d 436 (4th Cir.), cert. denied, 355 U.S. 827 (1957) (no attribution where proceeds were payable to the partnership). For the application of the regulations to split-dollar life insurance (i.e., the employer-corporation and the employee-insured share the cost of the policy premiums), see Rev. Rul. 76–274, 1976–2 C.B. 278, as modified by Rev. Rul. 82–145, 1982–2 C.B. 213; Dimen's Estate v. Commissioner, 72 T.C. 198 (1979), affd. mem., 633 F.2d 203 (2d Cir. 1980) (corporation's incidents of ownership attributed to decedent who was the sole shareholder).

4. *Life insurance purchased with community funds.* The regulations recognize the general rule that life insurance purchased with community funds is an asset of the community, rather than separate property of the insured-decedent. Thus, if the proceeds are payable to the decedent's estate but are community assets, the decedent's one-half interest is includible in the decedent's gross estate under § 2042(1); the other half belongs to the surviving spouse. Reg. § 20.2042–1(b)(2); but cf. Street's Estate v. Commissioner, 152 F.3d 482 (5th Cir. 1998) (full amount of proceeds payable to insured-decedent's estate included under § 2042(1)). Similarly, if the proceeds are payable to a third person as beneficiary and the decedent possessed incidents of ownership in the policy (as manager of the community assets or as agent for the other spouse), only half of the proceeds are includible in the decedent's gross estate under § 2042(2). Reg. § 20.2042–1(c)(5); Rev. Rul. 2003–40, 2003–1 C.B. 813. If the death of the insured makes a previously revocable transfer of the policy final, the surviving spouse is treated as making a taxable gift of his or her half of the proceeds. Reg. § 25.2511–1(h)(9); Commissioner v. Chase Manhattan Bank, 259 F.2d 231 (5th Cir. 1958), cert. denied, 359 U.S. 913 (1959); Kaufman v. United States, 462 F.2d 439 (5th Cir. 1972) (*Chase Manhattan Bank* case not applicable where surviving spouse received at least half of the proceeds; amount passing to third person attributed to the decedent).

As a corollary of these rules, if the noninsured spouse dies first, the value of his or her one-half interest in the policy is includible under § 2033. United States v. Stewart, 270 F.2d 894 (9th Cir. 1959), cert. denied, 361 U.S. 960 (1960); Rev. Rul. 75–100, 1975–1 C.B. 303 (includible amount determined by reference to terminal reserve, not cash surrender value); cf. Cavenaugh's Estate v. Commissioner, 51 F.3d 597 (5th Cir. 1995) (at subsequent death of insured spouse, one-half of proceeds includible under § 2042(1), where all proceeds were payable to decedent-insured's estate); Cervin's Estate v. Commissioner, 111 F.3d 1252 (5th Cir. 1997) (same result under § 2042(2), where proceeds were payable to other beneficiaries).

If the decedent assigned the policy to the surviving spouse so that it became the spouse's separate property under state law, § 2042 is inapplicable, even if premiums were paid with community funds. Compare Kern v. United States, 491 F.2d 436 (9th Cir. 1974) (under Washington law, presumption of community ownership overcome), with Madsen's Estate v. Commissioner, 690 F.2d 164 (9th Cir. 1982) (under Washington law, designation of surviving spouse as beneficiary and owner not sufficient to convert policy into surviving spouse's separate property).

5. *Estate tax apportionment.* Where life insurance proceeds payable to beneficiaries other than the decedent's estate are includible in the gross estate under § 2042(2), § 2206 gives the executor a right to recover the resulting federal estate tax from the beneficiaries, unless the decedent's will directs

otherwise. This provision, which originally appeared in the Revenue Act of 1918, is intended to prevent the tax burden generated by the life insurance proceeds from being inadvertently shifted to the recipients of the decedent's probate assets. See infra page 638.

6. *Time when a gift of life insurance becomes complete for gift tax purposes.* Consistent with the approach developed in Burnet v. Guggenheim, supra page 83, and Sanford's Estate v. Commissioner, supra page 89, a transfer of a life insurance policy is complete and subject to gift tax when the donor is divested of all dominion and control—i.e., the incidents of ownership—over the policy. See, e.g., Goodman v. Commissioner, 156 F.2d 218 (2d Cir. 1946). Reg. § 25.2511–1(h)(8) indicates that the gift tax is not imposed when the donor has relinquished all the incidents of ownership except the power to designate a new beneficiary of the policy. If in that situation the donee were to turn the policy in for its cash surrender value, a completed gift would occur at that time, and the donor would then become liable for a gift tax.

7. *Proposals for reform.* The ABA Tax Section Task Force was unable to reach a consensus on how best to tax life insurance. Report on Transfer Tax Restructuring, 41 Tax Law. 395, 416 (1988). It did, however, attach to its report a study paper that discusses alternative approaches. Id. at 436–41. See also Gutman, A Comment on the ABA Tax Section Task Force Report on Transfer Tax Restructuring, id. at 653, 665–71 (recommending a premium payments test, coupled with retention of § 2042(1) and some form of the incidents of ownership test).

2. INTERPLAY BETWEEN §§ 2035 AND 2042

Under § 2035(a), the gross estate includes the proceeds of a life insurance policy if (1) within three years before death the decedent transferred an interest or relinquished a power with respect to the policy, and (2) the interest or power would have given rise to inclusion under § 2042 had it been retained by the decedent until death. Thus, for example, if within three years before death the decedent took out a policy on his own life and thereafter transferred all incidents of ownership in the policy to another person, the proceeds are includible in the gross estate, even though the transfer may have been subject to gift tax. Rev. Rul. 82–13, 1982–1 C.B. 132 (distinguishing transfer of new policy from renewal of preexisting group term policy). The result is the same if the decedent transferred the policy more than three years before death but retained incidents of ownership which were relinquished within the three-year period. By contrast, if the decedent possessed no incidents of ownership at any time during the three-year period, § 2035 has no application. If the decedent paid premiums to keep a previously transferred policy in force, the premium payments may be subject to gift tax but they do not cause the proceeds to be drawn back into the gross estate.

The Commissioner initially enjoyed substantial success in arguing that § 2035, as in effect before the 1981 amendment, brought back into the gross estate life insurance proceeds in situations where the decedent controlled the transfer of the policy within three years of his death, even if he was not the formal owner of the policy. For example, if within three years of death the decedent had taken out a policy in his own name and then immediately transferred it to his children, the proceeds would have been included in the gross estate under § 2035(a). It was argued that the same result should follow in the case of an indirect transfer, where the decedent paid the premiums and caused the policy to be taken out in the name of the children as owners and beneficiaries. In the leading case of Bel v. United States, 452 F.2d 683 (5th Cir. 1971), cert. denied, 406 U.S. 919 (1972), the court stated:

> We think our focus should be on the control beam of the word "transfer." The decedent, and the decedent alone, beamed the accidental death policy at his children, for by paying the premium he designated ownership of the policy and created in his children all of the contractual rights to the insurance benefits. These were acts of transfer.... Without [the decedent's] conception, guidance, and payment, the proceeds of the policy in the context of this case would not have been the children's.... Had the decedent, within three years of his death, procured the policy in his own name and immediately thereafter assigned all ownership rights to his children, there is no question but that the policy proceeds would have been included in his estate. In our opinion the decedent's mode of execution is functionally indistinguishable. Therefore, we hold that the action of the decedent constituted a "transfer" of the accidental death policy within the meaning of section 2035.... [452 F.2d at 691–92.]

Accord, Detroit Bank & Trust Co. v. United States, 467 F.2d 964 (6th Cir. 1972), cert. denied, 410 U.S. 929 (1973) (policy taken out by trustee of irrevocable trust at decedent's direction and with funds furnished by decedent); First Natl. Bank of Oregon v. United States, 488 F.2d 575 (9th Cir. 1973) (decedent paid all premiums on policy taken out by his wife).

These cases, however, were decided when § 2035 generally reached all transfers made within three years of death, including outright gifts of property. The 1981 amendment curtailed the operation of the three-year rule and introduced the explicit reference to § 2042 (and other enumerated sections). In cases arising after the 1981 amendment, the courts have held that § 2035 no longer applies to life insurance on the decedent's life unless the decedent possessed incidents of ownership (within the meaning of § 2042) at some point during the three-year period before death. Leder's Estate v. Commissioner, 893 F.2d 237 (10th Cir. 1989); Headrick's Estate v. Commissioner, 918 F.2d 1263 (6th Cir. 1990); Perry's Estate v. Commissioner, 927 F.2d 209 (5th Cir. 1991). In the wake of these decisions, the Service has conceded that it will no longer litigate the issue of whether life insurance proceeds are includible in the gross estate "where, even though the decedent was never listed as owner on the policy, the policy was procured at his instance, he paid the insurance premiums and he died within three years of taking out the policy." AOD 1991–12 (Jul. 3, 1991) (acquiescence in *Headrick's Estate*).

NOTES

1. *Third party as decedent's agent.* Suppose that within three years before death the decedent created an irrevocable trust and directed the trustee to take out a policy on the decedent's life; the trust was funded with cash equal to the amount of the initial premium. Under § 2035(a) in its present form, is it open to the government to argue that the decedent, who never made a formal transfer of the policy, nevertheless had a degree of control that was functionally equivalent to incidents of ownership? See Kurihara's Estate v. Commissioner, 82 T.C. 51 (1984) (trustee acted as decedent's agent, under pre–1981 law); cf. Clay's Estate v. Commissioner, 86 T.C. 1266 (1986) (premiums paid by decedent's wife from joint bank account were not attributable to decedent, under pre–1981 law).

2. *Premiums paid by donee within three years of death.* If the decedent died within three years after transferring a life insurance policy on his or her own life, the proceeds are generally includible in the gross estate under § 2035(a). The includible amount may be reduced, however, if the donee paid premiums to maintain the policy between the time of the transfer and the decedent's death, on the theory that a portion of the proceeds is attributable to the donee's premium payments. See Silverman's Estate v. Commissioner, 61 T.C. 338 (1973), affd., 521 F.2d 574 (2d Cir. 1975) (excludable portion based on ratio of donee's premium payments to total premium payments, under pre–1981 law); Friedberg's Estate v. Commissioner, 63 T.C.M. (CCH) 3080 (1992) (following same approach under post–1981 three-year rule). For an argument that the adjustment should be limited to the dollar amount of the post-transfer premiums paid by the donee, see Kahn & Waggoner, Tax Consequences of Assigning Life Insurance—Time for Another Look, 4 Fla. Tax Rev. 381 (1999).

3. *Incidents of ownership held by controlled corporation.* If a corporation holds all the incidents of ownership of a policy on the life of its controlling shareholder, the corporation's incidents of ownership are attributed to the shareholder to the extent the proceeds are payable to a third party for a non-business purpose. See Reg. § 20.2042–1(c)(6), supra page 385, Note 3. Suppose that, within three years before the controlling shareholder's death, the corporation assigns the policy to the third party, who receives the proceeds at the shareholder's death. In Rev. Rul. 82–141, 1982–2 C.B. 209, the Service concluded that "the principle underlying the attribution rule of section 20.2042–1(c)(6) of the regulations mandates that the incidents of ownership possessed by [the corporation] be attributed to [the controlling shareholder] for purposes of section 2035 of the Code." Suppose that the shareholder makes a gift of stock within the three-year period, retaining no more than 50 percent of the voting power in the corporation. In Rev. Rul. 90–21, 1990–1 C.B. 172, the Service ruled that the three-year rule preserves attribution of the corporation's incidents of ownership to the shareholder.

3. POLICIES OWNED OR PAID FOR BY DECEDENT ON LIFE OF THIRD PERSON

Section 2042 is concerned exclusively with "policies on the life of the decedent," and has no application to a policy on the life of another person, even if the decedent owned or paid for it. If the decedent owns such a policy at the time of his death, its value is includible in the gross estate under § 2033. See DuPont's Estate v. Commissioner, 233 F.2d 210 (3d Cir.), cert. denied, 352 U.S. 878 (1956), rejecting the theory that the amount includible under § 2033 is limited to the policy's cash surrender value and applying instead the gift tax valuation principles of Guggenheim v. Rasquin, supra page 363.

Assume that *H* takes out an insurance policy on his own life and designates his wife *W* as beneficiary if she survives him or his children if she does not. *H* then assigns the policy to *W*, retaining no incidents of ownership, so that the proceeds are removed from *H*'s gross estate under § 2042. *W* has the power to change the designated beneficiaries, to surrender the policy, to borrow against it, etc. More than three years later, *H* and *W* die together in a plane crash or other accident. Are the proceeds includible in *W*'s estate? The proceeds would clearly come within § 2033 (property owned at death) if paid to *W*'s estate on the ground that she survived *H*; but in the absence of sufficient evidence concerning the order of death, state law may treat *W* has having predeceased *H*, with the result that the proceeds become payable to the children as contingent beneficiaries. Nevertheless, because *W* owned the policy until her death, the value of her "interest" in the policy is includible under § 2033. But is its value the full amount of the proceeds—on the ground that the policy had virtually "matured" in the agonizing moment before death—or some lesser amount, e.g., its cash surrender value, the amount of the interpolated terminal reserve, or zero? In Old Kent Bank & Trust Co. v. United States, 292 F.Supp. 48 (W.D. Mich. 1968), revd., 430 F.2d 392 (6th Cir. 1970), the district court held that nothing was includible on the ground that the wife had at her death nothing to transfer to her heirs because her rights over the policy were extinguished by her death. By contrast, in Chown's Estate v. Commissioner, 51 T.C. 140 (1968), revd., 428 F.2d 1395 (9th Cir. 1970), the Tax Court held that the policy matured at the moment of the husband's death, and since this was also the moment of the wife's death, the full amount of the proceeds was includible in her estate under § 2033. On appeal, it was held in both cases that the includible value was measured under the terminal reserve method set forth in Reg. § 25.2512–6(a). Accord, Wien's Estate v. Commissioner, 441 F.2d 32 (5th Cir. 1971); Rev. Rul. 77–181, 1977–1 C.B. 272 (same principle applied where each decedent owned a policy on the other's life).

If the owner of an insurance policy on the life of another person transfers it or rights under it during his life, it may be includible in the transferor's gross estate under §§ 2036 to 2038, as illustrated by the following case.

PYLE v. COMMISSIONER

313 F.2d 328 (3d Cir. 1963).

HASTIE, CIRCUIT JUDGE.

The Tax Court has held that the proceeds of an insurance policy on the life of Wallace Pyle are includible in the gross estate of his widow, Ida Pyle, who has since died, as property which she transferred, reserving a life estate, within the meaning of section 2036 of the 1954 Internal Revenue Code. This ruling resulted in a determination of an estate tax deficiency. The executor of Mrs. Pyle's estate has brought the case here for review.

Mrs. Pyle applied for and obtained a $30,000 insurance policy on her husband's life, payable on his death to her. The policy granted Mrs. Pyle all the rights accorded the "insured" under the policy and she was the named beneficiary. Thus, it is clear that when the policy was issued Mrs. Pyle alone enjoyed the various incidents of ownership, including the rights of borrowing, assignment and cash surrender. She also had the right to change the beneficiary and to elect among settlement alternatives.

At Mrs. Pyle's request, during the life of her husband, a rider was attached to the policy providing that, upon the death of the insured husband, the proceeds would be retained by the company which would pay Mrs. Pyle 3% interest thereon, plus dividends, for the remainder of her life. Thereafter, the earnings, and ultimately the proceeds of the policy, were to be paid to her children. Mrs. Pyle reserved the right to revoke and change this revised method of settlement until the death of her husband, but did not do so. Upon the husband's death, the revised scheme of settlement became irrevocable.

Section 2036 of the 1954 Code requires that there shall be included in the gross estate of a decedent the value of "any interest [in property] . . . of which the decedent has at any time made a transfer . . . under which he has retained for his life . . . the right to income from, the property. . . ." The Tax Court concluded that, in the circumstances outlined above, Mrs. Pyle's action during the lifetime of her husband in changing the disposition to be made of the proceeds of the life insurance policy upon maturity constituted a transfer of property under which she retained a life estate.

Challenging this conclusion, the petitioner argues that it was the death of the insured husband rather than the earlier action of Mrs. Pyle which in legal contemplation effected the transfer of property. The fact that Mrs. Pyle's election as to the disposition of proceeds at maturity was revocable until her husband died and that interests in such proceeds were contingent or inchoate until her husband's death are thought to support this contention.

We think petitioner's argument is unsound. The only transfer of property with which we are concerned is the transfer of the right to receive proceeds upon maturity. That transfer could be accomplished only through the exercise of ownership rights created by the terms of the policy and vested exclusively in Mrs. Pyle from the date of issuance until her husband's death. The fact that the husband's death was the event which caused the policy to mature and made Mrs. Pyle's election as to changes in the disposition of the proceeds irrevocable did not make him a transferor. For he had no power over the disposition of the proceeds during his lifetime and no interest in them which could pass to another at his death. An instructive analogy is provided by Goodnow v. United States, Ct. Cl., 1962, 302 F.2d 516, where a wife was held not to have been the transferor of the proceeds of a policy on her husband's life because he was the legal owner of the policy, with a vested right to elect among optional dispositions of the proceeds. As concerns the proceeds, the position of the husband there was essentially the position of the wife here.

Petitioner also points out that some of the premiums on the policy were paid by the husband. But certainly this gave him no interest in and no power over the disposition to be made of the proceeds upon his death. That is the only transfer which is relevant here. There are other cases, notably Estate of Susie C. Haggett, 1950, 14 T.C. 325, acq., 1950–2 Cum. Bull. 2, upon which petitioner relies, in which the original purchase of insurance or an annuity was a transaction constituting a transfer of property which was to become effective in some degree only upon the purchaser's death. The present case is different because it was neither the original purchase of insurance nor the payment of premiums which in fact or law accomplished the decisive shifting of the right to proceeds. Those transactions are simply irrelevant.

Here again, Goodnow v. United States, supra, is helpful. For in that case the wife paid certain premiums on policies on her husband's life, but the husband was vested with ownership rights in the policies, including control over the disposition of proceeds. In these circumstances, the wife's payment of premiums did not make her a transferor of any property interest in the policies.

It remains only to consider whether Mrs. Pyle's election of an alternative disposition of the proceeds was such a transaction as amounts to a transfer of property with a retained life estate, within the meaning of section 2036. Mrs. Pyle was the beneficiary originally named in the policy and as such was entitled to receive the entire proceeds of the policy on her husband's death. Then, as was her right under the terms of the policy, she caused the dispositive provisions of the policy to be changed so that she would receive only interest on the proceeds during her life, with ownership and enjoyment of this property passing to other designated persons upon her death. If it had been after maturity that Mrs. Pyle gave up her absolute right to the proceeds of the policy and elected instead to receive income for life with remainder to others, the transaction would clearly have been a transfer of property within section 2036.... This case is different only in two respects. Mrs. Pyle acted while enjoyment of her right to the proceeds was still prospective and contingent upon her husband's death. Thereafter, so long as her husband lived, she could have revoked her action. While such circumstances may affect the time when in legal contemplation the transfer is accomplished, they do not make the actor any less a transferor of an interest in property. . . .

The decision of the Tax Court will be affirmed.

NOTE

Payment of premiums by decedent. Suppose Mr. Pyle took out a policy on his own life and transferred it in trust naming Mrs. Pyle as life income beneficiary. If Mrs. Pyle then paid the premiums, would anything be includible in her estate under § 2036(a)? In Goodnow v. United States, 302 F.2d 516 (Ct. Cl. 1962), cited in the *Pyle* case, nothing was included in the wife's estate despite her payment of the premiums on policies so transferred:

> It is clear, of course, that Mrs. Goodnow transferred, either directly or indirectly, the requisite funds for the payment of premiums. She was also entitled, under the express terms of the trust instrument, to the income from the insurance proceeds for life. The relevant inquiry here is, granting the transfer of property, whether her life estate under the trust amounts to a *retention by her* of a life estate *in the property she transferred.* It does not. She herself retained no interest in the funds she transferred. She did have a contingent life interest in the income from the insurance proceeds. This interest, however, was not retained by her in the funds she provided for the payment of premiums. It was granted to her by the express terms of the trust instrument executed by her husband. Further, there is no indication that the Goodnows agreed sub rosa that she should have a life estate in the trust income if she would make the requisite premium payments. This is particularly true in view of the fact that the trust instrument, as originally written, provided that Mrs. Goodnow's interest would terminate upon her subsequent remarriage.
>
> In addition to the necessity of finding that Mrs. Goodnow *herself* retained a life interest in the property she transferred, it is also necessary to find, under section 2036(a)(1), that she retained the life interest in the *same* property she transferred. In other words, assuming arguendo that Mrs. Goodnow herself retained a life interest, the question then becomes whether she had a life interest in the premium payments she transferred. In order to justify such a conclusion, we would have to hold that, as a matter of law, the premium payments and the income from the insurance proceeds are one and the same. That this is obviously not the case may be seen from the fact that there is no necessary relationship between the premiums and the ultimate investment income. The premiums were not simply funneled through the insurance companies and returned to Mrs. Goodnow in another form. Rather, they were received by the insurance companies as the consideration for the promises contained in the insur-

> ance contracts. If there was any funneling process at all, it ceased when the funds were received by the companies. [302 F.2d at 520–21.]

The trust in *Goodnow* was revocable by the husband throughout the period of his wife's premium payments and until his death. Would this fact have been a more persuasive reason for reaching the court's result? Cf. Margrave's Estate v. Commissioner, infra page 398. If the trust in *Goodnow* had been irrevocable, would the *Pyle* rationale have led to a different result?

Should the payment of premiums by either spouse in *Pyle* have been treated as gifts for gift tax purposes? See Commissioner v. Berger, 201 F.2d 171 (2d Cir. 1953).

G. POWERS OF APPOINTMENT: § 2041

1. INTRODUCTION

Unlike virtually all of the preceding material, which deals with property owned by the decedent at death or transferred during life by quasi-testamentary disposition, this section concerns itself with the taxability of property that the decedent never owned but that he or she could control by exercising a power of appointment. The Revenue Act of 1916 said nothing about property over which the decedent had a power of appointment. In an early case the Supreme Court held that such property was not the "property" of the decedent and therefore was not includible in the gross estate either under the predecessor of § 2033 or under the postponed-possession-or-enjoyment clause. United States v. Field, 255 U.S. 257 (1921).

The Revenue Act of 1918. The 1916 omission was remedied by the Revenue Act of 1918, providing for inclusion in the decedent's gross estate of "any property passing under a general power of appointment exercised by the decedent (1) by will, or (2) by deed executed in contemplation of, or intended to take effect in possession or enjoyment at or after, his death." Because the property was not subject to the estate tax under the 1918 provision unless the power was exercised, the holder of the power[39] could enjoy a large measure of beneficial enjoyment and control with impunity. For example, *A* could transfer property in trust, giving her son *B* a life income interest coupled with a testamentary general power of appointment over the corpus and designating *B*'s issue as takers in default. Although *A*'s initial transfer in trust would be subject to gift or estate tax, the trust property would not be included in *B*'s gross estate, despite his dominion and control over it, if he was content to let it pass to the takers in default. See Helvering v. Safe Deposit & Trust Co., supra page 181. Moreover, if *B*'s power was not a "general" power of appointment, he could exercise it without incurring estate tax liability. Thus, if *B*'s power was a power to appoint only to his wife or children, the property would

---

39. In the traditional lexicon of property law, a power of appointment is created by a "donor" and held by a "donee"; the appointive property passes to an "appointee" if the power is validly exercised, or to a "taker in default" if it is not; prior to exercise of a power, the potential appointees are referred to as "objects" of the power.

not be included in his estate even if he exercised the power. In Clauson v. Vaughan, 147 F.2d 84 (1st Cir. 1945), a son was given a power to appoint to anyone except his wife (from whom he was later divorced) and her family. Admitting that "a trivial or fake limitation obviously imposed for the purpose of tax evasion" might be ignored, the court held that the power in question was not "general" even though the son could appoint to himself or to anyone in the world other than to his first wife or her family.

Statutory reform: The 1942 legislation. In 1942, the power of appointment provision was completely revised. The 1942 legislation made economic power or dominion, rather than actual exercise of the power, the criterion for taxing property subject to a power of appointment: The property was includible if the decedent possessed a power of appointment at the time of his death, whether he exercised it or not. In reaching unexercised powers, the 1942 legislation was analogous to § 2038, which reaches powers held at death over property transferred by the decedent during life. The 1942 provision also taxed the decedent if he exercised or released a power of appointment in contemplation of death or by other quasi-testamentary disposition.

In addition to abandoning the dichotomy between exercised and unexercised powers, Congress in 1942 adopted a statutory definition of the term "power of appointment," instead of leaving to the courts the determination of what powers were sufficiently "general" to be subject to tax. Under the 1942 law, the term "power of appointment" meant any power to appoint exercisable by the decedent alone or in conjunction with another person unless (a) the decedent could appoint only to certain members of his own family or the donor's family or to charities, or (b) the power was a quasi-fiduciary power exercisable only in favor of a "restricted class" and not for the decedent's own benefit. Special provision was made for powers created on or before October 21, 1942, the date of the new law's enactment.

The Powers of Appointment Act of 1951. The power of appointment area was again sweepingly revised by the Powers of Appointment Act of 1951, whose rules were carried forward into § 2041 of the Code. The reasons for the extensive changes in 1951 were set out as follows in Guterman, The Powers of Appointment Act, 29 Taxes 631, 632 (1951):

> The 1942 amendments were designed to give recognition to the fact that broad powers of appointment, even though not within the common law definition of a general power of appointment, were substantially equivalent to ownership. The amendments came about as a result of the incongruity of treatment of this type of right of disposition of property as against other rights under the estate tax which had been swept into the category of substantial equivalent of ownership. The form of the 1942 amendments created certain burdens in dealing with powers of appointment which were not consistent with

> the general recognition of their importance and utility in the disposition of property. Thus, for example, the amendments granting immunity from taxation to a nonbeneficial power exercisable by a fiduciary were found to preclude in many cases, except under the most awkward limitations, the naming of executors and trustees who might be closely related to the decedent. Because such fiduciaries frequently had some kind of contingent interest in property subject to the power, there was a possibility of estate tax on the property subject to the power in the fiduciary's estate. In some cases, will draftsmen were impelled to exclude the participation of such close relatives in the exercise of any power and to confine the exercise of such power to so-called disinterested trustees, that is, usually persons unrelated to the decedent. This problem was aggravated by the fact that a mere right to invade principal in favor of a beneficiary was by regulation swept within the category of a power of appointment, so that the common provision in a will of this kind created serious dangers of taxation, unless the particular beneficiary came within the limited statutory group in whose favor powers could be held without estate taxation or, as indicated above, unless the right to act in favor of the beneficiary was confined to disinterested trustees. The question of how remote an interest a fiduciary might have and still be subject to the danger of estate tax on a fiduciary power became a subject of much discussion and controversy. This area obviously called for a statutory change.

On the 1951 legislation, see Craven, Powers of Appointment Act of 1951, 65 Harv. L. Rev. 55 (1951).

2. GENERAL POWER OF APPOINTMENT

Responding to these complaints about the 1942 legislation, the 1951 Act liberated powers of appointment from the estate tax except for general powers, defined by § 2041(b)(1) to mean powers exercisable in favor of the decedent, the decedent's estate, the decedent's creditors, or creditors of the decedent's estate. Although this is more restrictive than the 1942 definition, the 1951 Act carried forward an important part of the 1942 legislation by requiring the property subject to a general power, if it was created after October 21, 1942, to be included in the gross estate if the power was retained until death, even if it was not exercised and hence lapsed when the decedent died. To this extent, the 1951 Act accepted the premise of such other sections of the Code as §§ 2038 and 2036(a)(2) that the estate tax should concern itself with the decedent's control over property, whether the control was exercised affirmatively or not. Powers created on or before October 21, 1942, however, are subject to tax only if they are exercised. Thus, under current rules, taxability requires a determination that a "power of appointment" exists and that the power is "general."

MARGRAVE'S ESTATE v. COMMISSIONER

618 F.2d 34 (8th Cir. 1980).

HENLEY, CIRCUIT JUDGE.

This is an appeal from a decision of the United States Tax Court involving the difficult question whether the proceeds of an insurance policy on the life of the decedent, owned by decedent's wife but payable to The United States National Bank of Omaha as trustee of decedent's revocable inter vivos trust, are includible in the decedent's gross estate for estate tax purposes. The Tax Court, in a well reasoned opinion, held that the proceeds are not taxable to the estate of the decedent because he possessed no "incidents of ownership" with respect to the policy and possessed "no power of appointment" over the policy or proceeds. We affirm.

Robert B. Margrave died on April 29, 1973 survived by his wife, Glenda Ardelle Margrave, and children. Prior to his death and on June 16, 1966 the decedent had executed a will and established a trust known as the Robert B. Margrave Trust. The will provided in part that all his personal and household effects would go to his wife if she survived him for a period of thirty days and the remainder of his estate would be "poured-over" into the Robert B. Margrave Trust. The United States National Bank of Omaha was named executor of the will.

The Bank was also named trustee of the Robert B. Margrave Trust. Under the terms of the trust decedent retained an unqualified right to modify or revoke the trust and was the income beneficiary.

The trust agreement also provided for the creation of two other and separate trusts after the death of the decedent. One trust, the Glenda Ardelle Margrave Trust, consisted of approximately half of his estate and was largely for the benefit of the widow who had a general power of appointment. The other trust, the Robert B. Margrave Residuary Trust, was for the benefit of Margrave's children. Margrave died leaving as the only assets of the Robert B. Margrave Trust certain insurance policies on his life.

On January 29, 1970 decedent's wife applied for an insurance policy on the life of her husband. The policy, a twenty year decreasing term life insurance policy with a $100,000.00 face value, was later issued on March 12, 1970 by the Western Life Insurance Company. Mrs. Margrave was the owner of record of the policy and she paid the premiums with her own funds. Under the terms of the policy, all benefits, rights, options and privileges available or exercisable during the insured's life were vested in the owner. Furthermore, the bank, as trustee of the trust created by Robert B. Margrave on June 16, 1966 was named primary beneficiary of the policy.

Following decedent's death, the proceeds of the insurance policy in the amount of $84,583.00 were paid to the bank as trustee of the trust.

The estate tax returns filed by the bank, however, did not include this amount. The Commissioner, relying largely on 26 U.S.C. § 2042(2) and 26 U.S.C. § 2041, determined that the insurance proceeds were includible and thus added the amount of the insurance proceeds to the decedent's gross estate and issued a notice of deficiency. The executor of decedent's will then petitioned the Tax Court for a redetermination of the deficiency. The Tax Court by divided vote held that the decedent possessed neither an "incident of ownership" under 26 U.S.C. § 2042(2) nor a "power of appointment" under 26 U.S.C. § 2041, and concluded that the insurance proceeds were not includible in the gross estate.[40]

On appeal the appellant first argues that the Tax Court erred in finding that the insurance proceeds were not includible in decedent's gross estate under 26 U.S.C. § 2042(2). Section 2042 provides that the gross estate shall include the value of life insurance proceeds receivable by other beneficiaries to the extent that the decedent possessed at his death any of the "incidents of ownership." The appellant argues that the decedent possessed at his death "incidents of ownership" as to the insurance policy because of the decedent's ability to change the beneficiary of the policy through his power to modify or revoke the trust. Appellant claims that the fact that Mrs. Margrave had the ultimate power to change the beneficiary of the policy does not warrant exclusion of the proceeds of the policy under § 2042(2). Noting that at the time of decedent's death Mrs. Margrave could no longer deprive Mr. Margrave of his power to change the beneficiary, the appellant concludes the decedent possessed "incidents of ownership" at the time of his death. We do not agree. . . .

We note that there was never an instant when Mr. Margrave possessed more than a mere power over an expectancy. During his life, decedent's power was subject to the absolute whim of Mrs. Margrave who could completely eliminate decedent's ability to designate the beneficiary through her own power to modify or revoke the insurance policy. At his death, Mr. Margrave's power to designate the beneficiary, by the terms of the trust, ceased to exist. In such circumstances we are unable to find "incidents of ownership" sufficient to include the proceeds of the insurance policy in decedent's gross estate under § 2042(2).

Appellant next contends that the Tax Court erred in concluding that the insurance proceeds are not includible in decedent's gross estate under 26 U.S.C. § 2041. That section provides that the gross estate includes the

---

40. Seven members of the sixteen member Tax Court vigorously objected to Judge Tannenwald's analysis for the majority in three separate dissenting opinions. Judge Fay, joined by four other judges, contended that the insurance proceeds were in fact includible in decedent's gross estate because decedent's unqualified power to modify the trust terms constituted a general testamentary power of appointment under 26 U.S.C. § 2041. Judge Chabot concluded that the insurance proceeds were includible reasoning that the decedent's unqualified power to modify or revoke the trust falls within the ambit of 26 U.S.C. § 2042(1). Judge Quealy took the position that the insurance proceeds are not only includible in decedent's gross estate under 26 U.S.C. § 2041 and 26 U.S.C. § 2042(1), but also under 26 U.S.C. § 2042(2). He felt that decedent's power to modify or revoke the trust was an "incident of ownership" and that a decedent's power need not be vested or absolute to constitute such an "incident of ownership." Judge Goffe concurred generally agreeing with the Tax Court majority, but emphasized that the present case does not involve a prearranged plan of tax avoidance.

value of all property to which the decedent has at the time of his death a "general power of appointment." Appellant insists that the decedent's power to modify or revoke the trust constitutes a "general power of appointment." Again, we do not agree.

A "general power of appointment" is defined by the Code as "a power which is exercisable in favor of the decedent, his estate, his creditors, or the creditors of his estate. . . ." 26 U.S.C. § 2041(b)(1).

In order for such a power to result in the inclusion of an item in decedent's gross estate under § 2041, the decedent must at least (1) possess a power within this definition of "a general power of appointment," and (2) there must be a property interest to which this "general power of appointment" attaches.

While it is clear that the decedent possessed a "general power of appointment" by virtue of his ability to modify or revoke the trust, Maytag v. United States, 493 F.2d 995 (10th Cir. 1974); 26 C.F.R. § 20.2041–1(b)(1), we do not believe that any property interest attached to that power.

As the Second Circuit noted in Connecticut Bank & Trust Co. v. United States, 465 F.2d 760 (2d Cir. 1972), "at the very least, property subject to a § 2041 power of appointment must be in existence prior to the time of decedent's death." Id. at 764. See also Lang v. United States, 356 F. Supp. 546 (S.D. Iowa 1973); Rev. Rul. 79–117, I.R.B. 1979, 15, 12; Rev. Rul. 75–126, 1975–1 C.B. 296; Rev. Rul. 75–127, 1975–1 C.B. 297. Prior to his death, Margrave possessed only a power over an expectancy because the rights of the trustee to the proceeds were subject to Mrs. Margrave's power to change the designation of the trustee as beneficiary. Although the death of Mr. Margrave caused the trustee's right to the proceeds to vest and create a property interest to which Mr. Margrave's power of appointment might attach, Mr. Margrave's death simultaneously terminated his ability to modify or revoke the trust. Thus, Mr. Margrave's "general power of appointment" was at all times merely a power over an expectancy. In such circumstances, we do not believe the proceeds of the life insurance policy can be included in decedent's gross estate under 26 U.S.C. § 2041.

Affirmed.

NOTE

Aftermath of Margrave's Estate. The Service announced in Rev. Rul. 81–166, 1981–1 C.B. 477, that in the future it will not seek to include life insurance proceeds in the insured's gross estate under either § 2041 or § 2042 in circumstances like those presented in the *Margrave* case. The ruling went on, however, to state that the wife made a taxable gift of the insurance proceeds to the trust when, at her insured husband's death, the proceeds became payable to the trust. Further, to the extent that she was the income beneficiary of the trust, the transfer required the transferred assets to be included at her death in her gross estate under § 2036.

JENKINS v. UNITED STATES

428 F.2d 538 (5th Cir.), cert. denied, 400 U.S. 829 (1970).

GOLDBERG, CIRCUIT JUDGE.

We consider here the application of federal estate tax provisions to an unexercised and evanescent power of appointment. The executors of the estate of Martha O. Jenkins seek approval of the decision below excluding from the decedent's estate the value of certain property subject to a power of appointment. Though equitable considerations invite us to affirm the ruling below in an effort to ameliorate the apparent harshness of the tax in this particular case, legal imperatives leave us no choice but to reverse and hold that the tax must be paid.

This case grew out of the lives—and deaths—of two sisters, Ada Lee Jenkins and Martha O. Jenkins. These sisters, both of whom were unmarried, lived together in Midland, Georgia, for many years prior to their deaths. Although they owned a substantial amount of property, they lived in a simple, frugal manner. On December 23, 1958, both sisters, who were then in their seventies, executed wills. These wills were very similar in wording and provisions, each sister leaving the other a life estate coupled with a power of invasion or consumption over the testatrix's property.

On September 24, 1962, Ada Lee Jenkins died. Shortly after her sister's death Martha O. Jenkins decided that she did not wish to serve as executrix under her sister's will, and on October 4, 1962, she executed a document renouncing her designation as executrix. She apparently took no other action with regard to the will of her sister. Although she had previously been in good health, on October 10, 1962, Martha suffered a heart attack, and on the following day she died. Because of the short period of time—only seventeen days—between the deaths of the two sisters, Ada's will had not been probated at the time of Martha's death. The wills of both sisters were filed and admitted for probate on October 25, 1962. Two nephews of the sisters, Alonzo Wimberly Jenkins, Jr., and McLendon Wash Jenkins, qualified as the executors of both estates.

The will of Ada Lee Jenkins contained several provisions leaving her surviving sister a life estate coupled with a power of invasion or consumption over certain real and personal property located in Muscogee County, Georgia. Each of the relevant provisions of the will included language substantially identical to the following:

> Should my sister, Martha O. Jenkins, survive me, then in that event, I give, bequeath and devise to Martha O. Jenkins all my right, title and interest in and to ... [certain named property] ... to have, hold, use and enjoy for and during her natural life, *with full and unlimited power and authority to dispose of the same in fee simple by gift or otherwise at any time during her life without accountability to anyone*, ... and should my sister not dispose of my interest in said [property]

during her lifetime, then on her death the same shall pass to and become the absolute property of [a certain named remainderman].... (Emphasis added.)

These provisions of the will led to a disagreement between the Commissioner of Internal Revenue and the executors of the estate of Martha O. Jenkins as to the amount of estate taxes due. When the executors computed and filed an estate tax return for the estate of Martha O. Jenkins, they excluded from her gross estate the value of the property in which she received a life estate with powers of invasion by her sister's will. The Commissioner, however, ruled that the value of this property must be included because Martha's powers of invasion constituted a general power of appointment over such property. After paying the additional estate taxes required by the Commissioner's ruling, the executors filed a claim for a refund. When this claim was disallowed, the executors filed suit in the United States District Court for the Middle District of Georgia, seeking a refund in the amount of $26,962.73.

As plaintiffs in the district court the executors advanced four alternative contentions in support of their position that the value of the property in dispute should not be included in Martha O. Jenkins' estate for estate tax purposes. First, they contended that Martha did not have a general power of appointment because she could dispose of the property only inter vivos and not by will. Second, they contended that her power of appointment was not a general power because it was "limited by an ascertainable standard relating to the health, education, support, or maintenance of the decedent." Int. Rev. Code of 1954, § 2041(b)(1)(A), 26 U.S.C.A. § 2041(b)(1)(A). Third, they contended that Martha did not possess an exercisable general power of appointment at the time of her death because Ada's will had not yet been probated. Finally, plaintiffs contended that requiring Martha's estate to pay the amount of estate taxes in dispute would amount to a deprivation of property without due process of law in violation of the Fifth Amendment.

The district court, hearing the case on stipulated facts, entered judgment for the plaintiffs. In its opinion the court accepted plaintiffs' first and third contentions, rejected their second contention, and did not reach the fourth. Jenkins v. United States, M.D. Ga. 1968, 296 F. Supp. 203. The government appeals to this court. For the reasons hereinafter given, we are compelled to reject each of the plaintiffs' contentions, and we therefore reverse the judgment of the district court.

I

Plaintiffs' first contention is that decedent did not have a general power of appointment because her power could be exercised only inter vivos and not by will. We reject this contention because it involves a patent misconstruction of the relevant provisions of the Internal Revenue Code.

Section 2041 of the Code provides that the value of the decedent's gross estate shall include the value of property over which the decedent at the time of his death possessed a "general power of appointment." For estate tax purposes, therefore, property over which a decedent possessed such a power is treated as if the decedent actually "owned" the property in the conventional sense. Section 2041(b)(1) defines a "general power of appointment" as "a power which is exercisable in favor of the decedent, his estate, his creditors, or the creditors of his estate." The statutory definition is thus cast in the disjunctive. A power of appointment is a general power under § 2041(b)(1) if the donee of the power can exercise it in favor of himself *or* his estate *or* his creditors *or* the creditors of his estate....

In the case at bar the decedent received by virtue of her sister's will a life estate in the property involved with an unlimited power of disposition. Thus she had the power to make inter vivos dispositions of the property, but she could not dispose of the property by will. In statutory terminology, she had the power to appoint the property to herself or to her creditors, but she did not have the power to appoint the property to her estate or to the creditors of her estate. In view of the definition contained in § 2041(b)(1), the fact that decedent could appoint to herself or to her creditors was sufficient to make her power of appointment a general power. Her inability to make appointments either to her estate or to the creditors of her estate was irrelevant....

II

Plaintiffs next advance the contention that decedent's power of appointment was not a general power because it came within the "ascertainable standard" exception found in § 2041(b)(1)(A). This section provides:

> A power to consume, invade, or appropriate property for the benefit of the decedent which is limited by an ascertainable standard relating to the health, education, support, or maintenance of the decedent shall not be deemed a general power of appointment.

Plaintiffs make much of the fact that decedent had a substantial amount of property of her own and of the fact that she lived in an exceedingly frugal manner. Because of these facts, which are undisputed, plaintiffs contend that "there was no likelihood" that decedent would ever have exercised any of her powers of disposition over the property involved. Therefore, plaintiffs ask us to conclude, decedent's power of appointment was limited by an ascertainable standard within the meaning of the Code. We reject this contention, as did the court below. 296 F. Supp. at 208–210. The district court's analysis of this issue was eminently correct, and we quote with approval from the opinion below:

> In this connection the evidence shows that at the time of her sister's death Martha O. Jenkins was 82 years of age and was possessed of a substantial estate in her own right consisting of real and personal property having a value of approximately $150,000.00.

The evidence further shows that the two sisters lived in a very conservative manner, growing their own vegetables and raising their own chickens and spending not more than about $5.00 a week for groceries. They wore black cotton dresses and would spend money on nothing unless it was absolutely necessary. It is interesting to note that they resisted until the end the urgings of their relatives that they buy themselves a television set, which fact may be regarded not only as evidence of their frugality but as a monument to their discretion.

The Court is convinced that Martha O. Jenkins would never have encroached upon her sister's estate to satisfy any of her own meager wants or needs, first because she had no need to do so, and second because the remaindermen named in her sister's will were the same remaindermen who were the beneficiaries under her own will later probated, but the question is not what she *would* have done with the property, but rather what she *could* have done with it. 296 F. Supp. at 209 (emphasis in original).

The district court was correct in holding that the relevant inquiry is not what the decedent may have *planned* to do with the property, but rather what she was *empowered* to do. An ascertainable standard must be a *prescribed* standard, not a post-prescriptive course of action. The acting out of the standard is irrelevant, for it is the script rather than the actor which controls a decision concerning the existence of an ascertainable standard. In determining what the decedent was *empowered* to do, courts must look to the express language of the instrument creating the power, or to the language of the instrument as modified by state law....

In the instant case the instrument creating the power—the will of Ada Lee Jenkins—gave Martha O. Jenkins "full and unlimited power and authority to dispose of the [property] in fee simple by gift or otherwise at any time during her life without accountability to anyone." It is difficult to imagine a more unlimited, open-ended, freewheeling power than this. Moreover, Georgia law does not modify such language by *implying* any "support and maintenance" limitation. See Williams v. Jones, 1963, 219 Ga. 45, 131 S.E.2d 553; Townsley v. Townsley, 1952, 209 Ga. 323, 72 S.E.2d 289.

In the words of the district court, "we can only conclude that the will gave Martha O. Jenkins an unlimited right to consume or give away inter vivos any or all of her sister's property regardless of whether such encroachment was for support and maintenance or for some other purpose." 296 F. Supp. at 210. Her complete power over the property during her lifetime was not modified by any standard other than one she might impose on herself. Thus her power was not limited by any "ascertainable standard" within the meaning of § 2041(b)(1)(A).

III

Plaintiffs' third contention is that decedent did not possess an exercisable general power of appointment at the time of her death because the will of Ada Lee Jenkins had not then been probated or filed or offered for probate. Plaintiffs prevailed on this issue in the district court. 296 F. Supp. at 206–208. Our examination of this contention, however, leads us to the conclusion that it must be rejected.

We note at the outset that there is no language in the will itself which evidences a desire on the part of Ada that Martha's possession of the power of appointment was to be postponed until some time after Ada's death. On the contrary, the relevant provisions of the will are couched in terms of the moment when Martha survived Ada, i.e., the moment of Ada's death: "Should my sister, Martha O. Jenkins, survive me, then in that event, I give, bequeath and devise to Martha O. Jenkins all my right, title and interest. . . ."

The district court, however, found significance in the language of Item Sixteen of the will, which provides in part:

> *Upon the probate and admission to record* of this my will, it is my desire that my executrix, executors or executor administer my estate with [sic] the control or supervision of any Court or other authority and to that end, reposing special confidence in them, I relieve them and each of them of accountability to any Court or other authority in the administration, management and final distribution of my estate. (Emphasis added.)

The district court placed special emphasis on the first seven of the quoted words. We cannot agree, however, with the court's apparent conclusion that these words expressed a desire on the part of the testatrix to postpone her surviving sister's possession of the power of appointment. On the contrary, when these words are read in the context of the entire sentence, it is clear that they have reference only to the procedure of probating the will, and not to the timing of the passage of the power of appointment to Martha O. Jenkins.

Moreover, we find nothing in Georgia law which leads us to conclude that Martha's possession of the power would have been postponed until probate or until any other point in time later than the death of Ada. In the absence of any contrary provision in the will itself, we think it is clear that Martha received an exercisable general power at the moment of Ada's death. . . .

We are compelled to reject plaintiffs' contention that Martha O. Jenkins could not have exercised her power of appointment prior to the probate of her sister's will. Under Georgia law she could have made conveyances of the property involved in this case at any time after her sister's death, subject only to subsequent perfection of the record title. The fact that she did not then possess a fully perfected record title is not controlling for federal estate tax purposes. The substantive powers she received at the time of her sister's death clearly came within the definition of a general power of appointment in § 2041(b)(1) of the Internal Revenue Code, and these powers were clearly exercisable at the time of her death. . . .

IV

Plaintiffs finally contend that including the value of the property here involved in the gross estate of Martha O. Jenkins constitutes a deprivation of property without due process of law in violation of the Fifth Amendment. The district court did not reach this issue because of its findings favorable to the plaintiffs on two other issues. 296 F. Supp. at 210. We find it necessary to consider plaintiffs' constitutional argument, however, in view of the fact that on each of the preceding issues we have reached a decision adverse to the plaintiffs' position.

Plaintiffs base their constitutional argument on two premises. First, they contend that the property here involved passed directly from the estate of Ada Lee Jenkins to the remaindermen "without decedent at any time receiving the right to the use or benefit of those properties, or of the power or right to dispose of those properties." This argument is nothing more than a reiteration of plaintiffs' contention that Martha O. Jenkins received nothing by her sister's will at the time of her sister's death. In the light of our holding that Martha O. Jenkins *did* receive powers and rights at the time of her sister's death, this argument is untenable.

Secondly, plaintiffs contend that decedent was denied an opportunity to exercise her statutory right to disclaim or renounce the power of appointment. Section 2041(a)(2) grants to every donee of a post–1942 power the right to disclaim or renounce the power. If a decedent exercises this right, the value of the property as to which he has renounced the power will not be included in his gross estate. Moreover, the exercise of the right is not itself a taxable event.

Plaintiffs direct our attention to Treas. Reg. § 20.2041–3(d)(6), which provides:

> A disclaimer or renunciation of a general power of appointment is not considered to be a release of the power. The disclaimer or renunciation must be unequivocal and effective under local law. A disclaimer is a complete and unqualified refusal to accept the rights to which one is entitled. There can be no disclaimer or renunciation of a power after its acceptance. In any case where a power is purported to be disclaimed or renounced as to only a portion of the property subject to the power, the determination as to whether or not there has been a complete and unqualified refusal to accept the rights to which one is entitled will depend on all the facts and circumstances of the particular case, taking into account the recognition and effectiveness of such a disclaimer under local law. Such rights refer to the incidents of the power and not to other interests of the decedent in the property. If effective under local law, the power may be disclaimed or renounced without disclaiming or renouncing such other interests. In the absence of facts to the contrary, the failure to renounce or disclaim

> within a reasonable time after learning of its existence will be presumed to constitute an acceptance of the power.[41]

Relying on the final sentence of the quoted provision of the regulation, plaintiffs contend, in effect, that every donee of a general power of appointment is entitled to a reasonable time to disclaim or renounce before he can be charged with possession of the power. Applying this principle to the facts of this case, plaintiffs argue that Martha O. Jenkins did not have a reasonable time in which to exercise her right to disclaim or renounce.

Even if we were to assume arguendo that the principle for which plaintiffs contend is correct, they still would fail in their attempt to apply such a "reasonable time" principle to the facts of this case. In the first place, if plaintiffs' contention in this regard is based on the theory that decedent had not yet received any power because her sister's will had not yet been probated, then the contention is untenable for the reasons previously given. In addition, plaintiffs' contention must be rejected even if it is not based on the time-of-probate argument. The sentence of the regulation upon which plaintiffs heavily rely provides that "[i]n the absence of facts to the contrary, the failure to renounce or disclaim within a reasonable time *after learning of its existence* will be presumed to constitute an acceptance of the power." Treas. Reg. § 20.2041–3(d)(6) (emphasis added). Martha O. Jenkins was obviously aware of the existence of her power of appointment as soon as it came into her possession at the time of her sister's death. After all, she was not unfamiliar with the provisions of her sister's will. Moreover, after her sister's death she had sufficient time to execute a document renouncing her designation as executrix under her sister's will. Had she desired to disclaim or renounce her power of appointment, she could have done so at that time. We would ignore reality if we were to accept plaintiffs' argument that decedent was somehow robbed of her right to renounce.

Plaintiffs' constitutional argument, like their other contentions, is completely devoid of merit. The power of appointment possessed by Martha O. Jenkins had taxable existentiality at her death and was untainted by any constitutional disablement. The Commissioner's inclusion within her estate of the value of the properties embraced by the power is fully sanctioned by law.

The judgment of the district court is reversed.

NOTES

1. *"Power of appointment."* A power need not be labeled as a "power of appointment" to qualify as such under § 2041, as is demonstrated in the *Jenkins* case by the court's treatment of the surviving sister's unlimited power of disposition. Reg. § 20.2041–1(b)(1) states that the term "includes all

41. This regulation was revised in 1986 to reflect the provisions of § 2518 (relating to qualified disclaimers of interests and powers created by post–1976 transfers). See infra page 415, Note 1.—EDS.

powers which are in substance and effect powers of appointment regardless of the nomenclature used in creating the power" and cites as examples a power to invade or consume trust property, a power to affect beneficial enjoyment by altering, revoking or terminating the disposition, and a power to remove a trustee holding a power and to substitute oneself. The cases are substantially in accord. See Wolf's Estate v. Commissioner, 29 T.C. 441 (1957), affd. and revd. on other issues, 264 F.2d 82 (3d Cir. 1959) (unlimited power to designate beneficiaries of employee benefits); Maytag v. United States, 493 F.2d 995 (10th Cir. 1974) (trustee-beneficiary's power to compel termination of trust). The powers to amend administrative provisions, exercise fiduciary powers, or assent to a trust accounting are not treated as general powers under the regulations. See, e.g., Rolin's Estate v. Commissioner, 68 T.C. 919 (1977), affd., 588 F.2d 368 (2d Cir. 1978) (broad fiduciary power over investments was not a general power); Rev. Rul. 77–460, 1977–2 C.B. 323 (parent's right under local custodianship statute to petition court for review of third-party custodian's exercise of discretion was not a general power). A third-party trustee's virtually unfettered discretionary power to invade corpus for the decedent's benefit cannot be imputed to the decedent even if the trustee is directed to exercise its discretion liberally in decedent's favor. Rev. Rul. 76–368, 1976–2 C.B. 271. If, however, the trustee is required by the instrument to distribute corpus on the decedent's demand, the decedent's power is general.

2. *"General" power of appointment.*

a. *Power to defray decedent's legal obligations.* Reg. § 20.2041–1(c)(1) treats a power as general to the extent it is exercisable to discharge a decedent's legal obligations. Thus, for example, a parent to whom property is transferred as trustee for a minor child has a general power to the extent that the parent has discretion to use the trust property to discharge his or her own obligation to support the child. Cf. Rev. Rul. 79–154, 1979–1 C.B. 301 (decedent's power to appoint insurance proceeds retained by insurer under settlement option for health, education, support, and maintenance of adult children whom she was not obligated to support held not general; however, if duty to support existed, decedent's power would be regarded as general to extent that fund could have satisfied decedent's obligation).

b. *Power to consume construed under local law as unlimited.* Not infrequently, a poorly drafted will devises property to a beneficiary in a form that is neither a fee nor a life estate, coupled with a broad power of sale and followed by a gift over to a secondary beneficiary of any balance remaining at the primary beneficiary's death. Ordinarily, such a devise is construed under local law as creating an unrestricted power to dispose of the property during life, which in turn constitutes a general power of appointment for federal tax purposes. See, e.g., de Oliveira v. United States, 767 F.2d 1344 (9th Cir. 1985); Condon Natl. Bank v. United States, 349 F.Supp. 755 (D. Kan. 1972); Rev. Rul. 243, 1953–2 C.B. 267. The power may be immune from tax, however, if it is subject to implied restrictions under local law that prevent it from being exercised by the holder for his or her own benefit. See Rev. Rul. 54–153, 1954–1 C.B. 185; Rev. Rul. 76–502, 1976–2 C.B. 273 (Maryland law). As illustrated in the *Jenkins* case, it is often necessary to turn to local law to determine whether a power is sufficiently broad to meet the federal criteria for taxability under § 2041. For the "proper regard" to be given in federal tax proceedings to a state court's prior determination of these issues, see Commissioner v. Bosch's Estate, supra page 26.

c. *Power over property in the decedent's estate.* The "or" in § 2041(b)(1) is construed as disjunctive, so that a power is general if it can be exercised in favor of the holder, or his creditors, or his estate, or the creditors of his estate. Thus the power to dispose of property by gift in *Jenkins* was taxable, although the decedent had no power to transfer the property by will. By the same token, a power exercisable only by will meets the test. See Edelman's Estate v. Commissioner, 38 T.C. 972 (1962). What if at decedent's death the property becomes part of his or her probate estate and devolves accordingly?

In Second Natl. Bank of Danville v. Dallman, 209 F.2d 321 (7th Cir. 1954), the proceeds of a life insurance policy on the decedent's father were payable to the decedent for life and at her death to her estate. The court held that the proceeds were not includible in the decedent's gross estate because at her death she neither had an interest in them (see supra page 184, Note 3) nor (under pre–1951 law) possessed a general power of appointment over them:

> [The statute] defines a general power of appointment thus: "For the purposes of this subsection the term 'general power of appointment' means a power which is exercisable in favor of the decedent, his estate, his creditors, or the creditors of his estate...." ... We think it obvious that decedent had no general power of appointment and certainly she was not endowed with power to dispose of the insurance proceeds by will. This power of appointment of which the statute and the cases speak is not something to be plucked out of the air; it must be created before it can be exercised. Decedent's power, such as it was, must be found in the insurance contract between her father and the insurance company and not elsewhere.
>
> The salient provisions of this contract have heretofore been noted and need not be repeated in detail. It is sufficient to state that the sole and only power reposed in decedent was the right to appoint a contingent beneficiary. If this power had been exercised, which it was not, the beneficiary thus appointed would have been entitled to take the insurance proceeds. And even the exercise of this meager power was limited, that is, it was required to be made in "writing and filed at the Home Office of the Company (accompanied by the Policy for suitable endorsement) prior to or at the time this Policy shall become payable." It thus appears plain that as a prerequisite to any valid change of beneficiary, decedent was required not only to nominate but also to take the prescribed steps in order to make such nomination effective, all to be performed prior to her death. This was not done, and as a result the proceeds were payable at decedent's death not by her direction but by that of her father as contained in the contract. There is not so much as an intimation in the contract of any right possessed by decedent to dispose of the proceeds at her death, by will or otherwise. Every vestige of right or interest which decedent had in these proceeds was extinguished by death; nothing passed from her to the executor of her estate. Any exercise of power in this respect by decedent in her testamentary capacity must have been of her own creation; it certainly was not that of her father.

> We have examined the many cases called to our attention and we find none where the right to make a disposition of property, testamentary or otherwise, by power of appointment was not derived from a donor. [209 F.2d at 323–24.]

The Service announced that it would not accept the *Dallman* case as precedent in disposing of similar cases. Rev. Rul. 55–277, 1955–1 C.B. 456. Its view prevailed in Keeter v. United States, 461 F.2d 714 (5th Cir. 1972), where the court stated:

> It appears to this court that the settlors in *Dallman* and in our case granted absolute powers of appointment to their respective donees subject only to the proviso that the donees were to exercise their powers of appointment by means of a will. We know of no state in which the executor is empowered to do whatever he chooses with a decedent's estate. Certainly Florida law required Mrs. Shaw's executors to do precisely what Mrs. Shaw directed in her will.... Thus, under the state law that defines the *substance* of Mrs. Shaw's directive authority over the insurance proceeds, the executor could not act as an insulator preventing Mrs. Shaw from spreading the insurance bounty as she chose, nor was the executor an independent agent with respect to her estate. She specifically directed that any powers of appointment be exercised in a certain way, and the executors, as required by law, complied. Therefore, the substance of the settlement option was to grant an absolute power of appointment of the insurance principal and interest to Mrs. Shaw, exercisable at her death by her will. [461 F.2d at 719.]

Does the Service's acquiescence in *Margrave* (see Note, supra page 400) represent a retreat from the position it successfully pursued in *Keeter*? In *Margrave*, the court found that Mr. Margrave had a general power, but nevertheless held § 2041 inapplicable because there was no "property interest attached to that power" at any time before Mr. Margrave's death. On substantially the same theory that § 2041 applies only to property that was "in existence" before the decedent's death, the Second Circuit has held that the gross estate does not include a wrongful death recovery that is distributed, pursuant to state law, under the decedent's will. Connecticut Bank & Trust Co. v. United States, 465 F.2d 760 (2d Cir. 1972). The Service has accepted this construction. Rev. Rul. 75–126, 1975–1 C.B. 296 (recovery under wrongful death statute); Rev. Rul. 75–127, 1975–1 C.B. 297 (recovery under survival statute). Wrongful death recoveries are also immune from inclusion under § 2033. See supra page 195, Note 2.

3. *Power subject to an "ascertainable standard."* A power held by the decedent to consume, invade or appropriate property for his own benefit is exempt by virtue of § 2041(b)(1)(A) if it is exercisable only under "an ascertainable standard relating to the health, education, support or maintenance of the decedent." Reg. § 20.2041–1(c)(2) expands on the statutory language by giving examples of standards that qualify, but, in practice, the cases have achieved no greater precision on the point than the cases applying the judge-made "external standard" rules under § 2038. That experience is described in the Note, supra page 258. The results have not borne out the drafters' prediction that the 1951 legislation would make the law "simple and

definite enough to be understood and applied by the average lawyer." S. Rep. No. 382, 82d Cong., 1st Sess. 3 (1951). For example, compare Brantingham v. United States, 631 F.2d 542 (7th Cir. 1980), holding that a decedent's power to invade trust corpus for her own "maintenance, comfort and happiness" was limited by an ascertainable standard, with Rev. Rul. 82–63, 1982–1 C.B. 135, reaching a contrary result and refusing to follow *Brantingham*; both trusts were governed by Massachusetts law.

The standards that were to govern the power to invade corpus in the following cases were held not sufficiently limited to qualify for the exemption under § 2041(b)(1)(A): Independence Bank Waukesha v. United States, 761 F.2d 442 (7th Cir. 1985) ("whatever purpose she desires"); First Virginia Bank v. United States, 490 F.2d 532 (4th Cir. 1974) ("for her comfort and care as she may see fit"); Miller v. United States, 387 F.2d 866 (3d Cir. 1968) ("other expenses incidental to her comfort and well-being"); Strite v. McGinnes, 330 F.2d 234 (3d Cir.), cert. denied, 379 U.S. 836 (1964) ("reasonable needs and proper expenses or the benefit and comfort"); Little's Estate v. Commissioner, 87 T.C. 599 (1986) ("proper support, maintenance, welfare, health and general happiness in the manner to which he is accustomed"); Rev. Rul. 77–194, 1977–1 C.B. 283 ("proper comfort and welfare"). On the other hand, limits impliedly imposed by local law have been used as the basis for finding open-ended powers to be exercisable only for the holder's health, education, support, or maintenance. See Vissering's Estate v. Commissioner, 990 F.2d 578 (10th Cir. 1993) ("continued comfort, support, maintenance, or education"); Sowell's Estate v. Commissioner, 708 F.2d 1564 (10th Cir. 1983) ("emergency or illness"); Pittsfield Natl. Bank v. United States, 181 F.Supp. 851 (D. Mass. 1960) ("as he may from time to time request, he to be the sole judge of his needs"); Berg v. United States, 47 A.F.T.R.2d 1612 (D. Minn. 1981) (power to sell property "in case of necessity").

Although the Senate Finance Committee report, supra, states that a power is not a "general power" if the holder "is legally accountable for its exercise or nonexercise," this does not mean that legal accountability alone creates a sufficient shield. See Peoples Trust Co. v. United States, 412 F.2d 1156 (3d Cir. 1969) (fiduciary obligation to exercise power in good faith insufficient to establish exemption).

4. *Joint powers.* A post–1942 joint power is exempt under § 2041(b)(1)(C) if exercisable by the decedent only in conjunction with the creator of the power or a person having a substantial adverse interest. If the person whose consent is required falls into neither of these categories but is a potential appointee, the decedent is treated as having a general power over only a ratable share of the appointive property. Reg. § 20.2041–3(c). The concept of a substantial adverse interest—unknown to the estate tax prior to the 1951 Act—is sketched out by § 2041(b)(1)(C)(ii), but its meaning has been developed for the most part by analogy to the gift tax law. See, e.g., Towle's Estate v. Commissioner, 54 T.C. 368 (1970) (substantial adverse interest requires "at the very least ... that the third person have a present or future chance to obtain a personal benefit from the property," citing Commissioner v. Prouty, supra page 101, Note 1); Rev. Rul. 79–63, 1979–1 C.B. 302 (joint holder has substantial adverse interest if he is also taker in default, but not if he is merely a potential appointee); Rev. Rul. 76–503, 1976–2 C.B. 275 (joint

holder has substantial adverse interest if he can exercise power for his own benefit after decedent's death, but not if he must continue to share it with decedent's successor). For other rulings dealing with the adverse interest rule, see Maytag v. United States, 493 F.2d 995 (10th Cir. 1974) (co-trustee's right to fiduciary compensation is not an adverse interest within the statutory meaning); Rev. Rul. 75–145, 1975–1 C.B. 298 (joint payees of uncashed Social Security checks have interests adverse to each other).

5. *Limited power held by taker in default.* As noted earlier, § 2041(b)(1) defines the term "general power of appointment" to mean "a power which is exercisable in favor of the decedent, his estate, his creditors, or the creditors of his estate." Suppose the power is exercisable only in favor of a restricted class, such as the holder's nieces and nephews, but in default of appointment, the property will go to the holder's estate. The holder of such a power has as much control as if he were expressly empowered to appoint to his estate. Is the power taxable as a general power? See Martin v. United States, 780 F.2d 1147 (4th Cir. 1986). Alternatively, if the holder dies without exercising the power, can the property be included in his gross estate under § 2033 on the theory that he had an "interest" in the property at his death?

6. *Successive powers.* There is one exception to the principle that § 2041 taxes only general powers of appointment. Section 2041(a)(3) requires property to be included in the gross estate if the decedent, by will or by quasi-testamentary disposition, exercised a post–1942 power to create another power that under local law may be employed to postpone vesting of an interest in the property (or to suspend ownership or alienability) for a period of time that is unrelated to the date of creation of the first power. An example is a power held by *A* and exercisable in favor of *A*'s issue, if under local law *A* can exercise the power by authorizing a child to appoint among his or her issue (whether born before or after the creation of *A*'s power), and so on for successive generations. The provision was enacted because of the possibility that under the law of a few states (Delaware was given as the example at the time) the underlying property might escape federal gift and estate taxes for an indefinite period after the creation of the first power. See Leach, Powers of Appointment, 24 A.B.A.J. 807 (1938); see also Murphy's Estate v. Commissioner, 71 T.C. 671 (1979) (under Wisconsin law, power could be exercised to suspend alienability only for period running from creation of power; § 2041(a)(3) analyzed but held inapplicable).

3. TAXABLE EVENTS: POSSESSION AT DEATH, EXERCISE, RELEASE, AND LAPSE

Property subject to a general power of appointment, as defined in § 2041(b)(1), is includible in the decedent's gross estate if the power was created after October 21, 1942,[42] and was either (1) exercisable at the time

42. Section 2041(a)(1) states that a general power of appointment created on or before October 21, 1942 is subject to tax only if it is exercised by the decedent by will or by quasi-testamentary disposition. For the meaning of "exercise," see Minot's Estate v. Commissioner, 45 T.C. 578 (1966) (will contest did not exercise power of appointment; cases reviewed). For the date of "creation" of a power, see § 2041(b)(3) (power created by will); Reg. § 20.2041–1(e) (power created by inter vivos instrument).

of decedent's death, or (2) exercised or released during the decedent's life in a manner that would have subjected a similar transfer of the decedent's own property to inclusion under §§ 2035, 2036, 2037, or 2038. A lapse of a power without exercise is ordinarily treated as a release of the power, subject to an exception for "5–and–5" powers.

a. Unexercised Power Held by Decedent at Death

ROLIN'S ESTATE v. COMMISSIONER

588 F.2d 368 (2d Cir. 1978).

KAUFMAN, CHIEF JUDGE.

In this case, we must determine the effectiveness, for estate tax purposes, of an instrument by which the executors of the estate of Genevieve Rolin purported to renounce her interest in a trust created by her late husband, Daniel. The Tax Court held the renunciation effective. 68 T.C. 919 (1977). We affirm.

Daniel established the trust in 1958, retaining for life the income plus the power to amend or revoke the trust at any time. Upon his death, the corpus was to be divided into two parts: "Trust A" would receive an amount equal to the maximum marital deduction available to Daniel's estate under I.R.C. § 2056, and "Trust B" would receive the remainder. Genevieve would receive the income of both trusts for life. In addition she was granted the right to invade the corpus of Trust A at any time and in any amount during her life, and she also received a general testamentary power of appointment over its assets. If she failed to exercise the power, Trust A would be merged into Trust B at her death and the assets distributed to the Rolins' issue.

Daniel died on September 30, 1968. Genevieve, who was then 72 years old and suffering from a heart ailment, died four months later. Between Daniel's death and her own, Genevieve had not received the income from either trust, nor had she attempted to invoke the power of appointment over Trust A. As soon as Genevieve's executors qualified, they attempted to renounce her interest in the trust. Even without the Trust A assets, her estate was larger than Daniel's; consequently, the progressive rate structure of the federal estate tax would render inclusion of those assets in her estate disadvantageous to the Rolins' heirs. Thus, the tax saving to Daniel's estate created by the marital deduction of I.R.C. § 2056(b)(5) would be more than offset by the increased liability of Genevieve's estate under § 2041, which taxes property over which the deceased held a general power of appointment at death. If the renunciation is held effective, Daniel's estate will pay about $35,000 more estate tax than otherwise, but Genevieve's will pay approximately $99,000 less.

We agree with the Tax Court that the renunciation was effective in this case. New York law permits executors, within a reasonable time, to disclaim legacies to which their testator was entitled. Estate of Dreyer v. Commissioner of Internal Revenue, 68 T.C. 275 (1977), acq., 1978–12

I.R.B. 6; Estate of Hoenig v. Commissioner of Internal Revenue, 66 T.C. 471 (1976), acq., 1978–12 I.R.B. 6. Moreover, disclaimers "relate back" to the date of the gift (here, September 30, 1968, the date of Daniel's death) and prevent title from ever vesting. Albany Hospital v. Albany Guardian Society, 214 N.Y. 435, 441, 108 N.E. 812 (1915).

The Commissioner does not dispute this, nor does he now contend that the Tax Court erred in holding that the power to disclaim is not limited to legatees, and extends to inter vivos gifts taking effect at death. See 68 T.C. at 925 (citing cases). Rather, he argues that because a power of appointment is not a descendable property right but a personal privilege that expires at death, Mastin v. Merchants National Bank, 278 Ala. 261, 264, 177 So. 2d 817, 820 (1965), there was nothing for the executors to disclaim. How, he asks, could they renounce a power they could not exercise?

We are of the view, however, that New York courts would permit executors to renounce powers and other interests held by their testator at death to the same extent they permit disclaimers of legacies. Outright ownership necessarily includes both a life estate and a general testamentary power of appointment. It is not any more anomalous to permit retroactive renunciation of those rights when they stand alone than it is when they are merely part of the bundle of rights constituting a fee simple. Furthermore, since the principle of retroactive renunciation is that a disclaimer of an interest may be treated as relating back in time, it seems irrelevant to the efficacy of that principle that the interest has expired. It is agreed on all sides that *Hoenig* and *Dreyer* correctly stated the law of New York with respect to legacies; accordingly, we conclude that a New York court would find the disclaimer in the instant case effective.

Nor does § 2041 require a different result. That provision cannot be viewed in isolation from the rest of the Code. Section 2033 includes in the gross estate "the value of all property to the extent of the interest therein of the decedent," and the predecessor to § 2041 was first enacted because Congress was doubtful whether the forerunner of § 2033 would reach property as to which decedent did not hold fee simple title but merely a testamentary power of appointment. United States v. Field, 255 U.S. 257, 265 (1921). Moreover, the statute was amended in 1942 in response to Helvering v. Safe Deposit & Trust Co., 316 U.S. 56, 59–62 (1942), which held that only *exercised* powers were taxable. See, e.g., H.R. Rep. No. 2333, 77th Cong., 2d Sess. 160–61 (1942). See generally B. Bittker & L. Stone, Federal Income, Estate and Gift Taxation 1093–96, 1240–48 (4th ed. 1972). The clear congressional purpose in enacting § 2041 was merely to ensure that, since the possessor of a general testamentary power of appointment may control the disposition of the property after his death as fully as the owner of a fee simple title, such powers are taxed in the same manner as outright ownership. Because, as *Hoenig* and *Dreyer* held, an executor's power to make a timely retroactive renunciation does not transgress the policy of § 2033, neither is it inconsistent with § 2041.[43]

Indeed, this result comports well with more general considerations of estate tax policy. So long as assets do not escape taxation entirely and no specific provision of the Code is contravened, taxpayers are generally permitted to arrange their affairs to minimize estate tax liability. See, e.g., Estate of Charles W. Smith v. Commissioner of Internal Revenue, 565 F.2d 455, 457–58 (7th Cir. 1977) (per curiam). Here, the trust agreement gave Genevieve the right to renounce her interest in the trust within 14 months of Daniel's death, and it specifically provided that her executors might exercise that right should she die before accepting the benefits of the trust. Since New York courts would uphold her executors' renunciation, and since the Trust A assets will be taxed as part of Daniel's estate, I.R.C. §§ 2036, 2038, we see no reason to deny effect to this provision of the trust agreement. Accordingly, the judgment of the Tax Court is affirmed.

NOTES

1. *Disclaimer of unexercised power.* Compare the Second Circuit's reasoning in *Rolin* with that of the Fifth Circuit in the *Jenkins* case, supra page 401. Consider the Commissioner's contention, set out in the court's footnote, that a holding for the taxpayer in *Rolin* "would read § 2041 out of the Code." The Service has accepted the *Rolin* holding. Reg. § 20.2041–3(d)(6), as revised in 1986, states that a qualified disclaimer of a post–1976 power that meets the requirements of § 2518 is not to be considered a taxable release, nor is the disclaimer of a pre–1977 power if it is unequivocal, valid under local law, and made within a reasonable time after the donee learns of the power's existence. The requirements for a qualified disclaimer under § 2518 are discussed supra at page 165.

In many jurisdictions, a decedent's surviving spouse is entitled to claim an elective share of the decedent's property; if not exercised by the spouse while still living and within a prescribed time following the decedent's death, this right is automatically extinguished. Does the right to claim an elective share constitute a general power of appointment, the lapse of which may be subject to gift or estate tax? See Rev. Rul. 74–492, 1974–2 C.B. 298 (widow died without exercising right, which was, "in effect, renounced by operation of law"; § 2041 not applicable).

2. *Power subject to a condition.* Section 2041(a)(2) requires property to be included in the gross estate of a decedent who "has at the time of his

43. The Commissioner has argued that a holding for the taxpayer in this case would read § 2041 out of the Code, because the executor of a donee of an unexercised general power would almost always disclaim, leaving in doubt only whether the disclaimer was timely. The timeliness limitation, however, is a substantial one. Transfers made before December 31, 1976 are subject, in addition to the timeliness requirements of local law, to the "reasonable time" limitation of Treas. Reg. § 20.2041–3(d)(6). And for transfers occurring after that date, I.R.C. § 2518(b)(2) requires, in the case of an adult, renunciation within nine months of the creation of the power.

Indeed, it is apparent that there can be effective posthumous disclaimers of powers only when the donee dies shortly after the donor, for otherwise the power will vest irrevocably through passage of time.

death" a general power of appointment over the property. The statute further provides that a power "shall be considered to exist" on the date of the decedent's death even if its exercise is subject to a condition of prior notice or takes effect only after a specified period of time, whether or not notice has been given or the power has taken effect at the time of death. For similar language in § 2038, see supra page 253, Note 3. This sort of restriction is to be distinguished from a provision that a power will become exercisable only upon the occurrence of a specified condition or event during the decedent's life, such as attaining a prescribed age or surviving another person. If the decedent dies before the condition has been met, the power does not "exist" at the date of decedent's death and § 2041 does not apply.

In Kurz's Estate v. Commissioner, 101 T.C. 44 (1993), affd., 68 F.3d 1027 (7th Cir. 1995), the decedent's husband created a marital trust and a family trust. The decedent had an unrestricted power to withdraw the principal of the marital trust, as well as a power to withdraw up to 5 percent of the principal of the family trust in any calendar year after the marital trust was completely exhausted. The taxpayer argued that the decedent's power to withdraw 5 percent of the family trust was not "exercisable" at death because the power was subject to a condition (i.e., complete exhaustion of the marital trust) which did not in fact occur during her life. The Tax Court rejected this argument:

> We hold that, if by its terms a general power of appointment is exercisable only upon the occurrence during the decedent's lifetime of an event or contingency that has no significant nontax consequence independent of the decedent's ability to exercise the power, the power exists on the date of decedent's death, regardless of whether the event or contingency did in fact occur during such time. Because petitioner has failed to demonstrate any significant nontax consequence independent of decedent's right to withdraw principal from the family trust fund, we hold that, on the date of her death, decedent had a general power of appointment over 5 percent of the family trust fund that causes that portion to be includable in her estate under section 2041. [101 T.C. at 61.]

In order to exercise her power over the family trust, the decedent would have had to exhaust the marital trust, thereby losing the benefits of trust management and protection from creditors with respect to the marital trust property. In the Tax Court's view, these collateral effects did not amount to "significant nontax consequences." Compare the situation where a retained § 2038 power is subject to a contingency within the decedent's control, discussed supra at page 252, Note 2. Without adopting the Tax Court's rationale, the Seventh Circuit affirmed its conclusion, noting that the decedent could have withdrawn all of the marital trust and 5 percent of the family trust upon notice to the trustee.

3. *Capacity to exercise power.* A line of decisions holds that a power remains exercisable within the meaning of § 2041 even though the decedent has been adjudged legally incompetent. See Alperstein's Estate v. Commissioner, 613 F.2d 1213 (2d Cir. 1979), cert. denied, 446 U.S. 918 (1980) (extensive analysis); Boeving v. United States, 650 F.2d 493 (8th Cir. 1981) and cases cited therein; Rev. Rul. 75–350, 1975–2 C.B. 366 (power exercisable

only by will was subject to tax even though holder lacked legal capacity to execute will due to mental illness); Rev. Rul. 75–351, 1975–2 C.B. 368 (same result where holder died during minority before attaining legal capacity to execute will). This general principle has been extended to the situation where a conservator has been appointed to manage an incompetent's property even though the conservator's exercise of the power has become subject under local law to an ascertainable standard that would have immunized the power had it been incorporated in the instrument creating the power. Gilchrist's Estate v. Commissioner, 630 F.2d 340 (5th Cir. 1980). Nor may a general power be disregarded because the decedent was unaware of its existence and had no opportunity to exercise it. Freeman's Estate v. Commissioner, 67 T.C. 202 (1976). See also Jenkins v. United States, supra page 401 (holder died before will creating power was admitted to probate).

4. *Estate tax apportionment.* Where appointive property is includible in the gross estate, § 2207 gives the decedent's executor a right to recover the resulting federal estate tax from the person receiving the property, unless the decedent's will directs otherwise. This provision is intended to prevent the tax burden generated by the appointive property from being inadvertently shifted to the recipients of the decedent's probate assets. See infra page 638.

5. *Income tax basis.* Under § 1014(b)(9), property acquired from a decedent "through the exercise or nonexercise of a power of appointment" and includible in the decedent's gross estate takes a stepped-up (or stepped-down) basis in the recipient's hands for income tax purposes. Does this provision apply to property acquired through the decedent's release of a power?

b. Quasi–Testamentary Exercise or Release of Power

If the decedent exercised a general power of appointment during life, the property is includible in the gross estate under § 2041(a)(2) if a similar transfer of the decedent's own property would have brought §§ 2035, 2036, 2037, or 2038 into play. For example, suppose that *D* exercised a general power of appointment over property during her life, directing that the property be held in trust to pay income to *D* for life with remainder to her issue. The property is includible in *D*'s gross estate under § 2041(a)(2), just as a similar transfer of her own property in trust subject to a retained life estate would be includible under § 2036.

Section 2041(a)(2) treats the release of a post–1942 power the same as an exercise of the power. For example, assume that a settlor left property in trust to pay income to *D* for life with remainder to *D*'s issue; *D* also holds a presently-exercisable general power of appointment over the trust property. If *D* releases the power, the effect is to confirm her life estate, much as if she had appointed the property outright to herself and then retransferred it subject to a retained life estate. Because the hypothetical alternative would be taxable under § 2036, the release is treated as a quasi-testamentary disposition and the property is includible in *D*'s gross estate.

In taxing the quasi-testamentary exercise or release of a general power of appointment, § 2041(a)(2) refers not only to §§ 2036 through 2038 but also to § 2035, relating to transfers of property within three years of death. In its current form, the three-year rule generally does not apply if the holder of a general power exercises or releases the power in a manner that leaves the holder with no interests or powers with respect to the underlying property. Such a disposition falls outside the limited scope of § 2035(a), discussed supra at page 224.[44] However, the three-year rule remains applicable if the decedent, having exercised or released a general power in a quasi-testamentary manner, attempts at the last minute to cut the taxable string. Thus, if *D* exercises a general power during life, directing that income be paid to her for life with remainder to her issue, and then within three years before death makes a gratuitous assignment of her outstanding life estate, the underlying property is drawn back into her gross estate.

c. Lapsed Powers and the "5-and-5" Exemption

Section 2041(b)(2) sets out the general principle that the lapse of a power of appointment is to be treated as a release of the power, but provides an exemption for lapses during any calendar year up to the greater of $5,000 or 5 percent of the value of the assets from which an exercise of the lapsed power could have been satisfied (the "5-and-5" exemption). Consider the impact of § 2041(b)(2) in the following circumstances. A settlor creates a trust of $200,000 to pay income to *A* for life with remainder to *A*'s issue, and gives *A* an unrestricted power to withdraw $50,000 of corpus, which will lapse if not exercised by the time *A* reaches age 40. *A* reaches age 40 and then dies without having exercised the power. What portion of the trust property is includible in *A*'s gross estate under § 2041? What would be the result in the absence of § 2041(b)(2)? Section 2514(e) provides parallel gift tax treatment for lapsed powers. What would be the gift tax consequences of allowing the right of withdrawal to lapse at age 40?

The provisions of §§ 2041(b)(2) and 2514(e) have become widely used by settlors who make regular annual contributions to trusts that are structured to qualify for one or more annual exclusions. As discussed in Chapter 2, Section D, a gift qualifies for the exclusion only if the donee receives a present interest in the transferred property. A "*Crummey*" power satisfies the present-interest requirement by conferring a noncumulative lapsing power to withdraw all or a specified portion of the transferred amount. Consider the tax consequences of such a power in the following circumstances. *A* transfers $10,000 in trust for her minor nephew *B*, and plans to make similar annual contributions in the future. The trustee has discretion to apply income and corpus for *B*'s benefit, but any unexpended income is to be accumulated and added to corpus. When *B* reaches age 25 the trust will terminate and the trust property will be

44. The 1981 amendment to § 2035 originally included a cross-reference to § 2041, but this was removed by the Technical Corrections Act of 1982, P.L. 97-448, § 104(d)(1)(C).

paid to *B*; if *B* dies before reaching age 25, the trust property will pass to *A*'s other nephews and nieces, for whom identical trusts have been set up. To qualify the annual $10,000 contributions for the gift tax annual exclusion, *B* is given the right (exercisable personally or through a guardian) to withdraw the amount contributed by *A* at any time during the calendar year in which the contribution is made; the power, however, is noncumulative, so that it lapses at the end of the calendar year if it has not been exercised.

Under §§ 2041(b)(2) and 2514(e), the exempt amount is equal to the greater of $5,000 or 5 percent of the aggregate value (measured at the time of lapse) of the assets that could have been used to satisfy an exercise of the power. In the early years, the exempt amount is limited to $5,000; only when the value of the trust property exceeds $100,000 will the 5 percent test yield a larger amount. Thus, when *B*'s power to withdraw $10,000 lapses at the end of the first year, $5,000 of the lapsed amount is exempt, and the balance of $5,000 is treated as if *B* had withdrawn it and then immediately recontributed it to the trust. For gift tax purposes, *B*'s deemed transfer in trust is only partially complete, since *B* is treated as retaining an income interest as well as a future interest in corpus (conditioned on surviving until age 25). The gift is complete with respect to the future interests of *A*'s other nephews and nieces who will receive the trust property if *B* dies before reaching age 25. No matter how small the actuarial value of the other beneficiaries' interests,[45] *B* must report them on a gift tax return because the annual exclusion is not available for gifts of future interests. If *B* has the misfortune to die before reaching age 25, a fractional portion of the trust property attributable to his annual deemed $5,000 contributions will be includible in his gross estate.[46]

A has several options[47] by which she may avoid these entanglements, but they may come at the price of compromising other planning objectives.

1. She may limit her annual contribution to $5,000 a year or limit the *Crummey* power to $5,000, instead of claiming the full $10,000 exclusion.

---

45. The actuarial value of these interests is small, corresponding to the low probability that *B* will die before reaching age 25. However, if the other beneficiaries include *B*'s siblings, the special gift tax valuation rules of § 2702 will apply, producing a taxable gift equal to the full amount of *B*'s $5,000 deemed transfer. See supra pages 78–83.

46. Note that the entire $10,000 contributed to the trust by *A* in the year of *B*'s death and subject to his unexercised power of withdrawal will be includible in his gross estate under § 2041.

47. A more sophisticated device is a so-called hanging or suspended power which lapses in annual increments equal to the exempt amount under § 2514(e). See Adams & Bieber, Making "5 and 5" Equal 20: *Crummey* Powers After ERTA, 122 Tr. & Est. 22 (Sept. 1983); Rothberg, *Crummey* Powers Enhance the Usefulness of Trusts for Minors and Life Insurance Trusts, 15 Est. Planning 322 (1988).

Withdrawal powers may also raise generation-skipping transfer and income tax problems. For example, irrevocable life insurance trusts frequently include withdrawal powers to qualify premium payments for one or more gift tax annual exclusions, but such trusts may fail to qualify for an automatic zero inclusion ratio under § 2642(c)(2). See infra page 564. On the income tax implications of lapsed powers of withdrawal, see Westfall, Lapsed Powers of Withdrawal and the Income Tax, 39 Tax L. Rev. 63 (1983).

2. She may curtail the interests of the other beneficiaries and give *B* the equivalent of complete ownership by directing that in the event of his premature death the trust property will pass to his estate or as he may designate by a general power of appointment (with the other beneficiaries named as takers in default). Alternatively, *B* could be given a separate nongeneral power, supplementary to the *Crummey* power, to prevent any portion of his annual deemed contributions from constituting a completed gift.
3. She may fund the trust with an initial contribution of $200,000, giving *B* a noncumulative right to withdraw $10,000 each year from the trust corpus.

Note that the 5–and–5 exemption applies to "the lapse of *powers* during any calendar year." In Rev. Rul. 85–88, 1985–2 C.B. 201, the Service interpreted this clause to mean that a person who holds more than one lapsed general power over the same trust in a calendar year is allowed only one 5–and–5 exemption; the 5–percent limitation is calculated based on the maximum amount subject to any such power at the time of lapse during the calendar year. The ruling reaches the same result in the case of multiple powers over identical separate trusts created by the same settlor, and applies the 5–percent limitation to the aggregate amount subject to such powers at the time of lapse. Is only one 5–and–5 exemption allowed to a person who holds lapsed powers over several trusts created by different settlors? What if the trusts were created by the same settlor but have different terms?

The original purpose of the 5–and–5 exemption was to permit flexible trust drafting, without tax cost, where the settlor was concerned that the net trust income alone might not be sufficient for the income beneficiary's needs. Query: Can this tax-free flexibility be reconciled with the Code's general policy of treating the holder of a general power of appointment as an absolute owner? The ABA Tax Section Task Force has called for the repeal of the 5–and–5 exemption, with appropriate grandfathering provisions, commenting that the exemption has "no conceptual justification." Report on Transfer Tax Restructuring, 41 Tax Law. 395, 412 (1988).

d. Powers of Appointment and the Gift Tax

Before 1942 there was no express statutory provision addressing the gift tax treatment of powers of appointment. In that year, the statute was amended to treat the "exercise or release of a power of appointment" as a "transfer of property by the individual possessing such power," subject to an exception for the types of powers that were immune from estate taxation under the 1942 law (i.e., a power to appoint only to members of the creator's or holder's family or to charities, and so-called fiduciary powers). Quite naturally, when Congress revised the estate tax treatment of powers of appointment in 1951, it adopted parallel gift tax provisions in what is now § 2514. Accordingly, the gift tax, like the estate tax, applies only to a "general power of appointment," and this term is defined in the same way for both taxes. Under § 2514(b), the exercise or release of a post–1942 general power is treated as a "transfer of property by the individual possessing such power"; § 2514(a) makes special provision for pre–1942 powers. Section 2514(e) conforms the gift tax treatment of lapsed powers to the estate tax provisions of § 2041(b)(2).

NOTES

1. *"Reverse powers."* If a power is exercisable only in favor of the holder's children but the holder's estate is the taker in default, is the exercise of the power in favor of a child treated as a gift? On the question whether the power is a "general power of appointment," see supra page 412, Note 5. The "reverse power" also poses gift tax questions parallel to the estate tax questions already raised. If an income beneficiary is given a power to appoint the underlying property during life in favor of the remainderman, does the income beneficiary's exercise of the power give rise to a taxable gift? See Regester's Estate v. Commissioner, 83 T.C. 1 (1984) (exercise of power treated as indirect transfer of income interest); but cf. Self v. United States, 142 F.Supp. 939 (Ct. Cl. 1956) (contra). If so, how is the amount to be measured? What of a remainderman who exercises a power to advance principal to the income beneficiary?

2. *Creation of power of appointment.* The statute does not state whether the *creation* of a power of appointment is a taxable gift. If *A* creates in her son *B* a power to appoint to himself, or if she gives *B* a power to appoint to others and names *B* as the taker in default, has *A* made a gift? If *A* confers on *B* the power to appoint to *C* or *D*, naming *E* as the taker in default, has *A* made a completed gift? If so, are one or more exclusions available under § 2503(b)?

Recall that under § 2041(a)(3) a nongeneral power of appointment is subject to the estate tax if it is exercised to create another power in a state in which the rule against perpetuities permits the indefinite suspension of ownership by the creation of successive powers. See supra page 412, Note 6. In keeping with the special estate tax rule for such powers, § 2514(d) provides that the lifetime exercise of such a power to create another power in such a state is subject to the gift tax.

3. *References.* See Federal Transfer Tax Consequences to the Donee of Annually Lapsing Powers of Withdrawal, 22 Real Prop., Prob. & Tr. J. 693 (1987); Natbony, The *Crummey* Trust and "Five and Five" Powers After ERTA, 60 Taxes 497 (1982).

CHAPTER 5

DEDUCTIONS AND CREDITS

■ ■ ■

The gross estate comprises all of the property described in §§ 2033 through 2042, which are examined in Chapters 3 and 4; for the inclusion of qualified terminable interest property under § 2044, see infra page 514. The taxable estate, to which the tax rates set out in § 2001 are applied, is defined by § 2031 as the gross estate less the deductions authorized in § 2053 (funeral and administration expenses, claims, and debts), § 2054 (casualty losses), § 2055 (charitable deduction), § 2056 (marital deduction), and § 2058 (state death taxes).[1] After the estate tax has been determined, certain credits are computed and allowed against the tax under § 2010 (the "unified credit"), § 2012 (credit for gift tax on pre-1977 gifts included in the gross estate), § 2013 (credit for tax on prior transfers), and § 2014 (credit for foreign death taxes).

A. EXPENSES, CLAIMS AND DEBTS: § 2053

1. FUNERAL EXPENSES

Section 2053(a)(1) allows a deduction for funeral expenses to the extent allowable by the law of the jurisdiction under which the estate is being administered. The term "funeral expenses" is not precisely defined but includes such obvious items as the undertaker's charges and the costs of a funeral service. In addition, Reg. § 20.2053–2 provides that the phrase includes a "reasonable expenditure for a tombstone, monument, or mausoleum, or for a burial lot, either for the decedent or his family, including a reasonable expenditure for its future care." See Gillespie's Estate v. Commissioner, 8 T.C. 838 (1947) (bequest for perpetual care of family burial plot not deductible if decedent not interred therein); Rev. Rul. 57–530, 1957–2 C.B. 621 (same); Berkman's Estate v. Commissioner, 38 T.C.M. (CCH) 183 (1979) (deduction allowed for decedent's daughter's

1. The deduction for state death taxes in § 2058 took effect in 2005, replacing a credit for such taxes previously found in § 2011, as discussed infra at page 546. Section 2057 is presently inoperative, but at various times it authorized a deduction for "qualified family-owned business interests" (from 1998 to 2003), a deduction for one-half of the proceeds from certain sales of "qualified employer securities" (from 1986 to 1989), and a so-called "orphan's deduction" for certain transfers to a decedent's minor children (from 1976 to 1981).

expenses in traveling to funeral and, six months later, to cemetery for tombstone setting; no deduction for travel expenses incurred by daughter's family).

In Rev. Rul. 66–234, 1966–2 C.B. 436, the Service held that payments by the Veterans Administration or Social Security Administration earmarked for funeral expenses reduce the amount deductible under § 2053(a)(1), even though those payments are not includible in the gross estate under § 2033. This result follows because only the net outlay is "actually expended" by the estate as required by Reg. § 20.2053–2. See also Rev. Rul. 77–274, 1977–2 C.B. 326 (same principle applies to portion of wrongful death recovery allocable to funeral expenses).

2. ADMINISTRATION EXPENSES

HIBERNIA BANK v. UNITED STATES

581 F.2d 741 (9th Cir. 1978).

WALLACE, CIRCUIT JUDGE.

The Hibernia Bank (Hibernia) appeals from a judgment of the district court denying its claim for a refund of federal estate taxes. This appeal squarely presents an important issue of estate tax law which has engendered a crisp conflict among the circuits. We affirm.

I

In May 1965, Celia Tobin Clark died testate leaving an estate worth several million dollars. Mrs. Clark's will provided for several specific bequests of personal property. The will also directed that the residue, which included the bulk of the estate, be divided among four testamentary trusts. The income of each trust was to be paid to one of Mrs. Clark's children with the remainder to be divided equally among Mrs. Clark's grandchildren. The residue of Mrs. Clark's estate included two principal components: a mansion situated on 240 acres in Hillsborough, California, and approximately 10,000 common shares of Hibernia Bank stock.

Mrs. Clark's will named Hibernia as trustee for the four testamentary trusts. The will also nominated two individuals to act as co-executors. These individuals declined to serve, however, and ultimately Hibernia was appointed administrator with the will annexed of the Clark estate.

On June 2, 1965, Mrs. Clark's will was admitted to probate. By December 1967, all of the specific bequests and virtually all claims against the estate had been paid. Apparently, at this time, Hibernia, acting as the administrator, could have sought permission to distribute the remaining assets, including the mansion and the Hibernia stock, to the testamentary trusts and to close the estate. Rather than do so, however, Hibernia elected first to liquidate the Hillsborough mansion.

Hibernia encountered substantial difficulty in disposing of the mansion, and it was not finally sold until the spring of 1972. During this period, the administrator was required to spend some $60,000 per year in order to maintain the residence. Thus, Hibernia believed that it was necessary either to sell the estate's share of Hibernia stock or, alternatively, to borrow the funds required to maintain the mansion. Hibernia elected to borrow.

In each of the years from 1966 through 1969, Hibernia executed a substantial loan from a commercial bank. The net proceeds from these loans equaled $775,000. Hibernia itself acted as lender for two of the four loans, the proceeds of which totaled $625,000. The interest payments for the four loans totaled $196,210.[2]

In June 1971, Hibernia filed with the Commissioner a claim for a refund of part of the estate taxes paid on the Clark estate. As part of this claim, Hibernia asserted that it was entitled to deduct from the gross estate as expenses of administration the amount it had paid in interest on the four bank loans. The Commissioner disallowed the claimed deduction for the interest and denied the corresponding refund.

In March 1974, Hibernia brought suit in the district court asserting that it was entitled to deduct the loan interest and claiming a corresponding refund. Hibernia argued that the interest payments were deductible expenses of administration within the meaning of 26 U.S.C. § 2053(a)(2). The district judge disagreed and entered judgment in favor of the Commissioner. Hibernia renews its contentions on appeal; we also disagree.

II

Hibernia's argument is straightforward. Section 2053(a)(2) provides:

> For purposes of the [estate] tax ... the value of the taxable estate shall be determined by deducting from the value of the gross estate such amounts ... for administration expenses ... as are allowable by the laws of the jurisdiction, whether within or without the United States, under which the estate is being administered.

In addition, Treas. Reg. § 20.2053–1(b)(2) provides in part:

> The decision of a local court as to the amount and allowability under local law of a claim or administration expense will ordinarily be accepted if the court passes upon the facts upon which deductibility depends.

Therefore, the essence of Hibernia's argument is that the deductibility of administration expenses is exclusively a question of state law. Since

2. Although the ethical quality of Hibernia's conduct as the estate's administrator does not bear on our disposition of this case, we do observe that Hibernia allowed itself to be placed in positions fraught with potential for abuse. First, Hibernia's decision to borrow funds and thereby subject the estate to substantial interest payments rather than sell the Hibernia stock carries at least the outward appearance of an attempt by Hibernia to avoid placing a large block of its own stock on the market at the expense of the Clark estate. Second, is Hibernia's decision to borrow from itself. This act placed Hibernia in a position where its interest sharply conflicted with that of the estate. As long as the loans remained unpaid, Hibernia received substantial interest payments at the expense and diminution of the estate. Of the $196,210 paid in total interest for the four loans, $133,241 was paid to Hibernia.

in this case the California probate court expressly approved the $196,210 interest payments as administration expenses, Hibernia contends that the Commissioner was required to permit a corresponding deduction.

Hibernia's contention is supported by Estate of Park v. Commissioner of Internal Revenue, 475 F.2d 673 (6th Cir. 1973), in which the Sixth Circuit expressly rejected the cases to the contrary and held "that the deductibility of an expense under 2053(a) (or its predecessor) is governed by state law alone." Id. at 676.

The district judge rejected Hibernia's argument and expressly declined to follow *Estate of Park*. The district judge ruled that in addition to showing that the claimed expense is allowable under state law, "the taxpayer must show that the claimed administrative expense was a reasonable, necessary administrative expense within the meaning of federal law."

There is no dispute in this case as to whether the interest rate was reasonable or as to the total amount of interest payments. Thus, the dispute centers around whether or not the interest payments were expenses of administration within the meaning of federal estate tax law. In order to resolve this issue, the district judge focused on Treas. Reg. § 20.2053–3(a), which provides in part:

> The amounts deductible from a decedent's gross estate as "administration expenses" . . . are limited to such expenses as are actually and necessarily incurred in the administration of the decedent's estate; that is, in the collection of assets, payment of debts, and distribution of property to the persons entitled to it. The expenses contemplated in the law are such only as attend the settlement of an estate to individual beneficiaries or to a trustee. . . . Expenditures not essential to the proper settlement of the estate, but incurred for the individual benefit of the heirs, legatees, or devisees, may not be taken as deductions.

Viewing the issue in this light, the district judge found that the estate had been kept open *much* longer than necessary, thereby rendering the loans and interest payments made during the excess period also unnecessary. Specifically, the judge found as a matter of fact that "[w]ithin fifteen months of the testator's death [Hibernia], in its capacity as administrator of the estate, had sold all the assets of the estate except the mansion with its surrounding acreage and the Hibernia Bank stock." In addition, the district judge concluded that Hibernia had failed "factually [to] demonstrate an existing necessity to keep the Clark estate open for seven years." The district judge reasoned that since it was wholly unnecessary to keep the estate open during the period of the loans, the loans and interest payments were therefore also unnecessary to the administration of the estate. The implication is that the estate was left open in order to sell the mansion not because the sale was necessary for the administration of the estate, but rather because the heirs preferred to have cash distributed to the trusts rather than an undivided interest in the mansion. Thus, the expenses were not deductible.

III

We agree with the district judge that allowability under state law is not the sole criterion for determining the deductibility of a particular expenditure under section 2053(a)(2).

In Pitner v. United States, 388 F.2d 651 (5th Cir. 1967), the Fifth Circuit held that

> [i]n the determination of deductibility under section 2053(a)(2), it is not enough that the deduction be allowable under state law. It is necessary as well that the deduction be for an "administration expense" within the meaning of that term as it is used in the statute, and that the amount sought to be deducted be reasonable under the circumstances. These are both questions of federal law and establish the outside limits for what may be considered allowable deductions under section 2053(a)(2).

Id. at 659.[3] See also Estate of Smith v. Commissioner of Internal Revenue, 510 F.2d 479 (2d Cir.), cert. denied, 423 U.S. 827 (1975).

We agree with the Fifth Circuit. We cannot read section 2053(a)(2) as permitting the deduction of expenditures which simply are not expenses of administration within the meaning afforded that term by federal estate tax law. Our holding is firmly supported by prior decisions as well as sound principles of policy. . . .

Policy considerations also militate in favor of our holding. The federal estate tax is not a tax on the decedent's property, but rather a tax on *the transfer* of that property. See 26 U.S.C. § 2001(a); 26 C.F.R. § 20.0–2 (1976); see also United States Trust Co. v. Commissioner of Internal Revenue, 307 U.S. 57, 60 (1939); see generally C. Lowndes, R. Kramer & J. McCord, Federal Estate and Gift Taxes § 1.1 (3d ed. 1974). The mechanics of the estate tax give meaning to this distinction by permitting deductions from the decedent's gross estate for debts, administration expenses, and certain other liabilities. The resulting "taxable estate" on which the estate tax is calculated is the amount actually transferred to the heirs. Although fairness dictates that the taxable estate not include assets which will not be available for transfer to the heirs, fairness does not require the deduction of amounts which are not true liabilities of the estate. Thus, "[e]xpenditures not essential to the proper settlement of the estate, but incurred for the individual benefit of the heirs, legatees, or devisees" are not expenses of administration within the meaning of section 2053. 26 C.F.R. § 20.2053–3(a).

---

3. In *Pitner*, the court did observe, and we agree, that in most instances "the state law may be relied upon as a guide to what deductions may reasonably be permitted for federal estate tax purposes." 388 F.2d at 659. As the court explained, however, deference to state law as a guide cannot justify the deduction of expenses which simply are not "administration expenses" within the meaning of federal estate tax law.

The district judge's conclusion that the Clark estate was left open much too long is amply supported by the record. Fed. R. Civ. P. 52(a). Since it was unnecessary to leave the estate open during the period of the loans, it is clear that the loans were not necessary to the administration of the estate. Accordingly, the district judge was correct in disallowing an administration expense deduction for the amount of the interest payments.[4]

Affirmed.

DUNIWAY, CIRCUIT JUDGE (concurring).

I concur. I write only to point out that there are sound practical reasons, in addition to those stated by Judge Wallace in his opinion, which require that we construe § 2053(a)(2) of the Internal Revenue Code as permitting the deduction of those expenditures only which are expenses of administration within the meaning of federal estate tax law.

First, in California, and I suspect in most other states, probate proceedings are essentially ex parte in character. While the Probate Code requires an executor or administrator wishing to borrow money to obtain an order of court authorizing the borrowing, see California Probate Code § 830, and while an executor or administrator must account to the court for all receipts and expenditures, see California Probate Code §§ 921 and 922, there is no requirement that personal notice be given to any party interested in the estate. Notice is given by posting a notice by the clerk at the courthouse (Probate Code § 1200) and is required to be mailed to an interested party only if that party has filed a request for a special notice (Probate Code §§ 1200 and 1203). Publication in a newspaper of general circulation is also required if the petition is for leave to borrow (§ 1201). The court can require additional notice (§ 1204) but generally does not do so. In this case only one person interested in the estate filed a request for notice and the administrator, because of that notice, regarded that person as "uncooperative." The petitions for orders of the court authorizing the administrator to borrow, and the accounts of the administrator, were not contested by anyone. There is no inducement to a California state court to restrict the allowance of claimed administrative expenses in order to prevent improper reductions of the federal estate tax. Indeed, many state judges would probably be pleased to assist the representative of the estate and the heirs in thus reducing the estate tax.

Second, as is pointed out in Judge Wallace's opinion, . . . the Hibernia Bank was on every possible side of the probate proceedings in this case. It

4. The district judge did not specifically indicate at what point the estate should have been closed. This creates the possibility that some of the interest payments might be deductible if the corresponding loans were executed during the period the estate was properly open. We do not believe, however, that this question requires us to remand. First, the district judge disallowed all of the interest payments. Thus, we may properly infer that he found none of the loans necessary to the proper administration of the estate. Second, although he did not base his ruling on this finding, . . . the district judge did find that Hibernia "was not prevented from disposing of its Hibernia Bank securities due to a lack of interest in the marketplace, and that consequently [Hibernia] need not have borrowed money in lieu of selling the Hibernia securities." We see no reason to believe that this finding does not pertain to all of the loans.

was the administrator with the will annexed of the decedent's estate; it was the trustee of the three testamentary trusts that were each to receive one quarter of the residue of the estate; it borrowed $625,000 from itself, and paid itself over $130,000 in interest. A large block of its stock was the most valuable single asset of the estate, and Hibernia's management had an interest in not having that stock sold. As administrator, Hibernia had a duty to hold down expenses. As the lender, it had a duty to its shareholders to obtain the highest interest rate that it could lawfully obtain. As the trustee, it had a duty to compel itself as administrator to close the administration of the estate as soon as practicable. As lender, its interest was to have the estate kept open and continue to borrow money and pay interest. As administrator, it owed beneficiaries a duty to minimize estate taxes. No matter which way it turned, it met itself. There was nobody actually before the probate court to question the validity or propriety of any of its expenditures, or to object to any phase of its administration of the estate. Certainly the interest of the United States in collecting its estate tax was not represented before the probate court, and it is doubtful that the United States would have been recognized had it attempted to appear before that court. California Probate Code § 1203 permits the United States to request notice and to appear in a probate proceeding "[w]hen compensation, pension, insurance or other allowance is made or awarded by the United States government, or a department or bureau thereof, to estates of decedents. . . ." There is no other California statute that I know of that authorizes the government of the United States or the Internal Revenue Service to appear in a probate court. Moreover, the United States would be likely to find itself in a hostile forum if it did appear.

I cannot believe that it was the intention of the Congress in adopting § 2053(a)(2) of the Internal Revenue Code to place the federal fisc at the mercy of an essentially ex parte probate proceeding in a California court in which it is possible for one institution to play so many and such inconsistent roles. I do not believe that Congress intended to give the game away in that fashion.

NOTES

1. *Federal definition of administration expenses.* In order to qualify as a deductible administration expense under § 2053(a)(2), the regulations require not only that an item be allowable under local law but also that it be "actually and necessarily incurred in the administration of the decedent's estate; that is, in the collection of assets, payment of debts, and distribution of property to the persons entitled to it." Reg. § 20.2053–3(a). Thus, for example, if a probate court orders that a support allowance be paid to the decedent's surviving spouse, the amount of the allowance does not constitute an administration expense within the meaning of the regulations even if it is so designated by applicable state law. Taxpayers have challenged the validity of the regulation, arguing that it goes beyond the statutory language, which

refers only to local law. Courts have repeatedly upheld the independent federal definition of administration expenses. In addition to *Hibernia Bank* and cases cited therein, see Grant's Estate v. Commissioner, 294 F.3d 352 (2d Cir. 2002); and Millikin's Estate v. Commissioner, 125 F.3d 339 (6th Cir. 1997), in which the Sixth Circuit repudiated its earlier holding in *Park's Estate* and accepted the majority view. See also Love's Estate v. Commissioner, 923 F.2d 335 (4th Cir. 1991), involving a payment made by the decedent's estate to obtain clear title to a foal which was conceived after the decedent's death by a mare owned by the decedent. Although the payment was allowed by the local probate court as an administration expense, the court held that it was not deductible under § 2053(a)(2) because the payment represented an investment in the foal rather than a cost of preserving or maintaining an asset of the estate.

2. *Nonprobate assets.* Section 2053(a)(2) allows a deduction for expenses incurred in administering property subject to claims, which encompasses, generally speaking, the decedent's probate estate. Section 2053(b) supplements § 2053(a)(2) by allowing a similar deduction for expenses of administering property not subject to claims which is included in the gross estate (e.g., property held in an inter vivos trust or passing by right of survivorship). To be deductible under § 2053(b), expenses of administering such property must be of a type that would have been deductible under § 2053(a)(2) if the property were subject to claims, and the expenses must be paid before the time for assessing an estate tax deficiency has expired (normally three years after the filing of the return). See Reg. § 20.2053–8. In a case involving a revocable trust that terminated on the settlor's death and was includible in her gross estate under § 2038, the Tax Court construed § 2053(b) as requiring that expenses be "of the same nature as administration expenses deductible under [§ 2053(a)(2)], i.e., that the expenses must be incurred in winding up the affairs of the deceased." Burrow Trust v. Commissioner, 39 T.C. 1080 (1963), affd., 333 F.2d 66 (10th Cir. 1964) (trustee's fees in winding up trust held deductible under § 2053(b)).

3. *Commissions and fees.* The most common administration expenses are the executor's or administrator's commissions, which are deductible to the extent that they have actually been paid or at the time of filing the estate tax return are "ascertainable with reasonable certainty and will be paid." Reg. § 20.2053–1(d)(4). An amount specified in the will as the executor's compensation is deductible up to the amount allowable by local law or practice; a bequest to the executor "in lieu of commissions," however, is not deductible. Reg. § 20.2053–3(b)(2). The application of these principles requires a distinction between a payment made as a gratuitous bequest and a payment made for services to be rendered as executor. Cf. United States v. Merriam, 263 U.S. 179 (1923) (for income tax purposes, a payment is a tax-free bequest if the executor is required to do no more than comply in good faith with "the implied condition that he shall clothe himself with the character of executor," but it is taxable if "he must perform the service to earn the compensation"). If the executor claims a statutory commission in lieu of the amount specified in the will, the statutory commission is deductible. See Underwood v. United States, 407 F.2d 608 (6th Cir. 1969).

The Service may require documentation of legal fees paid to the estate's attorney, but rarely does so if the amount is approved by the local probate court. See United States v. White, 853 F.2d 107 (2d Cir. 1988), cert. dismissed, 493 U.S. 5 (1989) (Service entitled to inspect attorney's records relating to administration of decedent's estate, despite probate court decree allowing attorney's fees); O'Neal v. United States, 258 F.3d 1265 (11th Cir. 2001) (deduction denied for lack of substantiation where estate refused to disclose invoices for attorney's fees). Reg. § 20.2053–3(c)(3) states that attorney's fees incurred by beneficiaries in litigation brought to establish their respective interests in the estate are not deductible if the litigation "is not essential to the proper settlement of the estate," even if approved by the probate court for payment or reimbursement by the estate. Because will contests and similar proceedings, even though instituted by individual claimants, usually determine the amounts to be distributed by the executor to the contending parties, the courts often treat the expenses of such litigation as essential to the proper settlement of the estate. See Pitner v. United States, 388 F.2d 651 (5th Cir. 1967) (deduction allowed for legal fees incurred by beneficiaries in establishing their right to receive decedent's property under oral will contract, even though there was no probate of will or formal administration of estate); Dulles v. Johnson, 273 F.2d 362 (2d Cir. 1959), cert. denied, 364 U.S. 834 (1960) (legal expenses of beneficiaries in will construction proceedings initiated by executors were reimbursed by estate and were deductible); cf. Heckscher's Estate v. Commissioner, 63 T.C. 485 (1975) (legal fees incurred by beneficiary for separate representation in suit brought by trustee for instructions on distribution of trust assets held not deductible); Landers' Estate v. Commissioner, 38 T.C. 828 (1962) (no deduction for legal fees incurred by decedent's widow to establish right to support allowance).

At the time the estate tax return is filed, the amounts of the executor's commissions and attorney's fees will often be as yet undetermined. The regulations allow the deduction only if the amount is "ascertainable with reasonable certainty and will be paid," and warn that no deduction may be taken based on "a vague or uncertain estimate." If the amount to be paid becomes ascertainable only after the estate tax return has been filed, "relief may be sought by filing a claim for refund." Reg. § 20.2053–1(d)(4).

If an estate contests a deficiency or sues for a refund of federal estate tax, a final judgment will bar the estate from subsequently suing for a refund based on the expenses of the original litigation. To protect itself, the estate can follow the procedure prescribed by Reg. § 20.2053–3(c)(2), viz., claim a deduction for estimated litigation expenses at the time of the original litigation concerning the deficiency or refund claim. See Bohnen v. Harrison, 232 F.2d 406 (7th Cir. 1956); see also Rev. Rul. 78–323, 1978–2 C.B. 240 (overpayment of estate tax attributable to otherwise deductible attorney's fees paid after a Tax Court decision becomes final and more than three years after the filing of the estate tax return will not be refunded except to the extent allowance of the fees is reflected in the Tax Court's final decision).

4. *Interest payments.* In the *Hibernia Bank* case, the interest payments made by the estate were not deductible because the bank loans were found not to be necessary for the administration of the estate. See also Black's Estate v. Commissioner, 133 T.C. 340 (2009) (no deduction allowed for

interest on loan from partnership to deceased partner's estate; loaned funds came from partnership's sale of stock that could have been distributed in kind and estate had no source of repayment other than future partnership distribution or redemption; the arrangement "constituted an indirect use of [the] stock to pay the debts of [decedent]'s estate and accomplished nothing more than a direct use of that stock for the same purpose would have accomplished, except for the substantial estate tax savings"). For an analysis of circumstances that justify keeping an estate open beyond the normal period without jeopardizing the deductibility of administration expenses, see Papson's Estate v. Commissioner, 73 T.C. 290 (1979) (negotiation of a long-term lease of estate's shopping center was proper, administration was not unduly protracted).

If the estate has insufficient liquid assets to pay death taxes, taking out a loan may be the only available alternative to a forced sale of assets. In this situation, the interest payments on the loan, to the extent "necessarily incurred," constitute a deductible expense of administration under § 2053(a)(2). Todd's Estate v. Commissioner, 57 T.C. 288 (1971) (interest on funds borrowed to pay federal or state death taxes). Furthermore, the Service acknowledges that a deduction is generally allowed for interest paid to the government on late or deferred death taxes, regardless of whether the estate could have made timely tax payments without selling assets at a sacrifice. Rev. Rul. 79–252, 1979–2 C.B. 333 (interest on estate tax deficiency); Rev. Rul. 81–154, 1981–1 C.B. 470 (deduction allowed for interest on late payment of federal estate tax, but not for penalties for failure to file or pay); Rev. Rul. 81–256, 1981–2 C.B. 183 (same for state death taxes); Rev. Rul. 83–24, 1983–1 C.B. 229 (same for late payment of foreign death taxes); Bahr's Estate v. Commissioner, 68 T.C. 74 (1977) (acq.) (interest on federal estate tax deferred under § 6161).[5] Ordinarily, such interest becomes deductible only as it accrues. Rev. Rul. 80–250, 1980–2 C.B. 278 (deduction allowable for accrued interest on deferred estate tax but not for future interest payments, where executor has option to accelerate payment); Rev. Rul. 84–75, 1984–1 C.B. 193 (same for interest on funds borrowed to pay federal estate tax); but cf. Graegin's Estate v. Commissioner, 56 T.C.M. (CCH) 387 (1988) (allowing immediate deduction for balloon payment of interest due at maturity of 15–year non-prepayable promissory note). If the executor elects to defer the federal estate tax under § 6166 (relating to closely held business interests), the deferred tax payments bear interest at a special low rate, but the interest payments are not deductible for federal estate or income tax purposes. §§ 2053(c)(1)(D) and 163(k). Section 6166 is discussed infra at page 635.

5. What is the policy justification for allowing interest expense, even if necessarily incurred, as an estate tax deduction? Consider the following:

> The deduction for interest incurred by the estate should be repealed. It is difficult to see any rational reason for allowing interest incurred by the estate to be deducted in computing the taxable estate. The estate tax is imposed on the net value of the decedent's assets at the date of death. That date-of-death net value is not reduced by interest accruing after that date any more than it is increased by income earned or appreciation occurring after that date. Not only is the deduction for interest analytically mistaken, but ... by radically reducing the effective interest rate paid with respect to estate tax deficiencies, it has the perverse effect of creating a very significant incentive for representatives of estates to string out estate tax controversies as long as possible to defer the payment of, and thereby reduce the real cost of, the estate tax. [Brockway, Comprehensive Estate and Gift Tax Reform, 67 Tax Notes 1089, 1104–05 (1995).]

Interest on debts incurred by the decedent during life is deductible as a claim against the estate under § 2053(a)(3), but Reg. § 20.2053–4 limits the deduction to amounts accrued at the time of death. In Wheless' Estate v. Commissioner, 72 T.C. 470 (1979), however, the Tax Court held that this provision does not preclude a deduction for post-mortem interest as an administration expense under § 2053(a)(2), if the executor keeps the debt outstanding because payment would require a forced sale of assets and if payment of the interest is allowable under local law.

5. *Expenses of selling estate assets.* Expenses of selling assets of the estate are deductible if the sale is necessary (1) to pay debts, administration expenses or taxes, (2) to preserve the estate, or (3) to effect distribution. Reg. § 20.2053–3(d)(2). For an application of these principles involving sales commissions paid by a deceased sculptor's estate to a gallery in selling off the decedent's works, see Smith's Estate v. Commissioner, 57 T.C. 650 (1972), affd., 510 F.2d 479 (2d Cir.), cert. denied, 423 U.S. 827 (1975), allowing a deduction for commissions on sales that were necessary to raise funds to pay debts, taxes and administration expenses, but not for commissions on additional sales. Cf. Vatter's Estate v. Commissioner, 65 T.C. 633 (1975), affd. mem., 556 F.2d 563 (2d Cir. 1976) (deduction allowed for expenses of selling real estate in order to make distribution in cash rather than in kind); Posen's Estate v. Commissioner, 75 T.C. 355 (1980) (no deduction for expenses of selling cooperative apartment; though allowable under state law, expenses were incurred for heir's benefit and were not necessary for estate administration).

In valuing an unusually large block of stock or other property included in the gross estate, the expenses of a hypothetical sale are sometimes taken into account; the so-called blockage adjustment is discussed infra at page 596. It has been held that such a valuation adjustment does not preclude a deduction under § 2053(a)(2) for expenses actually incurred in selling the property, if the sale is necessary to generate funds to pay administration expenses, debts or taxes. See Joslyn's Estate v. Commissioner, 500 F.2d 382 (9th Cir. 1974) (allowing deduction for expenses of selling large block of stock, even though stock was valued below quoted market price in the gross estate due to blockage adjustment); Joslyn's Estate v. Commissioner, 566 F.2d 677 (9th Cir. 1977) (applying same principle to underwriter's "spread"); Jenner's Estate v. Commissioner, 577 F.2d 1100 (7th Cir. 1978) (same). In response to these decisions, the Service takes the position that any selling expenses that qualify for a deduction under § 2053(a)(2) cannot also be taken into account in valuing the property under § 2031. See Rev. Rul. 83–30, 1983–1 C.B. 224 (underwriting fees); Gillespie v. United States, 23 F.3d 36 (2d Cir. 1994) (applying same principle to other selling expenses).

6. *Relationship to income tax deductions.* Expenses of administration that are allowable as estate tax deductions under § 2053(a)(2) may also qualify for an income tax deduction as "ordinary and necessary expenses" incurred in carrying on a trade or business (§ 162) or in producing or collecting income (§ 212). Under § 642(g), the executor may not deduct such expenses on the estate's federal income tax return unless he or she waives the right to claim them as an estate tax deduction. Such deductions may be split between the income and estate tax returns if this works to the estate's

advantage. Section 642(g) also applies to sales commissions and similar items, which can be offset against the amount realized on a sale of property for income tax purposes only if the executor waives the deduction under § 2053(a)(2).

Section 642(g) does not, however, prevent so-called deductions in respect of a decedent from being deducted for income tax purposes under § 691(b) by the estate or the heir who pays them, even if they have also been claimed as deductions for estate tax purposes under § 2053(a). An example is a § 162 or § 212 expense that was accrued but unpaid at the death of a decedent who used the cash method of accounting for income tax purposes. The opprobrious connotation of "double deduction" does not apply to these items, because if they had been paid by the decedent before death they would have reduced both his taxable income and his gross estate; allowing them to be deducted under both § 2053(a)(3) and § 691(b)(1) produces substantially the same result. See 3 Bittker & Lokken, Federal Taxation of Income, Estates and Gifts ¶ 81.2.6 (3d ed. 2001).

3. CLAIMS, DEBTS, AND MORTGAGES

LEOPOLD v. UNITED STATES

510 F.2d 617, 622–25 (9th Cir. 1975).

GOODWIN, CIRCUIT JUDGE.

[The first half of this opinion dealing with the trusts created for the decedent's two daughters by his first marriage appears supra at page 254.]

The second issue on this appeal involves the deductibility for estate tax purposes of a $264,000 payment by the executors of decedent's estate to Constance Trevor de Schulthess, as guardian for her daughter Beatrice Tina.

The decedent and his second wife, Constance, were married on February 2, 1958. On August 13, 1958, their daughter, Beatrice Tina, was born. One year later Constance filed an action for divorce. Following extensive negotiations, the decedent and Constance entered into a property-settlement agreement, one clause of which provided as follows:

> 12A. *Testamentary Gift to Child.*—The Husband shall promptly make and execute and keep in effect until his death a Will under which he shall devise and bequeath property to Beatrice Tina de Schulthess in an amount at least equal to the sum of the following:
>
> (a) $250,000, and
>
> (b) [a formula amount]. . . .

This property-settlement agreement was approved and incorporated into an interlocutory judgment of divorce entered on January 17, 1961.

Although the decedent did make a bequest to Beatrice Tina, the amount was uncertain. Constance filed a creditor's claim for $273,900 based on the quoted clause of the property-settlement agreement. The executors rejected the claim in part, but after Constance had filed suit in state court, the matter was settled, and $264,000 was paid to Constance in satisfaction of the claim filed on behalf of Beatrice Tina.

In their claim for refund, the taxpayers contended that this payment was a deductible claim against the estate under section 2053(a)(3) of the Internal Revenue Code, 26 U.S.C. § 2053(a)(3). The government replied that although Beatrice Tina had an enforceable claim under local law, the claim was not supported by adequate and full consideration in money or money's worth, as required by section 2053(c)(1)(A). See Lyeth v. Hoey, 305 U.S. 188, 194 (1938). The district court agreed with the taxpayers, finding that the $264,000 payment was based upon a promise by the decedent contracted bona fide and for an adequate and full consideration, and concluding that the payment was deductible.

Section 2053(a)(3) does authorize deductions from the gross estate for amounts paid to satisfy "claims against the estate." However, subsection (c)(1)(A) further provides that deductions "shall, when founded on a promise or agreement, be limited to the extent that they were contracted bona fide and for an adequate and full consideration in money or money's worth. . . ." One purpose of this limitation is to prevent testators from depleting their estates by transforming bequests to the natural objects of their bounty into deductible claims. United States v. Stapf, 375 U.S. 118, 130–133 (1963).

We begin our analysis by looking to two decisions of this court construing an analogous provision of the Internal Revenue Code.[6] In United States v. Past, 347 F.2d 7 (9th Cir. 1965), we scrutinized a property-settlement agreement made in anticipation of divorce. There the husband and wife jointly transferred certain community property into a trust, with the income payable to the wife for her life and the remainder payable to the couple's children. When the wife died, the Commissioner included the entire corpus of the trust in her gross estate. The district court held instead that none of the property was includible because the decedent had received adequate and full consideration from her husband for making the transfer. We reversed, holding that the fact that the transfer was part of a property-settlement agreement incident to a divorce was insufficient in itself to make the transfer one for an adequate and full consideration. The value of what the decedent received must be measured against the value of what she transferred. Since in *Past* the decedent received less than she transferred, we held that the trust property was not excludible from federal estate tax upon her death.

In Estate of Haskins v. United States, 357 F.2d 492 (9th Cir. 1966), we again were faced with a property-settlement agreement incident to a divorce. There, as part of the agreement, the husband placed money in a trust in which he reserved a life estate with the remainder to his children.

6. Although these two cases both involve inter vivos transfers and therefore were decided under section 2043 rather than section 2053, the taxpayers and the government agree that they are still in point, since the two sections are similar in purpose and language. See Hartshorne v. Commissioner, 402 F.2d 592, 595 n.4 (2d Cir. 1968).

We affirmed a district court decision holding that the corpus of this trust was includible in the decedent's gross estate. We noted that both parents were devoted to their children and keenly mindful of parental obligation. Testamentary provisions for the care of children, even though required by a property-settlement agreement, were not necessarily made for monetary consideration but could be viewed as a form of estate planning by the couple.

The government contends that *Haskins* requires us to reverse the judgment of the district court holding that the payment to Constance was a deductible claim against the estate. However, in *Haskins* the district court specifically found that there was no consideration for the transfer; here, the district court found that there was. Moreover, *Haskins* did not establish a per-se rule that a testamentary provision for one's own children could never be made for monetary consideration.

In Hartshorne v. Commissioner, 402 F.2d 592, 594 n.2 (2d Cir. 1968), the government did take the position that a bequest to one's own children can never be a "claim against the estate" within the meaning of section 2053 because such a bequest is simply an agreement to make a testamentary disposition to persons who are the natural objects of one's bounty. The Court of Appeals for the Second Circuit rejected this absolute position, and so do we. The Second Circuit noted, in language which conforms to the test laid down in *Past* and *Haskins*:

> ... Under exceptional circumstances ... it may be that a claim by someone who might otherwise inherit from the decedent should be deductible under section 2053. If the claim is not simply a subterfuge for a nondeductible legacy, if the claim is supported by "adequate and full consideration," and if the consideration is a non-zero sum which augmented the decedent's estate, then it would seem that the deduction should be allowed. Whether or not a particular claim is deductible, then, will depend on the facts in each case. [402 F.2d at 594–95 n.2.]

Constance's claim on behalf of Beatrice Tina meets this standard. The case presents the "exceptional circumstances" to which the Second Circuit alluded.

The testimony before the district court was sharply conflicting on the question whether the decedent's agreement to make the bequest to Beatrice Tina was bargained for or merely gratuitous. Because the taxpayers prevailed below, this court must view the evidence in the light most favorable to them. United States v. Disney, 413 F.2d 783, 787 n.2 (9th Cir. 1969). Viewing the evidence in this light, we affirm as not clearly erroneous the district court's finding that decedent's promise was contracted bona fide and for an adequate and full consideration.

Decedent's will suggests that Beatrice Tina might not necessarily have been a natural object of the decedent's bounty. His will established his first wife and her daughters as the residuary beneficiaries of his estate; by contrast, nothing was left to Constance and no more to Beatrice Tina than was required by the property-settlement agreement. His attorney testified that the decedent knew that his first two daughters' share of the residuary estate would be worth considerably more than the amount promised to Beatrice Tina. Moreover, these two daughters already had the inter vivos trusts which are the subject of the first issue on this appeal.

The record strongly suggests that the decedent and Constance were not equally concerned with the financial welfare of their daughter, and that Constance felt she had to wrench from her husband—or at least from her husband's lawyers—the promise to leave a bequest to Beatrice Tina. She feared that because of the circumstances concerning the marriage and the birth of their daughter, her child might not be treated equally with the children of the first marriage. The decedent's attorney testified that the decedent did give a preference in financial matters to his first two daughters, in part because he felt that Constance was more self-assertive than his first wife and would always manage to provide for her child.

Constance's initial demands for support payments for herself were within the range of California court awards in similar cases. Nonetheless, she accepted a substantially smaller sum, partly in consideration for her husband's promise to bequeath more than $250,000 to their daughter. Constance apparently felt that she could spend her support payments more freely and would not have to set aside part for her estate if she knew that her child would be taken care of in the event of her ex-husband's death. Thus, by accepting reduced alimony, Constance paid for her husband's promise to leave money to their daughter; in effect, she diverted to her daughter that consideration which otherwise would have flowed to herself. Although the property-settlement agreement might have spelled out more precisely what Constance relinquished in exchange for her husband's promise to leave their daughter a bequest, the record supports the finding that the promise was contracted for in good faith for value which augmented the decedent's estate. . . .

NOTES

1. *Payments on occasion of marriage or divorce.* Section 2043(b)(1) provides generally that a relinquishment or promised relinquishment of any "marital rights in the decedent's property," including dower, curtesy, or statutory rights in lieu thereof, does not qualify to any extent as consideration in money or money's worth. This provision complements § 2053(c)(1)(A), which disallows deductions for claims "founded on a promise or agreement" to the extent they were not contracted for adequate and full consideration in money or money's worth. As a result of these provisions, no deduction is allowed under § 2053 for a decedent's obligation under a typical antenuptial agreement to make payments to a surviving spouse in exchange for the spouse's relinquishment of marital rights in the decedent's property. See Herrmann's Estate v. Commissioner, 85 F.3d 1032 (2d Cir. 1996) (no deduction for interest left to surviving spouse, pursuant to antenuptial agreement, in exchange for spouse's relinquishment of her "contingent right to an

equitable distribution of [decedent's] property in the event of a divorce that never occurred").

The estate tax treatment of payments made to a former spouse under a property settlement agreement incident to divorce is now regulated by statute. In 1984, Congress enacted § 2043(b)(2), which creates an exception to the general rule that the relinquishment of marital rights does not qualify as consideration. Under § 2043(b)(2), transfers between spouses in settlement of their marital or property rights are deemed to be supported by adequate money's-worth consideration if the requirements of § 2516(1) are met. Thus, if husband and wife enter into a written agreement settling their marital or property rights and divorce occurs within the three-year period specified in § 2516, any payments required by the agreement to be made at the death of one spouse to the survivor are fully deductible under § 2053(a)(3), even if the amount of the payments exceeds the value of the marital or property rights relinquished by the survivor.

A divorce agreement may fail to qualify for the safe harbor of § 2516 because, for example, the divorce does not occur within the statutory time period. An executor in such a case may attempt to justify the deduction by reference to the decision in Harris v. Commissioner, supra page 121, that a transfer incident to divorce was based on a judicial decree and hence was not "founded on a promise or agreement" within the meaning of § 2053(c)(1)(A). Under this rationale, consideration is not required, but the transfer must be pursuant to an agreement that has been approved in a divorce proceeding by a court with jurisdiction to accept, reject, or modify the agreement. See Fenton's Estate v. Commissioner, 70 T.C. 263 (1978) (*Harris* not applicable because Mexican divorce court did not have power to disregard terms of agreement); Gray v. United States, 541 F.2d 228 (9th Cir. 1976) (same for California divorce court unless agreement is tainted by fraud); Rev. Rul. 76–113, 1976–1 C.B. 276 (deduction allowed for amount payable pursuant to a divorce decree issued by a court having full power to settle marital rights).

In the alternative, the executor may claim that the obligation was incurred for consideration. In this connection, the Service acknowledges that one spouse's release of the right to be supported by the other is not a "marital right" within the meaning of § 2043(b)(1) and therefore qualifies as consideration. Cf. Rev. Rul. 68–379, 1968–2 C.B. 414 (gift tax), supra page 117. Because the legal obligation to support a spouse terminates at death, a claim based on the decedent's contractual obligation to make payments after death is supported by consideration only to the extent that the value of the support rights relinquished by the spouse exceeded the payments required to be made by the decedent during life. In the *Leopold* case, this argument was used to justify the deduction for the payment to the decedent's daughter. See also Kosow's Estate v. Commissioner, 45 F.3d 1524 (11th Cir. 1995) (spouse accepted reduced support payments in exchange for decedent's promise to provide for their children in his will); Satz's Estate v. Commissioner, 78 T.C. 1172 (1982) (no evidence that value of support rights of minor children and ex-spouse exceeded amount to be paid by decedent during life).

Community property rights also fall outside the definition of "marital rights" in § 2043(b)(1), with the result that a relinquishment of community property rights qualifies as consideration. See Carli's Estate v. Commissioner, 84 T.C. 649 (1985) (spouse's relinquishment prior to marriage of her community property rights in decedent's future earnings accepted as consideration, because the rights to her share of his earnings would have been enforceable prior to his death). If under local law each spouse becomes entitled to an equal one-half vested interest in marital property upon divorce, does a relinquishment by one spouse of his or her interest qualify as money's-worth consideration for a promised payment by the other spouse? See Waters' Estate v. Commissioner, 48 F.3d 838 (4th Cir. 1995).

Section 2516(2), pertaining to support of minor children, was not incorporated into § 2043(b)(2), presumably on the theory that a parent's obligation to support a child ordinarily terminates at the parent's death. Thus, in order to secure the deduction for a payment of the kind made to Beatrice Tina in the *Leopold* case, it continues to be necessary, as described above, to argue either that the obligation is founded on a divorce decree which makes consideration unnecessary or that consideration was present in the form of the decedent's spouse's forbearance at the negotiating table.

2. *Requirement of full consideration.* As stated in the *Leopold* case, § 2053(c)(1)(A) provides that claims against the estate, unpaid mortgages, and other indebtedness may be deducted, if "founded on a promise or agreement," only "to the extent that they were contracted bona fide and for an adequate and full consideration in money or money's worth." Thus, the requirement of consideration does not apply to tort claims or obligations imposed by law, such as taxes or support of legal dependents; the statute also provides that consideration is not necessary to support a deduction for a charitable pledge that would qualify for the charitable deduction under § 2055 if it constituted a bequest. Test these rules where the estate pays claims arising out of the following circumstances:

1. A loan taken out by the decedent to fund a $100,000 gift to a niece.
2. A state court judgment enforcing decedent's promise to pay $100,000 to a niece on her graduation from college without drinking hard liquor or smoking.
3. Decedent's oral promise to a niece to leave her a $100,000 bequest if she took care of the decedent in his old age.

HUNTINGTON'S ESTATE v. COMMISSIONER

16 F.3d 462 (1st Cir. 1994).

COFFIN, SENIOR CIRCUIT JUDGE.

Charles and Myles Huntington claim that their stepmother, the decedent, promised as part of a reciprocal will agreement with their father that she would devise her estate in equal shares to them and their stepsister. Decedent died intestate, leaving the sons without an inheritance. Their claim against her estate ultimately led to a $425,000 settlement. The question posed by this appeal is whether the estate may deduct the settlement amount for purposes of the federal estate tax. The answer depends upon whether the mutual will agreement was "contracted bona fide and for an adequate and full consideration in money or money's worth," as required by 26 U.S.C. § 2053(c)(1)(A). After careful review of the facts and precedent, we affirm the Tax Court's determination that the claim is not deductible.

I. Factual Background

[The decedent, Elizabeth Huntington, was married to Dana Huntington from 1955 until Dana's death in 1980. They had one daughter, Nancy. Dana also had two sons from his previous marriage, Charles and Myles. On January 3, 1978, Dana executed a will leaving $25,000 to each of his three children and the rest of his estate in trust with Elizabeth as life income beneficiary and the three children as equal remainder takers. This will was superseded by his last will, executed on May 8, 1979, which left the entire estate outright to Elizabeth. After Dana's death on April 6, 1980, his last will was initially challenged by Charles and Myles, but was finally admitted to probate.

In 1981 Charles and Myles sued to impose a constructive trust on the property that Elizabeth received from Dana, arguing that Dana had executed his last will in reliance on Elizabeth's oral promise that she would execute a will leaving her own estate to the three children in equal shares. This lawsuit was finally settled in December 1986, when Elizabeth agreed to execute a will leaving 20 percent of her estate to Charles and 20 percent to Myles. Two weeks later, however, Elizabeth died intestate. Charles and Myles filed a claim against her estate, and also filed a second lawsuit to enforce the settlement terms. The second lawsuit was finally settled in 1989, when Elizabeth's administrator paid $425,000, representing 40 percent of the estate, to Charles and Myles. The estate claimed a deduction for the $425,000 payment, which the Commissioner disallowed. The Tax Court upheld the Commissioner.]

On appeal, the estate argues that Elizabeth received substantial consideration in exchange for her promise to provide for Charles and Myles in her will—the excess amount over what she would have received under Dana's revoked 1978 will—and that this consideration made the sons' claim fully enforceable and deductible. In addition, the estate contends that Elizabeth also received valuable consideration when she agreed in December 1986 to settle the constructive trust lawsuit. In exchange for her promise to execute a will in which she would devise 40 percent of her estate to Charles and Myles, her stepsons released their claim to two-thirds of her estate. The estate contends that either or both of these considerations is sufficient to support its claim to a deduction under section 2053....

II

At the risk of stating the obvious, we think it worth noting at the outset that any analysis of estate tax issues must be sensitive to "the general polic[y] of taxing the transmission of wealth at death," United States v. Stapf, 375 U.S. 118, 134 (1963). Section 2053 of the Internal

Revenue Code, which allows deductions from a decedent's gross estate for certain claims, has been carefully crafted to promote that policy. In a series of revisions to the statutory language early in the century, increasingly formal requirements were imposed on claims based on promises or agreements, see Taft v. Commissioner, 304 U.S. 351, 355–56 (1938);[7] Estate of Pollard, 52 T.C. 741, 744 (1969), "to prevent deductions, under the guise of claims, of what were in reality gifts or testamentary dispositions," Carney v. Benz, 90 F.2d 747, 749 (1st Cir. 1937).

In other words, Congress wanted to be sure that bequests to family members and other natural objects of the decedent's bounty were not transformed into deductible claims through collaboration and creative contracting. See Bank of New York v. United States, 526 F.2d 1012, 1016–17 (3d Cir. 1975); Carney, 90 F.2d at 749; Estate of Satz v. Commissioner, 78 T.C. 1172, 1178 (1982); Pollard, 52 T.C. at 744. Thus, a "claim against the estate" is deductible only if the agreement giving rise to the claim was "contracted bona fide and for an adequate and full consideration in money or money's worth," 26 U.S.C. § 2053(c)(1)(A).

Thus far, this case has focused primarily on whether Elizabeth Huntington received sufficient consideration, within the meaning of section 2053, for her promise to include Charles and Myles in her will. The Tax Court concluded that the Huntingtons' reciprocal will agreement was supported only by donative intent, and that this was not enough to establish a deductible claim. In its notice of appeal and in its brief, the estate specifically challenges the Tax Court's failure to credit as consideration Elizabeth's enhanced inheritance—the immediate $75,000 representing the bequests previously earmarked for Charles, Myles and Nancy, plus absolute rights in the balance of Dana's estate (in contrast to simply a life estate). Alternatively, it offers as "adequate and full" consideration the financial benefit conferred on Elizabeth when Charles and Myles dropped the constructive trust lawsuit in exchange for her second promise to include them in her will.

Our view of the caselaw, reflected against the backdrop of section 2053(c)(1)(A)'s limiting purpose, persuades us that the real issue here is not whether Elizabeth received a financial benefit from the reciprocal will agreement—clearly, she did—but whether the mutual promises made by Dana and Elizabeth created the sort of "bona fide" contractual obligation for which section 2053 allows a deduction. We have little difficulty in concluding that they did not.

---

7. The history of section 2053 was detailed in *Taft* as follows:

The Revenue Act of 1916 permitted the deduction of the amount of claims against the estate "allowed by the laws of the jurisdiction . . . under which the estate is being administered." . . . The Act of 1924 altered existing law and authorized the deduction of claims against an estate only to the extent that they were "incurred or contracted bona fide and for a fair consideration in money or money's worth." Congress had reason to think that the phrase "fair consideration" would be held to comprehend an instance of a promise which was honest, reasonable, and free from suspicion whether or not the consideration for it was, strictly speaking, adequate. The words "adequate and full consideration" were substituted by § 303(a)(1) of the Act of 1926. [304 U.S. at 356 (footnotes omitted).]

Two threshold propositions inform our inquiry. First, transactions among family members are subject to particular scrutiny, even when they apparently are supported by monetary consideration, because that is the context in which a testator is most likely to be making a bequest rather than repaying a real contractual obligation. See Bank of New York, 526 F.2d at 1016; Estate of Morse v. Commissioner, 69 T.C. 408, 418 (1977), affd. per curiam, 625 F.2d 133 (1980); Estate of Woody, 36 T.C. 900, 903 (1961). Second, we need not be concerned with whether a tax avoidance motive was present here, "because it is the substance of the arrangement as a potential device for defeating the estate tax that is of controlling significance," Estate of Pollard, 52 T.C. at 745. See also Young v. United States, 559 F.2d 695, 703 (D.C. Cir. 1977).

Thus, while the record in this case provides no evidence that the Huntingtons sought to defeat estate taxes through their reciprocal will agreement, this fact does not assist the estate's effort to overturn the deficiency judgment. The record is equally barren of evidence indicating that the agreement was other than a collaborative effort to pass on the family's assets. From all that appears in the record, it is most plausible that Dana and Elizabeth discussed their respective desires for disposing of their property, and concluded that everyone's needs would be met by the simple will ultimately executed by Dana on May 8, 1979, and the will Elizabeth was expected to complete shortly thereafter. Such a purely voluntary, testamentary arrangement is not the product of a bona fide contract, and consequently does not provide a basis for a deduction under section 2053.

The estate suggests that, because Dana had a firm commitment, evidenced by his prior wills, to make direct bequests to his sons, the change in his last will must have been the product of bona fide bargaining between the couple. Neither the fact that Elizabeth received an immediate advantage, relative to the earlier wills, nor Dana's longstanding intention to make his sons beneficiaries of his estate is enough, however, to transform an apparently cooperative agreement into a bona fide contract. See Estate of Morse, 69 T.C. at 418.

Dana simply may have changed his mind about the best way to provide for his family, either before or after discussion with Elizabeth. By passing on his entire estate to his wife, who was substantially younger than himself, he could ensure that she would be fully provided for as long as she lived. He may have felt that Charles and Myles, both well into adulthood, had no immediate need for the money. By securing his wife's agreement that the balance of both of their estates would be divided equally among the couple's three children, he still could fulfill his moral obligation to Charles and Myles.

There is no evidence that Dana and Elizabeth reached agreement on the asserted reciprocal wills only after a period of give-and-take bargaining. Indeed, Dana's sister testified that her brother's lawyer suggested that "he not discuss every last detail of his estate plan [with Elizabeth] because ... she would probably want to argue over every point." Elizabeth's wishes may have played a substantial role in Dana's decision to change his will—she was, after all, his wife—but the record is silent as to any form of negotiations.

This is not to say that "hard bargaining as would occur between hostile parties is an absolute prerequisite to a deduction under section 2053," Estate of Morse, 69 T.C. at 419. But when family members adopt a course of action whose object is to pass on their collective wealth, a deduction for the amount ultimately transferred is not permitted under section 2053 unless there is some showing of a bargained-for exchange. Any other conclusion would seriously undermine the policy of taxing the transfer of wealth at death. Where, as here, there is no evidence of any type of negotiations, the claim to deductibility unquestionably fails for lack of proof.

The language of the Third Circuit in Bank of New York v. United States, 526 F.2d at 1017, is equally applicable here:

> When the interests of family members are not divergent but coincide so that the elements of a transaction advance the separate concerns of each, we are unable to find the arm's length bargain mandated by the Code. This Court has adhered to the distinction between family arrangements bargained for at arm's length and family arrangements that reflect a community of interests. Tax advantages are not permitted when an agreement between members of a family could be regarded as a cooperative attempt to make a testamentary disposition rather than as an arm's length bargain.

... Some courts have suggested that a bona fide, deductible claim can be differentiated from one that fails to meet the requirements for deductibility by examining whether the claim is *against* the estate or *to* a portion of the estate. See, e.g., Latty v. Commissioner, 62 F.2d 952, 953 (6th Cir. 1933); Estate of Lazar v. Commissioner, 58 T.C. 543, 552 (1972). In other words, if the debt underlying the claim has its origin in a discretionary desire to pass on wealth to specific individuals—giving those individuals a claim "to" a portion of the estate—it is unlikely to be the sort of bona fide, arm's-length obligation that is deductible under the statute. Deductible claims will have arisen from transactions that created true debts "against" the estate.

The estate, of course, insists that there *was* a debt here once Elizabeth made her promise and received a financial benefit, but then reneged on the deal. It may be that, under state law, the reciprocal will agreement was an enforceable contract that, when violated, created a debt in favor of Charles and Myles against the estate. A valid contract is not necessarily enough, however, to establish a deductible claim for purposes of section 2053. Bank of New York, 526 F.2d at 1015; see also Stapf, 375 U.S. at 131.... A claim derived solely from Dana Huntington's desire to share some portion of his estate with his sons, carried out through cooperative estate planning, is precisely the sort of "debt" section 2053(c)(1)(A) was designed to exclude. See Bank of New York, 526 F.2d at 1018 ("The policy of section 2053 is to deny a deduction where the underlying transaction was 'essentially donative in character.' ") (citing H. Rep. No. 2333, 77th Cong., 2d Sess. 169 (1942) (reprinted in 1942–2 Cum. Bull. 372, 493); S. Rep. No. 1631, 77th Cong., 2d Sess. 238 (1942) (reprinted in 1942–2 Cum. Bull. 504, 679)).

Nor does the subsequent court-approved settlement with Elizabeth's estate transform the claim into an arm's-length transaction within the meaning of section 2053. The *Bank of New York* case again is directly on point:

> To effectuate the policy underlying the federal estate tax requires that courts look beneath the surface of transactions to discover the essential character of each transfer. Even where a claim is ultimately satisfied by the operation of law, the courts will determine the nature of the claim for federal tax purposes by examining the particular status of the claimant that enabled him to impose his claim on the estate. [526 F.2d at 1017]. . . .

Our examination of the issue of arm's-length bargaining helps bring into focus the parties' dispute over consideration. If the reciprocal will agreement did represent collaborative estate planning by the Huntingtons, the fact that Elizabeth received a larger direct bequest than she would have received under Dana's prior will is of no consequence. In such circumstances, the increase would reflect changed priorities rather than a bargained-for "consideration." ... The problem with the Huntington sons' claim therefore may be characterized alternatively as a failure of proof of "full and adequate consideration."

We need not decide today whether there may be some factual circumstances in which a claim that began with a wholly discretionary desire to make a bequest can fulfill the requirements of section 2053 for a "bona fide" contract supported by "an adequate and full consideration in money or money's worth." It suffices to say that, in this case, the requisite attributes of a deductible claim were not shown.

The decision of the Tax Court is affirmed.

NOTES

1. *Services as consideration.* For several years prior to her death, decedent received assistance in various personal and financial matters from two cousins of her predeceased husband. Decedent promised the cousins that she would leave each of them a one-third share of her estate. At her death decedent left an estate of $4,500,000, but her will provided a bequest for each cousin of only $100,000. The cousins sued to enforce the will contract and eventually received $400,000 and $550,000 in settlement of their respective claims. Assume that each cousin actually performed services worth $75,000. Should the estate be allowed a deduction for all or part of the amounts paid to the cousins? See Wilson's Estate v. Commissioner, 76 T.C.M. (CCH) 350

(1998) (deduction allowed for amounts paid; services deemed adequate and full money's-worth consideration). See also Stern's Estate v. United States, 81 A.F.T.R.2d (RIA) 501 (S.D. Ind. 1998).

2. *Consideration benefiting decedent.* Decedent's son Charles owed decedent's daughter Rhoma $14,000, part of a debt incurred to purchase a seat on the New York Stock Exchange. Decedent agreed to assume Charles' $14,000 debt, and in return Rhoma discharged Charles' obligation. At decedent's death, his estate paid the $14,000 debt to Rhoma and deducted this amount as a claim under § 2053. The Tax Court allowed the deduction in Woody's Estate v. Commissioner, 36 T.C. 900 (1961):

> The Commissioner presses upon us the argument that the statutory requirement [of consideration under § 2053(c)(1)(A)] was intended to prevent one from diminishing his taxable estate by creating obligations which are not correspondingly offset by the consideration received in exchange for such obligations.... But the fundamental error in the Commissioner's position here is the assumption that the decedent or his estate did not benefit by Rhoma's release of her $14,000 claim against her brother. The evidence shows that the decedent intended to and did make an inter vivos gift to his son. Had he made that gift out of his own funds, his estate would have been depleted by $14,000. He achieved the same result by inducing Rhoma to cancel Charles' $14,000 debt to her in exchange for his undertaking to pay a like amount to her.... In every real sense, therefore, the decedent's obligation was supported by "adequate and full consideration in money or money's worth," and the principle relied upon by the Commissioner is inapplicable to the facts of this case. [36 T.C. at 904.]

Compare the Tax Court's reasoning in Davis' Estate v. Commissioner, 57 T.C. 833 (1972), denying a deduction for a claim made by decedent's son against her estate, based on a promissory note that was executed under seal, secured by a mortgage, and enforceable under local law. The court pointed out that there was no evidence of any consideration passing to the decedent "which augmented her estate, granted her a right or privilege she did not possess before, or operated to discharge an existing claim," and noted that the common law seal did not constitute consideration in money or money's worth. 57 T.C. at 836. Is there any substantive difference between the winning claim in the *Woody* case that the decedent received consideration and the losing claim in the *Davis* case?

3. *Accommodation guarantees.* The courts have allowed the deduction of claims that are based on the decedent's accommodation guarantee or endorsement of a debt contracted by a third party, whether or not the decedent derived any financial benefit from the underlying transaction. The deduction is subject to the proviso that at the time the guarantee was made the primary obligor must have been solvent and the decedent must have had a reasonable expectation of reimbursement if he were called on to make payments under the guarantee. See Scofield's Estate v. Commissioner, 41 T.C.M. (CCH) 227 (1980) (and cases cited therein). In these cases, the decedent's right of subrogation against the primary obligor at the time the guarantee was made is deemed to be full and adequate consideration. Does this consideration

compensate the decedent for having accepted the risk? For whom and for what reasons will a person provide an accommodation guarantee? A sampling of cases suggests that the transaction is almost always quasi-donative in character. See Commissioner v. Wragg, 141 F.2d 638 (1st Cir. 1944) (decedent was accommodation endorser of notes issued by son for funds used, at least in part, to finance family corporation that decedent had organized); Commissioner v. Porter, 92 F.2d 426 (2d Cir. 1937) (borrower was decedent's son-in-law). No deduction is available for unmatured potential claims against the accommodation guarantor; thus, the deduction is allowed only to the extent the decedent has become liable upon the primary obligor's default. Furthermore, the amount of the deduction will be reduced by the value of any right of reimbursement against the primary obligor. See Theis' Estate v. Commissioner, 770 F.2d 981 (11th Cir. 1985) (no deduction allowed because husband-wife decedents signed only as accommodation parties and would have had rights of reimbursement if they or their estates had been required to pay); Rev. Rul. 84–42, 1984–1 C.B. 194 (same).

4. *Sham debts.* In Flandreau's Estate v. Commissioner, 994 F.2d 91 (2d Cir. 1993), decedent's two sons and their wives made 14 interest-free loans to decedent over a three-year period, in exchange for decedent's unsecured promissory notes. Each loan was preceded by a gift in an identical amount from the decedent to the lenders, and all but two of the gifts were fully covered by the annual exclusion. The notes, totaling $102,000, remained unpaid at the decedent's death and were ultimately paid from estate assets. In disallowing a deduction for the payment of decedent's notes, the court noted that the contemporaneous gifts were "highly relevant evidence that the notes [did] not reflect bona fide debts contracted for adequate and full consideration." 994 F.2d at 94. Cf. Rev. Rul. 83–54, 1983–1 C.B. 229 (no deduction for estate's payment of claim arising from collusive law suit brought by decedent's child against decedent on the advice of a "financial planner").

5. *Mortgages and other debts secured by includible property.* Section 2053(a)(4) authorizes a deduction for unpaid mortgages and other debts in respect of property to the extent the value of the property (undiminished by the mortgage or debt) is included in the gross estate. Under this provision, a deduction was allowed for a husband's obligation, arising out of a divorce decree, to keep in force a policy of life insurance naming his divorced wife as beneficiary, where the insurance proceeds were included in his gross estate under § 2042. See Robinson's Estate v. Commissioner, 63 T.C. 717 (1975); Rev. Rul. 76–113, 1976–1 C.B. 276 (same).

Section 2053(a)(4) is subject to the same statutory limits as § 2053(a)(3), viz., debts must be "allowable" under local law and, if founded on a promise or agreement, must meet the consideration requirement of § 2053(c)(1)(A). In the case of a nonrecourse debt, Reg. § 20.2053–7 recognizes that the executor may obtain the same result without reference to § 2053(a)(4) by limiting the amount included in the gross estate to the value of the decedent's equity in the property. Thus, if the decedent owned land worth $100,000 subject to a nonrecourse mortgage of $40,000, the executor apparently may either include $100,000 under § 2033 and claim a $40,000 deduction under § 2053(a)(4), or simply include the $60,000 net equity value under § 2033. Although the taxable estate is the same under either method, the size of the gross estate will be smaller if the executor includes only the net equity value, and this could affect ancillary matters such as the duty to file a return under § 6018(a)(1), see infra page 632, which depends on the size of the gross estate.

6. *Taxes.* Federal, state, and municipal taxes that are due and payable when the decedent died are deductible as claims against the estate under § 2053(a)(3). See Reg. § 20.2053–6(d), (e), and (f) (gift, excise, and income taxes); but see Proesel v. United States, 585 F.2d 295 (7th Cir. 1978), cert. denied, 441 U.S. 961 (1979) (decedent's executor consented, as authorized by decedent's will, to split gifts made by decedent's spouse during decedent's life; deduction denied, because decedent was not subject to any enforceable obligation at death). No deduction is allowed under § 2053 for "[a]ny income taxes on income received after the death of the decedent, or property taxes not accrued before his death, or any estate, succession, legacy, or inheritance taxes." § 2053(c)(1)(B). State death taxes on property included in the gross estate, however, are eligible for a deduction under § 2058, discussed infra at page 546. In a special situation described in § 2053(d), the executor may elect to take foreign death taxes as a deduction (thus waiving the right to claim them as a credit) as long as the benefit of the deduction inures solely to the benefit of qualified public, charitable, or religious organizations. For a discussion of the meaning of "estate, inheritance, legacy, and succession taxes," see Rev. Rul. 82–82, 1982–1 C.B. 127 (Canadian tax on appreciation in value of decedent's property before death is not a death tax; deduction allowed). Taxes that are not deductible as claims against the estate because they were not obligations existing at death may nevertheless be deductible as administration expenses under § 2053(a)(2), unless the deduction is barred by § 2053(c)(1)(B).

McMORRIS' ESTATE v. COMMISSIONER

243 F.3d 1254 (10th Cir. 2001).

BRISCOE, CIRCUIT JUDGE.

The Estate of Evelyn M. McMorris appeals a tax court decision in favor of the Commissioner of Internal Revenue. The tax court held that the Commissioner properly considered an event occurring after the death of Evelyn McMorris in disallowing her estate's deduction pursuant to 26 U.S.C. § 2053(a)(3) for payment of federal and state income taxes owed at the time of her death. Exercising jurisdiction under 26 U.S.C. § 7482(a)(1), we reverse and remand with directions to vacate the deficiency assessment at issue here and to recalculate any remaining unrelated deficiencies owing.

I

The facts are undisputed. Donn McMorris, Evelyn's husband, died in 1990, and Evelyn received 13.409091 shares of stock in NW Transport Service, Inc., from his estate. The stock was reported in Donn's estate tax return at an appraised value of $1,726,562.50 per share as of the date of his death and that value became Evelyn's basis in the stock. Evelyn, through her conservator Jerry McMorris, entered into an agreement with

NW Transport to redeem the stock for $29,500,000.00 (approximately $2,200,000.00 per share), payable over 120 months at ten percent interest.

Evelyn died in 1991, a resident of Colorado. In her federal estate tax return, her estate claimed deductions of $3,960,525.00 and $641,222.00, respectively, for her 1991 federal and state income tax liabilities. Federal income tax in the amount of $3,681,703.00 and Colorado income tax in the amount of $639,826.00 actually were paid with Evelyn's 1991 individual tax returns. A large part of the income reported on Evelyn's income tax returns resulted from the gain on redemption of the NW Transport stock.

In January 1994, the Commissioner issued a deficiency notice to Donn's estate disputing, among other things, the value of the NW Transport stock. Specifically, the Commissioner valued the stock at $3,618,040.00 per share. Donn's estate contested the Commissioner's determinations and, after lengthy negotiations, the parties reached a settlement in January 1996 for an increased value of the NW Transport stock at $2,500,000.00 per share as of Donn's death. This value became the new basis for the NW Transport stock redeemed by Evelyn. As a result of her increased basis, the taxable gain from Evelyn's redemption of the stock was eliminated and she realized a loss.

Evelyn's estate filed an amended 1991 federal individual income tax return seeking a refund of $3,332,443.00. The amended return reflected a loss from redemption of the NW Transport stock and eliminated certain dividend income reported on the original return. Meanwhile, Evelyn's estate was challenging a deficiency notice received in November 1994 concerning an unrelated gift deduction in the amount of $140,000.00 in her estate tax return. The estate contested the deficiency in tax court and that litigation was ongoing when Evelyn's amended 1991 federal income tax return was filed in January 1996.

In March 1996, the Commissioner filed an amended answer in Evelyn's estate tax litigation, asserting an increased deficiency in estate taxes. According to the Commissioner, the estate was no longer entitled to deduct Evelyn's 1991 federal and state individual income taxes because those liabilities were subject to refunds. Indeed, the Commissioner approved a $3,330,778.00 refund of Evelyn's 1991 federal income taxes in 1997, but the record filed with this court does not indicate that her estate filed an amended 1991 state income tax return or a protective refund claim with the Colorado Department of Revenue.

Evelyn's estate later conceded the Commissioner's original deficiency determination in its entirety (including disallowance of the $140,000.00 gift deduction). However, the estate refused to accept the Commissioner's view that the estate's deduction for Evelyn's income tax liabilities should be limited to the amount ultimately found to be due and owing by Evelyn. The estate instead took the position that post-death events may not be considered in determining the amount of its deduction for Evelyn's individual income tax liabilities because those liabilities were valid and enforceable claims against the estate at the time of Evelyn's death. Unable to resolve their differences, the parties submitted the case to the tax court on a fully stipulated basis.

The tax court held that the estate's deduction for Evelyn's 1991 federal income tax liability must be reduced by the amount actually refunded in 1997. According to the tax court, it was proper for the Commissioner to consider events occurring after Evelyn's death in calculating this deduction because the estate challenged Evelyn's individual income tax liability through her amended return. The tax court also held that the estate's deduction for Evelyn's 1991 Colorado income tax liability should be reduced to reflect the proper amount of tax after being adjusted downward as a result of her decreased federal taxable income. Although the record revealed that Evelyn's estate had not filed an amended Colorado income tax return and Evelyn had not received a refund of any 1991 state income taxes, the tax court reasoned that nothing prevented the estate from seeking such a refund on Evelyn's behalf. The tax court determined there was an estate tax deficiency of $1,581,593.00 based on the amounts set forth in (1) the original notice of deficiency, and (2) the increased deficiency arising from disallowance of the estate deductions for Evelyn's 1991 individual income tax liabilities. The estate appeals the latter deficiency determination.

II

We review decisions of the tax court "in the same manner and to the same extent as decisions of the district courts in civil actions tried without a jury." 26 U.S.C. § 7482(a)(1). Because this case was submitted to the tax court on a fully stipulated basis, we review the purely legal question presented by this appeal de novo. See Duke Energy Natural Gas Corp. v. Comm'r, 172 F.3d 1255, 1258 (10th Cir. 1999).

III

Section 2053(a)(3) of the Internal Revenue Code authorizes a deduction for "claims against the estate" in calculating the value of a decedent's taxable estate. There is no dispute in this case that unpaid income taxes incurred by a decedent prior to death may be deducted as a claim against the estate. See Treas. Reg. § 20.2053–6(f). Rather, the disagreement centers on whether events occurring after a decedent's death may be considered in calculating that deduction. In particular, the parties debate the effect of the 1996 settlement between Donn's estate and the Commissioner on the value of the section 2053(a)(3) deduction taken by Evelyn's estate for her 1991 income taxes. The estate argues the settlement is not relevant because the value of its deduction should be determined as of Evelyn's death. The Commissioner counters that the settlement was properly considered because the deduction is limited to the actual amount of taxes Evelyn ultimately owed....

... Neither section 2053(a)(3) nor the tax regulations clearly indicate whether events that occur after a decedent's death are relevant in calculating a deduction for a claim against the estate.[8] The statute is silent on this issue. The regulations, on the other hand, contain language which arguably supports the positions of both parties. For instance, one regulation cited by the estate provides: "The amounts that may be deducted as claims against a decedent's estate are such only as represent personal obligations of the decedent existing at the time of his death." Treas. Reg. § 20.2053–4. But, another regulation relied upon by the Commissioner permits estates to deduct a decedent's tax liabilities as a claim against the estate even if the exact amount is not known, as long as the deduction "is ascertainable with reasonable certainty, and will be paid." Treas. Reg. § 20.2053–1(b)(3). In light of these apparent inconsistencies, the most we can discern "from these Regulations is that the situation we now face is not expressly contemplated." Estate of Smith v. Comm'r, 198 F.3d 515, 521 (5th Cir. 1999).

We therefore begin our analysis with the leading case on this issue, Ithaca Trust Co. v. United States, 279 U.S. 151 (1929). In *Ithaca Trust*, the decedent left the residue of his estate to his wife for life, with the remainder to certain charities. To ascertain the amount of the charitable deduction for estate tax purposes, the wife's residual was calculated with a mortality table and subtracted from the principal of the estate. However, the wife died much sooner than expected. The question for the Court was whether the value of the estate's deduction should be calculated according to the wife's life expectancy as of the date of the testator's death or by applying the wife's actual date of death. In a unanimous opinion, the Court adopted a date-of-death valuation rule: "The estate so far as may be is settled as of the date of the testator's death." Id. at 155. The Court acknowledged that "[t]he first impression is that it is absurd to resort to statistical probabilities when you know the fact," but it stated that "the value of the thing to be taxed must be estimated as of the time when the act is done," i.e., the passing of the decedent's estate at death. Id. The Court therefore concluded by stating that, as "[t]empting as it is to correct uncertain probabilities by the now certain fact, we are of opinion that it cannot be done." Id.

Several courts have relied on the date-of-death valuation rule announced in *Ithaca Trust* to hold that events occurring after a decedent's death are irrelevant in valuing an estate's deduction under section 2053(a)(3). See Estate of Smith, 198 F.3d at 520–26 (allowing estate to deduct date-of-death value of claim against it even though estate later settled for lesser amount); Propstra v. United States, 680 F.2d 1248, 1253–56 (9th Cir. 1982) (same); Estate of Van Horne v. Comm'r, 78 T.C. 728, 732–39 (1982) (same), affd., 720 F.2d 1114 (9th Cir. 1983); Greene v. United States, 447 F. Supp. 885, 892–95 (N.D. Ill. 1978) (declining to consider creditor's failure to comply with statute of limitations for filing claim after decedent's death in allowing estate's deduction for claim); Russell v. United States, 260 F.Supp. 493, 499–500 (N.D. Ill. 1966) (same);

8. The regulations were amended in 2009 to require expressly that post-death events be taken into account. See Reg. §§ 20.2053–1(d) and 20.2053–4, discussed infra at page 456, Note 2.—EDS.

Winer v. United States, 153 F. Supp. 941, 943–44 (S.D.N.Y. 1957) (same). While most of these courts acknowledged that *Ithaca Trust* involved a different section of the federal estate tax statute, i.e., charitable bequest deductions under the precursor to 26 U.S.C. § 2055, they interpreted the opinion as announcing a broad principle that the value of a taxable estate should be determined as closely as possible to the date of the decedent's death.

Other courts, however, have refused to extend the principle of *Ithaca Trust* beyond charitable bequest deductions, holding that postmortem events may properly be considered in calculating the value of a claim against the estate deduction. See Estate of Sachs v. Comm'r, 856 F.2d 1158, 1160–63 (8th Cir. 1988) (holding that Commissioner could rely on retroactive tax forgiveness legislation enacted four years after decedent's death in disallowing estate deduction for paying those taxes); Comm'r v. Estate of Shively, 276 F.2d 372, 373–75 (2d Cir. 1960) (holding that decedent's estate could not deduct full date-of-death value of spousal support obligations because ex-wife re-married before estate filed return); Jacobs [v. Commissioner, 34 F.2d 233, 235–36 (8th Cir. 1929)] (holding that husband's estate could not deduct amount of claim against it arising from antenuptial agreement as a result of wife's waiver of claim after husband's death); Estate of Kyle v. Comm'r, 94 T.C. 829, 848–51 (1990) (disallowing estate's deduction for date-of-death value of litigation claim against it because case was resolved in estate's favor six years after decedent's death); Estate of Hagmann v. Comm'r, 60 T.C. 465, 466–69 (1973) (refusing to allow estate to deduct valid claims against it because creditors never filed those claims after decedent's death), affd. per curiam, 492 F.2d 796 (5th Cir. 1974). Although these courts have offered a variety of reasons why *Ithaca Trust* should be limited to charitable bequests, three recurring themes emerge.

One explanation for not extending *Ithaca Trust* to claims against the estate is that the congressional purpose underlying that deduction is different from that of deductions for charitable bequests. According to this rationale, the date-of-death valuation rule does not apply to section 2053(a)(3) because the purpose of that deduction is to appraise the decedent's actual net worth at death, while the purpose of section 2055 is to encourage charitable bequests by ensuring that if a testator makes a charitable gift in a prescribed form, a deduction will be allowed in a specified amount. See, e.g., Sachs, 856 F.2d at 1162 ("there is no legislative interest behind the § 2053(a)(3) deduction in encouraging claims against the estate in the same way that date-of-death valuation encourages charitable bequests").

Another justification for not applying *Ithaca Trust* to section 2053(a)(3) is based on the other deductions in the section. This approach places heavy reliance on the fact that section 2053(a) allows a deduction not only for claims against the estate but also for funeral and estate administration expenses. Under this view, since these expenses are calculated after death, Congress must also have intended that claims against the estate be ascertained by post-mortem events. See, e.g., Jacobs, 34 F.2d at 236 ("funeral expenses, administration expenses, and claims against the estate, under this paragraph, were intended by Congress to be determined in the course of an orderly administration of the estate").

The third reason these courts reject a date-of-death valuation approach is they do not consider it sensible to allow an estate to deduct a claim it does not ultimately owe or pay. See, e.g., Shively, 276 F.2d at 375 ("To permit an estate such a deduction under these circumstances would be to prefer fiction to reality and would defeat the clear purpose of [the precursor to section 2053(a)(3)].").

We do not find any of these explanations particularly persuasive. Even assuming Congress had different motives for allowing deductions under section 2053 than it did for deductions under section 2055, this distinction "fails to explain why deductions for claims against the estate should be computed [any] differently from charitable bequests." Propstra, 680 F.2d at 1255 n.11. Further, we find it insignificant that Congress placed funeral and estate administration expenses, which are calculated after death, with claims against the estate in section 2053(a), because that section also contains a deduction for unpaid mortgages, which may be calculated without reference to post-death events. Finally, we note that the emphasis on actuality in valuing claims against the estate is at odds with the Supreme Court's admonition that as "[t]empting as it is to correct uncertain probabilities by the now certain fact, we are of opinion that it cannot be done." Ithaca Trust, 279 U.S. at 155. Thus, instead of facing compelling arguments why we should reject date-of-death valuation for claims against the estate, we are left with ambiguous interpretations of the appropriate method for calculating section 2053(a)(3) deductions.

These ambiguities, of course, do not automatically lead to the conclusion that events occurring after a decedent's death may never be considered in valuing a claim against the estate. But neither do they provide us license to ignore the Supreme Court's pronouncement that "[t]he estate so far as may be is settled as of the date of the testator's death." Ithaca Trust, 279 U.S. at 155. We therefore agree with the Fifth Circuit that a "narrow reading of *Ithaca Trust*, a reading that limits its application to charitable bequests, is unwarranted." Smith, 198 F.3d at 524. Accordingly, we hold that the date-of-death valuation rule announced in *Ithaca Trust* applies to a deduction for a claim against the estate under section 2053(a)(3). As a result, in this circuit, events which occur after the decedent's death may not be considered in valuing that deduction.

Sound policy reasons support our adoption of the date-of-death valuation principle for section 2053(a)(3) deductions. Specifically, this principle provides a bright line rule which alleviates the uncertainty and delay in estate administration which may result if events occurring months or even years after a decedent's death could be considered in valuing a claim against the estate.... Our holding resolves these problems by bringing more certainty to estate administration, an ideal which has long been promoted by judge and commentator alike. . . .

Although our holding ultimately benefits the estate in this case, application of the rule we announce today just as easily can favor the Commissioner. . . . For example, in Estate of Lester v. Commissioner, 57 T.C. 503 (1972), the estate was obligated by a divorce decree to pay $1,000.00 per month to the decedent's ex-wife. The estate made twenty-four payments and then settled with the ex-wife by purchasing an annuity policy for her benefit for $78,700.00. The estate argued it was entitled to deduct at least $102,700.00, the total of its payments and the annuity policy, as a claim against the estate. Invoking *Ithaca Trust*, the Commissioner insisted the deduction was limited to $92,456.16, the actuarial value of the ex-wife's life expectancy as of the decedent's death. The tax court agreed with this position:

> We think there is no reason in this case to go beyond the principle of Ithaca Trust Co. v. United States, supra—that the value of the judgment in the divorce proceedings is to be determined as of the date of the husband's death by the use of the tables employed here by the Commissioner, which take into consideration the contingency of the wife's death prior to final payment of the installments to become due.
>
> There is no need to go into the effect of events subsequent to the husband's death, i.e., how the estate finally freed itself of a continuing and admitted liability. [Id. at 507.]

Thus, as the facts of *Lester* demonstrate, whether our holding benefits the government or the taxpayer depends on the particular circumstances of each case.

In this case, the tax court concluded it was appropriate to consider post-mortem events because the estate later sought a refund of Evelyn's 1991 federal income tax and could have done the same with regard to her state income tax. Emphasizing that "a claim that is valid and enforceable at the date of a decedent's death must remain enforceable in order for the estate to deduct the claim," McMorris v. Commissioner, 77 T.C.M. (CCH) 1552, 1554 (1999), the tax court reasoned that once the estate challenged Evelyn's tax liabilities, they were "no longer a valid and enforceable claim against the estate," id. at 1555. As support, the tax court cited its prior holding in Estate of Smith v. Commissioner, 108 T.C. 412 (1997), revd. and vacated, Smith, 198 F.3d 515, which distinguished cases involving the *valuation* of claims that are certain and enforceable on the date of a decedent's death from cases where the *enforceability* of the claims [was] unknown at death because they were disputed or contingent. Under this approach, the former claims are calculated as of the date of death, while the latter claims are calculated by considering post-death events. See id. at 419.

In examining the "enforceable" nature of the estate's claims in this case, the tax court did not have the benefit of the Fifth Circuit's subsequent decision in *Smith*, which concluded that "this dichotomy, which distinguishes between enforceability on the one hand and valuation on the other, . . . is not a sound basis for distinguishing claims in this context." 198 F.3d at 525. As the Fifth Circuit explained:

> There is only a semantic difference between a claim that may prove to be invalid and a valid claim that may prove to have a value of zero. For example, if given the choice between being the obligor of (1) a claim known to be worth $1 million with a 50 percent chance of being adjudged unenforceable, or (2) a claim known to be enforceable with a value equally likely to be $1 million or zero, a rational person would discern no difference in choosing between the claims, as both have an expected value $500,000. [Id.]

Because the tax court in *Smith* improperly relied on the "contingent" nature of the estate's claim to consider post-death events, the Fifth Circuit remanded the case with instructions that the tax court "neither . . . admit nor consider evidence of post-death occurrences when determining the date-of-death value of [the] claim." Id. at 526.

In this case, instead of focusing on whether the estate's section 2053(a)(3) deduction for Evelyn's income tax liabilities "remained enforceable" for an infinite period of time, the tax court should have examined whether the estate properly calculated that deduction as of the date of Evelyn's death. Had the tax court done so, it would have recognized that the increased deficiency at issue in this appeal was not premised on a date-of-death miscalculation. The increased deficiency was based solely on the fact that the federal and state income taxes incurred by Evelyn in 1991 became subject to a refund as a result of a settlement between another estate and the Commissioner in 1996. Therefore, the tax court erred when it considered that settlement in calculating the total tax deficiency for Evelyn's estate.

IV

We reverse the tax court's ruling that events occurring after death may be considered in valuing a claim against the estate deduction. We remand to the tax court with directions to vacate the determination of the estate tax deficiency at issue and to recalculate any remaining unrelated deficiencies owing.

NOTES

1. *Date-of-death valuation rule.* In the principal case, the estate was allowed to deduct the full amount of the decedent's income tax liability originally reported on the estate tax return, even though most of that amount was subsequently refunded to the estate. Was it reasonably foreseeable at the time of the decedent's death that her basis in the stock inherited from her husband might be adjusted upward, eliminating her taxable gain and generating an income tax refund? If so, should that possibility be reflected in the amount allowed as a deduction under § 2053? Cf. Smith's Estate v. Commis-

sioner, 198 F.3d 515 (5th Cir. 1999) (potential income tax deduction for payment of disputed claim taken into account in valuing claim under § 2053). Upon filing for an income tax refund, should the estate have been required to accept a corresponding adjustment of the amount previously claimed as a deduction on the estate tax return? Cf. Letts' Estate v. Commissioner, 109 T.C. 290 (1997), affd. mem., 212 F.3d 600 (11th Cir. 2000) (discussing "duty of consistency" in marital deduction setting).

For many years, in the absence of definitive guidance in the statute or the regulations, courts struggled to determine whether events occurring after the decedent's death could be considered in determining the amount of claims deductible under § 2053. Relying on the Supreme Court's *Ithaca Trust* decision, several courts held that claims must be determined as of the date of the decedent's death, without regard to subsequent events. In addition to the principal case and cases cited therein, see O'Neal v. United States, 258 F.3d 1265 (11th Cir. 2001). In *Ithaca Trust*, Justice Holmes's cryptic opinion for the Court concluded that a deductible bequest of a charitable remainder following a life estate in the decedent's widow was properly valued under the actuarial tables set forth in the regulations, notwithstanding the fact that the widow died less than six months after the decedent. (Note that under current law such a bequest would be nondeductible by virtue of the split-interest rules of § 2055(e)(2), discussed infra at page 473.) Does *Ithaca Trust* support the "bright line rule" announced in *McMorris* that "events which occur after the decedent's death may not be considered" in computing the deduction for claims under § 2053, or does it stand for the narrower proposition that individual characteristics may not be considered in using actuarial tables to value partial interests such as life estates, remainders, and reversions? On grounds of administrative convenience, such interests generally must be valued based on actuarial life expectancies rather than actual events, even though an investigation of individual characteristics would undoubtedly yield more accurate results in particular cases. Thus, in *Ithaca Trust*, the widow's medical history before the valuation date, her condition on that date, and her death thereafter were all properly disregarded in determining her actuarial life expectancy under the tables. See Gerzog, Actuarial Tables Versus Factually Based Estate Tax Valuation: *Ithaca Trust* Revisited, 38 Real Prop., Prob. & Tr. J. 745 (2004).

In Marshall Naify Revocable Trust v. United States, 106 A.F.T.R.2d (RIA) 6236 (N.D. Cal. 2010), the decedent had incurred a substantial California income tax liability on capital gains realized by his corporation before his death. On the federal estate tax return, the executor initially claimed a deduction of $61 million, the estimated amount of the liability at the date of death; the estimate was subsequently revised down to $47 million. The Internal Revenue Service allowed a deduction of $26 million, the amount actually paid by the estate in settlement of the state income tax liability four years after the decedent's death. The court held that the deduction was limited to the $26 million settlement amount and explained its reasoning as follows:

> But it cannot be that simply because one can assign a probability to any event and calculate a value accordingly, any and all claims are

reasonably certain and susceptible to deduction.[9] To so hold would read the regulatory restriction out of existence. The regulation clearly provides that one can deduct a claim on a return only if it is "ascertainable with reasonable certainty, and will be paid. No deduction may be taken upon the basis of a vague or uncertain estimate." 26 C.F.R § 20.2053–1. The regulation therefore explicitly contemplates that some claims will be simply too uncertain to be taken as a deduction, regardless of the fact that it is always possible to come up with some estimate of a claim's value.

Indeed, the disputed claim in this case seems tailor-made for the second part of § 20.2053–1, which provides that for uncertain claims "[i]f the amount of a liability was not ascertainable at the time of final audit of the return by the district director and, as a consequence, it was not allowed as a deduction in the audit, and subsequently the amount of the liability is ascertained, relief may be sought by petition to the Tax court or claim for a refund." In other words, this regulation provides that, for uncertain claims, an estate may obtain the appropriate deduction either during the audit or after the audit via a petition or claim for a refund. Despite the Estate's invocation of equitable arguments, it is apparent to this Court that this regulation adequately provides for an equitable outcome. Had the Estate availed itself of this provision, it would have ultimately been entitled to the value of the settlement. It could have simply informed the IRS that California had an uncertain claim, but that it was not yet ascertainable with reasonable certainty. If the state audit never happens, then the claim is worthless. If the audit occurs and [the decedent] is determined to owe taxes, then the Estate can deduct the value of the claim, whatever it may be. Instead, the Estate went for broke, arguing that it has always been entitled to a deduct a sum that it never paid: $47 million. . . .

The language [of Reg. § 20.2053–1 requiring that a claim "will be paid"] appears to be directed at the sort of claim that, although its value is reasonably certain, may or may not be paid. In other words, the language excludes claims like this one: had [the decedent's] tax plan been successful (i.e. had California either failed to audit him or concluded that [his corporation] was a legitimate Nevada business), he would not have paid any state tax. On the other hand, if his plan failed, he might pay $61 million in taxes. Therefore, at the time of death, it was uncertain as to whether the claim "would be paid." Furthermore, the one calculation of value that almost certainly would not be paid is the value the Estate now seeks to deduct: $47 million.

---

9. To illustrate, imagine an individual is given a lottery ticket for a drawing with a prize valued at $100. Imagine further that only one other lottery ticket was sold, and that the odds of winning stand at 50%. The expected value of that ticket is therefore $50. However, this Court does not conclude that the "reasonabl[y] certain[]" value of that ticket is therefore $50. On the contrary, whatever happens, the owner of the ticket will never end up with $50. She will have either $0 or $100, and there are equal odds on both. This Court therefore concludes that a "reasonably certain" value for purposes of this regulation is not the same thing as an expected value. If it were, the regulation would make no provision for "uncertain" claims because an estate could postulate an expected value for any and all claims.

Some courts, seeking to steer a middle course between a rigid date-of-death valuation rule and an open-ended consideration of post-death events, distinguished claims that were "for sums certain" and "legally enforceable as of the date of death" from those that were "disputed or contingent." See Propstra v. United States, 680 F.2d 1248 (9th Cir. 1982) (post-death events relevant in valuing the latter but not the former); Van Horne's Estate v. Commissioner, 78 T.C. 728 (1982), affd., 720 F.2d 1114 (9th Cir. 1983), cert. denied, 466 U.S. 980 (1984). Does this distinction make sense?

2. *Final regulations.* The regulations under § 2053 were amended in 2009 to provide more detailed guidance concerning the deductibility of claims against a decedent's estate. In addition to requiring that a claim be bona fide and enforceable, the regulations limit the deduction to amounts actually paid. In general, a claim may not be deducted until it is actually paid or "the amount to be paid is ascertainable with reasonable certainty and will be paid." No deduction is allowed based on a "vague or uncertain estimate." To the extent a claim is "contested or contingent," it is treated as not ascertainable and hence not deductible. Reg. § 20.2053–1(d)(4). If a claim is still contingent when the estate tax return is filed, the executor must forgo an immediate deduction and wait until it is actually paid or becomes ascertainable; at that point, the executor may file for a refund. If there is a possibility that a claim may remain contingent beyond the deadline for refund claims (generally three years from the filing of the return), the executor may preserve the right to a refund by filing a protective refund claim. Reg. § 20.2053–1(d)(5).

A claim that consists of an obligation to make recurring payments is deemed to be ascertainable if the claim is "enforceable and certain" and the payments are "not subject to a contingency." Reg. § 20.2053–4(d)(6). For this purpose, contingencies relating to the death or remarriage of the claimant do not prevent an immediate deduction but are taken into account "according to actuarial principles" in measuring the amount of the claim. For example, suppose the decedent was obligated, pursuant to a divorce settlement which remains enforceable against the estate, to make periodic payments to a former spouse until the latter's death or remarriage. Standing alone, the contingencies of death or remarriage affect the value of the claim but do not preclude an immediate deduction. If the former spouse dies before the estate tax return is filed, the deduction is limited to the amount actually paid. Suppose, however, that the former spouse dies one year after a deduction is allowed for the full amount of estimated payments reported on the estate tax return (and before the end of the limitation period for assessment). Must the executor file an amended return showing a reduced deduction limited to the amount actually paid? Note that if the payment obligation is subject to any contingencies in addition to death or remarriage, the claim is unascertainable and the deduction will become available only as payments are actually made or become ascertainable.

The regulations expressly reverse the judicial date-of-death valuation rule. In determining the deductibility of a claim, events occurring after the decedent's death "will be taken into consideration" until the end of the limitation period for assessment (or thereafter in connection with a refund claim). Reg. § 20.2053–1(d)(2). One obvious application of this rule involves the situation where a claim against the estate becomes unenforceable after death because the creditor fails to present it within the period specified by the local non-claim statute. Among the prerequisites for deductibility, the regulations provide that a claim must be "a personal obligation of the decedent existing at the time of the decedent's death" and must remain "enforceable against the decedent's estate" until it is paid or becomes ascertainable. Reg. § 20.2053–4(a)(1). Thus, no deduction is allowed for a claim that is paid after it has become unenforceable. Reg. § 20.2053–4(d)(4). Uncertainty may arise from state-to-state variations in the scope of the non-claim statute and in the relevance of estoppel, waiver, misrepresentation, and other defenses in determining whether claims are enforceable despite noncompliance with the local rules. See Greenberg's Estate v. Commissioner, 76 T.C. 680 (1981) (deduction allowed for settlement of claim; presentment not necessary where executor led creditor to believe that formality was not necessary); Rev. Rul. 75–24, 1975–1 C.B. 306 (deduction allowed for claim that was paid without formal presentment; payment was proper under Mississippi law because approved by beneficiaries); cf. Rev. Rul. 75–177, 1975–1 C.B. 307 (contra where payment not proper under state law).

To the extent that a claim may be eligible for reimbursement from insurance proceeds, third-party contributions, or other sources, the amount of the deduction must be reduced accordingly. Reg. §§ 20.2053–1(d)(3) and 20.2053–4(d)(3). For example, the deductible amount of bona fide, enforceable medical expenses incurred by the decedent and paid by the executor must be offset by any actual or potential reimbursement under the decedent's medical insurance policy. Nevertheless, no offset is required if the executor reasonably determines that "the burden of necessary collection efforts in pursuit of a right of reimbursement would outweigh the anticipated benefit from those efforts." Reg. § 20.2053–1(d)(3). Suppose that an immediate deduction is allowed for the full amount of a medical expense based on the executor's reasonable determination that the expense was not covered by the decedent's insurance policy. If the executor subsequently succeeds in collecting insurance proceeds before the end of the limitation period for assessment, must the executor file an amended return?

Despite the general requirement that claims must be actually paid or ascertainable to qualify for immediate deduction, the regulations provide limited relief in the form of two safe harbor exceptions. The first safe harbor allows an immediate deduction for claims against the estate that are closely related to other claims or assets included in the gross estate. The related claims or assets must have an aggregate value of more than 10 percent of the gross estate, and the deductible amount cannot exceed the value of the related claims or assets. Reg. § 20.2053–4(b). Under this provision, an immediate deduction may be allowed for a contested $1 million claim against the estate if the estate has a $2 million counterclaim arising from the same matter and the gross estate is worth less than $20 million. The second safe harbor allows an immediate deduction for claims with an aggregate value of no more than $500,000, regardless of the size of the estate. The total amount of each claim, reduced only by any amount deductible under the general rule or the first safe harbor, must fit within the $500,000 limit. Reg. § 20.2053–4(c). Under this provision, if there are three contested claims against the estate in the amounts of $100,000, $200,000, and $300,000, an immediate deduction may be allowed for any two of the claims (but not for any portion of the third claim). Under both safe harbors, the claims must be valued by a "qualified appraiser" based on a "qualified appraisal" (as defined in § 170(f)(11) and the regulations thereunder), and the deductible amount may not exceed the "current value" of the claim, adjusted to reflect events occurring after the decedent's death.

For a detailed discussion of the regulations, see Blattmachr, Gans & Zeydel, Final Regs. on Deducting Expenses and Claims Under Section 2053 (Parts 1 and 2), 37 Est. Planning 3 (May 2010); id. at 15 (June 2010).

B. CASUALTY LOSSES: § 2054

Section 2054 allows a deduction for "losses incurred during the settlement of estates arising from fires, storms, shipwrecks, or other casualties, or from theft," to the extent not compensated by insurance or otherwise. The specified causes are identical with those in § 165(c)(3). If a loss is claimed as an estate tax deduction, however, the same loss may not also be deducted on the estate's income tax return. § 642(g).

Section 165(c)(3) is explicitly restricted to losses of *property*. Is § 2054 similarly restricted, or could a loss of potential profits, brought on by shipwreck or fire, be deducted from the value of the gross estate? The deduction under § 165(c)(3) may not exceed the "basis" of the lost property, by virtue of § 165(b). In the case of a loss under § 2054, may the full value of property at the time of the loss be deducted, even if by reason of inflation it exceeds the estate tax value? If the property declined in value between the date of death and the date of the loss, how is the amount of the deduction to be computed?

In Leewitz v. United States, 75 F.Supp. 312 (Ct. Cl.), cert. denied, 335 U.S. 820 (1948), the court made this comment on § 2054:

> At the outset it should be observed that we are here concerned with losses for estate tax purposes where the only losses allowable are those above mentioned, as contrasted with losses allowable for income tax purposes, which include business losses, such as from bad debts, and losses on transactions entered into for profit as well as losses of the kind allowed for estate tax purposes. Only one estate tax return is filed and therefore, once a deduction is allowed, there is no chance for adjustment in another estate tax return in the event there should be some recovery on account of the item for which the deduction was allowed. On the other hand, income tax returns are filed on an annual basis and any recoveries with respect to a deduction allowed in one year will be reflected in income adjustments in a subsequent year. This comparison becomes significant as indicating the nature of the losses which are allowable for estate tax purposes; namely, losses from which no recovery would ordinarily be expected, such as from fires or storms. In addition, these losses have reference to destruction of or damage to physical property where the extent of the loss can be fully

measured as of the time the loss is allowed without the necessity for future readjustment. [75 F.Supp. at 317.]

A similar problem arises with respect to proof that the loss is not compensated by insurance or otherwise. The extent of compensation is often undetermined in the year the casualty occurs; in the income tax field, it is only a matter of timing whether the taxpayer holds the item in abeyance until the claim for compensation is settled or deducts the full amount of the loss in the earlier year and reports the insurance or other recovery as income in the year of settlement. If the amount of a loss was uncertain when the estate tax return was filed, can it be claimed on an amended return when finally liquidated? Must a loss, to be deductible under § 2054, occur before the estate tax return is due?

C. CHARITABLE BEQUESTS: § 2055

The original federal estate tax statute, enacted in 1916, did not contain a deduction for charitable bequests, but this omission was rectified by the Revenue Act of 1918, which included a deduction for charitable and similar bequests closely resembling § 2055 of current law. Although the wide range of public, charitable, religious, and educational organizations that qualify for the deduction under § 2055 largely parallels the lists entitled to deduction under § 170(c) (income tax) and § 2522(a) (gift tax), the three provisions are not identical in every detail. See, e.g., the difference in eligibility of cemetery associations under § 2055(a)(2) and § 170(c)(5), as described in First Natl. Bank of Omaha v. United States, infra. It should also be noted that § 2055 does not impose a dollar or percentage limit on the amount that may be deducted; thus, no estate tax is payable if an estate is left entirely to qualifying organizations. For a review of the arguments for and against imposing such a limitation, see Bittker, Charitable Bequests and the Federal Estate Tax: Proposed Restrictions on Deductibility, 31 Rec. A.B. City N.Y. 159 (1976) (concluding that a limitation should not be enacted).

1. QUALIFYING ORGANIZATIONS

FIRST NATIONAL BANK OF OMAHA v. UNITED STATES

681 F.2d 534 (8th Cir. 1982), cert. denied, 459 U.S. 1104 (1983).

HENLEY, SENIOR CIRCUIT JUDGE. . . .

McIninch died in 1975 and left the bulk of his estate to charity. One of his bequests was of $100,000.00 to the Walnut Grove Cemetery Association[10]

10. [The Walnut Grove Cemetery Association] is a non-profit association organized and operated for the purpose of maintaining the Walnut Grove Cemetery in Brownville, Nebraska. It is governed by a Board of six trustees who serve without pay. It is non-sectarian and is not affiliated with any municipal or state governmental unit. It sells burial lots to the public at

> to be maintained as a Perpetual Care Trust Fund pursuant to Section 12–510 of the Revised Statutes of Nebraska, 1943, on condition, however, that the officers of the Association select the Omaha National Bank as trustee of said Fund to serve in manner provided by Sections 12–509 through 12–512.08, inclusive, of the Revised Statutes of Nebraska, 1943. The earnings on the Fund established by this bequest to the extent permitted by Nebraska law shall be applied first toward maintenance of the McIninch family plot and the balance of the earnings shall then be used for the general beautification and maintenance of the entire cemetery.

The will further stated:

> It is my hope that the Walnut Grove Cemetery, with the assistance provided by this bequest, can be preserved as an historic spot in recognition of the early settlers of Nebraska buried there.

The executor contends that the bequest is deductible as a bequest to a trust for charitable purposes under 26 U.S.C. § 2055(a)(3). The executor also asserts that the imposition of a tax on this bequest, where similar bequests made to church-owned, not-for-profit cemeteries are routinely exempted from taxation, constitutes a denial of equal protection of the law.

The cases relied upon by the United States have dealt primarily with the deductibility of bequests under 26 U.S.C. § 2055(a)(2). This subsection allows an estate tax deduction of the value of all bequests "to or for the use of any corporation organized and operated exclusively for . . . charitable . . . purposes," and its focus is on the purposes for which the ultimate beneficiary of the bequest operates.

There is no direct authority in this circuit regarding the charitable status under subsection (a)(2) of cemetery associations such as Walnut Grove, and the decisions from other jurisdictions dealing with this issue are by no means uniform. Those jurisdictions holding that bequests to or for the use of cemetery associations are "charitable" have focused primarily on the public nature of the services performed by such associations. Thus, in Estate of Edwards, 151 Cal. Rptr. 770 (1979), the California Court of Appeals stated:

> Cemetery's fundamental responsibility is the proper disposal of human remains. That function is critically important to society because it insures that society is not subject to disease from decomposing human remains. Absent Cemetery's presence in the private marketplace, and the presence of other similarly situated cemeteries, government would be required to provide that crucial service. Hence, in our view, Cemetery's presence and continued operation in the private

---

reasonable price and makes provision for maintenance of the cemetery grounds. It sells perpetual care contracts at a price of $50 for each grave space but does not require the purchase of such a contract as a precondition for burial. It once maintained a paupers' field but no longer does so. The only prerequisite for burial is to purchase a grave space outright or make arrangements for installment payment. There have been a few occasions when full payment was never received.

> marketplace effectively lessens the burden of government. [151 Cal. Rptr. at 776.]

That court concluded that cemetery associations are charitable within the meaning of the inheritance tax portion of the California Revenue and Taxation Code. . . .

Those cases holding that cemetery associations such as Walnut Grove are not charitable within the meaning of subsection (a)(2) have focused on the fact that such associations do not provide free burial space for the indigent, nor is less than fair value ever charged for maintenance. Child v. United States, [540 F.2d 579, 583–84 (2d Cir. 1976), cert. denied sub nom. National Bank of Northern New York v. United States, 429 U.S. 1092 (1977)]; Gund's Estate v. Commissioner, 113 F.2d 61, 62 (6th Cir. 1940), cert. denied, 311 U.S. 696 (1941); Bank of Carthage v. United States, 304 F. Supp. 77, 80 (W.D. Mo. 1969). The underlying logic of this approach is that "[a]n organization which does not extend some of its benefits to individuals financially unable to make the required payments reflects a commercial activity, rather than a charitable one." Federation Pharmacy Services, Inc. v. Commissioner, 625 F.2d 804, 807 (8th Cir. 1980). Further, the argument that such associations are charitable because they perform a "public" function has been rejected by these courts. In Child v. United States, supra, Judge Oakes, writing for the majority, stated:

> Our view is that relief for the public fisc is more symptomatic than evidentiary regarding whether an activity is charitable: charity often results in an absorption of a burden otherwise falling upon the state, particularly where the social welfare is a principal purpose of the state. But this does not mean that activities lessening public expense in any of a myriad of areas of public interest are perforce charitable. [540 F.2d at 583.] . . .

With this background in mind, we turn to the executor's contention that the bequest is deductible under 26 U.S.C. § 2055(a)(3). This contention essentially stems from the provision in the will that all income earned by the trust fund established by the bequest is to be used for the maintenance of the cemetery. The executor asserts that all income earned by the trust is thus deductible for income tax purposes as a charitable contribution under Sections 642(c) and 170(c)(5) of the Internal Revenue Code, and that the bequest establishing the trust therefore qualifies under Section 2055(a)(3) as a bequest "to a trustee . . . to be used by such trustee . . . exclusively for . . . charitable . . . purposes. . . ." Id.

Unlike subsection (a)(2), subsection (a)(3) focuses on the use for which a bequest is to be applied, and not upon the eleemosynary nature of the ultimate beneficiary of the funds. See National Savings and Trust Co. v. United States, 436 F.2d 458, 460 (Ct. Cl. 1971). In addition, even if the cemetery association cannot qualify as a charitable organization under subsection (a)(2), the cases are divided as to whether the word "charitable" should be used in the same sense throughout subsection 2055(a). Compare, e.g., Child v. United States, 540 F.2d at 581 n.4 ("[O]ur decision

. . . depend[s] on the meanings of 'charitable' and 'religious' as those words are used throughout § 2055(a), and not on the different wording of subsections (2) and (3). . . . ") with National Savings and Trust Co. v. United States, 436 F.2d at 460–61 (Even where a bequest to a foreign governmental body does not qualify as a bequest to a domestic governmental subdivision under subsection (a)(1) or as a contribution to a charitable organization under subsection (a)(2), it can nevertheless qualify for a deduction under subsection (a)(3) if the gift is clearly restricted to charitable purposes.) and Kaplun v. United States, 436 F.2d 799, 801–04 (2d Cir. 1971) (to the same effect).

We have carefully considered both of the approaches outlined above, and we believe the approach taken by the Court of Claims in National Savings and Trust Co. v. United States is the better one. As we have stated, the focus of subsection (a)(3) is entirely different from that of subsection (a)(2), in that subsection (a)(3) focuses on the use of the funds, rather than the character of the beneficiary of the funds. And we are not prepared to hold that the charitable or noncharitable characterization of the ultimate beneficiary of the funds as determined under subsection (a)(2) is necessarily determinative of the characterization of the use to which such funds are put under subsection (a)(3). Such a construction seems at odds with Congress' purpose of encouraging charitable contributions, and would arguably eliminate much of the independent effect that subsection (a)(3) may have. . . .

Neither, however, are we able to agree with the executor that the availability to the trust of an income tax deduction for "charitable" contributions should control the estate tax consequences of such contributions. One of the income tax sections relied upon by the executor, 26 U.S.C. § 170(c)(5), provides:

> (c) Charitable contribution defined.—*For purposes of this section*, the term "charitable contribution" means a contribution or gift to or for the use of— . . .
>
> (5) A cemetery company owned and operated exclusively for the benefit of its members, or any corporation chartered solely for burial purposes as a cemetery corporation and not permitted by its charter to engage in any business not necessarily incident to that purpose, if such company or corporation is not operated for profit and no part of the net earnings of such company or corporation inures to the benefit of any private shareholder or individual.

(Emphasis supplied.) Similarly, the other income tax statute relied upon by the executor, 26 U.S.C. § 642(c), allows an income tax deduction to a trust for any income set aside for "a purpose specified in section 170(c) or . . . to be used exclusively for . . . charitable purposes, . . . or for the establishment, acquisition, maintenance or operation of a public cemetery not operated for profit." There is nothing in either of these sections or in Section 2055 indicating a legislative intent that the income tax definitions of charitable contributions are to be used for estate tax purposes as well....

In these circumstances, we must do as subsection (a)(3) suggests, and look to the use to which the funds are to be put by the trustees.... The question thus becomes: Is the use of the bequeathed funds pursuant to the provisions of the will a use "exclusively for charitable purposes"? ...

We have already determined that the fund does not benefit the poor, and we also think it clear that the bequest does not advance education or religion.[11] Nor do we think the *maintenance* of a cemetery is an activity that may be considered a governmental function or a function that protects health. Cf. Child v. United States, 540 F.2d at 583–84 ("Charity often results in an absorption of a burden otherwise falling upon the state. But this does not mean that activities lessening the public expense ... are perforce charitable.").

It remains to be determined whether the fund has a purpose which is beneficial to the community. One argument is that the fund is beneficial to the community in that it serves the community's interest in having available plots of land for the burial of the deceased. The purpose of this particular fund, however, is not to provide such plots, but rather to maintain them. Further, although the maintenance of such plots is arguably in the community's interest, we are unable to conclude that this particular bequest acts primarily to serve such an interest.

We observe that the funds "to the extent permitted by Nebraska law shall be applied first toward maintenance of the McIninch family plot." Such language does not indicate that the benefit to the testator is merely incidental....

In the instant case, the trust income is to be applied *first* to the maintenance of the McIninch plot, and the *balance* to the general maintenance of the cemetery. This language is indicative of an intention to give absolute precedence to non-public beneficiaries (the McIninch family), and not a mere preference to such beneficiaries as members of a permissible class of general beneficiaries.

Further, although the will purports to restrict the noncharitable use of the trust income by reference to Nebraska law, the parties have not cited, and we have not found, any Nebraska statutes or cases which impose meaningful or substantial restrictions on such private uses.[12] In the absence of such restrictions, we are not prepared to hold that the

11. The language in the will expressing a hope that the cemetery will be maintained for historical purposes will not aid the executor in this regard. That language is precatory in nature, and thus cannot be said to be a clear restriction to use for an historic purpose....

12. It is well settled that state law cannot govern the federal tax consequences of a particular transaction or event unless the applicable federal statute "by express language or necessary implication makes its own operation dependent on state law." Mississippi Valley Trust Co. v. Commissioner, 72 F.2d at 200. Here, however, we are not looking to Nebraska law for the purpose of applying its definitions to Section 2055. Rather, we look to the state law in these limited circumstances solely for the purpose of determining whether the reference to such law *in the testator's will* imposes any meaningful, substantial restriction on the use to which the bequeathed funds may be applied.

noncharitable uses to which the trust income may be applied are merely incidental.... Accordingly, the judgment of the district court, as it relates to this bequest, is affirmed.[13]

We also affirm the district court's judgment as it relates to the bequest to the Fontenelle Chapter of the Order of the Eastern Star. The Order is a Masonic Order, and such Orders cannot be said to be operated exclusively for charitable purposes, as they carry out social and fraternal, as well as charitable purposes. First National Bank in Dallas v. Commissioner, 45 F.2d 509, 511 (5th Cir. 1930), cert. denied, 283 U.S. 845 (1931). Consequently, the bequest to the Fontenelle Chapter may qualify as a charitable bequest only if the testator has limited the use of the bequest to exclusively charitable purposes....

In the case at bar, the testator has not placed any restrictions on the use of the bequest by the Fontenelle Chapter. Accordingly, the bequest cannot be said to have been made exclusively for charitable purposes. Mississippi Valley Trust Co. v. Commissioner, 72 F.2d at 199. The judgment of the district court, as it relates to this bequest, is also affirmed.

Affirmed.

NOTES

1. *Qualified beneficiaries.* Section 2055(a) identifies four main categories of beneficiaries that are qualified to receive tax-deductible contributions for estate tax purposes.[14]

a. *Governmental agencies.* This category consists of the United States, any state, any political subdivision thereof, or the District of Columbia, provided the contribution is made "for exclusively public purposes." Thus, for example, a bequest to a municipal cemetery may qualify for a deduction under § 2055(a)(1). Rev. Rul. 79–159, 1979–1 C.B. 308. Section 2055(g) augments § 2055(a)(1) with cross references to various statutes not included in the Internal Revenue Code which explicitly qualify various quasi-governmental agencies, such as the Library of Congress and the National Park Foundation. As noted in the principal case, the courts have held that gifts to foreign governments can qualify for deduction under § 2055(a)(2) or (a)(3) if the contributions are to be used exclusively for the charitable or other purposes specified therein, even though § 2055(a)(1) is limited to domestic govern-

13. We note that the executor's equal protection argument is meritless. In passing on the constitutionality of the statute in these circumstances, the appropriate standard is a "relaxed scrutiny" standard, "under which a statutory classification will not be disturbed 'if any state of facts may reasonably be conceived to justify it.' " Merchants National Bank v. United States, 583 F.2d 19, 24 (1st Cir. 1978), quoting McGowan v. Maryland, 366 U.S. 420, 426 (1961). In the case at bar, the interment of deceased persons in church-owned property can obviously have a religious significance that is quite independent of any charitable considerations. Child v. United States, 540 F.2d at 584. Further, Congress could properly consider religious groups as being beneficial and stabilizing influences in community life, and Congress could also consider a classification of cemeteries as "religious" or "non-sectarian" to be useful, beneficial, and in the public interest. See Walz v. Tax Commission of the City of New York, 397 U.S. 664, 673 (1970).

14. In addition, § 2055(a)(5), added in 1997, allows a deduction under narrowly circumscribed conditions for certain transfers of stock to an employee stock ownership plan.

ments and their political subdivisions. See Old Colony Trust Co. v. United States, 438 F.2d 684 (1st Cir. 1971) (Canadian municipal-owned hospital); Kaplun v. United States, 436 F.2d 799 (2d Cir. 1971) (coins to Israel to be exhibited in museum); National Savings & Trust Co. v. United States, 436 F.2d 458 (Ct. Cl. 1971) (German town to build home for the aged); Rev. Rul. 74–523, 1974–2 C.B. 304 (foregoing decisions will be followed provided that the use is limited to exclusively charitable purposes).

b. *Charitable, religious, etc., organizations.* Section 2055(a)(2) qualifies corporations organized and operated exclusively for "religious, charitable, scientific, literary, or educational purposes," including the encouragement of art, for fostering national or international amateur sports competition (excluding the provision of athletic facilities or equipment), or for preventing cruelty to children or animals, provided (1) the organization's net earnings do not inure to the benefit of any private stockholder or individual, (2) it is not disqualified for tax exemption under § 501(c)(3) by reason of attempting to influence legislation, and (3) it does not participate or intervene in any political campaign on behalf of (or in opposition to) any candidate for public office.

Purposes which qualify as "charitable" for tax purposes generally include "the relief of the poor, the advancement of religion, the advancement of education, or 'erecting or maintaining public buildings or works or otherwise lessening the burdens of government.' " Rev. Rul. 59–310, 1959–2 C.B. 146. Thus, for example, a nonprofit organization that was formed to provide swimming and recreational facilities without charge for the use of local residents was held to be organized and operated exclusively for charitable purposes. Peters v. Commissioner, 21 T.C. 55 (1953) (income tax case); accord, Rev. Rul. 59–310, 1959–2 C.B. 146. Several courts have also held bequests to local or state bar associations deductible for estate tax purposes on the ground that the associations' activities were primarily scientific, educational and charitable, and that their nonconforming activities were merely incidental. Dulles v. Johnson, 273 F.2d 362 (2d Cir. 1959), cert. denied, 364 U.S. 834 (1960); St. Louis Union Trust Co. v. United States, 374 F.2d 427 (8th Cir. 1967); cf. Kentucky Bar Found. v. Commissioner, 78 T.C. 921 (1982) (income tax case); but see Association of the Bar v. Commissioner, 858 F.2d 876 (2d Cir. 1988), cert. denied, 490 U.S. 1030 (1989) (bar association's rating of judicial candidates was prohibited campaign activity, notwithstanding public benefit).

As a condition for tax-favored status, the Service may require that an organization adopt and implement a policy of nondiscrimination. For example, if an organization's charitable activities consist of providing public recreational facilities, it cannot exclude a portion of the general public on the basis of race. Rev. Rul. 67–325, 1967–2 C.B. 113. Furthermore, the Service has denied tax-exempt status to private schools that fail to adopt racially nondiscriminatory policies as to students, and the courts have upheld the Service's action against statutory and constitutional challenges. Rev. Rul. 71–447, 1971–2 C.B. 230; Bob Jones University v. United States, 461 U.S. 574 (1983); see also Calhoun Academy v. Commissioner, 94 T.C. 284 (1990). These cases and rulings interpret the statutory requirements in the light of an overriding public policy against racial discrimination. Although similar considerations might be invoked in other contexts, the Service has shown no signs of denying tax-exempt status to organizations that restrict access to services or facilities on grounds such as age, sex, or religion.

c. *Trusts for charitable purposes.* Trusts and fraternal orders qualify under § 2055(a)(3) as recipients if the contribution is to be used exclusively for "religious, charitable, scientific, literary, or educational purposes, or for the prevention of cruelty to children or animals," provided the trust or order satisfies conditions (2) and (3) summarized above. In Buder v. United States, 7 F.3d 1382 (8th Cir. 1993), the decedent left a bequest in trust "to be used solely and exclusively in fostering and promoting the cause of patriotism, loyalty and fundamental constitutional government in the United States of America, and in combating subversive activities, socialism and communism." Rejecting the government's contention that the trustees had discretion to distribute funds to organizations engaged in prohibited lobbying or campaigning activities, the court allowed a charitable deduction based on language in the will which specified that recipients must be "charitable, benevolent or educational organizations or entities."

If the executor or another person is given a power to designate the recipients of a charitable bequest, an estate tax deduction is allowed only if under local law the power is mandatory and cannot be exercised in favor of any beneficiary beyond the limits of § 2055(a). Compare Delaney v. Gardner, 204 F.2d 855 (1st Cir. 1953) (denying deduction where executors had "absolute discretion" and were not bound by memorandum listing charitable beneficiaries); Rev. Rul. 71–200, 1971–1 C.B. 272 (discretion to select beneficiaries qualifying for income, estate or gift tax deduction; deduction denied), with Rev. Rul. 69–285, 1969–1 C.B. 222 (bequest to executor "to be distributed to whatever charities she may deem worthy"; deduction allowed); State Street Bank & Trust Co. v. United States, 634 F.2d 5 (1st Cir. 1980) (deduction salvaged by artful construction).

Suppose a testator leaves property in trust to provide scholarships for needy students—clearly a charitable purpose—but then directs the trustee to give preference to the testator's own relatives in awarding benefits. Should a deduction be allowed based on the testator's expressed charitable intent, or denied on the ground that the real beneficiaries are members of the testator's family? See Sells' Estate v. Commissioner, 10 T.C. 692 (1948) (allowing deduction for bequest to provide scholarships "first to relatives or other boys or girls"). Should it matter whether the testator's relatives are given "absolute precedence" or "a mere preference . . . as members of a permissible class of general beneficiaries"? Cf. First Natl. Bank of Omaha v. United States, supra.

d. *Veterans' organizations.* Section 2055(a)(4) qualifies veterans' organizations if incorporated by Act of Congress, as well as their departments and local chapters or posts, provided no part of the organization's net earnings inures to the benefit of any private shareholder or individual. This section does not contain the prohibition found in the two preceding sections, relating to charitable organizations and trusts for charitable purposes, against lobbying and other political activity. See Regan v. Taxation with Representation, 461 U.S. 540 (1983) (rejecting constitutional challenge to similar preferential treatment in § 501(c)(3), and noting that Congress could rationally decide to subsidize lobbying by veterans' organizations in light of longstanding policy to compensate veterans for their past contributions to the nation).

2. *Disqualified recipient organizations.* Section 2055(e)(1) disallows the deduction for certain contributions if the beneficiary organization is described in § 508(d) (relating to private foundations incurring a tax on termination) or § 4948(c)(4) (relating to foreign organizations engaging in prohibited transactions). Furthermore, § 508(a) requires that a newly created organization claiming tax-exempt status under § 501(c)(3) must notify the Service of its application for such status. This requirement, however, obviously does not apply to organizations such as cities, states, fraternal societies, and veterans' organizations which derive their eligibility to receive tax-deductible contributions from provisions other than § 501(c)(3) and accordingly have no reason to claim exemption thereunder.

2. QUALIFYING TRANSFERS

BURGESS' ESTATE v. COMMISSIONER

622 F.2d 700 (4th Cir. 1980).

BRYAN, SENIOR CIRCUIT JUDGE.

This is an appeal by Kenneth D. Thomas, executor of the estate of Grafton G. Burgess of North Carolina, from a decision of March 12, 1979, by the United States Tax Court, upholding a deficiency of $43,775.85 determined by the Commissioner of Internal Revenue in assessment of the Federal estate tax upon the Burgess estate. The determination was the result of the disallowance of a charitable deduction claimed by the executor under section 2055 of the Internal Revenue Code of 1954, as amended in 1969 and as in effect at the time of decedent's death.

The bulk of the estate consisted of 11 tracts of real property which had been conveyed to Grafton by his mother. Although she conveyed a full interest in fee simple in eight of the tracts, she retained a life estate in the other three—18 acres surrounding her home and two one-acre tracts of business property. On June 23, 1973, Grafton died, and by his will made a few specific bequests and devises. Among them he devised two small parcels to his brother, Ralph, for life. The rest of his property passed into a residuary trust created for the benefit of his mother for her lifetime. The trustees were instructed to be generous and were given the power to invade the corpus for her support. At the mother's death, the trust would terminate and the remainder interest in the entire property, after paying five specific bequests, would pass in fee simple to two Lutheran churches in North Carolina.

Soon after Grafton's death, Ralph initiated suit against the executor of Grafton's estate in the Superior Court of Alexander County, North Carolina, the court probating the will, to set aside his mother's conveyances to Grafton. He charged that Grafton had obtained the real estate from their mother through the imposition of undue influence. Before this litigation came on for trial, all parties in interest, including the mother, by her guardian ad litem, and the churches, reached an agreement in compromise of the claims in suit. The agreement was effectuated by the court's final decree on July 31, 1974.

Specifically, the decree provided: that the mother's life interest in the trust be dissolved; that she continue to hold a life interest in her business properties and residence, but with a diminished amount of acreage surrounding her house; that a tract of 42.5 acres be allotted to Ralph in fee, with the understanding that he would support his mother for the rest of her life; and that the estate continue to be liable on a $30,000 note secured by real estate involved in the litigation. The effect was that the fee title to all of the remaining property was at once invested in the two churches. However, the will was never revoked or set aside in any respect whatsoever.

In the tax return for Grafton's estate, the executor claimed a charitable deduction under I.R.C. § 2055 in the amount of $158,237.15, the value of the property received by the churches. On the Commissioner's adverse ruling, the executor petitioned the Tax Court for a redetermination. After reviewing the facts (as to which the parties were in complete accord), the Court sustained the determination of the Commissioner. The executor appeals.

The ground of the Tax Court's decision was that the churches' fee simple interest in the residue of the estate was obtained by purchase, not inheritance. Under the will, to repeat, the residue passed first in trust to Grafton's mother for life, and upon her death to the churches in fee. Had this testamentary scheme eventuated, the churches would have received their interest as an inheritance. The estate, however, would not have been able to take a charitable deduction under I.R.C. § 2055(a) because the will created non-deductible "split interests" by investing a life estate in decedent's mother and the remainder in the churches. I.R.C. § 2055(e)(2). Instead of adhering to the testamentary plan, however, the beneficiaries redistributed the property of the deceased when they settled the suit aimed at striking down the questioned conveyances. As a result, the churches received the immediate enjoyment of the fee simple interest in the residue of Grafton's estate but, of course, not through inheritance. In addition, as more particularly explained in a moment, the deductions which the executor claimed under the exceptions to the "split interest" rule, stated in subsection (e)(2) (for property in which Grafton had only a remainder interest), were not allowed because these exceptions do not apply to property passing through a nonqualifying trust, such as that before us.

Despite the fact that the redistribution of decedent's property was directed by a State court order, presumably under State law, we think we must apply Federal law in determining Federal tax questions. Lyeth v. Hoey, 305 U.S. 188, 193–94 (1938). In this application, we, like the Tax Court, cannot accept the argument of the executor that *Lyeth* permits the churches to take their interest by inheritance. That decision permitted the benefits of a compromise settlement agreement to be treated as property acquired by inheritance, but the circumstances there were altogether diverse from those presently. To begin with, the case involved an heir in a *will* contest, and, thus, was framed from the beginning to end in a testamentary setting. Here, unlike in *Lyeth*, the agreement and the decree settled a suit challenging the validity of *deeds* signed, sealed and delivered before death and without reference to a testamentary environment or context. The character of that law suit determines the tax treatment.

Alternatively, as previously noted, the executor claims that the exceptions in § 2055(e)(2), permitting deductions for "split interests" where the property passing is "a remainder in a personal residence or farm or an undivided portion of the decedent's entire interest in property . . . ," would, nevertheless, allow the deductions claimed for property in which Grafton owned only the remainder interest (the three tracts in which his mother retained a life estate). This property included the residence he shared with his mother, land said to be farm land adjacent thereto, and additional business property. He left his entire remainder interest in these properties in undivided portions to his mother in the residuary trust. That which the churches could have obtained under the will thus had to pass first through the trust. Since the devises were, therefore, neither outright nor via a qualifying trust, we accept the Tax Court's construction placed on the statute, as clarified by the regulations, and conclude that the deductions claimed under the exceptions created by subsection (e)(2) were properly disallowed. 26 C.F.R. § 20.2055(e)(2)(i)–(iii).

While those persons mentioned in the will had the power to divide the property by agreement inter se, they could not maneuver their interests so as to rewrite the will and, thereby, achieve a tax savings. The State court order did not free the estate, as shaped in the will, from the Federal tax laws. Hence, the dispositions under the will stand subject to the Internal Revenue Act; the estate has not been discharged of the inheritance taxes assessed by the United States. . . .

Affirmed.

NOTES

1. *Transfers in settlement of will contests.* The deduction allowed by § 2055(a) encompasses "bequests, legacies, devises, or transfers," which means that the contribution must be made by the decedent whose estate claims the deduction. Thus, if the children of a parent who dies without a will turn the parent's property over to the family church "because that's the way Mother wanted it," the children and not the mother are making the gift, and the estate is not entitled to a deduction. When the settlement of a will contest includes a payment to a charity, it is often necessary to decide whether the charity owes its good fortune to the decedent or to the decedent's heirs.

Courts have used the rule in Lyeth v. Hoey, discussed in the principal case, to determine that the charity has received the settlement payment by inheritance from the decedent and that the estate is eligible for the § 2055(a) deduction. See, e.g., Dumont's Estate v. Commissioner, 150 F.2d 691 (3d Cir. 1945). The court in *Burgess* distinguishes *Lyeth* on the ground that the contest challenged the validity of the mother's deeds rather than the decedent's will. From which set of papers did the two churches receive their status as legatees? As the court points out, had there been no contest, the remainder to the churches in the trust created by Grafton Burgess for his mother would not have qualified for the deduction due to the restrictions on split-interest bequests (discussed infra at page 473).

At one time it seemed fairly clear that a settlement agreement could not make deductible a bequest that was nondeductible in its original form. See Robbins v. Commissioner, 111 F.2d 828 (1st Cir. 1940) (deduction denied because the settlement agreement, whereby a bequest to a college in an amount to be determined by testator's daughter was converted to a definite amount, did not alter the fact that the payment was not made "through any act of the testator"); see also Bach v. McGinnes, 333 F.2d 979 (3d Cir. 1964) (since bequest to charity was not deductible as of date of decedent's death, settlement "could not breathe life into a stillborn non-existent eligibility"); Underwood v. United States, 407 F.2d 608 (6th Cir. 1969) (deduction denied where settlement provided outright payment to charity in lieu of contingent remainder under will). The Service adopted this approach in Rev. Rul. 77–491, 1977–2 C.B. 332 (no deduction for an outright charitable transfer that resulted from a post-mortem modification pursuant to a compromise agreement). In Rev. Rul. 78–152, 1978–1 C.B. 296, however, the Service distinguished Rev. Rul. 77–491 and allowed a deduction for an amount that became payable to charity under decedent's will by virtue of a widow's election against the will, although the original bequest would not have been deductible. In Flanagan v. United States, 810 F.2d 930 (10th Cir. 1987), the court allowed a deduction for an outright payment made to charity in settlement of a will contest, even though the will provisions gave the charity a nonqualifying remainder interest. The court rejected the Service's attempt to distinguish a surviving spouse's right to elect against a will from the right of heirs or legatees to contest a will as "a distinction without a difference," and concluded that "the settlement of a bona fide will contest is no more a post-mortem amendment of the will than a spouse's election." See also Strock's Estate v. United States, 655 F.Supp. 1334 (W.D. Pa. 1987).

Following these decisions, the Service reconsidered its position, revoked Rev. Rul. 77–491, and ruled that if an estate, in settlement of a bona fide will contest, makes an outright payment to charity in lieu of a split-interest remainder under the will, the estate is entitled to a charitable deduction even though no deduction would have been allowed for the bequest in its original form. Rev. Rul. 89–31, 1989–1 C.B. 277. The ruling warns, however, that the Service will scrutinize settlements to guard against collusive attempts to circumvent the provisions of § 2055(e)(2) concerning split-interest transfers. See Burdick v. Commissioner, 979 F.2d 1369 (9th Cir. 1992) (deduction denied where church accepted commuted value of nonqualifying remainder, in absence of bona fide will contest; sole purpose was to avoid split-interest rules); La Meres' Estate v. Commissioner, 98 T.C. 294 (1992) (post-death modification that had "no nontax purpose" failed to secure deduction for otherwise nonqualifying bequest).

2. *Disclaimers.* If in the *Burgess* case there had been no other complicating factors, could the decedent's mother have renounced her interest in the trust by a qualified disclaimer that met the requirements of § 2518 and thereby rendered the remainder interests of the churches deductible under § 2055(a)? Recall that under § 2518 a disclaimed interest in property is treated as if it "had never been transferred" to the person making the disclaimer. See Chapter 2, Section E.

In some situations, a disclaimer may not only salvage a deduction for an otherwise nondeductible bequest, but also generate tax savings for the testator's family that greatly exceed the value of the disclaimed interest. Suppose that the testator leaves $1 million in trust for charitable purposes, subject to a power of invasion to provide support for the testator's mother in case of need, and directs that the rest of the estate, amounting to $5 million, be distributed to the testator's children. The power to invade, which disqualifies the trust for the charitable deduction, may be of minor importance if the mother is elderly and has substantial resources of her own. A qualified disclaimer by the mother of her interest in the trust will produce a $1 million deduction for the charitable bequest and increase the children's legacy by the resulting estate tax savings. Even if the mother does not disclaim her interest but dies within nine months after the testator and before the power of invasion has been exercised, the "complete termination" of the power is treated as a qualified disclaimer. § 2055(a).

3. *Indirect transfers.* Occasionally a parent leaves a bequest to a child who upon becoming a member of a religious order has taken a solemn vow of poverty and renounced all interests in property in favor of the order. The courts have consistently denied a charitable deduction, even though the child's bequest passes to the order, on the ground that the transfer to charity is effectuated not by the parent's will but by the child's vow of poverty. Cox v. Commissioner, 297 F.2d 36 (2d Cir. 1961); Callaghan's Estate v. Commissioner, 33 T.C. 870 (1960); Barry's Estate v. Commissioner, 311 F.2d 681 (9th Cir. 1962); Lamson's Estate v. United States, 338 F.2d 376 (Ct. Cl. 1964). By similar reasoning, it has been held that no deduction is allowed for intestate property that passes to the state by escheat. Senft v. United States, 319 F.2d 642 (3d Cir. 1963). See also Engelman's Estate v. Commissioner, 121 T.C. 54 (2003) (deduction denied for unrestricted bequest to Israel, despite donee's official act directing use exclusively for charitable purposes; "The donor, not the donee, must restrict use of the gift to charitable purposes.").

In Pickard's Estate v. Commissioner, 60 T.C. 618 (1973), affd. mem., 503 F.2d 1404 (6th Cir. 1974), the decedent left her residuary estate in trust to pay an annuity to her mother for life, with remainder to the decedent's stepfather. The stepfather died shortly before the decedent, leaving his own residuary estate in trust to pay income to the decedent's mother for life with remainder to two charities. Thus, at the time of the decedent's death, the two charities received an indefeasibly vested remainder interest in her residuary estate. The Tax Court denied a charitable deduction because the decedent's will contained no indication of charitable intent: "at the very least, the instrument of testamentary disposition must sufficiently articulate, either directly or through appropriate incorporation by reference of another document, the manifestation of decedent's charitable bounty." 60 T.C. at 622.

4. *Death taxes and other charges against charitable bequests.* Section 2055(c) provides that if any death taxes are payable out of the charitable bequest, the deduction is limited to the net amount receivable by the charity. This provision overrules the holding of Edwards v. Slocum, 264 U.S. 61 (1924), which allowed a deduction for the gross amount of a residuary bequest to charities even though the net value of the bequest received by the charities was reduced by federal and state death taxes. For a review of the legislative history, see Bush's Estate v. United States, 618 F.2d 741 (Ct. Cl. 1980). Since the taxes that are due depend on the size of the charitable deduction and vice versa, computation of the taxes payable in such cases requires trial and error or the use of algebraic formulas, details of which may be found in I.R.S. Publication 904 (May 1985); see also Taussig, Kimball & Sprague, Iterated Equations for Vicious Circle Tax Problems: Manual and Computer–Assisted Solutions, 49 Taxes 538 (1971).

The courts have imposed a similar limitation without statutory authority where a charitable bequest is reduced by other types of charges, such as administration expenses and claims against the estate. Luehrmann's Estate v. Commissioner, 287 F.2d 10 (8th Cir. 1961) (requiring that deduction for charitable residuary bequest be reduced to reflect administration expenses paid out of the residue, even though executor elected to deduct the expenses on the estate's income tax return rather than on the estate tax return); Burke v. United States, 994 F.2d 1576 (Fed. Cir.), cert. denied, 510 U.S. 990 (1993) (same where expenses were charged to income rather than corpus). This issue was revisited in Commissioner v. Hubert's Estate, 520 U.S. 93 (1997), where the Supreme Court allowed a charitable deduction without any reduction for administration expenses that were paid from post-mortem income generated by the assets allocated to the charitable share.

In response to the *Hubert* decision, the Treasury promulgated new regulations concerning the effect of administration expenses on the charitable deduction. The regulations divide administration expenses into two categories: "estate management expenses" and "estate transmission expenses." The former category includes expenses incurred in investing, preserving, or maintaining estate assets during a reasonable period of administration. The latter category covers all other administration expenses, including those incurred in collecting the decedent's assets, paying debts and death taxes, and distributing the remaining assets to beneficiaries. In general, estate management expenses attributable to the charitable share can be paid from the charitable share with no adverse effect on the charitable deduction, but estate transmission expenses paid from the charitable share give rise to a dollar-for-dollar reduction in the charitable deduction. Reg. § 20.2055–3(b). See also infra page 535, Note 2, discussing a similar issue in connection with the marital deduction.

3. SPLIT-INTEREST BEQUESTS: TRANSFERS FOR BOTH CHARITABLE AND PRIVATE PURPOSES

Section 2055(e)(2), enacted in 1969, imposes severe restrictions on the deductibility of charitable transfers if an interest in the same property passes or has passed (for less than adequate and full consideration in money or money's worth) from the decedent to a private individual or for any other noncharitable use. The decedent's will in Burgess' Estate v. Commissioner, supra page 467, provides an example of the kind of trust that is the target of the legislation. It directed that decedent's mother have the use of the property for life and that the remainder at her death be paid to two churches, with a discretionary power in the trustees to invade the corpus for her support. The legislation also applies to the converse situation, the so-called charitable lead trust, where the income is payable to a charity for a term of years and the remainder to noncharitable beneficiaries (e.g., children) designated by the decedent. The restrictions, which also apply to the deductions allowed by §§ 170 and 2522 for income and gift tax purposes, are designed to prevent powers over investments and discretionary distributions from being exercised in a manner that benefits the noncharitable beneficiaries at the expense of the charity's interest, and thus to ensure that the amount deducted is commensurate with the benefit actually received by the charity. The restrictions seek to accomplish this result by disregarding traditional fiduciary accounting distinctions between principal and income, which are subject to manipulation through investment decisions and discretionary allocations, and by treating the underlying property and its income as, roughly speaking, a single fund.

In reading the following case, consider in what ways, if any, the trustee can manipulate the trust fund to the disadvantage of the charities.

EDGAR'S ESTATE v. COMMISSIONER

74 T.C. 983 (1980), affd. mem., 676 F.2d 685 (3d Cir. 1982).

IRWIN, JUDGE.

Respondent determined a deficiency in petitioner's estate tax of $28,074.21. Due to concessions, the only issue remaining for our consideration is whether petitioner is entitled to a charitable deduction for the value of the remainder interest of a trust which was bequeathed to qualifying institutions (within the meaning of sec. 2055(a)(2)).

All of the facts have been stipulated, and the stipulation of facts is incorporated herein by this reference. At the time the petition was filed herein, Century National Bank & Trust Co., Executor of the Estate of Clara E. Edgar (hereafter estate), was a national banking corporation, organized under the laws of the United States and having its principal place of business at New Brighton, Pa.

By trust agreements dated August 29, 1961, Clara E. Edgar (hereafter sometimes referred to as decedent) and her sister, Jean Edgar Vaughan, created reciprocal revocable inter vivos trusts.

Pursuant to the terms of her trust agreement, decedent transferred stocks, bonds, notes, and other assets to the Union National Bank, as trustee.

According to the terms of decedent's trust agreement, the income of the trust was to be paid to her during her life. After her death, the income was to be paid to Jean Edgar Vaughan. The agreement provided that the trustee had the power, in its discretion, to "distribute to or apply for the benefit of the Donor, Clara E. Edgar, and her sister, Jean Edgar Vaughan, such amounts out of the principal of the trust estate held for said beneficiaries, as shall in the judgment of the trustee be necessitated by reason of illness or other emergency or inadequacy of the income, for the adequate support and the necessities of such beneficiaries." Upon the death of the survivor of the two sisters, the trust was to terminate. Several specific dispositions from the trust's principal were required, but the residue of the principal, and any accrued income, were to be poured over into Jean Edgar Vaughan's trust fund and be distributed "in accordance with the terms and conditions as in said Trust Agreement."

According to the terms of the Jean Edgar Vaughan Trust Agreement, the income of said trust was to be paid to Jean Edgar Vaughan. After her death, the income was to be paid to Clara E. Edgar. This trust agreement also contained the following provision:

> The Trustee named may, from time to time, in its discretion distribute to or apply for the benefit of any beneficiary, from time to time, entitled to the receipt or application for his or her benefit of income hereunder, such amounts out of the principal of the trust estate held for such beneficiary, as shall in the judgment of the Trustee be necessitated by reason of illness or other emergency, or inadequacy of income, for the adequate support and the necessities of such beneficiary.

Upon the death of the survivor of the two sisters, the trust was to terminate. Several specific dispositions from the trust's principal were required, but the residue of the principal was placed in trust with the Union National Bank as trustee. The agreement further provided that from the net income of the latter trust, these would be paid during each of their lives: $75 per month to Harriet T. Norris; $100 per month to Anna M. Ott; $150 per month to Virginia I. Reinehr; and, by means of the supplement to the agreement of August 29, 1961, $50 per month to Martha Powers. The remaining income was to be distributed equally among several religious, educational, or charitable institutions, all of which qualified within the meaning of section 2055(a)(2). The agreement provided that, as each of the four life beneficiaries died, her share of the income of the trust would pass to the institutions.

Jean Edgar Vaughan died on December 9, 1965.

Clara E. Edgar died testate on March 22, 1973. By decedent's last will and testament, dated April 21, 1966, she bequeathed the residue of her testamentary estate to the Jean Edgar Vaughan trust created by agreement of August 29, 1961, "for the uses and purposes set forth herein." At the time of Clara Edgar's death, the Jean Vaughan trust fund's principal was valued at approximately $249,000. During 1973, the trust generated income of $13,149. The property previously transferred by decedent to the Clara E. Edgar trust had a value of $138,170.24 at the time of her death.

On December 30, 1975, petitioner applied to the Orphans Court Division of the Court of Common Pleas of Beaver County, Pa., seeking to obtain a construction of the Clara E. Edgar Will and Trust Agreement and the Jean Edgar Vaughan Trust Agreement. The court decreed, in pertinent part, as follows:

> 2. That paragraph of the Jean Edgar Vaughan trust created August 29, 1961, reading as follows, and thus incorporated by reference in the decedent's trust as set forth above:
>
>> The Trustee named may, from time to time, in its discretion distribute to or apply for the benefit of any beneficiary, from time to time, entitled to the receipt or application for his or her benefit of income hereunder, such amounts out of the principal of the trust estate held for such beneficiary, as shall in the judgment of the Trustee be necessitated by reason of illness or other emergency, or inadequacy of the income, for the adequate support and the necessities of such beneficiary.
>
> is hereby construed to apply only to the life estates reserved and/or granted to or for the benefit of Jean Edgar Vaughan and Clara E. Edgar, such reservation and/or grant being contained in the two paragraphs immediately preceding the principal invasion clause quoted above in full.
>
> 3. Following the deaths of Jean Edgar Vaughan on December 19,[15] 1965 and Clara Edgar on March 22, 1973 no beneficiaries of the decedent's trust had any interest in the principal thereof except the five named charitable beneficiaries, viz: Passavant Homes (Rochester), First Presbyterian Church (New Brighton), The Lighthouse (New Brighton), Hillsdale College and The Salvation Army (Beaver Falls Barracks).
>
> 4. Following the deaths of the above-named life tenants, the trustee neither had nor has any power to invade principal for the benefit of any beneficiary, specifically including the following annuitants or income beneficiaries: Hariett [sic] Townsend North, Anna M. Ott, Virginia Inman Reinehr and Martha Powers.

In its estate tax return, petitioner claimed as a charitable deduction under section 2055(a)(2) the entire net balance of the decedent's estate,

15. The parties stipulated that the date is Dec. 9, 1965.

amounting to $179,982.89. Petitioner has conceded that the correct amount should be $142,000.[16]

Respondent contends that the transfer in question is a split interest and subject to the provisions of section 2055(e) because interests in the same property (the income of the trust) passed both to qualifying institutions (within the meaning of sec. 2055(a)(2)) and to nonqualifying individuals. In such cases, no deduction is permitted unless, in the case of a remainder interest, the interest passes to a charitable remainder annuity trust, a charitable remainder unitrust, or a pooled income fund, or, in the case of all other interest, the interest is in the form of a guaranteed annuity or is a fixed percentage, distributed yearly, of the fair market value of the property.

Petitioner argues to the contrary that the nonqualifying beneficiaries have no interest in the income of the trust and, therefore, section 2055(e)(2) does not apply to disallow the charitable deduction. This argument is based upon petitioner's contention that the trust fund created by Jean Edgar Vaughan will generate enough income to fully satisfy the income interests of the individual, noncharitable beneficiaries, and that decedent's residuary estate, considered as a separate trust, will, therefore, never be invaded for the benefit of the nonqualifying beneficiaries.[17] Petitioner points out that at the time of decedent's death, the Jean Vaughan trust was valued at $249,000 and generated income of $13,149 in 1973.

The essence of petitioner's argument, thus, is that where the economic facts concerning a transfer which provides for nonqualifying beneficiaries to receive a part interest in property are such that those beneficiaries will never receive any portion of that part interest, section 2055(e) is inapplicable. We disagree. Section 2055(e)(2) was enacted in 1969, effective with respect to decedents dying after December 31, 1969 (with certain exceptions, not here relevant), Pub. L. 91–172, sec. 201(d)(1), 83 Stat. 487, 549, in order to correct perceived abuses in the charitable contributions area. One of these abuses was the manner in which trust assets might be invested: for example, maximizing income interests by investing in high-income, high-risk assets, thus enhancing the value of the income interest but decreasing the value of the charity's remainder interest. To provide a closer correlation between the charitable contributions deduction and the ultimate benefit to charity, Congress provided rules which have to be met before a gift can qualify for a deduction. H. Rept. 91–413 (1969), 1969-3 C.B. 200, 237–239. Although this specific situation may not have been regarded as abusive by Congress when it enacted this legislation,[18] as

16. Net amount passing from decedent's estate less the value of the nonqualifying individuals' life estates in the trust income.

17. The discretionary authority of the trustee to invade principal was held, in a county court proceeding, inapplicable after the death of decedent and her sister.

18. We note, however, that the annual distribution from such a charitable remainder trust must be an amount equal to at least 5 percent of the value of the trust's assets in order to qualify as either a charitable remainder annuity trust or a charitable remainder unitrust. Sec. 664(d)(1)

petitioner contends, permitting economic factors to be considered would directly contradict Congress' intent to establish specific rules in this area. It is clear that the trust document created, in legal terms, a remainder interest in favor of the charitable institutions. We hold that such an interest must in all events conform to the statutory requirements.

Petitioner apparently concedes that the trust fails to meet the statutory requirements set forth in sections 2055(e)(2)(A) (which are, in turn, set forth in secs. 664 and 642(c)(5)) and 2055(e)(2)(B).

In the alternative, petitioner contends that because the value of the annuitants' interests in the trust can be definitely ascertained and valued using the standard tables for valuing annuities, the trust qualifies under section 2055, relying on sec. 20.2055–2(a), Estate Tax Regs.

Prior to the enactment of section 2055(e)(2), a deduction was allowed for the charitable remainder in a trust created for private purposes if the remainder was readily ascertainable and hence severable from the noncharitable interest. Sec. 20.2055–2(a), Estate Tax Regs.; Henslee v. Union Planters National Bank & Trust Co., 335 U.S. 595 (1949), rehearing denied, 336 U.S. 915 (1949); Merchants National Bank of Boston v. Commissioner, 320 U.S. 256 (1943). As stated above, however, the law in this area was changed for decedents dying after December 31, 1969, and the regulation upon which petitioner relies is, by its own terms, inapplicable to decedents dying after December 31, 1969. . . .

NOTES

1. *Power to invade for noncharitable purposes.* The regulations have long provided that where property is transferred for both charitable and noncharitable purposes, no deduction is allowed for an interest passing to charity unless that interest is "presently ascertainable, and hence severable from the noncharitable interest." Reg. § 20.2055–2(a). Furthermore, if a trustee or a beneficiary has a power to invade or consume the property or otherwise divert it from charitable purposes, the deduction is limited to "that portion, if any, of the property or fund which is exempt from an exercise of the power." Reg. § 20.2055–2(b)(1).

Prior to the enactment of § 2055(e)(2), the courts were often called on to determine whether a charitable remainder qualified for the deduction where the underlying property was subject to a power of invasion in favor of an

---

and (d)(2). This provision was enacted to prevent a charitable remainder trust from being used to circumvent the current income distribution requirement imposed on private foundations. S. Rept. 91–552 (1969), 1969–3 C.B. 481. In the absence of these rules, a charitable remainder trust could provide for a minimal payout to the noncharitable income beneficiary (substantially less than the amount of the trust income). Since the trust generally is exempt from income taxes, see sec. 664(c), this would allow it to accumulate trust income in excess of the payout requirement of the unitrust or annuity trust without tax for the future benefit of charity. It is not at all clear, therefore, that such a trust was not considered to be potentially abusive. This reason, alone, is sufficient to find that the trust fails to meet the remainder annuity trust requirements, sec. 664(d)(1), even if we were to consider the two trusts to be separate (although by its terms decedent's trust poured over to Jean Edgar Vaughan's trust). Sec. 664(d)(3), which provides an exception to the "5 percent" rule if certain requirements are met, is not applicable here.

individual income beneficiary. In Ithaca Trust Co. v. United States, 279 U.S. 151 (1929), a landmark case decided before the promulgation of the "presently ascertainable" standard in the regulations, the Supreme Court allowed the deduction because the income was more than sufficient to maintain the life tenant and the life tenant's power of invasion was limited by an ascertainable standard that precluded any real uncertainty in valuing the charitable remainder. In two later cases, the Court applied the regulations and denied the deduction where the trustees were given such broad discretion to invade corpus for the income beneficiaries that the value of the charitable remainders could not readily be ascertained. Merchants Natl. Bank v. Commissioner, 320 U.S. 256 (1943); Henslee v. Union Planters Natl. Bank & Trust Co., 335 U.S. 595 (1949). The difficulty encountered by the courts in applying these principles, due to wide variations in the standards governing powers of invasion and in the personal and financial circumstances of income beneficiaries, was a major cause of the dissatisfaction that led to the enactment in 1969 of § 2055(e)(2) concerning split-interest transfers.

In Marine's Estate v. Commissioner, 990 F.2d 136 (4th Cir. 1993), the decedent left his residuary estate of more than $2 million to two charities, but in a codicil authorized his personal representatives "in their sole and absolute discretion, to compensate persons who have contributed to my well-being or who have been otherwise helpful to me during my lifetime." Although the amount payable to any single recipient was limited to one percent of the estate, the number of possible recipients was virtually unlimited. In fact, the personal representatives made only two awards, one for $10,000 and the other for $15,000. The court disallowed the entire charitable deduction because on the date of decedent's death there was no standard by which the amount of the charitable bequests could be ascertained. See also Johnson's Estate v. United States, 941 F.2d 1318 (5th Cir. 1991) (decedent left entire estate in trust for support of her sisters, maintenance of family graves, and education of Catholic priests and nuns; no deduction allowed, despite subsequent funding of separate shares; decedent's will established "no upward limit" on sisters' support needs and there was "no way to divide the entire estate between the charitable and noncharitable beneficiaries" due to their conflicting interests).

2. *Conditional charitable bequests.* Charitable bequests are sometimes conditioned on post-mortem events, such as the charity's success in raising matching funds, a child's death without issue, naming a building after the testator, or continued use of property for a specified purpose. Because the property can pass to the decedent's other beneficiaries or intestate successors if the prescribed condition does not occur or is subsequently broken, it is impossible to be certain at the date of death that the bequest will be used exclusively for charitable purposes. The regulations adopt a common-sense approach to this problem by disregarding possibilities that are excessively speculative: "no deduction is allowable unless the possibility that the charitable transfer will not become effective is so remote as to be negligible." Reg. § 20.2055–2(b)(1). For applications of this approach, see Rev. Rul. 67–229, 1967–2 C.B. 335 (bequest to existing orphanage conditioned on continued operation in county of decedent's residence; deduction allowed in absence of any evidence of intent to move or cease operations); cf. Woodworth's Estate v.

Commissioner, 47 T.C. 193 (1966) (deduction disallowed for a bequest contingent on the establishment of a Catholic hospital in the county where decedent resided, since there was more than a negligible possibility that such a hospital would not come into existence). The deduction may be saved if under local law the cy pres doctrine ensures that the funds will be used for another charitable purpose in the event the decedent's specific objective cannot be achieved. See Rev. Rul. 72–442, 1972–2 C.B. 527 (deduction allowed where funds were insufficient to establish a nonprofit retirement home, but cy pres doctrine required that funds be used for other charitable purposes).

Where a charitable remainder is subject to conditions that can be measured actuarially, the Service has established a 5–percent threshold for determining whether there is a significant possibility that the charitable remainder may fail. Thus, if a charity will receive property at the death of the life tenant only if the life tenant's sibling is not then living, no deduction is allowed if the probability of the sibling's survival is greater than 5 percent. Rev. Rul. 85–23, 1985–1 C.B. 327; see also Rev. Rul. 70–452, 1970–2 C.B. 199 (probability that annuity payments to individual beneficiary will exhaust fund before charitable remainder becomes possessory); Rev. Rul. 77–374, 1977–2 C.B. 329 (same, with illustrative computation); United States v. Dean, 224 F.2d 26 (1st Cir. 1955) (no deduction for charitable bequest that would be defeated if 82–year–old woman outlived two women age 67 and 68; 9–percent probability of survival was not negligible).

3. *"Same property" requirement.* Section 2055(e)(2) applies only if "an interest in property ... passes or has passed from the decedent [to or for charitable purposes] and an interest in the same property passes or has passed (for less than an adequate and full consideration in money or money's worth) [to or for noncharitable purposes]." By this test, a transfer that splits decedent's entire interest in the property between two or more charities is entitled to the deduction under § 2055(a) without meeting the special requirements of § 2055(e)(2). Does the exemption similarly apply to a transfer of the entire interest that the decedent ever owned in property, even though it consists of an interest that would not be deductible if the decedent had carved it out of a larger property? For example, assume that a deceased parent created a trust to pay the income to child *A* for life with remainder at *A*'s death to child *B*. *B* dies during *A*'s lifetime, bequeathing the remainder interest to charity. Is the remainder to charity, to the extent includible in *B*'s gross estate, deductible without reference to § 2055(e)(2)?

The "same property" requirement seeks to prevent the division of a single property into two bundles of rights, one of which can be administered in such a way as to enhance the value of the other, thus benefiting the noncharitable beneficiary at the charity's expense. For example, if the decedent left property in trust to pay income to *A* for life with remainder at *A*'s death to charity, the trustee might be inclined to favor *A* in selecting investments and allocating items to income or principal. The same problem could arise if the decedent created an inter vivos trust to pay income to *A* for life and retained a reversionary interest which decedent then left to charity by will. In both cases, the decedent created charitable and noncharitable interests in the same property, thus bringing the requirements of § 2055(e)(2) into force. Cf. § 2055(e)(4), which treats a work of art and the copyright thereon as separate properties for purposes of § 2055(e)(2) if certain conditions are met.

If the foregoing threshold conditions of § 2055(e)(2) are met, the charitable interest does not qualify for the deduction unless it comes within one of the statutory safe harbors for (1) charitable remainder trusts or pooled income funds, (2) charitable lead trusts, (3) transfers of an undivided portion of the decedent's entire interest in property, (4) remainder interests in the decedent's personal residence or farm, or (5) so-called qualified conservation contributions. Under certain conditions set forth in § 2055(e)(3), a charitable interest that would have been deductible but for the split-interest rules of § 2055(e)(2) may be reformed so that it complies with those rules and qualifies for the deduction. See Tamulis' Estate v. Commissioner, 509 F.3d 343 (7th Cir. 2007) (no deduction allowed for charitable remainder following income interest in family members, even though trust was administered as if it were a qualified charitable remainder unitrust, in absence of qualified reformation).

4. *Charitable remainder trusts and pooled income funds.* If a charitable remainder interest is subject to § 2055(e)(2), it qualifies for the deduction under § 2055(a) only if it is in a charitable remainder annuity trust (as defined in § 664(d)(1)), a charitable remainder unitrust (as defined in § 664(d)(2)), or a pooled income fund (as defined in § 642(c)(5)).

In general, a charitable remainder trust is a trust which provides for distributions (payable at least annually) to one or more noncharitable beneficiaries for life or a term of not more than 20 years, followed by a charitable remainder interest. The remainder interest must be irrevocable and not subject to invasion for the benefit of any noncharitable beneficiary (except for the required periodic distributions). Furthermore, the value of the remainder interest must initially be at least 10 percent of the net fair market value of the underlying trust property. The periodic distributions to noncharitable beneficiaries may be either in the form of an annuity (i.e., a fixed amount equal to at least 5 percent but not more than 50 percent of the initial net fair market value of the trust property) or a unitrust interest (i.e., a fixed percentage—at least 5 percent but not more than 50 percent—of the net fair market value of the trust property, valued annually).

Unlike an annuity trust, which requires fixed annual payments, a unitrust automatically apportions annual increases (or decreases) in the value of the trust assets between the charitable and noncharitable beneficiaries. This advantage is counterbalanced, however, by the administrative burden of valuing the trust assets each year to determine the amount of the unitrust payments. Annual valuations may be especially burdensome if the trust is funded with real estate or closely held business interests.

A detailed exposition of the statutory requirements for both types of charitable remainder trusts appears in Reg. §§ 1.664–2 and 1.664–3. See also 3 Bittker & Lokken, Federal Taxation of Income, Estates and Gifts ¶ 82.1.2 (3d ed. 2001). Sample forms of charitable remainder annuity trusts are set forth in a series of revenue procedures beginning with Rev. Proc. 2003–53, 2003–2 C.B. 230; similar forms for charitable remainder unitrusts appear in a series of revenue procedures beginning with Rev. Proc. 2005–52, 2005–2 C.B.

326. A charitable remainder trust must function exclusively as such from the time of its creation; it is not enough that the trust instrument includes the required provisions if they are flouted in practice. See Atkinson's Estate v. Commissioner, 115 T.C. 26 (2000), affd., 309 F.3d 1290 (11th Cir. 2002), cert. denied, 540 U.S. 946 (2003) (no estate tax deduction for charitable remainder where trust failed to make required distributions to settlor during life).

For estate tax purposes, charitable remainder interests are valued on the assumption that the periodic annuity or unitrust payments will begin as of the date of death, but in practice a testamentary trust cannot begin to make the required distributions until the trust is funded with assets received from the executor. For this reason, Reg. § 1.664–1(a)(5) allows the time for making actual payments to be deferred, but the Service requires that the governing instrument provide for corrective payments to remedy any underpayment or overpayment of the required amounts. Rev. Proc. 2003–57, 2003–2 C.B. 257; Rev. Proc. 2005–56, 2005–2 C.B. 383.

Query: If the split-interest rules are intended to protect the charity from manipulation of the fund to its detriment, why establish a minimum amount that must be paid out each year to noncharitable beneficiaries? For a partial answer, see the Tax Court's opinion in Edgar's Estate v. Commissioner, supra page 476, footnote 18.

A pooled income fund is a trust or other fund maintained by a charitable organization as a vehicle for contributions by donors who wish to retain for themselves, or for one or more designated beneficiaries, a life income interest in the property. The donor must irrevocably assign the remainder interest to the charitable organization that maintains the fund; the contributions of all donors are commingled in a single fund, and the payout to income beneficiaries is determined by the rate of return earned by the fund as a whole. Furthermore, as each income beneficiary dies, a ratable portion of the corpus is removed from the fund and becomes the property of the charity. See 3 Bittker & Lokken, supra, ¶ 82.1.3. Sample provisions for the governing instruments to obtain these benefits are set out in Rev. Rul. 82–38, 1982–1 C.B. 96; see also Rev. Rul. 85–57, 1985–1 C.B. 182; Rev. Rul. 90–103, 1990–2 C.B. 159; Rev. Rul. 92–81, 1992–2 C.B. 119.

5. *Charitable lead trusts.* In a charitable lead trust, the charitable interest precedes distributions to private individuals. For the taxpayer, a charitable lead trust offers the satisfaction of making a tax-deductible contribution to charity, even though all or a substantial part of the trust corpus will ultimately pass to children or other noncharitable beneficiaries. The charitable lead interest is valued under the actuarial tables prescribed by § 7520. Fluctuations of a few percentage points in the annual rate of return can have a dramatic impact on the amount of the charitable deduction, as illustrated in the following examples.

Testator leaves $10 million of 10–percent bonds in trust to pay Yale University an annuity of $800,000 per year for 24 years. Using a 6–percent annual rate of return, the value of this annuity exceeds the amount transferred, and thus the full amount of the bequest is covered by the deduction. Reg. § 20.2031–7(d)(6) (Table B). (Since the factor for a 24–year annuity of $1 is 12.5504, an annuity of $800,000 is worth $10,040,320 ($800,000 ×

12.5504), but the deduction cannot exceed the amount transferred.) The trust will earn $200,000 per year more than it is required to pay Yale and can reinvest this excess, after taxes, and pay over the accumulation plus the bonds to the remainder beneficiaries at the end of the 24–year period.

Using a 10–percent annual rate of return, the annuity factor for a 24–year annuity of $1 is 8.9847. Thus, the value of a 24–year annuity of $800,000 is only $7,187,760 ($800,000 × 8.9847), leaving $2,812,240 ($10,000,000 − $7,187,760) subject to tax. Reg. § 20.2031–7(d)(6) (Table B). A taxpayer who seeks to eliminate the tax by increasing the annuity amount will discover that it requires an annuity of slightly more than $1,113,000 in the above example to obtain a full deduction. An extension of the annuity's life will also increase its value, but the increases are small and come at a high cost in additional years. For example, at a 10–percent annual rate of return, a 48–year annuity of $800,000 is worth $7,917,520, meaning that a 100–percent increase in the number of years increases the value of the annuity by approximately 10 percent.

The testator's estate is entitled to a deduction under § 2055(e)(2) for a charitable lead trust only if the charity's interest is either a guaranteed annuity or a unitrust interest (i.e., annual distributions equal to a fixed percentage of the fair market value of the property, calculated annually). Sample forms of charitable lead annuity trusts are set forth in Rev. Proc. 2007–45, 2007–2 C.B. 89, and Rev. Proc. 2007–46, 2007–2 C.B. 102; similar forms for charitable lead unitrusts appear in Rev. Proc. 2008–45, 2008–30 C.B. 224, and Rev. Proc. 2008–46, 2008–30 C.B. 238. Many taxpayers prefer the annuity arrangement because the corpus need not be valued each year and any appreciation in the value of the corpus will pass with the remainder to the noncharitable beneficiaries. The requirements for a charitable lead trust are generally a mirror image of those for a charitable remainder trust, except that the payout is not subject to minimum or maximum percentages, and the term of a lead trust may be for any specified term of years (not limited to 20 years) or for the life of one or more individuals who are living and ascertained at the testator's death. The permissible measuring lives are limited to the testator's spouse and the ancestors (or spouses of ancestors) of the remainder beneficiaries, in order to discourage the use of "vulture" lead trusts in which a seriously ill individual, unrelated to the testator or the remainder beneficiaries, is selected as the measuring life.

6. *Charitable lead annuity trusts and the GST tax.* It is, of course, possible to create a charitable lead trust in which the remainder passes at the end of the lead term to beneficiaries two or more generations below the transferor's generation. For purposes of the generation-skipping transfer tax, a charitable organization is assigned to the transferor's generation. Thus, if a settlor creates a trust to pay an annuity to a charity for 20 years and then to distribute the remaining trust property to the settlor's grandchildren, a generation-skipping transfer tax will be imposed at the end of the 20–year term. Under § 2642(e), the "inclusion ratio" (representing the portion of the trust that is subject to GST tax) is computed at the end of the 20–year term, by reference to an "applicable fraction" (representing the portion of the trust that is exempt from GST tax) equal to (1) the amount of the GST exemption allocated to the trust increased by an interest factor based on the annual rate

of return used in determining the charitable deduction and the actual duration of the lead term, divided by (2) the value of the trust property at the end of the lead term. This provision is intended to prevent taxpayers from using charitable lead trusts to leverage the tax benefit of the GST exemption. The GST exemption, the inclusion ratio, and the applicable fraction are discussed infra at page 563.

7. *Undivided portion of decedent's entire interest in property.* Section 2055(e)(2) contains a parenthetical exception for interests described in § 170(f)(3)(B), relating to income tax deductions for charitable contributions. Under this provision, a bequest or other transfer, not in trust, of "an undivided portion of the [decedent's] entire interest in property" can qualify for a charitable deduction under § 2055 without regard to the split-interest rules of § 2055(e)(2). For example, if a decedent leaves property to a charity and decedent's child as tenants in common, the value of the charity's interest is deductible. Although the bequest creates both a charitable and a noncharitable interest in the same property, it does not permit the abuses that § 2055(e)(2) was enacted to prevent. Recall, however, that the safe harbor is limited to non-trust transfers. Thus, no deduction is allowed if the decedent leaves property in trust to pay income in equal shares to charity and to a child during the child's life, with half the remainder payable to charity and half to the child's heirs. Rev. Rul. 77–97, 1977–1 C.B. 285; Galloway v. United States, 492 F.3d 219 (3d Cir. 2007). Is this the type of abusive split-interest transfer at which § 2055(e)(2) is aimed?

8. *Personal residences, farms, and conservation interests.* A charitable devise of a remainder interest in the decedent's personal residence (including a vacation home) or in a farm is deductible without regard to the split-interest rules. This exemption results from the incorporation by reference into § 2055(e)(2) of § 170(f)(3)(B), which applies only to contributions that are not made in trust. Is the deduction allowed if by the terms of the transfer the personal residence is to be sold at the life tenant's death and the proceeds paid to charity? See Rev. Rul. 77–169, 1977–1 C.B. 286 (deduction denied); Blackford's Estate v. Commissioner, 77 T.C. 1246 (1981) (acq.) (deduction allowed); Rev. Rul. 83–158, 1983–2 C.B. 159 (deduction allowed where charity had option to receive residence instead of sale proceeds).

Similarly, the split-interest rules do not apply to a charitable devise of a "qualified conservation contribution," which is defined in § 170(h)(2) as a remainder interest in real property granted to a charitable organization for such purposes as preserving land for public outdoor recreation or educational use; protecting habitats for fish, wildlife, or plants; or preserving open space for scenic enjoyment.

9. *Gift tax treatment of split-interest gifts.* Lifetime gifts to charities are deductible in the same manner as testamentary transfers. They also provide opportunities for income tax deductions and for the transfer of appreciated assets to members of the donor's family and other private beneficiaries without incurring a tax on the capital gain. Section 2522, which authorizes the gift tax charitable deduction, parallels the estate tax provisions of § 2055 except for a few minor differences in wording. Specifically, § 2522(c)(2) imposes the same restrictions as § 2055(e)(2) on the deductibility of charita-

ble contributions if an interest in the same property either is retained by the donor or is transferred by the donor to a private individual or for any other noncharitable purpose. Where § 2522(c)(2) applies, the donor can deduct the value of the interest transferred to charity only if (1) in the case of a remainder interest, it is in a charitable remainder annuity trust, a charitable remainder unitrust, or a pooled income fund, or (2) in the case of any other interest, it is a guaranteed annuity or a unitrust interest. As in § 2055(e)(2), certain contributions are deductible without satisfying these special rules, either because they are not covered by the threshold conditions that bring § 2522(c)(2) into play or because they are exempted by its parenthetical reference to interests described in § 170(f)(3)(B).

Special rules enacted in 2006 limit the availability of the gift tax charitable deduction when a donor contributes an undivided portion of his or her interest in tangible personal property. No deduction is allowed for such a gift unless immediately before the gift "all interests in the property" are held either by the donor alone or by the donor and the donee. § 2522(e)(1). Thus, if two siblings own a painting as tenants in common and one of them donates an undivided one-half portion of her interest to charity, the gift is nondeductible. In contrast, the deduction would not be disallowed if the sibling donated her entire interest in the painting to charity or if the sole owner of the painting donated an undivided fractional interest to charity.[19] Even if a gift of a partial interest in tangible personal property initially qualifies for a charitable deduction, the deduction is subject to recapture (with interest and a 10–percent additional tax) if (1) the donor fails to donate all of the donor's remaining interest in the property to charity within the earlier of ten years after the initial gift or the donor's death, or (2) the charitable donee does not receive "substantial physical possession of the property" or fails to use it in a manner related to the donee's charitable purpose or function during the recapture period. § 2522(e)(2).

D. MARITAL DEDUCTION: §§ 2056 AND 2523

In determining the amount of the decedent's taxable estate, a deduction is available for the value of all property included in the gross estate that passed during the decedent's life or passes at death to the decedent's surviving spouse. In addition, a gift made by one spouse to the other is deductible in determining the amount of the donor's taxable gifts. The evolution of the marital deduction from a deduction of one-half the adjusted gross estate or amount of the gift to an unlimited deduction has been described in an earlier section (see supra page 206). The deduction, however, remains subject to the qualifications and limitations prescribed by § 2056 (estate tax) and § 2523 (gift tax). This is to ensure that the

19. Similar rules apply to the income tax. In addition, for purposes of the income tax charitable deduction, if a donor makes a deductible contribution of a partial interest in tangible personal property and subsequently donates additional interests in the same property, the value of the subsequent contributions must be based on the fair market value of the property at the time of the initial contribution or the subsequent contribution, whichever is less. § 170(*o*)(2). As originally enacted, this additional limitation applied for income, gift and estate tax purposes, but it was removed from the gift and estate tax provisions in 2007 with retroactive effect.

property qualifying for the deduction, if not consumed by the surviving spouse, will be subject to either the gift tax or the estate tax when it is subsequently transferred to the couple's children or other beneficiaries.

The unlimited marital deduction permits spouses to transfer property to one another free of both gift and estate taxes, regardless of which spouse earned, inherited, or otherwise acquired the property. Accordingly, the couple can protect the property owned by the first spouse from estate tax until the survivor dies, or they can split their property so that part is taxed to the estate of the first to die and the balance is taxed at the death of the surviving spouse. On the other hand, if both spouses are independently wealthy so that there is no advantage in shifting transfer tax liability from one to the other, they can arrange for each spouse to be taxed solely on his or her own property.

1. THRESHOLD REQUIREMENTS

Section 2056(a) authorizes the marital deduction in plain language: The amount deductible is the value of any interest in property that (1) "passes or has passed from the decedent," (2) to his or her "surviving spouse," (3) "but only to the extent that such interest is included in determining the value of the gross estate." Even if property satisfies these three basic requirements, however, it may be disqualified by the complex "terminable interest" rule (see infra page 488), which is designed to ensure that marital deduction property will be taxed if and when the surviving spouse transfers it by gift or bequest.

a. Surviving Spouse

The executor has the burden of establishing the requisite marital status and survivorship of the spouse. Both issues can entail an interplay between federal and state law and, when the validity of an earlier divorce is at stake, between the law of two or more states.

The marital status at the date of death is controlling in applying § 2056(a). Thus, property transferred by gift to a donee who was not married to the decedent when the gift was made can be deducted if they are married at the date of death (provided the property is included in the decedent's gross estate and otherwise qualifies); conversely, property given to the decedent's spouse does not qualify if the spouse predeceases the decedent or if they are divorced. See Rev. Rul. 79–354, 1979–2 C.B. 334. It is likely that a legal separation or an interlocutory decree of divorce will not be sufficient to terminate a marriage if these events do not terminate the survivor's marital property rights under local law.

Marital status, like other aspects of family law, generally is determined by state law. However, the Defense of Marriage Act, enacted in 1996, defines marriage for purposes of federal law as "a legal union between one man and one woman as husband and wife." 1 U.S.C. § 7. Thus, a marriage between two men or two women is not recognized for purposes of federal law, even if the couple is legally married under applicable state law. As a result, a same-sex married couple is not entitled to file a joint federal income tax return and transfers from one spouse to the other do not qualify for a marital deduction under the federal estate and gift taxes.

In an era when divorce is commonplace, the survivor's status as the decedent's "spouse" can depend on whether at the time of their marriage the decedent, the survivor, or both were validly divorced from a prior mate. This question at times cannot be answered without choosing among the conflicting laws of two or more states or foreign countries. In Steffke's Estate v. Commissioner, 538 F.2d 730 (7th Cir.), cert. denied, 429 U.S. 1022 (1976), the court held that property passing to decedent's "wife" did not qualify for the marital deduction because the wife's Mexican divorce from a prior husband was held invalid after decedent's death. The court reviewed the authorities and set the following as its test:

> When there are conflicting judicial decrees regarding the validity of a divorce, the decision should be followed for federal estate taxation purposes that would be followed by the state which has primary jurisdiction over the administration of a decedent's estate, i.e., the jurisdiction in which the decedent was domiciled at the time of his death. [538 F.2d at 735.]

See also Goldwater's Estate v. Commissioner, 539 F.2d 878 (2d Cir.), cert. denied, 429 U.S. 1023 (1976) (decedent remarried after a Mexican divorce; held, first wife, not second, was decedent's "surviving spouse").

Deference to the law of the state of domicile does not answer all the questions, however. In Spalding's Estate v. Commissioner, 537 F.2d 666 (2d Cir. 1976), the Second Circuit held that the husband was the surviving spouse of the decedent, a second wife whom he married in California, even though a lower New York court had found the husband's Nevada divorce invalid. The court emphasized that the husband's Nevada divorce was not challenged in California, the state where decedent's property was being administered. In so holding, however, the court did not deal with the Tax Court's conclusion that the California courts would have been required by the Constitution to give full faith and credit to the New York judgment invalidating the Nevada divorce decree. Consider the complications that result if it becomes necessary to have an ancillary proceeding in New York to administer decedent's property located there. The *Spalding* opinion implies that the Nevada divorce should be honored unless explicitly invalidated in the jurisdiction where the decedent was domiciled at death—a principle that would generally recognize "the living marriage and not the atrophied one." 537 F.2d at 669.

Local law is also relevant in determining whether the decedent left a "surviving" spouse, especially where it is impossible to determine the order of the spouses' deaths. Many states have enacted "simultaneous death" legislation which presumes, in the absence of sufficient evidence to the contrary, that the spouse failed to survive the decedent. This presumption, however, can be overridden by a contrary provision in the decedent's will, and it has become common practice in drafting wills to include express provisions concerning survivorship. Under Reg. § 20.2056(c)–2(e), "[i]f the order of deaths of the decedent and his spouse cannot be established by proof, a presumption (whether supplied by local law, the decedent's will, or otherwise) that the decedent was survived by his spouse will be recognized ..., but only to the extent that it has the effect of giving to the spouse an interest in property includible in her gross estate...."

In 1988, Congress enacted two new sections, §§ 2056(d) and 2523(i), concerning transfers to a spouse who is not a citizen of the United States. For estate tax purposes, § 2056(d) disallows the marital deduction for property transferred to a surviving noncitizen spouse unless the transfer is made in the form of a "qualified domestic trust."[20] Section 2056A sets forth a definition of a qualified domestic trust, and provides for a deferred estate tax to be imposed on distributions of corpus during the surviving spouse's lifetime and on the value of the property remaining in the qualified domestic trust at the surviving spouse's death. In addition to the usual conditions of § 2056, a qualified domestic trust must meet three further requirements: (1) at least one trustee must be an individual United States citizen or a domestic corporation, with express authority to withhold the deferred estate tax from any distributions of trust corpus; (2) the trust must comply with requirements prescribed by regulation to ensure collection of the deferred estate tax; and (3) the executor must make an irrevocable election to treat the trust as a qualified domestic trust. These restrictions on the marital deduction do not apply, however, for transfers from a nonresident alien decedent to a spouse who is a United States citizen. § 2106(a)(3). For gift tax purposes, § 2523(i) disallows the marital deduction for gifts of property to a noncitizen spouse (whether or not in the form of a qualified domestic trust), but at the same time increases the annual exclusion from $10,000 to $100,000 for such gifts (indexed for inflation since 1998 and reaching $136,000 in 2011). For a discussion of related provisions concerning marital joint tenancies, see supra page 213, Note 3.

20. H.R. Rep. No. 795, 100th Cong., 2d Sess. 592–93 (1988), gives the following explanation for the new provisions:

> The marital deduction defers the estate tax on the assumption that the deductible property if not consumed will ultimately be includible in the surviving spouse's estate. This assumption is generally correct for citizen spouses, since to avoid U.S. taxation on his or her worldwide estate, the surviving spouse must have both renounced U.S. citizenship and given up U.S. residence. In addition, the likelihood that property passing to U.S. citizen spouses will escape estate taxation is reduced by the special estate tax imposed in the event of tax-motivated expatriation.
>
> Property passing to an alien surviving spouse is less likely to be includible in the spouse's estate, since to avoid taxation on the worldwide estate, the spouse need only give up U.S. residence. Accordingly, the committee believes that allowing the marital deduction for such property is inconsistent with the assumption underlying the marital deduction and, consequently, that the marital deduction should be allowed only where the property passes to a spouse who is a U.S. citizen.... Finally, in order to avoid imposing a gift tax upon common financial arrangements between spouses, an exclusion would be created for the first $100,000 of gifts to alien spouses each year.

b. Property Passing From the Decedent and Included in Decedent's Gross Estate

Under § 2056(c), the requirement that property "pass" from the decedent is met by virtually any method of deathtime transfer (e.g., by will, intestacy, right of survivorship, power of appointment, etc.), as well as by transfers made "by the decedent at any time," which implies that any lifetime gift by the decedent to the spouse can qualify for the marital deduction. This sweeping authorization is limited, however, by the requirement of § 2056(a) that the interest passing to the surviving spouse must be included in the decedent's gross estate. Thus, a lifetime gift to the spouse satisfies the "passing" requirement only if the property is drawn back into the gross estate by the operation of §§ 2035 to 2042.

The regulations provide that the "passing" requirement is met where the surviving spouse receives property from an election to take against the will or from a will contest in "bona fide recognition of enforceable rights of the surviving spouse in the decedent's estate." Reg. § 20.2056(c)–2(c) and (d)(2). Is it sufficient that the surviving spouse receives property in settlement of a colorable claim advanced in good faith, or must the settlement reflect the spouse's "enforceable rights" under a proper interpretation of state law? In light of the Supreme Court's decision in *Bosch*, supra page 26, it has been held that a private settlement agreement, like a lower state court judgment, must "be based on an enforceable right, under state law properly interpreted." Ahmanson Found. v. United States, 674 F.2d 761 (9th Cir. 1981); accord, Brandon's Estate v. Commissioner, 828 F.2d 493 (8th Cir. 1987); Rev. Rul. 83–107, 1983–2 C.B. 159. Property relinquished by the surviving spouse in electing against the will or in settling a will contest is not treated as passing to the surviving spouse. Reg. § 20.2056(c)–2(c) and (d)(1). For further discussions of the "passing" requirement in connection with an election against a will and a family settlement agreement, respectively, see *First Natl. Exchange Bank of Roanoke*, infra page 494, and *Carpenter's Estate*, infra page 504. See also Schroeder v. United States, 924 F.2d 1547 (10th Cir. 1991) (to avoid conflict with stepdaughters, widow relinquished property received by right of survivorship and elective share, and transferred it in trust retaining only an income interest; held, relinquished property did not pass to widow).

2. DISQUALIFICATION OF TERMINABLE INTERESTS

Section 2056(b)(1) denies the marital deduction for an interest in property passing from the decedent to a surviving spouse if (1) an interest in the same property passes from the decedent to another person, (2) the surviving spouse's interest may "terminate or fail" on the lapse of time or on the occurrence of a contingency, and (3) possession or enjoyment of the property will thereupon shift to the other person. The gift tax counterpart of this provision appears in § 2523(b). The terminable interest rule can be illustrated as follows: If the decedent's will creates a trust to pay income to the surviving spouse for life, with remainder at the spouse's death to their children, the bequest is disqualified by § 2056(b)(1) because it creates interests in both the spouse and their children, the spouse's interest will terminate at her death, and the children will then receive possession and enjoyment of the trust property.

Consider the application of these principles to the hypothetical situations set out below. What is the statutory basis for the conclusion in each case that the arrangement does or does not qualify for the deduction?

1. Decedent's will creates a trust to pay income to his widow for life, with remainder to the widow if she survives *X*, otherwise remainder to *X*. *X* is decedent's aged parent who dies, as expected, soon after the decedent. (Deduction not allowed.)
2. The widow in the first hypothetical purchases *X*'s interest, thus converting her beneficial interest into a fee simple. (Deduction not allowed.)
3. Decedent's will includes a bequest to his widow of decedent's entire interest in a patent that will expire in five years. (Deduction allowed.)
4. Decedent's will creates a trust to pay income for the support of decedent's children until the youngest child reaches age 25, whereupon the trust is to terminate with corpus payable to decedent's widow. The youngest child is 15 years old at decedent's death. (Deduction allowed.)
5. A few years before decedent's death, his aunt created a trust to pay income to decedent or his estate for a fixed 25–year term, with remainder to *X*. Decedent's will leaves the income interest for the remainder of the 25–year term to his widow. (Deduction allowed.)

The statute contains two provisions designed to prevent a testator from using the executor as a conduit for the transfer of disqualified interests to a surviving spouse. First, § 2056(b)(1)(C) denies the marital deduction where the executor or a trustee acquires a terminable interest for the surviving spouse at the decedent's direction. Under this rarely encountered rule, the value of the patent in the third case above would not be deductible if acquired for the spouse by the executor pursuant to a direction in the will, even though it is deductible when bequeathed directly to the spouse. The deduction would also be available if the executor purchased the patent pursuant to a general investment power authorizing the acquisition of both terminable interests and other property rather than pursuant to the decedent's direction.

Second, if the interest passing to the spouse may be satisfied from a pool of assets that includes any nondeductible assets, § 2056(b)(2) requires a pro tanto reduction in the value of the spouse's interest in determining the amount of the marital deduction. This reduction is mandatory even if the executor actually distributes to the spouse only assets that are fully qualified for the deduction. Section 2056(b)(1)(C), described above, disqualifies *terminable* interests acquired by the executor; § 2056(b)(2) is aimed at an asset that would be *nondeductible* if transferred directly to the surviving spouse. Thus, the fact that the estate includes a terminable interest like a patent is not fatal; the interest must be a nondeductible terminable interest (e.g., a term of years reserved by the decedent in connection with an earlier gift of the underlying property to a child).

As the following materials illustrate, the terminable interest rule and its statutory exceptions have given rise to more than their fair share of interpretive problems.

a. Support Allowance for Surviving Spouse

JACKSON v. UNITED STATES

376 U.S. 503 (1964).

MR. JUSTICE WHITE delivered the opinion of the Court.

Since 1948 [§ 2056(a)] has allowed a "marital deduction" from a decedent's gross taxable estate for the value of interests in property passing from the decedent to his surviving spouse. [Section 2056(b)] adds the qualification, however, that interests defined therein as "terminable" shall not qualify as an interest in property to which the marital deduction applies. The question raised by this case is whether the allowance provided by California law for the support of a widow during the settlement of her husband's estate is a terminable interest.

Petitioners are the widow-executrix and testamentary trustee under the will of George Richards who died a resident of California on May 27, 1951. Acting under the Probate Code of California, the state court, on June 30, 1952, allowed Mrs. Richards the sum of $3,000 per month from the corpus of the estate for her support and maintenance, beginning as of May 27, 1951, and continuing for a period of 24 months from that date. Under the terms of the order, an allowance of $42,000 had accrued during the 14 months since her husband's death. This amount, plus an additional $3,000 per month for the remainder of the two-year period, making a total of $72,000, was in fact paid to Mrs. Richards as widow's allowance.

On the federal estate tax return filed on behalf of the estate, the full $72,000 was claimed as a marital deduction under [§ 2056]. The deduction was disallowed, as was a claim for refund after payment of the deficiency, and the present suit for refund was then brought in the District Court. The District Court granted summary judgment for the United States, holding, on the authority of Cunha's Estate v. Commissioner, 279 F.2d 292, that the allowance to the widow was a terminable interest and not deductible under the marital provision of the Internal Revenue Code. The Court of Appeals affirmed, 317 F.2d 821, and we brought the case here because of an asserted conflict between the decision below and that of the

Court of Appeals for the Fifth Circuit in United States v. First National Bank & Trust Co. of Augusta, 297 F.2d 312. 375 U.S. 894. For the reasons given below, we affirm the decision of the Court of Appeals.

In enacting the Revenue Act of 1948 ... with its provision for the marital deduction, Congress left undisturbed § 812(b)(5) of the 1939 Code, which allowed an estate tax deduction, as an expense of administration, for amounts "reasonably required and actually expended for the support during the settlement of the estate of those dependent upon the decedent." ... As the legislative history shows, support payments under § 812(b)(5) were not to be treated as part of the marital deduction allowed by [§ 2056]. The Revenue Act of 1950, ... however, repealed § 812(b)(5) because, among other reasons, Congress believed the section resulted in discriminations in favor of States having liberal family allowances. Thereafter allowances paid for the support of a widow during the settlement of an estate "heretofore deductible under section 812(b) will be allowable as a marital deduction subject to the conditions and limitations of [§ 2056]." S. Rep. No. 2375, 81st Cong., 2d Sess., p. 130.

The "conditions and limitations" of the marital deduction under [§ 2056] are several but we need concern ourselves with only one aspect of [§ 2056(b)(1)], which disallows the deduction of "terminable" interests passing to the surviving spouse. It was conceded in the Court of Appeals that the right to the widow's allowance here involved is an interest in property passing from the decedent within the meaning of [§ 2056(c)], that it is an interest to which the terminable-interest rule of [§ 2056(b)(1)] is applicable, and that the conditions set forth in [(A) and (B) of § 2056(b)(1)] were satisfied under the decedent's will and codicils thereto. The issue, therefore, is whether the interest in property passing to Mrs. Richards as widow's allowance would "terminate or fail" upon the "lapse of time, upon the occurrence of an event or contingency, or upon the failure of an event or contingency to occur."

We accept the Court of Appeals' description of the nature and characteristics of the widow's allowance under California law. In that State, the right to a widow's allowance is not a vested right and nothing accrues before the order granting it. The right to an allowance is lost when the one for whom it is asked has lost the status upon which the right depends. If a widow dies or remarries prior to securing an order for a widow's allowance, the right does not survive such death or remarriage. The amount of the widow's allowance which has accrued and is unpaid at the date of death of the widow is payable to her estate but the right to future payments abates upon her death. The remarriage of a widow subsequent to an order for an allowance likewise abates her right to future payments. 317 F.2d 821, 825.

In light of these characteristics of the California widow's allowance, Mrs. Richards did not have an indefeasible interest in property at the moment of her husband's death since either her death or remarriage would defeat it. If the order for support allowance had been entered on the day of her husband's death, her death or remarriage at any time within two years thereafter would terminate that portion of the interest allocable to the remainder of the two-year period. As of the date of Mr. Richards' death, therefore, the allowance was subject to failure or termination "upon the occurrence of an event or contingency." That the support order was entered in this case 14 months later does not, in our opinion, change the defeasible nature of the interest.

Petitioners ask us to judge the terminability of the widow's interest in property represented by her allowance as of the date of the Probate Court's order rather than as of the date of her husband's death. The court's order, they argue, unconditionally entitled the widow to $42,000 in accrued allowance of which she could not be deprived by either her death or remarriage. It is true that some courts have followed this path, but it is difficult to accept an approach which would allow a deduction of $42,000 on the facts of this case, a deduction of $72,000 if the order had been entered at the end of two years from Mr. Richards' death and none at all if the order had been entered immediately upon his death. Moreover, judging deductibility as of the date of the Probate Court's order ignores the Senate Committee's admonition that in considering terminability of an interest for purposes of a marital deduction "the situation is viewed as at the date of the decedent's death." S. Rep. No. 1013, Part 2, 80th Cong., 2d Sess., p. 10. We prefer the course followed by both the Court of Appeals for the Ninth Circuit in *Cunha's Estate*, supra, and by the Court of Appeals for the Eighth Circuit in United States v. Quivey, 292 F.2d 252. Both courts have held the date of death of the testator to be the correct point of time from which to judge the nature of a widow's allowance for the purpose of deciding terminability and deductibility under [§ 2056]. This is in accord with the rule uniformly followed with regard to interests other than the widow's allowance, that qualification for the marital deduction must be determined as of the time of death.

Our conclusion is confirmed by [§ 2056(b)(3)], which saves from the operation of the terminable-interest rule interests which by their terms may (but do not in fact) terminate only upon failure of the widow to survive her husband for a period not in excess of six months. The premise of this provision is that an interest passing to a widow is normally to be judged as of the time of the testator's death rather than at a later time when the condition imposed may be satisfied; hence the necessity to provide an exception to the rule in the case of a six months' survivorship contingency in a will. A gift conditioned upon eight months' survivorship, rather than six, is a nondeductible terminable interest for reasons which also disqualify the statutory widow's allowance in California where the widow must survive and remain unmarried at least to the date of an allowance order to become indefeasibly entitled to any widow's allowance at all.

Petitioners contend, however, that the sole purpose of the terminable-interest provisions of the Code is to assure that interests deducted from the estate of the deceased spouse will not also escape taxation in the estate of the survivor. This argument leads to the conclusion that since it is now clear that unless consumed or given away during Mrs. Richards' life, the entire $72,000 will be taxed to her estate, it should not be included in her husband's. But as we have already seen, there is no provision in the Code for deducting all terminable interests which become nonterminable at a later date and therefore taxable in the estate of the surviving spouse if not consumed or transferred. The examples cited in the legislative history make it clear that the determinative factor is not taxability to the surviving spouse but terminability as defined by the statute. Under the view advanced by petitioners all cash allowances actually paid would fall outside [§ 2056(b)(1)]; on two different occasions the Senate has refused to give its approval to House-passed amendments to the 1954 Code which would have made the terminable-interest rule inapplicable to all widow's allowances actually paid within specified periods of time.

We are mindful that the general goal of the marital deduction provisions was to achieve uniformity of federal estate tax impact between those States with community property laws and those without them. But the device of the marital deduction which Congress chose to achieve uniformity was knowingly hedged with limitations, including the terminable-interest rule. These provisions may be imperfect devices to achieve the desired end, but they are the means which Congress chose. To the extent it was thought desirable to modify the rigors of the terminable-interest rule, exceptions to the rule were written into the Code. Courts should hesitate to provide still another exception by straying so far from the statutory language as to allow a marital deduction for the widow's allowance provided by the California statute. The achievement of the purposes of the marital deduction is dependent to a great degree upon the careful drafting of wills; we have no fear that our decision today will prevent either the full utilization of the marital deduction or the proper support of widows during the pendency of an estate proceeding.

Affirmed.

MR. JUSTICE DOUGLAS dissents.

NOTES

1. *Nondeductible terminable interests.* The Supreme Court's opinion in *Jackson* makes clear that the widow's allowance in that case was a terminable interest because it would "terminate or fail" if the widow died or remarried within two years after the decedent's death. Furthermore, the requirements of subparagraphs (A) and (B) of § 2056(b)(1) were concededly met because any assets not needed to pay the widow's allowance would pass under the residuary clause of decedent's will to a trust for the decedent's daughter. Thus, the widow's allowance fell squarely within the definition of a nondeductible terminable interest. Note, however, that the widow's allowance would have qualified for the marital deduction if the widow had been the sole beneficiary under her husband's will. See Reg. § 20.2056(b)–1(g) (Example 8).

2. *Statutory allowances for the support of a surviving spouse.* The California widow's allowance in *Jackson* is typical of many state probate

statutes authorizing payments from a decedent's estate for the support of a surviving spouse. Suppose that a surviving spouse who applies for a support allowance automatically becomes entitled to a fixed sum if the spouse is living at the time of the court decree awarding the allowance. Viewing the spouse's rights from the time of the decedent's death, several courts have followed the Supreme Court's lead and held that even this limited survivorship requirement renders the spouse's interest terminable for purposes of the marital deduction. See, e.g., Abely's Estate v. Commissioner, 489 F.2d 1327 (1st Cir. 1974) (Massachusetts law); Hamilton Natl. Bank of Knoxville v. United States, 353 F.2d 930 (6th Cir. 1965), cert. denied, 384 U.S. 939 (1966) (Tennessee law); see also Rev. Rul. 72–153, 1972–1 C.B. 309 (Washington law).

In some states, however, the applicable statute is interpreted as creating an unconditional right which vests in the surviving spouse immediately at the decedent's death and cannot be defeated by the spouse's subsequent death or remarriage. In these circumstances, the spouse's support allowance has been held not to be a terminable interest, even though the amount of the allowance depends on the probate court's exercise of discretion. See, e.g., Green's Estate v. United States, 441 F.2d 303 (6th Cir. 1971) (Michigan law); Radel's Estate v. Commissioner, 88 T.C. 1143 (1987) (Minnesota law); Watson's Estate v. Commissioner, 94 T.C. 262 (1990) (Mississippi law). What if a state enacts a statute that gives the probate court discretionary authority to award a lump sum support allowance which is to "vest in [the surviving] spouse retroactively as of the moment of [the decedent's death] so that it will be a fixed sum certain as of said date of death and shall not terminate with the subsequent death or remarriage of the surviving spouse"? Conn. Gen. Stat. § 45a–320(b). In Rubinow's Estate v. Commissioner, 75 T.C. 486 (1980), affd. mem., 679 F.2d 873 (2d Cir. 1981), the court held that such an allowance was a terminable interest because at the time of the decedent's death the surviving spouse's rights were "wholly contingent on future judicial action and committed to the discretion of the [probate] judge." The statute did not achieve its intended purpose of qualifying the allowance for the marital deduction.

b. Post–Mortem Elections

FIRST NATIONAL EXCHANGE BANK OF ROANOKE v. UNITED STATES

335 F.2d 91 (4th Cir. 1964).

BUTZNER, DISTRICT JUDGE.

The District Court held that the commuted value of a widow's dower in the estate of her husband qualified for the marital deduction allowed by § 2056 of the Internal Revenue Code of 1954. We affirm.

Josephus Daniels Pell died on September 2, 1958. His will left his entire estate in trust for the benefit of his widow for her life.

The widow renounced her husband's will pursuant to § 64–13, Code of Virginia, 1950. She thus became entitled to one-half of the decedent's net personal estate and a life estate in one-third of his realty.

The statutes of Virginia provide that the widow has a right to elect commutation of her dower if it appears that her dower may not be conveniently laid off and assigned in kind.

The Circuit Court of Franklin County, Virginia found as a fact that dower could not be conveniently laid off and assigned in kind and that the widow was entitled to have her commuted dower interest paid to her in cash. The Court ordered a sale of the real estate. From the net proceeds the widow was paid in cash her commuted dower interest in the sum of $33,167.70.

The Executor claimed as a part of the marital deduction the commuted dower interest paid to the widow. The Government disallowed this amount. It is the Government's position that the interest which passed from the decedent to the widow as of the date of death was a dower life interest although it was never assigned to her in kind. The Government contends that the money she received upon commutation and sale of the property was simply a conversion of this interest into another form which did not change the terminable attributes of the dower interest.

The cash received by the widow will not qualify as a part of the marital deduction if it is a terminable interest passing from the decedent to the widow or the conversion of a terminable interest. The cash received by the widow, however, will qualify for the marital deduction if it is a nonterminable interest. Qualification for the marital deduction must be determined as of the time of the husband's death. Jackson v. United States, 376 U.S. 503 (1964).

The problem which is involved in this case has been considered in the Fifth, Sixth and Eighth Circuits. United States v. Hiles, 318 F.2d 56 (5th Cir. 1963); Dougherty v. United States, 292 F.2d 331 (6th Cir. 1961); United States v. Crosby, 257 F.2d 515 (5th Cir. 1958); United States v. Traders National Bank of Kansas City, Executor, 248 F.2d 667 (8th Cir. 1957). Each of these cases held that the cash received by the widow was not a terminable interest and that it qualified for the marital deduction. We agree with the results reached in these cases. No case has been found which supports the Government's position.

The statutes of Virginia pertaining to dower and its commutation do not significantly differ from the statutes of the several states considered by the Courts of Appeals in the above mentioned cases. The District Court correctly interpreted the Virginia law as follows:

> It is well settled that until the widow's dower has been assigned to her her dower right is merely a right to sue for and compel the setting aside to her of her dower interest. It is not an estate in itself.... When assigned it becomes a life estate in the lands assigned. But prior to that time it has attached to nothing, although it is a right vested in the widow.

The statutes of Virginia accorded the widow a number of rights which became effective at the moment of the decedent's death. She had the right to take under the decedent's will, which conferred upon her only a life estate. She had a right to renounce the will and upon doing so she had a right to dower.[21] The right to dower, sometimes called dower consummate, was a vested right. Her dower, however, was not an estate or an interest in any specific land. It could not become a life estate in realty until it was laid off and assigned in kind. At the time of the decedent's death dower could not be assigned in kind since the land was not susceptible to assignment. Thus, at the time of the decedent's death the widow did not have an estate or interest for life in one-third of the decedent's realty, nor could she ever acquire such an interest for the reason that it was impossible to assign her dower in kind. In the final analysis, it appears that at the time of the decedent's death the widow had a right to the commuted value of her dower. The commutation of her dower was not a conversion or sale of her life interest. Her commuted dower was paid to her in cash. Her right to it is absolute and non-terminable. It qualifies as a marital deduction.

Jackson v. United States, 376 U.S. 503 (1964) does not require a different conclusion. In that case the Court held that a widow's allowance under California law did not qualify for the marital deduction....

The characteristics of the widow's allowance described in *Jackson* differ materially from the right of the widow in this case. The right to a widow's allowance in *Jackson* is not a vested right and nothing accrues before the order granting it. Here the right to dower, however, vested at the time of the husband's death. As the Supreme Court pointed out, if the order in *Jackson* for the widow's allowance had been entered on the day of her husband's death, her death or remarriage at any time within two years would terminate a portion of the allowance. In this case, to the contrary, if the order paying the commuted dower had been entered on the day of the decedent's death, the widow's death or remarriage would not divest her or her estate of the money which she had received.

The inclusion of the commuted value of the widow's dower in the marital deduction is consistent with the intent of Congress to achieve uniformity among married taxpayers in common law states and community property jurisdictions....

Affirmed.[22]

NOTES

1. *Election between alternative bequests.* If the will offers the decedent's surviving spouse a choice between a nondeductible terminable interest (e.g.,

21. The election of the widow to renounce the will did not prevent her dower and the personal property which she received from being an interest passing to her from her husband. [Reg. § 2056(c)-2(c).] The Government concedes that the widow's election to take against her husband's will and to take her dower relates back to the date of the husband's death. No claim is made that the personal property which the widow received upon renunciation of the will failed to qualify for the marital deduction.

22. The Service has acquiesced in the holding in First Natl. Exchange Bank of Roanoke v. United States. Rev. Rul. 83-107, 1983-2 C.B. 159.—EDS.

an income interest in a testamentary trust) and a deductible interest (e.g., a cash bequest), and the spouse elects to take the cash, does the bequest qualify for the marital deduction? The courts generally have allowed the deduction, on the theory that

> there is no substantial difference between an elective testamentary bequest of a non-terminable interest that relates back to the testator's death, and a widow's election against a will pursuant to state statutes, which qualifies for the marital deduction so long as the interest actually passing to the spouse is nonterminable.... The statutory policy governing the disposition of the "elective share" cases is applicable to the testamentary election situation ... and compels a similar result.

Neugass' Estate v. Commissioner, 555 F.2d 322 (2d Cir. 1977) (widow entitled under will to a life estate in decedent's art collection or to absolute ownership of items selected by her within a specified period). Accord, Mackie's Estate v. Commissioner, 545 F.2d 883 (4th Cir. 1976) (choice between interest in discretionary trust and outright ownership of other property selected by the spouse); Tompkins' Estate v. Commissioner, 68 T.C. 912 (1977) (choice between income interest in trust and $40,000 cash). After losing these cases, the Service finally conceded that "[a] cash bequest in lieu of a life estate, payable unconditionally at the election of the surviving spouse within a reasonable time after the decedent's death qualifies for the estate tax marital deduction under § 2056." Rev. Rul. 82–184, 1982–2 C.B. 215.

2. *Conditions and restrictions.* A purely formal procedural condition that the surviving spouse choose between alternative bequests does not convert an otherwise deductible bequest into a terminable interest. Cf. Rev. Rul. 76–166, 1976–1 C.B. 287 (surviving spouse's otherwise vested interest in homestead not terminable merely because spouse is required to signify formal acceptance and may die before then); Rev. Rul. 76–199, 1976–1 C.B. 288 (marital deduction allowed for amount paid to decedent's widow to settle dower claim, where payment conditioned on Service's allowance of marital deduction). Nevertheless, the marital deduction may be lost if the bequest is subject to additional conditions or restrictions. For example, in Edmonds' Estate v. Commissioner, 72 T.C. 970 (1979), the decedent's will gave a life estate in the family home to his widow as well as a right to release the life estate and receive up to $100,000 to purchase a new home. Several years after the decedent's death, the spouse exercised her right to take the $100,000 cash. The court denied the marital deduction, noting that "there was no way of knowing, at the time of decedent's death, whether the surviving spouse would purchase a new home, or how much of the $100,000 would be needed to effect such a purchase." For similar outcomes where the surviving spouse takes property subject to conditions or restrictions under the terms of the decedent's will or under a settlement of a will contest, see Allen v. United States, 359 F.2d 151 (2d Cir.), cert. denied, 385 U.S. 832 (1966) (bequest to widow conditioned on her agreement to leave the property, along with her own estate, to decedent's four children; marital deduction disallowed); Tebb's Estate v. Commissioner, 27 T.C. 671 (1957) (will bequeathed property outright to widow, who settled will contest by agreeing to use property only for her normal living expenses and to leave the balance to stepchildren; held, no marital deduction for terminable interest received by widow); Rev. Rul. 82–

184, 1982–2 C.B. 215 ("a cash bequest payable on the condition that the spouse purchase a new home is a nondeductible terminable interest for purposes of section 2056").

3. *Joint and mutual wills.* Spouses sometimes execute joint and mutual wills providing that at the first spouse's death their combined property will go to the survivor for life, with a power to use or consume it freely, and that any property remaining at the survivor's death will go to their children or other designated beneficiaries. Although a joint and mutual will typically purports to give the survivor absolute ownership of the decedent's assets, the survivor may be bound by an agreement, express or implied, to leave any unconsumed property at death to the designated beneficiaries. If such an agreement is enforceable against the survivor under local law, the interest that passes at the death of the first spouse to the survivor is terminable and the marital deduction is lost.[23] Why is this? See Opal's Estate v. Commissioner, 450 F.2d 1085 (2d Cir. 1971) (under New York law, binding will contract left survivor with only a life interest in property passing from decedent, coupled with limited power of disposition); see also Bartlett v. Commissioner, 937 F.2d 316 (7th Cir. 1991) (Illinois law); Batterton v. United States, 406 F.2d 247 (5th Cir. 1968), cert. denied, 395 U.S. 934 (1969) (Florida law); Abruzzino's Estate v. Commissioner, 61 T.C. 306 (1973) (West Virginia law); but see Vermilya's Estate v. Commissioner, 41 T.C. 226 (1963) (under Minnesota law, widow took fee simple in property passing from decedent subject to binding obligation to leave property remaining at death to named relatives; marital deduction allowed because agreement created no "interest" in relatives). Consider whether the executor can avoid this type of litigation and salvage the marital deduction under current law by making a QTIP election (see infra page 514).

If the property is held by husband and wife as joint tenants with right of survivorship, it has been held that the survivor acquires outright ownership of the property by virtue of the joint tenancy, that the contract contained in the joint and mutual will does not reduce the survivor's rights to a terminable interest because the property passes outside the will, and that the survivor's obligation to bequeath the property to designated beneficiaries is imposed by the survivor rather than by the first spouse to die. United States v. Ford, 377 F.2d 93 (8th Cir. 1967) (joint tenancy and life insurance). Based on this reasoning, the Service has ruled that the interest passing to the survivor at the death of the first spouse qualifies for the marital deduction; the ruling goes on, however, to state that reduction of the survivor's interest from absolute ownership to a life estate (pursuant to the terms of the contract contained in the joint and mutual will) constitutes a transfer of property by the survivor subject to a retained life estate within the meaning of § 2036(a).

---

23. Consider the problem that arises if a decedent leaves property outright to a surviving spouse with no restrictions set forth in the will, but subject to an oral agreement that the spouse will give the property to a designated beneficiary (e.g., the decedent's child by a prior marriage). Should the marital deduction be denied on the theory that the spouse's interest is terminable, or should it be allowed on the theory that the agreement is unenforceable? (In many states, an agreement to make, or not to revoke, a will must be in writing.) Is it fraudulent for the executor to claim a marital deduction without disclosing the existence or terms of the agreement? See Redke v. Silvertrust, 490 P.2d 805 (Cal. 1971), cert. denied, 405 U.S. 1041 (1972) (oral agreement enforceable under state law, not void as a fraudulent device to obtain the marital deduction).

Rev. Rul. 71–51, 1971–1 C.B. 274. Compare Grimes v. Commissioner, 851 F.2d 1005 (7th Cir. 1988) (surviving spouse made a taxable gift to remainder beneficiaries when contractual obligations under joint will became irrevocable at first spouse's death), with Lidbury's Estate v. Commissioner, 800 F.2d 649 (7th Cir. 1986) (no taxable gift where contract imposed no substantial restrictions on surviving spouse's power to consume property). See Hess, The Federal Transfer Tax Consequences of Joint and Mutual Wills, 24 Real Prop., Prob. & Tr. J. 469 (1990).

4. *One "property" or two?* Occasionally it becomes necessary to determine whether interests passing from a decedent to a surviving spouse and to another person relate to a single property or to separate properties. If there is only one underlying property, the terminable interest rule may preclude the marital deduction; whereas, if there are two separate properties, the deduction may be available even if the spouse's interest is terminable. For example, in Rev. Rul. 77–130, 1977–1 C.B. 289, a policy of insurance on the decedent's life provided for payments of $600 per month to the decedent's surviving spouse for life and $300 per month to *C*, another beneficiary, until age 21 or *C*'s earlier death. The Service ruled that the surviving spouse's interest qualified for the marital deduction:

> [W]ith the happening of the decedent's death, two distinct rights came into being, each separate and independent of the other.... The mere fact that the two interests derived from the same insurance contract is insufficient to fuse these independent interests in such a way that *C* should be deemed to have received an interest in the property that passed to the decedent's surviving spouse and a part of which property *C* may possess or enjoy after the spouse's death.

In Meyer v. United States, 364 U.S. 410 (1960), however, the Supreme Court rejected the notion that a life insurance policy comprised two separate properties where the proceeds were payable in monthly installments to the insured's widow for life, with 240 installments guaranteed, and if the widow died during the 240–month period the rest of the guaranteed installments were payable to the decedent's daughter:

> Whether a policy of life insurance may create several "properties" or funds, either terminable or nonterminable or both, we need not decide, for we think the policy here involved constituted only one property, and made only so much of its proceeds payable to the wife as she might live to receive in equal monthly installments, and made any guaranteed balance payable to the daughter....
>
> We think petitioners' argument—that the insurer's bookkeeping division of the proceeds of the policy into two parts created two properties—cannot withstand the provisions of the policy and the actual facts respecting the insurer's bookkeeping division of its proceeds, under the clear terms of the statute and its legislative history. The policy made no provision for the creation of two separate properties—one a property sufficient to provide payments for 240 months, to the wife while she lived and any remainder to the daughter, and another property sufficient to provide an annuity to the wife for the period of her actuarial expectancy beyond the 240 months—and no such separate properties were in fact

created. The allocations made were merely actuarial ones—mere bookkeeping entries—made by the insurer on its own books for its own convenience after the insured, the other party to the contract, had died. The wife and the daughter were, respectively, primary and contingent beneficiaries *of the policy* alone. Neither of them had any title to, nor right to receive, any special fund, and indeed none was actually created. The bookkeeping entries made by the insurer no more created or measured their rights than the insurer's erasure of those entries—which it was free to make at any time—would destroy their rights. Their rights derive solely from the policy. [364 U.S. at 413–15.]

Might the result in *Meyer* have been different if the decedent had purchased two policies, the first directing that installments be paid to the widow for life, with no guaranteed term, and the second paying similar installments to the daughter for the remainder of a specified term of years but only if the widow died within the period? Note that in *Meyer* the surviving spouse would have received the entire proceeds of the policy if she lived long enough, while in Rev. Rul. 77–130 the length of the spouse's life had no effect on the value of *C*'s interest.

5. *Survivorship conditions.* Section 2056(b)(3) provides that an interest is not to be considered as terminable solely because it will terminate or fail if the surviving spouse dies within six months of the decedent's death (or dies with the decedent in a common disaster), as long as such death does not actually occur. Thus, if the other requirements of § 2056 are met, a standard survivorship condition imposed by an express provision in the will or by local law (e.g., a bequest conditioned on the spouse's surviving the decedent by 120 hours, or by 30 days) does not defeat the marital deduction if the spouse actually survives for the specified time period.

Unlike the six-month survivorship rule, the common disaster rule does not prescribe a time period within which the surviving spouse's interest must either mature or terminate. This omission means that the ownership of the property might remain in limbo for years after the decedent's death if the surviving spouse's life remains in jeopardy as a result of the common disaster. Reg. § 20.2056(b)–3(c) provides that the marital deduction will not be allowed in the final audit of the estate tax return if there is "still a possibility" that the common disaster provision may operate to deprive the surviving spouse of the interest.

Conditions of survivorship that are not limited to six months or a common disaster may prove fatal to the marital deduction. For example, in Harmon's Estate v. Commissioner, 84 T.C. 329 (1985), the court held that a bequest to the decedent's husband conditioned on his surviving the distribution of the decedent's estate was a nondeductible terminable interest. See also Bookwalter v. Lamar, 323 F.2d 664 (8th Cir. 1963), cert. denied, 376 U.S. 969 (1964) (bequest to widow contingent on her surviving administration of decedent's estate); Fried v. Commissioner, 445 F.2d 979 (2d Cir. 1971), cert. denied, 404 U.S. 1016 (1972) (bequest to widow contingent on her surviving probate of decedent's will); Heim's Estate v. Commissioner, 914 F.2d 1322 (9th Cir. 1990) (bequest to widow with gift over to children if the widow should "fail to survive distribution"); Rev. Rul. 88–90, 1988–2 C.B. 335

(spouse's interest in testamentary trust conditioned on survival to date trust became funded).

The courts have sometimes used local rules governing the devolution of title to rescue taxpayers who strayed from the narrow path charted by § 2056(b)(3). For example, in Bond's Estate v. Commissioner, 104 T.C. 652 (1995), the decedent's will left his residuary estate to his widow, provided that she "survive distribution." Based on its finding that the widow's interest in the real property (but not the personal property) included in the residuary estate became indefeasibly vested immediately at the decedent's death under local law, the Tax Court allowed a marital deduction for the real property; the personal property passing under the same clause of the will, however, was held to be a nondeductible terminable interest. Accord, Horton's Estate v. Commissioner, 388 F.2d 51 (2d Cir. 1967); see also Tilyou's Estate v. Commissioner, 470 F.2d 693 (2d Cir. 1972) (marital deduction allowed for an amount passing under a clause terminating the spouse's interest in the event of her death "before she shall have become entitled to any part or share of my residuary estate," on ground that she became equitably "entitled" to her share at decedent's death even though she was not entitled to receive it until the distribution date); Kellar v. Kasper, 138 F.Supp. 738, 744 (D.S.D. 1956) (allowing marital deduction for bequest to widow conditioned on her surviving distribution of decedent's estate, based on construction of ambiguous language in light of testator's intent; testator, "astute lawyer that he was, can be presumed to have understood the marital deduction provision of the law, and the record shows that he redrew his will for the sole purpose of taking advantage of such marital deduction").

In Rev. Rul. 54–121, 1954–1 C.B. 196, the Service ruled that life insurance proceeds payable to the decedent's widow would not qualify for the marital deduction if she was required to survive until the insurance company received due proof of the insured's death, because that might occur more than six months after his death. But see Eggleston v. Dudley, 257 F.2d 398 (3d Cir. 1958), holding that a policy containing a similar clause, construed with regard to the parties' intent under local law, created a nonterminable interest eligible for the marital deduction.

3. DEDUCTIBLE TERMINABLE INTERESTS: STATUTORY SAFE HARBORS

As already noted, the marital deduction may be available for an interest passing to the surviving spouse that is technically terminable (e.g., the patent in the third case given at page 489). In most cases, however, a terminable interest is nondeductible unless it falls within one of the statutory safe harbors set forth in § 2056(b)(5) through (b)(8).

a. Life Estate With Power of Appointment

Until the introduction of "qualified terminable interest property" in 1981, the most important statutory exception to the terminable interest rule was § 2056(b)(5), which makes the marital deduction available for an interest in property passing from the decedent if the surviving spouse is entitled for life to all the income from the interest (or from a specific portion thereof) and possesses a power to appoint the entire interest (or such specific portion) to the spouse or the spouse's estate. This combination of life income interest and general power of appointment makes the surviving spouse "the virtual owner of the property" for purposes of the marital deduction. S. Rep. No. 1013, 80th Cong., 2d Sess. (1948), reprinted in 1948–1 C.B. 285, 342. The policy requirements of the statute are satisfied because the interest, if not consumed, will be subject to the gift or estate tax when the surviving spouse disposes of it or dies. The § 2056(b)(5) exception is available whether the surviving spouse is the income beneficiary of a trust or merely the legal life tenant of the property; Reg. § 20.2056(b)–5(e) states that the same principles apply to both trust and nontrust dispositions. See Rev. Rul. 77–30, 1977–1 C.B. 291 (allowing marital deduction for legal life estate coupled with unrestricted power to consume and dispose of property under Virginia law).

(1) Right to Income

Section 2056(b)(5) requires that the surviving spouse be "entitled for life to all the income from the entire interest, or all the income from a specific portion thereof, payable annually or at more frequent intervals." The regulations flesh out this rather skeletal statutory language in considerable detail, providing that in the case of an interest transferred in trust: (1) the trust must give the surviving spouse "substantially that degree of beneficial enjoyment of the trust property during her life which the principles of the law of trusts accord to a person who is unqualifiedly designated as the life beneficiary of a trust"; (2) it is immaterial whether the spouse's enjoyment of the property is ensured by specific provisions of the trust instrument or by the rules of fiduciary administration prescribed by state law; (3) reasonable rules allocating receipts and expenses between income and corpus do not disqualify the interest unless they deprive the spouse of the requisite beneficial enjoyment; (4) administrative powers granted to the trustee do not disqualify the interest unless they evidence an intent to deprive the spouse of the requisite beneficial enjoyment; and (5) the interest does not qualify if "the primary purpose of the trust is to safeguard property without providing the spouse with the required beneficial enjoyment." Reg. § 20.2056(b)–5(f).

In Rev. Rul. 69–56, 1969–1 C.B. 224, the Service examined a series of four governing instruments vesting the fiduciary with specified administrative powers and concluded that the instruments were consistent with § 2056(b)(5), either because the fiduciary was required by state law to balance fairly the interests of the income beneficiary and remainder beneficiaries or because the instrument did not preclude the local courts from imposing reasonable limitations to protect the surviving spouse's income interest. In conjunction with the regulations, this ruling provides useful guidelines for the drafter insofar as it validates a broad range of conventional fiduciary powers (e.g., power to treat ordinary cash dividends as income when received without regard to the declaration or record date, to allocate stock dividends and extraordinary cash dividends to principal, and to apportion trustees' commissions between income and principal).

The surviving spouse's right to current income distributions is buttressed by Reg. § 20.2056(b)–5(f)(7), which provides that an interest is disqualified if the income may be accumulated in the discretion of any person other than the spouse or if distributions of income are conditioned on the consent of any other person. Thus, the deduction is jeopardized if a trustee has discretion to withhold income or if the trust instrument links income distributions to the spouse's support needs. The courts, however, have shown considerable flexibility in construing trust language in a manner that preserves the deduction. See, e.g., Mittleman's Estate v. Commissioner, 522 F.2d 132 (D.C. Cir. 1975) (reference to "proper support, maintenance, welfare and comfort" of surviving spouse described purpose of trust, but did not qualify spouse's right to receive income at least annually, even though the instrument made no mention of income distributions); Davis' Estate v. Commissioner, 86 T.C. 1156 (1986) (boilerplate fiduciary powers did not impair right to income where spouse was entitled to "the entire net income"); Rev. Rul. 85–35, 1985–1 C.B. 328 (no disqualification where trustee has power, if spouse becomes legally disabled, to pay income to relative or representative for spouse's benefit or to apply income directly for spouse's benefit).

Even if a trust does not provide for periodic payments of income to the surviving spouse, the deduction is still allowable if the spouse has an unrestricted power, exercisable each year, to draw down income that will otherwise be accumulated and added to corpus. The surviving spouse must have "such command over the income that it is virtually hers." Reg. § 20.2056(b)–5(f)(8).

The trust instrument may contain a saving clause stating that any discretionary authority given to trustee is void if it would result in disallowance of the marital deduction. See Rev. Rul. 75–440, 1975–2 C.B. 372 (saving clause used as "an aid in determining the testator's intent," indicating that testator did not intend to give disqualifying power to trustees); but cf. Rev. Rul. 65–144, 1965–1 C.B. 442 (saving clause in charitable remainder trust void because it imposed "condition subsequent" on unambiguous disqualifying provision).

(2) Power of Appointment

In addition to a right to income, the surviving spouse must have a power to appoint the entire interest (or a specific portion thereof), exercisable during life or by will in favor of the spouse or the spouse's estate, and the power must be exercisable by the spouse "alone and in all events." The regulations amplify the statutory language, stating that a power of appointment does not qualify if it can be exercised only with the consent of a person other than the spouse, if it can be terminated during the spouse's life by any event other than a complete exercise or release by the spouse (e.g., remarriage), or if it is exercisable only for a limited purpose (e.g., support). Reg. § 20.2056(b)–5(g)(3).

In referring to a power of appointment, § 2056(b)(5) is concerned with substance, not with labels. Thus, an unlimited power to invade property is a power to appoint it. Reg. § 20.2056(b)–5(g)(1). Similarly, the unrestricted right of a joint tenant with right of survivorship to obtain an undivided one-half share of the property by severing the joint tenancy without the other tenant's consent is a power to appoint that portion. Reg. § 20.2056(b)–5(g)(2). If a trust contains ambiguous language—for example, if the surviving spouse is empowered to "use," "consume," "sell," or "dispose of" the property—it may take a lawsuit to determine whether under local law the spouse has the requisite power of appointment or only a life estate with broad managerial powers.

CARPENTER'S ESTATE v. COMMISSIONER

52 F.3d 1266 (4th Cir. 1995).

MOTZ, CIRCUIT JUDGE.

This appeal involves the widowed beneficiary of a trust created pursuant to her husband's will, who accepted certain funds as part of a settlement agreement after a dispute arose over the terms of the trust. The tax court found that because the widow's interest under the trust was a life estate unaccompanied by a general power of appointment, the decedent's estate was not entitled to a marital deduction for funds paid to the widow as part of the settlement. We affirm.

I

Stanley M. Carpenter, a resident of North Carolina, died on October 2, 1987. He was survived by his wife, Ernestine Carpenter, who was 63 years old at his death, and his daughter by a previous marriage, Nancy Carpenter Reid, who was 50 at his death.... Several years prior to his death, on May 5, 1981, Stanley executed a holographic will. He also executed a codicil to his will on December 17, 1986. The validity of these documents is uncontested.

Under the terms of the will, Stanley left to his daughter, Nancy, $50,000 in cash and three parcels of real property. Stanley Carpenter devised to Ernestine his "personal cars, trucks, tractors, mowers, farm equipment, guns and everything I own at the farm." The will further provided that certain real property from the estate was to be placed in trust for the benefit of Ernestine as follows:

> 3. ... My wife is to select the Trust Dept. She is also to take an equal part as an executor with the Trust in all decisions regarding this trust [sic].
>
> This Trust is to work with my wife + to give her all money necessary to give her a good life and happiness.
>
> I chose to use a Trust so that no one can dominate or take advantage of her for her entire life....

> The Trust working with my wife may sell any property at anytime if necessary for cash for the Trust in case my wife wants cash for her personal health, needs, trips or anything relating to my wife....
>
> As stated this Trust is to protect my wife only. I hope she will use it wisely for her happiness....

The trust created by Stanley Carpenter's will further provided that any remaining trust assets upon Ernestine Carpenter's death should be transferred to Nancy Reid:

> Since I am leaving practically all of my life's assets for my wife's benefit while she lives, I think and want anything left in the Trust to go to my daughter Nancy....

The will contained no residuary clause and, as a result, Stanley died intestate with respect to his remaining assets unidentified in the will....

Apparently after some negotiation, on May 20, 1988, Ernestine and Nancy executed a Family Settlement Agreement, which was thereafter filed in, and approved by, the General Court of Justice, Superior Court Division, Durham County, North Carolina. Pursuant to the agreement, Ernestine and Nancy waived their respective rights under the terms of the trust. Instead, they agreed that all of the property designated in the will as trust assets, and all remaining property not mentioned in the will, should be divided equally between the two of them as tenants in common. In order to demonstrate that a good faith dispute had arisen as to the proper interpretation of Stanley Carpenter's testamentary trust, the agreement provided:

> And Whereas, said holographic will is vague and indefinite and a Declaratory Judgment action would be necessary to interpret said will in order to clarify the status of legal title to much of the property of said estate at great expense to the estate, and a genuine dispute has arisen between the Wife and Daughter as to the true intent of Stanley Manning Carpenter with respect to the selection of a trustee or trustees as set forth in Item 3 of said Last Will and Testament and with respect to the property to be left in trust, to wit: whether the Wife may sell the property comprising the corpus of the proposed trust for her support without reference to a standard of support, or whether said property may be sold for payment of the Wife's necessities of life only.

[The federal estate tax return showed a marital deduction in the amount of $464,795, the purported value of Ernestine's share of the property divided between Ernestine and Nancy pursuant to the terms of the settlement agreement. The Commissioner disallowed $422,464.50 of the claimed deduction, and the Tax Court sustained the Commissioner's determination.]

II

The Estate's initial argument is that Ernestine's "rights under the testamentary trust were not terminable interests." The Estate concedes that generally a "marital deduction is not allowed for a terminable interest" and that a "life estate is a terminable interest." See 26 U.S.C. § 2056(b)(1); 26 C.F.R. § 20.2056(b)–1(b). Furthermore, it acknowledges that the language of the governing instrument—here the will—and the law of the state of the decedent's domicile—here North Carolina—determine the nature of an interest and how it should be taxed. See Commissioner of Internal Revenue v. Estate of Bosch, 387 U.S. 456, 465 (1967); Morgan v. Commissioner of Internal Revenue, 309 U.S. 78, 80–81 (1940). See also 26 C.F.R. § 20.2056(b)–5(e).

Stanley Carpenter's will clearly provides that Ernestine is to receive a life interest in the trust assets.... Moreover, Stanley Carpenter's intent to convey to Ernestine an interest for her life is further supported by the fact that he created a remainder interest in favor of his daughter with respect to the trust assets.... Thus, it seems clear that Ernestine's interest under the testamentary trust was a life estate, a concededly terminable interest.

The Estate does not claim to the contrary, nor does it claim that Ernestine was given the power to "turn her interest into a fee simple interest." Rather, it claims that in addition to the life estate, Ernestine also received "a general power of appointment." The Internal Revenue Code provides a life estate accompanied by such a power can qualify for a marital deduction. See 26 U.S.C. § 2056(b)(5). The general power of appointment must, however, include five features. Id.; 26 C.F.R. § 20.2056(b)–5. Among these are the requirements that:

> (3) The surviving spouse must have the power to appoint the entire interest to either herself or to her estate; [and] (4) The power in the surviving spouse *must be exercisable by her alone* and (whether exercisable by will or during her life) *must be exercisable in all events*[.]

26 C.F.R. § 20.2056(b)–5(a)(3) and (4) (emphasis added).

The Estate asserts that the "only factor that would seem to be in question in this case is whether Mrs. Carpenter had the power to appoint the entire interest to either herself or her estate" i.e., the sole issue is whether the power given to Ernestine Carpenter complies with the requirement set forth in 26 C.F.R. § 20.2056(b)–5(a)(3). The Estate then devotes its attention to attempting to demonstrate that in order to qualify for the marital deduction, the only power that Ernestine needed to have been given was the power to appoint her entire interest to herself, so that the fact that she admittedly was not given the power to appoint her interest to her estate was not fatal to her claim. It is true that in order to qualify for a marital deduction, a widow need not be given a life estate with the power to appoint to her estate, provided that she is given the power to appoint to herself. See 26 U.S.C. § 2056(b)(5); 26 C.F.R.

§ 20.2056(b)–5(a)(3). However, that power must also be "exercisable by her [the widow] alone and in all events." See 26 U.S.C. § 2056(b)(5); 26 C.F.R. § 20.2056(b)–5(a)(4). Thus, we must examine North Carolina law to determine if the power given to Ernestine under the will permitted her (1) to appoint her entire interest to herself *and* (2) to exercise this right alone and in all events.

The Estate relies on four North Carolina cases in support of its position that the powers given Ernestine were sufficient to qualify her life estate for a marital deduction.... That reliance is misplaced.

The crucial issue in each of these cases was whether the nominal life tenant had been given broad enough powers of disposition so that her life estate was really a fee simple interest, or could be converted into a fee simple interest.... This determination is simply not an issue in the case at hand. Here, the Estate concedes that Ernestine was not given a fee simple or powers sufficient to convert her life estate into a fee simple interest, i.e., to convey it to a grantee who "takes an indefeasible fee." ...

Furthermore, and perhaps more significantly, not one of these cases upon which the Estate so heavily relies involves a life estate held in trust, let alone one held in a trust administered by a neutral co-trustee. Thus, the fact that Ernestine's interest was in a trust to be administered by an institutional co-trustee is not even addressed by the Estate's argument. Yet this obviously constitutes an important limitation on powers given to Ernestine by the will. There is, moreover, a North Carolina case that deals with the rights of a life tenant whose interest was held in trust, which, although heavily relied on by the tax court, is not cited in either of the Estate's appellate briefs. See Campbell v. Jordan, 162 S.E.2d 545 (N.C. 1968).

In *Campbell*, the court construed a trust in which the trustees were empowered to convey a portion of the trust assets to a life tenant in *fee simple*—free of the trust—if the trustees deemed it "necessary or best for the welfare of the [beneficiaries], and consistent with the welfare of [the testator's] family and estate...." 162 S.E.2d at 547. A life tenant brought suit asserting the trustees had a mandatory duty to terminate the trust and convey the trust assets to her in fee simple. The Supreme Court of North Carolina categorically rejected this contention, reasoning:

> We think it abundantly clear that *testator did not intend to give his trustee the unbridled discretion to divide his estate in contravention of his testamentary plan* or to invade the corpus in behalf of any beneficiary except in case of necessity or circumstances clearly denoting that such invasion was best for the beneficiary's personal welfare. The beneficiary's necessity or welfare does not include the personal satisfaction she might derive from owning the property in fee and being able to devise it to persons of her choice. [Id. at 551 (emphasis added).]

Although in this case Ernestine herself is a co-trustee and the trustees are given broader rights to invade the corpus, i.e., for Ernestine's "happiness ... personal health, needs, trips or anything else relating to" her, the *Campbell* rationale is nonetheless applicable. As in *Campbell*, to hold that the life tenant was given the interest she claims—here a life estate with general power of appointment which would qualify for a marital deduction under § 2056(b)—would be to ignore the testator's intended testamentary plan. The language of Stanley Carpenter's will clearly demonstrates his intent that the trust benefit his daughter, Nancy, as well as his wife, Ernestine.... Moreover, the will clearly reflects Stanley Carpenter's intention not to convey a life estate directly to his wife, but rather to create a trust to "protect" her so that "no one can dominate or take advantage of her for her entire life." To conclude that he conveyed to Ernestine a life tenancy with a qualifying general power of appointment would be to disregard all of these specific and deliberate manifestations of testamentary intent....

Indeed, concluding that the will gave Ernestine a qualifying general power of appointment over the life estate would be contrary to the plain language of § 2056 that she be able to exercise the power "alone and in all events." 26 U.S.C. § 2056(b). In fact, the regulations promulgated pursuant to this statutory requirement specifically provide that if the widow is not permitted to dispose of her interest "in any manner, including the power to dispose of it by gift[,]" or if exercise of the power requires the "joinder or consent of any other person[,]" it is "not considered to be a power exercisable by a surviving spouse alone and in all events...." 26 C.F.R. § 20.2056(b)–5(g)(3). See also Wisely [v. United States, 893 F.2d 660, 663 (4th Cir. 1990)] (noting when "the consent of persons other than [the surviving spouse] is required as a condition precedent to distribution of the marital trust income[,]" the interest should not qualify under § 2056(b)(5) for a marital deduction); United States v. Lincoln Rochester Trust Co., 297 F.2d 891, 892–93 (2d Cir.) ("[u]nless the surviving spouse has the right to dispose of the principal by gift or otherwise in her absolute discretion" there is no entitlement to the marital deduction), cert. denied, 369 U.S. 887 (1962).

In sum, although there is no North Carolina case directly on point, a review of the relevant authority indicates that, faced with the testamentary language in this case, the Supreme Court of North Carolina would likely conclude that the will did not empower Ernestine to appoint the trust assets to herself and to the deprivation of the remainder holder. Accordingly, Ernestine was not given enforceable rights in a life estate with a general power of appointment to qualify under § 2056(b)[24] for a marital deduction.

---

24. In its reply brief, the Estate argues that 26 C.F.R. § 20.2056(b)–5(g)(2) is inconsistent with § 2056(b)(5) of the Internal Revenue Code in that § 20.2056(b)–5(g)(2) requires the surviving spouse to have the power "to appoint the entire interest or a specific portion of it as part of her estate (and free of the trust if a trust is involved) that is, in effect, to dispose of it to whomever she pleases." 26 C.F.R. § 20.2056(b)–5(g)(2). The Estate contends that requiring the creation of a power "to dispose of [the trust assets] to whomever she pleases" is contrary to

III

Even if the interest that passed to Ernestine under the will was a terminable interest, and so did not qualify for the marital deduction, the Estate insists that it was nevertheless entitled to the deduction. This is assertedly so because "the distribution of ... assets to Mrs. Carpenter pursuant to the Family Settlement Agreement ... passed to her in recognition of her enforceable rights in an arms-length settlement of a legitimate will controversy."

Only property that "passes ... from the decedent to his surviving spouse" qualifies for the marital deduction. 26 U.S.C. § 2056(a). Thus, critical to this argument is whether the funds Ernestine Carpenter received pursuant to the settlement agreement with Nancy Reid "passed from" Stanley Carpenter to her. The relevant regulation provides:

> If as a result of the controversy involving the decedent's will, or involving any bequest or devise thereunder, a property interest is assigned or surrendered to the surviving spouse, the interest so acquired will be regarded as having "passed from the decedent to his surviving spouse" *only if the assignment or surrender was a bona fide recognition of enforceable rights of the surviving spouse in the decedent's estate*.... If the assignment or surrender was pursuant to a decree rendered by consent, or pursuant to an agreement not to contest the will or not to probate the will, it will not necessarily be accepted as a bona fide evaluation of the rights of the spouse. [26 C.F.R. § 20.2056(c)–2(d)(2) (emphasis added).]

Relying on this language, the Estate contends that the Family Settlement Agreement constitutes the good faith resolution of an arm's length, adversarial dispute between Ernestine Carpenter and Nancy Reid and, for this reason, represents a "bona fide recognition of Ernestine's enforceable rights ... in the decedent's estate." The difficulty with this argument is that the "test" of whether assets pass from the decedent for estate tax purposes is "whether the interest reaches the spouse pursuant to state law, correctly interpreted—not whether it reached the spouse as a result of good faith, adversary confrontation." Ahmanson Found. v. United States, 674 F.2d 761, 774 (9th Cir. 1981). Accord Estate of Brandon v. Commissioner of Internal Revenue, 828 F.2d 493, 499 (8th Cir. 1987). Even good faith settlements of genuine adversarial will disputes do not establish that under state law, a settling party is entitled to rights under the will itself for estate tax purposes. Estate of Hubert v. Commissioner of Internal Revenue, 101 T.C. 314, 319 (1993). Rather, a court must examine

---

§ 2056(b)(5), which provides that a general power of appointment may qualify a surviving spouse for the marital deduction "whether or not in each case the power is exercisable in favor of others...." In fact, these two provisions are consistent: § 20.2056(b)–5(g)(2) alludes to the surviving spouse's ability to dispose of the trust assets *after* exercising a general power of appointment in favor of herself, while § 2056(b)(5) deals with the ability to exercise the power of appointment in the first place. Moreover, any alleged inconsistency would be irrelevant in this case because both provisions require that an unlimited power of appointment be exercisable in favor of the surviving spouse. Ernestine Carpenter's interest therefore fails to qualify under either the statute or the accompanying regulations.

the basis for the settlement to ensure the claims on which it is grounded are valid, enforceable rights under the will. Brandon, 828 F.2d at 499; Ahmanson Found., 674 F.2d at 774.

Furthermore, the enforceability of a widow's rights is to be determined based on her claims existing against the estate "at the time the settlement was reached." Brandon, 828 F.2d at 499. Therefore, the proper focus is on the rights a widow received under the terms of the testamentary trust, not on any subsequent rights she may have received from the settlement agreement itself. See First Natl. Exchange Bank of Roanoke v. United States, 335 F.2d 91, 92 (4th Cir. 1964) ("[q]ualification for the marital deduction must be determined as of the time of the [decedent's] death").

Because, as we have held above, pursuant to state law, Ernestine did not inherit from Stanley a life estate with a general power of appointment, qualifying under § 2056(b) for a marital deduction, such an interest could not have passed to her in the Family Settlement Agreement. Property transferred pursuant to a settlement agreement—even a bona fide arm's length settlement agreement—will not qualify for a marital deduction if the surviving spouse did not, *prior* to the settlement, have an enforceable right under state law to an interest deductible under § 2056.[25]

IV

... Finally, the Estate contends that disallowance of the marital deduction in this case would violate public policy by putting Ernestine Carpenter in jeopardy of double taxation. However, this argument assumes that there will be funds remaining from the settlement agreement in her estate at the time of her death. This need not necessarily be the case. Furthermore, this double taxation argument has been consistently rejected. See Jackson v. United States, 376 U.S. 503, 509–510 (1964); Estate of Pipe v. Commissioner of Internal Revenue, 241 F.2d 210, 214 (2d Cir.) ("the possibility of double taxation is not a sufficient basis for allowing a marital deduction if the bequest does not comply with the specific statutory requirements ..."), cert. denied, 355 U.S. 814 (1957).

Affirmed.

NOTES

1. *Disqualified general power of appointment.* Consider the possibility that the surviving spouse may be given a power that does not meet the

25. The Estate's reliance on our decision in *First Natl. Exchange Bank of Roanoke* to support its argument that Ernestine's share of the settlement agreement qualifies for the marital deduction is misplaced. In *Roanoke*, a widow renounced her husband's will and exercised her absolute right under Virginia law to claim her dower interest. Our decision in *Roanoke*, permitting the widow to claim the marital deduction with respect to the proceeds of her dower election, hardly controls the present case, which involves neither Virginia law, nor the election of dower. To the extent *Roanoke* is relevant here, it is consistent with our decision in this case. In *Roanoke*, we upheld the allowance of a marital deduction for the amount of the dower interest because the surviving spouse had an "absolute and non-terminable" right to dower. 335 F.2d at 93. Here, Ernestine has no such "absolute and non-terminable" right to the trust assets.

requirements of § 2056(b)(5) but nevertheless constitutes a "general power of appointment" within the meaning of § 2041. If this occurs, the marital deduction may be denied in the decedent's estate, notwithstanding the eventual inclusion of any unconsumed property in the spouse's gross estate. See, in addition to the principal case, Walsh's Estate v. Commissioner, 110 T.C. 393 (1998), where the marital deduction was lost because the spouse's general power would lapse in the event of the spouse's incompetency. Would it make sense in such a case for the spouse to disclaim the nonqualifying power?

2. *Life estate with power to consume.* In Field's Estate v. Commissioner, 40 T.C. 802 (1963), the Tax Court held that a surviving spouse's power under a trust "to consume my entire estate for any purposes which she shall deem advisable," which was construed by the local probate court to include the power to dispose of the property by gift, did not qualify for the marital deduction:

> We are not unmindful of the fact that the decree of the Probate Court construed the will to give [the surviving spouse] the unrestricted power to dispose of the trust property in any manner, "including the power to dispose of it by gift," and that there is some inference from language in the opinions in decided cases and the language in the last sentence of section 20.2056(b)–5(g)(3), Estate Tax Regs., that the inclusion of the power to dispose of the trust corpus by gift raises an otherwise limited power of invasion to an unlimited power to invade and thus qualifies the spouse's interest as a life estate with power of appointment under section 2056(b)(5) of the Code. We have found no cases which so hold and we think the language used in the regulations pertains only to whether a power of invasion is exercisable "in all events." While a power to dispose of by gift may be a prerequisite to qualify a power of appointment as one exercisable by the spouse "in all events," it does not follow that the power to dispose of trust corpus in any manner, including the power to dispose of it by gift, necessarily qualifies the spouse's interest as a life estate with power of appointment within the meaning of the statute. Under the language of the statute and section 20.2056(b)–5(g)(1), Estate Tax Regs., the interest of the spouse does not qualify for the marital deduction unless the spouse has the power to appoint the trust corpus to herself during her lifetime or to her estate at her death free of the trust. We do not find that either the will of the decedent in this case, as construed under Ohio law, or the decree of the Probate Court goes that far. [40 T.C. at 809–10.]

Accord, Foster's Estate v. Commissioner, 725 F.2d 201 (2d Cir. 1984) (power to consume limited by good faith standard). The taxpayers in these cases are contending that the surviving spouse's interest qualifies for the marital deduction under § 2056(b)(5) because the language of the will can be construed to give the spouse a life estate with a general power of appointment over the remainder. If the testator in *Field's Estate* had died after 1981, the executor could have obtained the marital deduction by electing to treat the trust property as "qualified terminable interest property" under § 2056(b)(7). See infra page 514. Was this option available in *Carpenter's Estate*, where the testator died in 1987? In an omitted portion of the opinion in that case, the court refused on procedural grounds to address the taxpayer's argument that the marital deduction should be allowed because the deduction could have been obtained under § 2056(b)(7), and noted that no attempt was made to elect QTIP treatment.

(3) Specific Portion Rule

The statutory language of § 2056(b)(5) requires that both the income interest and the power of appointment held by the surviving spouse relate either to the entire interest passing from the decedent or to a "specific portion" thereof. The regulations define the term "specific portion" as "a fractional or percentage share" of the underlying property interest. Reg. § 20.2056(b)–5(c). Under this definition, a right to receive one-half (or some other specified percentage) of the trust income would qualify, but a right to receive annual income distributions limited to a fixed dollar amount would not. Similarly, a power of appointment over a fractional share of the trust property would qualify, but a power limited to a fixed dollar amount or to specific trust assets would not. The purpose of the fractional or percentage share requirement is to ensure that the spouse's income interest or power of appointment "reflects its proportionate share of the increase or decrease in the value of the entire property interest to which the income rights and the power relate." Reg. § 20.2056(b)–5(c)(2).

In Northeastern Pennsylvania Natl. Bank & Trust Co. v. United States, 387 U.S. 213 (1967), the decedent created a testamentary trust to pay his widow a fixed monthly sum for life and granted her a power of appointment over the entire trust property remaining at her death. Although the monthly payments to the widow did not constitute a fractional or percentage share of the trust income, a majority of the Court saw no difficulty in treating the payments as equivalent to the income from a "specific portion" of the trust corpus, and concluded that Reg. § 20.2056(b)–5(c) "improperly restrict[ed] the scope of the congressionally granted deduction." 387 U.S. at 218. The majority opinion noted that the decedent's trust posed no risk of tax avoidance because the widow had a qualifying power of appointment over the entire trust property. As pointed out in the dissenting opinion, however, the Court's reading of the "specific portion" requirement could easily give rise to a tax avoidance scheme in a separate-property jurisdiction that would be unavailable in a community-property jurisdiction:

> Assume a trust estate of $200,000, with the widow receiving the right to the income from $100,000 of its corpus and a power of appointment over that $100,000, and the children of the testator receiving income from the balance of the corpus during the widow's life, their remainders to vest when she dies. Now suppose that when the widow dies the trust corpus has doubled in value to $400,000. The wife's power of appointment over $100,000 applies only to make $100,000 taxable to her estate. [387 U.S. at 227.]

Thus, if a marital deduction of $100,000 is allowed in the decedent's estate, the $100,000 appreciation in the deductible half of the trust will escape tax in both spouses' estates and pass tax free to the children. By contrast, in a community-property jurisdiction, any appreciation in the surviving spouse's one-half share of the community property would automatically be reflected in the spouse's gross estate.

After the decision in *Northeastern Pennsylvania Natl. Bank & Trust Co.*, the Service continued to resist attempts by taxpayers to expand that decision to other situations. See, e.g., Rev. Rul. 77–444, 1977–2 C.B. 341 (surviving spouse not entitled to income from specific portion of trust where trustee required to accumulate $40,000 of income for grandchildren before making payments to surviving spouse); Rev. Rul. 79–86, 1979–1 C.B. 311 (same where trustee had power to divert amounts considered advisable to support decedent's parent in customary standard of living). See also Rubin's Estate v. Commissioner, 57 T.C. 817 (1972), affd. mem., 478 F.2d 1399 (3d Cir. 1973) (no deduction allowed where testamentary trust directed payments to widow of $100 per week for life from income or principal, remainder to children). In Alexander's Estate v. Commissioner, 82 T.C. 34 (1984), affd. mem., 760 F.2d 264 (4th Cir. 1985), however, the taxpayer succeeded in obtaining the marital deduction on facts similar to those outlined in the dissenting opinion in *Northeastern Pennsylvania Natl. Bank & Trust Co.* Finally, in 1992, Congress prospectively overruled the holding in *Northeastern Pennsylvania Natl. Bank & Trust Co.* by enacting § 2056(b)(10), which expressly defines the term "specific portion" as "a portion determined on a fractional or percentage basis."

(4) Estate Trusts

An estate trust is created by a transfer of property under which the corpus and accumulated income are payable at the surviving spouse's death to the spouse's estate. This means that the property will pass (subject to claims of the spouse's creditors) to the persons designated by the spouse's will or, if there is no will, to the spouse's intestate successors under the local law of descent and distribution. An estate trust does not require a statutory exemption from the terminable interest rule in order to qualify for the marital deduction. It does not violate the rule because the surviving spouse's interest does not terminate or fail with the lapse of time or the occurrence of an event; moreover, there is no interest passing from the decedent to another person which could confer possession or enjoyment of the trust property upon termination or failure of the spouse's interest. Rev. Rul. 68–554, 1968–2 C.B. 412. The principal advantage of an estate trust, as compared with a § 2056(b)(5) trust, is that income need not be distributed currently but can be accumulated; similarly, the trust can provide for the retention of unproductive assets.

(5) Proceeds of Life Insurance, Endowment, and Annuity Contracts Subject to Power of Appointment in Surviving Spouse

Section 2056(b)(6) provides an exception to the terminable interest rule for proceeds of life insurance, endowment, and annuity contracts, subject to requirements resembling those prescribed by § 2056(b)(5) for life-estate-with-power-of-appointment trusts. Under § 2056(b)(6), the following conditions must be satisfied:

1. The proceeds must either be payable in installments or be held by the insurer subject to an agreement to pay interest thereon, and all (or a specific portion) of the amounts payable during the surviving spouse's life must be payable solely to the spouse.
2. The installments or interest must be payable to the surviving spouse annually or more frequently, commencing not later than 13 months after the decedent's death.
3. The surviving spouse must have the power, exercisable by the spouse alone and in all events, to appoint all (or a specific portion) of the amounts payable under the contract to the spouse or to the spouse's estate.
4. No person other than the surviving spouse may have a power to appoint the amounts payable under the contract to any person other than the spouse.

Section 2056(b)(6) represents only one of several alternative methods of obtaining the marital deduction for proceeds of a life insurance, endowment, or annuity contract. It applies not only to insurance on the decedent's life, but also to insurance on the life of a person who predeceased the decedent, as well as to endowment and annuity contracts maturing before the decedent's death.

b. Qualified Terminable Interest Property

In 1981 Congress created another exception to the terminable interest rule by enacting § 2056(b)(7), which makes the marital deduction available for "qualified terminable interest property" (QTIP) at the election of the decedent's executor.[26] In general, property must meet three require-

---

26. The House Committee on Ways and Means gave the following explanation of the reasons for introducing QTIP:

> [T]he committee believes that the present [i.e., pre-1981] limitations on the nature of interests qualifying for the marital deduction should be liberalized to permit certain transfers of terminable interests to qualify for the marital deduction. Under present law, the marital deduction is available only with respect to property passing outright to the spouse or in specified forms which give the spouse control over the transferred property. Because the surviving spouse must be given control over the property, the decedent cannot insure that the spouse will subsequently pass the property to his children. Because the maximum marital deduction is limited under present [i.e., pre-1981] law to one-half of the decedent's adjusted gross estate, a decedent may at least control disposition of one-half of his estate and still maximize current tax benefits. However, unless certain interests which do not grant the spouse total control are eligible for the unlimited marital deduction, a decedent would be forced to choose between surrendering control of the entire estate to avoid imposition of estate tax at his death or reducing his tax benefits at his death to insure inheritance by the children. The committee believes that the tax laws should be neutral and that tax consequences should not control an individual's disposition of property. Accordingly, the committee believes that a deduction should be permitted for certain terminable interests [i.e., qualified terminable interest property]. [H.R. Rep. No. 201, 97th Cong., 1st Sess. 159–60 (1981), reprinted in 1981–2 C.B. 352, 377–78.]

What assumptions underlie the Committee's contention that the decedent needs dispositive control to insure that the children are not disinherited? In what ways does the enactment of QTIP protect (or fail to protect) the decedent's children from disinheritance?

ments to qualify as QTIP: (1) the property must pass from the decedent; (2) the surviving spouse must have a "qualifying income interest for life" in the property; and (3) the decedent's executor must make a valid election to treat the property as QTIP. § 2056(b)(7)(B)(i). If these requirements are met, the marital deduction is available for the entire value of the underlying property, even though the surviving spouse receives only a life income interest. See § 2056(b)(7)(A). (The gift tax counterpart of this provision is § 2523(f), which affords parallel treatment for lifetime transfers.) To ensure that the value of the underlying property will ultimately be subject to estate or gift tax in the hands of the surviving spouse, §§ 2044 and 2519 treat the spouse as making a transfer of the underlying property upon the termination or transfer of the spouse's income interest. In the years since 1981, the QTIP provisions have become the most widely used exception to the terminable interest rule and have largely eclipsed the practical significance of § 2056(b)(5).

(1) Qualifying Income Interest for Life

Property passing from the decedent can qualify as QTIP only if the surviving spouse receives a "qualifying income interest for life." This requirement is met if (1) the spouse is entitled to all (or a specific portion) of the income from the property, payable at least annually, for life, and (2) during the spouse's life, no person (including the spouse) has a power to appoint any part of the property to any person other than the spouse. § 2056(b)(7)(B)(ii). The requirement that the spouse receive a life income interest is substantially identical with the parallel provision of § 2056(b)(5) discussed above. Indeed, in determining whether a life income interest confers the requisite degree of beneficial enjoyment under § 2056(b)(7), the regulations incorporate by reference the rules developed under § 2056(b)(5). Reg. § 20.2056(b)–7(d)(3). Property treated as QTIP is typically held in trust to pay income to the surviving spouse for life, but a legal life estate may also qualify. See Reg. § 20.2056(b)–7(h) (Example 1) (devise of residence to spouse for life, remainder to children); Cavenaugh's Estate v. Commissioner, 100 T.C. 407 (1993), affd. on this issue, 51 F.3d 597 (5th Cir. 1995) (devise of residence to spouse for life; sale proceeds to be held in trust to pay income to spouse for life). Of course, the property cannot qualify as QTIP if the spouse's income interest is subject to termination on remarriage or is limited to amounts necessary for support. See, e.g., Reg. § 20.2056(b)–7(h) (Example 5) (remarriage contingency); Nicholson's Estate v. Commissioner, 94 T.C. 666 (1990) (income limited to amounts needed to maintain widow in "usual and customary standard of living"); Davis v. Commissioner, 394 F.3d 1294 (9th Cir. 2005) (distributions for widow's "health, education, or support, maintenance, comfort and welfare" in accordance with her "accustomed manner of living"). Similarly, the property does not qualify if a trustee has a power to accumulate trust income without the spouse's consent. On the other hand, an accumulation power may be neutralized by other terms of the trust which ensure that the spouse has an unrestricted right to receive current income. See, e.g., Reg. § 20.2056(b)–7(h) (Examples 2 and 3) (spouse's power, exercisable each year, to withdraw trust income that would otherwise pass to other beneficiaries); cf. Ellingson's Estate v. Commissioner, 964 F.2d 959 (9th Cir. 1992) (disregarding trustee's power to accumulate income in excess of spouse's "needs, best interests and welfare," in light of decedent's expressed intent to qualify property as QTIP).

Property is also ineligible for QTIP treatment if any person (including the surviving spouse) has a power exercisable during the spouse's life to appoint any part of the property to any person other than the spouse. See, e.g., Manscill's Estate v. Commissioner, 98 T.C. 413 (1992) (trustee's power to invade corpus "for the support" of decedent's daughter); Bowling's Estate v. Commissioner, 93 T.C. 286 (1989) (trustee's power to invade corpus for "emergency needs" of "any beneficiary," including decedent's son and brother). This restriction is intended to foreclose the possibility that the property might be diverted from the surviving spouse in a manner that escapes estate and gift tax altogether (e.g., under a nongeneral power of appointment). Powers exercisable only at or after the spouse's death, however, are permitted because the property remaining at the spouse's death will ordinarily be includible in the spouse's gross estate by virtue of § 2044, whether the power is exercised or not. Thus, for example, the spouse may be given a power of appointment, exercisable by will in favor of the decedent's issue. Moreover, the statute does not prevent any person from holding a power to invade the property for the spouse's benefit during life. Thus, for example, a trustee may be granted a power to distribute corpus to the spouse, either in the trustee's absolute discretion or subject to a standard (e.g., for the spouse's support). Query whether the spouse may be given a general power of appointment exercisable during life in favor of "any person" (including the spouse)? Cf. Cavenaugh's Estate v. Commissioner, 100 T.C. 407 (1993), affd. on this issue, 51 F.3d 597 (5th Cir. 1995) (surviving spouse had "5 and 5" power over QTIP).

Under § 2056(b)(7)(B)(iv), a "specific portion" of property is treated as "separate property." The definition of "specific portion" in § 2056(b)(10), discussed above in connection with § 2056(b)(5), applies equally here. Hence, an otherwise qualifying income interest for life is not disqualified merely because it relates to a fractional or percentage share of the underlying property. Similarly, a disqualifying power (e.g., a power to invade property for a person other than the surviving spouse) that is limited to a fractional or percentage share of the underlying property does not prevent the balance from qualifying as QTIP.

One major difference between § 2056(b)(5) and § 2056(b)(7) is that the latter provision does not require that the surviving spouse be given a general power of appointment over the underlying property. This feature, along with the flexibility provided by the QTIP election, explains why QTIP has become so widely used: It makes the marital deduction available in the decedent's estate while permitting the decedent to control the ultimate disposition of the property after the spouse's death. The QTIP provisions may also be particularly helpful in obtaining the marital deduction where an ambiguous power to invade or consume property fails to meet the technical requirements of § 2056(b)(5). See supra page 511, Note 2.

Another significant departure from the rules of § 2056(b)(5) concerns the treatment of survivor annuities. Section 2056(b)(7)(C) expressly authorizes QTIP treatment for "an annuity included in the gross estate of the decedent under § 2039" (or under § 2033, in the case of an annuity that constitutes community property), provided that the surviving spouse is the sole beneficiary during the spouse's life. Such an annuity qualifies for QTIP treatment unless the executor "otherwise elects" on the estate tax return. Thus, for example, a survivor annuity payable under a qualified pension plan to a deceased employee's surviving spouse for life with remainder to other beneficiaries automatically qualifies as QTIP unless the executor affirmatively elects to forgo the marital deduction.

(2) QTIP Election

Unlike the marital deduction under § 2056(b)(5), which applies automatically if the statutory requirements are met, the deduction for QTIP is elective. Under § 2056(b)(7)(B)(v), the QTIP election is made by the decedent's executor on the estate tax return. The regulations interpret the "specific portion" rule of § 2056(b)(7)(B)(iv), discussed above, to permit the executor to elect QTIP treatment for a fractional or percentage share of the underlying property. See Reg. § 20.2056(b)–7(b)(2). As a result, if the spouse has a qualifying income interest for life in the entire trust property, the executor may elect to claim a marital deduction for a fractional portion of the trust, with the result that only a corresponding portion of the trust property will be included in the spouse's gross estate under § 2044. Moreover, the fractional portion may be defined by a formula based on the final estate tax value of the underlying property. See Reg. § 20.2056(b)–7(h) (Examples 7 and 8). Although the election is made by the executor, not the surviving spouse, the spouse may nevertheless defeat the marital deduction by making a qualified disclaimer of the qualifying income interest for life. See Rev. Rul. 83–26, 1983–1 C.B. 234 (no marital deduction allowed where spouse disclaimed property for which executor had already made proper QTIP election).

SHELFER'S ESTATE v. COMMISSIONER

86 F.3d 1045 (11th Cir. 1996).

KRAVITCH, CIRCUIT JUDGE:

The Commissioner of the Internal Revenue Service ("Commissioner") appeals the Tax Court's decision in favor of the estate of Lucille Shelfer. The court held that Lucille's estate was not liable for a tax deficiency assessed on the value of a trust from which she had received income during her lifetime. The estate of Lucille Shelfer's husband, Elbert, previously had taken a marital deduction for these trust assets, claiming that the trust met the definition of a qualified terminable interest property trust ("QTIP") pursuant to 26 U.S.C. § 2056(b)(7).

This case presents an issue of first impression for this circuit: whether a QTIP trust is established when, under the terms of the trust, the surviving spouse is neither entitled to, nor given the power of appointment over, the trust income accumulating between the date of the last distribution and her death, otherwise known as the "stub income." The Commissioner interprets the QTIP statutory provisions to allow such trusts to qualify for the marital deduction in the decedent's estate; accordingly, the value of the trust assets must be included in the surviving spouse's estate. We agree with the Commissioner and reverse the Tax Court.

I

Elbert Shelfer died on September 13, 1986 and was survived by his wife, Lucille. Elbert's will provided that his estate was to be divided into two shares, that were to be held in separate trusts. The income from each trust was to be paid to Lucille in quarterly installments during her lifetime. The first trust was a standard marital deduction trust consisting of one-third of the estate. It is not at issue in this case. The second trust, comprising the remaining two-thirds of the estate, terminated upon Lucille's death. The principal and all undistributed income was payable to Elbert's niece, Betty Ann Shelfer.

Elbert's will designated Quincy State Bank as the personal representative for his estate, and on June 16, 1987, the bank filed a tax return on behalf of the estate. The bank elected to claim a deduction for approximately half of the assets of the second trust under the QTIP trust provisions of 26 U.S.C. § 2056(b)(7). The IRS examined the return, allowed the QTIP deduction, and issued Quincy Bank a closing letter on May 10, 1989. The statute of limitations for an assessment of deficiency with respect to Elbert's return expired on June 16, 1990.

On January 18, 1989, Lucille died; Quincy State Bank served as personal representative for her estate. The bank filed an estate tax return on October 18, 1989 and did not include the value of the assets in the trust, even though the assets previously had been deducted on her husband's estate tax return. The IRS audited the return and assessed a tax deficiency for the trust assets on the ground that the trust was a QTIP trust subject to taxation. Quincy State Bank commenced a proceeding in tax court on behalf of Lucille's estate, claiming that the trust did not meet the definition of a QTIP trust because Lucille did not control the stub income; therefore, the Bank argued, the estate was not liable for tax on the trust assets under 26 U.S.C. § 2044. The Tax Court agreed. The Commissioner appeals this decision.

II

. . . Lucille's estate contends, and the Tax Court held, that the phrase "all of the income" [in § 2056(b)(7)(B)(ii)(I)] includes income that has accrued between the last distribution and the date of the spouse's death, or the stub income. They argue that "all" refers to every type of income.

Stub income is a kind of income, and thus the surviving spouse must be entitled to stub income in order for the trust to qualify as a QTIP trust. They conclude that because Elbert's will did not grant Lucille control over the stub income, the QTIP election fails.

In contrast, the Commissioner and amicus argue that the statute is satisfied if the surviving spouse controls "all of the income" that has been distributed. They contend that the requirement that income be, "payable annually or at more frequent intervals," limits "all of the income" to distributed income, namely those payments that have been made to the surviving spouse during her life. See Estate of Howard v. Commissioner, 910 F.2d 633, 635 (9th Cir. 1990) (concluding that "if [the surviving spouse] has been entitled to regular distributions at least annually, she has had an income interest for life").

The estate replies that the phrase "payable annually or at more frequent intervals" is separated from the preceding clause by commas, and thus is a parenthetical clause. Because parenthetical clauses are non-restrictive, it contends that the clause is merely a description of the distribution process and does not in any way limit the preceding requirement that the spouse must be entitled to "all of the income."

Both parties insist that their reading of the statute is "plain." We do not agree. Although the use of commas around the clause "payable annually or at more frequent intervals" does indicate a parenthetical clause, we refuse to place inordinate weight on punctuation and ignore the remainder of the sentence. It is equally plausible that the next clause is designed to provide a context from which to define "all of the income."[27]

. . .

Accordingly, we must look beyond the "plain language" of the statute for guidance. When faced with a similarly ambiguous tax code provision, the Supreme Court thoroughly examined the history and purpose of the tax provision at issue, past practices, and the practical implications of its ruling. Commissioner v. Engle, 464 U.S. 206 (1984). We follow suit, beginning with the history and purpose of the marital deduction.

III

. . . An essential goal of the marital deduction statutory scheme "from its very beginning, however, was that any property of the first spouse to die that passed untaxed to the surviving spouse should be taxed in the estate of the surviving spouse." Estate of Clayton v. Commissioner, 976 F.2d 1486, 1491 (5th Cir. 1992). In accordance with this intent, the statute proscribed deductions for terminable property interests. Terminable prop-

27. We accept the possibility that the second clause—"payable annually or at more frequent intervals"—may be an important context for understanding the first phrase, "all of the income." See Smith v. United States, 508 U.S. 223, 230–32 (1993) (noting that surrounding terms may clarify the meaning of a word). We reject, however, the Commissioner's assertion that the second clause necessarily limits the preceding clause. If this clause were indeed a restrictive clause, then the surviving spouse would only be entitled to that which had been paid out annually or more frequently; another person could receive income distributed less frequently. This result was clearly not intended by Congress.

erty interests are those interests that will terminate upon the occurrence of an event, the failure of an event to take place, or after a certain time period. Because these interests could terminate prior to the death of the surviving spouse, they posed a risk that the assets would escape taxation in the spouse's estate tax return.

The original statute allowed three exceptions to the terminable property rule for interests that would not escape taxation in the spouse's estate. Property interests would qualify for the marital deduction under any of the following conditions: (1) the interest of the spouse was conditional on survival for a limited period and the spouse survived that period; (2) the spouse had a life estate in the property with the power of appointment over the corpus; or (3) the spouse received all life insurance or annuity payments during her lifetime with the power to appoint all payments under the contract. To take advantage of these exceptions, however, the decedent had to relinquish all control over the marital property to the surviving spouse.

As divorce and remarriage rates rose, Congress became increasingly concerned with the difficult choice facing those in second marriages, who could either provide for their spouse to the possible detriment of the children of a prior marriage or risk under-endowing their spouse to provide directly for the children. In the Economic Recovery Act of 1981, Congress addressed this problem by creating the QTIP exception to the terminable property interest rule. According to the House of Representatives Report, the QTIP trust was designed to prevent a decedent from being "forced to choose between surrendering control of the entire estate to avoid imposition of estate tax at his death or reducing his tax benefits at his death to insure inheritance by the children." H.R. Rep. No. 201, 97th Cong., 1st Sess. 160 (1981). Thus, the purpose of the QTIP trust provisions was to liberalize the marital deduction to cover trust instruments that provide ongoing income support for the surviving spouse while retaining the corpus for the children or other beneficiaries.

In addition to creating the QTIP trust provisions, the 1981 Act also substantially changed the marital deduction by lifting the limitations on the amount of the deduction. The Senate Report for the 1981 Act states the reason for the change: "The committee believes that a husband and wife should be treated as one economic unit for purposes of estate and gift taxes, as they generally are for income tax purposes. Accordingly, no tax should be imposed on transfers between a husband and wife." S. Rep. No. 144, 97th Cong., 1st Sess. 127 (1981), reprinted in 1981 U.S.C.C.A.N. 105, 228.

Although the legislative history of the 1981 Act sets forth Congress's reasons for enacting the statute, it does not directly address the stub income issue. When "neither the statutory language nor the legislative history are dispositive of the issue, we guide ourselves generally by the purposes" of the Act and Congress's intent in enacting it. Rickard v. Auto Publisher, Inc., 735 F.2d 450, 457 (11th Cir. 1984). Accordingly, we must decide which interpretation of the statute best comports with the two general goals discussed above: expanding the marital deduction to provide for the spouse while granting the decedent more control over the ultimate disposition of the property, and treating a husband and wife as one economic entity for the purposes of estate taxation.

Under the Commissioner's interpretation of the statute, the decedent would gain the tax benefit, retain control of the trust corpus, and provide the spouse with all of the periodic payments for her personal support. The stub income, which accrues after her death and is thus not used for her maintenance, could be appointed to someone else. This result is consistent with the statutory goals of expanding the deduction while providing for the spouse's support. In contrast, the Tax Court's reading of the statute would condition the tax benefit for the entire trust corpus on ceding control over a much smaller amount that is not needed for the spouse's support.

The statute's second goal, treating a married couple as one economic entity, was effected in a comprehensive statutory scheme. In addition to the QTIP provisions of § 2056(b)(7), Congress added § 2044, which requires the estate of the surviving spouse to include all property for which a marital deduction was previously allowed, and § 2056(b)(7)(B)(v), which states that a QTIP "election, once made, shall be irrevocable." Taken together, these sections of the code provide that assets can pass between spouses without being subject to taxation. Upon the death of the surviving spouse, the spouse's estate will be required to pay tax on all of the previously deducted marital assets. The Commissioner's position comports with the statutory scheme because it compels the surviving spouse to abide by the irrevocable election of a QTIP trust and to pay taxes on property that had previously been subject to a deduction....

Following the logic of the regulations, ... [t]he trust corpus and the stub income would be taxable pursuant to § 2044, which requires the spouse to include all previously deducted property in which she has a qualifying interest for life.[28] This comprehensive scheme, like that of the power of appointment trust, allows an initial deduction and later taxation of the property.[29] ...

28. We acknowledge that § 2044 does not expressly apply to stub income because it provides that the surviving spouse's estate must include all property over which the spouse had a qualifying income interest for life. Although we have already shown that the trust property can be a qualifying income interest for life even if the surviving spouse is not given control of the stub income, we have not determined whether the stub income can be part of the qualifying income interest for life. The Commissioner's regulation, now finalized at 26 C.F.R. [§ 20.2044–1(d)(2)], clarifies the issue by specifically including the stub income in the spouse's gross estate. We note that although the regulation was not finalized at the time of this action, it is the most consistent interpretation of the statute for the same reason that the regulations for the power of appointment trust are reasonable. Both regulations ensure that previously deducted property is taxed at the death of the surviving spouse. Moreover, both regulations are faithful to the statutory scheme. In the power of appointment regulations, the stub income is rendered subject to the power of appointment and becomes taxable. In the QTIP provisions, the stub income is included in the spouse's estate along with the trust corpus, both of which are not controlled by the spouse.

29. Our reading of the regulation does not disqualify a trust instrument that provides for the surviving spouse to have the power of appointment over the stub income or to receive the stub

Examining the legislative history of the 1981 Act, we conclude that Congress intended to liberalize the marital deduction, to treat a husband and wife as one economic unit, and to allow the stub income to be treated in the same manner as the trust corpus for taxation purposes. These goals favor a broad interpretation of the statute that would allow the QTIP election in this case. Having assessed the legislative history and purpose of the statute, we turn to the practical implications of this interpretation.

IV

Our construction of the statute has several practical advantages over the Tax Court's position. First, it would assure certainty in estate planning.... The status of trust instruments that were set up in accordance with the Commissioner's advice will not be in question and the validity of the Commissioner's final regulation on this matter will be affirmed.[30]

Second, our result comports with standard trust practices. Under the Tax Court's approach, a trust fund that made daily payments to the surviving spouse would qualify for the deduction because there would be no undistributed income; in contrast, one that made quarterly payments would be ineligible. In *Howard*, the Ninth Circuit noted that "no trust pays its beneficiaries on a daily basis. The statute did not impose such an unrealistic requirement for a trust to become a QTIP." Howard, 910 F.2d at 635....

Finally, a broad reading of the marital deduction provisions benefits the federal Treasury and furthers Congressional intent to ensure taxation of all previously deducted property. In the instant case, for example, the corpus of $2,829,610 would be subject to taxation, for a gain of over $1,000,000 in tax deficiencies. The Tax Court's opinion would grant similar estates a substantial windfall, encouraging other executors of wills to disclaim the previously taken deduction.

For all of these reasons, we conclude that our interpretation of the statute will better serve the practical realities of trust administration and estate taxation.

V

After determining that the statutory language is ambiguous, we looked beyond the statute to additional sources of information, such as the legislative history. Careful consideration of these documents led us to discern two purposes for the 1981 Act: treating the married couple as one economic unit, and expanding the deduction to include arrangements that divest the surviving spouse of control over property. These congressional

---

income as part of her estate. Under those circumstances, congressional goals will be served because the stub income will clearly be taxable and the couple will be considered one economic unit. We merely hold that the estate planning document at issue here also qualifies for the deduction because Congress provided a statutory scheme which will require taxation of the stub income if it reverts to the trust remainderman.

30. The Commissioner's position has been promulgated in a final regulation, 26 C.F.R. § 20.2044–1(d)(2), which is substantially the same as the position taken by the Commissioner here.

goals are best served by allowing the deduction in the decedent's estate and requiring subsequent inclusion in the surviving spouse's estate when trust documents do not grant control over the stub income to the surviving spouse. Accordingly, we reverse the Tax Court.

NOTES

1. *Inclusion in surviving spouse's gross estate.* The court in *Shelfer's Estate* finds that the statutory requirement that the surviving spouse be entitled to "all the income" is not violated merely because the "stub income" earned between the last distribution date and the date of the spouse's death is distributable to other beneficiaries. The regulations confirm this result. Reg. § 20.2056(b)–7(d)(4). The same expansive definition of QTIP carries over to § 2044, which requires inclusion in the surviving spouse's gross estate of property for which a QTIP deduction was allowed in the first spouse's estate and in which the surviving spouse had a qualifying income interest for life. The court in *Shelfer's Estate* indicates that § 2044 should reach not only the trust corpus but also the stub income earned between the last distribution date and the date of the surviving spouse's death. Again, the regulations agree. Reg. § 20.2044–1(d)(2) (requiring inclusion of stub income under § 2044 to the extent not already included under any other provision).

2. *Duty of consistency.* The courts have long recognized that in some circumstances a taxpayer who made a representation or reported an item on a tax return may be barred by equitable principles from adopting an inconsistent position on a subsequent tax return after the statute of limitations has run on the earlier return. See Johnson, The Taxpayer's Duty of Consistency, 43 Tax L. Rev. 537 (1991) ("At its core, the doctrine reflects a distaste for a taxpayer's attempt to have his cake after already having eaten it."). Suppose that a decedent leaves property in trust for the surviving spouse and the executor elects to treat the trust as QTIP. After the limitation period for assessing additional estate tax has run, it is discovered that the surviving spouse's interest in the trust does not in fact meet the definition of a "qualifying income interest for life" under § 2056(b)(7)(B)(ii). Is the nonqualifying trust property includible in the surviving spouse's estate, or does it escape estate and gift taxes altogether? See Letts' Estate v. Commissioner, 109 T.C. 290 (1997), affd. mem., 212 F.3d 600 (11th Cir. 2000) (property deducted in first spouse's estate was includible in surviving spouse's estate; duty of consistency prevented surviving spouse from repudiating implied representation made in claiming deduction on first spouse's estate tax return); Buder's Estate v. United States, 436 F.3d 936 (8th Cir. 2006) (allowing equitable recoupment); but cf. Posner's Estate v. Commissioner, 87 T.C.M. (CCH) 1288 (2004) (duty of consistency inapplicable to "mutual mistake on the part of a taxpayer and the Service concerning a pure question of law").

3. *Income interest contingent on election.* At one time the Service took the position that property did not qualify for QTIP treatment if the spouse's income interest was contingent on the executor's QTIP election. For example, suppose a testator leaves property in trust, with income payable to the surviving spouse for life if the executor elects to treat the trust property as QTIP; if no QTIP election is made, however, the property will be held in trust

for other beneficiaries. The Service denied the marital deduction for the trust property, regardless of whether an election was actually made. In the Service's view, the statutory definition of QTIP was not met because the spouse's right to receive income from the property depended on a post-mortem exercise of discretionary authority by the executor; in effect, the executor held a prohibited power to appoint the property away from the spouse. The Service's argument initially met with success in the Tax Court, but was repeatedly rejected on appeal. Clayton's Estate v. Commissioner, 976 F.2d 1486 (5th Cir. 1992), revg. 97 T.C. 327 (1991); Robertson's Estate v. Commissioner, 15 F.3d 779 (8th Cir. 1994), revg. 98 T.C. 678 (1992); Spencer's Estate v. Commissioner, 43 F.3d 226 (6th Cir. 1995), revg. 64 T.C.M. (CCH) 937 (1992). Faced with this string of reversals, the Tax Court announced that it would no longer adhere to its earlier rulings, and the Service finally conceded defeat. Clack's Estate v. Commissioner, 106 T.C. 131 (1996) (acq. in result). The regulations now provide that an otherwise qualifying income interest that is contingent on the executor's QTIP election "will not fail to be a qualifying income interest for life because of such contingency or because the portion of the property for which the election is not made passes to or for the benefit of persons other than the surviving spouse." Reg. § 20.2056(b)–7(d)(3); see also Reg. § 20.2056(b)–7(h) (Example 6).

4. *Individual retirement accounts.* The balance in a decedent's individual retirement account (IRA) must be paid out to the surviving beneficiaries in annual installments over a specified period. § 408(a)(6). The IRA may also qualify as QTIP if all the income is payable to the surviving spouse at least annually and no distributions can be made to any other beneficiary during the spouse's life. For example, suppose the decedent's IRA is payable to the surviving spouse in annual installments consisting of all the income earned on the IRA plus a ratable share of the remaining principal balance; at the spouse's death, any remaining balance will be paid to the couple's children. The annual distributions to the surviving spouse meet the requirements of both § 408(a)(6) and § 2056(b)(7), and the executor can elect to treat the IRA as QTIP. See Reg. § 20.2056(b)–7(h) (Example 10).

What if the IRA is payable not directly to the spouse but instead to a trust in which the spouse has a life income interest? In Rev. Rul. 2000–2, 2000–1 C.B. 305, the Service ruled that both the IRA and the trust qualify as QTIP where "the trustee of the trust is the named beneficiary of the decedent's IRA, the surviving spouse can compel the trustee to withdraw from the IRA an amount equal to all the income earned on the IRA assets at least annually and to distribute that amount to the spouse, and no person has a power to appoint any part of the trust property to any person other than the spouse." In these circumstances, the Service views the trust as "a conduit for payments equal to income from the IRA to [the spouse]" and indicates that the decedent's executor must make the QTIP election for both the IRA and the trust. Note that the spouse need not actually receive all the IRA's income each year; it is sufficient that the spouse can compel the trustee to withdraw that amount. Thus, any income in excess of the minimum distributions required by § 408(a)(6) can be left in the IRA. See also Rev. Rul. 2006–26, 2006–1 C.B. 939 (illustrating power of withdrawal under three alternative methods of determining income).

5. *Redundant election.* A QTIP election, once made, is irrevocable. § 2056(b)(7)(B)(v). Nevertheless, the Service will disregard an otherwise valid QTIP election "where the election was not necessary to reduce the estate tax liability to zero." Rev. Proc. 2001–38, 2001–2 C.B. 124. Thus, if the executor purports to elect QTIP treatment for a marital trust even though it is clear that no estate tax will be imposed in any event—because, for example, the decedent's available unified credit is sufficient to eliminate any estate tax without regard to the marital deduction—the QTIP election is superfluous and will be disregarded. As a result, the decedent's estate will still pass free of tax, and the marital trust property will not be taxable under §§ 2519 or 2044 in the surviving spouse's hands. What if some amount of estate tax would be payable in the absence of an election, but the executor elects QTIP treatment for more property than is necessary to reduce the estate tax liability to zero?

6. *Reformation.* In Rapp's Estate v. Commissioner, 140 F.3d 1211 (9th Cir. 1998), the decedent's will created a trust to pay discretionary income and corpus to his widow for life, with remainder at her death to other beneficiaries. On its face, the bequest did not qualify for the marital deduction because the widow's right to receive income depended on the trustees' exercise of their discretion. In an attempt to cure this defect, the widow obtained a probate court order which modified the terms of the trust to provide for annual distributions of all the trust income to the widow for life. No appeal was taken from the probate court order, which accordingly became final and binding on the parties. Nevertheless, relying on the holding in *Bosch*, supra page 26, the Tax Court and the Ninth Circuit found that the probate court order was contrary to state law and therefore not binding for federal estate tax purposes. Accordingly, no marital deduction was allowed for the trust property. What difference would it have made if the probate court's order had been affirmed by the highest state court? Cf. Loeser v. Talbot, 589 N.E.2d 301 (Mass. 1992) (approving reformation of trust to provide surviving spouse with a qualifying income interest for life, but "pass[ing] no judgment on the actual tax consequences of the trust as reformed"). Does a court-ordered reformation of a trust instrument have retroactive effect not only for the parties but also for non-parties such as the federal government? See Van den Wymelenberg v. United States, 397 F.2d 443 (7th Cir.), cert. denied, 393 U.S. 953 (1968) ("not even judicial reformation can operate to change the federal tax consequences of a completed transaction"); Rev. Rul. 93–79, 1993–2 C.B. 269; but cf. Flitcroft v. Commissioner, 328 F.2d 449 (9th Cir. 1964).

(3) Termination or Disposition of Spouse's Income Interest

To ensure that QTIP does not escape estate or gift tax in the hands of the surviving spouse, §§ 2044 and 2519 treat the termination or transfer of the spouse's income interest as a transfer of the underlying property. Under § 2519(a), "any disposition of all or part of a qualifying income interest for life" made by the spouse during life is treated as "a transfer of all interests in [the QTIP] other than the qualifying income interest." Since the income interest itself is already subject to gift tax under § 2511, there is no need to include it again under § 2519. All other interests in the QTIP, however, are included in the spouse's constructive transfer, even if the spouse disposes of only a portion of the income interest. For example, assume that *H* created a QTIP trust to pay income to his wife *W* for life, with remainder at her death to their children. If *W* releases the entire income interest, she will be treated as making a gift of the full value of the trust property to the remainder beneficiaries. See Reg. § 25.2519–1(g) (Example 1). If *W* releases only one-half of the income interest, she will still make a constructive gift of the entire remainder interest and an actual gift of one-half of the income interest. Note also that *W*'s retention of part of the income interest may have two disagreeable consequences: (1) the retained income interest may be valued at zero under § 2702 (see supra page 78), with the result that *W* incurs a gift tax on the full value of the trust property; and (2) the constructive transfer subject to a retained life interest in one-half of the income may cause one-half of the value of the trust to be drawn back into *W*'s gross estate at death under § 2036(a). See Reg. § 25.2519–1(g) (Example 4).

If the spouse does not dispose of the income interest during life, the value of the underlying property will be included in the spouse's gross estate (and treated as passing from the spouse) at death under § 2044. Frequently the spouse has no testamentary power to appoint the remainder. To prevent the estate tax burden from falling on the spouse's other assets, § 2207A(a) grants the spouse's estate the right to recover the estate tax attributable to QTIP from the recipients of the property, unless the spouse's will (or revocable trust) directs otherwise. The recoverable amount is equal to the incremental increase in the estate tax caused by inclusion of QTIP under § 2044, i.e., the difference between the amount of tax actually paid and the amount that would have been paid if the property were not included in the gross estate. Section 2207A(b) provides a similar right of recovery for the gift tax imposed under § 2519. If the spouse exercises a right of recovery under § 2207A(b), does the recovery reduce the amount of the spouse's deemed gift under § 2519? See Reg. § 25.2519–1(c)(4) (net gift calculation). If the spouse (or the spouse's executor) fails to exercise a right of recovery under § 2207A, does the forgone benefit constitute a deemed transfer to the persons from whom recovery could have been obtained? If so, who is the transferor and when does the transfer occur? See Reg. §§ 20.2207A–1(a) (executor's failure to exercise § 2207A(a) right of recovery triggers deemed transfer by persons who would benefit from recovery, unless recovery waived pursuant to spouse's will) and 25.2207A–1(b) (deemed transfer by spouse who fails to exercise § 2207A(b) right of recovery). Suppose the spouse makes a lifetime disposition of the income interest and exercises the right of recovery under § 2207A(b). If the spouse dies less than three years later, is the gift tax recovered from the recipients of the property includible in the spouse's gross estate under § 2035(b)? See Morgens' Estate v. Commissioner, 133 T.C. 402 (2009) (requiring gift tax gross-up). What is the income tax basis of the property in the hands of the recipients? See supra page 40 and page 236, Note 7.

REVENUE RULING 98–8

1998–1 C.B. 541.

. . . The decedent, *D*, died in 1993 survived by *S*, *D*'s spouse. Under the terms of *D*'s will, a trust (the QTIP Trust) was established under which *S* was to receive all of the trust income, payable at least annually, for *S*'s life. On *S*'s death, the remainder was to be distributed outright to *C*, *D*'s adult child. *S* was not given a general power of appointment over the trust property.

On the federal estate tax return filed for *D*'s estate, the executor made an election under § 2056(b)(7) to treat the trust property as QTIP, and a marital deduction was allowed to *D*'s estate for the value of the property passing from *D* to the QTIP Trust.

Subsequently, *S*, *C*, and the trustee of the QTIP Trust entered into the following transaction: (1) *S* acquired *C*'s remainder interest in the QTIP Trust; (2) *S* gave *C* a promissory note in the face amount of *x* dollars (the value of the remainder interest) for the remainder interest; (3) the trustee distributed all of the QTIP Trust assets (having a value of $x + y$ dollars) to *S*; and (4) *S* thereupon paid *x* dollars from those assets to *C* in satisfaction of the promissory note.

At the conclusion of the transaction, the QTIP Trust was terminated; *S* held QTIP Trust assets having a value of *y* dollars (which was equal to the value of *S*'s life interest in the trust); and *C* held assets having a value of *x* dollars (which was equal to the value of the remainder interest in the trust). *S* contended that the transaction was not subject to gift tax because *S* received full and adequate consideration (the *x* dollar remainder interest in the QTIP Trust) in exchange for the *x* dollar promissory note given by *S* to *C*. . . .

The estate tax marital deduction provisions are intended to provide a special tax benefit that allows property to pass to the surviving spouse without the decedent's estate paying tax on its value. Tax is deferred on the transfer until the surviving spouse either dies or makes a lifetime disposition of the property. Under either circumstance, a transfer (estate or gift) tax is paid. . . .

The statutory scheme of the QTIP provisions is consistent with this congressional intent. Thus, a marital deduction is allowed under § 2056(b)(7) for property passing from a decedent to a QTIP trust in which the surviving spouse possesses a lifetime income interest. Sections 2519 and 2044 act to defer the taxable event on the marital deduction property only so long as the surviving spouse continues to hold the lifetime income interest.

Under § 2519, if a surviving spouse disposes of any part of the qualifying income interest, the spouse is treated as making a gift of the remainder interest in the underlying property (i.e., all interests in the property other than the income interest). Correspondingly, under § 2511, the disposition of the income interest by the spouse is treated as a gift, to the extent the income interest is transferred to another for less than adequate consideration.

The term "disposition," as used in § 2519, applies broadly to circumstances in which the surviving spouse's right to receive the income is relinquished or otherwise terminated, by whatever means. See H. Rep. No. 201, 97th Cong., 1st Sess. 161 (1981) that states:

> The bill provides that property subject to a [QTIP election] will be subject to transfer taxes at the earlier of (1) the date on which the spouse disposes (either by gift, sale, or otherwise) of all or part of the qualifying income interest, or (2) upon the spouse's death.

A commutation, which is a proportionate division of trust property between the life beneficiary and remainderman based on the respective values of their interests is, in the context of a QTIP trust, a taxable disposition by the spouse of the qualifying income interest, resulting in a gift under § 2519 of the value of the remainder interest. The commutation of the spouse's income interest in the QTIP trust is essentially a sale of the income interest by the spouse to the trustee (or the remainderman) in exchange for an amount equal to the value of the income interest. Sales and commutations are expressly characterized as dispositions in the applicable legislative history and regulations. [Reg. §§ 25.2519–1(f) and (g) (Example 2).] . . .

There is little distinction between the sale and commutation transactions treated as dispositions in the regulations and the transaction presented here, where *S* acquired the remainder interest. In both cases, after the transaction the spouse's income interest in the trust is terminated and the spouse receives outright ownership of property having a net value equal to the value of the spouse's income interest. Similarly, the remainderman receives ownership of property equal in value to the remainder interest. Thus, the transaction in the instant case essentially effectuates a commutation of *S*'s income interest in the trust, a transaction that is a disposition of *S*'s income interest under § 2519. Therefore, under § 2519, *S* is regarded as making a gift of *x* dollars, the value of the remainder interest in the QTIP Trust. Section 25.2519–1(f).

This conclusion that *S* has made a gift is also supported by an additional analysis. *S* acquired an asset (the remainder interest in the QTIP Trust) that is already subject to inclusion in *S*'s transfer tax base under § 2044. In analogous situations, the courts have recognized that the receipt of an asset that does not effectively increase the value of the recipient's gross estate does not constitute adequate consideration for purposes of the gift and estate tax. See Commissioner v. Wemyss, 324 U.S. 303 (1945). . . .

A companion case to Commissioner v. Wemyss, Merrill v. Fahs, 324 U.S. 308 (1945), and the cases that preceded it, involved situations where *A*, an individual, transferred property to *B*, *A*'s spouse (or future spouse), in exchange for *B*'s relinquishment of marital rights in *A*'s property. The

Court held that *B*'s relinquishment of the marital rights did not constitute adequate and full consideration for *A*'s transfer because the assets subject to the marital rights were already includible in *A*'s taxable estate. The property subject to dower and marital rights is clearly included in the gross estate of the property owner. Thus, to conclude that the relinquishment of dower and marital rights by the spouse of the property owner constituted adequate and full consideration for a transfer by the property owner for gift tax purposes would effectively subvert the legislative intent and statutory scheme of the gift tax provisions. . . .

Likewise, in the present situation, property subject to the QTIP election was intended to be subject to either gift or estate tax. *S*'s receipt of the remainder interest does not increase the value of *S*'s taxable estate because that property is already subject to inclusion in *S*'s taxable estate under § 2044. Rather, *S*'s issuance of the note results in a depletion of *S*'s taxable estate that is not offset by *S*'s receipt of the remainder interest. Thus, for estate and gift tax purposes, *S*'s receipt of the remainder interest cannot constitute adequate and full consideration under § 2512 for the promissory note transferred by *S* to *C*. As was the case in Merrill v. Fahs, any other result would subvert the legislative intent and statutory scheme underlying § 2056(b)(7). Therefore, under § 2511, *S* has made a gift to *C* equal to the value of the promissory note *S* gave to *C*.

In addition, a gift tax would be imposed under the above alternative rationales even if *S* acquired only a portion of *C*'s remainder interest; e.g., *S* acquired 60 percent of *C*'s remainder interest. If, under applicable state law, such a transaction results in a partial termination of the trust, *S* would be treated as disposing of part of *S*'s income interest in the trust, and the commutation analysis would apply. See [Reg. § 25.2519–1(g) (Example 4)]. If the trust does not terminate, *S* would nonetheless be treated as making a transfer under §§ 2511 and 2512 for less than adequate and full consideration to the extent of the value of the property or cash *S* transfers in exchange for the partial remainder interest.

Further, the conclusion of this revenue ruling would be the same if *S* transferred to *C* property or cash rather than the promissory note. The economic effect of the transaction is identical, regardless whether *S* uses *S*'s own funds to finance the transaction or gives a promissory note and discharges the note using some of the QTIP Trust assets received in the transaction. Thus, the result is the same for transfer tax purposes. . . .

If a surviving spouse acquires the remainder interest in a trust subject to a QTIP election under § 2056(b)(7) in connection with the transfer by the surviving spouse of property or cash to the holder of the remainder interest, the surviving spouse makes a gift both under § 2519 and §§ 2511 and 2512. The amount of the gift is equal to the greater of (i) the value of the remainder interest (pursuant to § 2519), or (ii) the value of the property or cash transferred to the holder of the remainder interest (pursuant to §§ 2511 and 2512).

NOTE

Commutation. The transaction in Rev. Rul. 98–8 does not involve a formal transfer of *S*'s income interest in the QTIP Trust, but it could easily be recast as a sale of *S*'s income interest to *C* in exchange for a portion of the trust assets to be received by *C* immediately thereafter upon termination of the trust. The latter version of the transaction clearly gives rise to a deemed gift of the remainder interest under § 2519. See Reg. § 25.2519–1(g) (Example 2). The regulations require the same result if *S* and *C* receive the commuted value of their respective interests upon termination of the trust. Reg. § 25.2519–1(f) ("the sale of qualified terminable interest property, followed by the payment to the donee spouse of a portion of the proceeds equal to the value of the donee spouse's income interest, is considered a disposition of the qualifying income interest"). In effect, Rev. Rul. 98–8 ensures that the full value of the trust property, for which a deduction was previously allowed in *D*'s estate, will eventually be subject to gift or estate tax in *S*'s hands. Should § 2519 apply if the trustee, pursuant to a discretionary power granted in the trust instrument, terminates the trust by distributing all of the trust assets to *S*?

(4) Lifetime QTIP Transfers

The gift tax counterpart of § 2056(b)(7) is § 2523(f), which permits a donor-spouse to elect QTIP treatment for a lifetime transfer of property in which the donee-spouse is given a qualifying income interest for life. If the donor elects QTIP treatment, the transfer escapes gift tax in the donor's hands and becomes subject to estate or gift tax under §§ 2044 or 2519 upon the subsequent termination or transfer of the donee's income interest. One feature of § 2523(f) that is peculiar to lifetime transfers concerns the treatment of interests retained by the donor; obviously, there is no need for a parallel provision in § 2056(b)(7). Under § 2523(f)(5), the donor's retained interest is disregarded for both estate and gift tax purposes as long as the donee remains alive and retains the qualifying income interest for life. In effect, tax ownership of the QTIP property is shifted entirely to the donee until the property becomes subject either to gift tax under § 2519 on a lifetime disposition of the income interest or to estate tax under § 2044 at the donee's death. For example, assume that *H* transfers property in trust to pay income to his wife *W* for life, then income to *H* for life if he survives her, with remainder to their children. *H* elects to treat the trust property as QTIP, and *W* receives the trust income until her death. If *H* dies before *W*, § 2523(f)(5)(A) prevents the trust property from being drawn back into his gross estate under § 2036. (But for this special rule, the value of the remainder would ordinarily be includible in *H*'s gross estate under § 2036, see supra page 275, Note 3.) At *W*'s death, the property is includible in her gross estate under § 2044; thereafter, *W* is treated for estate tax purposes as the transferor of the trust property. Thus, if *H* survives *W* and receives the trust income until his death, the property will not be includible in his gross estate under

§ 2036. If *W*'s executor made a valid election to treat the trust property as QTIP, however, the property would be includible in *H*'s gross estate under § 2044. See Reg. § 25.2523(f)–1(f) (Examples 10 and 11).

c. Charitable Remainder Trusts With Life Interest in Surviving Spouse

In 1981 Congress enacted § 2056(b)(8), which makes the marital deduction available for property passing from the decedent to a charitable remainder annuity trust or a charitable remainder unitrust (see supra page 480, Note 4), if the surviving spouse is the only noncharitable beneficiary of the trust. A parallel gift tax provision appears in § 2523(g). Because an outright transfer to either a spouse or a charity would qualify for a marital or charitable deduction, Congress concluded that there is no justification for imposing a tax when complete beneficial ownership is split between a spouse and a charity. Are there circumstances in which the requirement that the surviving spouse be the *sole* noncharitable beneficiary is overbroad? Consider a trust to pay an annuity in equal shares to the decedent's surviving spouse and child for the spouse's life, with remainder to charity. Does the spouse's one-half interest in the annuity qualify for the marital deduction, or would the decedent have been well advised to use two trusts rather than one?

4. VALUATION OF INTEREST PASSING TO SURVIVING SPOUSE

UNITED STATES v. STAPF

375 U.S. 118 (1963).

MR. JUSTICE GOLDBERG delivered the opinion of the Court....

Lowell H. Stapf died testate on July 29, 1953, a resident and domiciliary of Texas, a community property jurisdiction. At the time of his death he owned, in addition to his separate estate, a substantial amount of property in community with his wife. His will required that his widow elect either to retain her one-half interest in the community or to take under the will and allow its terms to govern the disposition of her community interest. If Mrs. Stapf were to elect to take under the will, she would be given, after specific bequests to others, one-third of the community property and one-third of her husband's separate estate. By accepting this bequest she would allow her one-half interest in the community to pass, in accordance with the will, into a trust for the benefit of the children....

In fact Mrs. Stapf elected to take under the will. She received, after specific bequests to others, one-third of the combined separate and community property, a devise valued at $106,268, which was $5,175 less than she would have received had she retained her community property and refused to take under the will....

By electing to take under the will, Mrs. Stapf, in effect, agreed to accept the property devised to her and, in turn, to surrender property of greater value to the trust for the benefit of the children. This raises the question of whether a decedent's estate is allowed a marital deduction under [§ 2056(b)(4)(B)] where the bequest to the surviving spouse is on the condition that she convey property of equivalent or greater value to her children. The Government contends that, for purposes of a marital deduction, "the value of the interest passing to the wife is the value of the property given her less the value of the property she is required to give another as a condition to receiving it." On this view, since the widow had no net benefit from the exercise of her election, the estate would be entitled to no marital deduction. Respondents reject this net benefit approach and argue that the plain meaning of the statute makes detriment to the surviving spouse immaterial.

Section [2056(a)] provides that "in general" the marital deduction is for "the value of any interest in property which passes . . . from the decedent to his surviving spouse." [Section 2056(b)(4)] then deals specifically with the question of valuation:

> [(4)] *Valuation of Interest Passing to Surviving Spouse.*—In determining for the purposes of [§ 2056(a)] the value of any interest in property passing to the surviving spouse for which a deduction is allowed by [§ 2056]— . . .
>
> [(B)] where such interest or property is incumbered in any manner, or where the surviving spouse incurs any obligation imposed by the decedent with respect to the passing of such interest, such incumbrance or obligation shall be taken into account in the same manner as if the amount of a gift to such spouse of such interest were being determined.

The disputed deduction turns upon the interpretation of (1) the introductory phrase "any obligation imposed by the decedent with respect to the passing of such interest," and (2) the concluding provision that "such . . . obligation shall be taken into account in the same manner as if the amount of a gift to such spouse of such interest were being determined."

The Court of Appeals, in allowing the claimed marital deduction, reasoned that since the valuation is to be "as if" a gift were being taxed, the legal analysis should be the same as if a husband had made an inter vivos gift to his wife on the condition that she give something to the children. In such a case, it was stated, the husband is taxable in the full amount for his gift. The detriment incurred by the wife would not ordinarily reduce the amount of the gift taxable to the husband, the original donor.[31] The court concluded:

---

31. See, e.g., Commissioner v. Wemyss, 324 U.S. 303. There the Court stated that under the Revenue Act of 1932 mere detriment to the transferee did not constitute the requisite "consideration in money or money's worth" to the transferor so as to relieve him of gift tax liability. Respondents' reliance on this case ignores that it involved neither a determination of who was to be considered the beneficial donee nor a valuation of the gift received by such donee.

> Within gift tax confines the community property of the widow passing under the will of the husband to others may not be "netted" against the devise to the widow, and thus testator, were the transfer inter vivos, would be liable for gift taxes on the full value of the devise. 309 F.2d 592, 598.

This conclusion, based on the alleged plain meaning of the final gift-amount clause of [§ 2056(b)(4)(B)], is not supported by a reading of the entire statutory provision. First, [§ 2056(a)] allows a marital deduction only for the decedent's gifts or bequests which pass "to his surviving spouse." In the present case the effect of the devise was not to distribute wealth to the surviving spouse, but instead to transmit, through the widow, a gift to the couple's children. The gift-to-the-surviving-spouse terminology reflects concern with the status of the actual recipient or donee of the gift. What the statute provides is a "marital deduction"—a deduction for gifts *to the surviving spouse*—not a deduction for gifts to the children or a deduction for gifts to privately selected beneficiaries. The appropriate reference, therefore, is not to the value of the gift moving from the deceased spouse but to the net value of the gift received by the surviving spouse.

Second, the introductory phrases of [§ 2056(b)(4)(B)] provide that the gift-amount determination is to be made "where such interest or property is incumbered in any manner, or where the surviving spouse incurs any obligation imposed by the decedent with respect to the passing of such interest...." The Government, drawing upon the broad import of this language, argues: "An undertaking by the wife to convey property to a third person, upon which her receipt of property under the decedent's will is conditioned, is plainly an 'obligation imposed by the decedent with respect to the passing of such interest.'" Respondents contend that "incumbrance or obligation" refers only to "a payment to be made *out of* property passing to the surviving spouse." Respondents' narrow construction certainly is not compelled by a literal interpretation of the statutory language. Their construction would embrace only, for example, an obligation *on* the property passing whereas the statute speaks of an obligation "*with respect* to the passing" gift. Finally, to arrive at the real value of the gift "such ... obligation shall be taken into account...." In context we think this relates the gift-amount determination to the net economic interest received by the surviving spouse.

This interpretation is supported by authoritative declarations of congressional intent. The Senate Committee on Finance, in explaining the operation of the marital deduction, stated its understanding as follows:

> If the decedent bequeaths certain property to his surviving spouse *subject*, however, *to her agreement*, or a charge on the property, for payment of $1,000 to *X*, the value of the bequest (and, accordingly, the value of the interest passing to the surviving spouse) is the value, reduced by $1,000, of such property. S. Rep. No. 1013, 80th Cong., 2d Sess., Pt. 2, p. 6. (Emphasis added.)

The relevant Treasury Regulation is directly based upon, if not literally taken from, such expressions of legislative intent. Treas. Reg. [§ 20.2056(b)–4(b)]. The Regulation specifically includes an example of the kind of testamentary disposition involved in this case:

> A decedent bequeathed certain securities to his wife in lieu of her interest in property held by them as community property under the law of the State of their residence. The wife elected to relinquish her community property interest and to take the bequest. For the purpose of the marital deduction, the value of the bequest is to be reduced by the value of the community property interest relinquished by the wife.

We conclude, therefore, that the governing principle, approved by Congress and embodied in the Treasury Regulation, must be that a marital deduction is allowable only to the extent that the property bequeathed to the surviving spouse exceeds in value the property such spouse is required to relinquish.

Our conclusion concerning the congressionally intended result under [§ 2056] accords with the general purpose of Congress in creating the marital deduction. The 1948 tax amendments were intended to equalize the effect of the estate taxes in community property and common-law jurisdictions. Under a community property system, such as that in Texas, the spouse receives outright ownership of one-half of the community property and only the other one-half is included in the decedent's estate. To equalize the incidence of progressively scaled estate taxes and to adhere to the patterns of state law, the marital deduction permits a deceased spouse, subject to certain requirements, to transfer free of taxes one-half of the non-community property to the surviving spouse. Although applicable to separately held property in a community property state, the primary thrust of this is to extend to taxpayers in common-law States the advantages of "estate splitting" otherwise available only in community property States. The purpose, however, is only to permit a married couple's property to be taxed in two stages and not to allow a tax-exempt transfer of wealth into succeeding generations. Thus the marital deduction is generally restricted to the transfer of property interests that will be includible in the surviving spouse's gross estate. Respondents' construction of [§ 2056] would, nevertheless, permit one-half of a spouse's wealth to pass from one generation to another without being subject either to gift or estate taxes.[32] We do not believe that this result, squarely contrary to the concept of the marital deduction, can be justified by the language of [§ 2056]. Furthermore, since in a community property jurisdiction one-

32. The Court of Appeals recognized the effect of its decision:

> Here estate taxes are due now on the property of the husband with the devise to the widow excluded. It is a part of the marital deduction or exclusion on which taxes are deferred to the estate of the widow to be assessed on so much of it as survives on another day. The net of the transfer by the widow became subject to gift taxes at the time of the transfer. The property transferred by the widow will, to the extent of an amount equal to the devise to her, escape both gift and estate taxes. [309 F.2d 592, 598.]

For an illustration of the tax effects of the decision, see the dissent of Judge Wisdom. 309 F.2d at 608–609.

half of the community normally vests in the wife, approval of the claimed deduction would create an opportunity for tax reduction that, as a practical matter, would be more readily available to couples in community property jurisdictions than to couples in common-law jurisdictions. Such a result, again, would be unnecessarily inconsistent with a basic purpose of the statute.

Since in our opinion the plain meaning of [§ 2056] does not require the interpretation advanced by respondents, the statute must be construed to accord with the clearly expressed congressional purposes and the relevant Treasury Regulation. We conclude that, for estate tax purposes, the value of a conditional bequest to a widow should be the value of the property given to her less the value of the property she is required to give to another. In this case the value of the property transferred to Mrs. Stapf ($106,268) must be reduced by the value of the community property she was required to relinquish ($111,443). Since she received no net benefit, the estate is entitled to no marital deduction.

NOTES

1. *"Net value" limitation.* Section 2056(b)(4) explicitly requires that death taxes, encumbrances, and certain other obligations be taken into account in determining the value of a deductible interest passing to the surviving spouse. Accordingly, the amount of the marital deduction is limited to the "net value" of the spouse's interest, determined as of the date of the decedent's death (with appropriate adjustments if the executor elects the alternate valuation date under § 2032). Reg. § 20.2056(b)–4(a). For example, if the spouse receives a devise of Blackacre with a fair market value of $1 million, subject to a mortgage of $200,000, the resulting marital deduction is $800,000. In *Stapf*, the marital deduction was reduced to zero because the obligation assumed by the spouse actually exceeded the value of the property she received under the decedent's will.

In applying the net value limitation, the issue is not whether death taxes, encumbrances or other obligations are actually paid from the spouse's share, but whether they are chargeable against that share. Thus, where an executor was empowered to pay death taxes from a marital trust if he considered it prudent from a business standpoint to do so, the marital deduction was reduced even though the executor did not exercise this discretionary authority. Wycoff's Estate v. Commissioner, 506 F.2d 1144 (10th Cir. 1974), cert. denied, 421 U.S. 1000 (1975); Reid's Estate v. Commissioner, 90 T.C. 304 (1988) (marital deduction reduced by amount of death taxes that could have been charged against marital bequest, even though trustees actually exercised discretionary power to pay taxes from other assets).

2. *Administration expenses.* If the decedent's will names the surviving spouse as residuary beneficiary, the marital share is likely to bear the burden of estate administration expenses under local law. As a result of the net value limitation discussed above, the marital deduction is ordinarily reduced by the amount of administration expenses payable from the residuary estate. Suppose, however, that the decedent's will or local law gives the executor

discretion to pay administration expenses from income earned by the residuary estate during the period of administration, and the executor does so. Should the amount of the marital deduction depend on whether administration expenses appear in the executor's accounts as charges to corpus or to income? Several courts have held that the marital deduction must be reduced regardless of whether the expenses are charged to corpus or to income, since the impact on the net value of the spouse's interest is the same in either case. See Street's Estate v. Commissioner, 974 F.2d 723 (6th Cir. 1992); Ballantine v. Tomlinson, 293 F.2d 311 (5th Cir. 1961). In Commissioner v. Hubert's Estate, 520 U.S. 93 (1997), however, the Supreme Court allowed a marital deduction without any reduction for administration expenses that were paid from post-mortem income generated by the assets allocated to the marital share.

In response to the *Hubert* decision, the Treasury promulgated new regulations concerning the effect of administration expenses on the marital deduction. The regulations divide administration expenses into two categories: "estate management expenses" and "estate transmission expenses." The former category includes expenses incurred in investing, preserving, or maintaining estate assets during a reasonable period of administration. The latter category covers all other administration expenses, including those incurred in collecting the decedent's assets, paying debts and death taxes, and distributing the remaining assets to beneficiaries. In general, estate management expenses attributable to the marital share can be paid from the marital share with no adverse effect on the marital deduction, but any estate transmission expenses paid from the marital share give rise to an automatic dollar-for-dollar reduction in the marital deduction. Reg. § 20.2056(b)–4(d). As a practical matter, a smaller marital deduction does not necessarily result in a larger taxable estate, since many items classified as estate transmission expenses qualify independently for a deduction under § 2053(a)(2). An estate tax deduction under § 2053(a)(2), however, comes at the price of forgoing an income tax deduction for the same item. See § 642(g), discussed supra at page 432, Note 6. Thus, the regulations curtail the "double benefit" of using the marital deduction to shelter estate transmission expenses from the estate tax while claiming the same expenses as an income tax deduction. See August, Final *Hubert* Regs. Fix Boundaries for Deducting Administration Expenses, 27 Est. Planning 195 (2000); Budin, Final *Hubert* Regulations Will Require Review of Many Estate Plans, 92 J. Taxn. 225 (2000); Gans, Blattmachr & McCaffrey, The Anti–*Hubert* Regulations, 87 Tax Notes 969 (2000).

3. *Effect of death taxes.* The apportionment of death taxes is determined by local statutory and case law in light of the testator's expressed or inferred intent (see infra page 641). If death taxes are chargeable against the residuary estate and the spouse is the sole residuary beneficiary, the marital deduction must be reduced by the full amount of the death taxes. Reg. § 20.2056(b)–4(c). On the other hand, if the decedent's will or local law provides for "equitable apportionment" of death taxes among the various beneficiaries in proportion to the amount of tax generated by their respective shares, a deductible marital bequest ordinarily generates no estate tax and accordingly no adjustment in the amount of the marital deduction would be necessary.

In determining how death taxes are to be apportioned, the courts often resolve ambiguities in favor of the surviving spouse, particularly if the decedent's will manifests a desire to maximize the marital deduction. See, e.g., Dodd v. United States, 345 F.2d 715 (3d Cir. 1965) ("[w]e may impute to the testator the intention that his estate and his wife alike should have the fullest benefit of the marital deduction"; held, federal estate tax not chargeable against widow's share of residuary estate); Milliken's Estate v. Commissioner, 70 T.C. 883 (1978) ("Although [the Massachusetts Supreme Judicial Court] may have stretched the meaning of language in [testamentary instruments] to reach conclusions that might not ordinarily be reached in other circumstances, we must nevertheless take the law of Massachusetts as we find it applied by that court"; will and pourover trust interpreted to exonerate marital share from state death taxes); Haskell's Estate v. Commissioner, 58 T.C. 197 (1972), affd. mem., 485 F.2d 679 (3d Cir. 1973) (New Jersey inheritance tax not charged against bequest to surviving spouse of amount equal to maximum marital deduction); Rev. Rul. 81–165, 1981–1 C.B. 472 (Virginia estate tax not chargeable against marital bequest under applicable apportionment statute); but see First Natl. Bank of Atlanta v. United States, 634 F.2d 212 (5th Cir. 1981) (marital portion of residuary estate was chargeable with ratable share of federal estate tax where will directed payment from residue; court rejected contention that testator intended a contrary result).

A special problem arises where the federal estate tax (or a similar state tax) is chargeable in whole or in part against the surviving spouse's share. Under § 2056(b)(4)(A), the amount of the marital deduction depends on the net amount received by the spouse; at the same time, the latter amount depends on the amount of the tax, which in turn depends on the amount of the marital deduction. To break out of this circle of interdependent variables, the executor may have to resort to cumbersome trial-and-error computations or to algebraic equations. Alternatively, the executor may refer the matter to the Service. See I.R.S. Publication 904 (May 1985) (suggested procedures for interrelated computations, with explanations and examples); Taussig, Kimball & Sprague, Iterated Equations for Vicious Circle Tax Problems: Manual and Computer–Assisted Solutions, 49 Taxes 538 (1971).

5. PLANNING CONSIDERATIONS

The unlimited marital deduction often makes it possible for a married couple to defer all or part of the estate tax on their combined assets until the death of the surviving spouse. Even if a zero estate tax at the first spouse's death can be achieved simply by an outright bequest of all the decedent's property to the surviving spouse, this approach is rarely advisable. From an estate planning perspective, the amount and form of the marital deduction depend on several factors, including the availability of the decedent's unified credit, the amount likely to be subject to estate tax at the surviving spouse's death, and, by no means of least importance, the decedent's preferences concerning the disposition of the property.

a. Interplay Between Unified Credit and Marital Deduction

One important goal of marital deduction planning has traditionally been to make the best possible use of each spouse's unified credit. At the death of the first spouse the unified credit, to the extent not used during life, automatically eliminates the estate tax on property in the decedent's taxable estate up to the ceiling amount specified in § 2010. The amount of taxable transfers sheltered from gift and estate tax by the unified credit, often referred to as the "exemption" or the "exclusion," was set at $5 million in 2010 (indexed for inflation beginning in 2012). For an example illustrating the operation of the unified credit, see supra page 20. To make use of the available unified credit at the decedent's death, it is essential that there be a taxable estate after all qualifying marital bequests and other deductible items (e.g., charitable bequests, administration expenses and claims) have been deducted from the gross estate. This is usually accomplished by limiting the marital bequest to the portion of the decedent's estate that exceeds the exemption amount, and by making a nondeductible bequest that generates a taxable estate equal to the exemption amount while avoiding inclusion in the spouse's gross estate (e.g., a bequest in trust to provide for the spouse's support during life, with remainder at the spouse's death to children or other beneficiaries). This bifurcation of the decedent's property into a nondeductible bequest (often referred to as a "credit shelter" or "by-pass" bequest) and a deductible marital bequest eliminates all estate tax at the decedent's death, while making full use of the decedent's unified credit and limiting the property that must ultimately be included in the spouse's gross estate.

Consider the interplay between the unified credit and the marital deduction in the case of a hypothetical married couple, assuming that neither spouse has made any taxable gifts and that the amount and current ownership of the couple's combined assets are as follows:

1. Combined assets worth $5 million;
2. Combined assets worth $10 million—
   (a) all owned by one spouse, or
   (b) half owned by each spouse;
3. Combined assets worth $20 million—
   (a) all owned by one spouse, or
   (b) half owned by each spouse.

How might the couple be advised to arrange their property in order to minimize the aggregate federal estate tax burden? Keep in mind the difficulty of predicting which spouse will die first, the need to provide financial security for the survivor, and the strong reluctance of most testators to relinquish control over their property.

NOTES

1. *Impact of other taxable transfers on exemption amount.* To the extent not used during life, the unified credit is allowed against the estate tax, which is imposed on the sum of the decedent's taxable estate and "adjusted taxable gifts" (i.e., post–1976 taxable gifts which are not drawn back into the gross

estate). § 2001(b). Accordingly, the decedent's adjusted taxable gifts must be taken into account in determining the amount of the taxable estate that can pass free of estate tax. To produce a federal estate tax of zero, any reduction in the available exemption amount may be offset by a corresponding increase in the marital bequest. For example, if *D* dies in 2012 with a gross estate of $8 million, having made adjusted taxable gifts of $2 million, the available exemption amount is reduced from $5 million to $3 million. Assuming that there are no other deductions or credits, the federal estate tax on *D*'s estate can still be reduced to zero if *S*, *D*'s surviving spouse, receives a deductible marital bequest of $5 million (rather than $3 million).

In drafting wills, it is common practice to include a nondeductible bequest to a credit shelter trust, which is intended to take advantage of any available exemption amount without giving rise to any federal estate tax. The amount of such a bequest may have to be adjusted not only for adjusted taxable gifts, as described above, but also for other taxable transfers under or outside the will. The following bequest is typical:

> If my spouse survives me, I give to [the trustee of the credit shelter trust] an amount equal to the excess, if any, of (1) the largest amount, if any, that can pass free of federal estate tax on my estate after taking into account the federal unified credit, over (2) the value of any other property passing under this will or outside this will that is includible in my federal gross estate and does not qualify for any deduction allowable under the federal estate tax law in effect at my death.

2. *Benefits for the surviving spouse in a credit shelter trust.* Testators are often reluctant to provide for maximum funding of a credit shelter trust because this appears to deplete the marital share and prejudice the interests of the surviving spouse. The problem is more apparent than real, however, because the credit shelter trust may contain liberal provisions for the surviving spouse. For example, the spouse may be given an income interest for life, as well as a power to compel distributions of corpus for the spouse's health, education, support or maintenance, and a noncumulative power to withdraw up to $5,000 or 5 percent of the corpus each year. Care must be taken, however, to ensure that the provisions for the spouse's benefit will not cause the trust property to be includible in the spouse's gross estate.

b. Portability of Unified Credit

If both spouses are to make full use of their respective unified credits, it has traditionally been necessary to make sure that each spouse leaves a taxable estate at least equal to the exemption amount. To achieve the desired result, two conditions must be met. First, each spouse must have a sufficiently large estate to make an appropriate credit shelter bequest. If the couple's combined wealth is concentrated in the hands of one spouse, there is a risk that the less wealthy spouse may die first, leaving an estate worth less than the exemption amount and forfeiting a corresponding portion of his or her unified credit. To forestall this unhappy outcome, the couple may rearrange their affairs, using inter vivos gifts (sheltered by the marital deduction) to bring the less wealthy spouse's estate up to the exemption amount. Even if both spouses have sufficiently large estates, however, there is a second condition which must be met, namely, each spouse must leave a taxable estate, after deductions, at least equal to the exemption amount. If one spouse dies and all of his or her property passes to the surviving spouse in a form that qualifies for the marital deduction, there may be no taxable estate and the decedent's unified credit may be lost. To prevent this from happening it is customary to limit the size of the marital share by means of a formula bequest, as discussed below. If the marital share is overfunded as a result of property passing outside the will (for example, by a marital joint tenancy with survivorship rights or as life insurance proceeds), it may be possible to bring the decedent's taxable estate up to the desired amount if the surviving spouse makes a qualified disclaimer.

The risk that a spouse's unified credit may be wasted, either through lack of sufficient property owned at death or through inadvertent overfunding of the marital share, has been significantly reduced by the advent of "portability." Beginning in 2011, if one spouse dies without using all of his or her unified credit, the unused amount may be used by the surviving spouse, in addition to his or her own unified credit, if the decedent's executor so elects on a timely filed estate tax return. § 2010(c). The portability provision, despite its limitations (see infra page 549), offers married couples considerable flexibility in tax planning. Since the deceased spouse's unused unified credit can be passed on to the surviving spouse, it has become far less important to make sure that the decedent makes full use of his or her unified credit. As a result, the need for a credit shelter bequest (or for lifetime gifts to ensure adequate funding of such a bequest) has become less pressing.

One effect of portability may be to encourage estate plans that leave most or all of the deceased spouse's property outright to the surviving spouse. Although a credit shelter trust is no longer needed to make optimal use of the unified credit, many married couples may continue to find such a trust attractive for other reasons. For example, because a credit shelter trust is not subject to estate tax at the surviving spouse's death, such a trust may be used to hold property that is expected to appreciate substantially in value (albeit at the cost of forgoing a stepped-up income tax basis at the surviving spouse's death). Furthermore, a credit shelter trust may play a crucial role in sheltering a portion of the deceased spouse's estate from the generation-skipping transfer tax; the GST exemption, unlike the unified credit, is not portable. Finally, a credit shelter trust may serve important planning goals entirely apart from tax savings, such as allowing the decedent to control the ultimate disposition of his or her property and protecting the trust property from creditors.

c. Tax Deferral or Tax Equalization?

In a system that subjects transfers in excess of the exemption amount to progressively higher marginal tax rates, the goal of deferring the payment of estate taxes until the death of the surviving spouse may be in tension with the competing goal of minimizing the couple's overall estate tax burden. Under a progressive rate schedule, a marital bequest that produces a zero estate tax liability in the estate of the first spouse to die may ultimately produce a heavier aggregate tax burden on the family fortune than a bequest of a smaller amount.[33] Thus, the tradeoff between estate tax deferral and equalization of marginal rates has traditionally loomed large in the planning of marital bequests.

Today, the tax advantages of "estate splitting" have been severely curtailed. Beginning in 2010, the estate tax is in effect imposed at a flat rate of 35 percent on all taxable estates in excess of the $5 million exemption amount. Consequently, the differential in marginal rates for large estates has all but disappeared.[34] For example, suppose that *D* dies in 2011 with a gross estate of $12 million, having made no adjusted taxable gifts. *D*'s will makes a credit shelter bequest of $5 million to the children and a deductible marital bequest of $7 million to his surviving spouse *S* (who has negligible assets of her own), producing an estate tax of zero. (Assume there are no other deductions or credits.) Later in 2011 *S* dies leaving the $7 million to the children, and her estate pays an estate tax of $700,000. On the other hand, suppose that *D*'s will divides the $12 million estate equally between the children and *S*, with a direction that all taxes be paid from the children's portion. There is an estate tax of $350,000 at *D*'s death, followed by another tax of $350,000 when *S* dies later the same year leaving $6 million to the children. The aggregate estate taxes are $700,000—precisely the same as the single tax imposed on *S*'s estate where *D* took a larger marital deduction. The principal remaining tax advantage of estate splitting is to ensure that each spouse is able to make full use of his or her unified credit, but, as the above example suggests, this goal is accomplished as long as each spouse's estate is at least equal to the exemption amount; above that amount, the estate tax consequences are essentially identical if the couple's wealth is concentrated in the hands of one spouse or divided equally between both of them. Moreover, as discussed earlier, the "portability" provision enacted in 2010 greatly reduces the risk that either spouse's unified credit will be wasted, regardless of how the couple's combined wealth is allocated.

Still, it is no simple matter to quantify the relative advantages of leaving all, half, none, or some intermediate portion of the decedent's property to the surviving spouse. Any attempt to compare the estate tax consequences necessarily rests on highly speculative assumptions concerning future events: the duration of the spouses' lives; the order of their

33. For example, assume that the estate tax is imposed at a marginal rate of 35 percent on taxable estates up to $10 million and at 45 percent on estates over $10 million, subject to a $5 million exemption amount. A married couple with combined wealth of $20 million could arrange to avoid paying any estate tax at the death of the first spouse by means of a $5 million credit shelter bequest, giving rise to a $4 million tax on the remaining $15 million at the death of the surviving spouse ($5,750,000 tentative tax less $1,750,000 unified credit). In contrast, if each spouse left a taxable estate of $10 million, their combined estate tax liability would be only $3,500,000. The $500,000 tax saving represents the benefit of shifting $5 million from a 45-percent bracket in the survivor's estate to a 35-percent bracket in the first spouse's estate.

34. A differential may persist, however, where state death taxes are imposed at graduated rates.

deaths; the value of property acquired, retained, and consumed by each; and the rate of return on investments. These and other factors are likely to have a far greater impact than rates or exemptions on the impact of tax deferral or tax equalization.

In retrospect, it may appear that a full marital bequest would have minimized the family's aggregate estate tax burden, if the surviving spouse would have used the property for such nontaxable purposes as personal consumption, annual exclusion gifts, exempt payments of tuition and medical expenses, charitable and political contributions, or in the event of remarriage, deductible gifts to a new spouse. Conversely, it might turn out that the couple's aggregate tax burden would have been minimized if less than half of the first spouse's property had been transferred to the survivor. The property might have become unexpectedly valuable after the first spouse's death; or the surviving spouse might have lived frugally, made no gifts, and inherited a large fortune. The calculus might also be affected by changes in the unified credit or in the tax rates.

After pondering these and other variables, a married couple may understandably choose to reduce the estate tax at the first spouse's death to zero and let the future take care of itself. Tax deferral is attractive to many taxpayers because it permits *S* to retain for life the use of the amount of estate tax that would otherwise be payable at *D*'s death under an equalization strategy. It does not follow, however, that by investing this amount *D* and *S* will reduce their aggregate estate tax burden. If *S* invests the deferred tax and the property inherited from *D* at the same rate of return, *S*'s enlarged estate will generate a correspondingly higher estate tax.

If the decision is made at the planning stage to use an equalization strategy, the spouses' wills must be drawn to create a parity between the estimated future values of their respective estates. If one spouse is wealthy and the other has only negligible assets, the propertied spouse's will may leave half the estate to the nonpropertied spouse and half to a family trust.[35] Fluctuations in the estimated future values of the two estates will trigger corresponding changes in the percentages needed to achieve parity. The results are obviously only rough approximations because the true values cannot be known until both spouses are dead. A testator may attempt to bring more precision to the process by including in his or her will a so-called estate equalization clause, which requires that the marital bequest be calculated based on the actual value of the testator's estate and the assumed value of the surviving spouse's estate as if the spouse had survived the testator but died later on the same day as the testator. See Rev. Rul. 82–23, 1982–1 C.B. 139 (allowing marital deduction for property passing under estate equalization clause).

35. The propertied spouse might consider making lifetime gifts to the nonpropertied spouse to ensure that the donee can take full advantage of the estate tax unified credit. Recall that the lifetime QTIP provisions of § 2523(f) permit the donor-spouse to obtain a marital deduction without giving up control over the disposition of the property at the donee-spouse's death (see supra page 530).

Finally, if the first spouse's will does not impose an equalization limit on the marital bequest, an independently wealthy surviving spouse can reduce or nullify an overfunded marital bequest by making a qualified disclaimer under § 2518. Property passing to another beneficiary as the result of a qualified disclaimer is treated as passing directly from the decedent to the ultimate recipient rather than through the surviving spouse's hands. Accordingly, the spouse is treated neither as receiving the property under § 2056 nor as retransferring it under § 2511. See Chapter 2, Section E.

d. Marital Deduction Formula Clauses

As described above, the testator may use the marital deduction to defer estate tax on the spouses' combined assets until the death of the surviving spouse or, in the alternative, to split the combined assets between the estates of the two spouses. In either case, the size of the marital bequest is typically determined under a formula clause that describes the necessary computations to achieve the desired result.[36] Formula clauses fall into two basic categories—pecuniary clauses and fractional share clauses.[37] Under a pecuniary clause, the marital bequest is expressed as a general bequest of assets having an ascertainable dollar value, leaving the residuary estate to pass to other beneficiaries. By contrast, under a fractional share clause, the marital bequest is expressed as a fractional share of the residuary estate, with the balance passing to other beneficiaries.

Consider the following example of a pecuniary formula clause, which describes the amount of the deductible marital bequest needed to produce an estate tax of zero while taking advantage of the unified credit:

> If my spouse survives me, I give to my spouse an amount equal to the minimum marital deduction necessary to eliminate (or reduce as far as possible) the federal estate tax on my estate, after taking into account all other property passing to my spouse under this will or outside this will that is includible in my federal gross estate and qualifies for the federal marital deduction, and after taking into account the federal unified credit.

The reference in this formula clause to property passing outside the will embraces joint tenancy property, life insurance proceeds, and other non-probate assets that are included in the gross estate and that pass to the surviving spouse in a manner qualifying for the marital deduction. The formula clause operates only to the extent that these nonprobate assets, together with any other marital bequests under the will, do not generate a

36. Where the objective is to defer the estate tax until the death of the surviving spouse while making use of the first spouse's GST exemption, it may be necessary to create two separate marital trusts. See infra page 558, footnote 4.

37. Each category has spawned many variations. See Casner & Pennell, Estate Planning § 13.7 (6th ed. 2001); Mulligan, Marital Deduction Planning and Drafting to Reflect Changes in the Law, 26 Est. Planning 339 (1999); Covey, Marital Deduction and Credit Shelter Dispositions and the Use of Formula Provisions (1984); Polasky, Marital Deduction Formula Clauses in Estate Planning—Estate and Income Tax Considerations, 63 Mich. L. Rev. 809 (1965).

sufficiently large marital deduction to eliminate the federal estate tax on the decedent's estate. The interplay of the marital deduction and the unified credit is discussed supra at page 537.

The value of a pecuniary formula bequest is readily converted into a specific dollar amount once the values of the formula components are ascertained. If such a bequest is satisfied with appreciated or depreciated property, the estate may realize gain or loss for income tax purposes. See 2 Bittker & Lokken, Federal Taxation of Income, Estates and Gifts ¶ 40.4.2 (3d ed. 2000). As explained below, this problem does not arise if the testator employs a fractional share formula instead of a pecuniary formula.

The use of a pecuniary formula marital bequest creates another problem if the will permits the bequest to be funded with assets selected by the executor and valued as of the date of death (or alternate valuation date) rather than the date of distribution. In this situation, the Service was concerned that the executor might attempt to minimize the surviving spouse's future estate tax liability by funding the marital bequest with assets that had declined in value between the relevant valuation date and the distribution date, leaving appreciated assets for the nonmarital share. To prevent this sort of scheme, the Service issued Rev. Proc. 64–19, 1964–1 C.B. 682, stating that the amount of the bequest will be considered unascertainable (and hence disqualified for the marital deduction) unless the executor is required by the terms of the will or by applicable state law (1) to fund the bequest with assets having a date-of-distribution value that is not less than the amount of the bequest, or (2) to fund the bequest with assets that are "fairly representative of appreciation or depreciation in the value of all property" available to satisfy the bequest. Note that the problem addressed by Rev. Proc. 64–19 does not arise if the executor has no discretion to select the assets used to fund the bequest, or if the will requires that the bequest be funded solely with cash or with assets valued as of the date of distribution; the problem can also be avoided by using a bequest of specific assets or a fractional share of the residuary estate rather than a pecuniary amount.

The estate tax can be reduced to zero by using either (1) a pecuniary formula marital bequest followed by a residuary credit shelter bequest or (2) a pecuniary formula credit shelter bequest followed by a residuary marital bequest. (For an example of a pecuniary credit shelter formula clause, see supra page 538, Note 1.) Why might a testator prefer one form rather than the other? If the will provides a pecuniary credit shelter bequest followed by a residuary marital bequest, and the pecuniary bequest is to be funded with assets valued as of the date of distribution, does the possibility of post-death fluctuations in the value of the residuary estate make the marital bequest nondeductible? See Rev. Rul. 90–3, 1990–1 C.B. 174 (no adverse effect on marital deduction).

Consider the following example of a fractional share formula clause, which is designed to produce an estate tax of zero while taking advantage of the unified credit:

> If my spouse survives me, I give to my spouse a fractional portion of my residuary estate, determined as follows: the numerator of the fraction shall be an amount equal to the minimum marital deduction necessary to eliminate (or reduce as far as possible) the federal estate tax on my estate, after taking into account all other property passing to my spouse under this will or outside this will that is includible in my federal gross estate and qualifies for the federal marital deduction, and after taking into account the federal unified credit; and the denominator of the fraction shall be an amount equal to the value of my residuary estate.

Note that under a fractional share formula clause the marital bequest is not a fixed dollar amount, but reflects a proportionate share of any appreciation or decline in the value of the residuary estate between the estate tax valuation date and the date of distribution. Accordingly, the distribution of appreciated or depreciated property in satisfaction of a fractional share marital bequest generates no gain or loss for income tax purposes; furthermore, such a bequest is not subject to the constraints of Rev. Proc. 64–19. As a practical matter, however, a fractional share bequest may create considerable administrative difficulties. The executor must either distribute each item to the surviving spouse and the other residuary beneficiaries in proportion to their prescribed fractional shares, or adjust the prescribed fraction to reflect any disproportionate partial distributions made during administration.

6. SPLIT GIFTS BY MARRIED COUPLES TO THIRD PERSONS

As explained supra at page 25, § 2513 permits gifts made by a husband or wife to a third person to be treated as if each spouse made one-half of the gift, provided they consent to this treatment for all gifts made by either spouse during the same calendar year while they remain married. This split-gift procedure doubles the number of annual exclusions available in determining the amount of the taxable gift, and may further reduce the aggregate gift tax by making a second unified credit available.

To elect split-gift treatment under § 2513, both spouses must be citizens or residents of the United States; they must also be married to each other at the time of the gift and neither must remarry during the remainder of the calendar year. An election applies to all gifts made by either spouse during the calendar year, but does not carry over to gifts made in earlier or later years. Because the consent applies only to gifts made while the spouses are married to each other, it does not embrace transfers that become complete only when the actual donor dies (e.g., a revocable trust) because the marriage terminates at the "exact instant" when the transfer occurs. Rev. Rul. 73–207, 1973–1 C.B. 409 (proceeds of insurance policy owned by wife on husband's life became payable to designated beneficiaries at husband's death; split-gift treatment not available because wife's gift became complete at same instant that husband's death terminated marital relationship).

Split gifts are attributed one-half to each spouse by § 2513 solely for gift tax purposes; for purposes of determining whether the transferred property is drawn back into the gross estate at death, the actual donor is treated as the transferor of the entire property. For example, if the donor spouse dies within three years after assigning a life insurance policy on his own life, the entire proceeds are drawn back into the donor spouse's gross estate at death under § 2035, even if the gift of the policy was split for gift tax purposes. Conversely, nothing is drawn back into the gross estate of the consenting spouse. When the proceeds are drawn back into the donor spouse's gross estate, the split gift is excluded from the adjusted taxable gifts of both spouses (§ 2001(b) and (e)), and the full amount of the gift tax imposed on the split gift is allowed as an offset in computing the donor spouse's estate tax (§ 2001(b)(2) and (d)). However, any portion of the consenting spouse's unified credit that offset the gift tax on her half of the split gift is lost and cannot be restored, even though the entire value of the property has been taxed in the donor spouse's estate. Cf. Ingalls v. Commissioner, 336 F.2d 874 (4th Cir. 1964) (no restoration of consenting spouse's specific exemption used on pre–1977 gifts included in donor spouse's gross estate); Norair v. Commissioner, 65 T.C. 942 (1976), affd. mem., 556 F.2d 574 (4th Cir. 1977) (same).

E. DEDUCTION FOR STATE DEATH TAXES: § 2058

For many years § 2011 allowed a credit against the federal estate tax for estate, inheritance, legacy, or succession taxes paid to a state or the District of Columbia with respect to property included in the decedent's gross estate. Congress enacted the credit in 1924 and enlarged it in 1926, in response to claims that death taxes were properly the province of the states and that the federal government should withdraw from the field or, at least, share it equitably with the states. The amount of the credit was subject to dollar limitations, based on a special base (the "adjusted taxable estate") and a schedule of graduated rates set forth in § 2011(b). This special base and rate schedule preserved without substantive change the dollar limits on the credit that were established in 1926.

The § 2011 credit was also designed to reduce interstate competition for wealthy decedents. See Advisory Commission on Intergovernmental Relations, Report on Coordination of State and Federal Inheritance, Estate and Gift Taxes 32–35 (1961). In due course, all fifty states and the District of Columbia enacted death taxes specifically designed to collect the maximum amount eligible for the § 2011 credit. By 2001, nearly forty states had come to rely exclusively on such "sponge" or "pick-up" taxes, and the remaining states had developed hybrid systems in which the death tax was set equal to the greater of the § 2011 credit amount or a separate inheritance or estate tax. For the states, the main attractions of a pick-up tax were its simplicity and convenience. A pick-up tax required only a few sentences in the statute books, permitted the state revenue officials to ride piggyback on the federal estate tax audit in determining the value of assets and the amount of allowable deductions, and channeled to the states a portion of the estate taxes that would otherwise have gone to the federal government without increasing the total amount of tax payable.

Although the § 2011 credit provided a high degree of uniformity and stability at the state level, it also functioned as a form of revenue sharing at the expense of the federal fisc. Motivated by a desire to recapture some of the revenue lost as a result of the estate tax cuts enacted in 2001, Congress decided to phase out the § 2011 credit and replace it with a less costly deduction for state death taxes. Accordingly, the federal credit for state death taxes was fully repealed in 2005; in its place, § 2058 now allows an unlimited deduction for "any estate, inheritance, legacy, or succession taxes" paid to a state or the District of Columbia with respect to property included in the gross estate. The deduction is allowed only for taxes that are "actually paid," and the deduction generally must be claimed within four years after the filing of the estate tax return.

The most immediate consequence of replacing the § 2011 credit with the § 2058 deduction for state death taxes is that the federal government will recapture a substantial portion of the estate tax revenue that it formerly shared with the states. The effects on state death tax systems in the longer term are more difficult to predict. Even before 2001, several states had already set the level of their pick-up taxes by reference to the § 2011 credit as it existed on a specified date, thereby preserving estate tax revenue that would otherwise have been lost due to future increases in the federal unified credit. See, e.g., N.Y. Tax L. §§ 951 and 952. In the years since 2001 a substantial number of additional states have moved to "decouple" their pick-up taxes from the repealed § 2011 credit. See, e.g., Mass. Gen. L. ch. 65C, § 2A. However, in states that rely exclusively on pick-up taxes and adjust automatically to changes in federal law, those taxes have simply disappeared along with the § 2011 credit. (Some state constitutions expressly prohibit any form of death taxation other than a pick-up tax. See, e.g., Fla. Const. art. VII, § 5.) It remains to be seen whether the states will completely abandon their death taxes in an attempt to attract wealthy residents or whether, given the inexorable pressure to raise revenue, they will restore some form of free-standing inheritance or estate tax. For the time being, the states have the opportunity to experiment with alternative systems of death taxation without interference or support from the provisions of the federal estate tax.

NOTES

1. *Property included in the gross estate.* The deduction under § 2058, like the former § 2011 credit, is allowed only if the property subject to state death taxes is included in the decedent's gross estate for federal estate tax purposes. See Second Natl. Bank of New Haven v. United States, 422 F.2d 40

(2d Cir. 1970) (no credit allowed for state death taxes paid with respect to trust property that was excluded from the federal gross estate because the value of the decedent's reversionary interest did not exceed 5 percent of the value of the trust property).

2. *State gift taxes.* Although state gift taxes do not qualify for the § 2058 deduction, they may be deducted under § 2053(a) as a claim against the estate to the extent they are still unpaid at death; the disallowance of § 2053(c)(1)(B) extends only to death taxes. See supra page 446, Note 6. This distinction causes difficulty in the case of a state gift tax that is later credited against a state death tax and thus serves as a down payment on the death tax. In Lang's Estate v. Commissioner, 613 F.2d 770 (9th Cir. 1980), one issue involved the deductibility of such a "hybrid" tax which was paid after the decedent's death. The court refused to treat the gift tax as a death tax, and held that it was deductible as a claim against the estate as expressly provided in Reg. § 20.2053–6(d). In 1981, the Service accepted the *Lang* court's treatment of the gift tax as a deductible claim but also indicated that only the portion of the state death tax in excess of the deductible gift tax would qualify for the § 2011 credit. Rev. Rul. 81–302, 1981–2 C.B. 170. In First Natl. Bank & Trust Co. v. United States, 787 F.2d 1393 (10th Cir. 1986), the estate paid an Oklahoma gift tax on gifts made by the decedent during the last year of her life. The gifts were drawn back into the decedent's gross estate for Oklahoma estate tax purposes, and the gift tax was treated as a down payment on the resulting Oklahoma estate tax. Relying on *Lang*, the executor claimed both a federal estate tax deduction under § 2053 and a federal estate tax credit under § 2011 for the amount of the Oklahoma gift tax. The Tenth Circuit rejected the "erroneous analysis and result" of *Lang*, and treated the gift tax as a death tax which qualified for the credit but not the deduction. 787 F.2d at 1395.

3. *References.* For discussions of the implications of replacing the § 2011 credit with the § 2058 deduction, see Michael, State Responses to EGTRRA Estate Tax Changes, 103 Tax Notes 1023 (2004); Steiner, Coping With the Decoupling of State Estate Taxes After EGTRRA, 30 Est. Planning 167 (2003).

F. CREDITS AGAINST THE TAX

To arrive at the amount of estate tax payable by the executor, certain credits are allowed against the tax computed under § 2001. These credits consist of: (1) the unified credit (§ 2010); (2) the credit for federal gift taxes paid on pre–1977 transfers of property included in the gross estate (§ 2012); (3) the credit for federal estate taxes paid with respect to property transferred to the current decedent by another decedent who died within ten years before or two years after the current decedent's death (§ 2013); and (4) the credit for death taxes paid to a foreign country with respect to property situated in that country and included in the gross estate (§ 2014).

1. UNIFIED CREDIT: § 2010

The unified credit automatically offsets the gift and estate taxes imposed on cumulative taxable transfers made during life or at death up to the "applicable exclusion amount" specified in § 2010. This amount, often referred to as the "exemption" or the "exclusion," was set at $5 million in 2010 and is indexed for inflation beginning in 2012. For a computation illustrating the operation of the unified credit, see supra page 20.

In general, the unified credit is not transferable; if a taxpayer's cumulative taxable transfers at the time of death are less than the applicable exclusion amount, the unused unified credit cannot be used by any other taxpayer. Nevertheless, a special provision added in 2010 allows a surviving spouse to make use of a deceased spouse's unused unified credit if the deceased spouse's executor so elects on a timely filed estate tax return. § 2010(c). Technically, the surviving spouse's applicable exclusion amount consists of a "basic exclusion amount" of $5 million (indexed for inflation beginning in 2012), increased by a "deceased spousal unused exclusion amount." The additional amount available to the surviving spouse is computed by subtracting the deceased spouse's cumulative taxable transfers from his or her own basic exclusion amount. Consequently, the deceased spouse's unused unified credit need not be wasted but instead can be used to augment the surviving spouse's own unified credit. The "portability" feature, which took effect in 2011, applies for purposes of the gift and estate taxes but not the generation-skipping transfer tax.

NOTES

1. *Election by deceased spouse's executor.* The portability feature requires an election by the deceased spouse's executor on a timely filed estate tax return. § 2010(c)(5)(A). How likely is it that this requirement will be met? Note that no estate tax return need be filed unless the sum of the decedent's gross estate and adjusted taxable gifts exceeds the basic exclusion amount. § 6018. If an estate tax return is filed, is there any reason why the executor might elect *not* to allow the surviving spouse to make use of the decedent's unused unified credit? Should the portability feature apply automatically unless the decedent's executor elects otherwise? Why is portability limited to married couples? Should the unified credit be freely transferable?

2. *Multiple predeceased spouses.* Ordinarily the computation of the surviving spouse's additional exclusion amount presents little difficulty. For example, suppose that *H* dies in 2011 survived by his wife *W*, having made cumulative taxable transfers of $2 million, and his executor elects to pass on his unused exclusion amount of $3 million to *W*. *W* can now make $3 million of taxable transfers, in addition to her basic exclusion amount of $5 million, without incurring any gift or estate tax. (Note that *W*'s basic exclusion amount is indexed for inflation beginning in 2012, but the additional amount carried over from *H* is not.)

The outcome may be more complicated in cases involving multiple marriages. In the preceding example, suppose that *W* subsequently remarries and survives her second husband, whose executor elects to pass on the second husband's unused exclusion amount of $4 million to *W*. Is *W* now allowed to transfer $4 million free of gift and estate taxes, in addition to the $3 million derived from her first husband and her own $5 million basic exclusion amount? See § 2010(c)(4) (limiting additional exclusion amount to the lesser of the basic exclusion amount or the unused exclusion amount of the "last" deceased spouse). What if the second husband left an unused exclusion amount of only $1 million? See id.

Suppose instead that *W* dies before her second husband, having used up $4 million of her $8 million exclusion amount (including $3 million derived from her first husband). How much of *W*'s remaining $4 million exclusion amount can she pass on to her second husband, if her executor so elects? See id.

3. *Statute of limitations.* The filing of an estate tax return generally marks the beginning of a three-year limitation period for the assessment of tax. § 6501(a). Even after the statutory period has expired, however, the government may examine the decedent's estate tax return to determine the amount of the unused unified credit available to the surviving spouse. § 2010(c)(5)(B).

4. *References.* For further discussions of proposals to make the unified credit portable between spouses, see ABA Tax Section Task Force, Report on Transfer Tax Restructuring, 41 Tax Law. 395, 398–400 (1988) (arguing that portability would obviate the need for "complex credit shelter trust clauses" and "lifetime transfers to the nonpropertied spouse to permit consumption of her exemption if she dies first"); Turnier, Three Equitable Taxpayer–Friendly Reforms of Estate and Gift Taxation, 87 Tax Notes 269 (2000); Task Force on Federal Wealth Transfer Taxes, Report on Reform of Federal Wealth Transfer Taxes, 58 Tax Law. 93, 200–03 (2004); Gans, Blattmachr & Bramwell, Estate Tax Exemption Portability: What Should the IRS Do? And What Should Planners Do in the Interim?, 42 Real Prop., Prob. & Tr. J. 413 (2007); Staff of Joint Comm. on Taxation, Taxation of Wealth Transfers Within a Family: A Discussion of Selected Areas for Possible Reform 9–12 (2008). The interplay between the unified credit and the marital deduction is discussed supra at page 537.

2. CREDIT FOR PRE–1977 GIFT TAXES: § 2012

Where the decedent made a pre–1977 taxable gift of property that is drawn back into the gross estate—because, for example, the decedent retained a life income interest in the transferred property—the federal gift tax paid on the gift is allowed as a credit against the federal estate tax, subject to the limitations prescribed by § 2012. This protection against double taxation of the same property led the Supreme Court to observe in Smith v. Shaughnessy, 318 U.S. 176 (1943), that "the gift tax amounts in [these] instances to a security, a form of down payment of the estate tax," although the credit is sometimes less than the full amount of the down payment. Section 2012 applies only to pre–1977 gifts; for gifts made after

1976, the unified gift and estate tax computation under § 2001(b) automatically takes gift taxes on post–1976 gifts into account, making a separate credit unnecessary. For an illustration of a computation under § 2001(b), see supra page 20.

Stripped to its bare bones, § 2012 allows a credit for the federal gift tax paid on a pre–1977 gift if "any amount in respect of such gift is required to be included" in the decedent's gross estate. The amount of the credit is limited to the lesser of (1) the gift tax paid on the gift (referred to in Reg. § 20.2012–1(c) as the "first limitation"), or (2) the estate tax attributable to inclusion of the gift in the gross estate (referred to in Reg. § 20.2012–1(d) as the "second limitation"). By conditioning the credit on inclusion of the gift, or a portion thereof, in the donor's gross estate at death, § 2012(a) makes the credit available only when necessary to prevent double taxation; no credit is warranted if the donated property is not subjected to estate tax in the donor's estate. The first and second limitations are similarly concerned with the prevention of double taxation; in effect, by limiting the credit to the lower of the gift tax or the estate tax, they ensure payment of the higher of the two taxes.

3. CREDIT FOR TAX ON PRIOR TRANSFERS: § 2013

If the decedent (the "transferee") received property from another decedent (the "transferor") who died within ten years before, or two years after, the date of the transferee's death, the transferee's estate is allowed a credit under § 2013 for the estate tax paid (as defined and adjusted by § 2013) by the transferor's estate with respect to the property. This credit is the descendant of a provision that came into the estate tax law in 1918, as a result of a recommendation by the House Committee on Ways and Means:

> It has come to the attention of the committee that persons closely related have died within such a short space of time that the same estate passing within a short period of time has been subjected to the estate tax and thereby diminished unreasonably because of the short period within which the two levies have been made. For example, a husband dies leaving a large amount of property to his wife, an elderly woman, who dies within a few weeks after her husband's death. Under existing law the entire estate is taxed on the transfer from husband to wife and on the transfer from wife to other beneficiaries. [H.R. Rep. No. 767, 65th Cong., 2d Sess. (1918), reprinted in 1939–1 C.B. (Part 2) 86, 102.]

To prevent the undue depletion of a family fortune by two estate taxes within a brief period of time, § 2013 permits the transferee's estate to take a credit for an appropriate portion of the estate tax paid by the transferor's estate. The basic amount of the credit is limited to the lesser of (1) the amount of federal estate tax attributable to the transferred property in the transferor's estate (referred to in Reg. § 20.2013–2 as the "first limitation"), or (2) the amount of federal estate tax attributable to the transferred property in the transferee's estate (referred to in Reg. § 20.2013–3 as the "second limitation"). If the transferor died within two years before the transferee, the allowable credit is equal to this basic amount. If the transferor died more than two years before the transferee, however, the allowable credit is reduced on a sliding scale: only 80 percent of the basic amount is allowed if the transferor died within the third or fourth years before the transferee, with further reductions to 60 percent (transferor died within fifth or sixth years before transferee), 40 percent (seventh or eighth years), and 20 percent (ninth or tenth years). No credit is allowed if the transferor predeceased the transferee by more than ten years.

The credit (determined by applying the "first" and "second" limitations described above) is also allowed if the transferor dies within two years after the transferee. For example, assume that in 2005 *A* created a trust to pay income to *A* for life with remainder to *B*. If *B* dies in 2011, survived by *A*, the actuarial value of the remainder interest is includible in *B*'s estate, and if *A* dies in 2012, the trust assets will be includible in *A*'s estate under § 2036. Section 2013 mitigates the resulting double taxation by allowing a credit to *B*'s estate, which may be claimed on an amended return if necessary.

To qualify for a credit under § 2013, the previously taxed property itself need not be owned by the transferee at the time of his death, nor need it be otherwise includible in his gross estate, since the "second limitation" is applied by computing the difference between the net estate tax payable on the transferee's estate and the net estate tax that would be payable if the value of the transferred property were excluded from the gross estate. In effect, it is assumed that the transferee's estate is augmented by the value of the previously taxed property, whether the transferee actually saved that property and consumed other assets or vice versa. Moreover, this no-tracing principle applies even if the property would not, in any event, be included in the transferee's estate. See, e.g., Rev. Rul. 59–9, 1959–1 C.B. 232 (decedent, life income beneficiary of a trust established by his father, may take a credit for tax paid by father's estate on actuarial value of life estate at father's death, even though transferred income interest was not includible in decedent's gross estate).

There are limits, however, to the allowance of a credit where it is difficult or impossible to appraise the value of the interest that passed to the transferee at the transferor's death. Compare Holbrook v. United States, 575 F.2d 1288 (9th Cir. 1978) (credit not allowed where transferee's life income interest could not be valued as of transferor's death, because trustees were authorized to invest in unproductive property); Pollock's Estate v. Commissioner, 77 T.C. 1296 (1981) (same where income was payable in the discretion of trustees), with Weinstein's Estate v. United States, 820 F.2d 201 (6th Cir. 1987) (transferee's interest in discretionary trust held capable of valuation where discretion was governed by ascertainable standard); Rev. Rul. 75–550, 1975–2 C.B. 357

(illustrating method of valuing transferee's income interest where discretionary power to invade corpus for other beneficiaries is limited by definite standard).

No credit is allowed for any gift tax that may have been paid on a gift of property to the decedent, no matter how short the interval between the time of the gift and the transferee's death.

The value of the transferred property is the same as its value in the transferor's gross estate, reduced by the following amounts: (1) any federal estate tax and any state or foreign death taxes that were payable out of the property or payable by the transferee in connection with the property; (2) any encumbrances on the property or obligations imposed by the transferor with respect to the property; and (3) any marital deduction allowed to the transferor's estate, if the transferee was the transferor's surviving spouse. The first two adjustments ensure that the amount taken into account reflects the net value received by the transferee rather than the gross value transferred by the transferor. The third adjustment recognizes that any marital deduction allowed to the transferor's estate mitigated the estate tax burden on property passing to the transferee, and ensures that only the excess value received by the transferee over the deductible amount is taken into account under § 2013.

NOTES

1. *Valuation of transferred property.* In imposing the first and second limitations, §§ 2013(b) and 2013(c)(1) refer to the "value" of the transferred property, which is defined in § 2013(d) as the value used in determining the transferor's federal estate tax liability. If the transferee received a partial interest (e.g., a life estate) in property included in the transferor's gross estate, the estate tax value of the property must be apportioned, ordinarily by reference to actuarial principles. See Reg. § 20.2013–4(a). Suppose the transferor died leaving property to the transferee for life with remainder to another beneficiary, and the transferee died shortly after the transferor. May the transferee's executor claim a § 2013 credit based on the actuarial value of the life estate at the time of the transferor's death, even if at the time of the transferor's death the transferee was "terminally ill"? The Service takes the position that the actuarial value of the life estate may be taken into account for purposes of § 2013 only if that value was actually and necessarily used in determining the transferor's estate tax liability. See Reg. § 20.7520–3(b)(3)(ii); cf. Continental Illinois Natl. Bank & Trust Co. v. United States, 504 F.2d 586 (7th Cir. 1974) (actuarial tables applicable where transferee had incurable cancer and died within a month after the transferor). What if the transferee dies simultaneously with the transferor, so that the life estate expires at the very instant it comes into existence? Here, the Service takes the position that the mortality assumptions prescribed in § 7520 are not controlling, and the courts have upheld the Commissioner's determination that the life estate has no value for purposes of § 2013. See Reg. § 20.7520–3(b)(3)(iii); cf. Carter's Estate v. United States, 921 F.2d 63 (5th Cir.), cert. denied, 502

U.S. 817 (1991) (simultaneous deaths); Lion's Estate v. Commissioner, 438 F.2d 56 (4th Cir.), cert. denied, 404 U.S. 870 (1971) (same).

2. *Reference.* See Rudick, The Estate Tax Credit for Tax on Prior Transfers, 13 Tax. L. Rev. 3 (1957).

4. CREDIT FOR FOREIGN DEATH TAXES: § 2014

For this credit, and the related possibility that an estate tax treaty may prevent double taxation, see supra page 39, Note 4.

CHAPTER 6

THE GENERATION-SKIPPING TRANSFER TAX

■ ■ ■

A. OVERVIEW

Congress first enacted a tax on generation-skipping transfers in 1976 to supplement the newly unified estate and gift taxes. According to the legislative history, the basic purpose of the GST tax is to ensure that wealth is subject to transfer tax as it passes from one generation to the next.[1] To illustrate the problem at which the GST tax is aimed, suppose that *A* leaves her residuary estate in trust to pay income to her child *B* for life, with remainder at *B*'s death to *B*'s descendants then living. Although the initial transfer at *A*'s death is subject to estate tax, no estate tax is imposed at *B*'s death when the income interest terminates and the property is distributed free of trust to the remainder beneficiaries. Indeed, no further gift or estate tax is imposed until the remainder beneficiaries transfer the property to their own descendants during life or at death. The result is the same even if *B* has a power to designate the remainder beneficiaries, as long as that power does not amount to a general power of appointment.

The original GST tax was intended to produce approximately the same transfer tax result as if the underlying property were transferred

1. The House Ways and Means Committee offered the following explanation:

> The purpose of the Federal estate and gift taxes is not only to raise revenue, but also to do so in a manner which has as nearly as possible a uniform effect, generation by generation. These policies of revenue raising and equal treatment are best served where the transfer taxes (estate and gift) are imposed, on the average, at reasonably uniform intervals....
>
> Present [i.e., pre–1976] law imposes transfer taxes every generation in the case of families where property passes directly from parent to child, and then from child to grandchild. However, where a generation-skipping trust is used, no tax is imposed upon the death of the child, even where the child has an income interest in the trust, and substantial powers with respect to the use, management, and disposition of the trust assets....
>
> Generation skipping results in inequities in the case of transfer taxes by enabling some families to pay these taxes only once every several generations, whereas most families must pay these taxes every generation. Generation skipping also reduces the progressive effect of the transfer taxes, since families with moderate levels of accumulated wealth may pay as much or more in cumulative transfer taxes as wealthier families who utilize generation-skipping devices. [H.R. Rep. No. 1380, 94th Cong., 2d Sess. 47 (1976), reprinted in 1976–3 C.B. (Vol. 3) 735, 780–81.]

outright to the beneficiaries at each generation. Thus, in the above example, a tax would be imposed at the termination of *B*'s interest, calculated as if *B* had owned the trust property and transferred it at death to the remainder beneficiaries. This approach turned out to be unduly cumbersome in operation and limited in scope. For instance, *A* could achieve substantially similar results, while avoiding the GST tax, by making separate transfers directly to *B* and to *B*'s descendants.

In 1986 Congress repealed the original statute and replaced it with a completely revised GST tax, which appears in Chapter 13 of the Code (§§ 2601 to 2663). The revised GST tax continues to reach trusts (and similar arrangements) that shift beneficial enjoyment of property to persons two or more generations below the transferor while sidestepping estate and gift taxes at the level of the intervening generations. For example, assume that *A* transfers property in trust for the benefit of *A*'s child *B* and *B*'s descendants. Any distribution of trust income or corpus to a descendant of *B* while *B* is alive will constitute a "taxable distribution," and *B*'s death will constitute a "taxable termination" with respect to any property remaining in trust. In addition, unlike its predecessor, the revised GST tax reaches transfers made directly to persons two or more generations below the transferor. A typical instance of such a "direct skip" is a gift or bequest made by a grandparent to a grandchild.

Under the revised GST tax, each individual transferor has a GST exemption equal to the estate tax exemption ($5 million in 2011, indexed for inflation beginning in 2012), which may be freely allocated to any property transferred during life or at death. The amount of GST exemption allocated to particular property affects the rate of GST tax imposed on generation-skipping transfers occurring with respect to the property. If there is no allocation of GST exemption, the GST tax is imposed at a flat rate equal to the maximum estate tax rate (35 percent). By contrast, if sufficient GST exemption is allocated to cover the full value of the transferred property, the applicable rate of GST tax is reduced to zero; in effect, generation-skipping transfers involving the property are exempted from GST tax.

Although the GST tax is intimately connected with the estate and gift taxes, it stands apart from those taxes. In operation, the GST tax has its own separate exemption and rate structure, as well as its own criteria for determining the timing and amount of taxable transfers. Furthermore, the GST tax has its own distinctive terminology which merits close attention.

B. GENERATION-SKIPPING TRANSFERS

The GST tax applies to "generation-skipping transfers" that shift beneficial enjoyment of property to persons two or more generations below the transferor without attracting estate or gift taxes at the level of the intervening generations. There are three types of generation-skipping transfers: (1) direct skips; (2) taxable terminations; and (3) taxable distributions. § 2611(a). Direct skips, which may be outright or in trust, occur in connection with a completed lifetime gift or at the transferor's death. Taxable terminations and taxable distributions always involve a trust[2] with beneficiaries two or more generations below the transferor. In analyzing any generation-skipping transfer, it is essential first to identify the transferor and then to determine the generational relationship between the transferor and the beneficiaries.

1. TRANSFEROR

In general, when an individual makes a transfer of property subject to gift or estate tax, that individual becomes the "transferor" of the property for GST tax purposes. § 2652(a)(1). For example, a donor who makes a completed gift of property is the transferor of that property,[3] and a decedent is the transferor of all property included in his or her gross estate. The statutory definition applies equally to transfers that are technically "taxable" and to those that qualify for an exclusion or deduction. Thus, a donor is the transferor not only of his or her gifts that are taxable but also of those that qualify for the annual exclusion. Similarly, a donor or decedent who makes a transfer that qualifies for a marital or charitable deduction is the transferor of the transferred property.

An individual remains the transferor of particular property only as long as there is no subsequent transfer of the same property subject to gift or estate tax. Upon such a subsequent transfer, the new donor or decedent becomes the transferor of the property. For example, if a parent transfers property in trust to pay income to a child for life, then to the child's children until the youngest reaches age 21, with remainder to the child's descendants then living, the parent remains the transferor throughout the entire term of the trust. If, however, the child held a general testamentary power of appointment, the child would become the new transferor at death as a result of the inclusion of the trust property in the child's gross estate. In the case of a lapsed general power of appointment, the holder of the power is treated as a new transferor only to the extent that the lapse exceeded the "5 and 5" exemption (see supra page 418). Reg. § 26.2652–1(a)(5) (Example 5).

When an individual makes a transfer that qualifies for a marital deduction, he or she ordinarily remains the transferor only until the property becomes includible in the spouse's completed gifts or gross estate. In the case of qualified terminable interest property (QTIP),

2. For GST tax purposes, a "trust" includes any arrangement (other than a decedent's estate) which has "substantially the same effect as a trust." § 2652(b)(1). Reg. § 26.2652–1(b) provides that a trust includes "arrangements involving life estates and remainders, estates for years, and insurance and annuity contracts," as well as transfers where the identity of the beneficiary depends on a contingency that might not be resolved within six months. Furthermore, § 2654(b)(2) provides that for GST tax purposes "substantially separate and independent shares of different beneficiaries in a trust shall be treated as separate trusts." See also Reg. § 26.2654–1.

3. A gift-splitting election is effective for GST tax purposes: Each spouse is treated as the transferor to the same extent that he or she is treated as the donor under § 2513. § 2652(a)(2).

however, the statute permits the original donor or his or her executor to elect to disregard the QTIP election for GST tax purposes. § 2652(a)(3). The effect of this so-called "reverse QTIP" election is simply that the original donor or decedent continues to be treated as the transferor of the property for GST tax purposes, notwithstanding the subsequent inclusion of the property in the spouse's completed gifts or gross estate. The reverse QTIP election offers married couples considerable flexibility in allocating their individual GST exemptions.[4]

2. GENERATION ASSIGNMENT

Once the transferor is identified, it is necessary to determine the generational relationship between the transferor and the individual beneficiaries. The transferor's spouse (including a former spouse) is assigned to the same generation as the transferor. § 2651(c)(1). Each beneficiary who is a descendant of a grandparent of the transferor (or the transferor's spouse) is assigned to a generation level based on the degree of relationship.[5] § 2651(b). Under this scheme, the transferor's (and his or her spouse's) siblings are all assigned to the transferor's generation; the transferor's (and his or her spouse's) children, nieces and nephews are all assigned to the next lower generation; the transferor's (and his or her spouse's) grandchildren, grandnieces and grandnephews to the next lower generation; and so on.[6] Moreover, the generation assignment of each relative also applies to that relative's spouse. § 2651(c)(2).

Chronological age is taken into account only if the rules based on family relationships do not apply. In such a case (i.e., a beneficiary related to the transferor remotely or not at all), a beneficiary who was born within 12½ years after the transferor is assigned to the transferor's generation; a beneficiary who was born more than 12½ years but not more than 37½ years after the transferor is assigned to the next lower generation; and so on, with a new generation beginning every 25 years. § 2651(d).

Under the "look-through" rule of § 2651(f)(2), an entity such as a trust, partnership, or corporation generally is treated as an aggregation of its individual beneficiaries, partners, or shareholders. However, charitable organizations, which have no beneficial owners, are assigned to the transferor's generation. § 2651(f)(3).

4. Section 2652(a)(3) requires that a reverse QTIP election apply to "all of the property in [a QTIP] trust." Thus, although partial reverse QTIP elections are not permitted, an election may be made with respect to one trust and not made with respect to a separate trust.

5. Relationships by legal adoption or by half-blood are treated the same as full-blood relationships. § 2651(b)(3); Reg. § 26.2651–2.

6. In certain circumstances a grandchild or other descendant of the transferor (or the transferor's spouse) may be reassigned to a higher generation pursuant to the "predeceased parent" rule of § 2651(e), discussed infra at page 560.

3. SKIP PERSONS

A generation-skipping transfer, by definition, involves a transfer to or for the benefit of a "skip person," defined as any individual who is assigned to a generation two or more generations below the transferor. § 2613(a)(1). For example, a transferor's grandchild is a skip person; the transferor's spouse or child is not.

A trust may or may not qualify as a skip person, depending on the generation assignment of its beneficiaries. The statutory definition of a skip person includes a trust only if (1) "all interests in such trust are held by skip persons," or (2) no person holds "an interest in such trust" and at no time in the future may any distribution of income or corpus be made to any person other than a skip person. § 2613(a)(2); Reg. § 26.2612–1(d)(2) (disregarding potential future distribution to non-skip person if probability of such a distribution is "so remote as to be negligible"). For GST tax purposes, an individual generally holds an "interest" in trust property if he or she is presently entitled to receive trust income or corpus or is a permissible current recipient of trust income or corpus. § 2652(c)(1).[7] Thus, for example, a trust qualifies as a skip person if the trustee is presently required or permitted to distribute income or corpus to a class of beneficiaries consisting solely of skip persons (e.g., the transferor's grandchildren). A trust also qualifies as a skip person if there are no permissible current recipients of income or corpus and the only possible recipients of any future distributions are skip persons (e.g., a trust to accumulate income for 21 years and then distribute the corpus and accumulated income to the transferor's grandchildren then living). An individual is treated as holding an interest in trust property if the trust income or corpus may be used to satisfy his or her support obligations (e.g., to support a spouse or child), unless such use is within the discretion of a fiduciary or is pursuant to a state law resembling the Uniform Transfers to Minors Act. § 2652(c)(3); Reg. § 26.2612–1(e)(2).

The statutory definition of a skip person excludes any trust in which a non-skip person holds an interest. For example, if the trustee has discretion to distribute trust income to the transferor's descendants, the trust is not a skip person as long as any child of the transferor is living, even if the child never receives any trust income.[8] Treating a trust as a non-skip person may affect both the timing and the type of generation-skipping transfers involving the trust.

4. DIRECT SKIPS

A direct skip is defined simply as "a transfer subject to [estate or gift tax] of an interest in property to a skip person." § 2612(c)(1). The transfer may be outright or in trust. The simplest instance of a direct skip

---

7. A charitable organization holds an interest in trust property only if the charity is presently entitled to receive trust income or corpus or is the remainder beneficiary of a charitable remainder annuity trust, a charitable remainder unitrust, or a pooled income fund (see supra page 480, Note 4).

8. An interest may be disregarded, however, if it "is used primarily to postpone or avoid [GST] tax." § 2652(c)(2).

is a gift or bequest made by a grandparent to a grandchild. In the case of an outright transfer, it is usually obvious whether the transferee is a skip person, and hence whether the transfer is a direct skip. In the case of a transfer in trust, however, a direct skip occurs only if the trust itself qualifies as a skip person.[9] For example, a transfer in trust for the benefit of the transferor's grandchildren and their descendants is a direct skip; all interests in the trust are held by skip persons, and so the trust itself is a skip person. If a child of the transferor also holds an interest in the trust, however, the trust is not a skip person and the creation of the trust is not a direct skip. (In this case, the trust property may still be subject to GST tax upon a subsequent termination or distribution.) See Reg. § 26.2612–1(f) (Examples 3 and 4).

In determining whether a transfer is a generation-skipping transfer, a special rule applies if the transferor (or the transferor's spouse) has a descendant whose parent (also descended from the transferor or the transferor's spouse) is dead at the time of the transfer giving rise to estate or gift tax. In this situation, the descendant is reassigned to the deceased parent's generation, and the process is repeated if necessary to eliminate any remaining vacancies in the line of living descendants.[10] § 2651(e)(1); Reg. § 26.2651–1. For example, if *A* makes a gift or bequest to *C*, the child of *A*'s predeceased child *B*, *C* is reassigned to *B*'s generation for GST tax purposes, and any descendants of *C* also move up one generation. As a result, *C* becomes a non-skip person, and the transfer to *C* (or to a trust in which *C* holds an interest) is not a direct skip. In the case of a transfer in trust, the generation reassignment remains applicable in determining whether a subsequent termination or distribution is subject to GST tax. See Reg. § 26.2651–1(c) (Example 1).

A direct skip always involves a transfer that is subject to estate or gift tax, and usually occurs at the same time as the transferor's death or the completed lifetime gift. A special timing rule applies, however, where the transferor makes a completed gift of property that may be drawn back into the gross estate of the transferor (or the transferor's spouse) at death, without regard to the three-year rule of § 2035. In this situation, the direct skip does not occur until the transferor's death (or the earlier termination of potential inclusion in the gross estate of the transferor or the transferor's spouse). § 2642(f); Reg. § 26.2632–1(c). For example, assume that *A* purchases land in the name of *A* and *A*'s grandchild *B* as joint tenants with right of survivorship, and *A* subsequently dies survived by *B*. Although the creation of the joint tenancy constitutes a completed gift from *A* to a skip person, a direct skip occurs only at *A*'s death. As a result, no allocation of *A*'s GST exemption to the land can be made until *A*'s death.

---

9. The "look-through" rule of § 2651(f)(2), which attributes ownership of an entity's property to the individual holders of beneficial interests in the entity, does not apply in determining whether a transfer of property in trust is a direct skip. § 2612(c)(2).

10. The "predeceased parent" rule of § 2651(e) also applies to collateral relatives descended from the parents of the transferor (or the transferor's spouse), but only if the transferor has no living descendants at the time of the transfer. § 2651(e)(2).

5. TAXABLE TERMINATIONS AND TAXABLE DISTRIBUTIONS

Taxable terminations and taxable distributions occur only with respect to property held in trust. In general, no GST tax is imposed as long as any interest in the trust property is held by a non-skip person.

A taxable termination occurs whenever an interest in trust property terminates, unless (1) "immediately after such termination, a non-skip person has an interest in such property," or (2) "at no time after such termination may a distribution ... be made from such trust to a skip person." § 2612(a); Reg. § 26.2612–1(b) (disregarding potential future distribution to skip person if probability of such a distribution is "so remote as to be negligible").[11] For example, assume that *A* transfers property in trust and authorizes the trustee to make discretionary distributions of income or corpus to any one or more of *A*'s children or grandchildren, with remainder at the death of the last surviving child to the grandchildren then living. *A* has two children, *B* and *C*. Shortly after the creation of the trust, *B* dies survived by *C*. No taxable termination occurs at *B*'s death because *C*, a non-skip person, continues to hold an interest in the trust property. A taxable termination does occur with respect to the property remaining in trust at *C*'s death, because all interests in the trust property are then held by skip persons.[12]

A taxable distribution occurs whenever trust income or corpus is distributed to a skip person, unless the distribution constitutes a direct skip or a taxable termination.[13] § 2612(b). In the above example, any distributions of trust income or corpus made to *A*'s grandchildren before *C*'s death would be taxable distributions.

6. MULTIPLE SKIPS

If property remains in trust following a generation-skipping transfer, the statute provides a mechanism to prevent a subsequent termination or distribution from triggering a second GST tax within a single generation.[14] This is accomplished by a special rule which reassigns the transferor to the generation immediately above the highest generation of any

11. If a transfer that qualifies as a direct skip also satisfies the statutory definition of a taxable termination, Reg. § 26.2612–1(b)(1) gives controlling effect to the former classification. Thus, for example, if a revocable trust terminates at the settlor's death and distributes property to skip persons, the transfer is treated as a direct skip rather than a taxable termination.

12. Note that the "predeceased parent" rule of § 2651(e) does not cause the transferor's grandchildren to move up one generation. Since *B* and *C* were alive at the time of the initial transfer in trust, their respective children are not subsequently reassigned to a higher generation. See Reg. § 26.2651–1(c) (Example 2).

13. A distribution of a specified portion of trust property to skip persons is treated as a taxable termination (rather than a taxable distribution) with respect to that portion of the trust property, if (1) the distribution occurs at the termination of an interest in the trust property, and (2) the termination occurs by reason of the death of a descendant of the transferor. § 2612(a)(2); see Reg. § 26.2612–1(f) (Example 11).

14. A related problem arises where a generation-skipping transfer of property triggers a GST tax and the same property is subsequently transferred to a person in a generation not lower than person who holds an interest in the trust property immediately after the generation-skipping transfer. § 2653(a). For example, assume that a trust pays income to the transferor's child for life, then to the transferor's grandchild for life, with remainder to the transferor's great-grandchild. The first generation-skipping transfer involving the trust is a taxable termination which occurs at the death of the transferor's child. Immediately after that taxable termination, the transferor is reassigned to the child's generation (i.e., one generation above the grandchild, who has become entitled to receive the trust income). As a result, the transferor's grandchild is no longer a skip person, and subsequent income distributions to the grandchild are not taxable distributions. The next generation-skipping transfer will be a taxable termination which will occur at the death of the transferor's grandchild.

C. COMPUTATION AND PAYMENT

The GST tax imposed on a generation-skipping transfer is equal to the "taxable amount" multiplied by the "applicable rate." § 2602. The applicable rate may range from zero to the maximum estate tax rate (35 percent), depending on the amount of GST exemption allocated to the property involved.

1. TAXABLE AMOUNT AND TAX LIABILITY

The taxable amount of a generation-skipping transfer generally is equal to the value of the property involved, subject to various adjustments. The person primarily liable for paying the GST tax varies according to the type of generation-skipping transfer.

In the case of a direct skip, the taxable amount is the value of the property received by the transferee (§ 2623), and the transferor is generally liable for paying the GST tax (§ 2603(a)(3)). The combined effect of these rules is to impose a "tax-exclusive" GST tax on the direct skip: The GST tax payable by the transferor is not included in the taxable amount received by the transferee.[15]

In the case of a taxable termination, the taxable amount is the value of the property involved in the taxable termination, reduced by the types of items allowable as estate tax deductions under § 2053 (e.g., administration expenses, debts). § 2622. The GST tax is payable by the trustee from the trust property. § 2603(a)(2). Since the GST tax is not deductible from the value of the trust property in determining the taxable amount, the GST tax on the taxable termination is "tax-inclusive."

that of the prior transferee. In this situation, as long as the transfers do not have the effect of avoiding GST tax, the later transfer is disregarded for GST tax purposes. § 2611(b)(2).

15. Nevertheless, to prevent the transferor from reaping the cumulative benefits of a tax-exclusive GST tax and a tax-exclusive gift tax, § 2515 treats the GST tax imposed on a lifetime direct skip as an additional gift for gift tax purposes. The result is analogous to imposing two levels of gift tax on the property, with the amount of the second gift tax included in the amount of the first gift. See Example 1, infra page 566.

In the case of a taxable distribution, the taxable amount is the value of the property received by the transferee, reduced by expenses incurred by the transferee in connection with the GST tax. § 2621(a). The GST tax is payable by the transferee. § 2603(a)(1). Since the GST tax is included in the taxable amount, regardless of whether it is paid from the transferred property or other property of the transferee, the GST tax on the taxable distribution is "tax-inclusive."[16]

2. APPLICABLE RATE AND GST EXEMPTION

Each transferor has a GST exemption which may be freely allocated to any property transferred by him or her during life or at death. § 2631. The GST exemption, originally set at $1 million, subsequently was increased to match the estate tax exemption. Accordingly, the GST exemption is now $5 million (indexed for inflation beginning in 2012). In the absence of any allocation of GST exemption, the GST tax is generally imposed at an applicable rate equal to the maximum estate tax rate (35 percent). An allocation of GST exemption to transferred property, however, produces a blended rate, which may range from zero to the maximum rate, for generation-skipping transfers involving the property.

The statute provides a mechanism linking the allocation of GST exemption with the applicable rate. In general, the amount of GST exemption allocated to transferred property is divided by the adjusted value of the property to arrive at an "applicable fraction." § 2642(a)(2); Reg. §§ 26.2642–1 and 26.2642–2. An "inclusion ratio" is then calculated by subtracting the applicable fraction from 100 percent. § 2642(a)(1). The applicable rate is equal to the maximum rate multiplied by the inclusion ratio. § 2641. For example, assume that a transferor dies when the maximum rate is 35 percent, leaving $5 million outright to a grandchild (a skip person). An allocation of $5 million of the transferor's GST exemption to the bequest would produce an applicable fraction of 100 percent, an inclusion ratio of zero, and an applicable rate of zero. An allocation of only $1 million of GST exemption would produce an applicable fraction of 20 percent, an inclusion ratio of 80 percent, and an applicable rate of 28 percent (80 percent of 35 percent).[17]

The statute provides for deemed allocations of a transferor's GST exemption to transferred property in a prescribed order of priority. First of all, the GST exemption is deemed allocated to the transferor's lifetime direct skips and to certain lifetime transfers in trust, in chronological order, to the extent necessary to produce an inclusion ratio of zero. § 2632(b) and (c). Any GST exemption remaining at death is deemed allocated first ratably to the transferor's deathtime direct skips, and then

16. A beneficiary might be tempted to achieve a tax-exclusive result by having the trustee pay the GST tax on the taxable distribution directly from the trust. The statute forecloses this gambit by treating any such payment as an additional taxable distribution. § 2621(b).

17. If a trust has an inclusion ratio of more than zero but less than 100 percent, a "qualified severance" may be used to divide the original trust into two or more new trusts, each having an inclusion ratio of either zero or 100 percent. § 2642(a)(3); Reg. § 26.2642–6.

ratably to any trust property that might subsequently be involved in a taxable termination or a taxable distribution. § 2632(e). The transferor (or his or her executor) may opt out of the deemed allocations and make different allocations of the GST exemption. § 2632(a)(1), (b)(3), (c)(5), and (d); Reg. § 26.2632–1.

In the case of trust property, an allocation of GST exemption may be made long before any generation-skipping transfer occurs. For example, if *A* transfers $5 million in trust to pay income to *A*'s child *B* for life, with remainder at *B*'s death to *B*'s descendants then living, the creation of the trust constitutes a taxable gift but not a direct skip. *A* may nevertheless shelter the entire trust from GST tax by allocating $5 million of GST exemption to the trust property upon the creation of the trust. Even if the value of the trust property increases to $10 million at *B*'s death, the inclusion ratio remains fixed at zero from the time of the allocation.[18]

A special rule prevents any allocation of GST exemption from being made to property transferred during life as long as the same property may be includible in the transferor's gross estate. § 2642(f); Reg. § 26.2632–1(c). This rule in effect requires that a transfer of property be complete for both estate and gift tax purposes before the inclusion ratio is determined for GST tax purposes.[19]

Another special rule prescribes an automatic inclusion ratio of zero for direct skips that are excluded from taxable gifts under § 2503.[20] § 2642(c)(1). In the case of property transferred in trust, however, the zero inclusion ratio is available only if distributions of trust income and corpus are limited to a single individual beneficiary during life and any trust property remaining at death is includible in the beneficiary's gross estate. § 2642(c)(2). See Reg. § 26.2642–1(d) (Examples 2–4).

D. PLANNING CONSIDERATIONS

The GST tax serves as a backstop to the estate and gift taxes. It applies to generation-skipping transfers that would otherwise incur no transfer tax at any generation level between the transferor and the beneficiary. If the GST tax applies at the maximum rate, the total transfer tax cost may be greater than if a gift or estate tax were imposed at each generation. From a planning perspective, therefore, the tax consequences of generation-skipping transfers deserve careful analysis. Even a brief overview of the GST tax reveals several opportunities to avoid or mitigate the impact of the GST tax.

---

18. The inclusion ratio of trust property generally remains constant following a generation-skipping transfer. § 2653(b)(1). For adjustments reflecting transfers of additional property or allocation of additional GST exemption, see § 2642(d).

19. Another special rule applies in determining the inclusion ratio for a charitable lead trust. See supra page 482, Note 6.

20. The definition of generation-skipping transfers also excludes any transfer which, if made by the transferor during life, would qualify for the § 2503(e) gift tax exclusion relating to payments for tuition or medical care. § 2611(b)(1). Under this exception, qualifying payments are exempt from GST tax even though made from a trust rather than by a living individual.

One technique for avoiding GST tax is to expose the property involved to gift or estate tax in the hands of a beneficiary one generation below the transferor. This technique is most useful where the transferor has no available GST exemption and the beneficiary's estate and gift tax rate is less than the rate that would apply to a generation-skipping transfer. For example, assume that *A* (having previously exhausted any available GST exemption) transfers property in trust to pay income to *A*'s child *B* for life, with remainder at *B*'s death to *B*'s descendants then living. If *B* has a general power of appointment, the trust property will be subject to gift or estate tax in the hands of both *A* and *B* but will escape GST tax. If *B*'s effective gift or estate tax rate is less than the applicable GST tax rate (e.g., as a result of the gift tax annual exclusion or *B*'s unified credit), the total transfer tax cost will be less than if the trust were subject to GST tax at *B*'s death. Moreover, if the trust continues after *B*'s death for subsequent generations of beneficiaries, *B*, as the new transferor, may be able to allocate her own GST exemption to the trust property.

Where the GST tax applies, optimal allocation of the transferor's GST exemption may produce significant GST tax savings. An allocation of GST exemption to property held in trust in effect exempts a fractional portion of the trust property from GST tax until the property becomes subject to gift or estate tax in the hands of a new transferor. Accordingly, an allocation of GST exemption to trust property that appreciates substantially in value will shelter increasing amounts from GST tax. Furthermore, the value of a single allocation of GST exemption, in terms of the number of generation-skipping transfers sheltered from GST tax, tends to be greater in the case of a long-term trust for successive generations of beneficiaries than an outright direct skip.

Further GST tax savings may be reaped by skipping multiple generations in a single generation-skipping transfer. Since the GST tax does not discriminate among skip persons of different generations, a transferor may wish to skip as many generations as possible at the cost of a single GST tax. For example, a generation-skipping transfer to the transferor's great-grandchild is taxed no more heavily than a similar transfer to the transferor's grandchild.

An allocation of GST exemption to trust property may be wasteful if the trust beneficiaries include non-skip persons as well as skip persons. Distributions to non-skip persons are wholly exempt from GST tax in any event; an allocation of GST exemption is superfluous. Conversely, distributions to skip persons normally require an allocation of GST exemption to escape GST tax. Thus, a well-advised transferor may create a "non-exempt" trust for non-skip persons and a separate "exempt" trust for skip persons, so that any available GST exemption can be allocated exclusively to the latter. See Fleet Natl. Bank v. Marquis, 771 N.E.2d 133 (Mass. 2002).

In the case of a married couple, it may be important to make full use of each spouse's GST exemption.[21] If one spouse is disproportionately wealthy, gift-splitting may be used to ensure that the other spouse's GST exemption is not wasted. Spouses may also find the reverse QTIP election useful. For example, assume that *A*, married to *B*, creates a QTIP trust and allocates *A*'s GST exemption to the trust property. If *A* makes a reverse QTIP election, *A* will continue to be treated as the transferor of the trust property, and the trust will retain its initial inclusion ratio, even after the trust property becomes subject to gift or estate tax in *B*'s hands. As a result, *B*'s GST exemption remains available for allocation to other property.

Finally, even at the maximum applicable rate, the GST tax does not hit all generation-skipping transfers with equal force. The GST tax applies to direct skips (whether occurring during life or at death) on a tax-exclusive basis, but it applies to taxable terminations and taxable distributions on a tax-inclusive basis. Accordingly, direct skips are taxed less heavily than other generation-skipping transfers. Moreover, because the gift tax (unlike the estate tax) is tax-exclusive, a lifetime direct skip is the cheapest type of generation-skipping transfer in terms of total transfer tax cost. To illustrate the point, assume that *A* wishes to put $100,000 (after taxes) into the hands of *B*, a skip person, and that all transfer taxes are imposed at a flat 35 percent rate. The total amount of transfer taxes will vary depending on whether the transfer occurs during life or at death and whether it is made outright or in trust, as follows:

1. *Lifetime direct skip. A* makes a taxable lifetime gift of $100,000 to *B*, incurring $47,250 of gift tax and $35,000 of GST tax.

a.	net amount received by *B*	$100,000
b.	GST tax on direct skip (35% × *a*)	35,000
c.	gift tax (35% × (*a* + *b*))[22]	47,250
d.	total out-of-pocket cost to *A*	$182,250

The total transfer tax cost is the same as if *A* made a gift of $135,000 to *B*'s parent, incurring a gift tax of $47,250, and *B*'s parent then made a gift of $100,000 to *B*, incurring a gift tax of $35,000.

2. *Testamentary direct skip.* A leaves a taxable estate of $207,692 to B, incurring $72,692 of estate tax and $35,000 of GST tax.

a.	taxable estate (total out-of-pocket cost to *A*)	$207,692
b.	estate tax (35% × *a*)	(72,692)
c.	GST tax on direct skip (35% × *d*)	(35,000)
d.	net amount received by *B*	$100,000

The total transfer tax cost is the same as if *A* left a bequest of $207,692 to *B*'s parent, incurring an estate tax of $72,692, and *B*'s

21. The provision allowing limited portability of the unified credit (see supra page 549) does not apply to the GST exemption; therefore, a decedent's unused GST exemption cannot be passed on to a surviving spouse.

22. The amount of the gift is grossed up by the amount of GST tax under § 2515.

parent then made a gift of $100,000 to *B*, incurring a gift tax of $35,000.

3. *Taxable distribution from inter vivos trust.* *A* creates an inter vivos trust of $153,846, incurring $53,846 of gift tax; the trust subsequently makes a taxable distribution of $153,846 to *B*, incurring $53,846 of GST tax. (The GST tax cost would be identical in the case of a taxable termination, but the tax would be paid by the trustee from the trust property.)

a.	net amount received by *B*	$100,000
b.	GST tax on taxable distribution (35% × (*a* + *b*))	53,846
c.	gift tax on creation of trust (35% × (*a* + *b*))	53,846
d.	total out-of-pocket cost to *A*	$207,692

The total transfer tax cost is the same as if *A* made a gift of $153,846 to *B*'s parent, incurring a gift tax of $53,846, and *B*'s parent then left a bequest of $153,846 to *B*, incurring an estate tax of $53,846.

4. *Taxable distribution from testamentary trust.* *A* leaves a taxable estate of $236,686 in trust, incurring $82,840 of estate tax; the trust subsequently makes a taxable distribution of $153,846 to *B*, incurring $53,846 of GST tax. (The GST tax cost would be identical in the case of a taxable termination, but the tax would be paid by the trustee from the trust property.)

a.	taxable estate (total out-of-pocket cost to *A*)	$236,686
b.	estate tax (35% × *a*)	(82,840)
c.	GST tax on taxable distribution (35% × (*a* − *b*))	(53,846)
d.	net amount received by *B*	$100,000

The total transfer tax cost is the same as if *A* left a bequest of $236,686 to *B*'s parent, incurring an estate tax of $82,840, and *B*'s parent then left a bequest of $153,846 to *B*, incurring an estate tax of $53,846.

Thus, although *B* ends up in each case with $100,000 after taxes, there are substantial differences in the total amount of transfer taxes, and hence in the out-of-pocket cost to *A*. The out-of-pocket cost to *A* of a taxable distribution (or a taxable termination) from a testamentary trust is $236,686, compared to $182,250 for a lifetime direct skip. The out-of-pocket cost of a taxable distribution (or a taxable termination) from an inter vivos trust ($207,692) is the same as that of a deathtime direct skip ($207,692).

NOTES

1. *Disclaimers.* If the beneficiary of a transferred interest makes a qualified disclaimer, the disclaimed interest is treated for gift, estate and GST tax purposes as passing directly from the transferor to the ultimate beneficiaries. § 2518(a). If, however, the ultimate beneficiaries are skip persons, the GST tax may be applicable. § 2654(c). For example, assume that *A*'s parent dies intestate and *A* makes a qualified disclaimer of *A*'s share of the estate, causing the disclaimed share to pass directly to *A*'s child *B*. The amount passing to *B* is treated as a direct skip, and the estate of *A*'s parent is liable for the resulting GST tax.

2. *Basis adjustments.* When a generation-skipping transfer occurs, the income tax basis of the property involved generally is increased (but not above fair market value) by any portion of the GST tax attributable to the excess of the property's fair market value over its adjusted basis immediately before the transfer. § 2654(a)(1). This adjustment occurs after taking into account the analogous adjustment under § 1015(d) for property acquired by gift.

In the case of a taxable termination triggered by a beneficiary's death, the basis of any portion of the trust property not covered by an allocation of GST exemption is stepped up (or down) to fair market value. § 2654(a)(2). This adjustment is analogous to the adjustment under § 1014(a) for property acquired from a decedent.

3. *Perpetual trusts.* By statute or judicial decision in most states, the duration of private trusts traditionally has been limited by some version of the Rule Against Perpetuities. In recent years, however, several states have moved to abolish the Rule in the hope of attracting new trust business. In these states it is already possible for a transferor to create a perpetual "dynasty" trust. To the extent such a trust is covered by the transferor's unified credit and GST exemption, the trust property will pass from one generation to the next free of all estate, gift and GST taxes. Assuming this sort of arrangement is permissible, is it desirable as a matter of policy? Is it advisable as a practical matter? For commentary on the interplay of the GST tax and the Rule Against Perpetuities, see Bloom, The GST Tax Tail Is Killing the Rule Against Perpetuities, 87 Tax Notes 569 (2000); Dukeminier & Krier, The Rise of the Perpetual Trust, 50 UCLA L. Rev. 1303 (2003); Sitkoff & Schanzenbach, Jurisdictional Competition for Trust Funds: An Empirical Analysis of Perpetuities and Taxes, 115 Yale L.J. 356 (2005); Schanzenbach & Sitkoff, Perpetuities or Taxes? Explaining the Rise of the Perpetual Trust, 27 Cardozo L. Rev. 2465 (2006); Staff of Joint Comm. on Taxation, Options to Improve Tax Compliance and Reform Tax Expenditures 392–95 (2005).

4. *Effective date.* In general, the GST tax applies to generation-skipping transfers made after October 22, 1986, the date of enactment. Lifetime transfers that became complete for gift tax purposes after September 25, 1985 are also subject to the GST tax, but trusts that were "irrevocable" on September 25, 1985 are exempt from the GST tax. Detailed transitional rules appear in Reg. § 26.2601–1.

5. *References.* For further discussion of the GST tax, see Dukeminier, Dynasty Trusts: Sheltering Descendants From Transfer Taxes, 23 Est. Planning 417 (1996); Gallo, Estate Planning and the Generation–Skipping Tax, 33 Real Prop., Prob. & Tr. J. 457 (1998); Blattmachr & Pennell, Adventures in Generation–Skipping, or How We Learned to Love the "Delaware Tax Trap", 24 Real Prop., Prob. & Tr. J. 75 (1989).

Chapter 7

Valuation of Property

■ ■ ■

A. GENERAL PRINCIPLES

The valuation of property raises issues that cut across the income, estate, gift and GST taxes. In theory, separate methods of valuing property might be adopted for purposes of the different taxes, reflecting the special policy underpinnings of each tax.[1] As a practical matter, however, general valuation principles have developed along remarkably homogeneous lines. The resulting rules tend to be double-edged in application: A victory for the government in one context may be turned to the taxpayer's advantage in another, and vice versa. In several situations, the Code aims to alleviate hardship or prevent abuse by imposing special rules that modify or override general valuation principles.

The Code repeatedly refers to the "value" of property, but does not purport to prescribe a valuation method of general application. §§ 2031(a) (estate tax), 2512(a) (gift tax), and 2624(a) (GST tax). That task is taken up by the regulations, which generally require that property be included in the gross estate at its "fair market value." Fair market value in turn is defined as "the price at which the property would change hands between a willing buyer and a willing seller, neither being under any compulsion to buy or to sell and both having reasonable knowledge of relevant facts." Reg. §§ 20.2031–1(b) (estate tax) and 25.2512–1 (gift tax).

The valuation date generally coincides with the time of the transfer: the date of death, for estate tax purposes (§ 2031(a)); the date of the gift, for gift tax purposes (§ 2512(a)); or the time of a generation-skipping transfer, for GST tax purposes (§ 2624(a)). Under § 2032 (discussed infra

1. In the 1930s, James Bonbright, a leading theorist of property valuation, advocated such a functional approach. He argued that in the estate tax context the "ideal basis" for valuing property lies in its "value to the owner," i.e., the beneficiary, and that "market value, in the strict sense of the price at which it might be sold to any outside party, is irrelevant save as a possible measure of the value of the property to those who inherit it." He conceded, however, that "[b]ecause a valuation based on market price is so *generally* the best available measure of the value of the assets to the beneficiaries themselves, its adoption is justified as a matter of administrative convenience even in many instances in which the assessor has reason to believe that the assets will not in fact be liquidated and that they will come into the possession of beneficiaries to whom they will have a value in excess of their sale price." Bonbright, The Valuation of Property 694–96 (1937).

at page 629), if certain conditions are met, a decedent's executor may elect to value property for estate tax purposes as of an alternate valuation date up to six months after death. See also § 2624(b) and (c) (alternate valuation date for certain generation-skipping transfers).

The special valuation rules of Chapter 14 (§§ 2701–2704), where applicable, override general valuation principles. Section 2701, relating to certain transfers of interests in corporations and partnerships (see infra page 591), and § 2702, relating to certain transfers in trust (see supra page 78), apply solely for gift tax purposes. Section 2703 (see infra page 608) and § 2704 (see infra page 622) require that certain rights and restrictions be disregarded in valuing property for purposes of the estate, gift and GST taxes.

UNITED STATES v. CARTWRIGHT

411 U.S. 546 (1973).

MR. JUSTICE WHITE delivered the opinion of the Court. . . .

[Under the Investment Company Act of 1940, open-end investment companies ("mutual funds") are permitted to market their shares continuously to the public, and are also required to be prepared to redeem outstanding shares at any time. The public offering or "asked" price is based on the per-share value of the company's net assets, and may also include a charge or "sales load" representing compensation to the underwriter who acts as the company's selling agent. In contrast, the redemption or "bid" price is limited to the per-share net asset value. Because there is virtually no private trading in mutual fund shares, there are in effect two prices for identical shares at any given time: the asked price paid by investors on initial purchase, and the bid price paid by the company on redemption.

Decedent died in 1964 owning mutual fund shares with a public offering price of around $133,300 and a redemption price of around $124,400. Reg. § 20.2031–8(b), as promulgated in 1963 and in effect at the decedent's death, required that the shares be valued at the public offering price.]

In implementing 26 U.S.C. § 2031, the general principle of the Treasury Regulations is that the value of property is to be determined by its fair market value at the time of the decedent's death. "The fair market value is the price at which the property would change hands between a willing buyer and a willing seller, neither being under any compulsion to buy or to sell and both having reasonable knowledge of relevant facts." Treas. Reg. § 20.2031–1(b). The willing buyer-willing seller test of fair market value is nearly as old as the federal income, estate, and gifts taxes themselves, and is not challenged here. Under this test, it is clear that if the decedent had owned ordinary corporate stock listed on an exchange, its "value" for estate tax purposes would be the price the estate could have obtained if it had sold the stock on the valuation date, that price being, under Treas. Reg. § 20.2031–2(b), the mean between the highest and lowest quoted selling prices on that day. Respondent urges that similar treatment be given mutual fund shares and that, accordingly, their value be measured by the redemption price at the date of death, the only price that the estate could hope to obtain if the shares had been sold.

Respondent's argument has the clear ring of common sense to it, but the United States maintains that the redemption price does not reflect the price that a willing buyer would pay, inasmuch as the mutual fund is under a statutory obligation to redeem outstanding shares whenever they are offered. According to the Government, the only market for mutual fund shares that has both willing buyers and willing sellers is the public offering market. Therefore, the price in that market, the asked price, is an appropriate basis for valuation. The central difficulty with this argument is that it unrealistically bifurcates the statutory scheme for the trading in mutual fund shares. To be sure, the fund is under an obligation to redeem its shares at the stated price. 15 U.S.C. § 80a–22(e). But, at the time of the original purchases, both the fund and the purchasers are aware of that duty and both willingly enter into the sale transactions nonetheless. As Judge Winner correctly observed in Hicks v. United States, 335 F. Supp. 474, 481 (D. Colo. 1971):

> Viewing the contract in this light meets every test of the "willing buyer-willing seller" definition usually applied in the determination of market value. The "willing buyer" is the fully informed person who agrees to buy the shares, agreeing at that time to sell them to the fund—the only available repurchaser—at the redemption price. The "willing seller" is the fund which sells the shares at market value plus a load charge, and which agrees to buy the shares back at market less the load charge. That is the market, and it is the only market. It is a market made up of informed buyers and an informed seller, all dealing at arm's length.

In the context of the Investment Company Act, the redemption price may thus be properly viewed only as the final step in a voluntary transaction between a willing buyer and a willing seller. As a matter of statutory law, holders of mutual fund shares cannot obtain the "asked" price from the fund. That price is never paid by the fund; it is used by the fund when selling its shares to the public—and even then the fund receives merely the net asset value per share from the sale, with the sales load being paid directly to the underwriter. In short, the only price that a shareholder may realize and that the fund—the only buyer—will pay is the redemption price. In the teeth of this fact, Regulation § 20.2031–8(b) purports to assign a value to mutual fund shares that the estate could not hope to obtain and that the fund could not offer.

In support of the Regulation, the Government stresses that many types of property are taxed at values above those which could be realized during an actual sale. For example, ordinary corporate stock is valued at its fair market price without taking into account the brokerage commission that a seller must generally pay in order to sell the stock. Respondent does not contend that that approach is inappropriate or that, for example, the value of ordinary stock in an estate should be the market price at the time less anticipated brokerage fees. But § 20.2031–8(b) operates in an entirely different fashion. The regulation includes as an element of value the commission cost incurred in the hypothetical *purchase* of the mutual fund shares already held in the decedent's estate. If that principle were carried over to the ordinary stock situation, then a share traded at $100 on the date of death would be valued, not at $100 as it now is, but at, say, $102, representing the "value" plus the fee that a person buying the stock on that day would have to pay. It hardly need be said that such a valuation method is at least inconsistent with long-established Treasury practice and would appear at odds with the basic notions of valuation embodied in the Internal Revenue Code. . . .

Even if it were assumed that the public offering price were somehow relevant to the value of mutual fund shares privately held, there would still be the difficulty that shares so held are, in important respects, similar to ordinary corporate stock held subject to a restrictive agreement (such as a first-refusal right at a specified price). With respect to the value of such stock, the Treasury Regulations have provided that the price that may be obtained in the marketplace does not control. Rather, so long as the restriction is a bona fide one, the value of the shares in the hands of the restricted stockholder is determined in accordance with the terms of the restriction. Treas. Reg. § 20.2031–2(h). Outstanding mutual fund shares are likewise held subject to a restriction, as the Court of Appeals noted. 457 F.2d, at 571. Those shares may not be "sold" at the public offering price. By statute, they may be "sold" back to the mutual fund only at the redemption price. We see no valid justification for disregarding this reality connected with the ownership of mutual fund shares.

The Government nevertheless argues that Treas. Reg. § 20.2031–8(b) reasonably values the "bundle of rights" that is transferred with the ownership of the mutual fund shares.[2] For this argument, heavy reliance is placed on this Court's decisions in Guggenheim v. Rasquin, 312 U.S. 254 (1941); Powers v. Commissioner, 312 U.S. 259 (1941); United States v. Ryerson, 312 U.S. 260 (1941), which held that the cash-surrender value of a single-premium life insurance policy did not necessarily represent its only taxable value for federal gift tax purposes. In *Guggenheim*, the lead case, the taxpayer purchased single-premium life insurance policies with an aggregate face value of one million dollars for approximately $852,000 and, shortly thereafter, gave the policies to her children. On the gift tax return, the policies were listed at their cash-surrender value of about $717,000—admittedly the only amount the donor or the donees could

2. The Government argues that, as a practical matter, an estate would rarely be hurt by valuation of mutual fund shares at the asked price, because Treas. Reg. § 20.2053–3(d)(2) permits an estate to deduct the difference between the asked and bid prices if the shares are sold to pay certain enumerated expenses. By its terms, however, that regulation applies only if "the sale is *necessary*" to pay those expenses. (Emphasis added.) In any event, the regulation is inapplicable altogether if the shares are transferred in kind to an heir or legatee.

receive, if the policies were surrendered. But the Commissioner valued the gift at the cost of the policies, and this Court upheld that valuation: "the owner of a fully paid life insurance policy has more than the mere right to surrender it; he has the right to retain it for its investment virtues and to receive the face amount of the policy upon the insured's death. That these latter rights are deemed by purchasers of insurance to have substantial value is clear from the difference between the cost of a single-premium policy and its immediate or early cash-surrender value...." 312 U.S., at 257. Because the "entire bundle of rights in a single-premium policy" is so difficult to give a realistic value to, the Court deferred to the Commissioner's determination and permitted valuation to be based on cost: "Cost is cogent evidence of value." Id., at 258. But as the District Court observed, 323 F.Supp., at 773, shares in mutual funds are quite unlike insurance policies, particularly in light of the policy owner's right to receive the full face value of the policy upon the insured's death. Moreover, mutual fund shares present no analogous difficulties in valuation. On any given day, their commercial value may be determined by turning to the financial pages of a newspaper. Obviously, with respect to mutual funds, there are "investment virtues" and the prospects of capital gains or dividends. But that is true of any corporate security. Nonetheless, shareholders in mutual funds are singled out by the Regulation and their holdings valued at an unrealistic replacement cost—which includes "brokers' commissions"—while other shareholdings are valued without regard to such commissions.

The unrealistic nature of this difference in treatment may be demonstrated by comparing the treatment of shares in load funds, such as the decedent's, with shares in no-load funds. Obviously, even if it could be argued that there are relevant differences between mutual fund shares generally and corporate stock, there are no differences in terms of "investment virtues" or related interests between no-load and load fund shares. Indeed, as the terms imply, the only real distinction between the two is that one imposes an initial sales charge and the other does not. Nonetheless, under the Regulation, a share in a no-load fund is valued at its net asset value while a share in a load fund is valued at net asset value plus sales charge. To further illustrate, consider a decedent who had purchased one share in each of two no-load mutual funds, at $100 per share. The decedent died before either appreciated, but after one of the funds had changed to a load fund. Although both shares are still worth $100, and could be redeemed for only that amount, the Regulation would require that one be valued at $100 and the other at $100 plus the new load charge. A regulation that results in such differing treatment of identical property should be supported by something more than a transparent analogy to life insurance.

[The Court concluded that Reg. § 20.2031–8(b) was "unreasonable and unrealistic," and held it invalid.]

MR. JUSTICE STEWART, with whom THE CHIEF JUSTICE and MR. JUSTICE REHNQUIST join, dissenting....

At the outset, it may be well to note the basic general rule with respect to valuation that prevails under our estate tax laws. This rule is embodied in Treas. Reg. § 20.2031–1(b), and provides that the value of property includable in a decedent's estate shall be the fair market value of such property at the date of the decedent's death. "The fair market value is the price at which the property would change hands between a willing buyer and a willing seller, neither being under any compulsion to buy or to sell and both having reasonable knowledge of relevant facts." 26 C.F.R. § 20.2031–1(b).

The difficulty in applying this rule to mutual fund shares—a difficulty which, no doubt, led the Commissioner to promulgate Regulation § 20.2031–8(b)—is that such shares *once issued* are not subject to disposition in a market of "willing buyers" and "willing sellers." Indeed, as both the District Court and the Court of Appeals noted, the only practical means of disposing of mutual fund shares once acquired is redemption, and redemption cannot be deemed a sale of the sort described in the general rule (26 C.F.R. § 20.2031–1(b)), since the party purchasing (the issuing company) is under an absolute obligation to redeem the shares when tendered, and the party selling has no practical alternative, if he wishes to liquidate his holdings, other than to offer them to the issuing company for redemption.

This being the case, the Commissioner was faced with the problem of establishing a method of valuing the shares most nearly equal to their inherent worth. In doing so, he chose not to treat their redemption value as dispositive of this question. In promulgating his Regulation, he might rationally have considered that "on demand" redemption at net asset value is but one of many rights incident to the ownership of mutual fund shares.

For example, in the case of [decedent's] shares, her estate had not only the right to redeem them "on demand," but also to retain them; and if it had done so it would have possessed not only the normal dividend and capital gains rights associated with most investments, but also the right to have such dividends and capital gains as accrued applied toward the purchase of additional shares at a price *below* that which a member of the general public would have had to pay for such shares. In addition, under the investment contracts involved here, [decedent's] estate would have had the right to exchange her shares in any one of the three mutual funds involved for those of either or both of the other funds managed by [the company]—without paying the usual sales charge or load.

The Commissioner has determined that the proper method of valuing *all* the rights, both redemptive and otherwise, incident to the ownership of mutual fund shares is to determine what a member of the general public, acting under no constraints, would have had to pay for these rights if purchased on the open market. And, as noted earlier, although no such market exists for mutual fund shares *once issued* to an investor, a perfectly normal market of willing buyers and sellers does exist with respect to such shares prior to their issuance. Thus, the Commissioner took the price at which the shares would have sold on this market as fairly reflective of their inherent worth. I cannot say that this method of valuation adopted by the Commissioner, and embodied in Regulation § 20.2031–8(b), is so unreasonable and inconsistent with the statute as to render it invalid.

The respondent's claim that the regulation is invalid is grounded upon two principal arguments. First, he says, the estate is being taxed on an amount in excess of what it can, as a practical matter, realize from the disposition of the mutual fund shares. But this is equally true of many other assets subject to taxation under our estate tax laws. For example, real property passing into an estate is taxed upon its full fair market value, despite the fact that as a practical matter the estate must usually pay some percentage of that sum in brokerage fees if it wishes to dispose of the property and receive cash in its stead. This attack upon the Regulation thus amounts to no less than an attack upon the whole system of valuation embodied in the Treasury Regulations on Estate Tax, based as it is upon fair value in an open market. I am not ready to hold that this long-established and long-accepted system is basically invalid.

The respondent's second argument is that the Regulation places a higher valuation on mutual fund shares than is placed upon registered common stock shares and other similarly traded securities. This argument assumes that the redemption or net asset value of a mutual fund share is identical to the fair market value of a traded security, and, by a parity of reasoning, that the sales charge or load associated with mutual fund purchases is equivalent to the commission that a stockbroker charges a purchaser of securities. Under this view, the Commissioner would be entitled to tax mutual fund shares passing into an estate only on their net asset value, since in the allegedly comparable situation of common stock shares no consideration may be given to brokers' commissions in arriving at an appropriate valuation for estate tax purposes. See 26 C.F.R. § 20.2031–2(b).

Although this argument has a certain superficial appeal, the analogy on which it relies is hardly an exact one. For an estate in disposing of marketable securities must pay a brokerage commission on their *sale*, and will thus realize less than the amount at which the securities have been valued, while an estate turning in mutual fund shares for redemption pays no commission or other surcharge whatever. Moreover, unlike traditional securities, there is no open trading market for mutual fund shares once issued and in the hands of an investor. If such a market of willing buyers and sellers did exist, the Commissioner would doubtless be bound to treat mutual fund shares exactly like other securities. But where no market for an asset exists, there simply is no market price to provide a readily identifiable standard for valuation. Under these circumstances, it is the Commissioner's duty under the statute to establish criteria for determining the true worth of the totality of rights and benefits incident to ownership of the asset. This the Commissioner has done in Regulation

§ 20.2031–8(b) by providing that the value of a mutual fund share for federal estate tax purposes shall be the price a member of the general public would have to pay to acquire such share. Such an approach to the valuation of assets not regularly traded in a market of willing buyers and sellers has already been sustained by this Court in a case closely akin to the case before us. See Guggenheim v. Rasquin, 312 U.S. 254.

Given the peculiar characteristics of mutual fund shares, it is arguable that the Commissioner might reasonably have adopted a method of valuation different from that which he has chosen. But that is a question that is not for us to decide. . . .

NOTES

1. *Aftermath of Cartwright.* Following the *Cartwright* decision, the regulations were amended to conform to the result in that case. Reg. §§ 20.2031–8(b) and 25.2512–6(b) now require that shares of an open-end investment company be valued at the public redemption price.

2. *Fair market value.* The regulations define fair market value by reference to a hypothetical sale between a willing buyer and a willing seller, both parties having reasonable knowledge of relevant facts. The regulations contemplate a transaction occurring in the market "in which such item is most commonly sold to the public, taking into account the location of the item wherever appropriate." Thus, for example, in the used car market, value is the price at which the dealer sells rather than the one at which he or she buys. Reg. §§ 20.2031–1(b) and 25.2512–1.

The regulations also provide that value is not to be determined by a "forced sale" price. Is an owner an unwilling seller if forced to sell by his or her creditors? If the sale follows a well-advertised auction at Sotheby's? What constitutes "reasonable knowledge of relevant facts"? This concept evidently includes not only facts that are publicly available, but also those that a reasonable buyer or seller would elicit by inquiry or investigation before coming to an agreement as to price. See Rev. Rul. 78–367, 1978–2 C.B. 249 (describing "the reality of the market place" relating to disclosure and investigation, and concluding that gift tax valuation of stock should take into account public announcement of company's merger plans). What if value has been affected by false financial statements that are not known to the owner? See Johnson v. Commissioner, 74 T.C. 89 (1980), affd., 673 F.2d 262 (9th Cir. 1982) (stock market quotes established fair market value; shareholder could have realized quoted price, even though the market was inflated by false financial statements).

The search is not for the property's "fair," "normal," or "inherent" value, but for its "fair market value." In American Natl. Bank & Trust Co. v. United States, 594 F.2d 1141 (7th Cir. 1979), the court offered the following comparison between inherent and market value:

> Two conceptions of value are possible. First it is apparent that an asset always has some theoretical, underlying value which is revealed or made apparent by subsequent events. For example, an unsigned painting by

Botticelli languishing in a second hand art shop with a minimal price tag always had the same inherent value which it acquires when the creator of the painting is later discovered. In a second sense, however, value is a practical process, always changing in accord with the price that it will yield on the market at a given time. In this sense, the undiscovered Botticelli has a value far less than its "inherent" value. The Code and the Regulations clearly enshrine this second sense of value.... [594 F.2d at 1144 n.2.]

3. *Built-in capital gain.* The income tax "basis" of property is ordinarily irrelevant in determining its fair market value. In the case of a closely held corporation that holds appreciated assets, however, a purchaser of the corporation's stock might well demand a valuation adjustment to reflect the corporation's potential income tax liability on its built-in gain. Several courts have allowed such an adjustment on the ground that the built-in gain will eventually be taxed when the corporation sells or distributes its assets. See Davis' Estate v. Commissioner, 110 T.C. 530 (1998); Eisenberg v. Commissioner, 155 F.3d 50 (2d Cir. 1998); Jameson's Estate v. Commissioner, 267 F.3d 366 (5th Cir. 2001).[3] How should such a valuation adjustment be calculated? Should the answer depend on whether the stock represents a controlling or a minority interest in the corporation? On the nature of the corporation's assets? On whether there is a plan to liquidate the corporation or sell its assets in the near future?

In Dunn's Estate v. Commissioner, 301 F.3d 339 (5th Cir. 2002), the decedent owned a majority block of shares in a closely held operating corporation. The court held as a matter of law that the built-in capital gain tax attributable to appreciated corporate assets must be taken into account as a dollar-for-dollar reduction in calculating the corporation's "asset-based value" but that the tax did not enter into the calculation of "earnings-based value." The court went on to say that the likelihood of liquidation had no place in either the asset-based approach or the earnings-based approach, but that it did affect the relative weights to be accorded to the two approaches in determining the value of the decedent's shares.

In Jelke's Estate v. Commissioner, 507 F.3d 1317 (11th Cir. 2007), cert. denied, 129 S.Ct. 168 (2008), the decedent owned a minority interest in a family holding company whose assets consisted entirely of marketable securities with substantial unrealized appreciation. Reversing the Tax Court, which had computed the present value of the built-in tax liability based on a hypothetical gradual liquidation of the company's portfolio over a 16-year period, the Eleventh Circuit adopted the rationale of *Dunn's Estate* and allowed the full amount of the built-in tax liability as an offset against the value of the company's assets based on a hypothetical immediate liquidation. According to the court, the dollar-for-dollar offset reflected "the reality of the depressing economic effect that the lurking taxes have on the market selling price":

---

3. These cases arose after the 1986 repeal of the so-called *General Utilities* doctrine (see General Utilities & Operating Co. v. Helvering, 296 U.S. 200 (1935)), which for many years allowed a corporation to distribute appreciated property to its shareholders without recognizing gain. Under current law a corporation generally must recognize gain on a distribution of appreciated property. §§ 311(b) and 336(a).

> The hypothetical willing buyer is a rational, economic actor. Common sense tells us that he or she would not pay the same price for identical blocks of stock, one purchased outright in the marketplace with no tax consequences, and one acquired through the purchase of shares in a closely-held corporation, with significant, built-in tax consequences. [507 F.3d at 1333.]

How persuasive is the court's reasoning? The holding company in *Jelke's Estate* had long-term capital appreciation as its primary investment goal and maintained a low annual asset turnover rate of around 6 percent. Is it reasonable to assume an immediate liquidation of the company as a valuation premise? While a hypothetical *purchaser* would welcome a dollar-for-dollar offset for the potential capital gain tax, a hypothetical *seller* would resist such an adjustment on the ground that there was no plan to liquidate the company and under current conditions a complete asset turnover would require 16 years. Is it not likely that the parties would ultimately compromise on something less than a dollar-for-dollar offset? Recall the admonition in Reg. § 20.2031–1(b) that fair market value "is not to be determined by a forced sale price." Invoking "the virtue of simplicity," the court explained that its approach provides "a welcome road map" for judges "not formally trained in the art of valuation" and "bypasses the unnecessary expenditure of judicial resources being used to wade through a myriad of divergent expert witness testimony." A dissenting opinion rebuked the majority for taking the easy way out: "To avoid the effort, labor, and toil that is required for a more accurate calculation of the estate tax due, the majority simply assumes a result that we all know is wrong. We can do better than that. The tax court did."

In allowing these valuation adjustments for shares of corporate stock, the courts have emphasized that a corporate-level income tax will ultimately be imposed when appreciated assets are sold or distributed, even though the timing and amount of the tax may be uncertain. In contrast, no adjustment is allowed for appreciated assets owned directly by an individual, presumably because the potential income tax liability can be expunged if the assets are held until death and receive a stepped-up basis at that time. See § 1014, discussed supra at page 40. Recall, however, that the basis step-up does not apply to items of "income in respect of a decedent," and that such items accordingly come into the beneficiary's hands with a built-in income tax liability. See §§ 691(a) and 1014(c). Does it follow that a valuation adjustment should be available for items of income in respect of a decedent? In Smith v. United States, 391 F.3d 621 (5th Cir. 2004), the decedent left two retirement accounts funded with marketable stocks and bonds which constituted income in respect of a decedent. Observing that a hypothetical buyer "would not consider" the income tax consequences "since he is not the beneficiary and thus would not be paying the income tax," the court held that the accounts must be included in the gross estate at the fair market value of the underlying assets, with no adjustment for the built-in income tax liability. Accord, Kahn's Estate v. Commissioner, 125 T.C. 227 (2005).

4. *Effect of restrictive agreements.* Partnership agreements often require that a deceased partner's interest be purchased by the surviving partners at a specified price. Suppose that the partners are a parent and her two children,

and the specified purchase price is $1—or some other amount substantially below fair market value. How should the value of the parent's partnership interest be determined at her death for estate tax purposes? Does the rationale of the *Cartwright* case suggest that the value of the interest should be limited to $1? See § 2703, discussed infra at page 608.

B. VALUATION METHODS AND APPLICATIONS

1. VALUATION METHODS

Several different methods may be available for determining fair market value. In theory, if the relevant facts and circumstances are accurately identified and properly taken into account, the end result should be the same no matter which method is used. In many cases, however, the type of property being valued and the availability (or unavailability) of relevant factual data will influence both the method used and the results obtained. Several commonly encountered valuation methods are summarized below:

a. *Historical cost.* If the property to be valued was bought or sold in an arm's-length transaction at or about the valuation date, the price actually paid is ordinarily the best evidence of the property's fair market value. See Guggenheim v. Rasquin, supra page 363 (holding that the amount paid by the taxpayer for several single-premium life insurance policies was the "proper criterion" in determining their value for gift tax purposes), discussed and distinguished in *Cartwright*, supra page 571. The passage of time or a change in the nature of the property may diminish the evidentiary force of the actual transaction, raising an issue as to whether it can be rehabilitated by an adjustment that takes account of these factors. See United States v. Ryerson, 312 U.S. 260 (1941) (79-year-old donor assigned single-premium life insurance policies five years after they were issued; policies valued at replacement cost rather than original cost); cf. Publicker v. Commissioner, 206 F.2d 250 (3d Cir. 1953), cert. denied, 346 U.S. 924 (1954) (gift of jewelry valued at price paid by donor five years earlier, with a 20-percent adjustment to reflect the increased value of large diamonds).

b. *Prices paid for comparable property.* Courts frequently seek guidance in current transactions of comparable property, "determining the indicated value of the subject property by considering actual sales prices of similar properties located in the general area and which were sold within a reasonable time before or after [the valuation date]." Fawcett's Estate v. Commissioner, 64 T.C. 889 (1975). If the sales are few in number or distant in time, they may lose probative value. See Fitts' Estate v. Commissioner, 237 F.2d 729 (8th Cir. 1956) (sales three years before and five years after valuation date were "too remote" to establish estate tax value; moreover, taxpayer did not prove they were arm's-length transactions); Kinney's Estate v. Commissioner, 80 F.2d 568 (9th Cir. 1935) (sales in 1930 not relevant in determining 1927 estate tax value, because economic depression intervened). Another issue that may arise is whether an adequate adjustment can be made to take into account dissimilarities in the properties. See Nail's Estate v. Commissioner, 59 T.C. 187 (1972) (court reviewed adjustments made to reflect differences in size, access to highway, availability of water, and several other features).

c. *Capitalization of income.* The courts often determine the fair market value of property by estimating the present value of its anticipated income and of its salvage value, if any, at the end of its income-producing life. If the property is expected to produce a constant amount of annual income in perpetuity, the value of the property can be estimated by discounting the income stream to present value at an assumed discount rate; the same result can be obtained by dividing the amount of annual income by the assumed discount rate. Thus, the present value of a perpetual stream of $1,000 annual payments, assuming a 5–percent discount rate, is $20,000 (i.e., $1,000 ÷ .05). If the discount rate is 8 percent, the present value of the same income stream is $12,500 (i.e., $1,000 ÷ .08).

Capitalization of income may be the principal or only way to value property in the absence of relevant market transactions; moreover, it is a useful way to test the assumed comparability of actual sales, and it may be used as a supplement where the probative value of actual sale prices is debatable. The value produced by this method is only as accurate as the underlying financial data. The key variables involve estimates of future earnings, salvage value, and capitalization or discount rates. See 5 Bittker & Lokken, Federal Taxation of Income, Estates and Gifts ¶ 135.2.3 (2d ed. 1993).

d. *Appraisals by experts.* Reg. § 20.2031–6(b) requires an expert's appraisal to be filed with the estate tax return for household and personal items totaling more than $3,000 in value. Elsewhere in the regulations, the taxpayer is asked to submit complete data underlying the valuation of stock and business interests. Reg. §§ 20.2031–2(f), 25.2512–2(f), and 301.6501(c)–1(f).

In litigated cases, the parties typically rely on expert testimony and appraisals to support their respective valuation claims. The Tax Court has described the role of valuation experts as follows:

> Expert testimony sometimes aids the Court in determining valuation. Other times, it does not. The Court is not bound by an opinion of an expert. We weigh an expert's testimony in light of his or her qualifications, as well as with regard to all other credible evidence in the record. Depending on what we believe is appropriate under the facts and circumstances of the case, we may reject an expert's opinion in its entirety, accept it in its entirety, or accept only selective portions of it.

[Mandelbaum v. Commissioner, 69 T.C.M. (CCH) 2852, 2862–63 (1995), affd. mem., 91 F.3d 124 (3d Cir. 1996).]

Litigation of valuation disputes often produces a result that might have been reached far more quickly and cheaply by an out-of-court settlement. The heavy burden of such unnecessary litigation has elicited words of warning from the Tax Court:

> [E]ach of the parties should keep in mind that, in the final analysis, the Court may find the evidence of valuation by one of the parties sufficiently more convincing than that of the other party, so that the final result will produce a significant financial defeat for one or the other, rather than a middle-of-the-road compromise which we suspect each of the parties expects the Court to reach. [Buffalo Tool & Die Mfg. Co. v. Commissioner, 74 T.C. 441, 452 (1980).]

In the event of a controversy involving the valuation of a gift reported on a gift tax return, the donor may petition the Tax Court for a declaratory judgment. § 7477. On a factual issue such as valuation, the burden of proof generally rests with the taxpayer, but in certain circumstances the burden shifts to the government if the taxpayer introduces "credible evidence" in support of his or her position. § 7491. The Senate Finance Committee report states that this standard refers to "the quality of evidence which, after critical analysis, the court would find sufficient upon which to base a decision on the issue if no contrary evidence were submitted (without regard to the judicial presumption of IRS correctness)." S. Rep. No. 174, 105th Cong., 2d Sess. 45 (1998). Furthermore, § 7517 requires the Service, on request, to provide a statement explaining the basis of its valuation for estate, gift, or GST tax purposes. The House Ways and Means Committee report indicates that this requirement was designed to encourage resolution of valuation disputes at the earliest possible time through full disclosure of valuation methods. H.R. Rep. No. 1380, 94th Cong., 2d Sess. 61 (1976), reprinted in 1976–3 C.B. (Vol. 3) 738, 795.

Section 6662 imposes penalties if the value of property reported on an estate or gift tax return is substantially lower than the amount ultimately determined to be correct, unless the resulting underpayment of tax is $5,000 or less. A 20–percent penalty applies to a "substantial" valuation understatement where the reported value is 65 percent or less of the correct amount. An enhanced 40–percent penalty applies to a "gross" valuation misstatement where the reported value is 40 percent or less of the correct amount. Neither penalty applies, however, if the underpayment was due to "reasonable cause" and the taxpayer acted "in good faith." § 6664(c)(1). A separate penalty applies to any person who prepares an appraisal, knowing that it will be used in connection with a tax return or a refund claim, if the appraisal results in a substantial or gross valuation understatement. § 6695A.

2. APPLICATIONS TO SPECIFIC TYPES OF PROPERTY

a. Real Estate

In valuing real estate, experts routinely use the comparable sales and capitalization-of-income methods, the latter method being particularly common for rental properties such as office buildings and apartment houses. Historical cost carries some weight if the property was recently purchased; replacement or reproduction costs may be relevant in the case of buildings. The regulations state that property shall not be valued at the value at which it is assessed for local tax purposes unless the assessed value represents fair market value. Reg. §§ 20.2031–1(b) and 25.2512–1.

b. Tangible Personal Property

The valuation of works of art, antiques, manuscripts, and similar unique items is done by experts, who employ most of the general valuation principles discussed above. Historical cost, for example, is ordinarily accepted as a presumptive if not conclusive criterion of market value. The capitalization-of-income method may seem ill adapted to the valuation of works of art, but it can be employed for motion pictures, novels, and other income-producing properties. The prices paid for comparable works, however, are the most commonly encountered criteria for value, even though they almost always leave room for debate about such imponderables as the aesthetic quality, physical condition, and authenticity of the works being compared.

The regulations provide that property (e.g., a decedent's automobile) is to be valued at the price that a member of the public would have to pay to purchase the item rather than the amount that the estate would receive from a sale to a dealer. Reg. §§ 20.2031–1(b) and 25.2512–1. See Publicker v. Commissioner, 206 F.2d 250 (3d Cir. 1953), cert. denied, 346 U.S. 924 (1954) ("public" for high-quality, set diamonds consists of individual purchasers, not jewelers); cf. Anselmo v. Commissioner, 80 T.C. 872 (1983), affd., 757 F.2d 1208 (11th Cir. 1985) ("public" for low-quality, unset gems consists of jewelers, not individual retail customers). If jewelry, furs, or other items that are subject to an excise tax on purchase are given to a donee within a reasonable time after purchase, the amount to be declared on the gift tax return is the purchase price, including the excise tax. Reg. § 25.2512–7; Publicker v. Commissioner, supra. If the interim between purchase and gift exceeds a reasonable time, the excise tax is to be taken into account to the extent that it affects the market value. Reg. § 25.2512–7; see also Rev. Rul. 55–71, 1955–1 C.B. 110 (federal excise tax is a "relevant factor" in determining fair market value for estate tax purposes because it is "an item which will tend to increase the amount at which an individual or an estate would be willing to sell such property").

c. Actively Traded Stocks and Securities

The regulations provide that stocks and bonds for which there is a market—on a stock exchange, over the counter, or otherwise—shall be valued by taking the mean between the highest and lowest selling prices on the valuation date or, if there were no sales on that date, by taking a weighted average of such means on the nearest dates before and after the valuation date. If actual sales are not available within a reasonable period from the valuation date, the mean between bid and asked prices may be used instead. Reg. §§ 20.2031–2 and 25.2512–2.

The regulations go on to provide that if the value of the stocks or bonds as thus determined "does not reflect the fair market value thereof, then some reasonable modification of that basis or other relevant facts and elements of value are considered in determining the fair market value." Reg. §§ 20.2031–2(e) and 25.2512–2(e). Furthermore, the regulations acknowledge that the size of the block of securities to be valued may be relevant (see infra page 596).

As explained in the *Cartwright* case, supra page 571, mutual fund shares are valued at the public redemption price as of the valuation date. Reg. §§ 20.2031–8(b) and 25.2512–6(b).

d. Income Interests, Remainders, and Annuities

Section 7520 generally provides that the value of a partial interest—e.g., an income interest for life or a term of years, a remainder, a reversion, or a private annuity—must be determined under valuation tables promulgated by the Service.[4] The tables, which appear in abridged form in the regulations, reflect prescribed actuarial assumptions concerning life expectancies and rates of return on investments. Reg. §§ 20.2031–7, 20.7520–1, 25.2512–5, and 25.7520–1. The applicable rate of return is determined on a monthly basis by reference to the average market yield of midterm U.S. Treasury obligations.[5] Furthermore, the tables are required to be revised at least every ten years to reflect the most recent available national mortality experience. § 7520(c)(3). The tables greatly simplify valuation of the most commonly encountered interests, where possession will begin or end upon some future event that is certain to occur (i.e., the end of a fixed term of years or the death of a particular individual). In situations involving an interest dependent on the duration of two or more lives, special actuarial factors may be obtained from the Service. Reg.

---

4. In the case of a commercial annuity (i.e., an annuity contract issued by "a company regularly engaged in the selling of [such] contracts"), the valuation tables do not apply. Instead, the value of a commercial annuity is established through the issuer's sale of "comparable contracts." Reg. §§ 20.2031–8(a) and 25.2512–6(a).

5. Section 7520(a)(2) prescribes "an interest rate (rounded to the nearest $\frac{2}{10}$ of 1 percent) equal to 120 percent of the Federal midterm rate in effect under section 1274(d)(1) for the month in which the valuation date falls." (If any part of the transfer qualifies for a charitable deduction, the taxpayer may elect to use the federal midterm rate for either of the two months preceding the month of the transfer.) Section 1274(d)(1) defines the federal midterm rate as "the rate determined by the Secretary based on the average market yield on outstanding marketable obligations of the United States with remaining periods to maturity over 3 years but not over 9 years."

§§ 20.2031–7(d)(4) and 25.2512–5(d)(4). The following examples illustrate how a remainder, an income interest, and an annuity are valued under the tables.

A *remainder* is a right to receive property at some future time, e.g., at the death of an income beneficiary or after a fixed term of years. The present value of a remainder can be determined by discounting the value of the property (which is assumed to have a constant principal value) using a discount rate equal to the prescribed annual rate of return. To discount a future payment to present value, divide the amount of the future payment by a factor of $(1 + r)^n$, where r is the rate of return (compounded annually) and n is the number of years until the payment date. For example, assuming a 7–percent annual rate of return, the present value of $1,000 payable in five years is $1,000 ÷ 1.07^5, or $712.99. According to the tables, this is also the value of a remainder in property worth $1,000 following a fixed 5–year term. Reg. §§ 20.2031–7(d)(6) (Table B) and 25.2512–5(d)(2)(ii).

An *income interest* is a right to receive the stream of income generated by property for a specified period of time, e.g., during the life of the recipient or for a fixed term of years. The present value of an income interest can be determined by discounting each annual installment of income to present value (using a discount rate equal to the prescribed annual rate of return) and calculating the sum of those amounts. For example, assuming a 7–percent annual rate of return, the present value of a five-year stream of income from property worth $1,000 is $287.01:

Year	*Current Income*	×	*Discount Factor*	=	*Present Value*	*Cumulative Present Value*
1	$70.00		0.934579		$65.42	$65.42
2	70.00		0.873438		61.14	126.56
3	70.00		0.816297		57.14	183.70
4	70.00		0.762895		53.40	237.10
5	70.00		0.712986		49.91	287.01

Note that the same result can be reached by subtracting the present value of a remainder following the income interest (determined as described supra) from the full value of the underlying property. In effect, the tables apportion the value of the property between the income interest and the remainder: The full value of the property ($1,000) is equal to the sum of the present values of the income interest ($287.01) and the remainder ($712.99), respectively. Reg. § 25.2512–5(d)(2)(iii).

An *annuity* is a right to receive fixed periodic payments over a specified period of time. Unlike an income interest, the payments under an annuity are fixed without reference to the current income earned on the underlying property. Thus, to the extent that the payments exceed the current income, they consume the principal value of the underlying property. A gift of an annuity is typically expressed in terms of a stream of level annual payments. The present value of such an annuity, payable at the end of each year, is $(a \div r) \times [1 - (1 \div (1 + r)^n)]$, where a is the amount of the annual payment, r is the annual rate of return on the outstanding principal, and n is the number of years in the annuity term.[6] For example, assuming a 7–percent annual rate of return, the present value of a $100 annuity, payable annually for a fixed five-year term, is $(\$100 \div .07) \times [1 - (1 \div 1.07^5)]$, or $410.02. The same result can be obtained by discounting each annuity payment to present value and calculating the sum of those amounts:

Year	*Annuity Payment*	×	*Discount Factor*	=	*Present Value*	*Cumulative Present Value*
1	$100.00		0.934579		$93.46	$93.46
2	100.00		0.873438		87.34	180.80
3	100.00		0.816297		81.63	262.43
4	100.00		0.762895		76.29	338.72
5	100.00		0.712986		71.30	410.02

The present value of an annuity represents the principal amount which, together with income at the prescribed rate of return (compounded annually), will produce exactly the amounts needed to make the scheduled payments, leaving no remaining principal at the end of the annuity term:

Year	*Beginning Principal*	+	*Income (7 Percent)*	−	*Annuity Payment*	=	*Ending Principal*
1	$410.02		$28.70		$100.00		$338.72
2	338.72		23.71		100.00		262.43
3	262.43		18.37		100.00		180.80
4	180.80		12.66		100.00		93.46
5	93.46		6.54		100.00		0.00

Reg. § 25.2512–5(d)(2)(iv).

For further details on the operation of the tables, see Hastings, The Treasury Department Valuation Tables: How They Work and How to Make Them Work for You, 46 N.Y.U. Inst. on Fed. Taxn. ch. 53 (1988).

The actuarial tables evidently provide convenience and certainty, but they often do so at the expense of accuracy in particular cases. For example, in the case of a trust to pay income to *A* for life and then remainder to *B*, the tables may grossly overstate the value of the income interest compared to the remainder interest if *A* has an abnormally short life expectancy or if the trust is funded with unproductive property. Prior to the enactment of § 7520 in 1988, the courts held that the tables were generally binding on the government as well as on taxpayers unless they produced "a substantially unrealistic and unreasonable result." O'Reilly v. Commissioner, 973 F.2d 1403 (8th Cir. 1992); Weller v. Commissioner, 38 T.C. 790 (1962). Section 7520 mandates the use of the tables in valuing "any annuity, any interest for life or a term of years, or any remainder or

6. Special adjustments may be required if the scheduled payments vary in amount, or occur more frequently than annually, or are made at the beginning rather than the end of the compounding period.

reversionary interest," except as otherwise specified in regulations. The regulations in turn authorize departures from the tables in cases where the interest being valued is subject to a special "contingency, power, or other restriction," where the governing instrument fails to ensure an adequate degree of beneficial enjoyment for the holder, or where the individual who is a measuring life dies or is "terminally ill" at the time of the transfer. Reg. §§ 20.7520–3(b) and 25.7520–3(b).

Notwithstanding the express command of § 7520 and the limited exceptions in the regulations, courts have not completely abandoned the doctrine of the pre–1988 case law allowing departures from the tables if necessary to avoid unrealistic and unreasonable results. In several cases involving a deceased lottery winner's interest in a stream of future annual payments, courts have refused to value the stream of payments under the tables on the ground that the tables produce unrealistic and unreasonable results because they fail to take account of restrictions on transferability under state law. Shackleford v. United States, 262 F.3d 1028 (9th Cir. 2001) (allowing discount); Gribauskas' Estate v. Commissioner, 342 F.3d 85 (2d Cir. 2003) (same). Other courts, however, have reached the opposite conclusion, finding that the tables do not produce unrealistic or unreasonable results. Anthony v. United States, 520 F.3d 374 (5th Cir.), cert. denied, 129 S.Ct. 115 (2008); Negron v. United States, 553 F.3d 1013 (6th Cir. 2009). If transfer restrictions warrant a departure from the tables in valuing lottery payments, should the same rationale apply with equal force to other non-assignable interests such as a retirement annuity payable to a deceased employee's surviving beneficiary? See Reg. § 20.7520–3(b)(1) (distinguishing "ordinary" from "restricted" beneficial interests).

Interests are often conditioned on uncertain future events—e.g., marriage, divorce, or birth of issue—that are not reflected in the actuarial tables. Nothing in the regulations prohibits the use of other actuarial data to calculate the probability of such events. Indeed, the Service itself has sanctioned the use of the American Remarriage Table in valuing a decedent's obligation under a separation agreement to make support payments to a surviving spouse until death or remarriage. Rev. Rul. 71–67, 1971–1 C.B. 271 (estate tax deduction); cf. Rev. Rul. 76–472, 1976–2 C.B. 264 (decedent's vested remainder subject to open should be valued with "due regard" for probability that 53–year–old woman might bear or adopt additional children). An element of unreliability is obvious, however, when the event at issue involves a volitional act (e.g., marriage or procreation), particularly if the act will be rewarded by the receipt of a handsome inheritance or deterred by its denial. Accordingly, it is recognized that actuarial tables are not the only way to predict the occurrence of contingencies involving marriage, birth of children, or similar events. See Rev. Rul. 61–88, 1961–1 C.B. 417 (decedent's remainder interest, contingent on the death without issue of a childless woman age 44, "may be of considerable value" and is to be valued on the basis of "all known circumstances relative to the particular [woman], rather than to women aged 44 in general"). If a taxpayer fails to establish the likelihood that a crucial event will (or will not) occur, a deficiency based on a worst case assumption will be upheld. See, e.g., Robinette v. Helvering, supra page 75, Note 3 (in valuing gift in trust, no value assigned to donor's reversionary interest that would become possessory only if the donor survived her daughter and the daughter died without issue who reached age 21).

Section 2702, enacted in 1990, imposes special gift tax valuation rules where a donor transfers property in trust for the benefit of a family member while retaining an interest in the same property. The special rules, where applicable, supersede the tables and in effect shift value from the retained interest to the transferred interest for gift tax purposes. Section 2702 is discussed supra at page 78.

e. Closely Held Business Interests

In valuing shares of stock or securities for which there is no recognized market, the regulations enumerate several factors to be taken into account: in the case of stock, "the company's net worth, prospective earning power and dividend-paying capacity, and other relevant factors"; in the case of securities, "the soundness of the security, the interest yield, the date of maturity, and other relevant factors." Reg. §§ 20.2031–2(f) and 25.2512–2(f). The regulations go on to list "[s]ome of the 'other relevant factors' ":

> the good will of the business; the economic outlook in the particular industry; the company's position in the industry and its management; the degree of control of the business represented by the block of stock to be valued; and the values of securities of corporations engaged in the same or similar lines of business which are listed on a stock exchange. However, the weight to be accorded such comparisons or any other evidentiary factors considered in the determination of a value depends upon the facts of each case. In addition to the relevant factors described above, consideration shall also be given to nonoperating assets, including proceeds of life insurance policies payable to or for the benefit of the company, to the extent such nonoperating assets have not been taken into account in the determination of net worth, prospective earning power and dividend-earning capacity.

The regulations are supplemented by Rev. Rul. 59–60, § 4.01, 1959–1 C.B. 237, which states that the following factors, "although not all-inclusive are fundamental and require careful analysis in each case":

(a) The nature of the business and the history of the enterprise from its inception.

(b) The economic outlook in general and the condition and outlook of the specific industry in particular.

(c) The book value of the stock and the financial condition of the business.

(d) The earning capacity of the company.

(e) The dividend-paying capacity.

(f) Whether or not the enterprise has goodwill or other intangible value.

(g) Sales of the stock and the size of the block of stock to be valued.

(h) The market price of stocks of corporations engaged in the same or a similar line of business having their stocks actively traded in a free and open market, either on an exchange or over-the-counter. [1959–1 C.B. at 238–39.]

The same ruling also recognizes that the death of a key person in the management of a company may affect the value of the company's stock:

> The loss of the manager of a so-called "one-man" business may have a depressing effect upon the value of the stock of such business, particularly if there is a lack of trained personnel capable of succeeding to the management of the enterprise. In valuing the stock of this type of business, therefore, the effect of the loss of the manager on the future expectancy of the business, and the absence of management-succession potentialities are pertinent factors to be taken into consideration. On the other hand, there may be factors which offset, in whole or in part, the loss of the manager's services. For instance, the nature of the business and of its assets may be such that they will not be impaired by the loss of the manager. Furthermore, the loss may be adequately covered by life insurance, or competent management might be employed on the basis of the consideration paid for the former manager's services. These, or other offsetting factors, if found to exist, should be carefully weighed against the loss of the manager's services in valuing the stock of the enterprise. [Id., § 4.02(b), 1959–1 C.B. at 239–40.]

After shares have been valued in accordance with the foregoing principles, the resulting amount may be subject to adjustments for blockage, marketability, control, transfer restrictions, and the like. See Sections C and D of this chapter.

Unincorporated business interests, such as interests in partnerships or proprietorships, generally are valued by applying the valuation principles used for shares of closely held businesses. The regulations recognize this parallel by providing that the net value of such interests is to be determined "on the basis of all relevant factors," including an appraisal of all assets (tangible and intangible, including goodwill), of demonstrated earning capacity, and of the other factors listed as applicable to shares of closely held businesses. Reg. §§ 20.2031–3 and 25.2512–3; see also Rev. Rul. 68–609, 1968–2 C.B. 327 (principles set out in Rev. Rul. 59–60 apply in valuing "business interests of any type, including partnerships and proprietorships"). The estate tax regulations also recognize that partnership agreements frequently provide that each partner's interest shall pass at retirement or death to the active or surviving partners on specified terms, often for less than the interest's fair market value. On the valuation of interests subject to restrictive agreements, see infra page 608.

Section 2701, enacted in 1990, imposes special gift tax valuation rules where a donor transfers stock or a partnership interest to a family member while retaining a senior equity interest in the corporation or partnership. The special rules, where applicable, tend to depress the value of the retained interest, thus indirectly increasing the value of the transferred interest for gift tax purposes. Section 2701 is discussed infra at page 591.

In valuing business interests, it is seldom necessary to value the underlying business assets (machinery, equipment, inventory, goodwill, etc.) separately, particularly if the appraiser employs the capitalization-of-income or comparative market price approach. If a separate appraisal of business assets becomes necessary, establishing the value for intangible assets such as goodwill and going concern value may be difficult, since a translation of these assets into data for conventional valuation methods is seldom available. Rev. Rul. 68–609, 1968–2 C.B. 327, suggests the following method for estimating the value of the intangibles:

> A percentage return on the average annual value of the tangible assets used in a business is determined, using a period of years (preferably not less than five) immediately prior to the valuation date. The amount of the percentage return on tangible assets, thus determined, is deducted from the average earnings of the business for such period and the remainder, if any, is considered to be the amount of the average annual earnings from the intangible assets of the business for the period. This amount (considered as the average annual earnings from intangibles), capitalized at a percentage of, say, 15 to 20 percent, is the value of the intangible assets of the business determined under the "formula" approach.

Experts using this method can arrive at quite divergent conclusions, and their estimates may be even further apart if they use book value, values of allegedly comparable businesses, and other factors as a guide. See Kelly's Estate v. Commissioner, 14 T.C.M. (CCH) 476 (1955), in which the shares of common stock of a closely held publishing company were variously valued at $516 (estate tax return), $1,000 (revenue agent), $4,000 (ninety-day letter), $980 (taxpayer's first expert), $822 (taxpayer's second expert), $1,320 (taxpayer's third expert), $4,000 (government's first expert), $3,400 (government's second expert), and $2,200 (court).

On the valuation of closely held business interests, see generally Pratt, Valuing a Business (5th ed. 2007); Laro & Pratt, Business Valuation and Taxes (2005).

3. VALUATION FREEZES INVOLVING CORPORATE STOCK AND PARTNERSHIP INTERESTS: § 2701

Section 2701 was added to the Code in 1990, in response to various estate freezing techniques involving closely held corporations and partnerships. The type of transaction at which § 2701 is aimed can be illustrated by a simple example. Assume that *A* owns all the stock of a corporation, consisting of one share of voting common stock and 99 shares of voting preferred stock. *A* makes a gift of the common stock to her child *B*, retaining the preferred stock. In addition to 99–percent voting control, the preferred stock carries a noncumulative 8–percent annual dividend, a liquidation preference of $10,000 per share, and a "put" right that entitles the holder to compel redemption by the corporation on demand for $10,000 per share. The total value of the corporation is $1 million. Under general valuation principles, a value of $990,000 might plausibly be attributed to *A*'s retained preferred stock based on its voting control and liquidation preference.[7] According to the "subtraction method," the value of the preferred stock would be subtracted from the total value of the corporation to arrive at a residual value of $10,000 for the common stock given to *B*.[8] Subsequently, *A* may be able to shift substantial value to *B* free of gift tax simply by failing to maximize the return on the preferred stock through exercise of her voting or other discretionary rights.[9] Although the preferred stock will ultimately be subject to gift or estate tax on a subsequent disposition, *A* will have retained control of the corporation while excluding subsequent appreciation in its value from her transfer tax base. For cases involving analogous transactions, see Anderson's Estate v. Commissioner, 56 T.C.M. (CCH) 553 (1988); Lewis Hutchens Non–Marital Trust v. Commissioner, 66 T.C.M. (CCH) 1599 (1993).

Section 2701 attacks estate freezing techniques like the one described above by prescribing special gift tax valuation rules for the initial transfer. In general, the special rules apply where a donor transfers an interest in a

7. Prior to the enactment of § 2701, the Service took the position that if the preferred stock had a fixed dividend rate and was nonparticipating, the common stock usually had "substantial value" because it was entitled to the benefit of future appreciation in the value of the corporation. Rev. Rul. 83–120, 1983–2 C.B. 170. In one estate freeze case, however, the Tax Court found that preferred stock accounted for more than 99.96 percent of a corporation's value, leaving a residual value of less than 0.04 percent for the common stock. Snyder v. Commissioner, 93 T.C. 529 (1989).

8. The subtraction method assumes that the total value of the corporation is equal to the sum of the values of the various classes of stock. For a case rejecting this assumption on unusual facts, see Newhouse's Estate v. Commissioner, 94 T.C. 193 (1990).

9. Where a parent receives noncumulative preferred stock and children receive common stock in a corporate recapitalization, a failure to distribute earnings in subsequent years may in effect shift value from the parent's stock to the children's stock. If the failure to declare dividends is supported by valid business reasons and the parent has no legally enforceable right to compel a distribution, the Tax Court has been reluctant to find indirect gifts from the parent to the children. See, e.g., Daniels v. Commissioner, 68 T.C.M. (CCH) 1310 (1994); cf. Snyder v. Commissioner, 93 T.C. 529 (1989) (deemed gift where preferred shareholder failed to exercise conversion right).

family corporation or partnership to a younger-generation family member while retaining a preferred equity interest in the same entity. In operation, the special rules tend to depress the value of the retained interest and indirectly to increase the value of the transferred interest for gift tax purposes. Under the special rules, most retained interests (other than narrowly defined "qualified payment" rights) are valued at zero. Thus, if the donor retains no qualified payment rights, the entire value of the corporation or partnership may be allocated to the transferred interest and treated as a taxable gift. The special rules apply solely for gift tax purposes in the initial transfer; a subsequent transfer of the retained interest during life or at death is governed by general valuation principles. To mitigate the resulting risk of double taxation, the regulations provide for a reduction in the donor's taxable gifts upon the subsequent transfer.

Section 2701 is built around a network of specially defined terms and detailed technical requirements which sometimes obscure the basic statutory structure. The following thumbnail sketch of § 2701 is not intended as a substitute for a close reading of the statute and the regulations. In general, the statute comes into play when an interest in a corporation or partnership is transferred to a younger-generation family member (a "member of the transferor's family," defined in § 2701(e)(1) to include the transferor's spouse, descendants of the transferor or of the transferor's spouse, and spouses of those descendants), if the transferor or an older-generation family member (an "applicable family member," defined in § 2701(e)(2) to include the transferor's spouse, ancestors of the transferor or of the transferor's spouse, and spouses of those ancestors) holds an "applicable retained interest" immediately after the transfer. § 2701(a)(1). Note that the statute does not apply where an interest is transferred to a collateral relative such as a sibling, niece, or nephew. The transfer may occur directly (e.g., an outright gift) or indirectly (e.g., a capital contribution, redemption, or recapitalization). § 2701(e)(5). The statute also provides for attribution of ownership where an interest is held indirectly through a corporation, partnership, or trust. § 2701(e)(3). The statute applies to transfers occurring after October 8, 1990.

An "applicable retained interest" is defined as an equity interest in a corporation or partnership that confers an "extraordinary payment right" or (in the case of an entity that was subject to family control immediately before the transfer) a "distribution right." § 2701(b)(1). An extraordinary payment right generally includes a right to compel liquidation or a put, call, or conversion right, if the exercise (or nonexercise) of the right affects the value of the transferred interest. § 2701(c)(2); Reg. § 25.2701–2(b)(2). A distribution right generally includes a right (other than an extraordinary payment right) to receive distributions on a preferred interest in the corporation or partnership. § 2701(c)(1). Broadly speaking, an applicable retained interest gives the holder discretionary rights to claim a share of the entity's assets or earnings in the future; if the discretionary rights are not exercised, the net effect may be to enhance the value of the transferred interest.

The special rules do not apply if the applicable retained interest is "of the same class as" or "proportionally the same as" the transferred interest, or if market quotations are readily available for the applicable retained interest (or the transferred interest) on an established securities market, since in such cases the risk of value shifting is not considered significant. § 2701(a)(1) and (a)(2); cf. § 2701(c)(1)(B)(iii), (c)(2)(B), and (c)(2)(C). In determining whether the retained and transferred interests are of the same class, nonlapsing differences in voting rights are disregarded. Reg. § 25.2701–1(c)(3). Thus, for example, the special rules do not apply if the transferor gives nonvoting common stock to a child while retaining voting common stock. The statute is also inapplicable if the transferor retains only a debt obligation of the entity; any failure to enforce the obligation would constitute a taxable gift under general gift tax principles.

Under the "subtraction method" set forth in the regulations, the gift tax value of the transferred interest is determined by subtracting the value of the applicable retained interest (and certain other family-held equity interests) from the total value of all family-held equity interests in the entity. The special rules govern the valuation of some—but not necessarily all—rights conferred by applicable retained interests. Under the special rules, extraordinary payment rights and distribution rights (other than "qualified payment" rights) are valued at zero if they are retained by the transferor or held by an applicable family member under an applicable retained interest. § 2701(a)(3)(A). A qualified payment is defined as a cumulative dividend payable at least annually at a fixed rate on preferred stock or a comparable payment under a partnership interest. § 2701(c)(3).[10] Some rights conferred by an applicable retained interest, however, may be neither extraordinary payment rights nor distribution rights: for example, mandatory payment rights; liquidation participation rights; and nonlapsing rights to convert equity interests into a fixed number or percentage of equity interests of the same class as the transferred interest. Reg. § 25.2701–2(b)(4). These rights, as well as qualified payment rights, are generally taken into account at fair market value (i.e., without regard to the special rules of § 2701), except that zero-valued rights are assumed not to exist. Reg. § 25.2701–2(a)(4). Furthermore, under a special "lower-of" rule, an extraordinary payment right held in conjunction with a qualified payment right is valued as if the extraordinary payment right would be exercised to minimize the aggregate value of the combined rights. § 2701(a)(3)(B); Reg. § 25.2701–2(a)(3).

The method set out in Reg. § 25.2701–3(b) involves four steps. In Step 1, the total fair market value of all "family-held" equity interests in the entity (i.e., interests held by the transferor, applicable family members, and descendants of the parents of the transferor or the transferor's

10. The statute permits a transferor to elect to treat a qualified payment right as a nonqualified distribution right, or vice versa. In the case of an applicable family member, a distribution right is treated as a qualified payment right only if the holder so elects. § 2701(c)(3)(C); Reg. § 25.2701–2(c).

spouse) is determined under general valuation principles. In Step 2, this amount is reduced by the value of applicable retained interests held by the transferor and applicable family members, determined under the special rules,[11] and by the fair market value of certain other family-held equity interests. In Step 3, the residual amount is allocated among the transferred interest and other subordinate equity interests. In Step 4, the value allocated to the transferred interest is reduced by specified items (e.g., limited minority discounts and consideration received by the transferor). A variant of the four-step method applies in the case of a transfer resulting from a capital contribution.

Under an overriding "minimum value" rule, in determining the value of a transferred junior equity interest (e.g., common stock), the aggregate value of junior equity interests cannot be less than 10 percent of the sum of the total value of all equity interests in the entity and the total amount of the entity's indebtedness to the transferor or applicable family members. § 2701(a)(4); Reg. § 25.2701–3(c). The minimum value rule reflects the notion that a junior equity interest may have a substantial "option value" because it is entitled to any future appreciation in excess of amounts needed to satisfy indebtedness and claims of senior equity interests.

If value is accorded to qualified payments under an applicable retained interest in the initial transfer and subsequently the qualified payments are not made as scheduled, the statute provides for a deemed taxable transfer upon the holder's death (or earlier transfer of the applicable retained interest). § 2701(d); Reg. § 25.2701–4.[12] The amount of the deemed transfer[13] is the amount of the delinquent payments compounded at a yield equal to the discount rate that was used in determining the present value of the payments in the initial transfer. § 2701(d)(2)(A). A special cap, however, limits the amount of the deemed transfer by reference to appreciation in the value of subordinate equity interests in the entity occurring after the initial transfer. § 2701(d)(2)(B). The statute also allows a grace period for payments made within four years of the due date, on the ground that business exigencies may justify a limited delay in making qualified payments. § 2701(d)(2)(C).

The special rules apply only in the initial transfer; in a subsequent transfer during life or at death, an applicable retained interest is valued

---

11. The regulations provide a special adjustment where the percentage of any class of applicable retained interests held by the transferor and applicable family members exceeds the "family interest percentage" in subordinate equity interests. Reg. § 25.2701–3(b)(5). This adjustment mitigates the impact of the special rules to the extent that value would otherwise be shifted to interests other than family-held subordinate equity interests.

12. If the applicable retained interest is transferred to the holder's spouse in a manner qualifying for a marital deduction, the deemed transfer is deferred and the spouse steps into the holder's shoes. § 2701(d)(3)(B) and (d)(4)(A). If the interest is transferred to an applicable family member, the deemed transfer is not deferred, but the compounding rule continues to apply to the interest in the applicable family member's hands. § 2701(d)(4)(B).

13. Upon the payment of a delinquent amount, the holder of the qualified payment right may elect to accelerate the deemed transfer of the right, with respect to such payment. § 2701(d)(3)(A)(iii).

under the general fair market value standard. To mitigate the risk of double taxation arising from valuing the applicable retained interest under different methods in the initial and subsequent transfers, the regulations provide for a reduction in the transferor's taxable gifts upon the subsequent transfer. § 2701(e)(6); Reg. § 25.2701–5. In general, the amount of the reduction is limited to the lesser of (1) the artificial increase in the transferor's taxable gifts that was caused by applying the special rules in the initial transfer, or (2) the increase in the transferor's taxable gifts or gross estate caused by failing to apply the special rules in the subsequent transfer. Reg. § 25.2701–5(b).

To illustrate the operation of § 2701, consider the impact of the special rules on the estate freezing transaction described supra at page 591. *A*'s gift of the common stock is a "transfer" of "an interest in a corporation" to *B*, a member of *A*'s family. *A*'s preferred stock meets the definition of an "applicable retained interest," both because it carries "extraordinary payment rights" (i.e., the rights to compel liquidation and to put the preferred stock) and because it carries a "distribution right" (i.e., a noncumulative dividend) with respect to a corporation controlled by *A*'s family. Moreover, none of the statutory exceptions applies: The preferred stock is not "of the same class" or "proportionally the same" as the common stock, and neither class of stock is traded on an established securities market. Accordingly, the nonqualified distribution right and the extraordinary payment rights conferred by the preferred stock are valued at zero under the special rules.[14] As a result, the entire value of the corporation is allocated to the common stock, producing a taxable gift of $1 million. If *A* subsequently makes a taxable transfer of the preferred stock during life or at death, a reduction will be allowed in calculating *A*'s taxable gifts; the reduction is limited to $990,000 (the amount of the earlier increase in taxable gifts resulting from application of the special rules) or, if less, the fair market value of the preferred stock at the time of the subsequent transfer.

The Senate Finance Committee explained the primary goals of § 2701 as follows:

> (1) to provide a well defined and administrable set of rules;
>
> (2) to allow business owners who are not abusing the transfer tax system to freely engage in standard intrafamily transactions without being subject to severe transfer tax consequences; and
>
> (3) to deter abuse by making unfavorable assumptions regarding certain retained rights. [136 Cong. Rec. 30,488, 30,538 (Oct. 18, 1990).]

---

14. Under the regulations, *A*'s ability to compel liquidation of the corporation is an "extraordinary payment right" which is valued at zero. Reg. § 25.2701–2(a)(1) and (b)(2). In contrast, the liquidation preference is a "liquidation participation right" which is valued "as if [*A*'s] ability to compel liquidation . . . [d]id not exist." Reg. § 25.2701–2(b)(4)(ii). In theory, some minimal value could be attributed to the latter right.

Consider how § 2701 balances these goals. To what extent is the scope of the special valuation rules shaped by their anti-abuse function? Can a working definition of nonabusive, "standard intrafamily transactions" be extrapolated from the exceptions to § 2701?

C. PREMIUMS AND DISCOUNTS

1. BLOCKAGE

In the case of actively traded stocks, the regulations recognize that a block of stock may be sufficiently large in relation to the usual trading volume to justify a departure from the quoted market price per share:

> If the executor can show that the block of stock to be valued is so large in relation to the actual sales on the existing market that it could not be liquidated in a reasonable time without depressing the market, the price at which the block could be sold as such outside the usual market, as through an underwriter, may be a more accurate indication of value than market quotations. [Reg. § 20.2031–2(e).]

Under the so-called blockage rule, a discount may be allowed in order to reflect more accurately the price at which an exceptionally large block of stock would change hands in a hypothetical sale on the open market. The blockage rule thus suggests that a large block of stock may be worth less per share than a smaller block of the same stock. Blockage discounts are usually applied to the property being valued, but in applying the comparable sales method of valuing property, the price paid for a large block or tract of otherwise comparable property may already have been discounted to reflect the impact of its size on the market. In such a case, the property being valued may be worth relatively more than an equally sized portion of the comparable property.

The blockage rule is recognized in valuing property for gift as well as estate tax purposes. Where a donor simultaneously gives several blocks of identical stock to different donees, each gift must be valued separately. Reg. § 25.2512–2(e) (blockage rule applied "with reference to each separate gift" for gift tax purposes). In Rushton v. Commissioner, 498 F.2d 88 (5th Cir. 1974), the court rejected the taxpayers' attempt to obtain a blockage discount based on the aggregate amount of stock transferred to several donees on the same day:

> We note that by its explicit terms § 25.2512–2(e) permits the application of a blockage discount for any shares only upon a showing that "the block of stock to be valued, *with reference to each separate gift*, is so large" that its liquidation would depress the market price. Hence, the blockage concept must be triggered in the first instance by the size of each particular gift, without consideration of companion donations. This is a strange prerequisite indeed for a regulatory scheme which allegedly contemplates the ultimate aggregation for valuation purposes of all gifts of a single stock made in one day. It is equally clear, and equally damaging to taxpayers' position, that the regulation

requires the production of expert evidence on the price which each gift would bring if sold, not in some hypothetical market, but under the conditions actually obtaining at the time of gift. An aggregation principle, however, directly contradicts the regulatory intent of appraisal in a realistic market; for, under such a system, the question becomes not what would each block have returned if sold in the market existing at the time of valuation, but rather what would that same block have brought in a fictitious market, one flooded by the other gifts. [498 F.2d at 92–93.]

Although the blockage rule was originally developed in valuing blocks of stock or securities, courts have extended the rule to other property, such as a large collection of a particular artist's work. For example, in determining the value of a gross estate that included 425 pieces of sculpture created by the decedent, the Tax Court noted that "at the very least, each willing buyer in the retail art market would take into account, in determining the price he would be willing to pay for any given item, the fact that 424 other items were being offered for sale at the same time," and found a "useful analogy" in the blockage rule applicable to securities. Smith's Estate v. Commissioner, 57 T.C. 650 (1972), affd. on other grounds, 510 F.2d 479 (2d Cir.), cert. denied, 423 U.S. 827 (1975). See also Auker's Estate v. Commissioner, 75 T.C.M. (CCH) 2321 (1998) (extensive discussion of "absorption discount" in valuing three apartment complexes owned by decedent).

A blockage discount may be calculated by several different methods, depending on the circumstances of the particular case. The burden of justifying both the existence and the amount of the discount rests with the taxpayer. In the case of stock or securities, the regulations contemplate a hypothetical sale "outside the usual market, as through an underwriter." Does this mean that no blockage discount is allowed if a skillful broker could liquidate a large block of stock over a short period of time at a price approaching the quoted market price for a large block of stock? See Rushton v. Commissioner, 498 F.2d 88, 92 n.10 (5th Cir. 1974). In a case involving a collection of art works, a blockage discount was taken into account by discounting to present value the estimated proceeds from a hypothetical liquidation of the collection over a specified time period. Calder v. Commissioner, 85 T.C. 713 (1985).

Suppose that a decedent dies owning a large block of stock having a quoted market price of $101 per share. Although no actual sale of the block is contemplated, it is determined that the most advantageous method of disposing of the stock would be a secondary offering to the public through an underwriter. Such an offering would result in a public sale price of $100 per share, of which the underwriter would retain $2 per share as compensation and the estate would receive the balance of $98 per share. Assuming a blockage discount is appropriate, should it be limited to $1 per share (i.e., the difference between the $101 quoted market price and the $100 public sale price), or should it include an additional $2 per share representing the underwriter's compensation? In Gillespie v. United

States, 23 F.3d 36 (2d Cir. 1994), it was held on similar facts that the blockage discount is limited to $1 per share; the $2 per share underwriting fee (like any other selling expense) does not affect fair market value, whether or not it is deductible as an administration expense for estate tax purposes. See also Rev. Rul. 83–30, 1983–1 C.B. 224 (same result where public sale actually occurred).

2. LACK OF MARKETABILITY

A discount for lack of marketability is not expressly authorized by the Code or by the regulations, which merely direct that unlisted stock be valued by taking "relevant factors" into account, including the value of listed stocks of corporations in a similar line of business. See § 2031(b); Reg. §§ 20.2031–2(f) and 25.2512–2(f). Cf. Rev. Rul. 59–60, § 4(h), 1959–1 C.B. 237 (emphasizing importance of "active, free public market" for stock of comparable companies). Nevertheless, in valuing closely held business interests or other property having limited marketability, courts frequently allow a discount "to reflect the fact that there is no ready market" for the property. Andrews' Estate v. Commissioner, 79 T.C. 938 (1982); see also Piper's Estate v. Commissioner, 72 T.C. 1062 (1979) (closely held stock); Propstra v. United States, 680 F.2d 1248 (9th Cir. 1982) (decedent's interest in community real property).

A discount for lack of marketability is not automatically allowed merely because it might be difficult to locate bidders or negotiate sale terms for the property being valued. Such a discount would not be allowed, for example, in valuing a tycoon's mansion, an illuminated manuscript, or a prize racehorse. Indeed, if a valuation discount were automatically allowed for difficulty, delay and expense in selling property, it would make little sense to restrict the deductibility of carrying costs and selling expenses for estate tax purposes. Cf. Reg. § 20.2053–3, discussed in the *Hibernia Bank* case, supra page 423. Instead, the discount represents an adjustment for the fact that the property being valued is less readily marketable than otherwise comparable property.

3. CONTROL PREMIUMS AND MINORITY DISCOUNTS

Although the regulations do not explicitly authorize control premiums or minority discounts, they do recognize that "if the block of stock to be valued represents a controlling interest, either actual or effective, in a going business, the price at which other lots change hands may have little relation to its true value." Reg. §§ 20.2031–2(e) and 25.2512–2(e). In short, a controlling block may have a higher per-share value than the otherwise comparable noncontrolling shares. This principle is relied on by the Service and accepted by the courts. See Rev. Rul. 59–60, § 4(g), 1959–1 C.B. 237; Trenchard's Estate v. Commissioner, 69 T.C.M. (CCH) 2164 (1995); Salsbury's Estate v. Commissioner, 34 T.C.M. (CCH) 1441 (1975).

By the same token, a downward adjustment to the per-share price (the so-called minority discount) is frequently allowed when valuing noncontrolling shares. See, e.g., Newhouse's Estate v. Commissioner, 94 T.C. 193 (1990) (although amount of discount is a question of fact, "it is unreasonable to argue that no discount should be considered for a minority interest in a closely held corporation"); Andrews' Estate v. Commissioner, 79 T.C. 938 (1982) (combined discount for lack of control and lack of marketability, noting that the two discounts are "conceptually distinct").

What is the theoretical basis for control premiums and minority discounts? Aside from the allure of control for its own sake, why would a rational investor pay a higher price for controlling shares than for noncontrolling shares? One possible explanation is that investors may believe that control will enable them to increase corporate profits by replacing management or setting new policies. This explanation assumes that investors believe that a company has prospects that have not yet been fully discovered or exploited; it provides no basis for a control premium unless the company's performance leaves room for improvement. See Ahmanson Found. v. United States, 674 F.2d 761 (9th Cir. 1981) (no premium allowed for control group's alleged power to replace management of company that was already well managed).

A second, less benign explanation is that control represents the power to divert value from the minority shareholders. As a practical matter, controlling shareholders may be able to pay generous salaries to themselves, employ their relatives, and buy from and sell to the corporation on advantageous terms. The courts, however, have not been willing to recognize value in such opportunities for self-dealing. See Ahmanson Found., supra (no control premium allowed for controlling shareholder's alleged ability to "exploit corporate assets for personal advantage," since industry was highly regulated and "numerous legal restraints" deterred self-dealing); Trenchard's Estate v. Commissioner, 69 T.C.M. (CCH) 2164 (1995) (rejecting controlling shareholder's alleged power to liquidate corporation at will and set own compensation as basis for control premium).

These alternative explanations suggest two quite different approaches for identifying the circumstances in which control premiums and minority discounts are appropriate and for calculating their amount. To the extent that a control premium reflects potential gains from more efficient management, the amount of the premium per share should remain more or less constant regardless of the size of the control block: A purchaser who pays a premium of $1 per share to acquire a 51–percent control block should be willing to pay the same premium for each additional share. By contrast, the self-dealing rationale suggests a different result: A purchaser intending to siphon value away from minority shareholders would seek to acquire control through the smallest possible block, and would derive no benefit from purchasing additional shares.

If a controlling block of stock commands a premium, does it follow that the minority shares should be discounted by an equal aggregate amount? Or is the sum of the values of all interests in a closely held business not necessarily equal to the value of the business as a whole? Cf. Chenoweth's Estate v. Commissioner, 88 T.C. 1577 (1987) ("[w]hile we would tend to agree that the sum of the parts cannot equal more than the whole ... it might well turn out that the sum of the parts can equal less than the whole"); Newhouse's Estate v. Commissioner, 94 T.C. 193 (1990) (common and preferred stock valued separately may be worth less than their proportionate shares of the entire company's value; "subtraction method" not appropriate on particular facts).

BRIGHT'S ESTATE v. UNITED STATES

658 F.2d 999 (5th Cir. 1981).

ANDERSON, CIRCUIT JUDGE.

This case presents to the en banc court an important question involving the principles of federal estate tax valuation. Mary Frances Smith Bright died on April 3, 1971. During her lifetime, she and her husband, Mr. Bright, owned 55% of the common stock of East Texas Motor Freight Lines, Inc., 55% of the common stock of twenty-seven affiliated corporations, and 55% of the common and preferred stock of Southern Trust and Mortgage Company (the stock of all such corporations is hereinafter referred to collectively as the "stock").

During her lifetime, Mr. and Mrs. Bright held the 55% block of stock as their community property under the laws of the State of Texas. The remaining forty-five percent is owned by parties unrelated to the Brights; a thirty percent block of stock is owned by H. G. Schiff, and the remaining fifteen percent is owned by two or three other individuals. None of the stock was publicly traded and no market existed for any of the stock on the date of Mrs. Bright's death. Mr. Bright is executor under the will of his wife. The will devised Mrs. Bright's interest in the stock to Mr. Bright as trustee of a trust for the primary benefit of Mrs. Bright's four children.

After audit of the estate tax return, the government assessed a deficiency, which was paid by the estate, and the instant suit for a refund of over $3 million in federal estate taxes and assessed interest was brought in the district court. The sole issue before the district court was the value of the estate's stock. Before the bench trial on the fair market value issue, the district judge ruled as a matter of law that "no element of control can be attributed to the decedent in determining the value of the decedent's interest in the stock ... for estate tax purposes. The parties are hereby ordered to proceed with preparation for trial and trial of this case on that basis." At the trial the district court found that the value of the stock was consistent with the testimony of the estate's expert witnesses, and entered judgment for the estate. The government filed a timely notice of appeal. A panel of this court vacated the judgment of the district court and remanded with instructions, holding that the district court erred in entering the pretrial order relating to the element of control. 619 F.2d 407 (June 18, 1980). The estate's petition for rehearing en banc was granted, and the panel opinion was vacated. 628 F.2d 307 (Oct. 2, 1980). We now affirm the judgment of the district court.

The only issue facing the en banc court is whether the district court erred in entering the above-quoted pretrial order relating to the element of control. We reject the heart of the government's arguments, and also reject a secondary government argument because it was raised for the first time on appeal.

Two principal arguments constitute the heart of the government's case, the first based on its description of the property transferred as an undivided one-half interest in the control block of 55% of the stock, and the second based on family attribution between the estate's stock interest and the stock interest held individually by Mr. Bright.

First, the government argues that the property to be valued for estate tax purposes is an undivided one-half interest in the control block of 55% of the stock, and that the proper method of valuation would be to value the 55% control block, including a control premium, and then take one-half thereof. Both parties agree that the estate tax is an excise tax on the transfer of property at death, and that the property to be valued is the property which is actually transferred, as contrasted with the interest held by the decedent before death or the interest held by the legatee after death. United States v. Land, 303 F.2d 170 (5th Cir. 1962).... Both parties agree that, under Texas law, the stock at issue was the community property of Mr. and Mrs. Bright during her life, that Mrs. Bright's death dissolved the community, that upon death the community is divided equally, that each spouse can exercise testamentary disposition over only his or her own half of the community, and that "only the decedent's half is includable in his gross estate for federal tax purposes." Commissioner v. Chase Manhattan Bank, [259 F.2d 231, 239 (5th Cir. 1958)]....

In its brief the government argued that, because the interest to be valued was an undivided one-half interest in the full 55% control block, the proper method would be to value the whole, including its control premium, and then take one-half thereof to establish the value of the estate's undivided one-half interest. The estate points out that the government's argument overlooks the fact that the block of stock is subject to the right of partition under Texas law at the instance of either the surviving spouse or the estate of the deceased spouse. Tex. Prob. Code Ann. § 385 (Vernon 1980). The government has not argued that partition would not be freely granted in a case involving fungible shares, such as this case. Thus, the estate has no means to prevent the conversion of its interest into shares representing a 27½% block, and we conclude that the estate's interest is the equivalent of a 27½% block of the stock. Accordingly, we reject the government's approach of valuing the 55% control block, with its control premium, and then taking one-half thereof. Accord Estate of Lee v. Commissioner, 69 T.C. 860 (1978).

Having determined that the property which is to be valued for estate tax purposes is the 27½% block of stock owned by the estate, we turn to the government's second argument, which is based on the doctrine of family attribution between the successive holders of interest to be taxed, the decedent, the executor, and the legatee, on the one hand, and the related party, Mr. Bright, on the other. The government argues that the following facts are relevant and should have been considered by the district court in valuing the 27½% block: the fact that Mr. and Mrs. Bright were husband and wife and held their stock during her lifetime as a control block of 55%; the fact that Mr. Bright held the estate's 27½% block after her death as executor and subsequently as trustee of the testamentary trust for their children, while he simultaneously held another 27½% block in his individual capacity, thus continuing the control block after death; and the fact that the government might be able to adduce evidence that Mr. Bright, as executor or trustee, would not be willing to sell the estate's 27½% block as a minority interest, but would be willing to sell it only as part of the block of 55% including his individually-owned stock so that a substantial control premium could be realized. Such facts and evidence, the government argues, would have formed the basis of expert testimony that the value of the estate's stock includes some control premium. For several reasons, we reject the government's attempt to import into this area of the estate tax law this kind of family attribution, and we hold that the foregoing evidence proffered by the government is not admissible to prove the value of the stock at issue.

First, we reject any family attribution to the estate's stock because established case law requires this result. A recent case directly in point is Estate of Lee v. Commissioner, supra. There Mr. and Mrs. Lee held as community property 4,000 of the 5,000 outstanding shares of the common stock of a closely held corporation. They also held all 50,000 shares of the preferred stock. Upon the death of Mrs. Lee, the community was dissolved, leaving Mr. Lee and the estate of Mrs. Lee each with an undivided one-half interest in each item of the community property. 69 T.C. at 873. The Tax Court held that this was the equivalent of 2,000 shares of common stock and 25,000 shares of preferred stock, and that the estate's interest was a minority interest. 69 T.C. at 874.

In United States v. Land, supra, this court held that a restrictive agreement, which depressed the value of a partnership interest but which by its terms expired at decedent's death, did not affect value for estate tax purposes because the estate tax is an excise tax on the transfer of property at death and accordingly valuation is to be made at the time of the transfer, i.e., at death, and the valuation is to be measured by the interest that actually passes. 303 F.2d at 172. It follows necessarily from our *Land* holding that the fact that Mr. and Mrs. Bright held their stock during her lifetime as a control block of 55% is an irrelevant fact. It is a fact which antedates her death, and no longer exists at the time of her death....

Beginning at least as early as 1940, the Tax Court has uniformly valued a decedent's stock for estate tax purposes as a minority interest when the decedent himself owned less than 50%, and despite the fact that control of the corporation was within the decedent's family.... Our research has uncovered no cases, and the government has cited none, which have attributed family owned stock to the estate's stock in determining the value thereof for estate tax purposes.[15]

[The court surveyed analogous cases in the gift tax area and found that the weight of authority rejected family attribution, noting the exception of Driver v. United States, 38 A.F.T.R.2d 6315 (W.D. Wis. 1976).[16]]

We conclude that the case law reflects long established precedent that family attribution should not apply to lump a decedent's stock with that of related parties for estate tax valuation purposes. This constitutes our first reason for rejecting family attribution in the instant context.

Our second reason for rejecting this kind of family attribution is our conclusion that the doctrine is logically inconsistent with the willing buyer-seller rule set out in the regulations. . . .

It is apparent from the language of the regulation that the "willing seller" is not the estate itself, but is a hypothetical seller. In Revenue Ruling 59–60, the Internal Revenue Service has so held: "Court decisions frequently state in addition that the *hypothetical* buyer and seller are assumed to be able, as well as willing, to trade and to be well informed about the property and concerning the market for such property." 1959–1 C.B. at 237 (emphasis added). . . .

The notion of the "willing seller" as being hypothetical is also supported by the theory that the estate tax is an excise tax on the transfer of property at death and accordingly that the valuation is to be made as of the moment of death and is to be measured by the interest that passes, as contrasted with the interest held by the decedent before death or the interest held by the legatee after death. Earlier in this opinion, we noticed that our United States v. Land, supra, decision logically requires a holding that the relationship between Mr. and Mrs. Bright and their stock is an irrelevant, before death fact. Thus, it is clear that the "willing seller" cannot be identified with Mrs. Bright, and therefore there can be no family attribution with respect to those related to Mrs. Bright. Similarly, the dictum in *Land*—that valuation is not determined by the value of the interest in the hands of the legatee—means that the "willing seller" cannot be identified with Mr. Bright as executor or as trustee of the testamentary trust. Therefore, there can be no family attribution based on identity of the executor and trustee, Mr. Bright. The *Land* dictum is established law. . . . The *Land* dictum also comports with common sense. It would be strange indeed if the estate tax value of a block of stock would vary depending upon the legatee to whom it was devised. . . .

15. [The court distinguished lower court cases involving real property on the ground that "real estate, unlike fungible shares of stock, is not freely subject to partition."]

16. In *Driver*, the sole shareholder of a corporation made gifts totaling around 42 percent of the stock to eight donees on December 31, 1968, and made virtually identical gifts to the same donees on January 2, 1969. None of the donees received a majority interest as a result of the transfers. The court refused to allow either a minority discount or a control premium in valuing the gifts.—EDS.

Accordingly, we affirm the district court's ruling to the extent that it defined the interest to be valued as equivalent to 27½% of the stock, to the extent that it excluded as evidence of value the fact that the estate's stock had, prior to decedent's death, been held jointly with Mr. Bright's interest as community property, and the fact that, after death, the particular executor (Mr. Bright) and legatee (Mr. Bright as trustee) was related to another stock holder (Mr. Bright individually), and to the extent that it excluded any evidence that Mr. Bright, as executor or trustee, would have refused to sell the estate's 27½% block except in conjunction with his own stock and as part of a 55% control block. We hold that family attribution cannot be applied to lump the estate's stock to that of any related party, but rather that the stock is deemed to be held by a hypothetical seller who is related to no one.

Having rejected the heart of the government's arguments, we turn finally to a secondary argument raised by the government for the first time on appeal. The district court ruled before trial that "no element of control can be attributed to the decedent in determining the value of the decedent's interest in the stock" and that the parties must try the case on that basis. (R. 115.) We have held that decedent's interest did not constitute control, and that there can be no family attribution to lump the estate's stock with that of related parties. However, the government complained at oral argument that the district court's order sweeps more broadly, and that the order prevented the introduction of evidence which would have been proper. For example, although the "willing buyer" is also hypothetical, both he and the "willing seller" would have "reasonable knowledge of relevant facts." Reg. 20.2031–1(b). Thus, both the "willing seller" and the "willing buyer" would know that Mr. Bright individually owned, as of the date of death, 27½% of the stock, that Mr. Schiff owned 30%, that the 27½% being offered by the "willing seller" would provide the margin of control for either Mr. Bright or Mr. Schiff, and that the "willing buyer" might negotiate a resale to either Mr. Bright or Mr. Schiff. The government contends that the foregoing facts constitute admissible evidence, and that such facts might affect the value of the 27½% minority interest which is to be valued. The relevance of such facts, the government argues, is contemplated by the willing buyer-seller rule, which presupposes that they both have "reasonable knowledge of relevant facts." Such facts are to be distinguished from the kind of facts which we have held to be irrelevant on account of their derivation from family attribution based on the identity of the decedent, the executor or the legatee. Family attribution facts are irrelevant because the valuation is based on a sale by a *hypothetical seller*—not Mrs. Bright, not Mr. Bright as Executor and not Mr. Bright as trustee—who is related to no one. The "willing buyer-seller" rule renders irrelevant only the real seller and buyer, not the other stockholders. Thus, while the identities of decedent, the decedent's estate and the decedent's legatee are irrelevant, the remaining stockholders in the corporation are in no sense hypothetical. Thus, the government argues that such facts are among the "relevant facts" of which the hypothetical seller and buyer have knowledge. Although this particular application of the willing buyer-seller rule has not been widely recognized, a few cases have acknowledged the relevance of such facts. Marian Otis Chandler, 10 T.C.M. (P–H) ¶ 41,193 at p. 41–392 (1941); Estate of Bernon Prentice, 25 T.C.M. (P–H) ¶ 56,003 (1956) ("There is evidence that a block of stock of Fulton Trust of the size owned by the decedent could not have been sold at one time on the over-the-counter market at prevailing prices, and that the holder of such a block would probably be forced to take the lower price in order to dispose of it. On the other hand, there is testimony that such a block might bring a higher price than market, if a buyer could be found who wanted to acquire control of the bank." At p. 16). Estate of Marjorie Gilbert Brush, 32 T.C.M. (P–H) ¶ 63,186 (1963) ("And these statements may further tend to indicate that the substantial number of shares held by the decedent's estate may for such reason have had greater value as a single block, because of their potential for affording 'leverage' to a potential buyer or buyers in acquiring a controlling stock interest." At p. 1032)....

Although we assume arguendo that such facts are admissible, as the government urges, we need not reach the issue of whether the district court's pretrial order in this case was too broad, i.e., whether the order precluded the introduction of such facts. We have searched the record carefully, and have concluded that the government did not raise this issue in the court below....

[Of the 23 members of the en banc court, 18 joined the majority opinion and five dissented. The two dissenting opinions are omitted.]

NOTES

1. *Family control.* After losing several cases involving transfers of minority interests in family corporations, the government conceded that it will no longer "assum[e] that all voting power held by family members may be aggregated" in valuing transferred shares for estate and gift tax purposes. "Consequently, a minority discount will not be disallowed solely because a transferred interest, when aggregated with interests held by family members, would be a part of a controlling interest." Rev. Rul. 93–12, 1993–1 C.B. 202. See also Ward v. Commissioner, 87 T.C. 78 (1986) (gift tax); Propstra v. United States, 680 F.2d 1248 (9th Cir. 1982) (estate tax); Andrews' Estate v. Commissioner, 79 T.C. 938 (1982) (estate tax). In light of Rev. Rul. 93–12, consider whether a minority discount is appropriate in the following cases:

1. *D*, the sole shareholder of a corporation, gives all of her stock to her four children in equal 25–percent blocks. See Whittemore v. Fitzpatrick, 127 F.Supp. 710 (D. Conn. 1954) (gifts valued as separate minority blocks).
2. Four siblings, equal 25–percent shareholders of a corporation, acting in concert, contribute all of their stock to an irrevocable long-term trust for the benefit of their respective descendants. See Citizens

Bank & Trust Co. v. Commissioner, 839 F.2d 1249 (7th Cir. 1988) (discussing effect of restrictions imposed by terms of transfer).

3. *D*, the sole shareholder of a corporation, gives a 49–percent block of stock to her child. One year later, upon being diagnosed with a terminal illness, *D* gives another 2–percent block of stock to her child. *D* dies shortly afterward, leaving her remaining 49–percent block to the same child. See Murphy's Estate v. Commissioner, 60 T.C.M. (CCH) 645 (1990) (no minority discount where sole purpose of bifurcated transfer was to obtain valuation discount; arrangement "lacked substance and economic effect").

4. *D* dies owning 40 percent of the stock of a corporation, which is included in her gross estate under § 2033. A second 40–percent block of stock held by a QTIP trust created by *D*'s predeceased spouse is included in *D*'s gross estate under § 2044. See Bonner's Estate v. United States, 84 F.3d 196 (5th Cir. 1996) (no aggregation); Mellinger's Estate v. Commissioner, 112 T.C. 26 (1999) (same). What if the second 40–percent block of stock is held by a marital trust in which *D* had a life income interest and a general power of appointment? See Fontana's Estate v. Commissioner, 118 T.C. 318 (2002) (aggregation required where decedent had "control and power of disposition over the property").

5. *D* and her child acquire all of the stock of a corporation as joint tenants with right of survivorship, each furnishing 50 percent of the purchase price. *D* dies survived by her child, and 50 percent of the stock is included in *D*'s gross estate under § 2040(a). See Young's Estate v. Commissioner, 110 T.C. 297 (1998) (no fractional interest discount for joint tenancy of real property).

2. *"Swing" value.* In *Bright's Estate*, the court declined on procedural grounds to consider the government's argument concerning the "swing" value of the decedent's stock. Evidently, if Mr. Bright held a 27½–percent block and Mr. Schiff held a 30–percent block, a hypothetical purchaser of Mrs. Bright's 27½–percent block might be able to form a controlling alliance with either of the other major shareholders, or to steer a course between them. On the other hand, Mr. Bright and Mr. Schiff might instead form their own control group, relegating the purchaser to minority status. Should a minority discount have been allowed in valuing Mrs. Bright's stock? Should the stock have been valued as part of a potential control block to reflect its swing value? See Winkler's Estate v. Commissioner, 57 T.C.M. (CCH) 373 (1989) (denying minority discount in valuing "a 10 percent block of voting stock that could be pivotal as between the two families" holding a 40–percent block and a 50–percent block); but cf. Simplot's Estate v. Commissioner, 249 F.3d 1191 (9th Cir. 2001) (divided court denied premium in valuing voting shares relative to nonvoting shares, where decedent and three siblings owned all voting shares in roughly equal blocks).

3. *Fragmentation at death.* When a decedent's controlling interest is divided among several beneficiaries under the terms of a testamentary transfer, taxpayers have argued that the resulting conversion into minority interests should be reflected in valuing the gross estate. The courts, however, have

rejected the argument, reasoning that the estate tax is imposed on value transferred rather than value received. See Ahmanson Found. v. United States, 674 F.2d 761 (9th Cir. 1981); Curry's Estate v. United States, 706 F.2d 1424 (7th Cir. 1983).

On the other hand, the fragmentation of property at death may be relevant in valuing a bequest for purposes of the estate tax marital or charitable deduction. Assume the sole shareholder of a corporation dies leaving 49 percent of the stock to charity and 51 percent to a child. Although the stock is valued as a single 100–percent block for purposes of inclusion in the gross estate, the amount of the charitable deduction may reflect a minority discount for the 49–percent block passing to charity. See Ahmanson Found. v. United States, 674 F.2d 761 (9th Cir. 1981) (applying minority discount in determining charitable deduction for bequest of nonvoting interest); see also Chenoweth's Estate v. Commissioner, 88 T.C. 1577 (1987) (bequest of controlling interest entitled to premium for purposes of marital deduction); but see Provident Natl. Bank v. United States, 581 F.2d 1081 (3d Cir. 1978) (requiring uniform valuation in calculating adjusted gross estate and marital deduction).

4. *Reform proposals.* Several reform proposals have emerged in recent years with the goal of curbing abuse and reducing uncertainty concerning valuation discounts. One proposal advanced by the Joint Committee on Taxation in 2005 adopts a two-pronged approach. The first prong consists of an "aggregation rule" which would value any transferred interest as a ratable portion of the transferor's entire interest as it existed immediately before the transfer (or, if the interest forms part of a controlling interest in the transferee's hands, as a ratable portion of the value of the transferee's entire interest immediately after the transfer). The aggregation rule would limit the use of minority discounts when a transferor breaks up a controlling interest into several smaller interests and transfers those interests separately (see supra Note 1). The second prong of the proposal consists of a "look-through rule" which would deny a lack-of-marketability discount in valuing a transfer of an interest in an entity, to the extent of the entity's marketable assets, if the transferred interest was part of a controlling interest in the hands of the transferor (before the transfer) or the transferee (after the transfer). Finally, to prevent the use of marital transfers to circumvent these rules, each transferor or transferee would be treated as owning any interest held by his or her spouse. See Staff of Joint Committee on Taxation, Options to Improve Tax Compliance and Reform Tax Expenditures 396–404 (2005).

5. *References.* For further discussions of control premiums and minority discounts, see Feld, The Implications of Minority Interest and Stock Restrictions in Valuing Closely Held Shares, 122 U. Pa. L. Rev. 934 (1974); Fellows & Painter, Valuing Close Corporations for Federal Wealth Transfer Taxes: A Statutory Solution to the Disappearing Wealth Syndrome, 30 Stan. L. Rev. 895 (1978); Repetti, Minority Discounts: The Alchemy in Estate and Gift Taxation, 50 Tax L. Rev. 415 (1995); Reilly & Rotkowski, The Discount for Lack of Marketability: Update on Current Studies and Analysis of Current Controversies, 61 Tax Law. 241 (2007); Pennell, Wealth Transfer Taxation: "Transfer" Defined, 128 Tax Notes 615 (2010).

D. RESTRICTIONS ON TRANSFER, VOTING, OR LIQUIDATION

1. RESTRICTIVE AGREEMENTS: § 2703

Often the owners of a closely held business enter into a restrictive agreement governing the transfer of their interests. For example, a common form of buy-sell agreement provides that any shareholder desiring to sell stock to an outsider must first offer it to the other shareholders at a specified formula price; the agreement may also provide that any deceased shareholder's stock is subject to mandatory or optional purchase by the surviving shareholders at the same price. Such transfer restrictions may serve valid business objectives, such as maintaining cohesive ownership and control, preventing transfers to outsiders, creating liquidity at an owner's death or retirement, and eliminating the need for costly and intrusive appraisals. At the same time, an agreement that provides for purchase of an interest by a related party at an artificially low price may also operate as a device for avoiding transfer taxes.

a. Section 2703

In 1990 Congress added § 2703 to the Code to deter the use of restrictive agreements as a valuation freezing technique. The basic rule of § 2703(a) requires that property be valued for estate, gift and generation-skipping transfer tax purposes without regard to "any option, agreement, or other right to acquire or use" property at a below-market price, as well as "any restriction on the right to sell or use such property." The principal target of § 2703 is a buy-sell agreement that creates a *right* in a third party to purchase a closely held business interest at a below-market price or imposes a *restriction* on the owner's ability to sell the interest at its full market price. The statute also has potential application to restrictions on the use of property. See Note 3, infra page 621.

To illustrate the effect of § 2703(a), assume that the stock of a family corporation is owned equally by *A* and her child *B*, who have entered into a buy-sell agreement. The agreement restricts transfers of stock while both parties are living and provides that upon the death of either party the survivor must purchase the decedent's stock for $100,000 (the fair market value of each party's stock when the agreement was made). When *A* dies survived by *B*, her stock has an unrestricted fair market value of $500,000. Under § 2703(a), *A*'s stock must be included in her gross estate at a value of $500,000 even though the estate is required to sell the stock to *B* for $100,000. The estate tax result is the same as if *A* had made an enforceable promise to leave *B* a bequest of $400,000, the difference between the unrestricted value of the stock and the mandatory purchase price. (For the estate tax treatment of *B*'s claim against *A*'s estate, see § 2053(c)(1)(A), discussed supra at page 438, Note 2.)

Section 2703 is intended to reach disguised gifts and bequests, not bona fide business transactions. Accordingly, § 2703(b) carves out an exception to the basic rule of § 2703(a) for a restrictive agreement that meets each of the following requirements: (1) the agreement must be a "bona fide business arrangement"; (2) it must not be a "device to transfer such property to members of the decedent's family for less than full and adequate consideration in money or money's worth"; and (3) its terms must be "comparable to similar arrangements entered into by persons in an arms' length transaction." If any one of the requirements is not met, the underlying property is valued without regard to the transfer restrictions imposed by the agreement. Conversely, if all three requirements are met, the transfer restrictions may be taken into account in valuing the property. Because the safe harbor provisions of § 2703(b) determine whether a restrictive agreement will have any effect on transfer tax valuation, those provisions merit close attention.

The first two requirements of § 2703(b) are taken almost verbatim from a 1958 estate tax regulation concerning restrictive agreements, and the case law interpreting that regulation remains highly relevant in determining whether a restrictive agreement constitutes a "bona fide business arrangement" and not a testamentary "device" under § 2703(b). Reg. § 20.2031–2(h). The third requirement, that the terms of a right or restriction must be "comparable" to an arm's-length transaction, has no direct counterpart in Reg. § 20.2031–2(h), but it too echoes the analysis developed by courts under that regulation. The "comparability" requirement of § 2703(b)(3) is met if the right or restriction "could have been obtained in a fair bargain among unrelated parties in the same business dealing with each other at arm's length," i.e., if it "conforms with the general practice of unrelated parties under negotiated agreements in the same business." Reg. § 25.2703–1(b)(4). In comparing the actual right or restriction with a hypothetical fair bargain, "the expected term of the agreement, the current fair market value of the property, anticipated changes in value during the term of the arrangement, and the adequacy of any consideration given in exchange for the rights granted" are to be taken into account. Id.

The provisions of § 2703 reinforce the well-established requirements of Reg. § 20.2031–2(h). As one court noted, § 2703 "for all intents and purposes codifies [the] pre-existing regulatory language" and is "instructive as to how such language should be applied to agreements entered into even before 1990." Gloeckner's Estate v. Commissioner, 152 F.3d 208 (2d Cir. 1998); see also True's Estate v. Commissioner, 390 F.3d 1210 (10th Cir. 2004) (§ 2703 "essentially codified the rules laid out in § 20.2031–2(h)"). By the same token, the case law under Reg. § 20.2031–2(h) has continuing relevance even after the enactment of § 2703. Not all restrictive agreements are disregarded under the basic rule of § 2703(a); if the terms of an agreement meet all three requirements of § 2703(b), the valuation of restricted property is still governed by the principles developed by courts under prior law. See Blount's Estate v. Commissioner, 87 T.C.M. (CCH) 1303 (2004), affd. and revd. on other grounds, 428 F.3d 1338 (11th Cir. 2005) ("regardless of whether section 2703 applies to a buy-sell agreement, the agreement must meet the requirements of the pre-section 2703 law to control value for Federal estate tax purposes''). Given the widespread use of restrictive agreements in business and estate planning, those principles remain as important as ever.

b. Agreements Outside § 2703(a)

The Service has long recognized that a restrictive agreement generally constitutes "a factor to be considered, with other relevant factors, in determining fair market value," and may even be sufficient in some cases to "fix the value" of restricted property for estate tax purposes. Rev. Rul. 59–60, § 8, 1959–1 C.B. 237. In several early cases, the courts held that an enforceable option to purchase a decedent's interest for a specified price established a ceiling on the value of the interest for estate tax purposes where the interest could not have been sold for a higher price during life. The courts reasoned that "the property could not be sold for more than the option price," and dismissed as "too extravagant to require further refutation" the notion that the property might have a greater fair market value because of the possibility that the option would not be exercised. Wilson v. Bowers, 57 F.2d 682 (2d Cir. 1932); see also May v. McGowan, 194 F.2d 396 (2d Cir. 1952) (option to purchase stock at formula price that turned out to be zero); Brodrick v. Gore, 224 F.2d 892 (10th Cir. 1955) (mutually binding restrictions on transfer of partnership interest). In Weil's Estate v. Commissioner, 22 T.C. 1267 (1954), the Tax Court summarized the prevailing doctrine as follows:

> It now seems well established that the value of property may be limited for estate tax purposes by an enforceable agreement which fixes the price to be paid therefor, and where the seller if he desires to sell during his lifetime can receive only the price fixed by the contract and at his death his estate can receive only the price theretofore agreed on. [22 T.C. at 1273–74.]

With the promulgation of Reg. § 20.2031–2(h), the courts began to look more closely at whether, in the words of the regulation, a restrictive agreement represented "a bona fide business arrangement and not a device to pass the decedent's shares to the natural objects of his bounty for less than an adequate and full consideration in money or money's worth." As a threshold matter, taxpayers ordinarily encounter little difficulty in demonstrating a valid business purpose, at least in the context of an active business operation. See Bischoff's Estate v. Commissioner, 69 T.C. 32 (1977) (maintaining "family ownership and control" of pork processing business). A vehicle for holding passive investments, without any clearly articulated investment strategy, may be subject to more searching scrutiny. For example, in Holman v. Commissioner, 601 F.3d 763 (8th Cir. 2010), a husband and wife made gifts in trust for their children of interests in a family limited partnership that was funded solely with shares of Dell, Inc., "a highly liquid and easily valued company." In holding that transfer restrictions in the partnership agreement must be disregarded under § 2703, the court noted that the restrictions did not constitute a bona fide business arrangement but instead were adopted primarily for purposes of "estate planning, tax reduction, wealth transference, protection against dissipation by the children, and education for the children."

Courts also look at several other factors: whether the parties are related; whether the formula price was reasonable at the time the agreement was entered into; whether the same rights and restrictions apply uniformly to all parties; and whether the agreement has been consistently enforced. An agreement is likely to withstand scrutiny if the parties are unrelated, or if related and unrelated parties are subject to the same rights and restrictions. See Bischoff's Estate, supra (mandatory sale reduced proportionate partnership interest of decedent's family); Seltzer's Estate v. Commissioner, 50 T.C.M. (CCH) 1250 (1985) (two of five parties unrelated to decedent); Gloeckner's Estate v. Commissioner, 152 F.3d 208 (2d Cir. 1998) (intended beneficiary of redemption agreement was neither related to decedent nor in "a relationship with decedent such as to be effectively considered a member of his family"); see also Reg. § 25.2703–1(b)(3) (requirements deemed met if more than half of restricted property is owned directly or indirectly by individuals other than specified family members and natural objects of transferor's bounty). Occasionally, even closely related family members may negotiate an agreement at arm's length. See Commissioner v. Bensel, 100 F.2d 639 (3d Cir. 1938) (protracted negotiations between father and estranged son).

A more difficult problem arises where all the parties to a restrictive agreement are closely related and do not negotiate at arm's length. Courts have recognized that an agreement may serve a valid business purpose and at the same time constitute a testamentary device. Indicia of a testamentary device include a formula price that does not bear a reasonable relationship to the unrestricted value of the interest; an arbitrary formula price arrived at without independent appraisals or negotiation; and the lack of a mechanism for adjusting the formula price. See True's Estate v. Commissioner, 390 F.3d 1210 (10th Cir. 2004) (book value formula price without adjustment mechanism, arrived at without negotiation between decedent and children); St. Louis County Bank v. United States, 674 F.2d 1207 (8th Cir. 1982) (decedent's ill health at time of agreement, coupled with family relationship of parties, supported inference of testamentary device; formula produced purchase price of zero at decedent's death, and agreement had not been enforced on earlier occasion). Accordingly, courts carefully scrutinize agreements that provide for sale of a deceased party's interest to younger-generation family members at a bargain price.

Nevertheless, courts have occasionally treated an agreement among family members as a bona fide business arrangement despite strong testamentary overtones. For example, Littick's Estate v. Commissioner, 31 T.C. 181 (1958), involved a newspaper company owned by the decedent and his two brothers in approximately equal shares. Under a buy-sell agreement entered into when the decedent was terminally ill, the stock of any deceased shareholder was required to be sold to the company for $200,000, and in the decedent's case a portion of the stock was to be held in escrow for his son "in order that 'he may have some interest' in the company." The court noted that the agreement was binding on all three brothers, and that it was possible (though unlikely) that one of the other brothers might die before the decedent. In the absence of evidence "that the $200,000 figure was not fairly arrived at by arm's-length negotiation or that any tax avoidance scheme was involved," the court concluded that the agreement fixed the value of the decedent's stock at $200,000 for estate tax purposes. 31 T.C. at 186–88.

An agreement has no conclusive effect for estate tax purposes, and is treated merely as a factor to be taken into account in valuing the decedent's interest, if it fails to restrict lifetime transfers, see Hoffman v. Commissioner, 2 T.C. 1160 (1943), affd., 148 F.2d 285 (9th Cir.), cert. denied, 326 U.S. 730 (1945), or if it fails to create an enforceable obligation to sell the interest at death, see Worcester County Trust Co. v. Commissioner, 134 F.2d 578 (1st Cir. 1943); Baltimore Natl. Bank v. United States, 136 F.Supp. 642 (D. Md. 1955).

By the same reasoning, a restrictive agreement that leaves the owner free to sell or retain property generally has no conclusive effect on the property's value for gift tax purposes, even if the agreement requires a sale at some future time. See James v. Commissioner, 3 T.C. 1260 (1944), affd., 148 F.2d 236 (2d Cir. 1945); Ward v. Commissioner, 87 T.C. 78 (1986). Such an agreement is treated as a factor to be taken into account in valuing the restricted property for transfer tax purposes. See Curry's Estate v. United States, 706 F.2d 1424 (7th Cir. 1983) (right of first refusal relevant even if formula price currently exceeds unrestricted value, since unrestricted value might rise in future); Commissioner v. McCann, 146 F.2d 385 (2d Cir. 1944).

Lauder's Estate, which follows, arose before the enactment of § 2703, but the valuation analysis would not change under current law. In reading the case, consider how § 2703 might affect the planning and drafting of similar restrictive agreements.

LAUDER'S ESTATE v. COMMISSIONER

64 T.C.M. (CCH) 1643 (1992).

HAMBLEN, CHIEF JUDGE:

[The decedent, Joseph H. Lauder, died in 1983 at the age of 81, survived by his wife Estee and two sons, Leonard and Ronald. At the time of his death decedent owned stock in EJL Corporation, a holding company for Estee Lauder, Inc. and another Lauder family corporation engaged in the manufacture and distribution of cosmetics, fragrances, and related products.[17]

A shareholder agreement executed in May 1974 restricted a shareholder (or his or her estate) from transferring common stock to a third

17. For convenience, the court refers to both EJL Corporation and Estee Lauder, Inc. as EJL.

party by providing that, prior to such a transfer, the stock must first be offered for sale to the other shareholders or to the corporation at a formula price based on adjusted book value per share, excluding goodwill and other intangible assets. The 1974 agreement was Leonard's idea. He arrived at the book value formula after consulting with a close family financial adviser, but without obtaining an appraisal of the corporation or its stock and without comparing the stock prices and book values of publicly traded cosmetics companies. In arriving at the pricing formula, Leonard considered that companies listed in the Standard & Poor's 400 were selling at approximately book value, even though an index within the Standard & Poor's 400 showed an average price-to-book-value ratio of approximately 2 to 1 for cosmetics companies during 1974.

In December 1976, EJL and its shareholders executed a new agreement which superseded the 1974 agreement and provided essentially identical restrictions on transfers of common stock. Again, neither the Lauders nor EJL obtained an appraisal of EJL or its stock, nor did they compare the stock prices and book values of publicly traded cosmetics companies. In determining the pricing formula, Leonard did not examine the Standard and Poor's 400, but an index within the Standard & Poor's 400 reflected an average price-to-book-value ratio of approximately 3 to 1 for cosmetics companies during 1976.

On several occasions the corporations and their shareholders waived their purchase rights under the 1974 and 1976 agreements in order to facilitate the transfer or retention of shares by Lauder family members. A few months after Joseph's death, his estate sold his EJL shares to EJL for $4,111 per share, the formula price determined under the 1976 agreement.]

The issue for decision is whether the formula price contained in restrictive shareholder agreements, to which decedent was a party, controls the valuation of stock in a closely held corporation for purposes of the Federal estate tax. . . .

The courts . . . have long recognized that the value of corporate stock may be limited for Federal estate tax purposes by an enforceable buy-sell agreement or option contract which fixes the price at which the stock may be offered for sale to the remaining shareholders. See May v. McGowan, 194 F.2d 396 (2d Cir. 1952); Lomb v. Sugden, 82 F.2d 166 (2d Cir. 1936); Wilson v. Bowers, 57 F.2d 682 (2d Cir. 1932); see also Commissioner v. Bensel, 100 F.2d 639 (3d Cir. 1938), affg. 36 B.T.A. 246 (1937). Such agreements are also recognized as restricting the value of partnership interests. Brodrick v. Gore, 224 F.2d 892 (10th Cir. 1955); Fiorito v. Commissioner, 33 T.C. 440 (1959); Estate of Weil v. Commissioner, 22 T.C. 1267 (1954).

Several requirements have evolved for testing whether the formula price set forth in such restrictive agreements is binding for purposes of the Federal estate tax. It is axiomatic that the offering price must be fixed and determinable under the agreement. In addition, the agreement must be binding on the parties both during life and after death. See Wilson v. Bowers, supra at 683; see also United States v. Land, 303 F.2d 170, 173 (5th Cir. 1962); Brodrick v. Gore, supra at 896; Estate of Matthews v. Commissioner, 3 T.C. 525, 528–529 (1944). Finally, the restrictive agreement must have been entered into for a bona fide business reason and must not be a substitute for a testamentary disposition. See sec. 20.2031–2(h), Estate Tax Regs.; Dorn v. United States, 828 F.2d 177, 181–182 (3d Cir. 1987); St. Louis County Bank v. United States, 674 F.2d 1207, 1210 (8th Cir. 1982); see also Slocum v. United States, 256 F. Supp. 753, 755 (S.D.N.Y. 1966).

Petitioner contends that the formula price set forth in the shareholder agreements is controlling for purposes of determining the estate tax value of decedent's stock. Petitioner maintains that the shareholder agreements establish a fixed and determinable price for the stock, that the obligation to offer the stock to the remaining shareholders is binding both during life and at death, and that there is a bona fide business purpose for the agreements. Petitioner argues that the formula reflects a fair, objective measure of the value of the stock, which approximated fair market value on the dates that the shareholder agreements were executed.

Respondent concedes that the shareholder agreements establish a fixed and determinable selling price for decedent's stock. However, respondent contends that various transfers of EJL stock by the Lauders during the period in question reveal that the Lauders themselves did not consider the agreements binding. Respondent further contends that the formula price grossly undervalued the EJL stock on the dates the shareholder agreements were executed. Respondent argues that the formula price was derived without an appraisal of EJL, that the value of intangibles is not taken into account under the formula, that the parties to the agreements did not negotiate with respect to the formula, and that the agreements do not provide for a controlling interest premium with respect to the shares held by Estee.

We are convinced that the shareholder agreements created enforceable obligations against decedent both during his life and after his death. See Wilson v. Bowers, supra at 683, and cases cited therein. Moreover, we conclude that the Lauders considered the agreements to be binding, notwithstanding that EJL stock was transferred to nonshareholders both contemporaneously with and subsequently to the execution of the agreements. In particular, the Lauders executed formal waivers, consistent with the agreements, with respect to [exchanges of voting stock for nonvoting stock as well as transfers of nonvoting common stock in trust for the Lauder grandchildren and charitable contributions of nonvoting common stock]. In addition, each transferee was explicitly bound by the terms of the agreements. On the whole, we cannot agree with respondent that these transfers were inconsistent with the Lauders' intent to maintain family control over EJL. . . .

The foregoing aside, we are left to decide whether: (1) The restrictive shareholder agreements served a bona fide business purpose; and (2) the agreements were intended as a testamentary device to transfer decedent's stock to the natural objects of his bounty for less than adequate and full consideration. Specifically, section 20.2031–2(h), Estate Tax Regs., provides in pertinent part:

> Even if the decedent is not free to dispose of the underlying securities at other than the option or contract price, such price will be disregarded in determining the value of the securities unless it is determined under the circumstances of the particular case that the agreement represents a bona fide business arrangement and not a device to pass the decedent's shares to the natural objects of his bounty for less than an adequate and full consideration in money or money's worth....

Section 20.2031–2(h), Estate Tax Regs., was first adopted over 34 years ago. See T.D. 6296, 23 Fed. Reg. 4529 (June 23, 1958). Contrary to petitioner's position, the regulation requires not only that the agreement meet the business purpose prong of the test but also that the agreement not be a testamentary device. See St. Louis County Bank v. United States, supra; see also Dorn v. United States, supra at 182; Estate of Bischoff v. Commissioner, 69 T.C. 32, 41–42 (1977); Estate of Reynolds v. Commissioner, 55 T.C. 172, 194 (1970).

In discussing the issue presented in this case, one commentator has observed that legitimate business purposes are often "inextricably mixed" with testamentary objectives where, as here, the parties to a restrictive stock agreement are all members of the same immediate family. 5 Bittker, Federal Taxation of Income, Estates and Gifts, par. 132.3.10, at 132–54 (1984). More specifically, it has long been recognized that restrictions placed on the transfer of stock in order to maintain exclusive family ownership and control may serve a bona fide business purpose. Estate of Bischoff v. Commissioner, supra at 39–40; Estate of Littick v. Commissioner, 31 T.C. 181, 187 (1958); Slocum v. United States, 256 F. Supp. 753 (S.D.N.Y. 1966). At the same time, however, the family may achieve testamentary objectives to the extent that the agreement allows for the possibility (and generally the probability) that stock held by members of a more senior generation will be sold to subsequent generations (children and grandchildren) at a bargain price. Bittker, supra at 132–57 through 132–59.

With these considerations in mind, it is evident that intrafamily agreements restricting the transfer of stock in a closely held corporation must be subjected to greater scrutiny than that afforded similar agreements between unrelated parties. Dorn v. United States, 828 F.2d at 182; Harwood v. Commissioner, 82 T.C. 239, 259 (1984), affd. without published opinion 786 F.2d 1174 (9th Cir. 1986); Estate of Kelley v. Commissioner, 63 T.C. 321, 325 (1974); Estate of Tiffany v. Commissioner, 47 T.C. 491, 499 (1967); Hoffman v. Commissioner, 2 T.C. 1160, 1178–1179

(1943), affd. sub nom. Giannini v. Commissioner, 148 F.2d 285 (9th Cir. 1945) ("[T]he fact that the option is given to one who is the natural object of the bounty of the optionor requires substantial proof to show that it rested upon full and adequate consideration.").

Turning to the case at hand, there can be no question that the shareholder agreements, on their face, serve the legitimate business purpose of preserving family ownership and control of the various Lauder enterprises. We are persuaded that these concerns were a motivating factor in the Lauders' decision to enter into the agreements....

Notwithstanding the business purpose for the agreements, petitioner also bears the burden of proving that the agreements were not intended as a device to pass decedent's shares to the natural objects of his bounty for less than an adequate and full consideration in money or money's worth. Suffice it to say that Leonard's testimony that the agreements were not so intended is insufficient to satisfy petitioner's burden of proof on this most critical point. Davis v. Commissioner, 88 T.C. 122, 141, 144 (1987), affd. 866 F.2d 852 (6th Cir. 1989).

Petitioner asserts that the agreements are not testamentary in nature on the grounds that: (1) Decedent was not in poor health or apprehensive of imminent death at the time the agreements were executed; (2) there was an interval of several years between the execution of the agreements and decedent's death; (3) the parties adhered to the terms of the agreements; and (4) any one of the Lauders could have predeceased the others.

In contrast, there are compelling circumstances suggesting that decedent, who was in his seventies when the agreements were signed, entered into the agreements as a substitute for a testamentary disposition to pass on his interest in the business to the members of his family for less than adequate consideration. We are most concerned with the arbitrary manner in which Leonard, an experienced businessman, adopted the adjusted book value formula for determining the purchase price of the stock under the agreements. Leonard admitted that he arrived at the formula without a formal appraisal and without considering the specific trading prices of comparable companies. Nor does it appear that Leonard obtained any significant professional advice in selecting the formula price. Leonard settled on the book value formula himself after consulting with Arnold M. Ganz (a close family financial adviser now deceased). Notably, there is no mention of Mr. Ganz in Leonard's affidavit submitted along with petitioner's original motion for partial summary judgment. We further note that Shutzer, petitioner's expert, declined to evaluate decedent's stock on the basis of book value because he did not believe that "real world" investors would value the stock in this manner.

In arriving at the book value formula in 1974, Leonard testified that he considered that companies listed in the Standard & Poor's 400 generally traded for book value. Assuming that Leonard considered the Standard & Poor's 400, we find it somewhat incredible that Leonard, as president and director of EJL, was unaware or overlooked the fact that the Standard

& Poor's 400 indicated that the average price to book value ratio of cosmetic companies ranged between 2 to 1 and 3 to 1 during the period in question.

We are also concerned by Leonard's testimony that he did not have EJL appraised out of anxiety over the confidentiality of EJL's financial statements. Such testimony seems contrived in light of the engagement of the Warburg investment banking group in 1975 for the purpose of investigating the feasibility of raising capital for the company through the private placement of $15 million in long-term notes. Although Leonard was evasive on the point, it is clear that in carrying out its "due diligence" investigation Warburg was privy to detailed financial information regarding EJL's operations and projected revenues. Further, Warburg was permitted to release a private placement memorandum to at least one insurance company before the Lauders withdrew from the transaction in 1976.

No less significant is the fact that the record is devoid of any persuasive evidence that the Lauders negotiated with respect to the formula price. To the contrary, the record indicates that Leonard unilaterally decided upon the formula price. Ronald could not remember who decided upon the formula and only recalled that Leonard had explained the formula to him. Estee had no specific recollection of either of the agreements. Given these circumstances, it appears that the parties never intended to negotiate the matter, fully recognizing that an artificially low price would provide estate tax benefits for all.[18]

As a final matter, we question the propriety of expressly excluding the value of all intangible assets from the book value formula. In our view, the cosmetics industry is somewhat unique in that intangible assets, such as trademarks and trade names, represent a significant component of the aggregate value of total assets. Moreover, there can be no doubt that much of the value in EJL is attributable to the name "Estee Lauder" and to the goodwill generated over the years by virtue of the Lauders' creative and novel marketing of EJL products. This point is supported in the record by the fact that Estee was compelled to transfer the "Estee Lauder" trademark to EJL to enable the latter to negotiate for loans and other credit in the public market. Thus, while we appreciate that an adjusted book value formula may provide a simple and inexpensive means for evaluating shares in a company, we cannot passively accept such a formula where, as here, it appears to have been adopted in order to minimize or mask the true value of the stock in question. See Estate of Trammell v. Commissioner, 18 T.C. 662 (1952).

Considering the foregoing factors in conjunction, an inference may fairly be drawn that the agreements were designed to serve a testamentary purpose. To finally resolve whether the agreements are binding for

18. Presumably, if decedent and Estee were pursuing an identical agreement with unrelated parties in the place of Leonard and Ronald, they would have been motivated, by virtue of their advanced age, to negotiate a formula ensuring as high a price as possible for their shares balanced against their desire to maintain continuity of management and control.

estate tax purposes, we turn to the question of whether the price to be paid for decedent's stock under the agreements reflected adequate and full consideration in money or money's worth.

With respect to the issue of the adequacy of the consideration, we begin with petitioner's alternative argument that:

> Mutual promises, made when any one of the shareholders could have predeceased the others, themselves provide full and adequate consideration for the Shareholder Agreement.

From petitioner's point of view, there is no need to demonstrate any nexus between the formula price and the fair market value of the subject stock.

. . . [W]e fully appreciate the utility and merit of shareholder agreements in maintaining family ownership and control of business organizations. We agree that the mutual promises of the parties to a restrictive shareholders agreement generally provide full and adequate consideration for the agreement where the parties deal at arm's length. See, e.g., Cartwright v. United States, 457 F.2d 567, 571 (2d Cir. 1972), affd. 411 U.S. 546 (1973); Fiorito v. Commissioner, 33 T.C. 440, 446 n.1 (1959). In particular, it can be assumed that unrelated parties will tend to negotiate a formula serving their best interests and reflecting a fair price. Where the parties to a restrictive shareholders agreement are truly unrelated and there is no indication that the agreement was intended as a testamentary device, there generally is no basis for respondent to seek to value the stock at a price higher than that paid under the agreement. See Estate of Seltzer v. Commissioner, T.C. Memo. 1985–519. In short, the gross estate will include the actual amount paid by the remaining shareholders to the deceased shareholder's estate.

In contrast, the assumption that the formula price reflects a fair price is not warranted where, as here, the shareholders are all members of the same immediate family and the circumstances show that testamentary considerations influenced the decision to enter into the agreement. In such cases, it cannot be said that the mere mutuality of covenants and promises is sufficient to satisfy the taxpayer's burden of establishing that the agreement is not a testamentary device. Rather, it is incumbent on the estate to demonstrate that the agreement establishes a fair price for the subject stock. Where the estate fails in its burden of proof and the Court finds that the restrictive agreement sets an artificially depressed price for the subject stock, it follows that the estate of the deceased shareholder will be required to pay additional Federal estate tax based on the fair market value of the stock as determined by the Court.

In light of the circumstances present in the instant case, we must consider the adequacy of the consideration in terms of the price to be paid for decedent's stock as of the dates the agreements were executed. As previously indicated, petitioner maintains that the adjusted book value formula reflects a fair, objective measure of the value of the stock, which approximated fair market value on the dates that the shareholder agreements were executed. Respondent argues to the contrary.

We have considered whether such formulas reflect full and adequate consideration in our prior cases. In particular, in Bensel v. Commissioner, 36 B.T.A. 246, 252–253 (1937), affd. 100 F.2d 639 (3d Cir. 1938), the Board of Tax Appeals (our predecessor) concluded that an option price, negotiated between a father and son who at the time were estranged, was controlling for estate tax purposes.[19] The Board held that the option price was not lower than that which would have been agreed upon by persons with adverse interests dealing at arm's length. The Board concluded that the consideration was full and adequate in money or money's worth at the time the option contract was entered into.

We followed the *Bensel* analysis in Estate of Bischoff v. Commissioner, 69 T.C. 32, 41 n.9 (1977). In short, we rejected respondent's argument that the buy-sell agreement in question was merely a substitute for a testamentary disposition in part on the ground that the formula price to be paid for a partnership interest represented the fair market value of the assets of the partnership.

Notably, the phrase "adequate and full consideration" is not specifically defined in section 20.2031–2(h), Estate Tax Regs. In defining the phrase, we begin with the proposition that a formula price may reflect adequate and full consideration notwithstanding that the price falls below fair market value. See, e.g., Estate of Reynolds v. Commissioner, 55 T.C. 172, 194 (1970). In this light, the phrase is best interpreted as requiring a price that is not lower than that which would be agreed upon by persons with adverse interests dealing at arm's length. Bensel v. Commissioner, supra. Under this standard, the formula price generally must bear a reasonable relationship to the unrestricted fair market value of the stock in question.

With the foregoing in mind, we turn to the expert reports and the question of whether the book value formula price reflected adequate and full consideration for decedent's stock on the date the shareholders agreements were executed....

[In valuing the EJL common stock, the court adopted a comparative market valuation method using price/earnings multiples of 11 and 12.5 for May 1974 and December 1976, respectively. The court also allowed a 40-percent discount for lack of liquidity.]

Applying these multiples and discounts to the earnings used in Shutzer's computation, we conclude that decedent's EJL common stock would have sold for $1,485.13 and $2,153.02 per share as of May 1974 and December 1976, respectively. In contrast, the prices for the stock as determined in accordance with Article 6 of the agreements were $614.70 and $1,212.07 per share, as of May 1974 and December 1976, respectively.

---

19. In Bensel v. Commissioner, 36 B.T.A. 246, 252–253 (1937) affd. 100 F.2d 639 (3d Cir. 1938), the father and son were hostile to one another. The father granted the son an option to buy his stock, exercisable upon the father's death, as an inducement to retain the son (considered a valuable employee) in the corporation's employ. There is no comparable evidence of arm's length dealing here.

Comparing these two sets of figures, we are unable to conclude that the formula price reflects the price that would be negotiated between two unrelated parties. Consequently, we cannot agree with petitioner that the formula price reflects full and adequate consideration on the dates the agreements in question were executed. Considering all of the circumstances, particularly the arbitrary manner in which the formula price was selected, we conclude that the agreements were adopted for the principal purpose of achieving testamentary objectives. Thus, the formula price is not binding for purposes of valuing the EJL stock held by decedent on the date of his death....

As a consequence of our holding that the formula price is not binding for purposes of the Federal estate tax, further proceedings will be necessary to determine the fair market value of the EJL stock held by decedent on the date of his death. Secs. 2031, 2033. While we do not here render the agreements invalid per se, we hold that for Federal estate tax purposes they have no viability and that the valuation provisions are, simply put, an artificial device to minimize such taxes....

NOTES

1. *Aftermath of Lauder.* In a subsequent proceeding, the Tax Court ultimately valued Joseph Lauder's EJL stock at $7,474 per share, resulting in an estate tax deficiency of more than $20 million. Lauder's Estate v. Commissioner, 68 T.C.M. (CCH) 985 (1994). The taxpayer argued that, even if the formula price set forth in the 1976 agreement did not fix the value of the stock for estate tax purposes, various other terms of the agreement should be recognized as having a depressing effect on the fair market value of the stock. The court rejected this argument: "[W]e cannot agree that particular aspects of such an agreement can be employed to depress the fair market value of the subject stock (and thereby avoid Federal estate tax) where it is evident that the agreement was adopted primarily as a testamentary device." Nevertheless, the court acknowledged that the existence of the agreement demonstrated the Lauders' "commitment to retain family control," and noted that this element was taken into account in allowing a 40–percent discount to reflect the lack of a public market for the stock. Id. at 999. Accord, True's Estate v. Commissioner, 390 F.3d 1210 (10th Cir. 2004) (terms of tainted restrictive agreement disregarded, but existence of agreement reflected in marketability discount).

2. *Creation of restrictions.* The valuation principles governing restricted property have been developed largely in the estate tax context, since buy-sell agreements commonly require that property be offered or sold at death. The creation of transfer restrictions, however, may also have gift tax consequences. Suppose that *A* grants *B* an enforceable option to purchase property owned by *A* for $100,000 at any time during the next five years. The unrestricted value of the property is $150,000, and *A* receives no money's-worth consideration for granting the option. The Service has ruled that the grant of the option constitutes a completed gift by *A* in an amount equal to the value of the option. Rev. Rul. 80–186, 1980–2 C.B. 280 (noting factors to

be considered in valuing the option: the property's current fair market value, the option price, any potential increase or decrease in value, and the time period of the option). If *A* dies owning the property within the five-year option period, the property may be includible in *A*'s gross estate at its full unrestricted value. See Dorn v. United States, 828 F.2d 177 (3d Cir. 1987).

If a buy-sell agreement requires that each party's interest be offered at death to the surviving parties at the same formula price, should differences in the age or physical condition of the parties be taken into account in determining the effect of the agreement on the value of each party's interest for gift tax purposes? See Littick's Estate v. Commissioner, 31 T.C. 181 (1958) (assuming mutual restrictions constituted adequate and full consideration for purposes of §§ 2035 through 2038). If the buy-sell agreement can be terminated or amended with the consent of all parties, has any party made a completed transfer for gift tax purposes? See Lauder's Estate v. Commissioner, 68 T.C.M. (CCH) 985 (1994) (finding options not intended to be irrevocable).

3. *Restrictions on use of property.* Section 2703 applies not only to buy-sell agreements but also to similar rights and restrictions concerning the use of property. Such rights and restrictions may be imposed by laws and regulations, by corporate articles or bylaws, by a partnership agreement, or by private agreement. Reg. § 25.2703–1(a)(3). Thus, unless the requirements of § 2703(b) are met, arrangements that have traditionally been recognized as value-depressing factors—e.g., long-term, low-rent leases; corporate loan agreements forbidding the payment of dividends while the debt is outstanding; and irrevocable proxies to vote the stock of a closely held corporation—may be disregarded in valuing the underlying property for transfer tax purposes. For a discussion of use restrictions under prior law, see O'Connell's Estate v. Commissioner, 640 F.2d 249 (9th Cir. 1981) (bank loan, subject to agreement not to sell assets, pay dividends, or alter corporate capital structure).

Courts and appraisers also take into account the effect on value of various governmental controls, including zoning ordinances, state and federal securities regulations, and taxes. See, e.g., Gilford's Estate v. Commissioner, 88 T.C. 38 (1987) (discount for transfer restrictions imposed by federal securities law); McClatchy's Estate v. Commissioner, 147 F.3d 1089 (9th Cir. 1998) (same). Does § 2703 affect the transfer tax valuation of property subject to such restrictions?

4. *Testamentary device.* Section 2703(b) represents a renewed attempt to distinguish a "bona fide business arrangement" from a testamentary "device." Previous attempts have met with mixed success. See Reg. § 25.2512–8, discussed in the *Anderson* case, supra page 132; True's Estate v. Commissioner, 390 F.3d 1210 (10th Cir. 2004) (restrictions not negotiated at arm's length or free of donative intent; transfers not made in ordinary course of business). The principal innovation of § 2703 is the "comparability" requirement of § 2703(b)(3), discussed supra at page 609. As a practical matter, it may be difficult to locate a similar business and nearly impossible to discover the terms of a restrictive agreement negotiated by unrelated parties at arm's length. Assuming that these obstacles can be overcome, how likely is it that

the terms of the arm's-length agreement will be "comparable" to those of an agreement between family members?

5. *Restricted management accounts.* Suppose an investor deposits cash and marketable securities with a bank as custodian of a "restricted management account." By the terms of the deposit agreement, the bank has sole management authority and complete investment discretion regarding the assets in the account for a fixed term of years. The investor retains complete beneficial ownership of the account, including the right to assign the account to a permitted transferee but not the right to withdraw any assets from the account during the fixed term. In Rev. Rul. 2008–35, 2008–2 C.B. 116, the Service held that the investor's interest in the account is determined for estate and gift tax purposes by reference to the fair market value of the underlying assets without any reduction or discount to reflect restrictions imposed by the deposit agreement. "Any restrictions on the ability to withdraw assets, terminate the agreement, or transfer interests in the [account] do not impact the price at which those assets would change hands between a willing buyer and a willing seller and, thus, do not affect the value of the assets in the [account]." Are the restrictions disregarded under § 2703(a) or do they come within the safe harbor of § 2703(b)?

6. *Effective date of § 2703.* Section 2703 applies to any right or restriction created or "substantially modified" after October 8, 1990. A discretionary modification is ordinarily treated as "substantial" if it changes "the quality, value, or timing of the rights of any party" to an agreement or adds a family member as a party. A modification is not "substantial," however, if it is required by the terms of a preexisting right or restriction or produces an option price that more closely approximates fair market value. Reg. § 25.2703–1(c).

7. *References.* See Adams, Herpe & Carey, Buy–Sell Agreements After Chapter 14, 132 Tr. & Est. 22 (May 1993); Fross, Estate Tax Valuation Based on Book Value Buy–Sell Agreements, 49 Tax Law. 319 (1996); Zuckerman & Grall, Corporate Buy–Sell Agreements as Estate and Business Planning Tools, 28 Est. Planning 599 (2001).

2. LAPSING RIGHTS AND RESTRICTIONS: § 2704

Closely held business interests are sometimes structured so that valuable rights automatically lapse, or temporary restrictions automatically take effect, at the holder's death. Prior to the enactment of § 2704 in 1990, such arrangements produced conspicuously low estate tax valuations in a few cases. Congress responded by adding § 2704, which requires that certain lapsing rights and restrictions be disregarded for transfer tax purposes.

a. Prior Law

A decedent's interest in a corporation or partnership generally is valued for estate tax purposes without regard to a right or restriction that automatically expires at the holder's death. A leading case, United States

v. Land, 303 F.2d 170 (5th Cir.), cert. denied, 371 U.S. 862 (1962), involved the valuation of a decedent's partnership interest which was required to be offered at death to the surviving partners at its full value; if the decedent had wished to withdraw from the partnership during life, the other partners would have been entitled to purchase his interest at two-thirds of its "calculated value." In a cryptic but often-quoted passage, the court observed:

> Brief as is the instant of death, the court must pinpoint its valuation at this instant—the moment of truth, when the ownership of the decedent ends and the ownership of the successors begins. It is a fallacy, therefore, to argue value before-or-after death on the notion that valuation must be determined by the value either of the interest that ceases or of the interest that begins. Instead, the valuation is determined by *the interest that passes*, and the value of the interest before or after death is pertinent only as it serves to indicate the value *at* death. [303 F.2d at 172.]

The court then rejected the taxpayer's argument that the estate tax value of the decedent's interest should be limited to two-thirds of its calculated value:

> [V]alue looks ahead. To find the fair market value of a property interest at the decedent's death we put ourselves in the position of a potential purchaser of the interest at that time. Such a person would not be influenced in his calculations by past risks that had failed to materialize or by restrictions that had ended. Death tolls the bell for risks, contingencies, or restrictions which exist only during the life of the decedent. A potential buyer focuses on the value the property has in the present or will have in the future. He attributes full value to any right that vests or matures at death, and he reduces his valuation to account for any risk or deprivation that death brings into effect, such as the effect of the death on the brains of a small, close corporation. These are factors that would affect his enjoyment of the property should he purchase it, and on which he bases his valuation. [303 F.2d at 173.]

Moreover, the court carefully distinguished the facts before it from superficially similar cases in which transfer restrictions taking effect only at death were held not to establish a ceiling on the estate tax value of a decedent's interest:

> [W]hen a decedent retains complete freedom to prevent the property being subjected to a restriction or contingency his inaction constitutes a passive transfer of an interest in the property to the person who stands to benefit by the limitation on the value of the property passing to the decedent's heir or legatee. [303 F.2d at 173.]

In Harrison's Estate v. Commissioner, 52 T.C.M. (CCH) 1306 (1987), the Tax Court purported to apply the *Land* rationale in valuing a decedent's partnership interest without regard to liquidation rights that automatically lapsed at death. The decedent in *Harrison* owned a 1–

percent general partnership interest and a 77.8–percent limited partnership interest; each of his two sons was a 10.6–percent general partner. As a general partner, the decedent had the right during life to compel a liquidation of the partnership, but that right expired at death. The decedent's general partnership interest was subject to purchase by his sons at death for around $750,000, which was stipulated to be its value for estate tax purposes. The valuation dispute focused on the decedent's limited partnership interest, which had a stipulated value of around $59 million immediately before death (i.e., before the liquidation right lapsed) and $33 million immediately after death (i.e., after the liquidation right lapsed). Relying on the *Land* court's notion that "value looks ahead," the Tax Court valued the decedent's limited partnership interest at $33 million. Did the lapse of the decedent's liquidation right at death constitute a "passive transfer" of $26 million?

b. Section 2704(a)

Section 2704(a), enacted in response to *Harrison* and similar cases, seeks to curb the use of lapsing rights as a transfer tax avoidance technique. In general, the statute treats the holder of a voting or liquidation right in a family corporation or partnership as making a deemed transfer upon a lapse of the right during life or at death. § 2704(a)(1). The amount of the deemed transfer is equal to the difference between the value of all the holder's interests in the entity before the lapse (determined as if the voting and liquidation rights were nonlapsing) and the value of the same interests after the lapse. § 2704(a)(2). In accordance with its focus on intrafamily transfers, the statute applies only if the corporation or partnership is controlled by the holder of the lapsed right and members of the holder's family both before and after the lapse. § 2704(a)(1); see also § 2704(c)(1) ("control"), (c)(2) ("member of the family"), and (c)(3) (attribution); Reg. § 25.2704–1(c)(2)(i) (statute not applicable to lapse that deprives holder and family members of ability to liquidate interest).

A "voting right" includes a general partner's right to participate in management, and a "liquidation right" includes a right to compel redemption of an equity interest whether or not in connection with a complete liquidation of the entity. Reg. § 25.2704–1(a)(2)(iv) and (v). Normally, a lapse occurs when a presently exercisable voting or liquidation right is restricted or eliminated, whether by operation of law, by the terms of corporate articles or bylaws, by agreement, or by any other means. Reg. § 25.2704–1(a)(4), (b), and (c)(1). A lapse also occurs if the holder transfers one interest and retains a separate, subordinate interest, thereby relinquishing the ability to compel liquidation of the retained interest. Reg. § 25.2704–1(c)(1).

To illustrate the operation of § 2704(a), consider a partnership structured like the one in *Harrison*. The father's ability as a general partner to compel the partnership to redeem his general and limited partnership interests at any time during life constitutes a liquidation right which lapses at death. The statutory requirement that the partnership be controlled by the father and members of his family (i.e., his two sons, who are the other general partners), both before and after the lapse, is met. The exception in Reg. § 25.2704–1(c)(2)(i) does not apply because after the father's death the two sons can compel the partnership to redeem the decedent's partnership interests. Therefore, the lapse of the father's liquidation right is treated as a deathtime transfer. The amount included in his gross estate under § 2704(a) is the difference between the combined value of his general and limited partnership interests before the lapse and the value of those interests after the lapse. See Reg. § 25.2704–1(d) (Example 5). Note that if the father's personal services constituted a key element in the value of the partnership, any decrease in the value of his partnership interests resulting from his death (independently of his lapsed liquidation right) would be unaffected by the valuation rule of § 2704(a). See Reg. § 25.2704–1(d) (Example 1).

c. Section 2704(b)

Section 2704(b) requires that certain restrictions on liquidation of a family corporation or partnership be disregarded for transfer tax purposes. The statute applies in valuing an interest in a corporation or partnership that is transferred to a member of the transferor's family, if the corporation or partnership is controlled immediately before the transfer by the transferor and members of the transferor's family. § 2704(b)(1); see also § 2704(c)(1) ("control"), (c)(2) ("member of the family"), and (c)(3) (attribution).

Under § 2704(b), the transferred interest is valued without regard to any "applicable restriction," which generally includes any temporary restriction that "effectively limits the ability of the corporation or partnership to liquidate." § 2704(b)(2)(A).[20] A restriction is temporary if it either will lapse by its terms at some time after the transfer or is subject to removal by the transferor and members of the transferor's family immediately after the transfer. § 2704(b)(2)(B). A restriction imposed by federal or state law is not an applicable restriction. § 2704(b)(3)(B). Thus, the statute applies only to the extent that limitations on liquidation are more restrictive than those generally imposed by law. Reg. § 25.2704–2(b). The statute also provides an exception for "commercially reasonable" restrictions arising from financing undertaken by the entity with an unrelated party. § 2704(b)(3).

To illustrate the type of arrangement at which § 2704(b) is aimed, assume that *A* and her children *B* and *C* are equal partners in the *ABC* general partnership. Under state law, a partnership ordinarily can be dissolved and liquidated by any general partner. *ABC*'s partnership agreement, however, provides that the partnership can be liquidated during the

---

20. The Tax Court has held that § 2704(b) does not apply to a restriction on a partner's ability to withdraw from a partnership unless such withdrawal would cause the partnership to liquidate. Kerr v. Commissioner, 113 T.C. 449 (1999), affd. on other grounds, 292 F.3d 490 (5th Cir. 2002).

first ten years of its existence only with the consent of all the partners. Since the requirement of unanimous consent is more restrictive than the provisions of state law, and will lapse after ten years, it constitutes an applicable restriction. If *A* transfers her partnership interest to her children during life or at death, the interest will be valued under § 2704(b) without regard to the restriction, i.e., as if the interest carried the right to liquidate the partnership. See Reg. § 25.2704–2(d) (Example 1); cf. Watts' Estate v. Commissioner, 823 F.2d 483 (11th Cir. 1987) (under prior law, value of decedent's general partnership interest was based on going concern value rather than higher liquidation value because partnership agreement provided for continuation of partnership after general partner's death).

According to the Conference Committee report, the provisions of § 2704 "do not affect minority discounts or other discounts" available under prior law. H.R. Rep. No. 964, 101st Cong., 2d Sess. 1137 (1990). Is there a qualitative difference between applicable restrictions under § 2704(b) and the implicit restrictions on a minority shareholder's interest? Recall the Tax Court's observation in Newhouse's Estate v. Commissioner, 94 T.C. 193 (1990), that a minority discount reflects "inability to compel liquidation and inability to realize a pro rata share of the corporation's net asset value."

Reference. See August, Artificial Valuation of Closely Held Interests: Sec. 2704, 22 Est. Planning 339 (1995).

E. SPECIAL USE VALUATION: § 2032A

Real property is ordinarily included in a decedent's gross estate at fair market value based on its "highest and best use." If certain requirements are satisfied, however, § 2032A, which was first enacted in 1976 and then liberalized by several amendments, permits real property used for farming or other business purposes to be included at its current or special use value.[21] The resulting reduction in the includible value of the property is

---

21. The House Ways and Means Committee report explained the rationale of § 2032A as follows:

> Your committee believes that, when land is actually used for farming purposes or in other closely held businesses (both before and after the decedent's death), it is inappropriate to value the land on the basis of its potential "highest and best use" especially since it is desirable to encourage the continued use of property for farming and other small business purposes. Valuation on the basis of highest and best use, rather than actual use, may result in the imposition of substantially higher estate taxes. In some cases, the greater estate tax burden makes continuation of farming, or the closely held business activities, not feasible because the income potential from these activities is insufficient to service extended tax payments or loans obtained to pay the tax. Thus, the heirs may be forced to sell the land for development purposes. Also, where the valuation of land reflects speculation to such a degree that the price of the land does not bear a reasonable relationship to its earning capacity, your committee believes it unreasonable to require that this "speculative value" be included in an estate with respect to land devoted to farming or closely held businesses.
>
> However, your committee recognizes that it would be a windfall to the beneficiaries of an estate to allow real property used for farming or closely held business purposes to be valued for estate tax purposes at its farm or business value unless the beneficiaries continue to use the property for farm or business purposes, at least for a reasonable period of time after the decedent's death.

limited to $750,000 (indexed for inflation since 1998 and reaching $1,020,000 in 2011).

To qualify for special use valuation, the real property must satisfy several statutory tests designed to ensure that the property was being used for farming or other business purposes prior to and at the time of the decedent's death and that the property constituted a substantial part of the gross estate. Moreover, if the decedent's heirs dispose of the property or cease to use it for farming or other business purposes within a ten-year period following the decedent's death, the estate tax benefits flowing from special use valuation may be forfeited through the imposition of a recapture tax. Special use valuation is available only if the following requirements are met:

1. The decedent must be a citizen or resident of the United States at the time of death, § 2032A(a)(1)(A), and the real property must be located in the United States, § 2032A(b)(1).
2. The real property must be used for a "qualified use" by the decedent or a member of the decedent's family at the time of death. § 2032A(b)(1). A "qualified use" means use "as a farm for farming purposes" or use in any other trade or business. § 2032A(b)(2). Members of an individual's family include the individual's ancestors, spouse, and lineal descendants, as well as lineal descendants of a spouse or parent and spouses of such lineal descendants. § 2032A(e)(2). For example, a parent, brother, sister-in-law, stepchild or niece would each be a family member, but an uncle or first cousin would not.
3. For at least five of the eight years preceding death, the real property must have been owned and used in a qualified use by the decedent or a family member, and there must have been "material participation" by the decedent or a family member in the operation of the farm or other business. § 2032A(b)(1)(C); Reg. § 20.2032A–3. A lease to a family member, or to a "closely held business" (as defined in § 6166) owned and operated solely by the decedent and family members, is permitted. Reg. § 20.2032A–3(b)(1). However, a lease to a non-family member does not qualify unless the rent or other income is "substantially dependent upon production" from the leased property. See Brockman v. Commissioner, 903 F.2d 518 (7th Cir. 1990) (fixed cash lease did not qualify); Heffley v. Commissioner, 884 F.2d 279 (7th Cir. 1989) (same); cf. Schuneman v. United States, 783 F.2d 694 (7th Cir. 1986) (adjustable cash lease did qualify).

Also, your committee believes that it would be inequitable to discount speculative values if the heirs of the decedent realize these speculative values by selling the property within a short time after the decedent's death.

For these reasons, your committee has provided for special use valuation in situations involving real property used in farming or in certain other trades or businesses, but has further provided for recapture of the estate tax benefit where the land is prematurely sold or is converted to nonqualifying uses. [H.R. Rep. No. 1380, 94th Cong., 2d Sess. 21–22 (1976), reprinted in 1976–3 C.B. (Vol. 3), at 735, 755–56.]

4. The real property must have been "acquired from or passed from the decedent to a qualified heir." § 2032A(b)(1). A "qualified heir" is a member of the decedent's family, as described above. § 2032A(e)(1). If the decedent created successive interests in the property (e.g., a life estate and remainder), Reg. § 20.2032A–8(a)(2) permits an election only for the portion of the property in which all the successive interests are held by qualified heirs. The courts, however, have refused to apply the regulation rigorously in all situations. See Davis' Estate v. Commissioner, 86 T.C. 1156 (1986) (contingent remainder to charity did not disqualify property); cf. Thompson's Estate v. Commissioner, 864 F.2d 1128 (4th Cir. 1989) (2–percent income interest received by nonqualified heir did not disqualify remaining 98 percent of property); Clinard's Estate v. Commissioner, 86 T.C. 1180 (1986) (remote possibility that qualified heir might exercise testamentary power of appointment in favor of nonqualified heirs did not disqualify property).

5. At least 50 percent of the adjusted value of the gross estate must consist of real or personal property meeting requirements 2 and 4 above, § 2032A(b)(1)(A); and at least 25 percent of the adjusted value of the gross estate must consist of real property meeting requirements 3 and 4 above, § 2032A(b)(1)(B). The "adjusted value" of property is its fair market value, net of mortgages and other indebtedness with respect to the property. § 2032A(b)(3). Moreover, for purposes of the 50–percent and 25–percent tests, property transferred by the decedent within three years before death is taken into account. § 2035(c)(1)(B). Certain residential buildings and "structures and improvements functionally related to the qualified use" are treated as "real property devoted to the qualified use." § 2032A(e)(3). See Sherrod's Estate v. Commissioner, 774 F.2d 1057 (11th Cir. 1985), cert. denied, 479 U.S. 814 (1986) (where only a portion of a farm was used in qualified use, rest of farm property not aggregated as "functionally related").

6. A notice of election and a recapture agreement must be attached to a timely filed estate tax return. § 2032A(a)(1)(B) and (d). The notice of election must contain specified information concerning the availability and computation of special use valuation. Reg. § 20.2032A–8(a)(3). The recapture agreement must be executed by all persons in being who have a present or future interest in the specially valued real property, and must consent to the payment of an additional estate tax in the event of a premature disposition or cessation of qualified use. Reg. § 20.2032A–8(c).

If these requirements are met, § 2032A(e)(7) and (e)(8) sets out methods for establishing the special use value of farm or other business property. Under § 1014(a)(3), the income tax basis of the qualified real property in the heir's hands is equal to its special use value.

The benefits of § 2032A are not unconditional. In general, the statute imposes an "additional estate tax" if within ten years after the decedent's death the qualified heir disposes of the specially valued real property outside the heir's family or ceases to use the property for the qualified use. § 2032A(c)(1) and (c)(6). In the case of a disposition to a member of the qualified heir's family, the family member steps into the heir's shoes with respect to the real property. § 2032A(e)(1). The decedent's surviving spouse or descendants may lease the real property to a family member on a net cash basis without incurring the additional tax. § 2032A(c)(7)(E). However, if a qualified heir leases the real property to a non-family member, the cessation of the heir's qualified use triggers the additional tax. Martin v. Commissioner, 783 F.2d 81 (7th Cir. 1986). The amount of the additional tax generally is equal to the estate tax savings resulting from the special use valuation, calculated without any interest charge. Under § 1016(c), the qualified heir may elect to increase the income tax basis of the specially valued property by the difference between the property's fair market value and its special use value as of the date of the decedent's death (or the alternate valuation date, if applicable). If such an election is made, the income tax basis of the property is stepped up as of the day before the event that triggered the recapture tax, reducing the gain on any disposition that causes the recapture. As a trade-off for the stepped-up basis, however, the heir is required to pay interest on the recapture tax computed from the estate tax due date to the date of payment, using the prevailing rates for tax deficiencies during such period.

For an explanation of the details of § 2032A and of the several formulas used to value qualified real property, see 5 Bittker & Lokken, Federal Taxation of Income, Estates and Gifts ¶ 135.6 (2d ed. 1993); see also H.R. Rep. No. 201, 97th Cong., 1st Sess. 165–79 (1981), reprinted in 1981–2 C.B. 352, 380–87; Penry, A Practitioner's Guide to Current Use Valuation Under § 2032A, 19 Real Prop., Prob. & Tr. J. 998 (1984).

F. ALTERNATE VALUATION DATE: § 2032

Section 2032 permits the executor to value the estate as of an alternate valuation date up to six months after the decedent's death, instead of using the value on the date of death.[22] This provision, originally enacted in 1935, is intended to prevent the confiscation of estates when market values decline abruptly after the decedent's death. Under § 2032, as amended in 1984, the alternate valuation date cannot be elected unless its effect is to decrease both the value of the gross estate and the amount of the tax liability. (Under pre–1984 law, executors could elect the alternate valuation date even if the assets had increased in value since the date

22. The alternate valuation date also applies for GST tax purposes in two situations: (1) under § 2624(b), any direct skip of property that is included in the transferor's gross estate is automatically valued at its estate tax value, with regard to §§ 2032 and 2032A; and (2) under § 2624(c), if a taxable termination occurs at the same time as and as a result of the death of an individual, an election may be made to value the underlying property as of the alternate valuation date.

of death, and would commonly do so when the election caused little or no increase in estate tax liability but substantially increased the basis of the property for income tax purposes.)

If the executor makes an election under § 2032, all property included in the gross estate must be valued as of the alternate valuation date; the election cannot be made selectively for some assets and not for others. Reg. § 20.2032–1(b)(2). Under § 2032(a)(2), the alternate valuation date is six months after the decedent's death; but with respect to any property that is "distributed, sold, exchanged or otherwise disposed of" within the six-month period, § 2032(a)(1) fixes the date of disposition as the alternate valuation date. For this purpose, a "disposition" encompasses any transaction by which property ceases to be part of the gross estate, such as a surrender of stock in a corporate liquidation, but the term does not extend to a mere change in form such as a tax-free incorporation or recapitalization. Reg. § 20.2032–1(c)(1). If the value of specific property is "affected by mere lapse of time," § 2032(a)(3) requires that the property be valued as of the date of death, "with adjustment for any difference in its value as of the later date not due to mere lapse of time."

Proposed regulations under § 2032 provide that a change in value during the alternate valuation period is taken into account only to the extent it results from "market conditions," which are defined as "events outside of the control of the decedent (or the decedent's executor or trustee) ... that affect the fair market value of the property being valued." By contrast, "[c]hanges in value due to mere lapse of time or to post-death events other than market conditions will be ignored in determining the value of decedent's gross estate under the alternate valuation method." Prop. Reg. § 20.2032–1(f)(1). As examples of property "affected by mere lapse of time," Prop. Reg. § 20.2032–1(f)(2) lists patents, life estates, remainders, and reversions. Thus, a patent that has ten years to run at the date of death is valued for the full ten years rather than nine and a half years. Examples of "post-death events other than market conditions" include "a reorganization of an entity (for example, corporation, partnership, or limited liability company) in which the estate holds an interest, a distribution of cash or other property to the estate from such entity, or one or more distributions by the estate of a fractional interest in such entity." Prop. Reg. § 20.2032–1(f)(3). Suppose that a decedent dies owning stock in a family corporation and, two months later, his executor exchanges the original stock for new stock pursuant to a tax-free reorganization. Due to transfer restrictions imposed in the reorganization, the new stock is worth considerably less than decedent's original stock. For purposes of alternate valuation, should the change in value be taken into account? See Prop. Reg. § 20.2032–1(f)(3)(ii) (Example 1); but cf. Kohler v. Commissioner, 92 T.C.M. (CCH) 48 (2006).

Reg. § 20.2032–1(d), implementing the decision in Maass v. Higgins, 312 U.S. 443 (1941), excludes from the gross estate any "property earned or accrued (whether received or not) after the date of the decedent's death." Conversely, "all property interests existing at the date of decedent's death which form a part of his gross estate" are included even if they are not collected until after death. Under this principle, rents and interest earned after the decedent's death and cash dividends payable to stockholders of record after that date are not made subject to the estate tax by an election to use the alternate valuation date. When distributions by a corporation are not made in cash, but in additional shares of its own stock, the regulations treat the transaction in the same manner as a cash dividend. If, however, the effects of the corporate distribution are so drastic that the stock does "not reasonably represent the same" property before and after the distribution (i.e., a partial liquidation of the corporate assets), the distribution, except for any part that is attributable to corporate earnings after the decedent's death, will be included in the gross estate and subject to tax. Reg. § 20.2032–1(d)(4).

For further discussion of alternate valuation under § 2032, see Blattmachr & Lo, Alternate Valuation—Now, Perhaps, More Important than Ever, 111 J. Tax'n 90 (2009).

CHAPTER 8

PAYMENT, COLLECTION, AND APPORTIONMENT

■ ■ ■

A. ESTATE TAX

1. TAX RETURNS AND ELECTIONS

An estate tax return (Form 706) is due nine months after death (§ 6075) and must be filed for the estate of every citizen or resident of the United States whose gross estate exceeds the basic $5 million exemption (indexed for inflation beginning in 2012) for the year of death less the amount of the decedent's adjusted taxable gifts (i.e., taxable gifts made after 1976 that are not drawn back into the gross estate). For filing purposes, therefore, the statute (§ 6018) treats the estate as though it were not entitled to any deductions and requires a return, unless the amount of the estate is fully offset by the decedent's remaining basic exemption.

The statutory intent is to require a return whenever there is a possibility that an estate tax will be due. For example, the estate of a person who dies in 2011, having previously made adjusted taxable gifts of $1 million, must file a return if the value of the gross estate at death exceeds $4 million; the necessity of filing is not excused by the existence of deductions under §§ 2053 (administration expenses and debts), 2054 (casualty losses), 2055 (charitable bequests), 2056 (marital bequests), or 2058 (state death taxes) which might reduce the net estate below the taxable threshold. Deductions become a factor in the computation of the tax only if claimed on the return.

The executor or administrator of the estate has primary responsibility for filing the return; if, however, the fiduciary fails to act or no fiduciary has been appointed, every person in actual or constructive possession of any of the decedent's property situated in the United States is considered an executor and is required to file a return. If the executor values the gross estate below the exemption equivalent, but the estate contains assets that are difficult to value, such as a closely held business, works of art, or real estate, the executor may be well advised to file a return in order to start the three-year statute of limitations running; there is no limitation on the time for assessing the tax if no return is filed. A filed return has the further advantage of providing a record of each asset's basis, which is necessary for the computation of the income tax on a future sale or exchange of the asset. Section 6662 imposes a 20–percent penalty if property is undervalued by 35 percent or more on an estate or gift tax return or its basis is overstated by 50 percent or more on an income tax return, subject to a $5,000 threshold; an enhanced 40–percent penalty applies in the case of a "gross valuation misstatement" (i.e., estate or gift tax undervaluation of 60 percent or more, or overstatement of income tax basis by 100 percent or more).

Section 6651 imposes a penalty for failure to make a timely filing of the return, which may run as high as 25 percent of the tax if the delay exceeds four months. The executor may avoid the penalty by establishing that the late filing was "due to reasonable cause and not due to willful neglect," and the question has frequently arisen whether the executor's reliance on expert counsel constitutes reasonable cause. For example, in United States v. Boyle, 469 U.S. 241 (1985), the executor, being unfamiliar with the estate tax law, had retained an experienced tax attorney. The Supreme Court held that the failure to file a timely estate tax return was not excused by the taxpayer's reliance on an attorney and such reliance is not "reasonable cause" under § 6651(a)(1).[1] The Court observed:

> The Government has millions of taxpayers to monitor, and our system of self-assessment in the initial calculation of a tax simply cannot work on any basis other than one of strict filing standards. Any less rigid standard would risk encouraging a lax attitude toward filing dates. Prompt payment of taxes is imperative to the Government, which should not have to assume the burden of unnecessary ad hoc determinations. [469 U.S. at 249.]

Under § 6081(a), the Service may grant an extension of time to file the return on a showing of good cause, but this itself does not extend the time for payment. An extension for filing is not to exceed six months except in a case where the executor is abroad. There are no hard and fast rules regarding what constitutes "good cause," but problems involving value or ownership of property, the executor's illness, controversy over the terms of a marital or charitable bequest, and similar matters usually justify a postponement. An extension of time may also be helpful by giving

1. In a footnote, the Court set out the reasons that have been accepted as "reasonable cause":

> The Internal Revenue Service has articulated eight reasons for a late filing that it considers to constitute "reasonable cause." These reasons include unavoidable postal delays, the taxpayer's timely filing of a return with the wrong IRS office, the taxpayer's reliance on the erroneous advice of an IRS officer or employee, the death or serious illness of the taxpayer or a member of his immediate family, the taxpayer's unavoidable absence, destruction by casualty of the taxpayer's records or place of business, failure of the IRS to furnish the taxpayer with the necessary forms in a timely fashion, and the inability of an IRS representative to meet with the taxpayer when the taxpayer makes a timely visit to an IRS office in an attempt to secure information or aid in the preparation of a return. Internal Revenue Manual (CCH) § 4350, (24) ¶ 22.2(2) (Mar. 20, 1980) (Audit Technique Manual for Estate Tax Examiners). [469 U.S. at 243 n.1.]

the executor a longer and more informed view of how various elections that must be made on the estate tax form will affect the estate's taxes and the taxes of the beneficiaries. For instance, under the qualified terminable interest property provision of § 2056(b)(7), the executor may elect to claim a marital deduction with respect to all, part, or none of the property in which the surviving spouse has a life income interest. Because a decision to qualify the property will impose possible estate or gift tax liability on the surviving spouse, the executor may wish to strike a balance, claiming only so much of the property for the marital deduction as is necessary to give the estate and surviving spouse the maximum tax advantage. See supra page 537.

A decision to extend the filing date is likely to be only the first of many decisions that the executor will be called on to make. The estate tax places responsibility on the executor to make elections in various contexts, and each election involves trade-offs of the kind described above. For example, an election to qualify the family farm or closely held business for special use valuation under § 2032A will reduce the estate tax but, in so doing, it will subject the beneficiaries to a possible recapture tax if the property is sold or put to other use within ten years.

In order to start the statute of limitations running for taxable gifts made during the calendar year in which the decedent died, as well as for unreported taxable gifts made in earlier years, the executor must file gift tax returns reporting such gifts. § 6501(a) and (c)(3). In this regard, the executor is required to attach copies of all gift tax returns to the estate tax return and to disclose (subject to penalties for perjury) information about transfers made by the decedent during life. If the decedent was married at the time of death (and if the surviving spouse has not remarried before the end of the taxable year), the executor may consent on the final gift tax return to treat gifts made to third persons as having been made one-half by each spouse. Split-gift treatment is presumably also available for gifts made in an earlier year for which no return was previously filed, if the statutory requirements were met during that year and the Service has not sent out a deficiency notice.

If a married decedent's cumulative taxable transfers made during life and at death do not exhaust the available exemption, the decedent's unused exemption amount may be passed on to the surviving spouse if the executor so elects on a timely filed estate tax return. The "portability" of the exemption between spouses is discussed supra at page 549.

The executor is also responsible for filing any income tax returns that the decedent would have been required to file if living, including any delinquent returns. § 6012(b)(1). Section 6013(a) authorizes the use of a joint return if the decedent was married; the final joint return may include the decedent's income until the date of death and the income of the spouse for the entire year. The executor must exercise care not to put assets of the estate at risk by assuming liability without indemnification for the accuracy of the spouse's declarations and for payment of the spouse's share of the tax. In preparing the final return, the executor has the option of using medical expenses, incurred during the decedent's final taxable year and paid by the estate within one year after the decedent's death, either as deductions on the final income tax return or as § 2053 deductions on the estate tax return.

During the administration of the estate, the executor is required to file fiduciary income tax returns (Form 1041). To the extent that the executor claims an administration expense or casualty loss as an income tax deduction, § 642(g) requires that a statement be filed waiving the right to claim a deduction for the same item on the estate tax return under §§ 2053 or 2054. See supra page 432, Note 6.

The executor, who may become personally liable for distributing assets of the estate if the taxes are not paid (see infra page 639), has the right to request an early determination of the decedent's estate tax and a release from personal liability therefor. Under § 2204, the Service has nine months from the date of the request or the filing of the estate tax return, whichever is later, to notify the executor of the amount of the estate tax. Upon payment of that amount, the executor is released from personal liability for any deficiency that may later be found to be due. This immunity does not extend to the estate itself or to any transferee who succeeds to the estate's assets. An early determination is available even if an extension of time for payment of the estate tax has been granted, provided the executor furnishes a bond, if requested by the Service. For a parallel provision concerning the decedent's income and gift taxes, see § 6905.

2. EXTENSION OF TIME FOR THE PAYMENT OF THE ESTATE TAX: §§ 6161, 6163, AND 6166

An extension of time for filing the estate tax return is no excuse for late payment of the tax. The statute requires that the tax be paid within nine months of death unless (1) an extension of time has been granted under § 6161, (2) payment has been deferred under § 6163 for the portion of the tax attributable to a reversion or a remainder, or (3) the executor has elected to pay the tax attributable to certain closely held business interests in installments pursuant to § 6166.

On a showing of "reasonable cause," the executor may obtain an initial extension of up to 12 months (§ 6161(a)(1)) and successive annual extensions of up to ten years (§ 6161(a)(2)). For example, reasonable cause for an extension may be found where assets would have to be sold at a sacrifice price in order to raise funds to pay the tax. Interest accrues during the period of the extension, as provided in § 6601. The § 6161 extension procedure is also available for the payment of any installment pursuant to an extension granted on account of a closely held business under § 6166, with the proviso that the extension not exceed 12 months from the due date of the last installment, and for estate tax deficiency payments, with the proviso that the period not exceed four years.

Section 6163, originally enacted in 1932, authorizes the executor to elect to postpone the time for payment of any estate tax on a reversionary or remainder interest included in the gross estate (and not created by the decedent's own testamentary act) for six months after the termination of the preceding interests in the property. An additional extension of three years may be granted on a showing of reasonable cause.

In 1958 Congress enacted § 6166 to allow the executor to pay the estate tax attributable to certain closely held business interests in up to ten annual installments. The primary purpose of this provision is to save the estate from being forced to sell or liquidate a closely held business in order to raise funds to pay the estate tax. The statute was subsequently revised to relax the requirements for eligibility and to permit an initial deferral period preceding the installment payments. Under the current version of § 6166, the executor may elect to defer paying the tax attributable to a closely held business interest for up to five years, and then to pay the deferred tax in up to ten annual installments. The first year of the ten-year installment period overlaps with the final year of the five-year deferral period, resulting in a maximum extension of 14 years. Notice of the election must be attached to the estate tax return. If a deficiency is assessed, the amount of the deficiency is prorated over all the installments, except in cases of negligence, intentional disregard of rules and regulations, or fraud. A § 6166 election is allowed regardless of whether an election is also made to value property at its special use value under § 2032A.

Interest is payable annually during both the five-year deferral period and the ten-year installment period. § 6166(f). The rate of interest is set at 2 percent on a portion of the deferred tax, and the balance bears interest at 45 percent of the rate for underpayments of tax. The 2–percent portion is limited to the amount of tax imposed on the first $1 million (adjusted for inflation, $1,360,000 in 2011) of taxable transfers exceeding the amount sheltered by the unified credit. § 6601(j). Interest on the deferred tax is not deductible for estate or income tax purposes.

The § 6166 election is available only if the decedent was a citizen or resident of the United States at the time of death. Furthermore, more than 35 percent of the value of the "adjusted gross estate" (i.e., the gross estate, less deductions allowable under §§ 2053 and 2054) must consist of an "interest in a closely held business." The minimum value requirement must be satisfied both with and without the inclusion of transfers made within three years of death. § 2035(c)(2). As a result, deathbed gifts of other property are not effective to push the value of closely held business interests over the 35–percent threshold. The closely held business may take the form of (1) a proprietorship, (2) a partnership in which at least 20 percent of the total capital interest is included in the gross estate or in which there were no more than 45 partners, or (3) a corporation in which at least 20 percent in value of the voting stock is included in the gross estate or in which there were no more than 45 shareholders. § 6166(b). The closely held business must be "carrying on a trade or business," and the statute imposes special restrictions in the case of holding companies and passive investment assets. See Rev. Rul. 2006–34, 2006–1 C.B. 1172 (guidance concerning trade or business requirement with respect to real property). Interests in two or more closely held businesses may be aggregated in order to cross the 35–percent threshold as long as at least 20 percent of the total value of each such business is included in the gross estate. § 6166(c). The values used for the estate tax control the computations under § 6166. Thus, if the executor elects special use valuation under § 2032A, the same value must also be used for purposes of § 6166.

In the event of a controversy involving an estate's eligibility for estate tax deferral under § 6166, the executor may petition the Tax Court for a declaratory judgment. § 7479.

The § 6166 extension may be terminated and unpaid portions of the tax may become due if there is a disposition or withdrawal of at least 50 percent of the value of the closely held business interest, or if any payment of principal or interest is not made within six months of the due date. § 6166(g). In addition, if the estate has any undistributed net income for a year in which an installment is due (i.e., after the five-year deferral period), such income must be applied to reduce the unpaid portion of the tax.

For a discussion of eligibility requirements and planning opportunities under § 6166, see Blattmachr, Gans & Madden, Untangling Installment Payments of Estate Tax Under Section 6166, 36 Est. Planning 3 (July 2009).

3. REDEMPTION OF STOCK TO PAY THE ESTATE TAX: § 303

Section 303, relating to stock redemptions, offers the executor a method by which to pay the estate tax at what is for practical purposes a discount. Under the statute, subject to certain conditions described below, property distributed by a corporation in redemption of its stock is treated as payment in exchange for the stock, even if the distribution would otherwise be taxed as a dividend under § 301. To the extent the fair market value of the redeemed stock exceeds its basis, the resulting gain generally will be eligible for preferential capital gain treatment. This provision, like § 2032A (special use valuation) and § 6166 (deferral and installment payment of estate tax), is intended to save the estate from being forced to sell or liquidate a closely held business in order to raise funds to pay the estate tax. Section 303 contains the following conditions and limitations:

1. The value of the redeemed stock must be included in the decedent's gross estate.
2. Stock of the redeeming corporation must constitute more than 35 percent of the "adjusted gross estate" (i.e., the gross estate, less deductions allowable under §§ 2053 and 2054); for this purpose,

transfers made within three years of death are includible in the gross estate under § 2035(c)(1)(A). The stock of two or more companies can be aggregated under § 303(b)(2)(B) to satisfy the percentage requirement. The decedent may be a minority stockholder in a large corporation (e.g., 36 percent of the adjusted gross estate consists of General Motors stock), but, as a practical matter, only closely held corporations will redeem their stock pursuant to § 303.

3. The amount of distributions eligible for § 303 treatment is limited to the sum of the death taxes (state as well as federal) and the funeral and administration expenses allowable as deductions for estate tax purposes.

4. Distributions eligible for § 303 treatment must be made within a specified period (three years plus 90 days, with an extension allowed for a Tax Court proceeding or installment payments under § 6166) after the death of the decedent.

Section 303 may be used to obtain cash for the payment of estate taxes and funeral and administration expenses. Because the redeemed stock is given a stepped-up basis under § 1014, the estate usually will realize little or no gain by the redemption and thus will incur minimal income tax liability.

See generally Kahn, Closely Held Stocks—Deferral and Financing of Estate Tax Costs Through Sections 303 and 6166, 35 Tax Law. 639 (1982).

4. PAYMENT AND COLLECTION

The executor pays the estate tax from the assets of the estate. There are, however, several provisions that may be invoked to require contributions from certain beneficiaries, even though the assets they receive are not part of the probate estate and are not subject to administration by the executor.

Section 2206 (see supra page 387, Note 5) states that the executor shall be entitled to recover from the beneficiary of any life insurance included in the gross estate such portion of the total estate tax payable as the proceeds of the policies bear to the taxable estate. The executor has similar rights to recover a proportionate share of the tax from the recipient of property over which the decedent had a general power of appointment (§ 2207, see supra page 417, Note 4) and from the recipient of property transferred by the decedent during life subject to a retained life estate (§ 2207B, see supra page 328, Note 2). No reimbursement is allowed under these provisions against the surviving spouse for property received that qualified for the marital deduction. Unless the decedent's will directs otherwise, the executor has a fiduciary duty to enforce these rights of recovery as a necessary step in the conservation of the estate's assets. Section 2207A (see supra page 526) authorizes the surviving spouse's estate to obtain reimbursement for the estate tax imposed by

§ 2044 from the beneficiaries who succeed to qualified terminable interest property at the spouse's death; the statute contains a parallel provision concerning the gift tax imposed by § 2519 on a lifetime disposition of the spouse's qualifying income interest for life. The Code does not provide rights of recovery with respect to property included in the gross estate under other provisions (e.g., due to a § 2038 power to revoke, a § 2039 survivor annuity, or a § 2040 joint tenancy). Under § 6324(a)(2), however, the beneficiaries, along with all other persons who are in possession of property from the estate, may be subject to "transferee liability" up to the value of the property received, if the tax is not paid when due. Armstrong v. Commissioner, 114 T.C. 94 (2000). Although it is clear that transferee liability for unpaid estate taxes is limited to the date-of-death value of the property received, there is a split of authority over whether the same limitation applies to liability for interest. Compare Baptiste v. Commissioner, 29 F.3d 1533 (11th Cir. 1994) (limitation not applicable) with Baptiste v. Commissioner, 29 F.3d 433 (8th Cir. 1994), cert. denied, 513 U.S. 1190 (1995) (contra, on identical facts).

To assist the collection process, the Code authorizes several liens on transferred property. In addition to the general tax lien of § 6321 (the scope of which is described by §§ 6322 and 6323), a special lien for estate taxes is created by § 6324 and is valid for ten years against the gross estate. If property is transferred to a bona fide purchaser for full consideration, the lien attaches to the proceeds. Additional special liens are imposed to ensure payment of the postponed estate tax attributable to a § 6166 election (§ 6324A) as well as the additional estate tax imposed by § 2032A(c) upon a premature disposition or cessation of qualified use of real property for which special use valuation was elected (§ 6324B). Section 6325 gives the Service authority to release any federal tax lien (e.g., to facilitate a sale of property) if the owner deposits an equivalent amount of money or furnishes a bond, or if the value of the remaining property is at least double the unpaid tax.

The executor may become personally liable for an unpaid estate tax by virtue of 31 U.S.C. § 3713, which imposes such liability if the executor pays any debt of the estate before satisfying debts due to the United States. Reg. § 20.2002–1 construes the term "debt" to include a beneficiary's distributive share of the estate. But cf. Leuthesser v. Commissioner, 18 T.C. 1112 (1952) (construing statutory language narrowly). Funeral and administration expenses, including fees, are not debts of the decedent and may be given priority over the federal tax claims. As explained earlier in this section, the executor can secure protection from personal liability by requesting a prompt determination of the tax pursuant to § 2204.

See generally Liability of Fiduciaries and Transferees for Federal Estate and Gift Taxes, 2 Real Prop., Prob. & Tr. J. 250 (1967); Miller, The Fiduciary's Personal Liability for Deficiencies in Federal Income, Estate and Gift Taxes of a Decedent or Decedent's Estate, 11 Gonz. L. Rev. 431 (1976).

NOTES

1. *Equitable adjustments.* The executor stands in a fiduciary relationship to the beneficiaries, and is under an obligation to conserve the assets of the estate, which presumably includes minimizing the overall tax burden. At the same time, the executor is required to treat all beneficiaries impartially and to refrain from self-dealing. The exercise of any of the various tax elections available to the executor will almost invariably result in a benefit to some beneficiaries at the expense of other beneficiaries. Thus, an election may put the executor, particularly one who is also a beneficiary, in breach of basic fiduciary duties. In such circumstances, is the executor under a fiduciary duty to compensate for the resulting disproportionate tax burden by effecting an equitable adjustment among the beneficiaries?

This issue has received both judicial and legislative attention in the context of an election under § 642(g) to deduct administration expenses, claims, and casualty losses on the fiduciary income tax return rather than on the estate tax return. It may be that by this election the estate's total tax burden is reduced, but because administration expenses and casualty losses are ordinarily charged against principal whereas the fiduciary income tax is charged against income, the election forces the principal beneficiaries to subsidize a windfall for the income beneficiaries. In 1955, the New York Surrogate's Court broke new ground by holding that the principal account must be reimbursed by the amount of the estate tax savings that would have resulted had the deductions been taken on the estate tax return. In re Warms' Estate, 140 N.Y.S.2d 169 (Sur. Ct. 1955); see also In re Bixby's Estate, 295 P.2d 68 (Cal. App. 1956); In re Rappaport's Estate, 467 N.Y.S.2d 814 (Sur. Ct. 1983) (in the reverse situation, the court directed the executors to deduct the administration expenses on the estate tax return, provided that the nonmarital beneficiaries make reimbursement of the income tax savings that could have been realized by deducting the expenses on the fiduciary income tax return). Several statutes have followed the *Warms* lead. See, e.g., N.Y. E.P.T.L. § 11–1.2; cf. Uniform Principal and Income Act § 506(a)(1) (1997) (discretionary adjustment). Because the number and variety of conflicts that may result from tax elections are practically limitless, prudent practice suggests that specific directions be included in the will absolving the executor from liability for breach of duty and making explicit the conditions, if any, under which an equitable adjustment is required. See generally Carrico & Bondurant, Equitable Adjustments: A Survey and Analysis of Precedents and Practice, 36 Tax Law. 545 (1983); Dobris, Limits on the Doctrine of Equitable Adjustment in Sophisticated Postmortem Tax Planning, 66 Iowa L. Rev. 273 (1981).

2. *Statutes of limitations.* Section 6501(a) generally requires that estate, gift, and income taxes be assessed within three years after the filing of the return. The three-year period is increased to six years if the gross estate is understated by more than 25 percent (§ 6501(e)). There is no statute of limitations on assessment or collection if no return is filed or if the return is fraudulent (§ 6501(c)). Once a timely assessment is made, § 6502 permits the tax to be collected by levy or court proceeding begun within ten years after

the assessment. Section 6511(a) requires that a claim for a refund of the estate or gift tax be made within three years after filing of the return or two years after payment of the tax, whichever occurs later.

3. *Appeals.* Disputes between the executor and the Internal Revenue Service are usually resolved administratively following a conference between the executor and a Treasury representative. For a description of this process, see 4 Bittker & Lokken, Federal Taxation of Income, Estates and Gifts ¶ 112 (3d ed. 2003). If the administrative appeal procedure does not settle the matter, the executor has a choice of courts in which to pursue the dispute. The executor may pay the tax and sue for a refund in either the federal District Court or the Claims Court; or the executor may refuse to pay the tax (in which case interest will accrue) and challenge the deficiency by petition to the Tax Court. Trial by jury is available only in the District Court. Appeals from the District Court and the Tax Court go to the appropriate Circuit Court of Appeals; appeals from the Claims Court go to the Court of Appeals for the Federal Circuit. The United States Supreme Court has discretion to review cases from the appellate courts by granting a writ of certiorari. For a detailed description of tax litigation, see 4 Bittker & Lokken, supra, ¶ 115.

5. APPORTIONMENT OF THE ESTATE TAX

Although Congress presumably could establish a comprehensive system for apportioning the burden of the federal estate tax among some or all of the persons sharing in the gross estate, it has not done so. Consequently, the federal estate tax, like administration expenses, debts, and other charges, ordinarily must be paid out of the residuary estate. See Annot., Ultimate Burden of Estate Tax in Absence of Statute, Will, or Other Provision, 68 A.L.R.3d 714 (1976). If the residue is insufficient, specific devises, legacies, and other interests will abate in the same manner as when debts exceed the residue. Contrariwise, state inheritance taxes, which are levied on the recipients of the estate, usually come out of the recipients' shares; thus, residuary legatees are burdened only with the inheritance tax attributable to their own shares.

It has always been possible for the testator to nullify this default method of charging the estate tax against the residue by providing in the will that the tax shall be apportioned among all, or some, of the beneficiaries. However, wills sometimes fail to include an apportionment clause, even when it is reasonably clear that the decedent would not have wanted the residuary legatees to bear the entire tax burden. In view of this problem, the New York State Commission to Investigate Defects in the Laws of Estates recommended in 1930 that a statute be enacted to apportion the burden of the tax:

> The great complaint against the estate tax has been that this burden falls upon the residuary legatees, who are, under most wills, the widow, children, or nearer or more dependent relatives. Cases have arisen where the residue has been greatly depleted by the imposition of the Federal Estate tax. Moreover, the residuary legatee under the

> present system is compelled not only to pay the tax assessed against the transfers passing by operation of the will, but is also compelled to pay the tax on other transfers to persons not participating in the decedent's estate. Thus, if ... a transfer under an inter vivos trust becomes effective by reason of the death of the settlor, the tax on all such transfers is imposed upon the residuary legatees. This new law provides for an equitable apportionment of all these transfers by the surrogate in an accounting or other appropriate proceeding on notice to all the parties. Thus the donee of a gift taking effect at death will be compelled to bear his fair share of the tax upon the amount of the property which he derived and which was included in the general estate subjected to taxation. It is believed that this plan will present a fair, just and equitable method of the allocation of the estate tax, both Federal and State. [Legis. Doc. No. 69, 197–98 (1930).]

Pursuant to the Commission's report, New York became the first state to enact a comprehensive estate tax apportionment statute, which in its current form appears as N.Y. E.P.T.L. § 2–1.8. Most states have followed New York's lead and require, either by statute or judicial decision, that the estate tax be apportioned among the beneficiaries unless negated by the decedent's will. Some states require apportionment between the probate estate and property passing outside the will but do not order apportionment within the probate estate, so that the death taxes on probate assets must be paid out of the residue. See Annot., Construction and Application of Statutes Apportioning or Prorating Estate Taxes, 71 A.L.R.3d 247 (1976).

The hardship on residuary legatees, described in the New York Commission's report above, is accentuated if there is an unexpected decline in the value of the estate's assets, or if the taxable estate is swollen by the inclusion of inter vivos gifts, joint property, life insurance proceeds, or property subject to a general power of appointment. The executor is entitled to recover a ratable share of the federal estate tax from the recipients of the latter two classes of taxable property under § 2206 (life insurance proceeds) and § 2207 (property subject to a general power of appointment), unless the decedent directs otherwise. Although these federal provisions cover only a small portion of the problem, their existence gave rise to a challenge to the constitutionality of the New York apportionment statute on the ground that Congress had preempted the field. In Riggs v. Del Drago, 317 U.S. 95 (1942), the Supreme Court held that "Congress intended that state law should determine the ultimate thrust of the tax" and that the New York statute did not contravene the supremacy clause of the Constitution.

Many states have enacted one version or another of the Uniform Estate Tax Apportionment Act, which was initially promulgated in 1958 and was subsequently revised in 1964 and 2003 in response to changes in tax laws and estate planning practices. Broadly speaking, the uniform act provides a rule of equitable apportionment for federal and state estate taxes (but not state inheritance or gift taxes), so that the burden of the tax falls on the beneficiaries of the taxable estate in proportion to the value of their interests. Because property qualifying for a marital or charitable deduction does not give rise to any estate tax burden, the benefit of those deductions inures to the recipients of such property. In the case of a transfer involving successive beneficial interests (e.g., a life estate followed by a remainder), any resulting tax is generally charged to the corpus of the property without apportionment, even if this reduces the amount of a deduction that would otherwise be allowable (e.g., in the case of a charitable remainder trust). The statutory rules are default rules which can be overridden if the decedent directs a different method of apportionment. For a discussion of recent revisions to the uniform act, see Kahn, The 2003 Revised Uniform Estate Tax Apportionment Act, 38 Real Prop., Prob. & Tr. J. 613 (2004).

NOTES

1. *Federal impact of state apportionment.* Apportionment is primarily concerned with allocating the burden of a fixed amount of death taxes, but the allocation may affect the amount itself, not merely its allocation. For example, if the residue of an estate is left to the decedent's surviving spouse or to charity, the amount of the marital or charitable deduction will be affected by whether the tax is to be paid out of the residue or apportioned among the beneficiaries of the estate. See §§ 2055(c) and 2056(b)(4)(A). For this reason, the federal courts sometimes have to pass on questions of state apportionment law in federal tax proceedings. See, e.g., Penney's Estate v. Commissioner, 504 F.2d 37 (6th Cir. 1974) (applying Ohio law, holding marital and charitable bequests exonerated from liability for death taxes, thereby saving almost $2,350,000 in taxes); Robinson v. United States, 518 F.2d 1105 (9th Cir. 1975) (holding Montana law required equitable apportionment, thereby exonerating marital share of residuary estate); Second Natl. Bank v. United States, 351 F.2d 489 (2d Cir. 1965), affd., 387 U.S. 456 (1967) (under Connecticut law, direction in will against apportionment caused federal estate tax to be charged against residuary estate, including marital share). Federal courts may also be called on to decide troublesome questions of state apportionment law in connection with proceedings to compel reimbursement under § 2205. See, e.g., Doetsch v. Doetsch, 312 F.2d 323 (7th Cir. 1963) (conflict of laws concerning apportionment when gross estate includes out-of-state inter vivos trust).

2. *Testamentary clauses affecting apportionment.* Estate tax apportionment is generally governed by state statutes unless the decedent's will "otherwise provides." The federal statutes providing for apportionment with respect to specified types of property also give way to a contrary provision in the will. See §§ 2206 (life insurance proceeds), 2207 (property subject to a general power of appointment), 2207A (qualified terminable interest property), and 2207B (property transferred subject to a retained life estate). It is sometimes necessary, therefore, to determine whether an ambiguous provision of a will negates apportionment. For example, the decedent in In re Mills' Will, 70 N.Y.S.2d 746 (App. Div. 1947), affd. mem., 80 N.E.2d 535 (N.Y. 1948), directed that all death taxes "imposed upon my estate or any part thereof, or

the transfer thereof or any right of succession thereto" be paid out of the residuary estate. The court held that this direction was not sufficiently clear to negate the New York equitable apportionment statute; the testator—a former Secretary of the Treasury—had created certain inter vivos trusts that were outside the probate estate but were subject to estate tax, and the court held that the reference in his will to death taxes "on my estate" referred only to his probate estate. The court implied that a simple direction that "all inheritance, estate, transfer and succession taxes be paid out of my residuary estate" would be sufficient to negate apportionment. Cf. In re Fischer's Will, 162 N.Y.S.2d 495 (Sur. Ct. 1957) (no apportionment where will directed that all death taxes "upon my estate or any portion thereof" be paid from residuary estate); In re Holst's Estate, 433 A.2d 1284 (N.H. 1981) (will directing executor to pay from the residuary estate "all ... taxes as may become due or payable by reason of property passing as a consequence of my death so that the sum and amounts specifically set forth, reserved, bequeathed and distributable to a beneficiary shall not be reduced by any tax chargeable to the same" required all death taxes on testamentary and nontestamentary property to be paid out of the residuary estate). In McLaughlin v. Green, 69 A.2d 289 (Conn. 1949), however, a direction of this character was held insufficient under a similar Connecticut law, and the court suggested that a more elaborate formula be employed. See generally Annot., Construction and Application of "Pay–All–Taxes" Provision in Will, as Including Liability of Nontestamentary Property for Inheritance and Estate Taxes, 56 A.L.R.5th 133 (1998); Annot., Construction and Effect of Will Provisions Expressly Relating to the Burden of Estate or Inheritance Taxes, 69 A.L.R.3d 122 (1976).

In the absence of a specific clause relating to the apportionment of death taxes, the state courts turn to other provisions in the will to discover the testator's intent on the subject. The numerous cases are collected in Annot., Construction and Effect of Will Provisions Not Expressly Mentioning Payment of Death Taxes But Relied On as Affecting the Burden of Estate or Inheritance Taxes, 70 A.L.R.3d 630 (1976), and Annot., Construction and Effect of Provisions in Nontestamentary Instrument Relied Upon as Affecting the Burden of Estate and Inheritance Taxes, 70 A.L.R.3d 691 (1976). The courts have shown a tendency to construe clauses negating apportionment (or, in the absence of any tax clause, other provisions in the will) in a manner that exonerates interests passing to a surviving spouse or charity from liability for death taxes generated by other interests. On marital bequests, see, e.g., In re Ericson's Estate, 377 A.2d 898 (N.J. 1977) (testator's intent to obtain maximum marital deduction exonerated marital share from tax liability, despite contradictory clause in will); Swallen's Estate v. Commissioner, 98 F.3d 919 (6th Cir. 1996) (ambiguous "boilerplate" provision did not override equitable apportionment statute). On charitable bequests, see, e.g., In re Rankin's Estate, 404 A.2d 1200 (N.J. Super.App.Div. 1979) (although clause directed that taxes be paid from residue, charitable bequest of one-third of residue was exonerated from tax burden on equitable principles); In re Slade's Will, 360 N.Y.S.2d 803 (Sur. Ct. 1974) (charitable bequest not required to pay share of tax since it generated no part of tax); but see In re Wilson's Estate, 315 P.2d 451 (Cal. App. 1957) (clause directed taxes to be paid from residue; charitable share of residue must bear ratable share of tax because residue is computed after payment of taxes).

A tax apportionment clause must be drafted with extreme care to make clear (1) which federal and state taxes are covered, (2) which beneficiaries or property are to be exonerated from the tax burden, and (3) which beneficiaries or property are to bear that burden. The testator ordinarily will wish to ensure not only that the marital and charitable bequests are not liable for any taxes but also that gifts of specific property or of small amounts of money to family, friends or employees are kept intact and are not diminished by a ratable share of the taxes. The drafter's task becomes more complicated when additional considerations are taken into account. How are the death taxes on the family business to be allocated among the beneficiaries? Is there a desire to alter the provisions of § 2207A, which places the estate tax burden attributable to qualified terminable interest property on the beneficiaries who succeed to it at the surviving spouse's death? Is it a wise precaution to set aside a fund to pay any recapture estate tax that might be imposed with respect to property for which special use valuation was elected under § 2032A? Are the taxes on a generation-skipping transfer to be paid out of the transferred property, or should an alternative source of payment be provided to preserve the full value of the transferred property? Does a "boilerplate" provision directing that "all taxes payable as a result of my death are to be paid from my residuary estate" apply to any of the above situations?

3. *Nonstatutory apportionment.* Even without statutory authority, the courts, when applying state law, have been increasingly willing to apply a doctrine of equitable apportionment to relieve the residuary legatees of the tax burden generated by lifetime gifts and by deathtime transfers of nonprobate assets. See Penney's Estate v. Commissioner, 504 F.2d 37 (6th Cir. 1974) (tracing development of equitable apportionment doctrine in Ohio, requiring contribution from nonprobate assets to pay share of death taxes); see also Dodd v. United States, 345 F.2d 715 (3d Cir. 1965), holding that the New Jersey rule requiring that the federal estate tax be paid from the residue in the absence of a contrary direction by the testator permitted apportionment within the residue, which was divided between the testator's children and his widow; the court held that the tax was payable in full out of the children's share because the wife's share qualified for the marital deduction and did not generate any tax liability. Note the effect of this result on the amount as well as the distribution of the tax burden. Would it have been more equitable to charge the children's share of the residue with the tax attributable to them, and to divide the balance of the tax between the children and the widow?

B. GIFT TAX

Section 6019 requires that a gift tax return (Form 709) be filed for each calendar year in which an individual makes any gift that is not fully covered by the annual exclusion for gifts of present interests (§ 2503(b)), by the exclusion for tuition or medical payments (§ 2503(e)), or by the marital deduction (§ 2523). In addition, certain gifts qualifying for the charitable deduction (§ 2522) do not require the filing of a gift tax return.

Note that the exception for interspousal gifts does not apply to gifts of qualified terminable interest property, since the donor spouse must file a gift tax return in order to make a valid QTIP election under § 2523(f). If a married couple elects to treat a gift by one of them to a third person as made half by each of them under § 2513, the donor spouse must file a return on which the other spouse consents to split-gift treatment.

Under § 6075(b), the gift tax return generally is due by April 15 following the close of the calendar year in which the gifts were made. If the donor obtains an extension to file his or her income tax return, the extension automatically applies to the gift tax return as well. However, if the donor dies during the calendar year of the gift, the gift tax return must be filed no later than the due date of the estate tax return. Under § 6081(a), the Service may extend the filing date by up to six months (or longer, if the donor is abroad), on a showing by the donor of good cause.

Postponement of the filing date does not excuse failure to pay the tax, but the donor may apply under § 6161(a)(1) for an extension of the time for payment. The grant of an extension (subject to interest) of up to six months is discretionary with the Service, which requires a showing that timely payment would result in "undue hardship." Reg. § 25.6161–1(b) states that more than a showing of inconvenience to the taxpayer is required and cites as an example the prospect of a substantial financial loss resulting from the sale of property at a sacrifice to raise funds to pay the tax. The additional extension allowed for the payment of the estate tax on a closely held business under § 6166 is not available to defer payment of the gift tax.

The donor is primarily liable for the gift tax, but if payment is not made by the due date, the donee becomes personally liable under § 6324(b) up to the value of the property received. The donee's liability, however, is not limited to the amount of the donor's unpaid tax attributable to the gift received by the donee. Thus, in Baur v. Commissioner, 145 F.2d 338 (3d Cir. 1944), the donee of a nontaxable gift (e.g., a gift fully covered by the annual exclusion) was held liable for an unpaid tax on a gift made by the same donor to another donee in the same calendar year, even though the donor was not insolvent at the time of the gifts and was not made insolvent thereby.

C. GENERATION-SKIPPING TRANSFER TAX

Section 2603(a) imposes personal liability for the payment of the GST tax on the transferee for a taxable distribution, on the trustee for a taxable termination or a direct skip from a trust, and on the transferor for all other direct skips. Section 2662(a) directs the Treasury to prescribe by regulations the person who is required to file the return and the time by which the return must be filed. See Reg. § 26.2662–1. In general, the persons who are liable for the payment of the tax under § 2603(a) are also responsible for filing the return, as follows: in the case of a direct skip (other than from a trust), the return must be filed on or before the due date of the estate or gift tax return for the transfer; and, in all other cases, the return must be filed on or before April 15 of the year after the calendar year in which the generation-skipping transfer occurs.

INDEX

References are to Pages

References are to Pages

References are to Pages

†